D1162416

LONGMAN

ILLUSTRATED ENCYCLOPEDIA OF

WORLD HISTORY

LONGMAN

ILLUSTRATED ENCYCLOPEDIA OF

WORLD HISTORY

IVY LEAF

First published in 1976 under the title
Longman Illustrated Companion to World History
by Longman Group Limited

Published in 1989 by
Ivy Leaf
Michelin House
81 Fulham Road
London SW3 6RB

This edition produced exclusively for
Bookmart Limited

ISBN 0 86363 000 6

Printed in Austria

Contents

Editor: Grant Uden
Revised material: Guy Arnold
Associate Editor: John S. Wingate-Saul

Illustrations: Anthony Colbert
Cartography: Volume I, John Flower
Volume II, Keith Morton
Index: Sally Bicknell

Picture Research: Sandra Assersohn
with Anne Fisher
and Jane Dorner
Book Lists: R. J. Hoare

CONTRIBUTORS

W. J. Baker
Frederick Buckle, D.S.C., M.A.
Philip A. Burgoyne
Aileen Hamilton Burslem
Charles Chenevix Trench, M.C., B.A.
R. J. Claye, B.A.
P. Collister, M.A.
Tom Corfe, M.A.
Marcus Crouch, B.A., F.L.A.
John Dobie
Phyllis A. Downie, M.A., F.L.A.
Wilfred J. Fance, F.Inst.B.B.
Paul Fincham, B.A.
R. S. Fitton, Ph.D.
W. W. French, M.A.
A. W. Fuller
Max H. Fuller, M.A.
R. M. Gard, M.A.
John F. Goodchild
Hugh Gregor, M.A.
E. E. Y. Hales, C.B.E.
Fernau Hall
Sylvia Haymon
Mark Haymon
E. G. Heath
A. G. L. Hellyer, M.B.E., F.L.S.
J. W. Hunt, M.A.
John F. Leech, M.B.E.
John Marsh, M.A.
Zoë Marsh, B.A., M.Ed.
Brigadier P. W. Mead
Winifred F. Pretty, M.A.
David V. Proctor, M.A., D.I.C.
Peter H. Rogers, B.A., Dip.Ed.
Joan M. Saunders
Hugh Shearman, Ph.D.
Christine Smale, A.R.C.A.
Ernest W. Sockett, B.A.
Frank Staff
H. M. Stedman
B. G. Stone, O.B.E., M.A.
J. J. Sullivan, K.S.G., B.Sc.(Econ.)
Elfrida Vipont
Annesley Voysey, B.Sc.
Arthur H. Waite
Marjorie Weemys
Barry Williams, B.A.
John S. Wingate-Saul, M.A.
Barbara Winstanley, B.Sc., F.M.A.
B. K. Workman, M.A.
Dorothy F. H. Wrenn
Paul Zec, M.A.

Secretary: Mary Chick

Preface

This encyclopedia is not intended to be primarily a work of quick reference though it may often serve this useful purpose. Rather, it is hoped that it will be congenial to browse in, sometimes for instructional purposes, sometimes simply because it is interesting to do so.

In pursuit of these aims, contributors of very varied background and experience were invited to collaborate under the direction of the editor, Grant Uden and the first edition was published in two volumes in 1976. The contributors came from a wide range of occupations: school and university, commerce, the law, the old colonial service, agriculture, libraries, museums and technical organisations.

A short encyclopedia of this nature can not cover every subject and the editor therefore deliberately followed a policy of selecting those subjects which would make it both as balanced and as interesting as possible.

The index provides a detailed system of cross-referencing. As well as listing the entries themselves, it also lists people, events etc. which appear within entries, but which do not have entries to themselves. The cross-referencing system used within the text has deliberately been kept simple. For instance, cross-references to other entries are grouped together at the end of an entry and appear thus:

See also AUSTRIA: CHARLES V: etc.

In the Index references to names articles are shown in **bold.** Where suggestions for further reading are made they appear as follows:

¶ JONES, DAVID and PAULINE, *Hadrian's Wall* (Jacdaw). 1958.

The suggestions for further reading are intended mainly for young people, though adult books are not excluded.

Guy Arnold

A

Abbeys: homes of monastic communities. In early Christian times there were people who felt the need to live in lonely places and devote their time to prayer. Known as hermits or anchorites, they were often revered for their holy lives, and their admirers would sometimes follow their example. Thus, small groups of hermits came to live in the same place.

Eventually the members of these groups realised that they would benefit by organising their lives for the common good, and the first monastic communities appeared in Egypt, in the 4th century AD. Their living quarters were arranged like small villages, with several monks in each hut, or cell. The monks spent most of their time in prayer, but they also worked as farmers or craftsmen, selling their produce to buy food and to obtain money for the poor. The leader of each group was called the abbot, from a Syrian word *abba*, father. New communities grouped their buildings together for convenience around a central church. Certain buildings were essential – a refectory, a dormitory, a kitchen, a guest house, cells for the monks and a cloister. The whole area was often surrounded by a defensive wall and was called an abbey because its ruler was the abbot.

St Benedict of Nursia, born in Italy in AD 480, became a monk. He felt that the lack of organisation in the abbeys wasted time and ability, so he drew up rules by

Artist's reconstruction of a typical abbey complex, showing the purpose of the various parts and their relationship to one another.

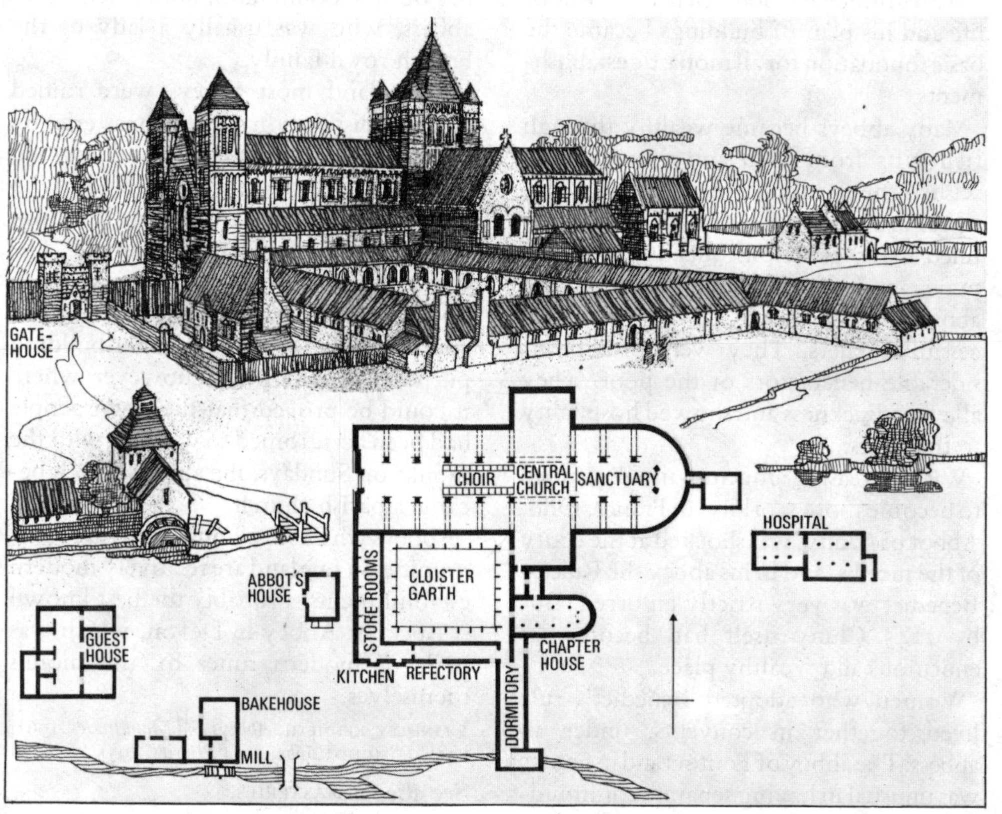

which a monk's day was planned from the time he rose until he went to bed. Benedict founded a monastery at Monte Cassino in Italy, where he had the buildings arranged in a way most convenient for community life. The central building was the church. Adjoining it was the chapter house, where daily business meetings were held, and the dormitory, where the monks slept. This was connected to the church by a stairway so that they could easily get to early services. Enclosing a square garden (the garth) was an arched cloister. The refectory and the kitchen with its cooking smells were well away from the church. Detached from the main block, though within the surrounding wall, were the abbot's dwelling, a hospital, a guest house and farm buildings. If possible, the abbey was situated near a stream for drainage purposes.

With minor variations, Benedict's rule of life and his plan of buildings became the basic foundation for all monastic establishments.

Many abbeys became wealthy through rich gifts from men and women who wished the monks, in return, to say continual prayers for their souls. Monks fulfilled many functions outside the life of prayer and the necessary labour in and about the monastery. Some were successful teachers. They were often considerable benefactors of the poor. They alleviated sickness and showed hospitality to travellers.

With increasing affluence, monks tended to become more worldly. In France, Odo, Abbot of Cluny, was shocked at the laxity of the monks, and in his abbey the Rule of Benedict was very strictly enforced. But by 1245 Cluny itself had become an enormous and wealthy place.

Women who adopted Benedict's rule lived together in convents, under an abbess. The abbey of Fontevraud in France was unusual in having separate communi-

Buckfast Abbey, Devon.

ties of monks and nuns, both ruled by an abbess, who was usually a lady of the French royal family.

In England most abbeys were ruined after the dissolution of the monasteries by Henry VIII. Their lands and buildings fell into the hands of the king's friends, who usually converted part into a dwelling-house and left the rest to crumble. The process of destruction was hastened when lead was removed from the church roof and stones were taken for other building purposes. In some places, however, where it could be proved that the townspeople had been accustomed to worship with the monks on Sundays, the abbey church became a parish church.

Abbeys which now house monastic communities in England are relatively modern establishments. Probably the best known is Buckfast Abbey in Devon, which was built in modern times by the monks themselves.

¶ LINDLEY, KENNETH. *Abbeys and Monasteries*, 1961; VALE, EDMUND. *Abbeys and Priories*, 1955

See also MONASTERIES.

Abdication (from the Latin *abdicare*, to disown): the renunciation, usually voluntary, of office before the end of the term for which it was assumed. The word is usually applied to the abdication of sovereign power. Military disaster, political difficulties and personal reasons have all caused abdications. The Habsburg emperor Charles V (1520–55), worn out by the problems of his huge empire, pronounced his abdication on 25 October 1555. Napoleon I of France (1804–14) abdicated after his defeat in 1813–14. Defeat and revolution preceded the abdication in 1917 of Nicholas II of Russia (1894–1917). In Germany, on 28 October 1918, the sailors at Kiel mutinied. Twelve days later a republic was declared and next day the Kaiser drove to Holland where he abdicated.

In 1936 Edward VIII of England was told by his ministers that he must renounce either his proposed marriage or his throne. As a constitutional sovereign he was obliged to accept his ministers' advice and, after a brief period of indecision, the King abdicated. Other modern examples have been the abdication of Wilhelmina of the Netherlands in favour of her daughter Juliana (1948); and of Leopold III of Belgium in favour of his son Baudouin (1951).

Abdul Hamid.

Abdul Hamid (1842–1918): sultan of Turkey 1876–1909. A despotic and ruthless ruler, aptly nicknamed "the Damned", among whose major infamies was the massacre of some 80,000 Armenians. His resistance to reform, his perennial misgovernment and use of espionage and wholesale arrest finally brought about his deposition by the Young Turks in 1909. *See also* TURKEY and YOUNG TURKS.

Aborigines: the native or earliest known inhabitants of a country, particularly before colonisation by another people (from Latin *ab origine*, "from the beginning"); e.g. Australian Aborigines (full-blooded as distinct from half-castes) now number about 140,000 out of a total population of 15,265,000 (1983) on the continent.

¶ GAMACK, RONALD S. *What Became of the Australian Aborigines?* 1969

Accolade: the conferring of knighthood, usually by the sovereign, signified by a touch on shoulder or neck, or in some cases by embrace or touch of hand (from Latin *collum*, "neck"). In earlier times every knight had the right to create other knights, especially on the field of battle.

Acre: a port of Israel on the Mediterranean, of military and commercial importance from very early times. Renamed St Jean d'Acre by the Crusaders, retaken by Saladin and again by Richard I, it remained the chief seaport of the Christian kingdom of Jerusalem until the Muslim conquest. In 1791 Napoleon's attack was repulsed with the assistance of British seamen. Acre had become independent of the Turkish Pashas in 1749, but in 1840 a fleet under the British admiral Sir Robert Stopford expelled the Egyptians and restored it to the Turks. Israel took it from the Arabs in 1948 and has expanded the city with massive housing and industrial projects, including steel manufacture.

Acts: literally, things done or accomplished, as in the Acts of the Apostles in the Bible. In ancient Rome a daily gazette called the *Acta Diurna* was published containing a summary of proceedings in the courts, public assemblies and events of popular interest. The same word is used in many countries for the laws made by parliaments and other ruling bodies.

Adams, John (1735–1826): second president of the USA (1797–1801). A conscientious and courageous lawyer, he led the opposition to British rule and helped draft the Declaration of Independence. He was a distinguished ambassador to Britain from 1785 to 1788 and was chosen president succeeding Washington in 1796.

Adams, John Quincy (1767–1848): sixth president of the USA (1825–29) and son of the above. His presidency, owing to the sustained opposition of Andrew Jackson and his supporters, was the least successful part of a distinguished career. As Secretary of State under President Monroe, he drew up the famous Monroe Doctrine (*see* separate entry).

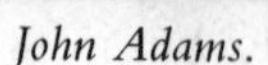

John Adams. *John Quincey Adams.*

Adams, Samuel (1722–1803): statesman and another member of the redoubtable family which played such a major role in 18th- and 19th-century American history. A shrewd and adroit politician, he was a major influence on public opinion, organised the "Boston Tea-Party" and signed the Declaration of Independence.

Aden Protectorate: This term formerly included a strip of the south-eastern coast of Arabia from the Red Sea for some 800 miles [1300 kilometres] towards the Persian Gulf and enclosed the town and colony of Aden. Since 1967 all this land (which includes the former East Aden Protectorate) and the old Federation of Southern Arabia has been incorporated under the Republic of South Yemen.

Aden itself is a small area of land near the southern exit of the Red Sea. The old town is situated in a steep-sided crater, while the old port is somewhat detached from it. Aden developed as a focus of caravans engaged in the exchange of goods between the eastern and western worlds. Sea trade began to supplant the caravans in Roman times: though ships could not sail into the wind, Arab dhows could easily be carried eastward by the south-west monsoons in summer and could return westward in winter under the north-east monsoons. When the Suez Canal opened, Aden was an easily protected site guarding the route to India, well placed as a store for coal and later for oil. Population in 1983: 2,086,000.

Adenauer, Konrad (1876–1967): chancellor of the Federal Republic of Germany (West Germany) from 1949 to 1963. At

the head of a Christian Democrat government, he led the West Germans out of complete defeat in World War II towards economic recovery, based on friendship with the West, especially France and the USA.

Adrian IV (Nicholas Breakspear, d. 1159): the only Englishman to become pope. His pontificate is marked by at least two causes of future trouble in English and European history – his grant to Henry II of the sovereignty of Ireland in 1155 and his bitter struggle with the Emperor Frederick which began the long quarrel between the popes and the Hohenstaufen emperors.

Adrian IV (Nicholas Breakspear).

Aegean Civilisation: the prehistoric civilisation of Greece and the Aegean basin. The lands and islands of the Aegean Sea always had a certain unity. From Troy to Crete and from Cyprus to Corinth, all places were subject to the same influences. The earliest palaces at Troy and Knossos in Crete can be dated to before 3000 BC, and many of the Cyclades Islands produced excellent primitive sculpture. The pre-Greek peoples were gradually supplanted by Greek-speaking tribes from about 2000 BC and the effect of the successive waves of colonists can clearly be seen in all centres. The Greek language formed a very strong link. The Aegean was also influenced by Egyptian art and religion as well as by the records of the civilisations of the Near East. The result was a dynamic society which was always ready to accept new ideas.
See also ATHENS, GREECE (ANCIENT), MINOAN and MYCENAEAN CIVILISATIONS.

Aeroplane: *see* AVIATION.

Afghanistan: bordering on north-west Pakistan and a political entity since 1747. The country has had a turbulent history, its importance being that it lies on the invasion route into India by the Khyber and Bolan Passes. Disputes for control between Britain and Russia were a feature of 19th century Afghan politics. In 1979 a Marxist regime asked for Soviet military assistance to maintain it in power.

Africa: the second largest continent, with an area of 11,600,000 square miles [30,041,740 square kilometres] and a population in 1982 of 504,000,000.

The first creatures who made and used tools were probably born in Africa; and it was probably here that man first walked the earth. Much later, about 5,000 years ago, one of the most advanced peoples in the world lived in Africa; these were the Egyptians who later were to form part of the Roman Empire which stretched along the north coast of Africa. Here Christianity spread and reached down to Ethiopia. Later, in the 7th century AD, the Arabs invaded Africa and introduced another great dynamic religion, that of Islam, which spread down the east coast of Africa and across the north to Morocco.

From about AD 800 for some 500 years the Muslim or Islamic civilisation was as advanced as any in the world: during the same time there was a succession of large states or empires in the grassland area on the southern border of the Sahara. At the time of the Hundred Years War in England (*c.* 1350–1450) a visiting Arab wrote of the people of Mali, "they are seldom unjust, their Sultan shows no mercy to anyone who is guilty of the least act of it. There is complete security in their country." Mali was eventually absorbed by Songhai with its fine university of Timbuktu. Meanwhile on the East African coast there was a flourishing trade in gold, ivory and slaves based on coastal settlements in which the Swahili people lived. In the interior, mass migrations of people were taking place which continued throughout the sixteenth and seventeenth centuries.

A typical Kikuyu village with traditional grass-roofed huts.

Once Europeans had explored the coastline of Africa it was not long before they began to trade with the people on the coast, and over the next 400 years European governments came to control most of Africa. In 1482 Portugal's discovery of the estuary of the River Congo gave her control of Angola and put her in contact with the Congo, which was one of the few large African states near the coast. In her overseas empire in Brazil there was a huge demand for slaves, for which Angola was the supply base, and the Congo was torn apart. Later Denmark and Holland also established slave stations on the west coast and England played a leading part in this hideous traffic. On the east coast Arabs were prominent slavers. Slavery was not new to Africa, but exploitation on this scale was, and it was made easier by the introduction of firearms. The slave trade continued until the 19th century when England took the lead in stopping it (*see* SLAVERY).

Unloading peanuts in a modern processing plant in Senegal.

After the Napoleonic wars Britain took over the Cape from the Dutch, and friction soon arose with the Afrikaaners. Many trekked inland to get away from the government, and friction between Britain and the Afrikaaners resulted in two wars. Today South Africa is an independent republic.

In Europe very little was known of the interior of Africa, which was difficult to reach, until the 19th century, when the exploration of Africa became the adventure of the age. The journeys of Mungo Park, Livingstone and Stanley excited intense European interest in Africa. After them came traders and missionaries,

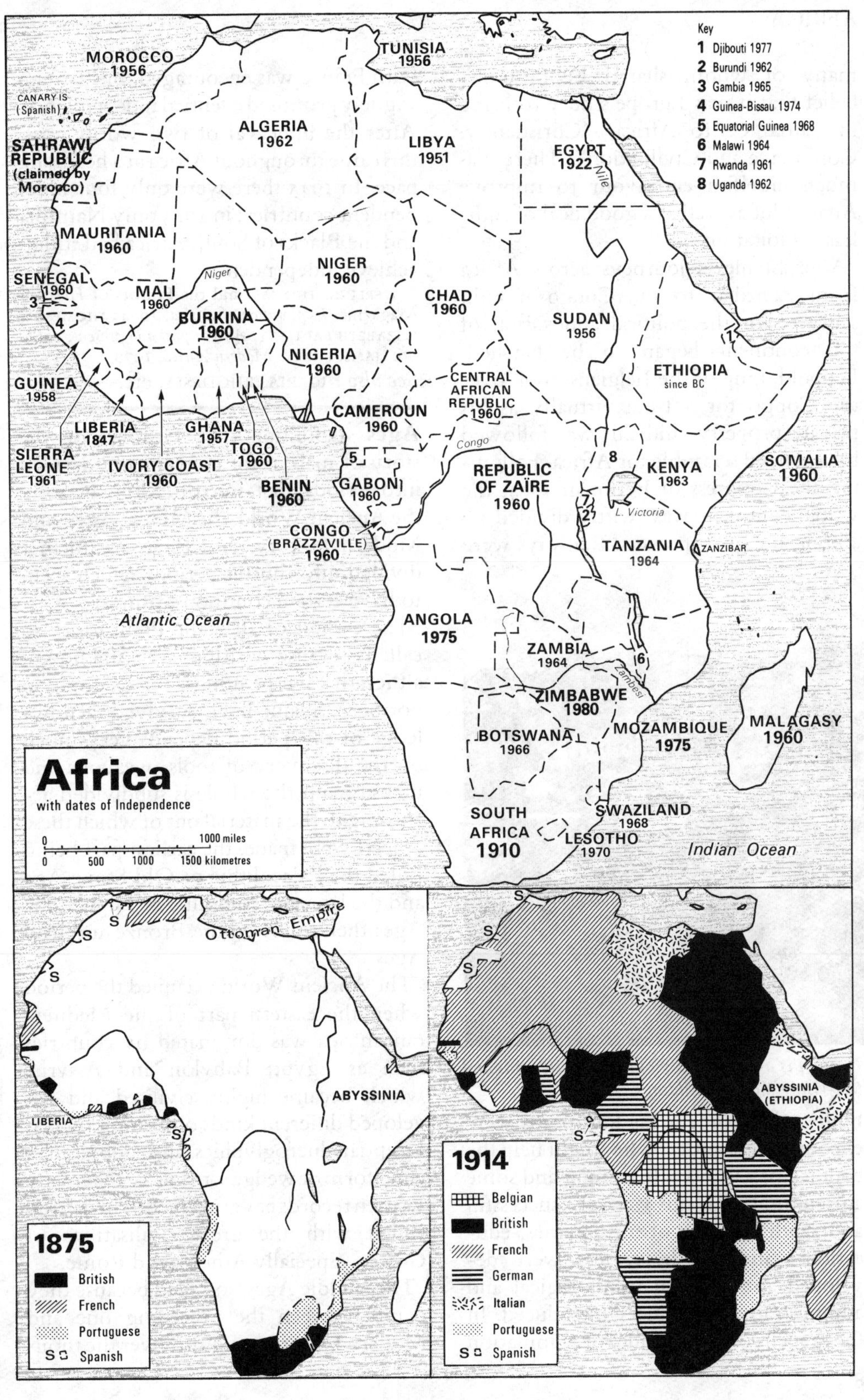

Africa
with dates of Independence
0 1000 miles
0 500 1000 1500 kilometres
Key
1 Djibouti 1977
2 Burundi 1962
3 Gambia 1965
4 Guinea-Bissau 1974
5 Equatorial Guinea 1968
6 Malawi 1964
7 Rwanda 1961
8 Uganda 1962
MOROCCO 1956
CANARY IS (Spanish)
SAHRAWI REPUBLIC (claimed by Morocco)
TUNISIA 1956
ALGERIA 1962
LIBYA 1951
EGYPT 1922
Nile
MAURITANIA 1960
SENEGAL 1960
MALI 1960
Niger
NIGER 1960
CHAD 1960
SUDAN 1956
ETHIOPIA since BC
BURKINA 1960
NIGERIA 1960
GUINEA 1958
CENTRAL AFRICAN REPUBLIC 1960
CAMEROUN 1960
LIBERIA 1847
GHANA 1957
SIERRA LEONE 1961
IVORY COAST 1960
TOGO 1960
BENIN 1960
Congo
GABON 1960
REPUBLIC OF ZAÏRE 1960
KENYA 1963
SOMALIA 1960
L. Victoria
CONGO (BRAZZAVILLE) 1960
TANZANIA 1964
ZANZIBAR
Atlantic Ocean
ANGOLA 1975
ZAMBIA 1964
Zambesi
ZIMBABWE 1980
MALAGASY 1960
BOTSWANA 1966
MOZAMBIQUE 1975
SOUTH AFRICA 1910
SWAZILAND 1968
LESOTHO 1970
Indian Ocean
1875
British
French
Portuguese
Spanish
Ottoman Empire
LIBERIA
ABYSSINIA
1914
Belgian
British
French
German
Italian
Portuguese
Spanish
ABYSSINIA (ETHIOPIA)

many of whom shared Livingstone's belief that it was Europe's duty to bring the three Cs to Africa, "Christianity, Commerce and Civilisation". There was much unselfish endeavour to improve Africa's lot as well as a good deal of ruthless exploitation.

After Stanley's journeys across Africa from Zanzibar to the Congo mouth, schemes for the political annexation of the continent began to be hatched. Leopold, king of the Belgians, took over the Congo for a time virtually as his private property, and this was followed by a general scramble for Africa. Following the Congress of Berlin in 1884, the whole continent was swiftly divided up among the great powers. Railways were

Nairobi is a thriving city of broad boulevards and fast-rising modern buildings.

built and in some areas Europeans were encouraged as settlers who might help the country pay its way. In mining and some agricultural areas this was very successful and, with the help of missionaries, educational and health services were developed and modern technological and administrative machinery introduced. In the French colonies the idea of assimilation with France was encouraged, but Britain vaguely promised eventual independence. After the upheaval of two world wars, this came throughout Africa at a headlong pace. In 1945 there were only four independent countries; in 1985 only Namibia and the Blacks of South Africa had still to achieve independence.

¶ STERLING, THOMAS, and the Editors of *Horizon* Magazine. *Exploration of Africa,* 1964; THOMPSON, ELIZABETH BARTLETT. *Africa: past and present*, 1968; WILLIAMS, BARRY. *Modern Africa*, 1970

See also NIGERIA, RHODESIA, etc.

Ages (definition of)**:** History, or the story of man, is for convenience divided into periods; first, into three long periods, the Ancient World, the Middle Ages, and Modern History, and these are further divided into shorter periods which seem to have certain common features.

The earliest of all is the Prehistoric; so called because writing was unknown, although cave paintings, for example in northern Spain, have survived. Knowledge of this period depends very much on the discovery of tools, weapons and utensils, and the whole is subdivided according to the material out of which these objects were made, the earliest part being called the Palaeolithic or Old Stone Age and the later the Neolithic or New Stone Age; then followed the Bronze and Iron Ages.

The Ancient World occupied the period when the eastern part of the Mediterranean Sea was dominated by countries such as Egypt, Babylon and Assyria, which became highly civilised and developed different kinds of writing such as Egyptian hieroglyphics and Babylonian cuneiform or wedge writing, so that many written records have survived. This period ended with the great civilisations of Greece, especially Athens, and Rome.

The Middle Ages, so called because they come between the preceding one and Modern History, roughly cover the thousand years between the occupation of Rome by the Goths in the early 5th century until the middle of the 15th century. The first part of this era, from about AD 400 to 800, is called the Dark Ages because, as a result of the Barbarian invasions of Europe, the learning of the Greeks and Romans seemed to have disappeared, though it was in fact preserved by the monasteries and, at the end of the period, revived by the emperor Charlemagne. Later there followed two periods when a great revival of learning took place, both known as Renaissance periods, the earlier one as the 12th century Renaissance and the more extensive one, known simply as the Renaissance, extending from the mid-14th to the 16th century, so overlapping the Middle Ages and the Modern period.

In the Modern period, the 16th century is often called the Age of the Reformation, when the unity of the Catholic Church in the West was broken by reformers such as Martin Luther and John Calvin.

Many things can give rise to the name of an age: a dominant character, as in the Age of Louis XIV, the Victorian Age, etc.; a climate of thought and social change, as in the Age of Reason and the Age of Revolution; economic and industrial upheaval, as in the Age of Steam. The great period of oceanic voyages and exploration of the late 15th and the 16th centuries is widely known as the Age of Discovery; and the landing of the American astronauts on the moon on 20 July 1969 has set indelibly the name Space Age on a new era of adventure and experience – an era epitomised by Neil Armstrong's words as he took the first tentative steps outside the lunar module *Eagle*: "That's one small step for a man, one giant leap for mankind."

Two important points must, however, be borne in mind; one is that historians hold differing views about the dating of periods and it is clear that exact dates cannot mark their beginning and end; and, second, that the rate of change has been much more rapid in some countries than in others; for example, the highly civilised Romans under Julius Caesar invading Britain in 55 BC found the Britons still living in the Iron Age, and in Australia today a very small group of Aborigines belongs, in some respects, to the Stone Age.

Agincourt, Battle of (24 October 1415): one of the most memorable battles in European history and a classic example of the failure of the medieval knight to adapt himself to changing modes of warfare. Fought between Henry V of England, with about 9,000 men, and the French array of nearer 60,000, at Agincourt in northern France, the battle resulted in a devastating defeat for the French who lost the greater part of their nobility. The encounter took place on rain-sodden ground with the French so confined that they were an easy target for the ruthless English longbowmen, then at the height of their power and efficiency (*see* ARCHERY).

A noble of Artois who was present at the battle tells how "the French had been all night on horseback, and it rained, and the pages, grooms, and others, in leading about the horses, had broken up the ground, which was so soft that the horses could with difficulty step out of the soil... The sad French were so loaded with armour that they could not move forward; and so heavy was their armour that, together with the softness of the ground, they could with difficulty lift their weapons."

¶ HIBBERT, CHRISTOPHER. *Agincourt*, 1964

Agricola, Gnaeus Julius (AD 37–93): Roman general whose achievements are chiefly remembered because of his life, written by his son-in-law Tacitus. He was governor of Britain for seven years and completed the conquest of the country. He was an active propagator of Roman civilisation and encouraged the education of chieftains' sons.

Agricultural Improvers, The: Farming and gardening began when the human race discovered how to grow plants for food instead of having to rely on gathering wild ones, and when men learnt how to breed domestic animals in place of being obliged to hunt wild ones. Ever since then the more enterprising men and women have sought new and better ways of farming and gardening.

The first book on farming to be published in England was the work of Sir Anthony Fitzherbert and his brother John. It appeared in 1523 and gave much practical advice. The authors recommended *mixed* farming (livestock and crops) in preference to crops alone; and today there is still argument about this.

Sir Richard Weston travelled in Flanders during the 17th century and came home enthusiastic about the "new" clover he had seen growing and would himself grow. Great faith is still put in clover for soil improvement.

In Jethro Tull's time (1674–1740) all seed was scattered (broadcast) by hand. He invented a machine that, like the modern

Tull's seed-planting drill from The Farmer's Tools.

drill, places the seed in parallel rows between which it is possible to hoe the soil, thus destroying weeds. He built the drill in 1701 and wrote *Horse-hoeing Husbandry* in 1733.

By means of a book that he called *England's Happiness Increased* (1664) John Forster recommended the "new" crop, potatoes, first brought to the British Isles in 1585 or 1586 by colonists returning from North Carolina. The cultivation of another "new" crop, turnips, was so enthusiastically supported by Lord Townshend (1674–1738) that he got the nickname of "Turnip" Townshend.

Breeders of livestock today honour the name of Robert Bakewell (1725–95). Using Leicester sheep he improved the breed by mating fairly closely related animals and by the use only of those rams whose value had been proved by the high quality of their offspring. In this he was far ahead of his time, for "inbreeding", "progent testing" and "proven sires" are still subjects for discussion.

Thomas Coke, Earl of Leicester (1752–1842) and Francis Russell, fifth Duke of Bedford (1765–1802) held huge gatherings of farmers on their estates when they demonstrated to their visitors some of the methods they believed in. These included row-crop work (following Jethro Tull), the use of bones as manure, rotations in which successive crops benefited each other and the land, the choice of good seed, and crops that fed livestock that produced manure that nourished crops. To Coke is attributed the saying: "Muck is the mother of money." These gatherings were called Sheep-shearings, being held in the month of shearing.

It is only during the present, 20th, century that a belief in the importance of tested seed has become general, and the National Seeds Testing Station was not established until 1917; yet in 1789 William Marshall wrote praising "Pacey's Rye Grass" which was seed collected from strong, leafy, native plants by William Pacey, a Gloucestershire farmer. This he sold to those who shared his belief that you cannot get good crops except from good seed.

Every farmer who cultivates the soil needs a plough, and its design and construction has attracted a lot of attention. Writers from the 16th century onwards have described their ideas about it, and craftsmen experimented with it. Walter Blith wrote at length about its principles of design in *The English Improver Improved* (1652). Today, plough manufacture is in the hands of a few commercial firms, and certain common principles have been adopted. Although every ploughman has strong views about what is a good plough, there have been no revolutionary changes (*see* PLOUGH).

Matters are very different with the harvesting of hay and corn, for the scythe has been slowly replaced by the mower, reaper and reaper-and-binder. Patrick Bell and an American, Cyrus McCormick, were the inventors chiefly concerned, and Joseph Mechi (1802–79) enthusiastically adopted the use of machinery and followed many of the latest practises. Other books must be consulted for information about the improvers of this century. Many of their problems are the same as those that exercised the minds of the early farmers.

In such a worldwide occupation as agriculture, there are few countries that cannot claim to have made some contribution to progress and development. As might be expected, and in view of its vast agricultural resources, the USA has played a vital part, and especially in the introduction of machinery that has revolutionised farming practice, such as the automatic grain binder and the combine harvester and thresher.

To France goes the honour of the first experimental agricultural station, established by Jean Boussingault about 1834 at his farm at Bechelbronn, Alsace. An important early school of scientists specialising in the structure and function of plants worked at Geneva in Switzerland. Germany had an agricultural college as far back as 1817. The Dutch have carried out invaluable research work, especially in the experimental gardens and laboratories at Buitenzorg in the East Indies. Every continent, every country, adds to the sum of knowledge and progress; just as every farm is a repository of thousands of years of inherited skills and past endeavours.

An 18th century engraving from Diderot's Encyclopaedia *showing various methods of ploughing.*

Agriculture: the science and practice of cultivating the land. As one of the earliest activities of man, its history extends much further back than written records. By the time these appear, agriculture was already a highly developed art. Much modern farming is based on the methods of the Romans whose influence can still be traced in a wide variety of practices including stock breeding, vine culture and the use of leguminous crops (peas, beans, etc.) as a means of gathering and conserving nitrogen preparatory to sowing wheat. Farming was, in fact, the only type of business in which an aristocratic Roman senator was allowed to engage, and some very sound advice on good management and on buying a farm can be found, e.g. in the writings of Cato, *c.* 170 BC. He mentions among other things the different types of plough suitable for light and heavy soils, detachable plough-shares, and the importance of siting, drainage, sound farming economy.

¶ LEE, NORMAN E. *Harvests and Harvesting through the Ages*, 1960

See also AGRICULTURAL IMPROVERS; PLOUGH, etc.

Airship: cigar-shaped, navigable, lighter-than-air craft, of which the first, in 1882, was the elongated balloon of Henri Giffard powered by a 3 h.p. engine; followed in 1884 by the electrically powered *La France*. In 1901 Santos-Dumont flew round the Eiffel Tower, and in 1903 the Lebaudy dirigible flew thirty-eight miles [61 km]. Count Ferdinand von Zeppelin had built his first airship in 1900 and, between 1900 and 1914, his "Zeppelins" carried 35,000 passengers without accident. During the First World War they were used for bombing London and the East coast. In 1919 the British R34 made the first Atlantic double crossing, but the crashes of the R101 in 1930 and of the *Hindenburg* in 1937 virtually closed the airship era, although the *Graf Zeppelin* flew for eleven years until 1939. Opinions have varied as to the best type of gas to use, the United States generally preferring helium and British and German experts choosing hydrogen. Structural failures and fire have been responsible for most airship disasters; but apart from essential safety factors a number of other technical problems remain to be solved before the airship can become a thoroughly reliable and economic proposition.

Model of Henri Giffard's airship, 1852.

¶ TOLAND, JOHN. *Ships in the Sky*, 1957

See also AVIATION.

Akbar (ruled 1556–1605): Mogul emperor of India. Grandson of Babar, he subdued northern and central India and extended his control as far south as the River Godavari. His administrative system gave real efficiency to Mogul sovereignty, and his Hindu minister, Todar Mall, carried through the first great land settlement, fixing rents due from cultivators to the Crown.

Akhnaten, Akhenaton, Ikhnaton, etc. (1398–1353 BC): Egyptian pharaoh. Crowned as Amenhotep IV, Akhnaten was the first monotheist, or worshipper of one god. He denied the numerous gods of Egypt, revering only *Aten*, which meant "brightness and heat of

the sun". He changed his name to Akhnaten in honour of his god, and in the sixth year of his reign left Thebes to found a new capital on the eastern bank of the Nile. He named this city Akhetaten, and encouraged artists and craftsmen to make it as beautiful as possible. They altered the formal style of Egyptian art so that the statues and paintings found there are life-like and natural. Not surprisingly, the priests hated the new religion. After Akhnaten's death they forced the court to return to Thebes and the new city was deserted.
See also PHARAOH; TEL EL AMARNA.

Alamein, Battle of (23 October–4 November 1942)**:** battle of World War II which resulted in an important victory for the British army, commanded by General Montgomery, over the Axis forces and led to the surrender of the latter in North Africa. Together with the Russian triumph at Stalingrad shortly afterwards, it marked the turning point of the war. "Before Alamein we survived; after Alamein we conquered," wrote Churchill.

¶ CARVER, MICHAEL. *El Alamein*, 1962; FARRAR-HOCKLEY, ANTHONY. *The War in the Desert*, 1969

Alaric (*c.* 370–410)**:** King of the Visigoths. He was a formidable warrior who ravaged Greece and the Byzantine empire and was the first Teutonic leader to conquer Rome (24 August 410). For a barbarian he sometimes showed considerable clemency and concern for beautiful buildings, etc. When he died, his warriors diverted the course of the River Busento, buried him in the river bed, then turned the water back into its old channel.

Alaska: state of USA in the far north-west of North America. Valuable fisheries, furs, lumber, etc., caused considerable exploitation of the native Indians in the 18th century. In 1824–25 treaties with the United States and Great Britain limited the boundaries of Russian possessions. These were later sold (1867) by the Russians to America for the comparatively trifling sum of $7,200,000. The most dramatic event in its later history was the great Klondike Gold Rush of 1896. In more recent times it has gained strategic importance owing to its position on the polar air route between the North American continent and the Far East. Oil has also been discovered and by 1982 provided the bulk of the state's revenues. In 1959 Alaska became the 49th state of the USA.

¶ MASTERS, ROBERT V. *Alaska in Pictures*, 1965

The Isabell Pass along the Richardson Highway, the only road between Fairbanks and Anchorage, Alaska.

Albert of Saxe-Coburg Gotha (1819–61): husband of Queen Victoria, and Prince Consort. His influence in politics was often resented, but he was a conscientious and self-sacrificing support to the Queen. He was greatly interested in the applications of science and art to industry and inspired the Great Exhibition of 1851.

A photograph by Roger Fenton of Queen Victoria and Prince Albert, the Prince Consort, in 1854.

Albion: probably the oldest name for Britain (from Latin *albus*, white) and suggested by the white chalk cliffs of the south-east coast. It occurs as early as the 4th century BC and some of the most powerful Anglo-Saxon kings were known as Kings of the Isles of Albion.

Alchemy: that branch of medieval chemistry chiefly devoted to finding the panacea, or universal cure; and also the so-called philosopher's stone, which was credited with the power of giving eternal youth and of transmitting base metals into gold. The study engaged the attention of serious men of science of both East and West for many centuries.

Alcuin or **Albinus** (*c.* 735–804): English scholar and theologian, who exercised a profound influence on European scholarship. As adviser to Charlemagne, he made the emperor's court a centre of culture and education. Among his contributions was the introduction of the style of handwriting known as the Carolingian minuscule, on which our Roman type is based.

Alexander III, called **"the Great"** (356–323 BC): king of Macedon. Son of the great Philip II (382–336 BC), Alexander was tutored by Aristotle and had considerable military experience when he came to the throne in 336 BC. Quickly crushing a Greek rebellion he marched at the head of 40,000 troops to invade Persia. Important battles on the River Granicus (334 BC), at Issus (333), Tyre (332) and Gaugamela (331) destroyed the Persian resistance, and Egypt was occupied in late 332 BC. After Gaugamela, Alexander moved east and north, visiting and subduing all parts of the Persian Empire, founding Greek cities and destroying the remnants of his opponents. Crossing the Hindu Kush he invaded India but, after defeating Porus, leader of

the Punjab princes, on the River Hydaspes (326 BC), his troops mutinied and he was forced to return. He was preparing to conquer Arabia when he died before his thirty-third birthday. Alexander was one of the great generals in history, excelling in the brilliant combination of heavy infantry (the phalanx) and heavy cavalry (the Companions). But he was more than

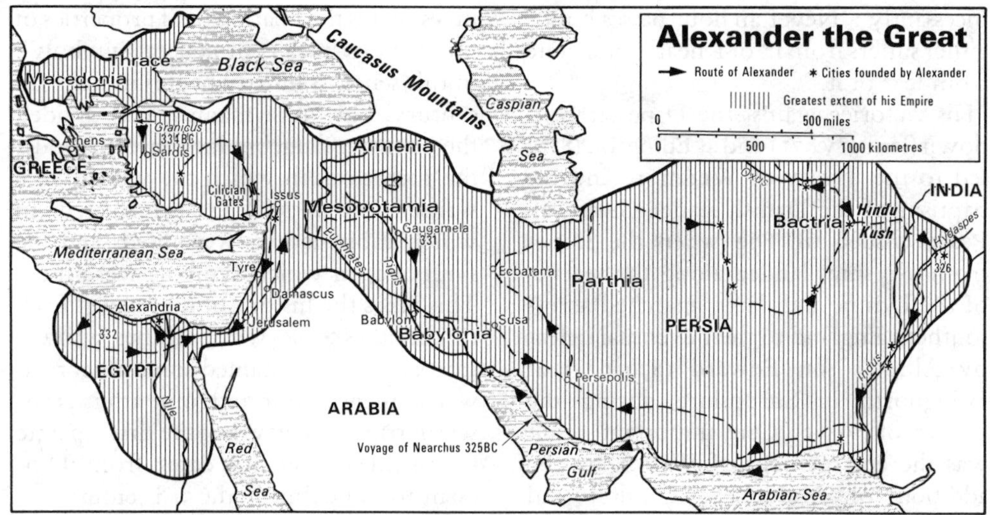

a general. Throughout the Persian Empire he introduced Greek ideas and was determined to fuse conquered and conquerors together into one people. His work gave a unity to certain parts of the Near East that was to be vitally important in later days.

¶ MERCER, CHARLES. *Alexander the Great*, 1964; MITCHISON, NAOMI. *Alexander the Great*, 1964

Alexander Nevski (*c.* 1220–63): Russian national hero, later made a saint, who received his additional name from his great defeat of the Swedish army on the banks of the River Neva (15 July 1240). He later defeated the Teutonic Order of knights at Lake Peipus (5 April 1242).

Alexandria: a city on the Nile delta, founded by Alexander the Great in 332 BC. It quickly became the capital of Hellenistic Egypt and developed into a vast commercial and artistic centre which flourished for over six centuries. After the decline of Athens, important literary men flocked there and had a great influence on Rome. It housed a famous library, burnt down in 48 BC, and one of the seven wonders of the ancient world – the lighthouse on the Island of Pharos. Antony and Cleopatra died at Alexandria, and under the Roman Empire it became a vital port for the export of corn. A cosmopolitan city, its population was a mixture of Semitic, Greek and Roman elements. Today it is Egypt's chief port. Population in 1980: 2,320,000.

The lighthouse at Pharos, built by Sostratus in the reign of Ptolemy II and later destroyed by earthquake.

Alfred (849–899), called **"the Great"**: king of the West Saxons. He was born at Wantage in 849 by his father Ethelwulf's first marriage. He suffered from a mysterious ailment which, according to his biographer, Asser, troubled him incessantly. "Never an hour passes but he either suffers from it, or is nearly desperate from fear of it."

His victories against the Danes at Ashdown (January 871) and at Edington (878) led to the Treaty of Wedmore and the baptism of the Danish leader Guthrum. Peace ensued till 892 when the Danes from 250 ships landed along the reaches of the Lympe and, later, marched across southern England to their eventual defeat by Alfred's son Edward (870–924) at Bridgnorth in Shropshire during the winter of 895–6. One important result was the enlargement of Wessex by the addition of Middlesex, London and Southern Mercia.

Alfred developed military power by building forts and by organising the militia of "fyrd" into interchangeable active service and farming sections. The forts were garrisoned full-time. The army was commanded by ealdormen. He debeloped naval power by using patrols off the East Anglian coast in 882 and 885 and by designing new ships.

His newly acquired Latin enabled him to supervise the compilers of the Anglo-Saxon Chronicles and the translators of Bede's Church History and the works of St Gregory. He planned universal education by founding schools and encouraging scholars at his court. His Christianity is shown by his rebuilding of churches and monasteries. He encouraged commerce and fine craftsmanship and rewrote the laws in the common speech. He is the greatest and noblest of English kings and the only one to have earned the title of "the Great", though this was not bestowed till the 17th century.

¶ OMAN, CAROLA. *Alfred, King of the English*, 1939; REEVES, MARJORIE. *Alfred and the Danes*, 1974

Algebra: according to the *Oxford Dictionary* "the part of mathematics which investigates the relations and properties of numbers by means of general symbols". In this sense its history begins in the 17th century, but Nesselmann (1842) divided the history of algebra into three periods: the rhetorical, in which the words were written out in full; the syncopated, in which abbreviations were used; and the symbolic, in which symbols were used. This takes the history of the subject back to about 1550 BC when Ahmes wrote a treatise which contained some algebra as well as mensuration and some attempt towards trigonometry, but the first separate treatment of algebra dates from Diophantus some time in the 3rd century.

The word itself appears to have originated about AD 800 as part of the title of a work by al-Khowârizmî, and its meaning appears to refer to the process known to some young students as "taking a quantity across to the other side of an equation and changing its sign".

Algeria: an independent republic in northern Africa, where the fertile coastal plain is protected by the Atlas Mountains from the hungry wandering peoples of the Sahara Desert. In Roman times wheat and fruit crops were irrigated by control of streams which flowed down the mountains. The area became part of the Byzantine Empire and from the seventh century was controlled first by the Arabs and then the Turks (1518–1830). Its harbours later became haunts of Barbary pirates until they were driven out by the French after 1830. Products of the plain became more valuable than ever and were protected by French troops in the mountain gaps. During World War II General de Gaulle made Algiers the headquarters of the French government in exile (1943–44). After seven years of bitter guerilla warfare by Algerian nationalists, independence was granted in 1962. Population in 1983: 20,695,000.

Alphabets: the letters of a language in their fixed order. The word is made up of the first two letters of the Greek alphabet – *alpha* and *beta*. Pre-alphabetic systems of written communication, such as the cuneiform ("wedge-shaped") signs of the Sumerians or the Egyptian hieroglyphics, used thousands of different symbols to convey meaning, but alphabetic writing needs only twenty-five or so letters to make any number of words. The ideal alphabet would have a single letter for each sound but the variety of accents and the constant changing of sounds in the speech of any given language would seem to render this impossible. The main alphabets in use have from twenty-two to thirty-five letters. English has twenty-six and about forty-two different sounds expressed by using, sometimes, the same letter to represent more than one sound, or by putting different letters together.

It is not known how the alphabet came to be formed. Its history goes back over 3,500 years when it is believed an alphabet was invented by the north-western Semites. This theory does not rule out the possibility that the older systems influenced its unknown creator, but any link between the alphabet and those systems has never been found.

The original alphabet developed through four main branches: (1) the Canaanite branch, subdivided into two secondary branches, viz the early Hebrew alphabet used by the Israelites of the Old Testament and the alphabet of the Phoenicians used also in that nation's colonies, of which Carthage was one; (2) the Aramaic branch used in western and central Asia, which spread to India, Java and Mongolia and gave rise to the Arabic and modern Hebrew alphabets; (3) the South Semitic branch used mainly in Arabia but which spread into Africa. The Ethiopic alphabet derives from it.

The fourth branch was the Greek alphabet and this was the most important of them all. Scholars are agreed upon its source from the north-west Semitic alphabet, but date its creation about 1000 BC. The shapes, values and sequence of the letters are essentially the same as the Semitic and so are the names, which are words taken from the Semitic languages but meaningless in Greek. The relationship, therefore, is clear, and, since the Semitic is earlier, there can be no doubt that the Greek derived from it. Because writing was not uniform among the many Greek states, there was a variety of local alphabets. These gradually approximated more and more to one another and, in 403 BC, the Ionic alphabet of Miletus was officially adopted at Athens. By the middle of the 4th century BC the Ionic became the common, classical Greek alphabet of twenty-four letters. The Greeks referred to it for many centuries, not as their "alphabet", but as *grammata* (letters) or *stoicheia* (elements or rudiments). The earliest record of the word "alphabet" is in a work attributed to Hippolytus of Rome which mentions "ex Graecorum alphabeto". If this attribution is accurate it places the date some time before AD 235 when Hippolytus died. The Greeks modernised and improved the Semitic script, introducing vowels and using some of the consonants for this purpose. They discarded some consonants and introduced others, improved the form of some of the letters and produced an alphabet which holds a unique place in the history of writing and through which a great many other alphabets derived, notably the Etruscan alphabet (through which came the Latin or Roman alphabet) and the Cyrillic, used in Russia and many of its satellites. Thus the Greek alphabet may be regarded as the ancestor of all European alphabets.

Of the many alphabets to which the

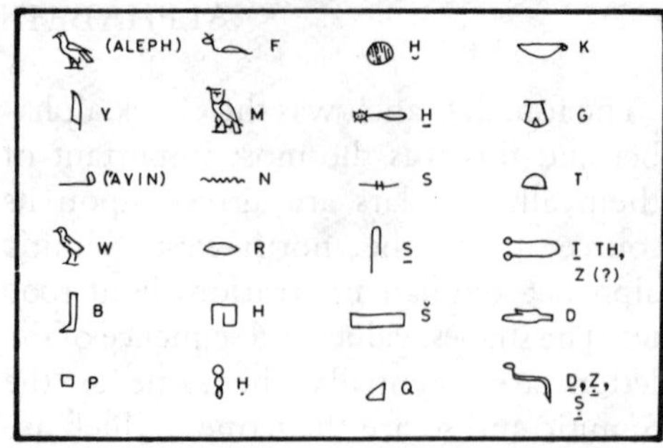

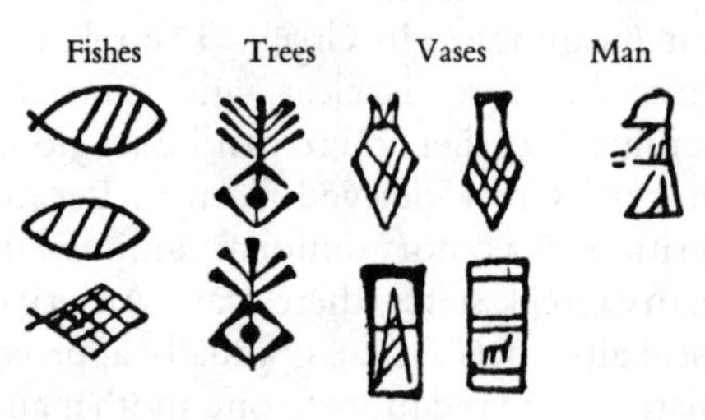

PICTOGRAMS

MAN, ANIMALS, AND PARTS OF THE HUMAN BODY

MAN	WOMAN	CHILD	MOUTH	NOSE	EYE	HAND	FOOT
HORSE	TIGER	DOG	ELEPHANT	DEER	SHEEP	SILKWORM	TORTOISE

	EGYPTIAN		PHOENICIAN	GREEK				GREEK NAMES	LATIN			HEBREW	HEBREW NAMES
1			𐤀	A	A	λ	α	Alpha	A	A	ꝺ ɑ a	א	Aleph
2			𐤁	8	B	B	β	Beta	B	B	B b	ב	Beth
3			𐤂	7	Γ	Γ	∫ γ	Gamma	<	C	C G ç ğ g	ג	Gimel
4			𐤃	Δ	Δ	Δ	δ	Delta	D	D	∂ δ d	ד	Daleth
5			𐤄	∃	E	Є	ε	Epsilon	E	E	e e	ה	He
6			𐤅	Y	YF		ϝ	(Digamma)	F	F	f f	ו	Vau
7			𐤆	‡	I	Z	ζ ζ	Zeta	‡	Z	z	ז	Zain
8			𐤇	日	H	H	h η	Eta	日	H	h h	ח	Cheth
9			𐤈	⊕	⊙	Θ	θ ϑ	Theta	⊗			ט	Teth
10			𐤉	≀	I	I	ι	Iota	I	I	i j	י	Iod
11			𐤊	K	K	K	κ κ	Kappa	K	K	k	כ	Caph
12			𐤋	V	Λ	λ	λ	Lambda	L	L	l l	ל	Lamed
13			𐤌	M	M	M	μ μ	Mu	M	M	m m	מ	Mem
14			𐤍	N	N	N	ν ν	Nu	N	N	n n	נ	Nun
15			𐤎	‡	Ξ	Ξ	ξ	Xi	⊞	+	x x	ס	Samech
16			𐤏	o	O	O	ο	Omicron	O			ע	Ain
17			𐤐	˥	Γ	Π	π ϖ	Pi	P	P	p	פ	Pe
18			𐤑	M	M				M			צ	Tzade
19			𐤒	Φ	Ϙ				Ϙ	Q	q q	ק	Koph
20			𐤓	P	P	P	ρ ρ	Rho	R	R	r r	ר	Resh
21			𐤔	Σ	Σ	C	c σ	Sigma	S	S	ſ ſ s	ש	Shin
22			𐤕	T	T	T	τ	Tau	T	T	τ t	ת	Tau
	I	II	III	IV	V	VI	VII		VIII	IX	X	XI	

Above left: Earliest hieroglyphic consonantal signs.
Middle left: Early Elamite pictorial symbols.
Below left: Chinese pictograms. All from The Alphabet, *by David Diringer (Hutchinson 1968).*
Above: Comparative alphabets.

Etruscan alphabet gave rise, the Latin was the most important and is the basis of the alphabets of western, central and northern Europe and, of course, of the English alphabet.

The Runic alphabet, thought to be derived from a North Etruscan alphabet, was used by the Teutonic peoples until displaced by Latin, and from about AD 500 to 1000 it was also used in England. In the 4th century AD a Gaelic alphabet in a peculiar script called Ogham was used for a time, but for the most part in southern Ireland, Wales and Scotland. An interesting theory about this script is that it was invented by the Druids as a secret code for private signalling. Another is that it was the signalling code of the Roman army and known to the native conscripts.

The superiority of the alphabet over all other systems of writing is such that it is used by nearly all civilised peoples. It passes easily from one language to another and thus many languages use the same alphabet, e.g. Croatian, Czech, Dutch, English, French, German, Hungarian, Italian, Polish, Portuguese, Spanish, Turkish (for official documents), Welsh and others.

¶ DIRINGER, DAVID. *Writing*, 1962

Ambassador: a high ranking official representing his government in the capital of another country and resident in the building or offices known as the Embassy. An Ambassador Extraordinary is one sent on a special mission. An Ambassador Plenipotentiary is one with full powers to sign treaties, etc., for his government.

Ambulance: a moving hospital unit following an army in the field or a specially fitted conveyance for invalids and the wounded. Surgical treatment on the scene of battle is a recent development in warfare and dates only from the end of the 18th century. Formerly it had been a follow-up arrangement, arriving a day or two after the engagement, and the rough-and-ready improvisations of the soldiery were a poor substitute.

The American Civil War saw a remarkable development of an efficient ambulance organisation, especially in the provision of properly equipped and staffed railway hospitals. An important landmark in the treatment of casualties in the field was the Geneva Convention of 1864 by which, subject to certain conditions, hospital and ambulance staff were declared neutral by both sides.

America, Discovery of: The continents of America were discovered by peoples from Asia of Mongoloid type about 13,000 years ago. The Bering Straits, which separate western Russia from Alaska, were crossed by these primitive hunters at the end of the last Ice Age. In the next 4,000 years they occupied all the different climatic regions of both continents, reaching the southernmost point of Patagonia before 7000 BC. Meantime these so-called "Indians" of America remained hunters, whether they lived in the tundra, the prairies or in the tropical forests. But on the high plateau of Mexico and the mountains of the Andes some Indians became farmers, growing maize as their main crop. Between 1500 BC and AD 1500 they developed their unique civilisation, while remaining cut off from the rest of the world.

As far as we know the Vikings from Norway were the only people who found their way to America during this period of 3,000 years. The Viking sagas tell the story of their expeditions. They had settled on remote Iceland in AD 874, and an expedition led by Eric the Red reached Greenland in 982. Eric's son Leif the Lucky reached the mainland of America about twenty years later, and called his discovery "Vinland". Remains of Viking settlements were discovered recently in Newfoundland, but the area Leif called "Vinland", with its wild grapes and mild climate, must have been further south on the mainland of North America. These settlements do not seem to have survived for long, and other Europeans, knew nothing about them (*see* VIKINGS).

In the 15th century, when Portuguese and Italian sailors were discovering various groups of islands in the Atlantic, such as the Canaries and the Azores, they knew nothing about America until it was rediscovered. There was talk of more islands across the Atlantic – "Atlantis" and "Brasil". John Cabot, an Italian seaman who sailed from Bristol in 1497, was the first European to see the North American mainland since the Vikings. He reached the island he named Newfoundland and then explored some of the mainland coast. Christopher Columbus, another Italian, had already in 1492 reached the islands in the Gulf of Mexico which he called the "Indies" and claimed them for Spain. Columbus thought he had found an easy route to the riches of the East. He called the natives Indians, and even after three more voyages he still claimed he was on the eastern edge of Asia. As a result, the newly discovered world was not named after Columbus.

Another Italian received this honour, though he deserved it less than Cabot or Columbus. Amerigo Vespucci had accompanied several expeditions along the coast of South America. His writings were widely published in Europe and he convinced people that a great new continent lay between Europe and Asia. A map of the world, printed in Germany in 1507, named this land after Amerigo.

¶ HOBLEY, L. F. *Exploring the Americas*, 1955

American Civil War (1861–65): The origins of the Civil War lay in the antagonism between the agricultural slave-owning South and the industrial non-slave North, both attempting to influence the development of the nation as it expanded westwards. The Civil War was fought largely by young civilians called from the fields and the factories to defend their respective causes. Some Northern soldiers (Yankees) fought to free the slaves, but most were interested in saving the Union of the country. The soldiers of the South (known as Johnny Rebs) fought to protect their homes and region against Northern invasion; some were greatly concerned about the right of a state or states to leave the Union; very few indicated that they were fighting for slavery, but most were deeply interested in maintaining the white man's supremacy over the Negro.

President Abraham Lincoln and General Wallace, photographed by Roger Fenton.

Seven Southern states (South Carolina, Georgia, Mississippi, Florida, Alabama, Louisiana and Texas) left the Union shortly after Abraham Lincoln was elected President (November 1860) on an anti-slavery programme. In February 1861 these states formed a "Confederate" government at Montgomery, Alabama. The war started when Lincoln tried to send supplies to Fort Sumter, which was a Federal garrison commanding the harbour of Charleston. Troops from South Carolina fired on the fort and captured it (14 April 1861). Lincoln appealed for 75,000 volunteers to quell the revolt. Faced with the decision of fighting for or against the Confederacy, Virginia, Tennessee and North Carolina then withdrew from the Union and thus united the South. Military operations begin in 1861 and were on a vast scale. During the war the North recruited over $2\frac{1}{2}$ million men and the South one million. During the four years of fighting 618,000 men died, though two-thirds of these deaths were caused by disease rather than by hostile bullets. The Union had all the advantages – an organised army, over twice the manpower of the South, command of the seas and the nation's industrial might – but it was not until Generals Grant and Sherman emerged to match the dashing leadership of the Southern generals, "Stonewall" Jackson and Robert E. Lee, that the North triumphed. The South finally surrendered in April 1865 at Appomatox Court House, Virginia. *See colour section.*

¶ ALINGTON, A. F. *The Story of the American Civil War*, 1964; ALLT, A. H. *The American Civil War*, 1961

See also CONFEDERACY; GRANT, ULYSSESS; LEE, ROBERT E.; LINCOLN, ABRAHAM; SLAVERY, etc.

American Colonies, The: Following the rediscovery of "America" by Columbus in 1492 several European countries made attempts to establish colonies in the "New World". In the 16th century a Spanish empire was established in

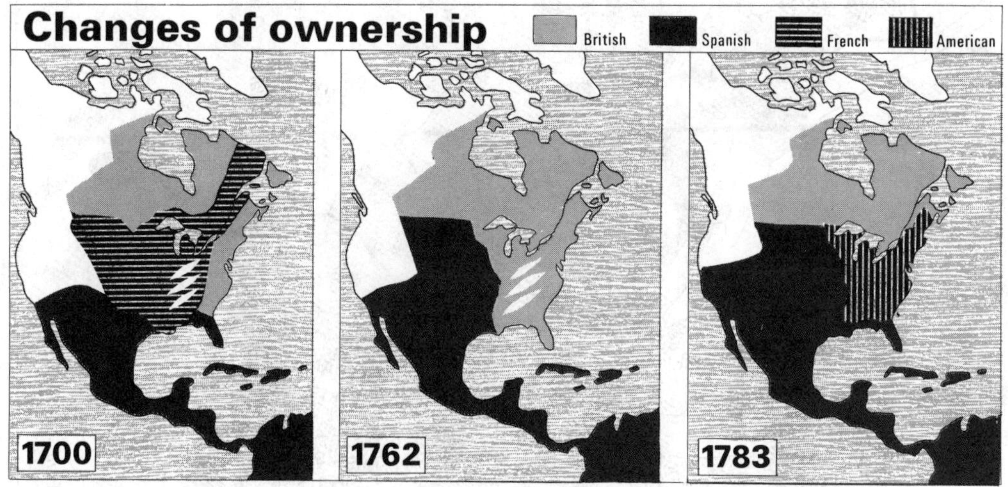

Central and South America and claim laid to the rest of the continent. The Spaniards' claim was upheld by a ruling of Pope Alexander VI in 1494, with the exception that Brazil was allotted to Portugal. But this supremacy was challenged, especially by the English and the Dutch, and after the defeat of the Spanish Armada in 1588 the power of the Spaniards declined. As a result, the English, Dutch and French established colonies on the eastern seaboard of North America. The French settled in the valleys of the St Lawrence, Mississippi and Ohio rivers. In 1614 the Dutch founded a settlement on the Hudson River which they called New Amsterdam (now New York) but, as a result of a military expedition during the second Dutch War in 1664, the area passed into English hands.

The significance of the conquest of the Dutch colony was that it rounded off the English possessions on the Atlantic seaboard and gave England a continuous line of colonies from the St Lawrence in the north to the northern boundary of Spanish Florida in the south. The early permanent English colonies had been made in what were loosely termed "New England" and "Virginia" and the right to conduct the government of these colonies had been granted by James I (ruled 1603–25) to the Plymouth Company and the London Company respectively. The first settlement in Virginia was made at Jamestown in 1609 and the initial one in New England followed eleven years later, when the Puritan refugees, the Pilgrim Fathers, sought religious freedom and commercial opportunities that they could not obtain in England. Their settlement became the colony of Massachusetts. This Puritan colony throve and grew very rapidly but, owing to religious disagreements, many people moved away to establish new settlements, such as Rhode Island, Maine, Connecticut, New Hampshire and Vermont, which subsequently became colonies. Other colonies developed to the south: in 1632 Lord Baltimore founded the colony of Maryland as a refuge for persecuted Roman Catholics; North and South Carolina were founded in 1663; in 1682 William Penn, a Quaker, established Pennsylvania, from which Delaware broke away in 1712; James Oglethorpe, soldier and philanthropist, founded the colony of Georgia in 1733. These were the Thirteen Colonies, administered by Governors appointed by the King of England, which continued to owe their loyalty to the mother country

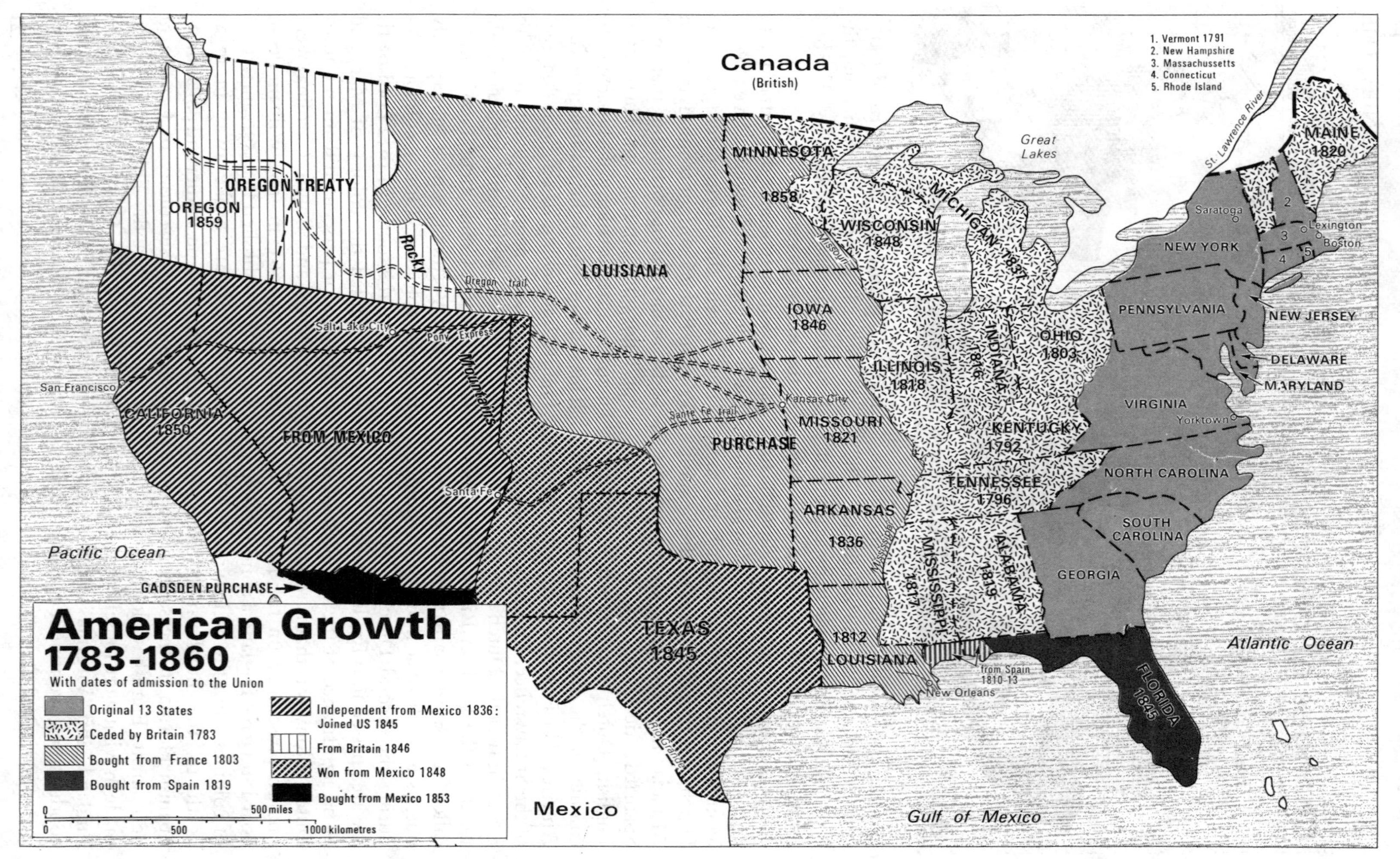
American Growth
1783-1860
With dates of admission to the Union
Original 13 States
Ceded by Britain 1783
Bought from France 1803
Bought from Spain 1819
Independent from Mexico 1836: Joined US 1845
From Britain 1846
Won from Mexico 1848
Bought from Mexico 1853
0
500 miles
0
500
1000 kilometres
Canada
(British)
1. Vermont 1791
2. New Hampshire
3. Massachussetts
4. Connecticut
5. Rhode Island
OREGON TREATY
OREGON
1859
Rocky
Mountains
Oregon trail
LOUISIANA
PURCHASE
MINNESOTA
1858
WISCONSIN
1848
MICHIGAN 1837
Great
Lakes
St. Lawrence River
MAINE
1820
Saratoga
Lexington
Boston
NEW YORK
PENNSYLVANIA
NEW JERSEY
DELAWARE
MARYLAND
VIRGINIA
Yorktown
NORTH CAROLINA
SOUTH
CAROLINA
GEORGIA
OHIO
1803
INDIANA
1816
ILLINOIS
1818
KENTUCKY
1792
TENNESSEE
1796
IOWA
1846
MISSOURI
1821
Kansas City
Missouri
Ohio
Mississippi
ARKANSAS
1836
MISSISSIPPI
1817
ALABAMA
1819
1812
LOUISIANA
New Orleans
from Spain
1810-13
FLORIDA
1845
Salt Lake City
Pony Express
Santa Fe trail
Santa Fe
San Francisco
CALIFORNIA
1850
FROM MEXICO
TEXAS
1845
Rio Grande
GADSDEN PURCHASE
Pacific Ocean
Mexico
Gulf of Mexico
Atlantic Ocean

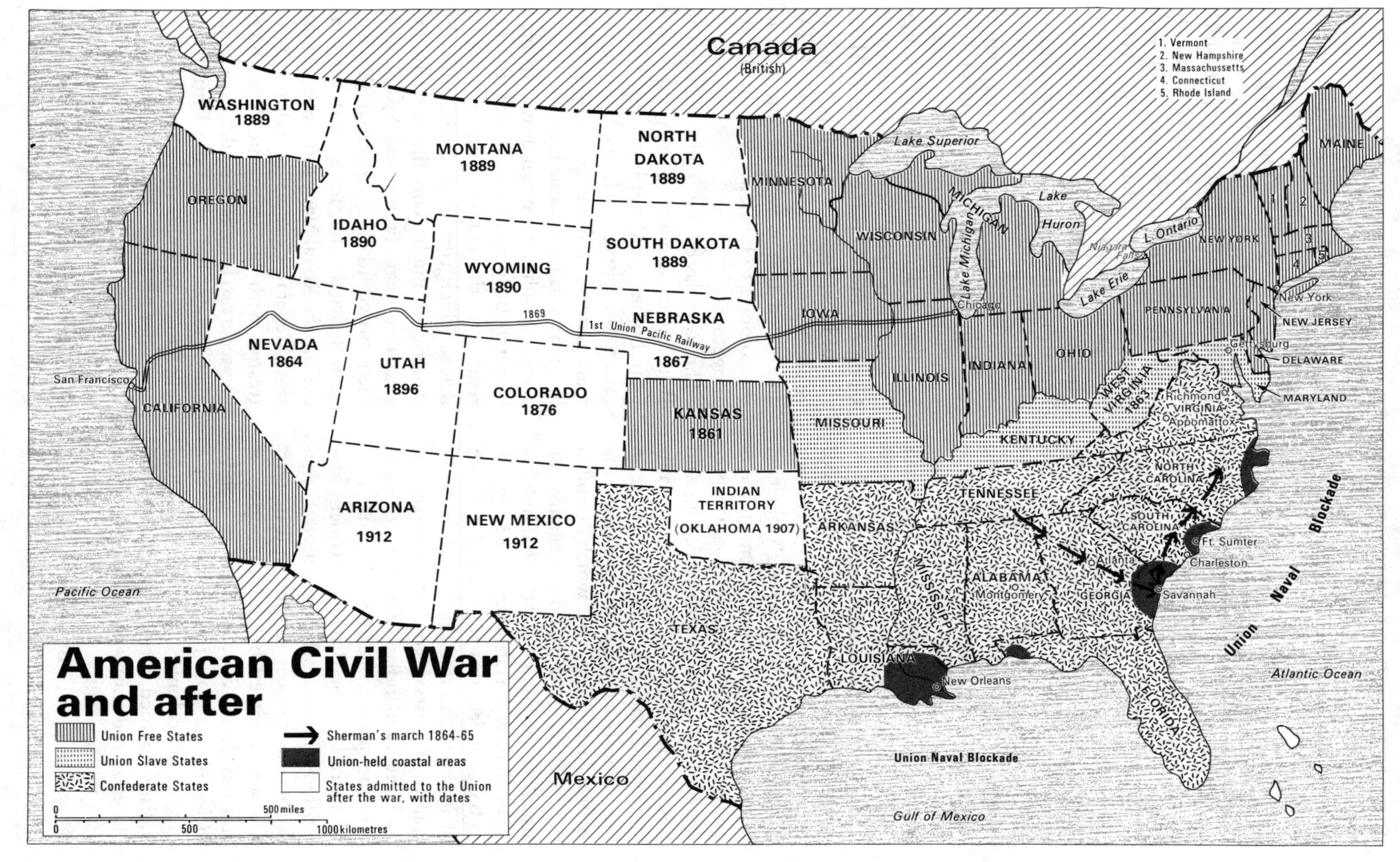
American Civil War and after
Union Free States
Union Slave States
Confederate States
Sherman's march 1864-65
Union-held coastal areas
States admitted to the Union after the war, with dates
0
500 miles
0
500
1000 kilometres
Canada
(British)
1. Vermont
2. New Hampshire
3. Massachussetts
4. Connecticut
5. Rhode Island
WASHINGTON
1889
MONTANA
1889
NORTH DAKOTA
1889
SOUTH DAKOTA
1889
IDAHO
1890
WYOMING
1890
NEBRASKA
1867
1869
1st Union Pacific Railway
NEVADA
1864
UTAH
1896
COLORADO
1876
KANSAS
1861
ARIZONA
1912
NEW MEXICO
1912
INDIAN TERRITORY
(OKLAHOMA 1907)
OREGON
CALIFORNIA
San Francisco
Pacific Ocean
Mexico
TEXAS
MINNESOTA
WISCONSIN
IOWA
MISSOURI
ARKANSAS
LOUISIANA
ILLINOIS
INDIANA
OHIO
KENTUCKY
TENNESSEE
MISSISSIPPI
ALABAMA
Montgomery
GEORGIA
Atlanta
Savannah
FLORIDA
SOUTH CAROLINA
Charleston
Ft. Sumter
NORTH CAROLINA
VIRGINIA
Richmond
Appomattox
WEST VIRGINIA
1863
MARYLAND
DELAWARE
NEW JERSEY
New York
Gettysburg
PENNSYLVANIA
NEW YORK
MAINE
1
2
3
4
5
MICHIGAN
Chicago
Lake Michigan
Lake Superior
Lake Huron
Lake Erie
L. Ontario
Niagara Falls
New Orleans
Union Naval Blockade
Gulf of Mexico
Atlantic Ocean
Union Naval Blockade

until the Declaration of Independence in 1776.

¶ BROWN, G. W., HARMAN, E. and JEANNERET, M. *The American Colonies: Canada and the U.S.A. before 1800*, 1962; WRIGHT, LOUIS B. *Everyday Life in Colonial America*, 1966

See also INDIVIDUAL ENTRIES.

American Independence, War of (1775–83): The immediate cause of the war between the British government and the American colonists was a series of quarrels over taxation. The real causes, however, went deeper. At that time the British government administered her colonies for her own benefit rather than for the good of the colonies. The colonists' trade was carefully controlled and they were not allowed to manufacture goods which might compete with British manufacturers. The colonists strongly objected to being taxed by a parliament in Westminster in which they were not represented. One of their earliest slogans said this very pointedly – "No taxation without representation". The taxes levied on the colonists were mainly to pay for the British Army (Redcoats) which defended the frontiers of the colonies against the attacks of the French and the Red Indians. Though there was still a legacy of expense to be recouped, this argument lost much of its strength after the French had lost control of most of North America during the French and Indian War (1745–63), and thus the quarrel over taxes became very bitter. In 1765 the British parliament passed the Stamp Act, which required all legal documents to bear stamps, and in 1767 this was followed by the imposition of customs duties on a number of goods, including tea. On 16 December 1773 a group of colonists disguised as Red Indians boarded three vessels in Boston Harbour and threw their cargoes of tea into the sea. After this so-called "Tea-party" the port of Boston was closed and the colony of Massachusetts deprived of many of its rights of government. Prompted by this, the Thirteen Colonies formed the First Continental Congress at Philadelphia in September 1774, at which they all agreed not to trade with Britain until their grievances were removed. Agitation in the meantime was being whipped up and volunteers were beginning to drill and arm themselves. War broke out on 19 April 1775 when a party of British troops who had been sent to raid a weapon store were attacked at Lexington. The Thirteen Colonies forgot their long-standing rivalries and joined together under the leadership of George Washington. The Second Continental Congress drew up the famous Declaration of Independence on 4 July 1776 (still celebrated as a National Day in the USA) and stated that it was the intention of the colonies to break away from Britain altogether.

The war lasted for eight years. The British commanders, poorly supported from home, could not bring the Americans to a decisive battle and Washington managed to avoid a major struggle until his army was fully trained and the British army's supplies were run down. In 1777 General Burgoyne was forced to surrender to the colonists at Saratoga – a defeat which convinced France that the Americans might win the war. In the next two years France and Spain, with their powerful fleets, entered the war against Britain and, for a short but vital period, the Royal Navy lost control of the seas. General Cornwallis, who had retreated with his army into Yorktown, was secure so long as he could receive supplies by sea; but when the British fleet failed to come to his aid he was forced to surrender his large army to the colonists. The news of this defeat led the British government to give up the struggle. At the Peace of Paris in 1783 the independence of the colonies was recognised and they developed their own forms of government, eventually uniting under the presidency of George Washington in 1789.

¶ CAMMIADE, AUDREY. *Franklin and the War of American Independence*, 1967; CLARKE, CLORINDA. *The American Revolution 1775–1783*, 1968

American Presidents: Every four years the American people go to the polls to elect a President. The man they choose serves not only as the head of state but also as the Commander-in-Chief of the Armed Forces and the leader of the Executive Branch of the United States Government (the equivalent in Great Britain being the Prime Minister). The American Constitution states that he must be a natural-born American citizen, at least thirty-five years old and have resided in the United States for at least fourteen years. The presidency is regarded today as the most important position in the world, but this has not always been so. When the War of American Independence ended in 1783 an American nation was not created, as it were, overnight. The war had merely achieved the separate independence of the Thirteen Colonies and it was to be another six years before the first President was elected and had conferred on him some of the powers that had been proposed in the first flush of enthusiasm in 1776, when the Articles of Confederation had been drawn up by the Second Continental Congress.

There have been forty presidents of the United States, from George Washington in 1789, who stood as a Federalist, to Ronald Reagan, a Republican, the present holder of the office; he defeated President Carter in 1980 and won a second term with a landslide victory in 1984.

Four Presidents have met with violent deaths whilst in office: Abraham Lincoln (held office 1861–65) assassinated by John Wilkes Booth in Ford's Theatre on Good Friday, 14 April 1865; and James A. Garfield (March–September 1881), William McKinley (1897–1901) and John F. Kennedy (1961–63), all of whom also died as a result of assassins' bullets. Four other Presidents died in office, though from natural causes: W. H. Harrison (held office March–April 1841), Zachary Taylor (1849–50), Warren G. Harding (1921–23) and Franklin D. Roosevelt (1933–45). Despite the fact that no fewer than one in five Presidents have, in one way or another, died in office, there has never been a shortage of politicians seeking the position. A President is first and foremost a member of a political party and, though he may if he so wishes choose his advisers from outside it, he is nevertheless very much influenced by the party's ideals. When George Washington became President in 1789 it was a triumph for those early Americans who believed in the need for a strong central government with a powerful President. This group were known as Federalists and were led by Alexander Hamilton. Opposed to this view were the Republicans who wanted to keep the powers of a federal government to a minimum and thus to maintain the rights of the individual states. This group was initially led by Thomas Jefferson (1743–1826) who became President in 1801. But these early political parties do not coincide with the modern Republicans and Democrats. These two parties, which have between them provided all the Presidents for the last hundred years, emerged in the years immediately before the Civil War (1861–65). The Republicans were founded as a Northern anti-slavery party in the 1850s and the Democrats have their historic roots in the South, though in the last forty years they have become associated with the Northern liberals and the trade unions. Each President, no matter to which party he belongs, tends to develop his own style and focus for his programme. Warren Harding (1865–1923) advocated a return to "Normalcy" after the First World War (1914–18); Franklin D. Roosevelt (1882–1945) promised, and achieved, a "New Deal" for Americans who had been shaken by the world-wide slump in the early 1930s; and, in recent years, we have had the appeals of John F. Kennedy (1917–63) for the "New Frontier" and of Lyndon B. Johnson (1908–73) for a "Great Society". A President sets aims and objects for the American people which tend to become lastingly identified with him.

Amphitheatre: the building provided in most Roman towns for gladiatorial and other shows. It normally had circular banks of stone seats round the sand arena, and might seat up to 60,000 as at the Colosseum in Rome. Famous surviving examples are also to be seen in Nîmes and Verona. Amphitheatres were sometimes flooded for naval spectaculars and were the scene of many of the martyrdoms of early Christians.

A detail of the classical facade of the Amphitheatre at Nimes, France.

Amundsen, Roald (1872–1928): Norwegian explorer. He made the first transit of the North-West Passage (*see* separate entry) and was the first to reach the South Pole (14 December 1911), arriving five weeks before the English explorer Robert Falcon Scott. Amundsen lost his life searching for the Italian air-ship *Italia*, wrecked on a polar flight.

¶ In WALTON, J. *Six More Explorers*, 1949

Anaesthesia: process by which a patient is kept unconscious during an operation. Greek and Egyptian doctors had a good knowledge of anatomy but found operations difficult to perform because the patient frequently died from pain, shock, and loss of blood. They could prevent this by drugging him with opium, but an overdose could prove fatal.

In medieval times surgeons were very unskilled, and it was not until the late 18th century that their knowledge approached anything resembling modern standards. But they were still reluctant to operate except in cases of grave necessity, as no one seriously believed that it was possible to render a patient insensible to pain.

In 1800 the scientist Sir Humphry Davy noticed that the gas nitrous oxide relieved him of the pain of a headache. Twenty-five years later a young Shropshire surgeon, Henry Hickman, was able to perform minor operations on animals made unconscious by carbon dioxide, but doctors ignored his claims. In 1844 an American dentist Horace Wells had a tooth painlessly extracted after inhaling nitrous oxide; in 1846 another American, Dr Morton, obtained the same results, using ether. Later that year a London surgeon, Robert Liston, amputated a man's leg while the patient was kept unconscious by ether. A Scottish doctor, James Simpson, discovered the use of chloroform in 1847. This could be mixed with oxygen so as to keep a patient insensible for long periods with little risk to his life.

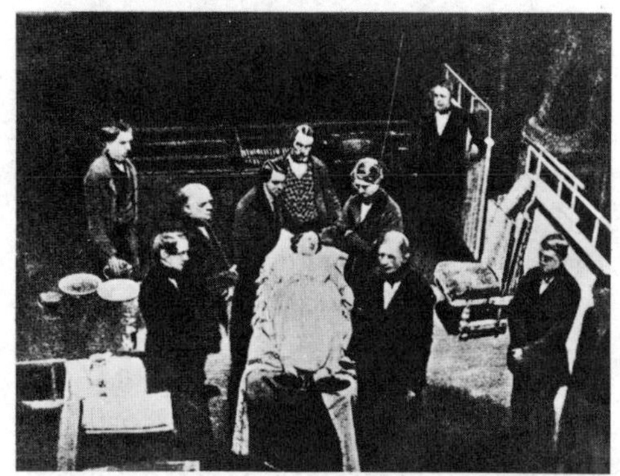

The first operation during which anaesthetics were used took place at Massachusetts General Hospital, 16 October 1896, with Dr Morton, the first anaesthetist, administering the ether.

Present day anaesthetists rarely use gases in order to produce unconsciousness; instead, drugs are injected into the patient's bloodstream. The drug used depends upon the time required by the surgeon to perform his operation. Dentists usually rely on local anaesthetics which temporarily prevent any feeling of pain in a small area of the body. These drugs are mixed with other substances which ensure that their effect does not spread or produce unpleasant after-effects. The most usual one is *Lignocaine*, which was first used in Sweden in 1942. It has replaced *Cocaine*, which could be habit-forming if used in the quantity required in modern dentistry. *See also* MEDICINE.

Ancestors: literally, those who go before; hence, those from whom a family or individual is descended. "Forefathers" was a term commonly used in other centuries. Ancestor worship forms a part of many world religions, in the belief that the souls of ancestors can still play their part in this world and are responsive to supplication and prayer.

Anchor: a heavily weighted hook for mooring a floating body to the seabed. All floating craft from the smallest dinghy to the largest ocean-going vessel need to carry an anchor with sufficient length of cable. A ship, having reached its desired mooring position, drops the anchor from the bows and then goes astern. As the cable tautens and the strain is put on the anchor, so the fluke or arm digs into the seabed and provides the necessary holding power.

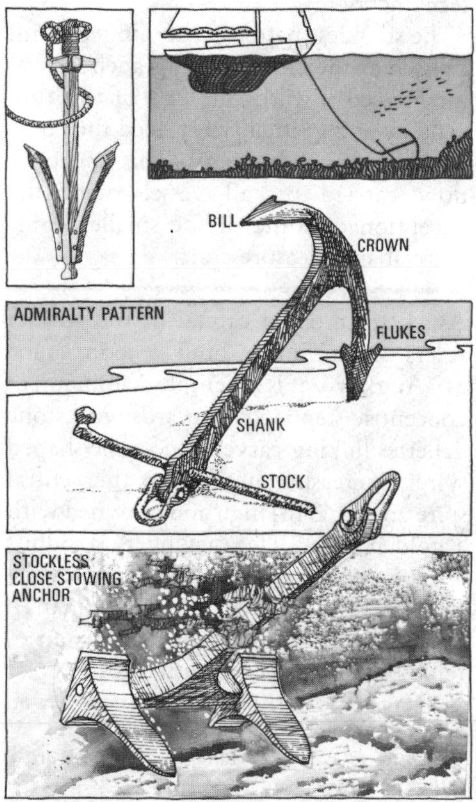

Although almost any form of heavy weight can serve as an anchor, the simplest being a large flat stone with a hole in it, the conventional form of iron anchor with twin flukes, long shank and stock crossing at right-angles can be traced back to Roman times, and this basic pattern with comparatively few variations was universally adopted as the standard type of anchor up to the 19th century. HMS *Victory* at Trafalgar carried five, the heaviest weighing 93 cwt [4,725 kg]. Varieties of the above are the wooden anchors, some weighted by stones, mainly used by native craft in India and in the Far East.

By 1850 much heavier anchors were necessary. A movable stock was also introduced on the smaller model for more convenient stowage on board. In Britain this became known as the Admiralty pattern anchor.

The stockless pattern with hinged arms, known as the close stowing anchor, was introduced towards the end of the 19th century and gradually replaced the cumbersome stocked variety. This anchor is now carried by all vessels with the exception of some of the smaller commercial and pleasure craft.

Angkor: moated capital of the Khmer rulers of Cambodia, built *c.* 900 to 1200 AD. Angkor Vat is a Temple-Mountain of concentric stepped courtyards with stone galleries linking carved pine-cone shaped spires, increasing in scale to the central spire 200 ft [60 m] high and crowned with a golden lotus. The carving is Buddhist and Hindu. It was dedicated to the worship of the God-King Suryavarman II (1112–52). Angkor Thom is a group of temples and palaces within a rectangular wall (1181–1201). The palaces were served by townsmen who lived by two reservoirs outside the walls.

Bayon towers, Angkor Thom, whose faces are as tall as a man.

Anglo-Saxons: the name given to three Germanic peoples (Angles, Saxons and Jutes) who raided and settled in Britain in the 4th and 5th centuries AD. The Angles were a sea-faring folk referred to by Tacitus (*c.* 55–118) in *Germania* (chapter 40) as "worshippers of Mother Earth in a sacred grove on a North Sea Island". They probably occupied southern Jutland. Bede's idea that the Jutes lived in northern Jutland is now untenable. The similarity of their pottery found in Kent and the Rhineland suggests their immediate homeland before migration. The Saxons occupied the area between the River Weser and the Zuyder Zee, living on artificial mounds or terpen.

Why the Angles gave their name to England (Angleland), since they were not the most numerous tribe, is difficult to understand. Bede (*c.* 673–735) used *Albion* or *Brittannia.* Alfred used *Englisc* to refer to an Englishman and his language. On the Continent "Anglo-Saxon" means a Saxon living in England and not one of the old Saxons who still lived on the Continent.

¶ LINDSAY, JACK. *Our Anglo-Saxon Heritage,* 1965; SELLMAN, R. R. *The Anglo-Saxons,* 1959

See also PLACE NAMES.

Anschluss: German for a union or joining together. With Hitler—an Austrian by birth—in power in Germany, the demand for Austria's union with Germany was stepped up within both that country and its German neighbour. At first the Italian dictator Mussolini resisted, but by March 1938 Hitler could ignore protests from Austrians and the outside world. German troops marched in, welcomed by Austrian Nazis and their followers. It was Hitler's first foreign conquest. Austria remained part of Germany until 1945.

Antioch: city on the left bank of the Orontes 12 miles [19 kilometres] from the sea. Founded in 300 BC by Seleucus I of Syria, it was once the seat of the Olympic Games; was embellished by Octavian (27 BC–AD 14) and fortified by the Byzantines; and was the seat of the first bishopric founded by St Peter. Successive wars saw it captured by Persians, Arabs, Turks and, in 1098, by the Crusaders. For 171 years, under Bohemond and his heirs, it became the most efficient and most ruthless of the Crusader kingdoms till Sultan Baibers took it in 1268. It declined when Mongol–Mameluke rivalry cut the trade route from the Mediterranean to Persia which had made it prosperous.

Apartheid: an Afrikaans word for segregation of the white, black and coloured peoples of the Republic of South Africa from each other. It was first used there by the Nationalist party in the 1948 election, but the policy of separation of the races goes far back in South African history. Under apartheid there are separate residential areas, schools and hospitals for white people, black people and coloured people; marriage between them is a criminal offence, and they may not mix socially; non-Europeans have to carry passes and are not represented in parliament or allowed to do a number of skilled jobs. In their own limited areas non-Europeans are promised opportunities of development.

Appeasement: the act of keeping the peace or pacifying. Before World War II it took on the special meaning of keeping peace at any price, as a result of the occasion when, in 1938, Neville Chamberlain, the British Prime Minister, persuaded Hitler to forgo war in return for a part of Czechoslovakia. This appeasement policy failed and therefore stood condemned.

Apprentices: those who learn an art or trade under the guidance of a master. Apprenticeship was known from very early times, e.g. in Babylon as early as 2100 BC. In England it developed in the 12th century. The boy was bound to his master, usually for seven years, by an indenture, an agreement drawn up by the master and the boy's father in the presence of an official of the Guild of his craft. The father paid a fee and the master undertook to feed, clothe and house the boy, to teach him the "art and mystery" of the trade and bring him up in sober ways, chastising him when necessary. The boy practised his craft under supervision, undertook some domestic duties and, at fair time, frequently slept beneath his master's stall. Until the last year of his apprenticeship he received no wages. After his apprenticeship he became either a journeyman working for wages or, on payment of an entry fee and completion of a "masterpiece", a master craftsman. There was no marked social distinction between master and apprentice, and the younger sons of gentlemen frequently became apprentices.

Apprentice engravers in the master's workshop, 1767. From Diderot's Encyclopaedia.

During the 15th century the Guilds fell increasingly into the hands of small groups and it was difficult for apprentices to become master craftsmen. The Elizabethan Labour Law (1563) laid down careful regulations and a set of property qualifications regulating entry to various occupations.

It was repealed in 1814.

Doctor Johnson used to hum an old song which included the words:

Up then rose the 'prentices all,
Living in London, both proper and tall.

They were, indeed, a formidable array when, incensed by some threat or injury to one of their number, they poured out of their shops in support. A reminder of this occurred during the disastrous 1969 rioting in Northern Ireland, when 600 apprentice boys made their annual march through the streets to commemorate the relief of Londonderry in 1689.

Aqueducts: a system of channels, pipes and conduits used to bring water over long distances. Aqueducts can be traced in the ancient Near East, and a famous Greek example ran through a hill on the island of Samos. It was the Romans who really exploited their use because of the increased demand in their large cities, especially for the public baths. The first Roman aqueduct was built in 312 BC, and at the height of the Empire more than twenty fed Rome. With no pressure pumps available, the water from the hills had to be gravity fed, and this accounts for the most obvious feature of Roman aqueducts, the channel raised high above flat ground or over gorges. Rome itself had many of these arched structures (parts of which still stand), and famous examples from the provinces are at Segovia in Spain and at the Pont du Gard in southern France.

The water channel was sometimes of masonry, sometimes lined with lead or earthenware, and was very carefully maintained and controlled. Vitruvius, in charge of the aqueducts at the beginning of the 1st century AD, has left us a detailed account of the structures, their capacity, and their distribution. For example one Roman aqueduct, the New Anio, measured 47 miles [76 kilometres], five-

sixths underground and one-sixth on arches. On arrival in the city the water was distributed through lead pipes, and there are some still in working order in Pompeii. According to records made by Sextus Julius Frontinus, who had charge of the Roman aqueducts towards the end of the 1st century AD, their capacity was such they could provide about 90 gallons [409 litres] a day for each inhabitant of the city of Rome.

Arabia: a rectangular peninsula of 1·5 million square miles [3·89 million square kilometres] in south-west Asia, bordered by three seas and the Fertile Crescent of Mesopotamia, Syria and Palestine. South Arabia (the Yemen) is fertile, producing myrrh, frankincense and spices – the "Arabia Felix" of classical writers – and was the settled kingdom of Saba (Sheba) by the 10th century BC. The centre of Arabia, a plateau of red soil, shifting sand or hard sandstone and lava, is a waterless desert punctuated by oases. It is the cradle of the Semitic race, breeding fierce hardy Bedouin who have in successive waves burst upon the Fertile Crescent and Egypt and Abyssinia. The heart of Arabia is so inhospitable that only rarely have its people been disturbed by the powerful empires on its borders. *See* MAP, page 32.

Arabs: the people of Arabia, thought to be the purest of the Semitic race. The southern Arabs were settled in the Yemen by the 10th century BC, building dams to conserve rainfall and seafaring to India and Indonesia. The northern Arabs were nomads (Bedouin), living by breeding camels and horses, grazing goats and, above all, raiding. They are said to have had a thousand words for the camel; they defined their life thus: "Our business is to make raids on the enemy, our neighbours and our brother – in case we find none to raid but a brother." They were grouped in tribes, holding pasture and water in common, governing themselves through a sheik and council of elders, carrying their tribal gods with them.

By 150 BC some of these nomads had settled in the Fertile Crescent and founded kingdoms which the Romans recognised as buffers against further nomad raids: the kingdom of Palmyra in Syria, and the Nabatean kingdom which wrought the rock-cut temples at Petra. Muhammad (AD 570–632), though himself a townsman of Mecca subjected to Jewish and Christian thought, fled to Medina (*see* HEGIRA, AD 622) and preached to the Bedouin. He gave them self-discipline, confidence and a sense of community, and their energy and land-hunger, which had hitherto been wasted in inter-tribal feuds and raids, were harnessed to a prolonged military offensive. They overthrew Byzantine rule in Syria in AD 636 and from their headquarters in Damascus, conquered Mesopotamia and Persia in 637, Egypt in 641, North Africa and Spain in 710 and Sicily in 827.

From their hard and simple life in the desert camps they brought lively imagination, a gift of poetry, and a feeling that the one true God demanded moral conduct, not elaborate ritual. They proved very receptive of the best in the cultures they defeated and became the great transmitters and interpreters to the modern world of Greek philosophy and science, Persian medicine, Indian mathematics and astronomy. Yet they remained impervious to the technical achievements of western Europe, retaining too long their originally justifiable contempt for that barbarous region.

Their military strength lay in their power to cross the desert and, later, the sea, and to appear suddenly and in force in the settled lands. Their capital cities were never far from the desert. They remained in warrior cantonments, using the existing officials, tolerating the infidel if he paid tribute money, collecting only a religious tax from the faithful. Their political and religious head was the Caliph (Deputy of the Prophet). The Arabic character of the Caliphate was diluted in the course of time. The truly Arab Umayyad Caliphate of Damascus was superseded in 747 by the Abbasid Caliphate of Baghdad, which was Persian in style. The Fatimid Caliphs of Egypt (969 onwards) depended more and more on Turkish or Circassian slave soldiers (Mamelukes), and in 1517 the Caliphate was transferred to the Ottoman Turks at Istanbul (*see* TURKEY).

The word "Arab", which in the Koran meant simply "nomad", is now used of any inhabitant of the former Ottoman Empire who speaks Arabic and takes pride

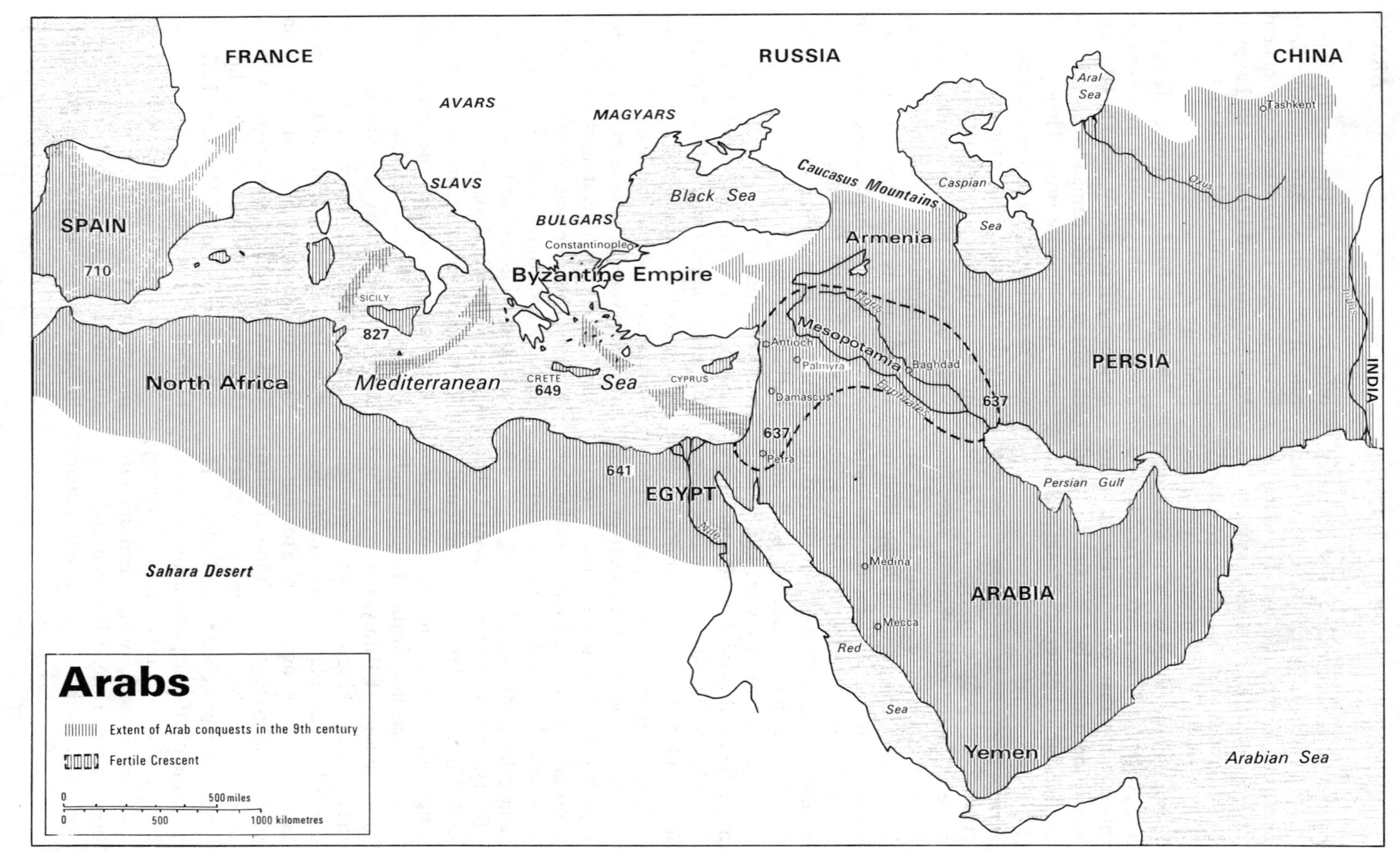
FRANCE
RUSSIA
CHINA
AVARS
MAGYARS
Aral Sea
Tashkent
Oxus
SLAVS
Black Sea
Caucasus Mountains
Caspian Sea
SPAIN
710
BULGARS
Constantinople
Armenia
Byzantine Empire
SICILY
827
Tigris
Mesopotamia
Antioch
Palmyra
Baghdad
Indus
PERSIA
INDIA
North Africa
Mediterranean
CRETE
649
Sea
CYPRUS
Damascus
Euphrates
637
637
Petra
641
EGYPT
Persian Gulf
Nile
Sahara Desert
Medina
ARABIA
Mecca
Red
Sea
Yemen
Arabian Sea
Arabs
Extent of Arab conquests in the 9th century
Fertile Crescent
0
500 miles
0
500
1000 kilometres

in the cultural achievements of the Arabs.

¶ ELLIS, HARRY B. *The Arabs*, 1960

Arbela, Battle of (331 BC): reckoned by Sir Edward Creasy (writing in 1851) as one of the fifteen decisive battles of the world. Fought between Alexander the Great and Darius III, it overthrew the Persian Empire and gave Asia to Alexander, beginning with Babylon, "the oldest seat of earthly empire".

Arbitration, International: a proceeding by which nations bring their differences to be heard by impartial judges and decided on the basis of generally accepted law among civilised communities. A landmark was the setting up of a permanent Court of Arbitration at The Hague (Netherlands) in 1899. There are at present no legal sanctions by which its decisions can be enforced.

Archaeology: the study of the past by the examination of its material remains. It therefore usually employs excavation of buried sites to add to the evidence of literature or to serve instead of written records. The scientific type of archaeology really started only in the Renaissance and for some centuries was chiefly devoted to the recovery of works of classical art, more antiquarianism than archaeology. Excavation was often careless, and the real history of an excavated site was frequently destroyed for the sake of a few beautiful objects. Typical of this amateur approach were the excavations of Schliemann (1822–90) at Troy and Mycenae in 1871 and 1876, where his excitement led him to date his valuable finds some 300 years too late.

In these early days burial sites received most attention, and the picture of the civilisation unearthed was one-sided. Only the rich and noble had costly funerals, and the written histories also tended to ignore the life of the common people. Over the past hundred years a new approach in archaeology has gradually emerged in which it has been seen that any object or building, however seemingly worthless, can add to our knowledge of the times or explain the relationship of one civilisation with kindred or contemporary cultures. The methods used have also been much improved. Unskilled labour is now nearly useless, and the accurate unveiling of the various strata in a site is held to be essential. Scientific aids have also been introduced, aerial photography, new cleaning techniques, and radio carbon dating. With the increase of knowledge, methods of comparative dating have greatly improved.

Almost the most significant archaeological advance has been the discovery and use of written records – the story of epigraphy. By the co-operation of archaeologists and linguistic experts the languages of the ancient Near East – Sumerian, Hittite, Babylonian, Egyptian – are now known and understood. The old Aegean method of writing, known as Linear B, is now proved to be Greek. The decoding of these scripts has been one of the most fascinating of all archaeological activities. The skill needed was well shown by work on the Rosetta Stone (*below*), a record in

three different languages, which gave the clue to the decipherment of Egyptian hieroglyphic writing.

Perhaps equally important has been the analysis of the Stone Age culture before writing was invented. Here archaeology reigns supreme. Every object found is of interest, from the shaped flint to the cave-painting, from animal bones to the remains of the earliest cities. Thus we can tell something of the lives of men in France and Spain 20,000 years ago, and Jericho is proved to have a history of over 10,000 years. Recent excavations on the Danube are claimed to push back the start of town life even further.

The most fascinating archaeology has centred on the Mediterranean lands and the Middle East. The excavation of the towns of Herculaneum and Pompeii records life as it was when they were destroyed by an eruption of Vesuvius in AD 79. The death pit at Ur shows the barbarous but splendid rites of the old Mesopotamians, and the work of Sir Arthur Evans (1851–1941) uncovered the vast royal palace at Knossos in Crete. Particularly in Egypt there has been spectacular success. Even the fragile papyrus is preserved in the dry sand. Nothing has been more exciting than the discovery in 1922 of the intact tomb of Tutankhamen with its enormously valuable collection of treasure. In Mesopotamia archaeology has thrown light on civilisations spanning 3,000 years, and in India an almost unknown civilisation has been unearthed. All we know of the Aztecs, Incas and Mayas in Central and Southern America in the time of the European Middle Ages comes from archaeology.

In North America, probably the most interesting – and certainly the most controversial – archaeological work has been the long search for authentic traces of the early Viking settlements. Hard evidence to substantiate the story of the five Viking voyages told in the sagas remains one of the greatest and most elusive of archaeological prizes.

In Britain finds have often been spectacular, as with the discovery of late Roman silverware at Mildenhall or the burial ship at Sutton Hoo. Painstaking research has elsewhere developed our picture of Celtic Britain or of the Roman occupation. The types of information to be gathered are very varied, ranging from burial customs and religious practices, through the lives and skills of the great men who owned costly possessions, to the ordinary life of the common man, what he ate and drank, what he wore, how he spent his time, how he made a living, and how he got on with his neighbour.

Apart from linguistic experts, archaeologists now have to call in the help of anthropologists, who by the comparison of modern primitive societies are able to shed light on unexplained relics from the past. This is especially important in explaining the development of beliefs and practices and of social conventions and arrangements. The orderly presentation of

Archaeologists carefully excavating the mosaic floors of the Roman Villa at Fishbourne, Chichester, Sussex.

the finds from the past has also been a significant feature of modern archaeology. The skilled restoration of ruined sites helps to illustrate what a place looked like, however controversial some of the restorations have been. Museums for the display of objects found were started in the Renaissance. From being almost lumber-rooms, museums are now carefully planned to give a clear and easily understood picture of a civilisation.

¶ ALLEN, AGNES. *The Story of Archaeology*, 1965
See also INDUSTRIAL ARCHAEOLOGY, SUTTON HOO; TUTANKHAMEN.

Archery: The bow is the earliest instrument we know in which mechanical power was used and, in its most primitive form, it was in use at least 50,000 years ago. Without doubt this simple but devastating device of stick and string became the principal implement used in the struggle for existence. Examination of prehistoric bows which have been unearthed in north-west Europe reveals bow design of a surprisingly high standard. Other archaeological finds of human and animal bones with arrow-heads of flint embedded in them indicate the lethal power of the bow and provide ample evidence of the use of archery as a hunting weapon or warlike arm over many thousands of years.

Historically there is ample evidence to show that the bow became a powerful implement of war amongst many nations. A unique form of bow was developed in Asia consisting of a core of wood strengthened by layers of animal sinew and horn. This resulted in a short and very powerful weapon capable of projecting an arrow which would penetrate tough leather and chain armour. This composite form of bow spread throughout the whole of Asia and the Middle East. The Romans employed units of mercenary bowmen in their armies, the Greeks used archery extensively in their battles, the bow was the principal weapon used by the Huns and Tatars in their ravages of Asia and Europe, and the great armies of China sent thousands of trained bowmen into battle armed with the composite bow. The Turks and Persians developed the composite bow for long-distance competitive shooting and distances of over half a mile have been recorded. The bow peculiar to Japan is up to 7 feet 3 inches [217 centimetres] in length, constructed of bamboo laminations and its most distinctive feature is the unsymmetrical positioning of the handgrip. Despite the apparently unwieldy nature of these implements the great war bows of Japan can claim a long and distinguished service.

The prehistoric bowyers of Europe established a pattern of bow construction from which was evolved the one-piece wooden bows of the Norman invaders, used with such disastrous effect at Hastings in 1066, and the famous English longbow, for 400 years the invincible weapon of the English armies. The first official recognition of the longbow as the weapon of the English appeared in 1252 when the Assize of Arms directed that soldiers should report equipped according to their status and bearing bows and arrows. Edward I introduced the scientific use of archery in battle, much as William the Conqueror had done at Hastings, employing the principle of co-operation between archers and the men-at-arms and cavalry for whom they gave covering fire. Numerous medieval battles give ample proof of the success of such co-operation but at Bannockburn (1314), where such tactics were disregarded, the result was dismal failure for the English. The Battle of Crécy (1346) was described by Sir Winston Churchill as one of the four supreme achievements of the British army and this conflict marks the beginning of the Hundred Years War. After this decisive victory, during which 6,000 Genoese crossbowmen were defeated and some 10,000 French were lost, the people of England were encouraged to practise regularly with the longbow to be ready in time of need. Royal proclamations insisted on regular training with the bow, and unlawful games such as football were forbidden.

It was during the campaigns of Edward III and the Black Prince in France, followed in 1415 by the historic Battle of Agincourt, that the longbow of yew in the hands of the English yeoman became recognised as the weapon *par excellence*. The clothyard shaft fletched with grey goose feathers and tipped with a vicious steel point, known as a bodkin, put terror into the hearts of the enemy.

The modern bowman shows correct stance.

After the Wars of the Roses the longbow began to decline in popularity as a weapon of war due to its replacement by the handgun, despite a spirited but unsuccessful attempt by influential military men to persuade the government to retain the bow as the official weapon of the army. Henry VIII encouraged the use of the bow by personal example and by the formation of an élite corps of bowmen, but during Elizabeth's reign an Order in Council (1595) directed that bows be withdrawn as approved weapons of war of the English armies.

The use of the longbow survived amongst a handful of enthusiasts who continued to practise in the fields near London and this led to a revival, patronised by the Prince Regent, towards the end of the 18th century. Exclusive societies attracted membership from the well-to-do and leisured classes. There was even a suggestion that the bow might be reintroduced into the British Army. As a sport archery became even more popular during Victorian times and many of the societies formed then are still in existence. The longbow was finally replaced in the 1940s by weapons of tubular steel and today archers use bows of fibre-glass and plastics designed on the principles of modern engineering.

¶ MILLIKEN, E. K. *Archery in the Middle Ages*, 1967

See also INDIVIDUAL ENTRIES.

Archimedes (*c.* 287–212 BC): Greek mathematician and inventor. He is chiefly remembered for the discovery in his bath of the hydrostatic law known as Archimedes' Principle, i.e. that when any substance is immersed in a fluid, its loss of weight equals the weight of the fluid displaced; but he made many other important discoveries, especially in the field of geometry, and was a successful inventor of mechanical contrivances and engines of war.

¶ BENDICK, JEANNE. *Archimedes and the Door of Science*, 1964

Archives and Records: the documents which any organisation, such as a government department, public authority, institution, business or family, produces in the ordinary running of its affairs, and which it subsequently preserves as evidence of its rights and activities, for reference in planning future action, or for historical research. Examples of archives are deeds proving ownership of property, financial accounts registering money transactions, and minutes recording executive decisions. Records, however, are generally understood to include all the documents created by the organisation, some of which may indeed be of enduring archive quality but many others merely of temporary use.

Britain has probably the most complete public archives in the world, the Public Record Office in London housing a practically unbroken series of legal documents and state papers beginning in the 12th century, as well as many older documents, including the Domesday Book (1087). Here, too, are kept the records of the Foreign Office, Treasury, Home Office, Admiralty and all other older government departments, and also those of the newer ministries which meet the needs of modern society. Elsewhere, other national records are preserved in the Scottish and Northern Ireland Record Offices, while the records of local government authorities are in County or Borough Record Offices throughout the country. Important collections of historical manuscripts are preserved in the British Museum, the Bodleian Library and the National Library of Wales, but many others are housed in libraries, institutions, private houses, churches and cathedrals. For instance, one copy of Magna Carta, the great statement of human liberties, is preserved in Lincoln Cathedral and there is another copy in Salisbury Cathedral.

There is in Britain no single authority responsible for supervising the whole of the country's archives. In France, and on the Continent generally, the agencies which control the national archives also supervise the care of local public records. Similarly, in the United States of America, the National Archives and Records Service set up in 1949 administers the Federal archives – among them the Declaration of Independence (1776), the Constitution, and the records of Congress – and maintains a number of Federal records centres, although each state looks after its own archives. This pattern is followed in Canada and in many Latin American, African, Asian and Commonwealth countries. The archives of international and world organisations are mostly cared for by the International Council of Archives created by UNESCO in 1948.

Arithmetic: a word which has changed its meaning. In ancient Greek times a distinction was made between Arithmetic, which was the theory of numbers, and Logistic, which was the art of calculating. It was not until about the beginning of the 16th century that the word Arithmetic was applied to the more practical parts of the subject. Even now the Germans use the word *Arithmetik* for the more theoretical parts of the subject, while the practical is called *Rechnung*.

Using the word in its more modern sense, little progress could be made until the Arabic numerals we now employ came into use. These seem to have developed from the Devangari numerals used in India in the 8th century, later modified by the eastern Arabs, and again altered by the western Arabs or Moors. From Spain they passed into western Europe and are found on a Sicilian coin of 1138. In England no use of Arabic numerals is found in parish registers or manorial rolls before the 16th century, although their first use in Scotland appears to have been in 1490.

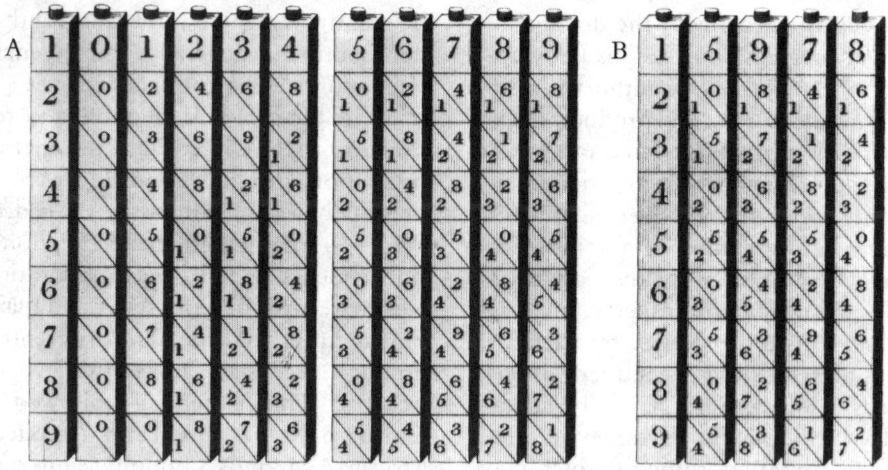

Napier's Bones: Group A shows the simple method of multiplying single digits and groups of digits devised by Napier. Group B is arranged to multiply 5978 by adding digits in adjacent triangles. Thus 3×5978 *is solved:* $1, 5+2, 7+2, 1+2, 4 = 17934$.

Apart from scientists and astronomers, who seem to have used the Arabic numerals in the 13th century, we appear to owe the more general use of the system to the merchants of Italy, who adopted it for general mercantile use during the 13th and 14th centuries. They also invented the system of double entry book-keeping.

Even after the general adoption of the Arabic numerals, the processes of arithmetic remained very clumsy, and in 1617 Napier invented a mechanical device, known as Napier's Rods or Napier's Bones, to assist in the process of multiplication. The main landmarks in the simplification of arithmetical processes were the introduction of symbols for the processes of addition, subtraction, multiplication and division, the invention of logarithms, and the use of decimals.

The origin of the symbols for "plus" and "minus" is still a subject for dispute, although it appears that they may have been first used as warehouse marks to indicate excess or deficiency in the weight of boxes or bales of goods. They first appeared in print in the fifteenth century but it was not until the beginning of the 17th century that their use became common. The sign = for "is equal to" was introduced by Record in 1557. The sign × for multiplication was developed in England about 1600, but its use in arithmetic became popular only in the second half of the 19th century. The sign ÷ for division first appeared in print in Rahn's *Teutsche Algebra* in 1659, and was introduced to England by a translation of this work in 1688.

The discovery of logarithms was made by Napier in 1614. By expressing all numbers as powers of a certain selected base number (usually 10), the processes of multiplication, division, involution and evolution are replaced by addition, subtraction, multiplication and division respectively, thus vastly simplifying complicated calculations.

The use of the decimal point came much later than the idea of the decimal fraction. A variety of ways of writing such fractions can be found. As an example, Henry Briggs (1561–1630) underlined the decimal figures, so that 2·639 appeared as 2<u>639</u>, but the point as used today appears in Napier's work of 1617. It was not until the beginning of the 18th century that its use became general and even now the notation varies in different countries.

¶ HOGBEN, LANCELOT. *The Wonderful World of Mathematics*, 1968

See also CALCULATING MACHINES.

Arkwright, Sir Richard (1732–92): English engineer and industrialist. Born at Preston in 1732, Arkwright received no formal education and, after serving his apprenticeship as a barber, went to Bolton where he worked as a wigmaker and publican. Moving to Nottingham in 1768, he became a partner with John Smalley of Preston and in 1769, after joining forces with Jedediah Strutt and Samuel Need, he patented the water-

frame, which produced the strong twist that led to a great expansion of the cotton industry. In 1771 the partners built at Cromford, Derbyshire, the first successful water-powered factory. After obtaining his carding patent in 1775 and ending the partnership, Arkwright built more mills in Derbyshire and Lancashire. Lancashire manufacturers were bitterly hostile to Arkwright's patent rights which he finally lost at a costly trial in 1785. Possibly, as his opponents asserted, Arkwright used the ideas of others, but he had a genius for organisation and more than anyone else created the modern factory system. Knighted in 1786, he built a mansion at Cromford, Derbyshire, and died in 1792 worth £500,000.

¶ In MCNICOL, H. *Seven Inventors*, 1943

Armada, Spanish: the term used especially of the fleet, the "Invincible Armada", sent by Philip II of Spain against England. The general word "armada" comes from the Spanish for "armed". "The Enterprise" or invasion of England was planned "to destroy the heretic queen", Elizabeth I, but was delayed by the continuation of the revolt of the Netherlands against Spain and by Philip's anxiety not to replace Elizabeth by Mary, Queen of Scots, because of her French connection. On 8 February 1587 Mary was executed at Fotheringay. No further delay was needed on this score, but Sir Francis Drake attacked Cadiz destroying about thirty large ships and as many smaller ("singeing the King of Spain's beard") and so delayed the invasion for a year. On 28 May 1588 the Spanish fleet of 130 ships set sail under the Duke of Medina Sidonia (the original commander, the Duke of Santa Cruz, had died) to invade England by coming up Channel, embarking a large army from the Netherlands under the Duke of Parma and sailing up the Thames estuary. Charles, Lord Howard of Effingham, was Lord High Admiral, and Drake was stationed at Plymouth to defend the Channel.

A running fight up the Channel lasted for eleven days. The Spanish lost three ships but never broke their crescent formation. On 27 July they put into Calais Roads, whence they were driven out by eight English fireships and, on 29 July, were heavily defeated off Gravelines. With a west-south-west wind blowing, they tried to sail home round northern Scotland and western Ireland, often in very rough weather, which cost them further ships. The English finally abandoned the chase owing to lack of powder. A shattered remnant of some 65 ships out of the original 130 reached Spain, while not a single English ship was

A contemporary painting by an unknown artist of the launching of the fireships against the Spanish Armada, 28 July 1588.

lost. England had decisively prevented invasion and, incidentally, ensured the success of the Dutch rebels.

¶ HORSCHFELD, BURT. *The Spanish Armada*, 1968; WILLIAMS, JAY. *The Spanish Armada*, 1968

See also FIRESHIPS.

Armenia: mountainous region between Lake Van and the Caucasus commanding the trade routes between Asia Minor and Persia, the Araxes running east and tributaries of the Euphrates running west. Thus it was the battlefield of Europe and Asia, fought for, or partitioned by, Persians, Byzantines, Arabs and Turks. It was the first state to adopt Christianity (AD 301), it developed an alphabet in AD 441, its architects used pointed arches and clustered columns by the 10th century. In periods of peace it prospered by the transit trade, by gold, silver, copper and salt mining, and by making carpets and brocades. Great ages were 94–56 BC under the Tigranid dynasty and in the 9th century AD under the Bagratunis. Armenia supplied the best troops, many administrators and even emperors to the Byzantine Empire. Under the Turks, Armenians kept their pride and sense of nationhood in spite of dispersal and persecution. Today Armenia is divided between the USSR, Turkey and Iran.

Armorial Bearings: heraldic material correctly used, under authorised control, by individuals and by communities; derived from the camouflage concealment and weather protection of the chain-mail wearer, by means of a surcoat. This was a shoulder-width and knee-length piece of "sendal" cloth. A central opening for the head enabled it to be slipped on, and the front and back portions held in, mainly by the sword-belt. The surcoat was frequently green in colour (see the 14th-century romance *Avowynge of King Arthur*) and its exact form may be seen on some few memorial brasses, *c.* 1280–1320. As these show, it was for mounted men. As times and fashions in battle changed, this garment assumed three successive forms: (1) Cyclas, *c.* 1325–35; (2) Jupon through remaining 14th century; (3) Tabard of Arms, originally derived from a short-sleeved coat worn by civilians, and still used by those privately appointed personal servants of the Sovereign who form the staff of the College of Arms (London), Lyon Office (Edinburgh) and the Office of Arms (Dublin). These tabards are worn officially on state occasions.

The coming of the closed helm at the turn of the 13th to 14th centuries, and the increasing close-combat mêlée of that time made mutual identification essential. This is the beginning of armorial bearings, and of the coat-of-arms, by the colouring, dividing, and patterning of the material. The limited range of available colouring matter, and the need for distant visibility without confusion, played a considerable part in the skill and ingenuity shown in producing a large number of unmistakable devices, and many forms of flag. These devices, at first, were simply areas of colour variously arranged.

With further passing of time, two important factors influenced armorial art: first, the increase of population, and the growing number of responsible people (not necessarily warriors) who really required a badge, coat-of-arms or crest by which they could be recognised; second, the discovery of more and more ways of using this method of "writing your name". These factors led to a great increase in the scope of heraldic craftsmanship. Instead of being almost exclusively concerned with the armoured knight and the battlefield, its uses were applied to domestic and peaceful pursuits. Armorial bearings find their place on gold and silver tableware, on china and glass, on wood and stone, or decorating hand written books. Cities, towns, schools, ecclesiastical bodies, banks and other industrial concerns all received legal grants of arms. Thus armorial bearings have not remained a thing of the past but still play an important part in many departments of modern life.

See also HERALDRY.

Armour: defensive cover for the body worn in fighting. Its use has been widespread since early times and undoubtedly the first armour was made from the skins of beasts. The evolution of body armour was governed by the need for extra pro-

Armorial bearings in modern life. Above left: The grasshopper crest of Martin's Bank, Lombard Street. Below left: The arms of Malvern Urban District Council, granted by letters of patent 1951. Below: The arms of the City of London.

tection against improved weapons, the changing tactics of war, the technological skill of the armourer and the limitations of the materials at his disposal.

Probably the first important innovation was to fasten scales or rings of metal to the outside of a simple basic garment of leather. In the later armour of this type the strengthening pieces were often riveted or quilted between layers of cloth or leather. This became known as the brigandine. As working large pieces of metal was difficult, to begin with the Greeks and many nations of the east wore scale armour, consisting of hundreds of specially shaped plates fastened to cloth or leather. This became very heavy, as it was necessary to have the plates overlapping each other to secure complete protection. The Greek soldier also wore a close-fitting helmet of bronze and protective pieces called greaves, which were carefully shaped to fit the legs. Sometimes a cuirass of bronze was worn, consisting of shaped back and breast plates.

Soldiers in the Roman army were provided with body armour of wide strips of leather specially hardened by boiling. Their helmets of bronze were similar to the Greek pattern and later types had visors which could be lowered for extra protection. Their commanders wore elaborately decorated back and breast plates moulded to the shape of the body. In gladiatorial combat a special form of helmet was developed which gave complete protection to the face. Amongst the Greeks and Romans the use of bronze was restricted by the scarcity of the tin required to produce it.

Mail armour, which consisted of thousands of interlaced or riveted links made up into a body garment, was in general use in Europe from the 10th to the 16th century. Its perishable nature has prevented much of an early date from surviving, but certainly in Europe mail was worn before plate and it has been made and used from very early times by almost every race that has used armour. The Bayeux Tapestry, which depicts the conquest of England by William of Normandy, illustrates fine examples of the mail shirt being worn by 11th-century warriors, who are also wearing the typical conical helmet of iron with an extension called the nasal which covered the nose. The mail shirt, or hauberk, was in general use throughout three centuries following the Conquest and this form of armour was so prominent in Europe that the period is often called the Age of Mail. Other forms of armour were used at the same time, but the higher classes wore mail almost exclusively.

The conical Norman helmet was replaced in the 12th century by the barrel helm which had curved sides and a flat top. A little later this was abandoned for the sugar-loaf helm with a pointed top which more easily deflected downward blows. The 13th century saw the final development in mail armour and the complete suit now included a mail coif, similar in design to a balaclava helmet, and this was frequently worn under a *chapel de fer*, or war hat of iron.

About the middle of the 13th century extra plates of steel, called ailettes, were added to protect vulnerable shoulders, and extra protection for the knees was devised in pieces known as poleyns. At about this time helmet visors were introduced and knights adopted the fashion of wearing surcoats over their armour. These were later to become emblazoned with heraldic arms for ease of recognition in battle. The period during which these additions and changes took place is generally referred to as the Transition Period, dating from the latter part of the 13th to the early 15th century. By the beginning of the 14th century many extra pieces of plate had been added: roundels to protect arm-pits and elbow joints; rerebraces to guard shoulders and upper arms; and vambraces encasing the lower part of the arms, including the elbow. Shoes of plate, called sabatons, were worn over mailed feet and gauntlets of steel replaced mittens of mail. Another major change early in the 14th century concerned the helmet. This became much more compact and the new pattern, known as the bascinet, had attached to its edge the aventail or collar of mail.

Towards the end of the Transition Period, in the early 15th century, knights rode into battle completely encased in plate except for the joints, which were covered by gussets of mail. During the next hundred years plate armour reached its greatest perfection. This was the period of Gothic armour which for beauty of form, dignity and perfect adaptation to its purpose has never been surpassed. The light bascinet of the 14th century soon gave way to the sallet which extended backwards to shield the neck and incorporated a movable visor. The end of the 15th century saw the appearance of fluting, which was designed to more easily deflect thrust weapons, and the use of a greater number of smaller plates, thus doing away with the need for the very large guards formerly worn at the joints. These changes resulted in the type of armour known as Maximilian, which is characterised by radiating fluted channels and the more rounded outlines of all its parts. The Maximilian Period lasted from about 1500 to 1540.

The ultimate in a suit of armour of the 16th century consisted of upwards of 130 highly finished and elaborately shaped pieces of tough steel skilfully assembled by means of innumerable articulated joints, often beautifully engraved, etched, gilded or damascened according to the fashion of the period. During the 15th

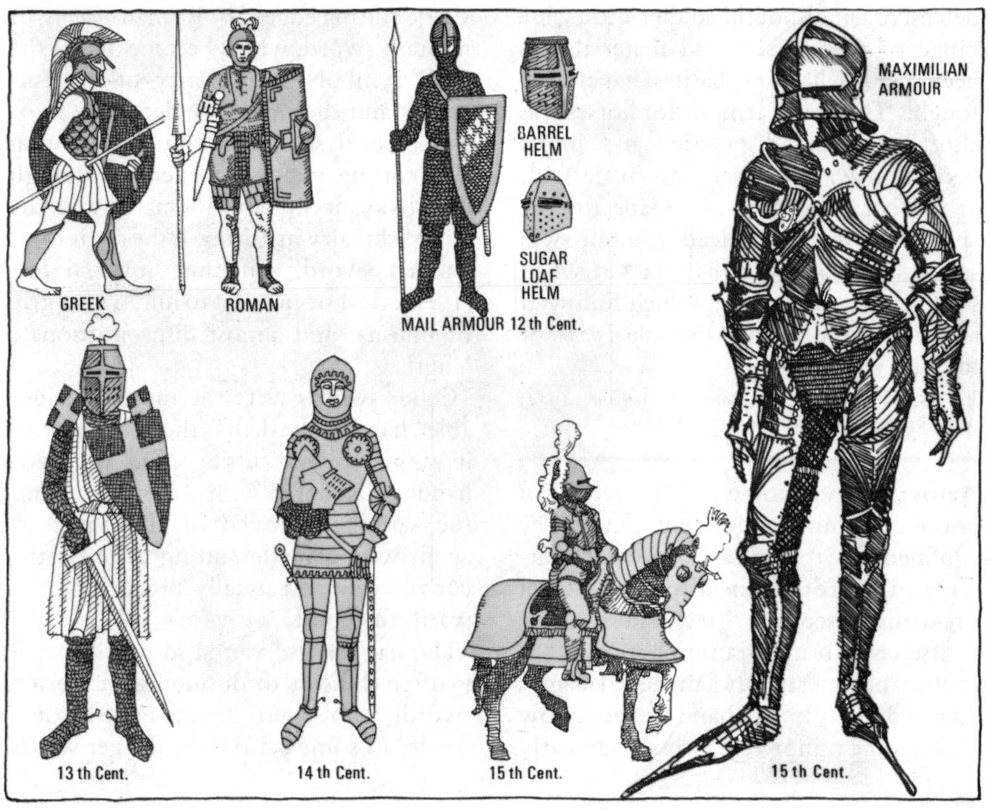

century armour was frequently adapted for the tournament, and in the 16th century special types of armour were evolved such as that made for pikemen, as well as special and costly parade armour.

The styles of European armour changed constantly and experts can confidently date examples to within ten or fifteen years. It is, however, quite different with oriental armours, the styles of which changed seldom and were worn for centuries. By the 10th century Japanese armour had assumed a characteristic form which it retained until armour was abandoned in the middle of the 19th century. In general, the armour of Japan is lighter and more flexible than that of Europe. It is characterised by the small size of the individual plates, the greater use of mail and leather and by the universal use of silk cords to fasten all the parts together.

The shield was essentially a part of the defensive armour of the soldier and a wide range of design, size and materials has been used wherever battles have been fought. The use of armour for horses was also a widespread practice and in its perfection was designed and made with as much care as the suits made for the armoured warrior. Head armour was revived in World War I (1914–18) when steel helmets were worn which followed a very similar pattern to the *chapel de fer* of the 14th century.

¶ PATRICK, NICOLLE. *A Book of Armour*, 1954; WILKINSON, FREDERICK. *Arms and Armour*, 1963

Arms: weapons of war. The term can cover all fighting equipment, but will be confined here to that carried by the fighting man before the general introduction of fire-arms (*see* separate entry). There was, of course, no abrupt transition. The 20th century bayonet is only a medieval dagger attached to a rifle; but hand weapons now play a very minor role, whereas in early centuries they were predominant. For an important type that does not rely entirely on man's muscle, *see* ARCHERY. Otherwise, early arms fall conveniently into three groups. There were some multi-purpose weapons: e.g. the halberd combining a spike and an axe-blade, and the most complicated types could trip and hook as well as pierce and slash. But a broad classification can be made into weapons with a cutting edge; weapons designed for thrusting and piercing at more than arm's length; and weapons for crushing.

Of the first type the most important were the sword and dagger. The dimensions and design of the sword have varied so much through the centuries that there is no such thing as a typical example. The ordinary sword of the ancient Greeks was two-edged, about 18 inches [456 millimetres] long and 2½ inches [63 millimetres] broad. The Spartans used a shorter type, slightly curved along its single cutting edge. The Roman *gladius*, or military sword, which became one of the chief symbols of authority of the emperors and their commanders, was two-edged, short, sharp and as much a thrusting as a cutting weapon. Generally (though not always accurately) associated with the age of chivalry in Europe is the great two-handed sword, sometimes over 6 feet [1·8 metres] from point to hilt, with a grip of unusual and almost disproportionate length.

Other swords were the more manageable "hand-and-a-half", the falchion with its single convex cutting edge, the two-handed flamberge with wavy edges, and the scimitar beloved of the Saracens, again with a single cutting edge on the convex side and usually broadening towards the point.

The dagger also varied so much that it is often difficult to distinguish it from a sword. Some were double-edged, some single. At some periods the dagger was as much a part of the conventional attire of civilians, including ladies, as of the soldier. The sharply tapering baselard or basilard, popular in the 13th and 14th centuries is an example. Other well known types were the kidney dagger, named after the kidney-shaped lobes at the base of the handle; the *main-gauche*, or left-handed dagger, held in the left hand at the same time as the right was wielding a sword; and the thin-bladed *misericorde* (literally "mercy"), used to give the final stroke to a fallen opponent.

The axe was another important cutting weapon. There was the great broad-bladed two-handed axe wielded by the Vikings; the francisca or throwing axe used with great effect by the Franks; and the pole-axe, often used by knights, set on a shaft 6 foot [1·8 metres] long. The axe was often a dual purpose instrument, used both as a tool and as a weapon.

For thrusting and piercing at a greater distance than that involved in hand-to-hand fighting there was the spear, in a knight's hands better known as the lance. The spear was the weapon of the formidable phalanxes (*see* separate entry) deployed in battle by such kings as Philip of Macedon. If the phalanx was eight ranks deep, every man, whatever his position, presented his 18-foot [5·5 metres] spear to the enemy, those of the front rank projecting 14 feet [4·2 metres] forward while those of the rearmost rank came level with, or a little in front of, the first rank—thus making an almost impenetrable hedge. The same type of formation was used by William Wallace at Falkirk (1298) and Robert the Bruce at Bannockburn (1314) with their "schiltrons" or circles of spearmen.

The lance as the chief weapon of the medieval knight. The type used in the joust and tournament was a simple tapering shaft, up to about 12 ft [3·6 metres] long, with a metal head and made of wood, such as ash, that would easily shatter. If the records are reliable, war lances were often much longer. We read that, at the Battle of Poitiers (1356), the French knights cut their lances down from 20 ft [6 metres] to 6 ft [1·8 metres] in length and fought on foot. In the 15th century the pike, in the hands of the Swiss infantry, became the most important weapon on the field. The Swiss pike usually consisted of an 18 ft [5·5 metres] wooden shaft topped by a 3 ft [90 cm] iron spike which could not be cut through by the cavalry's swords. Pikemen formed a bristling wall in defence and were also devastating in attack when they charged together. Pikemen remained important even after the invention of firearms. They were needed to protect arquebusiers and musketeers while they reloaded. When ring bayonets were fitted to muskets the pike was no longer needed.

Of the crushing weapons, the most primitive was the club, which developed into the more sophisticated war-hammer and mace, the latter particularly popular with some soldier-churchmen on the basis of the naïve argument that by using it they did not shed blood by the sword and were therefore not disobeying the Scriptures. The mace, nevertheless, was a terrible weapon in the hands of a powerful man. Somewhat similar in use was the flail, a hinged weapon, the shorter arm of which was a spiked bar or a ball on a chain. The medieval soldier sometimes displayed a grim humour in naming his weapons, one nickname for the flail being the "holy water sprinkler" and, for the mace, the "Morning Star". Basically, many arms were the homely tools and implements of field and farm—the fork, the axe, the flail, the scythe, the hedging knife—distorted and complicated for more terrible purposes.

¶ HALEVY, DOMINIQUE. *Armies and Their Arms*, 1963

Army: a large body of men, organised and equipped for warfare, usually on land. Throughout history many different types of armies can be traced, the chief being: (1) the general body of untrained citizens, pressed into service in some special emergency; (2) the citizen militia which has undergone a period of training; (3) the trained professional fighting men employed for the limited period of a war or campaign; and (4) the permanently employed members of a standing army. It is still possible to find representatives of all four types in warfare today, despite all the developments of military science and of highly technical resources. A special type of soldier has been the mercenary, fighting not for his own country but willing to be hired to serve another. One of the most famous mercenary companies was the White Brotherhood or White Company, led by the Englishman Sir John Hawkwood in the Italian wars of the 15th century. Mercenaries are still fighting, e.g. in recent times in Spain and the Congo.

At various times in history, different nations and countries have emerged as predominant in the practice of arms for a variety of reasons. Thus, the Roman legionaries were remarkable for their superb discipline; the victories of Epaminondas, Philip and Alexander of Macedon in the Ancient World can be largely attributed to their use of the troop formation known as the phalanx; John Ziska of Bohemia (1360–1424) brought his peasants to a terrible peak of efficiency by his use of armoured wagons – the first tanks – and by his highly developed deployment of artillery; and the great English victories of the Hundred Years War were achieved by the might of the English longbowmen. The Swiss won a great reputation with their heavy infantry, armed with pike and halberd. The Swabian *landsknechts* (German, "men of the plains"), organised by the Emperor Maximilian in the 16th century, in their administration, regimental organisation, discipline and etiquette provided the model for most modern armies. For a long period the army enjoying the greatest military reputation was that of Spain, till it was broken at Rocroi (1643) by the French under the twenty-two-year-old Prince de Condé ("the great Condé"). There are few nations of any size or importance that have not at some period or other emerged as great military powers. With his conception of the "nation in arms" as what has been called "a vast manufactory of cannon fodder", and the various schemes of conscription to provide the necessary men for his huge armies, Napoleon may be considered as the founder of the modern army.

As organisation, tactics, quality of leadership, etc., have varied so have the motives and driving force in the ranks. Often it has been simply the unquestioning general dedication to duty of highly trained and disciplined paid troops; sometimes the allegiance enjoyed by some great and magnetic commander; sometimes religious fervour or fanatical patriotism. Oliver Cromwell described the soldiers he most needed as "men as had the fear of God before them and as made some conscience of what they did." The small Swedish nation (helped by mercenaries) achieved surprising military and political stature under Gustavus Adolphus (d. 1632) because of its patriotic zest in the face of threats to its safety. And it was a confederacy of the noblemen and gentlemen of Holland contemptuously dismissed by the Spanish as "only a set of beggars" who adopted the famous war-cry "*Vivent les gueux*!" ("Long live the beggars") which "was so often to ring over land and sea, amid blazing cities, on blood-stained decks, through the smoke and carnage of many a stricken field" (John Lothrop Motley, *The Rise of the Dutch Republic*).

The battle of Camblan. Arthur's last fight with Mordred, from a Ms in The British Museum.

Arthur, King: British king and hero of the great cycle of Arthurian legends and romances. His authenticity as a historical character is difficult to establish or, at least, to disentangle; but the likelihood is that he was a successful Romano-British leader and general against the invading Saxons, born in the 5th century AD.

¶ ASHE, GEOFFREY. *All About King Arthur*, 1969; HIBBERT, CHRISTOPHER. *The Search for King Arthur*, 1970

Artillery: term used originally to denote any mechanical aid to the hurling of solid objects at an enemy. The Old Testament translator described Jonathan's bow and arrows as his "artillery" (I Samuel, 20:40). At an early age engines of war were constructed on the tension, torsion and counterpoise systems to project great stones at besiegers or besieged. Since the discovery of gunpowder in the 13th century the word artillery has been applied to the larger firearms – those too cumbersome to be carried by one man.

The earliest guns were rough tubes, with powder chambers behind them provided with touch-holes through which fire was applied to the powder. The explosion created a huge expansion of gas within the powder chamber, the only outlet for which was, if all went well, through the tube. There lay the projectile, to be expelled by the force of the expanding gases. These early guns, such as those used in all probability by Edward III at Crécy, were of wrought iron, longitudinal bars being bound together by iron hoops; they could fire their stone cannon balls a few hundred yards.

By the middle of the 16th century cast guns had begun to appear in bronze and iron – a big advance in the gunmaker's art, increasing range and accuracy and encouraging the study and development of the science of artillery.

For the next 300 years there was little development in the gun itself; new types of ammunition were designed, however, for engaging different types of target, while more attention was paid to the design of "carriages" on which the guns were moved in and out of battle. Gustavus Adolphus of Sweden was the first to appreciate the power of artillery as a tactically mobile battle weapon and introduced light "field" guns into service as early as 1630. Other nations were slow to follow, but by the end of the 18th century the mobile horse-drawn field gun had come to stay, side by side with the more static coast defence gun.

Between 1850 and 1914 artillery made perhaps the greatest strides in its history, with the introduction in turn of "rifling" of the gun barrel to impart spin to the projectile; of cylindrical in place of spherical shells; of breech-loading in place of muzzle-loading; of more effective measures to contain the gases generated by the explosion of the charge; and of new methods of gun construction to stand up to higher explosive forces. The range of a field gun rose by 1914 to 6,000 yards [5,486 metres] or more and that of the heavier guns to 13,000 yards [11,887 metres]; this led to a revolution in gunnery since fire was now brought to bear – far beyond the field of view from the gun itself – by the employment of observation posts, telephonic communications and various forms of optical instruments. Artillery was now the dominant arm and huge tonnages of ammunition was fired from guns which tended to become heavier and of longer range. The introduction of battle aircraft led to the development of specialised anti-aircraft artillery, and also of aerial observation of artillery fire, while the introduction of the tank led, rather more slowly, to the development of high velocity anti-tank guns. The period following this war saw the mechanical tractor gradually replacing the horse for towing guns.

During World War II the main artillery developments were in the field of technical gunnery which, with the aid of radio, allowed the fire of many guns to be concentrated within a few minutes on to a single target and, with the aid of radar and computers, enabled the anti-aircraft gun layers to follow and accurately engage enemy aircraft.

The free-flight rocket was used at the battles of Leipzig (1813) and Waterloo (1815), but was discarded soon afterwards on grounds of inaccuracy. It was reintroduced, however, during World War II as an area neutralisation weapon in the field and as an anti-aircraft device. It was the introduction of weapon guidance by the Germans in 1944 that led to the use of rocket propulsion on a large scale. Their "V2" rocket, with a range of 200 miles [322 kilometres] and a 1600 lb [726 kg] warhead, incorporated a simple inertial guidance system which, though inaccurate, enabled them, for example, to bombard London from Holland with some success.

Since World War II guided weapons have developed extensively by all the major powers to replace guns in the field, anti-tank, and air defence roles. In addition, the requirement to deliver a nuclear warhead has led to the development of large free-flight and guided rockets, and larger intercontinental ballistic weapons with improved inertial guidance systems. This in its turn is leading to the development of extremely complex anti-ballistic missile systems.

The gun still has many advantages over the guided and unguided missile. It is comparatively simple and reliable, and can deliver a heavy weight of fire accurately. The light air defence gun with its high rate of fire is still popular despite its lower effectiveness compared with the guided missile. An increasing number of tracked self-propelled guns are being introduced to enhance cross-country mobility.

Efforts are now being concentrated on increasing the reliability of target location, artillery communications, and the accuracy of fire by refinements in survey and prediction, with a view to engaging a target effectively without previous correction by observation. The response time of artillery weapons will thus be improved to compete with the increasing mobility of modern battle.

See also CRÉCY, BATTLE OF; WORLD WAR I; WORLD WAR II.

Ashurbanipal or **Assur-bani-pal** (d. *c.* 633 BC): the last great king of Assyria who, at the height of his power, ruled over a vast empire which did not long survive his death. Among his more constructive achievements was the building of the palace and library at Nineveh. The Bible is one source for his history.

¶ KAY, SHIRLEY. *Digging Into the Past*, 1974

See also ASSYRIA.

Bas-reliefs showing an Assyrian king being anointed by an eagle-headed priest figure. Now in the British Museum.

Asia: continent separated from Africa by the Red Sea and from Europe by the Urals, the Caspian and Black Seas and the Aegean, 17 million square miles [44 million square kilometres] in area, with a population in 1982 estimated at 2,718 million. It extends over 85 degrees of latitude and 164 of longitude and includes very different geographical features and climatic conditions. The northern lowlands are exposed to severe winters and are sparsely populated. The central plateau and its mountain ramparts suffer extremes of heat and cold. The south-west (Levant, Iran, West Pakistan) tends to be dry – an area of sheep and goats, of oases and date palms, of flat-roofed mud houses built round internal courtyards. In the south-east, Burma, Malaysia, Indo-China and the Indonesian islands are monsoon lands with high seasonal rainfall, forests at first cultivated on the "slash and burn" principle by tribes living in communal long-houses of bamboo and moving to fresh forest after two years cultivating yams and hill-rice. Later the people learnt to conserve the monsoon rains by reservoirs, canals and terraced rice-fields, and could extract four crops a year. Dense populations and rich civilisations like that of the Khmers of Cambodia (AD 850–1250) grew up in the river valleys.

Only outsiders – Europeans – ventured to give a single name to an area of such diverse landscapes and climates, or to peoples of many races and stages of development. The word "Asiatic" has become objectionable to Asians because it was often used disparagingly by Europeans confident of their superiority in technology, culture and political wisdom. Yet until 1400 it was the Europeans who felt dependent on Asia for silks and spices, for technical skills and religious ideas, for the arts of luxurious living, and for hope of rescue by Prester John (*see* separate entry) from the menace of Islam. Asia was the cradle of the great world religions and the home of the richest and most advanced civilisations. Asia contained all but one of the great river basins which fostered the growth of large-scale political units – Tigris, Euphrates, Indus, Ganges, Menam, Mekong and Yangtze. From Asia came the fierce nomadic conquerors – Huns, Turks, Mongols, Arabs. The Indus valley civilisation flourished *c.* 2000 BC. Sumerians irrigated the Euphrates plain *c.* 3500 BC. In China the Shang dynasty, flourishing in 1450 BC, already had written records. By 623 BC China was unified under the Tang, and from 202 BC to AD 226 the Han dynasty extended her frontiers as far as the Caspian. No dynasty in India was able to give that country political stability, and the mountain ramparts did not save the peninsula from Greek or Turk, but India made great contributions in astronomy, medicine and mathematics – the numerals we know as Arabic, the conceptions of the void, infinity, the atom and over one hundred surgical instruments.

Asians ignored the West: they needed

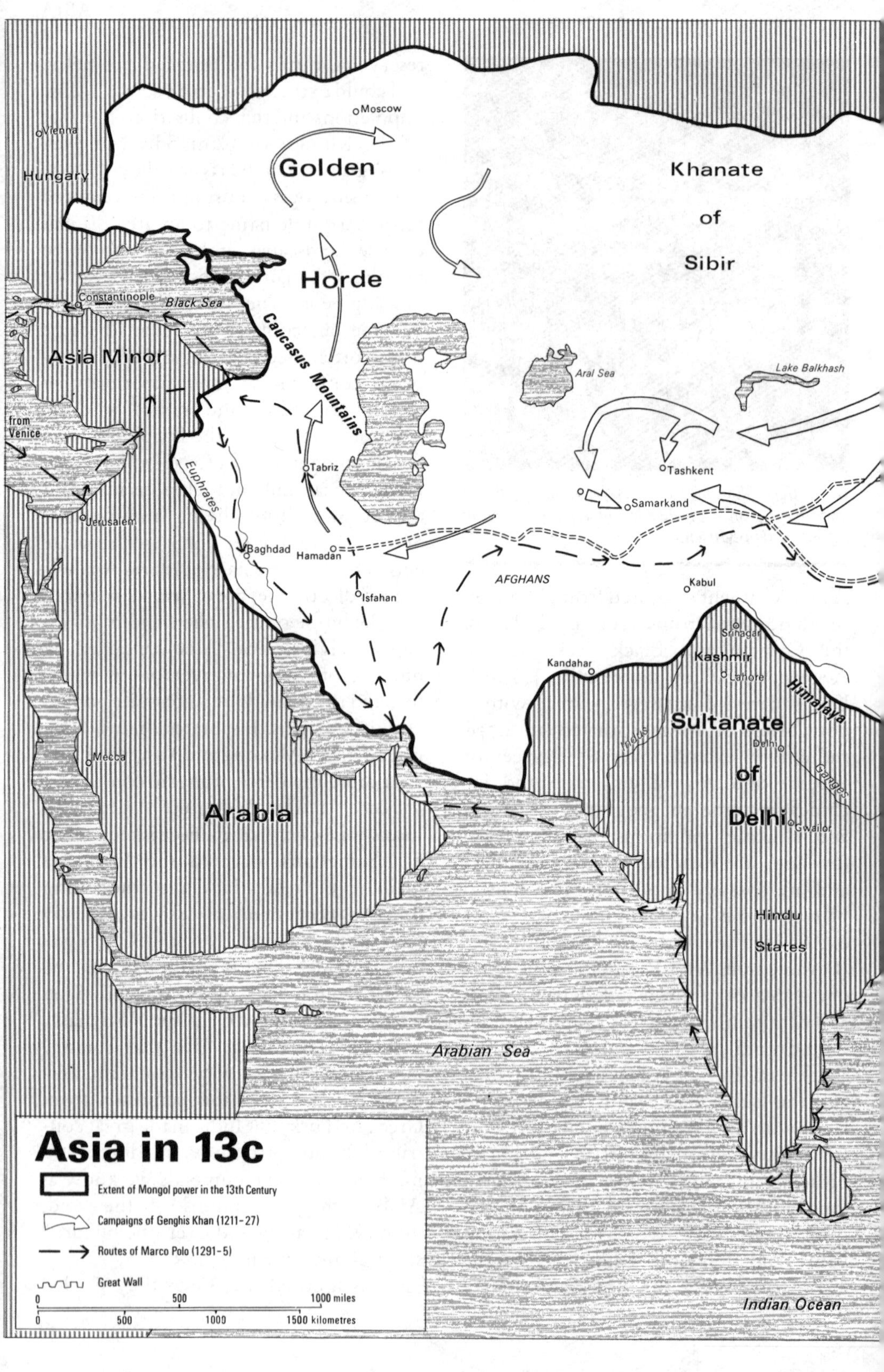
Asia in 13c
Extent of Mongol power in the 13th Century
Campaigns of Genghis Khan (1211-27)
Routes of Marco Polo (1291-5)
Great Wall
0
500
1000 miles
0
500
1000
1500 kilometres
Moscow
Vienna
Hungary
Golden
Horde
Khanate
of
Sibir
Constantinople
Black Sea
Caucasus Mountains
Asia Minor
from Venice
Jerusalem
Aral Sea
Lake Balkhash
Tabriz
Tashkent
Samarkand
Euphrates
Baghdad
Hamadan
Isfahan
AFGHANS
Kabul
Srinagar
Kashmir
Lahore
Kandahar
Himalaya
Sultanate
of
Delhi
Indus
Delhi
Ganges
Gwailor
Mecca
Arabia
Hindu
States
Arabian Sea
Indian Ocean

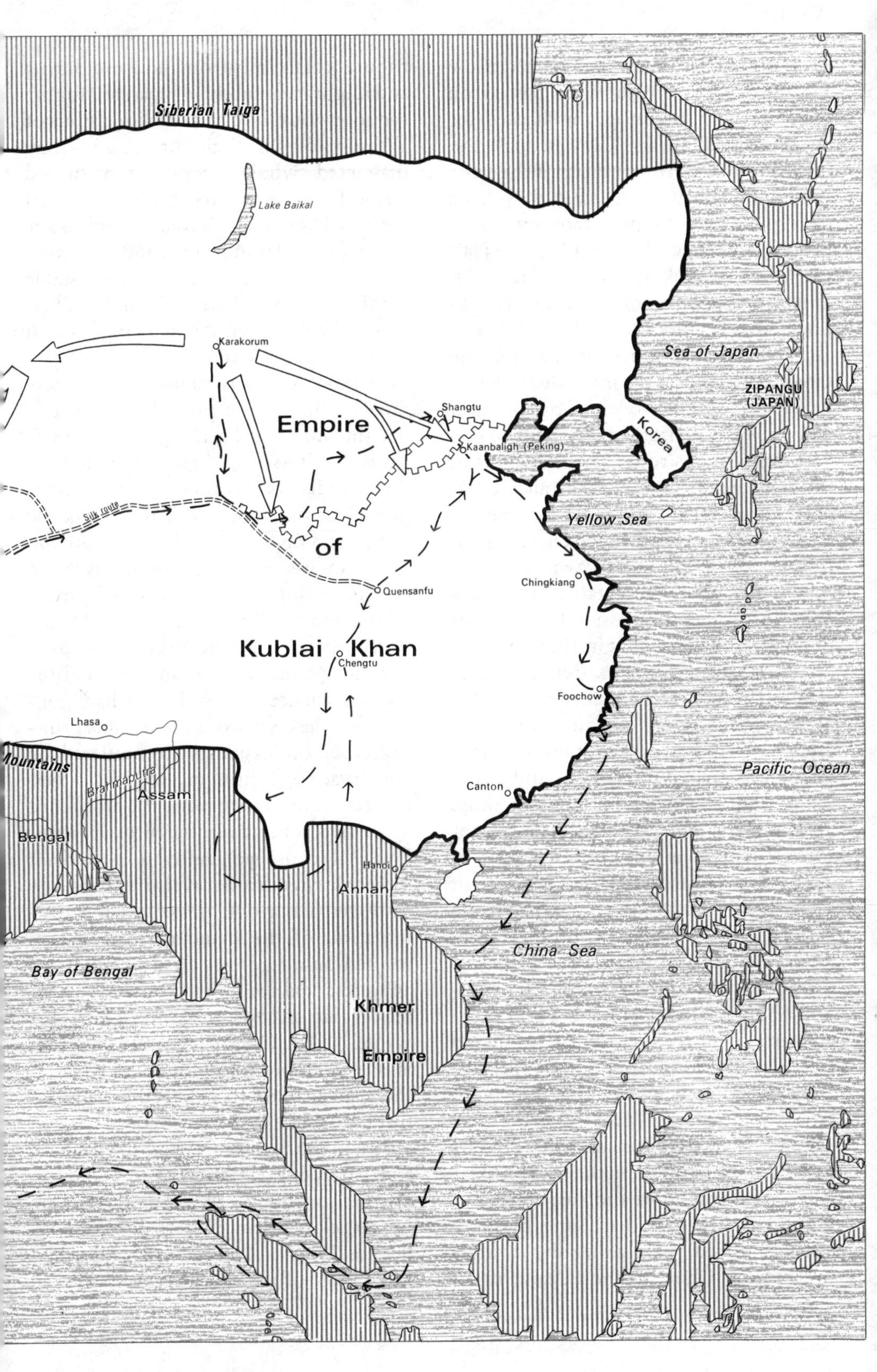
Siberian Taiga
Lake Baikal
Karakorum
Empire
of
Kublai Khan
Shangtu
Kaanbaligh (Peking)
Silk route
Quensanfu
Chengtu
Lhasa
Mountains
Brahmaputra
Assam
Bengal
Sea of Japan
ZIPANGU
(JAPAN)
Korea
Yellow Sea
Chingkiang
Foochow
Pacific Ocean
Canton
Hanoi
Annan
China Sea
Bay of Bengal
Khmer
Empire

no European product and rejected those European ideas which were forced on their notice. The Europeans thirsted for Asian spices and silks. They struggled to control the western terminals of the trade routes, but only twice have they been strong enough to penetrate into Asia proper. Alexander the Great (356–323 BC) carried the Greek Empire to the Indus and the kingdom of Bactrian Greeks lingered after him astride the Silk Road. But Asia rejected Greek civilisation. The Greek emphasis on the individual citizen, developing his personality by physical and intellectual effort, did not suit Asia's vast spaces, monstrous natural disasters of drought, famine and nomad raids, or its enervating climate and enforced idleness while crops ripen in the moist heat. Asians looked for a philosophy which valued meditation, passive acceptance of inescapable misfortune, compassion for all forms of life, and they found it in Buddhism. In 262 BC Asoka, of the Gupta dynasty which stemmed the Greek advance into India, accepted Buddhism, and in AD 400–800 Buddhism did much to unit the two greatest Asian civilisations – India and China; but the older religions of those areas revived and led them in divergent paths. Islam gave unity to large areas of Asia. Arab seafarers had traded with China before Muhammad, and they made many converts in Malaya and Indonesia. Arab conquest of Persia was less successful as the proud Persians adopted the unorthodox Shiite doctrine, but the Turks were converted and they carried Islam at the sword's point to India.

The third force which strove to unite Asia was the Mongol Empire. In the 13th century Genghis Khan and his descendants (chief among them the great Kublai Khan, of whose court and empire Marco Polo gave such a vivid account) by sheer terror enforced peace along the caravan routes from China to the Levant, drew tribute occasionally from India and Burma and might have subdued Japan but for the typhoon. But they had the limitations of all nomads. In their first onset they massacred whole peoples and turned fertile fields into sparse pasture or even desert. They contributed no ideas or techniques of lasting value, and they were unable to develop or maintain stable administrations of settled lands. Their empire broke up into feudal kingdoms of mainly Turkish war lords.

By 1500 Asia was subjected to a new shock – the second great European onslaught. Into seas hitherto navigated exclusively by Asians – Arabs, Dravidians of South India and Javanese – sailed Portuguese galleons. They, and after them the Dutch and English, drove Asian shipping off Asian seas. Asia's answer to this threat was to withdraw her centres of power inland and live in isolation. This failure to compete with the West is hard to explain. At the time Asians still held the lead in science. The Chinese had gunpowder, the compass, and movable printing type. But Asians were hindered by conservative forms of society. Their reverence for ancestors and the practice of a married son remaining in his parents' house discouraged innovation. Indians were inhibited from travel and change by caste restrictions, Chinese by the conservatism of the mandarin class which insisted on a rigorous classical education and preserved the script of 50,000 characters. As late as 1793 the Chinese Emperor wrote, "Our Celestial Empire possesses all things in prolific abundance. There is therefore no need to import the manufactures of outside barbarians." Lord Curzon wrote in the 20th century of the "superb and paralysing conceit" of the Chinese. By the late 19th century Asians could no longer close their eyes to Western influence. England and France occupied by force most of the southern peninsulas in their efforts to forestall each other. Russia joined them in the bid for Chinese markets, and the United States forced Japan to open her ports.

As early as the 1850s the Taiping Rebellion and the Indian Mutiny showed that Asian pride and nationalism could still be stirred; and Japan's defeat of Russia in 1904 marked the turning of the tide. Today, as the West falters, some of its youth is looking to Indian mystics or Chinese Marxists for the redeeming Word. Russia, as the only European power with a large empire in Asia, seems likely to bear the brunt of Asian resurgence.

See also INDIVIDUAL ENTRIES.

Asia Minor: western peninsula of Asia and its principal land link with Europe. 200,000 square miles (518,000 square kilometres) in area, it consists of the Anatolian plateau walled on north and south by limestone ridges which converge on the Taurus Mountains in the east. The centre of the plateau is desert and salt lake, but its fringes offer good grazing for goats and horses. The Mediterranean coast is precipitous, but the Aegean coast is open to the fertile valleys of the Meander and Hermus. The eastern rampart is pierced by passes into Armenia and by the Cilician Gate and has deterred migration from the east. The desolate heart of Anatolia and the lack of navigable rivers tend to isolate the fertile areas from each other, but unity has been imposed for long periods by great empires coveting this region for its strategic importance.

The first great empire was that of the Hittites, stocky invaders from the north, who dominated Anatolia from 1700 to 1200 BC. They gained from Armenia, and jealously guarded, the secret of making iron in large quantities, but were eventually driven towards the Euphrates by tribes entering Anatolia from the Balkans – Scythians, Phrygians, Achaeans from Greece, Galatians or Gauls. The Greeks established trading cities which made Phrygian wool into cloth, felts and blankets. The kingdom of Lydia became the frontier state of the Greeks, grew rich on the caravan trade and made the first stamped coinage from the electrum of Sardis.

In 546 BC Cyrus of Persia captured King Croesus of Lydia and made Anatolia a province of the Achaemenian Empire. The Persians built great roads, perhaps using Hittite routes. The Persian attack provoked reaction from the west and, in 334 BC, Alexander crossed into Asia Minor and passed eastwards to the Indus. On his death Anatolia fell, with Persia and the Punjab, to Seleucus. The Seleucids built cities on the Greek pattern and thoroughly Hellenised the region and, when the last Seleucid king of Pergamum bequeathed his province to Rome in 133 BC, the Greek language and culture were undisturbed. The Romans developed the metal and marble resources, and their Byzantine successors, after weathering Persian and Arab attacks, made Anatolia in the 9th century AD the basis of their military power and economic prosperity.

The defeat of the Byzantine Emperor by Seljuk Turks at Manzikert in AD 1071 heralded a wave of nomadic movement from Central Asia. Seljuk sultans established the Empire of Rum (Rome) based on caravan cities like Konieh and Sivas; but they failed to control the flood of nomads, Turks and Mongols, who came in search of land and booty. They were succeeded by one such band, the followers of Osman who had been granted a tract bordering the remnant of Byzantine territory and could therefore offer fighting, booty and infidel land. Taking Brusa in 1326 and crossing to Europe to take Adrianople in 1354 they founded the Ottoman Empire, and Anatolia declined, its people wasted by malaria and by demands for troops from sultans living and campaigning in Europe. Trade dwindled, and Europe was severed from contact with the region by which St Paul reached Macedonia. The Anatolians were not persecuted, and Greek-speaking Christians survived in large numbers, some of them being exchanged for Balkan Muslims when Kemal Ataturk overthrew the Ottoman Empire in 1921–23 and established Ankara as the capital of a Turkish Empire confined to Asia Minor and the small area surrounding Istanbul.

Asiento, The: the name, meaning "contract", given to the 1713 agreement for supplying the Spanish colonies in the West with Negro slaves. From 1702 a French company had had the exclusive contract, but by the Peace of Utrecht, following the War of the Spanish Succession (1702–13) the monopoly passed to Britain, who was authorised to supply a total of 144,000 slaves in thirty years, at the rate of 4,800 a year. Britain lost this degrading privilege for a time in the War of the Austrian Succession (1741–48) but had it restored for the four years remaining of the original contract. By the Treaty of El Retiro (1750) Britain agreed to the cancellation of the Asiento on the payment by Spain of £100,000.

Asoka (*c.* 273–232 BC)**:** Buddhist Emperor of India. Grandson of Chandragupta, founder of the Gupta dynasty, he ruled over a territory from the Hindu Kush to the northern boundary of Mysore. Impressed by the horrors of war, he attempted conquest by religion, which for him meant rule by the Buddhist code of morals. His empire fell to pieces after his death.

Assassination: originally the murder of Christians by chosen Muslim fanatics, from *Hashishiyun*, the drug they frequently took. It now has the general meaning of murder for political or religious reasons.

Assyria: kingdom on the Middle Tigris, its capitals successively at Asshur, Calah and Nineveh. The Assyrians were Semitic nomads who adopted the religion and good administration of the Sumerians. They rose to importance about 1350 BC; flourished under Tiglath-Pileser III (746–727) and Sennacherib (704–681); and were overwhelmed by the Medes and Babylonians in 612 BC. They prospered by trade (see Nahum, 3:16). Their donkey caravans, rafts and river boats exchanged the barley from their irrigated fields for Cappadocian copper, Armenian iron, Bactrian camels, Iranian horses or Lebanese timber. To safeguard these trade routes and interrupt those of its rivals, Assyria was tempted into the "policy of the unremitting offensive" (Toynbee). It developed, and constantly improved, a standing army of armoured infantry, cavalry, charioteers and siege engineers. Its kings gloated over the chilling terror they inspired and ruthlessly deported whole populations, including the lost ten tribes of Israel. They fought

Sculpture in bas-relief showing Asshurbanipal fighting lions on horseback and on foot. Now in the British Museum.

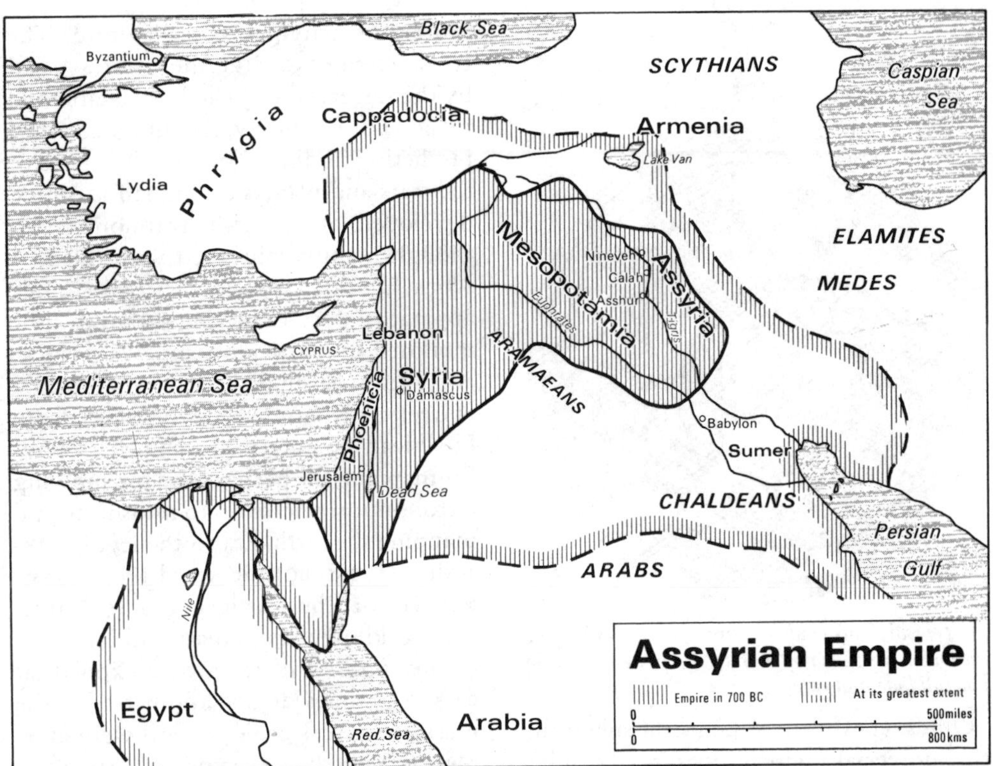

Egypt for control of Syrian trade, defended their homeland from Aramaean and Chaldaean nomads, and fought off waves of invaders from the North – Elamites, Scythians and Medes. The British Museum in London displays impressive Assyrian bas-reliefs of her armies and the royal lion hunts.

¶ PIKE, E. ROYSTON. *Finding out about the Assyrians*, 1963

Astrolabe: an instrument once used for observing and computing the positions and motions of the sun, stars and other heavenly bodies, also for calculating time and for survey work.

The astrolabe was probably invented by Greek astronomers working near Alexandria *c.* AD 350. After the 7th century the Arabs developed its manufacture and usage extensively. The astrolabe came to Europe with the Moorish occupation of Spain in the 8th century. By 1480 astrolabes were widely used in Europe and a special Mariner's Astrolabe had been designed for navigational purposes. Obsolescent in Europe by the end of the 17th century, astrolabes were used until the 19th century in the Middle East.

The astrolabe is drawn on a form of stereographic projection. The usual type is suspended by a ring shackled to the "throne" at the top of the body, or mater. The mater holds a fretted star map (or rete) and underlying plates, each of which is made for the latitude of place. The plates are engraved with lines for setting the rete. The back of European astrolabes has a zodiac/calendar scale, time scales and a shadow square. Islamic astrolabes usually have mathematical scales and a lunar/zodiac scale. The parts are held together by a pin, on which are mounted a sighting bar, an alidade and a rule.

A typical, suspended astrolabe showing the various parts; the mater, rete and plates, sighting bar, alidade and rule.

Other types of astrolabe are the spherical, the universal, which does not require separate plates, and the linear. Many fine examples are to be found in museums. *See also* MATHEMATICAL INSTRUMENTS.

Astronomy: the science dealing with the heavenly bodies and the earth in relation to them. It may be conveniently described under two headings: positional astronomy, which is concerned with observing, recording and predicting the positions and movements of the stars, planets and other celestial phenomena; and physical astronomy, which is concerned with investigation of their physical nature.

From excavations, we know that between 2000 and 200 BC the Babylonians had developed their habit of watching the stars into a mathematically based science, through which they had established a lunar calendar and a system of predicting the positions of the sun, moon and planets. This gave a fundamental framework of time and direction on which to base such important activities as agriculture. The zodiac circle of 360° (i.e. the zone traversed by the sun each year) had been established by 400 BC. Astrology, the supposed art of predicting or discovering the influence of the stars and planets on human fortunes, developed along with astronomy. Although mainly concerned with calendar work, Egyptian astronomers used a simple apparatus for observing transits, the merkhet, simple shadow and water clocks and a form of sundial.

Greek astronomers, benefiting from Euclidean geometry, developed systems for mapping the heavens and for applying astronomical references to measuring and mapping the earth. Erastosthenes of Alexandria (*c.* 250 BC) measured the circumference of the earth as 24,850 miles [39,990 kilometres], an astonishingly accurate figure. It is now reckoned at 24,850·53 miles [40,008 kilometres] at the meridian. Greek achievements were summarised in the *Almagest* (*c.* AD 150), Ptolemy's explanation of planetary motion, in which the earth is the centre of the universe and each planet moves about it in a mathematically calculated circular orbit. Roman astronomy is remembered chiefly because of the introduction by Julius Caesar, in 46 BC, of the Julian calendar of $365\frac{1}{4}$ days.

Humorous illustration comparing the relative merits of the Egyptian shadow and water clocks, from The Illustrated History of Science, *by Dr E. Sherwood.*

From the 7th century the Arabs and Persians developed astronomy and mathematics to a high degree. They founded observatories with organised study programmes. Their skill in masonry and metal work enabled them to build large sundials and quadrants, as well as portable instruments such as astrolabes. Following the Mongol invasion, the observatory at Samarkand (the present city of West Uzbekistan, USSR) became a centre for the exchange of knowledge with the Far East.

With the 8th-century Moorish Arab invasion, Spain became the western centre for the transmission of Arab astronomical knowledge, which reached much of south-west Europe by the 11th century. The invention of printing and the translation of the *Almagest* direct from Greek sources in the 15th century increased the spread of the science.

The publication (1543) of *De Revolutionibus* by Copernicus (1473–1543) brought a great advance in astronomical thought. Copernicus put the sun at the centre of the planetary system, though he retained the concept of circular orbits for the planets.

Tycho Brahe (1546–1601), an outstanding Danish observer, greatly improved the design of instruments and the cataloguing of stars. Before his observation of a supernova in 1572, it had been thought that stars existed in a changeless state.

Profiting from Tycho's results and through his own brilliant grasp of mathematics, the German Johannes Kepler (1571–1630) devised new laws stating that planets moved in elliptical orbits about the sun at a non-uniform speed. He also showed a relationship between periods of revolution and distances from the sun. Galileo (1564–1642) was the first to use a telescope for serious astronomical purposes (1609). His observations proved the existence of many more stars and confirmed the changing state of heavenly bodies.

From his observations of the moons of Jupiter, Roemer (1644–1710), another Danish astronomer, was the first to measure the speed of light accurately (1675).

Galileo's study of gravity paved the way to Sir Isaac Newton's study of universal gravitation. In his book *Principia Mathematica* (1687), Newton (1642–1727) showed how the planets are kept in their orbits by the same force as causes apples to fall to the ground. Not only did he solve a fundamental problem, but he explained the effects of gravity in scientific and mathematical terms. Although he sacrificed much of his own work to help Newton, Edmund Halley (1656–1742) completed his study of the paths of comets, giving further support to Newton's laws. Newton also investigated the properties of light and invented a new form of telescope, using mirrors as well as lenses. James Bradley (1693–1762), the clergyman who became Astronomer Royal, made an important contribution with his explanation of the aberration of light and nutation, or nodding, of the earth's axis. In 1787 Sir William Herschel (1738–1822) discovered a new planet, Uranus. Herschel also introduced a fresh concept of nebulae (cloud-like masses of gas, usually made luminous by radiation from nearby stars) and of the form of the sidereal system (i.e. the fixed stars and constellations), concluding that it was shaped like a lens with the Milky Way forming an edge.

The science of astrophysics was founded in the early 19th century with the first examinations of the nature of a star, through analysis of its spectrum by means of the spectroscope. William Wollaston (1766–1828) and then the German physicist Joseph von Fraunhoffer (1787–1826) showed there was a consistent connection between the rays of light emitted by a star and its matter. Later, Christian Doppler (1803–53) showed that the motion of a star could be measured by movements in its spectrum, and Sir William Huggins (1824–1910) applied this principle to the measurement of the speeds and directions in space of stars. The spectroscope also allowed astronomers to investigate the nature of the sun for the first time.

In the early years of the 20th century Hertzsprung and Russell made important discoveries in the field of the evolution of stars, using an application of spectroscopy. Since then, atomic physics has enlightened astronomers still further. Photography and radio astronomy (*see* separate entry) have provided improved tools for their work. Progress in space research enabled man to reach the moon in 1969.

See also MEASUREMENT.

Ataturk, Kemal (Mustafa Kemal, *c.* 1880–1938): Turkish soldier and statesman. One of the army officers who came to prominence after the overthrow of the Sultans, as general he expelled the Greeks from Smyrna (1922). As first President and "Father of his Country", he established the capital at Ankara and began the processes of emancipation and modernisation which made modern Turkey.

Athens: the most famous and important city of ancient Greece. It is still dominated by the Acropolis, the original citadel. The ancient city was centred around this hill, which served as a fort and a sanctuary probably as early as 1500 BC. Athens was insignificant till about 600 BC when serious trouble had been caused by the ownership of land becoming concentrated in the hands of a small privileged class, leading to virtual slavery and acute financial distress among the agricultural population.

In 594 BC Solon was given the task of reform. He changed Athens from a state based on birth to one based on wealth, and commercial prosperity grew under the "tyrants" Pisistratus and Hippias. After Hippias' expulsion in 510 BC Cleisthenes's democratic reforms prepared Athens for the major part she was to play in the struggle against Persia (490–479 BC).

With further reforms Athens had the most extreme democracy in Greece. All government posts were annually changed, and most were filled by lot. The main power rested in a vote by the whole citizen body, and only the generals were in any sense professionals. The fifty years from 480 to 430 BC saw the flowering of all the

The Parthenon, on the Acropolis, Athens, one of the world's most beautifully proportioned buildings.

arts, drama, painting, sculpture and architecture – an age associated with the genius of Pericles. Under his guidance the magnificent buildings, including the Parthenon, were started, and the Athenian Empire grew into the strongest power in Greece. Although Athens was defeated by Sparta in the Peloponnesian War (431–404 BC) she continued to produce great literary men, this time in comedy, oratory and philosophy. The roll-call is phenomenal – Aeschylus, Sophocles and Euripides as tragedians, Aristophanes the comic playwright, the sculptors Pheidias and Praxiteles, Ictinus the designer of the Parthenon, Socrates and Plato as philosophers, Thucydides the first scientific historian, Demosthenes and Isocrates as orators, and a host of others. All these were the products of a city of not more than 200,000 inhabitants which included perhaps 50,000 slaves. With the rise of Macedon under Philip II and Alexander, Athens lost her political importance, remaining a city of culture and beauty and one of the most important university centres of the Mediterranean. This tradition of teaching and learning was made international by Aristotle, and continued until the closing of the school of philosophy by Justinian in AD 529.

¶ ANDERSON, PATRICK. *Finding out about the Athenians*, 1961

Atlantic, Battle of the: the four-year struggle (1939–43) in World War II between German U-boats (*Unterseeboot* or undersea boat) and Allied merchant shipping carrying food and vital supplies. An important feature was the "wolf-pack" tactic by which numbers of U-boats hunted together, not always submerged. After tremendous Allied losses, the U-boat menace was finally defeated by the use of efficient escort and convoy systems and supporting aircraft.

Atlantic Cable: In the 1850s Cyrus West Field (1819–92) promoted the Atlantic Telegraph Company, to lay a transatlantic cable. Attempts in 1857 and 1858 were unsuccessful through deterioration of the electrical insulation. Improved cable of copper wire sheathed in gutta percha, hemp and iron wires, and sensitive equipment developed by William Thomson, later Lord Kelvin (1824–1907), enabled the *Great Eastern* to complete the first successful laying in 1866. Twenty telegraph cables now link Europe and the USA.

Telephone cables capable of transmitting 168 calls simultaneously were completed between Newfoundland and Scotland, and Newfoundland and France, in 1956 and 1959.

Atlantic Charter: the joint declaration of eight fundamental principles for a postwar settlement by Franklin D. Roosevelt, President of the USA, and Winston Churchill, Prime Minister of Great Britain, who met at sea 14 August 1941. The principles were concerned with the need for personal and national liberty and "freedom from fear and want".

Atlantis: a legendary island, group of islands, or continent in the Atlantic Ocean, now supposedly submerged. The story persists from the time of Plato (*c.* 429–*c.* 347 BC) till today and is still a subject for archaeological speculation. It is one of a group of legendary lost islands, including King Arthur's Avalon, the Greek Isles of the Blest, St Brendan's Island and the Portuguese Isle of Seven Cities, most of which are marked on early maps.

¶ O'CLERY, HELEN. *The Pegasus Story of Atlantis*, 1970

Atomic bomb: Its origins can be traced back to the work of Leucippus (*c.* 440 BC) and Democritus (*c.* 460 BC) whose atomic theory was further developed by the French scientist Henri Becquerel (the discoverer of radioactivity) in 1895, and the German chemist Otto Hahn (1879–1968), who discovered the fission process in which an explosion is caused by splitting the heart or nucleus of an atom. Therefore "nuclear" bomb is a more correct description than "atomic". More work was carried out at Cambridge, at the College de France and in Copenhagen, where Niels Bohr (1885–1962) reported on "chain reaction" set off by escaping neutrons.

The manufacture of the bomb concentrated on two types: either using 2½ lb [1·13 kg] of uranium 235, or plutonium. In Britain, Tube Alloys (actually Imperial Chemical Industries and Metropolitan Vickers) and, in the USA, the Manhattan Project, did the work. The result was the construction of a plutonium bomb ("Fat Man") which was exploded in the New Mexico desert at 5.30 a.m. on 16 July

The predecessor to the atom smasher, an apparatus for "the artificial disintegration of the elements".

1945. The uranium bomb ("Little Boy") was dropped by a B-29 Superfortress, *Enole Gay*, over Hiroshima on the morning of 6 August 1945, exploding at 800 feet [245 metres], destroying about 5 square miles [13 square kilometres] of the city and killing 70,000 people. On 9 August a second B-29 (*Bockscar*) dealt a similar blow to Nagasaki using "Fat Man" – the plutonium bomb.

¶ FERMI, LAURA. *All About Energy*, 1962

Augustine, St (Augustine of Canterbury, d. between 604 and 609): missionary to England and first Archbishop of Canterbury. Sent by Pope Gregory the Great, he arrived in England in 597 with forty monks, carrying a silver cross and a picture of the Crucifixion. Ethelbert of Kent received him with friendliness and was baptised by him in St Martin's Church, Canterbury. Augustine was named Bishop of the English and, it is said, baptised 10,000 converts to Christianity at Christmas. Because Ethelbert was the strongest king in England and Canterbury was his capital, that city has remained the seat of the primate or chief bishop.

See CANTERBURY; CANTERBURY, ARCHBISHOP OF.

Augustine of Hippo, St (354–430): African bishop and writer. Although of pure Roman birth, his father and mother were African provincials, probably with Numidian blood. He received a good education and adopted the normal moral standards of his time. Though there is no evidence of licentiousness and dissipation, he found much to reproach himself with in later years and tells some of the story in his *Confessions*. He became a convert to Christianity and was baptised in 387. Thereafter he attained a deserved reputation as a great scholar and Father of the Church, though fixed for life in the small seaport of Hippo, from which his letters, sermons and books exercised a vast influence over a much wider community.

¶ In DE SELINCOURT, AUBREY. *Six Great Thinkers*, 1958

Augustus, Gaius Julius Octavianus (63 BC–AD 14): first Roman emperor. Adopted by Julius Caesar (100–44 BC) as his heir in his will, the young Octavian in 44 BC immediately clashed with Mark Antony for the supremacy. Trouble was temporarily avoided by a coalition to defeat Brutus and Cassius at Philippi in 42 BC, but final conflict was inevitable, and Antony and Cleopatra were defeated and dead by 30 BC. Octavian then set about establishing the Empire and was given the title of Augustus in 27 BC. He left nominal control to the Senate and people, but in reality kept the power himself. All the frontier provinces and all but one of the legions were under him, and he managed the elections to favour suitable men. The Empire was therefore at the start almost a confidence trick, though it was clear that Augustus meant it to be an hereditary monarchy.

The contribution of Augustus to the Roman world was vast. The Civil Wars were ended and, under the Augustan peace, administration was enormously improved and a civil service was started. The provinces were well governed and regularly inspected. The frontiers of the Empire were fixed on natural lines (e.g. the rivers Rhine and Danube). His administrators were chosen from the knights as well as from the Senate. On the social side he tried to re-establish old standards and gave great encouragement to the arts. He relied on great men as helpers, e.g. Agrippa and Tiberius as generals, Virgil, Horace and Livy as writers to glorify Rome, and Maecenas in domestic affairs. The city was largely rebuilt.

Towards the end of his reign he seemed increasingly isolated and inactive. Trouble was always near on the frontiers, and his death left Rome still far from settled.

¶ In PRINGLE, PATRICK. *101 Great Lives*, 1964

See ROME, RULERS OF, for many other Caesars.

Australia: largest island and smallest continent of the globe, in the Pacific Ocean and entirely within the southern hemisphere. It takes its name from *Terra Australis*, the unknown great southland of the early geographers and map-makers.

Early navigators who explored Australia's coastline included the Dutchman Dirk Hartog, who landed on the west coast in 1616; Abel Tasman, also Dutch, who sailed the coast of Tasmania in 1642, naming it Van Diemen's Land; and the Englishman, William Dampier, who, in 1688 and 1689, sailed the western and north-western coastline. Captain James Cook, the English surveyor and circumnavigator, sailed along the east coast in 1770, landing at Botany Bay.

Governor Arthur Phillip founded the first penal settlement at Sydney Cove, New South Wales, in 1788. Other penal settlements were established in Van Diemen's Land (Tasmania) in 1803, and in 1824 at Morton Bay, Queensland. Western Australia was originally a free settlement, founded at Perth on the banks of the Swan River by Captain Stirling. It accepted convicts in 1849. In 1835 two colonists, Batman and Faulkner, founded Melbourne on Port Phillip Bay. South Australia, the only colony which never accepted convicts, was established by free settlers in 1836 at Adelaide under Governor Hindmarsh. George Bass and Matthew Flinders sailed the south coast of New South Wales and in 1798, in the sloop *Norfolk*, circumnavigated the whole continent.

The Great Dividing Range of mountains, which runs along the major part of the eastern coast, separates the coastal plain from the good pastoral land inland. The settlement at Sydney Cove was prevented from expanding by these mountains until three colonists, Blaxland, Wentworth and Lawson, found a way across in 1813. Land exploration then began. George Evans and John Oxley explored inland New South Wales, discovering the Lachlan and Macquarie Rivers; Allan Cunningham travelled north, finding the Darling Downs, one of the most fertile areas in Australia; in 1824 Hamilton Hume and William Hovell travelled overland from Sydney to Port Phillip Bay, Victoria, discovering the headwaters of the Murray River and establishing an important overland route; and Charles Sturt and Hume found the Darling River in 1829. In 1830 Sturt sailed down the Darling to the point where it joined the mighty River Murray, and then continued down the Murray to reach Lake Alexandrina. These are only a few in the long roll-call of men who endured hardship and sometimes lost their lives in the 19th-century exploration of the interior.

Discovery of good pastoral land led to the introduction into Australia of Spanish merino sheep by the early settlers. Merinos were found more suited to the climate than the English breeds, and their excellent fine fleece soon made Australia one of the world's leading wool producers. Thomas Mort installed refrigeration in ships to carry frozen lamb to other parts of the world. William Farrer experimented in 1902 with varieties of wheat suitable for Australia's hot, dry climate. He cultivated many types, notably the "Federation" strain. The

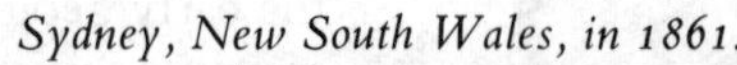
Sydney, New South Wales, in 1861.

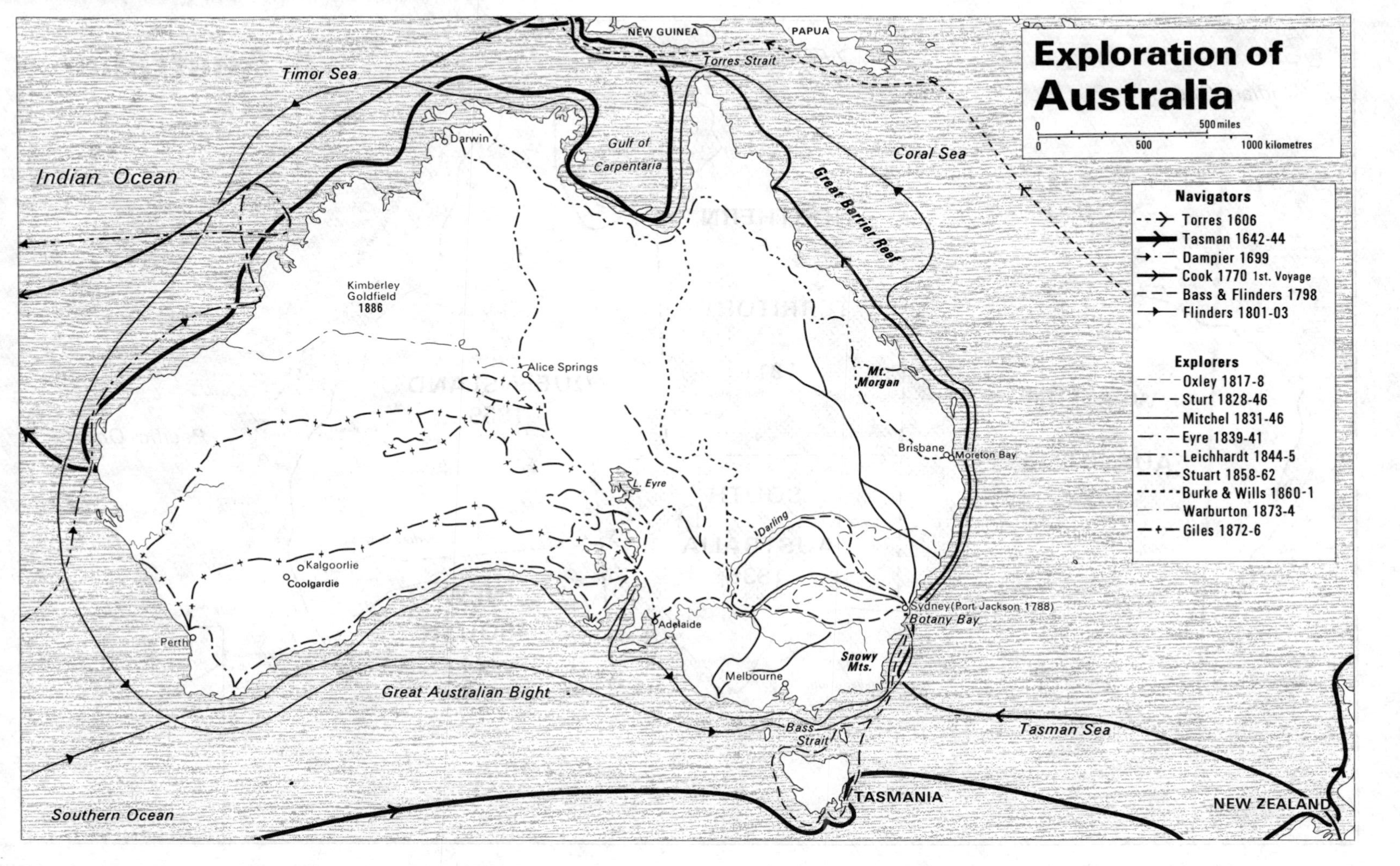
Exploration of Australia
0 500 miles
0 500 1000 kilometres
Navigators
Torres 1606
Tasman 1642-44
Dampier 1699
Cook 1770 1st. Voyage
Bass & Flinders 1798
Flinders 1801-03
Explorers
Oxley 1817-8
Sturt 1828-46
Mitchel 1831-46
Eyre 1839-41
Leichhardt 1844-5
Stuart 1858-62
Burke & Wills 1860-1
Warburton 1873-4
Giles 1872-6
NEW GUINEA
PAPUA
Torres Strait
Timor Sea
Coral Sea
Indian Ocean
Gulf of Carpentaria
Great Barrier Reef
Darwin
Kimberley Goldfield 1886
Alice Springs
Mt. Morgan
Brisbane
Moreton Bay
L. Eyre
Darling
Kalgoorlie
Coolgardie
Sydney (Port Jackson 1788)
Botany Bay
Adelaide
Perth
Snowy Mts.
Melbourne
Great Australian Bight
Bass Strait
Tasman Sea
TASMANIA
NEW ZEALAND
Southern Ocean

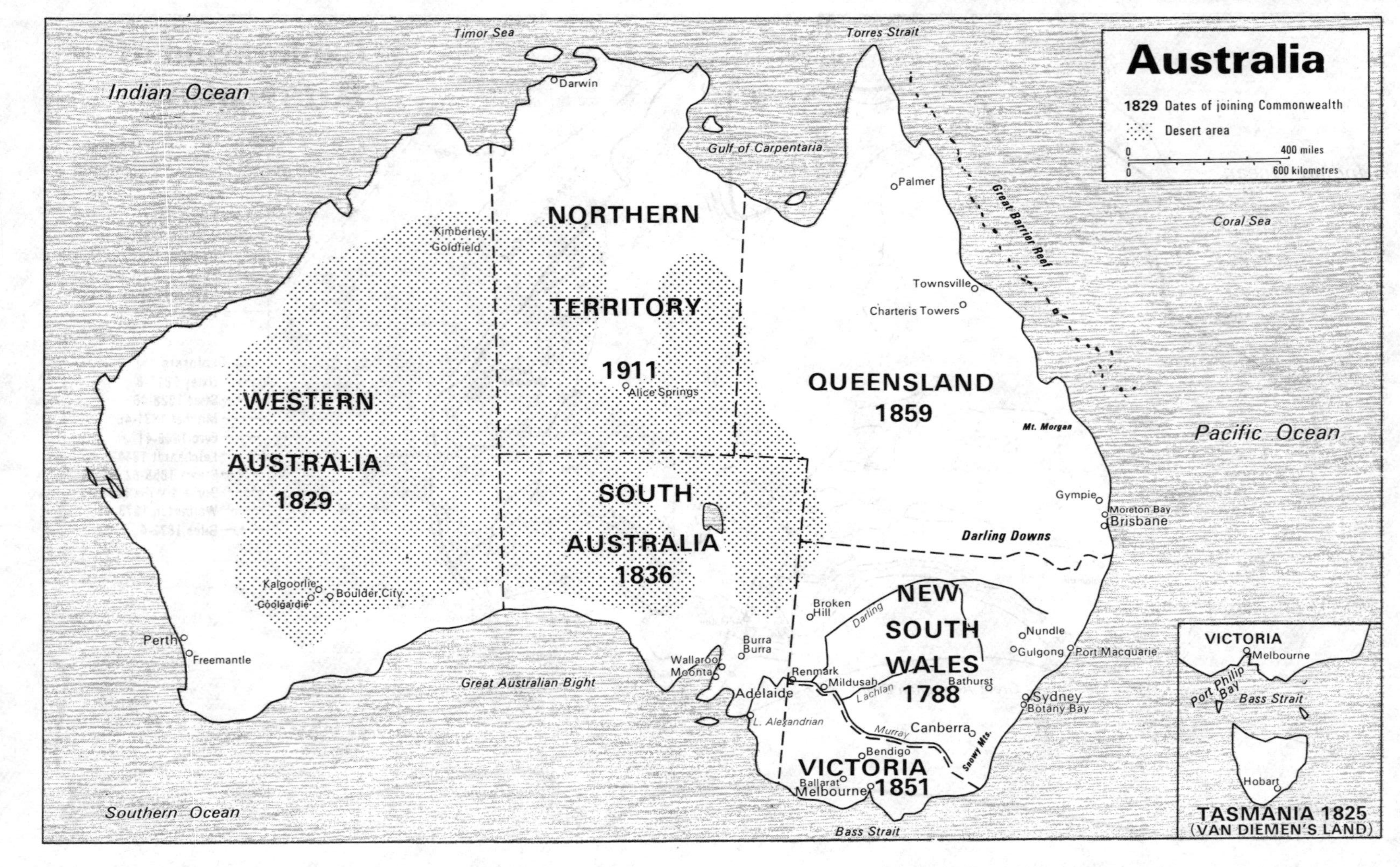

Australia
1829 Dates of joining Commonwealth
Desert area
0 400 miles
0 600 kilometres
Indian Ocean
Timor Sea
Torres Strait
Darwin
Gulf of Carpentaria
Palmer
Coral Sea
Great Barrier Reef
NORTHERN
TERRITORY
1911
Alice Springs
Kimberley Goldfield
WESTERN
AUSTRALIA
1829
Kalgoorlie
Coolgardie
Boulder City
Perth
Freemantle
Townsville
Charteris Towers
QUEENSLAND
1859
Mt. Morgan
Pacific Ocean
SOUTH
AUSTRALIA
1836
Gympie
Moreton Bay
Brisbane
Darling Downs
NEW
SOUTH
WALES
1788
Broken Hill
Darling
Nundle
Gulgong
Port Macquarie
Burra Burra
Wallaroo
Moonta
Great Australian Bight
Renmark
Mildusah
Lachlan
Bathurst
Sydney
Botany Bay
Adelaide
L. Alexandrian
Murray
Canberra
Snowy Mts.
Bendigo
VICTORIA
1851
Ballarat
Melbourne
Southern Ocean
Bass Strait
VICTORIA
Melbourne
Port Philip Bay
Bass Strait
Hobart
TASMANIA 1825
(VAN DIEMEN'S LAND)

main wheat-growing states today are New South Wales, Victoria, Western Australia and southern Queensland.

"Payable" gold (i.e. profitable to work) was found by Edward Hargreaves in 1851 near Bathurst, NSW. This and subsequent discoveries led to dramatic increases of populations: the new arrivals in Melbourne in 1852 averaged 2,000 a week, and the population of Victoria doubled in twelve months. In Western Australia, a pipe-line carrying water, 350 miles [560 kilometres] long, was built in 1903 from the Mundaring Weir near Perth to the goldfields of Kalgoorlie and Coolgardie. In 1845 copper had been found at Burra Burra, South Australia, making South Australia the most prosperous of the colonies in the late 1840s. Copper again revived South Australia's wealth with the mines at Moonta and Wallaroo in the early 1860s. Rich ore containing silver, lead and zinc was found at Broken Hill, NSW, in 1883. This was to become one of the world's wealthiest mines and is still in operation. Reports of rich nickel deposits in 1969–70 led to a rush of speculation almost as fevered as that which attended the gold strikes.

In a country with such a low annual rainfall, water conservation is important. In inland Australia, sheep and cattle stations depend on water obtained from bores sunk into the Great Artesian Basin. In the 1880s George and W. B. Chaffey started the first irrigation scheme on the Murray River at Mildura, Victoria, and Renmark, South Australia. Wine grapes, citrus and stone fruits are grown on the banks of the Murray by means of irrigation, making it one of the wealthiest areas in the country. Dams have been built on the coastal and inland rivers, helping to conserve water, and many other irrigation systems operate along the eastern coast. The largest of these embarked upon in 1949, is the Snowy Mountain Scheme, consisting of dams, diversion tunnels and hydroelectric power stations. In 1872 a cable was completed between Australia (Darwin) and Europe via Singapore and Java. Charles Todd supervised the construction of an overland telegraph line between Darwin, Northern Territory, and Adelaide, South Australia. This still remains an important link in Australia's telecommunications.

Australia sent troops to assist Britain in World War I. She was herself attacked by the Japanese in World War II, bombs being dropped on Darwin and Townsville and a submarine attack made on Sydney Harbour. In 1951 Australia signed the Anzus Treaty together with New Zealand and America. This is a declaration of self-help and mutual aid and an undertaking that the three countries will consult whenever security of any of them is threatened. Australia is a substantial aid donor country concentrating her efforts upon the developing countries of South East Asia.

Australia's present day exports are, from New South Wales, wheat, wool, coal, copper, dairy products; from Victoria, wheat, wool, dairy products; from Queensland, sugar, wool, beef, wheat, bauxite, copper; from Western Australia, iron ore, beef, wheat, gold; from South Australia, wine, dried fruits, iron ore, lead, zinc; from Tasmania, apples, aluminium, copper, zinc; from Northern Territory, beef, copper and uranium.

The six colonies of New South Wales (founded 1788), Tasmania (1825), Western Australia (1829), South Australia (1836), Victoria (1851) and Queensland (1859), became states forming the Commonwealth of Australia in 1901, with Canberra as the national capital. The Northern Territory and Australian Capital Territory were added in 1911. Population in 1983: 15,265,000.

¶ POWNALL, EVE. *Exploring Australia*, 1958; SHAW, A. G. L. *The Story of Australia*, 1967

Austria: now a republican area of central Europe. For centuries Austria played a decisive part in the history of Europe. In the 15th century foundations of Habsburg power were laid by a series of marriages until Charles V (1520–55) ruled a great empire which, however, was weakened by wars with France and the Turks, and by the rise of Protestantism culminating in the settlement of 1555 by which each prince decided the religion of his own state. In the 17th century Austria suffered a twofold attack: from the east by the Turkish revival which led to the siege of Vienna, from the west by the rising power of France. However, the Treaty of Utrecht weakened France and restored the balance of power. In the 18th century Austria was involved in long wars, 1740–48 and 1756–63, ending in the loss of Silesia. Internal reforms did little to strengthen her and she was further weakened by the revolutionary Napoleonic Wars in the course of which her armies suffered several crushing defeats, notably at Austerlitz (1805). Despite this, in 1815 Austria emerged still a great power and, under the influence of Metternich, played a leading part in the German Confederation.

The rise of Prussia brought a new threat and finally led to defeat in the Austro-Prussian war and Austria's exclusion from German affairs. The Peace of Prague established the supremacy of Prussia and led to the dual monarchy of Austria-Hungary, which lasted till 1918 and played an important part in European diplomacy. After World War I Austria became a Federated Republic. Too small to protect herself and weakened by internal dissension, the country fell an easy prey to Hitler in 1938 but, after Four Power occupation during 1945–55, finally regained independence with the 1938 frontiers re-established.

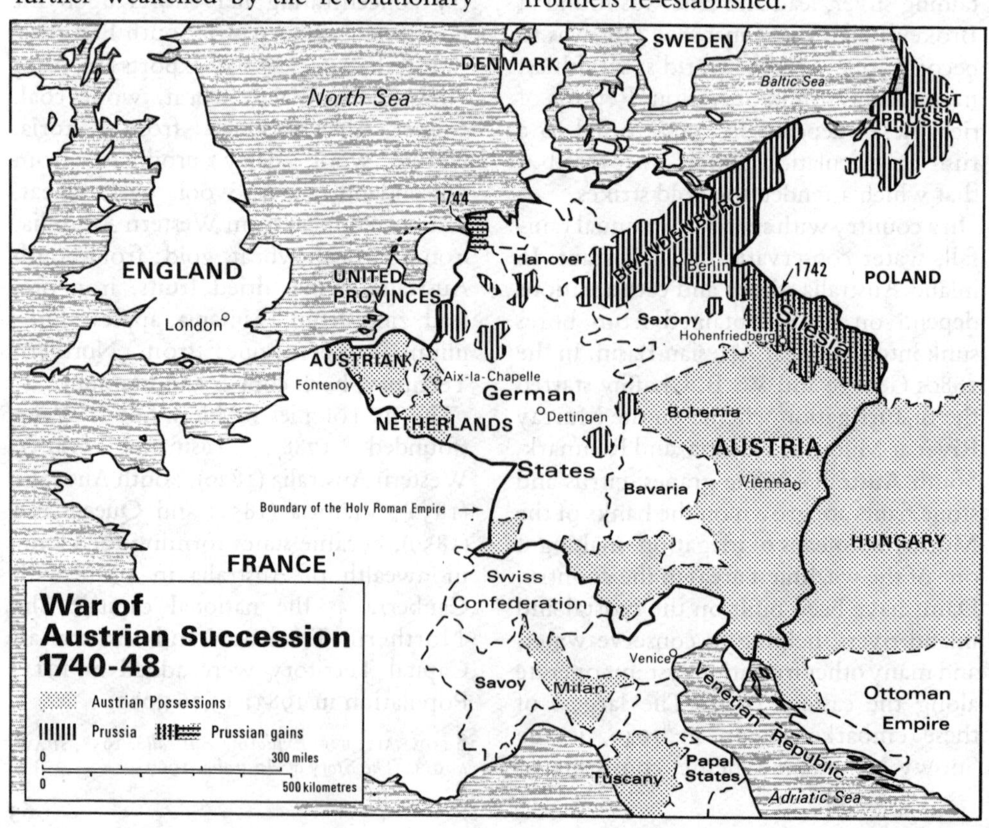

Austrian Succession, War of the (1741–48): the war fought after the death of Charles VI, Emperor of Germany, to determine the disputed succession to the Empire and the Austrian dominions. Since the two chief claimants (the Elector of Bavaria and Philip V of Spain) were both allies of France, it was necessary for Great Britain to resist this threat of supremacy. The struggle began when Frederick the Great of Prussia (1740–86) attacked Silesia in defiance of the Pragmatic Sanction (*see* separate entry) and started a continental and a colonial war. France, with Bavaria and other German states, joined Prussia. England supported Austria. Frederick won great prestige at Hohenfriedberg (1745). English forces fought at Dettingen (1743) and Fontenoy (1745), but their main efforts were in the colonial war in which they gained Louisbourg, but lost Madras.

The Treaty of Aix la Chapelle (1748) was little more than a truce. Prussia retained Silesia, and Louisbourg was exchanged for Madras. England was allowed by Spain to continue the slave trade for four more years (*see* ASIENTO), and had gone a long way to establishing the maritime supremacy that was to be demonstrated so formidably afterwards.

Auto-da-fe: literally an act of faith, or the carrying out of the sentence of death by burning passed by the Spanish Inquisition against heretics. Often a large number of victims were burnt at the same time, e.g. in 1559 at Seville twenty-one were burnt. The last burning was at Seville in 1781. The victims wore grotesquely embroidered yellow garments and yellow mitres.

Avebury: a British prehistoric monument, larger than Stonehenge, about five miles [8 kilometres] west of Marlborough, Wiltshire. The Great Circle, over 1,100

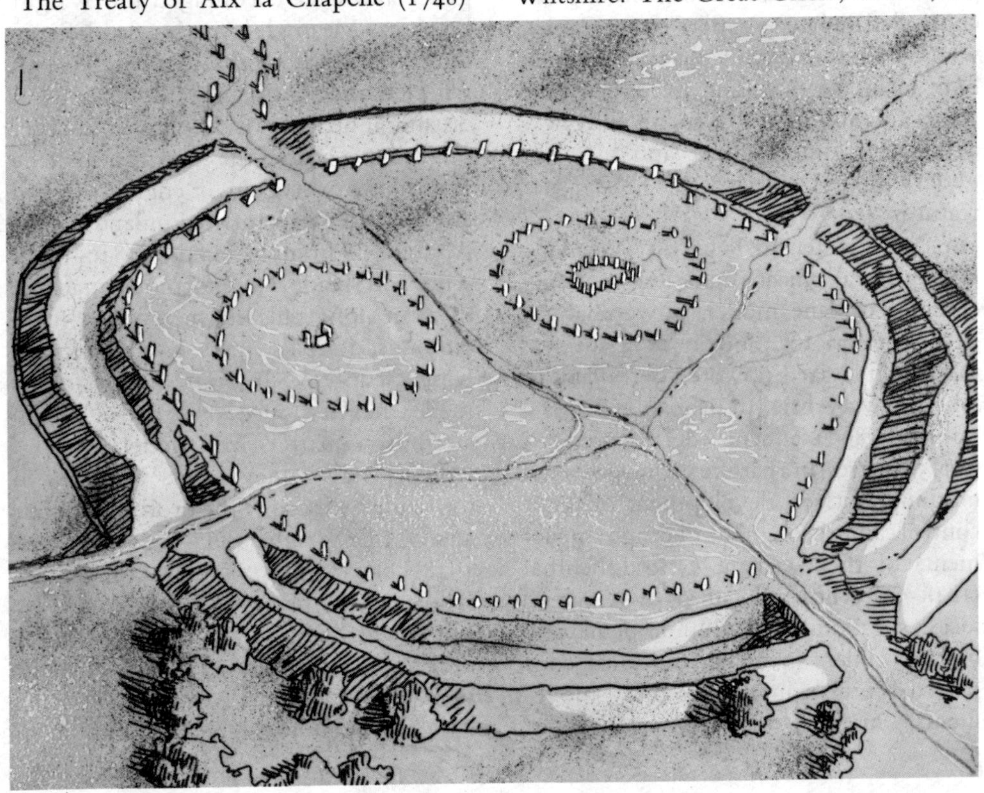

Avebury.

feet [335 metres] across, was made of 100 standing stones from a local source, each weighing about 39 tons [40 tonnes]. Inside were two or three smaller circles. Outside was a steep-sided, flat-bottomed ditch, the rubble from which was piled round in a huge mound. On the south the avenue of standing stones linked Avebury with the sanctuary, a mile away [1·6 kilometres]. The monument dates from about 1600 BC, being built by the Beaker people. Finds from Avebury are in the Avebury and Devizes Museum.

Aviation: manned flight. Although Roger Bacon (1214–92), amongst others, planned an ornithopter – a man-carrying machine with flapping wings – and Leonardo da Vinci (1452–1519), who made over 500 aeronautical sketches, drew plans for an almost workable semi-ornithopter and sketches of "falling leaf". glides, showing an understanding of controlled flight, it was Sir George Cayley who laid the foundations of aerodynamics, both in his writings and in his personal achievements. In 1809 he successfully flew a full-sized model glider and his 1852 glider design anticipated most later features.

In 1857 Lieutenant Felix du Temple, a French naval officer, made the first successful aeroplane model, powered by a clockwork motor, and in 1874 his was the first full-sized powered aeroplane to take off, very briefly, probably down a ramp. In 1890 Clement Ader covered 164 feet [50 metres] in a batlike steam-powered machine, but real development of flight control came through the gliding achievements of the German, Otto Lilienthal (1848–96) who, influenced by Cayley's ideas, successfully flew monoplane and biplane gliders in which the pilot controlled the machine by his body movements, his legs dangling in space.

Otto Lilienthal in flight. He has just thrown his legs backwards to restore the equilibrium of his glider.

Lilienthal, who had written "sacrifices must be made", was killed, but his writings influenced Octave Chanute, an American, who improved on Lilienthal's glider and later encouraged the Wright brothers. Meanwhile in Scotland Percy Pilcher flew a Lilienthal-type glider with wheeled undercarriage and towline take-off and, if he had not been killed in 1899, might have beaten the Wrights, since he was then working on an engine. He had also joined the team in England of the American, Hiram S. Maxim (1840–1916) who had made an enormous machine that ran along rails but never quite flew. Amongst its passengers was the future King George V. In 1901 S. P. Langley made the first successful petrol-driven aircraft – a quarter-sized model.

All previous achievements were put in the shade by those of the brothers Wilbur and Orville Wright (1867–1912 and 1871–1948), bicycle makers in Dayton, Ohio, whose 1899 biplane kit was followed by full-sized gliders of which No. 3 made nearly 1000 successful glides. Then came their famous Wright Flyer No. 1, powered by a 12 h.p. motor: a biplane with linen-covered wings, an elevator in front and a double rudder behind, launched off wooden rails. On Thursday 17 December 1903 Orville flew for twelve seconds at over 500 feet [152 metres] in the air and covering 120 feet [37 metres] of ground at a speed of 30 m.p.h. [48 km/h]. Later that day Wilbur flew for fifty-nine seconds, over half a mile through the air. This machine was followed by Flyers No. II and No. III which remained in the air for flights of over half an hour, banking, turning and circling. Then, for nearly three years, disappointed at the US government's lack of interest and general disbelief, the Wrights did not fly again.

Meanwhile in Europe others were experimenting, and in 1903 Captain Ferber in France flew the first Wright-type glider; in 1905 Santos-Dumont flew over 700 feet [213 metres]; Blériot flew a successful monoplane; and Henri Farman, an Englishman who lived in France, became the first man after the Wrights to be airborne for over a minute. Then in 1908 the Wrights flew again, demonstrating their enormous superiority over all rivals, and a year later there was a surge of activity inspired by the Wrights' techniques. Louis Blériot won the *Daily Mail* prize of £1,000 for flying the Channel, taking off from Calais at 4.41 a.m. on Sunday 25 July and landing near Dover Castle at 5·17½, a distance of 23½ miles [38 kilometres], in his No. XI monoplane powered by a 25 h.p. Anzani engine. In the same year the first great aviation meeting was held at Rheims when 23 machines took off. The longest flight was nearly 118 miles [190 kilometres] and the highest speed 48 m.p.h. [77 km/h]. In 1910 the *Daily Mail* prize of £10,000 for a London to Manchester flight was won by a Frenchman, Louis Paulhan in a Farman biplane. Claud Graham White (1879–1959), his English rival, tried desperately to catch him up by flying at night (the first man to do so), guided by the lights below of his friends' cars.

By 1914 Britain had 113 aeroplanes: sixty-three in the Royal Flying Corps (later, under the great leadership of Lord Trenchard, to become in 1918 the Royal Air Force) and fifty with the Navy. France had 120 and Germany 232. The early sorties over the trenches, with observers firing rifles and pistols at each other and dropping hand bombs, soon gave way to more sophisticated combat after the Germans had developed forward-mounted machine guns geared to fire between the revolutions of the propeller blades. Aerial combat between famous fighters such as the French Spads and British Sopwith Camels on the one side

The Wright aeroplane on its first flight, 17 December 1903. Orville Wright is piloting the machine, Wilbur watching him.

and the Fokkers on the other, led by aces such as Geynemer, Bishop (1894–1956) and Von Richthofen, passed into Western Europe's folk lore. Special bombing aircraft, such as the Handley Page, the Gotha and the J4, were developed, and these paved the way for civilian passenger flying. In 1919 a London to Paris service began and by 1927 many of today's great civil airlines, led by KLM in 1919, had been founded.

Many records were made between the wars: in 1919 John Alcock and Arthur Brown flew in a converted Vickers Vimy bomber from Newfoundland to Ireland in 16 hours 12 minutes, the first non-stop Atlantic flight; in 1925 Sir Alan Cobham flew to South Africa and back; the following year Admiral Richard Byrd of the United States Navy flew across the North Pole, and in 1927 Colonel Charles Lindbergh flew solo across the Atlantic in his monoplane Spirit of St Louis. In 1928 Charles Kingsford Smith made the first Pacific flight from America to Australia. In the same year Amelia Earhart flew the Atlantic with two companions in a Fokker seaplane, and in 1930 Amy Johnson flew solo from Croydon to Australia in 19½ days in a secondhand de Havilland Moth.

World War II saw an enormously increased use of air power: not only in aerial combat but for intensive bombing, the transport of men and supplies and for dropping parachutists and equipment. In the Pacific, aircraft carriers played a decisive role.

As early as 1942 the German Messerschmitt ME 262, the first turbojet, was constructed and became airborne in 1944, the same year as Britain's Gloster Meteor with an engine developed by Sir Frank Whittle. The research used on the V1 and V2 rockets which were sent by Germany against southern England was later used for the postwar development of rocketry and in 1947 the American Bell X-1, a rocket-powered research plane, was the first to fly faster than sound. In 1952 the Comet became the first jet-propelled passenger aircraft and the Vickers Viscount, the following year, the first turboprop. In 1954 the American Convair XFY-1 made the first winged vertical take-off. The fifties were notable for a great development in the use of helicopters, of which the first successful one had been the Sikorski as early as 1942. Then in the late fifties came the giant four-engined planes: Boeing 707s and Douglas DC 8s. The sixties saw the great space race between the USA and Russia, and the development of the supersonic Concorde and its Russian rival, which will make the remotest corners of the earth accessible in a matter of hours – all this less than seventy years since the first powered flight. The opening months of 1970 were marked by the first commercial flights of the giant Boeing 747 (the "jumbo" jet) capable of carrying more than 300 passengers.

Concorde taking off.

¶ ALLWARD, MAURICE. *Triumphs of Flight*, 1968; TAYLOR, J. W. R. *Aeroplanes*, 1961

See also AIRSHIP; CONCORDE.

Axis: the line around which a body revolves. The word was adopted to describe the alliance between Berlin and Rome created in 1936 and expanded into the German-Japanese-Italian Pact in 1937. Germany and Italy formed a solid block in central Europe from which they later attacked other countries in Europe.

Aztecs: The Aztecs of Mexico were a nomadic tribe until they settled down on some islands in Lake Texcoco at the beginning of the 14th century AD. They began to grow crops of maize on the shore and they copied the buildings of their neighbours, the Toltecs. In the 15th century the Aztec warriors began to conquer their neighbours until they dominated the whole of Mexico, collecting tribute of food and precious metals from over 300 cities.

In their capital city, Tenochtitlan, lived 300,000 people. Their cool stone houses surrounded wide shaded market squares above which rose pyramid-shaped temples and large palaces. The finest palaces in the city belonged to the Aztec emperor. Once he had been elected he was both commander-in-chief and high priest. Thus he would not only be trained in the use of swords, slings and arrows, but would also learn the picture writing which told of the Aztecs' religious duties.

The chief of these duties was to provide their gods with blood. They captured as many prisoners in war as possible so that

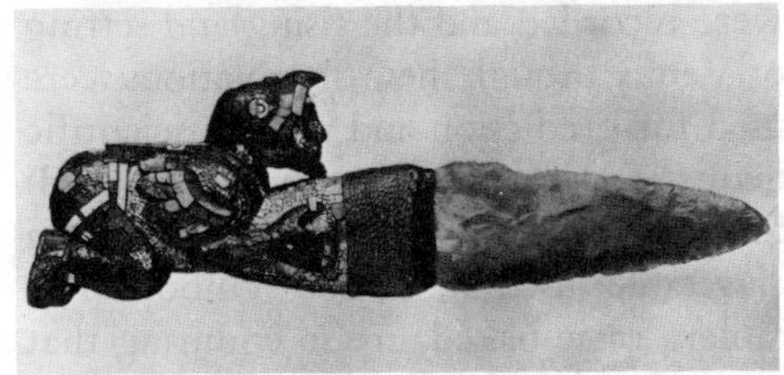

Aztec sacrificial knife inlaid with turquoise and shell, late 15th or 16th century, believed to be part of the treasure sent home by Hernán Cortés to the Emperor Charles V.

each one could be taken to the stone altar where his heart would be cut out with an obsidian knife and lifted up to the sun. The Aztecs were frightened of their gods, and this human sacrifice was the only way they knew of pleasing them. One emperor, after two years' fighting, dedicated a new temple with 20,000 victims.

Tiger-shaped sacrificial dish for the victim's heart.

The Aztec Empire was destroyed by the Spaniards at the beginning of the 16th century, but they helped to destroy themselves by their own superstitious fears and the hatred they created among their neighbours.

An example of an Aztec pictogram, showing the amusements of the nobility; a performance by musicians, a juggler, hunchbacks, and a dwarf (Codex Florentino).

¶ BRAY, WARWICK. *Everyday Life of the Aztecs*, 1968; BURLAND, C. A. *The Aztecs*, 1961

See also CORTÉS, HERNÁN.

B

Babar or **Babur** (Zahir Ud-Din Mohammed), called "the Tiger" (1483–1530): Prince of Farghana in Turkestan. He conquered Kabul and, between 1505 and 1526, led five expeditions over the north-western passes into India. In the fifth he defeated Sultan Ibrahim, the last of the Lodi kings of Delhi, at the battle of Panipat. He founded the Mogul Empire but died in 1530 before he could consolidate his power.

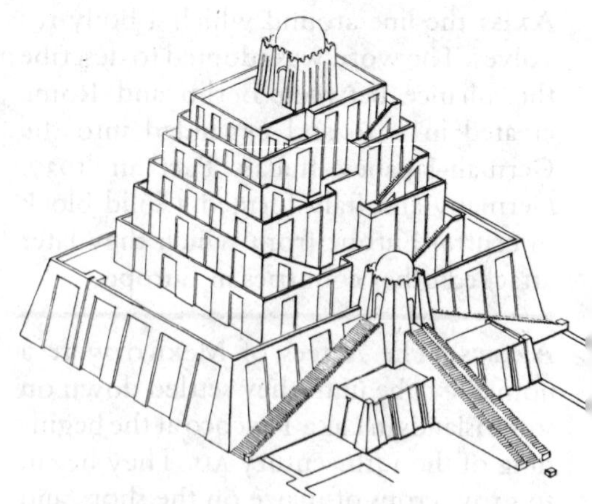

The ziggurat at Ur, as reconstructed by Sir Leonard Woolley.

Babylon and **Babylonia:** a city-state in the fertile alluvial plain between the Euphrates and Tigris and the neighbouring city-states which it absorbed. Babylon rose to prominence under its First Dynasty (1894–1595 BC), Semitic kings who absorbed the culture of the original Sumerian inhabitants. Hammurabi (1792–50 BC) extended his power over Elam, Assyria and Syria and published an enduring and comprehensive law code. The soil which, systematically irrigated, yielded two crops and grazing for beasts annually, governed Babylonian prosperity, institutions and religion. To people subject to disastrous and unpredictable floods, it seemed essential to propitiate the river gods. Each city belonged to its guardian god, the people existing to save him from the tedium of manual work. At the foot of the stepped pyramids (ziggurats) lay great temple buildings, accounting offices, grain stores, writing schools and barracks for canal engineers. All land and produce were the property of the god before whom even the king annually abased himself – in Babylon itself before Marduk, the Young Bull of the Sun. Babylonian religion has many parallels with the Old Testament: e.g. woman made from the rib of man in the Epic of the Creation; the expulsion from the Garden (perhaps a memory of the move to the valleys when the hills became desiccated after the Ice Age); the Flood in the Epic of Gilgamesh; and Sargon of Agade consigned to the river in a cradle of bulrushes.

The intricate systems of irrigation could not be operated without elaborate laws and courts of arbitration. Floods might obliterate field boundaries, and this made measurement important. The lack of timber, stone and metal made trade essential. Temple authorities kept careful accounts of crops and allotted the surplus to foreign trade, to rations for their artisans and to a reserve for famine years. The Babylonian system of numbers has given us the hour of sixty minutes or three thousand six hundred seconds. Eclipses were recorded and the rising and setting of Venus, though these observations were used for prediction and not for scientific deduction. A cuneiform (wedge-shaped) form of writing with a rush stylus on a clay tablet used about 600 symbols. The tablets, once baked, are so enduring that we have abundant written evidence of Babylonian life: kin lists, official letters, temple accounts, collections of proverbs and school exercises with the teacher's impatient corrections.

After 1595 BC Babylon succumbed to attacks by Hittites and by Cassites from the north-east, and then to a long period of Assyrian predominance. When Assyria was extinguished in 612 BC Babylon successfully contended with Egypt for the Assyrian Empire. In this struggle the Kingdom of Judah was caught up. In 597 BC Nebuchadnezzar took Jerusalem and carried King Jehoiachim and the Jewish nobles, troops and craftsmen into captivity in Babylon. When King Zedekiah of Judah aided a second Egyptian attack, he was blinded and carried into exile with his people.

In 546 BC Cyrus of Persia took Babylon and ruled it tolerantly and well. Later it fell to Alexander the Great, who died there in 323 BC. On his death and the break-up of his empire, Babylon became part of the successor empire of his general Seleucus. Before the Persian attack Babylon's prosperity had been checked by the silting of the rivers and her religion weakened by contact with the monotheism of her Jewish slaves. The whole area was finally impoverished when the Mongol Hulagu destroyed the irrigation system in the 13th century.

See also ALEXANDER THE GREAT.

Bacon, Francis, first Baron Verulam and Viscount St Albans (1561–1626): English statesman, Lord Chancellor, writer and natural scientist. Described as "of middling stature, his countenance . . . indented with age before he was old", he was a leader in the break from the medieval scholasticism and by his writings was largely responsible for the foundation of the Royal Society. He said of himself that he "rang the bell that called the wits together". He had a distinguished career of office but was disgraced and retired in 1621 for accepting bribes. While admitting the charge, he declared with some truth that he was "the justest judge in England these fifty years".

¶ FARRINGTON, BENJAMIN. *Francis Bacon: pioneer of planned science*, 1963

Bacon, Roger (1214?–94): English philosopher and experimental scientist; called "the wonderful doctor" because of the extent and range of his learning which embraced not only Latin, Greek and Hebrew, but mathematics, medicine, anatomy and optics. He foresaw the potency of gunpowder and the use of flying machines and power-driven boats. He insisted that a man ignorant of mathematics cannot master other sciences and he regarded experiment as "the lord of all sciences", the only reliable door to true knowledge. He entered the Franciscan Order of Friars and lectured in the universities of Oxford and Paris. He may be said to have had a considerable share in the rediscovery of America since Columbus, in his famous letter enlisting the support of Ferdinand and Isabella of Spain, quoted from the writings of Roger Bacon.

See also MATHEMATICS; ORDERS, RELIGIOUS.

Baghdad: "the City of Peace" founded in AD 762 by the second Abbasid Caliph on the Tigris near a canal to the Euphrates. The Abbasids were Muslims who claimed

descent from the Prophet's uncle Abbas. They led, under their black banners, a revolt of Persian peasants and underprivileged converts to Islam against the Caliphs of Damascus and their Arab oligarchy. The Abbasid Caliphs adopted not only Persian luxury and ceremonial, but also Persian culture, and under Caliph Mamun (*c.* 786–833) Baghdad gained a library, a School of Translation, which sent Greek scholars to Alexandria searching for manuscripts, and an observatory. Metal and textile crafts served the luxurious court (our tabby cat derives its name from the watered silk produced in the Attabiya quarter of Baghdad). Baghdad declined when eastern trade preferred the Cairo-Red Sea route, and when she was occupied by Persians in 945 and Seljuk Turks in 1055. These retained the Caliphs as puppet rulers, but in 1258 the Mongol, Hulagu, took Baghdad, destroyed the irrigation canals and slew the thirty-seventh Caliph and 80,000 of his subjects. By the 20th century, Baghdad had recovered its commercial and political importance and today it is the capital of Iraq. Population in 1975: 3,205,000.
See ARABS for map.

Bailey: the enclosed courtyard of a medieval castle, or sometimes the surrounding wall. Often there was an inner and an outer bailey. The Old Bailey, the Central Criminal Court in London, stands at the old outer boundary wall of the City.
See also CASTLES.

Baking: When man discovered ways of making fire, he acquired warmth and light. He also found that certain edible seeds became more digestible when broken, mixed with water and baked on hot stones. He built stone structures in which wood was burned as a better means of baking and ovens evolved. He sieved his broken grain through cloths and a finer flour resulted. Different grain yielded different flour, and soon wheat and rye were largely cultivated, both containing structural proteins that yielded better bread. Salt was introduced to bread, probably as a result of using sea water.

When dough is left for a sufficient time it ferments and becomes full of gas. For centuries it was thought that this change was spontaneous until Louis Pasteur (1822–95) discovered that it was due to yeast micro-organisms. Fermentation was known to the Babylonians and the early Egyptians. The earliest baker recorded in history is Luga, a temple baker in Babylon, who received a delivery of grain which was recorded on a cuneiform tablet. The language is Sumerian and dates from about 2366 BC. Twenty kinds of bread and cakes were made in Babylon, and sixteen are known to have been made in Egypt. From Egypt the Greeks learned the art of baking. Bread and cakes were improved and new types added. Aristophanes (450–385 BC) repeatedly mentions a wide variety of bread and cakes.

The Romans increased their knowledge of the art and craft of baking from Greece; it became a respected occupation, and bakers were held in high repute. As the Romans marched they took with them their customs and skills. Excavations of settlements in Roman provinces provide ample evidence of milling and baking.

There is little documentary evidence of organised baking in Britain after the Romans left. Bread was made in the castles and in the larger houses possessing an oven. In AD 1155 bakers were mentioned in the Account Rolls of the King's Exchequer. In 1266 the Assize of Bread, which continued until 1885, regulated the weight, type and price of bread. Authority was vested in the Worshipful Company of Bakers, who were also responsible for apprenticeship within the industry.

Housewives who had no oven made their doughs and took them to an established baker to be shaped and baked. This custom of public baking gradually dwindled as people bought their bread direct from the local baker.

For centuries bakers were skilled in cultivating their own yeast by means of ferments known as "barms", media in which yeast cells could multiply until they were of a quality to ferment a large dough. At the beginning of the 20th century, great changes took place as compressed yeast became available. Bread doughs could now be made in a one-stage process when all the ingredients were mixed together in one operation, instead of the historic two-stage process of barm and dough. Machinery was introduced and ovens were vastly improved. Large bakeries were developed where the production per man-hour of bread and cakes was greatly increased. Later, as a result of the application of science and technology to baking, complex physical, chemical and biological changes were largely brought under control.

Balaclava, Battle of (25 October 1854): an inconclusive battle of the Crimean War fought by the British, French and Turks against the Russians. The heroic, if militarily stupid, Charge of the Light Brigade had a lasting glamour thrown over it by Tennyson's poem. It was the subject of the French general Bosquet's famous remark: *C'est magnifique mais ce n'est pas la guerre* (It is magnificent but it is not war).

¶ In ALLEN, KENNETH. *Soldiers in Battle*, 1966

See also CRIMEAN WAR.

The Charge of the Light Cavalry Brigade, on the plain near Balaclava, 1854.

Balance of Power: a diplomatic device for preventing any one state becoming sufficiently powerful to endanger others. Practised by the Italian states in the 15th century, it became an accepted idea of European diplomacy, influencing the formation of leagues and the distribution of territory after wars. The application of the theory is clearly shown in the Vienna settlement of 1815 when France kept the frontiers of 1790 partly to preserve the balance. Before 1904 England, by her isolation, safeguarded the balance between the Triple Alliance of Germany, Austria and Italy on the one hand and the Franco-Russian alliance on the other. Since 1945 the world has thought of Russia and USA as the two great powers balancing each other (*see* COLD WAR).

Balance of Trade: in modern times, the difference in total value over a period between a country's imports and exports. There is a general theory that an excess of imports over exports is bad for economic wellbeing and that an excess of exports over imports is to be preferred. The term "balance of payments", concerned with the same theory, is now in much more common use.

Balkans, The: from the Turkish word for mountain, applied to the range extending from Sofia to the Black Sea and, by extension, to the peninsula projecting southward from Istria and the Danube mouth.

Arid mountains, poor roads, economic backwardness and political instability have made the inhabitants pessimistic and prone to extreme violence in politics but tenacious and loyal to their kin. In their history, long periods of foreign domination have alternated with times of turbulent rivalry between native races.

The Albanians are the purest survivors of the original Illyrian race, still rent by blood feud and brigandage. The Greeks were invaders, their maritime and commercial civilisation Aegean rather than Balkan. Macedonian hillmen succeeded to their power and subdued the Balkan tribes. In 168 BC Rome took Illyria and by AD 9 had expanded to the Danube. The Romans built towns and linked Albania, Salonika and Constantinople with roads. When the Han Dynasty in China repulsed the nomadic Huns, the Roman frontier was breached and the Balkans overrun between the 5th and 8th centuries AD by the Avars, who brought with them the Slavs, slow, stolid farmers. Finally, in the 8th century the Bulgars, horse-archers of central Asia, settled the steppes and plains bordering the Balkan range. They adopted the Slav language and Byzantine ideas of grandeur. In AD 811 they slew the Emperor Nicephorus I, and their king adopted the style of Tsar. In AD 870 the missionaries Cyril and Methodius brought Christianity and the Cyrillic script to Bulgaria and stimulated a flowering of art and literature which reached its height under Tsar Simeon (893–927), the greatest of Bulgarian kings. But the Bulgarians resisted the Byzantine attempts to treat them as vassals, and a wasting war from 977–1019 ended in the defeat of Bulgaria and the exhaustion of Byzantium. In the 13th century Serbia rose to prominence under kings of the Nemanjic line, and monasteries and churches adorned the land. Here, also, ambition led to disaster, and the great Serbian king Stefan Dusan was killed in 1355 trying to become emperor.

In their efforts to check the Serbs, the Byzantines had hired Turkish troops but were unable to persuade them to return to Anatolia. The Turkish troops defied Byzantium and defeated the Serbs on the River Maritza in 1371 and at the Field of the Blackbird in 1389. Thus the 500 years

Balkans
After the Treaty of Berlin 1878
Extent of the Ottoman Empire 1877
Extent of the Ottoman Empire 1878
Subsequent gains of others with dates
0 miles 200
0 300 kms
AUSTRIA - HUNGARY
Transylvania
Ukraine
RUSSIA
Bessarabia
Moldavia
Belgrade
ROMANIA
Wallachia
Dobruja
Constanta
Danube
BOSNIA
1878
SERBIA
1878
1878
Novi
Pazar
Nish
Kossovo
1878
Plevna
Varna
BULGARIA
Black Sea
Sofia
Adriatic Sea
MONTENEGRO
EAST RUMELIA
1885
Albania
Adrianople
Ottoman Empire
Macedonia
Thrace
Constantinople
ITALY
Illyria
Salonika
CORFU
(Greece)
THESSALY
1881
Aegean Sea
Anatolia
Smyrna
Ionian Sea
Athens
GREECE
Navarino
RHODES
CRETE
Mediterranean Sea
AUSTRIA HUNGARY
R
ROMANIA
SERBIA
M
BULGARIA
ALBANIA
I
TURKEY
GREECE
RHODES
CRETE
to Greece 1908
to Italy 1912
1913
A. Austria
Cz. Czechoslovakia
H. Hungary
I. Italy
M. Montenegro
P. Poland
R. Russia
A
H
Cz
P
R
I
ROMANIA
YUGOSLAVIA
BULGARIA
I
ALBANIA
TURKEY
GREECE
RHODES
CRETE
to Greece 1920
1923

of Balkan servitude to the Turks began. Tribute in money and slave-boys was demanded, but the Turks were more tolerant than the Byzantines, and the Turkish horse-soldiers who became non-hereditary landholders had no feudal jurisdiction and were often absent on campaign. As a result, the peasant community, the Slav Zadruga, remained a vigorous institution, easily changed to a co-operative society in the 19th century or to a collective farm in the 20th. As the Turkish empire lost its vigour, oppression by corrupt officials and brigandage inflamed the reviving nationalism of the Balkan peoples. The Serbs won independence 1804–16, the Greeks in 1821 and the Bulgarians in 1876. In the Balkan War of 1912 the Turks were confined to the area of Istanbul. But the Balkan states all hoped to restore the frontiers of their age of ascendancy. Even under present Russian domination, exercised in the Balkan countries in varying degree, strong nationalism survives.

Ballads: popular medieval narrative poems of unknown authorship, handed down by oral tradition. The original spelling of ballad was *balade*, a Norman-French word meaning "dance-song", because the first ballads were sung while people danced. But the words that were set to these tunes became so interesting that, by the 12th century, the audience listened to the singer instead of dancing, sometimes joining him in a refrain. Ballads told a story and many related the adventures of a popular hero.

¶ HODGART, MATT [illegible], ed. *The Faber Book of Ballads*, 1965

Balloons: round or pear-shaped envelopes inflated with hydrogen or filled with hot air. In 1783 Joseph Montgolfier (1740–1810) and his brother Etienne (1745–99) sent up sheep, a duck and a cockerel for an eight-minute flight, and in the same year the first manned flight was made across Paris in a gaily decorated Montgolfier hot air balloon, beneath which was suspended in a basket a crew of two, of whom one, Dr Pilatre de Rozier, was later killed trying to cross the Channel in linked hydrogen and hot air ballons. In 1783 also, J. A. C. Charles flew 27 miles [43 kilometres] from the Tuileries Gardens in a hydrogen balloon.

The first balloon-crossing of the Channel. Jeffries and Blanchard over the French coast.

In 1785 the American scientist Dr Jeffries (1744–1819) and J. P. Blanchard (1753–1809) crossed the Channel from Dover to Calais after throwing overboard much of their equipment in order to maintain height. In 1797 A. J. Garnerin (1770–1823) made the first parachute descent from a balloon, standing in a tub flying a

Tricolour. In 1836 a balloon was flown by a three-man crew from London to Germany. Balloons were used to carry delayed-action bombs by the Austrians attacking Venice in 1849, by the Federal Army in the American Civil War and to evacuate refugees during the siege of Paris (1871), and in Britain the Army Balloon School was founded in 1878. In 1897 three Swedish explorers lost their lives trying to fly across the North Pole. In this century captive balloons have been used for scientific, military and naval observation and for anti-aircraft defence. In 1931 Auguste Piccard (1884–1962) was the first man to reach the stratosphere, rising 95 miles [153 kilometres] above the earth in a balloon. Hydrogen and hot air balloons are still flown for sport.

¶ BURCHARD, PETER. *Balloons: from paper bags to skyhooks*, 1960; ROLT, L. T. C. *The Aeronauts*, 1966

Ballot: secret voting. The ancient Greeks used a pebble for certain elections and the Romans made secret voting compulsory in all public meetings. The word "ballot" comes from an Italian word *ballotta* meaning a little ball, which was used like the Greek pebble. Although the ballot is of such ancient origin, it was a surprisingly long time before adequate arrangements for secret ballot were introduced into modern democracies. South Australia (1846) can claim to be the first state to employ it. Not till 1872 was the secret ballot introduced into English parliamentary and local elections. In the USA the system was widely adopted after the presidential elections of 1884.

Bangladesh: previously the Eastern Province of Pakistan, covering 55,126 square miles [142,797 square kilometres] in the Ganges delta, and physically separated from the rest of Pakistan.

In 1970 a cyclone devastated the area, homes and crops were destroyed by floods, and over 220,000 lives were lost. The Province accused the central government of inaction following the catastrophe and, supported by Shaik Mujib Rahman's party, appealed for greater independence. Unrest in Dacca, the capital, was suppressed, but in 1971 civil war broke out. Thousands of refugees had meanwhile made their way into India. After protesting against the suppressive treatment of the Eastern Province, India declared war on Pakistan and helped Bangladesh achieve independence. In road communications this state is backward, but has the advantage of cheap water transport along the navigable channels of the Ganges, the Brahmaputra and the Maghna. Fishing is a thriving industry, and rice the most important food crop. Bangladesh also produces almost 50 per cent of the world's raw jute. Population in 1983: 94,651,000. *See* INDIA for map.

Bank of England: the central bank of England and Wales. It is a joint stock bank founded in 1694, when Whig financiers, in return for a Charter of incorporation, lent the government £1,200,000 at 8 per cent interest and so enabled it to overcome financial difficulties caused by the French War (1689–97). In the 18th century it became both the government's and the banker's bank and by the Bank Charter Act (1844) it gained the sole right to issue paper currency. The Bank of England was nationalised in 1946. Its nickname of "The Old Lady of Threadneedle Street" originated from a scornful remark by William Cobbett about the directors of the Bank.

Banks: establishments which receive deposits of money from customers, pay it out and invest it. In one form or another they have existed from very early times. Men who changed money sometimes became money-lenders and by 400 BC they were, in addition to their trading activities, receiving deposits, lending money in return for interest, transferring money from one customer's account to another and making loans on security – in short, acting as bankers.

Business organisation in medieval times reached its peak in Italian family firms such as the Medici of Florence. At its height this concern, though it always insisted that its trading business was its main interest, controlled a trading-banking house in Florence, had eight others scattered throughout Europe (one was in London), made loans to rulers and accepted deposits on which interest was paid. By the beginning of the 17th century there were public and private banks accepting deposits that could be transferred to others, sometimes by means of cheques, in important trading centres such as Barcelona, Valencia and Genoa. These banks made loans, the public ones only to city governments, the private banks to traders, landlords and others.

Northern Europe had such well-known public banks as the Bank of Amsterdam (1609), Bank of Hamburg (1619) and Bank of Sweden (1656). When, in 1694, England was at war with Louis XIV of France, a group of speculators led by William Paterson, a Scot, offered to lend the government £1,200,000 at 8 per cent interest, and were given the privilege of incorporation as the Bank of England. Before this time money scriveners (John Milton's father was one) had acted as intermediaries between those who lent and borrowed, but it seems that no true banking house ever grew out of a scrivener's office.

It was the goldsmith's who gave London its private banks. During the Civil War and Commonwealth period (1642–60) their strongrooms became the refuge of landowners' and merchants' cash and valuables. The goldsmiths paid interest on cash left with them and allowed the depositor to transfer money in his account to other persons, often by means of cheques.

After 1750 the number of private banks outside London rapidly increased, and they played a vital part in the finance of the Industrial Revolution. Nearly all issued their own notes and, as they were limited to not more than six partners, many, lacking sufficient reserves, collapsed in time of crisis. They were blamed for many of the monetary difficulties of the day, and their activities often embarrassed the Bank of England. Recurrent financial crises led to the Bank Charter Act, passed by Peel's government in 1844, which regulated the issue of notes and insisted on adequate reserves of specie (coin) being maintained, the beginning of central banking as we know it.

It was not until the three decades following 1890 that the English banking system came to consist of a small number of large banks each of which operated throughout the country. In the United States this movement took even longer; over 5,000 banks failed in the depression following the Wall Street crash of 1929.

Banks in recent years have developed rapidly, taking on new functions to reflect changing patterns of business. They have plunged into the hire purchase business and have formed unit trusts. The issue of travellers' cheques has extended, and credit cards have appeared; there has been the development of a business in stocks and shares and other ventures further away from the public eye.

Finally, there are the banking organisations that are involved in world, as opposed to national, financial affairs. These include the International Monetary Fund, the Export-Import Bank and the Bank for International Settlements.

¶ DANDY, JAMES. *Your Money and Its Life*, 1963

Banner: ensign of flag of the higher military commanders, nobility and greater knights which bore their arms. The banner of arms was freely used throughout the medieval period, not only in the field but on every occasion that called for armorial display. It provided a rallying point on the field of battle, and for ceremonial occasions its size was regulated according to the rank of its owner. Many different types of banners were devised but the most familiar is the banner of royal arms, mistakenly called the royal standard, which indicates the presence of the sovereign wherever it is flown.

Baptists: a major Protestant communion in Britain and America deriving their name from their insistence on adult baptism. In 1608 John Smith left Gainsborough, England, for Amsterdam. Believing the English Church to be no true Church, he baptised himself and rebaptised his followers. Baptists played an important part in England under Cromwell and in the American colonies. They claimed toleration on the grounds that all are spiritually equal and taught the duty of obedience to the civil government. Although most Baptists accepted the Restoration, many suffered imprisonment. There was a great revival in the late 17th century. In 1792 William Cary founded the Baptist Missionary Society.

Barbarians: a word coined by the Greeks to indicate people who could not speak their language and applied by them to the Persians in particular. The word has come to be used almost exclusively for the tribes, largely of Germanic origin, who invaded and eventually destroyed the western Roman Empire. Southern inroads of wild northerners were known in Greece in the 3rd century BC when the Galatians passed through to settle in Asia Minor. Rome herself suffered from invaders from north of the Alps from 106–101 BC, when the Cimbri and Teutones from Jutland caused great alarm in northern Italy.

The real threat to the northern frontiers of Rome dates from the 3rd century AD. The first tribe to come into conflict with Rome were the Goths, divided into the Visigoths (western) and Ostrogoths (eastern) from their original centres in the Ukraine. In the face of pressure from the Huns they were forced westwards and inevitably were pushed against the Roman Empire. For some time they were kept at bay, and an uneasy coexistence was established in spite of Arianism, the heretical brand of Christianity that they practised. Stupidity on the part of Rome led to the disastrous battle of Adrianople in 378, when the Gothic cavalry crushed the Roman legions. The Visigoths invaded Italy and eventually sacked Rome in 410 under Alaric (*c.* 370–410). They were then content to move off into Spain. Shortly afterwards the Ostrogoths came to an arrangement with the Romans and, based on Ravenna in north Italy, gave rise to a flourishing community of which the most notable figure was Theodoric (*c.* 454–526). Justinian (483–565) in his reconquest of Italy in the 6th century ousted the Ostrogoths, who then disappeared from history.

Very different were the Huns, a tribe which lived on horseback, led by their formidable warrior chief Attila (*c.* 406–453). Causing great danger to the Roman Empire in the 4th and 5th centuries, they rode across Europe into France but were defeated near Châlons in 451 by a combined force of Romans, Franks and Goths. Though they then invaded Italy, the death of Attila caused their rapid disappearance.

The Vandals were also pushed west and

south by the Huns, but they moved through Spain into North Africa from 406 onwards. Under Genseric (*c.* 395–477) they took over the rich Roman province and became expert in the construction of ships. They landed and sacked Rome in 455, but Justinian's general Belisarius defeated them in 534.

Two more tribes successively occupied northern Gaul in the 4th and 5th centuries. The Franks were able to settle in with the Romans, and Stilicho (*c.* 360–408) drew up a treaty with them in 396. They helped against Attila in 451, and their great king Clovis (*c.* 466–511) might almost be regarded as the founder of modern France. The Burgundians settled in the district still named after them.

On the perimeter of the Empire further Germanic tribes, the Angles, Saxons and Jutes, began to take over Britain. In the 4th century forts had been built against the Saxons on the east coast, and, when Rome evacuated her military garrison in 409, Britain was repeatedly invaded. The Saxons took over effective control of the island as a unit by the 7th century.

Lastly the Lombards, after the brief restoration under Justinian, moved into North Italy in the late 6th century and stayed. More than the other tribes, their idea was one of permanent conquest, and the conflict with the Papal power (the Lombards were Arians) lasted till their final overthrow by the increasingly civilised Franks under Charlemagne in 774.

¶ SOBEL, DONALD J. *First Book of the Barbarian Invaders*, 1963

See also INDIVIDUAL ENTRIES.

Barber-surgeons: The joint professions of barber and surgeon were in early centuries reckoned almost indistinguishable. Henry VIII of England (1491–1547) enacted that barbers should limit themselves to pulling teeth and blood-letting, while surgeons were not permitted to

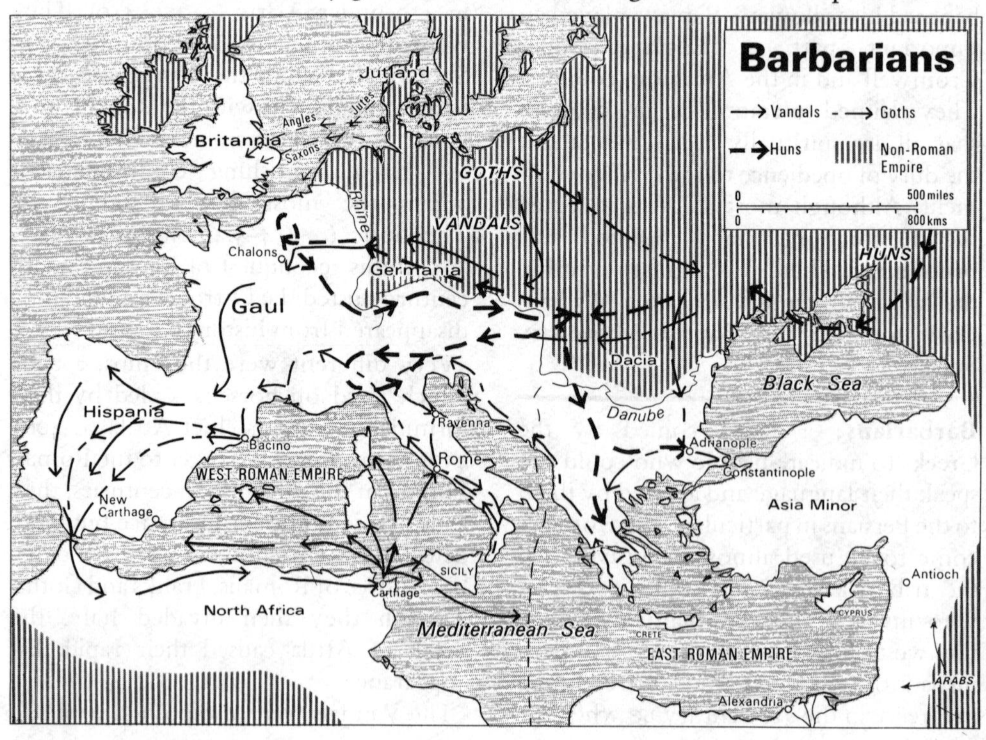

practise "barbery or shaving". The old barber's shop was a great centre for social meeting and the exchange of news, and musical entertainment was often provided. The dual function of the barber is still commemorated in the striped pole frequently displayed before his shop, a symbol of the bandages tied round the arm before and after blood-letting to reduce fever, etc.

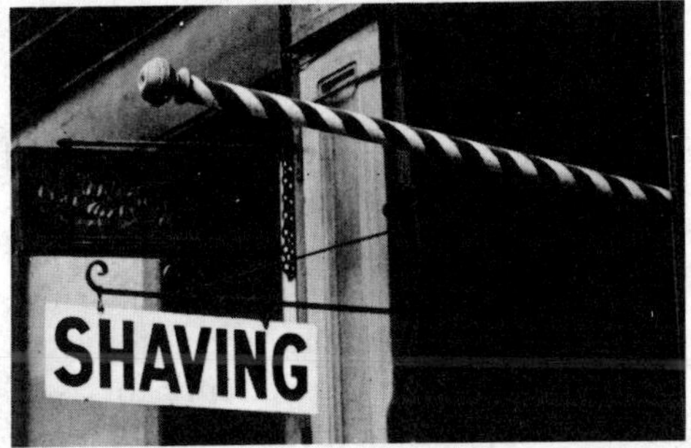

The traditional striped barber's pole.

Baron: originally meaning simply "man" or "freeman". Under the Norman Conquest in England the term came to stand for chief tenants holding land from a great lord, especially the king. Its early meaning still survives in the English legal term *baron and femme*, meaning "man and wife". It is now the lowest rank in the British peerage.

In Europe generally the word for a long time meant no more than man or husband and, later, a particularly powerful man. By the end of the 13th century in France the title had assumed much the same meaning as in Norman England, and the same process, with variations, may be traced in many other European countries. The title (Dan) was introduced into Japan in 1885 to denote the lowest class of territorial nobles and also as a title of honour, held without land.

Baronet: hereditary title created by James I of England in 1611 to obtain money for the support of the army in Ulster. It was offered to anyone willing to pay £1,095 in three annual instalments, this being the sum needed for the pay of 100 foot-soldiers for three years.

Baroque: a term, originally contemptuous and meaning "odd", for a style of architecture and ornaments developed in Italy about 1640 and flourishing in Spain and South Germany in the 17th century. It retained something of the forms of Renaissance Classical style, but lost much of its spirit: the column melted into barley-sugar shape; the circular, domed vault was strained into an oval; the pediment was broken to accommodate a statue or a painted plaque; the line of a cornice was blurred by decoration – cherubs, swags, cornucopias; windows became invisible sources of dramatic lighting. Such effects were used to stimulate faith in a Church which was challenged by heresy, and baroque flourished most in areas where the Counter-Reformation was active. Protestant England was little affected, and the French taste for order and moderation restrained the growth of baroque there. The pioneers of baroque in Italy were Bernini (1598–1680) and Borromini (1599–1667). The outstanding German architects were the Asam brothers, Cosmas Damian (1686–1739) and Evid Quirin (1692–1750), and Johan Balthasar Neumann (1687–1753).

See also RENAISSANCE, etc.

Bastille: the French name given to any castle with towers. As a proper name it signifies the old state citadel and prison of Paris. Built in the 14th century it came to be used as the prison for persons of rank or political importance. These included Fouquet, the Man in the Iron Mask, a Duke of Orleans and Voltaire. The fortress, which had become symbolic of the oppression of the *Ancien Régime*, was

attacked, captured and destroyed by the Paris mob on 14 July 1789, the event that marks the outbreak of the French Revolution. All that remains today is a commemorative column in the Place de la Bastille. On 14 July France observes a national holiday.
See also FRENCH REVOLUTION.

Baths and Bathing: used from very early times for the purposes of cleanliness, for the treatment of afflictions and for ceremonial reasons. The Bible contains a number of instances, e.g. the "multitude of impotent folk, of blind, halt, withered" visiting the pool of Bethesda, Jerusalem. Bathrooms were included in Egyptian palaces and many examples have survived of their incorporation in wealthy Greek and Roman houses, as well as of baths for public use. Efficient systems were in use for supplying both hot and cold water, and shower baths were an early innovation. In Rome especially the bath achieved splendid architectural form and the *thermae* became popular social centres, with club rooms, gardens and spaces for listening to lectures, etc. The designs of Pennsylvania Station, New York, and St George's Hall, Liverpool, England, were based on great halls in Roman baths.

In many early baths a progression was followed from a hot or steam room to warm and then to cold. In Muslim countries and in Russia the same practice was often followed, a more primitive system involving the bather making his final plunge into an icy pool or into piled snow. Many baths were built over wells and springs believed to have medicinal and curative properties. Not all baths, however, involve the use of water. Roman ladies had a preference for asses' milk. Sand, oils and mud are only a few of the other media used. A recipe of *c.* 1460 prescribes a medicinal bath made from, among other things, hollyhock, mallow, pellitory, brown fennel, dane-

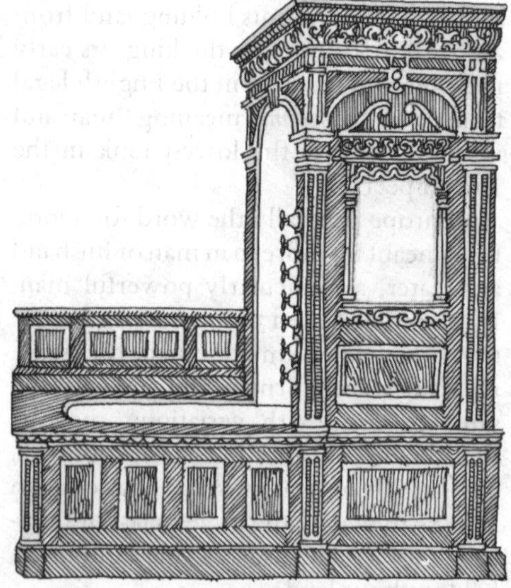

Above left: Romans bathing. Left: From a Franco-Flemish manuscript, late 13th century. Above: English domestic bath and shower unit, awarded a gold medal at the Health Exhibition of 1884.

wort, St John's wort, centaury, ribwort, camomile, herb-benet, bresewort, smallage, water speedwell, scabious, wild flax, withy leaves and green oats. ("Put your lord over it and let him endure it for a while as hot as he can, being covered and closed on every side.").

Although the Industrial Revolution brought a greater demand for personal cleanliness, it was not till the 19th century that bathrooms were installed in private houses in sizable numbers and, even then, the amenity was usually restricted to wealthier homes and the efficiency of the plumbing was doubtful. Not until much later in the present century has the provision of a bathroom in every house, however small, come to be regarded in many countries as an everyday necessity rather than a luxury.

Battering-ram: tree or other heavy length of timber, often with an iron head, swung to and fro by teams of men to breach the stone walls or break in the gates of fortified places. A variation, called the Bore, was equipped with an iron spike which stabbed mortar and stone till whole sections collapsed.

Battle of Britain: the attempt by Adolf Hitler (1889–1945), the German *Führer*, to destroy Britain's air force before proceeding with "Operation Sea Lion" – the invasion of Britain.

The German air attacks were known as "Operation Eagle" and were to have destroyed the RAF by 15 September 1940 so that the German Navy could take advantage of the right tidal conditions expected between 19 and 26 September 1940. The *Luftwaffe* (German air force) had about 2,500 planes initially, while the British Fighter Command had only about 650. Their defeat was mainly due to the air defence system of Great Britain which divided the area into five Fighter Command Group Areas. Each of these Groups had at its command an efficiently organised system of radar stations and Royal Observer Corps posts which kept contact with all enemy aircraft. This allowed Fighter Command to concentrate its forces where they could do most damage. In addition to this defence system, the British advantage lay in their equipment, especially the Supermarine Spitfire aircraft which could outmanouvre all German aircraft.

The battle falls into distinct phases. In July 1940 the Germans attacked Channel shipping and seaports in order to coax the RAF into battle and wear them down. In August they tried to destroy the radar stations, airfields and aircraft factories. By the end of August the RAF had suffered heavy losses and was close to cracking. Then in early September the *Luftwaffe* was ordered to switch its attack to London in response to British bombing of Berlin. This relieved the pressure on Fighter Command. Soon the *Luftwaffe*'s losses became so heavy that daylight bombing had to be abandoned.

In October Hitler cancelled "Sea Lion", and his invasion fleet dispersed.

See MAP page 86.

¶ SMITH, N. D. *The Battle of Britain*, 1962

See also WORLD WAR II.

Battles, Decisive: battles which changed the whole course of history. These battles often bear little relation to the numbers of men involved and the list of casualties, e.g. the Battle of Plassey, 1757, which "at a cost of 23 killed and 49 wounded . . . decided the fate of Bengal", compared with Borodino, 1812, in which there were 76,000 losses in an inconclusive battle.

There have been a number of attempts to enumerate the decisive battles of history. Henry Hallam (1777–1859) listed Marathon, Arbela, Metaurus, Châlons

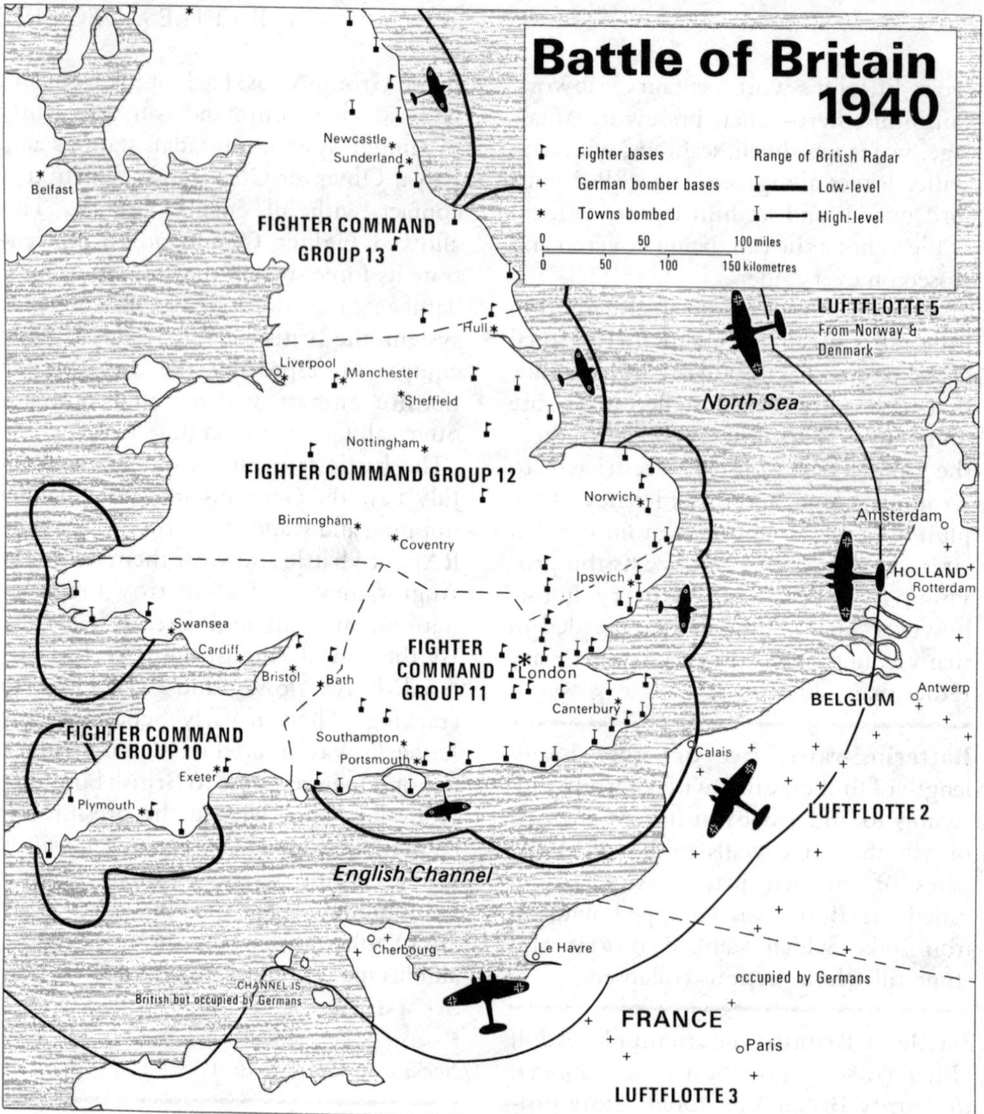

Battle of Britain 1940
Fighter bases
German bomber bases
Towns bombed
Range of British Radar
Low-level
High-level
0 50 100 miles
0 50 100 150 kilometres
FIGHTER COMMAND GROUP 13
FIGHTER COMMAND GROUP 12
FIGHTER COMMAND GROUP 11
FIGHTER COMMAND GROUP 10
LUFTFLOTTE 5
From Norway & Denmark
LUFTFLOTTE 2
LUFTFLOTTE 3
North Sea
English Channel
Belfast
Newcastle
Sunderland
Hull
Liverpool
Manchester
Sheffield
Nottingham
Norwich
Birmingham
Coventry
Ipswich
Swansea
Cardiff
Bristol
Bath
London
Canterbury
Southampton
Portsmouth
Exeter
Plymouth
Amsterdam
HOLLAND
Rotterdam
Antwerp
BELGIUM
Calais
Cherbourg
Le Havre
CHANNEL IS.
British but occupied by Germans
occupied by Germans
FRANCE
Paris

Defensive Systems
SECTOR CONTROL
British Fighters
RADIO STATION (AUTOMATIC)
ANTI-AIRCRAFT BATTERIES
SATELLITE STATION
HQ.
GROUP
RADAR STATION
HQ.
FIGHTER COMMAND
HQ.
ROYAL OBSERVER CORPS
OBSERVATION POST
German bombers

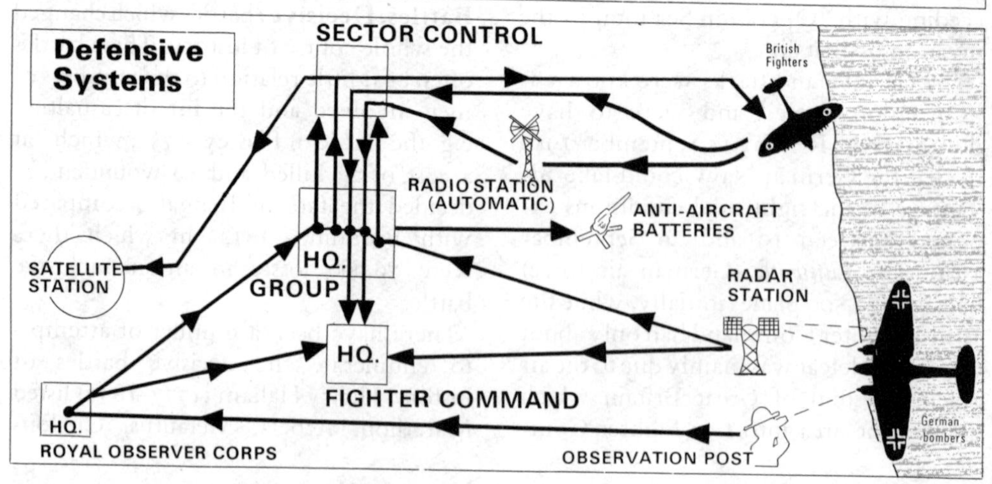

and Leipzig. Inspired by this, Sir Edward Creasy (1812–78) produced the most famous attempt in his *Fifteen Decisive Battles of the World* (1852). The fifteen were:

The Battle of Marathon, 490 BC
The Defeat of the Athenians at Syracuse, 413 BC
The Battle of Arbela, 331 BC
The Battle of the Metaurus, 207 BC
The Victory of Arminius over the Roman Legions under Varus, AD 9
The Battle of Châlons, AD 451
The Battle of Tours, AD 732
The Battle of Hastings, 1066
Joan of Arc's Victory over the English at Orleans, 1429
The Defeat of the Spanish Armada, 1588
The Battle of Blenheim, 1704
The Battle of Pultowa, 1709
The Victory of the Americans over Burgoyne at Saratoga, 1777
The Battle of Valmy, 1792
The Battle of Waterloo, 1815

Subsequent debate and disagreement have been inevitable. Brewer considered the Battle of Barnet (1471) "certainly one of the most decisive ever fought" because "it closed for ever the Age of Force, the potentiality of the barons, and opened the new era of trade, literature and public opinion". Naval historians will quarrel with the omission of Trafalgar (1805) which was "different from and more conclusive than any earlier battle under sail". Alternatives are endless; and there is, too, the whole period since Creasy wrote, with its ever-increasing canvas of world conflict. But there will probably be few to object to the inclusion, in any future list, of the Battle of Britain, immortalised in the words of Sir Winston Churchill in a speech to the British House of Commons, 20 August 1940: "Never in the field of human conflict was so much owed by so many to so few."

Bavaria: the southernmost and second largest state of the German Federal Republic, Bavaria has an ancient history. Some of its cities flourished in the Roman Empire and its medieval towns still attract many tourists. The former rulers of Bavaria, the Wittelsbachs, made the capital, Munich, a great centre of German culture.

In the past Bavarians showed little interest in a unified Germany and disliked the more determined Prussians. After 1918 Bavaria was a reluctant member of the Weimar Republic. Fanatics found a willing audience among the discontented citizens. Hitler made Munich his headquarters and chose Nuremberg, Bavaria's second city, as the meeting place for the big Nazi rallies.

Bayard, Pierre du Terrail (1474?–1524): the knight of France whose name has come down in history as symbolic of the ideals of chivalry and who was described as *sans peur et sans reproche* (without fear and without blame). Among his most famous exploits was the defeat of the army of Charles of Austria when he invaded France in 1521.

Bayeux Tapestry: the long, narrow strip of needlework, dating from *c.* 1088–92, depicting the Battle of Hastings and the events leading up to it. Strictly speaking it is not a tapestry, since the pictures are embroidered in wools on the linen material, not woven into it. Eight colours are used: yellow, grey, red, three blues and two greens; the stitch used is partly an outline stem-stitch and partly laid. The breadth is about 19½ inches [496 millimetres] and the total length – made up of several pieces joined together – is about 230 feet [70 metres]. Though it was long held to be the work of Queen Matilda and her ladies, more reliable evidence suggests that it was commissioned by

The Bayeux Tapestry. The English in flight, pursued by Norman horsemen.

Bishop Odo, half-brother of the Conqueror, and made by English craftsmen. The tapestry is preserved at Bayeux, France.

¶ DENNY, NORMAN, and FILMER-SANKEY, JOSEPHINE. *The Bayeux Tapestry: the story of the Norman Conquest 1066*, 1966

See also HASTINGS, BATTLE OF.

Beaufort, Margaret, Countess of Richmond (1433–1509): mother of Henry VII of England. She was one of the great women of her century, well educated, politically intelligent and, in the eyes of one of her contemporaries, of "sound sense and holiness of life". She was a generous benefactress of the Universities of Oxford and Cambridge and an early patron of the printers Caxton and Wynkyn de Worde.

Becket, St Thomas (1118–70): English archbishop and royal minister. He had considerable administrative gifts and as Chancellor to Henry II served him with conspicuous devotion and skill. His appointment as Archbishop of Canterbury in 1162 could have set the seal on a career marked by driving ambition and magnificent display; but in fact it broke the close intimacy with the king when Thomas turned his devotion to the church; and a series of bitter quarrels led to the Archbishop's murder in Canterbury Cathedral by four of Henry's knights. Becket had few qualifications for the position of archbishop. He became a priest only three days before his official enthronement and was deficient in his knowledge of Latin, of the scriptures and of the liturgy.

¶ DUGGAN, ALFRED. *Thomas Becket of Canterbury*, 1967

Bede (673–735), known as **"The Venerable"**: English monk, historian and scholar. Though he never stirred beyond the confines of his monastery at Jarrow, he was a leader of European intellectual thought and a powerful influence in the revival of learning under the Emperor

Charlemagne (*c.* 742–814). His writings, especially his *Ecclesiastical History of the English Nation,* are the chief source for English history up to 731, at which point he says: "Thus much . . . as far as I could learn either from the writings of the ancients, or the traditions of our ancestors, or of my own knowledge, has, with the help of God, been digested by me, Bede."

¶ PRICE, MARY R. *Bede and Dunstan,* 1968

Belgae: ancient Germanic and Celtic people who occupied northern Gaul and Belgium. Some established themselves in Britain in the 2nd and 1st centuries BC and brought about a political and commercial bond that was to have important results, such as Julius Caesar's invasion of Britain to suppress support for Gaul.

Belgium: constitutional monarchy in north-west Europe. This part of the continent has earned the nickname of "the cockpit of Europe", since it has been fought over interminably and has been the site of more major European battles than any other comparable area. After centuries of invasion, tangled alliances, occupation and revolution involving many European powers, Belgium and Holland joined in 1815 to become the Kingdom of the Netherlands; but the shortlived alliance ended in 1830, when Belgium broke away and was recognised as a separate kingdom, whose neutrality was guaranteed. It was overrun by Germany in both world wars, but has successfully re-established itself as an important member of Benelux, NATO and the European Common Market (*see* separate entries). Population in 1982: 9,854,600. *See* EUROPE for map.

Belisarius (*c.* 494–565): Byzantine general who as the servant of Justinian I conquered the Vandals in Africa and the Ostrogoths in Italy. He seems to have been a popular and lovable character, described by his companion Procopius as "a large man and attractive . . . so affable and easy to approach . . . that he seemed more like a really poor, humble fellow". Gibbon, however, has reluctantly to confess that "the fame and even the virtue of Belisarius were polluted by the lust and cruelty of his wife [Antonina]".

Alexander Graham Bell, left, and original Bell telephone.

Bell, Alexander Graham (1847–1922): inventor of the telephone. Educated in Scotland and England, he emigrated to Canada in 1870 and became a naturalised American citizen in 1874. His invention of the telephone in 1876 led to a US monopoly and to its introduction shortly afterwards into England and France. He should be remembered equally for his pioneer work for the deaf, in whose cause he lectured widely and trained many teachers, becoming the founder of the American Association to Promote the Teaching of Speech to the Deaf.

¶ In LARSEN, EGON. *Men who Changed the World,* 1962

Benedict Biscop (*c.* 628–89): an important figure in the development of European learning. He journeyed from England to Rome five times, bringing back many books and pictures. He is credited with introducing glass to England and used it in monasteries he built at Wearmouth and Jarrow, the home of Bede, who wrote his life.

Benedict of Nursia, St (*c.* 480–*c.* 544): Italian monastic founder and author of the rule followed by the Benedictine and Cistercian monks. Of noble family, he spent three years of early manhood in a cave forty miles from Rome, devoting himself to prayer and contemplation. In time he founded twelve monasteries in the neighbourhood, with twelve monks in each. Later he established the great monastery at Monte Cassino, destroyed in 1944 but since rebuilt.
See also ABBEYS.

Benefit of Clergy: exemption claimed by the Church from any jurisdiction of secular courts of law. The benefit was at first confined to genuine clerks in holy orders, but in the course of time it was extended to anyone who could read a verse in the Psalter. Usually this was the first verse of the fifty-first Psalm: "Have mercy upon me, O God, according to Thy loving kindness: according unto the multitude of Thy tender mercies blot out my transgressions." This was known as the "neck verse", since the offender who could successfully read it saved his neck. In time, benefit of clergy lost all its original meaning, since the successful pleader was no longer handed over to the Church, but had to face trial and sentence in the ordinary courts. Benefit of clergy was not finally abolished till 1827.

Benelux: the economic union between Belgium, the Netherlands and Luxembourg (Be/Ne/Lux). A customs union in January 1948, it led to much fuller economic union twelve years later. The Benelux countries were founder members of the EEC and have worked hard to make it succeed.

Benevolences: literally, gifts given with good will, but in practice far otherwise. They were forced loans extorted by a number of English kings from Edward II to James I, at first under the pretence that they would be repaid. Henry VII was probably the most expert operator. Henry VIII blandly called them "loving contributions".

Benin City: now capital and administrative centre of Bendel state of the Federation of Nigeria. Formerly it was the capital of the kingdom of Benin, which flourished in the 16th and 17th centuries, then declined owing to the disruptive effect of the Atlantic slave trade.

Benin brass. A warrior chief with attendants.

The first Europeans to reach Benin were the Portuguese in 1485, to whom its people, the Bini, probably owe much of their technical skill in the carving of wood and ivory, and in the casting of brass in which they excelled at the height of their fame. Examples of their 16th- and 17th-century art are now eagerly sought and very highly prized by museums and art collectors throughout the world.

The old kingdom was ruled by a theocracy of priests with the king, the Oba, as titular head of state. The city was divided into two parts: the palace and its precincts; and the town proper, which was in turn divided into forty wards, each associated with a craft or ritual.

The Bini practised a form of spirit and ancestor worship which involved fetishes and horrific human sacrifices which were ended after Benin was captured by the British in 1897.

Benin, which is today an important centre of the mahogany and rubber trades, and also exports cotton, palm oil and ivory, is now a typical African settlement of red clay houses, with a population of about 100,000.

Berlin: city of Brandenburg, Germany. Unlike other European capitals Berlin became important only in the 19th century. Until then it had been the capital of Prussia, which was only one of many German states. After Bismarck (1815–98) had created the German empire, Berlin quickly grew into a great city. From a population of 57,000 in 1709, and 160,000 in 1800, it multiplied to nearly two million in 1900. From Berlin, the Imperial government ruled a nation of over 60 million. It had splendour but little beauty, except in its surroundings of lakes and forests, where its working population could relax.

When, at the end of World War I, the Empire collapsed, there was much bitter and bloody street fighting between extremists of the (Communist) Left and the (Nationalist) Right. Gradually order was established; and in the "golden" 1920s Berlin was a city of over 4 million people, intent on having a good time. On 30 January 1933 Hitler became Chancellor of Germany, and that evening all Berlin seemed to welcome him with a spectacular torchlight procession. In 1936 the Olympic Games held in Berlin became a triumph for Nazi Germany. During World War II the city suffered heavily. Russian guns and tanks, in the street fighting of 1945, destroyed what British and American bombers had left standing in their frequent raids from 1943 onwards. The city surrendered to the Russians on 2 May 1945; the proud capital was a heap of rubble.

Since 1945 Berlin has been the focus where the disagreements between East and West appear most clearly. American, British and French forces have been in occupation of three-quarters of Berlin since July 1945 to "show the flag" far behind the Iron Curtain, the dividing line cutting Germany in two. The Berliners of the Western sectors quickly learnt to live according to Western ideas, while the Russian-occupied quarter became part of the German Democratic Republic – a Communist state. All traffic to West Berlin must go through Russian-controlled territory; aircraft have to fly in a corridor policed by Russia. These regulations inevitably caused trouble and have occasionally led to serious international tension. In 1948 Russia closed the rail and road links from the west to drive the Western powers out of Berlin. The Allied answer was the airlift. For eleven months the people of Berlin were kept going by relays of British and American 'planes. In May 1949 the Russians ended the blockade as suddenly as they had started it. In June 1953 a serious rising of workers shook the East Berlin government and Soviet tanks were called out to restore order. Until 1961 the inhabitants of Berlin could cross from one sector to the other without much difficulty; about 50,000 workers from its Eastern sector, in fact, worked in the more prosperous Western part. But in the middle of August of that year the East German government decided to end this contact and started to build the Berlin Wall – a grim construction of concrete, barbed wire and searchlights, with armed guards in watch towers.

This divided city could not remain the capital of all Germany. Occasionally West Germany makes a gesture of staging a ceremony (such as a formal meeting of its parliament) in Berlin; but Bonn now functions as the effective capital of West Germany and East Berlin as that of East Germany. *See* GERMANY for map.

Berlin, Congress of (1878): an international conference which settled, for a while, the power struggle in south-east Europe between Russia, Austria and the decaying Turkish empire. England, represented by Disraeli, played a leading role at this conference, forcing Russia to give up some of the gains she had made in the Russo-Turkish War of 1877.
See also EASTERN QUESTION.

Bernard of Clairvaux, St (*c.* 1090–1153): French Cistercian monk, preacher and reformer. In 1115 he founded the abbey of Clairvaux in north-east France and remained its abbot for the next thirty-eight years. He exercised vast influence by his preaching, his letters and other writings, and by his personal example of austere, dedicated monasticism. He preached the Second Crusade and was barely restrained from leading one himself. Erasmus described him as "an eloquent preacher, much more by nature than by art. He is full of charm and vivacity, and knows how to reach and move the affections."
See also ABBEYS.

Bessemer, Sir Henry (1813–98): British engineer and metallurgist who, among his other inventions, discovered the all-important process in 1856 of converting cast iron into steel by forcing air through the molten metal, thus decarbonising it.
See also STEEL.

The first form of Bessemer movable converter and ladle from the original drawings by Sir Henry Bessemer.

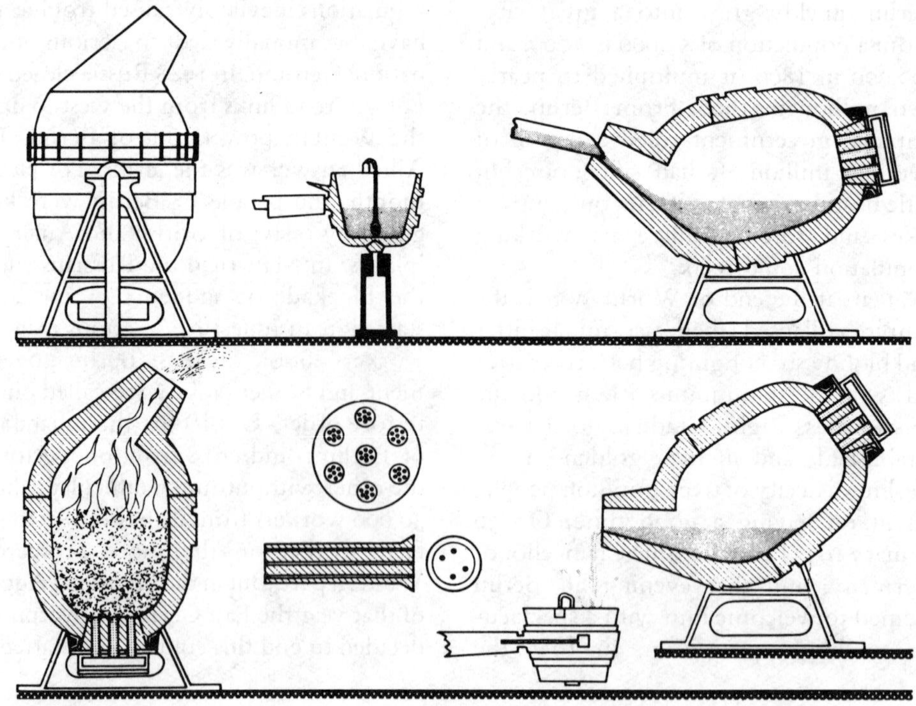

Bethlehem: town in Jordan, 5 miles [8 kilometres] south of Jerusalem now under Israeli occupation. The birthplace of Jesus Christ and earlier the home of David. Originally a walled and fortified city, its walls and towers were demolished in 1489. The 4th-century Church of the Nativity is on the assumed site of the holy birth.

Bethlehem's namesake in Pennsylvania, USA, founded in 1741, is not without its own distinctions. It had the first waterworks in the United States and has a distinguished musical history, including the first performance in America of Haydn's *Creation*.

Beveridge Report: a British government report by a committee with economist Sir William Beveridge (1879–1963) as chairman, issued in 1942. Its official title was *Social Insurance and Allied Services*. In the past, many people suffered great poverty when they were unemployed, ill, or too old to work. The Beveridge Committee examined these problems and recommended that there should be insurance against such misfortunes by providing a health service, unemployment and sickness benefits and retirement pensions for everybody. To help pay for this, workers and their employers were to pay insurance premiums to the state. The recommendations were made law and, because the state now undertakes to look after the wellbeing of all citizens in this way, Britain has been called the Welfare State.

Bible: the scriptures of the Old and New Testaments, as accepted and read throughout the Christian Church and used in Christian worship.

The word "Bible" is derived from a Greek word meaning "books". When the Bible was translated into Latin the same word – *biblia* – was used, but gradually it came to be thought of in the singular, as meaning *the* book. Yet is was and still is a collection of books, thirty-nine in the Old Testament and twenty-seven in the New Testament.

All sixty-six books of the Bible deal with the same theme, some directly, some indirectly. They tell of man's search for God, and of the ways of God towards man, in the experience of a single nation. They begin with the primitive idea of a tribal God who demands sacrifices, and they culminate in the idea of a God who is the loving Father of all mankind and who notices even the death of a sparrow. They begin with a Creator – "In the beginning God created the heaven and the earth" – and they culminate in a Saviour – "God sent not his Son into the world to condemn the world; but that the world through him might be saved".

The books of the Old Testament contain the scriptures of the Jewish people, beginning with the five books of Genesis, Exodus, Leviticus, Numbers and Deuteronomy. These were known as the Law, or the Torah; others were known as the Prophets – Joshua, Judges, the first and second Books of Samuel and of Kings, and all the writings of the great Jewish "prophets" or spiritual leaders. When Jesus said that he had not come to destroy the law and the prophets, but to fulfil them, it was of these books that he was speaking. Other books in the Jewish scriptures were called the "Writings"; these include religious poetry, philosophical writings, collections of wise sayings, historical records, and stories like Ruth or Jonah which were intended to teach people something new about God. The Law, the Prophets and the Writings cover a period in the life of the Jewish people of nearly a thousand years, beginning with myths and folk lore and continuing with written works.

The first Bible of the Christian Church was the Septuagint – the Greek version of

Above: Alcuin's revision of the Latin Vulgate, 9th century. Top right: A Wycliffite Bible, made by Wyclif's followers in 1380–84. This version belonged to Thomas of Woodstock, Duke of Gloucester, the youngest son of Edward III. Centre: Illustrations for the first page of the Coverdale Bible, 1535, showing the six days of the Creation. Below left: The Authorized Version, published in 1612 at the command of King James I. Below right: The New English Bible, the New Testament, published in 1961.

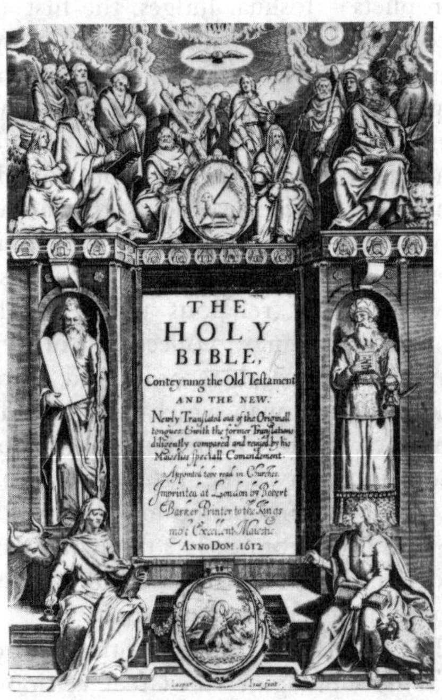

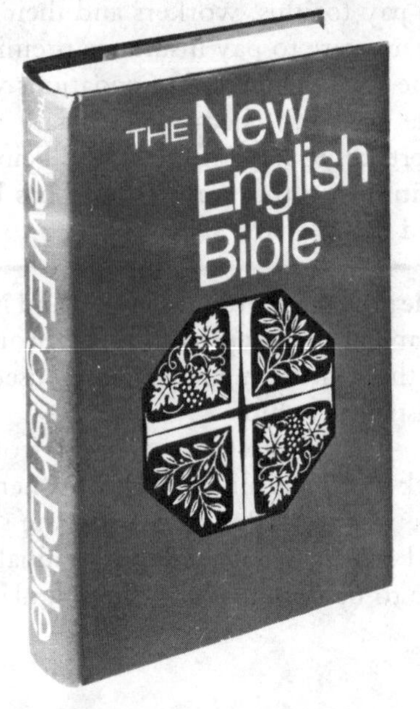

the Jewish scriptures. Gradually Christian writings were added, and these form the New Testament. As it was important to have a recognised version of the whole Bible, Pope Damasus (304–84) asked the scholarly St Jerome (342–420) to translate both the Old and the New Testament into Latin, and this great version is known as the Vulgate. It included some of the books which came to be rejected both by the Jews and by the Christian Church; these now form the Apocrypha. Other versions of the scriptures have been preserved in the Eastern Churches.

The New Testament consists of the four Gospels, the Acts of the Apostles, the Epistles (or letters) of the Early Church, many of which were written by St Paul, and the Book of Revelation. The first three Gospels, Matthew, Mark and Luke, are known as the Synoptic Gospels, meaning that in many ways they are similar. The fourth Gospel, ascribed to St John, is different; it is meant to convey the inner meaning of Christ's life and teaching. Mark is thought to be the oldest of the Gospels and John the latest, and the Epistles of St Paul are believed to be the earliest Christian writings which have survived.

The great English translations of the complete Bible came with the Reformation, but parts of it were translated in earlier times. Alfred the Great (849–99) is believed to have translated, or caused to be translated, the four Gospels and many of the Psalms, and other translations of parts of the Bible appeared in the Middle Ages, but the official Bible was still the Vulgate. The Bible story was familiar to the illiterate people of England through the spoken word, folk songs and legends, and the frescoes and stained glass windows in the churches.

John Wyclif (1329–84), the great reformer, and his followers believed that every man should be able to read and understand the Bible, but their translations were forbidden by the Church. William Tyndale (1494–1536) translated the greater part of the Bible from the Greek; most of his work was done in exile and he died a martyr's death in Holland. Miles Coverdale (1488–1568) used part of Tyndale's translation in his complete Bible, which was published in 1535. His version of the Psalms is still in use today in the services of the Anglican Church. In 1538 a royal injunction ordered that the Bible should be set up in every parish church; the edition used was the Great Bible, the work of Coverdale, first printed in 1539 and revised under Cranmer's direction. The Great Bible is sometimes called Cranmer's Bible, or the "Treacle Bible", because it refers to "treacle in Gilead" instead of "balm in Gilead". Another English version, first published in Geneva for the use of Protestant exiles, is the Geneva Bible; this is often called the "Breeches Bible" because it refers to "breeches" instead of "aprons" in the story of Adam and Eve.

In 1611 the Authorised Version was published at the command of James I (1566–1625): in the United States it is known as the King James Version. This is the best-loved book in the English language, and to many people it is *the* Bible beyond all others. A Revised Version was published in the 19th century. New authoritative versions have been published in recent years: the American Revised Standard Version, the New English Bible, and for the Roman Catholic Church the Westminster Version of the Holy Scriptures and also a translation by Monsignor R. A. Knox (1888–1957).

¶ SELBY-LOWNDES, JOAN. *Your Book of the English Bible*, 1964

See also ALFRED THE GREAT; CHRISTIANITY; CRANMER, THOMAS; ILLUMINATED BOOKS; INCUNABULA; VULGATE; WYCLIF, JOHN.

Bill, Parliamentary: in the British parliamentary system, the first form of a new law. It can be introduced by a minister or a private member in either the House of Commons or the House of Lords. This is called the first reading. It is then printed and sent to all members. At the second reading the chief features of the Bill are discussed and voted upon. In this way it may be changed in part or even brought to an end by a majority vote against it. If it passes the second reading it goes to a special committee, called a standing committee, which examines it in detail. Here again, changes, called amendments, may be made. The Bill is then examined by the whole House at what is called the report stage. Finally there is the third reading when the members vote whether or not to accept the Bill as a whole.

After a Bill has passed its third reading it goes to the other House (Commons or Lords) where it is treated in the same way. When a Bill has passed through both Houses and been approved by the monarch (the royal assent) it becomes an Act of Parliament and is part of the law of the land.

But members of the House of Commons are elected by the people: members of the House of Lords are not. A Bill passed by the House of Commons theoretically expresses the will of the people and in a democracy should become law, whether the House of Lords likes it or not. To ensure this, the House of Lords may send a Bill back to the House of Commons and so delay its passage but it cannot finally stop its becoming law.

Billeting: the quartering of soldiers in private houses. It was formerly a device much relied on for furnishing troops with food and lodging and was often a major grievance, e.g. in Stuart England, when troops were levied to relieve la Rochelle were a burden on the south. Billeting was an infringement of liberty, the soldiers were of the roughest type and disputes with them might involve civilians in trial by martial law. It was one of the grievances leading to the Petition of Right (1628). The Grand Remonstrance of 1641 repeated complaints against "charging of the Kingdom with billeted soldiers . . . that the land might either submit with fear or be enforced . . . to such arbitrary contributions as should be required of them".

Biography: from Greek *bios,* life, and *graphe*, writing. Biography deals with the lives of individual men and women. When the writer writes his own life, it is called *autobiography*.

The Old Testament has many biographies of the great Jewish prophets and kings. The Greeks and Romans produced a number of accounts of the lives of their great men. One of the earliest of these is the life of the philosopher Socrates (469–399 BC) written by his friend Xenophon (430–356 BC) the historian. The most famous of all the ancient biographers is Plutarch (AD 46–120). His book *Parallel Lives* related the lives of forty-six Greek and Roman heroes arranged in pairs for comparison. It was translated from Latin into French many hundreds of years later by Jacques Amyot (1513–93), and this French version was translated into English by Sir Thomas North (1535–1601). Shakespeare used North's translation when writing his classical plays.

During the Middle Ages many hundreds of biographies were written. They were not so often lives of great kings and generals as of the heroes of Christianity, the saints and other holy men and women. This was because the authors were mainly monks. One of the most famous was the Venerable Bede (673–735) who spent his life at Jarrow teaching Latin, Greek and

Hebrew. He wrote forty books, many of which were biographies of the saints. The *Life of Alfred* by Asser, Bishop of Sherborne, written in the 9th century, was the first biography of an English layman. Famous collections of lives are those by John Aubrey (1626–97), *Minutes of Lives,* usually known as *Brief Lives*; and Thomas Fuller (1608–61), *Worthies of England.*

John Aubrey.

The most famous biography in English is *The Life of Samuel Johnson* by James Boswell (1740–95), published in 1791. Boswell was a Scotsman who came to London and became a friend of Dr Johnson. He admired Johnson so much that he kept careful notes of many conversations with him so that in the biography we have a vivid picture of Johnson, with his weaknesses as well as his greatness clearly shown.

From the 18th century onward almost every man and woman of any importance became the subject of a biography. Such books as Southey's *Life of Nelson*, Forster's *Life of Dickens* and Morley's *Gladstone* really form a branch of history because the writers present their subjects within a framework of their times.

In the United States the writing of biography did not begin to assume an important place till the 19th century. In 1890 Abraham Lincoln's secretaries, Hay and Nicolay, produced one of the greatest American biographies, and there are now few major statesmen, soldiers and literary figures who have not received attention in this field. Special classes in biography have been included in a number of American colleges and universities.

Comprehensive works of national biography are among the most ambitious and valuable to be attempted. Sweden produced the first biographical dictionary in 1516–65. In Britain, *The Dictionary of National Biography* (first launched in 1885) now records the lives of over 30,000 British men and women. In America there is *The Dictionary of American Biography*, and other works of this type have been produced in, for instance, Holland, Austria, Germany and Belgium.

Bismarck, Otto Eduard Leopold, Prince von (1815–98): German statesman, known as the Iron Chancellor, and maker of the German Empire in 1871. An imposing figure physically, he made himself the master, first of Prussia, and then of Germany, by his outstanding political skill. Believing that "blood and iron" were necessary for achieving national greatness he provoked wars against Prussia's neighbours and rivals. As Prime Minister of Prussia he won victories over Denmark (1864), Austria (1866) and France (1870). As Chancellor of the new Germany he adopted a policy of peace through alliances. Few liked him; the world respected him. His work was largely undone within twenty-five years by the war of 1914–18.

With the death of his old master William I, in 1888, Bismarck's power was soon at an end. Unable to support the policies of the new and self-willed young emperor,

William II, the Chancellor offered his resignation in 1890 and went into retirement for the last eight years of his life.

Black Death: a plague which spread from the Far East and crept across Europe between 1347 and 1351. It ravaged the army besieging the Genoese port of Kaffa and was carried west by infected Genoese ships, reaching Sicily in 1347. It raged through Italy, France, Spain, Germany and Norway. A few countries, including the Netherlands, escaped. The disease appeared first in England in August 1348, brought from Calais by a merchant who landed in Dorset. From Dorset it spread westward through Somerset and Devon and north-east to London, and reached the North, Scotland and Wales in 1350. Few parts of the country escaped, though some villages in the midst of infected areas were strangely untouched. The worst was over by the end of 1349, but there were further visitations in 1361 and 1369. For the next three centuries the plague was endemic; the last major outbreak was the Great Plague of 1665.

There were two forms of the disease: the pneumonic, spread by direct contagion, and the bubonic, carried by fleas from infected rats, so called from the bubos or small black swellings which it caused. In this first visitation there was no acquired immunity and no known cure. Lack of sanitation combined with fear, which made families stay indoors, helped to spread the disease. The victims were usually dead within a few days, often within forty-eight hours, and they numbered about half the population of the infected areas. Townsfolk, tightly packed within walls, suffered most. The first outbreak struck mainly at the middle-aged, but the young and healthy were badly smitten by subsequent outbreaks, and that of 1361–62 was known as the *mortalité des enfants*. The clergy, by the nature of their profession, were seriously affected; in the diocese of Winchester 48 per cent died in a year, and in all parts of the country it was quite common for a secluded parish to have two priests in a single year. The monks, too, suffered acutely and some monasteries never recovered. A few villages disappeared completely; the battle of Bosworth was later fought on the site of one of these "lost" villages. Others, like Coombe in Oxfordshire, were resettled on new sites.

Everywhere the disease caused bewilderment and despair. Many, believing that it was a punishment for the ungodly, turned to penitence; in Tournai the dice-makers turned their dice into beads for prayer, and in 1349 the Flagellants, who underwent voluntary whipping, appeared in England and came each day to St Paul's and other parts of London, each carrying a scourge with three knotted tails. Others sought scapegoats, often the Jews, who were accused of spreading the infection by poisoning wells.

The disaster hastened great economic changes. Fields were left untilled and crops unharvested, land became relatively plentiful and labour scarce. Manorial records make frequent reference to fugitive villeins whose relatives were ordered to bring them to the next court. The shortage of labour encouraged lords to lease the demesne, sometimes with stock, or to turn to sheep farming which was economically sound since the export of raw wool to Flanders and the growing English cloth trade could take all the wool produced. In some cases landlords profited by the rising numbers of fees levied on tenants, but these gains were offset by disadvantages. Freemen and villeins who had already commuted their services for a money rent of one penny or a halfpenny for a day's work found new opportunities, but the villeins who had not done so now found the lords anxious to cling to their services and many ran away. In the end the lords realised that in order to keep the villeins on the lands they must lighten their services or accept a money rent. Labourers, taking advantage of the shortage of workers, were "so lifted up and obstinate" that they disobeyed the king's command to take no more than the accepted wage. Parliament passed the Statute of Labourers by which workers who demanded higher wages and employers who paid them were fined and tradesmen were forbidden to raise prices. Vigorous attempts were made to apply the law but as a result of the shortage of labour after the plague hired men had been able to demand an increase of anything up to 50 per cent in wages, and in the long run such enforcement was impossible.

Some manors remained remarkably peaceful but in others attempts were made to kill the Justices who enforced the law, and the bitterness caused by these conflicts was a direct cause of the Peasants' Revolt of 1381.

A vivid account of the Black Death occurs in the opening chapter of Conan Doyle's *Sir Nigel*.

¶ ZIEGLER, PHILIP. *The Black Death*, 1969

See also PEASANTS' REVOLT.

Black Hole of Calcutta (1756): a tragic episode during the Anglo-French fight for India. Suraj-ud-Daula, Nawab of Bengal, resolved to destroy European trading settlements and, on 16 June 1756, attacked Calcutta with an army of 50,000 men. The British with a force of only 515, including Indians, put women and children on board ships in the river, where they were joined by the governor, Drake, and the commander of the garrison, Minchin. An ex-surgeon, Holwell, took command in the city but was compelled to surrender on 20 June when his force was reduced to 170. One hundred and forty-six British, including one woman, were then shut in a military punishment cell about 18 feet [6 metres] square for a whole night; 123 perished. British reaction to this outrage led to the victory at Plassey the following year.

¶ BARBER, NOEL. *The Black Hole of Calcutta*, 1965

Blake, Robert (1599–1657): British admiral. Born at Bridgwater, Somerset, he became member of Parliament for the borough in 1640. He distinguished himself as a soldier in the Civil War; and, appointed as "General at sea" in 1649, scattered the Royalist fleet under Prince

Rupert within two years. With the outbreak of the Dutch Wars in 1652. Blake sustained a defeat by Tromp in the face of heavy odds, but won several notable victories including the virtual annihilation of Tromp's fleet in the three-day running battle of Portland in March 1653. In the Mediterranean, he enforced respect for the Commonwealth, destroyed the Tunis pirates and received the submission of Algiers. In April 1657, catching the Spanish fleet at Tenerife, he destroyed sixteen galleons without losing a single ship himself. He died entering Plymouth harbour on 7 August. Blake is described as only "of a middle stature, about five feet and a half, inclining to corpulence"; but he was one of the great leaders of history, "the copy of naval courage, and bold and resolute achievements".

¶ In BRENDON, J. A. *Great Navigators and Discoverers*, 1956

Blenheim, Battle of (13 August 1704): fought during the War of the Spanish Succession between the Allies under John Churchill, Duke of Marlborough, aided by Prince Eugène of Savoy, and the French and Bavarians under Marshal Tallard. The French planned to assault Vienna from the west while the Hungarian rebels attacked from the east. Marlborough marched south from the Netherlands, joined Prince Eugène and drew up his army opposite Blenheim at the junction of the rivers Danube and Nebel. Marlborough attacked across the marsh; after a tremendous struggle, the French were defeated and Tallard captured.

¶ TREVELYAN, G. M. *Blenheim*, 1965

Blockade: the closing of a port by naval action, or the denial of access to or departure from the enemy's coast; the

A tapestry depicting the Battle of Blenheim, now in Blenheim Palace. The Duke of Marlborough is on the right.

maritime equivalent of a siege and an undoubted right of a belligerent. Its aim may be to interrupt military or commercial activity.

The close blockade was adopted by Admiral Hawke in 1759, when he kept the Western Squadron cruising off Ushant from May to November, sheltering in Torbay only when south-westerly gales prevented the French leaving Brest. St Vincent resorted to the same policy, 1803–5. A close blockade exhausted crews and strained ships and, if prolonged into winter, exposed the fleet to destruction by storms. Above all it did not tempt the enemy out for a decisive battle. There was always the danger that he might slip out after a storm. On the other hand the constant watch improved seamanship, while the enforced idleness of the blockaded fleet lowered the morale of the men. Close blockade was most useful when invasion was threatened or when important fleet movements had to be protected.

Open blockade was preferred by Howe in 1779–80 when he decided to protect England from invasion by keeping his main fleet at Spithead. Toulon was watched by Mathews in 1744 and by Nelson in 1805 from a station which allowed the enemy to sail and be brought to action. By concealing the strength and disposition of the blockading fleet, and by relying on frigates to watch enemy movements, the open blockade could tempt the enemy out. The blockading fleet then hoped, in Nelson's words, "to follow him to the Antipodes" and bring him to battle before he achieved his aims. The Glorious First of June and Trafalgar were both made possible by open blockade.

In the 20th century, torpedo-boat, submarine, mine, radio and aircraft have made the close blockade impossible and the open blockade more effective. Light forces in the North Sea and the Straits of Dover, a cruiser screen watching from Scotland to Iceland, and a Grand Fleet at Scapa, proved effective for Britain against Germany in 1914–18, but less so in 1939–45 when Germany had the use of French and Norwegian ports.

Blockades directed against commerce affect neutrals and have caused many disputes. Britain, as a power fighting mainly at sea, has been reluctant to forgo the right to search, detain and confiscate cargo. Napoleon, by his Berlin and Milan Decrees (1806, 1807) imposed a self-blockade on his empire, hoping to cause unemployment and unrest in England by preventing her exporting her manufactures. England replied by Order in Council declaring a "paper blockade". Both sides broke their own rules: Napoleon winked at or licensed the import of English cloth for his army; England devised ingenious ruses for trading with Europe – forged French trade marks and ships' papers, a smuggling outpost on Heligoland and "pensions" for Rhenish customs officers.

Blockades have been used in peacetime. In the Cuba missile crisis in 1961 the USA turned away Russian ships bringing missiles. The United Nations sanctions on Rhodesia were partially reinforced by a British blockade of Beira.

Bloodless (or **Glorious) Revolution** (1688–89): the name in English history given to the overthrow of James II and the succession, without bloodshed, of William III and Mary. In the three years of his reign (1685–88) James II had alienated a large body of his subjects, particularly by his efforts to restore Romanism. The birth of a male heir to the King in June 1688 increased the threat of a Catholic dynasty, and a number of influential statesmen, their loyalties to crown and Church forced increasingly into conflict, decided to invite James's son-in-law, William of Orange, to England to secure the Protestant faith and his wife's right to the throne. It is important to realise that, at this stage, he had not been invited to take the throne himself.

On 5 November 1688 William's imposing fleet stood into Torbay, Devon, his flagship flying the colours of England with the motto, "The Protestant Religion and the Liberties of England" and, beneath it, "And I will maintain it". The army having deserted James, William's horse and foot (the largest invading force to set foot in England) advanced to London without opposition, "welcomed with loud acclamations by the people". The constitutional position was complicated but was greatly eased by the escape – connived at by William – of James II to France in December. The throne was declared vacant. Meanwhile, though he had arrived only as "husband of the heiress of England", William made it clear that he would not be content to remain "his wife's gentleman usher", and William and Mary were proclaimed King and Queen of England on 13 February 1689.

In the eyes of Englishmen there was something symbolic in the fact that the Protestant prince landed on "the fifth of November (a day never to be blotted out of the Englishman's heart)".

Boers: from the Dutch *Boer*, meaning farmer, husbandman; a name given to the Dutch settlers who from 1652 onwards established themselves in South Africa. From 1688 they were strengthened by the arrival of French Huguenots who were seeking religious freedom, and together they opened up and cultivated the vacant plains of South Africa. After about 150 years of expansion to the east and north-east, they began to encounter waves of black Bantu moving down from the north, and a situation developed very similar to that existing between the white immigrants in America and the indigenous Red Indians, though, in fact, the Bantu were no more indigenous than the white men. During the Napoleonic Wars the Cape was captured by the British. Some thirty years later the Boers, who had developed a fierce independence, trekked further north (the Great Trek, 1835–36) on to the high veld, establishing there, in due course, the Boer republics of the Orange Free State and the Transvaal. Constant friction with Britain led to two wars (1880–81 and 1899–1902) before the formation of the Union of South Africa in 1910.

Bohemia: an historic European kingdom and former province of western Czechoslovakia. Bohemia was for centuries an independent kingdom with a strong tradition of liberty. Prague had a Christian bishop in the 10th century and saw the foundation of its famous university in the 14th century. One of Bohemia's early heroes was the blind King John who fell gallantly at Crécy (1346) with his reins fastened to those of the knights who led him into battle. In 1415 John Huss challenged the authority of the Church and was burnt, but his views influenced other reformers, including Wyclif. The Bohemian silver mines were a source of great wealth. In 1526 Bohemia passed under Habsburg rule but enjoyed special privileges, including the right to elect her king. An attack on these privileges led to the "Defenestration of Prague" when Habsburg representatives were thrown from an upper window; and the subsequent election of Frederick of the Palatinate as king led to the beginning of the Thirty Years War (1618–48) in which Bohemia was devastated. In the next two centuries Bohemia played little part in European affairs. She joined in the revolutions of 1848–49 but was crushed.

After World War I Bohemia became (1918) part of the new republic of Czechoslovakia and, in 1949, an administrative region of that country.

Bolivar, Simon (1783–1830): Venezuelan liberator and statesman. The central South American republic of Bolivia was named after him and he created Greater Colombia from Colombia, Panama, Venezuela and Ecuador, former colonies of Spain, which he led in revolution. One writer says that he presents "one of history's most colossal personal canvases of adventure and tragedy, glory and defeat". At times a refugee and fugitive, he eventually led his forces to victory, after great physical hardships and, it is estimated, over 200 battles in some of which he was helped by a "foreign legion" of veteran English and Irish mercenaries.

¶ VAN LOON, H. W. *Jefferson and Bolivar: new world fighters for freedom*, 1966

Simon Bolivar, the Liberator, shown in a typically heroic pose.

Bolsheviks: the majority faction, led by Lenin, of the congress of the Russian Social Democratic Party which met in 1903, first in Brussels and then in London, because of trouble with the Belgian police. Less familiar is the term *Mensheviks* for the smaller and more moderate fraction, destroyed or absorbed after 1918 by the Communists. Bolshevik or Bolshevist is really the comparative adjective of the Russian *bolshoi*, meaning "large" – a word occurring in the present day internationally famous Bolshoi Ballet from Russia.

Bombay: former state of western India, now divided into the states of Gujarat and Maharastra, with Bombay as capital of the latter. It rose to importance as the best natural harbour on the west coast of India. A province of Gujarat from 1348, it was ceded in 1534 to Portugal, who handed it over to Charles II of England in 1661. It was transferred to the East India Company in 1668. There was swift development under Gerald Aungier (President of Surat 1669–77) who fortified the town, drained tidal swamps and gave protection to all religions. It superseded Surat as the chief settlement of the East India Company in 1687. Richard Keigwin, self-appointed Governor in 1683, stopped native warfare in Bombay waters before handing over to Sir John Child, 1690. Admiral Watson and Robert Clive suppressed piracy, 1756. Cotton trade with China opened in 1770, and replanning after a great fire in 1803 led to rapid development, accelerated by the coming of railways and the Suez Canal. By 1900 population was some 850,000 (10,000 in 1661) and passed eight million at the beginning of the 1980s.

Bonaparte family: The Bonapartes were descended from an Italian family originating in the 12th century and settling in Corsica in the 16th. It came into prominence in France in the 18th century. Charles Bonaparte (1746–85) had seven children, all born in Corsica, of whom the most famous was Napoleon I (*see* separate entry). There were four other sons: Joseph (1768–1844), Lucien (1775–1840), Louis (1778–1846) and Jerome (1784–1860), Each played a significant part both in the Napoleonic Wars and in the administration and diplomacy of the

The Bonaparte family. Left: Napoleon I, Emperor of France. Below left: Lucien. Below: Louis, King of Holland. Below right: Jerome, King of Westphalia. Right: Joseph, King of Naples and Spain.

Empire. With the exception of Louis, each supported Napoleon I during the Hundred Days (*see* separate entry). Although often differing in ideas from their illustrious brother, in their various ways they were instrumental in enabling Napoleon I to consolidate his hold on Europe, so necessary if he was to withstand the English menace.

Joseph, after taking part in various diplomatic negotiations including those preceding the Treaty of Amiens in 1802, was proclaimed King first of Naples and then of Spain. He also acted as head of the French government during his brother's absence in 1805. After the fall of the Empire in 1815 he retired to the USA, although he eventually returned to Europe and died in Italy. In 1830 he had unsuccessfully tried to establish the claims of the Duke of Reichstadt, the son of Napoleon I, to be considered as Napoleon II. Lucien helped his brother in the administration of France, partly as President of the Council of the Five Hundred and partly, in 1804, as one of his ministers. But fundamentally their ideas differed too much. Lucien was too democratic and left France to become minister in Spain. Louis was made King of Holland in 1806 but he also was too liberal-minded, and in 1810 he left France to live first in Bohemia and then in Rome. He was the father of Louis Napoleon, who later became Napoleon III. Lastly, Jerome gave naval assistance during the wars, was made a prince of France and, in 1806, by the Treaty of Tilsit, King of Westphalia. After 1815 he too left France, and lived in Switzerland and Italy. The youngest of the five brothers, he lived to see the accession to power of his nephew Louis Napoleon. He was the only one of the brothers to return permanently to France, where he became a Marshal and President of the Senate.

Louis Napoleon (1808–73) was the most prominent member of the family after Napoleon I. He became President of the Second Republic after the Revolution of 1848. In 1851, thanks to an astute and well planned *coup d'état,* he first prolonged his term of office as President and shortly afterwards, in 1852, despite his oath of allegiance to the Republic, and with the subsequent support of a plebiscite, constituted himself Emperor of the Second Empire and remained so until the disasters of the Franco-Prussian War in 1870. A strangely paradoxical character, by his well-meaning but inept foreign policy he led France to ruin when, outwitted by Bismarck and confronted by the famous Ems telegram, he found himself with no alternative but to declare war on Prussia. He was with his own forces at Sedan when the French were compelled to surrender and he himself was taken prisoner and obliged to accompany the German Emperor back to Germany. A short time later, after his release, he joined his wife, the Empress Eugénie, in exile in England, where he died three years later. Eugénie, who by her meddling in politics had helped to precipitate the ignominious end of the Second Empire, continued to live there until her death in 1919. Their only son was killed while fighting for England in the Zulu War in 1879.

The family name is often spelt "Buonaparte". This was the Italian form. Bonaparte is the French form, but was not much used, even by Napoleon I, until 1796.
See also NAPOLEON I.

Book of Common Prayer: the service book of Anglican churches. This is essentially the Prayer Book of 1559, modified in 1662. Proposals for a new Prayer Book were rejected by Parliament in 1928 and recent alternative forms of service are still experimental.

Books and the book trade: Books in one form or another are as old as civilisation, and book-selling was a commerical activity known, for example, to the Hebrews, the Greeks and the Romans. The Roman book-sellers displayed lists of books for sale on their doors or doorposts, and the poet Martial (*c.* AD 80) mentions that one of his books could be bought for five *denarii*. Many of the earliest book-sellers were scribes, who produced copies of manuscripts to order. By the 12th century the chief centres of book-selling were Paris and Bologna, probably because of the demand created by their universities, and book fairs at various places in Europe attracted buyers from many countries.

Late in the Middle Ages the demand from a more literate aristocracy, from the universities, and from the emerging middle class brought a change in method, and professional scriveners increased the output of manuscript books by something approaching mass-production techniques. (There had been something of this kind in the Roman Empire, when large numbers of manuscripts were produced by teams of trained slaves).

The development of printing with moveable types in the 15th century resulted in an enormous increase in books and made it possible, and necessary, to organise their sale systematically. One name for early book-sellers was *stationarii* because, unlike pedlars who carried their goods around the country, they remained in one place and sold from their stalls or shops. In England the control of book production was long in the hands of the Stationers' Company. In the 18th and 19th centuries travelling chapmen who sold cheap little books and pamphlets were often described as "running" or "flying" stationers.

Printing, which began in Germany, spread quickly through Europe, to Holland, France, Spain and especially to Italy, where the greatest centre for books was Venice. The new invention was brought to England by William Caxton, a businessman with a taste for literature who, having printed several books abroad, set up a press under the shadow of Westminster Abbey and produced a series of fine books, including works by Chaucer, Lydgate and Malory. The trade was comparatively slow to develop in

England. The book-sellers who opened up their businesses, mostly in the area around St Paul's Cathedral (which remained the home of English publishing until the Blitz of 1940), mostly sold books imported from the Continent, and Richard III had to introduce an Act to encourage foreign printers to come to England.

The spread of printed books accompanied the two great world movements of this age, the Renaissance and the Reformation. The Renaissance brought into Europe the great works of classical literature, and exquisite editions of Greek authors were published, notably by Aldus Manutius of Venice (1449–1515). The Reformation produced an enormous demand for translations of the scriptures, but it made publishing an exceedingly hazardous business. A change in religious opinion might bring the publisher suddenly into conflict with the authorities. Richard Grafton, who printed the English Great Bible in 1539, was imprisoned more than once, and others risked even greater penalties.

The next age brought political as well as religious difficulties. English publishers had to contend with the authority of the Stationers' Company which, after 1559, was responsible for licensing every book published, and with Queen Elizabeth I's habit of granting monopolies for certain kinds of book. During the struggle between King and Parliament in the 17th century publishers like William Prynne and John Lilburne, who held opinions at variance with the government, risked not only prison but whipping and physical mutilation. King and Parliament alike tried to limit the expression of opinion, and John Milton, opposing an ordinance "to prevent and suppress the license of printing", wrote in 1644 his great address to Parliament called *Areopagitica* in which he declared that "hee who destroyes a good Booke kills reason itselfe".

Towards the end of the 17th century the power of the Stationers' Company had declined, and as a result the rights of publishers and authors were often flouted by "pirates" who took other publishers' books and brought them out in unauthorised cheap editions. In an attempt to restore these rights a Copyright Act was passed in 1709; this, however, while it protected the author's rights, also imposed strict limits on them.

The Age of Reason in the 18th century was also the age of literature. Writers such as Pope and Dr Johnson became influential members of society. Publishers, too, played a part in the social life of the times. Many books were financed by subscription, and the wise publisher made sure that famous and fashionable names appeared on his list of subscribers. Until this time the publisher had usually been his own printer and his own book-seller; now the occupations of printer and publisher tended to separate.

Industrial and social revolutions at the end of the century had profound effects on the book trade. There was a new demand for books from classes of readers wanting to improve their education and their status. Technical inventions made it possible to produce paper more cheaply and to print books in larger editions. One result of this was a savage price war which threatened to bring the whole trade to ruin. Responsible men on both sides of the industry saw the danger and formed themselves into associations, in Britain the Associated Booksellers (later the Booksellers' Association) in 1890 and the Publishers' Association in 1896. These two bodies achieved the Net Book Agreement (1900), all the signatories to which agreed to sell books at established prices and not to undercut one another.

Since then there have been great changes in the world of books. Two world wars brought about fundamental revolutions in technology and thought. Paperbacks, long a familiar sight on the Continent and not unknown in Victorian England, were given a new look as "Penguins" in 1935, bringing the finest books of all ages within the reach of all readers. There were amalgamations and takeovers of booksellers and publishing houses. Despite all the prophecies of scientists that books would disappear in favour of television and tapes, books have continued to be written, published, sold and read in ever greater numbers. In 1962 the Restrictive Practices Court considered the Net Book Agreement and decided that this measure was in the public interest and that "the uniqueness of a new book" demanded for it consideration denied to other commodities.

¶ HARLEY, ESTHER S. and HAMPDEN, JOHN. *Books: from Papyrus to Paperback*, 1964

See also LIBRARIES; PRINTING.

Boone, Daniel (1734–1820): one of the most famous of American scouts and pioneers. Though he did not actually discover and found Kentucky, as is often claimed, he was an intrepid explorer and Indian fighter who established a number of border posts and well deserved the grant of land eventually confirmed to him as one who had "opened the way to millions of his fellow men".

Border States, The: the area between the Middle Atlantic and Old South regions in the eastern section of the United States, which includes the states of Kentucky, North Carolina, Tennessee, Virginia, and West Virginia. The region is divided in half by the Blue Ridge, Cumberland, and Great Smokey Mountains, which run roughly parallel to the Atlantic coastline. To the east of these mountains lie Virginia and North Carolina, areas of lowland and plateau, with many small rivers flowing into the Atlantic. In the inland section of the region, the major river is the Tennessee River, which drains much of that state.

It was at Jamestown in Virginia that the first permanent English settlement in North America was established in 1607. Throughout the colonial period, Virginia remained the most important of England's mainland colonies, and provided much of the political and military leadership in the American Revolution. Kentucky and Tennessee were the first sites of major settlement west of the Allegheny mountains. Led by men such as Daniel Boone, settlers began to trickle through the passes in the mountains during the 18th century, and both areas entered the new nation as states during the 1790s. West Virginia was the last state in the region to be formed. Originally it was the mountainous western region of Virginia. When the latter state seceded, the population of the mountains, among whom slavery had never taken root, remained loyal to the Union, and this area was recognized as a state in 1861.

This region, like the Old South, is primarily a rural, agricultural area. The major farm products are tobacco and cotton. Mining is also important, especially in West Virginia, which is the leading coal producing state in the United States. The effects of mining methods have left large areas of West Virginia and Kentucky scarred and rugged. Tourism, especially to such sites as Williamsburg and Mount Vernon in Virginia, is also an important feature of life in this region.

Borders, The: the lands lying on both sides of the ancient boundary between England and Scotland, comprising the English counties of Cumberland and Northumberland and the Scottish counties of Berwick, Dumfries and Roxburgh. The region is dominated by the wind-swept Cheviot Hills (highest point The Cheviot, 2,723 feet or 830 metres), along the watershed of which ran the border line itself for much of its 108 miles [172 kilometres] from Berwick to the Solway Firth. The bleak moorland pastures are broken by narrow, winding glens which open out into the wide valleys of the rivers Teviot, Tweed and Liddle in Scotland, and the Glen, Coquet, Rede and North Tyne in England.

In these quiet dales during the relative peace of the 13th century were built the English abbeys and priories of Alnwick, Brinkburn, Hexham and Lanercost and the Scottish abbeys of Dryburgh, Jedburgh, Kelso and Melrose. During succeeding centuries, however, from the opening of the Scottish wars of Edward I in 1290 down to the Union of the two Crowns in 1603, the Border was periodically the scene of armed invasions and pitched battles, Halidon Hill (1333), Otterburn (1388) and Flodden (1513) among the most memorable. Feuds between the Douglases, Percies and other noble families, and vendettas between the Charltons, Reeds, Armstrongs, Grahams and other clans in the rival dales were also fought out in savage raids and counter-raids. From early times the Border on both sides had been divided by mutual consent into East, Middle and West Marches, each with a respective English and Scottish warden whose duty it was to defend the frontier and to keep the peace. Even so, marauding bands of outlaws, called reivers or moss-troopers, continued to terrorise the border homesteads as late as the Union of the two Kingdoms in 1707.

The great castles of Norham, Alnwick, Bamburgh, Dunstanburgh, Naworth and Carlisle and the crumbling stones of countless fortified houses, known as bastiles and peel towers, still stand as silent witnesses of the violent past, while innumerable legends and ballads, many retold by Sir Walter Scott, immortalise the courage and endurance, the cruelty, chivalry and humour of the Border folk.

Borgia family: an Italian family of Spanish origin which came to considerable power in the 15th century and which, despite great abilities, has left behind it an unenviable reputation for treachery, cruelty and crime. The three most notorious were Rodrigo, Cesare and Lucrezia.

Rodrigo Borgia (1431–1503) became Pope in 1492 with the title of Alexander VI. He was the most corrupt and vicious of the Renaissance popes, bestowing unlimited patronage on his relatives, living in great splendour, falsely imprisoning and murdering his opponents or those on whose wealth he hoped to lay hands, and leaving behind him a number of illegitimate children.

Cesare Borgia (1476–1507), his son, was created, while still a youth, archbishop of Valencia and cardinal but was later released from his ecclesiastical obligations. He turned his attention to political intrigue and conquest in Italy and, with an army made up largely of French, Gascon and Swiss mercenaries, subdued a number of

The Borgia family. Roderigo, Cesare, Lucrezia, and Francis.

rebellious cities and states by a mixture of good fortune, ruthlessness and broken faith. He was capable of firm and just government when his ends had been achieved, but his subtlety and unscrupulousness gave him the doubtful honour of serving as a model for Machiavelli's *Prince* (*see* MACHIAVELLI).

Lucrezia Borgia (1480–1519), Cesare's sister, was described at the age of twenty as "of medium height and slender figure . . . She has a good profile, golden hair, light eyes. Her mouth is rather large, with dazzling teeth. Her throat is smooth and white and charmingly rounded and her whole being radiates gaiety and laughter." Four times married in her thirty-nine years and often the political tool of her father and brother Cesare, she has left behind as bad a reputation as they, particularly associated with the use of poison. But, while she was certainly no innocent, this is probably less than just and, especially during her later years, she was known for charitable work, for her devotion to the education of her children and as a patron of art and learning, gathering at her husband's court at Ferrara a number of illustrious poets, painters and scholars. It is not untypical of great Renaissance families to combine crime and greed with generous patronage of the arts and genuine appreciation of beauty.

From this tangled story it is something of a relief to turn to the dedicated life of: Francis Borgia (1510–72) who was ordained priest at the age of forty-one, refused a cardinal's hat and in 1565 became third general of the Order of Jesuits. His simple asceticism, devotion to penance and prayer and success as leader of his Order brought him canonisation in 1671.

Boston: capital of Massachusetts, USA, named after the town in Lincolnshire, England, the district from which the chief Puritan settlers came. Though the harbour was probably explored by the Norsemen and the locality had been mapped and inhabited years before, the official date of settlement is 17 September 1630. With its splendid commercial situation, it grew rapidly in importance till it became, in the view of its inhabitants and in Oliver Wendell Holmes's phrase, "the hub of the universe". Though it preserves much of the atmosphere of its early days, it is one of the most cosmopolitan cities in the USA, numbering French Canadians, Italians, Greeks, Armenians and Chinese among its inhabitants, as well as many Irish.

Boston was a centre of resistance to British rule during the War of Independence, witnessing, among other critical events, the "Boston Massacre" (5 March 1770) in which a number of townsfolk were killed by British troops, and the "Boston Tea Party" (16 December 1773) when the cargoes of three tea-ships were

"The Bloody Massacre Perpetrated in King Street", with the inscription "Engraved, printed and sold by Paul Revere".

thrown into the harbour as a protest against the British tax of threepence a pound on tea.

Boston can claim many "firsts". The earliest American newspaper, the *Boston News Letter,* was established there in April 1704. It is claimed that Boston blood was the first to be shed in conflict in the American Civil War; and a Boston man, Colonel Shaw, led the first negro regiment against the Federal armies in what has been called "the first black gesture of earned freedom"

Boston has also been the chief literary centre of the USA, numbering many of its most distinguished poets, historians, philosophers, essayists and novelists among its sons and daughters.

N. E. Numb. 1.

The Boston News-Letter.

Published by Authority.

From Monday April 17. to Monday April 24. 1704.

London Flying-Poſt from *De.emb. 2d to 4th.* 1703.

LEtters from *Scotland* bring us the Copy of a Sheet lately Printed there, Inſtituted, *A ſeaſonable Alarm for* Scotland. *In a Letter from a Gentleman in the City, to his Friend in the Country, concerning the preſent Danger of the Kingdom and of the Proteſtant Religion.*

This Letter takes Notice, That Papiſts ſwarm in that Nation, that they traffick more avowedly than formerly, & that of late many Scores of Prieſts and Jeſuites are come thither from France, and gone to the North, to the Highlands & other places of the Country. That the Miniſters of the Highlands and North gave in large Liſts of them to the Committee of the General Aſſembly, to be laid before the Privy-Council.

It likewiſe obſerves, that a great Number of other ill-affected perſons are come over from *France*, under pretence of accepting her Majeſty's Gracious Indemnity; but, in reality, to increaſe Diviſions in the Nation, and to entertain a Correſpondence with *France*: That their ill Intentions are evident from their talking big, their owning the Intereſt of the pretended King *James* VIII. their ſecret Cabals, and their buying up of Arms and Ammunition, wherever they can find them.

To this he adds the late Writings and Actings of ſome diſaffected perſons, many of whom are for the Pretender, that ſeveral of them have declar'd they had rather embrace Popery than conform to the preſent Government; that they refuſe to pray for the Queen, but uſe the ambiguous word Sove-

From all this he infers, That they have hopes of Aſſiſtance from *France*, otherwiſe they would never be ſo impudent; and he gives Reaſons for his Apprehenſions that the *French* King may ſend Troops thither this Winter, 1. Becauſe the *Engliſh & Dutch* will not then be at Sea to oppoſe them. 2. He can then beſt ſpare them, the Seaſon of Action beyond Sea being over. 3. The Expectation given him of a conſiderable number to joyn them, may incourage him to the undertaking with fewer Men if he can but ſend over a ſufficient number of Officers with Arms and Ammunition.

He endeavours in the reſt of his Letters to anſwer the fooliſh Pretences of the Pretender's being a Proteſtant, and that he will govern us according to Law. He ſays, that being bred up in the Religion and Politicks of *France*, he is by Education a ſtated Enemy to our Liberty and Religion. That the Obligations which he and his Family owe to the *French* King, muſt neceſſarily make him to be wholly at his Devotion, and to follow his Example; that if he ſit upon the Throne, the three Nations; muſt be oblig'd to pay the Debt which he owes the *French* King for the Education of himſelf, and for Entertaining his ſuppoſed Father and his Family. And ſince the King muſt reſtore him by his Troops, if ever he be reſtored, he will ſee to ſecure his own Debt before thoſe Troops leave *Britain*. The Pretender being a good Proficient in the *French* and *Romiſh* Schools, he will never think himſelf ſufficiently aveng'd, but by the utter Ruine of his Proteſtant Subjects, both as Hereticks and Traitors. The late Queen, his pretended Mother, who in

Bosworth Field, Battle of (22 August 1485): final battle of the Wars of the Roses (1455–85) in England. Henry Tudor's victory gave him a conqueror's title to the throne and opportunity to establish his rule. After landing in Wales he had marched into the Midlands, but support came slowly, and at Bosworth, Leicestershire, he was heavily outnumbered until Lord Stanley's force joined him. King Richard III (1483–85) fought heroically, killing Henry's standard-bearer and trying to attack Henry in person. Richard's body was slung across his horse's back and his golden circlet placed on Henry Tudor's head by Stanley. The victor knelt and thanked Almighty God, praying for grace to rule his "subjects and people".

Botany Bay: first landing place on the east coast of Australia in 1770 of Captain James Cook. First called Stingray Bay, it was changed to Botany Bay because of the plants found there by botanist Joseph Banks, who sailed with Cook in the *Endeavour*. With the loss of the American colonies England needed new settlements for convicts, and Botany Bay was chosen. On arrival with the first convicts in 1788 Governor Arthur Phillip found it unsuitable for settlement, lacking shelter for shipping and adequate fresh water. He established the first settlement at Sydney Cove, Port Jackson, where the city of Sydney now stands.

Botswana: formerly the Bechuanaland Protectorate; situated on the central plateau of southern Africa and incorporating a large part of the Kalahari Desert; bounded by Cape Province to the south, the Transvaal to the south-east, Zimbabwe to the north-east, the Caprivi Strip and Zambia to the north, and to the west, Namibia. The area is approximately 222,000 square miles (575,000 square kilometres) and the population one million in 1983. From 1885, when it became a British protectorate, until 1965 the territory was administered from Mafeking in the Cape Province of South Africa, and sixteen miles outside its own territory. In 1965 a new capital was established at Gaborone.

Little exploration took place until the early 19th century. In 1818 the London Missionary Society established a mission at Kuruman just south of the Molopo River in the northern Cape, and from there missionary explorers – including David Livingstone – ranged widely through the territory. After the Sand River convention in 1852 the Boers began to infiltrate, and the protection of British troops was sought in the 1870s. In 1885 the three main chiefs petitioned for British protection, which was granted. In 1896 the final stage of the Cape–Bulawayo railway line, which passes through the territory, was completed. In 1910, by an Order in Council, the Protectorate was placed under the wing of the United Kingdom High Commissioner in South Africa along with the two other African territories of Basutoland and Swaziland, the three then being known as the High Commission Territories, each with its own Resident Commissioner.

The Resident Commissioner of Bechuanaland was guided by an African advisory council, which eventually became a Legislative Assembly when the territory achieved independence as the Republic of Botswana within the Commonwealth in September 1966.

Boulton, Matthew (1728–1809)**:** British engineer who greatly assisted James Watt in the development of the steam engine, He was also a manufacturer of coins who produced a new copper coinage for Britain (1797) and struck coins for Russia, the Sierre Leone Company and the East India Company.

Bourbon, House of: ruling house of France whose family name originated in the 10th century with Adhémar, lord of the barony of Bourbonnais, a territory in central France. In 1272 the family became allied to the royal house of Capet by the marriage of Agnes, the Bourbon heiress, to a son of Louis IX, who received the title of duc de Bourbon. Although this branch had died out by the end of the 15th century, the title passed to Louis, duc de Vendôme, the grandfather of Henry of Navarre, who in 1589 became King of France. Thus established, the Bourbon dynasty ruled France until the Revolution in 1789, and again from 1815 to 1848. In 1700, on the death of Charles II of Spain, Louis XIV succeeded in establishing his grandson on the Spanish throne as Philip V. Except for a brief spell when Napoleon I made one of his brothers King of Spain, Philip's descendents ruled Spain until the abdication of Alfonso XIII in 1931. General Franco has now nominated a member of the Bourbon family as his own successor. The Orleanist branch of the family was descended from the brother of Louis XIV. Louis Philippe became the last King of France from 1830 until the Revolution of 1848 when he was compelled to abdicate. Charles III of Spain was the first

Bourbon to come into possession of the Two Sicilies. He passed on his rights to his second son, Ferdinand I, and they were retained by his descendants until the territory was incorporated into Italy during its unification in the 19th century.

Other branches of the family were the Parmese branch headed by the Dukes of Lucca and Parma, the Vendôme branch descended from Henry IV of France, and the prominent French families of Condé, Conti, and Montpensier.

Bow Street Runners: one of the early attempts to establish a regular detective force in England. Established in 1749 they operated from Bow Street Police Office, London, and, when specially required in cases of serious crime, acted as detectives, chiefly in London and the provinces. From their red waistcoats they were nicknamed "Robin Redbreasts". From them developed the modern Criminal Investigation Department.

Boyars: the old aristocracy of Russia with the privilege of holding land and owning serfs. They were originally the close friends and advisers of Russian princes and, later, the chief members of their councils. At first the rank was not hereditary but was won by merit.

Boycott: to refuse to have any dealings with; one of the interesting groups of words deriving from proper names in history (cf. Quisling), in this case Charles Cunningham Boycott (1832–97), a land agent in Ireland who came into conflict with the Land League agitators over his harsh treatment of tenants on Lord Erne's estates in County Mayo. An early use of the term occurs in an 1881 speech to the Land League by the Irish member of parliament James Dillon: "One word as to the way in which a man should be boycotted. When any man has taken a farm from which a tenant has been evicted . . . let everyone in the parish turn his back on him; have no communication with him; have no dealings with him. You need never say an unkind word to him; but never say anything at all to him."

Boyne, Battle of the (1 July 1690)**:** scene of the defeat some 40 miles [64 kilometres] north-west of Dublin, Ireland, of James II by William III, destroying the hopes of the exiled Stuarts. In 1690 James II landed at Kinsale with French support. William III (1689–1702) crossed to Ireland and, with a force of English, Dutch, Danes and Huguenots, attacked and defeated the Catholic forces. It is an instance of the importance of a battle being in no way commensurate with the casualties, since the English losses were only about 500.

Brahmins: members of the highest or priestly caste of Hindus, from *brahman*, worship. The other three chief castes are *Kshatriya* (warriors and rulers); *Vaisya* (farmers and merchants); and *Sudra* (manual workers).

Brass: (1) an alloy, or mixing together, of metals, usually copper and zinc. In early times the term was often applied to a combination of copper and tin, which we now know as bronze. It seems likely that the "brass" of the Bible, extensively used for domestic utensils, helmets, armour, shields and, e.g., in the building of the Temple, was in fact bronze, so worked that it was nearly as hard as steel. The Israelites learnt the art of casting from the Phoenicians. Roman coins of brass, containing just over 17 per cent zinc, have been found dating from the 1st century BC. The production became a flourishing industry in the Low Countries, beginning in the 3rd century AD.

(2) The term "brass" is also used to mean one of the memorial plates, found in

thousands of European churches, engraved with a representation of the person commemorated. While they cannot be relied on as portraits, being little more than conventional outlines, they do preserve to an outstanding degree details of contemporary costume, armour, weapons, etc., and are one of the finest sources of reference for this type of information. They cover a period of roughly 500 years, from the 13th to the 18th century. It has been calculated that at one time there were probably at least 150,000 in England alone; now something over 7,000 survive, ranging from life-size to small plates about a foot [0·09 metres] square. The earliest are often among the finest, being executed on thick metal and drawn with great boldness of style. From about 1450 the work tends to become progressively more conventional and of less artistic merit. As might be expected, because of the expense involved as well as the class distinction that found ample expression in churches as well as outside them, the early brasses are usually of people of the upper classes, nobles, knights, landowners and priests. Later, many more middle-class representatives, merchants, squires, lawyers, etc., arrive to show their increasing power and importance in the social scale. One of the earliest and best-known in England is that of Sir John d'Abernon, or d'Aubernon, in the church of Stoke d'Abernon near Guildford, Surrey. It dates from *c.* 1277 and its craftsmanship is such that every link of the chain mail is faithfully represented, along with the weapons and the rest of the armour.

These plates were often called "cullett" plates – a reminder that till about 1550 they were usually imported from Germany and Flanders, often coming from or through Cologne. Another early name for the metal was "latten" (from the French *laiton*, brass). It was, in fact, rarely true brass but an alloy of roughly 60–65 per cent copper, 10 per cent lead and tin and up to 30 per cent zinc.

Some of the most interesting types are the so-called palimpsest brasses, palimpsest deriving from Greek words meaning "rub" or "scrape" and "again"; in other words, brasses that have been used more than once. Shortage of material or economy sometimes led workmen to erase earlier inscriptions (which can, however, often be still traced) and to superimpose another; or to turn the plate over and use the reverse side. Sometimes they even used the earlier figure but slightly altered the costume detail to bring it more up to date. At Waterperry in Oxfordshire there is a brass first put down in *c.* 1450 when pointed footgear was in fashion. It was recut in 1540 when rounded toes were in vogue. The original points were not obliterated, so that the figure of Walter Curson is wearing two pairs of shoes.

Brass-rubbing has become an increasingly popular pastime and has sometimes been put to undesirable commercial use. This is a method of securing a copy of the brass by covering it with suitable paper and rubbing it evenly all over with black

The twice-used brass in Waterperry Parish Church, showing the second pair of figures, Walter and Isabel Curson, cut in 1540. Both the rounded and pointed ends can be seen on the knight's footgear.

wax, such as cobbler's "heel-ball". The etched lines on the brass are left white on the rubbing, so that a detailed reproduction can be obtained. Another method, which produces a positive rather than a negative copy, is to rub with white wax and then flood the paper with black ink which will not adhere to the wax but will fill in all the engraved lines the wax has not touched.

Many churches, in an effort to protect their treasured brasses from too much amateur rubbing, now charge a fee for the privilege. Fee or no fee, as a matter of courtesy, permission should always be sought before rubbings are taken.

¶ BUSBY, RICHARD J. *Beginner's Guide to Brass Rubbing*, 1969; MACKLIN, HERBERT W. *Monumental Brasses: together with a selected bibliography of county lists of brasses remaining in the churches of the United Kingdom*, 1953; NORRIS, MALCOLM. *Brass Rubbing*, 1965

Brazil: federal republic of South America, named after the valuable dyewood the early discoverers found growing in abundance.

Ships sailing from the Cape Verde Islands may sometimes have been carried westwards by storms in the south-east trade wind belt as early as the 1490s. The honour of discovering Brazil is generally given, however, to the Portuguese Cabral who, travelling towards the Cape of Good Hope, took a very westerly route and struck Brazil in 1500.

Except for the south-east, modern Brazil consists broadly of the area drained by the Amazon and its tributaries. It is covered with thick forest occupied by wild animals and harmful insects but few men. The people found by the Portuguese were an Indian type who interbred with their Portuguese conquerors and with the African Negroes brought to work as slaves on sugar plantations. Sugar was to some extent succeeded by gold and even diamonds after about 1700, but the slave trade continued up to 1888. Coffee flourished after the gold and still accounts for about 60 per cent of the country's export trade. Rubber was especially valuable until about 1910, when plantations sprang up in South-East Asia. Livestock has always been important. Among many minerals, manganese, iron and bauxite may be mentioned.

Brazil was proclaimed an independent empire in 1822 and became a federal republic in 1889. It is a rapidly developing country whose population rose from 51 million in 1950 to 129,660,000 in 1983. Its general growth has been spectacular and the capital of Brasilia, founded in 1957, had a population of 411,000 in 1980.

Breda, Declaration of: issued by Charles II of England, while still in exile, on 14 April 1660. The Royalist reaction against the Commonwealth was already developing rapidly. In March Pepys had seen "a great bonfire in the Exchange" and people called out "God bless King Charles II". The chief obstacle to his restoration was fear, and the King's declaration reassured his former enemies. Subject to Parliament's approval, he promised pardon, freedom for "tender consciences", a settlement of questions concerning sale and grants of land, payment of arrears due to the army and opportunities in the royal service for General Monk's men. Encouraged by this the Commons voted a grant of £50,000 and on 8 May Charles II was proclaimed King.

Breda, Treaty of (31 July 1667)**:** the treaty which ended the second Anglo-Dutch war, which, in spite of the Medway disaster, had gone slightly in England's favour. The main principle was that of return of conquests. England kept New York, New Jersey and Delaware, thus gaining a continuous line of colonies and control of an important trade route, but little else. The Dutch kept Pularoon and Dutch Guiana, and France retained Acadia and French Guiana. The Navigation Acts were slightly modified and "British Seas", for purposes of salute at sea, narrowed to the Channel. The Dutch never regained supremacy in the West Indies, but elsewhere rivalry continued.

Brewing: the manufacture of beer, ale, etc., the chief constituents being cereal (especially barley), malt, hops and water. Although now almost entirely in commercial hands, in early times it was a common domestic occupation. Beer was drunk extensively in ancient Babylon and Egypt; and a Roman housekeeping account of AD 1 in its provision of "beer for the weaver" shows that this cherished form of sustenance for workmen had early become an obligation. The monasteries were great brewers and set good standards of hygiene in their brew-houses. In the Middle Ages and later beer was drunk at every meal, so that brewing developed into an important trade. In 1419 there were 300 brewers in London alone. There were two chief strengths, strong ale and "small". In one medieval siege 260 quarters of malt were sent in to brew 520 gallons [2,364 litres] a day for forty days, this being a strong brew calculated to maintain a fighting spirit in the defenders.

Above: 18th century brewing techniques. Below: Continuous fermenting at Watney's Mortlake Brewery.

Bribery: giving and receiving gifts intended to influence official decisions or to obtain power. In the past it was a method frequently resorted to in the law courts and in politics. In 1289 several English judges were convicted of corrupt judgements. A song of the reign of Edward II (ruled 1307–27) related how a noblewoman could get a favourable court decision without saying a word, but a poor woman would go home unsuccesful. The most famous English judge to be accused of accepting bribes was Lord Bacon, who was impeached for the offence in 1621. He pleaded guilty but denied that his decisions had been influenced. The incorruptibility of British judges has now become almost proverbial.

In politics and local government, the public conscience has become increasingly sensitive and offences rarer, though they have persisted longer than in the administration of justice. Until comparatively recent times, bribery was a recognised device in elections. In a typical 1813 English election, expenses at a Somerset inn totalled over £300, which included the cost of 353 bottles of rum and gin and 792 dinners. The Secret Ballot Act of 1873 and the Corrupt Practices Act of 1883 went a long way to stamping out such bribery in Britain.

In certain countries, particularly those of a despotic and politically immature character, bribery is still a common feature. Its absence at all levels of public life is the aim of all civilised societies.

The USA has had its own bitter struggle against bribery and corruption. Surprisingly, if Russian documentary evidence be true, it was only substantial gifts of Russian money to members of the House of Representatives that induced the United States to make the controversial purchase of Alaska in 1867. According to one authoritative writer, the administration of President Harding (1921–23) is chiefly remembered as "a Saturnalia of corruption in high and medium places". During Truman's presidency (1945–53), as a result of a public outcry against corruption, more than 200 members of the Bureau of Inland Revenue resigned or were dismissed.

Bridges: constructions carrying human and other traffic across river, ravine, etc. The presence or absence of a bridge has often affected human history. Though the exploit is legendary, the story of Horatius defending the bridge across the Tiber, as retold by Macaulay in *The Lays of Ancient Rome*, gives a vivid picture of a situation that has occurred often enough in real life, even if the odds have not been so dramatically uneven.

Bridge building, primitive or sophisticated, has been a necessary activity from earliest times, and examples are known from thousands of years before the Christian era, e.g. across the River Euphrates. Probably the oldest surviving example is the stone single arch bridge over the River Meles in Turkey, which is estimated to date from nearly 1,000 years BC. The greatest of the early bridge builders were the Romans, who constructed them not only in Rome but everywhere the legions marched. One of the most famous, and one of the best preserved examples in the world, is the Pons Fabricius (62 BC) at Rome.

The earliest bridges were of wood, soon to be superseded by more durable stone. For military purposes there has often been a need for speedy and skilful improvisation. In 480 BC Xerxes, king of Persia, threw a one-mile bridge of boats across the Hellespont (now the Dardanelles Strait). Julius Caesar caused a remarkable trestle bridge to be built across the Rhine in ten days. A familiar type of bridge in recent warfare has been the Bailey bridge (named after the English inventor Sir Donald Bailey), made of latticed metal parts which can be easily transported and quickly erected.

In any study of the history of bridges it should be realised that, despite the early date of the first construction, there are very few early bridges that contain anything but fragmentary remains of their original materials. The ceaseless traffic of man and beast, whether at leisure, in commerce or war, has necessitated so much maintenance and repair through the centuries that it is often only the site that has any true claim to antiquity.

The use of iron, concrete and steel in modern times has greatly increased the scope of the bridge designer and builder. Over the last century the length of the longest bridge span has been multiplied by four and this process will undoubtedly go on. Most of the longest bridges are at present to be found in the USA, including the 4,200 feet [1,280 metres] San Francisco Golden Gate Bridge (1937) and the Verrazano-Narrows Bridge, New York City, (1965) of 4,260 feet [1,298 metres].

New and ever more impressive bridges appear regularly. A number were built during the 1970s and others, often spectacular in conception, are on the drawing board. Several have been completed in Japan; a magnificent suspension bridge now links Istanbul with Asiatic Turkey

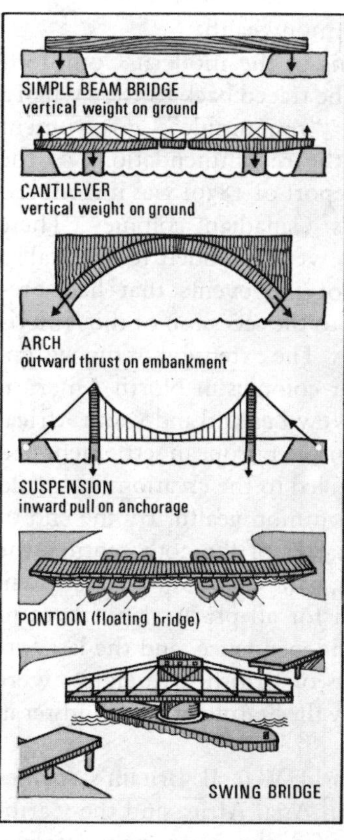

across the Bosphorus and in Britain the Humber Bridge spans the estuary of that name.

¶ DE MARE, ERIC. *Your Book of Bridges*, 1963; MURPHY, J. STEWART. *Bridges*, 1958

Bristol (England): the seventh largest city in England, though in the 15th century only London and Norwich were larger. Its population is now approaching the half million mark.

with France, Spain and Iceland until in the 1480s some ships sailed west across the Atlantic. Newfoundland may already have been discovered by the men of Bristol before John Cabot's famous voyage of 1497.

Bristol merchants played some part in the later voyages of exploration and actively encouraged the settlement of North America. During the 17th century imports of sugar and tobacco from American colonies became more important than Bristol's traditional trade in wine and cloth. These American imports were frequently financed by the sale of African slaves to American plantations, and so the infamous "triangle of trade" developed. By 1750 almost a hundred Bristol ships were involved, but the numbers declined before the abolition of the slave trade in 1807.

In the 19th century Bristol continued to look to America. I. K. Brunel planned to link London to New York via Bristol using a fleet of steam ships and his Great Western Railway. His *Great Britain* launched in 1843, was a propeller-driven iron ship of revolutionary design, but it was too large for Bristol's docks and was based instead on Liverpool, a port which grew much faster than Bristol.

The Bristol Aeroplane Company was a pioneer when the giant Brabazon airliner flew in 1949, but, like the *Great Britain*, it was not a commercial success. Nevertheless, the construction of the supersonic Concorde airliner does continue the story of Bristol as a city which links Britain and America across the Atlantic Ocean.

¶ BALLARD, MARTIN. *Bristol Seaport City*, 1966

British Commonwealth of Nations (since 1951 called the **Commonwealth**): the informal association of independent states which have in common the fact that they were formerly part of the British Empire. The word "commonwealth" was first applied to England during the Protectorate of Oliver Cromwell in the 17th century, and was first officially used in its modern sense at the Imperial Conference of 1926. The modern Commonwealth consists of forty-nine member states with their dependencies, most of which are now very small territories.

The countries of the Commonwealth extend over a quarter of the earth's land surface and include a quarter of the world's population. Three-quarters of the population of the Commonwealth is Asian, one-eighth African and, in origin, one-eighth European. Commonwealth trade accounts for between a quarter and a third of the total trade of the non-Communist world.

The formal link between Commonwealth countries is the British monarchy. In the old Commonwealth countries, and in a few of the new members states, the monarch is recognised as the head of state and is represented by a governor-general whose position is constitutionally equivalent to that of the British monarch in Britain. Most of the new Commonwealth states are republics with their own heads of state, and recognise the British monarch only as a symbol of association and as head of the Commonwealth.

The origins of the modern Commonwealth can be traced back to 1847 when a system of "responsible" government (based on the recommendations of the Durham Report of 1839) was introduced in Britain's Canadian colonies. These concessions were intended to forestall a repetition of the events that had previously led to the secession of the American colonies. The extension of this system to the other colonies in North America, Australia, New Zealand and South Africa, where extensive European settlement had taken place, led to the creation of the old "white" Commonwealth. By the end of the first quarter of the 20th century the Dominions, as they had come to be known, had moved for all practical purposes to complete independence, and the last formal vestiges of British sovereignty were removed by the Statute of Westminster in 1931.

Since World War II Britain's former territories in Asia, Africa and the Caribbean have for the most part attained independence as members of the Commonwealth. Beginning with the independence of India and Pakistan in 1947, this process has led to the extension of the Commonwealth concept of the tightly knit "family grouping" of the old dominions to the multiracial and economically diverse association of the "new" Commonwealth. Between 1947 and 1985 forty-five states gained independence from Britain and became members of the Commonwealth. It is worth noting that for the most part this process was a peaceful one, and the result of deliberate British policy. It is also true, in a wider context, that this was a consequence of the general decline of European world leadership in the 20th century and the growth of nationalism in the "third world" of peoples previously colonised from Europe.

The continued existence of the Commonwealth rests on trading connections, broadly similar ways of government and legal institutions, and the fact that English continues to be the language of government, business and education in all of the old and most of the new Commonwealth countries. But this legacy has not in all cases proved to be advantageous. The constitutions based on the "Westminster" model of parliamentary democracy and the rule of law which Britain bequeathed to her former colonial possessions were appropriate to the old European-settled Commonwealth, but not necessarily elsewhere; in Africa a number of member states, e.g. Tanzania, have formally or in practice amended their constitutions to provide for a system of "one party" democracy which they feel to be more relevant to their needs as developing countries. Also, Britain's attempts to launch federal Commonwealth states have in most cases been unsuccessful (*vide* the break-up of the Central African Federation in the 1960s).

The value of the Commonwealth in international affairs is that it is a force making for cohesion in a world where racial divisions and the gap between the rich, industrial nations and the poorer developing nations are becoming the most crucial problems that mankind has to face.

Table of members (with year of independence as of 1985)

Antigua and Barbuda (1983)
Australia (1901)
The Bahamas (1973)
Bangladesh (1972)
Barbados (1966)
Belize (1981)
Botswana (1966)
Britain
Brunei (1984)
Canada (1867)
Cyprus (1961)
Dominica (1978)
Fiji (1970)
The Gambia (1965)
Ghana (1957)
Grenada (1974)
Guyana (1966)
India (1947)
Jamaica (1962)
Kenya (1963)
Kiribati (1979)
Lesotho (1966)
Malawi (1964)
Malaysia (1957)
Maldives (1982)
Malta (1964)
Mauritius (1968)
Nauru (1968)
New Zealand (1907)
Nigeria (1960)
Papua New Guinea (1975)
St Kitts-Nevis (1983)
St Lucia (1979)
St Vincent (1979)
Seychelles (1976)
Sierra Leone (1961)
Singapore (1965)
Solomon Islands (1978)
Sri Lanka (1948)
Swaziland (1968)
Tanzania (1961)
Tonga (1970)
Trinidad and Tobago (1962)
Tuvalu (1978)
Uganda (1962)
Vanuatu (1980)
Western Samoa (1970)
Zambia (1964)
Zimbabwe (1980)

¶ HUSSEY, W. D. *British Empire and Commonwealth 1500–1961*, 1963

Britons: general name given by the Romans to the tribes of Britain, which included the Cantii, Belgae, Iceni and some twenty others. Caesar considered that the inhabitants of Kent were the most civilised of all the Britons, since they were seafarers and had many contacts with Gaul.

¶ IRVING, S. H. *The Ancient Britons*, 1967

Brittany: an ancient province forming the north-western part of France and covering the modern departments of Finistère, Côtes-du-Nord, Ille-et-Vilaine, Morbihan and Loire Inférieure. Inland, much of the landscape is bleak and windswept, while the coastline is wild and rugged. The roots of its history lie in prehistoric times, and there are many dolmens and menhirs giving evidence of this; the most notable are the *alignements de Carnac*, long lines of huge menhirs stretching over the moorland. The region is rich in legend and folk-lore, and numerous traditional customs and costumes are still in use today.

Brittany was conquered in 57–56 BC by Julius Caesar and called Armorica. In the 5th and 6th centuries, following a large influx of Celts from Britain fleeing before the Saxon invaders, it eventually came to be called Brittany. The language was a branch of Celtic allied to Welsh and old Cornish and is still spoken by the country people. In the 10th century it became an independent duchy and, later, a vassal province of France. During the Hundred Years War it sided alternately with England and France. Only in 1532 was it incorporated with France. During the French Revolution it supported the Bourbons and remained a stronghold of the Church. When priests were required to take the oath to the Civil Constitution of the Clergy, many of those in Brittany refused and remained loyal to their office.

During World War II, the geographical position of Brittany and its sea-ports of Brest, Lorient and St Malo gave it great strategic importance. It was one of the first areas to fall into Allied hands after the Normandy landings.

Bruce, Robert the (Robert I, 1274–1329): king of Scotland and national hero, called "the Liberator". Despite the fact that he never commanded a large army and was for long periods a fugitive, he is one of the great leaders of history. His career included murder in its darker passages, but by indomitable will and superb courage he brought his plundered and disunited people their greatest victory at Bannockburn (24 June 1314). King Robert died a leper at Cardross Castle. His heart was being carried to the Holy Land by Sir James Douglas when the Scottish knight became involved in a battle against the Moors of Granada. Mortally wounded, Douglas flung the silver

Seal of Robert the Bruce.

casket containing the heart into the Saracen host, with the shout, "Go first as thou wert wont to go!" The heart was later rescued and brought home to Melrose Abbey. Bruce was described as blue-eyed, yellow-haired and broad-shouldered, with a ready wit and fluent speech.

¶ DICKINSON, W. C. *Robert Bruce*, 1960

Brunel, Marc Isambard (1769–1849) and **Isambard Kingdom** (1806–59): civil engineers, father and son. Marc Isambard was educated for the church but later served in the French navy and emigrated to America where he built up a reputation as architect, surveyor and civil engineer. Among his other activities, he planned the defences of New York. He came to England at the age of thirty and the variety of his work and the volume of his energy can be gauged from the fact that he invented machinery for making ships' blocks, built sawmills, improved dockyard machinery and dock installations, experimented with steam navigation and built the Thames Tunnel.

His son inherited his father's genius; was the resident engineer at the Thames Tunnel, designed the Clifton Suspension Bridge at Bristol and many other bridges, docks, etc. Like his father he had a great interest in maritime affairs, applied the use of propellers to steam ships and built the famous *Great Eastern*. Another interest was the improvement of artillery. He is chiefly remembered as creator of the main line of the Great Western Railway in England, originally laid down by him to a 7-foot gauge between the rails. Many of the magnificent works which this entailed, such as the flat-arch brick bridge at Maidenhead, the Box Tunnel, and the Saltash Bridge over the Tamar, stand as a memorial to his genius.

¶ GARNETT, EMMELINE. *The Master Engineers*, 1954; ROLT, L. T. C. *The Story of Brunel*, 1965

Buccaneers: Europeans who, in the 16th and 17th centuries, emigrated to the West Indies, Isthmus and adjacent South American parts and who formed a confederacy to defend their interests against the colonising Spanish power. The confederacy gradually acquired more the character of a group of freebooters.

The buccaneers, the Brethren of the Coast, at first settled peacefully, following a strict code of "matelotage", sharing goods. Their name is of West Indian origin, from the manner in which they cooked meat on a wooden spit over an open fire. The English voyager and hydrographer William Dampier joined them for a brief period in 1679.

The grasping approach of the Spanish forced the buccaneers to band together and fight. Under Mansvelt, a Dutchman, they became a strong force with head-

Buccaneers' fort at Tortuga.

quarters at Port Royal, Jamaica. National interests and jealousies were always difficult to reconcile, but Mansvelt found an able lieutenant in Henry Morgan (1635–88). Morgan took over from Mansvelt and showed immense resource and power of leadership. Under him and his crafty lieutenant Boboadillo, the buccaneers captured the Spanish stronghold of Porto Bello and, in 1671, made an astounding march across the Isthmus, where they sacked Panama. Morgan was knighted for his services against the Spanish and retired to live a quieter and more respectable life as lieutenant-governor of Jamaica. Boboadillo formed a pirate confederacy. Van Horn commanded a successful buccaneer attack on Vera Cruz in 1683. The buccaneer confederacy ended when their headquarters at Port Royal was utterly devastated by an earthquake in 1692.

Today the term buccaneer is often used as being synonymous with pirate, but this is a misapplication (*see* PIRATES).

Buckingham Palace: the London home of the British sovereign. An earlier house on the site was built by the Duke of Buckingham in 1703 and purchased by George III in 1761. This was pulled down some sixty years later and the present palace erected by the architect John Nash at a cost of nearly one million pounds. It was occupied by Queen Victoria in 1837. Another London landmark, the Marble Arch, was removed from Buckingham Palace to its present site in March 1851.

Buddha and **Buddhism:** a religion and system of philosophy founded by Siddharta Guatama (563–483 BC), known as the Buddha or "the Enlightened One". He was the son of a raja of the Sakya clan from Kapilavastu in the Nepalese foothills. His class possibly resented the exclusiveness of the Brahmin religion introduced by the Aryan invaders. Till he was twenty-nine he lived the normal life of a noble: he married and had a son, he hunted and trained in martial exercises. Then, after seeing an old man, a diseased man, a dead man and a hermit, he left his family and his pleasures, shaved his head and put on rags, said farewell to his horse and his charioteer, and sought enlightenment as an ascetic. Fasting and mortification of the flesh brought no peace; but after six years' perseverance he defeated the Evil One and received enlightenment as he sat in the lotus posture under the Bo-tree at Buddh Gaya in Bihar. He conquered *Karma* (craving, desire) and so gained *Nirvana* (release from the necessity of rebirth after death). Soon afterwards he preached his first sermon to five other ascetics in the park at Sarnath near Benares. He preached the Middle Way between sensuality and asceticism and proclaimed the Eightfold Path of right thought and action. His ideas could be found in the Hindu scriptures, but he rejected the caste restrictions and exclusiveness of Brahminism. His early followers came from the rich and educated, and joined the Sangha (society) of saffron-robed monks who frequented the bamboo groves given by well-wishers. He left three "Baskets" – discourses, rules for monks, and metaphysics – which survive

only in versions compiled three centuries later. He claimed no divine powers: those who follow his rules could hope for similar enlightenment.

His movement gained impetus in India when the Emperor Asoka (273–232 BC) became a Buddhist, renounced war and devoted his life to building hospitals, wells, reservoirs and the pillars on which Buddhist doctrines were carved. Two schools of Buddhism soon emerged: the *Hinayana* (Lesser Vehicle) emphasised strict obedience to the rules for subduing the passions and throve in India, Ceylon and Burma; the *Mahayana* (Greater Vehicle) emphasised compassion and faith in the merits of Boddhisattvas – saints who delayed their attainment of Nirvana to help others. This more emotional and popular doctrine spread to China in AD 607. By allowing prayers for dead ancestors, Buddhists yielded to Chinese ancestor-worship, but the Chinese looked askance on the monk's abandoning of family responsibilities. Chan Buddhism, which strove for enlightenment by flashes of intuition induced by meditation, influenced the Sung style of painting in China. As Zen Buddhism in Japan, it did something to humanise the conduct of the Samurai class.

Buddhism survives vigorously in

Ceylon, Siam and Burma, and has made progress among Indian untouchables. In Communist China and Tibet it is persecuted, and in Japan is threatened by Western materialism. Its emphasis is on self-improvement and on a compassionate understanding that every act of virtue or sin affects others, as well as freedom from dependence on supernatural events.

¶ In PRINGLE, PATRICK. *101 Great Lives*, 1904

Budget: among its several meanings, the annual forecast of government revenue and expenditure. In Britain this is presented to parliament every year in April by the chief finance minister, the Chancellor of the Exchequer. He makes a speech in the House of Commons in which he gives an account of all the income (from taxes, etc.) and all the expenditure (on defence, education, housing, etc.) during the previous year. This shows whether the income has been enough to meet the expenses. He then sets out how much he thinks the nation will have to spend in the coming year and how he proposes to obtain the money. This may mean, for instance, an increase or decrease in income tax, or the introduction of a new tax or the repeal of an existing tax. These budget proposals are then debated and laws are passed to make it possible to carry them out. Though the House of Lords may delay or reject other types of legislation, it cannot oppose Budget proposals.

If during the year the nation is spending far more than the Chancellor expected, he may not wait until the following April but may introduce an interim Budget to restore the balance.

In the USA there was no central budget till 1921. It is now handled by a "bureau of the budget" in the Treasury Department, but is directly under the control of the President, who appoints its director. Subject to the President's overall financial policy, the main responsibility for framing the necessary legislation is in the hands of the Committee on Appropriations, which has a number of sub-committees corresponding to the main departments of government, e.g. agriculture, war, justice, etc. In addition, all States make provision for their own internal budgets.

Buffalo: the name given to various kinds of ox, including the American bison. It is one of the earliest animals known to history, wild or domesticated, found in ancient India, Malaya and Egypt, introduced into a number of European countries including Italy and Hungary, and playing an important role in American history. It is an animal reckoned of high intelligence and some species are among the most dangerous big game hunted by man, the wounded buffalo being proverbial for ferocity.

When he saw the buffalo on the plains of Texas in 1541, the Spanish adventurer Francisco de Coronado reported to the King of Spain: "It is impossible to number them, for while I was journeying through these plains . . . there was not a day that I lost sight of them." Through the centuries, observers in America recorded similar impressions and calculations; of, e.g., a herd that took three days to swim the Missouri, of another four million strong, of another ten miles long and eight miles wide.

The buffalo was the main source of food and household supply for the American Indian and the great hunts were the chief events in the calendar. The meat was eaten fresh or preserved. The hides were used for mittens, caps, footgear, robes, leggings, dresses, harness, tents, shields; the sinews for thread, bowstrings, etc.; the horns for cups, spoons and other domestic utensils. There was no part of the animal that was not put to some good

"Indian Chasing a Buffalo", a watercolour by Catlin, an early painter of life in the American West in the 19th century.

use. In addition, it became a valuable trading commodity with the white man.

Several factors contributed to the eventual disappearance of the enormous buffalo herds and, therefore, to the destruction of the Indian way of life. Chief among them, the coming of the railroad meant a vast increase in the slaughter and transportation of buffalo and its by-products. In 1872–73 one and a quarter million hides are estimated to have come from Kansas on freight cars. In the middle of the 19th century there were something like 50 million buffalo on the great plains. In the next forty years they virtually disappeared.

¶ In SILVERBERG, ROBERT. *The Auk, the Dodo and the Oryx: vanished and vanishing creatures*, 1969

Bull, Papal: from the Latin word *bulla*, a seal. A papal bull is so called because it is a letter issued by the Pope, written in Latin on a piece of parchment with a lead seal covered in wax. One of the most famous bulls is *Exsurge Domine* issued in 1520 against Martin Luther who burnt it in public in Wittenberg.

Bunche, Ralph Johnson (b. 1904): American sociologist and Nobel Peace Prize winner. The grandson of a slave, he worked as United States Mediator for Palestine (1948–49) and was the UN Secretary-General's personal representative in the Congo for a period. He received his Nobel Prize in 1950.

¶ In SPENCER, J. *Workers for Humanity*, 1962

Bunker Hill, Battle of (17 June 1775): the first considerable battle of the War of American Independence, fought at Charlestown, Boston, Massachusetts. The casualties were high in proportion to the numbers involved (1,054 killed and wounded on the British side; 420 on the American). Nominally a British victory, "it roused at once the instinct of combat in America" and produced important effects on the morale and confidence of the colonists. It was traditionally the occasion of the famous instruction: "Men, you are all marksmen. Don't one of you fire until you see the whites of their eyes."

Bunyan, John (1628–88): English writer and preacher. After working as a tinker, he served in the Parliamentary army during the Civil War of 1642–49. He left the High Anglican Church to join the Puritans and became a notable preacher, serving a long period of imprisonment because he was unlicensed. "If I were out of prison today," he said to his judge at the Bedford Assizes, "I would preach the gospel again tomorrow, by the help of God." Of his sixty books and tracts *The Pilgrim's Progress* has achieved immortality and is "probably the most widely read book in the English language and one which has been translated into more tongues than any book except the Bible".

One who knew him described him as "in countenance . . . of a stern and rough temper, but in his conversation mild and affable . . . tall of stature, strong-boned though not corpulent, somewhat of a ruddy face with sparkling eyes, wearing his hair on the upper lip in the old British fashion".

¶ REASON, JOYCE. *To be a Pilgrim*, 1961

Burgher: citizen or freeman of a burgh or borough, especially in Dutch, German and French towns. The corresponding word in England is "burgess", though Macaulay writes of the "burghers of Carlisle" and Shakespeare uses the word in a Venetian setting.

Burghers of Calais: the heroes of the famous incident (1347) in the Hundred Years War when Queen Philippa of England interceded with Edward III for the six principal citizens whose lives he had demanded as a price for sparing the rest of the town and as punishment for the trouble the siege had cost him. The French chronicler Jean Froissart describes how they knelt before the king with uplifted hands, saying: "Most gallant king, see before you six citizens of Calais who have been capital merchants, and who bring you the keys of the castle and the town," Philippa herself, though heavy with child, knelt to beg their lives and the King reluctantly yielded them into her hands.

Bronze group, The Burghers of Calais, *by Auguste Rodin.*

Doubts have been cast on the authenticity of the story. But it is well in keeping with the Queen's character, and Froissart apparently had it from the contemporary chronicler Jehan le Bel.

Burgundy: a province of eastern France. Its earliest inhabitants were a German tribe, the Burgundii, and during the Gothic invasions of the 5th century AD it became an independent kingdom. Later it was conquered by the Franks and later still regained its independence, but was finally absorbed into France. The Dukes of Burgundy were prominent from time to time, notably in the 14th century when Philip le Hardi, son of the King of France, was granted the Duchy of Burgundy. He linked it by family marriages to Flanders and the territory which is now Holland. The Burgundians became firmly established in the Low Countries and laid the foundations of modern Belgium.

Burgundy has always been noted for its wines, which include many famous names.

Burke, Edmund (1729–97): British statesman and orator, of Irish origins, of whom an observer wrote, "his figure is noble, his air commanding, his address graceful, his voice . . . clear, penetrating, sonorous and powerful; his language copious, various and eloquent, his manners attractive, his conversation delightful". Among the many exhibitions of his oratory were his great speech on Conciliation with America in 1775 and his nine-days' speech for the impeachment of Warren Hastings, 1794 (*see* separate entry). Not less powerful were his writings, which contain some of the greatest passages in the English language. H. J. C. Grierson estimated that "his is one of the greatest minds which have concerned themselves with political topics . . . and the form of his works has made him the only orator whose speeches have secured for themselves a permanent place in English literature beside what is greatest in our drama, our poetry and our prose."

Burma: state in south-east Asia on the rivers Chindwin, Irrawaddi, Sittang and Salween. The Burmese, of Tibetan race, invaded the region and in AD 1044 defeated the Mons who had developed rice-fields in the delta. From 1287 to 1535 they suffered defeats by Shan tribes of the northern hills but thereafter became the dominant race. Their kings took over Buddhism from the Mons, but it was the missionary journeys throught the villages by monks from Ceylon that gave Buddhism its popular appeal and vitality. The best Burmese kings have been devout Buddhists dedicated to peace, charitable works and pagoda building. But most Burmese kings have been bad, establishing themselves by murdering all rivals, oppressing the minority races, attacking their neighbours on frivolous pretexts and strangling trade by royal monopolies. In 1628, after a century of European contacts, they chose to return to Ava in the remote centre of the country, rather than establish a new capital at Syriam on the coast, thus condemning the country to ignorance and backwardness. Yet they provoked British India by raids on Bengal, Assam and Manipur. Britain occupied the coastal strips in 1826, the delta in 1852 and the remainder of the country in 1886. Till 1937 Burma was insensitively governed as a province of India and, though rice cultivation increased tenfold, the peasants were not protected from Indian moneylenders, and the workers suffered by the competition of low-paid Indian coolies. As a result the Burmese welcomed the Japanese army in 1942, though Aung San, the nationalist leader, helped to expel them in 1945 and showed moderation and vision in the negotiations in 1947. The country's politics have been troubled, alternating between civilian and military rule. A new constitution in 1974 made Burma a one-party state. Population in 1983: 37,982,000.

Byzantine Empire: the Empire of New Rome, founded by Constantine in AD 330 when he established his capital at Byzantium (*see* next entry), and ended when Constantine XI died in a gallant but vain defence of Constantinople against the Turks in AD 1453. Until the reign of Justinian (527–65) the emperors maintained the traditions and aims of the Roman Empire: they spoke Latin, they appointed consuls, they shaved their chins; they tried to retain the Augustan frontiers – North Africa, Spain, Italy, the Balkans. Thereafter they were forced to modify their aims. Heraclius (610–41), an Armenian himself, concentrated on Asia Minor as the heart of the Empire and introduced Greek as the official language. The isolation of Byzantium from the West was deepened by the loss of the Balkans to Avars and Bulgarians and by the struggles of the popes and emperors for control of the Church.

Constantine (323–37) took the title of the Thirteenth Apostle, and his successors claimed to be the representatives of Christ on earth charged with the duties of defining and defending right belief, and of using their power to extend the benefits of Christianity to Syrian, Bulgarian and Russian, indeed to an *imperium sine fine*, an "empire without limits". Both these attitudes were adopted by the Russian Tsars and, translated into Marxist terms, appear in Stalinism. The religious character of the Empire is of the first importance. It was the idea which united the many races and which was emphasised at great moments

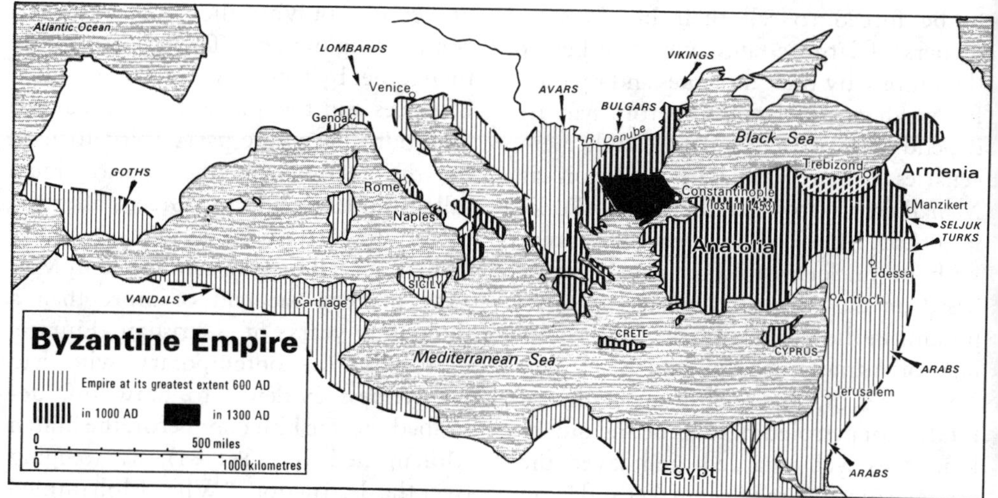

– when Heraclius in 628 announced the recapture of the True Cross from the Persians, and when the Mandylion, the Holy Towel bearing the imprint of Christ's features, was surrendered by the Arabs at Edessa in 944. The emperors contested, and finally in 1054 rejected, the claims of the Pope. As the Empire embraced many peoples of Semitic origin who saw idolatry in the use of carved or painted figures and could not accept that God could exist in Three Persons, there were bitter doctrinal disputes. The emperors tried to heal these divisions by calling councils, devising compromises, sometimes leaning towards the doctrines which pleased the Greeks of the capital, sometimes siding with the Anatolians and Armenians of the army. Persecution, assassination, massacre and deportation marked these disputes, the most bitter of which was the Iconoclast Movement against images (730–843).

Pressure on the Danube frontier and from Persia had dictated Constantine's move to Byzantium, and his successors were never free from military threats in the restless centuries of migration from Central Asia. The Balkan provinces were threatened by the Avars (570–615), the Bulgarians (811–1018) and the Vikings of Kiev (941). In the Mediterranean the Arabs took Crete, Cyprus and Rhodes, and when they were defeated the Normans occupied Sicily and South Italy. Venice, at first a western terminal of Byzantine trade, became a ruthless rival and in 1204, under the pretext of a crusade, in which she was joined by warriors from other parts of Europe, seized and sacked Constantinople.

The Byzantines met these threats by skilful diplomacy, an efficient army and navy and great resources of wealth. The civil service, trained in Greek grammar and rhetoric, supplied good diplomats and the emperors were reluctant to fight if they could achieve their ends by bribery or negotiation. The army was based by Heraclius on the free peasants of Anatolia, each family holding land on condition that one member served as a soldier. The Empire was divided into Themes, each under a military governor called a strategos, each responsible for its own defence. The cataphract, a cavalryman armed with lance and bow, dominated the battlefields till the coming of the Turks. Military engineering was far ahead of any rivals. But in spite of the efforts of the emperors of the Macedonian Dynasty (867–86) the free peasants tended to be forced to sell their holdings to owners of large estates, who weakened the Empire by their intrigues and revolts. For soldiers the later emperors had to depend on expensive and unreliable mercenaries. Their wholesale desertion at Manzikert in 1071 let the Seljuk Turks into Asia Minor. The Byzantine navy, with its nucleus of 1,000 naval guards based on the emperor's palace, was important in the defence of the long coastlines of Adriatic, Aegean and Black Sea. The secret of Greek Fire, an explosive mixture of petroleum, sulphur and quicklime, was well guarded, and saved the capital from an Arab fleet in 674 and from Prince Igor's Vikings in 941. These defence forces were expensive, but the Empire had great resources. The capital lay at a great crossroads of trade and a 10 per cent customs duty in such a position yielded well. Key industries and mines were run as state monopolies: silk-weaving was done in the palace area, there were Imperial stud farms and dye factories. All trade was closely regulated through guilds, and the state controlled prices and quality, Anatolia was fertile and, if any part of it was depopulated by war or religious persecution, the emperors hastened to people it again by forced migration from the Balkans.

When there was a respite from war these resources nourished great artistic achievement in the service of the Imperial Court, the Church, the officials and the richer landowners. Persian, Syrian, Greek and Roman influences blended to produce a style much admired and imitated by Charlemagne and Otto the Great in the West. Domed churches shone with glass mosaics which made barbarian visitors believe that "verily God there dwells among men". Ivory panels, silk brocades, silver dishes were the other outstanding products of Byzantine craftsmen.

The mass of the people had no political power, except when they were moved to riot by religious zeal. The emperors kept them quiet by lavish charity, close control of prices and the 40,000 free seats at the Hippodrome where party spirit focused on the factions in the chariot races called the Blues and the Greens after the costumes worn by the rivals.

The final fall of Constantinople in May 1453 marked the end of more than a thousand years of Christian Empire. Critobulos, a contemporary who had eye-witness evidence to draw on, described the Turkish conqueror, the Sultan Mohammed II (1451–81), as weeping over the destruction. "When Mohammed saw the ravages, the destruction and the deserted houses and all that had perished and become ruins, then a great sadness took possession of him . . . . And in truth it was natural, so much did the horror of the situation exceed all limits."

¶ RICE, TAMARA TALBOT. *Everyday Life in Byzantium*, 1967; WENZEL, MARIAN. *Finding out about the Byzantines*, 1965

Byzantium: a Greek city founded in 657 BC by Byzas of Megara. It was unimportant until Constantine chose it as his capital and it was dedicated as Constantinople on 11 May 330. It was ideally situated: central to the main military threats from the Danube and from Iran; on an easily defended peninsula between the Golden Horn and the Sea of Marmara; commanding the narrowest sea crossing to Asia and the sea route to the Black Sea. The landward approach was defended by the walls of Theodosius II (413–47). From the Golden Gate a wide street, the Mese, led to the Church of Holy Wisdom (537), the Imperial Palace and the Hippodrome. Water was brought by aqueducts and stored in underground cisterns. A university was extablished in 425. When the Turks took the city in 1453 they renamed it Istanbul.

C

Cabal, The (1667–73): a small group associated for some secret purpose or intrigue. The term was applied in the 17th century to any secret council, cabinet or junta. By coincidence, the initials of the five men who advised Charles II of England from 1667–73 (Clifford, Arlington, Buckingham, Ashley, Lauderdale) spelt Cabal, though the term did not originate with them. During these years England pursued a double policy, beginning with the Triple Alliance and ending with the Secret Treaty of Dover, by which the King, hoodwinking some of his advisers, committed himself to a pro-French and Catholic policy. Forced by financial difficulties to summon Parliament, he accepted the Test Act, which excluded all Catholics from office and, with the consequent resignation of Clifford and Arlington, broke up the Cabal.

Cabinet: a committee of government ministers under a chief minister or president; derived from French *cabinet*, a small room. Today, after a long period of evolution, the British cabinet, under the chairmanship of the Prime Minister, formulates the policies and decisions of the government. It is responsible to Parliament and, though there may be internal disagreement, attempts to present a united public image and accepts the principle of collective responsibility. In the USA the cabinet is the President's advisory body, made up of secretaries in charge of various government departments. These secretaries are not themselves members of Congress and are therefore directly responsible to the President.

¶ WALKER, PATRICK GORDON. *The Cabinet.* 1970

Cadiz, Spain: seaport of south-western Andalusia on the Isla de Leon, lying on a deep inlet forming two great natural harbours. Though known as a Phoenician trading settlement about 1100 BC, archaeological research has revealed only Carthaginian remains, dating from the 5th century BC. From 200 BC, the Romans developed it as a maritime centre. After occupations by Goths and Moors, Alfonso X of Castile took it in AD 1262. In 1587 Francis Drake's "singeing the King of Spain's beard" expedition destroyed the Spanish fleet there, and in 1596 the Earl of Essex burnt the city. From 1808 it was the headquarters of the Spanish patriots and endured a French blockade between 1810 and 1812. General Franco held Cadiz throughout the Spanish Civil War of the late 1930s.

Through the centuries, and especially in the 18th, its strategic importance was immense as a naval fortress lying near the sea routes from northern Europe to the Mediterranean, the African coast and South America. Cadiz suffered immeasurably from Spain's loss of her American colonies, especially Cuba. Recovery in commerce, shipping and shipbuilding, following improved rail and steamship communications, restored Cadiz as the centre of Spain's American trade.

The Old Port of Cadiz.

Caedmon, St (late 7th century): the first English Christian poet, who, according to the Venerable Bede, became a monk at Whitby late in life and, by the grace of God and under the guidance of the abbess Hilda, "sang the creation of the world, the origin of man, and all the history of Genesis".

Caesar, Gaius Julius (100–44 BC): soldier and dictator. As a young man, Caesar saw service in the East, where he defeated the Cilician pirates. As Aedile in 65 he spent lavishly and formed a political alliance with Crassus. Rumours connected him with the revolutionary ideas of Catiline in 63, but in the same year he was elected Pontifex Maximus. He went out in 61 to govern Further Spain, and returned in 60 to form the so-called First Triumvirate with Pompey and Crassus. In 59 he was Consul, and a violent year won for him the governorship of Gaul, which was to ensure his fame and recoup his fortune. A series of brilliant campaigns brought the whole country under Roman rule and led to invasions of Britain in 55 and 54. His interests in Rome were looked after by others, but on the death of Crassus in 53 relations with Pompey became increasingly strained, and civil war started when Caesar crossed the Rubicon in 49.

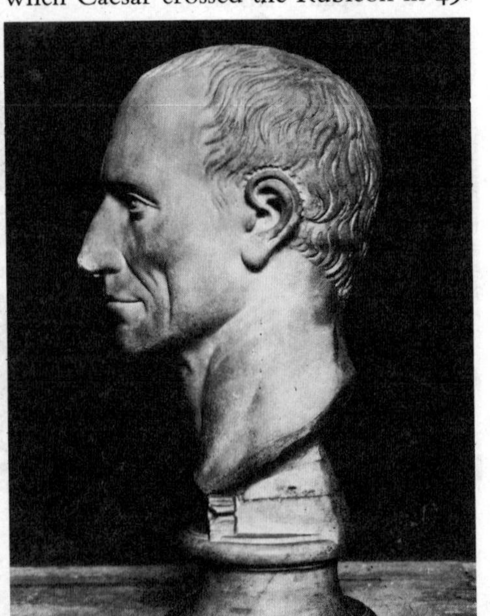

Again Caesar showed himself the master general, though his leniency forced him to fight the same enemies time and again. He still found time for extensive reforms, which included a change in the attitude to citizenship, financial measures, public works and the reform of the calendar. Honours were showered upon him, and in his last years he was permanent dictator. This above all led to his assassination by Brutus and Cassius on 15 March 44 BC.

¶ GUNTHER, JOHN. *All About Julius Caesar.* 1967; ISENBERG, IRWIN. *Caesar.* 1965

See also ROME, RULERS OF, for other Caesars.

Cairo: Egyptian city on the Nile, founded in AD 969 as capital of the Fatimid Caliphs by al'Muizz, in whose honour it was named al'Kahira, "the Victorious". It was near to al Fustat, the original tented capital of the Arab conquerors. The university of Al Azhar was founded in AD 988. The Saracen leader, Saladin, following an unsuccessful attack on the city by Crusaders, built a citadel on the Mokhattam Hills in 1176. Mameluke sultans ruled from 1260 till the Turkish conquest of 1517. Cairo declined when Portuguese seamen captured the Indies trade and when the Ottomans ruled from Istanbul. It revived when Mehmet Ali declared independence and introduced western industries in 1822. It is the capital of Egypt with a population of 5,650,000 in 1981.

Calais: historic port of northern France, eighteen miles [twenty-nine kilometres] from the English coast. Beginning as a fishing village with a natural harbour, it was fortified in the 13th century. Besieged by Edward III of England in the Hundred Years War, it was taken by him in 1347 and remained in English hands for more than 200 years. When it was finally lost in 1558 (the last English possession in France), Queen Mary is reported by Raphael Holinshed to have said: "When I am dead and opened, you shall find 'Calais' lying in my heart." It still occupies an important position as a cross-Channel port, and maintains several thriving industries, including lace and paper manufactures.

Calculating machines: machines for performing rapid arithmetical operations. Early number systems were not such as to make calculation easy, and this no doubt gave an impetus to the development of mechanical aids. The earliest was the abacus, which seems to have appeared first as a surface of sand or dust on which figures were traced with a stylus and erased when necessary, and was little more than a substitution for papyrus or paper. A more sophisticated form of the abacus was a table on which loose counters could be placed; and the most familiar type consisted of a number of beads, discs or counters placed on wires or in grooves, the successive lines or grooves representing units, tens, hundreds, etc. The abacus was used in ancient times in Egypt, Greece, Rome, China, Japan and Russia, as well as all over northern Europe.

Another device was Napier's Rods, sometimes called Napier's Bones. This dated from the year 1617. The rods or bones consisted of a number of square prisms. On one prism was inscribed one of the digits and the results of multiplying it by 2, 3, 4, 5, 6, 7, 8 and 9. To multiply 149 by 23, the rods bearing the numbers 1, 4 and 9 were placed side by side in that order. The results of multiplying by 3 and 2 could then be read off, and the required result obtained by addition.

The most important step towards the modern calculating machine was to replace the manual carrying of tens into the next column by a mechanical device consisting of a disc which engaged with a second disc, the first turning the second one unit after nine units have been turned on the first. This was invented by Pascal, who in 1649 received a royal charter for its manufacture. The replacement of manual operation by automation was first thought of by Babbage, who in 1822 produced a small working model of his "difference engine". His efforts to produce a satisfactory full-sized machine were defeated in his lifetime by the lack of techniques for machining the various metal parts to the fine tolerances required, and it was not until 1939 that his dream was finally realised when work began in the United States on a fully automatic calculator.

This was followed in 1942 by work on the modern electronic computer, which operates at a vastly higher speed as it lacks the inertia of moving metal parts. Development has been rapid and continuous since that date, and computers are now widely used in anything from space research to the control and ordering of stock for a chain store. These machines operate on the binary number scale; that is, a scale based on two, instead of the more familiar scale based on ten. It has been estimated that the electronic computer works five million times faster than a skilled operator using a manual calculator.

It remains to mention the slide rule. This depends on the discovery of logarithms by Napier in 1614. Suppose we draw up a table of powers of 2.

$$2^1 = 2$$
$$2^2 = 4$$
$$2^3 = 8$$
$$2^4 = 16$$
$$2^5 = 32$$

If we wish to multiply 8 by 4 we could use this table as follows: $8 \times 4 = 2^3 \times 2^2 = 2^5 = 32$. Thus the process of multiplication is replaced by addition of the

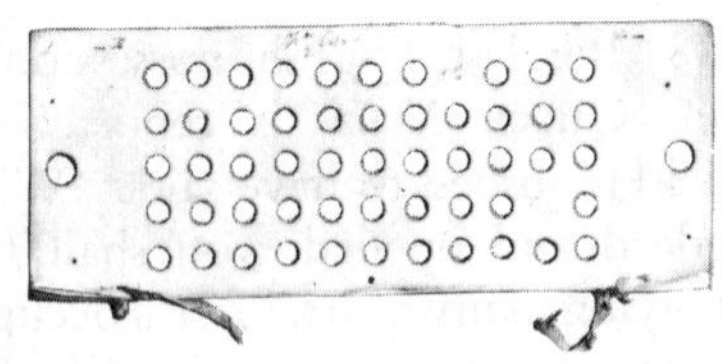
3. *Babbage's card.*

Calculating machines.
1. *Left, an abacus. Right, John Napier.*

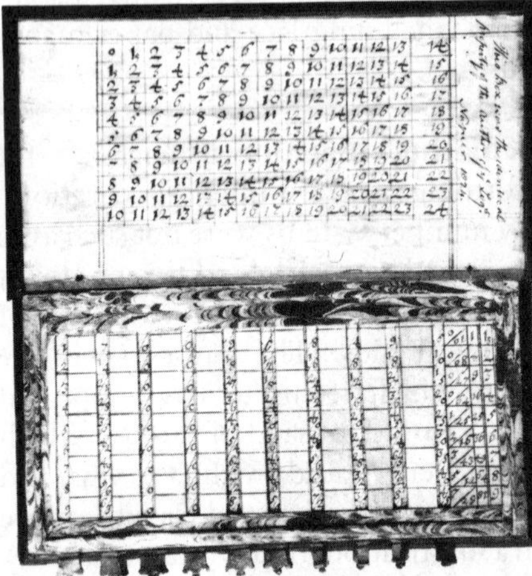
4. *Original Napier's Rods (cylindrical form).*

2. *Replica of Pascal's calculating machine.*

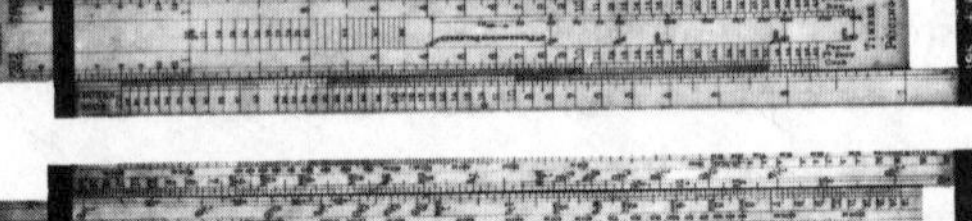
5. *(a) Hoare's plate and bar slide rule (bar side).*
(b) Builder's slide rule (timber side).

indices or logarithms. This table is a table of logarithms to base 2. The system most commonly used is based on 10, as suggested to Napier in 1616 by Briggs, Napier's original logarithms being based not on 10 but on a number approximately 2.71828, commonly called ε or epsilon. Logarithms are still very important for certain purposes. The slide rule is a mechanisation of this process, and its invention followed quickly on Napier's discovery of logarithms, the earliest example we know being employed by Oughtred in 1621. Before 1890 slide rules were in use only in England, France and Germany, but their use is now almost universal.

¶ PIPER, ROGER. *The Story of Computers.* 1970

Calendar: the arrangement of the time that the earth takes to go round the sun into a system of years, months and days. From earliest times, these three divisions were seen to have constant values (the month was originally the period from new moon to new moon), but the values could not be reduced to whole numbers. For instance, the actual length of the year is some eleven minutes short of 365 days 6 hours; the average length of the lunar month is just over 29½ days. All calendars have, therefore, been approximations to these awkward figures, and the most obvious solutions were adopted, especially the twelve-month year. Twelve months of 29½ days total 354 days, leaving a trifle over eleven days to fit in each year, and the normal method was one of intercalation, the insertion of an extra month when needed. At the same time, for the efficient conduct of affairs, the business and legal calendar needed a more uniform month and year, and so in early calendars we find the three systems together – solar, lunar and civil, i.e. based on the movements of the sun and the moon and on the business of the state.

The main exploratory work in the formation of a calendar was done by the Egyptians and Babylonians, who both started with lunar months. Egyptian religion attached great importance to the sun, and it was soon discovered that an extra quarter of a day had to be fitted in. This was officially allowed to accumulate until the calendar was once again "right" after a lapse of 1,460 years, or what was called a Sothic Period. In fact, the observance of the seasons was more important, and the months were simplified into thirty-day periods, which left only five days to intercalate. The problem of intercalation in Babylonia was solved by inserting an extra lunar month seven times in a cycle of nineteen years. The Greeks eventually followed the same system.

In Rome the year seems originally to have started in March and to have had ten named months – hence our names September, October, etc. What happened to January and February is obscure. In the changeover to a twelve-month system, months of varying lengths were proclaimed by the priests, and the first day of the month was a feast day called *Kalends*, or "Proclaimed". In this system, March, May, July and October had 31 days, February had 28 and the rest had 29, making a total of 355 days. A festival roughly dated to each full moon was held on the Ides. Intercalation was obviously needed, but this had got so out of control that, by 46 BC, the calendar was some eighty days out with the solar year. With help from Egyptian astronomers, Julius Caesar introduced the calendar which goes by his name, the Julian Calendar. With one minor exception, this is the one we use today. The names of our months are also Roman. The minor change was enacted by Pope Gregory XIII in 1582, by when it had been discovered that the solar year was not exactly 365¼ days. The Gregorian Calendar allowed leap years in centenary years only every 400 years. Thus 1900 was not a leap year, 2000 will be.

All calendars have eventually adopted some starting-point from which to reckon the years. The Jewish calendar is dated from the Creation, for which early scholars worked out, it has been estimated, some 140 different dates. The Greeks started from the first Olympic Games, 776 BC; the Romans began from the foundation of Rome in 753 BC. The changeover to the Christian system, using AD (Anno Domini) and BC (Before Christ), was introduced in the 6th century and adopted by most western countries by the 9th century.

The actual start of a year has also varied. The Greeks, for instance, began in midsummer. In England two systems worked alongside each other until 1752. Till that date the legal year began on 25 March, the calendar year on 1 January. In 1752 the Gregorian Calendar was also adopted, and this meant the "loss" of eleven days, which explains why the present financial year ends on 5 April, which represents 24 March in the Julian Calendar. The Gregorian Calendar was not adopted by some countries until this century. The only other change in modern times was the temporary calendar adopted by the

French revolutionary leaders in 1793, which went back to the Egyptian system of twelve thirty-day months which all had new names. The system lasted only till 1805.

The division of the month into sections had also been variously undertaken. The Egyptians and Greeks divided the month into roughly equal thirds. Rome started by a division into three feast days, the *Kalends* on the first of the month, the *Ides* on the 13th or 15th (depending on the length of the month), and the *Nones* on the ninth day (counting inclusively) before the *Ides*. Other days were reckoned backwards from these festivals. They also had a system of market-days, *nundinae*, held every eight days. Eventually this was easily changed into the seven day cycle of the week. The number seven is one of the oldest magic numbers. It is interesting to note that the names of the days of the week in English and, e.g., German are largely derived from the names of Norse gods, the French and Italian names from Roman gods.

The division of the day into hours was another early achievement, but the length of the hours sometimes varied. For instance, the Romans had twelve hours of day and twelve of night, and so at midsummer the hours of day were longer than they were at midwinter. The accurate division into twenty-four hours could not be done before accurate systems of measurement were invented. Midday has always been a clear reference point, and the twenty-four-hour clock is a product of recent times.

¶ In COLEMAN, LESLEY. *A Book of Time*. 1971
See also ARITHMETIC.

Calhoun, John Caldwell (1782–1850): American statesman. Coming from a prosperous slave-owning farming community of South Carolina, he entered politics in 1808 as a member of the South Carolina legislature and in 1817 became a member of the House of Representatives. A man of great integrity and powers of mind, he served as Vice-President and Secretary of State, declining nomination for the presidency itself. He opposed protective tariffs and endeavoured to legalise the appropriation of funds by the central government for such projects as canal and road building for the benefit of the country at large. He did not deviate from his defence of slave-owning interests, but treated his own slaves with kindness and justice.

Caliph, Calif or **Khalif:** from the Arab *Khalifah*, meaning successor or vice-regent; a title carried by the head of the Muslim, or Islamic, community as successor to Mohammed, the founder (*see* separate entry). The office of the caliph, not abolished till 1924 by the Turkish revolutionaries, was known as the caliphate. Despite the official abolition, there are still many Muslim theologians who hold that the Muslim world requires a caliphate, but support is small outside religious circles.

Calvin, John (Jean Cauvin, 1509–64): French reformer and theologian. A man of astonishing memory, eating and sleeping little, of judgment "so clear and correct that he often seemed almost to prophesy", his influence was of great importance in France and Switzerland (and afterwards in England, Scotland and the Netherlands). He held that biblical authority was above Church doctrine and tradition and that it was the duty of the State to aid and support the Church. Above all, his name is associated with the rigid theory of predestination – the doctrine that all human action is determined by God from the beginning and that, therefore, certain souls are pre-elected to salvation and others to perish.

Cambodia: a Buddhist country of Indo-China lying south-east of Thailand and west of Vietnam. Its greatest period of power was from the 9th century to the 12th, during which were built the royal city of Angkor-Thom (later lost to Thailand) and the great temple of Angkor-Vat. From the 14th century, power was lost and the country became a prey to the rivalry of Thailand and Annam until the French established protection in 1866. From then, though retaining a nominal independence, it remained a French colony until the abandonment of Indo-China by France after World War II. It endeavoured to preserve neutrality in the Vietnam war but when that ended the capital, Phnom Penh, fell to Red Khmer communist forces in 1975. The country changed its name to Kampuchea. Vietnam invaded it in 1978 and since then guerrilla forces have opposed the central government. Population in 1983: 5,996,000.

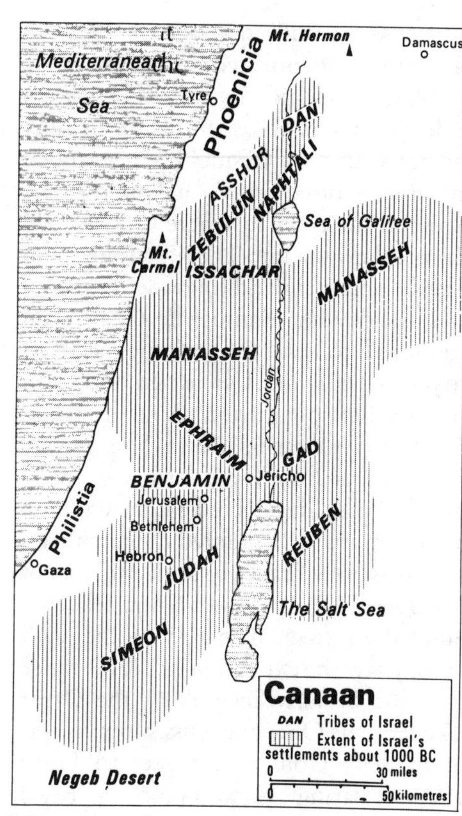

Canaan and the Canaanites: Palestine, the "Promised Land", and its indigenous inhabitants. Canaan was the land promised to Abraham – "Get thee out of thy country, and from thy kindred, and from thy father's house, unto a land that I will shew thee: and I will make of thee a great nation" (Genesis 12:1–2). A long narrow strip of land, stretching from the Mediterranean shore to the borders of the desert, and from Negeb in the south to the foothills of Mount Hermon in the north, it lay between the territories of two great powers of the ancient world, the kingdoms of the Nile and the kingdoms of Mesopotamia, on a great trade route which was also a military highway. It was a land of warring tribes, subject to attack from nomadic raiders, and studded with little strongholds where the tribesfolk could take refuge and repel their attackers. After years of wandering under their great leader, Moses, who never himself set foot in the Promised Land, the Israelites conquered it in stages during the second millennium BC. Many of the Canaanites were slaughtered or driven out, but some remained. The hatred for these original inhabitants, which is reflected in the Old Testament record, can be explained by the intense devotion felt by the Israelites for their God (their religion was monotheistic and at its best deeply spiritual), and by the horror with which they regarded the crude, immoral and often brutal practices carried out by the Canaanites in the name of their barbaric gods.

¶ In ROBINSON, C. A. *The First Book of Ancient Bible Lands*. 1963

Canada: largest country in the western hemisphere and largest member of the Commonwealth, with a population of more than 24 million in 1983.

The first authenticated discoveries were in Newfoundland by Bristol seamen under John and Sebastian Cabot in 1497 and 1498. In 1534 Jacques Cartier landed on what is now Gaspé, and in 1535 he explored the river to where Quebec and Montreal now stand. The Newfoundland fisheries and mainland fur trade were well established when Samuel de Champlain attempted to establish colonies at Port Royal in 1604 and Quebec in 1605. By 1615 he had penetrated as far as Lakes Huron and Ontario. Meanwhile, Henry Hudson, searching for a north-west passage to China, discovered Hudson's Bay. In 1627 Louis XIII granted the territories known as New France to the Company of One Hundred Associates. Montreal was founded in 1642. The rest of the 17th century saw the expansion of New France from the St Lawrence along the Great Lakes and the Ohio and Mississippi rivers; for in 1663 Colbert, minister to Louis XIV, declaring New France a royal colony, adopted a policy of development and exploration.

The founding of the Hudson's Bay Company in 1670 brought the English and French into conflict. The Treaty of Utrecht (1713) gave Britain Acadia (Nova Scotia), Newfoundland and French interests in the Hudson Bay area; but the fight for mastery in Canada continued until Wolfe's victory at Quebec in 1759, the surrender of Montreal the next year, and the Treaty of Paris which ended the Seven Years War in 1763. Problems of language, race and religion remained in spite of the Quebec Act of 1774 guaranteeing religious freedom. In the American War of Independence, Canadians were loyal to the Crown or neutral in the face of invasion. After the war, thousands of loyalists moved north from the States to the Canadian provinces, aggravating political problems. The 1791 Constitutional Act divided Quebec into Upper and Lower Canada. New Brunswick, Prince Edward Island and Nova Scotia were already separate colonies.

Meanwhile, the continent was being further explored, and Alexander Mackenzie reached the Pacific in 1793. Upper Canada prospered through immigration, a sensible policy of land grants and the inflow of capital from the United Kingdom. In Lower Canada advance was slower, for the French tended to stand aloof from commercial activities. Nova Scotia and New Brunswick also prospered through trade with the United States and the Caribbean. Antagonisms between the North West and Hudson's Bay Companies hampered development westwards until the two merged in 1821. Though the factions were ready enough to unite in resisting American invaders, internal political differences were deep-seated. Demands for more responsible government and rivalries between French-speaking and English-speaking Canadians led in 1837 to rebellions by English radicals under William Lyon Mackenzie in Upper Canada and by the French under Louis Joseph Papineau in Lower Canada. In 1840 the Act of Union, stemming from the Durham Report by the Governor General, joined Upper and Lower Canada, but did not grant full self-government. Some difficulties with the United States were settled in 1846 when the 49th Parallel was agreed as the Oregon Territory boundary. In 1858 British Columbia became a crown colony. Full self-government came to the major part of Canada with the 1867 North America Act, uniting Quebec, Ontario, Nova Scotia and New Brunswick into the Dominion of Canada. 1869 saw the western territory purchased from the Hudson's Bay Company, Louis Riel's first *métis* (= half-breed or cross-breed) rebellion, and Manitoba entering the

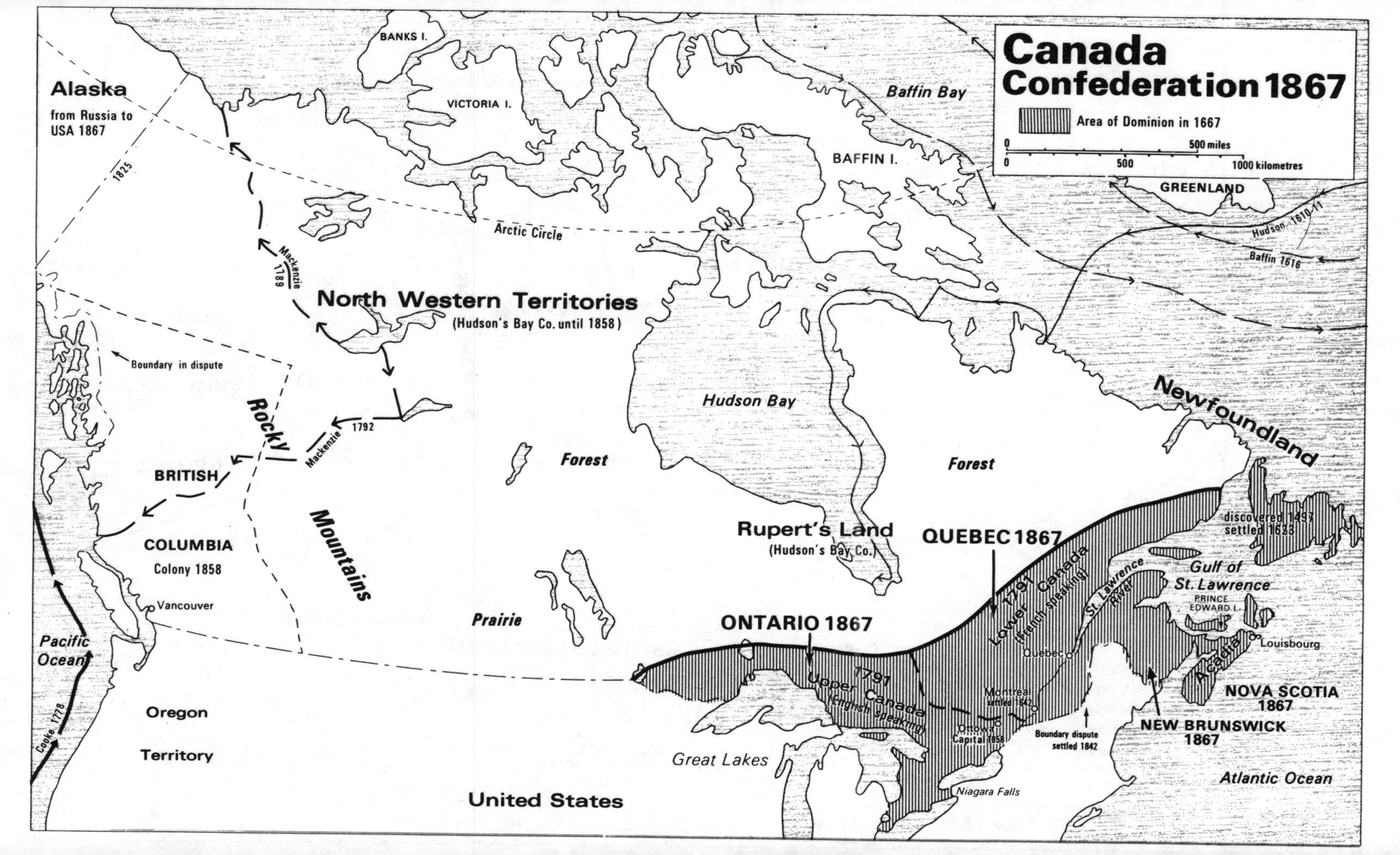

Canada
Confederation 1867
Area of Dominion in 1667
0
500 miles
0
500
1000 kilometres
Alaska
from Russia to USA 1867
1825
BANKS I.
VICTORIA I.
Baffin Bay
BAFFIN I.
GREENLAND
Hudson 1610/11
Baffin 1616
Arctic Circle
Mackenzie 1789
North Western Territories
(Hudson's Bay Co. until 1858)
Boundary in dispute
Rocky
Mountains
1792
Mackenzie
BRITISH
COLUMBIA
Colony 1858
Vancouver
Pacific Ocean
Cooke 1778
Oregon
Territory
Hudson Bay
Forest
Forest
Newfoundland
discovered 1497
settled 1623
Rupert's Land
(Hudson's Bay Co.)
Prairie
QUEBEC 1867
ONTARIO 1867
1791 Lower Canada
(French speaking)
1791 Upper Canada
(English speaking)
St. Lawrence River
Gulf of St. Lawrence
PRINCE EDWARD I.
Louisbourg
Acadia
Quebec
Montreal settled 1642
Ottowa Capital 1858
Boundary dispute settled 1842
NOVA SCOTIA 1867
NEW BRUNSWICK 1867
Great Lakes
Niagara Falls
Atlantic Ocean
United States

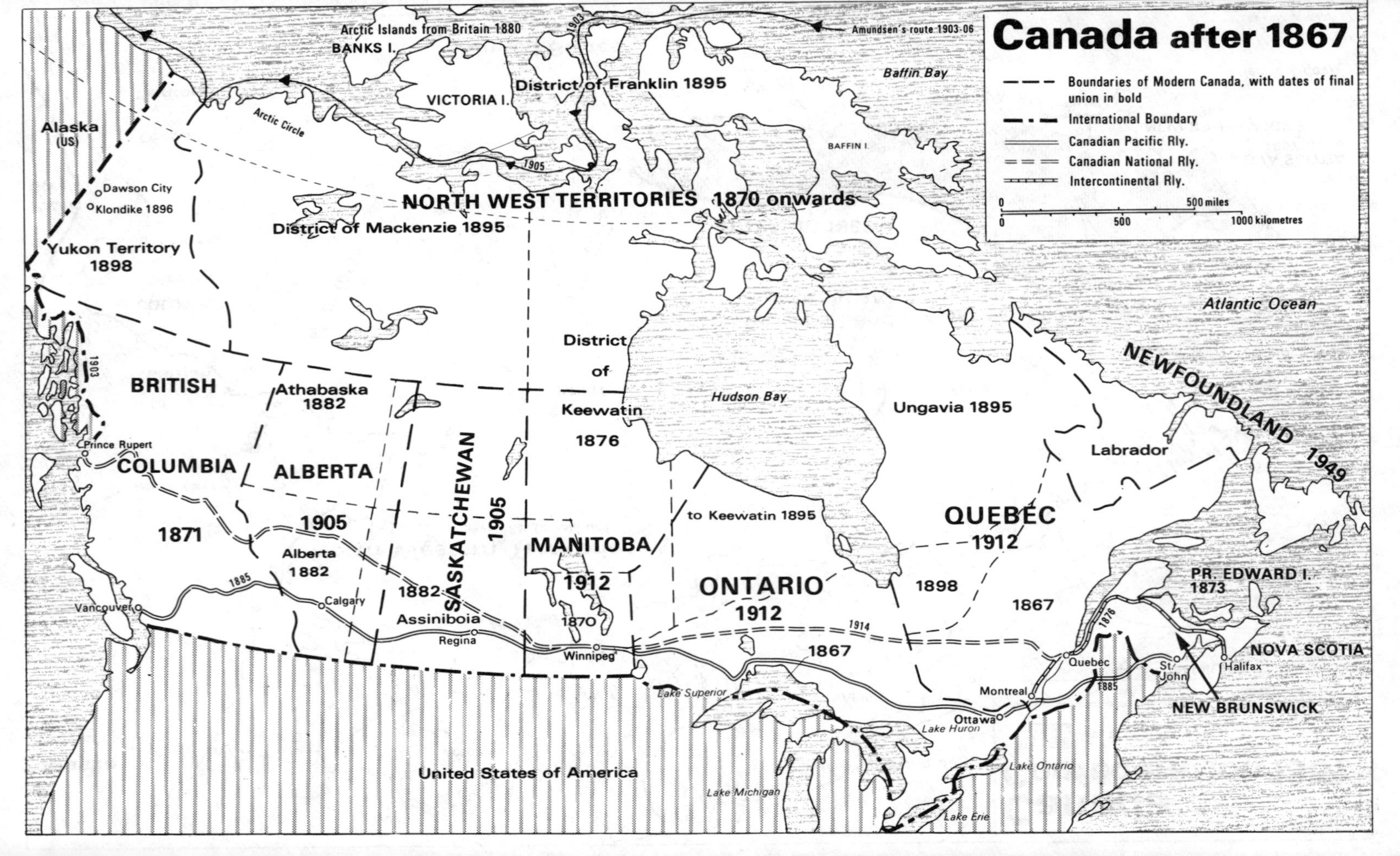

Canada after 1867
Boundaries of Modern Canada, with dates of final union in bold
International Boundary
Canadian Pacific Rly.
Canadian National Rly.
Intercontinental Rly.
0 500 miles
0 500 1000 kilometres
Arctic Islands from Britain 1880
BANKS I.
VICTORIA I.
District of Franklin 1895
Amundsen's route 1903-06
1903
1905
Baffin Bay
BAFFIN I.
Arctic Circle
Alaska (US)
Dawson City
Klondike 1896
Yukon Territory 1898
NORTH WEST TERRITORIES 1870 onwards
District of Mackenzie 1895
District of Keewatin 1876
Hudson Bay
Ungavia 1895
Labrador
NEWFOUNDLAND 1949
Atlantic Ocean
BRITISH COLUMBIA 1871
Prince Rupert
Athabaska 1882
ALBERTA 1905
Alberta 1882
SASKATCHEWAN 1905
Assiniboia 1882
MANITOBA 1912
1870
to Keewatin 1895
ONTARIO 1912
1867
1914
QUEBEC 1912
1898
1867
1876
1885
PR. EDWARD I. 1873
NOVA SCOTIA
NEW BRUNSWICK
Halifax
St. John
Quebec
Montreal
Ottawa
Winnipeg
Regina
Calgary
Vancouver
Lake Superior
Lake Huron
Lake Michigan
Lake Ontario
Lake Erie
United States of America

Miners in the Klondike. Old-timers used to tell Cheechakos (greenhorns) to dig in the hills knowing well that gold, being heavy, was usually deep in creekbeds. This time, however, the Cheechakos struck a rich lode.

Confederation. The other colonies followed, British Columbia in 1871, Prince Edward Island in 1873, Alberta and Saskatchewan in 1905 and, finally, Newfoundland in 1949. In 1870 the North West Territories, and in 1898 the Yukon, were transferred to the Government of Canada. Sir John A. Macdonald (d.1891) was the first Prime Minister. The Conservatives ruled till 1896, except from 1873 to 1878, on a programme of federal control of major provincial legislation and industrial expansion.

In 1885 the main line of the Canadian Pacific Railway was completed. A second *métis* rebellion failed and Louis Riel was hanged. Wilfrid Laurier (1841–1919), the first French-Canadian Prime Minister, and the Liberal Government which succeeded the Conservatives in 1896, not only promoted Canadian unity but, at the same time, developed a policy of freer trade and industrial expansion. The year 1896 also saw the Klondike gold rush. Between 1901 and 1911 the prairie provinces and British Columbia took in more than a million immigrants, and wheat production doubled.

In World War I, Canada supported the Allies to the uttermost, in spite of internal differences, especially over conscription. The reward was representation at the Paris Peace Conference and an independent place at the League of Nations. For twenty-seven years, from 1921 to 1948, Mackenzie King dominated Canadian politics. The Liberals ruled till 1957, except for five years after the 1929 depression, with a policy of national unity, lower tariffs, economic development and co-operation with Britain, especially in discussions which led to the Statute of Westminster, 1931, by which the full independence of the Dominions of the British Empire was recognised. In the 1930s new parties arose, mainly in the provinces (e.g. Social Credit in Alberta) but exercised little influence on federal affairs. In World War II, Canada was a main support of Britain for three years and effected a revolution in industrial methods and production. After the war she secured a place on the United Nations Security Council and joined NATO. Her troops served in UN forces in Egypt and Cyprus, she co-operated with the USA in NORAD and shared fully in the construction of the St Lawrence Seaway, opened in 1959.

Canada's resources are among the richest in the world and include wheat, dairy produce, pulp, paper, various metals, furs and oil. There is also a noteworthy heritage of literature, both in English and in French, its most outstanding contributions being in history and biography.

¶ TOTTON, S. J. *The Story of Canada.* 1960; WILLIAMS, B. *The Struggle for Canada.* 1967

Canadian National Railway: important railway system running for most of the way across Canada parallel to, and 200 miles [322 kilometres] north of, the Canadian Pacific Railway.

Canadian Pacific Railway: an undertaking controlling nearly 21,000 miles [34,000 kilometres] of railroad from Halifax, Nova Scotia, to Vancouver Island, coastal and Great Lakes steamships, chains of hotels and ocean-going liners and freighters. In 1871 British Columbia agreed to join the Confederation provided a trans-Canada railway was built, and 1874 saw a beginning. In 1880 the Canadian government contracted with a syndicate to take over lines already constructed, with 1 May 1891 as completion date, for subsidies of $25 million, land grants of 25 million acres [10 million hectares] and protection from competition. The main line was completed on 7 November 1885. It is now merged with the Canadian National Railway under the auspices of the government.

Canadian Pacific Railway.

¶ STUEBING, D., editor. *Building the Canadian Pacific Railway* (Jackdaw). 1969

Canals: artificial waterways for the purposes of irrigation and transport. The name comes from the Latin *canalis*, a water channel. Remains of the oldest known canal system, dating from about 5000 BC, were discovered by archaeologists in Iraq in 1968. Darius of Persia constructed one to link the Nile with the Red Sea, about 510 BC, and the Chinese were building them in the 3rd century BC. The earliest English canal, the Fossdyke, from Lincoln to the Trent, was built during the Roman occupation. In the Middle Ages canals were built in the Low Countries, Italy, Russia and India.

The invention of the lock, attributed to the Chinese, as early as AD 983 made it possible to lower or raise vessels afloat. Before this, ships were often hauled up or let down on a sloping plane of stonework.

Canal-building became important in England in the 18th century, when the Industrial Revolution called for greater mobility of coal and goods. Fifty-one

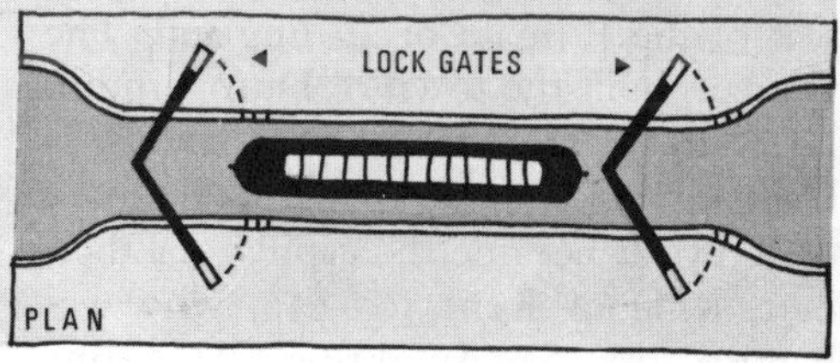

new canals were authorised by the British Parliament between 1791 and 1796 alone, and by 1830, when railway building began, there were 4,250 miles [6,825 kilometres] of navigable waterways in Britain.

All over the world canals have provided inland cities with access to the sea. Birmingham became the hub of a wheel of canal communications. In Germany, the raw materials of the Ruhr were made more accessible to industry. In the United States, the Erie Canal (1825), connecting New York with the Great Lakes, opened up a vast inland area and led to the rapid rise of such cities as Buffalo and Syracuse. Manchester, Strasbourg and Basle all owe their importance to inland waterways. The greatest canal system in the world is the Volga-Baltic Canal, opened in 1965 and covering 1,850 miles [2,995 kilometres].

The Suez Canal, 101 miles [162·5 kilometres] long and opened 17 November 1869 by the Empress Eugénie, was planned by Ferdinand de Lesseps (1805–94), a French engineer. The Panama Canal, 40 miles [64 kilometres] long, was begun in 1904. Opened in 1914, it is owned, operated and controlled by the United States under treaty.

¶ GREENWOOD, MARJORIE. *Roads and Canals in the Eighteenth Century*. 1953; WICKSON, ROGER. *Britain's Inland Waterways*. 1968; WYNYARD, JOHN. *Dams and Canals*. 1964

See also GRAND CANAL, PANAMA CANAL, SUEZ CANAL.

Candle: small column of wax or fat, with a central wick for illumination. Beeswax and tallow (usually beef or mutton fat) were often used in early times. A familiar type was the rushlight, made at home from the common rush and soaked in whatever kitchen grease was available. The 18th-century English naturalist Gilbert White, from observations in his village of Selborne, concluded that there were about 1,600 dry rushes to the pound; that a good rush would burn for an hour and more; and that "a poor family will enjoy five hours and a half of comfortable light for a farthing".

Cannae, Battle of (2 August 216 BC): fought in south-east Italy, near Barletta, between the Romans and the Carthaginian general, Hannibal (*see* separate entry). Hannibal's 40,000 troops almost annihilated an army of 70,000 Romans, and they never thereafter allowed him to bring them to pitched battle.

Canterbury, England: city of Kent and seat of the Primate of all England. The Romans built the town of Durovernum, later to be known by the Saxons as Cantwaraburh (= the town of the men of Kent). It became the capital of Ethelbert, King of Kent 560–616, who was baptised by St Augustine. Augustine thereafter chose the city as the centre from which to carry out his mission to the English. Among the chief events in the long history of the cathedral, dating from the 11th century, was the martyrdom of Thomas Becket in 1170.

Canterbury is also the name of an important region of New Zealand, producing wheat, lamb and dairy products.

¶ CROUCH, MARCUS. *Canterbury*. 1970

Canterbury, Archbishops of: holders of the highest office in the English Church. The Archbishopric of Canterbury has its origin in the mission sent by Pope Gregory the Great (Pope 590–604) in AD 597 under St Augustine (d. 604) to Ethelbert, King of Kent. The object of the mission was to reorganise, rather than to establish, in Britain the practice of the Christian religion, which had survived from Roman times despite the subsequent pagan invasions. The intention was to establish archbishoprics in two provinces based on London and York; but from the start Canterbury replaced London for the southern province, and Augustine became the first archbishop. It was not until the 14th century that it was finally established that York was subordinate to Canterbury, the archbishop of the former province being styled Primate of England and that of the latter Primate of all England, with the right of crowning the sovereign.

Canterbury is the larger province, its northern boundary including the dioceses of Lincoln, Leicester, Derby and Lichfield. The authority of the Archbishop of Canterbury extends also over certain overseas bishops; but in a large part of the Anglican Church he has no formal jurisdiction. Nevertheless the fact that, approximately every ten years, the bishops of the Church throughout the world meet in conference at Lambeth Palace, the London residence of the Archbishop of Canterbury, is a reminder of their common heritage in St Augustine's foundation.

In the 1,370-year history of the province there have been one hundred holders of the office of archbishop, seven of whom have been granted the title of Saint. There has been only one considerable gap in the line of succession, which occurred during the Commonwealth, when the vacancy caused in 1645 by the death of William Laud (see below) was not filled until, at the Restoration in 1660, Charles II appointed William Juxon (1582–1663) who, as Bishop of London, had attended his father on the scaffold.

The work begun by St Augustine was carried further by his sixth successor, Theodore of Tarsus (archbishop 669–90), a forceful and, indeed, somewhat ruthless character, to whom is owed the main outlines of the present English diocesan structure, although there has been much subsequent subdivision. The other name which should be remembered from the pre-Norman period is that of St Dunstan (archbishop 961–88), Abbot of Glastonbury. As archbishop he laboured to integrate the Danes with the English and encouraged the establishment of Benedictine houses in England.

Three of the medieval archbishops deserve notice for their resistance to the claims and pretensions of the kings. St Anselm (archbishop 1093–1109) spent, in consequence, much of his time in exile before finally achieving much of what he stood for. St Thomas Becket (archbishop 1162–70), the subject of a separate article, through his martyrdom and the subsequent pilgrimages to his shrine, brought immense wealth to the Abbey Church, until it was seized by Henry VIII at the Dissolution. Stephen Langton (archbishop 1207–28) is remembered for his part in the Great Charter of 1215. He was also famed as a poet and is thought to be the author of the hymn *Veni, Sancte Spiritus*, which is the subject of several translations in presentday hymn books.

With the Reformation the Archbishop of Canterbury assumed greater stature as head of a Church independent of Rome, but bound more closely to the state. Thomas Cranmer (archbishop 1533–56) helped to arrange the divorce of Henry VIII from Catherine of Aragon and took a leading part in the religious reforms of the reign of Edward VI. A master of English prose, he is responsible for some of the finest passages in the Book of Common Prayer. But, if Cranmer was the first Protestant archbishop, the turn of events restored the Roman religion under Mary and brought Cranmer to the stake. The last Roman archbishop was Reginald Pole (archbishop 1556–58) who died within hours of his cousin the Queen. Elizabeth's archbishop for many years was Matthew Parker (archbishop 1559–75), but she often treated him in ways that sorely tried

The Archbishop of Canterbury, Dr Ramsay, on a ceremonial occasion.

him. Moreover, she retained the Catholic objection to married clergy and would not acknowledge his wife.

History textbooks tend to stress the stubborn obstinacy of William Laud (archbishop 1633–45) as contributing largely to the troubles of Charles I which brought him, like his master, to the block. He deserves to be remembered as a great Chancellor of the University of Oxford and as one who brought much order and dignity into the services of the Church of England. William Sancroft (archbishop 1678–90), although leader of the Seven Bishops in their resistance to James II in 1668, considered himself precluded by his oath of allegiance to that monarch from taking a similar oath to William III. He was thus deprived of his office as a non-juror.

The 19th century and the present one have brought archbishops of sterling worth. Frederick Temple (archbishop 1896–1902), and his son, William Temple (archbishop 1942–44), both held the title and adopted the practice of retiring from office in old age. The present Archbishop is Dr Robert Runcie, the 102nd person to hold the office.

Canute or **Cnut** (994?–1035): King of the English, Danes and Norwegians. He was the first king to unite the English and the Danes. The two Danish invasions of England, of 1013 and 1015, culminated in the destruction of the "flower of the English Race" by Canute at Assandum (Ashington in Essex). The subsequent treaty of Olney gave Canute the north of England, while the English king, Edmund Ironside, kept Wessex and East Anglia; but the latter's death in November 1016, by sickness or assassination, left Canute sole ruler of England, with the agreement of the Witan, the highest council in the land.

He removed any opposition by executions, exile or marriage. He married Emma, the Norman widow of King Ethelred. His policies included the paying off of his Danish forces, with the exception of a standing bodyguard of forty ships and their crews (his *huscarls* or house carls, and freedom for any Englishman to occupy any state or ecclesiastical office in England or Denmark. He retained Edgar's Laws (959–75) and divided England into four earldoms, Wessex being occupied by Godwine as earl.

In his Christian settlement Canute, baptised before 1013, sought the goodwill of the Church by rich gifts to such great monasteries as Bury St Edmunds, Winchester and Glastonbury. Important churchmen influenced him (especially the Bishop of Crediton and the Archbishop of Canterbury) and his pilgrimage to Rome in 1026–7 brought substantial benefits not only for the Church but in commerce and in reputation for himself.

Abroad, Canute gained Denmark in 1019 and fixed its border with Germany by marrying his daughter Gunhild to the son of the Holy Roman Emperor. In 1028 Norway was added and Malcolm II, King of Scotland 1005–34, acknowledged his supremacy. Norman threats were countered by an alliance with Aquitaine.

He died at Shaftesbury 12 November 1035 and was buried at Winchester.

Cape Cod: peninsula, 65 miles [105 kilometres] long, in south-east Massachusetts, USA, where the Pilgrim Fathers landed in 1620. In 1914 the Cape Cod Canal was opened, cutting the distance from New York to Boston for waterborne traffic by over 75 miles [120 kilometres].

Cape Horn: promontory in southernmost Chilean Tierra del Fuego. It was discovered by the Dutch explorer Schouten in 1616 and named after his native town of Hoorn. The Cape Horn route to the Pacific played a major rôle in seafaring till the Panama Canal opened in 1914.

Cape Kennedy formerly **Cape Canaveral:** cape on the east coast of Canaveral Peninsula, USA, renamed after President John Kennedy (1917–63) and the chief centre for long-range rocket and earth satellite enterprises. *See page 145.*

¶ SASEK, M. *This Is Cape Kennedy.* 1963

Canute with his first wife, Queen Aelfgifu.

Rocket launching pad at Cape Kennedy.

Cape of Good Hope: the southern extremity of the Cape Peninsula in South Africa. It was first rounded by a European in 1487, when the Portuguese explorer Bartholomew Diaz named it Cape of Storms. King John II of Portugal renamed it Cape of Good Hope because its discovery seemed to offer hope that the Portuguese had found a new route to India. Cape Town, founded as a Dutch ship-victualling station in 1652 and a British colony from 1814, attained fully representative government in 1872 as capital of the Cape of Good Hope Province; it became the legislative capital of the Union of South Africa in 1910 and of the South African Republic in 1961. (*See* DISCOVERY, AGE OF.)

Cape Sagrés: cape of southernmost Portugal, near Cape St Vincent, famous for its association with Prince Henry of Portugal (1394–1460), who built an observatory there and other accommodation to further his work of exploration. The place became known as *Villa do Iffante*, Infante's Town, Infante being the title of a son (other than the eldest) of the king of Spain or of Portugal (*see* HENRY, PRINCE, called "the Navigator").

Cape St Vincent, Battle of (14 February 1797): fought off Cape St Vincent, southwest Spain, by Admiral Sir John Jervis (1735–1823) with fifteen British ships of the line, and the Spanish fleet of twenty-seven. Victory was mainly due to the initiative of Commodore Horatio Nelson in the *Captain*, of 74 guns. Nelson, last but two in line, left without orders to prevent a gap in the Spanish line closing and engaged the enemy van. He captured two of the four prizes taken, the *San Nicolas*, of 80 guns, and, across her decks, the *San Josef*, of 112 guns. Jervis's victory ensured British re-entry to the Mediterranean.

Capet Dynasty: third dynasty of French kings, founded by Hugues Capet, Comte de Paris (*c.* 940–996) in 987. He was head of one of the greatest feudal families and, upon the death of Louis V, last of the Carlovingian line, was strong enough to be elected king. He founded a remarkable dynasty which was to last for almost three and a half centuries in direct line; and, through the Valois and Bourbon branches, for over 800 years. When, during the French Revolution, the monarchy was abolished, Louis XVI became officially known as Louis Capet.

Firmly established in his capital, Paris, and the surrounding provinces, Hugues embarked upon a successful policy of territorial expansion and sound administration. He established a feudal system of government and, more important, converted the monarchy from an elected to an hereditary office. He and his successors instituted the custom of creating the elder son "Master of the Palace" and of crowning him during his father's lifetime. This, coupled with the fact that for over 300 years there was always a male heir, ensured undisputed succession.

The Capetians drew their strength also from the fact that they were not only chief of the feudal lords but the inheritors of the Roman tradition of empire which had been re-established by Charlemagne. They also had the support of the Church. The direct line came to an end in 1328, the succession passing first to the Valois and then to the Bourbon kings (*see* separate entries).

¶ FAWTIER, R. *Capetian Kings of France*. 1963

Capital Punishment: official punishment by death. This extreme form of punishment for offences or crimes is called "capital" (from Latin *caput*, head) because the usual method of carrying it out was chopping off the head or hanging. In more barbaric times its use was often wanton and indiscriminate; though, even in a civilised society such as 18th- and 19th-century England, it was retained for many comparatively trivial offences. In 1830, though the sentence was by no means always carried out, there were over 200 offences punishable by death, but during the following years this number was reduced to four: murder, treason (including attacks on the royal family), piracy and setting fire to naval ships. After 1868 executions were no longer held in public, no one under eighteen was executed, and a number of attempts were made to abolish capital punishment altogether. In 1965 capital punishment for murder was suspended in Britain for an experimental period of five years and was abolished in 1970; treason and attacks upon the royal family are still punishable by death.

Many European countries have either abolished capital punishment or never used it. These include Austria, Belgium, Denmark, Finland, West Germany, Holland, Norway, Portugal, Sweden and Switzerland. Six of the states in the USA have abolished capital punishment, and most of the other forty-two states may punish with life imprisonment instead. In many countries which have done away with capital punishment it has been found that the average number of murders has not increased.

Illustrated verses on the public hanging of a murderer.

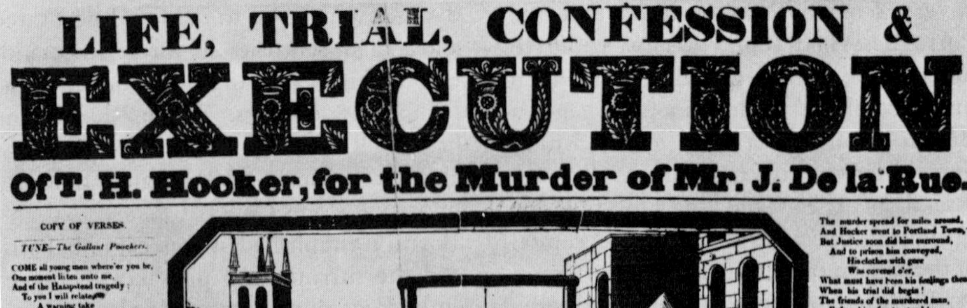

LIFE, TRIAL, CONFESSION &

EXECUTION

Of T. H. Hooker, for the Murder of Mr. J. De la Rue.

COPY OF VERSES.

TUNE—The Gallant Poachers.

COME all young men where'er you be,
One moment listen unto me,
And of the Hampstead tragedy:
To you I will relate,
A warning take
By Hocker's fate.
His days did end in shame and scorn:
Far better had he ne'er been born!
To leave his parents all forlorn,
And die in such disgrace!

To avarice he did give way,
A victim fixed upon to slay,
And who, upon the fatal day,
At Hampstead met his doom,
He his victim slew,
Poor De la rue,
He strugled hard his life to save,
But nought could stay the deadly stave
By Hocker's hand the wound received
That took his life away.

The sound of murder they did hear cry,
And to the spot did quickly hie,
Upon the ground they did descry,
The murdered De la rue,
In the prime of life he fell;
His sufferings none can tell.
Deep was the wound that Hocker gave,
No mortal man his life could save!
He now lies sleeping in the grave
Until the judgment day.

The murder spread for miles around,
And Hocker went to Portland Town,
But Justice soon did him surround,
And to prison him conveyed,
His clothes with gore
Was covered o'er,
What must have been his feelings then,
When his trial did begin!
The friends of the murdered man,
Before him for to stand!

When guilty found, the Judge did cry,
You must prepare yourself to die;
Your time is short, on the scaffold high
You'll end your wretched days,
Short is the time you'll live
To God your prayers, then give,
Down on your knees, without delay,
Pray to him both night and day,
For he alone your soul can save
From endless misery.

The execution now is o'er,
And Thomas Hocker is no more.
None on earth will him deplore,
For the murder he had done.
His glass is run,
His life is gone;
And while we in this world do stay,
Oh, let not passion get the sway;
Think on the dreadful judgement day,
And think of Hocker's end.

James Paul and Co., Printers,
2 & 3, Monmouth Court,
Seven Dials

Capitalism: economic system in which the main sources of production, etc., are privately owned and operated for private profit.

If a man has more wealth than he requires for his immediate needs, that sum is called his capital. This "spare money", or capital, is often used to produce more wealth. Every business, from a small shop to a great factory, has to spend money on raw materials, stock and machinery and in paying its workpeople before it can produce goods to sell. This money comes from people who have it to spare and are prepared to lend it. The goods are sold for more than they cost to produce. This extra money is called the profit, which is used to pay interest to those who have lent their capital. So, in what is called the capitalist system, there are said to be two main elements: the capital, which is used to pay for everything needed, and labour, which means the workpeople.

Countries such as Britain, France and the USA, in which the capital is largely owned by private persons, are said to have a capitalist system. Not all countries, however, have this system. Karl Marx (1818–83), a famous German economist and social philosopher, wrote a book called *Das Kapital* in which he described the system and showed how often labour got a much smaller share of the wealth it helped to create than the owners of the capital. From this book and others the idea of socialism spread: that is, all capital should be owned by society and all workers should be employed by the state. After a revolution in 1917 a system of this sort was adopted by Russia, now called the Union of Soviet Socialist Republics. Other countries are experimenting with a mixture of the two systems, e.g. in Britain at the present time certain major services, such as the railways and supply of water, are nationalised and are no longer operated by private companies.

Carbonari: literally, charcoal-burners, the name adopted by a secret society started in Naples in opposition to French rule, 1810. It survived in opposition to the despotic rule of the restored Bourbon kings, drawing members from landowners, soldiers, lawyers and officials dismissed in 1815. A rising under their banner – black, red and blue – was started in 1820, headed by General Pepe. King Ferdinand was frightened into granting a constitution which he denounced as soon as he was assured of Austrian aid. Lodges formed in other parts of Italy did much to stimulate the demand for Italian unity, though lack of unified direction made them ineffective in action.

Carnegie, Andrew (1835–1919): US steel magnate and philanthropist. Born in Scotland, he emigrated with his father to Allegheny, Pennsylvania, in 1848. After working in a variety of humble occupations, he became secretary, and then superintendent, of the western division of the Pennsylvania Railroad. He subsequently made a great fortune through foreseeing the demand for iron and steel and, by the time he was little more than fifty, controlled a vast plant, over 400 miles of railway and a line of steamships. He wrote *Triumphant Democracy* (1886) and *Gospel of Wealth* (1900) and gave practical demonstration of his belief in the responsibilities of wealth by large gifts and endowments, a particularly noteworthy benefaction being the provision of many public libraries in the United States and Britain.

¶ HARLOW, ALVIN E. *Andrew Carnegie*. 1963

Carolingian or **Carlovingian:** term applied to a dynasty of Frankish kings (751–987), from its most famous member, Charlemagne (Latin *Carolus*, Charles). *Caroline*, too, is used in connection with Charlemagne, but is also applied to the reigns of Charles I and Charles II of England (1642–49 and 1660–85).

Carthage and the **Carthaginians:** ancient city of North Africa, its empire and inhabitants.

Founded by Phoenicians as a trading post in 814 BC, Carthage quickly became the most important port on the coast of North Africa, and her international prestige increased when Phoenicia was overrun by Assyria. The continent of Africa offered uneasy peace but good mercenaries; progressive Carthaginians, however, saw their future to the north and west. An alliance with Etruria, the ancient country in central Italy, defeated the western Greeks off Alalia about 535 BC, and, after the decline of Etruria, Carthage took over control of Corsica, Sardinia and the west of Sicily. The attempt to gain the whole island was thwarted at the battle of Himera in 480 BC, and any success thereafter was only temporary. Alliances with Rome as early as 508 asserted Carthaginian mastery of the sea, and Carthage drove Pyrrhus from Sicily in 276.

In spite of this, conflict with Rome was bound to come, and the first so-called Punic War started in 264. Almost confined to Sicily and the seas around, the war ended Carthaginian sea power and she lost Sicily. Shortly afterwards she was cheated of Corsica and Sardinia. The Barcid family (Hamilcar, Hasdrubal and Hannibal) found new scope in Spain,

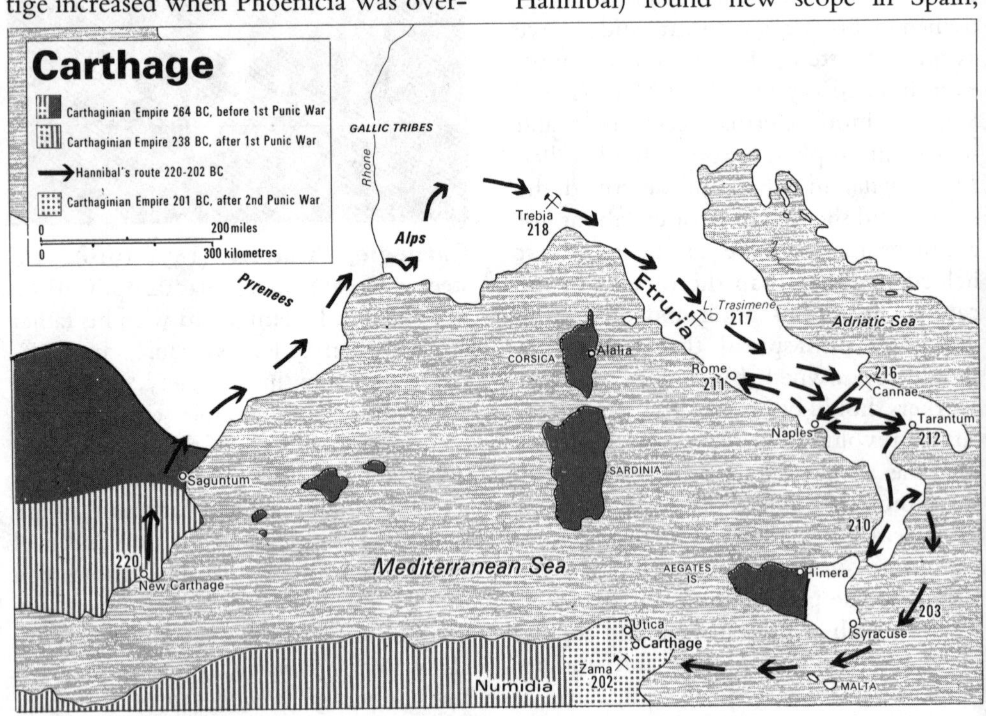

where New Carthage was founded in 228. A clash with Rome was welcomed by Hannibal, and this led to the second Punic War (218–201). Hannibal's successful invasion of Italy and his brilliant victories at Lake Trasimene and Cannae came to nothing because of the lack of support from home and the loyalty of Rome's allies. He was forced to return to Carthage in 203 to defend his homeland, where he was beaten at the battle of Zama (202). The terms imposed in 201 were harsh and forced Carthage to seek Roman permission for any new venture. Rome found an excuse to interfere in 149, and Carthage was totally destroyed in 146 BC. The city was eventually rebuilt and became an important Roman colony. A university centre, it was the capital of the wealthy and artistic province of Africa. Later still it became the capital of the Vandal chief Gaiseric.

Constitutionally, Carthage was an oligarchy, a form of government in which power rests in the hands of a small exclusive class. Two Suffetes were elected presidents, but their powers were severely limited by the oligarchical Councils of Five and the Court of the Hundred. Failure in battle was liable to lead to a general's execution. The true Carthaginian was brought up in fear of the old Phoenician gods, and it was his duty to lead the mercenary armies which were trained under the Spartan system (*see* SPARTA). It took a great man or family to rise out of this unrewarding society. Two such families were the Magonids in the 5th century BC and the Barcids in the 3rd.

Artistically, Carthage has little original to show, drawing most of her inspiration from Phoenicia, Greece and Egypt. In any case, very little survived the destruction in 146 BC and there are virtually no literary remains. If the impression left of Carthage is of a depressing, fear-ridden, militaristic caste system, it may be because of the violent hatred felt for Carthage by Roman writers.

¶ MELLERSH, H. E. L. *Carthage*. 1963

Cartier, Jacques (1491–1557): French navigator and explorer of Canada. During three voyages (1534, 1535–6 and 1541–2) he explored some way beyond the present Montreal, named the St Lawrence River and took possession of the country in the name of his king Francis (François) I.

¶ FERGUSON, R. D. *The Man from St. Malo*. 1959

Castile: historic kingdom of Spain, occupying most of the central plateau. It became an independent kingdom in the 10th century and, soon after Isabella of Castile married Ferdinand of Aragon in 1469, merged with that kingdom to become the Spanish state. Castile retains many features of medieval life, and Castilian remains the literary language of Spain.

Castles: fortified strongholds, usually within a defensive wall. In England castles, as private strongholds and the permanent residence of king or noble, were a product of the feudal system. This system did not exist before the Norman Conquest of 1066, and castles in the strict sense were not properly established until the arrival of the Norman conquerors. Duke William's first act on invading England was to build a castle at Hastings, and during the next generation a Norman garrison was to become established in every important lordship in the land.

The type of fortress with which all England was soon to become familiar was the motte and bailey castle. The motte was a high mound of earth with a wooden stockade round its flattened summit and standing in a levelled bailey, or courtyard, surrounded by a moat. An outer ditch with a fenced inner bank enclosed the whole. In the bailey were wooden sheds to shelter the garrison and their horses, and upon the mound itself stood the timbered tower which in due course became known as the keep. Access to the tower was possible only by means of a sloping bridge across the moat. This type of stronghold was practically universal in western Europe, and in England it became the normal type of fortress for the next hundred years.

The later great castles of stone were achieved by slow evolution from the more hurriedly built Norman strongholds, and after 1097, when the crusaders returned from the Middle East, a rapid development of fortification began. The palisade on the motte was reconstructed in stonework, the timber hall rebuilt with masonry and the sloping bridge replaced by an arch and steps of stone. Walls were increased in height and thickness and sprouted projecting turrets. Parapets were embattled or loopholed, and towers were provided with overhanging galleries, first of wood and later of stone, enabling missiles to be dropped through slits in the floor. These galleries became known as machicolations. Massive buttresses were built to distribute the weight over a larger area to resist undermining, and more resistant D-shaped or circular towers replaced the square plan.

Huge stone keeps were built of several storeys with walls of 12 to 20 feet [3·6 to 6·0 metres] thick and would include a great hall, the domestic quarters of the lord and his followers, and a chapel. Wide fireplaces and garderobes (latrines) were hollowed out in the walls, and a well was usually situated in the foundations. In England the square keeps of Hedingham, Rochester, Newcastle and Norwich are among the most famous. During the reign of Henry II (1133–89), the development of strong gate-houses became a main feature of castle building. These were called barbicans, and typically had two projecting circular towers on each side of the actual gate, compelling the enemy to advance on a very small front. The chamber on the first floor above the arch housed the portcullis, a heavy grating that could close the gateway instantly in an emergency. For extra security a heavy drawbridge was added which cut off the approach to the gateway. Sometimes the wooden palisade on the motte was replaced by a curtain wall of stone without a tower, and this type of mound defence, called a shell keep, encircled a broad central area in which there were small secondary buildings. Good examples of shell keeps are to be found at Launceston and Restormel in Cornwall, England, and Gisors in Normandy.

Another new principle of fortification, developed towards the end of the 12th century, was the concentric plan, the essential feature of which comprised a curtain wall defending a central stronghold. A fine example of this design can be studied at the Tower of London. A unified group of concentric castles was built by Edward I (1239–1307) during his campaigns against the Welsh, and such sites as Caernarvon, Harlech, Conway and Beaumaris remain as splendid examples of castles built on the concentric plan. This was the most advanced and effective type of defensive system and was probably brought home by the crusaders who had learnt to appreciate it in their attacks on Saracen strongholds. The crusaders built many new castles in the Levant and others were taken over, enlarged and improved. The walls of these great crusader bastions were immensely thick and strong; the best preserved of them all, the famous Krak des Chevaliers, is one of the finest examples of concentric castle building to be found.

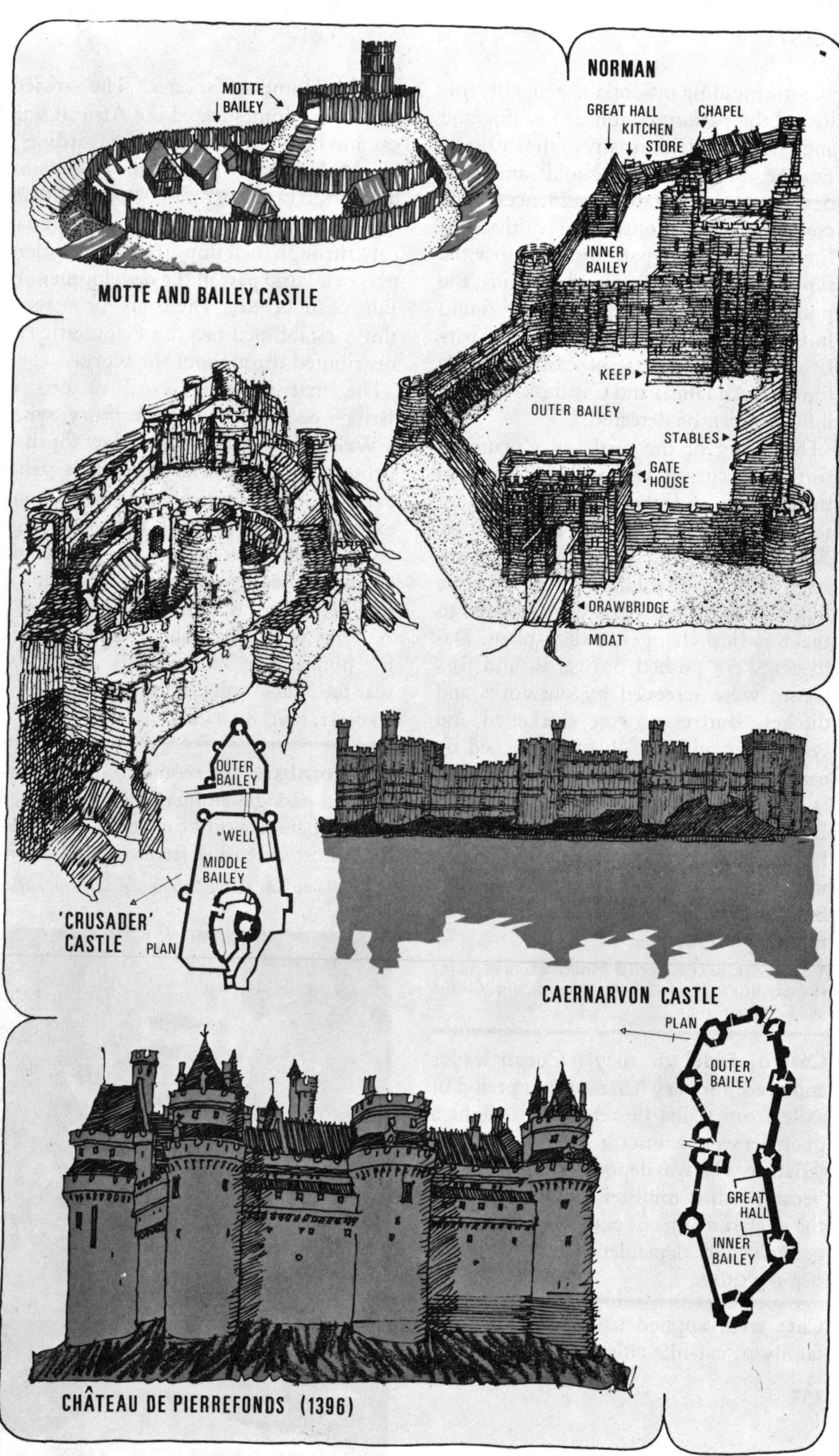
MOTTE
BAILEY
MOTTE AND BAILEY CASTLE
NORMAN
GREAT HALL
CHAPEL
KITCHEN
STORE
INNER BAILEY
KEEP
OUTER BAILEY
STABLES
GATE HOUSE
DRAWBRIDGE
MOAT
OUTER BAILEY
WELL
MIDDLE BAILEY
'CRUSADER' CASTLE
PLAN
CAERNARVON CASTLE
PLAN
OUTER BAILEY
GREAT HALL
INNER BAILEY
CHÂTEAU DE PIERREFONDS (1396)

Castle building in Scotland generally followed the pattern established in England and France, and, like many of the castles of Europe, began as strongholds and later developed into stately residences. The construction of continental castles followed a variety of patterns. In France the typical Norman stronghold abounds; the ponderous Gothic fortress is to be found in Germany; and in Spain, where a particularly rich variety of castles can be found in Andalusia and Castile, a Moorish influence can be detected.

The decay of the castle as a manorial fortress occurred when towns grew in importance and the new principles of fortification were applied to the city walls. Not until the 15th century, however, was siege artillery established on such a scale that fortification experts were obliged to make radical changes in their plans. Defences were pushed outwards, and fortresses were screened by outworks and ditches. Buttresses were thickened and walls were additionally strengthened by earth backings and arched galleries. The last stage of castle building on any scale in England took place during the reign of Henry VIII (1491–1547), when the ancient idea of a castle as an impregnable stronghold gave way to its use as a battery or gun emplacement.

¶ BROWN, R. ALLEN. *English Medieval Castles.* 1954; FRY, LEONORA. *Castles.* 1956; SELLMAN, R. R. *Castles and Fortresses.* 1963

Castro, Fidel (b. 1927)**:** Cuban leader and revolutionary hero. After a period of exile from Cuba he returned to fight a guerrilla war against the dictator Zaldivar y Batiste who was deposed in 1959. Castro became prime minister in his place, with the declared aims of ending injustice and poverty and dependence on the USA. *See also* CUBA.

Cat: term applied to any of the large family of cat-like animals, but especially to the domestic species. The ancient Egyptians domesticated the African wild cat and held it in veneration, regarding it as symbolising the moon. A possible derivation of the pet-name "puss" is from the Egyptian *pusht*, the moon. Egyptian cats, through their importation by traders, played a large part in the development of European breeds. There are now some thirty established breeds of domestic cat, distributed throughout the world.

The first written record of cats in Britain occurs in the 10th century, when a Welsh prince formulated a law for their protection, but there is considerable earlier evidence of domestication, from Roman excavations. A type of medieval siege engine, made of timber and hides and giving protection to soldiers attacking a fortified place, was christened "the cat". A whip with nine lashes, formerly used for punishment in the army and navy, was the "cat-o'-nine-tails".

¶ BURGER, CARL. *All About Cats.* 1967

Catacombs: interconnecting underground passages and galleries, often used in the ancient world for burial purposes. The most extensive (rediscovered 1598)

A catacomb in Rome, showing layered burial places.

were in Rome and consisted of an intricate labyrinth in several storeys. The galleries were 3 to 4 feet [0·9 to 1·2 metres] wide and sometimes opened into halls where numbers of people could gather. They were convenient places of refuge, e.g. during the persecution of the Christians. The catacombs of Rome still exist and parts can be visited.

¶ HERTLING, L. and KIRSCHBAUM, E. *The Roman Catacombs*. 1965

Cataphract: Greek for mail-clad, the heavy cavalryman who was the mainstay of the Byzantine Empire. Recruited from Anatolian farmers, the cataphracts wore chain-mail and carried bow, lance and sword. They dominated the field from AD 378, when Gothic cavalry defeated Roman legionaries, till AD 1258, when they failed before the more mobile Mongols and the better drilled Mamelukes.

Cathay: the name by which, in the Middle Ages, China was known to Europeans; from Khitai, the kingdom of the Khitan Tartars. Marco Polo, who knew the country at first hand (1271–75), limited the name to northern China, calling the southern part Manji. His account can be read in *The Travels of Marco Polo the Venetian*.

¶ STOKES, G. *Marco Polo and Cathay*. 1971

Cathedral: originally the church which contained the *cathedra*, or throne of a bishop. In France such a church was often termed the great or major church, and to this day the cathedral of Marseilles is known as *La Majeure*. In Italy the Latin phrase *Domus Dei*, meaning "the dwelling of God", was used, and for this reason most Italian cathedrals are referred to as the *Duomo*. The earliest Christian bishops travelled about in order to supervise their clergy, but gradually the custom grew of having as the cathedral a church in a fairly large town – principally to protect its treasures within a city wall. It was not until AD 1075 that, following the earlier work of, e.g., Theodore of Tarsus, a council organised English cathedrals and their dioceses, the districts which the bishops ruled in Church matters. Sometimes it was difficult to decide which church should be selected as a cathedral, and occasionally two shared the honour; this is why in England there is a Bishop of Bath and Wells.

A bishop needed an administrative staff to help him rule his diocese and look after the cathedral property. Often the cathedral was also the church of a monastery. In such cases organisation was simple, as the abbot was often also the bishop, and his monastic officials dealt with diocesan matters. Canterbury cathedral was of this type, which is why Thomas Becket was attended by monks. But many cathedrals were never attached to a monastery at all. The cathedral clergy lived near the building, either in separate houses or in one large house, called a college. But they never took monastic vows; they were a community of priests, governed by a set of laws called canons, which were usually drawn up by the bishop. In time, the word "canon" became the title of the clergy who lived under such laws.

These priests had special duties to perform. The bishop was frequently absent visiting parts of his diocese or attending the King's court. While he was away, the Dean ruled the cathedral, arranged services and appointed clergy. The Precentor attended to the choir, the Chancellor was in charge of the cathedral library and school, the Treasurer was responsible for the building and its upkeep and repair. These titles are still used by cathedral officials.

The largest cathedral in the world is St Peter's, Rome, built during the Renaissance and taking a hundred years to complete. It is huge, but so exactly pro-

1. *Above, the façade of St Peter's Rome. Below, Chartres Cathedral.*

2. *Above, Cologne Cathedral from the south. Below, Milan Cathedral, west front.*

3. *Canterbury Cathedral, west front.*

4. *Above, Coventry Cathedral from the east. Below, Washington Cathedral.*

portioned that its size is not obvious. Inlaid bronze strips in its floor show the relative sizes of several other cathedrals, and it is interesting to notice that St Paul's, London, Wren's masterpiece, is the second in area.

The Normans were great builders of churches and cathedrals, and the massive splendour of Durham is roughly contemporary with Palermo, in Sicily, and with Pisa, although the famous leaning tower is of slightly later date.

In France and Germany, Gothic architecture reached its peak, and soared towards heaven with spires, pinnacles, arches and carvings in graceful lines. Cologne and Chartres cathedrals are splendid with stained glass windows of glowing colours, and many Spanish cathedrals housed relics of saints in elaborate shrines, while their walls were adorned with pictures painted by the greatest artists of the time.

Milan cathedral in Italy is the third largest in the world and is the only notable Gothic cathedral in that country. It is an imposing building of white marble, glittering in the sun, with 2,000 statues of saints and martyrs and, on its roof, a forest of slender pinnacles amongst which one can walk. Inside are many paintings and sculptured figures. In the shrine of Carle Borromeo the mummified figure of the 17th-century bishop, gleaming with jewels and cloth of gold, may still be seen in its glass coffin.

Cathedrals, if they possessed relics of saints, became centres of pilgrimage. In England, many flocked to the shrine of St Thomas Becket at Canterbury, and in Spain the shrine of St James of Compostella was another building of renown. It is not easy for us, so accustomed to walls of unadorned stone, to realise the brilliance a medieval cathedral must have presented when its walls were decorated with frescoes and all its statues of saints and angels were painted in vivid colours. In Europe, there are cathedrals which retain much of this colour – at least inside the buildings. But in England the spoliation of monastic houses under Henry VIII, followed by the wholesale destruction of church pictures and statues by the Puritans, has made it normal for a cathedral to be the colour of the local stone.

Cathedrals are not always old buildings. In Liverpool, England, the Anglican Cathedral and the Roman Catholic Cathedral have both been built in the last half-century, while the beautiful new cathedral at Coventry links a very modern style of architecture with the ruins of the medieval one destroyed in an air raid during World War II. The cathedrals of the United States are all of comparatively recent date. In Washington, the cathedral of St Peter and St Paul (1908) is the burial place of many American statesmen, and in New York the remodelled cathedral of St John the Divine, begun in 1892, is still unfinished. The first Anglican cathedral in the USA was that of the Assumption of the Blessed Virgin Mary, Baltimore, 1806–21, though there are older Roman Catholic foundations, e.g. the Cathedral of St Augustine, Florida, built in 1793–97.

¶ OLDENBOURG, Z. *The Horizon Book of Great Cathedrals.* 1969; VALE, EDMUND. *Cathedrals.* 1957

Catherine II, called **"the Great"** (1729–96)**:** Empress of Russia 1762–96. A woman of strong personality – "prepossessing and affable" though, to one observer, with the eyes of a wild beast – she served her country single-mindedly, often working fifteen hours a day. She rebuilt the navy, reformed local government, increased Russian territory, continued the westernisation of the court and St Petersburg, was a brilliant conversationalist, read widely and conducted a correspondence with eminent foreigners such as Voltaire and

Catherine the Great of Russia.

Frederick the Great. Among her buildings was the Hermitage, designed to house her collection of European art treasures and today one of the great museums of the world.

¶ In CANNING, JOHN, editor. *100 Great Lives.* 1969

Cavalier: derived from Latin *caballarius*, a horseman, and in its most general sense any horseman, especially of the knightly class. The name was adopted by the supporters of Charles I of England (1625–49), though it was first used as a term of abuse during the London riots of December 1641, signifying *caballero*, i.e. Spanish trooper, and therefore oppressor of Protestants. Cavaliers included men of widely differing views: great noblemen, gentlemen, artists, poets and men who delighted in ancient customs, united as "men of honour" in complete devotion to King and Church. After 1660, disappointed in their hopes of reward and vengeance, they became fervent supporters of the Church rather than the person of the King. After the rise of Whigs and Tories the name was little used.

Because of his picturesque appearance and dashing horsemanship, the 17-century cavalier has always had a strong attraction for painters and poets. One of the most famous of Frans Hals's pictures is *The Laughing Cavalier*; and Robert Browning's *Cavalier Songs* are another typical example of the cavalier's place in literature.

¶ MURPHY, E. *Cavaliers and Roundheads.* 1965

Cavalry: mounted soldiers. In modern times the term is sometimes applied to motorised units that were formerly horsed.

In early times the use of cavalry was largely dictated by the nature and location of the countries involved. Thus the Romans were comparatively weak in horse soldiers because of the lack of suitable breeds of war-horse readily available to them. The Asiatic tribesmen, however, virtually lived on their horses. A Roman soldier, Ammianus Marcellinus, wrote a vivid account of the Huns from central Asia warming their food by putting it between their thighs and the backs of their horses. "The Huns remain on horseback day and night. . . . They are lightly armed for speed and surprise. . . . Charging in no definite ranks, they rush around dealing out widespread slaughter."

The most effective armies were those in which the foot soldier and cavalry were combined; the former to fight a solid disciplined battle or make firm inroads into hostile territory; the latter to protect the rear, to make forward skirmishes from the main base and to be used as a highly mobile force, thrown in at critical points during a pitched battle.

One of the first to combine successfully the use of both arms was Philip of Macedon (382–336 BC), father of Alexander the Great. Using the phalanx (*see* separate entry) armed with long pikes as the formidable core of his army, he reinforced the infantry with cavalry of three different types, heavily armoured for the assault, lightly armed for scouting work, or able to serve in a double capacity, fighting on horse or on foot as the situation demanded. The usual proportion was one mounted soldier to every six infantrymen.

Other eminently successful early users of cavalry were Alexander the Great and Hannibal. Hannibal crushingly defeated the magnificently disciplined Roman legions at the Trebia (218 BC) and Cannae (216 BC) by virtue of cavalry mobility and the capacity for surprise attack.

In more recent times, one of the greatest exponents of cavalry warfare was Gustavus Adolphus of Sweden (1594–1632) who, though he took the Roman legion as the model for his newly organised armies, insisted on adequate partnership with the cavalry wing. The horse regiments were organised in eight troops of 56 to 72 men. The dragoons carried musket, sword and axe; the cuirassiers sword and wheel-lock pistols. In battle his cavalry were normally marshalled on the flanks. They did some preliminary skirmishing; then, after a heavy artillery barrage, they crashed to the attack, riding knee to knee, on the enemy guns. These they often took over and blasted the enemy with his own artillery. Marlborough and Frederick the Great were other great exponents of the use of cavalry, though the latter, before he reorganised and built up his armies, said "the cavalry is not even worth the devil coming to fetch it away". His recipe for success was: "Move off at the fast trot and charge at the gallop." James Stuart, the famous Southern cavalry leader (better known as "Jeb") in the American Civil War, told his recruits: "Cavalry can *trot* away from anything, and a gallop is a gait unbecoming to a soldier unless he is going towards the enemy. Remember that. We gallop toward the enemy, and trot away, always."

The English cavalryman has not always enjoyed a reputation for reliability, though his courage and dash have not been in question. Wellington once said to the Prince Regent: "The cavalry of other European armies have won victories for their generals but mine have invariably got me into scrapes. It is true that they have always fought ... gallantly and bravely, and have got themselves out of their difficulties by sheer pluck."

There have been few examples of the use of horse soldiers since World War I when, it has been estimated, no less than 100,000 horsemen were assembled at the outset. Command in 1914–18 was still largely in the hands of cavalry generals who worked on the old theory of a thundering cavalry pursuit after infantry and artillery attacks. Even then success was limited and local, and the future held small place for the cavalryman. But he died hard, and its is perhaps fitting that his exploits should be commemorated in such somewhat incongruous terms as "armoured" and "mechanised" cavalry. *See colour section.*

Cave art: the art associated chiefly with the cave-dwellers in western Europe in Upper Palaeolithic times, but embracing cave paintings in North Africa, Australasia and elsewhere. The most commonly found work of art is painting or drawing on the walls or roofs of caves. Of the same date as many of these paintings are the small figurines modelled as the fertility symbol of a pregnant woman – the so-called Aurignacian Venuses. The European paintings date from about 20,000 BC.

Among the first cave paintings to be found were those at Altamira in the Cantabrian Mountains in Spain, though for many years they were held to be fakes. The discovery of others, especially near Les Eyzies in the Dordogne, convinced sceptics that the paintings were genuine, scientific tests in recent times have confirmed this. The most famous discovery was at Lescaux in 1940, and there have been extensive finds in the Sahara since then.

The subject matter of the paintings in France and Spain is very uniform. Most of the paintings are of animals, and the types drawn show the state of the climate at the end of the last Ice Age as well as indicating the animals valued or feared by primitive man. Prominently displayed are bison, mammoths, sabre-toothed tigers, deer and horses. Some very domestic-looking cows also appear. The very few representations of humans are little more than pin-men. The subjects were either incised or painted with hand, finger or stick, using ochre or an oxide of manganese. The uniformity of coloration is another notable feature of cave art, but it is possible to trace successive styles by the change from monochrome to polychrome techniques. Many of these paintings use the natural contours of the walls or roofs to give depth to belly or back or to serve for a leg or tail. Almost all must have been painted virtually in darkness, though remains of primitive lamps have been found.

In North Africa there is the same concentration on the portrayal of animals, and interesting examples show crocodiles and giraffes in places where it would now be impossible for them to live. The best known sites are just south of the Atlas range and in the Hoggar Mountains in the Sahara. The technique most commonly used is that of the outlined figure, but human figures are more realistic and the grouping of animals more sophisticated. Most of these paintings are thought to be of about the same date as those in southern Spain.

The purpose of cave art is far from clear. It may have been purely recreational. However, the general absence of human figures and small animals, and the almost total lack of vegetation, suggests that the cave men were painting what was either useful or dangerous to them. Many of the animals are obviously pregnant, and many paintings suggest hunting scenes. One of the mysteries is why the skill seems suddenly to have vanished. But even if there was some magical or totemic purpose, the sheer love of painting must often have carried the artist away.

¶ MARCUS, REBECCA B. *Prehistoric Cave Paintings.* 1970

Cave man: name usually associated with the cave-dwellers of the late Palaeolithic or Old Stone Age in south-western Europe and North Africa. The caves in Europe are mainly in limestone regions, and the most important of them date from about 20,000 to 10,000 BC. Something is known of the life of cave men from finds of flints, bones and works of art in the caves. Various periods of cave men are distinguished by names drawn from the centres in which remains were found – Mousterian, Aurignacian, Gravettian, Magdalenian. The eventual abandonment of the caves came probably with the final retreat of the last Ice Age.

¶ HOWELL, F. CLARK. *Early Man.* 1969

Cecil, William, Baron Burleigh (1520–98): English statesmen. He was the son of Richard Cecil, a courtier of Henry VIII's reign and owner of extensive lands including Burleigh, near Stamford, Lincolnshire. He was educated at Stamford Grammar School, St John's College, Cambridge, and Gray's Inn. His second wife, Mildred Cooke, was a very highly educated woman and daughter of Edward VI's governor, and their son Robert was to follow his father as Elizabeth's adviser.

In 1547 William Cecil became one of the Protector Somerset's secretaries and, on Somerset's fall from power, spent two months as a prisoner in the Tower in 1550. On his release he was appointed Secretary of State by the Duke of Northumberland. Under Mary, he was a conforming Roman Catholic but kept in close touch with Princess Elizabeth, on whose accession in 1558 he became Principal Secretary of State and in 1572 Lord Treasurer.

For forty years he was Elizabeth's chief adviser, and an American historian has said that his great achievement was the management of her. His policy was always one of moderation; for example, he strongly supported the Anglican Church settlement carried out by Archbishop Parker and opposed Archbishop Whitgift's attack on the Puritans. He wanted a policy of peace abroad, but when the Spanish Armada was imminent he was wholehearted in preparations for national defence. He advocated the expansion of trade and housed Flemish weavers on his property at Stamford. To Mary Queen of Scots he was an implacable enemy, because the plots in her favour threatened Elizabeth's life. He did indeed justify Elizabeth's words to him on her accession: "this judgement I have of you, that you will be faithful to the state and .... will give me that counsel which you think best". He was among the greatest of English statesmen. The Bodleian Library at Oxford contains a charming picture of him on "his little mule" on which he rejoiced to "ride privately in his garden".

Celts: an early people speaking the Celtic language. According to Herodotus (*c.* 450 BC) they lived in the Pyrenees. They were "barbarians" to the Greeks, and "Gauls with long hair" to the Romans. Their names suggest an Indo-European connection. They spread successively from south-west Germany to France, Spain and Britain; and later invaders reached through Europe as far as Asia Minor. Conquest and absorption by the Romans and barbarian tribes led to their loss of identity, until only Brittany and parts of the British Isles ("the Celtic fringe") remained predominantly Celtic.

¶ LINDSAY, JACK. *Our Celtic Heritage.* 1962; ROSS, ANNE. *Everyday Life of the Pagan Celts.* 1970

Censorship: the control or suppression of literature, films, etc., thought to be politically or morally undesirable. The "censor" was a Roman official whose duty was to supervise public behaviour. In time this work of censorship grew to cover official control over newspapers, books, plays and films. At various times in history anything which the ruler or the government thought was unsuitable for people to read or to see was banned. Pictures or books could be censored, either by being suppressed entirely or by having the offending parts cut out. In time of war, newspapers and letters are censored in case useful information is discovered by the enemy.

Today the amount of censorship varies

greatly from country to country. In Britain there is little censorship of books or the stage, and films are censored by the industry itself. Newspapers, too, exercise a good deal of voluntary censorship. In the Republic of Ireland there is much closer censorship, whilst in the USSR and in dictatorships such as Spain and Portugal the censorship is very strict indeed, in contrast with the complete freedom of Denmark and Sweden. In some states of the USA, almost anything can now be printed or seen on the stage. The idea that adults should decide for themselves what they shall read or see, without interference from a censor, is growing in the USA and Europe, but it is still generally felt that children should be protected from undesirable reading matter, and films.

Census: an official counting of a country's population, etc.

In the Old Testament we read of two "numberings of the people", the first ordered by Moses to ascertain the number of fighting men, and the second taken by David. The latter was followed by a pestilence, which perhaps gave rise to a long-standing superstition that a census was unlucky. Further, as all early censuses were directed to finding out those liable either to taxation or military service, and evasion or incorrect information was in the individual's personal interests, results were invariably inaccurate.

The word census is derived from the declaration, made every five years by every Roman citizen before two censors, of the name and age of himself and his wife and the number of his children and slaves. Livy tells us that the record also included the amount of his debts and the names of his creditors.

The great Domesday survey of 1086 in England was also dictated by fiscal motives. It is incomplete, since it omits the four northern shires and a number of towns, including Winchester and London.

The modern conception of a census as a complete count of all the people arose gradually during the 17th and 18th centuries. The United States took its first census in 1790, France in 1800 and England in 1801, followed by other countries at an increasing rate. The United Nations instigated a world census in 1950, and 150 countries collected data on more than 2,000 million persons.

Cervantes, Miguel de (1547–1616): Spanish writer whose best-known creation is Don Quixote de la Mancha, a parody of the knight-errant of chivalry. For many years Cervantes served as a soldier; he was wounded at the sea battle of Lepanto (*see* separate entry). In 1575 he was captured by Barbary pirates and for five years was held as a galley slave.

¶In THOMAS, H. and D. L. *Famous Novelists.* 1959

Chain shot.

Chain shot: cannon balls connected by a short length of chain. Introduced in the 17th century, chain shot could be used effectively in close range sea fights. When fired at the rigging of enemy ships, it worked considerable havoc and much reduced their speed and manoeuvrability.

Champion: literally, one who takes the field, or fights (Latin *campus*, field). In early times a champion was one who took the place of another who could not fight by reason of age or infirmity, or was exempted for some other special reason.

In England there was a special office of King's Champion for many centuries. His chief duty was to ride fully armed into the hall during the coronation feast and challenge to single combat anyone who disputed the right of succession. The ceremony was last carried out at the coronation of George IV.

Chancellor: an official title used by most peoples whose civilisation arose from the Roman Empire. It is associated with various duties and does not indicate any particular rank or dignity. The original chancellors were the *cancellarii*, or ushers of Roman courts of justice, who sat at the lattice-work screens or *cancelli* in the law courts.

In England the office of chancellor dates back to the reign of Edward the Confessor (1042–66). The chancellor was then an ecclesiastic who combined the functions of royal chaplain, king's secretary and keeper of the royal seal. The position of the Lord High Chancellor (to give him his full title) as Speaker of the House of Lords originated when the members of the royal Council customarily formed part of the parliament. Additionally the Lord Chancellor holds supreme judicial office, ranking above the Lord Chief Justice The title of chancellor without the predicates "High" or "Lord" is also applied in England to a number of other officials. Of these the most important is the Chancellor of the Exchequer, whose office was of little importance until the 19th century, but who is now Minister of Finance and one of the most influential members of the Cabinet. The title of chancellor is also given to the heads of English universities.

In Germany the title of *Erzkanzler*, or arch-chancellor, was borne by the Archbishop of Mainz and remained a reality until 1806, when the rank was abolished. In the German Empire of 1871–1918 the *Reichskanzler* was the Emperor's prime minister, directing foreign policy and superintending the internal affairs of the Empire. In the Austrian Empire the title was used in the same way, having its origin in the days of the Holy Roman Empire. Nowadays the federal prime ministers of West Germany and of Austria both hold the title of chancellor.

Charlemagne, Carolus Magnus, Charles the Great, Charles I of France (*c.* 742–814)**:** Emperor of the West. As soldier, statesman, champion of Christendom and patron of learning and education, he is one of the outstanding figures of history. Son of Pépin le Bref, on his father's death in 768 he became King of Austria and Neustria, his birthplace, and, on his brother Carloman's death in 771, of the whole Frankish kingdom. He fought many tribes until eventually his empire was bounded by the North Sea, the Elbe, Bohemia, the Garigliano in Southern Italy, the Ebro, the Pyrenees and the Atlantic. Ironically, amid so many great conquests one of Charlemagne's chief claims to remembrance is the largely legendary story of his fight against the infidels in 778 in the Pass of Roncevaux in the Pyrenees, when his nephew, the Paladin Roland, was killed – the theme of one of the most famous of the *chansons de* *geste*, epic poems which were among the earliest masterpieces of French literature.

Charlemagne had the ability to consolidate his empire, which he achieved by a system of assemblies and envoys with whom he kept in personal touch, by his code of laws and by the reform of justice. A devout Christian, he had the support of the Church, and on Christmas Day 800 was crowned Emperor by Pope Leo III. He thus became the founder of the Holy Roman Empire (*see* separate entry) and personified the revived conception of the Roman Empire in the west; from this derived the idea of a united Europe which has been repeated in various forms until our own time.

Charlemagne realised the importance of literacy and learning. His patronage of education and the arts was concerned less with creative work than with rediscovering and preserving what had been lost during years of barbarism. He introduced scholars to his court, including Alcuin from Northumberland and the French chronicler Einhard, who became his secretary and biographer. He founded schools, decreed that clergy and officials should be literate and encouraged the collection and preservation of books. In 1165 Charlemagne was canonised. He is the patron saint of the French education system, and his feast day, 28 January, is an annual school holiday.

Although remembered as Charles I of France, Charlemagne has been claimed as a national hero by both France and Germany, despite the fact that neither of these units had taken separate shape in his day. His capital was Aix-la-Chapelle, or Aachen, a city which, although more often German, has been from time to time in French hands. He was buried in its cathedral and a fine equestrian statue stands to his memory.

Unfortunately, Charlemagne's achievements did not long survive him. It was still for the Capetians (*see* CAPET) to establish the principle of hereditary monarchy. Charlemagne's successors were weak by comparison and in 843, on the death of his son, the empire was divided among his three gandsons. Yet Charlemagne had played an essential part in reviving the Roman conception of empire and its traditions and principles, with the added ideal of a united Christendom.

¶ In CANNING, JOHN, editor. *100 Great Lives.* 1969

Charles V (1500–58): King of Spain as Charles I, 1516–56, and Holy Roman Emperor, 1519–58. He ruled an empire which included the Netherlands, inherited from his father; Spain, the Spanish Netherlands, Naples, Sicily and the New World from his maternal grandfather Ferdinand; and the hereditary Habsburg lands from his paternal grandfather Maximilian I. In 1519 he was elected emperor. His problems have been described as "communications, heresy and debt". Worn out by attacks from outside and internal dissensions, Charles abdicated the empire to his brother Ferdinand I and his other lands to his son Philip II. He died in the little house to which he had retired, attached to the monastery at Yuste in Spain.

¶ GRANT, N. *Charles V.* 1970

Chart: map of a sea or ocean area specially prepared to meet the navigational requirements of seamen. The portulan chart is the oldest form and was designed for navigation by dead reckoning, i.e. estimated distance and compass direction sailed. Hand drawn and coloured on sheepskin, the portulan was plotted by measuring the magnetic bearings of, and courses between, coastal features, and estimating from a ship their distances apart. It gave the outline of a coast with place names written inland, a scale of distance and a radical network of direction or rhumb lines. The oldest surviving example dates from *c.* AD 1290.

In the 16th century navigators made long oceanic passages using plane (i.e. flat) charts based on latitude observations, estimated distances and true bearings (bearings corrected for magnetic variation) to enable them to navigate with the aid of nautical astronomy. In higher latitudes the curvature of the earth's surface made the plane chart very inaccurate over large areas. In 1569 Gerhard Mercator (1512–94) devised the so-called Mercator projection, which enabled courses and distances to be measured correctly. Edward Wright (1558–1615) gave the first mathematical explanation of this form of chart construction in 1599.

Further progress was made in 1615 when the Dutch mathematician Snellius first measured the length of a degree of latitude. The determination of longitude at sea to within about 130 miles [210 kilometres] was achieved with the lunar distance method developed by the Royal Observatory, Greenwich, England, and made practicable for seamen by the publication, annually from 1767, of the Nautical Almanac. With the concurrent development of the marine chronometer and the successful use of one by Captain James Cook on his second voyage (1772–75) longitude determination at sea by this method, to within a very few miles, also became practicable. The chronometer (*see* HARRISON, JOHN) enabled him to produce unprecedentedly accurate charts. The first charts illustrating compass variations were published in the first half of the 17th century.

In the late 18th century it became imperative to produce charts of uniform standards of accuracy for greater safety at sea. A French hydrographic service was established in 1720, and the Hydrographic Service of the British Royal Navy in 1795. From that date, uniformly accurate charts gradually became available on sale to sea-

World portulan, by Verrazzano, c. 1529.

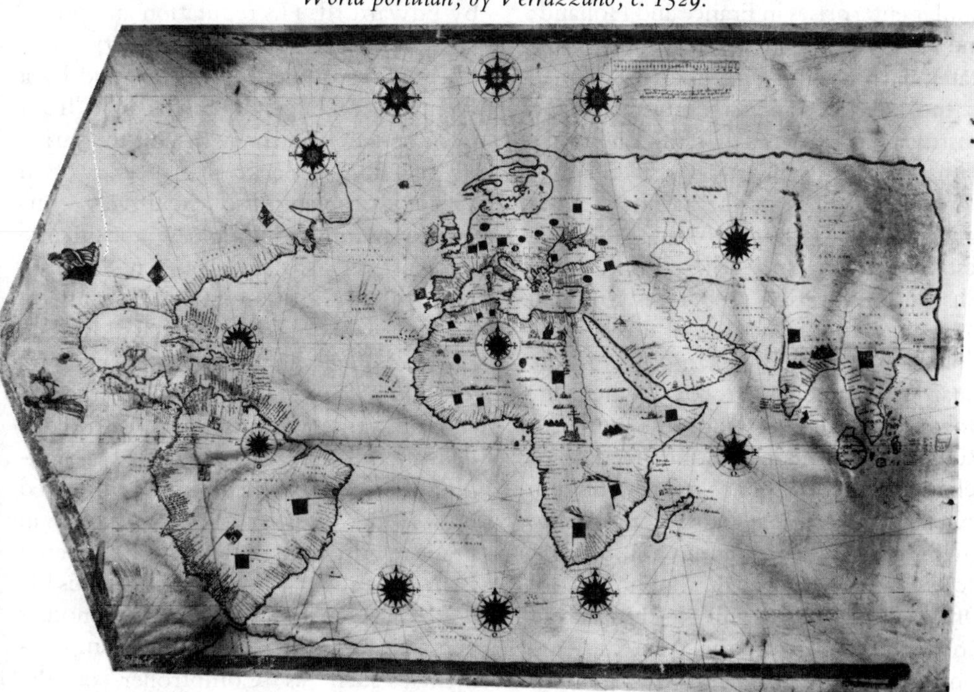

men of all nations.

British charts acquired an unquestioned reputation, which was one of the main reasons for the selection of the British Meridian at Greenwich as the Prime Meridian of the world at an international conference held at Washington in 1884. This move facilitated the production of uniformly accurate charts for the world.

Modern charts, in addition to features already mentioned, give other detailed information, such as the strength and direction of currents, magnetic variation, navigation marks and lights, and areas covered by radio and radar beacons.

Charter: written document granting, or confirming, status, rights and privileges. Sometimes charters were granted to boroughs, universities, guilds and religious foundations by the sovereign or other overlord; sometimes to trading companies, such as the Merchant Adventurers, the East India Company, the Hudsón's Bay Company, and various similar enterprises in France and Holland; and sometimes the term was applied to a statement of rights and liberties claimed in the face of oppressive authority and misrule. The classic case in English history is that of Magna Carta (Great Charter) drawn up in 1215 by the barons of King John; though, to some extent, this was a restatement of an earlier charter, the Charter of Liberties (1100) re-establishing in Henry I's reign the laws of Edward the Confessor. Another example was the Charter of Majesty (1608), when the Bohemians secured from the emperor Rudolf a document ensuring freedom of religious worship. The greatest English collection of original charters granted to towns, universities, religious houses, fairs, etc., is to be found at the Public Record Office, London, especially in the Charter Rolls, running from the time of King John to that of Henry VIII.

The most momentous "charter" of modern times was that of the United Nations, formulated at the 1945 Conference of the Great Powers at San Francisco. The charter, signed by fifty nations, laid down the prime responsibilities of the United Nations Organisation as the maintenance of world peace and security and the promotion of co-operation in all matters economic, social and cultural.

Chaucer, Geoffrey (1340?–1400): English poet. There is a painted portrait of him in a near-contemporary manuscript by the poet Occleve, inserted "to remind other men of his personal appearance"; and this fits with the word-portrait Chaucer drew of himself in the *Canterbury Tales (The Rime of Sir Thopas)*, where the innkeeper describes him as "small and fair of face", with "something elfish in his countenance" and "a beard the colour of ripe wheat".

As a young man he served in the French wars, was taken prisoner and ransomed by Edward III. His reputation and popularity rest largely on the *Canterbury Tales*, a sequence of tales supposedly told by a company of pilgrims on the road from London to Canterbury to visit the shrine of St Thomas Becket. Chaucer is often accused of being too exclusively concerned with the knightly and gentle sections of society, but he shows, nevertheless, a humour and warmth of humanity that make him much more than the poet of chivalry and the upper classes. His width of interests is shown by the fact that he wrote a treatise on the astrolabe, dedicated to "little Lewis", his ten-year-old son. He was also a diplomat employed on several missions of importance in France and Flanders. Though he suffered periods of adverse fortune, most of his life was passed in the enjoyment of modest pensions and in comfortable employments, such as Comptroller of the

Customs of the Port of London and royal Clerk of the Works. *See colour section.*

¶ STANLEY-WRENCH, MARGARET. *Chaucer: Teller of Tales.* 1967

Chess: one of the most ancient of indoor games, from *shâh*, a Persian word for "king" – the principal (though least powerful) piece on the board. The object of the game, played by two players, each with sixteen pieces on a chequered board, is to drive the king into such a position that he cannot escape capture, when "checkmate" or *shâh mât* ("the king is dead") is called. The origins of chess are lost in antiquity but, amidst many rival claims, the weight of evidence suggests that they may be found in India in the 6th or 7th century AD.

Chiang Kai-shek (1887–1975)**:** Chinese general and former president of China at the head of the Nationalist government. After the death of Sun Yat-sen in 1925, Chiang Kai-shek emerged as leader of the Kuomintang. His subsequent drive against the Communists, headed by Mao Tse-tung, failed. The Kuomintang forces were expelled from the mainland of China in 1949 and Chiang Kai-shek withdrew to obscure exile in Formosa. His wife occupied the limelight for a period as propagandist and fund-raiser for her husband, travelling far outside China. *See also* CHINA, KUOMINTANG, MAO TSE-TUNG, SUN YAT-SEN.

Generalissimo and Madame Chiang Kai-shek.

Chicago: third largest city of the USA situated at the south end of Lake Michigan. It takes its name from the Chicago river, an Indian word which perhaps comes from *she-kag-ong*, "wild onion place". It was visited by the French in 1673 and in 1804 became the site of a US fort, Fort Dearborn, which was captured by Indians in 1812 and finally abandoned in 1837. From being a mere village in 1830, Chicago achieved city status in the next decade. The most disastrous event in its subsequent history was the fire of 8–9 October 1871, which made 100,000

Marina City, Chicago.

people homeless. Chicago subsequently gained an unenviable reputation as a centre of labour troubles and, later, of ruthless gangster activities in connection with the illegal liquor trade during the years of prohibition. The city has always been a popular convention centre and has seen the making of a great deal of political history, including the nomination of Lincoln for President (1860). It is the chief railway centre of the USA and supports many industries, of which meat-packing is the largest. Chicago airport is the busiest in the world.

¶ WAGENKNECHT, E. *Chicago.* ★1967

China: country of central and east Asia, with an area of 3,691,521 square miles (9,561,000 square kilometres) and an estimated population of one billion in 1983. Historically the Chinese border has remained south of the mountain ranges that form the boundaries of the grass steppes of Mongolia. The southern boundary has been less distinct, and it has moved with the slow expansion of the Chinese cultural area. The main cultural division is provided by the mountains running north to south, the eastern extensions of the Himalayas, with the highland and lowland Chinese considering themselves quite distinct.

The earliest evidence of human activity comes from the so-called Peking man, found at Chou k'ou Tien, 26 miles [42 kilometres] south of Peking. Archaeologists date him at 500,000 years ago. Late Neolithic sites in China are numerous and show a gradual development, the village of Yang Shao being an important site.

The Chinese have numerous and uncertain myths concerning their early kings of the Hsia Dynasty, 2205–1766 BC; but for the Chang kings there is definite archaeological evidence at Anyang in North Honan, which was their ancient capital. These men used bronze, burned their dead with care and prophesied the future from the crack lines on burned bones. They ruled from 1766–1122 BC, to be followed by the Chou Dynasty, 1122–221 BC, whose written records enable historians to be much more exact.

The Chou organisation was feudal and without great central authority. Consequently China gradually deteriorated into a pattern of warring states, with little political stability, lasting from 481–221 BC. It was similar and almost coexistent with the state of anarchy in Greece and also produced its great philosophers, e.g. Confucius (550–480 BC) and Mencius (372–289 BC).

In 221 BC the powerful Shih-Huang Ti became Emperor and attempted to destroy the social and political system of ancient China. He burned as many classical books as possible. He completed the Great Wall by joining the stretches already built and extended it to 1,400 miles [2,250 kilometres] (*see* next entry). Shih-Huang Ti was succeeded by Lui Pang, the founder of the Han Dynasty, whose rulers created the first centralised Chinese state. The Han Empire lasted until AD 189, when it disintegrated, but before that time it had already been weakened by continuous plotting over the succession among the important Palace eunuchs. At the same time China was subjected to a succession of barbarian invasions and not until AD 618 did another unified administration emerge, this time under the Tang Dynasty.

Li Shih-min, the founder, had the advantage of noble birth – a deficiency that had caused considerable difficulty to the Han emperors. It has been said that the twenty-two years of his reign form the most wonderful era of Chinese history, a brilliant period of domestic reform, of encouragement of learning, of military and political skill, under a ruler who seems to have combined tolerance and mercy with a wide-ranging genius for government and who, amidst a coterie of able men around him, outstripped them all in ability. The Tang Dynasty survived until the 10th century, when provincial rebellions weakened central control, culminating in the abduction of the Emperor. AD 907–960 were years of chaos until a general, Chao Kuang-yin, founded the Sung Dynasty, which exerted political rather than military control over China.

In AD 1124 North China was overrun by the Nuchens, a nomadic tribe who in turn were overrun in 1210 by the Mongols under Genghis Khan. Their campaign of 1224 left North China desolate and devas-

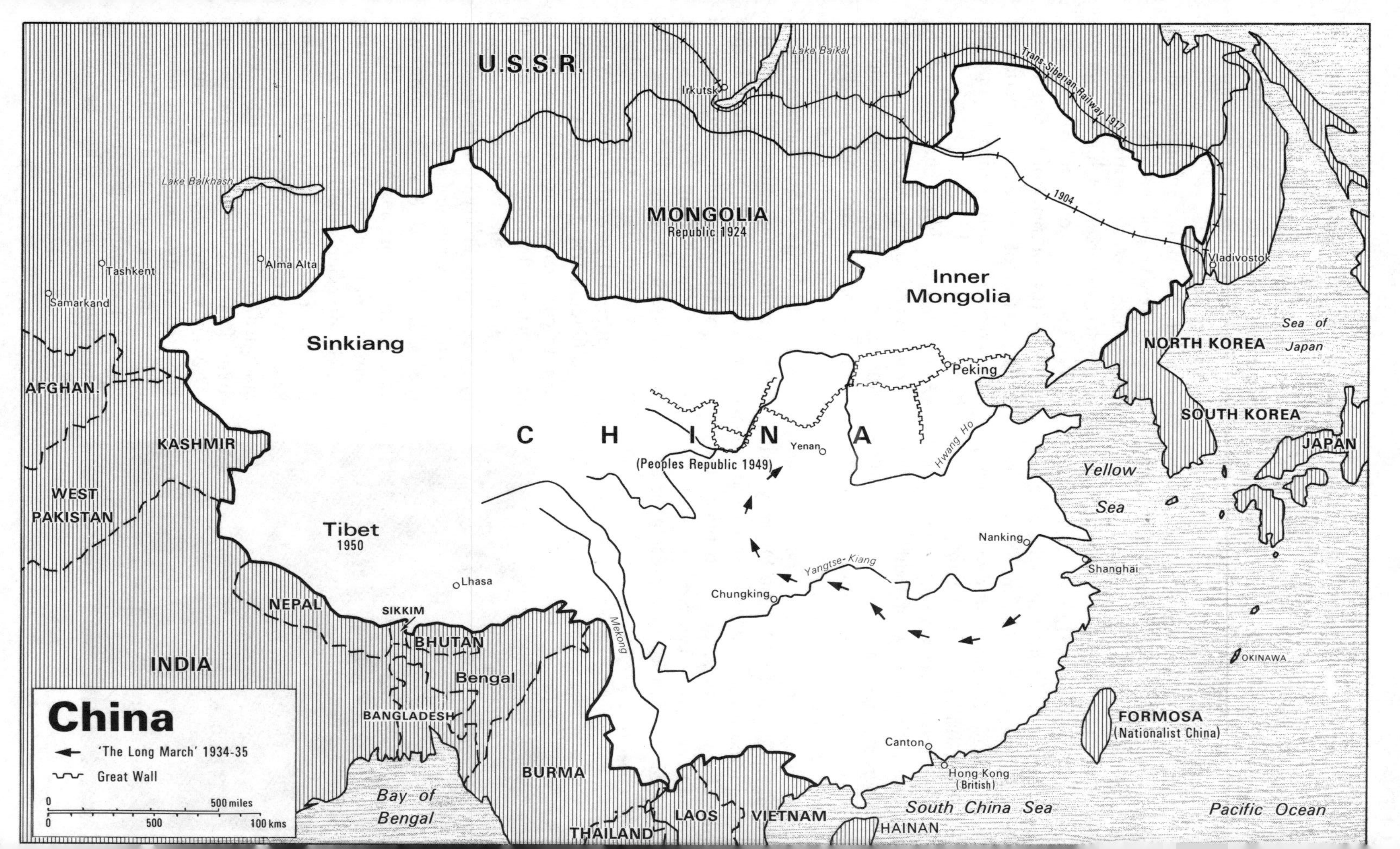

China
'The Long March' 1934-35
Great Wall
0
500 miles
0
500
100 kms
U.S.S.R.
Lake Baikal
Irkutsk
Trans-Siberian Railway 1917
1904
Vladivostok
Lake Balkhash
MONGOLIA
Republic 1924
Inner
Mongolia
Tashkent
Alma Alta
Samarkand
Sinkiang
AFGHAN.
KASHMIR
WEST
PAKISTAN
Tibet
1950
Lhasa
NEPAL
SIKKIM
BHUTAN
INDIA
Bengal
BANGLADESH
BURMA
Bay of
Bengal
THAILAND
LAOS
VIETNAM
HAINAN
C H I N A
(Peoples Republic 1949)
Yenan
Peking
Hwang Ho
Nanking
Shanghai
Yangtse-Kiang
Chungking
Mekong
Canton
Hong Kong
(British)
South China Sea
Pacific Ocean
FORMOSA
(Nationalist China)
OKINAWA
Yellow
Sea
NORTH KOREA
SOUTH KOREA
JAPAN
Sea of
Japan

tated. They would have destroyed the whole of China but for the advice to tax rather than kill the Chinese. The new Mongol Dynasty founded Peking in 1263, and their authority lasted till the mid-14th century.

The Ming Dynasty was founded by Chu Yüan-chang, a poor peasant who became a bandit chieftain and gradually overcame his rivals. He attacked the Mongols and extended the Chinese Empire further than ever before to include the whole of the Manchurian region. As Chu Yüan-chang had no state, he called his dynasty Ming, meaning brilliant. During this dynasty, the first trading relationships were established with the West, although the Portuguese left a very unfavourable memory and the nickname of "ocean devils" for Europeans in general.

By 1644 the Ming Dynasty had weakened and the Manchu Dynasty had conquered the provinces to the north of the Great Wall. A quarrel between the bandit emperor Tzu Ch'eng and his general Wu San-kuei over a singing girl

The Great Wall of China, near Peking.

resulted in the general inviting the Manchus into China in 1644. North China accepted them readily, but the South was conquered only after considerable fighting. This difference had important consequences later on.

In the 19th century Europeans adopted more aggressive policies towards China. In 1840 and 1860 the British fought two wars solely to force the Chinese importation of opium to continue. Also in 1860, the Sino-Russian treaty of Peking recognised the fact of Russian occupation of large areas of North China beyond the River Amur.

Amid the crumbling authority of the Manchus and foreign intrusions, Chinese nationalism began to develop; typified by the rebellion in 1900 organised by the anti-foreign secret society known as the Boxers, and the rise of Sun Yat-sen's party, the Kuomintang, meaning "the nationalist people's party". In 1911 the Manchus were overthrown but, for political reasons, General Yuan Shi-kai and not Sun Yat-sen became President. This produced a reversion to rule by war lords with large and powerful armies occupying different parts of the country. Popular resentment against foreigners was fed by the Japanese Twenty-one Demands in 1915, and by the neglect of Chinese interests in the Treaty of Versailles.

In 1921 the Chinese Communist Party was founded, and Mao Tse-tung was among its members. Moscow advised them to co-operate with the Kuomintang which, after Sun's death in 1924, was led by Chiang Kai-shek. But in 1927 Chiang Kai-shek turned on the Communists in Shanghai, killing an estimated 6,000 of them. Defeated, they withdrew to form a Soviet in the Chingkang mountains. The Red Army, formed from peasants and vagrants, was successful until Chiang's encirclement campaigns made Chingkang-Shan untenable. Thus began the epic struggle of the long march of 1934–35 to Yenan in North China. They crossed eighteen mountain ranges, twenty-four rivers and twelve provinces, capturing sixty-two cities on their route, but only a fraction of the original number survived. From Yenan, the Communists began to recover. They led the struggle against Japan during World War II and, finally overcoming Chiang Kai-shek in 1949, founded the People's Republic.

Two five-year plans, 1953–57 and 1959–62, have brought about rapid economic recovery. Mao Tse-tung, the political theorist and poet who had been chairman of the Communist Party (1943–76) launched the Cultural Revolution in 1966.

Chairman Mao died in 1976 and in the following years, China relaxed some of her policies towards the West. In 1979 China and the USA established formal diplomatic relations ending 30 years of overt hostility. By the 1980s China was slowly opening her doors to trade with western nations and was seeking increased western technology as she gave top priority to modernising her industry.

China, Great Wall of: defensive fortification running for about 1,500 miles [2,415 kilometres] from T'sin in the west across to the north-eastern sea. Average measurements are height 22 feet and width 20 feet, with 40-foot-high towers about every 100 yards [height 6·7 metres, width 6·1 metres, towers 12·2 metres, distance *c.* 91·4 metres]. Built largely by exiled criminals in the reign of Shih-Huang Ti (221–209 BC) and much restored during the Ming Dynasty (AD 1368–1644), every stone is reputed to have cost a human life.

Chivalry: in a limited sense, the knightly ranks of an army, e.g. the chivalry of Spain or France; in its wider meaning, the knightly system of the Middle Ages and the code of behaviour that controlled it. Though chiefly concerned with one class of society, the code of chivalric conduct, represented genuine aspiration to the brotherhood of all Christendom and to Christian conduct in military terms.

While there were never generally accepted rules, such as those prescribed for formally constituted Orders of Knights, there were certain common features which led a French scholar, Leon Gautier, to formulate the Decalogue, or Ten Com-

Robing a knight, a 13th-century ceremony.

mandments, of knighthood. The knight was first of all a Christian soldier, with unswerving faith in the Church; he must resolutely defend that Church; he must faithfully obey his feudal lord so long as that obedience did not conflict with allegiance to the Church; he must love his country; he must maintain unrelenting war against the enemies of Christendom; he must never retreat from the enemy; he must keep his pledged word; he must be generous in giving; he must show pity for the weak and steadfastness in their defence; he must at all times champion the good against the forces of evil.

Many men, in many countries, have amply demonstrated some of these virtues. A few have so embodied all the highest knightly qualities that their names have survived as exemplars. The Chevalier Bayard (Pierre du Terrail, Seigneur de Bayard, *c.* 1474–1524) has come down to us as the knight "sans peur et sans reproche" (without fear and without blame).

¶ BARBER, RICHARD. *The Knight and Chivalry*. 1971; UDEN, GRANT. *A Dictionary of Chivalry*. 1968

Christendom: the *Corpus Christianum* or ideal of a Christian society. Even in Shakespeare's day the term "Christendom" had become a geographical expression. In *Henry IV, Part I*, Hotspur says he would rather live on "cheese and garlic in a windmill" than endure Glendower's conversation "in any summer-house in Christendom". James I was described as "the wisest fool in Christendom". In this sense, Christendom is the Christian domain or habitat. To many devout souls in the Middle Ages it meant far more. It implied the ideal of a truly Christian society, with the Pope representing the spiritual authority and the Emperor the temporal authority, and Christ ruling over all.

Christianity: the religion of those who follow Jesus Christ and accept his teachings. "And the disciples were called Christians first at Antioch," wrote St Luke in the Acts of the Apostles. Before that, they were the brethren, the disciples, the believers, members of a small, persecuted Jewish sect centred in Jerusalem, inspired by the life and death and resurrection of Jesus of Nazareth and convinced that he was the promised Messiah, the Christ (from the Greek word meaning the anointed one) whose coming had been foretold in the Scriptures.

The early Christians at Antioch, in Syria, were mainly Gentiles (non-Jewish). It was to Antioch that St Barnabas summoned St Paul, who was to become the great Apostle to the Gentiles, and it was from Antioch that St Barnabas and St Paul transformed Christianity from a Jewish sect into a world religion.

Christianity spread rapidly as the early missionaries travelled along the excellent military roads of the Roman Empire into every Mediterranean country and beyond. Persecution could not quench it. The Christians would not acknowledge the existence of any of the multiplicity of gods who swarmed in the ancient world, nor would they offer divine honours to the Emperor. This gave them spiritual freedom and a fearless conviction that nothing could separate them from the love of God.

The Emperor Constantine the Great (*c.* 280–337) favoured Christianity, and eventually it became the religion of the state. Freed from persecution, it lost some of its vigour – "the blood of the martyrs is the seed of the Church" (Tertullian, 192–220) – and, allied with secular power, it lost some of its purity. But during the decline of the Roman Empire, the chaos of the barbarian invasions and the onset of the Dark Ages, it survived and, with it, civilisation.

The early Christian communities were ruled by *episcopoi* (overseers, now translated bishops), *presbyteroi* (elders, now translated presbyters or priests) and *diaconoi* (servants, now translated deacons). Some claim that their authority can be traced back to the days of the apostles, with St Peter as the first *episcopos*, or Head of the Church, in Rome: others think that the organisation developed later. would agree on a *spiritual* apostolic succession, which has survived unbroken from the days of the apostles until now.

Christianity has always been a missionary faith. The division of the Roman Empire into two parts, a Western, Latin-speaking part, dominated by Rome, and an Eastern, Greek-speaking half, dominated by Constantinople (or Byzantium), was reflected (and still is) in the development of the Christian Church, but the missionary tradition survived in both. The greatest expansion of Christianity, however, came eventually from the West.

Western Europe, overrun by barbarians, had to be reconverted. Though Rome was an important centre for missionary effort, another was Ireland, unconquered by Rome but early won to Christianity. The northern part of Britain was converted by missionaries from the Celtic Church in Ireland centred in Iona, the southern part by Rome, notably by St Augustine (d. 604), who was sent by Pope Gregory the Great (540–604). Though the influence of Rome eventually predominated, much that is best in Christianity in Britain is derived from the Celtic Church.

Christianity is not only a religious faith, it is a way of life. The early Christians spoke of *the Way*, and when Paul set off for Damascus before his conversion he asked for the necessary authority so that "if he found any of this way, whether they were men or women, he might bring them bound into Jerusalem" (Acts 9:2). Later, many felt they could not live their faith in the world, so they withdrew from it into communities where they accepted a disciplined life. Rules for these communities were set up by St Basil (330–379) in the Eastern Church and by St Benedict (480–550) in the Western Church, and thus the monastic orders developed. At their best, the monasteries became centres of piety, charity, learning, education, art and enlightenment.

Christianity was, and still is, constantly threatened from without and from within. The fall of the Roman Empire, the successive barbarian invasions and the rise of Islam (*see* separate entry) all seemed to spell disaster in the early days; the divisions within the Christian Church and the intolerance and violence of many so-called Christians were a constant and recurring threat. But always there have been saints and leaders to uphold the purity of the Christian Gospel and inspire others to return to it and to live by it.

Towards the close of the Middle Ages, efforts were made to reform the Western Church. Many abuses had crept in: high positions were held by men who sought wealth or power and had no aspirations towards purity of life or uprightness of conduct; there were scandals in some of the monasteries; the friars, vowed to a life of poverty and service, were accused by Chaucer (*see* separate entry) of preaching only "for profit of their bellies"; simony (the buying and selling of offices in the Church) was rife; and so-called "pardoners" made money from the sale of indulgences (forgiveness of sins) and spurious relics. The Prologue to Chaucer's *Canterbury Tales* gives a vivid picture of decadent churchmen, though it does not overlook the humble parson who "dwelte at hoom and kepte wel his folde":

But Cristes lore, and his apostles twelve,
He taughte, and first he folwed it
himselve.

The Christian symbols of the cross and fish, known as the Ichthus, cut in stone.

Some wanted to reform the Church from within; others attacked it from outside. The Lollards in England, inspired by John Wyclif (1329–84), and the Hussites in what is now Czechoslovakia, led by John Huss, martyr (1369–1415), heralded a movement which broke in full force upon Europe when Martin Luther (1483–1546) nailed his famous theses to the door of the church at Wittenburg. The Protestant Reformation resulted in the establishment of Reformed Churches in many of the north-western countries in Europe. John Calvin (1509–64) took the reforms a stage further; his strict "theocratic" rule in Geneva attracted exiles from other lands, influencing John Knox (1513–72) and the Scottish Reformation, the Huguenots in France, the reformed church in the Netherlands, and the Puritan sects in England.

Protestants and Puritans alike rejected the authority of the Pope. In England the King, Henry VIII (1491–1547), became Head of the Church, not without opposition from courageous and devout men, including the Lord Chancellor, St Thomas More (1478–1535), and the Bishop of Rochester, St John Fisher (1469–1535), both of whom suffered death on the scaffold rather than submit. Under Henry's successors, England swayed first towards Puritanism and then back to Roman Catholicism; the situation was stabilised under his daughter, Elizabeth I, whose *via media* (middle way) established the Anglican Church. The persecuted Puritan sects struggled for power and eventually gained it through the Civil War, which overthrew the monarchy and established a Commonwealth under Oliver Cromwell (1599–1658). This proved as intolerant as the previous regime – "Everyone desires to have liberty but none will give it!" said Cromwell accusingly to his ministers. After the Restoration (1660) the Anglican Church was restored and in 1689 the Toleration Act was passed, though there were still major exclusions, such as Roman Catholics and Unitarians.

Though the history of the Reformation and what followed is marred by intolerance, political intrigue and oppression, it brought new life and vigour to Christianity. Many of the Protestant and nonconformist churches and sects spring from this time; others developed later, and each in turn brought a distinctive contribution to the Christian Church. The geographical expansion which accompanied the age of discovery and the subsequent age of colonisation resulted in a tremendous expansion of the sphere of Christianity, which now embraced the whole world.

In many countries during the 19th century a rethinking of the Christian message resulted in an awakening of the social conscience, which was expressed eventually in practical measures of social reform, though the Christian ideal is far from being achieved. In recent years the Christian faith has been challenged by two world wars, by intolerant dictatorships, by industrial unrest, by violence, by scientific scepticism, by indifference and by the threat of world destruction. Many believe that these show the consequences of allowing scientific and technological development to outrun mankind's spiritual growth.

In an age of materialism on the one hand, and fear and insecurity on the other, Christians have been drawn closer to one another, and the modern ecumenical movement has brought a measure of spiritual unity into the diversity of the sects and churches.

¶ HOARE, ROBERT J. and HEUSER, ADOLF. *Christ Through the Ages*. Vols. 1 & 2. 1966; SELBY-LOWNDES, JOAN. *Your Book of the English Church*. 1963; YOUNGMAN, BERNARD R. *Into All the World: the story of Christianity to 1066 AD*. 1963

Christina (1626–89): Queen of Sweden 1644–54. Coming to the throne at the age of eighteen, she showed herself a ruler of brilliant gifts, marred by arrogance, selfishness, jealousy and wasteful spending. Her court became a centre of learning and she encouraged educational advance. Her wastefulness and neglect of the affairs of government eventually led to her abdication in 1654, and she left the castle of Uppsala, dressed as a man, under the name of Count Dohna. She made several attempts to regain the crown, but finally died in poverty and obscurity at Rome, into whose faith she had been received soon after her abdication.

She was one of the eccentrics of history, neglectful of her appearance, riding her horse boldly "in an outfit . . . not worth more than five ducats" and varying in mood and facial expression as often as the weather.

¶ In THOMAS, H. and D. L. *Famous Women*. 1959

Christmas: the annual Christian festival, on 25 December, commemorating the birth of Jesus Christ. There is little historical validity for the date and, in fact, 25 December was already being celebrated as a pagan feast in Britain before the arrival of Christianity. Dates in January, March, May and November have, at various times, been put forward as the true birthday.

Henry Cole's original Christmas card.

Christmas cards: greeting cards sent at Christmas. The first printed ones, hand-coloured, seem to have been sent to his friends by an Englishman, Henry Cole, in 1843 as a private venture, and the surplus copies were sold in a London shop for a shilling each. From this modest beginning a vast trade gradually developed till, in 1964, 650 million Christmas cards were posted in the United Kingdom alone. The poet Tennyson, when an old man, was invited to write a dozen Christmas card verses for 1,000 guineas but refused, adding, however: "Beyond doubt these verses would have found their way into many far corners of the earth where I cannot flatter myself even my name is known." A German named Hollinger once found an old painting of the Holy Family, wrote a Christmas greeting on the back and sent it to a friend. The picture was subsequently identified as a painting by Rembrandt. Hollinger tried to get it back, eventually taking the matter to court and losing his case at a cost of £11,800. This has been quoted as the highest price ever paid for a Christmas card.

¶ SANSOM, WILLIAM. *Christmas*. 1968

Chroniclers, Medieval: makers of chronicles (from Greek *chronos*, time), i.e. records of events in order of time. As monasteries were the chief means of communicating and recording events in the Middle Ages, many of the chroniclers were monks who wrote in Latin, but, as the monasteries declined in the later Middle Ages, the work of secular writers developed, written in the vernacular.

Bede (673–735), a monk of Jarrow, has been called "the father of English history" because of his *Ecclesiastical History of the English Church and People*, written in 731. "Thus much . . . I have with the Lord's help composed, either from ancient documents or from tradition of the elders or from my own knowledge".

The *Anglo-Saxon Chronicle* (892–1154) was the work of many monks and written in English; it was described as "a book of events and laws", and the keeping of such a record may have been inspired by Alfred (848–900). There were four main manuscripts of the *Chronicle*, of which the most important was written at Winchester and then moved to Canterbury, where the account of the Norman Conquest was added, showing the attitude of the English to this event.

Eadmer (1060–1124), a monk of Canterbury in the time of Lanfranc and Anselm and chaplain to the latter, wrote a contemporary account of the reigns of William I and II and Henry I, *Historia Novorum in Anglia*; and as he had been an eye-witness of much of what he described, e.g. Anselm's quarrel with William II, his work was particularly important and his descriptions were often dramatic.

William of Malmesbury (1080–1143) knew personally many of the great men of his time and aimed at filling the gap between Bede and his own time in *Gesta Regum*, while his *Historia Novella* was a contemporary account of part of Henry I's and Stephen's reigns. A distinguishing feature of his work was his use of named sources of information and, although his chronology was erratic, his judgments on people were often shrewd.

Gerald of Wales (1146–1223), Archdeacon of Pembrokeshire, is interesting as a writer who travelled abroad to France and Italy and had an interview with Pope Innocent III; he showed his prejudices clearly, e.g. he spoke of the English as "a people born to slavery" but praised "the noble Norman . . . and freeborn fearless Welshman". His chief works were *Description of Wales and Itinerary of Wales.*

Matthew Paris (d. 1259) dominated the historical writing of the 13th century; he presided over the scriptorium at St Albans Abbey for twenty-four years and was a superb journalist, deeply interested in his own times and holding strong views, e.g. he hated the foreigners with whom Henry III surrounded himself. His two most important works were *Chronica Maiora* and *Historia Anglorum*, which covered the period 1066 to 1253; novel features of his work were his use of illustrations, such as that of Henry III and Louis VIII of France embracing each other, and his use of maps.

With the invention of printing in the latter part of the 15th century, the post-medieval chroniclers reached a wider audience, e.g. Raphael Holinshed, a bookseller by trade, who wrote *The Chronicles of England, Scotland and Ireland*, published in 1578 in two volumes. One interest of his work lies in its use by Shakespeare for his historical plays and also for *Macbeth, King Lear* and *Cymbeline.*

William Camden (1551–1623), headmaster of Westminster School, may perhaps justifiably be called the last great English chronicler. Both his outstanding works were written in Latin and later translated into English. *Britannia*, published in 1586, was a detailed survey of the British Isles; and the *Annals of England and Ireland during the Reign of Elizabeth* was published in two volumes, one in 1615 and the other posthumously in 1627, for which he used documents lent to him by William Cecil, Lord Burleigh (1520–98). This work, and Bacon's *History of the Reign of Henry VII*, were described by the lawyer John Selden (1584–1654) as the only two serious works of history bringing events up to his day.

In France there were three outstanding chroniclers. Geoffroy de Villehardouin (*c.* 1160–1213), the first vernacular historian of France, wrote an account of the Fourth Crusade (1201–04). Jean Joinville (1224–1317), another chronicler of the Crusades, described the life of St Louis of France, Louis IX (1226–70), and ended with the King's canonisation. His writing was very personal and was a description of the events of his youth.

Jean Froissart (1338–*c.* 1410), a native of Hainault and fellow-countryman and secretary of Queen Philippa, wife of Edward III of England, wrote his *Chronicle* on the first part of the Hundred Years War between England and France (1337–1453). His aim was to record deeds of honour, and to him Edward III and the Black Prince were the noblest figures in Christendom. As the chief chronicler of chivalry, he was uncritical and had no real concern with historical development.

Churchill, John, 1st Duke of Marlborough (1650–1722): English general; son of Sir Winston Churchill of Dorset. He married Sarah Jennings (1678), and thirty-seven of their love letters survive. After helping to defeat the Duke of Monmouth at Sedgemoor (1685), he abandoned James II and joined William of Orange at the Revolution (1688), though he spent six weeks in the Tower (1692) for corresponding with the exiled James II.

His greatest achievements were during the Spanish Succession War (1702–13) as commander-in-chief of the Anglo-Dutch forces, having previously helped to form the Grand Alliance against France. His four great victories were at Blenheim (13 August 1704), which saved Vienna from the French and Bavarians; at Ramillies (23 May 1706); at Oudenarde (11 July 1708), followed by the expulsion of the French from the Netherlands; and at Malplaquet (11 September 1709). (*See* separate entries for these battles.)

John Churchill, 1st Duke of Marlborough, painted by Van der Werf.

After this career of success and resounding glory, a period of obscurity followed. His wife's close friendship with Queen Anne, which had formerly been a great help to his advancement, ended in a bitter quarrel; and the Tories, anxious for peace, replaced the Whigs. Marlborough was dismissed on a charge of embezzlement in 1711 and lived in exile at Antwerp until Anne's death in August 1714, when he returned to enjoy his remaining years amid the splendours of Blenheim Palace, Woodstock, built for him by Vanbrugh at a cost of £240,000 of public money.

Napoleon said that only Marlborough and Frederick the Great were fit to be his rivals. He "never fought a battle which he did not win, and never besieged a place that he did not take". His contemporaries, however, found him avaricious, and his loyalties and motives were not always above question.

¶ In CANNING, JOHN, editor. *100 Great Lives.* 1969

Churchill, Sir Winston Leonard Spencer (1874–1965): British statesman, author, historian; son of Lord Randolph Churchill and descendant of the great Duke of Marlborough. His mother, Jenny, was the daughter of Leonard Jerome of New York.

In early life, he served with the army in India and at Omdurman; as a newspaper correspondent in South Africa, he was captured by the Boers and made a spectacular escape. He entered Parliament as a Conservative for Oldham in 1900 but changed his allegiance in 1905 and held various posts in Liberal governments, notably First Lord of the Admiralty (1911–15), where he was responsible for the Fleet being fully prepared for war in 1914. He resigned on the failure of the Dardanelles campaign (*see* separate entry), but was back in the government by 1917. In 1924 he again changed party and became Conservative Chancellor of the Exchequer. From 1929 to 1939 he was out of office and repeatedly warned about the dangers of the new dictatorships and the need for re-armament.

At the outbreak of war in 1939 he became First Lord of the Admiralty, replacing Neville Chamberlain in May 1940 as Prime Minister of a coalition government. There followed his finest period when, as the German armies carried all before them, he rallied and inspired not only the British but also the subjected countries of Europe and led them towards victory.

In the general election of July 1945, his party was defeated but he was again Prime Minister from 1951 to 1955, when he finally resigned, remaining, however, M.P. for his Woodford constituency. When he died in 1965 he was given a state funeral.

Churchill received many honours but refused a peerage, being content with the Order of the Garter which enabled him to remain a "House of Commons man". Most important among his writings were his life of his ancestor the 1st Duke of Marlborough and his history of the Second World War.

¶ FARRELL, ALAN. *Sir Winston Churchill.* 1962

Winston Churchill, Prime Minister, visits Bristol after a bombing raid in April 1941.

Winston Churchill meets General Eisenhower, Supreme Commander of the Allied Expeditionary Forces, in France.

Cinque Ports, The: originally five "headports" in south-east England: Hastings, Romney, Hythe, Dover, Sandwich; and, later, Winchelsea and Rye. The Crown, in return for ships for coastal defence, granted them extensive local jurisdiction through their own Court of Shepway and exemption from various taxes. The oldest existing charter dates from 1278. Declining in strategic importance with the creation of the Tudor navy, the ports surrendered their charters in 1685. Acts of 1832 and 1835 abolished many privileges, and civil jurisdiction ended in 1869. The office of Lord Warden of the Cinque Ports still survives, and notable holders have included the Duke of Wellington and Sir Winston Churchill.

Circumnavigation: sailing completely round the world or a great land mass, e.g. Australia. Ferdinand Magellan (*c.* 1480–1521), a Portuguese navigator in the service of Charles I of Spain, led the first expedition to circumnavigate the globe, leaving Seville in September 1519 and seeking a passage through South America to the Pacific. In October 1520 he entered the strait which bears his name, losing two of five ships on the passage. Magellan was killed in the Philippines in April 1521, but Juan Sebastian del Cano brought his flagship, the *Victoria*, safely home in September 1522 with a cargo that more than paid for the voyage. Francis Drake (1541?–96) was the first English circumnavigator, 1577–80, sailing via Cape Horn in the *Pelican*, renamed *Golden Hind* en route. His harrying of Spanish settlements and capture of a treasure ship produced an estimated profit of 4,800 per cent. Thomas Cavendish (*c.* 1555–92) made a similarly profitable circumnavigation between 1586 and 1588. Lord George Anson (1697–1762) sailed in 1740 with eight ships to attack Spanish Pacific colonies. After incredible sufferings and with only the *Centurion* left, Anson captured a Spanish treasure galleon from Acapulco and in 1744 brought home treasure worth £500,000. Among other important voyages were those of Philip Carteret, commanding the *Swallow*, who followed a more southerly track, discovered Pitcairn Island, rediscovered the Solomons and completed an enterprising circumnavigation in 1769; and that of the Comte de Bougainville (1729–1811), French mathematician and member of the Royal Society, who sailed to the Falklands in 1767 to explore the Pacific and, following Carteret's southerly track in the Pacific, reached home in 1769. A vine, a strait in New Hebrides and a bay in the Magellan Strait are named after him.

James Cook (*see* separate entry) explored practically the whole Pacific and completed the circumnavigation on his first two voyages. Tobias Furneaux (1735–81) commanded the *Adventure* on

Above, Magellan's ship Vittoria. *Below, the* Golden Hind. *Top right, Sir Alec Rose in* Lively Lady. *Bottom right, Robin Knox Johnson in* Suhaili.

Cook's second voyage. Losing contact with Cook, he returned home in 1774, making the first easterly circumnavigation.

Robert Gray (1755–1806) made the first successful American circumnavigation from Boston, 1787–90, exchanging furs from the north-west Pacific coasts for tea in Canton. On his second voyage, he was the first navigator to enter the Columbia river. Joshua Slocum took a year building the *Spray*, 36 feet 9 inches [11·22 metres], from an old hull. He made the first single-handed circumnavigation from Nova Scotia in 1895. He wrote a classic account of this in *Sailing Alone around the World*.

The 1960s saw outstanding circumnavigations by yachts. In 1966–67 the sixty-two-year-old Francis Chichester in *Gipsy Moth IV*, assisted by commercial enterprises, completed the easterly passage single-handed. Alec Rose, at fifty-nine, from his own resources completed

the world voyage in 1967–68 in *Lively Lady*. Robin Knox Johnson in *Suhaili*, the only competitor to finish, won the *Sunday Times* Golden Globe in a race for the first ever non-stop circumnavigation in 1968–69.

Civil disobedience: actions taken by a political or social group to achieve an aim by causing embarrassment to the authorities without resorting to force or criminal activities. The spread of democracy in the 20th century, coupled with the growth of the problems and dangers facing society, made civil disobedience an essentially modern form of protest. The Suffragette movement before World War I was a good early instance; but the outstanding example was the campaign for Indian national independence, led by Mohandas Gandhi, whose methods of peaceful non-co-operation with the British authorities have been copied by many protest movements, notably antiwar groups in Europe and America in the 1960s.

Indian demonstrators greet the Royal Commission headed by Sir John Simon, 1928.

Civil liberties: the basic freedoms of the individual under the law, especially freedom from excessive state control and other oppression; the right to free speech; liberty to worship according to conscience; and democratic participation in government.

Civil rights: a term covering the claim of individuals in democratic societies to certain fundamental rights as free citizens, including some control, through the franchise, of the management of their own affairs, equality before the law, freedom of speech and writing and of political activity and association. Although the term is of recent origin, the principles are as old as ancient Athens and have been put forward often by minority groups such as the *Uitlanders* of the Rand in the 1890s, the Negroes of the United States and South Africa, and the Roman Catholics of Northern Ireland. In the USA these rights are established by amendments to the Constitution (1–8 and 13–15 inclusive). They are embodied in the United Nations Declaration on Human Rights. *See also* APARTHEID; ATLANTIC CHARTER; BALLOT; CIVIL DISOBEDIENCE; CONSTITUTION, AMERICAN; DRED SCOTT DECISION; EMANCIPATION OF WOMEN; FOURTEENTH AMENDMENT; HUGUENOTS; MAGNA CARTA; NORTHERN IRELAND, etc.

A Women's "Strike for Equality" march in New York, 1970.

Civil service: the secretariat or public servants of government, handling its paper work and day-to-day administration. "Civil" in this sense means relating to the citizens and their affairs (from Latin *civis*, citizens). The definition varies according to country. In Great Britain, the Civil service is concerned largely with central administration, playing a significant part in the formulation of policy and, at the highest level, getting legislation on to the statute book. In France it means every employee of the state. In earlier times, appointment, promotion and dismissal were usually in the hands of the crown, court favourites or powerful ministers (as they still are in many parts of the world) and were therefore dictated by political and social motives, not necessarily with any regard for qualification and ability. The surest safeguard against pressure and corruption has been found to be entry by competitive examination, irrespective of social background, creed or colour, a method increasingly adopted, e.g. in the USA and Britain, and serving to counter in some degree the effects of the "spoils system", whereby the political party in power distributes offices, appointments and privileges exclusively among its own supporters. In Britain the permanent head of the Treasury is the head of the civil service; in the USA government officers are appointed by the president, with some control by the Senate.

¶ CARSWELL, JOHN. *The Civil Servant and His World.* 1966

Cleopatra: the name of seven queens of Egypt, but almost invariably meaning Cleopatra VII (69–30 BC), best known for her association with Julius Caesar, Mark Antony and Octavian; and from the dramatisations, separated by 300 years, of her career by William Shakespeare and George Bernard Shaw.

¶ HORNBLOW, LEONORA. *All About Cleopatra of Egypt.* 1962

Cleopatra VII, from a bas-relief.

Cleopatra's Needles: popular name for two Egyptian obelisks of red granite, set up in Central Park, New York (1880) and on the Thames Embankment, London (1878). They date from about 1500 BC and have nothing to do with Cleopatra. The English example, weighing more than 186 tons [189 tonnes], had an adventurous voyage, being lost in a gale near Ferrol, before it was eventually recovered and brought to London. *See also* OBELISK.

Clipper ships: a class of sailing vessel with fine lines, specially built for speed. The demand for fast sailing vessels existed early in the 19th century. The Americans led the way by building large sailing craft of 750 tons [762 tonnes] on the lines of the Baltimore clippers. The opium trade of the 1830s, the Californian Gold Rush of 1847 and the discovery of gold in Australia in 1851, all stimulated the need for this type of vessel. The repeal of the Navigation Laws in 1849 brought American ships into the China tea trade, and British shipyards were quick to respond to the new challenge.

During the years 1855–70 considerable rivalry existed between shipowners in the China trade, and rich rewards were offered to the first vessels arriving in London with the new season's tea crop. The demand for speed heralded the advent of the China tea clipper. This was class of vessel designed with steep floors, a midship section far less than in the earlier American ships and a length eventually increased to 5·9 times the beam. Cargo-carrying capacity thus became of secondary importance to hull form.

The *Cutty Sark*, now permanently dry docked at Greenwich, England, is the only clipper to survive. Launched at Dumbarton in 1869, she was built to rival the *Thermopylae*, one of the fastest sailing vessels of her time. The *Cutty Sark*, in

The Cutty Sark *at sea.*

common with most of the tea clippers, was composite built, i.e. wooden planking on iron frames. Gross tonnage was 963 [978 tonnes] and total sail area about 32,000 square feet [2,972 square metres]. It has been stated that the fastest sailing merchantman ever built was the American *Flying Cloud*, though another claimant is the *Sovereign of the Seas*, built by Donald McKay at Boston, Massachusetts in 1852 and recording a speed of 22 knots [25·3 m.p.h.; 40·7 km/h]. The *Sea Witch* sailed from Hong Kong to New York in seventy-three days. The *Thermopylae* and *Cutty Sark* averaged eighty-eight days and eighty-two days (over a period of about ten years) from Australia to London.

¶ CLARK, ARTHUR H. *The Clipper Ship Era, 1843–1869.* *1969; JOHNSON, DAVID. *Clipper Ships and the Cutty Sark* (Jackdaw). 1971

Clive, Robert, Baron Clive of Plassey (1725–74): soldier and Governor of Bengal, who established the British East India Company as the dominant political and military power in India. His periods of service occurred when the British and French Companies were conducting armed rivalry as "allies" of native princes.

During his first period, 1743–53, he joined the army in the Carnatic after the fall of Madras (1746) and distinguished himself by seizing Arcot, capital of the Carnatic, and holding the citadel for fifty days against the army of the French puppet king, Chandar Sahib, thereby saving Trichinopoly and enabling the British to put their own nominee, Muhammad Ali, on the throne (1751).

He returned for his second period, 1756–60, as Lieutenant General and Governor of Fort St David, shortly before the fall of Calcutta and the "Black Hole" (*see* separate entry). He went to Bengal (1757), retook Calcutta, reduced the French settlement of Chandernagore, defeated the Nawab, Siraj-ud-Daula, at Plassey,

Robert Clive.

placed his own nominee, Mir Jafar, on the throne (receiving from him very substantial monetary rewards), and was appointed Governor of Bengal (1758). He then reduced the Dutch settlement of Chinsura, leaving the English with no rival in Bengal.

He was sent out again in 1765 to redress the corruption rife among the Company's officials and to deal with a dangerous political situation. Sir Hector Munro's defeat of the confederated princes of Hindustan at Buxar had, in fact, effectively dealt with the political peril before Clive arrived, so that he was able to secure for the Company, from the Emperor Shah Alam, the "Diwani" (finance administration) of Bengal, which meant real ruling power. But his reforms offended both army and civilians, and he returned to England in 1767, broken in health, to face attack in Parliament for accepting money from native princes. His defence was vigorous and the House, while agreeing that he had, with doubtful propriety, received £230,000 declared that he had "at the same time rendered great and meritorious services to his country".

¶ CLAIR, C. *Robert Clive.* 1963; SYLVESTER, D. W. *Clive in India.* 1968

Coal: a hard black rock, formed from the decayed vegetation of primeval swamp forests and compressed during the course of millions of years into seams now lying at varying depths in the earth's crust. It provides the world's main supply of fuel and is broadly classified into lignite, or soft coal; bituminous coal, the best suited for general industrial and domestic use; and anthracite, very hard coal used for special heating purposes. The main producing areas are north-west Europe, the eastern USA, China, the USSR, Australia, India and South Africa. The earliest mention of true coal, as distinct from charcoal, is probably about 370 BC, when a Greek writer speaks of fossil substances "called coals which kindle and burn" and which were found "in Liguria and in Elis, in the way to Olympias".

The coal industry in Britain began in the 13th century, an early landmark being a charter of Henry III in 1239 which enabled the burgesses of Newcastle to dig coal in the town fields. At first, coal was simply quarried from surface outcrops or excavated from shallow bell-shaped pits. Seams were also followed into the ground by drifts, or tunnels – a method still used today. By the 17th century little surface coal remained, and, to reach the lower seams, pits to depths of 100 feet [30·5 metres] had to be sunk, making simple manual or horse-driven pumping and winding equipment essential.

The North-East coalfield, because of its easy access by sea to the London market, gained a long lead in organisation and mining techniques over other fields, and the Newcastle coal trade was an important factor in the Civil War of 1642–49. Later, as the textile mills, iron works and factories of the Industrial Revolution began to consume coal in vast quantities, pits were sunk to depths of several hundred feet. The two usual methods employed in deep mining were the room and pillar system, in which columns of coal were left as roof supports, and the longwall system, in which the coal face was cut in lengths, stone filling being used to support the cleared section. Mining engineers also had to overcome enormous problems of drainage, ventilation, lighting, haulage and transport, while pitmen were exposed to terrible hazards from explosive and suffocating gases. The invention of the safety lamp in 1815 and controlled ventilation systems lessened these dangers, while, in developing steam power for pumping and winding engines, railways for easy transit of coal, and the locomotive for haulage, mining engineers made vital contributions to industrial progress.

Unlike the rest of Europe, where the state generally owned underground mineral rights, coal in Britain formerly belonged to private colliery owners. Pitmen at one time were engaged by the year, had to sign a bond regulating their terms of work and pay, and were otherwise largely dependent on the owners for their houses and general livelihood. Working condi-

Mid-19th century coal mining operation in Durham, showing miners descending in an iron tub from the mouth of the pit.

Miners' cottages in Wales.

tions were only slowly improved through a long history of strikes, union struggles and legislation, usually passed only after some terrible disaster or belated enquiry. An Act of 1842 ended the employment of women and young children underground, and subsequent legislation gradually reduced working hours, established safety and training standards and introduced basic welfare services.

Britain's coal mines were nationalised in 1946 and are now controlled by the National Coal Board. Whereas before 1800 Britain produced almost all the world's coal and exported vast quantities throughout the 19th century, present production represents a small fraction of the world's output and merely supplies the country's own needs. Loss of former markets, such as the railways and shipping, and competition from oil, natural gas and nuclear energy have compelled the industry to lower production, close uneconomic pits, reduce manpower and mechanise mining operations. Coal also has important byproducts, such as tar and basic chemicals, from which dyes, drugs, plastics, nylon, washing powders and countless other everyday goods are made.

In the USA some thirty states have plentiful coal resources. Up to about 1870 the bulk of the coal mined came from the vast anthracite fields of east Pennsylvania, which produced more than all the rest of the states together (17,083,134 tons [17,357,318 tonnes] in 1869 compared with 365 tons [370 tonnes] in 1829). Afterwards the exploitation of such deposits as those of west Pennsylvania, Illinois and Virginia altered the picture.

¶ TOMALIN, MILES. *Coal Mines and Miners.* 1960

Coalition: an alliance between two or more parties, usually temporary and for a definite and limited purpose. It may take the form of a combination of states at war, or an alliance between parties in government.

Coastguards: officials maintaining a lookout for smugglers, ships in trouble, illegal immigrants, etc. In Britain they originally formed an anti-smuggling force under the Customs. Increased customs duties in William III's reign encouraged equally increased efforts at evasion. Small armed boats, or "revenue cutters", proved ineffective, and smuggling continued unabated throughout the 18th century. From 1817 the navy reinforced the excisemen with guardships and boat patrols and stationed men in the Martello Towers (small circular forts built to guard against Napoleon's possible invasion), thus providing the beginnings of a more effective service. In 1854 the Board of Trade took over private life-saving companies, using coastguards for training. From 1856 the Admiralty assumed responsibility, enlarging coastguard duties to include coastal defence. In 1923 the service transferred to the Board of Trade. Now under the Ministry of Transport, its duties include assistance in case of wreck or distress, continuous coastal watch and co-operation with other search and rescue agencies.

In the USA in 1790 Congress authorised the construction of boats to assist the Customs – the Revenue Cutter Service. A military force from the beginning, the coastguards have fought in all US wars, as a 1799 Act requires. In 1915 Congress declared coastguards "part of the military forces" and merged the Revenue Cutter Service with the Lifesaving Service into the United States Coast Guard: the Lighthouse Service followed in 1939. In 1946 the USCG assumed certain safety-at-sea duties. The service is responsible for maritime law enforcement, military readiness, port security, safety at sea, and has its own Academy, a peacetime strength of 30,000 and equal reserves.

Many other seaboard countries maintain some sort of coastguard service, if only signalling stations and life-saving agencies.

Coat-of-arms: distinctive heraldic devices, consisting of the bearer's complete armorial achievement, which includes the shield, helmet, crest, mantling and, sometimes, supporters. (Mantling is the representation of the protective cloth fastened to the knight's helmet and hanging over his shoulders. Supporters are the animals or human figures placed on each side of the shield.) Medieval knights wore long and loose sleeveless coats over their armour, to which personal markings and special devices were often sewn. The use of such heraldic identification began in western Europe in the 12th century, although the modern system of recording personal coats-of-arms does not go back very far. The essential part of any armorial bearing is the shield, without which there cannot be a coat-of-arms.

See also ARMORIAL BEARINGS.

Cockpit of Europe: name given to Belgium because it has been the site of more battles between warring nations than any other country in Europe. The metaphor of the cockpit, from the small enclosed area used in the old sport of cockfighting, is also found in Shakespeare's *Henry V* when, referring to the theatre stage, the Prologue says: "Can this cockpit hold the vasty fields of France?"

Codes and ciphers: methods of secret communication. The art has been studied for centuries, and only the most superficial appreciation of it can be given in a short article. The earliest treatise on it was written by Aeneas Tacticus (360–390 BC), and we know that ciphers were used by Caesar. Charles I of England was foolish enough to take cipher notes (and the key to their use) to the battle of Naseby, where they came into the hands of Fairfax. We also have the cipher used by Marie Antoinette, consisting of eleven substitution alphabets used in succession. In addition to their serious use in war and in the secret communications of governments, ciphers have been of much interest to amateur cryptographers and to writers of fiction. Edgar Allan Poe's *The Gold Bug* and Conan Doyle's *The Dancing Men* are good examples of the latter class, and both give some insight into the methods involved in "breaking" a code or cipher.

One expert makes a distinction between cryptographs and ciphers. In this sense, a cryptograph uses letters or symbols in their normal sense but arranged so as to be unintelligible to anyone not possessing the key. The simplest example of this type is a message in which every word is spelt backwards. He then confines the word "cipher" to an arbitrary use of letters, words or figures in other than their ordinary sense and gives, as a simple example, the replacement of any letter by the one following it in the alphabet, A being replaced by B, B by C, and finally Z by A.

One of the best known ciphers is the Playfair cipher, which may be taken to give some idea of probably the most important and commonly used class. Suppose the key work is CRANLEIGH.

C R A N L
E I G H B
D F K M O
P Q S T U
V W X Y Z

A matrix is constructed of 25 letters, I standing for both I and J. The key word is written first, omitting any repeated letters in the key word, and followed by the remaining letters of the alphabet, in their usual order. Suppose we wish to send the message COME AT ONCE. This is broken into pairs, as CO ME AT ON CE. The letters C and O are found in the matrix at opposite corners of a rectangle and are replaced by those at the opposite corners, namely L and D. This holds throughout till we come to the last pair, C and E. These lie in the same column of the matrix and are replaced by those in the next column to the right, that is R and I. Thus, the message becomes LD DH NS ML RI. This would then be finally written as LDDHN SMLRI, i.e. in groups of five letters. In this case, there are two groups of five, but in a seventeen-letter message the final form would be three groups of five, followed by two letters only. Alternatively, the last group can be made up to five by the inclusion of random letters, which will be disregarded by the receiver.

The essential element of the code system is the code book, copies of which are held by sender and receiver. In the code book, there is a list of words, phrases or sentences, each accompanied by a code group replacing it. This code group may be another word (real or artificial) or a group of letters, figures or other symbols. Probably the best known code system is the Morse code, although in this instance the purpose of its use is not secrecy. This uses two signs only, the dot and the dash. Thus A is · –, B – · · ·, and so on.

The process of "breaking" a code or cipher is a difficult one. The first essential is to establish the language in which the message is written. As a general principle, the longer the message, the easier it will be to "break", as the normal frequencies at which the letters occur will have more chance to assert themselves. As early as 1742, D. A. Conrad gave tables of frequency for English, French, German, Italian, Dutch, Latin and Greek, and these have since been extended to other languages. In English the commonest letter is E and the least common Z, the order being E T R I N O A S D L C H F U P M Y G W V B X K Q J Z. In every thousand words, E appears on the average 126 times. A 72 times and Z only once. In a short message, the frequency of occurrence may, of course, differ widely from the average. We also have tables for the order of frequency of two letters and three letters. Other peculiarities, such as that Q must be followed by U and another vowel, may be of help in "breaking" a cipher.

¶ EPSTEIN, SAM and BERYL. *The First Book of Codes and Ciphers.* 1963; ZIM, HERBERT S. *Codes and Secret Writing.* 1965

Cold war: a state of diplomatic tension or a war of nerves, without resort to actual fighting. The term has been used particularly about the relations between the USA and the USSR, where there is constant manoeuvring for economic advantage and for the friendship of other countries.

Colombo Plan (May 1951): "The Colombo Plan for co-operative Economic Development in South and South-east Asia" grew out of a conference of Commonwealth ministers, presided over by Mr Senanayake of Ceylon, in January 1950, and a further conference at Sydney in May 1950. It was designed to develop the economy of the area, to increase food production and consumption, to overcome the industrial dislocation caused by the war, particularly in India, and generally to restore the key position of the area in world trade. Now called The Colombo Plan for Cooperative Economic and Social Development in Asia and the Pacific, its donors had provided $65.1 billion in aid by 1981.

Colonna: noble Roman family (their device a *colonna*, column), who defied popes and senate from their towers in Rome or their castles in the Sabine hills. Their determination to dictate the choice of popes and their feuds with the rival Orsini family often caused deadlock in the College of Cardinals. Boniface VIII destroyed their castles and exiled them, but, with French help, they captured him, hastening his death in 1303. To avoid their control, Clement V settled the papacy at Avignon in 1309. Similar struggles were fought with Sixtus IV (1471–84), Alexander VI (1492–1503) and Paul IV (1555–59). John Colonna was a saintly patron of St Francis in 1198; Vittoria Colonna, a devout poet and friend of Michelangelo.

Columbus, Christopher (*c.* 1446 or 1451–1506): Genoese navigator and discoverer. Columbus was the son of a cloth merchant from Genoa. After travelling widely, he settled in Portugal, where he worked out a plan for sailing west across the Atlantic to reach Japan and China. The Portuguese rejected his offer to lead such an expedition, being more interested in their African route to the East. The King of England also rejected the plan, but in 1492 King Ferdinand and Queen Isabella of Spain provided the money and the patronage needed "to discover and acquire islands and mainland in the Ocean Sea".

Christopher Columbus.

Columbus proved to be a skilful navigator. His three ships, *Santa Maria*, *Pint* and *Nina*, caught the north-east trad winds from the Canary Islands and, afte thirty-three days, they sighted the islan they named San Salvador. Columbu called the natives "Indians", since h believed he was now in Asia. He saile on to the larger islands of Hispaniola an Cuba, but could find no sign of Japan Nor did he find the gold everyone expected. Nevertheless, Columbus returne to an enthusiastic welcome in Spain.

Two thousand colonists volunteered t go with Columbus to Hispaniola. But h did not prove to be a tactful governor, an the terrified natives were unable to produce much gold. His colony was soon i disgrace. In 1498 he had discovered th mainland of South America, but he stil thought he had reached Asia. After final hazardous voyage to Hondura Columbus was kept in Spain, and die in obscurity in 1506.

¶ BLOCK, I. *Real Book of Christopher Columbu.* 1959; KNIGHT, FRANK. *Christopher Columbus.* 197 In BRETT, BERNARD. *Explorers and Exploring.* 197

See also AMERICA, DISCOVERY OF.

Commerce: trade and the exchange of goods. The ancient civilisations in the eastern Mediterranean and Mesopotamia could not supply all the goods and services they required. Inhabitants of the Nile and Tigris–Euphrates valleys, for example, had very little timber or ores, and no ivory, spices or precious stones; to obtain these they resorted both to peaceful commerce and to force. Egypt exported large quantities of grain as well as linen, glass, wool, vegetable oils and papyrus, in which writing material she had a virtual monopoly. Her imports included metals from Europe and gold and ivory from central Africa.

From the Nile delta, trade routes radiated through Asia Minor and by land and river to the Black Sea, the English Channel and the Baltic. Others went overland to the Euphrates and Tigris, to the Persian Gulf and through the mountain passes to India or on to China, famous for its silk. About the 1st century BC it was found that the monsoon winds would carry ships from the mouth of the Red Sea to India and back.

The growth of commerce and of a trading class went hand in hand. In Mesopotamia about 2100 BC the Code of Hammurabi shows that commercial organisation and the laws governing it had reached an advanced state.

It was about this time that Crete, a richly endowed island, became an important trader. Her merchants picked up Spanish metals and British tin. They traded in wine, oil, grain, lumber and manufactured goods, especially home-produced or foreign pottery. When Crete was overthrown her work was taken up by the Phoenicians.

Inhabitants of many Greek city states produced oil and wine and developed manufactures, surpluses of which were exchanged for imported grain, fish and other commodities. Large cities such as Corinth and Athens depended heavily on imported foodstuffs. Athens obtained her grain from Egypt and southern Russia, while Corinth turned to her colonies in Sicily and southern Italy.

The city of Rome, the centre of a far-flung empire, had few export industries; but her income was large and perhaps as many as 6,000 grain ships (most of them from Egypt) anchored in the Tiber each year. Many luxury goods, including spices, ointments and precious stones, came in from Asia, as did silk from China and wild beasts destined for the circus. It is not possible to calculate the amount of external trade or the trade within the empire itself, but in the cities there were sufficient prosperous people to create a market for oriental goods, and the grain trade was certainly a large one.

In the Middle Ages, as in earlier periods, it seems likely that trade between people and places in the same locality was greater in quantity than that carried out with distant countries. Yet there took place a considerable amount of commerce between widely scattered regions.

In Europe, rivers like the Rhine, Danube and Rhone–Saône were important highways of commerce, while Alpine passes such as the Brenner and St Gotthard served as links between the northern and Mediterranean trading areas. Various parts of the Mediterranean specialised in producing particular commodities, but the trade of the area also consisted in distributing merchandise brought from Asia; among the oriental goods spices, used by all who could afford them in the preparation of food, held the most important place.

North of the Alps, Europe produced wines in the vineyards of France and Germany and furs from the forest areas of Scandinavia and Russia, where the Novgorod Fair was a main gathering point. Other products were fish, especially the herring, timber and naval supplies from the Baltic, and metals such as copper and iron. By the 14th century Sweden had already become noted for her high grade iron and steel, a distinction she holds to this day. Salt, important for the preservation of meat and fish, was obtained by evaporating sea water along the Bay of Biscay and by working deposits in Cheshire, Salzburg and other places.

The trade of northern Europe was dominated, but not monopolised, by the Hanseatic League, which consisted of merchants of some eighty coastal and inland towns under the leadership of Lubeck and stretching from the Rhine to the Baltic. The League's great commercial power obtained them special privileges in the places where they traded. They lent money to kings and even, at one time, held the English crown jewels as security.

The Hansard merchants' power lay not so much in their military strength (although this was sufficient at one time for them to force the King of Denmark to hand over to them two-thirds of the dues he collected from ships passing through the Sound) as in the efficiency with which they traded in northern Europe and with the East via Kiev and Astrakhan. Cheap transportation was provided by the League's cargo ships, while lighthouses were built, pilots trained and maritime law improved and developed.

Trade with the East was stimulated by the crusades, and the rise of Venice as the chief trading city of Europe may partly be traced to this cause. Her fleets brought home previously unheard of luxuries, such as velvet, muslin and damask. Orange trees, rose trees and the art of making paper were introduced into Europe.

Markets and fairs held important places in medieval commerce. Markets were usually held frequently, with buyers and sellers travelling to them over relatively small distances. Fairs, on the other hand, were held less frequently, perhaps yearly, but usually lasted for several days or even longer and dealt in goods brought in from over a wide area. Some fairs, such as those of St Denis near Paris, Troyes, Bruges, Frankfurt and Salamanca, enjoyed a wide and even international reputation.

Of the events that mark the beginnings of modern times, Adam Smith, the great 18th-century pioneer of economic thought, considered that two – the discovery of America and of the Cape route

The Market-Place and Exchange, Nottingham, c. 1850.

to India – are among the most important in the history of mankind. Despite these discoveries Britain's trade continued to be almost exclusively with Europe. To Germany, the Baltic and the Low Countries went woollen goods, and to Spanish, African and Mediterranean ports went the "New Draperies", woollen goods more suited to warmer climates.

From about 1600 the northern trading area, under the influence of the great regulated companies – the Russia, the Eastland and the Merchant Adventurers – decreased in importance, while exports to Mediterranean ports by the Levant Company, a joint stock organisation, increased. By the eve of the English civil war the trading areas were of about equal importance, but this is not to say that the companies mentioned can be held solely, or mainly, responsible for the state of trade. It is worth noting that, in the early 17th century, some two-thirds to three-quarters of the nation's foreign trade was handled by London, and remarkably few English commodities other than raw or manufactured wool were exported.

By this time western European countries were trying to establish trade with America and the Far East. Both areas were not without their difficulties. English woollen cloth was too warm for widespread use in the East. In North America it was found that Red Indians and colonists were not sufficiently prosperous to buy large quantities of English cloth. For this reason, the most valuable parts of the New World were held to be the sugar islands of the West Indies and the tobacco-producing areas of North America, both of which produced goods enjoying a considerable market in Europe. By the end of the 17th century production for European markets was being carried on by means of slave labour imported from Africa as part of the notorious triangular trade.

Between the years 1760 and 1830 the Industrial Revolution created a new kind of economic situation. Britain's livelihood depended on her sales abroad of manufactured goods (cotton textiles in particular) and such services as those of shipping, insurance and banking. In exchange, Britain – and later, Germany, the United States and other countries – received increasing quantities of foodstuffs and raw materials from overseas, and the commercial wellbeing of many far-off supplying countries became dependent on the demand of the great industrial nations, a demand which could, and sometimes did, cease as quickly as it had developed. This could be specially serious for a country whose prosperity depended perhaps on the production and sale of copper or nitrates or, indeed, any single or narrow range of raw materials.

The trend towards specialisation has made increasingly rapid strides since about 1850, owing to the spread of industrialisation to new parts of the globe, a movement aided by the development of railways and, perhaps even more, by the coming of the steamship. It has now become possible to transport cheaply many types of raw materials and goods that it was previously not commercially profitable to move from one continent to another. Before 1879, for example, when the first successful shipments of frozen meat were sent from Australia to London, wool was the only important product of the sheep.

Over the past century there has come into being a world economy which, so far at least, has tended to benefit most the inhabitants of industrialised nations and perhaps especially those of North America and western Europe.

Committee of Public Safety: the *Comité du Salut Publique*, formed during the French Revolution (6 April 1793) and broken up about sixteen months later. It exercised formidable power during its short life and was responsible for the "Reign of Terror", which led to the execution of Louis XVI, Marie Antoinette and thousands of others.

Commons, The House of: the lower house of the Parliament of the United Kingdom and the one in which the greater share of business is conducted. It used to meet, first in the Chapter House and then the Refectory of Westminster Abbey, but Edward VI granted it St Stephen's Chapel (1547), which was destroyed by fire in 1834. The new Commons Chamber designed by Sir Charles Barry was destroyed by a German bomb (10 May 1941) and the present Chamber, opened on 26 October 1950, is the work of Sir Giles Gilbert Scott. Largely as a result of Churchill's insistence, it is a close replica of the former one.

At present (1985) there are 650 Members of Parliament, each representing a single constituency, 523 in England, 72 in Scotland, 38 in Wales and 17 in Northern Ireland. MPs must be British subjects, eighteen years of age and not disqualified by being a peer, a lunatic, a

The House in session. The Speaker is seated at the centre of the table, the Government benches on his right, the Opposition on his left.

criminal, a clergyman of the Anglican or a minister of the Scottish church. A general election is normally held every five years, and members receive an annual salary which is adjusted according to inflation.

The House is presided over by the Speaker, elected by members as the sole judge on points of order. The members of the majority party, forming the government, sit on the Speaker's right and the Opposition on his left.

The power of the House of Commons was finally recognised as being superior to that of the Lords when, by the Parliament Act of 1911, the latter could no longer reject or amend a money bill and their delaying power over legislation was limited to two years, reduced to one by the Act of 1949.

The scope and complexity of modern government have led to more and more parliamentary business being conducted outside the Chamber. In 1963 Richard Crossman, a very experienced parliamentarian, wrote of the resentment of members at both "the rapid decline in its [i.e. Parliament's] prestige and the process by which it is being stripped of any real rôle in the great decisions of state".

Much of the effective work is conducted in various Committees of the House. The chief groups are:

(*a*) Standing Committees. These take over Bills initiated in the House and save a great deal of time that would otherwise be spent in discussion there.

(*b*) Select Committees. These possess special powers and privileges, delegated to them by the House, in collecting evidence, etc., before presenting their conclusions and recommendations to members as a whole. Some, such as the Committee of Privileges and the Estimates Committee are virtually permanent; others are formed only to carry out a specified and temporary task.

(*c*) Joint Committees. These are formed of members from both the Lords and the Commons sitting together, usually on Bills on which there is a fair measure of agreement, and thereby saving time that would be lost in separate committees.

(*d*) Private Bill Committees which, as the name indicates, deal with Bills introduced in the House by private members rather than by the government.

The great problem is to streamline and speed up the conduct of business by delegation and, at the same time, to keep all members fully informed and satisfied that Parliament as a whole is still playing its full part in major decisions.

¶ In PRENTICE, D. M. *Your Book of Parliament.* 1967

Commonwealth, The (1649–60): the only republican period in English history. There were four distinct phases. From 1649–53, the Council of State and the Rump, or Remnant, of the Long Parliament governed the country until ejected by Oliver Cromwell, who sponsored the Little, or Barebones', Parliament. From 16 December 1653 to 3 September 1658 Oliver Cromwell was Lord Protector by the terms of the Instrument of Government (1653) and the Humble Petition and Advice (1657). For the next eight months, his son Richard governed as an ineffective successor till his resignation in May 1659. May 1659 to May 1660 was a period of anarchy, leading to the restoration of Charles II. *See* BRITISH COMMONWEALTH OF NATIONS for another use of the term "Commonwealth".

Communism: a view of society according to which all property is held by the community and all work is done for the common benefit. Although the theory of communism was set out in the 19th century, there are earlier examples of people who practised a "communistic" way of life or who held such beliefs. In ancient

Sparta the holding of a large private fortune was forbidden; the English Levellers of the mid-17th century wanted a society in which the poor would govern the rich and private property would be abolished.

In 1848 the Germans Karl Marx (1818-83) and his friend Friedrich Engels (1820-95) published the first document stating the aims of communism: the Communist Manifesto. Since then, communism in theory and practice has played an important part in European and world history.

The strength and popular appeal of communism sprang from two sources. First, its closeness to the spirit and needs of the time. Marx lived in an age of rapid developments and growing confidence in science, technology and industry. The universal belief that human progress was certain and constant gave impetus to new social sciences like economics, and enabled Marx to claim, along with others, that the historical forces which had shaped society up to his own time were open to a scientific interpretation and would continue to be so. Marx's analysis of these forces called into being the idea of the "class war". In his view, human history was the story of conflict between different social classes. In the Europe of his own day the conflict between the traditional nobility and the rising business or "capitalist" class would eventually give way to a fight to the death between the latter and the new industrial working class, or "proletariat", employed – and usually exploited – by the capitalists. The class war would end in the "dictatorship of the proletariat".

Second, both Marx and Engels were able to see at first hand the conditions of life and work in 19th-century industrial England. Their indignation at what they saw of poverty and misery among the factory workers made communism much more than a mechanical explanation of the world in which its founders lived; it was always a prescription for revolutionary action and in the early 20th century became a crusade.

As a blueprint for action classic communist doctrine has been interpreted in many different ways over the last hundred years – partly because of changing circumstances, partly because Marx himself is vague on many points. Just as each Christian church regards itself as the true interpreter of Christ's teaching, so there are different schools of communist thought. In the 20th century, however, because of the success of the Russian Bolshevik Revolution in 1917, the word communism has become generally identified with the ideas and achievements of the Russian Marxists, particularly Lenin (1870–1924). Unfortunately in Russia, as well as in those eastern European countries that have come under her influence since 1945, the achievement of a large measure of economic and social justice has been accomplished by very severe restrictions on what we in the West think of as important personal freedoms. In addition, the division of Europe after 1945 into American and Russian spheres of influence, bringing about a decade of "cold war", made communism in practice seem to many in the West to be nothing more than an instrument of subversion, suppression and terror. (It is only fair to add that a similar image of western capitalism prevails in the communist world.)

But it is now much more difficult to generalise about communism in practice. The success of the revolution in China led by Mao Tse-tung in 1949 has been followed by growing rivalry between that country and Russia for leadership of the communist world. This conflict really has little to do with communist doctrine; indeed, much that has been done in the name of communism in the last fifty years has been very remote from the letter and spirit of Marx's theories. However, one definite trend can be discerned: communism, or revolutionary socialism, has in the last two decades been gaining increasing acceptance among the underdeveloped countries of Asia, Africa and Latin America. This is partly the result of Russian and Chinese competitive strategy, but partly also because communism's basic message of economic justice and progress for the whole community is an attractive one for the millions of people in these regions living in poverty. The revolution in Cuba in 1959 and the war in Vietnam are both examples and consequences of this development.

¶ SAVAGE, KATHARINE. *Marxism and Communism.* 1968

See also LENIN; MARX; UNION OF SOVIET SOCIALIST REPUBLICS; etc.

Compass, Mariners': the navigational compass used by sailors. One of the greatest problems of the early navigator was to know North and South so that he could, e.g., use his chart or determine wind direction. He could sometimes use the Pole Star or the rising and setting sun, but in thick weather he needed an instrument. The answer was the Mariners' Compass.

An early mariners' compass.

At first this was only a magnetised needle floated on a straw, or other carrier, in a bowl of water. It was not kept permanently in position but was rigged only in case of necessity. Later the needle was balanced on a pivot, with a card beneath marked with the points of the compass.

It is not easy to find exactly when the change took place from the floating needle to the compass with a card. It was certainly happening in English ships at the beginning of the 15th century, for Exchequer accounts of the year 1411 show the *Marie* carrying two "seyling needles", while at the same time another ship, the *Christopher*, carried three compasses. This therefore seems to have been the period of transition.

The long progress from the "seyling needle" to the modern gyro compass was attended with many difficulties. One was that the compass needle does not in fact point true North but magnetic North. The difference between the two, which is known as the *variation of the compass*, was a considerable handicap to early navigators, especially since the variation at any one place is not constant. It increases every year to a maximum, then slowly decreases again.

The other eccentricity of early compasses was their liability to be affected by the presence of iron in a ship's guns, cargo, etc., causing the needle to give a false directional reading. This is called the *deviation of the compass*. The old British cruiser *Blenheim* had a telescopic funnel which caused a deviation of more than 6°, according to whether it was up or down. This sort of deviation caused many wrecks and great loss of life.

The eventual solution to all the old compass problems was the development of the gyro compass, which works on the principle that a rotating flywheel, if it spins rapidly enough, will set itself with its spindle parallel to the earth's axis. When this occurs, the ends of the spindle point true North and true South with no variation and no deviation.

¶ HITCHINS, CAPTAIN H. L. and MAY, COMMANDER W. E. *From Lodestone to Gyro-Compass.* 1955

See also ASTROLABE; ASTRONOMY; DIALLING.

Concentration camps: originally places where the civilian population of a district was accommodated in wartime, or where aliens were interned. The term was brought into common use by the British, who herded large numbers of civilians into camps towards the end of the Boer War (1899–1902), to prevent their helping Boer guerrillas. Cubans were held in concentration camps in 1898 by the Spanish. In the 20th century concentration camps were used by totalitarian governments seeking to crush opposition, and we find them in Russia after 1917, Italy from 1922 to 1943, Austria from 1934 to 1938, Germany from 1933 to 1945 and Spain after 1938. The camps established by the Hitler regime in Germany were especially notorious for the systematic extermination of millions of victims of Nazi racial doctrine.

Concorde: Anglo-French supersonic airliner sponsored by both governments. It is a mid-wing monoplane, 193 feet long [58·5 metres], with 84-foot [25·6-metre] wing span and a unique nose section that can be hinged downwards for greater visibility. Concorde is designed to carry up to 144 passengers at an altitude of between 50,000 and 62,000 feet [15,240 and 18,900 metres] and a speed of up to 1,400 miles [2,253 kilometres] an hour, crossing the Atlantic in three and a half hours. *See also* AVIATION.

Condottieri: from *condotta*, a contract; hence, contractors who supplied and led troops for hire to Italian despots who dare not arm their subjects or to republics rent by faction. The earliest were foreigners: e.g. Duke Werner's Great Company, 1343, and Sir John Hawkswood's White Company, 1360. The first Italian company was Barbiano's Company of St George, 1365. In their heyday, 1420–50, many condottieri usurped power in the states they served. Machiavelli condemned condottieri as the ruin of Italy – treacherous; avoiding night marches, trench digging and winter campaigns; neglecting infantry and preferring showy, but less decisive, cavalry encounters. At the battle of Zagonara in 1424 only one man died – suffocated in the mud.

Confederated States, The: a political organisation caused by the secession (breaking away) from the American Union of eleven Southern States as a result of the election of Abraham Lincoln as president. The states were Alabama, Arkansas, Florida, Georgia, Louisiana, Mississippi, North Carolina, South Carolina, Tennessee, Texas and Virginia. In the presidential election of November 1860 Lincoln had been successful in all the Northern States but hardly polled a single popular vote in the South. When the result was declared, South Carolina called a state Convention which, by the unanimous vote of its 169 members, resolved that "the Union now subsisting between South Carolina and the other states, under the name of the United States of America, is hereby dissolved". South Carolina thus resumed its position as an independent state, and within a short time the other states followed. The seceding states sent delegates to a meeting at Montgomery, Alabama, on 8 February 1861, and a provisional government was set up. The meeting chose Jefferson Davis (*see* separate entry) as president of the new Confederate States of America. In all the dissension, slavery was a basic issue.

The Confederacy comprised $5\frac{1}{2}$ million whites and $3\frac{1}{2}$ million Negro slaves. The constitution was based upon that of the United States, but stressed the independent character of each state, expressly permitted slavery, and elected the president for a period of six years with a ban on re-election. The capital of the Confederacy was established at Richmond, Virginia. The Confederacy remained in being until formally dissolved by Davis on 24 April 1865, when the Civil War ended.

¶ LEVENSON, D. *The Confederacy.* ★1968
See also AMERICAN CIVIL WAR.

Kong-Fû-Tsë (Confucius) Chinese philosopher.

Confucius (551–478 BC)**:** Chinese philosopher. He developed his philosophy during the period of anarchy in China known as the Period of the Warring States (481–221 BC). This was almost co-existent with the period of Greek anarchy that similarly produced philosophical attempts to solve current problems. Confucius looked back to a golden age in which loyalties and obligations received their true emphasis. He stressed the necessity for loyalty of son to father and recommended strict upbringing, not for the sake of harshness, but to counter the natural Chinese indulgence of children. In the interests of political stability he advocated similar loyalty to the Prince, a doctrine later used to justify conservatism.

¶ In CANNING, JOHN, editor. *100 Great Lives.* 1969

Congo, The People's Republic of the: a republic in west-central Africa, sometimes referred to as Congo-Brazzaville, which covers 130,000 square miles (336,700 square kilometres), formerly French or Middle Congo. The territory lies across the equator, much of it consisting of dense tropical forests containing valuable timber. Commercial exploitation is hampered by transport difficulties. The country's main exports consist of industrial diamonds, wood products, gold and oil. In 1970 Congo declared itself a communist state and is generally regarded as one of the more radical countries on the African continent although generally it maintains a low international profile. Population in 1983: 1,694,000.

Congregationalists: members of the nonconformist church which began in England in the reign of Elizabeth I, basing their belief on the words of Jesus: "Where two or three are gathered together in my name, there am I in the midst of them" (Matthew 18:20), i.e. any group of Christian believers can form a church, without any other religious or civil authority. Many of the early Congregationalists were called "Brownists", after their leader Robert Browne (1550?–1633). Attempts at suppression drove numbers of them abroad, and from one of the exiled groups, in Leyden, came the Pilgrim Fathers (*see* separate entry).

Congress, United States: the federal legislature of the USA. The American

Constitution (*see* separate entry) established two Houses of Congress, the Lower called the House of Representatives and the Upper called the Senate. These two bodies together are known as Congress and are responsible for making the federal laws for purposes defined by the Constitution, as distinct from state laws made by the individual states themselves. Congress, which means the formal meeting of delegates for discussion, met initially when the burgesses of Virginia proposed a Continental Congress which was held in the Carpenters' Hall, Philadelphia, on 5 September 1774. Thirteen years later, when a Federal Convention met under the chairmanship of George Washington to draw up a Constitution, the name Congress was officially adopted. The first sentence of the first article of the Federal Constitution reads: "All legislative powers herein granted shall be vested in a Congress of the United States, which shall consist of a Senate and a House of Representatives."

Above, the Senate Chamber. Below, the House of Representatives Chamber.

Senators are chosen at the election held in November of each even-numbered year, but only one-third of them are elected at any one time. Each state is represented in the Upper Chamber of Congress by two senators. The Vice-President of the USA is the presiding officer in the Senate. In the House of Representatives each state is allotted a certain number of members in proportion to its population. All members of the House of Representatives are elected for a two-year period and, once again, the election is held in the November of each even-numbered year. The presiding officer in this House is known as the Speaker. The life of Congress is considered to be two years. It normally convenes in regular session at noon on 3 January of each year in the Capitol building, Washington, DC.

¶ COY, H. *Congress.* *1968

Conquistadors: Spanish adventurers (from *conquistar*, conqueror) who emigrated to America in the early 16th century. Starting from the islands of the Caribbean, Diego de Nicuesa and Vasco de Balboa made expeditions to the mainland, which led to the discovery of the Pacific Ocean in 1513 and to rumours of vast empires where determined men could make their fortunes. Most of the Conquistadors came from the tough province of Estremadura and were able to endure hardship with great courage. They were always greatly outnumbered by the native tribes but were usually able to ally themselves with one tribe against another. Their few horses and firearms intimidated their enemies, and their steel swords were naturally more effective than the polished stone weapons of their adversaries. Thus, Hernán Cortés was able to defeat the Aztecs (*see* separate entry), and then Francisco Pizarro conquered the Incas. From the jungles of the Amazon (crossed by Gonzallo Pizarro) to the deserts of California (explored by Coronado), other soldiers continued to search for more rich civilisations to loot and destroy. They found it hard to settle down peacefully as landowners and frequently quarrelled among themselves, fighting over the wealth they had so suddenly acquired. Noblemen were sent from Spain as Viceroys to establish law and order, and tried unsuccessfully to protect the natives from exploitation.

¶ FRANCIS, PAMELA. *Spanish Conquest in North America.* 1964; INNES, HAMMOND. *The Conquistadors.* 1969

Conscientious objectors: those who object, on grounds of conscience, to participation in some form of human activity. The term is now applied almost exclusively to those who will not be conscripted into the armed forces, particularly into fighting units, because of their belief in the sanctity of human life.

Conscription: compulsory enlistment for military service. Early nomad raiders and migrating tribes expected every man to fight, but when the knight and bowman dominated the field only the wealthy, strong and skilful were needed. The dynastic struggles of the 18th-century despots were settled by mercenaries "in temperate and indecisive contests" (Gibbon). By 1800, democracy and nationalism in France produced the "nation in arms", conscripted, inflamed to sacrifice by the *Marseillaise*, roused by propaganda to a hatred of the enemy which made a just peace unlikely. Monarchies introduced conscription reluctantly, realising that an armed citizen must be placated by the abolition of serfdom. Prussia took these steps in 1809, to build up national unity and to train large numbers while she was limited by treaty to a small standing army. Soviet Russia and Nazi Germany saw the value of conscription for indoctrination purposes. Britain introduced conscription reluctantly in 1916, after great losses in trench warfare, reintroduced it on the eve of World War II in 1939 and continued it in peacetime until 1960. America relied on a selective call-up for the Korean and Vietnam campaigns. Today's more costly, intricate and destructive weapons require fewer soldiers but more careful direction of all men and women into the most vital jobs.

Constable: originally, "the count of the stable", a Byzantine royal officer, and hence, through the centuries, a term covering a wide variety of officers holding military and civil jurisdiction, from the highest officers of state in France and England down to the village policeman. In France, the *connétable* in the Middle Ages stood next to the king. In England, the Lord High Constable appeared in the 12th century and acted as "quartermaster-general of the court and army" and sometimes as a principal officer of the exchequer.

Constantine, known as **"the Great"** (*c.* 280–337)**:** Roman emperor. His military qualities brought him success after the abdication of Diocletian in 305, but the disputed inheritance kept him from the throne until his defeat of Maxentius in 312. Thereafter his chief rival was his

old colleague Licinius, whom he finally executed in 323. The empire was reunited under Constantine and the old city of Byzantium rebuilt and renamed Constantinople. A man of great administrative ability, he is especially famous for the Edict of Milan in 313, proclaiming religious toleration. Although not baptised a Christian until his death-bed, Constantine did much to establish Christianity, and the first Council of the Church was convened by him in 325 at Nicaea.

Constantinople: the old Greek town of Byzantium (*see* separate entry), now called Istanbul. It was refounded by Constantine in AD 324 and completed by 330. Its site was admirably suited to take advantage of trade from the Black Sea, and Constantine's wall completed naturally strong defences. With the division of the Roman empire in 395, Constantinople became the capital of the Eastern Empire and soon surpassed Rome in importance. The landward wall was extended westwards by Theodosius II between 413 and 447, and this still survives. Inside it, magnificent buildings were erected – e.g. the Imperial palace and the church of Hagia Sophia, the masterpiece of Byzantine art. Artists and scholars of East and West flocked there, and the fusion between them can be seen most clearly in Byzantine architecture. After the fall of the Western Empire in 476, Constantinople became the capital of the Roman world, reunited for a time under Justinian in the 6th century. In many ways it lived up to its planned name – New Rome. (To this day, the chief patriarch of the Greek Church signs as "Archbishop of Constantinople, New Rome".) The officials had Roman titles, and the same feuds occurred in the magnificent hippodrome. Christianity in the East developed along different lines from in the West, and the Patriarch of Constantinople was second only to the Pope until the breakaway of the Orthodox Church in 1054. The city repelled numerous sieges from Arabs, Slavs, Bulgars and, finally, Turks. One of these, in 677, was repelled by the first use of Greek Fire, a type of burning pot filled with a mixture of sulphur, naphtha and nitre. Constantinople eventually fell to the Turks in 1453, long after most of her empire. It then became the capital of the Ottoman empire. The Turks gave it its characteristic architecture of narrow streets and low roofs interspersed with the slender minarets of the many mosques. The modern city supports a number of important industries, including textiles, tobacco and shipbuilding, and had a population of 3,033,810 in 1980.

¶ FRY, PLANTAGENET SOMERSET. *Constantinople*. 1970

Constitution, British: the set of fundamental principles by which the British people are governed. Unlike, for example, the USA, Britain does not have an exact written constitution. It is sometimes referred to as an unwritten constitution, but this is not strictly correct because certain very important Acts which go to the making of the government are written, in the sense that they are clearly laid down in writing or in print; examples of this are the Magna Carta (1215), the Habeas Corpus Act (1679), the Bill of Rights (1689), the Act of Settlement (1701), and the Parliament Act of 1911. The greater part of the constitution is based on custom, experience and legal decisions, and not simply on Acts of Parliament. The constitutional head of the country is the monarch, who reigns but does not rule.

In Britain, in contrast to the USA, there is no separation of powers between those who make the laws and those who put them into effect. It is essential to the proper working of Cabinet Government in Britain that the Queen's ministers should be members of one or other House of Parliament. Parliament, and by that is usually meant the majority party in the House of Commons, is supreme; the practical necessities of parliamentary government make it necessary for Parliament to trust the Government (formed at the Queen's invitation by a member of the majority party in the Commons) to govern and to accept the direction of the Cabinet in regard to the programme of legislation. The Judiciary is, however, almost wholly separate and its independence strictly preserved: it interprets the constitution, but it cannot amend it.

¶ JENNINGS, SIR IVOR. *The British Constitution.* 1966

Constitution, United States: the set of principles adopted by the USA for the country's governance.

The Constitution, drafted between 14 May and 17 September 1787 by fifty-five men meeting in the city of Philadelphia, and made effective on 21 June 1788 by the vote of nine ratifying state conventions, is now regarded as the most successful written constitution in the history of modern man. The Constitution has, in fact, been all things to all men. Conservatives have hailed its effectiveness as a guarantee of vested rights. Liberals have held it in high esteem for its protection of civil liberties. All interests, all shades of American opinion, have acknowledged its prestige by seeking to prove their causes to be in support of, or at least not incompatible with, the Constitution.

The Constitution is based on a theory known as the Separation of Powers. When the Constitution was framed, people were afraid that too much power might be concentrated in the hands of a small group of people. Hence, there was adopted a scheme by which the people who made the laws (the legislators in Congress) were different from those who interpreted the laws (the judges of the Supreme Court) and also different from those who administered them (the Executive or President). Thus, the framers of the Constitution sought to achieve a "balance" of powers by means of checks and balances between the separate organs of government. How this works in practice can be seen from the following examples. Though all legislative powers are the responsibility of Congress, the President has power to veto its acts, and his veto can be overridden only by a two-thirds majority of both Houses. Although the executive power is vested in the President, he requires the consent of two-thirds of the Senate for the making of treaties and for important appointments. Although judicial power is vested in the Supreme Court, the Senate still has power to try "impeachments". There were only twenty-five amendments to the Constitution in the first 180 years: the first ten of these, known as the Bill of Rights, were passed within a year of the Constitution being ratified. They are known as the bedrock of individual liberties; the two most important to Americans being the First, which guarantees freedom of religious worship, of speech and of the press, and the rights of peaceful assembly and of petitioning the government; and the Second, which guarantees the people the right to keep and bear arms for the national security.

¶ MORRIS, R. B. *The Constitution.* ★1968

Consul: a head of the Roman state. Consuls served in pairs for a single year, elected by and from the whole citizen body. In theory, they were in command of the armies and presided at public meetings and senatorial gatherings. With the establishment of the Empire (27 BC), the consuls lost their importance, though the office continued to be filled. In modern usage, consuls are agents officially appointed by countries to look after their interests, and those of its citizens, in the foreign countries where consulates are based.

Continental System: Napoleon I's economic scheme to destroy Britain's revenues, credit and warlike potential, after his invasion plans failed. The Berlin Decree of 1806, excluding British goods from European countries under French control, was extended by the Decrees of Milan and Warsaw, 1807, and Fontainebleau, 1810. Britain's reply, the 1807 Orders in Council closing continental ports to neutral ships, ruined France's colonial and overseas trade. England's success in finding new markets, widespread hostility to the French in Europe, extensive smuggling in British commodities and manufactures and Napoleon's disastrous Russian campaign of 1812 combined to bring about the complete failure of the system.

Convoy system: the controlled sailing of merchant ships in groups under naval escort. Danger from pirates had driven merchant ships to carry arms and sail in company in medieval times. Venice and the Hanseatic League used convoy in this sense. Trans-oceanic convoy began for Britain with the Commonwealth (1649–60) parrying the privateers of the Royalists. In the mid-18th-century wars, merchantmen were escorted continuously by frigates and sloops, reinforced at focal points such as Cape St Vincent and Finisterre by fifth rate ships of 44 or 50 guns, while the terminal points – West Indies, Bay of Bengal, Channel Approaches – were patrolled by squadrons watching for enemy battle squadrons. These methods proved effective, insurance rates were low for ships in convoy and the writers on naval tactics emphatically advocated convoy. Sir Julian Corbett in 1911 explained its virtue with the graphic phrase: "Where the carcase is, there will be eagles gathered together."

View of a wartime convoy on its way to Gibraltar.

Yet in the 1914–18 war the British Admiralty was very reluctant to introduce convoys. One objection was that, with larger ships, turn-round was 30 per cent slower if port facilities were clogged with large numbers of ships arriving together. But the main objection was the prejudice of the naval profession against the monotony and frustrations of escort duty and the tying down of large numbers of warships in apparently passive defensive work. Until 1917 the Admiralty relied on patrolled shipping lanes and hunts and sweeps by light forces, and Britain lost $3\frac{1}{2}$ million tons [3·56 million tonnes] of shipping and sank only thirty-six U-boats. With the introduction of convoys later that year losses were halved and twenty-seven U-boats were sunk by escorts.

In spite of these successes, convoy was little discussed in Britain, nor were its drills practised between the two World Wars. In staff discussions in 1937 it was resolved to adopt it if the enemy practised unrestricted U-boat warfare, and convoys were instituted within days of the declaration of war in 1939. However, the escorts were still weakened to provide offensive sweeps, warships had not the range to escort the whole way across the Atlantic to America and, until escort carriers were built, heavy losses were suffered in mid-Atlantic from U-boats and aircraft operating from Norway. But by May 1943 the equipment and tactics of convoy escort had been perfected, and Germany withdrew her U-boats after losing forty-one in a month. In the air, as on the sea, it was found better to escort the convoys than to patrol the seas. Convoys to Russia in long Arctic daylight round German-held Norway were perilous. In July 1942 Convoy P.Q.17 was ordered by the British Admiralty to scatter for fear of attack by the battleship *Tirpitz*. Twenty-one isolated ships were sunk; of the thirteen which survived eleven had voluntarily kept in convoy with trawlers and corvettes of the escort force.

Other nations have been even slower to adopt convoy, notably the Japanese, who squandered their merchant fleet rather than dishonour their ships with merely defensive tasks.

Cook, Captain James (1728–79): British naval captain, explorer and navigator. After service with a firm of Whitby (Yorkshire) shipowners, he joined the Navy in 1755 as an able seaman. Quickly promoted master, his efficiency in charting the St Lawrence in 1759, his surveys of the Newfoundland coasts and his observation of the 1766 solar eclipse as the basis for calculating longitude established his reputation.

In 1768 he was commissioned and appointed to command the *Endeavour*, a collier purchased for an expedition for the Royal Society to Tahiti, to observe the transit of Venus across the Sun's face. This done on 3 June 1769, he sailed south and west to New Zealand, surveyed the North and South Islands and Cook Strait. He explored the whole length of eastern Australia, claiming it for Britain. Returning home in 1771, he was promoted commander.

Cook's second expedition, 1772, in *Resolution* and *Adventure* (Captain Furneaux), to survey the South Pacific and Southern Ocean all round the globe, proved that the supposed land mass, *Terra Australis Incognita*, did not exist in many latitudes short of 60°. Furneaux returned to England alone in 1774, completing the first easterly circumnavigation. Cook arrived home in 1775, was promoted post-captain, elected to the Royal Society and awarded the Copley Medal for his success in treating scurvy by insisting on adequate supplies of fresh food.

In June 1776 he began his third voyage in *Resolution*, with *Discovery* (Captain Clarke). He discovered the Sandwich Islands and charted the American coast from 44° 55′ N northwards. Returning to

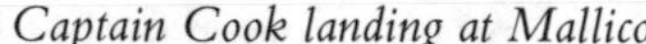
Captain Cook landing at Mallico.

Hawaii, he was killed by natives on 14 February 1779 while attempting to recover a stolen ship's boat.

¶ SWENSON, ERIC. *The South Sea Shilling: voyages of Captain Cook, R.N.* 1965; SYLVESTER, D. W. *Captain Cook and the Pacific.* 1971; WARNER, OLIVER. *Captain Cook and the South Pacific.* 1964

Coolidge, Calvin (1872–1933): 30th president of the USA (1923–9), often known as "Silent Cal" for his reserved character and habit of silence. Though not an outstanding leader, his insistence on thrift, obedience to law and order, and his belief that politics need not exclude some spiritual element, won him much popular confidence and support.

Co-operative societies: retail organisations in which the customers are members, providing capital and sharing in the profits by means of a dividend on their purchases.

Britain's special contribution to co-operation of this sort was retail grocery, the first successful shop being established at Rochdale in 1844. Rochdale worked on the principles of cash transactions, dividends on purchases and "one man one vote" adopted from earlier co-operative societies. The co-operatives spread and provided the first comprehensive retail service in dry goods and foodstuffs for working class people. In 1863 the Co-operative Wholesale Society was founded to produce goods to be sold by the retail societies. Such services as insurance, banking, housing and travel have been added, and in this century the movement has been the prototype of mass consumer marketing and multiple stores. Politically, the Co-operative and Labour Parties have close ties.

Co-operation is found throughout the world, though it does not always take the same form. The Rochdale consumer type is widespread, especially in north-western and central Europe. Another noteworthy development has been associations of peasant farmers. Both these types have the object of preventing profiteering by the middleman who buys from the producer and sells to the consumer. But whereas the first seeks mainly to secure a reduction in the cost of living for all its members, the second is chiefly concerned with increasing the gains of the farmers.

Right, Nicolaus Copernicus. Below, planets in orbit round the sun according to Copernican theory.

Copernicus, Nicolaus (1473–1543): Polish astronomer. He is chiefly remembered for his theory – revolutionary at the time – that the earth, rather than being the centre of the universe, orbits about the sun with the other planets. He was also a skilful painter, a physician, a currency reformer and a hard-working administrator.

¶ KNIGHT, DAVID C. *Copernicus: Titan of modern astronomy.* 1967

Coral Sea, Battle of the (May 1942): decisive battle of World War II in which US sea and air forces forced the withdrawal of a Japanese squadron from a movement towards Australia.

Coronado, Francisco Vasquez de (*c.* 1500–54)**:** Spanish explorer of southwest America. Though not reckoned among the greatest of the conquistadors, he accomplished one of the most surprising marches in the Spanish conquest of America, penetrating the plains of Texas and, with about thirty horsemen, continuing as far as central Kansas.

Coronation: the act or ceremony of crowning a sovereign and, in essence, the making of a public contract between monarch and people. In return for his subjects' allegiance, the king binds himself to govern with justice and mercy, according to the laws and customs of the land.

Strictly speaking, a king does not have to be crowned at all. Rulers have succeeded to their thrones by election, by conquest and by inheritance. King Edward VIII, during his brief reign of ten months in 1936, was no less King of England because he abdicated before the date fixed for his coronation. Nevertheless, people of all races, in all ages, have felt it desirable to confirm their rulers in their high office by means of some special ceremonial. The ritual of coronation has persisted because it touches feelings rooted deep in the consciousness of mankind.

Early kings were regarded as more than supreme rulers and lawgivers. Their powers were believed to extend to the forces of nature. Thus, the tribal rulers of primitive societies were often also the public magicians. The pharaohs of Egypt were worshipped as gods in their own lifetimes. The kings of ancient Mexico swore a coronation oath to make the sun shine, the clouds give rain, the rivers flow and the earth bring forth fruits in abundance. Kings who did not claim actual godhead officiated as high priests.

This concept of a king as in part priest underlies such coronation symbolism as the robing of the English monarch in the priestly vestments, the dalmatic, the alb and the stole. It is reinforced, in Christian countries, by Old Testament references to the anointing of kings. When Samuel, at God's direction, singled out Saul to be the first King of Israel, he "took a vial of oil and poured it upon his head . . . and said Is it not because the Lord hath anointed thee to be captain over his inheritance?" (I Samuel 10:1).

Anointing the new king came to be regarded as such an important part of the coronation ceremony that it gave rise to its own legends. In France, it was said, on the occasion of the coronation of Clovis the Great, a dove flew down from heaven bearing in its beak a container of holy oil for the royal anointing; and thereafter, at subsequent French coronations, a drop of the miraculous oil was always used along with the more mundane variety.

Not to be outdone, the English produced their own miracle. Their story was that the Virgin Mary had appeared to Thomas Becket and handed him a vessel of holy oil to be used for the consecration of English kings – a gift that unfortunately disappeared at the Reformation. It was by virtue of these miraculous oils that the kings of England and of France were thought to be able to cure the disease of scrofula by mere touch – though, long after the Reformation, Charles II in the course of his reign is said to have touched close on a hundred thousand people for the ailment. The proportion of cures is not known.

The crown, as an essential coronation feature, originated in a simple band made of blue silk or linen with white spots which was the diadem the Persian king Darius wore fastened round his headdress. When Alexander the Great conquered the Persians, he adopted the head-band as an emblem of royal power. Later, gold replaced linen, and further elaborations over the centuries produced the jewelled crowns which are sometimes too heavy for a monarch's head to bear.

Other items of coronation regalia are the sceptre and orb, signifying sovereignty; the rod, mercy; the ring, faith. Sword and spurs speak for themselves. When a king of England goes to his enthronement, he is preceded by four swords: the sword of mercy, the sword of justice to the spirituality, the sword of justice to the temporality, and the sword of state.

Coronations, when hopes for the new reign run high, have always been occasions for merrymaking. When, on the last day of September 1553, Mary Tudor, in a carriage drawn by six horses with trappings of cloth-of-gold, drove through London on her way to her coronation at Westminster, the City fountains and conduits ran wine, pageants were performed in her honour and "one Peter a Dutchman", holding a streamer five yards [4·6 metres] long, balanced on one foot on top of the weathercock of St Paul's, "to the great marvell of all people".

Though the details of ceremonial may vary locally and from age to age, the essential elements of a coronation are timeless. The only coronation recorded in the Bible, that of seven-year-old Jehoash, has a distinctly contemporary ring. "And he brought forth the king's son, and put the crown upon him, and gave him the testimony; and they made him king and anointed him; and they clapped their hands, and said, God save the king" (II Kings 11:12).

¶ TANNER, L. E. *The History of the Coronation.* 1953

The sceptre and orb, symbolising the sovereignty of the English monarch.

Cortés, Hernán (1485–1547): Spanish conquistador. He sailed in 1519 to the mainland of Central America with a force of 600 men, 16 horses, and 10 cannon. There he discovered and, with the help of local allies, conquered the rich empire of the Aztecs. At first he was welcomed by the Aztec emperor Montezuma (Moctezuma) and invited to visit the capital city, Tenochtitlan. Once inside Cortés seized Montezuma and held him prisoner but the Aztecs rose against the Spaniards, his force was almost trapped and he had to fight his way out of Tenochtitlan, suffering many losses. Cortés then showed great energy in organising a siege which, after eighty days and with great help from his Tlaxcalan allies, finally reduced the city. Subsequently, he organised the country as a province of Spain.

¶ BLOCKER, IRWIN R. *Cortes and the Aztec Conquest.* 1966

Cossacks (from Turkish *quzaq*, outlaw or adventurer): members of bands of light-horsemen who colonised the rivers in the Russian steppes – Ural, Don and Dnieper. These bands sprang up in the 16th century, attracting young men fleeing from serfdom, criminals, deserters and, later, Old Believers defying the reformed Orthodox Church. They governed themselves by free vote at the camp fire, electing annually a *hetman*, or chieftain, to lead them on forays. They lived by hunting, fishing, trading slaves and plundering, and by the annual subsidy of grain, arms and clothes given to them by the Czar for containing the Crimean Tartars. A Cossack who married was given a plot on the banks of the river. Peter the Great recruited them into regiments of irregular cavalry, in which their remarkable horsemanship could be used to advantage. Cossacks are now usually thought of only in terms of small bands of riders and dancers of incredible skill and colourful appearance. It must not be forgotten that they occupied a considerable part of the Russian empire, lived in settled communities and included substantial landowners.

Cossacks off duty during World War II.

Cotton and the cotton industry: Cotton (from an Arabic word meaning "a plant grown in conquered lands") is a white fibrous material which covers the seeds of a tropical shrub (*Gossypium arboreum*) growing from 3 to 6 feet [0·9 to 1·8 metres] high.

The Harappa civilisation of India grew cultivated cotton. Fragments of a cotton textile, dyed red with madder, were found at Mohenjo-daro adhering to a silver vase dated between 2500 BC and 1500 BC. Herodotus (*c.* 450 BC) mentions its use by the Greeks, and it was undoubtedly spread by the soldiers of Alexander the Great after the invasion of India (326 BC). In Egypt, cotton was grown in the 7th century AD, but an earlier date is suggested as possible from tomb paintings at Beni Hasan (2500 BC).

In America, the Anasazi culture (northern Pueblo) used cotton in Arizona (AD 700). In 1492 the Indians bartered it with Christopher Columbus (1451–1506). The Yucatan natives gave cotton clothes to Hernán Cortés (1484–1547). The Aztecs wore a body armour of brine-soaked quilted cotton, resembling a space suit. It was effective, cool and light. In 1498 Vasco da Gama (1460–1524) brought calicoes from Calicut (Calcutta) to Lisbon. Traditionally cotton as an article of commerce was brought to Europe by the Italian merchant princes. Flemish, Dutch and French protestant refugees then brought it to England. These refugees had a high degree of skill, which benefited both the cotton and woollen industries.

The cotton industry in England rose to prominence, particularly in Lancashire, during the Industrial Revolution, and factors such as the presence of water power from the Pennine streams, the nearness of coalfields and the major ports the humid climate and the established domestic system in that area have all been advanced to explain its growth there.

The derivation of some of the terms is interesting. Fustian (a linen warp with a cotton weft) was derived from Fustat (i.e. Cairo). Dimity, mentioned by Daniel Defoe (1661–1731), means "twice threaded", i.e. having a double thread woven into it. Calico is derived from Calicut in India, and muslin from Mosul in Iraq.

The early industry had two chief types of loom. The Dutch loom wove narrow fabrics and the hand loom broader ones. Four spinners were needed to keep one loom operational. This ratio was upset by the invention in England of the Flying Shuttle by John Kay of Bury in 1733, closely followed in 1760 by his son Robert's invention of a triple shuttle machine. The first improvement on the spinning side helped the domestic system, when James Hargreaves (1745–78) of Stanhill, near Blackburn, invented the Spinning Jenny in 1764. Other inventions were suitable for a factory system. In 1769 Richard Arkwright (1732–92) produced a spinning frame which could spin a great number of threads of any required degree of strength and fineness. In 1799 Samuel Crompton (1753–1827) produced a machine known first as the muslin wheel and later as the Mule, which could spin a fine yarn for the manufacture of muslin. In

Hargreaves' Spinning Jenny.

1758 the Rev. Edmund Cartwright (1743–1823) improved the loom, but the hand loom remained in use until 1830. Towards the close of the century industrial chemists invented a chlorine bleaching powder, and Thomas Bell's invention of revolving cylinders for pattern printing speeded up output. By 1789 the cotton industry was concentrated on the South Lancashire Coalfield, and steam power was replacing water power.

In America the industry can be considered as dating from 1793, when Eli Whitney (1765–1825) invented the saw gin – a machine which separated the cotton hairs (lint) from its seed at the rate of about 50 lb [22·7 kilograms] a day (*see* separate entry). The process was known as "ginning", "gin" being a contraction of "engine" and meaning a contrivance or trap. Whitney's invention soon brought America into the forefront of cotton-producing countries and, though the Civil War almost wiped out the crop and the freeing of the slaves produced great labour problems, it recovered its position by the end of the century.

Although the industry in Britain was also hit by the American Civil War, as it had been earlier by the Luddite Riots, it expanded until the end of World War I. From then unemployment, alleviated by the military needs of World War II, hit the industry badly and it began to contract – a process which was hastened by foreign competition and by the adoption of man-made fibres. In recent years many new nations have set up their own textile industries to meet home demands and compete in world markets so that the older established textile industries, such as Britain's, have been forced to concentrate upon quality exports to remain viable. Chief cotton producers are the USA, USSR, China, Egypt and Brazil.

¶ STYLES, SHOWELL. *The Battle of Cotton*. 1960

Councils of the Church: authoritative gatherings specially summoned to consider matters of Christian doctrine and discipline.

The first Ecumenical (universal) Council of the Church was the Council of Nicaea, summoned by Constantine the Great (*c.* 280–337). It met in 325 at Nicaea (Isnik in Asia Minor) to settle a controversy between two parties in the Church, the Arians and the Athanasians. The latter prevailed. A creed, known as the Nicene Creed, was approved by the Council; this was a forerunner of the more familiar Apostles' Creed, which was first used at Antioch in the 5th century.

There were six other Ecumenical Councils, held at Constantinople, 381; Ephesus, 431; Chalcedon, 451; Constantinople, 533 and 680; and Nicaea, 787. After this the Eastern Church ceased to be represented, so that later Councils are not regarded as Ecumenical in the strict sense, except by the Roman Catholic Church.

A series of Councils held over the centuries at the Lateran Palace in Rome dealt mainly with matters of heresy and reform. These are known as the Lateran Councils. The most important was the fourth Lateran Council, summoned by Pope Innocent III in 1215, when an effort was made to reform the Church by defining Christian doctrine, suppressing heresy, improving the education of the clergy and laying down more stringent rules for individual Christians – for instance, confession to a priest at least once a year.

Fresh efforts towards reform were made by the Councils of Constance (1414–18), which also put an end to the Great Schism, when there were two or even three Popes, each recognised by a different faction. This Council condemned the so-called heresies of John Wyclif (1329–84) and John Huss (1369–1415), ordering Wyclif's bones to be dug up and scattered and John Huss to be handed over to the secular authorities and burned at the stake.

The Council of Basle (1431–49) attempted to curb the authority of the Pope and also, unsuccessfully, to renew fellowship with the Eastern Church. The Greek Christians were anxious to obtain help from the West in their struggle against the Turks, who finally conquered Constantinople in 1453.

The Council of Trent, or Trento, in the Alto Adige, Italy (1545–63), was summoned by Pope Paul III. It met at intervals over the years and proved epoch-making. It repudiated Protestant doctrine, defined and reaffirmed the faith and practice of the Roman Catholic Church and the supreme authority of the Pope, recognised the (later) Nicene Creed as the basis of faith and established the Canon of the Scriptures – the Books of the Bible which were believed to have been divinely inspired, with the Vulgate as the authentic Latin version. Among more modern gatherings may be mentioned the Vatican Council of 1870, when the doctrine of Papal Infallibility was defined.

In recent years a new conception of the function of a Council of the Church in its widest sense has been developing. In the Conferences of the World Council of Churches, and in the Vatican Councils as inspired by Pope John XXIII, nearly all the branches of the worldwide Christian Church have been represented, either by delegates or by observers.

¶ *The Documents of Vatican II.* 1966; WATKIN, E. I. *The Church in Council.* 1961

Court: a word with several meanings, including an enclosed place; the place where a ruler keeps his state, attended by his retinue; a collective term for those attendant on a monarch; a tribunal of judges or other persons legally appointed to hear and determine a cause, whether civil, criminal, ecclesiastical or military; and the place where judicial trials are held. Disparate as they seem, all are connected, each growing out of the other.

Judicial tribunals originally met in temporary enclosures, or courts. Onlookers were kept beyond "the bar of the court", a term commemorated in the name and description of the practising barrister, one who has been "called to the bar".

The Germanic tribes that spread across the continent of Europe in the first centuries of the Christian era had no settled capitals. The royal headquarters might be no more than a ring of tents surrounded by a defensive earthwork or palisade – a court in its primary meaning. Castles came later, and these, too, were generally built round a courtyard. Wherever the king established himself was where he held court, where he surrounded himself with his *thegns*, the companions he could trust and those whose advice he could ask if he had a mind to.

As the business of government became more complicated kings found it expedient, from time to time, to discuss matters of policy with the leading men of the kingdom and to seek their help in framing laws. The Anglo-Saxon kings often summoned a *witenagemot*, a "court of wise men", for this purpose.

After the Norman Conquest the English court developed the two-pronged character to which we owe the institution of Parliament and the Courts of Law. The Great Council became the supreme law court of the kingdom and was the institution to which people could present petitions against an injustice or an inadequacy of the law: and that was the beginning of Parliament. From the *Curia Regis*, the King's Court, derive our High Court, Privy Council and Cabinet. While theoretically composed of the peers of the realm, the *Curia Regis*, in practice, included the chancellor, the justiciar and the king's judges, the men who did the work.

England early developed its common law courts. In medieval France, where the *Parlement* of Paris made no such distinction between legislative and judicial functions, such a backlog of judicial business built up that a number of provincial *parlements* had to be set up to cope with it, a system which lasted until the French Revolution.

In tracing the word "court" to its origins, one must be careful not to give the impression that no courts existed before medieval times. Every civilisation in history has had to develop some procedure for hearing civil disputes and bringing accused persons to trial. The ancient Hebrews had three courts, incorporating elaborate safeguards to ensure a fair hearing: the *Sanhedrin*, or supreme court, of seventy-one members, a court of twenty-three for criminal matters, and the *Beth Din*, a court of three which survives to this day, to deal with civil matters and act as a court of arbitration.

The ancient Athenians seem to have regarded going to law as a king of amateur sports. There were no professional lawyers, and the jurymen in one case alone might number thousands. The Romans built up a comprehensive judicial administration and a system of laws which has formed the basis of many modern legal codes.

Church, or ecclesiastical, courts have existed from at least the 5th century. William the Conqueror imported them into England. The papal *Curia*, which includes several judicial tribunals, is the government department of the Roman Catholic Church.

Courts-martial are special courts for the trial of military offences. The medieval *Curia Militaris* (also known as the Court of Chivalry, the Court of Knighthood and the Court of Honour) was not, despite its name, a court-martial but one dealing with matters arising out of medieval warfare.

Some countries (e.g. Turkey and the USSR) have Courts of Cassation to which application may be made that a decision of a lower court be nullified on the ground that it violates a rule of law. The French *Conseil d'Etat* is a court which redresses injustices committed by public authorities, and is thus a kind of communal ombudsman. The USA and the USSR federations of states have Supreme Courts at the pinnacles of their judicial systems. China has an extensive network of "People's Courts". All developed societies today possess law courts. How far justice is done in them is another matter.

Courts, International: courts which attempt to settle legal differences between nations.

If nations are to live at peace they must agree to a set of rules governing their relations and laying down an acceptable procedure for settling disputes.

Arbitration – i.e. referring a dispute to the judgment of a disinterested party – was frequently used by the city states of ancient Greece. In medieval Europe, disputes between rulers were often referred to the Pope for a decision, a practice that diminished with the emergence of sovereign states, the rulers of which insisted on being master in their own house.

The Jay Treaty of 1794, between Great Britain and the United States, was the beginning of modern international arbitration. It provided for arbitration machinery in boundary disputes and on matters arising out of the war with France.

The Permanent Court of Arbitration, established at the Hague in 1900, today has only a formal existence. It consists simply of an international panel from which, in case of need, arbitrators may be selected. After World War I the League of Nations set up a Permanent Court of International Justice which, in 1946, was reconstituted as the International Court of Justice, the principal court of the United Nations.

While these Courts have settled many disputes, their weakness lies in the fact that they can neither compel attendance nor enforce their judgments. At the Nuremberg Trials, after World War II, an international tribunal tried, condemned and carried out sentence on many leading Nazis as war criminals. Although they were courts of the conqueror judging the conquered, they represent nevertheless a completely new departure and may be a first step towards a truly International Court of Justice.

Covenanters: Scottish Presbyterians who, at various crises in the 16th and 17th centuries, subscribed to bonds or covenants in defence of their religion; for example, the National Covenant of 1638 to resist the imposition of an English Prayer Book. When the Restoration bishops returned (1660), Presbyterian "conventicles" (secret meetings) were forbidden. Both sides were violent. Covenanters murdered Archbishop Sharp; Episcopalians, led by Claverhouse, attacked Presbyterian worshippers at Drumclog. Three Covenanter rebellions were put down with great cruelty. Throughout the "killing time" the Covenanters remained convinced that they alone knew the will of God, who would punish their enemies. Relief for them came after the revolution of 1688, when support of the Covenant ceased to be a crime and the "outed ministers" returned to their pulpits.

Cranmer, Thomas (1489–1556): Archbishop of Canterbury 1533–56. Cranmer, a scholar, was drawn into affairs of state

after suggesting that the question of Henry VIII's divorce from Catherine of Aragon should be decided by theologians. As Archbishop he supported the Protestant reformers and the Act of Supremacy; wrote an introduction to the English Bible (1539); composed the English Litany and took the leading part in compiling the two English Prayer Books.

When Mary Tudor, a Catholic, came to the throne she could forgive neither his part in her mother's tragedy nor his religious beliefs. Arrested and brought to trial, he faced a conflict between his Protestantism and his belief in the subject's duty of obedience. Five times he recanted before his final courageous assertion of his Protestantism and his burning as a heretic, which did much to strengthen the opposition to Mary.

¶ In GARNETT, EMMELINE. *Tudors.* 1956

Crécy, Battle of (26–27 August 1346): English victory over the French in the Hundred Years War. The heavily armoured French nobility and knighthood fought with great gallantry but were notably disorganised; refusing to learn the

The Battle of Crécy. French horsemen, routed by the English longbow-men.

lessons of new methods of warfare they suffered humiliating defeat at the hands of the humble but highly mobile English longbow-men. At the lowest estimate, the French seem to have lost about 1,500 knights and 10,000 common soldiers; the English less than 100 all told. The most colourful account occurs in the *Chronicles* of Jean Froissart, who tells the famous story of the Black Prince winning his spurs in the battle.

¶ In VAN THAL, HERBERT. *Famous Land Battles.* 1964

Crimean War, The (1853–56): war declared on Russia by Turkey (1853), Britain and France (1854) and Sardinia (1855). It was caused basically by distrust of Russian influence in the Near East, but occasioned by a trivial quarrel between Russia and France over the guardianship of the Holy Places in Palestine. When the Sultan, advised by the British ambassador Stratford Canning, refused Czar Nicholas's claim to protect all Turkish Christian subjects, Russia occupied Wallachia and Moldavia (modern Romania), and Turkey declared war. After the destruction of a Turkish fleet off Sinope (1853) Britain joined France in demanding Russian withdrawal; war was declared and an Anglo-French army sent to Varna under the elderly Lord Raglan and the sickly St Arnaud (1854).

Shortly after, the Russians, threatened by Austria, withdrew; nevertheless the allies were shipped to the Crimea, a peninsula on the north shore of the Black Sea, to destroy the base of Sevastopol. They failed to follow up an initial victory on the River Alma and made their base at Balaclava, giving the Russians time to improve fortifications, under the direction of the brilliant engineer Todleben. As winter drew on, organisation of supplies was chaotic, there was little shelter, dysentery and cholera broke out and there were no adequate hospital arrangements. Despite all this, two Russian attempts to raise the siege were defeated at Balaclava and Inkerman.

Exposure of the conditions by the British war correspondent William Russell led to a change of government in Britain and to the arrival of Florence Nightingale to reform Scutari hospital.

Lord Raglan confers with the Allies. Photograph by Roger Fenton, 1856.

Deadlock in the Crimea, varied by a Sardinian success at Tchernaya, ended with the French capture of the Malakoff redoubt and the evacuation of Sevastopol; the new Czar, Alexander II, then consented to treat. By the Peace of Paris (1856) Russia surrendered her claims, the Black Sea was demilitarised, and Moldavia and Wallachia became independent under Turkish suzerainty. The war saw the award of the first Victoria Cross, the most coveted British decoration for gallantry.

¶ PEMBERTON W. B. *Battles of the Crimean War.* 1968

Criminal investigation: the inquiry into and detection of crime. Criminal investigators combine the use of scientific aids with the trained observation and reasoning powers of experts.

In cases involving death, pathologists are able to establish its cause and time its occurrence within narrow limits. In a case of violent death they can advise detectives what weapon to look for. If a gun, the make and calibre can be determined and if, presently, a weapon be produced, firearms experts are able to state with certainty whether it fired the fatal shot.

Fingerprints may furnish an important clue. Where documentary evidence is in question, photography can reveal alterations invisible to the naked eye. Typewriters, to the expert, are as uniquely individual as people, and a typewritten letter can be shown to have been typed on a particular machine. Attempts to disguise handwriting have little chance of deceiving the handwriting expert.

Each expert contribution is a piece in the jigsaw of factual data which must be put together by the detective in charge of the case. Further pieces may come from other sources, e.g. the statements of witnesses and informers. Information, however apparently trivial, has to be followed up and evaluated. Where appropriate, an identification parade may be held, though the hazards of this procedure have been highlighted by several cases of mistaken identity. The aim of the exercise is kept always in view – not merely to catch the law-breaker, but to establish his guilt beyond doubt and within the appropriate rules of evidence.

The foregoing is a summary of properly conducted criminal investigation in democracies, where the rights of the individual under the law are upheld and no subject may be interrogated under a show of force. It takes no account of the arbitrary arrests, the threats, torture, brainwashing and forced confessions which are among the police tools of totalitarian states.

Organisations to combat crime include England's CID (Criminal Investigation Department), France's Sûreté and the United States' FBI (Federal Bureau of Investigation). By means of Interpol (International Criminal Police Commission), national police departments co-operate to catch criminals who have fled the country of their crime.

Through the ages there have been wide variations in the standards of criminal investigation. In ancient Egypt accused persons were beaten on the hands and feet to encourage them to give evidence. At the other extreme, under the Code of Laws proclaimed by Hammurabi, king of Babylon (*c.* 2340 BC), suspicion was not enough. A thief, for example, could only be convicted if caught with the stolen property actually in his possession.

Investigation by ordeal, a practice that grew out of primitive beliefs in magic and in supernatural intervention in human affairs, was once widespread throughout the world. Carrying red-hot iron a prescribed number of paces, for example, was a method of establishing guilt or innocence prescribed equally in the ancient Hindu *Yajnavalkya Dharmasastra* and the laws of Anglo-Saxon Athelstan (895–940). This old accusatory procedure was gradually superseded by the *inquisitio*, the inquest or disinterested inquiry into the facts which is one of the great safeguards of individual liberty.

Croesus (560–547 BC): last King of Lydia. His great wealth, remembered in the phrase "as rich as Croesus", was gained from the caravan routes of Asia Minor. To further encourage trade, Lydia developed the first stamped coinage. Croesus conquered the Greek cities on the Ionian coast and allied himself with Babylon against the Persians. He gave rich presents to the Delphic oracle (*see* ORACLE), but was repaid with a prophecy of his defeat by Cyrus, King of Persia.

Cromwell, Oliver (1599–1658): Lord Protector of England. Oliver Cromwell, a Puritan squire, entered Parliament in 1628. As the creator and leader of the New Model Army, he played an important part in the defeat of Charles I. He subsequently signed the King's death-warrant; though, if tradition is to be believed, only in the bitter belief that it was "cruel necessity". What he believed to be the "testimony of events" led to his intervention in politics. He dissolved the Rump Parliament by force and, after an unsuccessful attempt to establish the rule of an assembly of "men fearing God and hating covetousness", nominated by congregational churches throughout the kingdom, he accepted the Instrument of Government by which he became Protector.

A portrait medallion of Oliver Cromwell.

At home he made important reforms and granted a high degree of religious toleration, but he failed to secure "government by consent" and for a time resorted to a military dictatorship, through the appointment of major-generals. He refused the crown but accepted the Humble Petition and Advice, receiving the title Lord Protector with power to nominate his successor. Abroad he gained great prestige. He found the Commonwealth threatened by enemies, but after nine months could tell Parliament "there is not a nation in Europe but desires a good understanding with you". His attempt to found a Protestant alliance failed, and his continuance of the Elizabethan policy of friendship with France and war with Spain led to financial difficulties. His belief that he was God's chosen instrument led to strange inconsistencies, but Clarendon, his enemy, admits that he had "a great spirit".

¶ LEVINE, I. E. *Oliver Cromwell.* 1967; MARTIN, BERNARD. *Our Chief of Men.* 1960

Cromwell, Thomas, Earl of Essex (1485?–1540): English statesman; son of Walter Cromwell, a brewer of Putney. After a varied career abroad, he entered the service of Cardinal Wolsey from 1520 to 1529 and gained great insight into political affairs.

He was a member of the Reformation Parliament (1529–36), a Privy Councillor (1531), Chancellor of the Exchequer (1533) and Secretary to Henry VIII (1534–40). His main achievement was drafting and steering through Parliament the legislation which separated England from Rome; and, as Vicar General, he was responsible for the dissolution of the monasteries, 1536–39. His fall was caused by his support of Church reform on lines more protestant than Henry VIII wanted and the failure of the King's fourth marriage to Anne of Cleves, which Cromwell had negotiated. After being charged with treason he was beheaded on Tower Hill, 28 July 1540.

Thomas Cromwell.

Cross: figure made by crossing one line with another. As a symbol or distinguishing mark the cross has been used since pre-Christian times in almost every part of the world. Early cross forms have been adopted and used in a variety of ways, such as the decoration of Coptic Christian monuments by the ankh cross, formerly the ancient Egyptian symbol of life, and the use of the pagan swastika by Nazi Germany in the mistaken fancy that it was a Nordic symbol.

The cross became the principal symbol of the Christian religion from the 4th century, recalling the crucifixion of Christ and indicating his victory over the powers of evil and death. On his conversion in 312, Constantine (reigned 306–337) had the sign of the cross exhibited on his standards and armour. This symbolic theme was revived by Urban II (pope 1088–99) who, as head of the council which proclaimed war on the infidels, said, "Let the cross glitter on your arms and standards, bear it on your shoulders and your breasts, it will become for you the emblem of victory or the palm of martyrdom". From this the name "crusades" was derived, and the support for the call to arms was immediate. The huge red cross sewn on the crusaders' clothes became a fine recruiting emblem, and the long conflict which followed became known as Cross *versus* Crescent (the crescent being the Muslim symbol). The various military and religious orders of knighthood founded at this time were distinguished by several forms of cross, of which possibly the best known is the Maltese cross of the Hospitallers, a white cross of eight points on a black ground. The Templars had as their distinctive mark a broad red cross, while the Knights of St Lazarus and St Maurice used a white cross with flowered points. This movement gave impetus to its use as an heraldic emblem, and it has long been one of the regular devices or "ordinaries" to decorate the heraldic shield.

There are nearly 400 varieties of the cross known, but only a dozen or so will

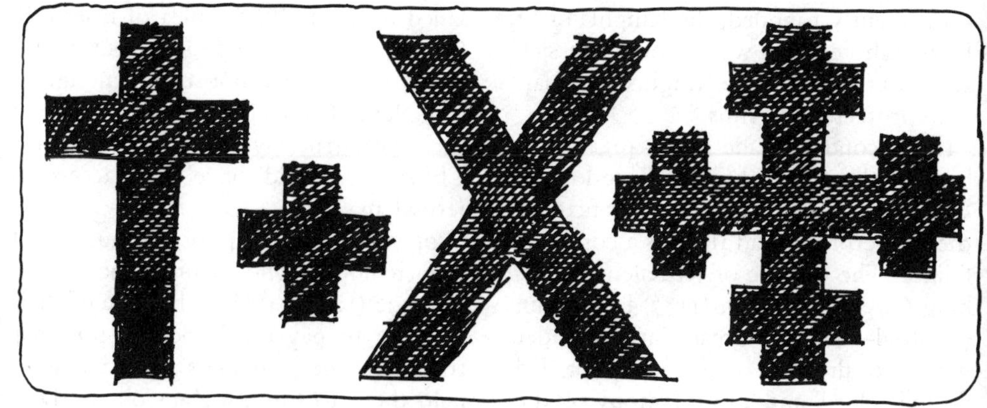

Left to right, Christian Cross, St George's Cross, St Andrew's Cross, and cross crosslet.

be found to occur regularly. The most common type has four arms of equal length, a typical example being the red cross of St George. A basic form whose lowest stem is longer than the other three arms is usually recognised as the principal symbol of the Christian religion. Another familiar type is the saltire, or cross of St Andrew, in the form of a Roman figure ten. The cross soon became decorated or ornamented, a good example being the cross crosslet, in which the four equal arms of the simple cross each have small cross pieces. A regular pattern of cross crosslets on a shield of arms is termed crusilly. Other decorated examples include the widely used cross patonce, the ends of which are splayed out or widened. Often the cross is used to divide the field on a shield of arms, and then it is sometimes subject to "lines of partition" where its outline assumes a wavy, ragged, indented or dovetailed pattern.

¶ BARBER, RICHARD. *The Knight and Chivalry.* 1971; UDEN, GRANT. *A Dictionary of Chivalry.* 1968

See also ARMORIAL BEARINGS *and* HERALDRY.

Crusades, The (from *crux*, cross): the series of eight military expeditions (11th–13th centuries) made by Christians of western Europe to rescue the Holy Land from the Saracens (Muslims).

In AD 637 the Arabs captured Jerusalem, but did not interfere with Christian pilgrimages to the Holy Sepulchre. The situation altered when, in 1076, Seljukian Turks captured the Holy City and maltreated pilgrims. The Eastern or Byzantine Empire was also threatened by the Muslim advance, and in 1095 the Emperor Alexius Comnenus appealed to Pope Urban II for help. The Pope proclaimed a Holy War at the Council of Clermont, and the result was the First Crusade (1096–99), which set off in two groups. A French knight, Walter the Penniless, and Peter the Hermit set off with a disorganised rabble of peasants, few of whom reached the Holy Land. The outstanding leaders of the knightly host were Godfrey de Bouillon, Duke of Lower Lorraine; Raymond, Count of Toulouse; Bohemund, Lord of Otranto; and Robert, Duke of Normandy, the Conqueror's eldest son.

An army of 150,000 gathered at Constantinople, Antioch was captured and, in the following year, Jerusalem fell with terrible slaughter of the Muslims. Godfrey de Bouillon became governor of Jerusalem, and the other lands taken from the Turks were divided among the leaders of the crusade. Two military orders were subsequently founded, the Knights of St John, whose duty was to help the sick and wounded, and the Knights Templar, who protected pilgrims.

The Second Crusade (1147–49), caused by the fall of the Christian Kingdom of Edessa and led by Louis VII of France and the Emperor Conrad III, was a complete failure. The capture of Jerusalem and its king Guy de Lusignan (1187) by Saladin (Salah-al-Din), the great Turkish leader who had already conquered Egypt, led to the Third and most famous of the Crusades (1189–92).

The emperor Frederick Barbarossa set out first and led his army to Asia Minor but was unfortunately drowned when swimming in the River Salef, after which his army disintegrated. Richard I of England and Philip Augustus of France sailed together from Marseilles, but reached the Holy Land separately, since Richard delayed to conquer Cyprus. The Crusaders captured the great fortress of Acre in 1191, but quarrels divided the leaders, and Philip Augustus, jealous of Richard's popularity, sailed home under the plea of ill-health. Owing to illness and desertions in his army, Richard was not strong enough to take Jerusalem. He therefore made a three-year truce with Saladin by which Christians should have free access to Jerusalem.

Pope Innocent III supported a number of French nobles who planned the Fourth Crusade (1202–04); but, because of their inability to pay the Venetians for their transport, the Crusaders agreed first to help them to capture Zara on the Dalmatian coast and to enthrone Alexius, pretender to the Byzantine Empire. Both attempts were successful; but, on the overthrow of Alexius in 1204, the Crusaders captured and ruthlessly plundered Constantinople. This Crusade never reached the Holy Land, but established a Latin empire on the Bosphorus which lasted till 1261.

The Fifth Crusade (1218–21) had been proclaimed by Innocent III in 1215, but this failed because the Crusaders were sidetracked into an Egyptian campaign,

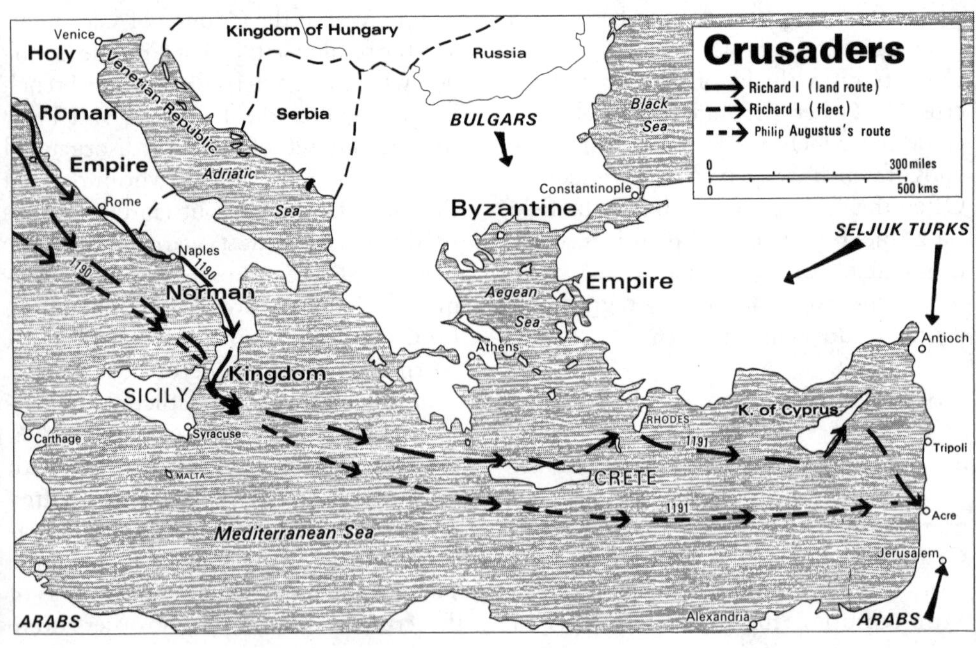

which failed ignominiously.

The Emperor Frederick II led the Sixth Crusade (1227–29), which, after very little fighting, resulted in a treaty by which Jerusalem, Bethlehem and other cities were restored to the Christians. The Turks recaptured Jerusalem (1244), and so Louis IX of France (St Louis) led the Seventh and Eighth Crusades (1248–54 and 1270–72). In the first, he was captured in Egypt, and in the second he died of plague in Tunisia, murmuring "Jerusalem, Jerusalem". Good and brave though he was, he brought little but hurt and disappointment to the Holy Land which he aspired to serve. The Holy City remained in Turkish hands until freed by General Allenby in 1917.

The most pathetic episode in the long story of these expeditions was the so-called Children's Crusade which was led by Stephen, a shepherd boy of Vendôme, in 1212. Witnesses told of 30,000 children of twelve years old or less. Hardship, the perils of the road and shipwreck wiped out thousands, and five shiploads were sold into slavery by unscrupulous merchants. Soon after, another army of 20,000 children led by Nicholas, a German boy, met an equally disastrous end.

Some of the results of the Crusades were very far-reaching. The Byzantine Empire never recovered from the disaster of the Fourth Crusade and fell in 1453 to the Turks, who continued to threaten south-east Europe until defeated by John Sobieski before Vienna in 1683. Trade with the East in luxury goods, such as perfumes, silks, spices and fruits, was stimulated. Concentric castles, adopted from the East, began to replace the old keep and bailey type, and the study of oriental languages, mathematics and poetic literature was much advanced in Europe. Despite individual gallantry and devotion, much of the history of the Crusades is an inglorious chronicle of jealousy, greed and treachery; and their chief modern historian (Sir Steven Runciman) has summarised them as "a long act of intolerance in the name of God".

¶ DUGGAN, ALFRED. *The Story of the Crusades.* 1963; KERR, A. J. C. *The Crusades.* 1966

Cuba: largest island of the West Indies covering 44,000 square miles [13,960 square kilometres] and with a population of 9,858,000 in 1983. The Spaniards are said to have been partly attracted to this island by the easily worked alluvial gold, though this was soon exhausted. Nickel, copper and manganese are minerals now of some importance; but, apart from the still valuable cattle pastures, plant commodities are Cuba's chief riches – sugar, tobacco, fruits, coffee, rice. They spring from the tropical warmth and generous, reasonably uniform, rainfall. Of these, sugar predominates.

Cuba gained independence from Spain in 1898. The USA then took most of her trade, but was blamed for later social difficulties during the revolution in 1959 led by Fidel Castro (*see* separate entry). Cuban trade was transferred to Russia and other communist countries. Russia established missile bases on the island in 1962, with serious strategic implications, but the bases were demolished when American resistance made war seem likely.

Castro's open avowal of communist beliefs, and the support he has received from Russia and Red China, have given Communism a strong base from which to foster revolution in other Latin American republics.

¶ In HUGHES, LANGSTON. *The First Book of the Caribbean.* 1965

Curfew (from French *couvrir*, cover, + *feu*, fire): fixed time after which no citizen may appear outdoors, often imposed under martial law. The term originates from the medieval precautionary custom of extinguishing fires at a stated time, signalled by a bell.

Customs and excise: duties imposed on goods imported or exported; and taxes levied on the manufacture, sale and consumption of certain goods. In Britain the Commissioners of Customs, appointed in 1671, were amalgamated with the Excise Department in 1909. In earlier times it was common for a government to "farm" the customs, i.e. let out to merchants and private individuals the right to collect taxes in return for a fixed sum or percentage. Systems of levying at times became so complex that, e.g., in 1784 a consignment of Russian linen coming into England paid duty under ten different heads in the regulations; and in 1801, despite much simplification by Pitt, Britain had 1,500 rates of custom duty, each imported article carrying several different rates.

Cuzco: city of south Peru, perched 11,000 feet [3,350 metres] high in a valley of the Andes. It has been inhabited continuously for nine centuries – longer than any other town in the Americas. In this valley the civilisation of the Incas developed. Roads from all parts of their empire centred on Cuzco, the home of the royal Inca and site of a towering temple to the sun sheathed in plates of gold. When the Spanish Conquistadors looted Cuzco in 1533, one of them wrote: "It has fine streets, except that they are narrow, and the houses are built of solid stones, beautifully joined . . . it must have been founded by a people of great intelligence."

Cyprus: island republic in the eastern Mediterranean. Its name indicates the presence of copper, and chrome ores and other minerals are also present. In early times Cyprus was densely forested, but the demand for ships and building materials along the north African and Levantine coasts caused the mountain slopes to be denuded, the soil to be washed away and thus the streams to flow less regularly.

The position of Cyprus has given it strategic importance over the eastern Mediterranean at all times. It guards the important gap made by the River Orontes in the Syrian mountains, through which trade with the Persian Gulf and beyond reached the Mediterranean. The Turks held the island from 1573 until Britain began to administer it in 1878, later annexing it when war against Turkey broke out in 1914. It was administered as a British crown colony from 1925 to 1959 when the struggle for independence headed by Archbishop Makarios, who became the first President of Cyprus in 1960, was brought to a successful conclusion. But communal strife between Greek and Turk led to a Turkish invasion of the north of Cyprus in 1974 and the island has remained partitioned since that date despite UN and Commonwealth efforts to find a lasting solution.

¶ SPYRIDAKIS, C. *A Brief History of Cyprus.* 1968

Czar: *see* TSAR.

Czechoslovakia: landlocked republic in central Europe. The main regions are Bohemia, Moravia and Slovakia, together with a small area of Silesia. The Bohemian plateau, enclosed by mountains in the west, contains the most intensive agricultural area of the country, as well as the important industrial centres. Prague, the capital, lies on the River Vltava in the centre of Bohemia. Moravia consists chiefly of the basin of the River Morava and is an important agricultural region. Slovakia is mountainous and, o the whole, more backward than Bohemia and Moravia.

Historically the Czechoslovak state, formed in 1919 under the Treaty of St Germain, is a continuation of Bohemia. From the 16th century the Czechs came under Habsburg rule and, after the battle of White Hill (1620), lost their religious and other liberties. Following the establishment of the Dual Monarchy of Austria–Hungary in 1867, the lands of Bohemia-Moravia came under Austrian rule, and Slovakia under Hungarian. Before 1914 many Czechs emigrated to America, where they played an important part in persuading President Wilson to urge the establishment, after the end of World War I, of an independent Czechoslovakia on the basis of national determination. The leaders of this movement were Masaryk, Beneš and Stefanik.

The constitution, drawn up in 1919, paid special attention to the treatment of the minority groups within the state, for, as well as the Czechs and Slovaks, more than three million were German, three-quarters of a million Hungarian and half a million Ruthenian. The first Republic was under the continuous rule of Masaryk and Beneš, who together formed the Czech National Socialist Party. Co-operation between the different nationalities began to break down in the early 1930s, when the world was suffering from the effects of economic depression. The Germans, one-third of the population, were more industrialised than the rest and therefore suffered more. Their grievances soon provided the basis for Nazi pressure from Germany – where Hitler had come to power in 1933. In the predominantly German district of the Sudetenland a Nazi party already existed under Konrad Henlein, and its representatives were attending the Nuremberg rallies. In 1938, having already occupied Austria, Hitler succeeded, at the Munich Conference, in forcing British and French agreement to the cession of the Sudetenland to Germany. Beneš promptly resigned, and his successor, Hacha, was forced by threat of massive bombing to place the whole of Czechoslovakia under the "protection" of Germany in March 1939. During World War II the Czechs and Slovaks suffered much from the brutality of Nazi occupation.

The Czechoslovak Communist Party emerged as an effective force after the country's liberation by the Russians in 1945. In 1948 the communists took power, with Russian backing, before an election

On 22 August 1968 Russian tanks entered Prague.

called for that year had taken place. From then, Czechoslovakia was one of the most reliable satellite states of Russia – especially after Antonin Novotny, an admirer of Stalin, became leader of the Communist Party. In January 1968 a reform movement led by Alexander Dubcek swept Novotny and his supporters from power, and a programme of liberalisation was successfully begun. But in August of that year troops from Russia and other communist countries invaded Czechoslovakia and the reform movement was crushed for the time being.

¶ BERNARD, K. *The Land and People of Czechoslovakia.* 1969

D

Dacia: Roman province north of the lower reaches of the Danube, roughly the modern Romania. Of little importance or threat to Greece or early Roman expansion, the Dacians became active enough to stir Julius Caesar to plan an attack and to persuade Antony and Octavian to form alliances with them. They found some unity under the leadership of Decebalus, especially in the war against Domitian between AD 85 and 89. Although defeated by Roman armies, the Dacians won from Domitian some recognition of independence, helped by the trouble to Rome of revolts elsewhere along the Danube. Trajan, who succeeded as emperor in 98, thought the Dacians a menace and, after two campaigns in 101 and 102, imposed peace terms. Three years later, he again invaded Dacia on the pretext of their non-compliance with the terms, and Decebalus escaped capture by suicide. Trajan commemorated his success by the magnificent reliefs on the column which he erected in a newly constructed forum in Rome. The area became a province.

Due to Gothic invasions Dacia was evacuated by Rome some time after 250. Lying north of the natural frontier of the Danube, it was bound to be the first part of the Roman empire to be relinquished. The two most important towns were Sarmizegethusa and Apulum.

Damascus: capital of Syria, the only surviving city mentioned in Genesis (14:15). Some of its trades are enshrined in our words damson, damask, damascened. It lies in fertile orchards between the Syrian mountains and the desert. It developed about 1200 BC under the Aramaeans and was a provincial capital of the Persian empire. Its natural beauty was such that Mohammed was reluctant to enter it as "he wished to enter Paradise only once". Its great age was between AD 661 and 750, when the Umayyad Caliphs made it their capital. Caliph Walid (705–15) built the mosque and palace, decorated with glazed tiles and mosaic by Greek craftsmen and grouped round fountains and courts of green marble. From 1516 to 1918 it was under Ottoman rule. Its population in 1982 was 1,129,000.

Dams: obstructions built to hold back water and raise its level. The dam may be only a few inches high, as in irrigation channels where water is forced over new ground by putting mud in one course and removing the blockage from another. Large dams were made even in early times in the courses of the Nile, the Tigris and other rivers.

Rockfalls down a valley side, or a lava flow, may obstruct the river flowing along the valley; or a glacier too deep to have yet melted may flow across a tributary river. But the lakes resulting from such natural dams can also be produced artificially. Storage of water is needed because civic and domestic demands are regular, while rainfall and evaporation are not, e.g. mill wheels had to grind corn at any time and not just at rainy periods, so damming was often necessary to form a mill pond. Hydroelectic power also varies with the season, though the need for electricity has a different pattern of variation. Electricity cannot be stored effectively, so the water must be stored instead.

Large lakes waste water by evaporation, and depth is therefore an advantage. But this increases pressure on the dam which needs great engineering skill in construction. Among these feats is the Aswan or Assuan Dam, built in 1902 on the first cataract of the River Nile. This is 176 feet [53·6 metres] high, with a road along the top, and runs for 1¼ miles [2 kilometres]. A new dam (the Aswan High Dam) caused protest from all over the world when it was learned that it involved the flooding of the ancient temple site of Abu Simbel (*c.* 1250 BC) with its great entrance statues of Rameses II. As a result of the outcry from scholars and historians, the temple has now been raised to safety. Another famous example is the Kariba hydroelectric dam on the Zambesi River, supplying power to both Zambia and Zimbabwe.

Among the world's most massive dams are the Fort Pack Dam, nearly 4 miles [6·4 kilometres] long and up to 251 feet [38 metres] high, across the Missouri river in Montana, USA; the Grand Coulee Dam, the largest concrete structure in the world, on the Columbia river, Washington State, USA; and the Tarbela Dam in West Pakistan, from 470 to 485 feet [143 to 147·5 metres] high and nearly 1⅔ miles [2·6 kilometres] long. The Grand Dixence Dam in Switzerland rises over 900 feet [274 metres], and two dams in the USSR, at Nurek and Ingurskaya, which are both about 1,000 feet [304 metres] high. The highest dam in the USA is the 726-foot [222-metre] Hoover Dam (1936) across the Colorado river.

¶ WYNARD, JOHN *Dams and Canals.* 1964

See also TENNESSEE VALLEY AUTHORITY.

Left, Kariba Dam, Zambia. Below left, Fontana Dam, North Carolina, USA. Below, Hoover Dam across the Colorado River, Nevada, USA.

Dance: rhythmic movement, or sets of movements, especially to music or drum-beat.

Many members of the animal kingdom perform movements which might be called dance. But man is the supreme dancer, in every age and in every type of society. A painting from the Old Stone Age shows the hunting dance of a shaman (priest-magician). He wears the horns, skin and tail of a deer and is clearly imitating the movements of a deer, presumably to make sure (by imitative magic) that the hunt will be successful. We find ritual ring dances from Neolithic times onwards among agricultural communities, with complex symbolism. The ring represents the wheeling of the sun, moon and stars and the cycle of the seasons. This cycle must be kept going by magical rites if man is to survive. The dancers hold each other's hands, shutting out the outside world and feeling a sense of confidence within their enclosed community.

There are many kinds of religious folk-dances, among them trance dances such as the Barong dances of Bali (in which dancers try unsuccessfully to pierce their bodies with sharp daggers), the Voodoo dances of Haiti (in which they become possessed by Afro-Christian gods), the Winter Dances of the Coast Salish Indians of British Columbia and the whirling dances of the dervishes. In India, the dance is right at the centre of culture, and all dances, whether folk or classical, have a basis in Hindu mythology – the greatest gods being worshipped as dancers. Indian influence is strong in the classical dances and dance-drama of most of south-east Asia and is to be felt in China, Japan and Korea in the Far East, as well as in the flamenco dance of Spain. Eastern classical dances belong to one family and differ from the classical ballet dance of the West in many ways: there is a great stress on contact with the ground (with rhythms beaten out by the feet), the arm and head movements are if anything more complex and highly developed than those of the legs, and the line of the limbs is often angular.

In Europe, during the Middle Ages and the Renaissance, social dances developed at the courts. Derived from rural folk dances, they were polished by dancing masters to suit a different milieu. This process continued in the ballrooms of the 18th and 19th centuries. In Victorian times the couple-dance became the norm, with the man holding and leading his passive partner – an admirable symbol of male attitudes to women at this time. But there was a revolutionary change in social dancing in the 20th century, along with corresponding changes in dance music. This revolution can be traced in a revived interest in traditional jazz and blues, jive and jitterbug dancing, the rise of rock

An illustration from a medieval manuscript showing the mystical circle dance.

music, the sudden explosion of the twist, and the victory of anarchic, improvised discotheque dancing, much closer to West African folk dancing in style than to the couple-dancing with set patterns of previous generations. (The link with West Africa is via the dances which Negro slaves brought with them to America.) This new type of dancing symbolises a demand for complete equality and independence by girls; the fact that it is often performed in semi-darkness, to very loud, repetitive music with a powerful hypnotic beat, brings it close to trance dancing.

The technique of ballet (developed out of that used in social dancing and in professional dancing in allegorical court entertainments) laid great stress on illusion: the arms were made to suggest smooth curves, the feet were pointed when in the air to continue the line of the legs, and landings from leaps were made soft to suggest weightlessness. (This suggestion of weightlessness was carried even further by female ballet dancing after the full pointe with blocked shoes was perfected.) Stories were first taken from Graeco-Roman mythology, but later covered a wide variety of subjects. Because no satisfactory dance notation had been perfected, nearly all ballets (including many masterpieces) were lost when taste changed and they fell out of the repertoire; but a handful of great romantic ballets was preserved through the second half of the 19th century within the court ballets of St Petersburg and Copenhagen (notably *La Fille Mal Gardée*, *La Sylphide*, *Giselle* and *Swan Lake*). The position is now different because of the world-wide spread of Benesh Movement Notation.

In the early years of this century the ballet became almost synonymous with the name of the Russian impresario Serge Diaghilev. Together with his choreographer Fokine, he created a style which emphasised the dramatic unity of the ballets they presented, which included *The Firebird, Petrouchka* and *Les Sylphides*. Although Diaghilev was opposed to the idea of ballet as a showcase for individual virtuosity, many of the star names in the history of ballet – for example, Nijinsky, Pavlova and Massine – were members of his company. The ideas of Fokine were superseded after World War II, when a romantic revival took place, but the lyrical approach of Frederick Ashton, and the classical and abstract development of George Balanchine, probably the two greatest choreographers in the world today, show that both interpretations of ballet can exist successfully side by side.

A new form of theatrical dancing, modern dance, was created by the American pioneers Isadora Duncan and Ruth St Denis in the early years of this century. This was barefoot, breaking away from the ballet technique, and absorbing many influences from the East. It flourished greatly in Germany in the aftermath of World War I, when defeat, despair, inflation and political chaos made only expressionist forms of art (breaking sharply with the past) meaningful to artists and public. The same sort of thing happened in the USA a decade later during the Great Depression, when as many as twelve million people were out of work and society seemed to be in process of disintegration. Great pioneers, like Martha Graham, Doris Humphrey, Charles Weidman and Helen Tamuris, perfected new forms of barefoot dance in which contact with the floor was stressed as well as angles and expressionist contractions. Another decade later, the American modern dance teachers and choreographers began to absorb a great deal from ballet; and today the best choreographers draw impartially on the traditions of ballet, modern dance and Eastern dance.

¶ HASKELL, A. C. *The Story of Dance*. 1969

Dante, or **Durante, Alighieri** (1265–1321): Italian poet and statesman, born of a noble Florentine family. In the troubadour tradition, his poems are silent about his wife and children, but sing his love for Beatrice, the unattainable beauty whom he first met when he was nine and who died when he was twenty-five. Her death drove him to philosophy. He served Florence as a soldier, ambassador and magistrate, and was a leader of the White faction, which opposed the bankers who wished to involve Florence in papal ambitions. In 1302 the rival faction sentenced him to death in his absence, and he lived in exile in Siena, Arezzo, Verona and, finally, Ravenna, where he died in 1321. Political defeat and exile gave him the incentive and the time to meditate on the nature of injustice and to write his epic poem, the *Divina Commedia* (1305–6), in which he visited the Inferno, Purgatory and Paradise. His *Convivia*, a philosophical encyclopedia, contains a defence of Italian as a literary language. His *De Monarchia* (1313) attacked Papal interference in temporal affairs and defended the divine authority of the emperors.

¶ In CANNING, JOHN, editor. *100 Great Lives.* 1969

Danzig (now called **Gdansk**), Poland: situated on the Baltic coast, the city of Danzig has for long periods been under German control. From 1454 to 1793 the city was Polish but was then ceded to Prussia in the second partition of Poland. In 1807 it became a free city linked with Napoleon's Duchy of Warsaw, being returned to Prussia in 1814. Under the Treaty of Versailles, 1919, Danzig was once more made a free city linked with Poland; but Hitler demanded its return to Germany and made this the excuse for the German attack on Poland in September 1939, which began the Second World War. In 1945 Danzig was restored unconditionally to Poland.

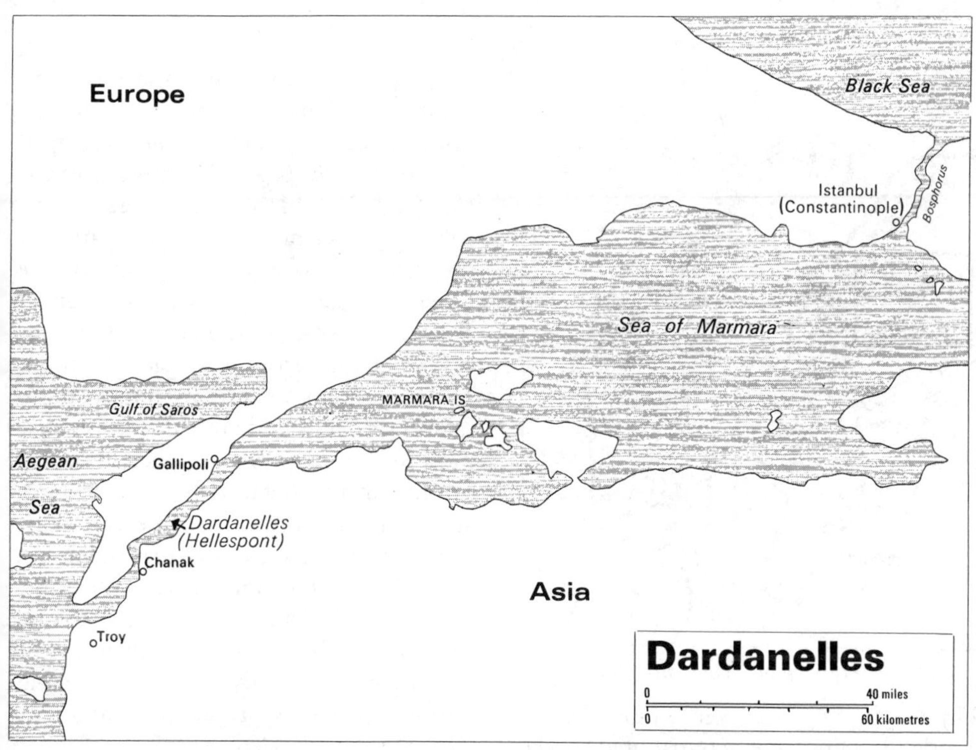

Dardanelles: the Hellespont of the ancient world; the narrow strait, forty-two miles long and from one to four miles wide, between Europe and Asia and connecting the Aegean and Black Seas. Command of it has always been a matter of strategic importance in any struggle between Europe and Asia, and it played a vital part in the Eastern Question (*see* separate entry). In legend, too, the Hellespont is familiar. In 1810 the English poet Byron swam the Hellespont in imitation of Leander who, in the ancient Greek love story, crossed it each night to visit Hero, a priestess of Aphrodite.

In World War I, in an effort to assist Russia by opening up communication between the Mediterranean and the Black Sea, Allied forces were landed (1915), but after heroic fighting in the face of strong Turkish resistance, were finally evacuated in December and January 1915–16 (*see* CHURCHILL, SIR WINSTON).

¶ In DUPUY, T. N. *The Campaigns on the Turkish Fronts.* ★1967

Darien scheme (1695–1700)**:** a plan by the Scots to establish a colony on the isthmus of Darien on the Atlantic coast of Central America. They had no colonies of their own, nor the right of free trade with England and her colonies; economically, therefore, they were very backward. In 1695 the Company of Scotland, trading to Africa and the Indies, was formed, having the monopoly of trade with Asia, Africa and America and the right to found colonies in these areas. Half the capital of £600,000 was to be raised in England and half in Scotland. William Paterson, a former director of the Bank of England and leading organiser of the scheme, suggested the site. From 1698 to 1700 three attempts at a settlement all failed owing to Spanish hostility, the unhealthy climate and diseases such as yellow fever and malaria, though the Scots blamed their failure on lack of English support. In the Act of

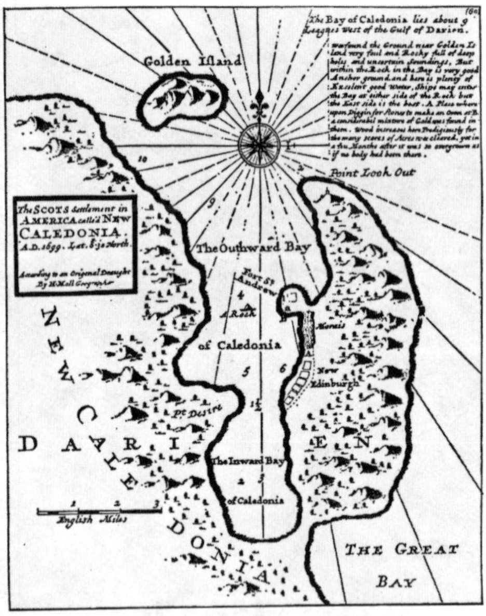

A contemporary map of New Caledonia.

Union (1707) between England and Scotland, England contributed over £219,000 to enable the shareholders of the Darien Company to be paid off.

Darius I, called **"the Great"** (*c.* 550–*c.* 485 BC)**:** King of Persia *c.* 521–*c.* 485 BC. Succeeding Cambyses, the conqueror of Egypt, after an interregnum, Darius put down rebellions and thoroughly reorganised the whole of the empire, regulating the provinces (or satrapies) and making the system efficient. An invasion of Scythia failed in about 513, but the revolt of Ionia in 499 was effectively crushed. Darius, incensed over Athenian help to the Ionians when they had burnt Sardis, launched two expeditions against the Greeks. In the course of the second, the Persians suffered disastrous defeat at the hands of the Athenians at Marathon (*see* separate entry). Darius planned a third expedition, but died before it could be carried out.

Darwin, Charles Robert (1809–82)**:** English naturalist. His career began when (1831–36) he accompanied a scientific expedition to South America in the *Beagle*, subsequently recorded in *The Zoology of the Voyage of the Beagle*. His most momentous (and, then, highly controversial) contribution to science was his formulation of the theory of evolution, set out in *The Origin of Species by Means of Natural Selection* (1859), i.e. the continuous process of change from a simple to a more complex form of life in which those species of plants and animals survive that most readily adapt themselves to their environment and therefore become stronger and more numerous than the rest. This involved the conclusion that man has evolved from the higher apes. "We must, however, acknowledge, as it seems to me, that man with all his noble qualities . . . still bears in his bodily frame the indelible stamp of his lowly origin" (conclusion of *The Descent of Man*, 1871).
section.

¶ KARP, W. *Charles Darwin and the Origin of the Species.* 1969; MELLERSH, H. E. L. *Charles Darwin.* 1964

Dauphin: title given to the eldest son of the kings of France from the 14th to the early 19th century. It originated from the *Dauphiné*, a former province of south-east France, purchased by the French crown in 1349 from its rulers, the Counts of Vienne.

Davis, Jefferson (1808–89)**:** American statesman and president of the Confederate States (*see* separate entry). Vacillating in his military policy, often a poor judge of men (to some of whom he was excessively loyal despite their manifest shortcomings) and unskilful in his relations with congress and foreign powers, he became a discredited figure with many of his contemporaries; though, when all is said, he managed to keep the South in the field for four years against far superior forces. The fact that he was held in cap-

tivity for two years by the Northern army and for a time treated with great severity, won back a good deal of sympathy for him in the South.

Dead Sea scrolls: ancient manuscripts discovered in a cave in Wadi Qumran, in Palestine, overlooking the Dead Sea.

In 1947 an Arab shepherd was seeking a lost sheep, when he discovered a cave. Returning with two of his friends, he explored the cave and found pottery jars containing ancient scrolls wrapped in linen. They had hoped for more obvious treasure, but they soon found a market for the scrolls. Some of the manuscripts eventually arrived in Jerusalem, where incredulous interest was aroused. At first it was impossible to investigate the site of the discovery, owing to the troubled state of Palestine. By the time scholars penetrated to the region, less careful searchers had been there before them, and the cave had been rifled of all save scattered fragments, which were carefully collected. Other caves were discovered, disclosing further scrolls.

The importance of the find was established when some of the original scrolls were conveyed to America and examined by the latest scientific methods. One was a complete scroll of the Book of Isaiah; examination of the wrappings proved that the linen had been woven of flax dating back to the lifetime of Jesus Christ. The scroll is older – probably a thousand years older – than the previous oldest Hebrew text (9th–10th century BC) yet it agrees with the texts in use today.

Nineteen books of the Old Testament have been found so far, with other documents throwing new light on Jewish history. They are believed to have belonged to the library of a Jewish community, the site of which has also been discovered, and to have been hidden at the time of the revolt against the Romans, when destruction was imminent.

¶ PALMER, GEOFFREY. *Quest for the Dead Sea Scrolls.* 1964

The Thanksgiving Scroll, before complete unrolling.

Deccan: an area of Hindu populations with Muslim rulers, the name being used either for the whole Indian peninsula south of the River Narbada or for the area between that river and the Kistna, which marked the southern limit of control of the Delhi emperors. In the 18th century the Mogul viceroys threw off their allegiance and became rulers of independent states, the most important being Poona, whose *Peshwa*, or ruler, became independent in 1706; Hyderabad (1724), whose *Nizam* is sometimes referred to as ruler of the Deccan; and Mysore, usurped by Sultan Haidar Ali in 1761, and one of the early British conquests in the region.

Declaration of Independence: document of 4 July 1776 in which the American colonists asserted their independence of Britain.

On 7 June 1776 a representative of the delegation of Virginia moved in the Continental Congress "that these united colonies are and of right ought to be free and independent states, that they are absolved from all allegiance to the British Crown, and that all political connection between them and the state of Great Britain is and ought to be dissolved". By 2 July this resolution was adopted, and a committee composed of John Adams, William Livingston, Roger Sherman and Thomas Jefferson was appointed to draw up a declaration.

The Declaration of Independence was chiefly the work of Jefferson (his original manuscript can be seen in the Library of Congress, Washington), and it contained a list of grievances against the King of England, a statement of radical philosophy of the 18th century and a formal declaration of independence.

The preamble to the Declaration begins:

"When in the course of human events, it becomes necessary for one people to dissolve the political bands which have connected them with another, and to assume among the powers of the earth, the separate and equal station to which the laws of Nature and of Nature's God entitle them, a decent respect to the opinions of mankind requires that they should declare the causes which impel them into separation.

"We hold these truths to be self-evident, that all men are created equal, that they are endowed by their Creator with certain unalienable rights, that among these are life, liberty and the pursuit of happiness. That to secure these rights, governments are instituted among men, deriving their just powers from the consent of the governed. That whenever any form of government becomes destructive of these ends, it is the right of the people to alter or abolish it, and to institute a new government, laying its foundation on such principles and organizing its powers in such form as to them shall seem most likely to effect their safety and happiness."

This "Unanimous Declaration of the Thirteen United States of America" was adopted on 4 July, the anniversary of which has ever since been celebrated as American Independence Day.

See also AMERICAN COLONIES; AMERICAN WAR OF INDEPENDENCE.

Delhi: capital of India, comprising the old walled city and New Delhi, on the Jumna River. It claims to have been the site of a capital city since prehistoric times and has, on many occasions, attracted attack. It was captured by Timur Lenk (Tamberlane) in 1398, by his descendant Babar in 1526, and by the Persian Nadir Shah in 1739. From 1771 the Mahratta chieftain Sindhia held control over a puppet emperor (Shah Alam) until the city was taken by Lord Lake in 1803 and subsequently passed under British rule. It was the centre of the Indian forces during the Mutiny in 1857. Many of the great buildings in Old Delhi are from a rebuilding of the city, 1638–58, by Shah Jahan.

New Delhi, an entirely new city, be-

The North block of the General Secretariat by Sir Edwin Lutyens.

came the capital after 1911 and remains the capital of independent India. The building of New Delhi is one of the most striking architectural achievements of the present century, not the least remarkable feature being that this great eastern city had an English architect, Sir Edwin Lutyens (1869–1944) as its chief planner.

Delian League or **Confederacy:** confederacy of over 200 Aegean cities and islands formed in 478 BC to counter Persian aggression. After the withdrawal of Sparta, the League was soon dominated by Athens, who forced reluctant members to co-operate. Tribute in military forces or money was exacted, and at first the treasury was established on the small island of Delos. In 454 the treasury was moved to Athens, and the League gradually developed into an Athenian empire. Uniformity of weights and measures was imposed, lawsuits favoured Athenians, democratic systems were supported. Revolts before 431 were few, but the League disintegrated after the Sicilian disaster in 431 BC. Most of the states reverted to Persian control.

Democracy: government by the people, usually by freely elected representatives (Greek *demos*, the people, and *kratos*, rule).

Democracy is one of many ways in which a country may be governed. (*See* OLIGARCHY, ELECTORAL SYSTEMS, TYRANNY, etc.) In some cases democracy has been replaced by a dictatorship in which one man, such as Hitler in Germany, Mussolini in Italy, and Stalin in Russia became in effect the sole ruler.

The terms "democrat" and "democratic" have become linked with political parties in various countries; e.g. the Christian Democrats and Social Democrats have been the most powerful parties in West Germany since World War II; and the Democratic Party (as opposed to the Republican party) is one of the two principal political parties of the USA.

Denmark: independent kingdom in northern Europe, situated between the North Sea and the Baltic, forming a part of Scandinavia. Denmark consists of the peninsula of Jutland and the islands of Zealand, Funen and Lolland, a total of 17,000 square miles [44,030 square kilometres] which supports a population of 5,124,700 (1982). Most of Denmark is lowland, its highest point being only 567 feet [182 metres] above sea level. West Jutland has large areas of infertile sandy heaths, but east Jutland and the islands contain rich farmland.

The Danes occupied their present territory in the 5th and 6th centuries AD, but they did not become associated with the rest of Europe until the 10th century, when Charlemagne's kingdom was extended to northern Germany. It was at this time that the Danes became united under one king, and an aggressive expansionist policy was launched, which resulted in large territorial gains in northern Germany and the conquest of part of the

British Isles during the reign of King Canute. This period was also marked by the increasing strength of the Roman Catholic Church, which, from wealthy monasteries, controlled large areas of Denmark.

During the 12th century the power of Denmark declined as the country degenerated into civil war and numerous struggles with Germany. She was of little importance until the 14th century, when the Hanseatic League was formed; an organisation of Danish and north German towns, which became the dominant political and economic power in the Baltic. At the same time there was a break in the direct line to the Danish throne and the succession passed to King Olaf of Sweden, who was also the heir to the Norwegian throne. This Scandinavian union lasted from 1375 to 1448. In 1450 Denmark concluded a permanent union with Norway which lasted until 1814. The union was broken by the cession of Norway to Sweden – a clause written into the Treaty of Vienna in recognition of Sweden's contribution to the Allied cause during the Napoleonic Wars.

Denmark maintained her independence throughout the 19th century, but came under increasing pressure from her near neighbour, Prussia, as that country grew in power and international stature. In 1864 a joint Austrian and Prussian expeditionary force occupied the Danish duchies of Schleswig and Holstein after a short and unequal war. The duchies were completely annexed by Prussia in 1866 after war with Austria and were returned to Denmark only at the end of World War I. Denmark took up a neutral position in the 1914–18 conflict, though she was obliged to make trade agreements with Norway and Sweden to protect her export market, which was being affected by the German blockade of Britain. During the war a new constitution was drawn up which included universal suffrage, ending the privileged position of the wealthy burghers who had held power since the Protestant Reformation of the 16th century, impoverishing the Catholic nobility and enriching the commercial middle class.

Denmark's neutrality was not accepted by Hitler during World War II, and the country was invaded in April 1940. Comparatively few people were killed or imprisoned by the Nazis, and the German occupation was grudgingly accepted by most Danes. Since the war Denmark has become a more active and committed member of the international community; she is a member of the United Nations Organisation; she is bound to the Western Alliance through her membership of NATO; and she is now a member of the European Economic Community.

¶ LOBSENZ, NORMAN M. *The First Book of Denmark*. 1970

Dentistry: the department of medicine dealing with the teeth. The oldest known book on dentistry was published anonymously in 1530. Among other information, it records the filling of defective teeth with gold foil by a physician to the caliph Haroun-al-Raschid in the 9th century AD. But the slow advance of preventive dentistry is evident from the fact that a queen as vain of her charms as Elizabeth I of England could be described by the French Ambassador as having teeth that were "very yellow and unequal. Many of them are missing, so that one cannot understand her when she speaks quickly."

It was not till 1840 that the first college for the education of dentists was established in Baltimore, USA. The refusal of early medical schools to give adequate training is the more remarkable in that caries, or dental decay, is said to have affected the human race more than any other disease. Some of the most important

Above, dental treatment in the 16th century. Below, modern dental craftsmanship.

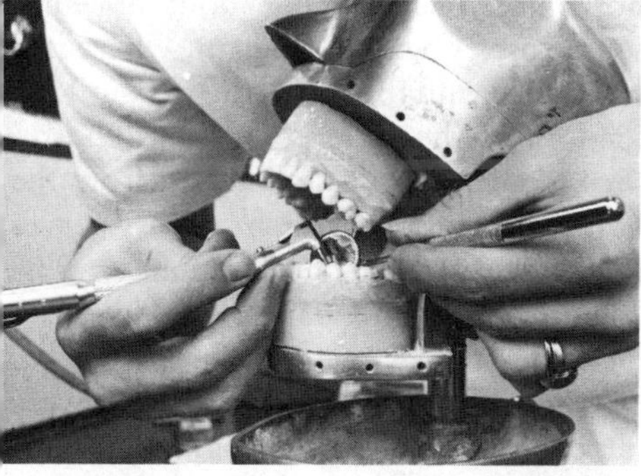

research in this field was accomplished in 1884 by W. D. Miller of Berlin.

The chief aims of modern dentistry are to preserve the teeth or, failing that, to remedy the loss by providing artificial substitutes. One of the greatest steps forward in dental health has been the establishment of school clinics, so that prevention can begin early. It has been proved that such treatment can have important effects on general physical development and mental efficiency.

See also ANAESTHESIA.

Depressions, Trade: periods of commercial slump. Before the Industrial Revolution most people were employed in agriculture, and the causes of depression lay largely in the smallness of the labour force needed to gather in a poor harvest. With the coming of factory production, alternating periods of boom and slump, known as trade cycles, occurred roughly every ten years. The world depression of the late 1920s and 1930s was most severe in the United States, Germany, Britain and other industrial countries. Following World War II the world experienced a period of rising prosperity and full employment which led politicians and economists to imagine they knew how to combat depressions. But the recession which began at the end of the 1970s and continued to the mid-1980s proved a major setback to such optimism.

Dewey, John (1859–1952): American educator and philosopher. As a teacher he set himself against authoritarian methods and insisted on the value of learning through personal practice and experience. As a philosopher, one of his main beliefs was that "the ever enduring process of perfecting, maturing, refining, is the aim in living. . . . The bad man is the man who, no matter how good he has been, is beginning to deteriorate, to grow less good. The good man is the man who, no matter how morally unworthy he has been, is moving to become better."

Dewey's influence has not been restricted to the USA, but has been widespread in Europe. As well, he lectured in the University of Peking (China) and was called in by the Turkish government to advise on educational reorganisation.

Dewey, Melvil (1851–1931): American librarian and originator of the Dewey Decimal System of classification currently in use in most public libraries.

Dialling: the construction and calibration of instruments that tell the time of day by reference to sun, moon or stars. The earliest known sundial is an Egyptian example dating from about 1500 BC.

Euclidean geometry dominated mathematics for the 2,000 years before Newton, and its most intricate and artistic expression may be seen in instruments for telling the time and for solving astronomical problems. The pedestal and wall dials that ornament gardens today are relatively simple residues of this art. The first British pedestal sundial is said to have been made for Richard III, and dialling continued to flourish for more than two centuries, during which several do-it-yourself books were published.

These dials, although called "azimuthal", actually indicate solar time from the sun's Right Ascension and require a style parallel to the earth's axis. Since the sun appears to turn round this once in twenty-four hours, if the shadow of the style is made to fall across a ring fixed symmetrically about the style, the time-scale on the ring advances one hour for each fifteen degrees. The sun crosses the plane of the ring at the equinoxes, so this is an equinoctial dial. The projection of the equal hour-calibrations onto a horizontal plane is a simple piece of geometrical drawing, the principles of which, like the astronomical basis of the instrument, were known to Hipparchus (150 BC) and developed by Ptolemy (AD 200) in Alexandria. A dial on a wall not facing due south is more complicated, and this is what most books on dialling were about.

After magnetic compass needles were commonly available (*c.* 1450), pocket versions of azimuthal dials appeared, with built-in compasses for setting the north-south axis. It is sometimes possible to date these because of the subsequent change in magnetic declination. Portable azimuthal dials were often adjustable for latitude. A distinct and older type of sundial depends only on the sun's altitude, so that it is not necessary for the user to know where north is. A Saxon version, in Canterbury Cathedral, takes the form of a small tablet of silver hanging from a gold chain. A gold pin plugs into a hole at the top to form a horizontal style, and the tablet is turned so that the pin casts a vertical shadow. The tip of the shadow then indicates the time of day. Seasonal variation is provided for by six different scales, with corresponding holes for the pin.

When the German Hans Holbein the younger painted "The Ambassadors" in 1533 he included two sundials, one of them a cylinder. A cylinder dial is continuously adjustable throughout the year. The cylinder hangs vertically. A date scale is marked round the upper rim. The horizontal style, pivoting about the centre top, projects beyond the rim, where it is set to date, and the dial is turned until the shadow of the style is vertical. The tip then indicates the time, read off from the hour-calibrations, which form curves round the surface of the cylinder. The "gentil monk" in Chaucer's *Schipmannes Tale* (line 206) knew it was time to go, "for by my chilindre it is prime of daye". He could not, of course, have known it was past prime of day, since on an altitude dial, morning and afternoon calibrations coincide.

Cylinder dials were still in use in the 19th century; but they were bulky, and no doubt the style readily broke or bent, and other designs of altitude dial fitted the pocket better. As usual, though, compactness brought complications.

The scratch, or "mass", dials sometimes found on the south walls of Saxon or Norman churches are neither true azimuthal nor true altitude dials. It is conjectured that the style was an iron pin driven into the wall horizontally: its shadow would then always be horizontal at sunrise and sunset. It may possibly have been knocked sideways into the north-south plane: if so, the noon shadow would be vertical. Lacking other means of measuring time intervals, a crude division of morning and afternoon by intermediate markings was probably adequate for determining the times for church services. The practice, current in Roman times, of dividing the period from sunrise to sunset into twelve "temporal hours" instead of the equal hours we now use, considerably simplified the design of a sundial and made it possible for portable Roman dials to be adjustable for latitude as well as time of year, all using a single time-scale. (A rare example, *c.* AD 250, is in the Old Ashmolean Museum, Oxford.) But equal hours, as measured by mechanical clocks, demand greater subtlety.

Above, plaster cast of the Saxon sundial on Kirkdale Church, Yorkshire. Below, "Butterfield" pocket sundial by Baradelle of Paris.

Touchstone's dial (*As You Like It*, Act II, scene vi) was probably what is usually called a Bauern Ring, and one of these has been acquired by the Stratford Museum in England. This is like a large finger ring, hung vertically, time being indicated by a bright spot on a scale inside the ring. The spot is the sun's image of a hole pierced in a plate that slides in a slot cut in the side of the ring opposite the scale. The plate needs to be set to date, and either several time scales or a special curved scale, usable throughout the year, are provided.

The most remarkable altitude dials measure equal hours and are adjustable over a wide range of latitudes. One was described by Regiomontanus (1436–76). The astrolabe could be used for telling the time, as well as for more complicated astronomical purposes, but was not, like a sundial, a direct-reading instrument.

"We, that take purses, go by the moon and seven stars, and not by Phoebus;" (*Henry IV, Part I*, Act I, scene ii). Nocturnals, made to tell time at night by reference to the circumpolar stars, were common in Shakespeare's time. A rarer device, a table for converting a sundial into a moondial, may be seen in Queens' College, Cambridge.

Solar time differs from mean time by an amount that may be as much as sixteen minutes. This difference, the "equation of time", first explained by Kepler, was calculated by Flamsteed (1670), and some later clocks, including some of Thomas Tompion's, indicated it on their dials. This enabled the clock to be set by sundial.

Diamonds: precious stones of crystallised pure carbon, the hardest and most durable of minerals.

In AD 100 the Roman Pliny described diamonds as "the most valuable of gems, known only to kings". In medieval times they were believed to protect the wearer from demons and death by poison and to preserve the love of husband and wife.

The first diamonds worn in Europe came from India, but in the 18th century gems from Diamantina in Brazil came on to the market. The most famous Brazilian diamond is the *Star of the South*. In 1847 the children of a South African farmer were seen playing with some unusual pebbles they had picked up. These were identified as diamonds, and so began the world-famous Kimberley mines. Diamonds are also found in Australia.

Many diamonds have names and histories. The *Koh-i-noor* ("Mountain of Light") diamond belonged originally to a Persian emperor. In 1813 the East India Company obtained it, and in 1850 presented it to Queen Victoria. It now adorns the Queen's crown.

Another famous gem, the *Orloff* diamond, was stolen from the eye of a gigantic figure in an Indian temple by a French soldier. During the journey home, the ship's captain stole it from the thief and later sold it for £90,000 to the Russian Prince Orloff, who gave it to the Empress Catherine II, when it became part of the Russian Crown jewels.

The *Sancy* diamond had a number of royal owners – Charles of Burgundy, Elizabeth I, Henrietta Maria, Louis XIV. Stolen during the French Revolution, it reappeared in Spain before passing into the possession of the Russian royal house.

The largest diamond ever found was the *Cullinan*, found in the Transvaal in 1905. It weighed one and three-quarter pounds [0·8 kilograms] before cutting, and was divided into nine gems, the most brilliant of which sparkles in the British Imperial State Crown.

¶ BRUTON, ERIC. *The True Book about Diamonds*. 1961

Dictionary: work in which all or a selection of the words in a language are arranged in alphabetical order and explained. A good dictionary also shows how to pronounce each word and gives information about its origins, i.e. its etymology. The first English dictionary of this kind was *The Universal Etymological English Dictionary*, published in 1721. Dr Johnson (1709–84) used this dictionary when compiling his famous *Dictionary of the English Language*, published in 1755. This attracted great interest because it gave very clear definitions and showed how words had been used by writers from the time of Queen Elizabeth I (1533–1603). Not very much was known at that time about what languages many English words had come from, and the etymologies (Greek *etumon*, first form of a word) in both dictionaries are their weakest part.

There have been many dictionaries since Dr Johnson's time. The greatest of all, the *Oxford English Dictionary*, was begun 100 year after Dr Johnson's, in 1858, and took seventy years to complete. It is in thirteen large volumes and gives the meaning, pronunciation and history of 414,825 words, with quotations showing wherever possible their earliest use in English. The *Shorter Oxford Dictionary* is an abridged version in two volumes.

The standard dictionary in the USA for more than a century was that by Noah Webster (1758–1843). His *Compendious Dictionary of the English Language* (1806) was followed twenty-two years later by his *An American Dictionary of the English Language* in two volumes, a work which, it is said, made his name "known familiarly to a greater number of the inhabitants of the United States than the name, probably, of any other individual except the Father of his Country" (George Washington).

The term "dictionary" has also come to be applied to any work of reference in which the entries are arranged in alphabetical order, e.g. *The Dictionary of National Biography*.

Diesel, Rudolf (1858–1913): German inventor and engineer who gave his name to the diesel oil engine, an internal combustion engine, the piston of which is driven by combustion and expansion occurring when fuel is injected direct into a cylinder of compressed air.

¶ In CROWTHER, J. G. *Six Great Engineers*. 1959

Dinosaurs: from Greek *deinos*, terrible, and *sauros*, lizard; the enormous reptiles that lived on the earth in Mesozoic times (120 to 200 million years ago). Representatives were the brontosaur, 65 feet or more long and 12 feet high [19·8 metres long, 3·7 metres high], and the diplodocus, up to 80 feet [24·3 metres] long. The size of their brain was negligible.

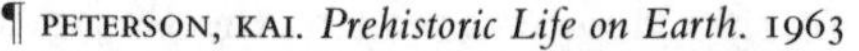
¶ PETERSON, KAI. *Prehistoric Life on Earth.* 1963

Diplodocus.

Diplomacy: the art of conducting negotiations, especially between nations. A diplomat is someone officially employed in international work of this kind, and the whole body of ambassadors, secretaries, etc., in foreign countries makes up the "diplomatic corps".

Diplomatic immunity: freedom enjoyed, under international law, by diplomats and their households serving in foreign countries. They are normally exempt from taxation and customs duties and often escape observance of minor police regulations. Their cars carry the diplomatic badge of their embassy, legation, etc.

Directories: guides to the names and addresses, usually in alphabetical order, of the inhabitants of a place or the members of a profession. The first English directory was published in London, probably in 1677. The English Post Office Directory was first published in 1800. The name Directory is also given in a special sense to the ruling body of five, 1795–99, during the French Revolution.

Disarmament: the giving up or limitation of military strength. The development of modern "total" warfare has meant that, in the search for peace, increasing emphasis has been placed on the need for nations to disarm; but, except where nations have been forced to do so following defeat in war (as with Germany in 1919), attempts to secure disarmament by international agreement have on the whole failed. The Hague Conferences of 1899 and 1907 and the Geneva Conference of 1932–33 are good, though depressing, examples. However, the development of nuclear weapons has led to more serious efforts. The treaty of 1963, banning the testing of such weapons in the atmosphere, is a definite, if limited, step in the right direction. This was signed in Moscow between Britain, the USA and the USSR, these three countries undertaking not to conduct tests in the atmosphere, in outer space and under water. Underground tests were not ruled out, though a future ban was seen as a desirable aim. In 1967 nuclear disarmament talks were resumed at Geneva at an eighteen-power conference. It became clear that France and China would not participate in any treaty, but by 1968 the draft test of an agreement between the USA and the USSR was submitted and a treaty has since been signed. Its main provisions aim at preventing the spread of nuclear weapons and safeguarding nuclear energy for peaceful applications.

Discovery, Age of: the period *c.* 1450–1600, characterised by an unusual number of significant voyages and discoveries.

Contact between East and West had been established by trade in luxury goods, such as spices and silk, and promoted by Marco Polo's visit to the Court of Kublai Khan at Peking in 1275, but a new unbroken sea route to the East was urgently needed in the 15th century. The cost of the goods brought to Europe overland and by sea was extremely high, owing to the number of tolls levied, and the Turkish advance west had to some extent interfered with the caravan routes at the eastern end of the Mediterranean. Scientific and technical knowledge had, by the late 15th century, considerably developed to aid voyages further afield. Ptolemy's belief that the world was a sphere was more widely accepted, and a Latin translation of his *Guide to Geography* was printed in 1470. Great improvements in shipbuilding were being made as galleys suitable only to the Mediterranean were replaced by sailing ships such as the Portuguese caravels, requiring at least 6 feet [1·8 metres] depth of water. Charts were more accurate as a result of the voyages down the West African coast organised by Prince Henry the Navigator, astrolabes were used to determine latitude, and the compass was improved and more widely used. Thus explorers could risk sailing out of sight of land, and Portugal and Spain, facing the open sea, were ideally placed to lead maritime exploration.

Prince Henry the Navigator (1394–1460) paved the way for Portuguese voyages round the West African coast to reach the Indian Ocean. From 1418 onwards he sent out expeditions which charted the coast, although at his death his sailors had gone little beyond Cape Verde. John II of Portugal (1481–95) gave command of two ships to Bartholomew Diaz in 1486 to sail along the African coast to Abyssinia, the supposed country of the legendary Christian ruler Prester John. Driven by violent storms, Diaz rounded the Cape of Good Hope (*see* separate entry), which he named the Cape of Storms, in 1487 and reached Algoa Bay. Because of the discontent of his crew he had to return, but this voyage and that of Pedro de Covilhao, who went overland from the Mediterranean to the Red Sea and then across the Indian Ocean to Calicut, paved the way for Vasco da Gama, commissioned by Emmanuel I of Portugal (1495–1521) to complete the sea route to India. Da Gama sailed on 3 August 1497 with four ships and 118 men and reached Calicut on 20 May 1498; he returned home with two ships and only half his crew but bringing an immensely rich cargo of pepper, ginger, cloves and precious stones, having completed 24,000 nautical miles [42,600 km/h]; thus Portugal established her claim to the monopoly of trade with the East, and the great Portuguese viceroy Alfonso da Albuquerque (1509–15) made Goa the capital of the Portuguese empire in the East, which included Ormuz on the Persian Gulf, Ceylon and the East Indies, as well as the settlements in India.

Meanwhile Christopher Columbus (1447–1506) had eventually persuaded Isabella of Spain to help him to cross the Atlantic to reach the East by sailing west. He set out on 3 August 1492 with five small ships, and reached San Salvador in the Bahamas. Although he made three later voyages (1494, 1498 and 1502), he always believed that he had found a direct route to Asia, hence the name West Indies for the islands in the Caribbean Sea. Amerigo Vespucci (1452–1512), a Florentine living in Seville, explored the north-east coast of South America in 1499 and discovered the mouth of the River Amazon. He later studied the local flora and fauna and decided that the continent could not be Asia. He therefore called it Mundus Novus (the New World), but the German geographer Martin Waldseemüller re-named it America.

Spanish soldiers followed up these voyages and so secured the great mineral wealth of South America for Spain. In 1519-21 Hernán Cortés conquered Mexico with a tiny force of Spanish soldiers and skilful use of local allies, and Francisco Pizarro was equally successful in annexing the great Inca empire of Peru in 1533. Meanwhile, Ferdinand Magellan (1480-1521), a Portuguese seaman employed by Spain, sailed from Seville with five ships in 1519 to try to reach the Indies by rounding South America. He navigated the dangerous and stormy straits which now bear his name and crossed the Pacific in ninety-five days, with supplies so short that his sailors ate rats. He was killed in the Philippines, but the *Vittoria* reached Spain in 1522, the first ship to have circumnavigated the world.

In order to avoid conflict between Spain and Portugal, the Treaty of Tordesillas (1494), based on papal Bulls of Alexander VI, established a north-south line of demarcation in the Atlantic, 370 leagues [about 1,110 miles: 1,700 kilometres] west of the Azores, recognising Spain's claim to the lands to the west and Portugal's to the east; this line enabled Portugal to claim Brazil, which Pedro de Cabral had reached in 1500.

England and France were late in embarking on voyages of discovery although John and Sebastian Cabot sailed from Bristol in 1497 with a commission from Henry VII to seek unknown lands. They reached Newfoundland and Nova Scotia and received £10 from the king for planting the English flag in Newfoundland. Cabot's voyages later encouraged English seamen such as Frobisher, Davis and Hudson to search for the North-West passage.

Francis I of France (1515-47) sent Giovanni di Verrazano in 1524 to try to find this passage. He sailed north along the east coast of North America and was followed in 1534 by Jacques Cartier, who reached the mouth of the St Lawrence and later penetrated to where Quebec and Montreal now stand (1534-35, 1541-42).

Thus, as a result of the explorations and discoveries of this period, the outline of the land masses of the world, except Australia, the Arctic and Antarctic and the northern edge of the Pacific Ocean, had largely been discovered.

¶ BERGER, J. *Discoverers of the New World.* 1969; RENAULT, GILBERT. *The Caravels of Christ, 1415-1498.* 1959

See also AMUNDSEN, COOK, *and end-papers.*

Disraeli, Benjamin, 1st Earl of Beaconsfield (1804-81): British statesman and writer. Born of Jewish parents, he became an Anglican in 1817. He had already won some reputation as a novelist before, in 1837, he entered Parliament, where his first speech was a failure. But he was soon to become a master orator, uttering "the polished and poisoned sentences, over which he had spent laborious hours" as though they were spontaneous (*see* the *Oxford Dictionary of Quotations*). As Prime Minister (briefly in 1868 and 1874-80) he managed Queen Victoria with great adroitness and showed considerable vision in foreign affairs, such as his purchase of a major interest in the Suez Canal.

¶ MAUROIS, ANDRE. *Disraeli: a picture of the Victorian Age.* 1962

District of Columbia: the seat of the national government of the USA, coterminous with the city of Washington; usually abbreviated to Washington, DC (*see* separate entry).

Divers: those who explore beneath the water. Man's capacity for remaining under water is restricted to about two minutes. With an artificial supply of air this period can be considerably extended. The harvesting of pearls and sponges, the examination of sunken wrecks and the recovery of precious cargoes are all a challenge for the diver.

Various forms of diving equipment to explore the underwater world have been known to exist for more than 2,000 years. The diving bell was one of the earliest known means of remaining under water for long periods. This had to be very heavy and large enough to take a man. When the bell was lowered beneath the surface, water would be forced up only a short way inside, thus allowing the occupant a sufficient supply of air to breathe. Alexander the Great is said to have used this method for exploring the seabed. In 1664, in the harbour at Stockholm, Swedish divers using the diving bell brought to the surface many of the cannon from the wreck of the warship *Vasa* from a depth of 100 feet [30·4 metres]. The whole vessel has recently been raised from the seabed. Larger diving bells, holding several men, have subsequently been developed with a supply of air being introduced by pipeline from above.

Also of ancient origin is a form of individual diving dress to give the diver freedom of movement under the water. The rudimentary efforts to get a supply of air to the submerged diver culminated in 1819 when Augustus Siebe, German by birth but later to become English, perfected a watertight suit with metal

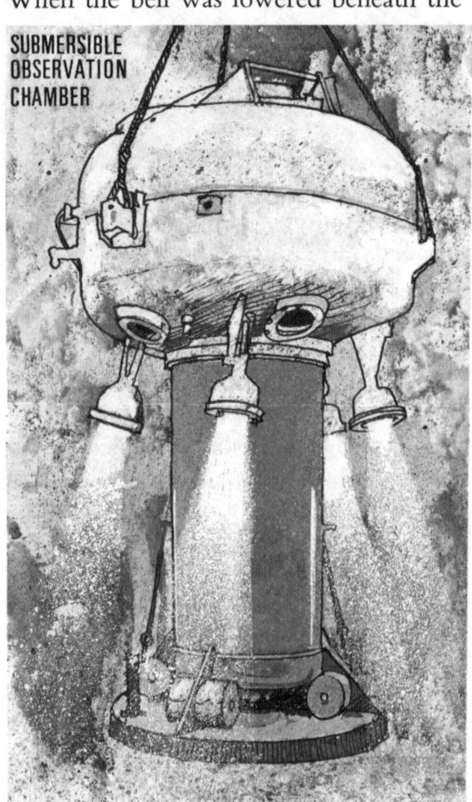

helmet and glass window. Fresh air was pumped into the suit through an air hose connected to the helmet. This became the standard form of individual diving dress throughout the world for many years. From 1834 to 1844 divers using Siebe's suits worked on the wreck of HMS *Royal George* sunk at Spithead, England, and brought up many items of the ship's equipment. The 20th-century version of this suit can take a man down to over 600 feet [182 metres].

Pressure becomes very great as the descent is made, and extreme care has to be taken when the diver is being returned to the surface. If brought up too fast he can suffer the "bends", caused by nitrogen dissolving into the blood supply and creating bubbles which, by blocking nerves, may lead to paralysis.

Twentieth-century advances include the introduction of the self-contained diving suit, in which the diver is completely independent of air from the surface. In the 1930s the French naval officer Jacques-Ives Cousteau developed the aqualung, using cylinders of compressed air which, when strapped to the back of the diver, maintain a controlled supply of air to the mouth. Vast possibilities of diving activities have been opened up by this technique. Frogmen and skindivers are exploring deeper into the ocean, and a depth of over 1,000 feet [305 metres] has been reached by American aquanauts using a mixture of oxygen and helium.

Greater depths still have been reached by means of the bathysphere, an immensely strong pressure-resisting craft. In 1960 Jacques Piccard in the *Trieste* descended to a depth of 35,800 feet [10,880 metres] in the Challenger Deep off Guam in the Pacific, the deepest known point in the world's oceans. *See also endpapers.*

¶ COOK, J. GORDON. *Exploring under the Sea.* 1964; ROMANOVSKY, VSEVOLOD. *Conquest of the Deep.* 1965

Divine Right: the idea that kings were appointed by God and responsible to him alone, first expressed during the Middle Ages and attaining a new importance at the Reformation. In England, the Tudors doubtless believed that they ruled by Divine Right, but James I (1603–25) went further, delighting in openly expounding his theories and writing a book *The Trew Law of Free Monarchies*, explaining that monarchy is the form of government ordained by God; that a king's right to the throne is strictly hereditary; that he is answerable to God alone and that rebellion is sinful. Charles I (1625–49) held similar views but talked less. Later Royalists talked more modestly of the duty of non-resistance, and the theory died out in the 18th century. One interesting offshoot of the doctrine was the belief that the sovereign's touch had divine power and could heal scrofula, known as the "King's Evil" (*see* separate entry).

Divining: the art of detecting the presence of water, metals and minerals underground by means of a rod or forked twig, often of hazel. The practice is very ancient, and the *virgula furcata* (forked rod) is described by the Roman Agricola, among other early writers. In England its use in mining was brought over in Tudor times by traders familiar with German methods, e.g. in the Harz Mountains of central Germany. The skill of the operator, or "dowser" (the origin of the term is unknown), has been greatly relied on by country folk, but scientists, in the face of a good deal of evidence, have remained divided in opinion about the basis for the successes claimed. More sophisticated apparatus, relying on electrical impulses, has been much employed by modern prospectors for oil and minerals.

Divining (divination) can also mean the foretelling of the future by omens and supernatural means.

Docks: artificially created basins into which ships are admitted for the purpose of loading or discharging cargo, or for repairs. In tidal harbours the level of the water in the basin is kept constantly high, and the entry and departure of ships is controlled by means of locks and gates.

On the dockside are cranes for loading and unloading thc ships, and behind these are warehouses and transit sheds to receive the cargoes. Extensive road and rail communications connect with the dockside and warehouses, bringing the goods for shipment or carrying them away to their final destination. In addition, a large fleet of lighters is available in the docks for loading and discharging cargoes overside.

Many commercial docks were planned and built in the early years of the 19th century, and, although extensively modernised, the basic layout has remained much the same. Since World War II, sweeping changes in the design of ships have necessitated the entire replanning of some of the docks and, more particularly, the wharves. The bulk carrier, the roll on/roll off ship, the container ship and the monster tanker all require special facilities for loading and discharging. For the large tankers of 100,000 deadweight tons [101,600 tonnes] and above, very deep water berths are required. These are usually situated away from the main harbours and docks, either in estuaries or, as in the case of Britain, in the naturally deep waters of the west coast at Milford Haven and the Clyde. The crude oil is pumped from the tanker into large circular storage tanks, and, in many of the larger ocean terminal ports, there are factories on the spot for processing and refining the oil into petrol and byproducts. The bulk carrier and the roll on/roll off ship have increased in size and number since 1945, and, while the former requires special gantry cranes for handling the cargo, the latter needs a special berth with ramps. The bulk grain carriers berth alongside the grain eleva-

The United States Lines' terminal at Tilbury Dock. Containers are unloaded here and stacked two or three high.

tors, their cargo being transferred by suction hose.

The introduction of the container ships of the 1960s has brought about the biggest changes in the layout and equipment of the docks. These are specially designed vessels fitted to take their entire cargo in large metal boxes or containers of standard dimensions. A container berth has to be a large area of dockside free of encumbrances and with no adjacent warehouses. The containers are brought to the quayside by rail or lorry and lifted off and stacked by straddle carriers. Large gantry cranes load the containers into the ship's hold and also stack them on deck. The reverse process is adopted for discharging. Many types of cargo, including frozen meat, are carried by this method, which enables a ship to be turned round with the minimum delay.

Ports with repair and maintenance facilities will have dry or graving docks, usually situated within the basin area. A caisson or gate is opened to admit the ship, after which it is closed and the dock pumped out. The ship will eventually settle on keel blocks, and supporting prongs are placed between the hull and the dockside. The ship is thus left dry for repairs.

The floating dock situated in deep water harbours also offers repair facilities outside the basin area. By flooding the tanks in the sides of the dock it can be sufficiently submerged to admit a vessel. The water then being pumped out, the dock will rise until the keel blocks are supporting the keel of the ship. Side shores are placed, and the ship is supported as in the dry dock.

¶ MURPHY, JOHN STEWART. *Docks and Harbours*. 1966

Dockyards: name generally applied to national establishments for building, equipping and maintaining warships. Owing to the nature of the work involved, it is necessary for them to be suitably defended against intrusion or attack, and they are usually situated near a garrison town. Unlike the commercial docks and harbours, the naval dockyard is mainly self-contained. The warship can be built, fitted out, completed with all necessary stores and ammunition and finally commissioned all within the confines of the dockyard. Naval barracks, usually situated near at hand, accommodate and train the crew until such time as the ship is ready to receive them.

In Britain the oldest of the three main dockyards is Portsmouth, situated on the southern shores and founded by King Henry VII when the first dry dock was constructed in 1496. Chatham followed *c.* 1560, and Plymouth became a royal dockyard in 1689. Very much later a demand for naval facilities in the north resulted in the establishment, in 1903, of the dockyard at Rosyth on the east coast of Scotland. Heavy demands on timber in the 17th, 18th and early 19th centuries required the dockyards to be situated within easy reach of forests. HMS *Victory*, building at Chatham dockyard between 1759 and 1765, required over 2,000 oak trees, most of which had to be brought in from the forests of Kent and Sussex. Another distinctive feature of the naval dockyards is the ropery, the long building where the yarns are twisted up to make the various sizes of rope required by a man-of-war. The ropery in Chatham dockyard has been in continuous service since it was built in the 18th century.

With the introduction of iron shipbuilding and steam propulsion in the mid-19th century, extensive replanning of the dockyards became necessary. Large machine shops, foundries and plate sheds were added. Later in the century, when electricity became available, generating stations to supply the necessary power were established in the dockyards.

Since World War II much of the actual warship building programme is undertaken by commercial shipyards, the main function of the naval dockyards being refitting, maintaining and generally keeping up to date the highly complex navigational, propulsion and operational systems of the 20th-century warship.

Outside Britain, the chief Commonwealth dockyards are at Gibraltar, Halifax (Nova Scotia), Singapore and Sydney (New South Wales).

In the USA these establishments are known as Navy Yards, three of the most important being at Norfolk, Virginia (where the first dry dock in the United States was opened in 1833), Charleston (the oldest city of South Carolina), and San Diego, South California.

Among the other great naval bases and dockyards of the world are Leningrad, Molotovsk, Kronstadt, Sevastopol, Nikolaiev and Vladivostok (USSR); Spezia, Naples and Taranto (Italy); Cherbourg, Brest, Lorient and Toulon (France); Yokohama, Osaka and Kobe (Japan).

Doges of Venice: the elected heads of the Venetian Republic. There were 120 Doges between the founding of Venice in AD 697 and the overthrow of the Republic by Napoleon in 1796. Their portraits are displayed on the walls of the Great Council Chamber – all except that of Marino Faliero, who was executed in 1355 for conspiring to make himself absolute. Until 1172 Doges were elected by the whole population; thereafter by the Grand Council. Between 1297 and 1319 further steps were taken to confine power to an oligarchy (*see* separate entry for definition) of merchant families. Only those whose ancestors had served on the Grand Council between 1172 and 1297 could be Councillors, and their names were inscribed in the Golden Book. Elaborate procedures were devised to prevent the election of a Doge being affected by personal ambition and family influence. Boys chosen at random from the crowds in St Mark's Square were invited into the Grand Council Chamber to pick the names of nine Councillors out of a box. These nine chose forty, twelve of

The Doge visiting a church on the Feast of St Roche, one of the many paintings by the Venetian, Canaletto, showing the Doge on a public occasion.

whom, chosen by lot, named twenty-five. Nine of these, again chosen by lot, named forty-five, from whom eleven chose the final forty-one, who chose the Doge. The Doge must receive twenty-five votes. Even this procedure did not prevent chicanery. Francesco Foscari was elected in 1423 because he had nine secret partisans among the final electors, who carefully defeated all possible rivals before nominating Foscari at the tenth ballot. Once elected, the Doge served for life, "a mere ceremonial idol", wearing his golden state mantle, his *vitta*, or cambric cap with strings, and his *corno*, or Dogal Cap, receiving ambassadors, entertaining popes and emperors. Every year on Ascension Day, to commemorate the departure of Doge Pietro Orseolo from the lagoon to subdue the Dalmatians in 997, the Doge was rowed in his gilded galley, the *Bucentauro*, to wed the sea "in sign of our true and everlasting dominion". Real power was denied to the Doge by restrictions which were imposed by the vigilant oligarchy. He could not refuse office or abdicate, he must never travel abroad, none of his sons or personal attendants might hold office in Venice, he must not receive an official guest or open an official letter alone, his letters to his wife must be censored. In 1229 a Senate was established which must sanction war, taxes and laws. In 1311 a Council of Ten, a body of examining magistrates, was set up, and they, in association with the Signoria, a cabinet of Doge and six Councillors, took all important decisions. Though the Doge alone was powerless against these councils, his influence could be great if he carried with him a substantial party. Foscari, for example, carried through the controversial policy of establishing a hinterland on the mainland which brought Venice into the conflicts with Milan and the Papacy during his long Dogeship, 1423–57. If a Doge had numerous enemies, his position was dangerous. Foscari himself was deposed, Antonio Foscarini was executed for treason though posthumously exonerated, nine were blinded and exiled, seven were assassinated.

The most famous Doge was Enrico Dandolo (1192–1205), who diverted the Fourth Crusade to take the Christian city of Zara, a trading rival of Venice in Dalmatia, and then, aged eighty-eight and blind, led them to the siege of Byzantium in 1204 and carried off as booty the four bronze horses which now adorn the façade of St Mark's Cathedral.

Dogs, Famous: Dogs probably first sought association with man as scavengers at nomad camp-fires. By 1500 BC they were domesticated by the Assyrians as guards and hunters. Marco Polo saw them used by the Chinese to draw sledges. Gradually bonds of affection grew between dog and man. Alexander the Great named a city after his dog, Peritas; the father of Pericles had a dog which swam beside his galley from fallen Athens to Salamis; the Bayeux Tapestry shows Harold of England carrying his dogs through the surf to embark for Normandy. "Smale ladies' popes that beere a way the flees", or lapdogs, appear in Renaissance Venice, Flanders and Spain. The dogs of great men seem sometimes almost to mirror their masters' character, swaggering, devoted, treacherous, courageous; Mathe, Richard II of England's greyhound, which is reputed to have deserted its fallen master and attached itself to his successor Henry IV (Bolingbroke); Kuntze, the white pug which gave the alarm and saved William of Orange from a Spanish raid near Mons; Boy, who disappeared, with Prince Rupert's luck, at Marston Moor and whose salutes for King Charles and King Pym were made with diagonally opposite legs; Bounce, who solaced Admiral Collingwood's months of lonely command; Tigger, whose snapping at ankles broke the ice at President Tito's first uneasy conference with a British General.

In a celebrated 14th-century case, Dragon, the dog of Aubry of Montdidier, who was found murdered in a forest in 1371, fought a judicial combat with his suspected murderer, Richard of Macaire. The enraged dog killed the murderer, who confessed before he expired.

Diamond, Sir Isaac Newton's dog, was responsible for the loss of years of scientific and mathematical research. Newton left him in his room while he was attending chapel in Trinity College, Cambridge, one day and returned to find the dog had overset a candle which had burnt the record of many years' experiments.

Dogs have saved innumerable lives. The most famous was Barry, the St Bernard from the hospice in the Great St Bernard Pass, who rescued forty travellers from the snow in the early 19th century, on one occasion digging a small boy out of an avalanche and carrying him on his back to the monks at the hospice.

St Bernard dogs with monks from the monastery.

Probably the most famous dogs in this century have been the Russian animals which pioneered space travel – Laika, the black and white fox terrier who died from lack of oxygen after orbiting the earth for seven days in 1957 in Sputnik 2, and Belka and Shelka (*below*) who were launched in Sputnik 5 in 1960 and retrieved from orbit, thus preparing the way for the first manned space flight.

Dole: from Anglo-Saxon, a share or portion; a charitable distribution. After a long and honourable history, the term has degenerated to mean a relief payment by a government to the unemployed. Shakespeare twice uses the expression, apparently current in Tudor times, "Happy man be his dole"; i.e. may his lot in life be happy.

Dolls: toy human beings. Egyptian children played with dolls, and they were common in ancient Greece. Greek dolls were made of clay, with movable limbs hinged to the body. When a Greek girl became old enough to marry, she left all her dolls in the temple of the goddess Artemis. Similar dolls have been found in the Roman catacombs. In Arabia, Ayesha, the child betrothed to the prophet Mohammed, coaxed him to play with her dolls.

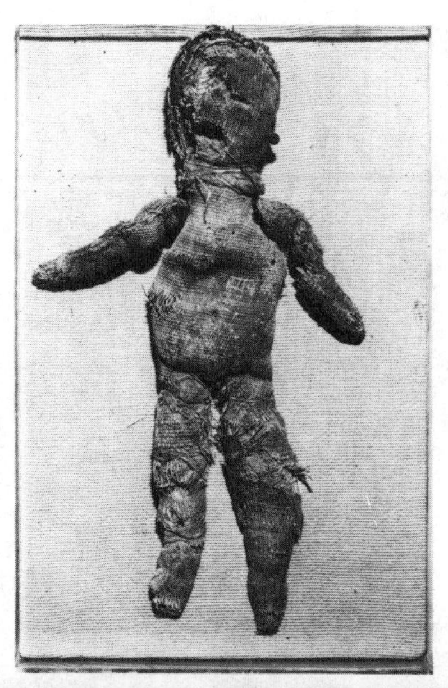

Right column above, Medieval woodcut, possibly representing doll makers at work. Below left, Doll with composition head and stuffed kid body wearing fashionable visiting dress 1792. Right, Wax doll with cloth body, English 1820.

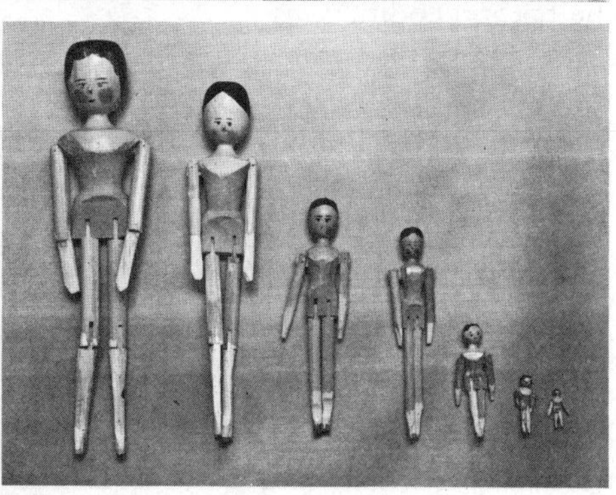

Dolls. Left column above, Roman Doll. Middle, Scandinavian dolls, made of straw. Below, Row of wooden "stick figure" dolls in varying sizes.

Right, Wax doll with carved wooden body and sleeping eyes. English about 1850. Far right, Alaskan Eskimo doll made from fox hair, parka wool, ticking and fox spin. Early 20th century.

Number 10, Downing Street.

The first English dolls were of wood, unjointed, and dressed exactly like their owners. In medieval days they were called "children's babies", but by Tudor times the word "doll" was used – an abbreviation of Dorothy, then a popular name. Nineteenth-century dolls were very elaborate, having stuffed bodies with beautifully modelled wax heads and real hair. Victorian dolls were made of porcelain, with jointed limbs, eyes that could open and close, and silk dresses. Jointed wooden dolls with painted faces – Dutch dolls – were dearly loved, but until recently the most lifelike dolls were of German manufacture.

A love for dolls appears to have been worldwide. Australian Aborigines made dolls of woven cane, and among Red Indian tribes a mother whose child died carried its dolls about as a sign of mourning. In Japan, elegantly dressed dolls were carried in religious processions, and a similar custom exists in parts of Sicily and Calabria, where a life-sized doll, the *bambino*, is carefully kept in a box and given to the girls of the family to play with on saints' days.

¶ HOKE, HELEN. *Dolls.* 1971

Domesday Book: the survey of England drawn up by command of William the Conqueror in 1086. Its purpose was to list the owners of estates and the amount of tax they had to pay. It was also intended to make a written record of the laws of England, amending where necessary, and not relying on memory or the spoken word, "so that every man, sure of his own right, should not usurp that of another".

One scholar has suggested the following method of compilation.

1. England was divided into a number of circuits.
2. The clerk of each circuit made a geographical roll at each village inquest (judicial enquiry).
3. The clerk then compiled a regional volume at his headquarters.
4. The regional volume was sent to Winchester and codified.

There are three surviving exemplars, as the documents are properly called. Volume I in the Public Records Office in London is the Winchester Volume. Volume II (Little Domesday) is the Clerk's Regional Volume for East Anglia. Exon Domesday, in Exeter Cathedral, looks like an "embryonic Volume II". No convincing reason for not including Northumberland, Cumberland, Westmorland, Durham and parts of Lancashire can be given.

At the village inquest, the clerk [illegible] the title of the estate, its owner in the time of Edward the Confessor (1005–60), its present owner and value.

¶ FINN, R. WELLDON. *Domesday Inquest.* 1965

Dominican Republic: independent state of the West Indies, occupying the major (eastern) part of the island of Hispaniola (*see* separate entry). The Republic was established in 1844 and suffered more than a century of periodic disorder and tyranny before the assassination of the dictator General Trujillo in 1961.

Downing Street, England: street in Westminster, London. The name is often used to mean the British government or the Cabinet, from the fact that the Prime Minister and the Chancellor of the Exchequer have their official residences there at Number 10 (*left*) and Number 11 respectively. It also houses the Foreign Office.

Drachma: a standard weight and coin in ancient Greece, originally meaning a "handful" (of metal spits or "obols"). The drachma was famous for the emblem of the owl on the obverse, a decoration also carried by the larger coins – the didrachm and tetradrachm. These were all silver coins. There were originally 6,000 drachmas in a talent. The drachma, divided into a hundred lepta, is still the monetary unit of Greece.

A housekeeping account of *c.* AD 1 shows a cloak costing 10 drachmas and, in each case for one drachma, a supply of turnips for preserving, some white loaves, and some olive oil. In 259 BC a painter estimated 53 drachmas for decorating the portico and two rooms of a house, or 30 drachmas if the owner supplied the materials.

Dragon: fabulous monster; indirectly, from the Greek word meaning sharp-sighted. Usually depicted and described as a winged serpent or fire-breathing scaly lizard, it is found in the legends and lore of many countries, usually in evil guise, though occasionally credited with kindly wisdom and powers of loyal guardianship.

St George Fighting the Dragon *by Carpaccio.*

The dragon as symbol, embroidered in silk on a Chinese royal robe.

Some of the greatest exploits of legendary heroes are concerned with the slaying of dragons, e.g. St George – the patron saint not only of England but of Greek soldiers and shepherds and of the Spanish province of Aragon.

The dragon was also an ancient symbol of power and regality. The Pendragon of early Britain was the chief leader, and a number of English kings fought beneath "the terrible standard of the dragon". The five-clawed dragon of China is an ancient and familiar symbol on royal robes and state costumes.

Dragoon: formerly a mounted soldier equipped to fight on foot and taking his name from the short musket or carbine he carried, called a "dragon". Later the term was often applied to cavalry regiments that had once been mounted infantry. The first British regiment of dragoons, was raised in the 1680s.

Drake, Sir Francis (*c.* 1543–96)**:** English admiral and circumnavigator; the greatest seaman of his age. A formidable leader and ruthless man of action, he could show generosity and tolerance in advance of his time, e.g. in his attitude towards coloured people. If he was testy and overbearing, it usually sprang from his clear conception of what was to be done and his impatience to be doing it, rather than wait for careful deliberation and planning. Even his enemies freely conceded his genius. His greatest exploits were his circumnavigation of the world (1577–80); his "singeing of the King of Spain's beard", when he destroyed more than thirty ships in the outer and inner harbours of Cadiz (1587) and so delayed the sailing of the Armada for a year; and his part in the destruction of that Armada when it finally reached the Channel in the summer of 1588. A Spaniard described him as of medium stature, "rather heavy than slender, merry. . . . He commands and governs imperiously. He is feared and obeyed by

Sir Francis Drake.

his men"; and an Englishman, as "round headed, brown hair, full bearded, his eyes round, large and clear, well favoured, fair and of a cheerful countenance".

He died at sea in January 1596 and was buried in Nombre de Dios Bay, off Puerto Bello, "in the waters of which the surge and thunder still seem to reverberate with the terror of his name".

¶ GIBBS, LEWIS. *The Silver Circle*. 1963; KNIGHT, FRANK. *That Rare Captain: Sir Francis Drake*. 1970

Drama: the composition, presentation and acting of plays. Drama grew out of the instinctive behaviour of primitive man in protecting himself against the wild, and it thus had an element of magic about it. These early dramatic activities stimulated the love for "dressing up" which has been common to mankind from the beginning of time. By believing that if he imitated anything he gained power over it, man performed mimic hunts, when some of the community pretended to be wild animals. In the "dress rehearsals" that followed, the "animals" were, of course, overpowered, and so the hunters gained confidence to kill the real animals when they hunted them.

As man progressed, these dramatic activities became more formalised into set patterns of movement and sound, and the dances that emerged were performed either for their own sake, or became religious ceremonies to invoke the god.

Some of the earliest records of these primitive rituals are Egyptian, dating from 2500 BC, and such ceremonies have lasted in most countries down to the present day.

The more sophisticated products of ancient Greece and Rome have a power and ageless freshness that still makes them capable of holding a modern audience. Most of the greatest Greek drama belongs to a comparatively short period, the 5th and 4th centuries BC, which saw the heroic tragedies of Aeschylus, the vivid contemporary commentaries of Euripides, the doom-ridden figures of Sophocles, brought low by their own weaknesses rather than by capricious gods, the wit of Aristophanes and of Menander. Much Roman drama stemmed from Greek origins, the high-spirited comedies of Plautus, the more polished productions of his successor Terence and, in part, the tragedies of Seneca.

It was not until after the Norman Conquest that a form of religious drama was introduced into England from France, and the presentations were called Miracles or Mysteries, which set out to portray the history of the fall of man and his redemption. This type of drama, which was performed at first in the churches and later on village greens or city streets, reached its peak in the 14th century at the festival of Corpus Christi, when the plays were often performed in cycles, for instance, at York and Coventry. Later came the Morality plays which, like the Miracles, set out to teach people about life; but the characters, instead of being biblical, were abstract personifications of moral qualities like Goodness and Envy.

Thus, up to the 16th century, the function of drama in England was to teach people the ways of God, but there soon followed experiments in playwriting, and the authors took as their models the works of early Greek playwrights, such as Plautus, Terence and Seneca. This resulted in the first real English comedy *Ralph Roister Doister*, written about 1550 by Nicholas Udall, the headmaster of Eton, for performance by his pupils; and later came the first real English tragedy *Gorboduc*. These two plays laid the foundation of theatre in England.

Meanwhile, the drama in the East, which had developed much earlier than in the West, was more concerned with dancing, pantomime and acrobatics than with religion; yet in India, as in England, it had been influenced by the Greek theatre. However, the Sanskrit drama of the 2nd century BC gradually developed into romantic plays about gods and princes, performed by wandering companies of professional actors in palaces and temples right up to AD 800. These plays later degenerated into various forms of classical dance, which became largely discredited, and it was not until this century that dance became once more a respectable art, which remains the chief dramatic activity of the country.

Similarly in China there were festivals of singing, dancing and acrobatics as early as 700 BC, but their serious drama dates from the 8th century AD and reached its peak in the 14th century. However, the traditional Chinese theatre, the Peking opera, did not emerge until the 19th century, and it has made little impact on the West.

In Japan, down to the 8th century AD, drama consisted of dancing and pantomime imported from China, and out of this developed the Nō theatre, the achievement of one family. By the 17th century it had been superseded by the more popular *Kabuki* and *Joruri*, a theatre of puppets. Today the Japanese theatre is almost entirely western in style, though the Nō theatre, with its classical heroic drama, still survives and has had a good deal of influence on some western dramatists.

Thus, while it was dancing and mime that flourished in the East, it was the playwright who dominated the European theatre. Drama reached a peak in England between 1575 and 1675, with Shakespeare and his contemporaries, followed by the Restoration dramatists, and in France with the classical plays of Corneille, Molière and Racine and the introduction of ballet. Italy saw the development of opera, which later spread to Germany, Austria and Spain.

This great activity resulted in the firs[t] permanent public theatres in the West In London those built during the reign of Elizabeth I and James I were eminentl[y] suited to the type of drama performe[d] and were among the most successful i[n] history. It has been estimated that, out o[f] a population of 160,000 in London at tha[t] time, some 20,000 visited them each week

After the Restoration period, the drama down to the end of the 19th century, wa[s] largely dominated by developments i[n] stage techniques which had been introduced from Italy in the form of changeable scenery within a proscenium, so tha[t] the theatre became chiefly notable for it[s] elaborate productions of Shakespeare an[d] its melodramas.

Later playwrights, such as Ibsen, Sha[w] and Chekhov in this century, swept awa[y] this artificiality with plays concerned wit[h] ideas rather than with elaborate scener[y] and sensational stories.

Since then there have been many experiments in methods of staging and creatio[n] of character, and perhaps Pirandello influenced the 20th-century theatre mor[e] than any other playwright with *Si[x] Characters in Search of an Author* (1921). I[n] America in the 1920s and 1930s the theatr[e] was dominated by Eugene O'Neill, wh[o] turned to the findings of psychology a[s] material for drama and who achieved h[is] best work in portraying man's endle[ss]

Scene from Michael Bakewell's 1973 production [of] O'Neill's A Long Day's Journey into Nigh[t]

Above, first page of the morality play Everyman. *Middle, The Globe Theatre, Southwark, in the time of James I. Below, Peter Daubeny's production of Pirandello's* Six Characters in Search of an Author.

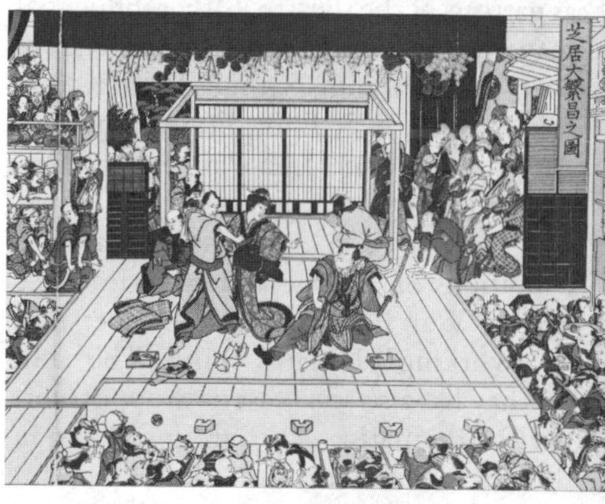

Above, Shakespeare's Swan Theatre, c. 1590. Middle, Inside a Japanese Kabuki theatre. Below, the ancient theatre of Epidauros, Greece, still in use.

struggle with his environment and the forces of evil. Tennessee Williams, preoccupied with decadence and life's failures, has been a notable successor to O'Neill in the realm of psychological studies. In Britain John Osborne for a time typified the "angry young man" of the 1950s. More recently the leading names among English playwrights have been those of the stylist Harold Pinter and Arnold Wesker, a committed socialist who has founded "Centre 42" with the aim of bringing the pleasures of art and the drama to sections of society not usually regarded as patrons of the theatre. Other influential playwrights in the modern scene have been Jean Anouilh, Samuel Becket, Bertold Brecht, T. S. Eliot, Eugene Ionesco, Arthur Miller and Jean-Paul Sartre. But, whatever the style, contemporary dramatists have tried to reflect the changing conditions of Europe and America since World War I and to probe deeper into the working of man's mind. The 20th century has also seen vast new opportunities for dramatist, actor and producer in the cinema and television studios, both of which have demanded a completely different approach. Not only have many memorable new dramatic pieces been specially created for these media, but a number of earlier plays have been given vivid life for greater audiences than the old theatre could ever command.

¶BRADBURY, J. *Shakespeare and His Theatre.* 1974; SAMACHSON, DOROTHY and JOSEPH. *Dramatic Story of The Theatre.* 1955

See also ATHENS; DANCE; HOMER; PANTOMIME; SHAKESPEARE, WILLIAM.

Dravidians: group of mixed races, mainly in southern India and the north of Ceylon. Strictly, the word "Dravidian" can be used only of the languages of southern India – Tamil, Telugu, Kanarese, Malayalam and Tulu – but it is generally used to describe the peoples themselves. They are some of the oldest of India, having been driven south by successive waves of invasion. Their racial characteristics vary from pure Aryan to near-negroid, and their culture from primitive practices, such as totemism and the erection of dolmens, to a high degree of civilisation with a remarkable literature. The name "Dravidians" is also used by Indians to denote simply the "southern" group of the Brahmins.

Dred Scott Decision (1857): the result of a legal test case brought before the US Supreme Court concerning slavery and its extension into the new territories. Dred Scott was a Negro who was taken from Missouri (a slave state) to "free soil" in Illinois and Wisconsin. After the death of his master he returned to Missouri where he was encouraged to claim that, as a result of his residence in free territory, he was no longer a slave. The case lasted eleven years. Eventually the Supreme Court ruled that, as a Negro was not an American citizen, Scott had no right to sue in the Federal Courts and that his status was determined by the laws of the state in which he first raised the case, i.e. in Missouri, which recognised slavery. The decision was hotly contested by Northern abolitionists and considerably intensified feeling over slavery throughout the Union.

Duels: combats between two persons armed with offensive weapons. They can be divided into two types: (1) judicial combats approved in earlier times by courts and kings as a method of settling disputes; and (2) private duels or "affairs of honour", fought to avenge insult, real or imagined.

The judicial duel was very common in Germany and France, but never became

The duel between the Count of Turin and Prince Henry of Orleans (19th century).

so firmly established in England. It appeared with the Norman Conquest and it was for long an accepted method for deciding quarrels about the ownership of land. Though the law was rarely invoked after Tudor times, as late as 1817 Lord Chief Justice Ellenborough pronounced in a murder trial, "the general law of the land is that there shall be trial by battle in cases of appeal unless the party brings himself within some of the exceptions". In this case, the court allowed the accused man to challenge the brother of the murdered girl to "wager of battle", though the challenge was refused. The ancient law was abolished in 1818.

Private duels began to gain in popularity in the 16th century as the old judicial combats were dropping out of use. In no country did they reach such near-mania proportions as they did in France where, according to an English ambassador to the court of Louis XIII (1601–43), "there is scarce a Frenchman worth looking as who has not killed his man in a duel". In Germany a special development was the *mensuren*, or student duels, common in

Withdrawal from Dunkirk, *from the painting by Charles Cundall (see article p. 254).*

all universities and conducted on a large scale by well-established *verbindungen*, or fighting corps, despite their illegality. In fact, the private duel has rarely been approved by law in any country and has been greatly frowned upon by the Church. Nevertheless, a blind eye was for long turned on all so-called "affairs of honour". In England a notable list can be compiled of men in high public office who fought duels, including Charles James Fox, Richard Brinsley Sheridan, William Pitt the Younger, Lord Castlereagh and the Duke of Wellington.

Dunkirk, Fr. **Dunkerque:** French North Sea port near Belgium. The port and surrounding countryside has been much fought over from the 10th century onwards. In 1940 (29 May–4 June) it was the scene of the heroic evacuation of 345,000 British and French troops ("Operation Dynamo") despite ferocious German bomb and artillery attacks. The official history of the war records that "the names of many small craft which took part were never reported or discovered". *See* illustration, p. 253.

¶ DIVINE, D. *The Nine Days of Dunkirk.* 1967
See also BATTLE OF BRITAIN; WORLD WAR II.

Dürer, Albrecht (1471–1528): German artist. One of the eighteen children of a Nuremberg goldsmith, he was apprenticed to Wolgemut, a well-known painter of the town and afterwards travelled in Europe. He had close contacts with printers and financed his travels by working on book illustration for printing presses in Basle and Frankfurt. After working for a time in Italy he returned in 1495 to Nuremberg to lead the Renaissance in Germany and establish himself as one of the most accomplished artists of any age. Luther described him as "one who was the best of men". He was a great painter, a superb copper engraver and a master of woodcut.

Drawing by Albrecth Dürer, possibly a self portrait, executed in 1521, seven years before his death.

Durham, England: the county town of Durham in northern England. The original site was Dunholm, a rocky promontory in a bend of the River Wear where the cathedral and castle were built. In 995 the monks of Lindisfarne, after long wanderings, rested the body of St Cuthbert here. In 1093 the present superb Norman cathedral was begun by Bishop William de St Carileph and completed in forty years. The cathedral library, once the monks' dormitory, contains the relics of St Cuthbert's grave but his body was buried where his shrine, destroyed in 1540, had stood. The fortifications of the castle, begun in 1072, were largely the work of Ranulf Flambard, Bishop of Durham (1099–1128). Durham was extremely

Durham Cathedral, looking into the nave from the south aisle. Below, St Cuthbert's stole.

important in the defence of the north and received its first charter in 1180. The Charter of the University was granted by William IV in 1837.

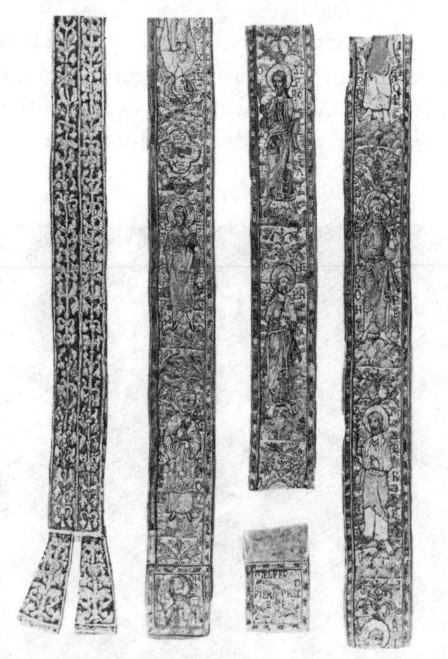

Durham Report (1839): report named after John George Lambton, 1st earl of Durham (1792–1840), British statesman and governor general of Canada, who recommended responsible government for the colonies and was instrumental in changing the British conception of empire.

Dwarfs: human beings of diminutive size. People have frequently derived amusement from abnormality, for example from the inmates of Bedlam, or St Mary of Bethlehem, the former priory which became a lunatic asylum in London. Today dwarfs entertain the multitude at the circus; earlier they diverted the members and guests of princely families. In most cases they enjoyed the affectionate protection of their patrons and were valued for their talents as acrobats or comedians. The Gonzaga dukes built in their palace at Mantua the Apartments of the Dwarfs, a suite of rooms, staircase and chapel for people three feet high. Isabella d'Este, who married a Gonzaga, once asked her father to send her the dwarf Fritello to divert her with dances and somersaults, and at another time sent her own dwarf Mattello to cheer her brother in his bereavement. The Spaniard Velasquez (1599–1660) conveys something of the sadness of abnormality in his paintings of the dwarfs of the Spanish Court under Philip IV: e.g. Don Antonio el Inglese, with a hound standing shoulder-high to him; and Don Sebastian de Morra, who diverted the Cardinal Infant in Flanders. In *Las Meninas* ("Ladies in Waiting") Velasquez shows himself painting, watched by two dwarfs, the German Marebarbola and the Italian Nicholas de Portosanto. Mary Tudor had a well-known dwarf, John Jarvis, but the most famous in English history is Jeffery Hudson, dwarf of Queen Henrietta Maria of England, who was once served up to Charles I in a pie. He fought two duels, one with a turkey-cock, the other with a captain of horse who paid

Detail from Las Meninas *by Velasquez.*

dearly for his contempt, and was himself a captain of horse in the Civil War. Until he was thirty he was no more than eighteen inches [460 millimetres] high.

Dyeing: the art of colouring materials, such as textiles. The earliest dyes were usually the product of plants, fruits and flowers. One of the oldest was indigo, a rich blue, found in garments as early as 3000 BC. Another was the famous Tyrrhene purple, for long associated with royalty, its manufacture being centred in Tyre, the ancient Phoenician seaport. The early Britons are recorded as having stained their bodies with the blue dye called woad. Various shades of blue are, in fact, the commonest of early dyes, though scarlet and yellow were also known. The range of natural dyes was greatly increased by the 14th-century Spanish conquests of South America and Mexico, which made available to Europe a wide range of plants indigenous to those countries. Most modern dyes are synthetic (or artificial), made from hydrocarbons.

Ancient methods of dyeing.

E

Earth, age of: some rocks contain uranium, which disintegrates at a measurable and constant rate, leaving lead as an end product. By measuring the proportion of lead and still unchanged uranium in a mineral, it is possible to calculate the approximate date at which the process started. The earliest rocks may have formed about 4,000 million years ago.

Though life in some elementary form may well have existed earlier, the first fossils were formed in the Cambrian period, in the region of 600 million years ago. Man appeared less than two million years ago.

¶ BEISER, A. *The Earth (Time-Life Young Readers' Library)*. 1969

See also GEOLOGICAL PERIODS.

Earthenware: articles made from natural clay, which, after heating, remains porous. For domestic use a thin coating of some non-porous substance is needed, and this is known as a glaze. People tend to think of earthenware objects as coarse and heavy, but many so-called "china" ornaments and vessels are really made of earthenware. A modern potter can turn out earthenware as thin and fine as china, but, because of the addition of chemicals and other substances, china is translucent and hard. One of these substances is crushed bone; hence the term "bone china".

When potters discovered how to use a glaze, they began to colour earthenware and then fire it a second time, so that the colour became permanent. This art was practised in ancient Egypt and was copied by Greek and Phoenician craftsmen, who exported their products all over the Mediterranean world. From a centre established at Faenza, Italy, glazed pottery is often known as *faience* ware. The people of Majorca used multicoloured decorations, and this pottery is known as *majolica.*

As the first potters did not glaze their vessels, these broke easily. If an archaeologist discovers quantities of unglazed pottery, he knows that the site is likely to have been occupied in very early times.

Primitive tribes and nations made distinctively shaped vessels, so that countries of origin and approximate dates of manufacture can be established through knowledge of types of earthenware. Glazed pots, decorated with flowing pictures of ordinary natural subjects, frequently squids, painted in bright colours under the glaze, were made in Minoan Crete. But similar patterns have been found at Tel-el-Amarna, the site of an earlier Egyptian city. It is possible that craftsmen from Egypt fled to Crete after their city fell. Greek and Egyptian earthenware occurs all over the Mediterranean area and is an indication of early trade links. Athenian ware, with its distinctive shapes and black paintings on the red clay, is easy to identify.

In the 17th century Dutch potters discovered how to cover clay with an enamel made principally of melted tin. This made

Pottery storage jar from Knossos, Crete. 1450–1400 BC.

the clay very hard. It would resist heat, and so was used for tiles. The process was invented in the town of Delft, and the tiles were often decorated in dark blue. Such pottery is still known as delft ware, or simply *delft*.

French earthenware is very hard because Breton potters mixed their clay with powdered flint, which explains why French cooking pots are so strong. It is an interesting example of word derivation that the French have given us the word *kaolin* for a type of fine clay, from Kao-ling, a hill in the Kiangsi province, China. Some of the greatest kaolin deposits are in Czechoslovakia.

In England, Cornwall and Devon are rich in clays suitable for pottery. The clay of the Cornish mines is white. It is not mined as coal is mined; a deep pit is dug, and the clay is hosed from the sides with jets of water. Eventually the water drains away, leaving the softened clay at the bottom of the pit.

The most famous English potter was Josiah Wedgwood (*see* separate entry), who worked in the Midlands during the early 18th century. The towns of this same area are called "the Potteries".

In the USA some china clays are found in Georgia, but American potters rely a great deal on imported clays.

¶ HAGGAR, R. G. *Pottery through the Ages*. 1966

Left: Attic red-figured cup, 400–390 BC. Dionysos and Ariadne escorted by Eros.

Earthquakes: shakings of the earth's crust due to natural causes. When rock masses abruptly shift their position, tremors spread out in all directions like the rings that spread outward through the water from a pebble dropped in a pond. These tremors, or vibrations, decrease in intensity in proportion to their distance from the seat of the disturbance until they can only be detected by a sensitive instrument called a seismograph.

So far from the earth being *terra firma*, the firm ground we like to think it, its crust is in a constant state of vibration. An earthquake occurs somewhere every few minutes, a severe one about once a fortnight; most of them, fortunately, in unpopulated areas or under the sea.

Not surprisingly, they occur predominantly in the geologically less stable parts of the world, areas where the process of mountain-building is still incomplete: that is, along the shoreline of the Pacific and in the region that stretches in a broadening wedge from the Azores to China, embracing the Mediterranean and the Alps, the Caucasus, Asia Minor and the Himalayas. The greatest recorded loss of life (estimated at 830,000) occurred in January 1556 in the Shenshi province, China.

From earliest times people who lived in earthquake-prone regions have tried to account for the terrifying phenomenon. The early Japanese believed a gigantic subterranean spider was responsible; the Mongolians blamed it on a pig, the Indians on a mole. The people of Kamchatka in Siberia thought earthquakes were caused by the dogs of their god Tuil scratching themselves to get rid of their fleas.

In Christian countries earthquakes were sometimes believed to be God's punishment for sin. In 1755, after a great earthquake had destroyed Lisbon and killed an estimated 15,000 people, many Protestant clergymen declared the catastrophe to be a judgment on the Portuguese for being Catholics. The survivors, on the other hand, ascribed their woes to the fact that they had tolerated Protestants in their midst.

The Lisbon earthquake was one of the earliest to be investigated scientifically, notably by John Mitchell (1724–93), who was the first to formulate the wave theory of earthquake transmission. It is asserted that the Lisbon earthquake temporarily stopped the medicinal springs at Karlsbad, 1,500 miles [2,414 kilometres] away.

One of the most destructive earthquakes to occur in the New World was that which, in San Francisco in 1906, killed 700 people and left a quarter of a million homeless. Broken gas mains led to fires that caused damage estimated at £400 million. As the water mains, too, had been destroyed little could be done to fight the fires. Many destructive earthquakes have been suffered in Chile, Peru and the Philippines.

Japan, over the centuries, has suffered so cruelly from earthquakes that it has been suggested that the tension of living always in the shadow of the next, inevitable, disaster may have affected the national character. It could account for an attitude to death that formerly elevated suicide into an honourable ritual and, more recently, encouraged pilots to crash-dive their planes to certain death on the decks of enemy ships.

In the earliest recorded earthquake in Japan, in AD 869, a thousand people died. In 1611 nearly 5,000 were drowned in Yamada Bay by the wave that followed an earthquake. When an earthquake struck Tokyo in 1923 the shock overturned the charcoal braziers in which the midday meal was being prepared; 700,000 houses burned to the ground, and the number of dead and missing reached the horrific total of 142,807. This earthquake resulted in the most extensive material damage on record.

Victims of a Turkish earthquake pick their way through the debris of their homes.

Another hard-hit country is Turkey, the most recent disaster, in which 2,000 lives were lost, occurring in Gediz and the surrounding area in March 1970.

Earthquakes in Great Britain are mostly of a minor nature. Only two lives are known to have been lost in British earthquakes, one on 6 April 1580, when a London apprentice was killed by a stone dislodged from a church tower, the other in 1884, near Colchester, when a child died in what was probably the worst earthquake in England in historic times. Church spires collapsed and hundreds of chimneys toppled. The damage was serious enough for the Lord Mayor of London to open a disaster fund to aid the victims.

In 1750, after shocks were felt in London in February and again in March, a madman prophesied that on the following 5 April a third earthquake would completely destroy the capital. Panic ensued, and refugees jammed the roads to the countryside.

An earthquake centred upon Tangshan in China during July and August 1976 led to the loss of thousands of lives and the destruction of a huge industrial and mining complex. And another in the Khurasan region of Iran in 1978 killed an estimated 20,000 people.

The greatest distance over which tremors have so far been recorded is over 200,000 miles [321,870 kilometres], i.e. from moon to earth. This was through a seismograph left on the moon by American astronauts. The seismograph, an instrument for measuring the period, extent and direction of earthquakes, was first set up in 1855 on Vesuvius, Italy. World maps of earthquakes show that these disturbances tend to follow certain well defined bands or circles, e.g. the lines of elevation dividing the great continental and oceanic areas.

Earthworks: man-made banks of earth for the purposes of civil and military engineering. Many earthworks began in Neolithic times as simple cattle enclosures reinforced by ditch and bank. Camps were usually divided into two parts, one for cattle and one for people. By the Iron Age, improvements had been made, consisting of additional earth banks and special precautionary constructions at the entrances, which were designed as ingenious mazes. When these arrangements developed into defensive forts, the tops of the banks were palisaded, and the ditches were filled with sharpened stakes.

To the archaeologist the most interesting earthworks are those which develop the natural features of the ground, such as are found in elaborate form at Maiden Castle and Badbury Rings in Dorset, England. The much more extensive earthworks constructed by the modern civil engineer for dams, canals, roads and railways have an equal claim on our interest.

Maiden Castle.

East India Company: "The Governor and Company of Merchants of London trading into the East Indies". The Company was incorporated in 1600 with Thomas Smythe as first Governor and received a charter from Queen Elizabeth I granting exclusive trade with India.

Early rivalry with Portuguese, Spaniards and Dutch (the last claiming a monopoly of the coveted Spice Islands trade) drove the Company to the mainland, where a "factory" was established at Surat in 1612. This was superseded by Madras (1640), Bombay (1668) and Calcutta (1690), founded by Job Charnock. This eventually became the seat of government.

The 18th century saw the development of the Company's governing power in India. Clive, who eliminated French and Dutch rivalry, took its responsibilities far beyond mere trade, a fact recognised by Lord North's Regulating Act, 1773 (developed further by Pitt's India Act, 1784), which gave a measure of government control over the Company and made the

Governor of Bengal Governor General of India. Warren Hastings (1773-85), Cornwallis (1786-93) and Wellesley (1798-1805) extended effective control, by conquest or treaty, over very large areas, and at home the President of the Board of Control became equivalent to the later Secretary of State for India.

During the 19th century the Directors of the Company became little more than advisers to the British government, and when in 1858, after the Indian Mutiny, the Company was wound up, no great change resulted. The last Governor General for the Company, Lord Canning, became the first Viceroy for the Crown.

¶ GARDNER, BRIAN. *The East India Company*. 1971

See also INDIVIDUAL ENTRIES.

East India Company, Dutch: chartered in 1602 by the States General (Netherlands) to trade with the East Indies. Its monopolistic charter empowered it to raise forces, wage war, make treaties, etc. Its headquarters were established at Batavia in 1619, and in the next half century it expelled the Portuguese from Ceylon and Malacca and the English from the Spice Islands, had established factories from the Persian Gulf to the Pacific and was paying a 40 per cent dividend. But enforcement of monopoly led to expensive wars, and in the 18th century the Company declined and became bankrupt, the chief causes of its dissolution in 1798 being the conquest of Holland by revolutionary France, and competition from Britain.

Easter Island: Pacific island roughly half way between the west coast of South America and the main islands of the Tuamotu Archipelago.

The Dutchmen who discovered the island in 1722 were amazed to find huge stone statues of men with long noses, large ears and heavy cylindrical crowns, arranged to correspond with the altitude

Colossal stone figure, Easter Island.

and bearing of the sun's rays at the equinoxes and solstices. The stone was quarried by skilled craftsmen from local rock, formed of compacted volcanic fragments and dressed so perfectly for building that mortar was not required. The sun-worshipping race which had created these images had been massacred about 1680 by the ancestors of the present inhabitants.

¶ HEYERDAHL, THOR. *Aku-Aku: the Secret of Easter Island.* 1958; MAZIERE, F. *Mysteries of Easter Island.* 1969

Eastern Question, The: fundamentally, the problem of Turkey in Europe and of the attitude of other powers to the spread of Russian influence round the Black Sea and in the Balkans and eastern Mediterranean.

The treaty of Kutchuk Kainardji, ending the Russo-Turkish war of 1768-74, gave Russia a footing on the Black Sea and the right of protecting Christians in Constantinople, extended later to the claim to protect all Christian subjects of Turkey. During the 19th century the problem became one of inheritance of the control of the Balkan provinces as Turkey ("the sick man of Europe") became weaker. Russian intervention in such events as the Greek revolt of 1821–30 and the Mehemet Ali crises indicated a desire to dominate Turkey which drew France and Britain together and caused the Crimean War (1853–6). After the Russian defeat of Turkey in 1877–8, followed by the treaty of San Stefano, which gave Russia overwhelming influence in the area, the Congress and Treaty of Berlin (1878), dominated by the British Prime Minister Disraeli, undid much of the treaty and closed the door of the Balkans to Russia.

The newly independent nations created by the Treaty of Berlin (Romania, Serbia and Montenegro), and their mutual quarrels and growing pan-Slavism, continued to cause diplomatic uneasiness. Austria had Balkan provinces as well as Danubian interests, and Germany, for strategic purposes, was very active in Turkey in the early 20th century. It was in the Balkans, at Sarajevo, that the shots were fired which occasioned the outbreak of war in 1914.

See also BERLIN, CONGRESS OF.

Eclipses: total or partial cutting off of light from a celestial body, especially the sun and moon.

In primitive times eclipses were regarded as portents, and we therefore find references to them in the ancient literature of China and Assyria and the works of Homer and Cicero. In the Bible, Amos 8:9, we find "I will cause the sun to go down at noon, and I will darken the earth in the clear day". An eclipse is recorded at Christ's Crucifixion, though scientific evidence suggests that the phenomenon would be impossible at the Paschal full moon. Herodotus mentions one (successfully predicted by Thales of Miletus), which took place during a battle between the Medes and Lydians and caused them to make peace.

A solar eclipse (*see* diagram) takes place when sun, moon and earth lie in a straight line, and a lunar eclipse when sun, earth and moon are in line. They would often occur if the orbit planes of earth and moon coincided, but these are inclined at an angle of 5° and hence cross only at two points (nodes), and an eclipse occurs only when the moon is near a node.

The moon's shadow is a cone approximately 233,000 miles [373,260 kilometres] long, and the moon's distance from the earth varies from 222,000 to 253,000 miles [357,280 to 407,170 kilometres], so that in a solar eclipse the apex of the full-shadow cone (umbra) may or may not reach the earth. In the first case the eclipse will be total in a circular area about thirty miles [forty-eight kilometres] in diameter, moving over the earth's surface on a track several thousand miles long. Observers in the half-shadow (penumbra) will see a partial eclipse. In the second case the moon does not obscure the sun completely but leaves a bright ring (annulus); hence the name annular eclipse.

In a lunar eclipse the earth's shadow is much larger (about 5,000 miles [8,050 kilometres] across), and the moon may thus be obscured for over an hour.

Full solar eclipse.

Astronomers take their equipment to places on the totality belt to use the brief seven minutes of a total solar eclipse to photograph the solar prominences. On 29 May 1919 an expedition to Sobral, Brazil, first obtained confirmation of Einstein's prediction of the deflection of light by a gravitational field. The next total eclipse visible in England will take place in Cornwall at 11 a.m. on 11 August 1999.

Economics: from Greek *oikonǫmia*, housekeeping. The mother of a family normally has her weekly allowance for housekeeping. If she spends it wisely on food and household goods without getting into debt we say that she is thrifty or economical; that is, a good manager. If we think of a country as one great household it is possible to study how the total wealth of the country is produced and how it is distributed, or shared out, among all the people. This study is called economics. Wealth is not money but all the things we need, such as food, clothes and shelter. Money is simply pieces of metal and paper that we use to make the exchange of goods and services easy. If a man buys a bicycle in a shop he has the bicycle in exchange for money, but in order to get that money to spend he had to do something for it. The shopkeeper

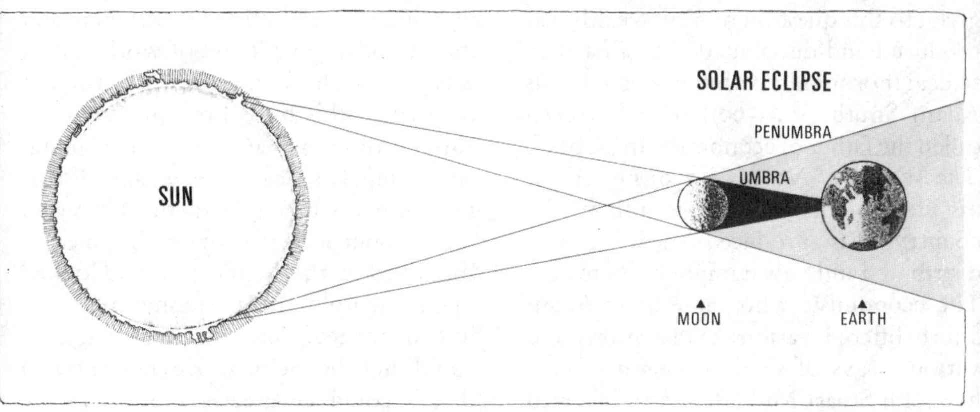

who has taken the money for the bicycle uses it to pay for the things he needs, and whoever gets the money from him uses it in the same way. So money goes round and round; and, all the time, everyone is working for money with which to pay for the things he needs, which have been made or grown by someone else in order to get money to pay for the things *he* needs.

Among those who thought about the production and distribution of wealth in this way were the ancient Greeks, which is why we use their word "economics" for this study. The Greeks, and the Romans after them, thought that wealth came only from growing food on the land. They believed that buying and selling goods was not as important as agriculture, and a famous Greek philosopher, Aristotle (384–322 BC), said that, because money did not grow and increase by itself, to charge interest for lending it was wrong. This idea continued into the Middle Ages, when charging interest on money lent was called "usury" and condemned as sinful. But, with the expansion of trade and the growth of towns, it became clear that the buying and selling of goods both at home and in other countries was an important part of the wealth of the country.

As trade increased in each country and between countries, more attention was given to this question of how wealth was produced and distributed. The first man to deal thoroughly with the problem was Adam Smith (1723–90), who has been called the father of economics. In his book *The Wealth of Nations* (1776) he set out his ideas of how all the wealth in the country was produced, how it was distributed and how it might be increased. The economists who came after Adam Smith offered various explanations and various ways of sharing wealth. Some, like John Stuart Mill (1806–73), believed that, if all men were allowed to try to get rich without any interference from the government, the whole country would benefit. Others, such as the German Karl Marx (1818–83), said that because all wealth is produced by man's labour it should all be shared among those who labour. He and other economists tried to show that those who produced the wealth were many, and often poor, while those who employed them were few and rich, and often did little, apart from providing the capital.

Meanwhile, governments in Germany, Britain and other countries began to make the poor less poor by providing old age pensions, sick benefits and unemployment benefits, so that, although the problem was not solved, some of the worst effects of poverty were reduced.

During the 20th century the greatest cause of poverty was seen to be unemployment. Most working men did not earn enough to save, and when they had no work they had no money. In England between 1921 and 1939 there was always one man in ten out of work, and in 1931 and 1932 it was more than one in five. An English economist, John Maynard Keynes (1883–1946), looked at this problem in a new way in his book *The General Theory of Employment, Interest and Money*. He pointed out that when men were out of work they had no money to buy goods that other people wanted to sell them and this put other people out of work also. It was possible, he said, for the government to prevent this by controlling the total amount of money available for spending and saving. His ideas were so valuable that governments in England, the USA and other countries acted upon the lines he suggested. Earlier economists had looked upon unemployment as something that just happened, like the weather, and could not be helped. Keynes showed that it could be greatly reduced if the government took appropriate action. For 30 years after 1945 the world enjoyed unparalleled prosperity which seemed to prove Keynes' theories to be correct.

Most countries now have a special branch of the government to deal with economic matters. Their business, like that of a good housewife, is to see that nations do not spend more than they earn. This means that they should not import (buy from other countries) more than they export (sell to other countries) and, if possible, should export more than they import. To secure such a position it is often necessary for governments to adopt special measures, such as price fixing, special taxes, etc.

The world-wide recession which occurred at the end of the 1970s and continued into the 1980s destroyed some of the easy assumptions which followed belief in Keynes' theories. At the beginning of 1985, for example, there were some 38 million unemployed in the rich countries of the OECD alone.

¶ BIRMINGHAM, WALTER. *Economics: an Introduction*. 1966

See also DEPRESSIONS, TRADE.

Ecuador: republic of north-west South America with a population of over 8 million. Perched 9,000 feet [2,745 metres] high in the Andes Mountains this territory has always linked the southern civilisations of the plateau with the lowlands of Venezuela and the highlands of Mexico. In the 15th century AD the powerful Incas conquered this land and made many of the inhabitants move to the Inca capital, Cuzco, while Inca settlers came to Quito. In fact the Inca Empire nearly split in half in 1525, when the illegitimate son of the king made Ecuador into his separate kingdom. This prince, Atahualpa, had just reunited the Inca Empire by capturing Cuzco from his brother when he was tricked into captivity by the Spanish conquistador Pizarro. The Spaniards proceeded to conquer the whole Inca Empire, including the territory now called Ecuador, and ruled it from a new capital city near the coast at Lima.

Ecuador continued to be part of the Spanish Viceroyalty of Peru until the end of the 18th century, when a separate province of Quito was established. Therefore, when the peoples of South America, under Bolívar, fought for freedom the people of Ecuador were not very interested in his ideas of confederation, as they did not think being ruled by Venezuela was likely to be any better than being ruled by Spain. In 1830 Ecuador became an independent state. In 1855 it was officially declared a republic and has remained so ever since.

See also BOLÍVAR, SIMON; SOUTH AMERICA for map.

Edinburgh: capital of Scotland and county town of Midlothian; a city that has often been called the Athens of the North because of its fame as a literary centre and because, in its site and the appearance of some of its buildings, it bears a superficial resemblance to ancient Athens. Surrounded by hills and crags, with a castle high on a windy ridge, the medieval fortress town is famed for its architectural beauty. Classical 18th-century Edinburgh of the New Town was a fitting background for the scholars, doctors, lawyers, printers, publishers and philanthropists who graced the age. Seat of learning and seat of government, the city has two universities. The Medical School, established in 1726, draws students from afar and gave asylum to refugee Polish doctors during World War II, when the Polish School of Medicine made history. There is an active Faculty of Law, and the Court of Session, established in the 15th century, is the supreme court of justice for the country. Less well

Houses in the New Town, Queen Street, Edinburgh.

known, but historically important, is the Court of the Lord Lyon King of Arms, the oldest heraldic court in Europe.

Warring factions and religious feuds governed life in the "auld toon", and within the narrow compass of the Royal Mile, which stretches from the Castle to Holyrood Palace, most of the dramatic events of Scottish history were enacted.

Edinburgh men have made great contributions to world history and literature, among them Dr J. Y. Simpson, pioneer of anaesthesia; Dr Guthrie, founder of the Ragged Schools, or free schools for the education of poor children; Sir Walter Scott and Robert Louis Stevenson, writers; Robert Chambers, publisher and author.

An annual festival of music, art and drama is now an international event.

¶ DOUGLAS, HUGH. *Edinburgh*. 1969

Edison, Thomas Alva (1847–1931): American inventor. He was a major contributor to the development of the cinema camera, the telephone and other electrical and electronic devices. He invented the electric light bulb and the phonograph, later to become the gramophone and record-player. He took out well over 1,000 patents for his inventions.

¶ THOMAS, H. *Thomas Alva Edison*. 1959

Above, Thomas Alva Edison.
Below left, early experimental Edison lamp, 1880.
Below right, commercial filament lâmp.

Edward, Prince of Wales, called "the Black Prince" (1330–76): England's greatest hero of the Middle Ages, called by Froissart "the chief flower of chivalry of all the world", though his career was marred by some acts of ruthless cruelty. There is no evidence to support the legend that he wore black armour. His fame rests chiefly on the English victories in France at Crécy (1346) and Poitiers (1356). His surcoat, helmet, shield, gauntlets and scabbard are preserved in Canterbury Cathedral, England, where his will directed he should be buried. The Black Prince's ruby, given to him in 1367 by Pedro of Castile, is now set in the Imperial State Crown worn by British monarchs on such great occasions as a coronation.

¶ BAKER, GEORGE. *Leopard's Cub: The Black Prince.* 1953

Effigy: a likeness, portrait or image. The head of a monarch incised on a coin is an effigy and so is a doll, and a scarecrow. The word has tended to be used more narrowly to refer to sculptured figures on tombs and to clothed figures such as the Guys that are still, every 5 November in England, consigned to the flames.

Waxworks, such as those at Madame Tussaud's in London, are effigies, and so were the little wax figures witches used to stick pins into in an effort to harm the person in whose image the figure was made. For many centuries it was the custom to represent royalty and other persons of renown at their funerals by life-sized robed effigies, made of wax or wood, carried on top of the coffin. The Undercroft Museum in Westminster Abbey houses a collection of these figures.

The ancient Egyptian mummy-case was at once a coffin and a stylised representation of the human form. The ancient Greek gravestone, or *stele*, was a pillar or upright slab, often decorated with a human figure in low relief. Another form of ancient monument was the sarcophagus, a box of clay or stone, with its lid often surmounted by painted statues. Some surviving examples of Etruscan sarcophagi are particularly attractive. They show the people commemorated very much alive, husbands and wives reclining on couches as at a banquet and obviously enjoying themselves. Often the figures hold in their hands an egg, the symbol of continuing creation, the seed of the future.

Edward the Black Prince in effigy.

The monumental effigies of medieval Christendom are among the greatest art treasures of the age. They provide a wonderfully detailed record of the changing fashions in costume, arms and armour. France was the innovator and had a thriving export trade in ready-made effigies, but each country developed its own characteristic work. Owing to the ravages of war and revolution on the Continent, more medieval tomb statuary has survived

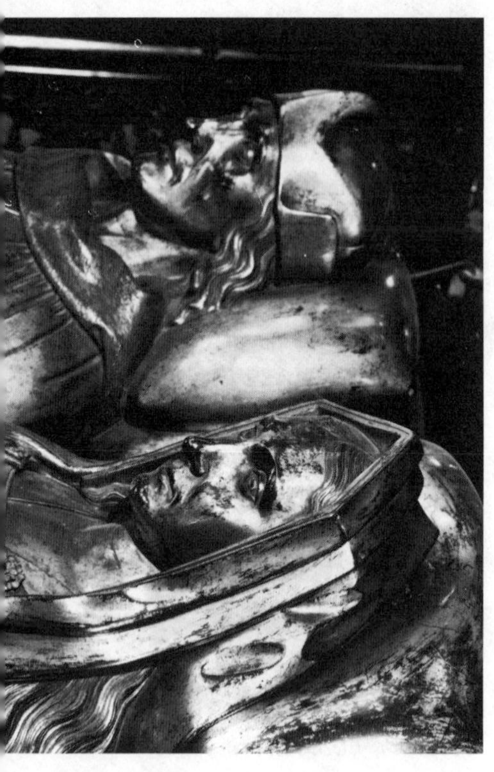

Above, Egyptian mummy case. Above right, Albert Memorial. Left, Henry VII and Elizabeth of York.

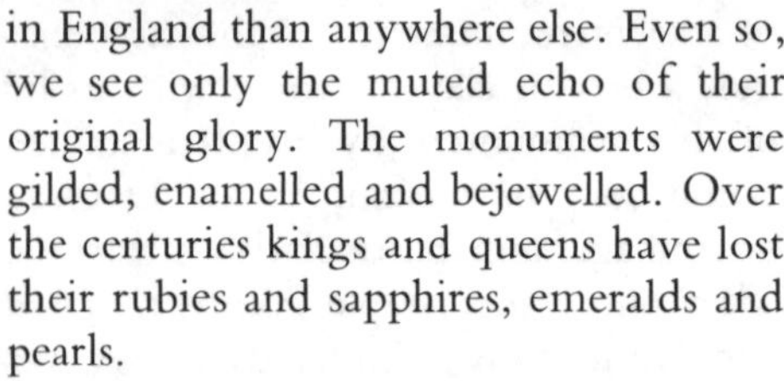

in England than anywhere else. Even so, we see only the muted echo of their original glory. The monuments were gilded, enamelled and bejewelled. Over the centuries kings and queens have lost their rubies and sapphires, emeralds and pearls.

Nevertheless, a splendid legacy remains in, for instance the effigies of King Henry IV (reigned 1399–1413) and his queen, Joanna of Navarre, in Canterbury Cathedral; Richard de Beauchamp, Earl of Warwick (1382–1439) in the collegiate church of Our Lady at Warwick; Bishop William of Wykeham (1324–1404) in Winchester Cathedral.

The bronze effigies of Henry VII (reigned 1485–1509) and his wife Elizabeth of York in Westminster Abbey were the work of an Italian, Pietro Torrigiano (1472–1522), and belong to the closing of the Middle Ages. In 1520, in Florence, Michelangelo began work on the monuments to Lorenzo and Giuliano Medici, which belong to a different world – the world of the Renaissance, the sculpture of which aimed at a classical detachment. The Baroque style of the 17th century was, by contrast, feverish and theatrical. The tomb of Pope Alexander II, designed by Giovanni Lorenzo Bernini (1598–1680), shows Death, a skeleton, rising out of the tomb to kill the pope.

Monumental effigies as an art form deteriorated into the sentimentalities of the 19th century; casualties, too, of our changing attitude to tombs as status symbols and to the ritualistic celebration of death. There remains, however, one marvellous Victorian example which tends to stun the critical sense – the Albert Memorial in Kensington Gardens, London, where Albert the Good, with the catalogue of the Great Exhibition in his hand, sits enshrined under his fantastic canopy.

EFTA (European Free Trade Association): organisation, with headquarters in Geneva, aimed at the abolition of tariffs on imports originating in the area covered by Austria, Norway, Portugal, Sweden and Switzerland. Britain, Denmark and in 1985 Portugal left to join the EEC.

Egypt: a region in the north-east corner of Africa and the Sinai peninsula, bestriding the lower reaches of the River Nile, with a population of 45,851,000 in 1983. The civilisation of Egypt is one of the oldest in history. Originally divided into two kingdoms, Upper and Lower Egypt, the land was united under the Pharaoh (or King) Menes in about the year 3000 BC. Subsequent pharaohs added to the strength of the kingdom. Cheops, who reigned 2,000 years before the time of Christ, built the Great Pyramid; Queen Hatshepsut (*c.* 1400 BC) ruled as powerfully as a king; Thutmose III, her successor, was a warrior Pharaoh who extended the boundaries of his kingdom.

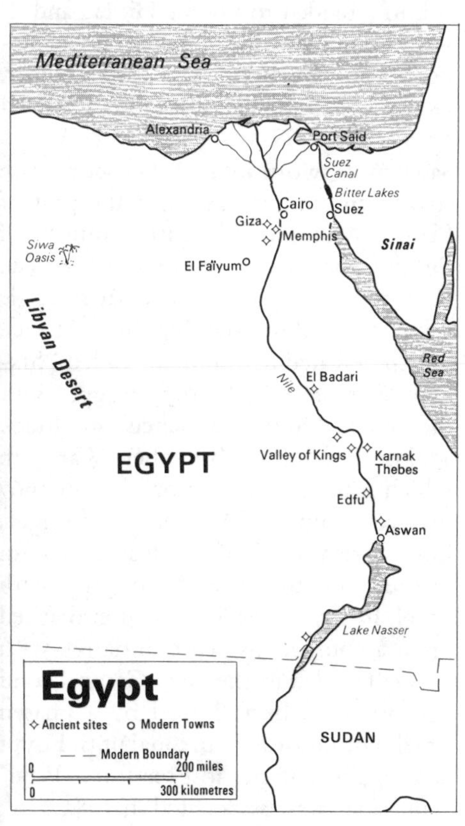

When important Egyptians died much of their property was buried with them. Models of servants, animals and boats were placed in the tomb, and its walls were decorated with paintings. Tombs were frequently looted by robbers, eager for treasure. Tutankhamen, whose tomb was discovered by the archaeologist Howard Carter in 1922, was an unimportant pharaoh, yet he was buried with great splendour. We can only guess what magnificent objects have been stolen from the tombs of greater kings.

The rule of the pharaohs became weaker, and Egypt was eventually conquered in 332 BC by the Greeks under Alexander the Great, who founded the city of Alexandria. On his death Egypt fell to one of his generals, Ptolemy, the ancestor of Queen Cleopatra whose charm fascinated Julius Caesar and his general, Marcus Antonius. Egypt became a part of the Roman Empire in 30 BC.

Egypt was a great grain-producing province. Its fertility was governed by the annual flooding of the Nile which deposited masses of fertile mud on the river banks. If the inundation failed there were no crops, and from very early times efforts have been made to control the water, which was the lifeblood of Egypt. The annual rise of the Nile is no longer an obvious phenomenon, as a series of great dams holds back the water, which is released as it is required.

After the fall of the Roman Empire, Egypt was eventually overrun by Arabs. Under Roman rule the majority of the Egyptians had adopted a form of Christianity, but by AD 640 a very mixed population lived in the cities – Greeks, Romans, Jews and Egyptians – while the Muslim Arabs occupied the desert beyond the

Weighing of the heart of the Scribe Ani in the After-life by the gods Anubis and Thoth. Egyptian XIX Dynasty.

Nile. Then the Muslim faith was adopted by the Ottoman Turks. This warrior race established its capital at Constantinople, and in 1517 Egypt became a province of the Turkish Empire. The Turks discouraged contact with people of other faiths, so that Egypt remained shut off from direct contact with the West for eleven centuries, until the invasion in 1798 of Napoleon Bonaparte.

Napoleon set out to conquer Egypt, accompanied not only by his army but also by scholars and archaeologists, whose task was to investigate the legendary monuments. They were fascinated by the pyramids, temples and tombs, but could only guess at their significance because they were unable to decipher the hieroglyphs engraved on them. It was not until 1822 that a French scholar, Jean François Champollion, discovered how to read hieroglyphic writing (*see* HIEROGLYPHICS).

European interest in Egypt increased, and wealthy travellers visited the country. Governments were also concerned, for Egypt occupied a strategic position on the Mediterranean coast and was a gateway to Africa and India. The Turkish Sultan was weak and his empire was breaking up. One of his officials, Mehemet Ali, made himself ruler of Egypt and tried to introduce Western culture. His grandson, the Khedive Ismael, made an agreement with France permitting the construction of the Suez Canal, which was completed in 1869. In 1874 Ismael raised money by selling Suez Canal shares and Britain purchased sufficient to give her effective control. For the next 80 years Britain regarded the Canal as the "lifeline" of Empire (India) and in consequence found numerous reasons to interfere in Egyptian affairs.

Gradually, the Egyptians came to resent this foreign interference. In 1922 the country achieved partial independence under Sultan Ahmed Fuad, but many Egyptians were not satisfied with this. During the Second World War the country tended to favour Hitler, and in 1952 Fuad's son, King Farouk, was deposed in favour of an army officer, General Neguib, who was soon succeeded by President Nasser. President Anwat Sadat was sworn in after Nasser's death (1970), and in 1973 assumed the post of Prime Minister. Recently much of Egypt's energy and resources have been absorbed by a bitter territorial struggle with its neighbour the Republic of Israel, which defeated her in the so-called "Six-Day War of 1967. In 1973 Egypt, with the aid of Syria, launched an attack against Israel (the "October War") in which some of the territory lost in 1967 was re-occupied. Dr Henry Kissinger, US Secretary of State, was active in negotiations to settle the dispute with Israel. In 1977 President Sadat embarked upon a courageous peace initiative with Israel. This led to the 1979 Camp David agreement to be followed by a phased Israeli withdrawal from Sinai until Egypt had regained all her lost territory. President Sadat was assassinated in 1982.

Eighteenth century: often called the Age of Enlightenment or the Age of Reason. These optimistic labels do not signify that, from AD 1700 onwards, people the world over suddenly began to be enlightened or reasonable. In most countries the lot of the common people was as hazardous as ever, poised on the knife edge between subsistence and starvation. Nevertheless in Europe, at least, a new spirit was stirring, one which was to have tremendous consequences for the whole world.

Previous centuries had laid the groundwork. The Reformation had opened the way to the view that there was more than one road to Heaven; upheavals like the English Civil War had nourished a growing conviction that government should be based on the consent of the governed. The voyages of the great explorers and the somewhat romanticised accounts of noble savages living in an idyllic state of nature prompted thinking people to reassess the values of their own self-styled civilisation.

Science had taken a great step forward in the second half of the 17th century, leading to the optimistic conclusion that the universe was a well regulated machine, functioning according to ascertainable, reasonable laws; a framework within which men of goodwill should be able to live in harmony with nature and each other. Practice, alas, fell far short of theory, and the difficulties of reconciling the two led eventually, in 1789, to the great explosion of the French Revolution.

England in the 18th century was governed by an aristocracy: the man in the street had no vote. Religious toleration was far from complete, and the Rebellions of 1715 and 1745 – attempts to bring back the deposed Roman Catholic Stuarts – failed as much for religious as dynastic reasons. In this century Britain both gained an empire and lost one. General James Wolfe's (1727–59) great victory over the French at Quebec in 1759 won Canada: the British Empire in India was founded, thanks largely to the efforts of Robert Clive (1725–74). In 1770 Captain James Cook (1728–79) landed on the coast of Australia and named it New South Wales. On the other side of the coin the American War of Independence (1776–83) (*see* separate entry) led to the loss of the American colonies and the emergence of the United States of America.

France, when the century opened, was an absolute monarchy, ruled over since 1643 by Louis XIV (1638–1715), often called the Sun King. His glory was achieved at dreadful cost to his subjects. They groaned beneath an unjust burden of taxation and died in their thousands in his vainglorious and unprofitable wars. By the time of his death in 1715 the seeds of the French Revolution were sown.

Germany as a national state may be said to date in spirit, if not in fact, from 18 January 1701, when the first king of Prussia crowned himself. His grandson Frederick the Great (1712–86), a military genius and a ruler who combined liberal principles with a cynical opportunism, raised Prussia to the status of an important European power.

Further east, too, another great modern state was taking shape. Peter the Great (1672–1725), a giant of a man in every sense of the word, was changing Russia from a barbaric, backward country into a European nation. Sweden was the chief sufferer from the process. St Petersburg (the modern Leningrad) was built by Peter on land seized from the Swedes.

In 1683 a Turkish army had stood at the walls of Vienna. By the 18th century Turkey was at the beginning of a slow decline. The vast, ramshackle Ottoman Empire, which included large areas of eastern Europe, Asia Minor and North Africa, began to fall apart, partly because of its own administrative inefficiency,

The Dream of Reason produces monsters *by Francisco Goya, 1797.*

partly because it came into conflict with the ambitions of Peter the Great, but chiefly because of the rise of a spirit of nationalism among the Greeks, Bulgars, Romanians, Syrians, Egyptians and other peoples who were held in subjection by the Turks.

Spain, which still held vast colonies in Central and South America, inadvertently hammered a nail in her own colonial coffin when, out of enmity to Britain, she supported the North American colonists in their struggle for independence. It was undoubtedly the successful example of the North Americans that inspired the South American colonies in the early years of the following century to make their own bid for freedom.

China, the great imperial power of the Far East, was, in the 18th century, ruled by conquerors, the Manchus, who had descended on the Celestial Kingdom from Tartary. The Emperor K'ien-lung, who reigned from 1735 to 1795, was an ambitious and aggressive man, who invaded Burma and Turkestan and overran Nepal and Tibet.

Perhaps the greatest events of the century were the three revolutions, two of which were not events at all but processes which are still continuing: the French Revolution; the Agricultural Revolution; and the Industrial Revolution.

The French Revolution raised the flag of liberty throughout Europe and opened the way to the social and political reforms of the 19th century. In the 18th century began that changeover from handicraft methods of work to modern technology that we call the Industrial Revolution, from cottage labour and the small workshop to the modern factory. Without an Agricultural Revolution it could not have happened. The Agricultural Revolution made industrial cities possible, for the growth of large urban populations

The French Revolution: The execution of Louis XVI, a satirical cartoon by James Gillray.

divorced from the land depended on the provision of sufficient food supplies. England and the Netherlands were pioneers in crop and livestock improvements and in devising improved agricultural implements. Add Agricultural and Industrial Revolutions together and the result, for better or worse, is today's mass-production world.

No survey of the 18th century, however brief, should conclude without mentioning some at least of the musicians, artists and writers whose lives were, in effect, important events of the period and whose works have continued to enrich the quality of life ever since. From musicians one may select Johann Sebastian Bach (1685-1750), Wolfgang Amadeus Mozart (1756-91) and Josef Haydn (1732-1809): from painters, Antoine Watteau (1684-1721), Thomas Gainsborough (1727-88) and Francisco de Goya (1746-1828). Writers of the 18th century include Johann Wolfgang von Goethe (1749-1832), Germany's greatest poet; Voltaire (1694-1778), whose writings did much to influence the course of European history; and Mikhail Lomonosov (1711-65), the first Russian writer to write in the ordinary spoken language of Russia instead of Old Slavonic, thus laying the foundation for modern Russian literature.

¶ ANDREWS, STUART. *Eighteenth Century Europe: the 1680s to 1815*. 1965

See also INDIVIDUAL ENTRIES.

Albert Einstein.

Einstein, Albert (1879-1955): mathematician and physicist, of German birth but, from 1940, a naturalised American.

Einstein was born at Ulm but soon moved to Münich. After occupying professorial posts at Prague and Zürich he became Director of the Kaiser Wilhelm Physical Institute in Berlin. After Hitler's rise to power Einstein, being of Jewish stock, left Germany and settled in the United States at Princeton, where he joined the Institute for Advanced Study.

One of the greatest mathematical physicists of all time, he made many contributions to science but is most widely known for his Theory of Relativity, developed between 1905 and 1916. This involves a four-dimensional space-time continuum, in which time is relative to the observer, as opposed to the older idea of a three-dimensional space with time as an independent "ever rolling stream", and explains gravitation as an error introduced by forcing a four-dimensional universe into a three-dimensional Euclidean frame.

Eisenhower, Dwight David (1890-1969): American general and statesman, 34th president of the USA. A professional soldier, he became successively commander of the American forces in Europe (June 1943), chief of the Allied forces in North Africa (November 1942), Supreme Allied Commander (1943-45) and, after World War II, commander of the land forces of the North Atlantic Treaty Organisation (1950-52). His chief asset was his gift for making the best use of the talents of subordinate officers and ensuring they worked together harmoniously. This conception of teamwork he carried into the presidency (1953–61) and maintained his national popularity, pursuing on the whole a middle course between conflicting views and interests.

¶ GUNTHER, JOHN. *Eisenhower*. 1952

El Dorado: legendary country, said to be in the middle of the South American jungle between the rivers Amazon and Orinoco and ruled by a king who was so wealthy that every year he was completely covered in gold. Such amazing treasures had, in fact, already been found in Mexico and Peru. But those who searched for El Dorado found only death or disappointment. Gonzalo Pizarro (1502–48) tried to copy his famous brother Francisco but found no empire to conquer. Sir Walter Ralegh explored the coast of Guiana in 1595 and in 1617 but failed to find any wealth and was later executed by King James for invading Spanish territory. El Dorado (Spanish, the golden man) has now come to mean any unattainable golden dream.

Electoral systems: ways of choosing representatives, members of parliament, etc. Electoral systems had their origins in ancient Greece and Rome. In Greece most public offices were filled by lot, but a few more important ones by election. Voting was usually by show of hands, but in some cases, notably that of ostracism (banishment of someone considered dangerous to the state), a secret vote was taken by the voters inscribing names on a potsherd (*ostrakon*). In Rome, after 139 BC, a voter for the *Comitia Centuriata* was required to use a tablet to indicate his choice, putting it into the appropriate box or urn. Elsewhere, pebbles or small wooden balls might be used, from which latter the word "ballot" is derived.

Until the 19th century, in countries where some form of elected government was in being, the number of voters was usually very small, but has steadily grown since that time as more and more countries have moved by stages towards universal suffrage. The minimum voting age varies from eighteen to twenty-four, but twenty-one remains the most common, despite the recent reduction from twenty-one to eighteen in Great Britain. Women have still not been given the right to vote in Switzerland, some Latin-American countries and various countries with largely Muslim populations.

There are three basically different electoral procedures in use at the present time: the majority system and two variations of proportional representation, i.e. the single transferable vote and the party list system. Under the majority system the candidate with the largest number of votes is elected, irrespective of whether or not he secures more than 50 per cent of the votes cast. In a single-member constituency under the transferable vote system, the voter does not mark his choice with a cross but numbers the candidates 1, 2, 3, etc., in the order of his choice. The returning officer then eliminates the candidates with the lowest number of votes in turn, distributing their votes to the remaining candidates according to the preferences shown on the ballot papers. The party list system operates in a similar way with much larger constituencies. The English Proportional Representation Society would like to see constituencies of at least 300,000 voters and at least five seats. Each party would produce its list of candidates, and the voter would mark his ballot paper with 1, 2, 3, etc., against the candidates of his choice. The candidates with the lowest number of votes would then be eliminated and their votes redistributed in the way described above.

The majority system is used in Great Britain and predominates throughout the Commonwealth and the United States. The single transferable vote was adopted by Australia for its House of Commons and is used in a small number of cities in the United States for municipal elections. The party list system is used in Switzerland, Israel, Italy and the Scandinavian and Benelux countries. Germany uses a mixed system. France introduced proportional representation in 1945 on a list system, based on the *Département* as a unit, but the system was modified in 1951 to give Gaullists and Communists less than their proportional share. In 1958 France reverted to the second ballot system, when an absolute majority was not obtained.

The supporters of proportional representation advocate it on the ground that it provides for the representation of minorities. In practice it has several grave disadvantages. Perhaps the most important of these is that it tends to produce a large number of small parties in the representative chamber, each incapable of forming a government by itself. Hence a coalition between parties is formed, and these coalition governments tend to be unstable and of short duration. Further, with larger constituencies the personal link between the representative and the members of his constituency is much reduced, and the representative becomes more a delegate of his party and less representative of his constituents irrespective of their political views.

Electricity: a basic form of energy. No one knows when electricity was discovered, but we do know that by 600 BC the Greeks found that a piece of amber, when rubbed, attracted light objects to it. The word "electricity", in fact, derives from *elektron*, the Greek word for amber. Some believe that the Chinese were the first to discover magnetism, but again the name comes from Greece, being derived from Magnesia, where the Greeks quarried their supplies of magnetic stone.

By the 13th century AD crude forms of magnetic compass were in use, but no further important discoveries were made until Dr Gilbert (or Gilberd), physician to Elizabeth I, published a book describing his work on magnetism. This stimulated others to experiment. In 1672 the German von Guericke built the first machine to produce electric charges, and this was followed by other similar devices, notably some by Hauksbee. In 1733 Du Fay became the first to show the existence of "positive" and "negative" electricity.

No way of storing electrical charges was known until 1746, when van Musschenbroek of Leyden University devised the so-called Leyden jar. This consists of a glass jar, coated inside and outside with metal foil; when a charge is applied by connecting the two foils to an electrical discharge machine it can be stored for a long period of time.

In the same year, 1746, Benjamin Franklin suggested that lightning was a form of electricity – a theory which few believed until Franklin proved it by the highly dangerous method of flying a kite in a thunderstorm and obtaining sparks from a metal key tied to the end of the string down at ground level.

The electrical cell, a chemical means of generating a steady electrical current, was invented by Volta around the year 1799. (An electrical unit, the volt, is named after Volta; other units named after eminent scientists of the day include the farad, the henry, the ampere and the ohm.)

Leyden jars.

Michael Faraday, by his discovery of the principles of the electric generator in 1831, made possible the giant electrical power stations of today. His first model produced only a feeble current, but soon other workers, including Wheatstone, Woolrich, Nollet, Wilde and Siemens, were building machines that could supply electricity in quantity. In 1881 Edison (*see* separate entry), the inventor of the carbon filament lamp, built the world's first public supply station for New York.

The early generating stations produced direct current (d.c.), but it was later realised that alternating current (a.c.) was more convenient. It is called alternating current because the supply flows first in one direction and then in the other.

The generators in modern power stations are driven by huge turbines; some of these operate directly from water power (hydroelectricity) and others from steam boilers. The steam has to be generated either by oil- or coal-fired boilers or from the heat derived from nuclear fission.

¶ CROWTHER, J. G. *Electricity*. 1961

See also EDISON; FRANKLIN, etc.

Emancipation of women: the freeing of women from restrictive social and political rules and conventions. The freedom of women to develop their whole personalities both as individuals and as citizens is still far from complete. Though there have been examples in history of matriarchal societies (i.e. societies where women were regarded as the head of the family), through the centuries women have tended to live under the dominance of men. The Bible relates that a woman, Deborah, was one of the Judges of Israel, but the position of a woman among the Hebrews, as among so many ancient peoples, was one of carefully preserved inferiority. Valued, even revered, as a potential or actual mother of sons, she was nevertheless a chattel, the property first of her father, then of her husband.

The Greek philosopher Plato (*c.* 427–348 BC) classed women with children and slaves as unreasoning creatures. Roman women, while allowed a good deal of personal independence, had no legal status. In most Eastern countries women were kept in a strict seclusion, from which they have not yet entirely emerged.

Christianity, for a time, took a different line. Jesus first proclaimed Himself as Messiah to the woman of Samaria, much to the astonishment of His disciples who "marvelled that He was speaking with a woman". Many women – such as Lydia, Damaris, Priscilla – are mentioned in connection with the early Church. But as the Church became a vast administrative machine and a power in the state, the early equality faded.

For all its proclamation of "Liberté, Egalité, Fraternité" the French Revolution, oddly enough, did next to nothing to improve the lot of the women of France. Influential writers such as Voltaire (1694–1778) and Rousseau (1712–78) were anti-feminists, who took the view that a woman's prime purpose in life was to give pleasure to men; and she should be educated only with this aim in mind. Just the same, the upheaval in France made people in other Western countries, women included, conscious of their own lack of freedom. Education, equal economic status, the right to enter the professions – all these were matters which could be put right only by the state; and consequently, in the 19th century, in countries where parliamentary democratic government promised some hope of success, movements began for obtaining for women the right to vote in elections, thus giving them some voice in the government of their country.

In the USA, Wyoming had given women the vote as early as 1869, but not for another fifty years was the Nineteenth

Amendment passed, declaring that the right of citizens to vote should not be "denied or abridged" on account of sex.

In Britain, after a hard fight, the outbreak of World War I in effect decided the issue. In the national emergency women were needed to play a full part in industry, replacing the men away in the trenches. In 1918 women over the age of thirty were enfranchised, and in 1928 women obtained the vote on the same terms as men. But, even in highly developed European democracies, not all women yet enjoy this basic right. In Switzerland, for example, there is still no universal female suffrage.

Today, in Britain, the movement for women's emancipation concentrates on equal pay for equal work and on the acceptance of an equal moral standard for both sexes.

¶ DUFFY, M. N. *The Emancipation of Women.* 1967; KAMM, JOSEPHINE. *Rapiers and Battleaxes.* 1966

Above, ladies dressed in bloomers, from Punch. *Below, American women on the march.*

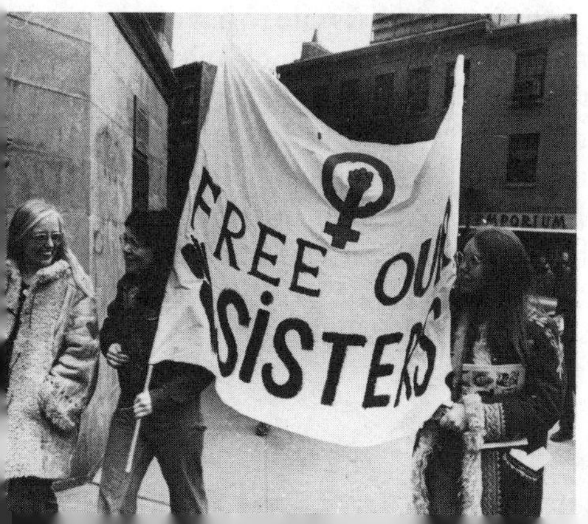

Emeralds: precious stones of bright green colour, from Greek *smaragdos*, a green stone. Emeralds were mined in Egypt in 1650 BC. The Greeks worked Egyptian mines in the time of Alexander the Great, and Cleopatra wore emeralds from Jebel Sikait on the Red Sea coast.

When the Spaniards conquered Peru in the 16th century they found that the Incas wore emeralds, but the conquerors never discovered the mines. Modern South America is, however, a source of emeralds, most of them mined at Bogota, Colombia. Russia, Australia and the United States produce small quantities.

People used to believe that emeralds had a medicinal value. Small amounts of powdered emerald were swallowed in wine to cure epilepsy and dysentery. When worn, the gem traditionally gave protection against evil spirits and strengthened women during childbirth. Because of its clear green colour, it was also valued as a cure for failing eyesight.

Hexagonal emerald prisms weighing up to 125 lb [57 kg] have been mined in the Urals, USSR. The largest cut specimen was carved by Dionysio Miseroni in the 17th century into a 2,680-carat jar, which belongs to the Austrian government. A carat is an international measure equivalent to 200 milligrams.

Empire: territories ruled over by an emperor. Though the term is used to describe a large and usually composite state, such as the German Empire from 1871 or the Russian before the revolution, it is more often applied to dependent territories ruled over by a government of a foreign people, as in the Roman or the British Empire. Such empires have usually been amassed by conquest – invariably so in ancient Asiatic empires, such as the Babylonian or the Assyrian or those of Alexander the Great and Rome. In modern times economic penetration, as that of the British in Egypt, has sometimes led to control, and "protectorates", hardly differing from colonies, have remained, in law, independent.

Of the great empires of history, the Romans and the British stand supreme in the West and the Chinese in the East. The first coloured all the thinking of medieval Europe, and even after the split in the 4th century AD the idea persisted of the empire one and indivisible. Christianity created the concept of one Holy Roman Empire, which lasted from the time of Charlemagne (800) until its formal dissolution by Napoleon in 1806.

Colonial territories have sometimes been ruled directly, as by the French and Portuguese, sometimes indirectly, making use of native institutions for administration, as by the Romans and the British. The ideal of an empire in which all colonial populations are citizens of the supreme country is as old as Alexander; St Paul could claim to be a Roman citizen, and every inhabitant of the British Empire at its height could claim effective protection from the British government.

¶ KOEBNER, RICHARD. *Empire*. 1961

Empire style armchair, French, c. 1820.

Empire style: term associated with Napoleon and the French Empire, particularly in the field of the decorative arts. Inspired by the classical grandeur of Rome, the clean crisp line of the style is found in architecture as in La Madeleine in Paris, in interior design and furniture, and in fashion as seen in J. L. David's famous painting of Mme Récamier.

The style has simplicity and grace in contrast to some of the greater flamboyance of the 18th century in France.

Enamel work: work in glass made opaque or translucent by an admixture of oxides, etc. Many will think of enamel as a hard, shining, coloured surface on saucepans, coffee pots and trays and not realise the aniquity of the art of enamelling which was used in ancient Egypt as early as the 12th and 13th dynasties (2000–1660 BC).

Enamel is composed of one or more layers of glass obtained by fusion to metallic surfaces. In the work of the 11th and 12th centuries AD the colours were separated' by thin metal strips which bound the areas or compartments (cloisons). This method is known as *cloisonné*. Later, the method of scraping and lowering the surface of the metal to form cavities to take the enamel is known as *champlevé*. Enamel painting on metal was introduced in the 15th century.

Enamelled decoration has been discovered on Celtic and Saxon ornaments, horse trappings and shields in the 6th to 9th centuries AD; this is said to have influenced the Byzantine enamel work which flourished between the 7th and 12th centuries and reached a great height of technical achievement and refinement. Because of the rich brilliance and durability of enamel it was often used for the embellishment of ecclesiastical articles, such as caskets, chalices, croziers and covers of sacred books.

Byzantine goldsmiths were invited to work in various countries, where others learnt from them. French and German schools were established, and famous examples were made in the Rhenish School at Limoges in the 12th and 13th centuries and in Siena in the 14th century.

In the 17th and 18th centuries enamelled small domestic articles, such as trinkets, clocks and ornaments, became fashionable. In the 19th century enamelling was brought into domestic use for culinary utensils. Enamelled interiors of cast iron pots and pans, and porcelain enamelled cast iron baths, became a flourishing industry. Enamelled plaques and lettered signs for shops and railway stations were also executed by this durable process.

Enclosures: the process of replacing open fields and common land by fenced farms; particularly the conversion of arable land (i.e. ploughed for crops) to grazing for sheep.

In medieval England many tenants held scattered separate strips of arable, with grazing rights on common land. Consolidation of these holdings by enclosure ensured better control of stock and tillage for the landlord. Where grazing rights were preserved, tenants found complaint difficult. With this proviso the Statutes of Merton 1236 and Westminster 1285 permitted enclosure by lords of the manor. After the Black Death (*see* separate entry) the demands of the wool trade encouraged intensive sheep farming; enclosures, while reducing labour costs, threw many ploughmen out of work, caused depopulation of the countryside, and increased the number of vagrants on the road.

Under the Tudors, with an increasing population and the need for greater productivity, enclosures were widespread. Anti-enclosure Acts under Henry VII, Henry VIII and Elizabeth I slowed the process but little. In the first half of the 17th century enclosures continued, generally by agreement or by money payments. In a trading nation it is understandable that men should seek financial profit rather than consider social consequences.

After 1750 further enclosures accompanied agricultural expansion and prosperity. Where the majority of the tenants agreed, enclosure was easily achieved by Act of Parliament, though the loss of common rights caused much dispute. Some historians condemn enclosures unequivocally for their economic injury to farmworkers. Others assert that economic benefits to the countryside far outweighed distress to individuals, since enclosures encouraged new techniques and increased efficiency. The process was complete in England by the 1860s.

In Europe generally enclosures made rapid progress after 1800, though in some countries, e.g. Czechoslovakia, changes did not come until after World War I.

¶ PARKER, R. A. C. *Enclosures in the Eighteenth Century*. 1960

England: southern part of the island of Britain, excluding Wales; the largest of the units of the United Kingdom, which contains the greater part of Britain's total population. The name is derived from the Angles, a Germanic people who invaded Britain in the 5th century AD. After the withdrawal of the Romans in AD 410 the history of the island is largely one of raids, conquest and settlement by various Germanic and Scandinavian peoples (*see* ANGLO-SAXONS, JUTES, etc.) until the arrival of the Normans, the last successful invaders, in 1066. Succeeding centuries saw a long preoccupation with wars in France and other external adventures but also, at home, the building up of a legal system and of parliamentary government that brought the nation to strong and united nationhood under the Tudors. For earlier aspects of English history see various articles on ruling houses (LANCASTER, NORMAN KINGS, PLANTAGENET, TUDOR, YORK) and on other topics, e.g. CRUSADES, FEUDAL SYSTEM, HUNDRED YEARS' WAR, MANOR. For the period from 1603 onwards see GREAT BRITAIN.

¶ UNSTEAD, R. J. *The Story of Britain.* 1969

English Channel: formed in Neolithic times by subsidence and by erosion of the Kent-Picardy chalk ridge, it has formed the "moat defensive" behind which the English could settle their religious and political quarrels without foreign intervention. Until the Tudors built a navy the Channel was the path of successful invaders, from the remote Celts and Iberians, through the Romans, Saxons and Norsemen to William I, Henry IV and Henry VII. Thereafter no foreign power has invaded successfully, and claimants of the throne only succeeded if Englishmen invited and supported them, e.g. Charles II, William III. Shore defences have mainly aimed to protect anchorages – whether the Roman forts of the Saxon shore, Henry's VIII's castles, the Martello Towers of the Napoleonic period or Palmerston's forts of the 1860s. In the 1939–45 war the Channel saw both triumphs of government planning and epics of private initiative and courage, as in the Normandy landings and the evacuation of Dunkirk. The Channel is now too shallow for the largest tankers.

¶ PUMPHREY, GEORGE. *Conquering the English Channel.* 1965

English language: language of the Germanic branch of the Indo-European family of languages, spoken by about 275 million people as their mother tongue; the chief language of world commerce and one of the greatest vehicles of literature.

In the 5th century Britain was invaded by three Germanic tribes, the Angles, Saxons and Jutes. It was not a concerted attack, but a process of conquest and colonisation that went on for almost 200 years. Gradually, the Celtic inhabitants of Britain were forced to give way. Those that kept up the fight retreated into Cornwall and Wales. The rest were absorbed so effectively that, place-names apart, only about a dozen Celtic words (among them "ass", "bannock" and "bin") were taken over into Old English, the language of their conquerors.

Old English, the foundation of the English we speak today, was vigorous and expressive, if somewhat unwieldy. But it was highly inflected: that is, many changes in word endings were used to denote differences of grammatical case, tense or mood. It was, however, a resourceful language, capable of assimilating new ideas. Thus, in the 7th century AD, when the English became converted to Christianity, although numerous Latin words relating to the new religion were taken over, many were not and, instead, existing Old English words were given new meanings (e.g. Easter, OE *eastron*, after Austro, pagan goddess of Spring); and new words were framed from native stems.

In the 9th century another race of continental invaders, the Danes, harried the shores of Britain and eventually settled in the district called the Danelaw. Their language was very similar to Old English, and many of their phrases and turns of speech were readily adopted. Danish legal terms were taken over into the English language, notably the word "law" itself.

Two centuries on, the Normans conquered England and changed not only the pattern of English life but the language, too. They introduced Norman-French words for all the machinery of power: words like "govern", "sovereign", "parliament", "people", "nation". Most English words relating to the nobility, to heraldry, feudalism, law and the arts of war are of Norman origin; so, too, are words relating to the arts, fashion and the pursuit of pleasure; but it is worth noting that, while the words for the flesh of various animals prepared for the table (e.g. beef, mutton, pork, veal) are Norman-French in origin, the plain Anglo-Saxon words remained for the beasts themselves – oxen, sheep, swine, calves.

Though the Normans were the masters, in the end English triumphed. It digested the new vocabulary, dropped most of its burdensome inflections and preserved its own special character. The invention of printing did much to standardise grammar and spelling.

With the Renaissance came a flood of terms derived from Latin and Greek. Wider contacts with other peoples, through trade and exploration, further enriched English with words culled from almost every country. Some examples are: "assassin", from a sect of Mohammedan fanatics who, during the Crusades, were sent out under the influence of the drug *hashish* to murder Christians: "alcove", from the Arabic *al-quabbah*, an arch or vault: "canoe", from a Haitian word recorded by Christopher Columbus: "buccaneer", from a Brazilian word meaning a gridiron, on which flesh was grilled by the original *boucaniers*. In more modern times "quisling" has passed into language to denote one who treacherously collaborates with the enemy, from the Norwegian Vidkun Quisling who worked with the Germans when they occupied his country, 1940–45. British government appointments now include "ombudsman" (borrowed from Swedish), a parliamentary commissioner first appointed in 1966 to investigate complaints by citizens against maladministration by ministers and government departments. *See also* FILIBUSTER.

¶ SPARKE, W. *The Story of the English Language*. 1966

Engraving: cutting of designs, etc., on a hard surface with a sharp tool. The origin of engraving appears to lie in man's inclination to score lines and patterns on a surface. This dates from primitive times. Prisoners, travellers, schoolboys and other people with time on their hands have left their mark on walls and other surfaces over the centuries. Ancient history has been revealed by the deciphering of rock cut inscriptions. Such writings are often called *graffiti*, from Italian *graffio*, a scratch.

Line engraving can be traced from the early decoration of precious metals and, later, the products of the armourers' workshops. Not until the 15th century were prints taken from designs, although

St Jerome in his cell, *a wood engraving by Albrecht Dürer, done in 1511.*

woodcuts were made in the Far East as early as the 9th century and wood blocks were used for printing on fabric in the Middle Ages. The earliest engraver known by his subject was "The Master of the Playing Cards". In the last part of the 15th century Germany was prolific in engravers, outstanding among them being Albrecht Dürer (1471–1528).

Perfection was attained in French engraved portraits in the 17th century. In the 18th and 19th centuries engraving tended to deteriorate from an original means of expression into a hack-work process of reproduction which has been supplanted today by the camera.

See also DÜRER; ETCHING.

Entente Cordiale: the 1904 friendly agreement between France and Britain, greatly helped by the exchange visits of Edward VII to Paris and the French President to London in 1903. In 1907 it was expanded to become the Triple Entente as a result of Anglo-Russian agreement. In essence this was a countermove to the Triple Alliance (1882) of Germany, Austria and Italy against France and Russia, which lasted until World War I.

Ephesus: old Greek city on the Aegean coast of modern Turkey, situated at the end of the east–west trade route down the Meander valley. Under the control successively of Lydia, Persia, Athens and then Persia again, Ephesus was liberated by Alexander the Great in 333 BC. On his death it became part of the Hellenistic kingdom of Pergamum, its population grew to over 100,000, and it rivalled Alexandria and Antioch in prosperity and as a cultural centre. When the district became the Roman province of Asia, Ephesus was in effect the capital of the province. Ephesus is chiefly famous for the great temple to Artemis (Cybele in Asia Minor, Diana to the Romans), which was considered one of the seven wonders of the ancient world. Rebuilt in the 4th century BC the temple housed the statue of Artemis-Cybele, and around it various groups of craftsmen made their living. "Great is Diana of the Ephesians," shouted the natives; the reaction of St Paul can be read in the Acts of the Apostles, chapter 20. In AD 262 the Goths destroyed city and temple and, though rebuilding followed, the old glory and power was never recovered. Malaria seems to have played a

Left, Diana of the Ephesians (Artemis). Above the theatre, Ephesus. Below, reconstruction of the Temple of Artemis, Ephesus.

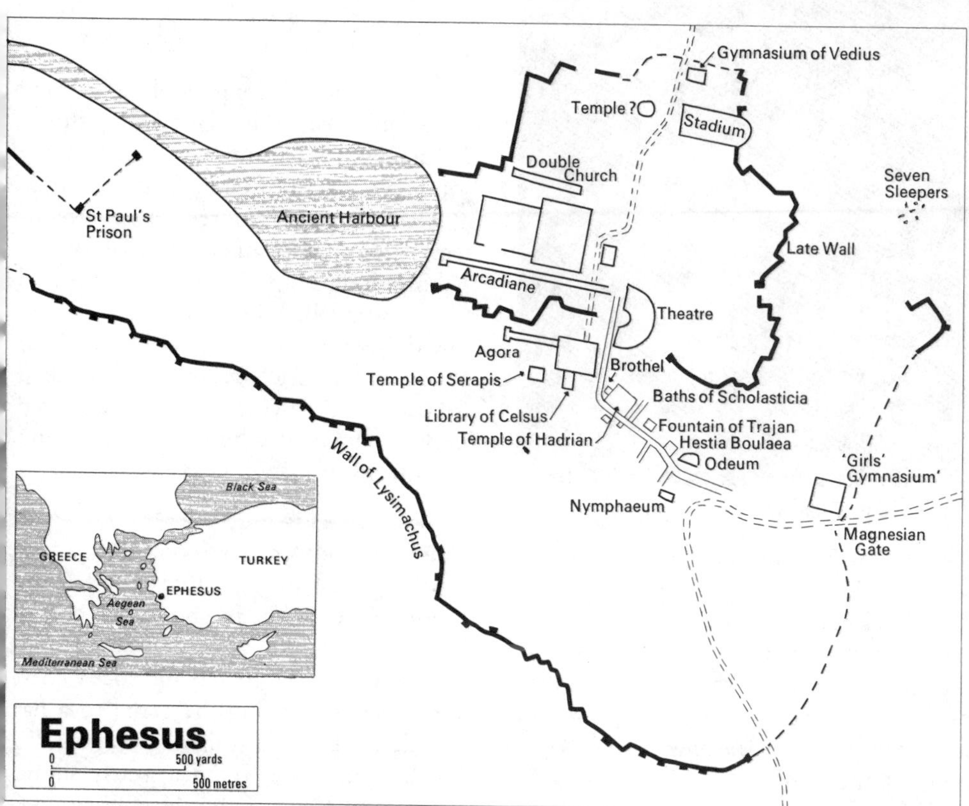

great part in the site being gradually depopulated and eventually deserted. It was not rediscovered and excavated till the 19th century.

Epics: long narrative poems on a grand scale about the exploits of heroes and nations. Originally formed from various works of unknown poets, they were sung or recited by minstrels. Examples of these folk epics are the great mythological poems such as, in Greek, the *Iliad* and the *Odyssey*, attributed to Homer (*see* separate entry), the first woven around the hero Achilles, the second chronicling the adventures of Odysseus, king of Ithaca, on his journey home from defeated Troy; in Sanskrit the very ancient East Indian *Mahabharata*, the longest known epic – 220,000 lines; in Spanish the *Poem of the Cid*; in Anglo-Saxon, or Old English, *Beowulf*, the earliest known epic in a non-classical language: in Finnish *Kalevala*, which gives an account of the origin of the world and a German translation of which is said to have suggested to Longfellow the form and epic style of his *Hiawatha*; in German the *Nibelungenlied*; and in French the *Song of Roland*, the most famous epic poem of medieval France.

Examples of the so-called art epic, distinctly the work of a single author, are, in Latin, Virgil's *Aeneid* (70–19 BC); Ovid's *Metamorphoses*, a series of tales dealing with mythological, legendary and historical figures (AD 1); in Italian, Dante's *Commedía* (*c.* 1308–20) and Ariosto's *Orlando Furioso*; in English, Milton's *Paradise Lost*, Scott's *Lay of the Last Minstrel*, Byron's epic satire *Don Juan*, and Tennyson's *Idylls of the King*.

Erasmus, Desiderius (*c.* 1465–1536): Dutch scholar, theologian and humanist. "In body he was thick-set and neat, but ... he was easily affected even by very small

Erasmus by Holbein.

changes of circumstance, such as food, wine, or the weather." He published the first Greek edition of the New Testament, taught in several European capitals, was the intimate friend of the greatest scholars of his day and exercised a profound influence on the learning of Europe, reviving the study of Greek and applying critical standards to the translation and interpretation of the Bible.

¶ JONES, R. D. *Erasmus and Luther*. 1968

Eric, called "the Red" (*c.* 940–*c.* 1010): Norse explorer. Having killed one of his neighbours in Iceland and been declared an outlaw, he sailed west looking for land that had once been sighted in a storm. Returning to Iceland he described the south-west coast of Greenland so favourably that several hundred settlers volunteered to join him, and in 982 twenty-five Viking long ships carried them round Cape Farewell, where they landed and raised sheep and cattle as well as catching abundant fish. Eric's settlements flourished for two hundred years but were destroyed in the 15th century by increasing ice and the attacks of Eskimos.

Ericson, Leif (*c.* AD 1000): Norse explorer, son of Eric the Red. Leif left the home of his father in about AD 1000 to look for a land to the west of Greenland. He soon sighted a frozen and rocky coast and sailed south until he came to a flat wooded place he called "Markland". Further south he found a grassy shore, where grapevines and wild wheat grew. His brother-in-law then organised an expedition of sixty men and five women to make a permanent home in this "Vineland", using the houses Leif had already built. These were the first Europeans to settle on the mainland of America, but the

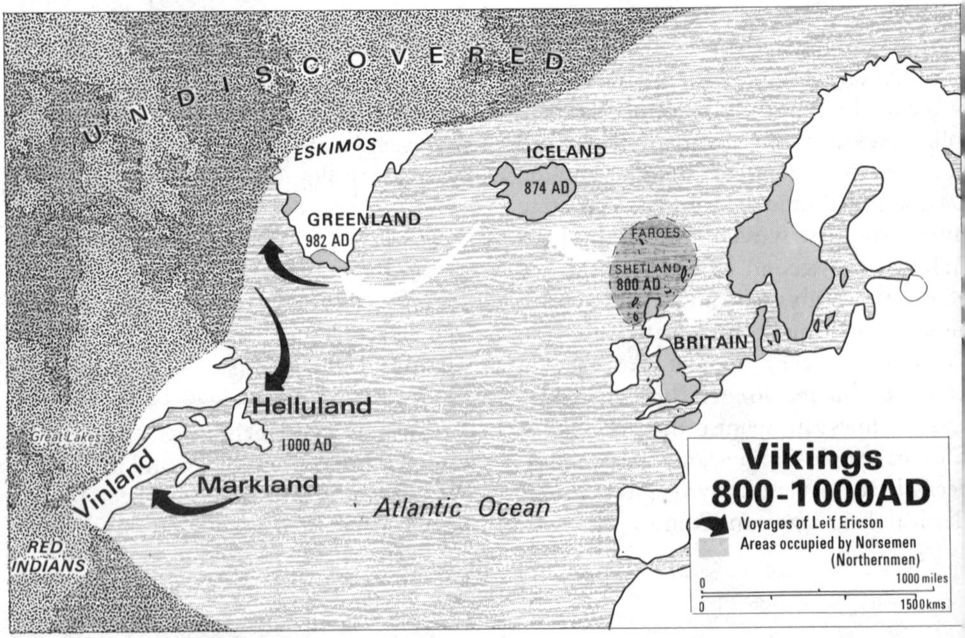

Gully erosion on Ashdown Beds, Sussex.

ıative "Skraelings" were hostile, and the ;ettlement lasted less than a hundred years.

¶ BENTLEY, J. D. *Leif Ericsson and the North Atlantic.* '967; ANDERSON, J. R. L. *The Vinland Voyage.* 1967; ANDERSON, J. R. L. *The Vikings.* 1974

Erosion: wearing away of the earth's ,urface by the action of water, wind and ce. It may be caused by simple weathering or, more violently, by transport of naterial which rubs or batters the surface over which it moves. Coasts not proected by deposition of sand offer specacular forms of horizontal erosion by sea waves. River bends, too, are often evilence of river's horizontal erosive power, ınd steep slopes are produced on the outside flank.

Rivers also erode vertically and deepen heir valleys. Sometimes the plain of a neandering river is uplifted and the river becomes entrenched in its old winding course with the former plain perched at a nigher level. Ice also can erode vertically, ınd shoulders can often be seen at the sides of valleys once occupied by a rapidly eroding glacier. They may form alps occupied by pasturing animals and buildngs for their owners.

Weathered rock plus humus is what we call soil. It is often only a few inches deep, and its removal by "soil erosion" may mean transformation of richly peopled regions into areas which are little better than bare rock.

¶ In WAYTE, M. E. *Mining the Soil.* 1963

Escorial or **Escurial:** the vast group of granite buildings erected 1563–84 by Philip II of Spain, thirty miles [forty-eight kilometres] north-west of Madrid, 3,500 feet [1,066 metres] above sea level. With more than a thousand doors and a hundred miles of passages, it combines palace, monastery, church, college, library, museum and royal tombs.

Courtyard of the Kings, the Escorial.

Esperanto: a manufactured language, made up in 1877 out of certain European languages, by Lazaro Zamenhof (1859–1917), a Russian physician, and designed for international use. Of the hundreds of artificial languages put together in the past three centuries, Esperanto attracts more adherents than any other. Esperanto, derived from the Latin *sperare*, to hope, was Zamenhof's pen-name.

Este, Family of: after Savoy, the oldest ruling family in Italy. They held the castle of Ateste near Padua in the Lombard invasions; they became linked by marriage with the Dukes of Swabia in the 11th century and leaders of the Guelph faction; in AD 1208 they became hereditary podestas (magistrates) of Ferrara and in 1288 added Modena and Reggio. Turbulence, passion and brilliance characterised them. Niccollo III (reigned 1393–1441) employed the humanist Guarino as tutor to his illegitimate sons Lionello (1441–50), who presided over the Classical Renaissance at its purest and freshest, and Borso (1450–71), who was a generous patron of painters. Duke Alfonzo (1505–34), who married Lucrezia Borgia, incarcerated his half-brothers Giulio and Ferrante for life in his palace after they had plotted against him for his leniency to another brother, Cardinal Ippolyto, who had ambushed and blinded Giulio. In 1597 Duke Alfonzo II died childless and Ferrara reverted to the Papacy. His cousin moved to Modena, where the Este ruled till Napoleon's time. Mary of Modena, second wife of James II of England, was an Este.

Estonia: a largely agricultural country on the eastern seaboard of the Baltic, now a constituent republic of the Soviet Union. Estonia once formed part of the three Baltic Provinces (Estland, Livland and Kurland), which were annexed to the Russian Empire in the 18th century. She received her independence at the end of the First World War, but held it only until 1940, when Russia reoccupied the Baltic states under the secret terms of the 1939 treaty with Germany. Hitler's attack on Russia in 1941 led to Nazi occupation of Estonia until 1944, when Soviet rule was fully re-established.

See EUROPE for map.

Etching: the process of printing designs and pictures from engravings on glass or metal, especially copper.

Some of the most outstanding examples of the art of etching originated in Germany, Italy, England, France and, especially, the Netherlands. The earliest etchers and engravers were probably goldsmiths who also worked on metal.

In contrast to the disciplined method of engraving by cutting a line on a metal plate, in etching the line is drawn with the easy flow of a needle on the waxed surface of the specially prepared plate. The plate is then dipped in acid, which eats into the metal where the needle point has scraped it clear of wax. Such a process had obvious relevance to the armourer's art since it provided decoration without impairing strength. Italian and German armourers employed this method as early as the 15th century. In the 16th century the artist and the armourer combined to produce outstanding examples. Daniel Hopfer of Augsburg is famous not only for his prints but for the etching of a suit of armour for Charles V (Holy Roman Emperor 1519–58). Interesting examples of etched armour can be seen in the Wallace Collection and the Tower Armouries in London and in other cities in Europe, one of the finest being Henry VIII's silvered armour for horse and man in the Tower.

Many painters have explored the medium of etching at some time in their careers. Albrecht Dürer (1471–1528) was

Above left, The Mill *by Rembrandt, 1641. Below left,* The Donkey *by Picasso, 1942. Above,* The detention as barbarous as the crime *by Goya, 1815.*

one of the first to print on paper from an etched plate. It was perhaps Rembrandt (1606–69) who discovered the fullest possibilities in this process. Others worthy of study are Piranesi (1720–78), Goya (1746–1828), William Blake (1757–1827), Whistler (1834–1903), Renoir (1841–1919) and Picasso (1881–1973).

In recent years great changes in the processes of print making show artists experimenting with hitherto untried ways of expression, often combining various processes, including etching.

See also ENGRAVING.

Ethiopia (formerly Abyssinia)**:** socialist state in north-east Africa, population 33,679,600 (1983). The Queen of Sheba went this way to visit King Solomon. Their son Menilek became Emperor of Ethiopia, and all later emperors claim to be descended from him. When the Greeks conquered Egypt, they began to trade with Axum, the capital city of Ethiopia, and by AD 330 missionaries from Egypt had begun to make the people Christian. In the 7th century AD Arab armies converted the rest of northern Africa to Islam, so that the Ethiopians were cut off from all other Christians. They have kept their original beliefs and customs ever since. A Muslim army conquered Ethiopia in 1541, but Portuguese explorers had already found their way to the fabulous Christian emperor they called "Prester John" (*see* separate entry), and 450 well-armed Portuguese soldiers drove the enemy away.

When the rest of Africa was being attacked in the 19th century, this time by Europeans who were carving out colonies for themselves, Ethiopia again escaped, though a British expedition under Sir Robert Napier in 1867–68 destroyed the capital before withdrawing. The Abys-

sinians defeated an Italian army at Adowa in 1896, and Italians had to wait for revenge until 1935, when Mussolini used bombs and poison gas against the mountain villages. Ethiopia became a free country again during the Second World War. Its modern capital Addis Ababa was chosen in 1963 to be the headquarters of the Organisation of African Unity.

¶ WATSON, JANE WERNER. *Ethiopia: Mountain Kingdom*. 1968

Etruria and the **Etruscans:** the name of the old district and its inhabitants, roughly the same as modern Tuscany, stretching from the north bank of the Tiber to the Po valley and beyond. At the height of Etruria's power in the 6th century BC, land under her control included Corsica, Elba and several places as far south as Campania. At the same time Etruscan kings, the Tarquins, held Rome, and an Etruscan fleet with Carthaginian help defeated the western Greeks off Corsica (about 535 BC). Throughout the 5th century Rome gradually began to get the upper hand, but it was not until 396 BC that the Etruscan stronghold of Veii, ten miles [sixteen kilometres] from Rome was captured. The Etruscans allied themselves with opponents of Rome from then on, but may be considered to be part of the Roman state from about 280 BC.

There are many mysteries about the Etruscans, in particular whence they came and what language they spoke. Tales of their arrival from Asia Minor are probably fictional. Their language was written in Greek characters, but it has not yet been deciphered. Their influence on Rome was considerable, especially in political and religious matters, and their artistic ability was great. They bequeathed the arch to Rome, and burial mounds in places like Tarquinia contain excellent murals, in which scenes of war, hunting and revelr

predominate. Metal work in bronze and gold was of a very high class, and Etruscan pottery, though owing much to Greek inspiration, was far superior to contemporary Roman ware.

¶ BLOCH, RAYMOND. *The Etruscans.* 1958

Etymology: the science of the development of words, how they have derived in form and sense. Every word in every language contains clues to its own history. The etymologist endeavours to uncover and record that history. The word etymology itself comes from Greek words meaning the true or real word.

Euclid: Greek mathematician. The 3rd century BC produced three great mathematicians, Euclid, Archimedes and Apollonius, of whom Euclid was the earliest. We know little of his life, except that he was born of Greek descent, was said to have been educated at Athens, became a successful teacher at Alexandria and died about 275 BC. He was the author of several works, but his best known book was the *Elements*, of which thirteen books survive. This soon established itself as the standard text on the elements of pure mathematics and dominated the elementary teaching of geometry until the end of the 19th century. English versions are mainly based on Simson's edition, published in 1758.

¶ DELACY, E. A. *Euclid and Geometry.* 1965

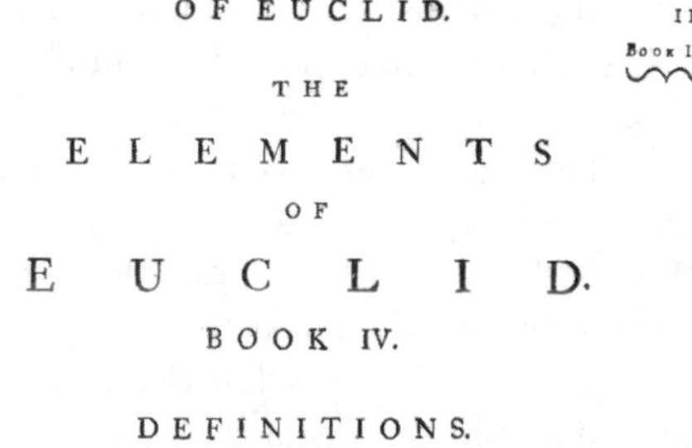
OF EUCLID. 115

Book IV.

THE

ELEMENTS

OF

EUCLID.

BOOK IV.

DEFINITIONS.

I.

A Rectilineal figure is said to be inscribed in another rectilineal figure, when all the angles of the inscribed figure are upon the sides of the figure in which it is inscribed, each upon each.

II.

In like manner a figure is said to be described about another figure, when all the sides of the circumscribed figure pass thro' the angular points of the figure about which it is described, each thro' each.

III.

A rectilineal figure is said to be inscribed in a circle, when all the angles of the inscribed figure are upon the circumference of the circle.

P 2 A rect-

A page from The Elements, Book IV.

Eugenics: the science concerned with methods of improving and protecting the quality of the human race by studying the qualities of mind and body that are handed down from parents to children. The word was coined by an English scientist, Sir Francis Galton (1822–1911), from two Greek words which mean "well-born".

Children often resemble their parents in some respects: strong, healthy parents tend to have strong, healthy children; clever parents are more likely to have clever children than stupid ones. Sir Francis Galton wrote many books to explain his ideas on eugenics, in the hope that men and women would be careful in their choice of wife or husband, so that children would be healthy and wise, and in time, the whole race would be improved.

The difficulty is that human beings are more than animals. Some of the greatest men and women intellectually have been very weak or sickly physically, while some of the strongest and healthiest people are dull and stupid. Also, we know that, in addition to the qualities that children inherit from their parents, much depends on their environment and the conditions in which they are brought up. In order for eugenists to bring about the improvements in the human race that they wish, it would be necessary to discover how qualities are passed on from parents to children, to decide on what qualities are required and how they are to be selected, and to control the environment of the children.

Euphrates River: one of the two great rivers of Mesopotamia, 1,700 miles [2,736 kilometres] in length. The Euphrates and the Tigris, together draining the highlands of Syria, Turkey and Persia, flow over the plain of Iraq into the Persian Gulf. Geography has had striking influences within the Euphrates lands, which themselves form an isthmus between the eastern and western world.

The Euphrates basin is largely desert, but melting of the northern mountain snows in spring produces floods in summer, enabling the inhabitants of the South to irrigate the plain when high temperatures favour fertility. By contrast, the Nile flows northwards and is fed by summer rains, which do not reach lower Egypt until the autumn fall of temperature. Irrigation of Euphrates lands was very advanced by about the 9th century BC

Cultivation with the aid of water and heat combined was associated with early settlement, especially south of Hit, where the river emerges from its valley course and becomes more accessible to farmers in the flat delta region.

The Euphrates was early used for transport of timber, stone, metals and olive oil downstream to the flat lands where these essential materials were absent but where corn could be offered in exchange. Trade upstream must presumably have been overland. From Hit a common route lay westwards to oases like Palmyra en route to Mediterranean ports.

See MESOPOTAMIA for map.

¶ MEADE, G. E. *The Tigris and the Euphrates.* 1963

Europe: the fifth largest continent, area 3,800,000 square miles [9,842,000 square kilometres]. The shores of the Mediterranean in the last thousand years BC gave the variety and the favourable climate in which, with written records and descriptive literature, the history of Europe began. In the small Greek cities, scattered on the mainland, on the islands of Greece and along the coast of the modern Turkey, a confident and intellectually fearless people created for themselves a distinctive European civilisation. Many of the Greek states had some degree of democracy or public consultation. It was slavery, however, which freed the most able Greeks from menial tasks, to give time to politics, art and philosophical speculation.

The unity and self-confidence of the Greek states grew through war with the great neighbouring Persian Empire. In 490 and 480 BC small Greek forces decisively defeated hordes of invading Persians at the battles of Marathon and Salamis. The golden age of Athens followed, with the building of an Athenian maritime empire in the eastern Mediterranean, and saw the dramas of Aeschylus and Sophocles, the political idealism of Pericles and the sculpture of Phidias. The later years of the 5th century BC, however, though they produced the dramas of Euripides, the writings of Plato and the histories of Herodotus and Thucydides, saw the brutal and ruinous Peloponnesian War between Athens and Sparta, involving most of the Greeks. In the 4th century BC Macedonia won predominance and, under Alexander the Great (356–323 BC), defeated Persia and built a great military empire, which extended from Greece and Egypt, across Mesopotamia and Persia, to the borders of India.

In another part of the Mediterranean the Latin-speaking Romans found their greatness through a long desperate war (264–146 BC) with the North African power of Carthage and created an empire which spread at least right round the Mediterranean, including most of the old Greek states. In 45 BC Julius Caesar finally replaced the Roman Republic by personal rule. His work was carried on by Augustus, who made the Roman Empire a centralised autocracy ruled by professional administrators.

The Empire's frontiers were at the Rhine, the Danube and the North African desert. It began to decline early in the 3rd century AD. The Romans had become almost a different people by the influx of population from the provinces. Along the frontiers the Germanic "barbarians" were exerting pressure. They wanted to enter the Empire, join its armies and enjoy its benefits; but in the end it broke in their inexperienced hands.

In addition to Greek intellectual vitality and Roman organisation, a new influence was now making itself felt in the Mediterranean world – the Christian religion. The Emperor Constantine was converted to Christianity in AD 312 and was later baptised.

Constantine divided the Empire administratively into East and West. A final separation came in 395. The western Empire was crumbling rapidly at the hands of migrating hordes of Germanic people. The Rhine frontier broke at the close of 406. The last western emperor was deposed in 476. But the eastern or Byzantine Empire lived on for a thousand years, enjoying periods of prosperity but generally dwindling, to fall to the Turks in 1453. Loss of Byzantine hold on Palestine called forth the Crusades of the 12th century to rescue the Holy Land.

From the ruins of the western Empire Germanic kingdoms rose and fell. People held to two sustaining ideals – Christianity and the memory of the Empire. Many of the best minds turned to the consolation of religion. The gap created by the collapse of Empire was partly filled by the Church, particularly by the Popes. In 800 the Pope crowned Charlemagne, king of the Franks, as emperor of a mid-European empire, including France, Germany, northern Italy and many borderlands. This Holy Roman Empire was later largely identified with Germany.

Further movements of peoples from the Scandinavian countries delayed peace in northern Europe; but after the year 1000 some order emerged through a graded series of bargains and understandings as to rights and obligations between kings and greater and lesser lords and knights. This was later called the feudal system.

In the later Middle Ages two influences which stimulated a rising level of civilisation were, first, the continued existence of the Byzantine Empire, still a living link with ancient Greece and Rome, and, second, the science and thought of the Islamic civilisation of North Africa and Spain. In the 15th century there occurred the rich blossoming of literature and art known as the Renaissance, owing its impetus to the rediscovery of Greek and Latin literature and of the human individual.

Along with the emergence of the national monarchies of France, England,

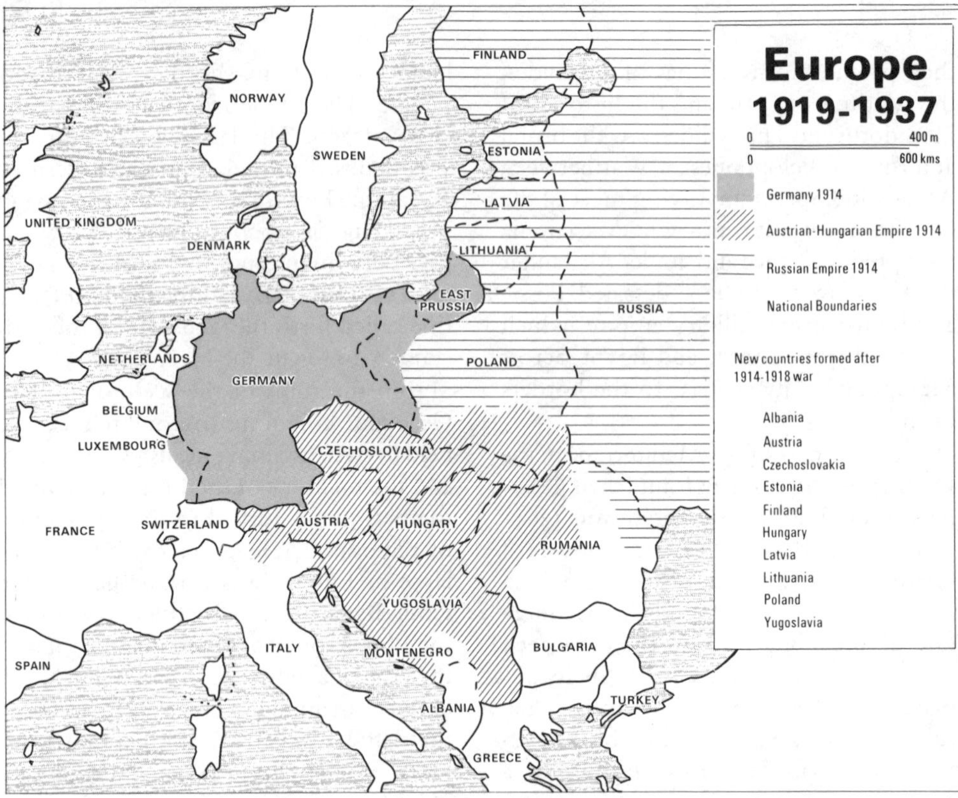

Europe 1919-1937

0 400 m
0 600 kms

Germany 1914
Austrian-Hungarian Empire 1914
Russian Empire 1914
National Boundaries

New countries formed after 1914-1918 war

Albania
Austria
Czechoslovakia
Estonia
Finland
Hungary
Latvia
Lithuania
Poland
Yugoslavia

FINLAND
NORWAY
SWEDEN
ESTONIA
LATVIA
UNITED KINGDOM
DENMARK
LITHUANIA
EAST PRUSSIA
RUSSIA
NETHERLANDS
GERMANY
POLAND
BELGIUM
LUXEMBOURG
CZECHOSLOVAKIA
FRANCE
SWITZERLAND
AUSTRIA
HUNGARY
RUMANIA
YUGOSLAVIA
SPAIN
ITALY
MONTENEGRO
BULGARIA
TURKEY
ALBANIA
GREECE

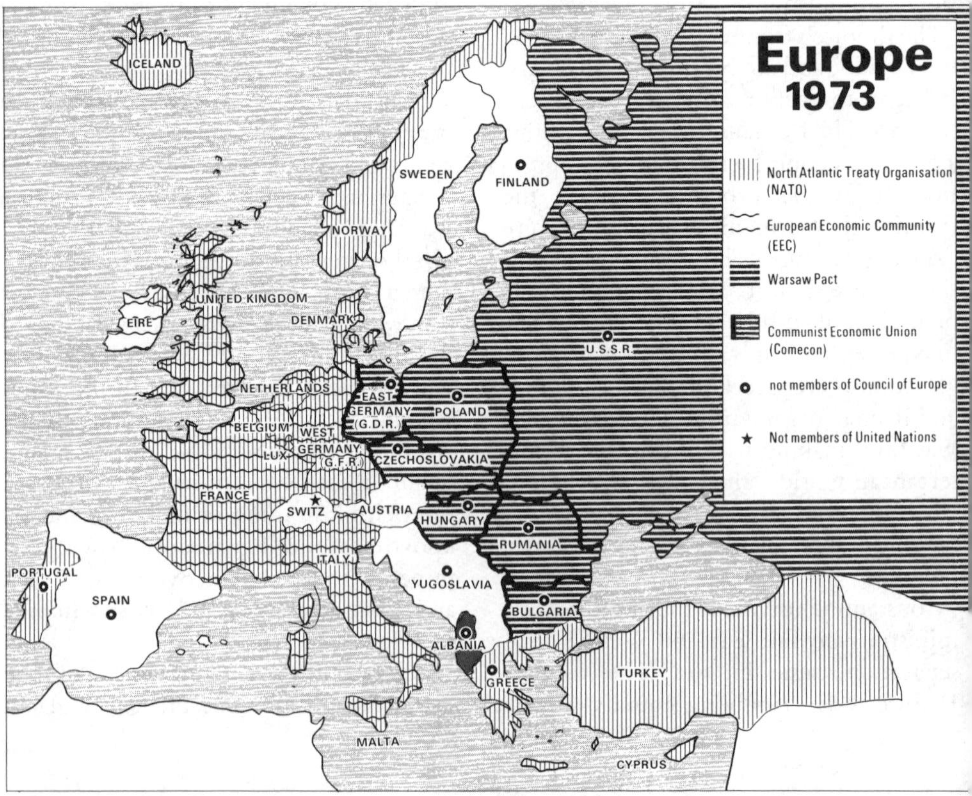

Europe 1973

North Atlantic Treaty Organisation (NATO)
European Economic Community (EEC)
Warsaw Pact
Communist Economic Union (Comecon)
not members of Council of Europe
★ Not members of United Nations

ICELAND
SWEDEN
FINLAND
NORWAY
UNITED KINGDOM
EIRE
DENMARK
U.S.S.R.
NETHERLANDS
EAST GERMANY (G.D.R.)
POLAND
BELGIUM
WEST GERMANY (G.F.R.)
LUX
CZECHOSLOVAKIA
FRANCE
SWITZ
AUSTRIA
HUNGARY
RUMANIA
PORTUGAL
ITALY
YUGOSLAVIA
SPAIN
BULGARIA
ALBANIA
GREECE
TURKEY
MALTA
CYPRUS

Spain and Portugal at the close of the 15th century, overseas exploration began. The Portuguese and Spaniards discovered and exploited America. Later the French, English and Dutch joined in the quest for overseas gain. The conflict of kingdoms in Europe was sharpened by this and by the Protestant revolt against the old order of western Catholic Christianity. European wars increasingly became struggles for overseas empire. From the 18th century a powerful intensifying factor in European conflict was the industrial revolution and the application of capital investment and scientific method to the production of goods, armaments and transport. Revolution in France led to more democratic government in many other countries. Overseas colonies began to gain their independence.

Long disturbed by movements of peoples from Asia, eastern Europe was later in development than the West. Russia became a strong European power but sought expansion into Asia rather than overseas. Germany, long divided, was also little involved in overseas imperialism, but the ambition of a united Germany to expand did much to bring about World War I (1914–18). Communist revolution in 1917 did not much alter Russian imperialist ambitions. A second World War (1939–45), in many respects a continuation of the first, left eastern Europe under Russian domination, while western Europe became a field for much American capital investment and influence. The overseas empires of the several European powers nearly all now became self-governing, and European countries, though prosperous and highly organised, lost much of their world role. A cause of much diplomatic activity was the search for a European unity, which would give Europe greater initiative in a world so much dominated by the USA and the USSR.

¶ FISHER, H. A. L. *A History of Europe*. 1936

European Common Market (**EEC** – European Economic Community): organisation set up in Brussels under the Treaty of Rome (1958) by France, the Federal Republic of Germany, Italy, Belgium, Luxembourg and the Netherlands ("the Six"). In January 1973 Britain, Denmark and Ireland also became members ("the Nine"). In 1981 Greece, which had enjoyed associate status, became a full member so making the EEC the Ten. Then in 1985, after lengthy negotiations, the EEC agreed to admit Spain and Portugal in January 1986 so bringing total membership to twelve. The EEC's principal organs are the Commission, its main executive body, the Council of Ministers (representing national as opposed to Community interests), the European Parliament whose members are delegated by the national parliaments of the member states, and the Court of Justice.

¶ KITZINGER, U. *The European Common Market and Community*. 1967

Everest, Mount: highest mountain in the world, in the Himalayas, southern Asia. The peak *Chomo Lungura* was named Everest in 1852, when Sir George Everest, Surveyor General of India, established it as the highest so far measured: 29,028 feet [8,847 metres]. No attempt to climb it could be made until the opening up of Tibet in 1921, when a reconnaissance of the north side, under Colonel Howard-Bury, explored the route for the 1922 expedition under General Bruce. Three attempts were then made on the summit, Bruce reaching 27,300 feet [8,300 metres], but on the third attempt an avalanche killed seven men. On the second expedition (1924) Norton and Somervell reached 28,000 feet [8,534 metres], and Irvine and Mallory were seen higher and may have reached the top, but never returned. Further expeditions in 1933, 1935, 1936 and 1938 were frustrated largely by adverse weather, but in 1933 Lord Clydesdale and Flight Lieutenant McIntyre made a flight over the summit.

With the Independence of India, 1947, the Nepalese route became open, and in 1951 Shipton led a reconnaissance of the southern side. This paved the way for a Swiss expedition in 1952, which reached 28,250 feet [8,610 metres] by the south ridge. In 1953 Colonel (now Lord) Hunt led the expedition on which Edmund Hillary and the Sherpa Tenzing Norkay at last reached the summit. Since then two Indian expeditions have succeeded, and in 1963 a highly equipped American party climbed several times to the top and made the first traverse of the mountain by the west shoulder and down by the south ridge. More recently the Chinese claim to have made a successful attempt by the north-east route.

¶ HUNT, SIR JOHN. *The Ascent of Everest.* 1954; WIBBERLEY, LEONARD. *Epics of Everest.* 1955

A judge, centre, presides over the Court of the Exchequer while clerks and officers count gold coins. Manuscript, period of Henry VI.

Exchequer: treasury of a state or government department in charge of public revenue and expenditure.

In feudal society every tenant had periodically to come to court to account to his lord and a tenant in chief to his overlord, i.e. the king. The administration of the country could not be carried out by these occasional meetings of the *Curia Regis*, and hence there grew up a permanent secretariat (also called *Curia Regis*) consisting of the chief justiciar, the chancellor (head of a body of clerks doing the secretarial work) and other officers of the royal household. When this body met for financial purposes it was called the Exchequer, from the chequered cloth on the table. Chequers, or counters, such as those used in various table games, were probably used to help in the counting of money.

After the chaos of Stephen's reign the Exchequer was reorganised by Richard Fitznigel (Richard of Ely, d. 1198) who wrote the *Dialogus de Scaccario* (1177). The money received was counted, weighed, assayed and stored in the Exchequer of Receipt, and the Sheriffs made their statements of account before the Exchequer of Account. Disputes between king and subject over the royal revenue were settled by the Barons of the Exchequer, sitting as a Court. By Edward I's reign the Exchequer had split off from the Curia Regis, as had also the Courts of King's Bench and Common Pleas, and the Exchequer succeeded in filching from the Common Pleas many civil cases between subject and subject by the Writ *Quominus*, by which a plaintiff alleged a fictitious debt to the king, which, by the defendant's default, he was unable to pay.

The modern Treasury is an offshoot of the Exchequer, and even down to 1875 the Chancellor of the Exchequer in Britain was entitled to sit as judge along with the Barons of the Exchequer.

F

Factories: building where goods are manufactured by collective effort. England, as the oldest industrialised country, still preserves many types of factory, from which much of the story can be learned.

The most famous early factory owner in England was John Winchcombe (d. 1520), better known as Jack of Newbury, the Berkshire clothier who is reputed to have led several hundred men equipped at his own expense, to fight at the battle of Flodden Field (1514), and whose house can still be seen in Newbury. But it was not till the 18th century that the main age of factory building began. The pioneers were Sir Thomas Lombe (1685–1739), who introduced the art of silk-throwing into England, and his half-brother, John (1693?–1722), whom he sent to Italy to learn the secret of the craft. Their mill, or factory, built at Derby (1718–22) must have been well known to Richard Arkwright and Jedediah Strutt, who, in 1771, built at Cromford in Derbyshire the first successful water-powered cotton spinning mill (the machinery in the partners' Nottingham factory, 1769, was turned by a horse). In 1776 Arkwright built a second mill, 120 feet long and seven storeys high, at Cromford, and in the same year Strutt built the first of his factories at nearby Belper. In 1781 Sylas Neville recorded in his diary that Arkwright employed "at least 950 [persons] day & night". Many of these were children, who, alongside adults, worked twelve hours a day for six days a week; in Manchester mills in 1816 the average working day was fourteen hours, including the time taken for meals.

The early English spinning mills were rectangular masonry boxes with timber beams and posts supporting several floors, a structural system that had descended through the centuries from Roman tenements, Hanseatic warehouses and metropolitan lofts.

Factories on the Arkwright scale were not usual. More typical were those at Keighley, which in 1816 had "twenty to thirty mills on one little brook", or at Oldham, where "many [mills] are made from cottages, a steam-engine attached to them, and rooms laid together". It was amongst these small factories that the worst working conditions were found. The early timber-framed mills, with machinery containing much wood, lit by oil lamps and candles and filled with highly combustible materials, were most vulnerable to fire.

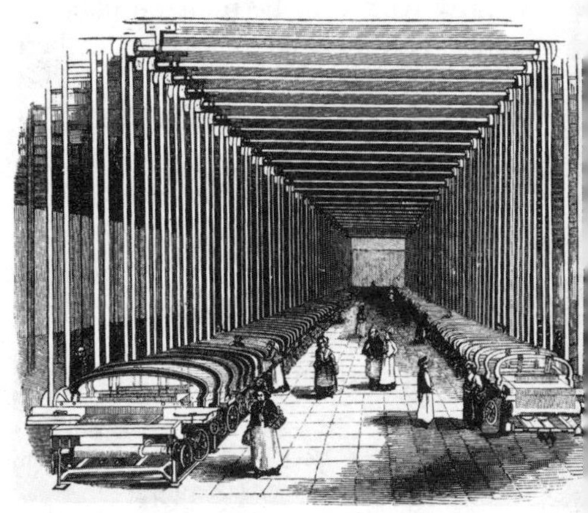

A cotton-weaving factory of the 1840s.

William Strutt, Jedediah's eldest son, pioneered the construction of the first multistorey fire-resistant buildings, with cast iron pillars and beams, hollow-pot and brick-arch floors. From Strutt's Derbyshire experiment, one of the most important technical innovations in building since medieval times, a continuous line of structural development reaches forward to the modern skyscraper.

By the 1790s the steam engine had become sufficiently efficient to be economically used to power mills. Factories

Cars on the production line at the Volkswagenwerk in Wolfsburg, West Germany.

became larger and more concentrated; few now tended to be built on country streams, although some of the earliest mills still survive.

The layout of factories has changed over the years, depending upon the form of power available. Whenever a country begins to industrialise, it is usual to adopt the latest factory design, but Britain, the oldest industrialised country, is fortunate, at least from the historian's point of view, in that all types are still to be seen.

¶ HENNESSEY, R. A. S. *Factories.* 1969; SPENCER, CORNELIA. *More Hands for Man.* 1963

Fahrenheit, Daniel Gabriel (1686–1736)**:** German physicist. Born in Danzig, he lived mainly in England, where he was a Fellow of the Royal Society in 1724, and in Holland. He is best known for his thermometer (1714), the first to employ mercury instead of alcohol. He took zero temperature as that of a freezing mixture of ice and salt and divided the range between that and blood heat into 96 degrees, making the freezing and boiling points of water 32 and 212 degrees. [The centigrade equivalents of these three temperatures are 35·5, 0 and 100 degrees.] Perhaps there were slight inequalities in the bore of his tube, as blood heat is now considered to be 98·4 degrees [36·6 degrees on the centigrade scale].

Fairs and trade exhibitions: large-scale displays to sell goods and promote trade. The word "fair" comes from the Latin *feriae*, a holiday. In the German language the word *Messe* means both a fair and a sacrament. Fairs, that is to say, were originally religious occasions, when people flocked to some particular church or shrine to honour the saint whose day it was.

Wherever people congregate in large numbers there is business to be done. Merchants seized their opportunity, and it was not long before religion at the fairs was running a poor second to trade. Booths were often set up in churchyards, the public scales were affixed to the church wall, and trading frequently overflowed into the church itself.

Shopping conditions in the Middle Ages were such that the fairs filled a very real need. There was a general scarcity of merchandise. No one, even in the cities, carried large stocks or could offer much selection. The fairs were, in effect, department stores where for a few days people had the chance to buy goods that ordinarily would never come their way.

No distinction was made between wholesale and retail. Smiths came to buy iron, clothmakers wool, millers corn. The poor made their modest purchases – a cooking pot, a length of hempen homespun, a bit of stockfish. Stewards of great houses laid in supplies of French wines and salt cod, wax and tallow for candles, rushes for the floor. Ladies bought needles and gold-wire frames for their towering headresses.

One advantage of the fairs was that in a dangerous age they held out the prospect of peaceful commerce. A fair was itself a valuable property, a privilege granted by

Bartholomew Fair, 1721.

the king to a nobleman, church or monastery or a town. Rents and taxes were levied on the traders, and in return the owner of the fair saw that the King's Peace was kept. A tribunal known as the Pie-Powder Court (from *pieds-poudrés*, the dusty feet of the travelling merchants) settled civil disputes arising out of the trading.

After business, entertainment. Acrobats, clowns, ballad-singers and puppeteers went from fair to fair, medieval equivalents of the Victorian vaudeville performers who made the rounds of the music halls. The amusement aspect is the one feature of the medieval open-air fair that still survives.

Fairs have a long ancestry and not only in Europe. The fair at Mecca, for example, that great gathering place of Muslim pilgrims, was famous throughout Islam. The earliest European fairs of which we have any record were those held at Champagne and Brie in France in the 5th century. Under the Emperor Charlemagne (742–814) the Troyes fair became one of the most important in Europe. Troy-weight, its system of weights, was adopted in England during the 14th century. The principal English fair, at Stourbridge, outside Cambridge, received its charter in 1211. The great Russian fair of Nijni-Novgorod dates from the 17th century.

The Leipzig fair, first held in the 12th century, came to specialise in furs and leather, linens, woollens and glassware. Later it became an annual showcase for the German book trade. Today, with the city situated in the Soviet satellite country of East Germany, its fair continues to be one of the surviving trade links between Eastern and Western Europe.

In England, the Fairs Act of 1871 led to the abolition of many fairs on the grounds that they had outlived their usefulness and encouraged "grievous immorality". They were, in any case, bound to decrease with the growth of industrial centres and the development of commerce and communications.

They have survived nevertheless, in changed form, and not only as fun fairs. They are now more often called exhibitions. On a small scale, exhibitions in this sense are trade promotions undertaken by a single industry or group of industries. On a large scale, they aim at covering a nation's activities – industrial, commercial and cultural – are government sponsored and are mounted for reasons that may be economic, political or even psychological. The 1951 Festival of Britain, for example, was devised, in large measure, as a morale booster for a population wearied by war and the grey years of rationing.

The French were the pioneers of industrial exhibitions: the first Paris *Exposition* took place in 1798. The first comprehensive national exhibition was the Great Exhibition of 1851, staged in London. It was also possibly the only one of its kind to make a profit. The Exhibition, which took place in Hyde Park, was housed in the glass and iron building that became known as the Crystal Palace. The plans for the building were drawn up by Joseph Paxton (1801–65), who, as head gardener to the sixth Duke of Devonshire, knew all about designing conservatories. The Crystal Palace was made of prefabricated

The opening of the Great Exhibition, 1851.

parts and is therefore doubly noteworthy as an early and inspired example of an industrial technique widely employed today. After the Exhibition the structure was removed to Sydenham Hill, in south-east London, where it was destroyed by fire in 1936.

The desire to include some exciting, eye-catching construction in plans for national exhibitions has resulted in a richly varied architectural legacy for the countries concerned. The Palace of the Trocadero originally housed the Paris *Exposition* of 1878, and the Eiffel Tower, that symbol of Paris, is a souvenir of the *Exposition* of

The Eiffel Tower, built in 1889.

1889. Wembley Stadium was erected for the British Empire Exhibition of 1924 and 1925, and the Festival Hall on the south bank of the Thames was built for the 1951 Festival of Britain.

The largest fair ever held was in 1939 at Flushing Meadows Park, Queens Borough, Long Island, New York. It covered over 1,200 acres [485 hectares] and attracted nearly twenty-six million visitors. The most spectacular example of recent years was "Expo 67", the Universal and International Exhibition which occupied a 700-acre [283 hectares] site at Montreal, Canada, and was mounted by sixty-two nations.

"Expo '70", staged in Osaka, Japan, provided striking evidence of Japan's emergence as a major industrial nation in the modern world.

¶ WILKINS, FRANCES. *Fairs.* 1967

Fakir: name commonly applied to Muslim or Hindu religious beggars, dependent on alms for their livelihood. Some, such as the Hindu Yogis or the Muslim Chishtis, belong to established religious orders; others are independent. They often practise remarkable austerities and have sometimes achieved the complete subjection of their body to their will.

Falconry: the art of training and flying hawks for the purpose of catching other birds and game. Falconry or hawking was introduced into England as early as the 8th century, and became a popular outdoor amusement for the upper classes. From the 11th century onwards the pursuit became particularly fashionable, and knowledge of its special vocabulary was essential for the nobleman.

The training of the birds was in charge of the falconers, who kept their charges in cages called mews. A list of the most favoured variety of hawks in the time of Charles I can be found in Izaak Walton's *Compleat Angler*. When a hawk was not flying at game, it was hoodwinked with a hood or cap. The decline of falconry was brought about by the perfecting of the hand-gun, and a few years after the end of the 17th century it was little practised.

Spasmodic attempts have been made to revive the sport, and recently it has been put to some practical use by flying falcons against gulls which, on occasion, have damaged fast-flying aircraft.

Falkland Islands: British colony in South Atlantic 800 km NE of Cape Horn claimed by Argentina and known as the Malvinas. Early in 1982 Argentine military forces occupied the islands; Britain reacted by sending a military (naval) task force and in the subsequent Falklands War (April–June 1982) the British defeated the Argentinians and regained control of the islands. The population is about 1800, the main occupation is sheep rearing.

Famine: extreme and widespread scarcity of food, generally following upon a failure of crops or their destruction before they can be harvested. History abounds in horrific examples, brought about by such natural catastrophes as droughts, floods, earthquakes and insect pests or by the man-made ravages of war.

India, dependent for its vital rice crop on the sometimes capricious advent of the monsoon rains has, over the centuries, been particularly vulnerable. In Bengal in 1943, one and a half million people died of starvation or of the epidemics that struck at the hunger-weakened population. The worst famine in recorded history is probably that which caused 9,500,000 deaths in northern China between February 1877 and September 1878.

In the past famine was by no means unknown in Europe. In AD 272 the British are recorded as being reduced to eating the bark of trees. The year 1016 saw a widespread famine throughout the continent of Europe. The French Revolution began in 1789, significantly a year of famine in France. The Irish famine of 1846, caused by a blight that attacked the potato crop, resulted in a million deaths and a great exodus of Irish people to the USA.

Improved methods of agriculture, irrigation and pest control have done much to reduce the incidence of famine. Thanks to modern communications, food can be rushed to famine areas. From August 1921 to July 1923 the American Relief Administration was reckoned to have saved 20 million people in the USSR from famine and ensuing diseases. Voluntary organisations, such as Oxfam and the Red Cross, have made great contributions. The United Nations, through its Food and Agricultural Organisation and its scheme for technical assistance to underdeveloped countries, has also done much and offers the best hope for the future.

A harder problem is presented by those famines – such as that arising out of the Nigerian-Biafran civil war (1967–69) – caused not by natural forces but by man's own deliberate act.

¶ EISENBERG, A. *Feeding the World.* 1966

Farnese, family of: robber-barons, Frankish or Lombard, from Farnese Castle on Lake Bolsena in central Italy. They led the Guelph faction in Orvieto and periodically commanded Papal armies. Giulia Farnese, mistress of Pope Alexander VI, secured a cardinal's hat for her brother Alessandro (1468–1549). He became Pope Paul III in 1534 and combined far-sighted reform of the Church with unblushing advancement of his family. His son Pier Luigi (1503–47) he made duke of Parma and lord of other Papal fiefs. His grandson Alessandro (1520–89) he made cardinal at the age of fourteen. His great-grandson Alessandro (1545–92), Duke of Parma and Governor of the Netherlands for Philip II of Spain, was a great soldier and statesman. The male line of Farnese dukes of Parma died out in 1731, but Elizabeth Farnese (1692–1766) used her influence as queen of Spain to install her son Philip in the Duchy.

Fascism: a political movement in Italy, which arose after the First World War. Its leader was Benito Mussolini (1883–1945), who was called the *Duce*. Italy had suffered greatly in the war, and Mussolini and his followers claimed that they would save her from Communism, provide employment for all and make Italy a great nation again. The Fascists adopted as their symbol the *fasces*, a bundle of wooden rods tied round an axe with a strap, which had been the symbol of authority in ancient Rome. They also gave the Roman salute with outstretched arm, wore a blackshirt uniform and used great violence on their opponents. In the election of 1921 they won only thirty seats. Next year, however, the Fascists marched, as an army, on Rome. The king and the premier were frightened by this show of force and gave way to Mussolini, who then became the dictator of Italy. Only one party was allowed, the Fascist party. This continued until the outbreak of the Second World War in 1939, when Italy became the ally of Germany and was ultimately defeated, and Mussolini was executed.

The idea of fascism was taken up by other countries soon after it became established in Italy. The Nazis under Hitler in Germany and the *Falange* under Franco in Spain followed the model of fascism. The word is now used to describe any political movement which aims to set up a dictatorship by force.

¶ CARSTEN, F. L. *The Rise of Fascism.* 1967

Fathers of the Church: the teachers of the Church in the early centuries of the Christian era. These were the men who by their writings, known collectively as Patristic Literature, laid the foundation of the accepted beliefs of the Western and Eastern Churches. Much of their time and thought was directed to refuting the various heresies, or opinions contrary to what the Church held to be the truth, which sprang up from time to time. The Patristic Age, as it is called, is generally reckoned as ending in the West with St Isidore of Seville (d. 636) and in the East with St John Damascene (d. 749). Several of the more important heresies belong to times later than the Patristic Age. (*See* entry on HERESIES.) It must be noted, too, that St Thomas Aquinas (1225–74), perhaps the most influential of all Christian writers, belongs to a much later period.

Probably the most famous of all the Fathers was St Augustine (354–430), Bishop of Hippo in North Africa, who fought against the Pelagian heresy concerning the nature of sin and of grace, said to have originated with Pelagius, monk of York. Augustine's writings, however, of which the principal are the *Confessions* and the *City of God*, touch on wider themes than simply the confrontation of heretics.

Feasts and festivals: days of general celebration and rejoicing, observed annually or at other fixed intervals. The two words are closely akin and of the same derivation, though "feast" has also the secondary idea of a gathering for eating and drinking by a more restricted group.

Observances of this kind are noted even in quite primitive societies, having as their object the winning of favour and protection from the deities who presided over the forces of nature and the means of human existence. The idea of commemorating some person or event is a later development.

Of the many festivals known to us from the pre-Christian era, only a few examples must suffice such as, at Athens, the Panathenaea, the occasion of the procession portrayed on the Elgin Marbles now in the British Museum, or the Saturnalia of the Romans, notorious for loose behaviour. In a purified form, however, the Saturnalia can be traced in some of the

The 1973 May Day celebrations in Red Square, Moscow.

traditional elements of our Christmas celebrations; and, in the same way, many of the old festivals of the pagan tribes of north-west Europe have connections with later observances of the Church. The clearest link of this kind is that between Easter and the Jewish Passover.

In Christian times, apart from the great festivals of Easter and Whitsun, which fall on Sundays, the rest of the week was frequently interrupted by the general observation of the more salient landmarks of the Church's year and of the days attributed to the more prominent of the saints, while local traditions brought round the commemoration of many a minor saint over a more restricted area. This clearly shows the derivation of the word "holiday" from "holy-day" and leads to the conclusion that, at least in medieval times, the working week was more frequently disturbed than is the case today. With the Reformation, the number of such observances was very much reduced in those communities which broke away from the older Churches, and even in those which retained their former loyalties the same process tended to evolve.

Many countries today celebrate festivals of secular as well as religious origin. Such festivals include the celebration of Independence Day (4 July) and Thanksgiving Day (the fourth Thursday in November, commemorating the first harvest of the Pilgrim Fathers) in the USA, and the observance of the November Revolution and of Labour Day (May Day) in the USSR. In England the Easter Monday Bank Holiday is still connected with the calendar of the Church, but from 1970 onwards the Spring Holiday became variable, not falling automatically on the day after Whit Sunday. Christmas Day, although a general holiday, is not, in law, a Bank Holiday.

¶ WATERS, DEREK. *A Book of Festivals.* 1970

Federal government: a form of government agreed on by a number of states who relinquish some sovereignty to a central authority but retain a measure of independence. The United States is governed by a form of federal government, in which power is shared between the member states and the central government. The central or federal government consists of three branches: the executive, the legislative and the judiciary. The first two, represented by the President and by Congress, have wide powers over foreign affairs, overseas trade and the armed forces and also control matters which are too big for any one state to manage by itself or which cut across the boundaries of individual states, such as unemployment, flood control and air traffic. The federal government is centred in Washington, which is not actually in any one of the states but in what is known as the District of Columbia.

Other examples of a form of federal government are the Federated Malay States (Malaya) and the United Arab Emirates (UAE).

Federal Reserve System: the central banking authority of the United States of America. It acts as a fiscal (revenue) agent for the US government and looks after the reserve accounts of commercial banks. It has many of the functions characteristic of the Bank of England. It was established as a result of the financial panic of 1907 and led to an inquiry, chaired by Senator Aldrich, to discover a sound monetary system for the country. In 1913 a Federal Reserve Act was passed, which in turn led to the organising of a central bank system in 1915. The system is controlled by the Federal Reserve Board, consisting of government nominees, first set up in 1936. The Reserve Banks, twelve in all, have the power to influence the member banks in matters of loans to customers.

See also BANKS.

Fenians: members of the Fenian Society (or Irish Republican Brotherhood), formed in the 19th century to overthrow British rule in Ireland by force. It took its name from the Irish word *fiann*, warriors.

During the years 1845 to 1849 Ireland suffered a terrible famine, known as the Great Hunger, in which one million died and nearly another million emigrated to the USA. It was there, in a country which had freed itself from British rule after the American War of Independence, that the Irish emigrants founded the Fenian movement. In 1858 John O'Mahony (1816–77) and his supporters called themselves the Irish Republican Brotherhood: one of them, James Stephens (1824–1901), was given the task of returning to Ireland to prepare for the rising. There was much secret activity for several years, but many English spies managed to get enrolled in the Fenians, and in 1865 the leaders in Ireland were arrested and sent to prison. In this way the Fenian movement failed at the time, but the spirit of revolt lived on and, many years later, its aims were achieved when the Republic of Ireland was declared in 1948.

Ferdinand V, called "the Catholic" (1452–1516)**:** king of Castile 1474–1504; king of Aragon and Sicily 1479–1516 (as Ferdinand II); king of Naples 1504–16 (as Ferdinand III). At the age of seventeen Ferdinand of Aragon married Isabella of Castile, and he worked all his life to make Spain into a single and powerful nation. He drove the Moors out of Granada and later conquered part of North Africa. To ensure loyalty to the true Catholic faith he introduced the Inquisition into Spain, and the first *auto-da-fé* took place in 1481. (The *auto-da-fé*, literally "act of faith", involved the burning of unrepentant heretics and penances for those who had recanted.) He achieved little by his various alliances with the Pope, with England and with Venice, against France and other Italian cities. But he left to his son Charles valuable territory in Italy and the Netherlands, as well as the first settlements on islands in the New World and an orderly and united kingdom in Spain.

Ferdinand V, detail from Adoration of the Madonna, *School of Castile.*

Ferrara, Italy: city-state, among canals and lagoons, in the fertile alluvial plain of the River Po. It was given by the Franks to the Popes but won its independence as a commune, or small administrative division, in the wars of Popes and Emperors. In 1208 it was the first free commune to surrender itself to a hereditary *podesta* (magistrate) when the Guelph family of Este was installed. Under its strong rule, Ferrara flourished as a centre of weaving, corn and cheese production. Its cathedral was built in 1135, the gloomy red, moated castle of the Este in 1385, its university was founded in 1391. Its squares are fringed by palaces of the Este and of the nobles whom they tamed to serve the state. Tournaments and epic poetry flourished in Ferrara. Ariosto (1474–1533) wrote *Or-*

The Este Palace, Ferrara.

lando Furioso there, Savonarola was born there and Guarino taught there. In 1607 the Papacy resumed control, and Ferrara decayed under the neglect and maladministration of Cardinal Legates. Its wheat fields and pastures reverted to swamp.

See also ESTE, FAMILY OF.

Feud: a state of bitter hostility between two families, tribes or clans, often passed down from generation to generation. The underlying cause, as with warfare on a more sophisticated scale, is usually economic. Feuds have always been rife – and still are not extinct – among isolated communities living in inhospitable country, where the possession of sufficient grazing or hunting territory can make all the difference between sustenance and starvation.

The Highland clans in Scotland nourished many notable enmities, culminating in the massacre by the Campbells of the Macdonalds of Glencoe. The feuding hillbillies of Arkansas, USA, have been celebrated in song and story. The *vendetta*, the family dedication to vengeance for a wrong done to one of its members, was – perhaps still is – a significant factor in Corsican life. Famous literary works based on the feud include Shakespeare's *Romeo and Juliet*, and *Lorna Doone* by R. D. Blackmore (1825–1900).

Feudalism: social, economic and political system, prevalent in Europe in the Middle Ages.

In the 19th century Carlyle said that money payments were "the universal sole nexus [i.e. link] of man to man". This is in strong contrast to feudalism, which Maitland defined as "a state of society in which the main social bond is the relation between lord and man, a relation implying on the lord's part protection and defence; on the man's part protection, service and reverence, the service including service in arms". This personal relationship was inextricably connected with the tenure of land, and the word feudalism is derived from the *feodus* or fee, the name given to the land held by a tenant.

The origins of feudalism can be seen in the patron and client relation of ancient Rome and in the organisation of the Germanic tribes described by Tacitus, where the chief (*princeps*) was surrounded by armed companions (*comites*), who were bound to fight for him. In troubled times, when the central government was too weak to protect him, the small landholder found it useful to surrender his land to a more powerful neighbour in return for protection; he then received it again on condition that he performed certain services for his lord. This process was known as commendation.

Feudalism was not a uniform system; its details differed from country to country and even from county to county, but in broad outline it has been likened to a pyramid, with the king at the apex. Immediately below came the tenants in chief, below them came their tenants, and so on in ever larger groups till the base of the pyramid was reached. Thus A might hold his land of B, who held of C, who held of the king. B was *mesne* (intermediate) lord of A but tenant of C; C was *mesne* lord of B but tenant in chief of the king. The service owed by tenant to lord depended on the nature of his tenure. In England there were six tenures: knight services, frankalmoign, grand serjeanty, petty serjeanty, free socage and villeinage.

Knight service was the principal form of tenure, under which the tenant was bound to perform military service for forty days a year within the realm. The tenant in chief held by the service of so many armed knights, which he must bring with him to serve in the king's host. The tenant owed homage and fealty to his lord, and breach of this sacred bond was felony in its earliest sense. If the tenant died, his heir paid a sum (relief) to the lord before entering on his inheritance, and, until this was paid, the lord had primer seisin (first ownership) of the land. If there was no heir the land escheated (reverted) to the lord. If the heir was a male under twenty-one, or a female under fourteen, the lord was entitled to wardship of the heir and also of the land and could sell the heir's hand in marriage to a suitor. Magna Carta confirmed this right but provided against "waste of the land or disparagement of the heir". The lord could also demand an aid (money payment) from his tenant. In 1215 John was compelled to promise that he would exact an aid without the consent of the council of the realm in three cases only: for the knighting of the tenant's eldest son, the marriage of his eldest daughter, or for his own ransom. A tenant also owed suit of court, i.e. he must attend his lord's court.

Frankalmoign was a religious tenure, whereby a monastery or a bishop held land without any service to the lord except that of praying for the soul of the donor.

The tenant in grand serjeantry was bound to do some particular service for the lord, e.g. carry his banner, be his champion, or constable. In petty serjeanty the tenant must provide the lord with a sword or so many arrows. A list of 13th-century serjeanties includes services from a preparer of herbs and from a naperer (who was to provide one tablecloth a year), the provision by a tenant of a roast pork dinner for the king when he hunted in Wychwood Forest, and the strewing of fodder for the king's beasts at Woodstock.

Socage and villeinage were non-military tenures. The service in these cases might consist of a rent payable in money or in kind, or the duty to plough the lord's land three days a year.

The chief defect of continental feudalism was the weakness of the king compared with his over-powerful vassals, with the result that there were frequent private wars between the great lords and even between them and the king. Henry II of England (reigned 1154–89), theoretically a vassal of Louis VII in respect of his French possessions, was in virtual control of a much greater area of France than the king, and there were frequent wars between them. Apart from the regrettable interlude of Stephen's reign, England escaped the worst features of feudalism.

¶ STRAYER, J. E. *Feudalism.* 1965

Field of the Cloth of Gold: the meeting between Henry VIII of England and Francis I of France near Calais in 1520. Both Francis and the emperor Charles V were seeking an alliance with England. Henry was accompanied by his wife Catherine of Aragon, his daughter Mary aged four and Cardinal Wolsey. The personal rivalry between Henry and Francis was considerable, and relations were not improved by Henry losing in a wrestling match with Francis. A Venetian onlooker said, "These sovereigns are not at peace, . . . they hate each other cordially." Despite lavish display and entertainment, from which the event took its name, nothing came of the meeting, principally because Charles V had previously visited England in preparation for an alliance, which soon followed.

¶ RUSSELL, J. G. *The Field of Cloth and Gold: men and manners in 1520.* 1969

Fifteenth Amendment: amendment to the US Constitution, adopted 30 March 1870, declaring that "the right of citizens of the United States shall not be denied or abridged by the United States or by any state on account of race, colour or previous condition of servitude". It was designed to prevent the old slave states excluding the Negro from having a say in the government of his state.

Fifteenth century: the years 1401–1500. It is not so long since historians, striving to impose some kind of order on the disorderly jostle of happenings we call history, were in the habit of parcelling the history of Europe into three neat and quite separate packages. The first package contained the classical history of Greece and Rome, the second, the period between the sack of Rome in 410 and the 15th century. This second period, labelled the Dark, and in its later centuries, the Middle, Ages was conceived of as coming to an abrupt end on 29 May 1453. On that day the Turks captured Constantinople, the scholars of the Eastern Roman Empire fled to Italy, and – according to the "parcels" school of history – modern times, the third package, came into being.

Today we are not content with such a simple view. History is full of loose ends, it spills untidily out of one century into the next. While such events as battles or the death of kings can be unequivocally dated, the less tangible forces that mould men's minds and shape their institutions are part of the gradual process of change that, now fast, now slower, goes on all the time.

"Modern times", then, did not begin in the 15th century. The most one can say with truth is that in that century the winds of change began to blow ever more strongly. The personal and interlocking loyalties of the feudal system gave way increasingly to ideas of nationalism and an impersonal centralised government. Commerce and industry became of greater economic importance than agriculture. Even the Roman Catholic Church, whose position had seemed so impregnable, found itself assailed. In religion, as in the arts and the sciences, people began to ask questions and to refuse to be fobbed off with evasions and half-truths.

All this adds up to what we call, inaccurately, the Renaissance, or "new birth", as if it had not evolved out of the preceding centuries. The Renaissance had been budding for more than a hundred years before the fall of Constantinople, but in the 15th century it came to flower. The Greek scholars who fled from the Turks diffused abroad a philosophy very different from the medieval Christian one that saw all human life as merely a preparation for the next world. The classical manuscripts they brought with them, like others already known in the West, put forward a point of view that has informed all civilised thought ever since – that of the dignity and importance of man.

Ideas, to make their maximum impact, must be widely disseminated. The invention of printing with movable type, therefore, must be accounted an outstanding event of the century. Johannes Gutenberg (*c.* 1398–1468) of Mainz, in Germany, printed his famous "Forty-Two Line

The true Effigies of Iohn Guttemberg Delineated from
the Original Painting at Mentz in Germanie.

Johannes Gutenberg.

Bible" (with forty-two lines to a page) in 1455 (*see* INCUNABULA). The first printed book in English – a collection of legends of ancient Troy – was printed by William Caxton (*c.* 1422–91) in 1476. In 1408, incidentally, on the other side of the world, the Chinese completed what must surely be the largest literary project ever attempted, the Great Encyclopedia of the Emperor Yung Lo. It consisted of no less than 11,100 bulky volumes. Although the Chinese had mastered much of the art of printing centuries before the Europeans, the Encyclopedia was handwritten. Understandably, only three copies were made.

The chief critics of the Church in the 15th century were the Lollards, the followers of the English religious reformer John Wyclif (*c.* 1320–84) and those of the Czech Jan Hus (John Huss, *c.* 1369–1415), the founder of the Moravian Church. Both sects, opposed to the worldliness and materialism inherent in a Church that had become a great political power, sought a return to the simple and spiritual faith of the Bible. For their pains they were denounced as heretics. In 1415 Hus was burnt at the stake, one of the human torches that lit the way to the Reformation. In 1483, in an attempt to stem the tide of history, Tomas de Torquemada (1420–98) was appointed Inquisitor-General of Spain, and the Inquisition became notorious for its refinements of cruelty to suspected heretics.

England entered the 15th century in the middle of its Hundred Years War with France. In 1415, under Henry V, thanks largely to the skill of the English archers, she won a great victory at Agincourt. But the day of the longbow was almost over. The French developed the cannon and fielded an additional and unique weapon in the person of Joan of Arc, the Maid of Orleans (1412–31), whose leadership inspired the French to great efforts and who, betrayed by jealous enemies, died at the stake as a heretic and a witch. In 1456 the verdict was reversed by papal decree, and in 1920, five hundred years later, Joan was declared a saint.

Trial of Joan of Arc from a 15th century mss. by an unknown artist.

By 1453, with the exception of Calais, England had lost all her French possessions and the overseas war was succeeded by the anarchy of civil strife, the Wars of the Roses (1455–85), which ended with the death of the Yorkist Richard III at the Battle of Bosworth Field and the accession of Henry VII, the first of the Tudor kings.

The year 1442 saw the beginning of modern colonialism. In that year the Portuguese established the first European warehouse on the west coast of Africa, at Cape Blanco. Soon they extended their foothold and their profitable trade in African slaves. In 1497 Vasco da Gama (*c.* 1460–1524) rounded the southern tip of Africa and sailed to India.

Leonardo da Vinci's design for a flying machine.

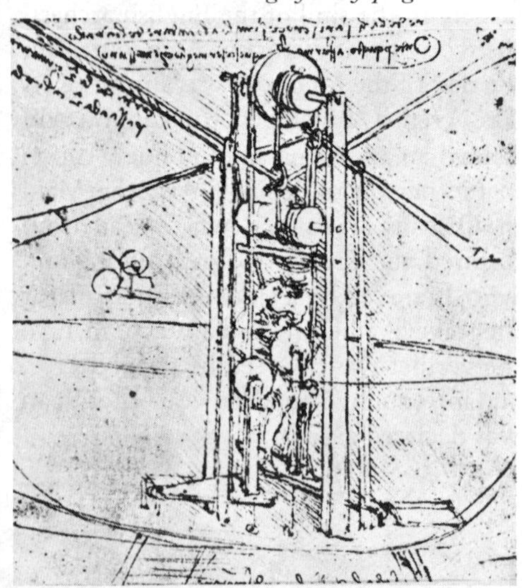

Five years earlier, under the patronage of Spain, an even more momentous voyage had taken place. In 1492 the Genoese Christopher Columbus (1451–1506), with 120 companions, set out westward in three small ships to sail to Japan, and inadvertently discovered the New World.

The century was wonderfully rich in artists, of whom may be especially mentioned the Florentine Sandro Botticelli (1445–1510); the Flemish Jan van Eyck (1390–1441); Albrecht Dürer (1471–1528), the great German painter and engraver; and Leonardo da Vinci (1452–1519), that universal genius, painter, sculptor, architect, musician, engineer and natural philosopher.

¶ HAY, DENYS. *Europe in the Fourteenth and Fifteenth*

See also BIBLE; OTTOMAN EMPIRE; PRINTING; REFORMATION; RENAISSANCE.

Figureheads: decorative carvings adorning the bows of ships.

To the sailor a ship is symbolic of a living creature, and some form of appropriate ornamentation of the prow has existed since very early times. Carved or painted eyes, or *oculi*, supposedly to guide a ship clear of danger, were an early form of bow decoration. Oculi are still to be seen in some craft of the Mediterranean, Indian Ocean and China Sea.

The fighting galleys of ancient Greece and Rome had their rams carved in the form of charging beasts, thus showing their warlike character. The Phoenicians chose a horse emblem, and the Norsemen in the early centuries AD had serpents on the high stems of their "long ships".

With the fitting of the fore and after castles in ships of the Middle Ages, the figurehead temporarily disappeared. In the 15th century bow rails began to be carried forward, forming a beakhead. They were highly decorated and sup-

ported a carved figure on the end. The lion figurehead appeared in Queen Elizabeth's reign and became the standard decoration in smaller ships almost consistently until 1725. Larger ships often had elaborate equestrian figures with supporting groups. The Dutch, Spanish and Scandinavian ships favoured the lion, and the French usually had classical figures. By the end of the 18th century whole figures were becoming popular. In the 19th century most nations displayed portrait figureheads, often female. With the introduction of the straight stem the figurehead disappeared, but surviving examples of the ship carvers' art are to be seen in the maritime museums of Europe and America.

Fiji: Commonwealth country in the south-west Pacific; population 650,000 (1982). Fiji consists of two main forested islands called Viti Levu and Vanua Levu, with a large number of much smaller ones, all situated roughly on latitude 18°S and longitude 180°. The islands were sighted by Tasman in 1643 and were visited by Cook in 1774. Fiji became a British colony in 1874, and standards of living and health were raised by improved transport and the development of cash crops, such as sugar cane, coconuts, and maize. But work on the sugar plantations was not popular, and Indians were brought in from 1879 onwards. They multiplied more rapidly than the Fijians, who are now outnumbered, though their rights are still protected. Fiji attained full independence in 1965.

Filibuster: from a Dutch word meaning a freebooter or pirate. In the USA the term is used colloquially to describe a deliberate obstruction of the business of a legislature by such tactics as the making of time-consuming speeches, sometimes spreading over several days. The term has now been taken over in England.

Fingerprints: impressions left by fingertips. The fine traceries of whorls and loops and lines which ridge the skin of our fingertips stay the same all through our lives. The chances that another's fingers have the same pattern as our own have been estimated at one in 64,000 million. For practical purposes, therefore, fingerprints are both enduring and unique to each individual. Thus they are an invaluable instrument for the identification of criminals. Television and films have made us all familiar with the evasive action of wearing gloves taken by criminals (although a recent advance in forensic science means that this will no longer afford the criminal protection).

In 1823 the Czech physiologist Johannes Purkinje produced a classification of nine types of impressions. In England the study was furthered by the researches of Sir Francis Galton (1822–1911), the founder of the science of heredity which he called eugenics (*see* separate entry). But some inkling of the special quality of fingerprints existed centuries earlier. In many early civilisations a king's thumbprint served for his signature, and, in humbler but equally valid style, the potter frequently thumbprinted his creations. In English legal practice today, the formal phrase that confirms a document under seal, "I deliver this as my act and deed", followed by the pressure of the forefinger on a paper seal, is a possible relic of this ancient practice.

A Finger Print Bureau was set up in Britain in 1901. Scotland Yard, today, has on record some two million sets of fingerprints of persons convicted of criminal offences. In the USA the Identification Division of the Federal Bureau of Investigation holds nearer six million.

Some countries employ fingerprints for wider purposes of identification. All immigrants to the United States, for example, are fingerprinted on their arrival as part of the immigration procedure.

¶ BLOCK, EUGENE B. *Fingerprinting*. 1969; ROWLAND, JOHN. *The Fingerprint Man: Sir Edward Henry*. 1959

Fingerprint records from the FBI in Washington.

Federal Bureau of Investigation
U. S. Department of Justice
J. Edgar Hoover, Director

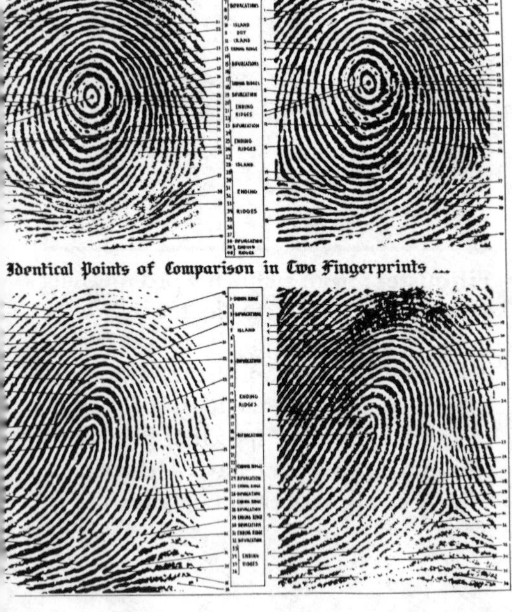

Finland: republic of northern Europe at the head of the Baltic Sea. Finland extends for 720 miles [1,159 kilometres] from north to south and about half that distance from east to west at the widest part; population 4,841,500 (1983). Situated between Sweden and Russia, with very limited access to the sea, it has a fairly wide range of temperature. Its northerly latitude caused a covering of ice until warmer conditions set in some 10,000 years ago. The uneven grinding of the ice resulted in innumerable hollows alternating with deposited matter; thus there are said to be 60,000 lakes, and bogs are widespread.

These physical conditions do not favour the growing of food grains, which have to be largely imported. Pasture, however, is good, and butter is exported. The lakes are connected by many canals, providing cheap but slow transport, except in winter. Timber is one of Finland's chief riches and accounts for a long history of shipbuilding which now includes, appropriately, ice-breakers especially exported to Russia for use along its northern coast. Finland's minerals have yielded little wealth except for the copper of Outokumpu. Her rich nickel resources went to Russia with the ceding of the port and corridor of Petsamo (Pechenga). Power is scanty, since much of the developed hydroelectric power was also lost to Russia, though new sources are springing up in the north.

Finland's intermediary position between Sweden and Russia has greatly affected her history. The Swedes conquered her in the 12th century and brought in strong cultural influences, though the Finns kept control of their own country. In the 19th century Finland was ruled by Russia and lost that control until it was restored after the 1914–18 War. In the Second World War the boggy and lake-strewn character of the country helped the four million Finns to put up a long and brave defence under the leadership of General Mannerheim (1867–1951) against the Russian hordes which invaded in 1939 when the USSR signed a non-aggression pact with Germany and joined in that country's policy of ruthlessly annexing other countries.

As a result of the war, Finland was obliged to surrender to Russia (1) the Petsamo Corridor and thus their outlet to the Arctic Ocean; (2) a wide band of country along the central eastern frontier; and (3) an important area of land in the south, west of Lake Ladoga. Finnish people living in these areas have naturally felt obliged to leave their homes and move into what is left of their own country.

In the circumstances described it is perhaps fortunate that Finns and Russians are not brought into close economic con-

Coffee table in laminated birch by the Finnish architect Alvar Aalto, 1947.

tact, and that social relations are not subjected to great strain. There is indeed a fairly strong Communist party, but the natural trade association is with the Scandinavian countries surrounding the Baltic – countries with which Finns also have the protestant religion in common. Indeed, Helsinki has two Lutheran churches side by side, one for Finnish-speaking worshippers and the other for Swedish-speaking. Thus, both languages are fully recognised. Finns also share with other Scandinavians great skill in craftsmanship and design and enjoy a far higher standard of living than the Russians.

See EUROPE for map.

Fire-arms: portable weapons firing shot or bullets. A "hand-gonne" was part of the armament of an English ship in 1338. It was an iron tube, fixed to a pole held under the arm and fired manually by a slowmatch applied to the touch-hole. By the mid-15th century the match was held in a "serpentine" which was lowered to the touch-hole by a trigger. This matchlock was the standard military musket until the late 17th century. It lacked the range, accuracy and rate of discharge of the longbow, but its ball penetrated plate-armour and a musketeer did not require years of practice. By the time of the Armada the longbow was obsolete.

The slowmatch was unreliable in rain,

its glow showed up at night and its sparks were dangerous near powder-barrels. The wheel-lock, producing sparks by a spring-rotated wheel scraping against a pyrite block, was much better but very expensive. By the 18th century both had been replaced by the flintlock (a type of gun-lock that ignites the charge of powder by means of sparks created by a piece of flint striking a metal striking plate). The flintlock was the supreme firearm in Europe from the late 17th until the early 19th century. The affectionate name "Brown Bess" is used to describe all types of British flintlocks made from 1720 to 1840.

Brown Bess was a smoothbore musket weighing about 11 lb [4·9 kilograms]. It fired lead bullets weighing one ounce [28·3 grams] and made by each soldier in his own bullet mould. A slow-burning coarse blac.. gunpowder was used which necessitated a large charge and also a long barrel 39 to 42 inches [1000 to 1070 millimetres]. To allow for deposits of half-burnt powder left inside, the barrel had to be made larger tha . the bullet. This meant that, although the weapon's maximum range was 300 yards [274 metres], it was inaccurate beyond 50 [46]. The rate of misfires averaged two in thirteen even in fine weather, and the flint had to be replaced every twenty rounds. Thus Brown Bess was only really effective when fired in volleys with the men shoulder to shoulder.

The percussion-cap lock, in which the spark is produced by the impact of the hammer on a small tube filled with fulminate of mercury, was invented about 1805. By the 1860s the cap was incorporated in the base of a fixed cartridge and detonated by a firing-pin.

A dead shot with a smooth-bore musket would be lucky to hit a single man 80 yards [73 metres] away. A rifled barrel was more accurate to a longer range, but difficult to load as the ball had to fit the grooves and be hammered down the barrel.

In theory the solution was to load at the breech, but the manufacture of a gastight breech defeated the gunsmiths of the 16th and 17th centuries. The ingenious dodge of wrapping the ball in a greased patch, which took the rifling but allowed easy loading, made the muzzle-loading rifle a practicable proposition in the 18th century. Early European rifles, with a bore of about 0·85 inches [31 millimetres] designed for smashing through a breastplate or a charging boar, were too heavy for the American frontier, where Pennsylvanian gunsmiths perfected a rifle with a long barrel, a small ball under 0·5 inches [3·85 millimetres], and a light charge. This was a wonderful weapon, deadly against an Indian, a redcoat or a deer up to 300 yards [274 metres].

Although the principle of the revolver was thought of three hundred years

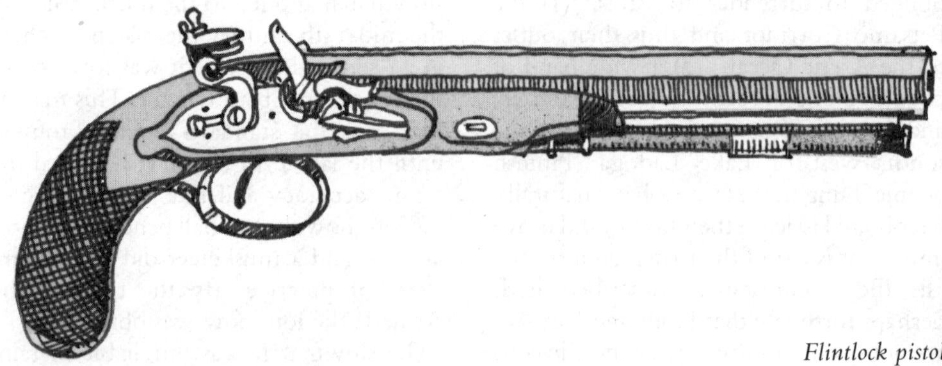

Flintlock pistol.

earlier, the difficulties of manufacture were first overcome by Samuel Colt of Connecticut in 1835. His Dragoon (1848) and later models were rugged, accurate, hard-hitting and cheap. Being mass-produced, broken parts could be replaced in any frontier store. The first efficient breech-loading, repeating rifle, the Winchester, also made its debut in the West.

The modern military rifle was produced in the late 19th century by a combination of the Mauser bolt-action, a smokeless propellent more powerful than gunpowder, and a nickel-coated bullet which did not, like lead, strip in the rifling when fired at a high velocity. The magazine-rifle with its flat trajectory, high rate of fire and no smoke to betray the rifleman's position revolutionised war. In two world wars various automatic loading devices further enhanced the deadliness of the "hand-gonne". *See also* ARTILLERY, etc.

Fire brigades (England)**:** bodies of men trained and equipped to fight fires. The formation of organised groups to fight fires as and when they occurred seems to be of remote antiquity. In AD 112 Pliny wrote from Bithynia, where he had been sent as governor, to the Emperor Trajan, discussing whether it was right to form fire brigades of up to 150 men; Augustus organised an official brigade in Rome, thus defeating an earlier ingenious swindle by Crassus, who ran a private fire brigade and used it to save burning property which he had just bought at give-away prices from the terrified owners. But, though fire fighting apparatus seems to have been in use as early as the second century BC, it had still not developed to any considerable extent almost two millennia later, when, for example, only hand-operated fire engines were available to fight the Great Fire of London in 1666. During the 18th century fire engines were mounted on wheels but were almost exclusively both

Modern fire brigade in action.

hand-pumped and hand-hauled, so that they were slow to reach fires and lacked a strong flow of water at fire sites. Steam power was applied to fire engines early in the 19th century, the power being applied to the water pump only and the engine itself being still drawn by men or horses, but early in the second half of the century steam fire engines were being manufactured in England and abroad, and the application of steam power to drive road vehicles was successfully experimented with in this as in other fields. The makers of such engines found a particularly good outlet for their products in the various international trade exhibitions which were popular during that period.

The introduction of the internal combustion engine for road transport purposes enabled the steam or horse-drawn engine to be replaced by a more adaptable and constantly ready vehicle, and the first of such fire engines, with both pumps and traction powered by petrol motors, appeared about 1903.

During the first quarter of the present century the centrifugal pump was recognised as being superior in efficiency to the piston or rotary-gear fire pump and was used in all the new larger fire engines. The use of mechanical fire extinguishers became popular for a time, although generally displaced by 1930 by ordinary water tanks, except for purposes requiring the use of special fire fighting equipment. Portable chemical extinguishers have become of much greater significance as emergency fire fighters. Most modern fire fighting apparatus contains some form of fire escape, and it is the duty of the firemen both to fight the fire and manipulate this and other life-saving equipment.

¶ BROWN, ROY and W. STUART THOMSON. *The Battle against Fire*. 1966; RICKARDS, MAURICE. *The World Fights Fire*. 1971

Fireships: small vessels, often merchantmen or prizes, which were filled with pitch, faggots and gunpowder, and grappled and burnt enemy ships. In action they sailed in the shelter of ships of the line awaiting a chance to descend on a disabled enemy. Frigates and ketches screened their approach to the enemy and covered the escape of their crews in boats. Their captains were expected to grapple the enemy and fire the ships before leaving and fully deserved the gold medal awarded for successful attempts. Enemy frigates and boats tried to grapple and tow the fireships clear. Used with dramatic effect by the Dutch at Antwerp in 1585 and by the English to dislodge the Armada from Calais in 1588, they became the most feared weapon of 17th-century sea warfare. Like torpedo boats they were small, destructive and vulnerable. As gunnery and ship-handling improved in the 18th century, fireships became less effective.

Flags: pieces of material, generally with a pattern or device, used for identification or display. From earliest times kings and peoples have used emblems to identify themselves for military or ceremonial occasions. The Greeks, for instance, were said to have used in battle ensigns or flags bearing devices associated with the city to which they belonged. From the 12th cen-

Fireships attacking the Spanish Armada, 1588.

tury, with the development of heraldry in Europe, the use of special symbols, devices and emblems on flags became widespread. Various types of flags displayed the arms of individuals, devices of cities and, most important of all, emblems of the sovereigns which became associated with the countries they ruled. The heraldic devices are now governed by precise rules, and there is a code which sets out the correct manner of displaying flags.

The term standard refers to the long tapering flag used in battle, under which the lord mustered his followers. The modern survival of the standard can be recognised in the various regimental colours with their badges and scrolls bearing the names of battle honours.

¶ CAMPBELL, GORDON and EVANS, I. O. *The Book of Flags*. 1971

See also BANNER, STARS AND STRIPES, UNION JACK, etc.

Flanders: former countship of Europe on the North Sea. Flanders is a vanished country whose ghost obstinately refuses to be laid. Today its name survives in two of the provinces of Belgium, East Flanders and West Flanders. Its chequered history is one of subjection to one great power after another until, in 1831, it became part of modern Belgium. Yet although Flanders has not, since 1382, existed as a separate state, 55 per cent of the people of Belgium speak Flemish (a language which, written, is the same as Dutch but is spoken with a different pronunciation), while a national pride in the brilliant cultural tradition of Flanders is still very much alive.

The ancient land of Flanders included, as well as the Belgian provinces, part of the Dutch provinces of Zeeland and a large area of north-west France, ruled by Counts who, apart from their formal homage to the French king, were virtually independent. The first Count, Baldwin Bras-de-Fer (Iron-Arm), is said to have introduced the industry that over the centuries brought Flanders fame and prosperity – that of cloth manufacturing.

Trade and art were the two great Flemish talents. In the Middle Ages bustling cities such as Bruges, Ghent and Leuven (Louvain) grew up, adorned with fine buildings. Flemish cloths, laces and tapestries became famous throughout Europe. Flemish painting in the 15th century was outstanding, combining uncompromising realism with a most exquisite delicacy of detail (*see* next entry).

Flanders came successively under the domination of Burgundy, Austria and Spain. The Flemings, talented and hardworking, by those very talents compromised their own freedom. They had made their country into a prize too valuable to be left to its own devices. Unfortunately,

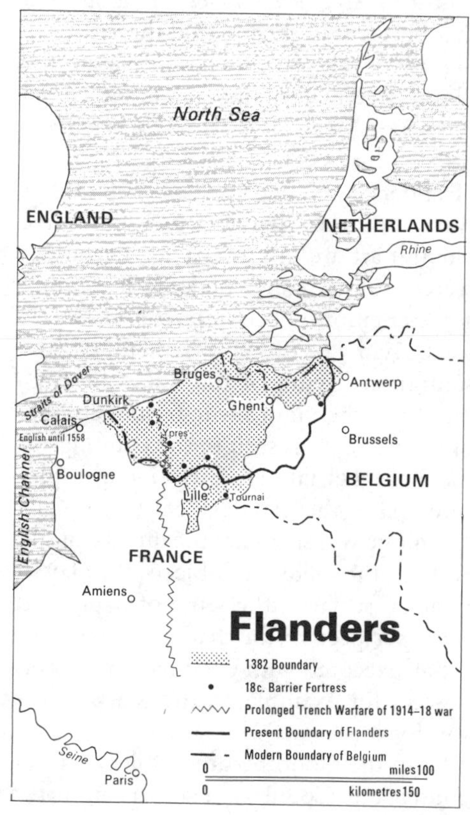

they weakened their national unity by local rivalries between the great cities. All attempts to free themselves from the foreign yoke came to nothing.

In 1648 the north-western portion of Flanders became part of what is now Holland. During the 17th century large areas were incorporated into France, which, during the French Revolution, swallowed the rest. After the fall of Napoleon Flanders, together with the other Belgic provinces, was united with Holland to form the Kingdom of the Netherlands. In 1830 a rising against Dutch rule led to the setting up of modern Belgium.

See also BELGIUM; BURGUNDY.

Flemish art: the work produced by the artists of Flanders. Flemish art flourished chiefly during the 15th, 16th and 17th centuries AD; nevertheless, it is known that before this great period the arts were highly developed, for example in the illuminated manuscripts and in the carved ivories of Liège, as early as the 11th and 12th centuries.

Flanders was overrun by continuous wars, but the characteristics of native Flemish art are unmistakable. The artists were realists concerned with faithful representation. Their interests in people were vividly recorded, whether it was the sumptuous living of the dukes of Burgundy or the vigorous festivities and life of the peasants as seen in the paintings of the Brueghel family. Early Flemish pictures have the richness of jewels. The technique was such that the quality of silk and fur, the solidity of objects, the play of light on surfaces, the sense of depth and aerial perspective, the characters of people, are all executed with great truth and skill, as seen, for example, in the work of Jan van Eyck (d. 1441).

Philip the Good became Duke of Burgundy and Count of Flanders in 1419. He was followed in 1468 by Charles the Bold. Both men were strong patrons of the arts. Artists on salaries were attached to their households and those of rich nobles and prelates. They were made *peintre et valet de chambre* and were expected not only to paint but to design anything necessary for ceremonial pageants and festive occasions. They were sent to foreign countries and might even play the rôle of secret agents, sometimes making, for example, drawings of fortifications. Some went on diplomatic missions as part of their duty. Hubert van Eyck (d. 1426) was employed by the Duke on several occasions; and in 1629 Peter Paul Rubens (1577–1640) was sent as an envoy to England to the court of Charles I, who knighted him.

Young artists were apprenticed to experienced painters and worked under them until they were qualified for the title of "Master" and could then practise their craft independently. The strict regulations of the Guilds helped to establish the quality of Flemish work and safeguarded its high standards in the prosperous international trade in objects of art.

Hubert van Eyck was court painter to Duke Philip and had an *atelier* (school) in Ghent. He started the famous altar piece now in S. Bavon, Ghent, *The Adoration of the Mystic Lamb*, which was finished by Jan van Eyck, who is known also for his painting of Jan Arnolfini and his wife, now in the National Gallery, London.

Among other outstanding artists were the versatile Hans Memling, or Memlinc (*c.* 1430–94); Dirk Bouts (*c.* 1415–75); Rogier van der Weyden (1400–64); Hieronymus Bosch (1450–1516), master of grotesque painting; the several members of the talented Brueghel family (living between 1525 and 1638); and Marcus Geeraerts (1561–1635), who came to England in 1568.

Rubens (1577–1640) was one of the

world's supreme painters. He studied in Italy and returned in 1609, setting up a thriving painting establishment in his elegant house in Antwerp. Among the artists who worked for him were Lucas van Uden (1595–1672), the landscape painter and engraver, and Anthony van Dyck (1599–1641), who came to England on the invitation of the Earl of Arundel and became court painter to Charles I. He too, was knighted. His portraits of royalty and the court are world-famous. It is interesting, as an example of teamwork, that van Dyck often used another Flemish painter, Hendrik van Steenwyck, well known for his skilful church interiors, to paint in his architectural detail.

While the Flemish painters of the 15th to 17th centuries are so renowned, the contributions of other craftsmen must not be forgotten: the skill of the sculptors, goldsmiths, tapestry weavers and wood carvers; the supreme achievements of the masons who built the town halls and guildhalls, including the Cloth Hall at Ypres; the soaring cathedrals and churches of Liège, Nivelles, Tournai, Brussels and Antwerp among many other places.

¶ LASSAIGNE, J. *Flemish Painting (2 vols.)*. 1957–8; MARTIN, GREGORY. *Flemish Painting*. 1964

Flints: pieces of hard silica, occurring in nodular form in chalk. The origin of flint has not been determined, but in certain instances it originates from the intake by marine organisms of silica from the water in which the chalk was laid down.

"Flints" is a term used colloquially of implements made from flint by men. The flint used can be of a variety of colours, depending upon its purity and the action of outside mineral agents. From a historical viewpoint, the most important characteristic of flint is that it is fractured easily by percussion, by pressure or by changes in temperature. When a piece of flint is struck a sharp blow on a limited part of its surface, it breaks so that a flake comes off; a continuing process of flaking can provide both a shaped core and a number of flakes which can themselves be chipped to provide a variety of working instruments. Nature is, of course, capable of providing the circumstances which chip flints, and it is sometimes difficult to differentiate between a very primitive man-made implement and one which is purely natural; but by the time of the later Palaeolithic (Old Stone Age) period in Europe very finely shaped flint instruments were being manufactured, probably on a commercial scale, and during the succeeding Mesolithic (Middle Stone Age) period minute implements of great exactitude and fineness of workmanship were produced, being succeeded in the Neolithic (New Stone Age) period by really beautiful specimens of workmanship, showing an advanced ability to manufacture and distribute on a complicated commercial scale.

The use of flint is not confined to primitive man. Before the commercial manufacture of matches in the 19th century, the spark struck from steel and flint and dropped on tinder was the normal domestic method of obtaining flame; and the flint lighter is still used by smokers.

Flint can also be split by pressure flaking: the Australian aboriginal, who, like numbers of primitive people, still uses flint tools, is able to use the sole of his foot to remove a small flake. Pressure flaking, again, is a process which can occur naturally. Flint can additionally be split by temperature changes, although this is a method seldom used in the making of flint implements.

While man used flint from a very early period for the manufacture of his tools, owing to its ability to produce a fine and wearing cutting surface, he did of course use stones of other varieties, although

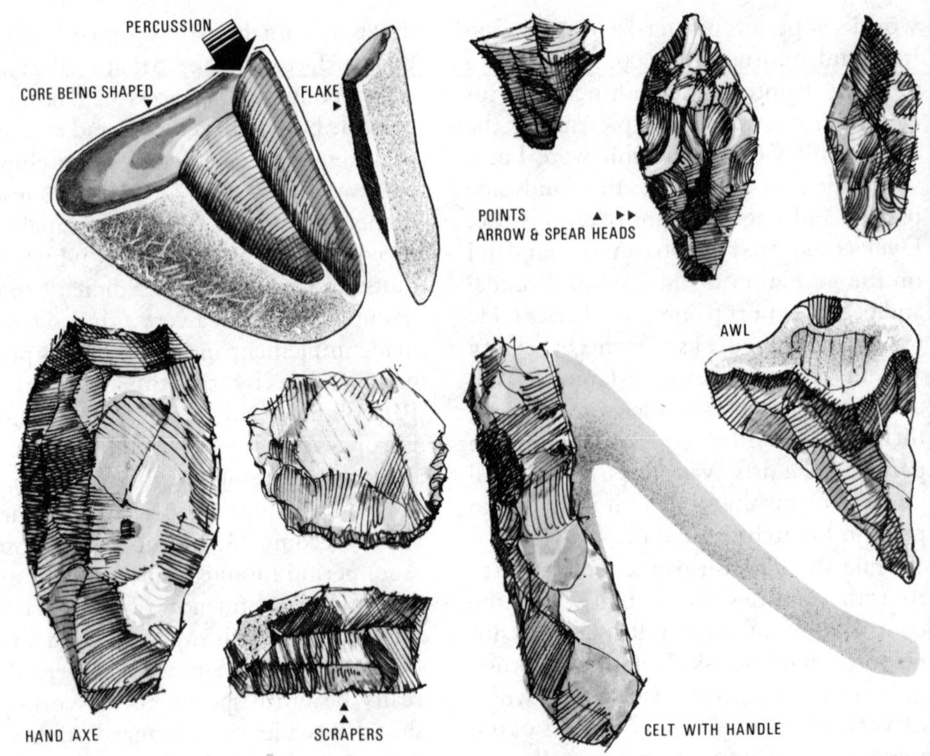

nothing quite approached flint in its ability to fracture.

Flints are divided by the archaeologist into a number of types, of which the following are the principal:

SCRAPERS, with sharp convex edges

POINTS, some possibly used for spear heads

AWLS, with a point carefully prepared all round

HAND AXES, varying from the earlier pear shape to the later flat and oval patterns

CELTS, using a grinding and polishing technique for the preparation of the tool and with only one cutting surface

ARROW HEADS, in which class some of the most beautifully executed of flint implements appear. The archaeologist has to be aware of the great numbers of arrow heads (in particular) which were manufactured during the 19th century for sale to credulous antiquaries of that period.

Florence: city of Tuscany, north central Italy, deriving its name from *Florentia*, town of flowers. It is one of the loveliest cities in the world, and its collection of art treasures is second only to those in Rome. Nowhere are there so many beautiful churches and fine buildings grouped in such a small area, set between narrow streets flanked with tall solid *palazze* built by rich Florentine families such as the Medici, the international bankers. In the 15th century, during the Renaissance, Lorenzo, the greatest of the family, gave generous encouragement to the arts.

The artists and craftsmen of Florence are the subject of the next article; among her other famous men were the poet Dante (1265–1321) and the Dominican religious reformer Savonarola (1452–98) (*see* separate entries).

Though declared an "open city" in World War II (and, therefore, immune from attack under international law), Florence did, in fact, suffer some damage, particularly to its bridges. A much greater disaster was the devastation of buildings and art treasures by the flooding of the River Arno in 1966.

¶ SCHEVILL, F. *History of Florence*. 1961
See also ITALY; MEDICI, etc.

Florentine art: the painting, sculpture and architecture characteristic of Florence.

As Florence became the strongest and richest town in the centre of Italy, it also became the centre of new ideas and the intellectual capital of the world in the 15th century. The early Renaissance, the age of re-awakening of thought, seeking after fresh ideals in literature, in sculpture, in architecture and in painting, was centred in Florence. The rich and powerful patrons, Cosimo de Medici (1389–1464) and his grandson Lorenzo the Magnificent (1448–92), encouraged artistic development and employed artists and craftsmen of every kind.

Painting in the 13th century was overshadowed by Byzantine formalism, and the first reaction against this is seen in the work of the Florentine painter Cimabue (1240–1303), who broke from the rigid traditions and gave understanding, humanity and strength to his figures and their setting, as can be seen in the fresco of the Basilica of St Francis of Assisi. Cimabue showed the way to Giotto (1266–1337), who went further and brought human expression and a spiritual quality to the people he portrayed. His frescoes in Assisi, Padua and in Santa Croce in Florence show that he was one of the world's greatest artists, whom many regard as the precursor of modern art. Although Andrea Orcagna (*c.* 1308–*c.* 1368) and Fra Angelico (1387–1455) must be singled out as great painters in the 14th and 15th centuries, for a hundred years after Giotto there was no one to equal him. He was an all-round genius, an architect and sculptor as well as a painter. One of the landmarks in Florence is the bell tower of the Cathedral, by Giotto and decorated with exquisite bas reliefs.

In northern Europe, architecture was dominated by what is known as the Gothic style, but Italy was not much affected by its influence. Rather, the study of ancient ruins throughout Italy made the Italians greatly interested in classical art. There was an outburst of architectural activity in the 14th and 15th centuries, and Filippo Brunelleschi (1377–1446) designed many famous buildings, including the cathedral of S. Maria del Fiori, with its masterly ribbed construction for the dome, the Medici Chapel of S. Lorenzo, the Palazzo Pitti and the Foundling Hospital. The other two great masters of the early Renaissance were Donatello and Masaccio. Donatello (1386–1466) was the greatest Florentine sculptor before Michelangelo. His achievements include the great statue of St George and his magnificent bronze figure of David. His greatest work, however, was probably done, not in Florence, but in Padua, where he spent ten years from 1443–53. His statues have a realism, dignity and power unknown before. Masaccio (1401–28) revived a grandeur in painting which had not been known since Giotto. In a short career he gave to Florentine painting a new mastery of linear perspective and a tonal quality that was at once inspired, restrained and full of humanity. This is nowhere better seen than in the church of S. Maria del Carmine in Florence.

The revolutionary thought of the early Renaissance resulted in great technical advances and encouraged a spirit of enquiry that the Florentine painters were ready to express in art. Among notable painters at the beginning of the 15th century were Fra Angelico (1387–1455), some of whose paintings can be seen in the cells of the monastery of San Marco in

Florence; Uccello (1400–75), known for his experiments with perspective as in his *Rout of San Romano* to be seen in the National Gallery, London; and Benozzo Gozzoli (1421–75), pupil of Fra Angelico and painter of the *Adoration of the Magi* in the Riccardi Chapel of the Medici family.

These painters were followed by others who studied in particular the movement of the naked male body, the important motive of much late Renaissance art, including that of the brothers Pollaiuolo (*c.* 1460). Sandro Botticelli (1444–1510) opened up a new world of painting with his lyrical compositions of *The Birth of Venus* and *Primavera*. He and Antonio Pollaiuolo (1429–98) and Verrochio (1435–88) began their careers as sculptors, carvers or goldsmiths.

As three great masters influenced the beginning of the century, so three others born in the second half and working into the 16th century achieved a worldwide reputation and influence – Leonardo da Vinci (1452–1519), scientist, engineer, architect, musician, writer and painter; Michelangelo (1475–1564), painter, sculptor, architect and poet; and Raphael (1483–1520), painter and architect.

Leonardo, the all-round genius and pupil of Verrocchio, has left few paintings, but his work shows a unity, a depth of understanding, a grace and feeling for atmosphere, as for example in the *Virgin of the Rocks*, that made Bernard Berenson declare, "He has left all of us heirs to one or two of the supremest works of art ever created". As a designer and engineer he had revolutionary ideas about the construction of bridges and catapults and other engines of war. Giorgio Vasari (1511–74), writing at the time, says: "The spirit of Leonardo, which was most divine, conscious that he could attain to no greater honour, departed in the arms of the monarch (King Francis I), being at that time in the seventy-fifth year of his age."

Michelangelo was another artist of great versatility, a sculptor unequalled for his powerful rendering of the human form, and commissioned to work for Lorenzo de Medici. His genius is also revealed in the remarkable frescoes in the Sistine Chapel – a stupendous work in which he painted scenes from the Old Testament, bringing sculptured form into painting. To quote Berenson again: ". . . in him, the last of his race, born in conditions artistically most propitious, all energies remaining in his stock were concentrated, and in him Florentine art had its logical conclusion."

Raphael was little more than thirty years old when he was appointed chief architect of St Peter's, Rome. His paintings and tapestry designs are marked by a masterly sense of composition and sensitive use of colour; and his portraits are among the earliest in European art to explore the character of the sitters as well as their external appearance.

¶ ANTAL, F. *Florentine Painting*. 1947; BERTRAM, A. *Florentine Sculpture*. 1969

See also FOURTEENTH CENTURY, etc.

Aurora, sculpture in the Medici Chapel, Florence, by Michelangelo.

Font: in churches and chapels, the basin holding the water used in the ceremony of baptism. This involves a symbolic washing away of sin, and in early times, when adult baptism by immersion (which still obtains in certain branches of the church) was the normal practice, a tank, cistern or natural pool was used. The word *fons* in Latin means a spring. As the habit of infant baptism, whether by immersion or, later, by affusion (the pouring of water onto the head), became more commonly adopted, it was necessary to provide a vessel to contain the consecrated water at a height convenient to the priest, holding the child in his arms and performing the ceremony in the presence of the parents, the godparents and, ideally, the general congregation.

Traditionally the font is placed near the door of the church as signifying that baptism is a ceremony of admission, but this is by no means always the case. With large churches and cathedrals the baptistery is sometimes a separate building.

Fontainebleau: French town some thirty-five miles [56 kilometres] south of Paris, with a population of about 23,000 people. It is closely associated with a château which began as a hunting lodge in the Forèt de Fontainebleau but became a fine royal residence in 1528 under Francis I. It was in this château that Hitler celebrated the fall of France in 1940 and, later, that the Western allies established their headquarters in 1945.

Food preservation: treatment of fruit, meat, fish, etc., to conserve it for future use.

In medieval times, ways of preserving food were few. Men slaughtered their cattle in autumn, packing the joints into barrels of salt. Spices and vinegar were used to make pickles, milk was preserved as cheese, grapes were fermented to make wine or dried as raisins, and fish was smoked over a wood fire.

It was known that ice could preserve food, but the difficulty was to preserve the ice. In the 18th century most landowners had an ice house in the coolest part of their grounds. It was a deep pit, roofed over. Quantities of snow were shovelled into it during winter, and food was buried in the snow.

In the 19th century François Appert, a French chemist, discovered how to preserve food by heating it to a high temperature and then sealing it in an airtight container of glass or metal. This method, known as "canning", became especially popular in America. Canned food keeps fresh for years – e.g., that taken by Scott on his Polar expedition in 1912 was still edible fifty years later.

Australian engineers began to experiment with refrigeration ships to keep meat fresh for long periods, so that it could be exported. In 1880 the first cargo of frozen mutton from Australia arrived in England on board the *Strathleven*. Viewed with suspicion at first, "Canterbury lamb" soon became popular.

In 1849 an English chemist named Horsford discovered how to preserve milk by heating it with sugar, then rapidly cooling it. Much evaporated, but the residue, tinned, kept indefinitely. Almost every type of food can now be preserved for short or long periods, and either a refrigerator or "deep freeze" is standard equipment in the modern home.

¶ FERGUSON, SHEILA. *Food.* 1971

Fool: professional jester, formerly attached to a court or great household. The fool has a long and farflung ancestry. He existed in Ancient Egypt, Greece and Rome. His quips and pranks, from earliest times, diverted the rulers of the Orient. When the Spaniards conquered Mexico they found court fools in the retinue of the Aztec emperor, Montezuma. The fool's traditional costume, which we associate primarily with the Middle Ages – the particoloured tunic hung with bells, hooded cap topped by ass's ears or cockscomb – may go back to Ancient Rome or even earlier.

Some of the early jesters were, to all intents and purposes, variety artists doing the rounds of the courts. Their fund of stories, their knockabout humour, made them always welcome in royal and noble households woefully starved of entertainment. Those in private employment were expected to raise their masters' spirits when melancholy, keep them from worrying too much over affairs of state and stimulate their digestive processes by enlivening mealtimes with their japes and witty conversation. They were, in effect, licensed anarchists in a society where every one else was accorded his strictly appointed place. Often they said what no one else dared to say. But if theirs was a privileged profession it had its dangers.

A whipping was the traditional reward for a jester who overstepped the mark.

Among court fools of influence and ability may be mentioned Henry I's jester Rahere (d. 1144), who founded the priory of St Bartholomew, London; Bahalul, jester to the Caliph Haroun-al-Raschid; and Chicot, jester and friend to King Henry III of France. Muckle John, fool to Charles I, was the last court fool of England.

Football: any one of a wide variety of games played throughout the world with a round or elliptical ball, usually made of an inflated bladder in a leather outer case. The most popular is ASSOCIATION FOOTBALL, often abbreviated to "soccer". Though games closely resembling it, some of them with a formal code of rules, were played very much earlier, Association Football proper dates from 26th October 1863, when the Football Association was formed in England. A World Cup Competition was instituted in 1930, Brazil having the best overall record to date. There is also a European

Nations Cup, competed for every four years, and an annual European Champion Clubs Cup Competition for the leading clubs from almost all European nations. In the first, winners have been the USSR (1960), Spain (1964) and Italy (1968). In the second, by far the most successful club has been Real Madrid, which had won the cup six times by 1971.

RUGBY UNION FOOTBALL is said to have had its origins in November 1823 at Rugby School, England, when William Webb Ellis, afterwards a clergyman, broke the rules and carried the ball. A code was gradually built up and the Rugby Union was founded in 1871. In 1895 twenty-two Lancashire and Yorkshire clubs broke away from the Union to form the Northern Rugby Football Union, the name RUGBY LEAGUE being adopted in 1922. Rugby Union football is now played fifteen a side and Rugby League thirteen. Both forms of the game are played in many countries outside Britain, including France, New Zealand and Australia. There are seven member countries of an International Rugby Football Board.

AMERICAN FOOTBALL is played with an H-shaped goal and handling, kicking and throwing permitted in any direction. There are eleven players a side, and an oval ball is used, rather smaller than the Rugby Football type. AUSTRALIAN FOOTBALL is unique in that it has eighteen a side, is played on oval grounds and has four posts, seven yards [6·4 metres] apart, at each end, kicks between the inner posts scoring higher than between the outer. Other varieties of the game are found in Canadian Football, Gaelic Football, etc., and some well known schools still perpetuate their own peculiar versions such as, in England, the Eton Field and Wall Games, the Harrow Base Game, and Winchester College Football.

See also SPORTS AND ATHLETICS.

Ford, Henry (1863–1947): American automobile engineer and manufacturer. He served as machine-shop apprentice in Detroit for five years and built his first "gasoline buggy" in 1892–3. In 1903 he organised the Ford Motor Company at Detroit, where he produced, in 1909, the first cheap standardised car, constructed on a mass-production assembly line. Within twenty years there were manufacturing plants and associated companies in twenty-five cities throughout the world. The famous Model T car was first produced in October 1908. By 1927, when it was discontinued in favour of the new Model A, 15 million had been sold.

Ford was in many ways a social pioneer, introducing in 1914 an eight-hour working day with a minimum daily wage equivalent to £1 and a profit-sharing scheme for his employees. He had the gift for the occasional saying that finds its way into the standard quotation works. One was: "They can have any colour so long as it's black." Best known was his comment in the witness box during a law case in 1919: "History is bunk."

¶ CALDWELL, CY. *Henry Ford.* 1955

Ford Model T Landaulette, c. 1920, now in the Montague Motor Museum, Beaulieu, England.

Foreign Legion: the *Régiments Etrangères* of France. The Legion was founded in 1831 by Louis Philippe, after the conquest of Algeria, as seven battalions, each of one nationality, partly to serve in Algeria, partly to protect the régime itself. These were handed over to Spain in 1835. Napoleon III recruited only Swiss for some years. In the Mexican War of 1861–7 Captain Dandon and sixty-two legionaries defied 2,000 Mexicans for ten hours and then charged with the bayonet. Dandon's wooden arm is paraded annually on 30 April. The Legion fought at Alma and Sebastopol, raised 53,000 men for the 1914–18 War, built roads and tunnels in Morocco between the wars and, in the 1939–45 War, fought at Narvik, in Eritrea and Syria and at Bir Hakeim in North Africa. Ten thousand legionaries were killed in Indo-China and over 1,200 in Algeria. One battalion was disbanded for complicity in the 1961 plot against de Gaulle, but the Legion still numbered 15,000 and included two parachute regiments two regiments of light tanks. The headquarters were at Sidi-bel-Abbés until Algeria gained independence, when they moved to Corsica.

Since 1855 green epaulettes and white cap covers have been worn. The Legion has traditionally been the asylum of those who want to begin life anew – the adventurer, the social outcast, the political refugee, the exiled prince. They may enlist under false names, they cannot be made to fight against their own country, and, though pay is low and discipline strict, they are entitled to a pension. Many Russian exiles joined after 1917, Spaniards after the Civil War of 1936, members of the German Afrika Korps after 1945, and Hungarians after the 1956 revolt. The disbandment of the Legion was announced in 1970.

¶ BLASSINGAME, WYATT. *All About the Foreign Legion.* 1960

Forgery: the making of a fraudulent imitation with intent to deceive; the counterfeit object itself. Among the extant literary works of both Greece and Rome are several known cases of forgery, including a diary (that of Dictys Cretensis) professedly written by a participant in the Trojan War. Sculptors in ancient Rome produced statuary in the ancient Greek style and passed it off as genuine.

There is a legend that Michelangelo (1475–1564), when young and unknown, imitated those ancient Roman forgers by making a statue of Eros in the Greek style and burying it in the earth until it had acquired the patina of age. The statue, acclaimed as an ancient masterpiece, was bought by a cardinal for his collection: whereupon Michelangelo confessed his deception, and his reputation was made.

There can be scarcely a museum which, with the development of scientific tests and the general rise in the standard of scholarship, has not quietly removed from its show cases some "ancient" object previously thought to be genuine. Sometimes the demotion has attracted widespread publicity, as when the terracotta statue of Mars, which had been the pride of the Etruscan collection of the Metropolitan Museum of Art in New York, was in 1961 shown to be not of the 5th century BC but 20th-century Italian. Chemical tests of its glaze showed the presence of manganese, a substance never used in ancient glazes. Tests on a bronze horse thought to be Greek of the 5th century BC, belonging to the same museum, revealed iron wires in its core, part of a casting process not invented until the 15th century. Piltdown in Sussex is associated with a forgery of a different kind, that of remains of an early type of man, "discovered" by an amateur palaeontologist. In 1953 it was conclusively shown that the skull of Piltdown

Man was a composite object which included the jawbone of a modern ape.

Paintings have been notoriously the forger's hunting ground. The forging of artists' signatures is extremely common. Between 1936 and 1942 Hans van Meegeren, an unsuccessful Dutch painter, painted seven paintings in the manner of Jan Vermeer (1632–72), a Dutch master whose works are very rare. During the German occupation of Holland, Van Meegeren sold these paintings to highly-placed Nazis and, in 1945, after Germany's defeat, was accused of collaborating with the enemy. To defend himself he revealed the forgery and painted another "Vermeer" in prison to prove his skill.

Furniture of the great periods and makers has been, and still is, being imitated. With some French furniture in the Louis XVI style even experts are often misled, for several French cabinet-makers, after the outbreak of the French Revolution (1789), used their own earlier designs. While the style associated with the monarchy fell into disfavour in France it was still in demand abroad. Consequently many pieces were made in the old style and exported as genuine Louis XVI furniture.

Of literary forgeries some outstanding examples must be mentioned. Thomas Chatterton (1752–72) pretended that poems which he himself had written were the work of an imaginary 15th-century monk called Thomas Rowley. For a while Chatterton succeeded in deceiving people as highly-placed and knowledgeable as the writer and connoisseur Horace Walpole (1717–97). Poor and in despair, Chatterton committed suicide at the age of seventeen. George Psalmanazar (?1679–1763), a Frenchman, published (1704) a *Description of Formosa*, a place which he had never visited, even going to the lengths of inventing a "Formosan" language. William Henry Ireland (1777–1835) claimed that, when one of his ancestors rescued Shakespeare from drowning, the poet, in gratitude, gave him many original manuscripts. Ireland's forgeries included a letter to Shakespeare from Queen Elizabeth I and a "Shakespearian" play, *Henry II*. Many well-known people were deceived before Ireland finally confessed his fraud.

A forgery that still leaves a question mark is that of the so-called Shapira Manuscript. In 1883 Moses Wilhelm Shapira (*c.* 1830–84), a Pole who kept an antiquities shop in Jerusalem, tried to sell the British Museum fifteen strips of sheepskin found, he said, by a Bedouin in a cave, and inscribed with a variant version of the Book of Deuteronomy. The asking price was said to be £1 million. Experts called in by the Museum pronounced the manuscript a forgery. In 1884 Shapira shot himself. In view of what we now know of the Dead Sea Scrolls, were the experts mistaken? There is no way of knowing: the Shapira Manuscript disappeared in 1887.

Forging (of metals): heating and hammering metal into shape. Iron, steel and certain alloys can be shaped by the art of forging. The most primitive blacksmiths were obviously aware of the way in which hot iron becomes sufficiently plastic to be bent and hammered into shape, and the forge, in fact, never uses iron in a molten state. Machinery was introduced into the process of iron forging at an early period. Machine forgings are produced in very large quantities for our modern mechanised society, although the ancient art of the blacksmith in his small forge is by no means lost.

The blacksmith at his anvil, like the operator of the most powerful forging machine, performs a number of processes

which can be broadly divided into: REDUCING from a larger to a smaller size (known as fullering and swaging); ENLARGING from a smaller to a larger size (upsetting); BENDING; JOINING one piece to another (welding); PUNCHING apertures; CUTTING.

The use of animal or water power in the mechanics of forging was known from early times. The forging press was, however, of 19th-century introduction and is operated either mechanically or hydraulically: the modern press can exert pressures of up to 50,000 tons [50,800 tonnes], although more modest presses are usual and naturally require less massive auxiliary equipment.

The blacksmith was one of the key figures of early society, his work in the manufacture and repair of implements and weapons and in such tasks as the shoeing of horses making his craft indispensable to the community. For this reason metaphor and simile derived from the craft are commonplace, and he holds an honoured place in literature as well as history. Some indication of his services through the centuries is provided by the fact that the commonest surname in the English-speaking world is Smith, with an estimated 1,300,000 in the USA and over 800,000 in England and Wales. Not all, of course, can point to blacksmith ancestry, since there are other types of smith, including goldsmith, swordsmith and the whitesmith, who worked in tin and white iron, or who did the finishing work on forged iron.

¶ LISTER, RAYMOND. *The Craftsmen in Metal*. 1966

Forum: the market-place of the old Roman town. Round a usually rectangular area, it was customary to group temples, public baths, law courts and market stalls. There would be a platform for public speeches, and the forum was often surrounded by a covered colonnade. It was the centre of civil business. In Rome itself the chief forum was the *Forum Romanum* below the Capitol, containing, among other features, the Senate House and the *Rostra*, or stage for public orations. Emperors built other fora, often to commemorate victories and containing some record of achievement, such as Trajan's Column in his forum. These additional sites did not detract from the importance of the *Forum Romanum*.

Fossils: from Latin *fodere*, to dig. Before the 17th century the term fossil was applied to any curious object extracted from the earth, whether or not it showed traces of plant or animal life. Today the term refers to the petrified traces of organisms, casts of shells (internal or external), footprints of mammals and mineral im-

Fossil trilobite.

pressions caused by chemical change. This study is known as Palaeontology. It helps palaeontologists and geologists to date the different strata of the earth and to gain knowledge of the evolution of all forms of life.

The recent work of Dr Louis Seymour Bazett Leakey (born 1903), a Kenyan anthropologist, and his wife Mary, demands special mention. Their researches in the Olduvai Gorge, Tanzania, have suggested that the earliest fossilised man forms are much older than was formerly believed, the so-called Zinjanthropus being at least one and a half million years old.

¶ CASANOVA, RICHARD. *Fossil Collecting: an illustrated guide.* 1960; KIRKCALDY, J. F. *Fossils in Colour.* 1970; MATTHEWS, WILLIAM H. *Wonders of Fossils.* 1968

Fourteen Points: statement of war aims made by President Woodrow Wilson of the USA in a speech on 8 January 1918. They included a renunciation of secret diplomacy; the removal, as far as possible, of economic barriers; freedom of the seas; and the formation of a general association of nations to guarantee the political independence of all states. These principles were accepted by the Allied Powers as a basis for peace in November 1918.

Fourteenth Amendment: amendment to the US Constitution, adopted 13 June 1866. The American Civil War had destroyed slavery and the civil status of the Negro subsequently became a controversial question. The Fourteenth Amendment gave a guarantee of citizenship and equal civil rights to "freedmen". The seceding states were required to ratify this amendment as a condition of being readmitted to the Union.

Fourteenth century: the years 1301–1400. In every sense except the purely physical one the world in the 14th century was at once a larger and a smaller place than it is today. Roads were few, poor and dangerous. The pace of travel was that of a man walking or, at fastest, on horseback. Distances of which we think nothing then seemed immense, and people tended to remain in the communities where they were born rather than brave the perils of the unknown world that began on the other side of the hill.

Even so, as in every century, there were people on the move, impelled by such age-old motives as hunger, greed and persecution; adventurousness, curiosity and the desire for power. The great conqueror of the period was Tamerlane (or Timur) (1336–1405), a Mongol ruler who, setting out from his capital of Samarkand, cut wide swathes of destruction across Asia. Looting and killing as they went, his followers invaded Persia, Russia and Mongolia. At Delhi alone, which they captured in 1397, they were alleged to have butchered 100,000 Indians. Tamerlane ranged as far west as Syria and Turkey, and was planning an attack on

China when death ended his terrible career. This period saw the establishment of Moscow as the chief Russian principality.

In the same century death came out of Asia in another form – in the shape of rat-carried fleas that spread bubonic plague through North Africa and Europe. In 1348 the Black Death, as it was called, reached England. There are no exact figures as to the number of deaths, but some historians estimate that by the time the plague was over half the population of Europe had perished. At least a third of the population of England was wiped out between 1348 and 1350 alone.

A country cannot lose so many of its citizens in such a short space of time without finding its affairs turned topsy-turvy. Suddenly there was a desperate shortage of labour, and a long-drawn-out struggle began between the peasants who wanted more wages and the great landholders who tried in every way to put the clock back to where it was before the Black Death. The repressive Statute of Labourers, passed in 1351, fixed rates of pay which bore no relation to the realities of the day.

Men were needed for war as well as for tilling the abandoned fields. Ever since 1336 England and France had been intermittently involved in what has come to be known as the Hundred Years War. At such battles as that of Crécy (1346) and Poitiers (1356) the English gained great victories, brought to perfection the use of the longbow and revolutionised the tactics of land warfare. But the resumption of war after a nine-year truce following on the Black Death drained England's depleted resources. In 1381 the discontents of the labouring classes came to a head in the unsuccessful Great (or Peasants') Revolt led by Wat Tyler (d. 1381).

The Black Death caused radical changes in the pattern of life in every country it ravaged. In England it accelerated the decay of the feudal system. Sheep-farming required less labour than the old system of open fields, and so more and more land was enclosed for the purpose. England was the foremost wool-producing country of the Middle Ages. Large quantities of wool were exported to the Low Countries, where it was made up into cloth. During the 14th century Flemish weavers were invited to settle in England and practise their craft there. As a result England began to develop a woollen industry of its own, instead of remaining purely a supplier of the raw material.

The 14th century saw the first dawning of that epoch in Western civilisation which we inaccurately term the Renaissance, or "rebirth", as if it were something that sprang to life all at once instead of evolving gradually out of the age preceding it. Giotto (1266–1337), born in Florence, may be truly called the earliest painter of the modern world. Dante (1265–1321), Petrarch (1304–74) and Boccaccio (1313?–1375) were the three great literary figures, who, writing in their native Italian instead of the Latin usual at the time, may be said to have founded Italian literature.

In England Geoffrey Chaucer (*c.* 1340–1400), author of the *Canterbury Tales*, was the first clearly identified poet of stature to use English as a literary language. John Wyclif (*c.* 1320–84), the religious reformer who asserted that the Bible, not the Church, must be a Christian's supreme spiritual authority, made, or supervised, the first complete translation of the Old and New Testaments into English.

In this century European architecture developed great richness of detail, variations of the Gothic style that are labelled today *Flamboyant* and *Decorated*. One of the most beautiful buildings in the world was built during the 14th century in quite another style – the Alhambra, the fortress-palace at Granada in Spain. Granada was the last Spanish possession of the Moors of northwest Africa who at one time had ruled a great part of Spain, and the Alhambra is a masterpiece of Moorish art.

In the 14th century the Moorish star was setting. Across the Atlantic, in Central America, another star, destined likewise to be extinguished by Spain, was in the ascendant. In 1325 (the date is more traditional than strictly accurate), on the site of the presentday Mexico City, the Aztec Indians founded their capital of Tenochtitlan, which grew into a splendid city full of stone temples erected on tall platforms shaped like pyramids with the tops cut off and with steep flights of steps leading up the sides. The Aztecs attained a high degree of social and military organisation and produced outstanding sculpture, pottery and work in precious stones. Their empire ended in 1521 when it was conquered by the Spaniards under Hernán Cortés (1485–1547).

¶ HAY, DENYS. *Europe in the Fourteenth and Fifteenth Centuries*. 1966

See also AZTECS, BLACK DEATH, HUNDRED YEARS WAR, TIMUR, etc.

Fox, Charles James (1749–1806): British statesman and orator, third son of Lord Holland. He was a man of great charm,

generosity and culture, often relaxing by reading the classics. His considerable personal financial difficulties were largely caused by heavy gambling. Among his friends was the future George IV, but George III disliked him, blaming him for his son's faults; consequently he seldom held high political office. In 1798 his name was erased from the Privy Council list for proposing the toast of "Our Sovereign, the People". On Pitt's death in 1806 Fox joined the Ministry of All the Talents (so called from the supposed collective wisdom and ability of its members), and had done much to ensure the eventual abolition of the slave trade before he died. Sir William Wraxall described his features as "dark, harsh and saturnine" but deriving "a sort of majesty, from the addition of two black and shaggy eyebrows, which sometimes concealed, but oftener developed, the workings of his mind".

¶ REID, L. *Charles James Fox*. 1969

Fox, George (1624–91): founder of the Religious Society of Friends. Appalled by the worldly lives of his acquaintances, he set out to find true religion and came to believe that man can approach God in silence and prayer, without intermediary, and obtain guidance by the "Inner Light". His interruption of services in "steeple houses", as he called ordinary churches, and refusal to conform to accepted customs, led to frequent imprisonment. His preaching in Britain, the Netherlands, northern Germany, the West Indies and America brought many converts, nicknamed Quakers, whom he organised in monthly and quarterly meetings, with yearly meetings of representatives in London. His output of letters and doctrinal works was considerable, but his writings, which were comparatively uncouth and illiterate, could never match the power of his presence and the spoken word. He is best known by his vivid

George Fox preaching in a tavern.

Journal, first edited in 1694 by Fox's co-worker Thomas Ellwood.
See also FRIENDS, RELIGIOUS SOCIETY OF, and QUAKERS.

France: republic in western Europe; population 54,346,000 (1983). Caves in the south-west show occupation by palaeolithic man, but France enters historic times as the home of a Gallic people, speaking a Celtic language. Greek colonies were established on its Mediterranean coast. France or Gaul was conquered for the Roman Republic by Julius Caesar between 58 and 51 BC. Through the more peaceful years of the Roman Empire, Gaul took on much of the civilisation, language, law and religions of Rome.

When the Roman Empire began to break up, Gaul became a bridgehead for invaders. In AD 406 the Suebes, Alans and Vandals crossed the Rhine and, after three years of pillaging, crossed the Pyrenees. The Salian Franks then occupied Belgium. the Ripuarian Franks took Trèves, the Alemanni occupied Alsace, and the Visigoths, who had been in Italy, moved into the south of France. Early in the 5th century the last Roman garrison left Britain, and British refugees later crossed into Gaul, where their descendants still live in Brittany. In 451 the Visigoths, the Salian Franks and the newly arrived Burgundians helped the Roman commander Aëtius to halt the invasion of Attila's Huns at the Battle of Châlons. Before the close of the 5th century the Franks, under their king, Clovis the Meroving, a Christian convert, became the dominant people in Gaul, defeating the Romans, the Alemanni and the Visigoths. Before his death in 511, Clovis had founded the French monarchy in close alliance with the Church.

The Merovingian dynasty lasted for nearly three centuries of civil wars and atrocities. The Merovings were retained as nominal kings even when all real power had fallen into the hands of their able Mayors of the Palace, an office held by the powerful house of St Arnulf. This dynasty of mayors defended France against the Arabs, aided the conversion of Germany to Christianity and became military protectors of the Pope. The last Meroving was deposed in 752, and Pépin the Short, mayor of the palace, reigned as king.

Pépin's son Charles the Great, or Charlemagne (742–814), built up an empire which included France, western Germany and a great part of Italy. In 800 he was crowned emperor in Rome by the Pope. This empire declined, suffering from the custom of division among heirs and from the raids and attacks of the Scandinavians. Scandinavian invasion established the powerful Duchy of Normandy in the north of France. Retaining their Norse energy but becoming Frenchmen, the Normans carried the French language and their own system of feudalism, law and administration to England, Sicily, Antioch and the Byzantine Empire and powerfully influenced France itself.

In 987 the Carolingians were replaced as kings of France by the house of Capet, a powerful feudal family, who held the island city of Paris and also Orléans. The uniting of the duchies of Normandy, Anjou and Aquitaine with the monarchy of England placed a great part of France under the rule of English kings until the beginning of the 13th century. Then the French kings again played a European rôle, making extended use of professional administrative officials. St Louis (reigned 1226-70) participated actively in the later Crusades. His less saintly grandson Philip IV (reigned 1285–1314) kidnapped Pope Boniface VIII and tortured, ruined and plundered the Knights Templar.

When lawyers held that under the laws of the Salian Franks a woman could not succeed to the French throne, Philip of Valois succeeded on the death in 1328 of the last Capet. Edward III of England (1312-77) claimed the French throne in 1338 through his mother. So began the Hundred Years War (1338-1453) with disastrous consequences for France, including naval defeat at Sluys (1340), military humiliation at Crécy (1346) and Poitiers (1356), the French king a prisoner in England, and the Peace of Calais in 1360, ceding Aquitaine, Ponthieu and Calais to England. As the war with England developed into its 15th-century phase there emerged those dramatic figures, Henry V of England, the victor of Agincourt (1415), and, on the French side, Joan of Arc (1412–31). After Joan's great service to Charles VII (reigned 1422–61), France slowly recovered.

In a series of wars from 1494 to 1559 French kings made claims to portions of Italy. This threatened the interests of the great Habsburg empire. While the Habsburg-Valois struggle absorbed the resources of France, Protestant beliefs spread freely. In 1559 Henry II of France (reigned 1547-59) ended the war in order to devote himself to stamping out Protestant heresy. This policy was bitterly pursued by his successors till 1598, when the Edict of Nantes gave the French Protestants a measure of toleration.

Henry IV (reigned 1589-1610) and Cardinals Richelieu (1585–1642) and Mazarin (1602-61) successively enhanced France's European position, broke the political power of the Protestants and subdued aristocratic rebels. During the long and superficially brilliant reign of Louis XIV (reigned 1643-1715) a series of wars in Europe, and attempted overseas expansion in America and elsewhere, undermined the prosperity of France and ended in 1713 with the humiliating Peace of Utrecht. Louis's persecution of the Protestants drove much talent from the country.

The reign of Louis XV (1715–74) saw heavy losses to Britain of overseas territory in North America and India. Unresolved social and financial problems and unreformed grievances led to Revolution, in which Louis XVI (reigned 1774-93) perished.

The Revolutionary and Napoleonic Wars, from 1792 to 1815, brought victorious French armies into a large area of Europe, carrying the effects of the French Revolution into many countries, especially in the breakdown of old aristocratic privilege, better life for common people and an improved legal system.

Between the collapse of Napoleon's empire in 1815 and the establishment of a Republic in 1870, after severe defeat by the Germans, there were three separate experiments in monarchy. Overseas imperial ventures in Africa, Indo-China and the Near East had limited success. The Republic survived World War I (1914-18) under severe strain, but in World War II (1939-45) France was overrun by German armies. A conservative stabilisation of French economy and politics was achieved in the 1960s under General Charles de Gaulle (president 1959-69). France played a leading role in creating the EEC which she has used as an instrument of her foreign policy.

¶ MAUROIS, ANDRE. *History of France*. 1956

See also CAROLINGIAN; CHARLEMAGNE; FRANCIS; FRANCO-PRUSSIAN WAR; FRENCH REVOLUTION; HUNDRED YEARS WAR; MEROVINGIAN; NAPOLEONIC WARS; NORMANDY; VALOIS, etc.

Francis I (1494-1574): king of France 1515-47. Francis was ambitious and intelligent; a lover of display and devoted to hard exercise and sport of all kinds. As a military leader he showed great bravery but little wisdom. On gaining the throne he led a successful campaign into Italy, but ten years later, in the same country, was taken captive by his rival, the Emperor Charles V, at Pavia. He did something to strengthen the French monarchy, but his record as a ruler was marred by boundless extravagance and his reliance on court favourites. He was at his best as a sincere lover of art and literature, and some of the greatest craftsmen, artists and writers of the time had cause to be grateful for his encouragement.

Francis Joseph I (1830-1916): emperor of Austria. He became emperor in 1848, when the empire and Habsburg monarchy seemed on the verge of dissolution. His stubbornness and sense of constitutional duty restored the situation, but throughout his reign of sixty-eight years he presided over an empire that was gradually declining in military power and internal coherence. His personal life was beset with misfortune, but his public and private difficulties seemed to strengthen the cold determination that was uppermost in his character. In 1914 the assassination of his nephew, the Archduke Franz Ferdinand, at Sarajevo in Yugoslavia led Austria into the attack on Serbia which began World War I and hastened the final collapse of the empire.

Francis of Assisi, St (*c.* 1181-1226): Italian founder of the Franciscan order of friars. The son of Pietro Bernadone, a merchant, Francis was given his name because his father was in France when the child was born. He became a pleasure-loving youth, fond of banquets and gaiety. In 1201 he spent some months in a Perugian fortress as a prisoner of war. When released he became more serious-minded. Eventually he left his home and friends to live with lepers and outcasts outside the city. His father disowned him, but many of his friends, impressed by his joyful serenity, joined him. They called themselves *friars*, meaning "brothers", and did not live in monasteries but travelled from place to place in imitation of Christ and His disciples. In 1220 he resigned his leadership of the Friars, probably because, in his humility, he did not consider himself suitable to rule the worldwide order the Franciscans were becoming. He was a tender, warm-hearted, joyous man and a lover of all nature as well as of his fellow man. One of his earliest followers described him as slender and delicate, wearing only an old patched tunic.

¶ BRUCE, J. *Life of St. Francis of Assissi.* 1965

St Francis Blessing the Birds, *by Giotto.*

Francis Xavier, St (1506–52): Spanish missionary, called "the Apostle of the Indies". The youngest son of a Spanish nobleman, Francis was born at the castle of Xavier, in the Pyrenees. He graduated at the University of Paris, became a Jesuit in 1537 and was sent as a missionary to Goa. During the voyage to India, he and many of the sailors contracted scurvy; Francis, in spite of his own sufferings, nursed his companions. From Goa he went to the East Indies and at Malacca met Yajiro, a Japanese Christian. Francis visited Japan, where he stayed until 1552, then journeyed to China, but died of a fever soon after his arrival. The countryside folk called him "the Great Father" and a fellow missionary has left a description of how, when followed by great crowds of as many as 6,000 people, he would climb into a tree and from there preach to them. He was buried in Goa, and is venerated by Eastern Christians.
See also JESUITS.

Franco, Francisco (1892–1975): Spanish general known as "El Caudillo" or leader of the Falangists, the Fascist movement founded in 1933 which defeated the republican forces in the Spanish Civil War (1936–39). He became head of state (dictator) in 1939, a position he retained until his death.

Franco-Prussian War, The (1870–71): war arising out of the candidature of a member of the Prussian ruling house for the Spanish throne, although its underlying cause was French jealousy of Germany's growing military strength. Bismarck managed to provoke France into declaring war (15 July 1870) knowing that the French army was ill-equipped and undermanned, while the Germans were ready for war. Both the main French armies were heavily defeated almost as soon as hostilities began; and following

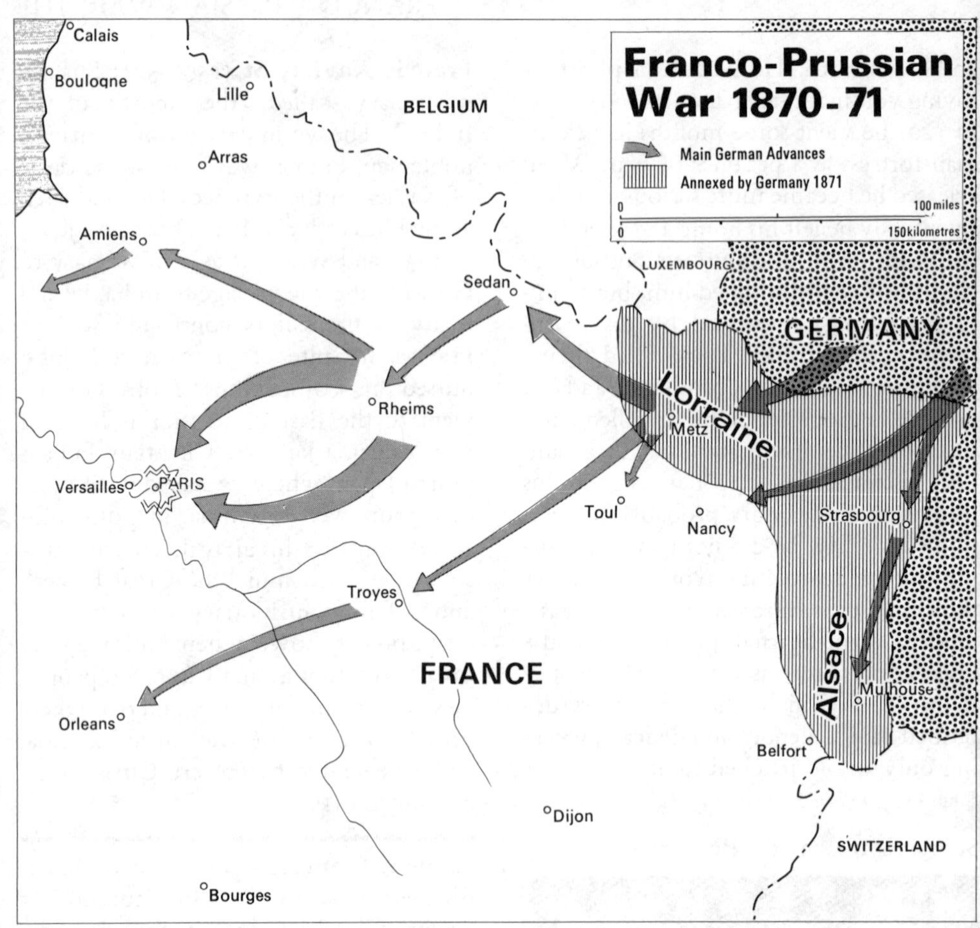

MacMahon's surrender at Sedan on 1 September Napoleon III was taken prisoner. On 27 October Bazaine surrendered at Metz with 100,000 men. On 28 January 1871 Paris fell after a siege of four months, and the war ended on 10 May with the signing of the Treaty of Frankfurt, by which France ceded Alsace-Lorraine to Germany and agreed to pay an indemnity of 5,000 million francs. Napoleon III died in 1873, an exile in England, where his widow survived him until 1920.

¶ HOWARD, MICHAEL. *The Franco-Prussian War.* 1961

Franklin, Benjamin (1706–90): American statesman, writer and scientist. Professor Bernard Faij wrote: "He was never led by his ambition to dishonesty or baseness. . . . Other men may have been greater, but very few have been more human." Another writer described him as "the first civilised American" an affectionate exaggeration which nevertheless gives a good indication of his width of interests and intellectual power. His writing is a remarkable combination of elegance, wit and trenchant argument. As a newspaper proprietor and as the first printer and bookseller in Philadelphia he influenced an ever-widening circle of readers; as a scientist he evolved the theory of positive and negative electrical forces and invented the lightning conductor; as statesman he helped draft the Declaration of Independence; and beneath these and many other achievements which brought him international fame remained a warm,

Franklin at the court of Louis XVI.

kindly and generous human being, justifying to the full G. E. Woodberry's description of him as "one of the great citizens of the world".

¶ MCKOWN, ROBIN. *Benjamin Franklin.* 1964

Franklin, Sir John (1786–1847): British admiral and arctic explorer. Franklin commanded explorations of the Canadian arctic coasts from 1819–22 and 1825–27. From 1837–43 he was lieutenant-governor of Van Diemen's Land (Tasmania) and did much for the welfare of the convicts there. His 1845 expedition to discover the North West Passage to Bering Strait from Lancaster Sound disappeared completely. Numerous search-explorations followed. In 1854 Dr Rae (1813–93) learnt of Franklin's death from Eskimos. Later McClintock (1819–1907) discovered the records of the expedition in a cairn on Point Victory. Franklin had died in 1847. Starvation and scurvy combined to destroy the survivors.

¶ SUTTON, ANN and MYRON. *The Endless Quest: the life of Sir John Franklin, explorer.* 1966

Franks: the Germanic people who gave their name to France. Their name "frank" or free seems to have distinguished them, while they were settled on the lower Rhine, from neighbouring peoples who were subject to the Roman Empire. They were a constant source of trouble to the Romans on the Rhine frontier during the 4th century AD. The Salian Franks were settled between the Zuyder Zee and the Main, and the Ripuarian Franks further south on the right bank of the Rhine. In 451 the Salian Franks joined with the Visigoths in helping the Roman commander Aëtius to halt the invading Huns. The Ripuarians were under one king but the Salians had several, the most powerful of whom was Clovis the Meroving (ruled 481–511). In two wars, in 496 and then in 505–7, he advanced into Gaul conquering all his opponents so that his kingdom reached to the Pyrenees. Owing to the influence of his wife Clotilda, he was baptised a Christian on Christmas Day 496, along with 3,000 other Franks; though this did not prevent him from using ruthless means, including assassination, to establish his supremacy. He aimed at co-operation between the Romans of Gaul and the Germanic newcomers, and in 508 the Eastern Emperor Anastasius gave him the title of proconsul. He codified the laws of the Salian Franks, and, in his later years, made his capital at Paris where he built the great church now known as St Geneviève. He died in 511, and, although his kingdom was divided among his four sons and much disorder followed, Clovis was the true founder of the Frankish monarchy. *See* GERMANY for maps.

Frederick I, called "Barbarossa" ("red beard") (*c.* 1124–90): Holy Roman Emperor 1155–90. A member of the powerful Hohenstaufen family, Frederick became German king in 1152 and was crowned Emperor three years later. Efforts to enforce his rule over the Lombard cities of northern Italy led to his excommunication by Pope Alexander III in 1160. Frederick set up a rival Pope. Torn between Italian ambitions and the need to protect his possessions in Germany, he was disastrously defeated by the Lombard cities at Legnano in 1176. Reconciliation with the Papacy followed. Drowned in Asia Minor while leading a great army on the Third Crusade, Barbarossa joined the ranks of national heroes in folklore who for centuries were believed to be still alive, ready to return in time of need.

Frederick II, called Frederick the Great (1712–86): king of Prussia 1740–86. After a harsh upbringing which brought him into open rebellion against his autocratic father Frederick William I, and at one stage involved the loss of his rank as crown prince, Frederick became king in 1740. He inherited an excellent army with which he promptly attacked Austria and won a large area of Silesia. In 1756 began the Seven Years War in which Frederick engaged in desperate struggle with Austria, France, Russia and Saxony, with Britain and Hanover as his only allies. Though most of Britain's military effort was exerted outside Europe, Frederick received much financial help from her. His brilliant generalship and indomitable will enabled him to save Prussia from annihilation, but the country was utterly exhausted when the war ended with the Peace of Hubertusberg in 1763. Though there was a brief renewal of war with Austria in 1779, Frederick devoted most of the rest of his life to rebuilding his devastated country. Brusque in manner and austere in habits, he took a particular interest in the administration of justice and was greatly loved by his people. He left a powerful army, a well organised and financially strong country and a heroic tradition of victorious survival in the face of crushing odds. He laid the foundation of Prussia's dominant position in Germany in the following century. A free-thinker, an admirer of French culture and a patron of Voltaire, he was indifferent to German literature; but he created the conditions of freedom of thought and self-consciousness which made possible the new German literature represented by Goethe, Schiller, Kant and their generation.

¶ In UNSTEAD, R. J. *Royal Adventurers.* 1963

Free trade: commerce between nations without the imposition of protective tariffs. In his *Wealth of Nations* (1776) Adam Smith argued that countries would benefit if they produced the goods they could make best and exchanged these for goods other countries could make more cheaply.

When Britain became a major industrial country, advocates of free trade agitated for the abolition of duties on the importation of corn and other goods. This, they believed, would lead to an increase in British exports of manufactured goods and a reduction in the cost of importing foodstuffs and raw materials. The Free Traders, who scored successes with the repeal of the Corn Laws (1846) and the Navigation Acts (1849), believed that European countries would follow Britain's example, and up to 1870 France, Germany, Holland, Scandinavia, Russia and Italy all moved toward freer trade. After 1870, however, the benefits of Free Trade began to be

Frederick the Great, of Prussia.

questioned. Britain's industrial supremacy was being challenged by Germany and the United States. Recent political events had strengthened nationalist sentiment in Europe and especially in Germany, Italy and France, while governments were looking for revenue with which to finance rising military expenditure or additional social services. One method of obtaining revenue was to impose or increase tariffs, and by about 1880 the low-tariff era had ended in Europe.

Today free trade is encouraged by the European Economic Community (the Common Market) and the European Free Trade Association (*see* EUROPEAN COMMON MARKET and EFTA) but only among themselves.

French Revolution: the series of violent events, 1789–99, which overthrew the French monarchy. Revolution came because crisis was impending in each of a wide range of aspects of French life, and all the crises began to blend into one. There was tension between the privileged and largely untaxed nobility and the unprivileged and overtaxed peasant farmers, businessmen and professional people. Philosophers such as Voltaire, Montesquieu and Rousseau had criticised much that was customary in social and political values and had offered many exciting new ideas.

Breakdown in government precipitated revolution. Grave financial difficulties caused the summoning of the States-General, a gathering of representatives of nobles, clergy and commoners, in the hope that taxation might be extended with their consent. They met in May 1789. The "third estate", i.e. the commoners, successfully demanded the formation of a National Assembly of the three estates together. The people of Paris organised a Civic Guard, soon to be the National Guard, and took the royal fortress of the Bastille. The Assembly set about drawing up a constitution. A project of national workshops drew mobs of unemployed and impoverished people into Paris. Louis XVI was a gentle, irresolute man, unwilling to use armed force. He became the prisoner of the revolution. Numbers of the nobility began to leave France.

A Declaration of the Rights of Man was adopted and the property of the Church was confiscated. The King tried to escape and failed. In September 1791 the new constitution was completed and accepted by the King.

Meanwhile the Emperor of Austria, whose daughter, Marie Antoinette, was Queen of France, issued, with the King of Prussia, the declaration of Pillnitz, stating that the restoration of order in France concerned all European states. In April 1792 France declared war on Austria. Prussia joined Austria, and the French suffered setbacks on their frontier. In the violent feelings now stirred up in France, the monarchy was ended. A reign of terror began. At the same time the new revolutionary French army defeated the Prussians at Valmy and the Austrians at Jemappes. In January 1793 King Louis XVI was executed.

During 1793 the Convention which had replaced the National Assembly quickly lost most of its power to special committees, of which the most important was the Committee of Public Safety. Together with a Revolutionary Tribunal, this Committee pressed on with the Reign of Terror, and large numbers of people were guillotined. Robespierre, the leader of the terror policy, created so much alarm among his own colleagues that he was in the end destroyed.

A new constitution was adopted, headed by a Directory of five men. The revolution was coming to an end. Public attention was increasingly attracted to the brilliant campaigns of Napoleon Bonaparte, the most able of the new young revolutionary generals. In November 1799 Bonaparte overthrew the Directory and established a Consulate of three, of whom he was First Consul. The way was open for the establishment of the Napoleonic Empire.

¶ DOWD, D. L. *The French Revolution.* 1966; ROSENTHAL, M. *The French Revolution.* 1968; SPENCER, CORNELIA. *The Song in the Streets.* 1965

See also BASTILLE; EIGHTEENTH CENTURY; NAPOLEON I; ROBESPIERRE; ROUSSEAU; VOLTAIRE, etc.

French revolutionary wars: the wars launched by France in April 1792, lasting to the Peace of Amiens, March 1802.

Attempts by Austria and Prussia to control the action of the French government encouraged revolutionary fervour, and in April 1792 the Girondins forced Louis XVI to declare war on Austria. The initial attack on the Austrian Netherlands was a fiasco, the French fleeing in panic, but vigorous organisation of national defence, under Danton, led to a check of the allied advance at Valmy (20 September), to French victory, under Dumouriez, at Jemappes, and to the capture of the Netherlands, while Custine cleared the middle Rhine, and Montesquieu and Anselme occupied Savoy and Nice. But the execution of the king (1793) and the occupation of Belgium brought Britain into the war.

Pitt's first coalition (Britain, Austria, Prussia, Holland, Spain, Sardinia) at first had some success, clearing Belgium after the battle of Neerwinden, besieging Dunkirk and even, under Admiral Hood, occupying Toulon. But the rise of the Jacobins (*see* separate entry), and Carnot's reorganisation of the army, using massed troops to attack vital points rather than spreading their strength, turned the tide. The allies were forced back across the Rhine, Napoleon Bonaparte made his first mark by forcing Hood from Toulon, and in 1794 Jourdan's victory at Fleurus led to the re-occupation of Belgium. The following year saw the French capture of Holland, and Prussia's retirement from the war, which ended the coalition.

In 1796, however, in a thrust for Vienna, Moreau on the Main and Jourdan on the Danube were defeated by the Archduke Charles; but Napoleon, in command of "the Army of Italy", after compelling Sardinia to a peace which ceded Savoy and Nice to France, forced the bridge of Lodi and entered Milan (16 May), thus gaining control of all Lombardy except Mantua. He defeated Austrian attempts to relieve Mantua at Brescia and Castiglione (August), Arcola (November) and Rivoli (January 1797) and on 2 February the great fortress surrendered. He then occupied Venice, organised northern Italy into the Cisalpine and Ligurian Republics and dictated the Peace of Campo Formio to Austria.

To deal with Britain, the only remaining enemy, whose success had been confined to naval victories and the capture of colonies, Napoleon now turned eastwards, landed an army in Egypt and won the battle of the Pyramids. But the annihilation of his fleet by Nelson at the Nile (August 1798) and the failure at Acre of his attack on Turkey altered his plans, and he returned to Paris to carry out the *coup d'état* which left him master of France (9 November) and to deal with a new coalition (Britain, Russia, Austria, Turkey, Naples, Portugal). French arms were successful in southern Italy, but at first unfortunate on the Rhine, in Switzerland and in northern Italy, where Suvaroff's brilliant campaign culminated at the River Trebia (June 1799). The position was redeemed by Masséna's defeat of the Russians at Zurich (September), Napoleon's victory at Marengo (June 1800) and

Moreau's at Hohenlinden (December), after which Austria signed the Peace of Lunéville (February 1801). Russia had left the coalition, but her "Armed Neutrality of the North" was broken up by Nelson's victory at Copenhagen (April).

After Abercromby's defeat of the French at Alexandria, peace was signed with Britain at Amiens (March 1802), France agreeing to evacuate southern Italy and Egypt, and Britain to return her conquests except Ceylon and Trinidad.

Fresco painting: painting on wet lime-plaster with a mixture of paint and water. This is not to be confused with tempera painting, i.e. painting on hard dry plaster.

Cennino Cennini, writing his autobiography in the 15th century, gave a vivid description of the method of fresco painting using pigment which penetrates the wet plaster and, when dry, hardens and becomes one with the wall surface.

The art of fresco painting was known to the Egyptians, Greeks and Romans, but the best known examples are those accomplished during the 13th to mid-16th centuries (the time of Cimabue to Michelangelo), such as the ceiling of the Sistine Chapel in Rome and murals in churches in Florence and in other Italian cities. One of the most famous fresco paintings in the world is Leonardo da Vinci's *Last Supper* at Milan.

See also FLORENTINE ART, etc.

Freud, Sigmund (1856–1939)**:** Austrian psychiatrist and founder of the technique of psychoanalysis, which seeks to help disturbed people by bringing to a conscious level the contents of the unconscious mind, chiefly by conversations between the analyst and his patient. Voluntary hypnosis often accompanies the treatment. Through his writings Freud has exercised profound influence on the modern treatment of some types of sick-

ness where mental conditions affect physical wellbeing, and his theories find echo in much contemporary literature and drama. The adjective Freudian, describing ideas that stem from Freud, has passed permanently into the language.

See also JUNG, CARL.

Friars: members of certain mendicant (begging) or preaching orders, who went out into the world, in contrast to the monks, who lived in religious houses. The word comes from Latin *frater*, brother.

In 1209 the Pope agreed that the followers of St Francis of Assisi be recognised as a religious order. Francis called them the "Friars Minor", meaning "the least of the brethren", but they were frequently known as Grey Friars, because of the colour of their habits. The original friars had no possessions and no houses. Like the Apostles, they travelled about, preaching, tending the sick and praising God. Their carefree attitude to life earned them the nickname "God's Jesters".

But even during the lifetime of Francis some of the friars began to feel that this way of life was not practical. During his absence in the Holy Land in 1219, a movement was started to reorganise the Order

Left, a Franciscan or Grey Friar. Right, a Dominican or Black Friar.

on something like monastic lines. After Francis relinquished the leadership, his successor, Brother Elias, introduced a Rule similar to that of St Benedict, and embarked on the construction of a vast Basilica at Assisi, much against the wish of Francis, who was nevertheless buried in its crypt in 1226. Elias, however, became so involved in worldly matters that he was deposed.

A period of unrest followed, some friars wishing to live as monks, others favouring the rule of Francis. Eventually, they were subdivided into three. The first lived like monks; the second, the Poor Clares, founded by St Clare, one of Francis's first disciples, was composed of women whose especial work was nursing; the third, the Tertiaries, whose members were mostly laymen, concerned itself with education and the care of orphans.

The other chief Orders are the Augustinian (or Austin) Friars, who followed the rule of St Augustine of Hippo; the Dominican (or Black) Friars, founded by St Dominic in 1212, which gave the Church some of her greatest scholars and thinkers; and the White (or Carmelite) Friars, founded about 1150 at Mount Carmel in the Holy Land.

See also AUGUSTINE OF HIPPO, ST; BENEDICT OF NURSIA, ST; FRANCIS OF ASSISI, ST.

Friendly Societies: voluntary associations of people paying contributions to provide for sickness, old age, etc. In England they were first formed in the early 17th century to help people save a little each week or month, so that, when they were in special need, some money would be available. In Scotland, an example is recorded as early as 1555. Friendly Societies became numerous in the 18th century, and a writer in 1801 estimated that there were more than 7,000 in existence. Many other countries developed similar associations. In America they are familiar under the name of "fraternal insurance" or "benefit societies". In past years, when people had money only when they were working and could save little, if at all. Friendly Societies played an important part in providing some relief in hard times. Nowadays, state insurances and welfare schemes have often removed the most urgent necessity for such schemes. But they continue to be popular, and many thousands are still in existence.

Friends, Religious Society of: a body of Christians, often known by their 17th-century nickname: Quakers. Quakerism arose during the 17th century at a time of religious ferment. George Fox (1624–91) (*see* separate entry) preached the immanence of God's spirit in people's hearts and of His guidance in their lives, the reality of Christ's presence, the need to live one's faith and for integrity in personal living, and the equality of all men and women before God.

After George Fox's visit to the northwest of England in 1652, the movement grew rapidly and became a missionary force, spreading throughout the British Isles and to Europe and North America. Friends (as they already called themselves, though the name Society of Friends came later) were bitterly persecuted, both under the Commonwealth and the restored

monarchy. They refused to take oaths, to pay tithes, to fight for Commonwealth or king, or to abandon their way of worship, which consisted of a period of silent waiting upon God, during which spoken ministry or prayer could be uttered by any of the group, man, woman or child. They needed no special buildings, no ordained ministers and no sacramental rites, and they had no creeds, believing that these set limits to truth. The Quakers would not avoid persecution by meeting in secret, so that thousands were arrested, brutally treated and imprisoned. Many died as a result, and in America three men and one woman were hanged on Boston Common. Later, in 1682, the Quaker William Penn (1644–1718) founded Pennsylvania, where religious liberty was enjoyed by all.

After the Toleration Act (1689) the Quakers tended to retire from public life. Their simple ways of living, of speech and of dress, adopted as protests against their inequality, became rigid customs. The distinctive Quaker dress was evolved and continued to be worn by most Friends who took their religion seriously – for instance, the saintly American Friend, John Woolman (1720–72), who testified effectively against slavery and other social evils, and Elizabeth Fry (1780–1845), the great English prison reformer.

Like other nonconformists, Friends were banned from public office and from entering universities. Many of them engaged in trade, commerce or industry, where their frugal habits and reputation for integrity won them success and often prosperity. In the 19th century the evangelical movement brought new, outward-looking ideas, and these were opposed by some Friends who clung to the old traditions. In the USA the resulting tensions caused disastrous Separations.

With the approach of the 20th century and the removal of barriers against nonconformists came a new era. Friends discovered their faith to be relevant in every department of life, including politics and the arts. Maintaining their separate identity, they now work more closely with other Churches. Their Yearly Meetings – the name given to the central organisation of each state or nationwide group – have become more vigorous and independent in thought. Varying in their interpretation of Quakerism, they unite in their insistence that faith must be lived. Friends from many countries have been active in social work and have undertaken relief service in times of war or disaster; they have also been constant in their search for a peaceful solution to the world's problems.

Froissart, Jean (*c.* 1337–*c.* 1410)**:** French chronicler and poet, often called the chronicler of chivalry, to the exploits and

Jean Froissart presenting his Chronicles *to the King, from an illuminated manuscript now in the British Museum.*

exponents of which his *Chronicles*, first published 1523–25, were chiefly devoted. He travelled widely and was three times in England, at one time as secretary to Philippa, queen of Edward III.

¶ UDEN, GRANT. *I, John Froissart.* 1968

Frontier: generally, the border separating one country from another. In the United States, the Frontier refers to those outlying regions which at different stages of the country's development were sparsely occupied by Indian traders, hunters, miners, ranchmen, backwoodsmen and adventurers of all sorts. This belt of territory formed the temporary boundary as the United States, stimulated in population growth by increasing waves of immigrants, expanded westwards from the Atlantic seaboard. The term "frontier" came to be used to describe a form of society where justice was rough and ready and living conditions somewhat primitive: the word is also used to describe an attitude of mind, common amongst the new Americans, which incorporated the pioneering spirit and the challenge of the vast, raw continent.

The lure of the West, rich in uncertainty and promise, led millions of Americans to migrate across the vast fertile plains in search of a new life. Disease, starvation and Indians wiped out whole wagon trains, and only the toughest pioneers survived to settle the land. The Civil War only temporarily affected this expansion, and after peace came (1865) they were free to exploit the natural abundance of the West and to push the Frontier still further westwards. Hundreds of millions of acres were brought under cultivation, and, aided by the linking of the Atlantic and Pacific by a railroad in 1869, this trend continued until by 1890 the Frontier no longer existed. But the Frontier lives on, not only in the numerous "Western" films but in the minds of the American people. When John F. Kennedy became President in 1960 he spoke of a New Frontier for Americans. This frontier was outer space, and the challenge was to put man on the moon.

Fugger, Family of: bankers to the Habsburg family. Johann, fustian weaver of Graben, founded the family fortune. His son moved to Augsburg. His grandsons Jakob and Andreas (called the "rich Fugger") extended operations to Venice and traded in spices, silk and woollen cloth. His great-grandson Jacob (1459–1525) lent money to Maximilian I and to Charles V in the Imperial Election of 1519 and received silver mines in Tyrol, Spain and Peru, copper mines in Hungary, quicksilver mines in Spain, and the Countships of Kirchberg and Weissenhorn in Austria. Half the proceeds of the Indulgences of 1517 were paid by the Archbishop of Mainz to the Fuggers. By

1547 they had amassed a capital of five million florins and had branches in Madrid, London, Antwerp, Danzig and Venice. The repeated bankruptcies of Philip II after 1557 eroded their fortune. The Fuggerei, almshouses for 106 poor families of Augsburg, recall their generosity. The Fugger Newsletters, written by and to members of the family, form one of the most important sources of commercial and political history of the 15th and 16th centuries.

Fur: the soft natural hair or dressed pelt of certain animals. Primitive man's need for food was closely linked with the use of animal skins for warmth. For the barbarian in northern climates this would have been a necessity. But throughout the ages fur has also been used as a mark of rank and as decoration on clothing. In medieval times certain furs were worn only by those of royal blood and were a masculine prerogative. Such luxury was forbidden by the Church to monks and to all but the highest ecclesiastical dignitaries. Fur became a badge of office, as seen in the judge's ermine and the decoration of academic robes.

Northern and central Europe were the main sources of supply in the Middle Ages, and the Hanseatic League actively promoted the trade in furs. The discovery of America gave it greater scope and impetus; in fact, fur trading can be considered one of the driving forces behind the exploration of North America. In the second half of the 17th century the Hudson's Bay Company was founded and long enjoyed a virtual monopoly in the region.

Wealth acquired in the 19th century as a result of the Industrial Revolution created new desires for luxury and comfort, which included the popularisation of furs. At the present time the fur trade flourishes in association with the dictates of fashion in clothes and interior decoration. For long, fur has been worn almost exclusively by women. Now the designers of men's fashion are also promoting its use. Fortunately for the conservation of increasingly rare fur-bearing animals, synthetic furs have become increasingly popular in recent years.

¶ CAMPBELL, M. WILKINS, *editor. The Fur Trade. (Canadian Jackdaw).* 1068

Furniture designers: Furniture designers and as old as furniture itself, but for centuries they remained anonymous. Even when, with the Renaissance, magnificent painted chests and richly inlaid cabinets were produced to the order of ruling families such as the Medici, the men who made them were esteemed as craftsmen rather than artists. This attitude began to change in 18th-century France, when a new word – *ébeniste* – was coined to supplement the old description, *menuisier*, which meant carpenter, or joiner. An *ébeniste*, originally, was a cabinet-maker who veneered furniture with ebony; but gradually the term widened to mean a skilled cabinet-maker generally, particularly one skilled in the delicate art of inlaying, known as marquetry.

One of the earliest and greatest of these French *ébenistes* was André-Charles Boulle (1642–1732). He is especially renowned for the inlay work in brass and tortoiseshell which today bears his name. (The spelling *buhl* is often used.) Boulle lived at a time when King Louis XIV (1638–1715) was bent on making France the centre of the civilised world. For years he was employed on work for the king's great palace at Versailles.

Boulle, who executed many of his own designs, also carried out designs made by Jean Bérain (1638–1711), a Belgian painter who was one of the first to treat furniture design as an art form in its own right. His designs, published in 1703, influenced

Above far left: Boulle armoire. Above left: McIntire chest on chest, 1796. Middle: French table, Empire style, c. 1800. Below: English cabinet, Victorian, 1868. Above: Chippendale ribbon back chairs. Middle: Hepplewhite bed. Below: Kaare Klint chair.

urniture designs throughout the century. Before him, the furniture of Louis XIV's eign, like the Sun King himself, had ended to be magnificent but overpower-ng. Under Bérain's influence it became ighter, gayer and altogether more ppealing.

French furniture of the 18th century eached a peak of excellence that has eldom been surpassed. Among outstand-ng *ébenistes* were Charles Cressent (1685-768), Jean Henri Riesener (1734–1806) nd David Roentgen (1743–1807).

The rollcall of English furniture designers egins with Thomas Chippendale (1718-'9), whose *The Gentleman and Cabinet Maker's Directory*, published in 1754, was he first important collection of furniture lesigns printed in England. Chippendale vas greatly influenced by French furni-ure of the reign of Louis XV (reigned 715-74) and also – like many other abinet-makers of the time – by the urrent fashion for pieces which imitated he Chinese or the Gothic style.

The fame of George Hepplewhite (d. 786) rests on the publication, two years fter his death, of *The Cabinet Maker and Ipholsterers' Guide*. Hepplewhite's de-gns – for chairs especially – were lighter nd more elegant than Chippendale's, vhich tended to be on the massive side. 'owards the end of the 18th century ooped skirts went out of fashion, and dies no longer needed such vast widths f chair to accommodate them.

Thomas Sheraton (1751-1806), the third f the great triumvirate of English furni-ure designers, was not, like the other two, cabinet-maker as well. His most impor-nt pattern book, *The Cabinet-Maker and Ipholsterer's Drawing Book*, first appeared n four parts between 1791 and 1794. Satin-vood was Sheraton's favourite wood.

In the middle of the 18th century the xcavation of the Roman city of Pompeii, uried under volcanic ash since AD 79, awakened a wide interest in classical art. Robert Adam (1728-92), one of four architect brothers, did much to popularise designs based on *motifs* borrowed from ancient Greece and Rome. Adam conceived of a house as a whole, designing its interior decoration, its furniture and even its carpets, as well as its architectural form. His furniture, with its use of rare woods, marbles and painted decoration, combines richness with simplicity of line.

The United States, in the days when it was a British colony and in the early years of its independence, naturally looked to Europe for a lead in taste and fashion. Duncan Phyfe (1768-1854), a Scottish immigrant who became the first cabinet-maker of importance in the US, obviously took his cue from Chippendale, Sheraton and Hepplewhite. Other famous early American cabinet-makers were John Goddard (1724-85) and Samuel McIntire (1757-1811).

In the 19th century, with the development of methods of mass production, standards of furniture design sadly declined. William Morris (1834-96), artist and poet, tried to revive the old pride in hand craftsmanship. Together with a group of like-minded artists and designers, he produced furniture, textiles, books and wallpapers. His error lay in trying to turn back the clock of history. For good or bad the age of machines had come to stay.

The Danish architect Kaare Klint was one of the founding fathers of modern Scandinavian furniture design. Alvar Aalto (b. 1898) of Finland, also an architect, is a world-famous designer of furniture, known particularly for his pioneer work with laminated wood. One of the best-known pieces of modern furniture is the chair first designed by the architect Mies van der Rohe (b. 1886) for the German pavilion at the Barcelona Exhibition of 1929.

¶ In LISTER, RAYMOND. *Great Craftsmen*. 1962

G

Galileo (Galileo Galilei) (1564–1642): Italian astronomer and scientist, whose achievements included the construction of telescopes, with which he observed the mountainous character of the moon and discovered Jupiter's satellites. He also enunciated a number of important laws in dynamics. Observation of a swinging lamp in the cathedral of Pisa led him to discover the isochronism of the pendulum, i.e. whatever the range of its swing it took exactly the same time to accomplish it. From the top of the Leaning Tower of Pisa he demonstrated that bodies of different weights fall with the same velocity. Although a convinced believer in the theory of Nicolaus Copernicus (1473–1543) that the earth is not at the centre of the universe but orbits about the sun with other planets, he was forced by the Inquisition to recant in 1633.

¶ GREGOR, A. S. *Galileo*. 1966

See also ASTRONOMY; COPERNICUS, NICOLAUS.

Sketches of the moon by Galileo, from the 1683 edition of Sidereus Nuncius.

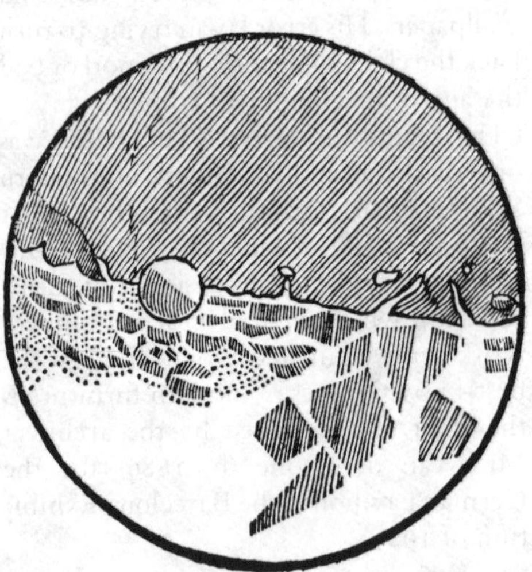

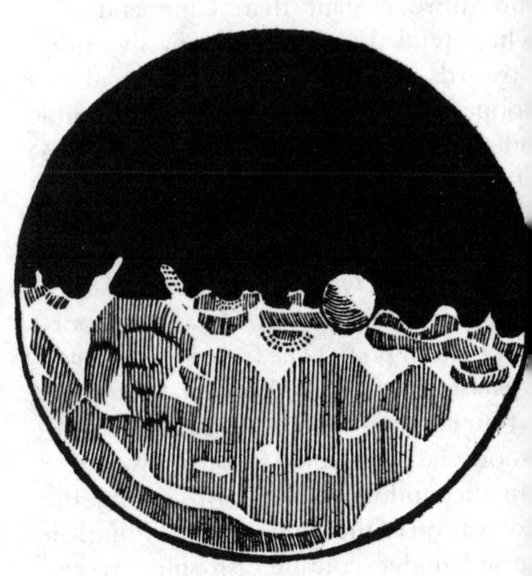

Galleon: from the Spanish word meaning a large galley. In the 16th century it became a large sailing warship; and in the 18th century was used for the Spanish treasure ships crossing the Pacific from Manila to Mexico. Galleons were usually built with a forecastle and a long beak; and an aftercastle with quarter deck and poop. They were fitted with three or four masts, square rigged except on the after masts. The galleon, armed with a broadside of heavy cannon, made an effective fighting unit.

In LANDSTROM, BJORN. *The Ship*. 1961

Galley: a vessel propelled principally by oars. Also rigged with lateen sails, the galley was popular in the Mediterranean, where weather conditions favoured its use. It developed from a lightweight craft of classical lines to become, in the 16th century, a fighting vessel, armed with cannon mounted in the bows and firing ahead over the spiked ram. Before the sea route to India from Portugal was established in 1497, trading galleys made yearly voyages to Southampton and western Europe, carrying spices brought by overland caravan to the Mediterranean from

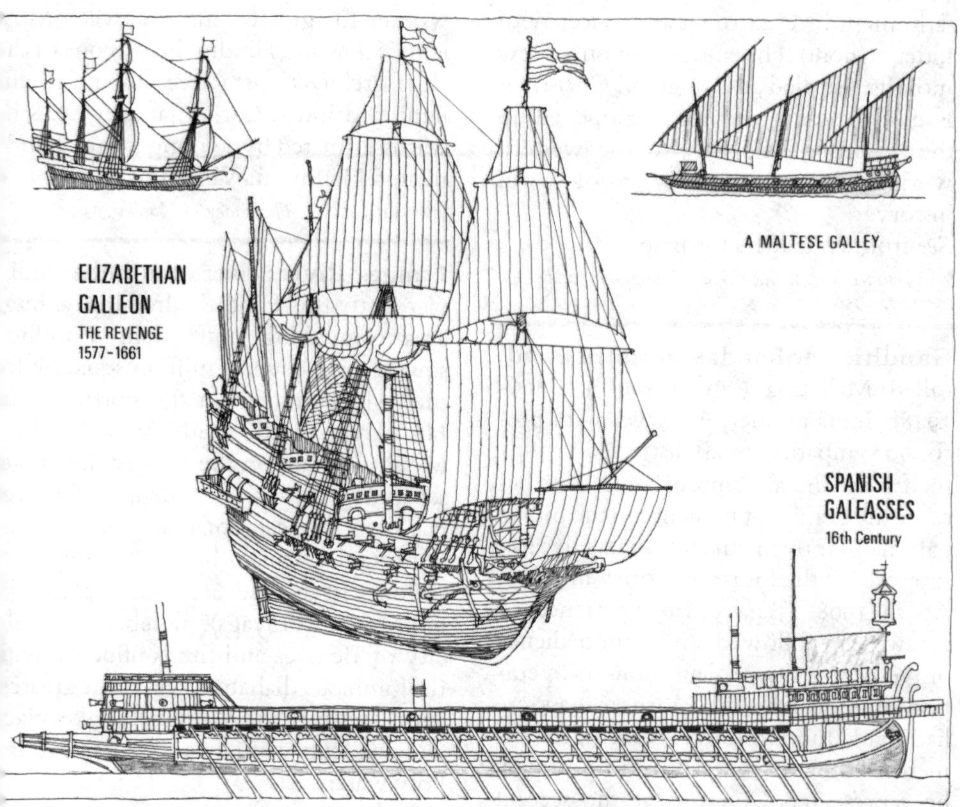

Asia. The later galleys were rowed by slave labour, criminals or prisoners of war. *See also* LEPANTO; SHIPS, TYPES OF.

Gallipoli: Turkish port on the Gallipoli peninsula. It was of great strategic importance to the ancient Greeks, who called it the Chersonese (or peninsula). The narrow exit for trade to and from the Black Sea region has at all periods placed great power in the hands of whoever commands the shores. The Turks captured the peninsula in 1356. It was a disembarkation point for the Allies in the Crimean War of 1853–56; and was the scene of a military operation in 1915, the attempt to knock out Germany's ally Turkey by a swift attack on Constantinople which, if it had succeeded, might have altered the whole course of the First World War.

JAMES, ROBERT RHODES. *Gallipoli.* 1965

Gama, Vasco da (*c.* 1469–1524): Portuguese navigator, chosen by Emmanuel I, king of Portugal, to lead the first European expedition to India. Using the newly discovered route around Africa, his four ships arrived at Calicut in May 1498. Though the Portuguese were unable to set up a factory because of the jealousy of the local traders, the expedition made a vast profit and da Gama was richly rewarded.

In 1502 he again led an expedition, this time to avenge the murder of a number of Portuguese traders left at Calicut by another explorer, Pedro Cabral. On this occasion da Gama behaved with unspeakable ruthlessness, but, as before, returned from the voyage with richly laden ships that earned him even greater honours. For the rest of his life he continued to advise Emanuel and was called out of retirement in 1524 to serve as viceroy of India, an honour he enjoyed for only a few months. He died at Cochin on Christmas Eve of the same year, having opened up the wealth of the East to the western world and, with it, a new era of world history.

See front endpapers for map.

¶ In BRENDON, J. A. *Great Navigators and Discoverers.* 1956

Gandhi, Mohandas Karamchand, called Mahatma ("great soul") (1869–1948): Indian leader. A lawyer with profound sympathy for all distressed groups, such as the Indian "untouchables", he became the dominant influence in the Indian nationalist movement after 1920. His early support for the Indian minority in South Africa (1908–15) gave him experience for his widely followed civil disobedience movement (non-violent non-co-operation) in India after the Amritsar massacre had made him hostile to British government. Although several times imprisoned, he represented Congress at the second Round Table Conference (1931–2) but continued his campaign on his return. As a leader in the independence negotiations with Britain, a vigorous opponent of the deeply entrenched caste system and a worker for greater unity between Moslems, Sikhs and Hindus, he was one of th chief architects of a free and more enlightened India. On 30 January 1948 h was assassinated by a young fanatic Hind named Nathuram Vinayak Godse.

Mahatma Gandhi.

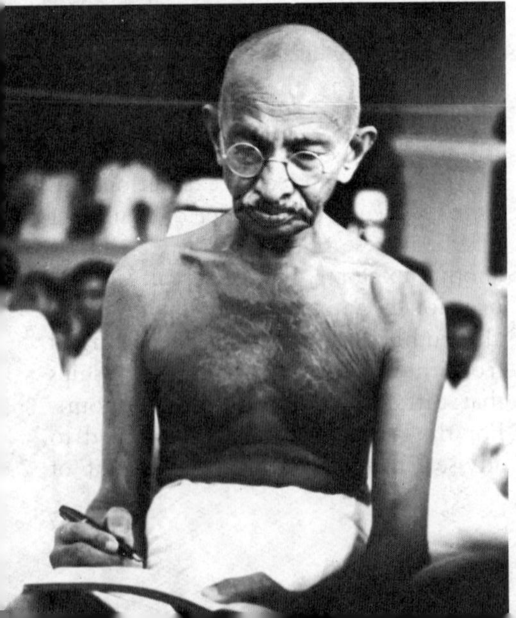

¶ ZINKIN, TAYA. *The Story of Gandhi.* 1965

Ganges River: river of northern India sacred to the Hindus, draining a hug area (something under half a millio square miles [over a million square kilo metres]), bounded on the north by th Himalayas, on the south by the Vindhy Mountains and on the east by the range separating Burma from Bengal. The are has been the scene of many of the mos important events in Indian history.

Along its course are many places o pilgrimage (Prayags), notably the hol city of Benares and the confluence wit the Jumna at Allahabad, where the greates annual festival, the Maghmela, takes plac and penitents wash away their sins in th holy waters.

¶ ZINKIN, TAYA and GANGAL, G. A. *The Gange* 1960

Gangsters: members of a band of violen criminals. Gangsters are the modern ver sion of what used to be known as outlaws The term was first used in the USA where in great cities such as Chicago and Nev York, groups of criminals gathered roun a leader, such as Al Capone, and mad themselves rich by certain kinds of law breaking. During the time of Prohibitio when the sale of alcoholic drink wa illegal, gangsters preyed upon the "speak easies" where such drinks were sold i secret. They demanded "protectio money" from the owners and, if this wa not paid, smashed up the premises ruth lessly and did not stop short of murde Many quite legal businesses were als blackmailed in this way.

Some of the gangs became very ric

and powerful and their leaders national figures. Although they were known to be criminals, they seemed to be above the law because when they were arrested and prosecuted few witnesses would speak against them either from fear or because they had been bribed to remain silent. Often the gangs made open warfare on one another. Though their leaders were named "Public Enemies", films made about them almost depicted them as heroes. Since the end of Prohibition less has been heard of the American gangster, but many such criminals still operate and are a constant menace to the police and to lawful citizens. The most notorious and widespread are members of the Mafia (*see* separate entry), the secret society of Sicilian origin whose terrorist network has spread far beyond its island home.

In recent years, gangsters of this kind have appeared in Britain, operating "protection rackets" in much the same way. The leaders of several such notorious gangs have been arrested and given long terms of imprisonment.

Gardens: pieces of ground, often near a house, for recreation and the growing of flowers and produce. There were gardens in the ancient civilisations of China, Persia and Egypt, but we know little about them. The famous hanging gardens of Babylon were terraces made in the artificial hill. Egyptian gardens appear to have been strictly formal with rectangular courtyards and beds and a free use of water, often in rectangular pools or tanks.

The Greeks planted groves and avenues of trees and ornamented them with statues, but they were valued primarily as public places in which to walk and discourse rather than for their design, seclusion or the plants which they contained.

The Roman concept of a garden came nearer to our own, which is not surprising since so much of Western gardening stems from the ideas of the Italian Renaissance, which itself drew heavily on classical literature and archaeology for its inspiration. In Roman times town gardens were usually made within a courtyard or peristyle, but the gardens of country villas were more outward looking, with terraces carefully planned and planted and sometimes commanding fine views of the countryside.

The particular contribution of the Italian Renaissance to garden making was to relate gardens more closely then ever before to the houses to which they were attached. Gardening, in fact, became highly architectural, and, since many Italian houses of this period were built on hillsides, the elevation often became as important as the plan. Differences in level were considered a virtue to be exploited by constructing series of terraces bounded by balustrades and linked by stone stairways which became an integral part of the design. These differences in level also encouraged the use of moving water, gushing, spouting and playing in elaborate cascades and fountains, often of great beauty.

The Moors, too, who had learned much from the Byzantine Empire and by the 8th century had colonised the whole of the southern Mediterranean coast and penetrated deep into Spain, loved water and used it in many ingenious ways, but often in still pools or canals rather than in the torrents and fountains beloved by Italian gardeners.

Italian garden-making reached its peak in the 16th century, French garden-making nearly a century later. At first the French style was based very closely on the Italian, but soon it developed on lines of its own, in part due to the comparative flatness of the land on which many of the finest gardens of the period were made, in part by a desire to impress by sheer size.

The long vista became a distinctive feature, closed in on each side by trees so that the eye was contained and directed onwards into the distance. The patterned beds, or parterres, with which considerable areas of these gardens were filled became ever more elaborate, and long stretches of formal water added to the sense of almost endless extension.

These canal-like pools had been developed by the Dutch, the flat and low-lying nature of whose land favoured such constructions, though on a smaller scale. The Dutch also made formal gardens of a more intimate nature than the French and used topiary (clipped shrubs, especially box and yew) in place of statuary, a style that was rapidly copied in Britain, especially after the accession of William of Orange.

The British were comparatively late starters in the art of garden-making. But where the Italians and the French got stuck in the rut of classicism, British gardening, once started, developed in extraordinarily varied ways. By the early 18th century the old formal styles of gardening were already being derided by many leaders of fashion and soon entirely new ideas were being applied to garden-making. Nature was to be the guide, pattern-making was to be swept away and gardens were to resemble beautiful pictures such as those painted by the most admired landscape artists, including Claude Lorraine, Gaspar Poussin and Salvator Rosa. At first these landscapes were adorned with buildings in the classical style, but soon romanticism crept in and ruins took the place of Palladian temples and bridges. Grass swept up to the very walls of the house and cattle were excluded by means of an invisible sunken wall, or ha-ha, so that gardens and countryside appeared to be continuous. A lake or artificial river became an essential feature for the middle distance, with clumps or belts of trees carefully disposed to channel and diversify the view. The most famous of these landscape gardeners was "Capability" Brown, who laid out the gardens of Kew and Blenheim.

By the 19th century new worlds were being explored and new plants introduced as never before. Formerly tender plants had been protected in orangeries, usually glazed on one side only and inadequately heated. Technical advances in greenhouse construction early in the 19th century, with greatly improved lighting and heating, made it possible to produce tropical and subtropical plants in great numbers, and many of these could be planted outdoors for the summer months. The practice of bedding out grew rapidly, with relays of plants produced under glass to be planted out as they were coming into flower and replaced directly they ceased to be decorative. The wide range of conifers, followed in the middle of the century by the rhododendrons and azaleas which poured into the country as a result of American and Asiatic exploration and plant-hunting expeditions, transformed the landscape. The rhododendrons would thrive in shade, and since many could be readily raised from seed and almost as

The grounds of the Nuneham Courtenay, laid out by "Capability" Brown.

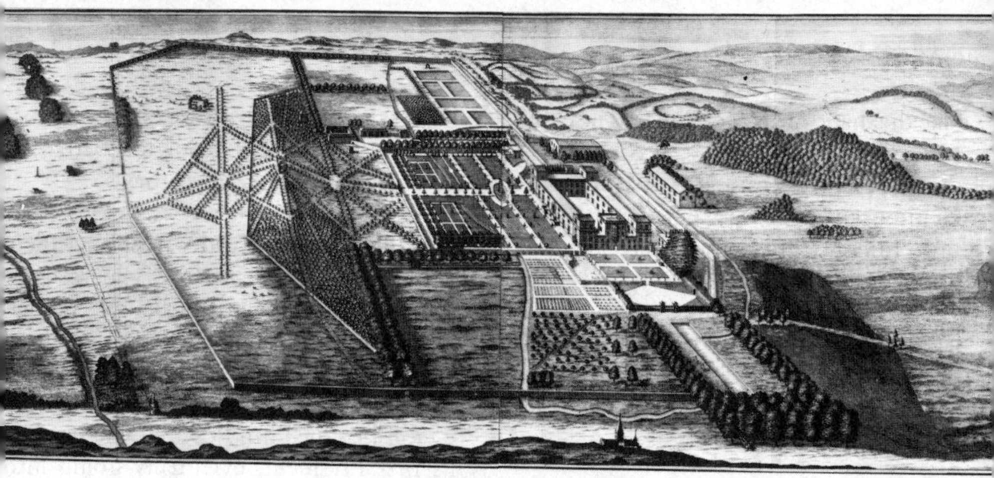

The original gardens of Wilton House.

readily hybridised, the nature planners found it possible to make their wild and woodland gardens almost as gay, at any rate for a few weeks each year, as the formal gardens filled with bedding plants.

But wild and woodland gardens require space and, with the changing economic conditions of the 20th century, gardens became steadily smaller. Already at the turn of the century a number of sensitive artists, architects and designers, among them Gertrude Jekyll, Edwin Lutyens, Harold Peto and Lawrence Johnstone, had been seeking to combine the best features of all the gardening styles that had gone before. British gardens such as Hidcote Manor in Gloucestershire and, a little later, Sissinghurst Castle in Kent were outstandingly successful examples of this kind.

In other countries different solutions have been sought. Scandinavian designers have produced gardens that in spirit at least seem closer to those of ancient Greece, with groves of trees and statuary, though usually of a very modern and abstract type. In some American gardens architectural solutions have been sought with plants themselves used in architectural ways to make patterns related in colour or form to those of the buildings or of the surrounding country. The highly stylished forms of gardening practised for centuries in China and Japan, in which nature is reduced to a formula and almost everything, plant, rock or building, has a symbolical significance, have also influenced American garden design, especially on the west coast.

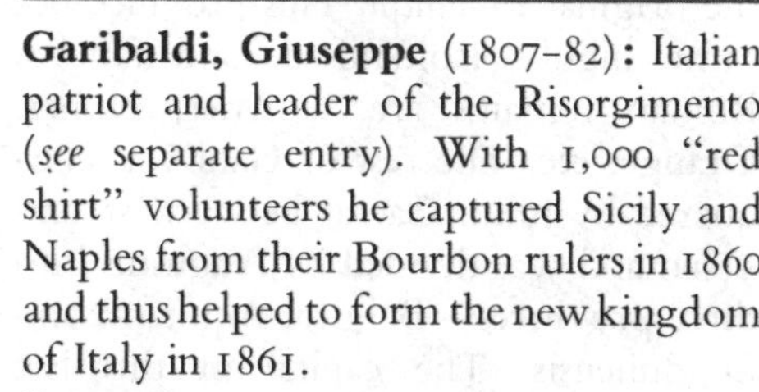

Garibaldi, Giuseppe (1807–82)**:** Italian patriot and leader of the Risorgimento (*see* separate entry). With 1,000 "red shirt" volunteers he captured Sicily and Naples from their Bourbon rulers in 1860 and thus helped to form the new kingdom of Italy in 1861.

¶ COOPER, LETTICE. *Garibaldi*. 1964

Gas: substance, often invisible, possessing perfect fluid elasticity and able to fill and take the shape of any container. The name, from Greek *chaos*, chaos, was coined by the Belgian chemist Jan Baptista van Helmout (1577–1644), who was the first man fully to grasp that there are gases distinct from ordinary atmospheric air.

For gas used for lighting purposes, *see* ILLUMINATION; in surgery, ANAESTHESIA. *See also* BALLOONS; LAVOISIER, ANTOINE-LAURENT; POISON GAS; SIMPSON, SIR JAMES; etc.

Gascony: former duchy and province of southern France. Gascony had been the Roman Gallic province of Novempopulania. Part of the shortlived Gothic kingdom, it fell to the Franks in the late 5th century but became largely independent on the death of the Frankish king Clovis (511), being invaded in 587 by Gascons or Basques from the Pyrenees who gave it its name. They were intermittently tributaries of the Meroving and Carolingian kings of France. The Duchy of Gascony was joined to that of Aquitaine in 1073 and, with Aquitaine, changed hands between French and English until finally restored to France in 1453. The inhabitants of Gascony were proverbially given to boasting, and a *gasconade* is an impressive boast or piece of bravado.

Gaul: Roman name for their provinces in France. Roman occupation began about 120 BC, and Provence gets its name from the original *Provincia*. This province became highly Romanised, and famous Roman remains are at Arles, Nîmes, Orange, etc. The rest of Gaul was conquered by Julius Caesar between 58 and 51 BC and was divided by Augustus into three provinces – Belgica, Aquitania and Lugdunensis. The capital of this last province was Lugdunum (the modern Lyons), which served as the centre of the Gallic road system and as the headquarters of the garrison. Apart from isolated rebellions, Gaul remained peaceful and prosperous and isolated from the barbarian invasions until the 4th century.

Gaulle, Charles André Joseph Marie De (1890–1970): French general and statesman. He organised the Free French forces after his country's surrender to Germany in 1940 and led the government-in-exile in Algiers, 1943–44. In 1958 he established the Fifth Republic and became its first President, eventually going into retirement in 1969.

In World War I he had proved himself a courageous soldier, being mentioned in despatches, thrice wounded and, as a prisoner of war, making five unsuccessful attempts to escape, his great height making concealment difficult. After the fall of the Vichy government in World War II he insisted that *La France Combattante*, which he headed, was not merely an allied auxiliary force but that it stood in the place of France itself. As a result of this persistence (to the point of arrogance), France was eventually accorded a full place amongst the victorious powers. De Gaulle's attitude in this symbolised his life, dedicated not to self-glory but to the historic greatness of France. Thoughtfully

General de Gaulle enters liberated Paris.

conscious of his role in history, a skilled military strategist and tactician, something of a philosopher and historian, a master of the spoken and written word, he was fundamentally a courteous and simple-living man whose abrupt retirement to the middle-class privacy of the small manor house at Colombey Les Deux Eglises a year before his death was more than a political gesture.

Gaza Strip: coastal region of south-west Palestine, about twenty-five miles long and four or five miles wide [forty kilometres long, eight wide]. It was given this name when the British mandate ended and the land went to Egypt in 1948. War between Arabs and Israelis broke out the same day. It was occupied by Arab refugees from Palestine, seized by Israel in 1956 during the Suez crisis but given back to Egypt by the UN. It was reoccupied by Israeli troops in 1967. Gaza was the home of the Philistines from the 12th century BC and, because of its importance as a highway between desert and sea, has been the scene of fighting by warlike nations for centuries.

Genealogy: a list of ancestors or the study of family history. Genealogy has been called the mother of history, in that lists of kings are among the earliest written sources. Early genealogies may give clues to tribal origins. The Bible contains many, e.g. in Genesis, Chapter 10, and St Matthew, Chapter 1. The Jewish concern for purity of race, above all for the priestly caste and after periods of exile, is seen in Ezra 11:62, and Nehemiah 7:5–61. The oldest source of Anglo-Saxon history was a genealogy tracing the kings of Wessex back to the god Woden. Private families in the Middle Ages used genealogies to further claims to lands, titles or arms (e.g. the Scrope-Grosvenor case of 1385, in which the poet Chaucer was a witness, over the use of a heraldic design, the "bend or"), but they depended on oral tradition or on monuments. A 19th-century Maori chief could quote thirty-four generations in a law suit. Genealogies in England began to be written in the 16th century, and "inaccuracy tainted with forgery" helped the "new men" of Tudor England to establish impressive pedigrees. J. H. Round in *Studies in Peerage and Family History* (1901) led to a more critical approach, and genealogical researches have often been turned to more serious purposes such as the study of hereditary disease (e.g. porphyria, the "Royal Malady"), inherited ability (e.g. the Cecils, the Darwins) and inherited criminal tendencies. The Mormons study genealogy so that they can baptise their ancestors by proxy.

Nevertheless, many people still derive much pleasure, without ulterior motive, in compiling a modest family tree and, as towns grow and people become more mobile, it is important that each generation records its origins. The Family Bible and the recollections of grandparents give a starting point. In Britain Civil Registration of Births, Marriages and Deaths takes one back to 1837. Before that Parish Registers, tombs, wills, school or college lists, embarkation lists of shipping companies, manor court rolls, may all give clues.

Geneva, Switzerland: the name given to the Swiss canton lying between the Juras and the Alps, to the lake fed by the muddy waters of the Rhône and joined below the lake exit by the milky River Arne, and finally, to the city of 327,000 population (1980).

The town has often been a home for refugees. It adopted Protestantism in 1535, and the reformer Calvin went to live there in 1536. Scholars and liberally minded people of many kinds have sought a haven in or near Geneva, including scientists, artists and writers. The town is also a natural gathering ground for home crafts from the surrounding mountains. Its watch-making is especially famous, and highly complex technical work has recently grown from native skill and the development of electric power. Switzerland avoids entangling alliances, and the country's liberalism has made Geneva an international centre for conferences, the Red Cross and for certain continuing activities of the old League of Nations.

Geneva Conventions: international conventions held in Geneva, Switzerland, in 1864, 1868 and 1929, to formulate a code of humanitarian observance of certain human rights in time of war. Though, from accident or design, there have been many exceptions, the Conventions have achieved considerable success in ensuring respect for the wounded, for medical personnel, hospitals and supplies, and adherence to accepted rules for treatment of prisoners of war. The most important agency in all this work has been the International Red Cross (*see* separate entry).

Genghis Khan (*c.* 1162–1227)**:** Mongol emperor. He was born in Outer Mongolia in a village of large oval-shaped tents. His father, an unimportant chief, soon died, so that he had to be clever and cunning to survive his childhood. He began to join the scattered nomadic tribes together and in 1196 was proclaimed "Genghis Khan" or "perfect warrior". Soon he led his mobile cavalry armies to conquer northern China, and by 1221 his empire stretched from Korea to the Persian Gulf. Northern India was subdued, and the Russian towns of Kiev and Moscow were destroyed. The invasion of Europe would probably have followed, had not Genghis Khan died in 1227. His most famous descendant was his grandson Kublai Khan.

¶ KING, CHARLES. *Genghis Khan.* 1971

Genghis Khan, in a typical Mongol tent, distributes arrows symbolising power through unity.

Genoa, Italy: port on Ligurian coast founded in the 3rd century AD by Romans. It developed as a republic under a Doge, with seven companies each supplying a quota of galleys for trade. To win the western Mediterranean islands – Corsica, Sardinia, Balearics – the Genoese combined with the Pisans to expel the Moors 1007–16, and then from 1019–1300 fought intermittently with the Pisans. Their enterprise soon took them to the Levant, Genoese engineers breached the walls of Jerusalem in the First Crusade, and Genoese troops helped defend Constantinople from the Turks in 1453. They sold Crimean slaves in Egypt, alum from Asia Minor in London and Antwerp, and Sicilian grain in France and Spain. Their black silk clothed the clergy and scholars of Europe. They fought Venice for control of the Levant trade, and, though they once captured the island of Chioggia in the Lido (1380), they were eventually defeated by the Venetians and turned to providing mariners, capital and marine insurance for the Portuguese and Spanish colonial empires. Their hinterland was too small, and in times of peril they submitted to Milanese or French rule, restoring the republic when the danger passed. Genoa was absorbed by Savoy in 1814 and is still an important seaport.

Genseric or **Gaiseric** (*c.* 395–477): king of the Vandals. An east German people, the Asding Vandals, migrated into Spain where in 428 Genseric became king of the Vandals and Alans. In 429 he led both peoples across into Africa, where they devastated the province and settled, cutting Rome off from its main supply of corn. Establishing a navy, Genseric harried the coasts of the western Mediterranean, conquering Sicily, Sardinia and Corsica and sacking Rome itself in 455. He also encouraged the invasion of Gaul by Attila the Hun in 451. The Vandal African kingdom lasted only a century.

Geological periods: stretches of time, dated from the nature of the earth's crust and from its different layers. Whatever their immediate appearance and less obvious qualities – whether of sandstone, chalk, clay, etc. – rocks are classified according to two dating principles:

1. When one sedimentary rock lies above another it can generally be assumed that it is younger than the rock below and older than any rock which may be above it. This makes dating of the rocks in relation to one another possible. However, if, for example, the south-east of England sank below the seas, marine deposits would cover only the submerged surface. If a later submergence affected the whole of the British Isles and the land eventually rose the south-east would have three kinds of rock one above another, while the remainder would have only two – the original rock and the second deposits. Thus, dating in the two areas would be different.

2. A second dating system depends on the fossil remains of animals or plants which can be related to a known stage in the world's history. The same fossil might be found in both chalk and sandstone; and although this may produce much confusion for a novice it helps scientists to identify, say, limestone in one place as a product of the same age as a clay in another.

Fossils, then, provide the main dating system; and according to this we have five main periods. The first, called Pre-Cambrian, is hardly a period at all because, although there was life at the time, no fossils were preserved. It is therefore a name attached to all rock before our classification system begins. This period is very vaguely estimated to have lasted from the first solidification of molten rock, probably over 4,000 million years ago, until about 600 million years ago.

There are four other main periods, called simply Primary, Secondary, Tertiary and Quaternary, and each of these is further subdivided. Thus, the Primary, or Palaeozoic, era (from about 600 million to 225 million years ago) includes the Carboniferous period when forests grew in swamps and by long compression became coal.

Although conditions changed a good deal within the main eras, it may be said that there was much disturbance of the earth's crust, accompanied by volcanic action, during the Primary and Tertiary eras, while the Secondary and Quaternary have been relatively inactive and have seen the deposition of material worn from the mountains formed during the Primary and Tertiary. Confusion sometimes arises because rocks formed in one era may only be recognised when brought to the surface in another.

Special emphasis must be placed on the Quaternary era because, although it has lasted only about $1\frac{1}{2}$ to $1\frac{3}{4}$ million years so far, it is still with us and its features are freshly marked in river deposits and other surface rocks. This era also includes the Ice Age, which has left its imprint on north-western Europe and the European mountains further south. It must be understood, however, that the temperature during this "age" has fluctuated considerably. There were four warm intervals alternating with four markedly cold periods, stretching from, say, $1\frac{1}{2}$ million years ago up to about 3000 BC, since when the cold has declined. We cannot be sure, of course, that we are not simply in another warm phase and that ice will not begin to advance again from the poles and that mountain glaciers will not descend to the plains. Country covered by one of the advances of the ice was eroded so that rock surfaces were smoothed, while glaciers cut pre-existing V-shaped valleys into a steep-sided cross-section more like a U. Eroded material was deposited at the ice edges or left widely spread when an ice sheet melted. Suitability of the soil for agricultural purposes is closely related to variations in these glacial deposits.

It is now thought that man rose from his earlier animal level at the very end of the Tertiary period. If this is so, he was soon confronted in many of his habitations by the rigours of the Ice Age. He discovered fire, learnt to protect himself in limestone caves and devised methods of hunting. *See also* FOSSILS.

¶ In CARTNER, WILLIAM C. *Fun with Palaeontology*. 1970

Geometry: literally, earth measurement. Originally concerned with what we would call "surveying", the word still has this meaning in some languages. Before Greek times geometry was intuitive and experimental. For example, the theorem of Pythagoras was known long before his time. In the *Chóu-peï* (a Chinese treatise of about 1100 BC) we find a diagram of the theorem but no proof, and the Hindus in the 5th century BC gave rules for making right angles by stretching cords of lengths three, four and five; five, twelve and thirteen, etc. Triangles formed with such cords would have a right-angle opposite the longest side. The great achievement of the Greeks, especially Euclid, was to systematise this knowledge. From certain basic assumptions (axioms or postulates) the theorems of geometry were developed in logical order. Next came the use of coordinates to apply algebra to geometry, with Descartes's publication in 1637 of the first treatise on Analytical Geometry. Projective Geometry was also developed in the period from 1639 to the end of the 18th century by Desargues, Pascal, Newton and Carnot. With the 19th century came a revival of interest in Pure Geometry. Perhaps the most notable feature of this period is the development of non-Euclidean geometries by Lobachevsky, Bolyai, Gauss and Riedmann, by varying Euclid's fifth postulate that through a point only one straight line can be drawn parallel to a given line. According to whether no line, one line or a pencil of lines can be so drawn, we obtain three geometries of two dimensions, known respectively as elliptic, parabolic (or Euclidean) and hyperbolic. These geometries have assumed importance in the 20th century, and Einstein considered that the universe is finite and that its geometry is elliptic.

George, St: patron saint of England, Aragon and Portugal, the Greek army, Greek shepherds, etc. He is listed by Pope Gelasius (AD 494) as one venerated by men "whose acts are known only to God". He was perhaps a native of Lydda, Palestine, who became a military tribune in a Roman Legion, may have served in Britain and was martyred at Nicomedia in AD 303 for protesting against Diocletian's revival of pagan worship. The Golden Legend (*c.* 1275) attached to him the story of overcoming the Dragon which exacted living tribute from the citizens of Silene, Libya – perhaps derived from the legend of Perseus and Andromeda. Edward III made him patron saint of England when he found the war cry "St George for England" efficacious. The year 1969, to the indignation of many, saw the removal of St George from the ranks of saints by the Vatican, though it is doubtful whether this will lead to any corresponding decline in his position in the legends and lore of Christendom. To many Englishmen it comes as a surprise to find that they have no proprietary claim on St George.

St George as symbol: The Red Cross Knight from Spensors Faerie Queene.

Georgia: republic of the USSR, adjacent to the Black Sea and the Turkish border. In ancient and medieval times the robust Georgian people survived conquest by Romans, Persians, Arabs, Mongols and Turks, but by the mid-19th century Russian domination of the region was complete. Towards the end of the century Georgia became an important centre of socialist and nationalist opposition to the Czar. After the Bolshevik Revolution (1917) the Georgians achieved a measure of independence, which came to an end in 1921 when the Red Army occupied the territory. In 1936 the Soviet dictator Stalin (1879–1953), a Georgian by birth, integrated Georgia fully with the Soviet Union.
See also USSR for maps.

Germany: region of north central Europe. *Germania* is the title of a book about Germany written by the Roman historian Tacitus in the 1st century AD. The Roman Empire embraced much of Germany, and Tacitus compares the tall, blond and virile Germans with the debauched and decadent Romans – who nevertheless maintained a high level of civilisation in Germany until the Empire itself collapsed. This collapse produced a vacuum which was only filled by the rise in the 6th century of the Franks. Under Clovis (481–511), then Charlemagne (768–814), the Frankish Empire sprawled from France to Austria. The Catholic faith was adopted, and on Christmas Day 800 Pope Leo III placed an imperial crown on Charlemagne's head, inaugurating that curious and longlived institution, the Holy Roman Empire.

In the 9th and 10th centuries Charlemagne's huge empire split into hundreds of small units, each with its own ruler, and the election of German emperors by electoral princes became established procedure. In the early Middle Ages emperors struggled to maintain royal authority against hostile and ambitious nobles and an interfering Papacy. In the 12th century the first great German dynasty, the Hohenstaufen, was established, and there was much eastward expansion. One feudal prince, Albert the Bear, attracted settlers to the area around the little village of Berlin, forming the nucleus of what was to become the great state of Prussia. During the next 200 years the political centre of gravity continued to shift towards the east; the Holy Roman (or German) Empire became relatively free of papal influence; and the towns grew in size and prosperity.

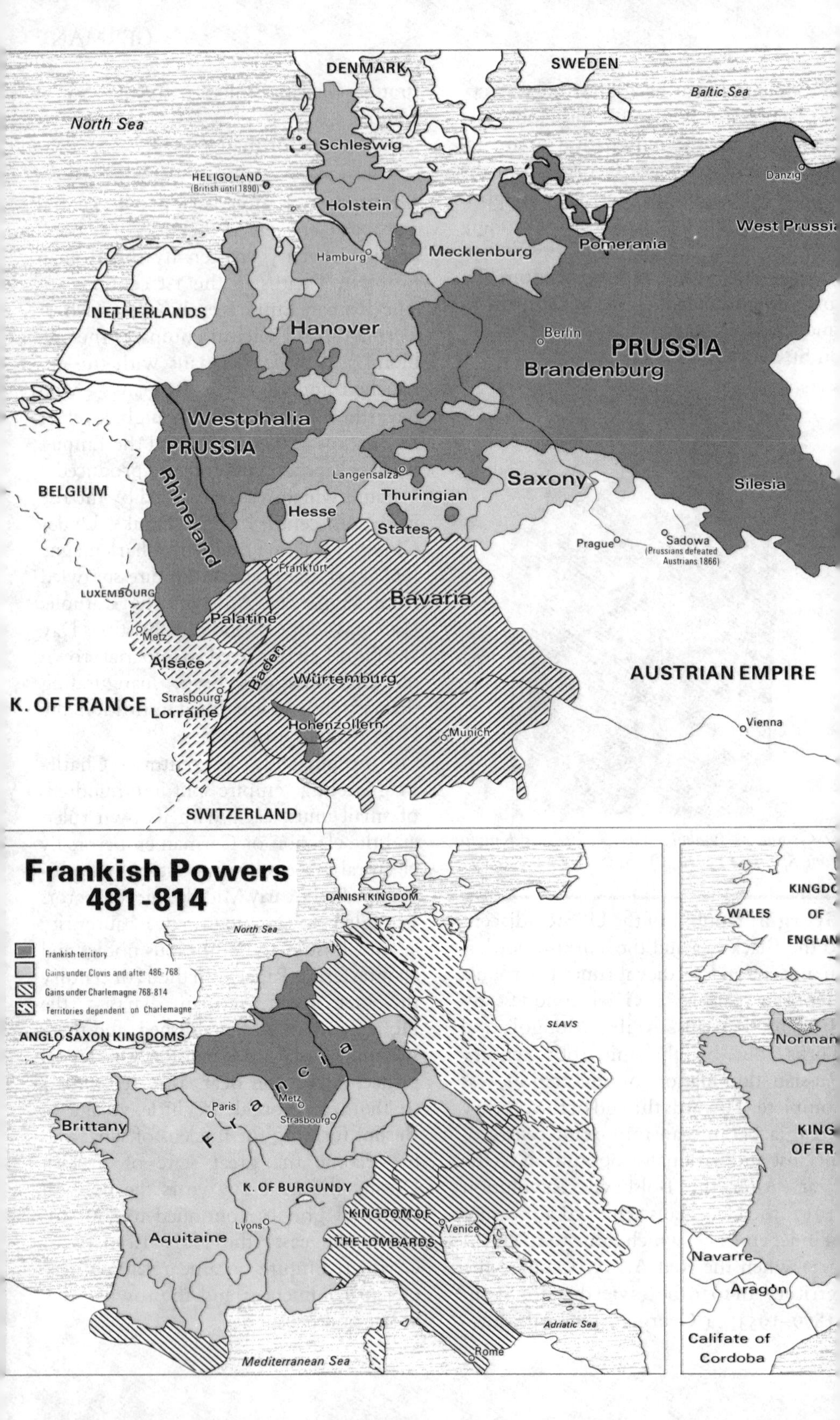
DENMARK
SWEDEN
Baltic Sea
North Sea
Schleswig
HELIGOLAND
(British until 1890)
Danzig
Holstein
West Prussia
Hamburg
Mecklenburg
Pomerania
NETHERLANDS
Hanover
Berlin
PRUSSIA
Brandenburg
Westphalia
PRUSSIA
Rhineland
Langensalza
Saxony
BELGIUM
Thuringian
States
Silesia
Hesse
Prague
Sadowa
(Prussians defeated Austrians 1866)
Frankfurt
LUXEMBOURG
Bavaria
Palatine
Metz
Alsace
Baden
Würtemburg
AUSTRIAN EMPIRE
K. OF FRANCE
Strasbourg
Lorraine
Hohenzollern
Munich
Vienna
SWITZERLAND
Frankish Powers
481-814
DANISH KINGDOM
North Sea
Frankish territory
Gains under Clovis and after 486-768
Gains under Charlemagne 768-814
Territories dependent on Charlemagne
SLAVS
ANGLO SAXON KINGDOMS
Francia
Metz
Paris
Strasbourg
Brittany
K. OF BURGUNDY
KINGDOM OF
THE LOMBARDS
Lyons
Venice
Aquitaine
Adriatic Sea
Rome
Mediterranean Sea
KINGDO
WALES
OF
ENGLAN
Norman
KING
OF FR
Navarre
Aragon
Califate of
Cordoba

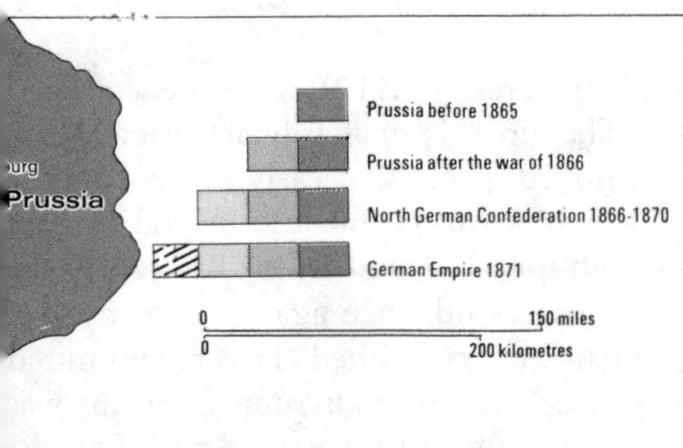

German Unification 1818-1871

By 1500 the Imperial throne had become the possession of the Habsburg family and remained so until the end of the Empire in 1806. Its greatest occupant was Charles V (1519–56), who through marriage treaties (a talent of the Habsburgs) ruled much of Europe besides Germany. Ironically it was in the latter that his power was least certain, in face of the religious and social upheavals of the Lutheran Reformation and the Peasants' Revolt. In fact, Germany was now to enter a period of internal chaos which reached its peak during the Thirty Years War (1618–48).

But the later 17th century saw the gradual achievement of a unified Prussian state under the Hohenzollern Frederick William, the "Great Elector" (1640–88), while the accession of Frederick II (1740–86) to the Prussian throne marks the beginning of the tussle for leadership in Germany between Prussia and Austria. By prodigious effort in war Frederick established Prussia's claim to be a recognised power and his own claim to the title "Great".

Although both Prussia and Austria were humbled by Napoleon at the peak of his success, his downfall in 1815 produced a long-overdue reorganisation of Germanic Europe. The number of German states was reduced to a Confederation of thirty-nine, under the leadership of Austria. In the 1830s and 1840s the states moved towards economic unity by signing a commercial treaty, or *Zollverein* (customs union), which excluded Austria and was dominated by Prussia, now the largest and richest north German state. But, despite the revolutionary outbreaks of 1848 throughout Germany (and most of Europe), Austria succeeded in restoring a supremacy which would henceforth be challenged only by force of arms.

Prussia's situation found the man it needed in Bismarck (1815–98), who became Prime Minister in 1862. An incomparably shrewd politician with a massive physical presence but a surprisingly gentle voice, Bismarck set out to make Prussia one again the leading German state. This he achieved in the war of 1866 against Austria, after which the latter no longer had a voice in German affairs. The Franco-Prussian War (1870–71) completed Bismarck's work of Prussian aggrandisement, and, when he proclaimed the second German Empire at Versailles in January 1871, Germany – almost incidentally – had become a united nation under a Hohenzollern Emperor. Bismarck remained German Chancellor until 1890, when he was dismissed by the new emperor, Kaiser Wilhelm II (1888–1941).

Wilhelm II, grandson of Queen Victoria on his mother's side, was determined to make of Germany – already an industrial giant – a world power with an overseas empire and a large navy. He succeeded, but at the price of alarming the rest of Europe, not least England. In 1914 the Kaiser allowed his generals to drag Germany into a conflict in support of Austria which led to a European war, with England, France and Russia against Germany.

The first World War of 1914–18 ended in the collapse of the German Empire and the humiliating peace settlement of Versailles. It also led to the first experiment in democratic government (the Weimar Republic). Although in the 1920s Germany at last seemed to have found stability and prosperity, the world economic crisis which began in 1929, coupled with the anti-democratic forces inside Germany, led to the break up of the Weimar Republic. In January 1933 Adolf Hitler, leader of the Nazi Party (*see* HITLER), became German Chancellor and proceeded to establish an iron dictatorship and to follow an ambitious foreign policy, with the declared object of restoring Germany's national honour and "racial purity". His attack on Poland in September 1939 led to the second World War in a generation.

The superbly professional German army enjoyed spectacular early successes in the war of 1939–45, but by the end of 1941 both the USA and Russia had joined the struggle, and once again Germany was finally overwhelmed. Hitler committed suicide, his country in ruins. Germany was divided into zones, under Anglo-French-American occupation in the west and Russian in the east. Berlin, though in the eastern zone, because of its political importance was put under four-power administration. In 1949 the western Federal Republic of Germany came into being; at the same time East Germany became the German Democratic Republic, remaining largely under Russian control. The much larger Federal Republic has since become the most prosperous state in Europe under the leadership of, among others, Konrad Adenauer (Chancellor 1949–63) and Willy Brandt.

While most western statesmen are committed in theory to the idea of German reunification, it is unlikely to come about in the foreseeable future. Russia lost perhaps twenty million people as a result of the German onslaught of 1941–44 and will probably long regard it as in her interest to maintain the present division. No peace treaty can yet be signed with Germany as a whole by the states that fought against her in World War II.

Germany – German Democratic Republic, commonly called East Germany: Republic of central Europe on the Baltic; population 16,732,500 (1982). The GDR came into existence in 1949 and consists of territory that was formerly the Russian zone of occupation after the Second World War. It has been ruled by a one-party constitution in which the Socialist Unity, or Communist, party provides the members of the parliament (*Volkskammer*) and the government. Since

1949 the real power has rested with the leader of the party and chairman of the Council of State.

From the beginning, the poverty of the GDR contrasted markedly with the prosperity of the Federal Republic (West Germany). Economic hardship, coupled with the lack of personal freedom, drove many to seek escape to West Germany. The western sector of Berlin provided an escape route in the 1950s for thousands of East German refugees. This exodus caused a further decline in the economy and led Ulbricht, with Russian support, to build the Berlin Wall in 1961, effectively cutting off the escape route. In the last few years there has occasionally been some slight relaxation, permitting relatives on either side of the Wall to visit each other at Christmas and Easter.

The GDR has achieved nothing like the degree of international recognition of her western neighbour, partly because of her smaller size and population, partly because of her domination by Russia. The basic treaty signed with West Germany (1972) opened the way for the GDR to establish diplomatic relations with western countries, and to be admitted to the UN.

Germany, Federal Republic of (West Germany)**:** republic of central Europe on the North Sea and the Baltic; population 61,469,500 (1983). Created a separate republic in 1949, following the Soviet blockade of Berlin (April 1948–May 1949), West Germany was recognised as a sovereign state in 1955 and plays an important rôle as a member of NATO and the European Economic Community. A landmark of the republic's new sphere of relationships was the treaty of friendship and co-operation with France, signed in 1963, thus ending a long traditional enmity. This, along with striking economic recovery, must be attributed largely to the work of Konrad Adenaur, Chancellor for fourteen years till his retirement in 1963. In 1972 a treaty between West and East Germany, ratified the following year, agreed on a basis for relationships between the two countries.

Gettysburg: small town in Pennsylvania, USA; the scene of a critical battle in the American Civil War, between the Confederates under Lee and the Federals under Meade (July 1863); and, a few months later, of the famous speech by Abraham Lincoln (the Gettysburg Address) which Edward Everett, who was present, prophetically declared would live through the ages. The final words were: "We here highly resolve that this nation, under God, shall have a new birth of freedom; and that government of the people, by the people, and for the people, shall not perish from the earth."

See also AMERICAN CIVIL WAR; LINCOLN, ABRAHAM.

Ghana: independent republic in West Africa; formerly the Gold Coast Colony; population 12,243,800 (1982). In 1482 the Portuguese established a fortified trading post at Elmina. Dutch, British, Danes, French and Germans followed, trading in gold and slaves, but by 1872 only the British remained, and the southern part of the country became a Crown Colony. The Ashanti empire was annexed in 1901, and in 1919 part of the adjoining ex-German territory of Togoland was placed under British mandate, becoming a trust territory after World War II and thus completing the geographical entity of Ghana.

The first effective moves towards independence were the formation of the United Gold Coast Convention in 1947 and of the Convention People's Party in 1949. Progress was aided by support of returning ex-servicemen after World

War II. Independence was granted on 6 March 1957. On 1 July 1960 President Nkrumah declared Ghana a sovereign republic and assumed dictatorial powers. In the period of serious mismanagement which followed, Ghana's reserves, which stood at NC490 million at independence, disappeared, and external debts of over NC520 million were incurred. In February 1966 a military coup ousted Nkrumah. In 1969 the military returned power to a civilian government (Dr Busia) but again seized power in 1972. The cycle was repeated at the end of the 1970s and Ft Lt Jerry Rawlings took power for a second time in 1982. Throughout this period the economy was stationary or in decline despite rich potential.

See also AFRICA for the early history of the continent, and map.

Gibraltar: British Crown Colony, occupying a peninsula at the tip of southern Spain. A largely barren rock, rather less than three miles by a mile in area (4·8 by 1·6 kilometres), it is separated from the mainland by a narrow strip of sand crossed by a frontier line. On the Gibraltarian side the strip now accommodates an airport, while the Rock shelters a town of 30,000 people. Until recently Spaniards came daily across the frontier to work in the town.

The Rock was captured by Admiral Sir George Rooke for Britain in 1704 and became a control point for entrance to and exit from the Mediterranean. It was besieged by the Spaniards between 1779 and 1783, but its precipitous sides and sea defences combined with the gallantry of the defenders under General Eliott (later Lord Heathfield) made it impregnable. In the last twenty-five years newly discovered natural caves and extensive tunnelling have provided extra cover and enormous storage space.

Gibraltar has no natural wealth and is therefore unable to maintain herself by growing her own food or exploiting minerals. Everything has to be imported. Water for domestic purposes comes from the rain falling on almost bare rock and channelled into underground reservoirs. Her port facilities have always been valuable to shipping, but tolerable prosperity depends increasingly on tourism.

In recent years Spain has demanded possession of Gibraltar, largely for prestige reasons. She has gained support in this from the United Nations, but Britain defends the overwhelming desire of Gibraltarians to remain British.

See EUROPE for map.

Gipsies or **Gypsies:** name used today to designate any people whose way of life is nomadic and who live in caravans. In a narrower sense it stands for a distinct race, the Romani, whose beginnings are obscure but who probably originated in India. "Gipsy" is a corruption of "Egyptian". Possibly the gipsies' skill at fortune-telling led to their being identified with a country that was associated with the magical arts.

Objects of suspicion and persecution – the Nazis alone put to death some 400,000 – they have nevertheless preserved their identity to a remarkable degree. Their language still survives, though with an inevitable admixture of foreign words. Their present day world population is estimated at between five and six million. Pure-blooded gipsies are called *Romanies*, those of half-blood *Posh-rats. Diddikais* have some gipsy ancestry. The gipsy name for Travellers, who have nothing in common with real gipsies other than their nomadic way of life, is *Barengré*.

Gipsies are known as musicians, horse traders, basket workers and menders of china. With the general decline of handicrafts their ancient skills as smiths have

English gipsies of the Fletcher tribe.

tended to decline, in Britain at least, into dealings in scrap metal, the unsightly accumulation of which, adjacent to their camps, is a potent cause of local ill will. Their reputation for dishonesty is founded on their light-hearted attitude to property rights in such things as pheasants. Major crime is rare among them; but, understandably, citizens burdened with the cares of home-owning, tax-paying, etc., tend to eye gipsies with distrust – and, perhaps, a little envy. Gipsies are found in Britain, the USA, Russia, Spain, Turkey, Poland and Hungary.

¶ SINCLAIR, O. *Gypsies*. 1967

Girl Guides: members of the World Association of Girl Guides and Girl Scouts. At the first Scout rally, held in London in 1909, girls arrived too, wearing Scout hats and neckerchiefs borrowed from their brothers. They were officially recognised in 1910, given the name of Guides and introduced to a modified form of Scout training sponsored by Agnes Baden-Powell. Emphasis is placed on domestic skills as well as on outdoor activities. The movement is now international.

¶ BRIMELOW, L. ELIZABETH. *The Guide Handbook*. 1968

Gladiator: originally a fighter with a sword, from Latin *gladius*; a criminal or slave, highly trained to fight in the Roman amphitheatres. Gladiators were matched against each other or against animals. Weapons varied from a net and trident to full armour, and matches with mixed weapons were favoured. The defeated gladiator might sue for mercy from the crowd. Gladiatorial shows were stopped by the Christian emperors (*see* page 364).

Gladiators (see page 363).

Gladstone, William Ewart (1809–98): British statesman and prime minister. He entered the House of Commons in 1832 and became leader of the Liberal Party in 1865. During his four terms as prime minister between 1868 and 1894 he devoted much of his energy to the problems of Ireland. Here, as in the field of foreign policy, he tried always to apply his own high Christian principles to politics. At home he promoted constitutional progress for the mass of the people, but was firmly opposed to social reforms which would involve government expenditure on a large scale. His economic philosophy of free trade and balanced budgets was not seriously challenged until the 1930s. Henry Duff Traill in *The New Lucian* (1884) gives a vivid word-picture of "that white-hot face, stern as a Covenanter's yet mobile as a comedian's; those restless, flashing eyes; that wondrous voice whose richness its northern burr enriched as the tang of the wood brings out the mellowness of a rare old wine; the masterly cadence of his elocution; the vivid energy of his attitudes; the fine animation of gestures . . .".

¶ COLLIEU, E. G. *Gladstone*. 1968

Glass: brittle translucent substance, produced by fusing a mixture of sand and soda or potash, to which certain other ingredients, such as carbonate of lime and red lead, may be added.

The earliest glass articles known to us are some glass-coated stone beads made in Egypt more than 5,000 years ago. Glass-making may have begun in Egypt or else in Syria which, besides the indispensable sand deposits, possessed ample forests to supply the large quantities of fuel needed for its manufacture.

The great glass-makers of the ancient world were the Romans, who perfected the art of glass-blowing and produced glassware that bears comparison with any that has been made since. Through the

Left, Venetian wineglasses. Above left, Spanish vase of transparent green glass, 16th century. Above right, English goblet of clear colourless lead-glass engraved with diamond-point, c. 1705.

Dark Ages the skills which they had dis- ;eminated throughout the Roman Empire were never entirely lost. In medieval :athedrals such as York Minster in Britain, Chartres in France and Cologne in Ger- nany, stained-glass windows glow like ewels. Glazed windows in the dwelling iouses of the upper classes began to come nto general use probably in the 12th :entury.

England, with the help of craftsmen rom Venice, Lorraine and the Low Countries, established its own glass-mak- ng industry in the 16th century. Its great ichievement was the development of 'flint-glass" – glass with lead oxide in its :omposition, an additive which made it iarder and more brilliant than any glass iitherto.

Modern industrial processes have made glass one of the most widely used man- nade products. Glass windows were used it Pompeii, but for centuries they were a arity and a luxury, so that it was not ınknown for people leaving their homes or a while to have the glass removed till heir return. Protective shutters were also :ommonplace. Today many tall buildings are virtually cages of glass and steel.

¶ EPSTEIN, SAM and BERYL. *The First Book of Glass.* 1964

Glorious First of June, Battle of the (1 June 1794): an operation off Ushant by the British fleet under Earl Howe (1726–99) against the French fleet under Admiral Villaret Joyeuse, convoying an American grain convoy. In severe fighting over four days Howe captured six enemy ships of the line and sank one, though the convoy escaped.

Glorious Revolution (1688): the replacement of James II, king of England, by his daughter Mary and her husband (his nephew), William of Orange, stadtholder of Holland. James fled to France on William's invasion, the throne was declared vacant and William and Mary were offered the crown on conditions laid down in the Bill of Rights (1689).

Godfrey of Bouillon (1060–1100): first Crusader ruler of Jerusalem. He was second son of Eustace II of Boulogne, and through his mother had a claim to the

Duchy of Lower Lorraine, but Emperor Henry IV confiscated it and installed Godfrey as his official there. He was fair, well built, brave, pious and of simple tastes, but a poor administrator and an indifferent commander, who concealed his lack of understanding and decision by obstinacy. In 1096 he sold his castles, pledged his lordships and set out by land to join the First Crusade. He was among the first to scale the walls of Jerusalem and was chosen Defender of the Holy Sepulchre (refusing the title of king), perhaps because Raymond of Toulouse and the patriarch Daimbert of Pisa thought he could be easily managed. Next year he died of typhoid after a visit to Venetian ships in Jaffa and was buried in the Church of the Holy Sepulchre.

Gold: heavy precious metal of bright yellow colour, easily worked. Gold has always been valued above other metals. It does not tarnish, is practically indestructible and can be melted down and remoulded without altering its qualities. The first known gold coins were made in Lydia, by King Croesus, who had them stamped with a lion and a bull to prove that they came from his treasury. Eventually, all civilised countries adopted gold as currency.

In ancient times, a king's gold was buried with him. From excavations at Mycenae and in Egypt we can guess at the treasure stolen long ago by tomb robbers.

In the 16th century Spanish explorers discovered that the Incas of Peru and the Aztecs of Mexico possessed vast quantities of gold. They plundered their cities and carried away shiploads of treasure, but never found the gold mines.

In the 19th century gold was discovered in California and the Yukon, and hundreds of men rushed to make their fortune. A few succeeded, but most returned as poor as before and many died in the hard winter of 1849.

Occasionally, gold is found near the earth's surface, but the mines of Johannesburg are over a mile deep. Gold was first

Gold mining in California.

seen there in stones lying on farmland. Prospectors hurried to the district, only to find that the rich gold seams were deeply buried in hard rock and could be reached only by the use of costly machinery, so that only wealthy companies could afford to sink shafts in the Rand.

Nowadays, gold bars, known as *bullion*, are used as an international currency, and are sent by banks from one country to another. Gold coins, however, have become generally too expensive for common use. The greatest monetary gold reserves in the world are held by the USA. In June 1983 gold and other reserves amounted to $32.6 billion. Most of the US gold reserves are stored in standard bars at Fort Knox, Kentucky.

¶ GIBBS, PETER. *The True Book about Gold.* 1959

Good Hope, Cape of: south-western tip of the African continent; discovered by Bartolomew Diaz, Portuguese navigator, in 1488 and called by him Cape of Storms, though a few years later Vasco da Gama, realising that the Cape marked the turning point after the long voyage south from Lisbon into the milder Indian Ocean, rechristened it Cape of Good Hope. The Dutch were the first to colonise it when in 1652 Jan van Riebeck with a party of nearly a hundred men established a settlement where Cape Town now stands, as a staging post for the Netherlands East India Company. *See* Endpapers.

Gordon, Charles George (1833–85): British general, born in Woolwich, SE London. He saw active service in the Crimean War and in 1860 was with the British expedition which reached Peking, then threatened with the Taiping rebellion. Li Hung-Chang appointed him leader of a Chinese force which temporarily repulsed the rebels, then joined with the Imperial Army, finally defeating the Taipings in 1864, after which he was known as "Chinese" Gordon. He was Governor of the Sudan 1873–80, returning in 1884 to deal with the revolt of Mohammed Ahmed, who called himself the Mahdi. Britain had advised Egypt to abandon the Sudan, and Gordon was instructed to evacuate as many Egyptians as possible; but he was surrounded and besieged by the rebels at Khartoum, where he held out against overwhelming odds for five months before the town fell and he was speared to death by the Mahdi's men.

Charles Gordon.

Gothic art and architecture: the type of art and architecture that flourished in Europe from the late 12th century to the time of the Renaissance. The term *Gothic*, as applied to art and architecture, was originally intended as an insult. It was used in this sense in the 18th century by people who considered the architecture of the Middle Ages rough and uncouth – in fact like the original Goths, one of the barbarian races which poured westward across Europe during the closing centuries of the Roman Empire. The richness and beauty of Gothic art make it hard to understand such a verdict. What the 18th-century critics objected to was that it was so unlike the classic art of Greece and Rome.

The Gothic period was one of intense religious faith. It was also one of intense interest in the material world. Out of this combination of qualities came the Gothic churches. The churches which preceded them, in the Romanesque (in England, Norman) style, were stocky-pillared, heavy-walled buildings with few windows, impressive but with something of a fortress look about them, temples of an unapproachable God. In part this was due to a limited knowledge of the principles of engineering, but only in part. Many of the great Romanesque churches were built as part of monasteries. They were austere, apart from the world.

The Gothic cathedrals were the creation of the growing towns: they belonged to the people, they housed the Son of Man. All their dominant lines were vertical, embodying man's striving for Heaven. Their structure depended on a great development in engineering skill and a vastly improved understanding of the laws of balance. Their builders found out how to construct vaulting that gave to the heavy stone ceilings an illusion of lightness and grace. They discovered how to concentrate the necessary supports in slender vertical shafts and exterior buttresses so that the old massive pillars were no longer needed, and large sections of wall could be opened up as windows, flooding the interior with the jewelled light of stained glass. The rounded arch of the Romanesque style gave way to the pointed arch which, flamelike, again tends to lead the eye upward.

The Cathedral of Nôtre Dame in Paris, consecrated in 1182, has been called the cradle of Gothic. Some of the earliest Gothic church-building in England is to be found in Lincoln Cathedral.

Gothic architecture did not remain static. There was a constant, gradual development. For convenience, three sub-periods are usually distinguished. The earliest period is called Early Gothic, except in relation to England, where the term Early English is used instead. The second period, when church interiors tended to become more elaborate and ornamented, is called Flamboyant (flamelike) in France and, in England, Decorated. In England, towards the end of the 14th century, the Decorated style gave way to the more severe Perpendicular.

Cathedral building was a long business, often taking centuries, so that one cathedral may contain work in several architectural styles. Among the great Gothic churches of Europe are the cathedrals of Chartres and Amiens in France; and, in England the chapel at King's College Cambridge, and the Henry VII chapel at Westminster.

The Gothic churches were treasure-houses of all the arts. Wood-carvers decorated bench-ends and misericords (the projecting brackets on the undersides of folding seats, against which the monks could lean during the long hours of standing enjoined by church ritual) with delightfully impudent carvings of animals and people. Many of the latter are obviously portraits, not to say caricatures. Norwich Cathedral in England possesses an outstanding series of misericords. The sculptured tombs of kings and queens, bishops and nobles, further enriched the interiors, and stained glass turned them into places of mystery and beauty. The colours of the great rose window at Chartres Cathedral are as pure and bright today as when the glass was made during the first half of the 13th century. The east window of York Minster, made in 1405–8, is the largest area of stained glass in the world. Much irreplaceable stained glass

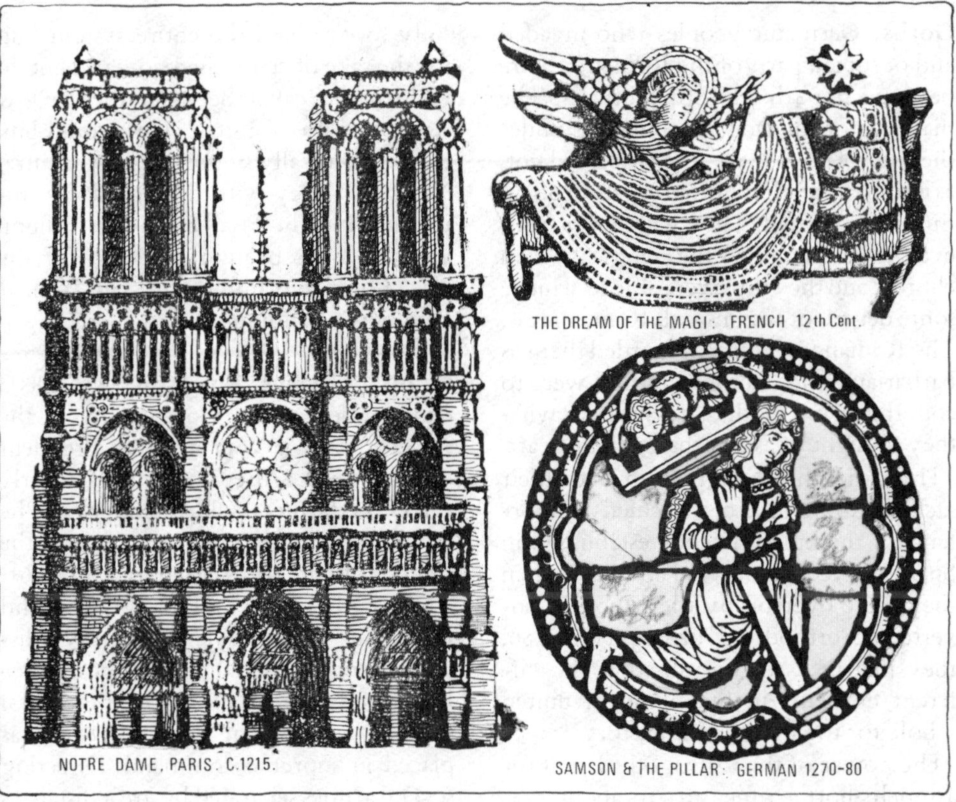
THE DREAM OF THE MAGI : FRENCH 12th Cent.

NOTRE DAME, PARIS. C.1215.

SAMSON & THE PILLAR: GERMAN 1270-80

was destroyed by the Puritans during the Civil War. That of York was saved by the citizens making it a condition of their surrender to the Parliamentary forces that the city's stained glass should not be harmed.

Ivory carving, an ancient art, flourished in the Gothic period. During the 13th and 14th centuries Paris was the chief centre. Little portable altars were carved with scenes from the Nativity, the Crucifixion, or the Last Judgment. Small statuettes were made of the Virgin and Child.

The encouragement of art is a byproduct of prosperity. With the growth of towns and the evolution of a monied merchant class, the demand grew for the kind of beautiful object that formerly was to be found only in the possession of the Church or a king or his nobles. The churches gained from this new class of connoisseurs. Out of piety or vanity or a combination of both, the latter enriched their parish churches with gifts, often of paintings. A typical painting of the Holy Family might show the donor kneeling respecfully at one side.

The Gothic style, with its accent on letting in the light, fitted best into northern Europe. Despite such marvellous examples as Milan Cathedral, it was not really suited to the Mediterranean sun. It was, too, an art of stone rather than of the brick and marble which were the predominant building materials of Italy. Perhaps for these reasons, with the coming of the Renaissance, Italy turned eagerly back to the classical models of Greece and Rome. The North, on the other hand, having found a mode of expression which suited it so well, was slow to change to the new fashion.

¶ BRANNER, R. *Gothic Architecture*. 1968; MARTINDALE, A. *Gothic Art*. 1967

Goths: Germanic peoples who invaded and occupied parts of the Roman Empire between the 4th and 8th centuries. The main historical facts are outlined under the entry BARBARIANS. The Goths did not, as is sometimes thought, bring the Roman Empire to an end. They were Christians, even if belonging to the heretical Arian church, and they thus were able to achieve some degree of fusion with Roman ideas. The Romans, of course, regarded them as barbarians, and later generations were to coin the term "Gothic" to apply to what they thought of as a barbaric form of art.

The Visigoths, though famous for their sack of Rome in 410, are chiefly important for the kingdom they established in Spain between about 500 and 711, when they were overrun by the Moors. Converted to orthodox Christianity in 589, they managed to fuse together the different elements in Spain into a united whole for the first time in history.

The power of the Ostrogoths lasted for a much shorter time, 493 to about 554. For over half that time they were ruled by Theodoric. He had been brought up in Constantinople, and the kingdom that he founded returned in many ways to the old Roman Empire. His capital at Ravenna was beautified by fine churches and mosaics, some of which can still be seen in the church of San Apollinare Nuovo. The Byzantine emperor Justinian reconquered Italy between 535 and 540. The Ostrogoths lasted a few more years, but on the invasion of the Lombards they disappear from history.

¶ In SOBOL, DONALD J. *The First Book of the Barbarian Invaders.* 1963

Grand Canal: chief canal of China. Water systems have always been important in China, both for irrigation and for transport, and consequently have been objects of political control. The Sui emperor, Yang Ti (610–17), decided not only to overhaul the entire system but, for the sake of centralised government, to construct a canal between the Yellow River and the Yangtze. This would link the economically important East-Central Yangtze Valley with the politically important North. Five-and-a-half million workers were brought together for the task. Over two million are said to have died while building it.

Grant, Ulysses Simpson (1822–85): commander of the Union army in the American Civil War and 18th President of the USA. After a chequered early career as farmer, soldier and clerk, he quickly came to prominence when the Union call to arms went out in 1861. Though the quality of his strategy and leadership was uneven he always displayed great personal courage, iron resolution and energy. He enjoyed the loyal support of Lincoln and in 1864 was placed in supreme command. Directing several armies separated by great distances and mustering a total of over a million men, he brought the federal forces to final victory. As President (1869–77), despite great personal qualities, he was less successful, placing too much faith in unworthy supporters and allowing corruption in administration to reach an alarming level.

General Grant.

Gravitation: force of attraction exerted by the earth and other bodies, independent of their chemical nature.

About 1604 Galileo discovered that a body falls under gravity with a constant acceleration, independent of its weight. In the *Principia* (published 1687) Sir Isaac Newton stated his Law of Gravitation and was able to deduce mathematically from this that a planet moving round the sun must conform to the laws laid down by Kepler (1609), as the result of observations made by himself and Tycho Brahe. Newton's system gives correct results in all but a few cases. In the 20th century Einstein, Milne and Birkhoff have advanced other theories to explain the few anomalies in Newton's system. The well known story of Newton and the apple receives no mention by Henry Pemberton, to whom Newton related the origin of his first ideas of gravitation. The anecdote in its popular form was given currency by Voltaire, who wrote: "One day, in the year 1666, Newton went into the country, and seeing fruit fall from a tree . . entered into a profound train of thought as to the causes which could lead to such a drawing-together or attraction".

¶ RONAN, COLIN, editor. *Newton and Gravitation. (Jackdaw).* 1967

Great Britain and Northern Ireland, The United Kingdom of: kingdom in north-west Europe, area approximately 94,500 square miles [244,700 square kilometres]; population 56,124,000 (1983)

Great Britain is the name of the whole island containing England, Wales and Scotland, together with the adjacent small islands ("Great" to distinguish it from Little Britain, or Brittany). The name Britain derives from the Brythonic Celts, the second wave of Celtic invaders of the island. The Romans called the country Britannia, but the medieval kings, though Wales was annexed in 1284, were styled Kings of England. When James I (1603–25), already King of Scotland, was crowned at Westminster, he had himself proclaimed "King of Great Britain", though in fact he ruled two separate countries, each with its own government. The two were merged into one state by the Act of Union of 1707, and this was called – now correctly – "the United Kingdom of Great Britain". The formerly separate kingdom of Ireland became part of it by the Act of Union of 1801, and its name then was "the United Kingdom of Great Britain and Ireland". The greater part of Ireland broke away in 1922, later to become an independent republic, leaving only the six northern counties, so finally the government at Westminster ruled "the United Kingdom of Great Britain and Northern Ireland" – its present name. The title of the sovereign is "Her Britannic Majesty", and a citizen of the country, which is called for short "the UK", is said to have British nationality. The national flag is the Union Jack, which combines the banners of St George (England), St Andrew (Scotland) and St Patrick (Ireland).

When the island of Great Britain was united in 1707 it had already been decided that there should be no royal absolutism as in nearly all the other powerful states of Europe. During the next two centuries the power of Parliament increased, and it also came to represent the mass of the people. In this way the problem was solved of building up an efficient government and at the same time securing popular control and individual freedom. Similar systems of parliamentary government were not only set up in other countries of the British Empire but widely adopted elsewhere, so that the Parliament at Westminster is known as "the mother of Parliaments".

From the 16th century more and more

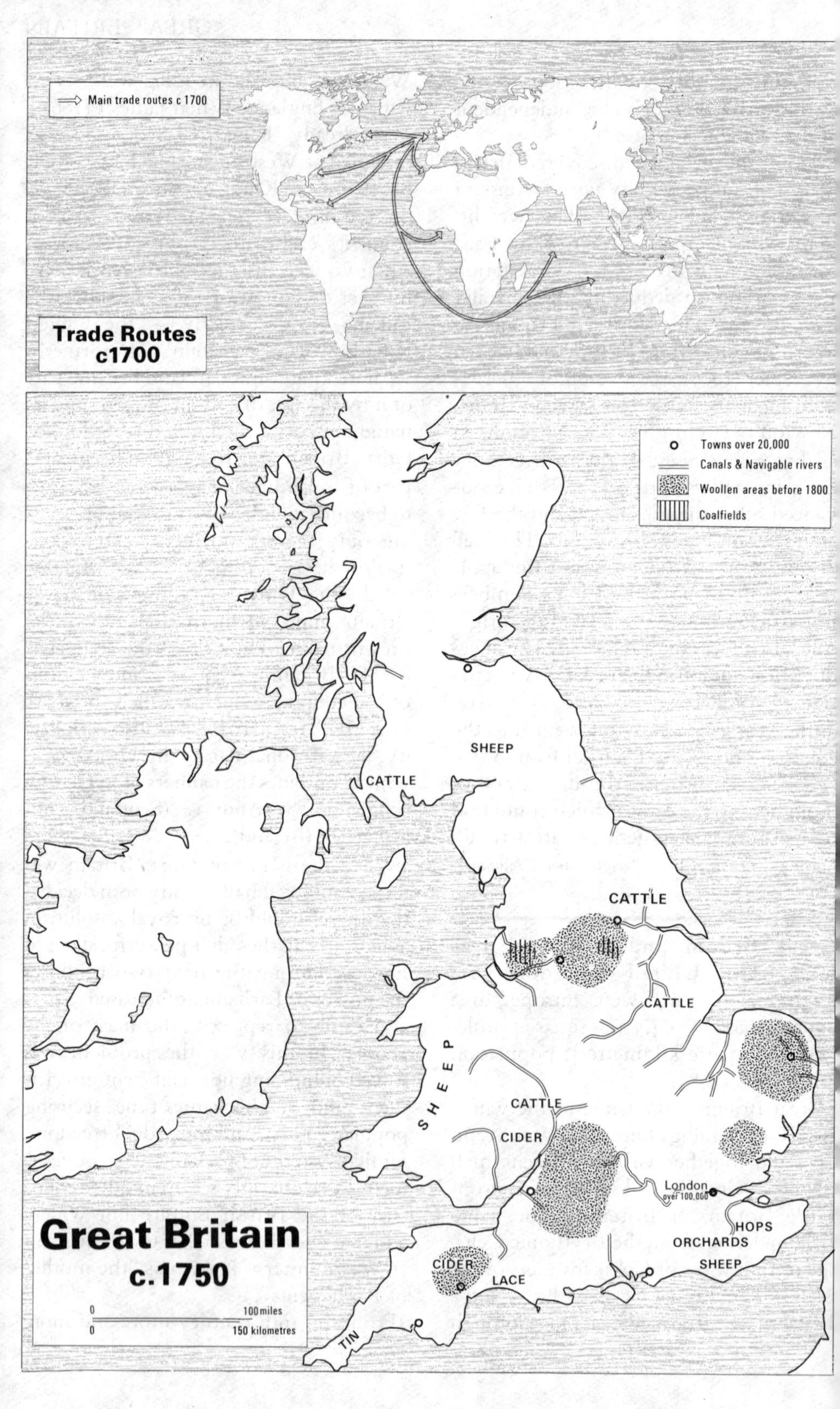
Main trade routes c 1700
Trade Routes c1700
Towns over 20,000
Canals & Navigable rivers
Woollen areas before 1800
Coalfields
SHEEP
CATTLE
CATTLE
CATTLE
SHEEP
CATTLE
CIDER
London
over 100,000
HOPS
ORCHARDS
SHEEP
CIDER
LACE
TIN
Great Britain c.1750
0
100 miles
0
150 kilometres

ships went out from Great Britain to trade, to fight and later to plant colonies. The main reason for this activity was that her position in the world had changed. Instead of being on the edge of a world map centred in the Mediterranean, the discoveries had placed this island most conveniently on the main seaways connecting Europe with other continents. Yet at the end of the 17th century the population of Great Britain was only about seven million, and she could not compare in wealth or power with her neighbour France. The great expansion of wealth and numbers began towards the end of the 18th century, through the combined effects of improved agriculture, rapidly growing trade, and above all the coming of technical changes in industry and transport, in which the British gained a big lead. These changes, as they continued to spread during the 19th century,

transformed the face of the countryside, the character of the towns and the lives of the people, and raised up new classes to take a share of political power. They also provided Great Britain with the wealth to build the great fleets and raise the armies – and to subsidise the larger armies of her continental allies – which overcame the power of France in the long series of wars from 1689 to 1815.

The final victory in these wars, the mastery of the seas which had ensured it, and the growing prosperity of the home base in these islands – these were the triple foundation on which was built in the 19th century the greatest empire the world had ever seen. It was acquired sometimes by conquest, as in India, sometimes by the settlement of large numbers of emigrants, as in Canada, sometimes by exploration and development of large areas of the tropics, as in Africa. The resources and trade of such vast and varied possessions and the sale of British manufactures the world over made the United Kingdom the most wealthy and powerful state in the world. While the subjugation of Ireland and India, as well as the inevitable domination of the colonists over the backward peoples of the Empire, darken the picture, two features of its history are notable if not unique: while so powerful abroad, a thoroughly civilian government at home allowed wide freedom to individuals and a growing share of power to the people through representation in Parliament; and both at home and in the colonies trade was free to merchants of all nations from the middle of the 19th century until after the First World War.

The loss of Great Britain's Empire since 1945 has not come through defeat, but through the growing up to independence of what were once the British colonies. Inspired partly by ideas of nationalism and self-government learned from Europe, the new nations no longer wanted to be ruled by Great Britain. Most of them remain linked with her, however, in the Commonwealth of Nations in ways largely undefined, perhaps by allegiance to the Crown, sometimes in defence or in trade, nearly always through language, law, education and general consultation on world affairs.

Great Eastern (1858)**:** an iron steamship of advanced design by Isambard Kingdom Brunel (1806–59), intended as a large capacity passenger and cargo vessel. A giant of 27,400 tons [27,800 tonnes] displacement, driven by paddles, screw and sail, she was, however, commercially a failure, probably because passengers found she had an uncomfortable roll, her engines did not provide enough speed, and it was not easy to find ports where she could berth. She had better success in another capacity, for in 1865–73 she laid the first Transatlantic cables.

¶ DUGAN, JAMES. *The Great Iron Ship.* 1953

First attempt to launch the Leviathan, *later renamed* Great Eastern.

Great Trek: the migration northwards in 1835 of Cape Dutch farmers in South Africa to escape from British rule. Known as *Voortrekkers*, they first occupied country between the Orange and Vaal rivers, whence venturesome spearheads probed into the unknown – men of faith and courage, battling against unpredictable hazards. Those in the Potchefstroom area were attacked by Mzilikazi and his impis. Louis Trichardt and his followers settled in the Zoutpansberg, but he and many of his people died of malaria on a journey into Mozambique. Piet Retief and Gert Maritz obtained a land concession from Dingaan, chief of the Zulus, across the Drakensberg, but the chief massacred Retief and some of his men whilst they were in his kraal. In a subsequent battle Dingaan was defeated at Blood River on 16 December 1838. These and other comparable epics are commemorated in the names of many South African towns, rivers and mountains.

Greece (Ancient): now a kingdom in south-east Europe, the country's history can be thought of as beginning when the mainland gained its independence from the Minoan power of Crete. But the early history and culture had so much in common with Crete that it is best to deal with the Mycenaean period separately (*see* MINOAN AND MYCENAEAN CIVILISATIONS), and to date the start of true Greek history from the invasions of the Dorians from the north after about 1200 BC. Greek history must also be held to include the history of places outside the mainland of Greece where Greeks had settled, especially in Ionia on the west coast of modern Turkey.

For some centuries the story is very confused. It took time for the Dorians to establish themselves in the Peloponnese, and for the other parts of Greece to re-form after the invasions. Some city-states declined dramatically in power, Mycenae among them. Others, such as Athens, only now began to emerge as important places. The general nature of the civilisation was of isolated city governments, at first under monarchies which soon gave way to aristocratic control. At some stage the Phoenician alphabet was adapted to the Greek language, and gradually Greek eyes looked further afield than the walls of individual cities. Ancient historians write of the amalgamation of numbers of smaller villages into a larger whole, especially at Athens and Sparta. But this was possibly a later phase. As the Greeks wandered, so prosperity increased with more trade, chiefly with the culturally more advanced areas of Asia Minor. Between 750 and 550 BC, there was a great move towards overseas colonisation (as far afield as the Crimea and Marseilles), and a temporary wave of "tyrannies", i.e. government by arbitrary rulers – not necessarily cruel or unjust – who seized power by force, such as the Cypselids at Corinth and Pisistratids at Athens. In some places monarchies continued, as at Argos and Sparta, but Argos faded in importance after her last great king, Pheidon, from about 650 BC, and Sparta's energies were inwardly directed as she sought territorial security and a revised constitution.

The next major upheaval in Greece was caused from outside. By 546 BC, when Persia under Cyrus the Great conquered Lydia and directly threatened the Greek cities of Ionia, the tyrannies had almost vanished. The advance in Greek civilisation can be seen in the first literature, epic poetry in the 8th and 7th centuries, lyric poetry in the 7th and 6th, and the first steps in history and drama towards 500 BC. Ionian philosophers had begun their exploration of natural science. Persia's presence on the Aegean was to last for over 200 years. The westward interests of Darius, king of Persia from 521 to 486 BC, eventually led the Ionians to revolt in 499 BC, embroiling Athens. Athens was by now the best organised democracy in Greece, and she needed all her strength and unity to resist the Persian attack of 490 BC, which was defeated at Marathon, and the sack of the city in 480 BC. This second invasion, after battles at Thermo-

pylae and Salamis, was finally defeated at Plataea in 479 BC, and the two most successful states were poised for disagreement. For the past fifty years Sparta had been the dominant city, head of the Peloponnesian League and unquestionably the strongest land power. She suffered, however, from isolationist tendencies, and, when Greece was looking for a leader after 479 BC, it was Athens that was chosen and Sparta who withdrew from the continuation of the war with Persia.

The time from 479 to 431 BC was the great age of Athens. The Delian League, formed to fight Persia, was gradually changed into her empire, with up to 250 individual member-states covering the north and east coasts of the Aegean and most of the islands. Her democratic constitution was developed into the most advanced known to the ancient world. At the same time all the arts came to fulfilment, especially in architecture, sculpture and tragic drama. It was no idle boast when the great planner of the period, Pericles, said that Athens was the "School of Greece". The age was not one of peace; Athens was at war with Sparta from 459 to 445 BC when she had to give up her idea of gaining a land empire in Greece. The war with Persia came to an end in 448 BC. The end of these two wars left her free to expand her influence into Italy and Sicily, and eastwards into the Black Sea.

In 431 BC the growth of Athenian power led to a major conflict with Sparta who was helped by Corinth and Boeotia among others. This so-called Peloponnesian War was running into stalemate when Athens launched a disastrous expedition to Sicily in 415 BC. Her own mismanagement and the skilful exploitation of her faults by Sparta led to its failure in 413 BC with enormous losses. Then with Persian money Sparta built ships which eventually (405 BC) inflicted the decisive defeat on the Athenian navy. Deserted by her allies and dependents, Athens was forced to surrender in 404 BC.

The next fifty years were marked by attempts by other states to dominate the mainland of Greece. First came the victorious Spartans. However, their harsh treatment of others led to the desertion of Corinth and Boeotia, and Sparta's reliance on Persia destroyed her pose as the champion of Greek liberty. By 395 she was on the defensive, and stupid provocation brought Athens and Thebes into alliance. Athens in 378 was actually strong enough to reform a League, but it was Thebes under her brilliant commanders Pelopidas and Epaminondas who defeated Sparta, the decisive battle being fought at Leuctra in 371 BC. Thebes now had a brief reign, which was notable for the first attempts at federal government in Greece, but this was cut short by the death of Epaminondas in battle in 362. Greece was now a vacuum. Inflation and the growing break-up of established beliefs and practices left her without energy or unity.

Into the gap came Philip II of Macedon, with an unscrupulous diplomacy and a highly trained, all-conquering army. Gradually he won firm frontiers for Macedon, and his infiltration southwards into Greece took full advantage of the chaos there. No sensible policy was formed against him, and futile opposition was ended at the battle of Chaeronea in 338 BC. Philip immediately tried to bring the Greeks together into an Hellenic League with the object of invading Persia. On his assassination in 336 he was succeeded by his brilliant son Alexander. (*See* separate entry.) Two years later he carried out his father's idea, and invaded Persia in a great campaign of revenge. Between 334 and 323 he conquered the old Persian Empire and extended Greek interests as far as India. He himself was the ruler of a vast Hellenistic kingdom in which an attempt was made to fuse all the different nations together. When Alexander died in 323, his conquests proved too unwieldy for any one man to handle.

The 4th century, though anarchic politically, abounded in new ideas. In it we find the great philosophers Plato and Aristotle, and meet with a new style of comedy that was to permeate European literature. The philosophical theories of Stoicism and Epicureanism were also started.

The immediate result of Alexander's death was a division of his Empire between five "successors". The strongest of these, Antigonus, was defeated at Ipsus in 301 BC, and some twenty years later things had settled down into three units. Greece itself formed one third, victim of the old troubles and now ravaged for a time by Gallic barbarians. The new Macedonian dynasty under Demetrius Poliorcetes was countered by both Pyrrhus, king of Epirus, and two increasingly powerful Leagues, those of Aetolia and Achaea. The Achaean League under Aratus steadily won ground with Egyptian help. A Spartan resurgence in 244 was ended when Sparta challenged the League and her king Cleomenes III was defeated in 222 BC by a combination of Macedon and the Achaean League. The second third was the Seleucid Empire ruling most of Asia Minor and Persia. Seleucus I and his successor Antiochus I started a dynasty that was to last till the Roman conquest in 64 BC. But they could not prevent the breakaway of small kingdoms, the most notable of which was Pergamum under Eumenes I and the Attalids. The third section was Egypt, the most stable and prosperous region, given to Ptolemy I and his successors. In it Alexandria grew to be the largest and wealthiest Greek city, a capital of commerce and a centre of brilliant intellectual achievements.

In 221 BC Philip V of Macedon came to the throne and his alliance in 215 with

Carthage brought Rome into conflict with Greece. After the Second Punic War, Philip V and Antiochus III decided to annex Egypt which, together with Rhodes and Pergamum, appealed to Rome. Rome accepted the invitation and was helped by the Aetolian and Achaean Leagues to drive Philip back into Macedonia. Rome thereupon withdrew, after proclaiming the independence of all Greek cities. The final stages of this independence centred round Philip's son, Perseus, whose actions against Eumenes II and Pergamum again brought in Rome who defeated him at Pydna in 168 BC. Harsh terms were imposed and many Macedonian sympathisers, especially in the Achaean League, were taken to Rome as hostages. Macedonia was split up and her actions were supervised, but she remained technically free. By 147 BC anti-Roman elements had brought on a crisis. Rome now invaded southern Greece, sacked Corinth, and formed Macedonia into a province in 146 BC. The south of Greece was controlled by the governor of Macedonia, nominally keeping her independence until the reign of Augustus, when Macedonia and Achaea were formed into two provinces governed by the Senate. Greece was much respected by the Romans, and Athens in particular remained an important university centre for centuries, but ancient Greek history as such was at an end.

¶ TAYLOR, DUNCAN. *Ancient Greece*. 1957

Greece (Modern): population 9,898,000 (1983). Under the Romans Greece declined into a largely neglected province, though the division of the Roman Empire in AD 395 and the establishment of the Eastern (Byzantine) Empire, did something to restore the use of the Greek language. The subsequent story of Greece is a tangled one of invasion from Slavonic and Balkan tribes, Sicilian Normans, Venetians, and French barons and knights. In 1466 came conquest b the Turks, who held the country till th successful War of Independence (1821 30) – a rising which stirred passionat enthusiasm among many European inte lectuals, including the English poet Byro who joined in the struggle and died fever at Missolonghi.

Peace and progress have not come easil to Greece, even in its regained indepe dence. Monarchies have come and gone abdication, deposition, banishment, assa sination, revolution, dictatorship (as we as occupation by German troops, 1940 44), have marked the path. But, despi all this, Athens is now a great city agai with a population of about 1½ millio Piraeus a flourishing port, along wit Patras and Salonica, and Athens an Salonica have their universities.

The scale of American aid has led som people to describe modern Greece as a American protectorate. But this suppo has not yet brought tranquillity to the 51,000 square miles [132,090 square kilo metres] that have seen so much of th achievement and tragedy of mankind. 1967 power was seized by a group army officers and King Constantine we into exile. The military dictatorship w brought to an end in 1974 and the ne year Greece adopted a new republica constitution (the people having vote against the restoration of the monarchy *See* EUROPE for map.

Greek art: artistic development in th Greek world in sculpture, painting, po tery and allied arts. The period is taken ending with the absorption into the ter tories of Rome of the Hellenistic worl that is to say the states surviving from th break up of the empire of Alexander th Great (d. 323 BC), a process which w largely completed by the end of the 2n century BC. The art and culture of Rom was for several centuries Hellenistic ɔirit and tradition, and that not a few of ɩe Greek statues which we know are, in ɩct, Roman copies.

In the earliest years of our period, in the land of Crete, a remarkable civilisation ꞉ems to have come to an abrupt end by ɪrthquake or invasion about the year 400 BC. The remains of the royal palace ꞉ Knossos have disclosed pottery and ·all-paintings of striking beauty. It is erhaps doubtful if we should reckon ɩese people as true Greeks. But it is clear ɩat they had considerable contact with ɩe islands to the north and possibly also ·ith the mainland, where the Mycenaean vilisation reached its final and flourish- ɩg stage in 1400–1150 BC. The name ɔmes from the palace and settlement of ɪycenae, a few miles from Argos on the ɪstern coast of Peloponnese, which was ɪomer tells us, the home of Agamemnon, ɩe Greek leader in the Trojan war. Ex- ɪvations here by Heinrich Schliemann ·822–90) yielded remains of the greatest istoric interest among them the magni- cent figures of two lions carved in the one which surmount the main gate and ɔme smaller objects such as daggers and rooches of exquisite design and work- ɪanship. Nearby, another palace, Tiryns, ɛlongs to the same period but has yielded ·wer artistic objects, while a third, Pylos, n the western coast is still being explored

ɔculpture was used by the Greeks in two ays, to produce free-standing statues (in- uding works in bronze) and to create *liefs* by carving away the surface of a ock of stone so that figures or other ɔjects are made to stand out. They used ·liefs to decorate the interiors and ex- riors of their temples, particularly the *·diments*, the large triangular spaces at ɩe ends of the buildings created by the vin-pitch roofs. The earliest Greek atues that survive date from about 650 ꞉, but the most of those known to us, ·me in a more or less mutilated con-

Cavalcade of horsemen from The Parthenon frieze, now in the British Museum.

dition, belong to the 5th century BC and later. Much of this material was brought to Western Europe by wealthy collectors in the 17th, 18th and early 19th centuries, an instance being the Elgin Marbles from the Acropolis at Athens, now in the British Museum, London. These are substantial fragments of a frieze displaying in relief a religious procession, including a cavalcade of youthful horsemen, which used to decorate the Parthenon, the temple of the goddess Athene. Phidias, the foremost sculptor of the 5th century BC, is said to have made the models, though he did not execute the actual figures, as he preferred to work in bronze: nothing of his work survives. Of Praxiteles (4th century BC), perhaps the most famous of all, we have some relics, but his *Aphrodite of Cnidos*, which was widely regarded as the most wonderful statue of the ancient world, is lost. The *Aphrodite of Melos (Venus de Milo)*, of much the same date but by an unknown hand, which is now in the Louvre, Paris, is perhaps the best known of all Greek statues.

Little or nothing survives of Greek painting, though some copies exist, such as the mosaic found at Pompeii of one of Alexander's battles, thought to be taken from a painting by Philoxenus (4th century BC).

It is in the decoration of pottery that we have the richest remains of Greek painting, since cups and vases are easily broken and their fragments are frequently found and put together. The shapes of the various drinking cups, vases and *amphorae* (two-handled wine jars) were in themselves an artistic delight; but the decorations, first in geometric patterns, then in foliage and later in human and animal figures, have a distinctive excellence which has never been surpassed. Athens was a particular centre for this craft, which at first used the "black-figure" style, in which the natural colour of the clay formed the background on which figures were painted in a black glaze. About 525 BC, however, the "red-figure" style was adopted, in which the figures were made to stand out from a background filled in in black. Some of the pieces we possess are signed by the craftsmen, and there are fine collections of Attic (Athenian) pottery in the museums of Europe and USA. In the Hellenistic age pottery was largely replaced by metal where anything but common earthenware was needed.

Greenland: the world's largest island 827,300 square miles [2,142,707 square kilometres] in area, lying mainly within the Arctic Circle; population 51,400 (1982). It has a polar climate, with more than three-quarters of it still covered by ice. Those parts of the coast now free from ice were once glaciated and have deep fjords between tundra-covered mountains. The south-western coast is inhabited chiefly by Eskimos, numbered in a recent census at 33,000. They still live by hunting polar bears, ermine, Arctic fox and hare for their skins and by fishing for seals and whales. Greenland was probably discovered by Eric the Red in AD 982. When the Union between Norway and Denmark was dissolved in 1814 it passed exclusively under the control of Denmark.

Greenwich Mean Time (GMT): the mean solar time for the meridian of what is now the Old Royal Observatory in Greenwich Park, within the boundaries of Greater London. In 1884 the Greenwich Meridian was chosen as the world's Prime Meridian; thus GMT became the basis of the international Time Zone System. Another name in Britain for Greenwich Mean Time was Railway Time since the Observatory's master clock synchronised all station clocks.

Gregory I, called "the Great" (540–604): Pope 590–604. A Roman of senatorial family, he sold his property for the relief of the poor and in his early thirties took monastic vows. As Pope he upheld the claims of the Papacy against those of the civil power. It was he who, in 597, sent St Augustine (d. 604) on his mission to Canterbury. The story told by Bede of Gregory's interest being aroused by seeing some British children exposed for sale in the slave market and exlaiming *"Non Angli sed angeli"* (not Angles but angels) is one of the traditional legends of English history. Gregory had considerable influence in the development of sacred music: the Gregorian chant is named after him. He was by popular demand canonised immediately after his death.

¶ SANDERLIN, GEORGE. *St. Gregory the Great Consul of God.* 1964

Gregory VII (1021–85): Pope 1073–85. Hildebrand, by which name he is often known in history, was a Tuscan of humble birth. After some years as the trusted adviser of his predecessors, he himself was elected at a time when the Papacy was resisting the Emperor in his claim to make his own ecclesiastical appointments (lay investiture). After humbling Emperor Henry IV (1050–1106) by making him do penance at Canossa in the winter snow of

077, Hildebrand himself was driven from Rome and died at Monte Cassino. He may be said to have saved the church from subjection to the feudal system.

The loss of the Revenge.

Grenville, Sir Richard (*c.* 1541–91): English sailor famous for his fight off the Azores in the *Revenge*, 500 tons, against fifty-three Spanish ships. Two enemy ships were sunk, two foundered, 2,000 men were killed. With the *Revenge* completely wrecked, her powder spent and Grenville mortally wounded, his crew finally capitulated. The story is immortalised in Sir Walter Ralegh's account and Lord Tennyson's poem.

Guatemala: republic in Central America, bounded by Mexico, El Salvador and British Honduras, with an estimated population of 6,394,100 (1983). The Maya Indians were decisively defeated in 1523 by Pedro de Alvardo, one of the lieutenants of Hernán Cortés (*see* separate entry) and the country remained under Spanish domination till it declared its independence in September 1821, only to be annexed almost at once by the Emperor Iturbide of Mexico. Independence was regained in 1839, since when Guatemala has been ruled by a series of dictators, a number of whom have been killed in battle, deposed or assassinated. The greatest was Rafael Carrera (1814–65), under whom the separate republic was formed in 1839. Guatemala City, the capital, was largely destroyed by earthquakes in 1917–18, but has been rebuilt. Agricultural products and minerals are the country's main resources.

Guelphs and Ghibellines: medieval factions of Italy. They arose in the disputed elections for the Holy Roman Empire on the death of Henry VI in 1197. Pope Innocent III first supported Otto of Brunswick of the Wölf (Guelph) family, then his rival Frederick II of the Hohenstaufen family, whose castle of Waiblingen in Swabia gave the name to the Ghibellines. The Ghibellines tended to support the Emperor and to be drawn from the Lombard or Frankish counts of the Italian countryside, often in league with the lesser guilds in the cities. The Guelphs tended to support the Pope and his allies the Angevins of Naples and were often citizens of the greater guilds.

Guerrillas: irregular troops, conducting sabotage and harassing action against invaders or occupying army. The word is derived from a Spanish word meaning "a small war" and is synonymous with "partisan" or "irregular". This type of warfare is as old as warfare itself, but was particularly noteworthy in the Peninsular War (1806–14), when Napoleon kept a large army in Portugal and Spain to combat the *guerrilleros*. The equivalent German word is *Banditen* or "bandits". Other examples of this kind of warfare occurred in the Arab Revolt (1916–18), the Bolshevik Revolution (1917–21) and the Chinese Revolution (1927–40). The resistance movements in occupied Europe (1940–45) were similar.

These forces, though strategic, are not entitled to the normal privileges accorded to prisoners-of-war. This position was defined by an American lawyer, Francis Lieber (1800–72), and confirmed by the

Hague Conferences of 1899 and 1907.

Among outstanding guerrilla leaders may be cited the English outlaw Hereward, who in 1070–71 led the revolt against William I in the marshes of Ely; Francis Marion, the "Swamp Fox", who took to the swamps round Charleston, South Carolina, in 1780; and Thomas Edward Lawrence ("Lawrence of Arabia") (1888–1935), who was the British liaison officer of the Arab Revolt against the Turks in World War I. In Greece, after World War II, the pro-Royalist National Republican Greek League (or EDES) harried the Communist-inspired National Popular Liberation Army (or ELAS). Fidel Castro (b. 1926) was exiled from Cuba in 1953 but returned to maintain guerrilla warfare against President Batista's regime until Batista fled the country, and Castro himself succeeded to the presidency in 1959. Che Guevara, another guerrilla and a disciple of Castro's, fomented trouble in Latin America until his capture and execution in Bolivia in 1967. Guerrilla warfare has played a major part in the frequent clashes between the Arab countries and the republic of Israel. A recent extension of activity has been the kidnapping of hostages and the hijacking of planes (*see* RANSOM).

Guesclin, Bertrand du (1320–80): France's greatest and most loved captain of the Middle Ages. The son of a Breton nobleman, despised in his youth for his ugliness and uncouthness ("uglier than any other between Rennes and Dinant . . . flat-nosed and swarthy, ill-formed and squat"), he rose to become a great soldier, a popular hero and Constable of France.

Guilds or **gilds**: medieval associations of craftsmen and merchants, from "geld" or "gild", meaning payment or tax. Guilds arose in the towns of western Europe in the early Middle Ages as associations for social, religious or economic purposes or for all three. In England they appeared after the Norman Conquest, first in the form of the guilds merchant, which flourished in the 12th and 13th centuries. When a town obtained freedom from tolls and charges levied by a lord or by the Crown, a guild would be set up to reserve this privilege for its members, the "freedom" of the guild. It was closely connected with the town government under its mayor, but remained separate though, when the merchants of the guild built a hall, it might be used by the town authorities, so that the guildhall became the seat of town government. The guilds drew up rules about such matters as the quality and price of goods, the place and time of selling them, apprenticeship and wages, the conduct of markets, and relations with "foreigners", which mean people from another town. They aimed to prevent competition in an age when every article was thought to have a "just price", when productive processes were very simple, when the maker and the seller were the same person and shop and workshop the same single room. People who had not paid to join the guild would find it difficult to make a living.

The guild merchant suited the very small country towns. When the 14th century towns began to grow larger and contained a number of craftsmen in each of the main trades, usually with their shops in the same street, craft guilds were formed, each regulating a particular trade. The bakers' and weavers' guilds were among the earliest. The craft guilds, gradually replacing the guild merchant, busily regulated the work of their members in the same way, ensuring that no one gained advantage over the others. Their most colourful activity was the performance of "mystery" plays, when each craft, or "mystery", produced its own scene in a religious play. The craft guilds were

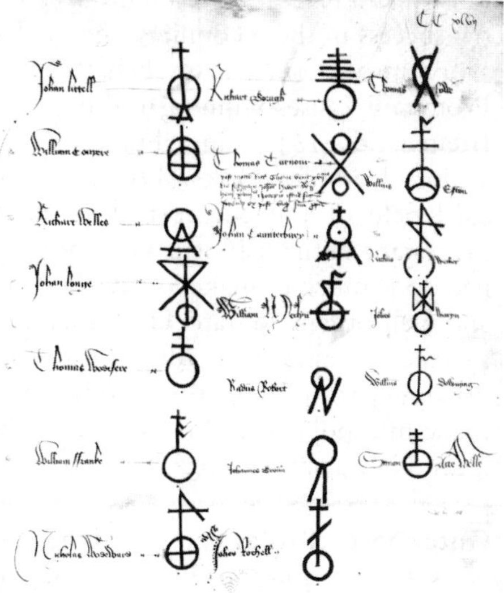

Trade marks of a coopers' guild.

sometimes called companies, and the best known survivors of these are the eighty or so livery companies which still exist as charitable and ceremonial bodies in the City of London.

The restrictive practices of the guilds proved to be their downfall. When trade expanded, men wanted to build up businesses on a larger scale than guild rules allowed. They either broke the rules or set themselves up in towns where there were no guilds, so that by about 1600 the guilds were losing their importance.

¶ PRICE, C. *Made in the Middle Ages.* 1962; RENARD, G. *Guilds in the Middle Ages.* 1969; SMITH, TOULMIN and SMITH, L. T., editors. *English Gilds.* 1962

Guise, House of: a powerful family prominent in 16th-century France. Francis, second Duke of Guise (1519–63), was a popular general. His brother Charles (1525–74) was Cardinal Archbishop of Rheims. Leading the extreme Catholic Party, they tried to control Catherine de' Medici and her three sons, who were successively kings of France. The Duke, who dominated France and commanded armies against the Protestants, was assassinated in 1563. His son Henry, third duke (1550–88), played a major part in the massacre of St Bartholomew (1572), tried to seize the French throne and was assassinated at the instigation of Henry III (1556–89).

Gunpowder: an explosive mixture of saltpetre, charcoal and sulphur. It is not "Greek Fire", which was a mixture of bitumen, sulphur and naphtha, sometimes with resin added, resulting in a type of napalm as recorded by the Byzantine princess Anna Comnena in the *Alexiad.*

Though the potential of gunpowder had been seen earlier, e.g. by the Franciscan Roger Bacon (*c.* 1214–92), its early use in Europe is said to be the work of an Augustinian monk and alchemist Berchtold Schwartz (*c.* 1320). But Thomas de Roldeston made it for Edward III (1312–77) for his Scottish wars in 1327, at Berwick in 1333 and at the Battle of Crécy in 1346. The burghers of Ghent also defended their city with it.

Documentary records attest the application of gunpowder to guns at Florence, 1324–26, and at Metz, 1324, as well as by Edward III. Small breech-loading guns of 14th-century date were called canon in France or gunnis (gonnes) in England. Large muzzle-loaders were known, e.g. Mons Meg at Edinburgh Castle, which dates from the 15th century, weighs nearly four tons [4·04 tonnes] and threw a stone shot of 300 lb [136 kilogrammes].

The proportions of saltpetre, charcoal and sulphur varied widely through the centuries and from country to country. Roger Bacon's recipe gave saltpetre 41·2 per cent, charcoal 29·4 per cent and sulphur 29·4 per cent. The amount of saltpetre in English powders increased until, e.g. in 1781, the proportions were saltpetre 75 per cent, charcoal 15 per cent and sulphur 10 per cent. German powder a hundred years later (1882) showed saltpetre 78 per cent, charcoal 19 per cent and sulphur 3 per cent. No explosive other than gunpowder was introduced till the 19th century.

Gunpowder Plot (November 1605): the plan by Roman Catholics to blow up the English Houses of Parliament at the opening by James I, create a Roman Catholic rising in the Midlands and secure toleration for Roman Catholics. The Princess Elizabeth, aged eight, was "to be surprised and proclaimed queen and married to a Roman Catholic gentleman". The plan was betrayed by a letter to Lord Mounteagle, generally believed to have been sent by one of the conspirators, his brother-in-law, Francis Tresham. The cellars beneath the House of Lords were searched, and Guy Fawkes was discovered ready to fire the gunpowder amounting to about thirteen tons [13·2 tonnes]. Eight of the conspirators, including Fawkes, were executed, and Tresham, who probably prevented the disaster, died in the Tower.

Gustavus I Vasa (1496–1560): king of Sweden. Born the son of a nobleman, his adventurous early career was marked by a tireless struggle against Denmark. For this he was proclaimed king by a Swedish parliament in 1523 and signed a peace treaty with Denmark in the following year. His concern for Sweden's independence was underlined by his break with the Roman Catholic Church in 1527; but his handling of domestic problems was less successful than his statecraft and there were four peasant rebellions during his reign. However, Gustavus undoubtedly strengthened the national identity of Sweden by founding a stable dynasty.

Gustavus Adolphus II (1594–1632): king of Sweden. He became king in 1611 when Sweden was at war with Denmark, Poland and Russia. He brought his country success in these conflicts, then led an army into Germany on behalf of the Protestant cause, winning the battles of Breitenfeld (1631) and Lützen (1632) against Catholic forces. Dying on the battlefield of Lützen, he had saved the Protestant faith in North Germany and had done much to make Sweden a strong and well-organised state. His brilliance as a soldier, his talent as an administrator and his ability to speak to the common man made him popular in his own day and a legend in ours.

Gutenberg Bible: possibly the first book to be printed in Europe. Johannes Gutenberg (*c.* 1398–1468) of Mainz, who is credited with the invention of movable type in Europe, produced this work about 1455. The text is that of the Vulgate, or Latin version of the Bible, in the form used before the Clementine revision of the next century. It is sometimes known as the Mazarin Bible, because the copy which first attracted attention was discovered in the library founded in Paris by Cardinal Jules Mazarin (1602–61). Forty copies are said now to survive, but only two or three of these are known to be complete. One, bound in three volumes, is in the United States Library of Congress.

Guyana: independent sovereign state within the Commonwealth, in the north-east of South America; population 944,000 (1983). The coast was sighted by Columbus in 1498 and Dutch settlements followed in 1596, 1625 and 1627. After a to-and-fro struggle for occupation by Dutch and British, the territory was finally ceded to Britain in 1814 as British Guiana. The country became fully independent in May 1966. As well as agricultural products, it has important resources of manganese, bauxite, copper, diamonds and gold.

H

Habeas corpus: in law, the operative words of the writ (*Habeas corpus,* "you must produce the body") commanding a person having another in custody to produce before a court the body of the person detained. Endangered when Charles I imprisoned five knights and the Royal Command was held to override the writ, the Habeas Corpus Act, 1679, was eventually pushed through the House of Lords by, it is said, counting one fat peer as ten. Now issued by any one of the readily accessible judges of the High Court, provided he is satisfied as to the merits of the application, this safeguard of liberty can be suspended only in time of serious emergency. The right is also written into the constitution of the USA. In totalitarian countries it does not exist.

Habsburg, or **Hapsburg, House of:** the former imperial house of Austria-Hungary. It takes its name from the ancestral castle of Habictsburg (Hawk's Castle) in Switzerland, built in the 11th century by Bishop Werner. Later owners of the castle became Counts of Habsburg and extended their territories. In 1273 the Emperor Rudolf founded the house that ruled as Dukes of Austria and Holy Roman Emperors. The Empire rested in Austrian hands from 1437 to 1740, when Maria Theresa (1717–80) married Francis of Lorraine, and the house of Habsburg-Lorraine continued to provide emperors until 1806. From then until the collapse of the Austro-Hungarian empire in 1918 Habsburg monarchs bore the title of Austrian Emperor. The Spanish Habsburg dynasty began with Charles V (1519–56), who was himself descended from Rudolf, and ruled Spain until 1700. The Habsburgs were perhaps the greatest masters in history of the art of marriage between related ruling houses, which enabled them to extend their power and influence throughout Europe in the 16th and 17th centuries. Unfortunately the in-breeding which this marriage policy often entailed produced a number of Habsburg rulers who were physically weak and mentally deficient, and despite their immense power and prestige they produced few rulers of corresponding ability.

See also AUSTRIA; CHARLES V; HUNGARY; MARIA THERESA, etc.

Hadrian (Publius Aelius Hadrianus, AD 76–138)**:** Roman emperor. Hadrian, perhaps the most capable of Roman emperors, was born in Spain at Italica near Seville, and in 117 succeeded Trajan, his cousin and former guardian. He served as an army officer and at the time of his accession was governor of Syria. A capable soldier and statesman, he was also a lover of architecture, painting and literature. After spending the first three years of his reign in Rome, in 120 he set out on the travels which were to occupy the next ten years of his life. He fortified the frontiers of the Empire in Germany and Britain, founded new towns and introduced legal reforms.

See also HADRIAN'S WALL.

Bust of Emperor Hadrian found in the Thames.

Hadrian's Wall: Roman defensive wall, north Britain. Hadrian arrived in Britain in AD 122 after the Romans had suffered a severe defeat by the Brigantes, a tribe or league of tribes in the north and north-west. He had already fortified the German frontier with a timber palisade, but in Britain he chose stone, though to begin with turf was used at the western end. The wall, of which much still remains, ran from Wallsend-on-Tyne to Bowness on the Solway Firth, a distance of about seventy-five miles (later extended by some ten miles [120 kilometres, later extended by 16.09 kilometres]) and consisted of a continuous stone wall with a vallum (earthwork) to the south of it. At intervals of a Roman mile were fortlets (mile castles) and, between each pair of these, two stone turrets for signalling. At irregular intervals were sixteen forts, built in contact with the wall, each housing an auxiliary regiment. In the next 300 years the wall was more than once overrun, and was finally abandoned some thirty years before the last Roman forces left Britain in AD 410.

¶ JONES, DAVID and PAULINE. *Hadrian's Wall* (Jackdaw). 1968; TAYLOR, DUNCAN. *A Soldier on Hadrian's Wall*. 1962

Hague, The: city on North Sea, southern Holland, fifteen miles [24.14 kilometres] north-west of Rotterdam; seat of the government of the Netherlands and, since 1922, of the International Court of Justice. It grew up round the castle built by Count William II in 1248, and the adjoining Knight's Hall (*c.* 1280) has been the scene of many conferences. The Triple Alliance between England, Sweden and the Netherlands was signed here in 1668. The Hague Conferences of 1899 and 1907 tried unsuccessfully to limit armaments but did much to establish more humane practices in the conduct of war, following up the work begun by the Geneva Convention of 1864.

Haiti: republic covering the western third of the West Indian island of Hispaniola, the rest of which consists of the Dominican Republic. Haiti was discovered by Columbus in 1492. Under Spanish and, from 1697, French rule, Haiti was populated largely by Negro slaves, brought in to work the rich sugar plantations. Under Toussaint L'Ouverture (*see* separate entry) they rose against their oppressors in 1791 and succeeded in establishing the first black republic in 1804, though it was not recognised by France for another twenty years. From 1915 to 1934 Haiti was under United States occupation. There have been many changes of government and much friction with the neighbouring Dominican Republic (*see* separate entry).

Hakluyt, Richard (*c.* 1552–1616)**:** English geographer. His interest was early awakened by a lawyer cousin of the same name whose conversation was enlivened by "certain bookes of cosmographie, an universall mappe and the Bible". After Westminster School and Christ Church, Oxford, Hakluyt served as chaplain in the Paris embassy from 1583 to 1588. Thereafter, as well as holding various ecclesiastical appointments, he wrote, collected and translated works on sea-voyaging and colonisation. He was friendly with seamen and discoverers such as Frobisher, Gilbert and Cavendish, and he was fortunate in having the patronage of Robert Cecil, Elizabeth I's powerful secretary of state. His fame rests chiefly on the *Principall Navigations, Voyages and Discoveries made by the English Nation* (1589), later extended to three volumes, which has been called "the greatest of all English epics" and is the first great collection of information we have about the sea voyages of the 16th century.

¶ HAKLUYT, RICHARD. In *Voyages and Discoveries*, ed. Jack Beeching. 1972

Halbert or **Halberd:** weapon which is a combination of battle-axe and spear; a long spike combined with an axe blade and a sharp hook or point mounted on a long shaft. It was used as early as the 13th century and was carried in the British Army until the end of the 18th century. This weapon replaced the pike in some continental armies in the 15th century, and it rapidly became one of the more widely used weapons in Europe. Early forms were simple and heavy but gradually became lighter and more elaborately decorated. Yeoman warders, or "Beefeaters", at the Tower of London still carry halberds ceremonially.

Halley, Edmund (1656–1742)**:** English astronomer. Among his many achievements were the publication at his own expense of Newton's *Principia*; the first catalogue, from his own observations, of stars visible in the southern hemisphere; the observation of the comet of 1682, now known as Halley's Comet; and the accurate prediction of the solar eclipse of 1715.

¶ In Crowther, J. G. *Six Great Astronomers*. 1961

Halley's Comet, 7 May 1910.

Hals, Frans (*c.* 1580–1666): Dutch painter. Many details of his life are still obscure and much that is known is discreditable. But as a portrait and character painter he ranks close to Rembrandt (*see* separate entry), and his pictures, for two centuries so little valued that the poet Byron was able to buy one for £28, are now among the greatest art treasures of the world. The best known is undoubtedly that usually, though wrongly, called "The Laughing Cavalier", now in the Wallace Collection, London. Others are "The Flute Player" (Amsterdam) and his paintings of the Officers of the Arquebusiers of St Andrew (Haarlem).

Hamburg: city in West Germany, the largest port on the river Elbe. It is said to have been founded in the early 9th century by Charlemagne, and a cathedral and castle were built in the 11th century. In the Middle Ages Hamburg became an important commercial centre for northern Europe. Its alliance with Lübeck in 1241 formed the nucleus of the Hanseatic League (*see* separate entry). In the early modern period Hamburg maintained its importance, but suffered a great deal from the Napoleonic Wars and World Wars I and II. Since 1945 the city has contributed much to West Germany's economic progress.

Hamilcar Barca (d. 228 BC): Carthaginian general and father of Hannibal (*see* separate entry). He successfully resisted the Romans in western Sicily towards the end of the 1st Punic War. Afterwards he went to Spain in 237 BC and quickly established a new Carthaginian empire there. He was an excellent soldier and a bitter enemy of Rome.

Hamilton, Alexander (1757–1804): American statesman. Hamilton was born in the West Indies and later studied law in New York. At the time of the American War of Independence (1775–83) he organised artillery regiments for George Washington. After independence was achieved he drafted the report which led

Duel between Aaron Burr and Alexander Hamilton, in which Hamilton was killed.

to the summoning of the Constitutional Convention of 1787, where he pressed for the establishment of federal (or strong central) government. He put his views on paper in contributions to the *Federalist*. As Secretary to the Treasury (1789–95) he established the Federal Bank. Subsequently Hamilton became the leader of the Federalists in New York and used his influence to stop the presidential hopes of Aaron Burr (the leader of the Democratic Republicans). In July 1804 Burr challenged Hamilton to a duel and fatally wounded him. Less than three years before, Hamilton's son Philip had also been mortally wounded in a duel with one of Burr's supporters.

Hammarskjöld, Dag (1905–61): Swedish Secretary-General of the United Nations Organisation. Educated as an economist, Hammarskjold represented his country at UNO and was elected Secretary-General in 1953, being re-elected in 1957. A gentle man who wrote poetry in his spare time, he took part in the Korean War truce negotiations in 1953, supervised the intervention of UNO in Egypt after the Anglo-French invasion of 1956 and worked untiringly to arrange a settlement of the crisis in the Congo in 1960–61. His death in an air crash came when he was on a mission to the Congo.

¶ LEVINE, I. E. *Dag Hammarskjöld: champion of world peace*. 1964

Carving from the top of Hammurabi's Column, 2000 BC.

Hammurabi (reigned *c.* 1792–50 BC): king of Babylonia. Ancestor of a famous line of rulers, he built one of the greatest empires of the ancient world and is especially remembered for the code of laws he proclaimed for use throughout it. The complete text of these laws was found by archaeologists on an eight-foot-high [2.44 metres] column, inscribed in twenty-one columns.

Hampton Court: palace at Hampton, Middlesex, some fifteen miles [24.14 kilometres] south-west of London. When Thomas Wolsey (*c.* 1472–1530), its first owner, found his position as King Henry VIII's Lord Chancellor becoming precarious, he vainly tried to save the situation by giving the palace to Henry. Henry built a great hall, decorated with the arms of Anne Boleyn (*c.* 1507–36), his second wife, but before it was completed she was beheaded, and Jane Seymour (*c.* 1509–37) became Queen of England. Her son, Edward VI (1537–53), was born at Hampton Court.

Catherine Howard (d. 1542), another of Henry's ill-starred wives, is said to haunt the palace. Held under arrest, she escaped

Dag Hammarskjöld.

View of Hampton Court showing the formal layout of the gardens.

and ran along a corridor in the hope of reaching the king. Guards seized her and dragged her away screaming – shrieks that are said still to resound through the Haunted Gallery.

Much rebuilding was undertaken by William III (1650–1702) and Mary (1662–94). William was killed in Hampton Court Park when his horse stumbled over a molehill. Thereafter Jacobites, the followers of the House of Stuart, drank grateful toasts to the mole responsible, "the little gentleman in black velvet".

¶ GUINNESS, GERALD, *editor. Hampton Court* (Jackdaw). 1969

Han Dynasty: emperors of China from *c.* 205 BC to AD 220. The Emperor Kao-tsu (ruled 202–195 BC), the first of the line, was of peasant origin, leader of a revolt against the Chou dynasty. The Emperor Wu (ruled 140–86 BC) impoverished China by schemes of expansion to the south-east and Korea. Associated with good administration and Confucianist philosophy, the dynasty reached its peak under Emperor Hsüan (ruled 74–48 BC). Later a number of weaker Han emperors were overshadowed by powerful court officials. The dynasty broke down in the early 3rd century AD, and China was split into three parts.

See also CHINA; POTTERY and PORCELAIN.

Han dynasty earthenware figures.

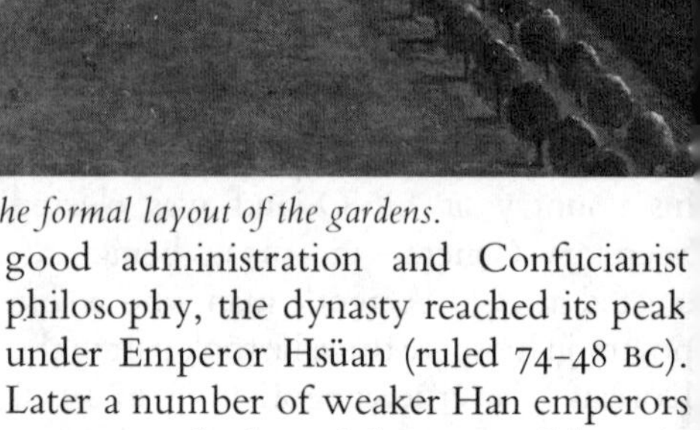

Handwriting: art and craft of penmanship. For many centuries man has tried to send his thoughts over distance and time, first by picture-writing – brief, wordless but full of meaning, as in his primitive cave-paintings. These we call pictograms. Then came a more rapid code using symbols, not pictorial representations. These we call ideograms, i.e. signs which convey the *idea* of an object, without expressing its name. To a limited extent the ideogram era overlapped the "sound-writing" or phonetic period which followed and in which we still live. People in different parts of the world have devised varied alphabets using letters which only occasionally resemble objects, e.g. "O" might be considered to resemble a shouting mouth. Alphabets differ only slightly throughout the Western world. From our own twenty-six letters hundreds of thousands of words may rapidly be represented and understood.

Writing materials have varied with time, place and conditions. For centuries the word "handwriting" has implied the use of some kind of pen, ink and a suitable writing surface. An earlier medium was wax written on by the Romans with a pointed stylus.

Paper was an Oriental invention, originally made from reeds, grass, etc., which passed westward. During the 12th century the Arabs used it; thence it gradually came into Europe, replacing parchment, made from the skins of various animals, and vellum, a particularly fine sort of parchment. Printers still sometimes print special copies of books on vellum.

Handwriting instruments through the centuries have altered with changing conditions. Our word "pen" comes from Latin *penna*, a quill feather, and many people still carry a pen-knife, a reminder of the days when its chief function was to trim quills. Wing-primaries from the

Specimens, engraved by George Bickham, from the Universal Penman, 1741.

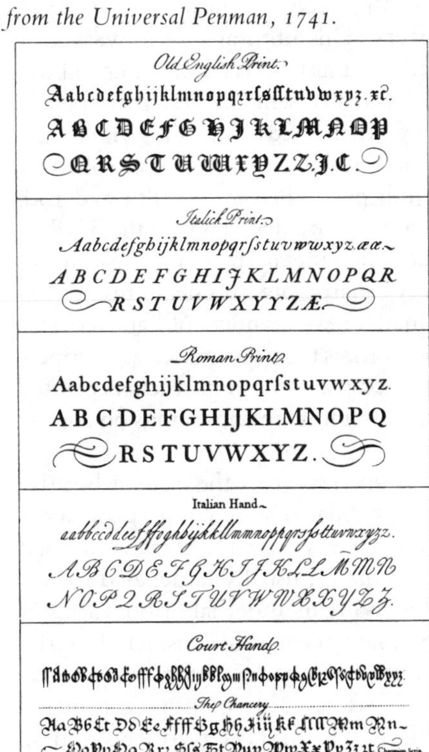

widely distributed and migrant geese were the most familiar quills, mainly because of their appropriate size. A trimmed goose-quill, if cut to a chisel-edge, stays unfrayed and serves well. This helped the development of a legible, space-saving form of handwriting known to us as Gothic, or compressed. This form lasted, with variations, through the Middle Ages till at last it was ousted, when demand outgrew the scope of medieval scribes, by the new art and craft of printing, which, however, continued many of the deeply rooted and much loved modes and manners of Gothic handwriting, e.g. abbreviations.

Various other forms of handwriting evolved, the Chancery hand *c.* 1400, the Court Hand, *c.* 1500–50, and the Stuart Secretary, *c.* 1650. In the 15th century Pope Eugenius IV (ruled 1431–47) caused a particularly beautiful and quick hand, which we now call *italic*, to be used in conducting the business of the papal chancery. This admirable form was introduced into England a century later and was used by many scholars and their pupils, among them Edward VI, Mary and Elizabeth I. All forms were controlled by the quill pen. Then in the 18th and 19th centuries came a new device – the flexible, replaceable metal pen nib. With its usually sharp but resilient point this originated new manners of handwriting, among others the style known as "copperplate" because some of its teachers printed examples of it from engravings on copper plates.

For about 150 years the elegant but (by today's standard) slow copperplate writing, and styles derived from it, continued and still linger, usually in debased forms. Within living memory laborious forms of copperplate were still considered as the only respectable handwriting. Good handwriting has had a stern struggle to wage at a time when the cry is for speed in all things and when the typewriter and ballpoint pen have come into universal use. But from time to time people with a love for the traditions and craftsmanship of fine penmanship make their voices heard and create a revival of interest, e.g. in this century Robert Bridges (the English poet laureate) and his wife, Edward Johnstone and Alfred Fairbank, and, in the USA, Paul Standard, have all used a fine hand based on 15th century italic.

¶ FAIRBANK, ALFRED. *The Story of Handwriting: origins and development.* 1970

Hangchow or **Hankow:** one of the first cities of inland China to be opened (1858) to foreign trade. Britain, France, Germany, Russia and Japan all had concessions there. With adjacent coal and iron, Hangchow produces steel, textiles, cereals and grain products. Captured by Chinese nationalists in 1926, it fell to the Japanese in 1937. The Chinese communists have merged it with the cities of Han-yang and Wu-ch'ang into the "tri-city" of Wu-han, capital of Hupeh province.

Hannibal (247–*c.* 182 BC)**:** Carthaginian general. He inherited from his father, Hamilcar, an undying hatred of Rome, and when he took over Spain in 221 BC he did everything to provoke war. Capturing Sagunitum in 218, he then marched through Gaul and across the Alps to invade Italy. This involved a famous journey across the Alps with a tattered horde of mercenaries – Spanish, African, Numidian and Gaulish soldiers, accompanied by horses and elephants. After victories in the Po valley he defeated major Roman armies at Lake Trasimene in 217 and at Cannae in 216, but on both occasions he failed to follow up his victories by a march on Rome. Until 203 he stayed in southern Italy, failing to cause rebellion among many of Rome's allies and lacking any real support from home. Recalled to Africa when Scipio invaded, he was defeated at Zama in 202 and spent the last years in Magnesia, where he finally took poison to save himself from the Romans. One of the greatest military geniuses of history, he found his match in the resilience of Rome.

COTTRELL, LEONARD. *Enemy of Rome*. 1965

Hanover, House of: British royal house. Its story dates from 1692, when Ernest Augustus, Duke of Lüneberg-Celle, received the title of Elector of Brunswick-Lüneberg (popularly called Hanover after its capital) from the Emperor Leopold I. His son George Louis was formally recognised as an Elector at the Imperial Diet of 1708. Through his mother, Sophia, granddaughter of James I, George Louis became the Protestant heir to the English throne by the Act of Settlement of 1701. He became king as George I on the death of Queen Anne in 1714.

From 1714 to 1837 the Electorate of Hanover was under British sovereignty George I (ruled 1714-27) and his son George II (ruled 1727–60) preferred Hanover to England, but both George III (ruled 1760–1820) and George IV (Prince Regent 1811-20, King 1820–30) regarded their German possession as more of an encumbrance than an asset.

Since a law ruling out female succession applied to what was now the Kingdom of Hanover, Queen Victoria could not succeed to the Hanoverian throne on the death of William IV (ruled 1830–37). The kingdom therefore passed to Ernest Augustus, Duke of Cumberland, the fifth son of George III. Both Ernest Augustus (ruled 1837–51) and his blind son George (ruled 1851–66) grew increasingly jealous of the rising power of Prussia in Germany. But the army of Hanover was defeated by the Prussians at the battle of Langensalza (1866) during the Seven Weeks War. In September 1866

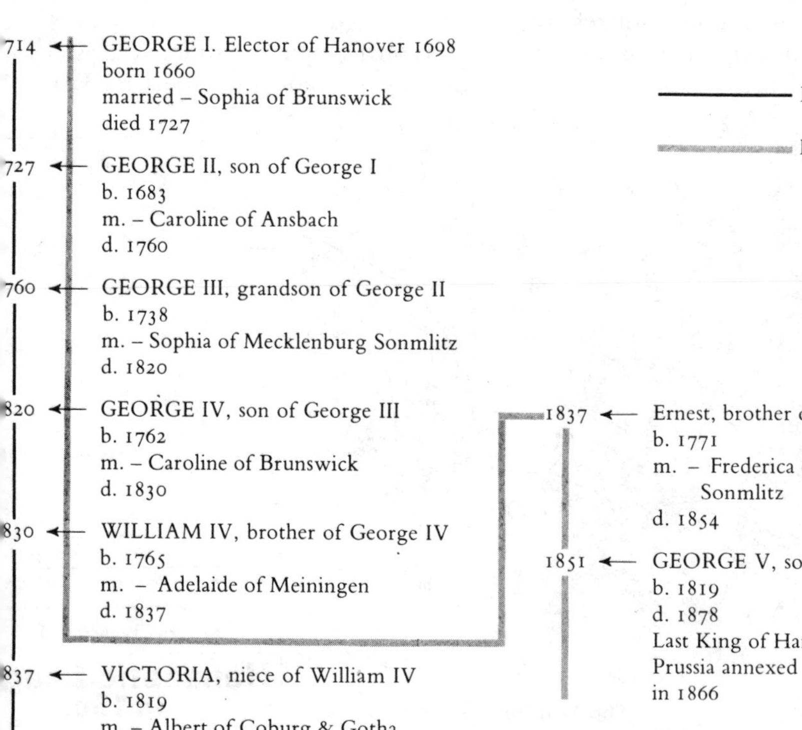

Hanover was formally incorporated into Prussia, and King George of Hanover went into retirement. Victoria grew up with very little contact with the surviving members of her father's family, and regarded herself as a Coburg rather than a Hanoverian, even to the extent of disapproving of the name George being given to the Prince who was later to rule as George V. The last slender tie was broken when George changed the family name to Windsor in 1917.

See also SAXE-COBURG GOTHA; WINDSOR, HOUSE OF.

Hansard: reports of the proceedings of the British Parliament. In 1803 William Cobbett began a series of unofficial reports of parliamentary debates. Thomas Curson Hansard (1776–1833) was the first printer and later took over the publication. In 1909 this publication first became an official verbatim report but is still referred to as Hansard, although now printed by the Stationery Office.

Hanseatic League: commercial league of north German towns. The Old High German word *Hansa* means "defensive alliance", and it was for mutual protection in international trade that the Hanseatic League, a medieval federation of north German towns, grew up. At the height of its power the League dominated German and Scandinavian trade, its influence extending from Novgorod in the east to London in the west. Its major city was Lübeck, where a Diet (or conference) met every three years. Eighty-five cities joined the League, as well as the districts of Lübeck, Cologne, Brunswick and Danzig. In addition there were four "factories" in Bruges, Bergen, Novgorod and London (the Steelyard, Deptford). The "factory" officials were responsible for the welfare, justice and trading rights of the German merchants' community. Factory in this earlier sense meant a headquarters for the transaction of commerce rather than a building where manufactures were carried on.

Originally a purely commercial association, by the mid-14th century the League

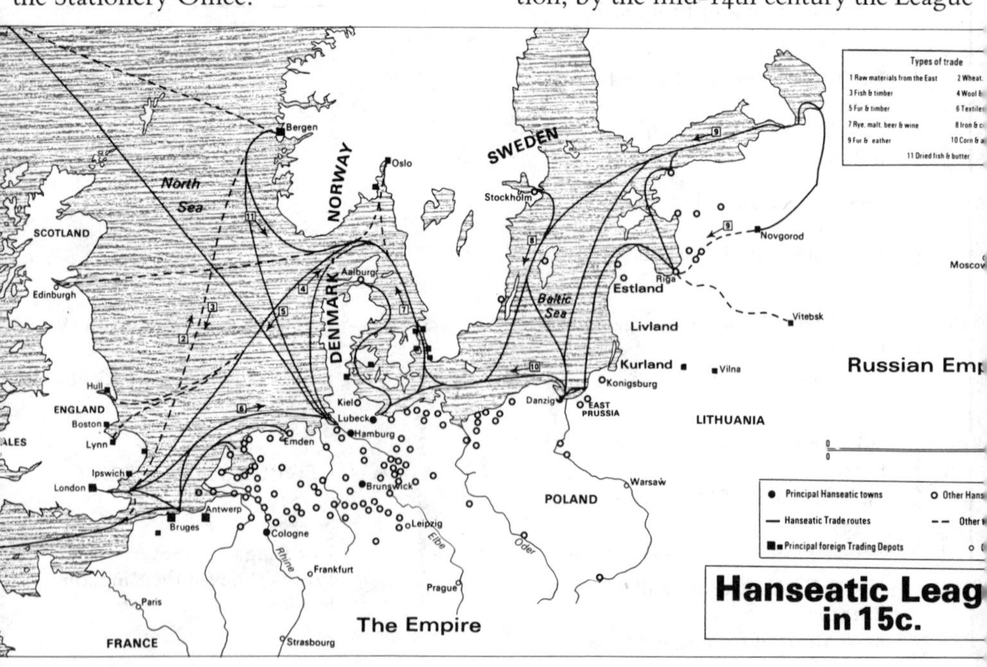

had developed its own political machinery, financial system and courts of justice. Its political strength is shown by its defeat of Waldemar IV of Denmark (1369), its economic strength by the fact that in the late 15th century the League's export of English cloth was forty times greater than that carried in English ships.

The League's decline was due to the exploration of sea routes to Asia and America by which England and Holland became superior commercial powers, to the falling off of the Baltic fishing industry, and to the political emergence of the German princedoms. The League's power was ultimately broken by the Thirty Years War. Lübeck, Hamburg and Bremen still retain the name *Hansestadte* – "Hansa towns".

Harding, Warren Gamaliel (1865–1923): twenty-ninth president of the USA. Harding was born in Ohio and became a lawyer and newspaper owner. After becoming a Republican senator he consistently advocated a policy of isolationism, opposing particularly United States intervention in Europe. In the 1920 presidential election Harding's pledge of a "return to normalcy" won him an overwhelming majority. His administration was very corrupt, and his private life was far from that which is normally expected from a modern head of state. He died suddenly in San Francisco in 1923 and was succeeded by Vice-President Calvin Coolidge (1872–1933).

Hargreaves, James (1745–78): British inventor of the spinning jenny. Hargreaves was a working Lancashire weaver when in 1764 he invented the first practical cotton spinning machine which quite rapidly replaced the spinning wheel. The "jenny" or "gin" (both words derived from "engine") was a hand-operated machine and an improved part of the "domestic" system of manufacture. A further developed form of jenny, Crompton's mule, was adopted in the powered textile mill.

Hargreaves obtained a patent for his jenny in 1770, but suffered through his remaining years both from the greed of rivals who wished to use the invention without proper payment to its inventor, and from the fierce opposition of the spinners who saw in the machine a threat to their livelihoods.

See also COTTON; INDUSTRIAL REVOLUTION.

Haroun al-Raschid (763–809): fifth of the Abbasid caliphs of Baghdad and hero of *The Arabian Nights*. Scholar, poet and warrior, he made his reputation before ascending the throne in successful campaigns, continued during his reign, against the Byzantine empire, carrying Persian arms to the Bosphorus and exacting tribute. During his brilliant reign (786–809) the empire reached its height, and he corresponded with Charlemagne on terms of equality. He was personally cruel, and much of his success was due to his ministers.

Harp: stringed musical instrument. It probably originated when man first discovered that the length and tension of a bowstring altered the pitch of its twanging sound, thus producing different notes. The earliest known harps, shown in Sumerian tomb-paintings, were bow-shaped.

Egyptian harps, which can be seen in pictures 3,000 years old, were about six feet [1.83 metres] in height, so that the musicians had to stand in order to play them. The Assyrians and the Greeks made small, triangular harps and from these the European harp developed. Anglo-Saxon minstrels called their harps "gligbeam", meaning "music-wood"

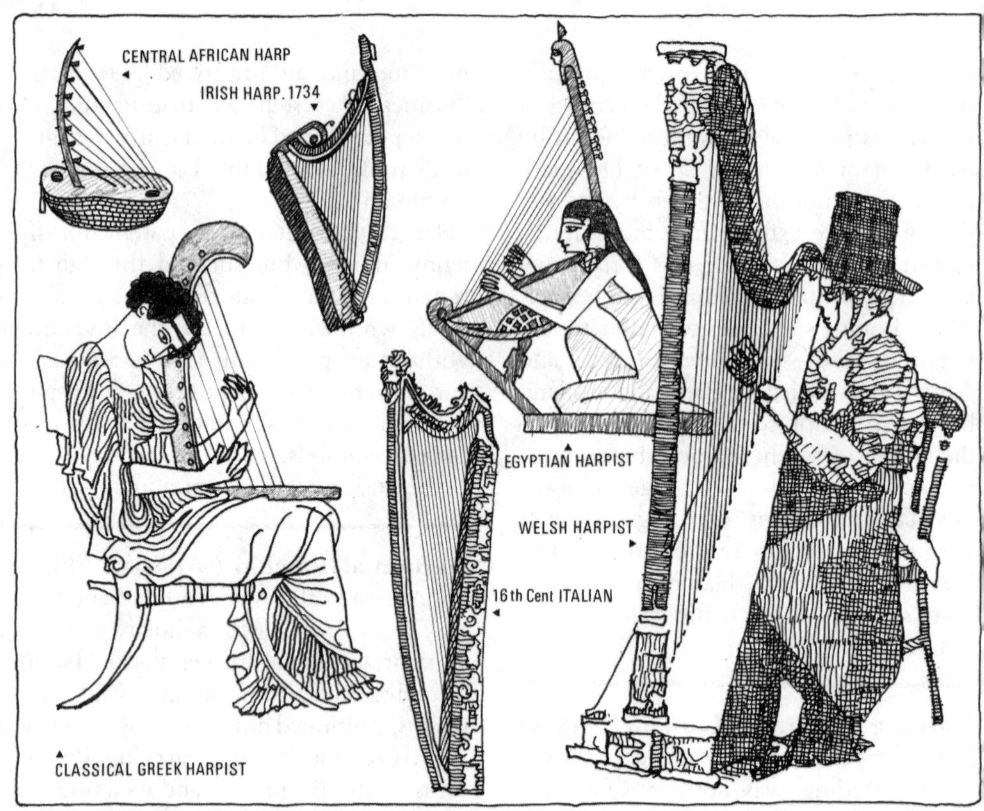

In the 15th century, harps were manufactured in London by a man named John Blore. In 1420, it is recorded, "13s 4d was paid for two new harps for King Henry, V and Queen Katherine", and the same king took his harp to France with him – complete with "chords and case". The minstrel, accompanying himself on a harp, was one of the chief sources of entertainment in the Middle Ages.

The chief steps in the development of the modern harp came with the invention of various pedal systems, by which the "stopping" (or modifying the tone) of strings can be achieved mechanically, leaving the hands of the harpist much more free. Though the playing of the harp as a source of domestic entertainment is now rarely met with, it has been increasingly used on the concert platform.

Harper's Ferry: river-crossing in west Virginia, where the Potomac and Shenandoah rivers meet; the scene of John Brown's dramatic raid on the Federal Arsenal between 16 and 18 October 1859. Harper's Ferry became an important settlement after the establishment of a federal armoury in 1796. John Brown, a fanatical believer in the emancipation of American slaves, conceived a plan for a slave rising in Virginia, which was to lead to the establishment of a "free" state in the southern Appalachian Mountains. The attack on the Federal Arsenal was to start the revolt, but no slaves joined Brown's raiding party, and after two days of fighting he surrendered to a force of marines, commanded by Robert E. Lee (1807–70). Brown was tried for treason and hanged (2 December). Brown's action made the dispute over slavery more bitter, the Southerners complaining that abolitionist propaganda was inciting Negroes to massacre their masters, while abolitionists regarded him as a martyr-hero, immortalising his action with a marching song, the first line of which is "John Brown's body lies a-mould'ring in the grave".

¶ KELLER, ALLAN. *Thunder at Harper's Ferry*. 1958

Harpsichord: keyboard musical instrument. The notes of a harpsichord are produced by the plucking of its strings by a small piece of metal known as the "jack". Harpsichords were originally known as virginals or spinets; large ones of the 18th century had several strings to each note and two, sometimes three, keyboards.

It was in the early 15th century that a keyboard was attached to a stringed instrument. In 1495 Italian musicians used "points of ravens' quills" to pluck the strings.

Large harpsichords were manufactured in the 16th century, the most celebrated designers being the Ruckers family, of Antwerp, who commissioned artists to decorate the wooden cases of their instruments.

English harpsichords were sturdier, and in the 18th century were fitted with pedals which raised the lid to produce *crescendo* effects. The Dolmetsch family still make harpsichords at Haslemere, England, and their pupil, Challis, has carried the art to the United States.

Harrison, John (1693–1776)**:** English maker of timepieces. Although only the son of a carpenter, he solved the problem (which had defeated many men of science, including Sir Isaac Newton) of keeping accurate time at sea and thereby finding longitude (*see* separate entry). Until the middle of the 18th century seamen out of sight of land had no accurate means of computing longitude, and errors often led to the wreck of ships and to great loss of life. Two examples are Anson's misadventure in 1741, when the *Centurion* lost between seventy and eighty men who

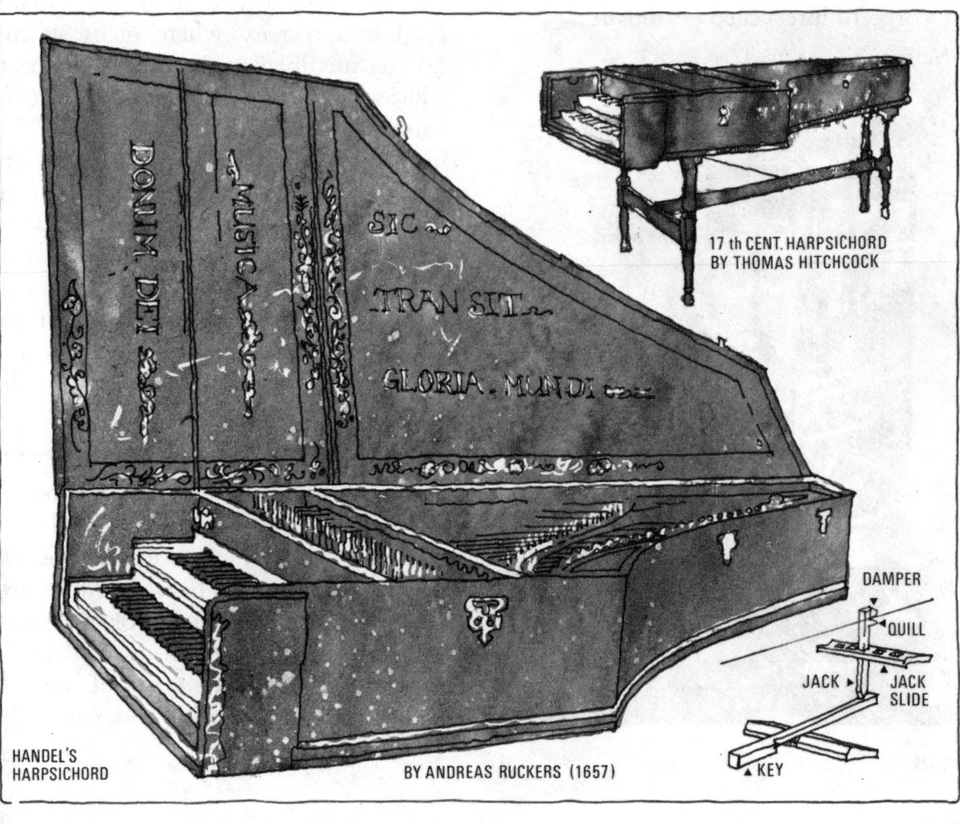

17 th CENT. HARPSICHORD BY THOMAS HITCHCOCK

HANDEL'S HARPSICHORD BY ANDREAS RUCKERS (1657)

were suffering from scurvy and who were prevented from getting the fresh vegetables that could have saved them because of error in navigation that kept the ship from land for nearly a fortnight; and the even worse disaster of 1707, when Admiral Sir Cloudesley Shovel's squadron, because of another error of calculation, was wrecked in the darkness on the Scilly Isles, with the loss of three ships, including the flag-ship, and some 2,000 men.

In 1714 the British government offered a reward of £20,000 for any "generally practicable and useful method of finding longitude at sea". Other nations had previously offered rewards, though not so large. John Harrison, without having served any apprenticeship to a clock-maker, acquired sufficient practical knowledge and skill to win this reward after it had been on offer for some fifty years – though the British government, despite repeated proofs of the accuracy of Harrison's timepieces, held off full payment till George III intervened personally.

Harrison's No 3 timekeeper.

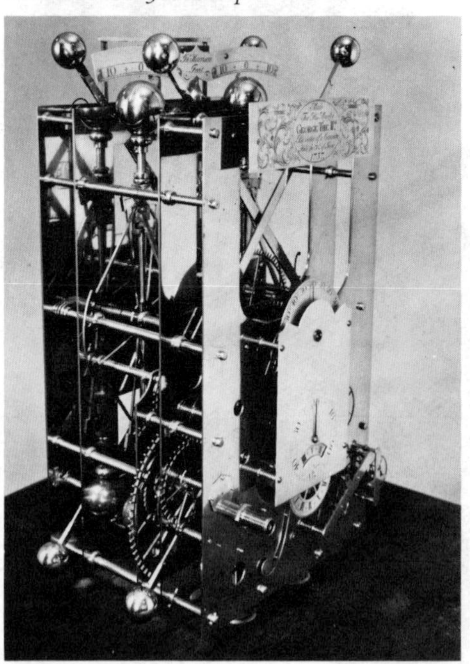

Harrison made five timekeepers for use at sea and "first of all men, showed the world that that annual tribute of ships, and treasures, and blood – that part of the heavy price of Admiralty – need be paid no longer . . . nor ever paid again. Such was this man's service to humanity." The words are those of Lieutenant-Commander Rupert Gould who, after an interval of more than 150 years, during which Harrison's timekeepers had been allowed to fall into disrepair, restored them to full working order. Most of them can still be seen at the National Maritime Museum, Greenwich, London.

Harvard University: the oldest and one of the foremost of American educational institutions, situated mainly in Cambridge, Massachusetts, but with sections in Boston and elsewhere. In 1636 the colony of Massachusetts voted £400 towards a new college which was to be built in "Newetowne". In memory of the English university where many of the leading members of the colony had been educated, the township was, in 1638, named Cambridge. Subsequently an immigrant Puritan minister, John Harvard, bequeathed money and books to the college, and in 1639 it was named Harvard College in his honour. Of its student body, drawn from all parts of the United States and abroad, approximately half are undergraduates; the rest study in the graduate schools of arts and science. The enrolment figure for 1970–71 was 20,297.

Harvey, William (1578–1657): English physician and discoverer of the circulation of the blood, announced in his book *De Motu Cordis* (1628). He achieved his discovery by the study of books, the dissection of bodies, experiment and detailed observation of many types of animal. Closely associated with the courts of

James I and Charles I, he was in charge of the royal children Charles and James at the battle of Edgehill (1642); and he himself recalled that "he withdrew with them under a hedge, and took out of his pocket a book and read" – a revealing picture of his devotion to study.

¶ MARCUS, R. B. *William Harvey: trailblazer of scientific medicine*. 1965

Hastings, Battle of (14 October 1066): Norman victory over the English at the outset of the Norman Conquest of England. William of Normandy landed at Pevensey only three days after Harold II of England had won a decisive victory over Harold III of Norway at Stamford Bridge. Harold hurried south with the English forces weakened by battle and forced marches. They took their position where the town of Battle now stands, fighting on foot in the shield-ring and using the long Danish battle-axe. The Normans fought from the saddle with spear and sword, using their force of archers in the intervals between cavalry charges. By nightfall Harold and his two brothers were dead, and the remnants of the English force were in retreat. *See also* BAYEUX TAPESTRY for illustration.

¶ GRAY, PETER. *The Battle of Hastings*. 1967; WARREN, W. L. *1066: The Year of Three Kings*. 1966

Hastings, Warren (1732–1818): governor-general of India, 1773–85. His policy of building up secure and friendly relations with Indian princes was thwarted by hostile members of the Council of the East India Company set up by the North's Regulating Act (1773), and with one member, Phillip Francis, he even fought a duel. Nevertheless, during the dangerous years of the war with France (1778–83) he successfully overcame a league under Hyder Ali in the Mysore war and kept the British Indian possessions secure without having to draw help from home.

Questionable expedients to raise money, such as the deposition of Chait Sing of Benares (1778) and the removal of their dowries from the Begums of Oudh, were used by Hastings's enemies, Burke, Fox and Sheridan, prompted by Francis. An impeachment was mounted against him, the trial lasting from 1788 to 1795, when Hastings was acquitted on all charges. The trial impoverished him, but drew attention to the duties of Britain towards subject races. *See illustration below*.

Hatshepsut (early 15th century BC): Egyptian queen (ruled *c*. 1489–*c*. 1469 BC). She is chiefly remembered for the magnificent terrace-temple built at Der el-Bahri beside the River Nile and for several

The Trial of Warren Hastings in Westminster Hall *by E. Dayes*.

obelisks at Thebes. Her tomb was discovered in 1841.

¶ In Holmes, W. *She Was Queen of Egypt.* 1959

Havana: capital city and chief port of Cuba. It was founded in 1514 by Diego Velasquez de Leon and often raided by English, French and Dutch. In the 17th century Havana was used as a place of assembly for convoys of Spanish ships sailing east and so attracted many attacks. It was captured by the British in 1762 but restored to Spain by treaty the following year. It became one of the chief ports and commercial centres of the Americas. As the administrative and political capital of Cuba it has shared fully in the vicissitudes of the island's history. *See also* CUBA.

Hawaii (formerly the Sandwich Islands)**:** state of the USA near the centre of the north Pacific Ocean, with its capital at Honolulu. The group of volcanic islands was discovered by Captain Cook in 1778. Hawaii was influenced by a wide variety of foreign traders, adventurers and missionaries, which its own primitive government under the Kamehameha dynasty could not exclude or control. A republic was established in 1894. The islands passed increasingly under United States domination, acquiring strategic importance in World War II. Hawaii became in 1959 the fiftieth state of the American Union. Most of the inhabitants are not now of native descent.

¶ BROWN, BILL. *People of Many Islands: the challenge of the Polynesians.* 1963

Hawkins, Sir John (1532–95)**:** English naval commander and administrator. As a merchant and shipowner he became a wealthy man before he was thirty and tried to make himself even richer by large-scale trading in Negro slaves – a practice not condemned by public opinion of his day. More creditable were his fine seamanship, his share in the defeat of the Spanish Armada (*see* separate entry) and, above all, his work as treasurer and comptroller of the English navy, in the course of which he removed many abuses and largely rebuilt the fleet with ships of improved design.

¶ In UNSTEAD, R. J. *Discoverers and Adventurers.* 1965

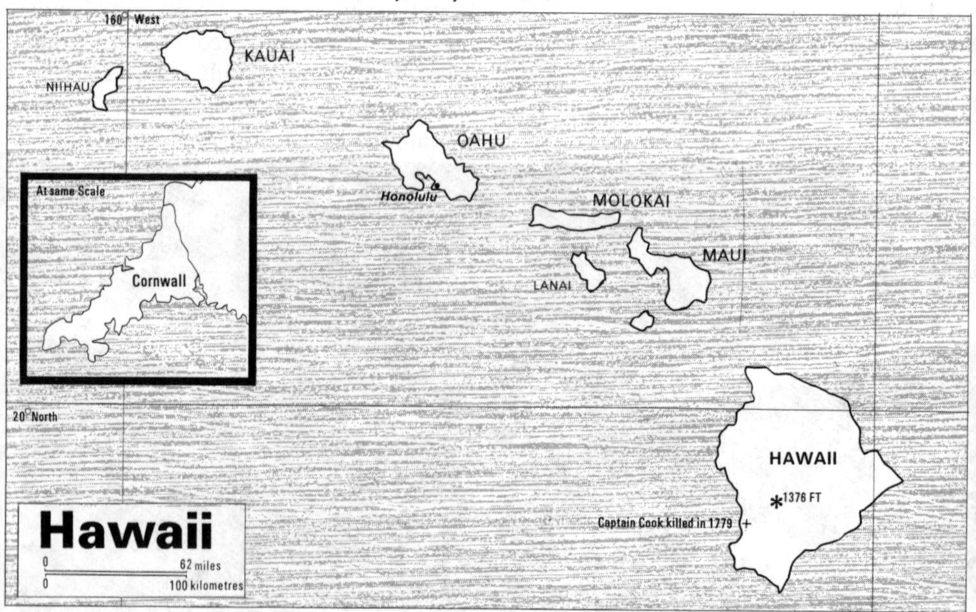

Hayes, Rutherford Birchard (1822–93): nineteenth president of the USA. Rutherford Hayes graduated from the Harvard Law School in 1845 and subsequently became the city solicitor at Cincinnati. During the Civil War (*see* American Civil War) he obtained rapid promotion in the Unionist Army and became a major-general of volunteers. In 1864 he was elected to Congress on a Republican "ticket" and in 1877, after a bitterly disputed election, became the nineteenth president of the United States (1877–81). His administration adopted a peaceful policy towards the Southern states, and the federal troops, which since the war had been stationed in the Southern capitals, were withdrawn. His policies were resented by the New York faction of the Republican Party, and as a result he was not nominated for a second period of office.

Health: fitness of body and mind. Primitive man believed that illness was sent by the gods. Good health could be preserved only by actions pleasing to them. The first health precautions, therefore, arose from superstition rather than knowledge or good sense, and for a long time, as mankind became more civilised, the priest still acted as doctor. The laws set out by Moses in Old Testament days contained many rules of diet and hygiene which were sensible for people living in a hot climate.

The Egyptians had intelligent ideas on the subject of hygiene. In 2000 BC the houses of the wealthy were equipped with bathrooms, and sanitary channels carried filth away. Earlier still cities with good drainage had been built in the Punjab, India, and the Indians of Peru had sewerage systems in their temples and towns.

Hippocrates, a Greek doctor of *c.* 460 – *c.* 377 BC, is acknowledged as the "father of medicine", and the so-called "Hippocratic oath" is still sworn by medical graduates at some universities. One of its provisions, often mentioned when doctors are required to give evidence in a court of law, is that they shall not divulge private information about their patients. Hippocrates attempted research into the causes of disease and was a pioneer of preventive medicine. The Greeks had advanced ideas of hygiene and believed, quite correctly, that many diseases can be kept at bay by attention to cleanliness and physical fitness. The precincts of the temple of Aesculapius, at Epidaurus, were almost like a hospital. The sick were brought there to be healed by the priests, who first gave them drugs which made them sleep and then prescribed medicines and suitable foods. This treatment of rest followed by nutritious diet undoubtedly helped many patients. Moreover, Greek doctors had some knowledge of setting fractures and dislocations.

4th century bas-relief of Aesculapius ministering to the sick.

The first people to have an efficient public health system on a large scale were the Romans. Like the Greeks, they were great believers in the virtues of cleanliness and built public baths and hospitals in all their major cities. They appointed officials whose duty was to inspect aqueducts in case the water became polluted, while others had to see that impure food was destroyed – to sell bad meat was a legal offence. In Rome itself, people were forbidden to throw rubbish into the Tiber. The Romans realised that swampy ground gave rise to malaria, although they did not understand how this came about, so they always built well away from marshes. They knew that people could carry infection; during an outbreak of plague in AD 532 the Emperor Justinian I made all travellers to Byzantium observe a period of quarantine.

But after the fall of the Roman Empire health precautions in Europe were forgotten. The cities of the Middle Ages were horribly insanitary – houses crowded together and frequently shared, during winter, by the pigs and cattle of the owners, to say nothing of the rats, carriers

A medieval water carrier.

of plague. Even in Tudor times there was little sanitation, apart from a gutter running down the street into which filth and garbage was thrown, to lie until heavy rain washed it away. Some people filled their cellars with refuse; a few ingenious men channelled it into the cellars of their neighbours. Bathing was an infrequent indulgence. Most of the major cities of Europe were built on the banks of rivers, which were sources of infection because all refuse eventually found its way into the stream. In London, Paris and Augsburg there were frequent edicts to forbid the pollution of the rivers by slaughtering cattle on the banks and casting offal into the water, while tanning was permitted only in certain districts. It was seldom that these rules were enforced: the citizens of medieval Europe had a fatalistic attitude to epidemics.

Epidemics there certainly were – indeed, they were almost an annual event. The Black Death of 1347–49 was the most notorious because it lasted for so long and killed so many, but leprosy, typhus and smallpox were all accepted as punishments inflicted by God for the sins of mankind. The Church had returned to the theory of primitive man. There was little attempt at cure as we understand it, though isolation and quarantine were enforced in times of pestilence, and special hospitals were set up to keep lepers apart from others. The understanding of hygiene was a slow process: in 1665 the citizens of London were fighting the Great Plague with the same remedies as had been used against the Black Death 300 years before.

The first settlers in North America had to reckon with epidemics. Almost half of the Pilgrim Fathers died during their first year in the New World. Disease spread from the settlers to the Indians, and as many Indians were destroyed by illness as were killed in territorial wars. The Americans quickly recognised the value of quarantine. In 1663, when plague was raging in the West Indies, ships were forbidden to enter Boston harbour, and travellers from areas where smallpox was rife had to spend a period in isolation before coming into New York.

The Industrial Revolution caused a great movement of population in England. People migrated from country areas to find work in the new factory towns. Many houses were needed, and they were built as quickly and cheaply as possible. Rows and rows were put up, tightly packed together, often with one pump and one lavatory shared by all the inhabitants of a row. Conditions in the

A typical East End court of the 19th century, with gas lighting and open drains.

factories were insanitary, and diseases, notably tuberculosis, spread rapidly amongst the workers. Those who worked in the cotton mills of Lancashire in England and the mines of South Wales and the Midlands were particularly subject to lung infection. The cotton-spinners worked in surroundings that were constantly damp and the miners suffered from long exposure to coal dust.

In the 1830s an epidemic of cholera swept through Europe, and the high death rate in industrial areas made it obvious that public health and sanitation were matters for grave concern. In London, much of the apparent indifference of the authorities arose from the fact that so many departments of local government were involved that it was not clear who was responsible for what. In 1830 there were over 100 Boards to deal with aspects of sanitation and health.

In the early years of the 19th century doctors concerned about the spread of disease amongst the poor in English cities had been bombarding their local councils with reports. In 1833 Parliament took note of these and a Factory Act was passed, the first of a series by which hours and conditions of work were regulated. In 1848 a General Board of Health was appointed by another Act. In 1851 a Housing Act became law, enforcing certain minimum standards of building and sanitation. Standards of housing are now the concern of local authorities.

England, however, lagged behind other nations in concern for public health. The French appointed a Comité de Salubrité during the Revolution. Its president was Dr Guillotin, and it is good that his name should be remembered for something other than his lethal invention, the guillotine. A German doctor, Johann Frank, suggested that the state ought to be responsible for the health and welfare of its workers. The American states of Massachusetts and Pennsylvania also passed laws which dealt with health and sanitation, but it was not until after the American Civil War that Congress dealt with such matters on a national scale.

But, if England was slower than many countries to begin to care for the health and welfare of workers, she eventually developed the most effective public health service in the world. In 1942, during World War II, Sir William Beveridge presented a report advocating a National Health Service, available to all, which should be maintained by contributions levied on all workers. This resulted in the National Health Service Act of 1946. Despite its disadvantages, the National Health Service does offer medical care to all sick persons and has relieved people's minds of the anxiety about the expense connected with illness.

In most countries, food is recognised as a source of infection. It is subject to strict inspection by officials, and the health of those who handle and sell it is frequently checked.

A very important development arising out of the formation of the United Nations Association after World War II was the establishment of the World Health Organisation. Member nations are agreed that the health of people living in underdeveloped countries is the responsibility of all. WHO sends out doctors and nurses to deal with epidemics and emergencies – earthquakes, for example – in countries unable to cope with such disasters; it also undertakes the medical training of members of the native population. In many parts of Africa and Asia progress is slow, but this awareness of collective responsibility is a new and important contribution to the health of mankind.

¶ DELGADO, ALAN. *A Hundred Years of Medical Care.* 1970; JOHNSON, R. W. *Disease and Medicine.* 1967; WATSON, ROGER. *Edwin Chadwick, Poor Law and Public Health.* 1969.

See also HOSPITALS.

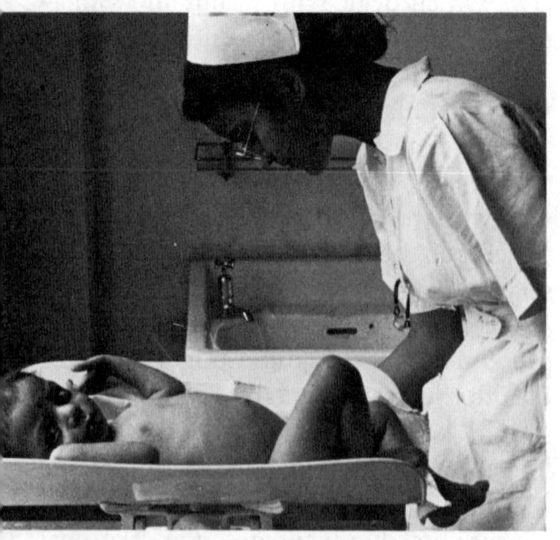

A young nurse in training at the WHO children's hospital in Karachi, Pakistan.

Heating: the first centres of Western civilisation were in areas with a warm climate. The Egyptians' problem was not to heat their houses, but to keep them cool. The Greeks also had no need to warm their houses, apart from introducing a portable iron brazier if the weather became cold. It was not until the Romans pushed the boundaries of their Empire northwards that the inhabitants of the temperate Mediterranean lands had to face long cold winters.

Roman engineers already had experience of heating water on a large scale. Their public baths had warm rooms to which water, heated by a furnace, was piped. When they built homes in colder countries, the Romans made increasing use of a hypocaust: the ground floor of the house was supported on piles of bricks standing in the foundations. In this low underground chamber charcoal fires were kept burning by slaves. The hot air rose, heating the floor and rooms above. It is interesting that a similar method was used in ancient Mongolia.

After the fall of the Roman Empire this efficient form of heating was forgotten. In the 9th and 10th centuries the wooden halls of chieftains had a central hearth of stone, and smoke found its way out through a hole in the roof. Later, fighting men built themselves stone castles which were extremely cold and draughty. Eventually someone hit on the idea of putting the hearth against a wall, with a hole behind it so that the smoke could escape. The wall opposite the fireplace was built to an extra thickness. It absorbed heat from the fire and retained it, so providing a second source of warmth. This method was adapted later by settlers in North America, who sometimes built two fireplaces in one wall and made the facing wall very thick.

In AD 1624 a Frenchman, Louis Savot, invented a fireplace which drew warm

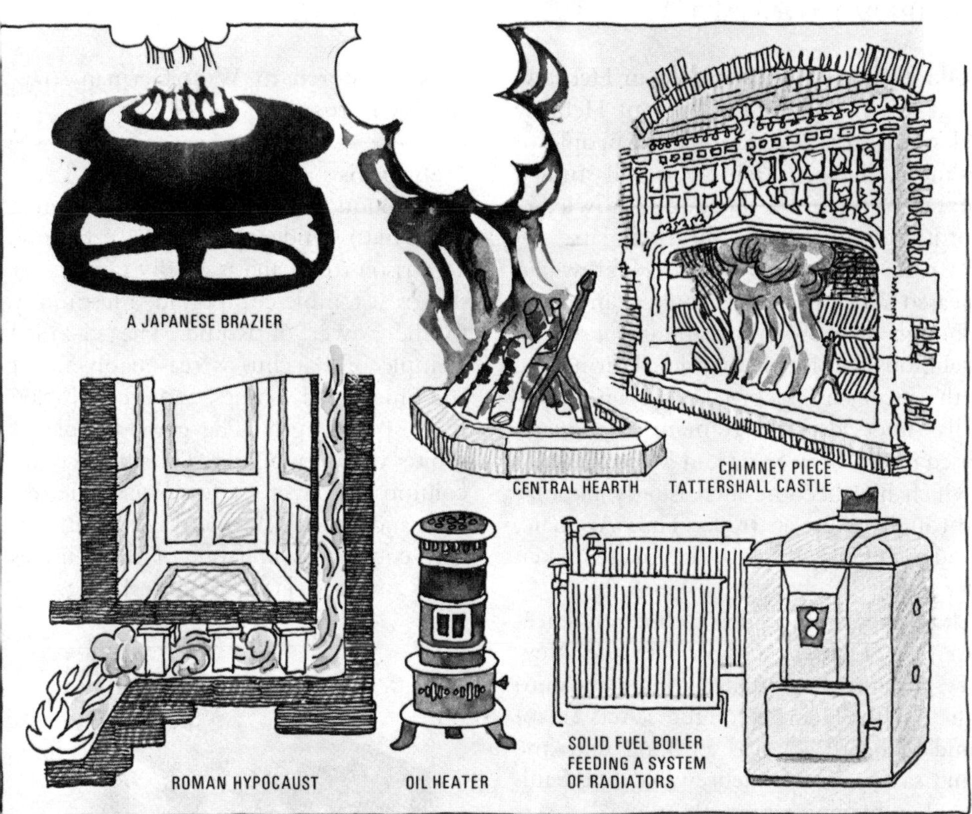

air from the room through passages under the hearth, carried it behind the grate and circulated it into the room again through a grille below the mantelpiece. About a hundred years later an Englishman, William Strutt, had the idea of passing hot air from a stove to other rooms in the house by channels in the walls. The same year, 1792, saw the installation of hot water pipes to warm the Bank of England.

A heating system of pipes and radiators carrying hot water was popularised in the United States in 1840 by an engineer named Robert Briggs. For years this remained the most popular form of heating in that country. In 1877 "district heating" was first tried, at Lockport, New York. Steam was piped from a central boiler house to several buildings. This system has been widely used in colleges and schools and in the 1930s some housing developments adopted it, though it has never become very popular. Recent years have seen a greater increase in the use of so-called "smokeless" fuels to lessen air pollution; and the development of domestic central heating systems fired by solid fuel, gas or oil. Electric storage radiators have also become very popular.

¶ WRIGHT, LAWRENCE. *Home Fires Burning: the history of domestic heating and cooking*. 1968

Hebrew language: the classical language of Israel. Long ago, people believed that Hebrew was the original language of mankind. "And the whole earth was of one language, and of one speech", we are told in Genesis 11:1 and, obviously, they thought that speech must be Hebrew. Scholars now know that certain other languages are older, and that no universal tongue can be traced.

Hebrew is one of the Semitic group of languages which includes, among others, Assyrian, Phoenician, Arabic, Aramaic and Ethiopic. Almost the whole of the

Old Testament was written in Hebrew, and this comprises the bulk of Hebrew classical literature, familiar to people of almost all races. Hebrew is still studied extensively, and a thorough knowledge of it is essential for Biblical scholars.

By the time Jesus was born, Hebrew had ceased to be a popularly spoken language, though it was still read and used in religious and learned circles. During the 4th century BC, Hebrew had been gradually superseded by Aramaic, a language used in northern Syria and Mesopotamia, which had become increasingly popular through its use in trade. Thus Aramaic, and not Hebrew, was the language spoken by Jesus.

It puzzles some readers to find references to "the Hebrew tongue" in the New Testament – for instance, "He spake unto them in the Hebrew tongue" (Acts 21:40) and "I heard a voice speaking unto me and saying in the Hebrew tongue, Saul, Saul, why persecutest thou me?" (Acts 26:14) – but here Aramaic is meant, and not classical Hebrew.

Modern Hebrew, as used by Jews in Israel today, was evolved in the 19th century. A special script is used, based on the ancient picture alphabet of the Phoenicians and read from right to left (*see also* ALPHABETS).

Hegira or **Hejira** (from Arabic *hijrah*, flight): the name given to the flight of Mohammed from Mecca to Medina in AD 622, a year of such significance in Muslim history that their calendar is dated from it.
See also MOHAMMED, etc.

Heligoland: small island in the North Sea. Heligoland was a British possession from 1807 to 1890, when it was given to Germany. Heavily fortified, the island was a stronghold in both world wars and was extensively bombed in the second. It was restored to West German sovereignty in 1952.

Heliopolis or **Baalbek:** town in Lebanon, conquered by Alexander the Great (d. 323 BC). Under the Romans it became a garrison town and is chiefly famous for the great temple compound, a testimony to the power of Rome. The so-called Temple of Bacchus is reasonably intact and measured some 220 feet [67.06 metres] in length. The great temple of Jupiter was even bigger. The six surviving columns are over 65 feet [19.81 metres] high and 7 feet [2.13 metres] in diameter. The courtyards in front of the temples were 200 yards [182.88 metres] long.

The Temple of Venus and Pillars of Jupiter, Baalbek.

Hellenism: term used to describe the civilisation of those countries influenced by Greek culture from the death of Alexander the Great (323 BC) to the battle of Actium (31 BC). This period is also known as the Hellenistic Age. Hellenism thus includes important developments in political practice, in literature, in philosophy, the arts and science. Geographically it embraced the whole area of Europe, Asia and Africa conquered by Alexander, but its most important centres were Athens, Alexandria, Antioch, Ephesus and Pergamum.

On Alexander's death his empire was divided up between three of his generals, and by 200 BC, after a century of trouble, there were four basic units. In Greece various leagues were trying to establish their independence from Macedonia, the Ptolemies ruled in Egypt, the Attalids around Pergamum, and the Seleucids in Syria and over the rest of the old empire. The three dynasties outside Greece presented a radically different political experiment in a fusion between an eastern monarchy of almost divine nature and the usual Greek democratic ideas. Thus, though the culture was Greek, the divine nature of the old kings was accepted by the new Greek rulers, and this was to be adopted later by the Roman emperors.

The Hellenistic Age is sometimes regarded as one of decadence in literature, and it is true that the grandeur of the old tragedies and oratory largely disappeared. But in their place came important innovations, the "New" comedy of Menander, the epigram, the pastoral idyll of which Theocritus was the master, the mime, the didactic poem. Much of this was to have great influence on Rome.

Important new philosophical theories started about 300 BC to meet the collapse of the old religion and the disillusionment that followed. The most famous were Stoicism and Epicureanism, both of which tried in very different ways to find a release from the worry of life, the Stoic being taught to endure hardship and ill fortune with patience and courage, the Epicurean to seek pleasure as the chief good, but only through virtue.

In the arts the age was one of great change, and western and Renaissance art were to be immeasurably influenced. It saw the start of grandiose building schemes (e.g. the Mausoleum at Halicarnassus) constructed to match the glory of the monarchs who ordered them. There also came a more naturalistic approach, especially in painting and sculpture. A vivid, dramatic picture now replaced the restrained if sometimes frozen portraiture of the Classical Age. The famous Laocoön group, which dates from the 1st century BC, is a good example.

Finally, the sciences flourished as never again until the Renaissance. The encouragement of scholarship, the fusion of ideas from Greece and the East and the foundation of major libraries all helped. Among famous names were Euclid, Archimedes, Hipparchus and Aristarchus. They were chiefly occupied with mathematics and astronomy, and Aristarchus's theory of the solar system pre-dated Copernicus by 1,800 years.

From 133 BC, when the last of the Attalids bequeathed his kingdom to Rome, the Hellenistic world was gradually absorbed into her dominions. Syria

The Laocoön Group, 1st century BC.

was conquered in 65 and Egypt annexed in 30. But the Roman poet Horace knew the truth when he wrote that "Greece, though captured, has taken prisoner its rough conqueror".
See also GREECE etc.

Helmet: armoured headpiece for protection in battle and for military display. Early types in Europe were probably derived from late Roman examples, first as simple crossed iron bands with a lining of horn or metal. A typical conical helmet with a nasal to protect the face traditionally belonged to St Wenceslaus (d. 935). In the 12th century a cylindrical flat-topped helm was introduced, and from 1180 a pierced face-guard was added. The kettle-hat, a broad-brimmed, open-faced helmet, then appeared, and remained in service as long as armour survived.

By the end of the 13th century the sugar-loaf helm had a skull shaped like a hazel nut to deflect blows more easily. Compact bascinets with high-pointed skulls, movable visors and mail neck-pieces, appeared in the 14th century, and these became the most popular form of helmet in Europe. In the 15th century the bascinet gave way to the salet, which had developed from the kettle-hat, extending backwards to shield the neck. Tournament helms with enlarged frog-mouthed chin-pieces were much larger and weighed as much as 20 pounds. The middle of the 15th century saw a new headpiece, the armet, which was the most perfect form of helmet, consisting of a hinged skull, removable visor and aventail. In the 16th century many fine examples of burgonets and casques were decorated solely for parade purposes. Helmets were disused for military purposes as armour was discarded. The modern steel helmet was introduced during the 1914–18 war as a general issue to foot soldiers, and simple forms, known

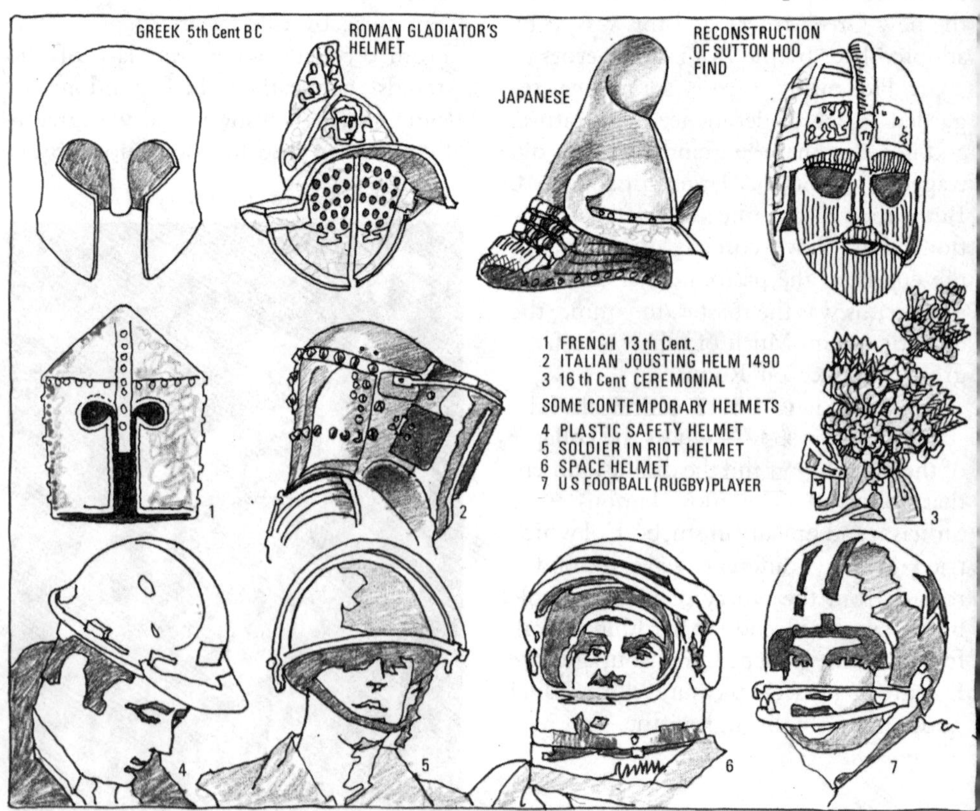

as crash helmets, are now often used for protective purposes by workmen, motorcyclists and certain sportsmen.

Helot: a slave in ancient Sparta. Most helots came from the conquest of Messenia. Treated as chattels, they fought in attendance on the Spartans and could win their freedom in return for bravery in battle. Revolts were frequent, and on several occasions Sparta was unable to undertake wars outside her boundaries because of trouble from them.

Henry, Prince, called **"the Navigator"** (1394–1460)**:** son of King John of Portugal and Philippa, daughter of John of Gaunt, Duke of Lancaster; honoured for his services to geographical discovery and navigation. At his Sagres school and observatory, near Cape St Vincent at the south-western tip of Portugal, he trained seamen and equipped expeditions to explore the west African coast, seeking a seaway to the east and a Portuguese empire, a dream accomplished in the century after his death. Madeira was discovered in 1418, but Cape Bojador proved impassable until Henry's decisive instructions drove Gil Eannes to sail beyond it. Senegal was reached in 1443. The resulting slave trade was a less happy result of Henry's expeditions.

BRADFORD, ERNLE. *Southward the Caravels: the Story of Henry the Navigator.* 1961

See also DISCOVERY, AGE OF; endpapers.

Heraldry: the art or science of devising, recording and interpreting armorial bearings. Heraldry is an unwritten yet unmistakable means, at first of individual and later of communal recognition. It is notable for precision of expression and description, with its own special terms known as blazonry.

It came into use for personal recognition in the mid-12th century, in Britain, France, Germany, Spain and Italy. A commonly held view is that allied forces taking part in the First Crusade needed distinctive devices. Tactically, in those battles fought only by daylight, and with the use of the enclosed helm, heraldic recognition became essential. The European nations mentioned above all produced their own devices, modes and styles, and each still has its own national heraldry.

Another opinion as to the origins and early popularity of heraldry emphasises the importance of the seal. A seal of specially coloured wax (a durable substance) became a means whereby an important but illiterate person could impress his or her assent on any document. King Edward the Confessor devised something even harder to forge than the complexity of the single seal; this was the double seal, attached by a cord and impressed on both sides (*see* SEALS).

A vital feature of personal heraldry is that it is hereditary, i.e. handed down from generation to generation. What is now called the heraldic "achievement" may have originated in a custom of hanging the war gear upon the wall above the fireplace, to keep everything dry and ready for immediate use. The proudly displayed, battle slashed "mantling" was possibly borrowed from the veil of the Arabs, used to keep off the fierce heat and the dust storms; the "torse" or twist perhaps derived from the Arab camel hair *arghal,* fastened round the forehead.

Next must be mentioned the sport, or sort of military training, known as the tournament. This sometimes became a brawl, until complicated and strict rules were made, initially under Edward I. The joust provided amusement, especially to the tenantry, who raised howls of delight upon seeing their seigneur, or his son, bring down his opponent (or, in the case of unpopular landlords, being themselves brought down). The livery-colours in which they were all clothed by their lord bore a surprising resemblance to football club colours of today (e.g. Hull city, in England, has interesting links with the Strabolgi family; both liveries and football club colours are red and white). Livery colours are still to be seen in Siena, Italy (*see* separate entry), upon *Il Palio*, 2 July and 15 August. Medieval liveries are worn by riders in the market-square horse race, and its ceremonies. By the end of the 15th century, battle tactics and methods had changed. With the increasing use of cannon, the surcoat and wooden war shield passed away, but the tournament continued for a time to display the colour and pageantry of the herald's art.

By this time heraldry (duly and rightly inherited) had roused the envy of the unprivileged and many claimed arms and the social standing that seemed to go with them. Control was needed to check abuse. The sovereign authority was the king or queen and continues to be so today, represented by a learned body of Heralds and Pursuivants with their artistic and clerical staff. In England their head is Garter King of Arms; in Scotland, Lord Lyon King of Arms, and in Ireland, Ulster King of Arms.

¶ MONCREIFFE, I. and POTTINGER, D. *Simple Heraldry*. 1953; SLADE, R. *Your Book of Heraldry*. 1967

See also ARMORIAL BEARINGS.

Herculaneum: Roman town on the bay of Naples, destroyed by the eruption of Vesuvius in AD 79. Covered by a mixture

A galleried courtyard at Herculaneum.

of mud and lava and by modern houses Herculaneum has proved difficult to uncover, but many of the excavations there have proved even more exciting than those at Pompeii. Modern restorations have been very successful.

Heresy: declared doubts of an orthodox religious principle. The word is Greek in origin and need not be confined to questions of Christian belief. Christ himself was regarded as a heretic by the Pharisees, though they called his teaching blasphemy.

To the historian the heresies which long disturbed the Western Church are of interest, as they often had wide and lasting repercussions. The teaching of the New Testament did not, in itself, supply a complete system of belief, and this led to speculation and thence to controversy and even physical violence. The two main causes of dispute were (1) the nature of the Trinity and particularly the nature of Christ as being both God and man, and (2) the seeming antithesis between God's purpose and man's exercise of his free will, which involved questions of the nature of sin and of eternal salvation or punishment.

The Arian heresy, the most notable in the early Church, concerned the nature of Christ, and was suppressed only after a long struggle led by Athanasius (*c.* 296–373), Bishop of Alexandria. Other heresies of the early centuries are mentioned in the article on FATHERS OF THE CHURCH.

In modern times questions of heresy have ceased to rouse the passions of the past, but as recently as 1925 a school teacher was condemned by a local court in Tennessee, USA, for teaching the theory of the Origin of Species.

Herod: the name of several Palestinian rulers. Herod the Great (73–4 BC) owed his position as King of Judaea and continued support from Rome to the good relations he established with the Emperor Augustus. A builder of towns and fortifications, he restored the temple at Jerusalem. He was also a patron of the arts and literature. His son Herod Antipas was governor of Galilee and built the city of Tiberias. John the Baptist's execution was brought about by Antipas's wife Herodias and his daughter Salome. Jesus was examined before Herod Antipas. Antipas was defeated and banished in the reign of Caligula. Herod Agrippa I, a grandson of Herod the Great, cast Peter into prison. The last of the Herods, his son Herod Agrippa II, who met Paul, died in Rome in AD 100.

¶ PEROWNE, S. *The Life and Times of Herod the Great*. 1956

Herodotus (*c.* 485–425 BC): Greek historian, often known as "The Father of History". Originally a Persian subject, he came of a wealthy family and was able to devote his time to the study of literature and to extensive travel, in the course of which he carried out much personal investigation into and recording of historic detail. When he wrote his *Histories* his chief aim was to give an account of the Persian war of invasion of Greece, but he interpolated much geographical and topographical detail and many interesting episodes outside the main narrative. His reliability as a historian is sometimes in doubt, but there is no dispute about the elegance of his style and his command of language.

¶ In PRINGLE, PATRICK. *101 Great Lives*. 1964

Hertzog, James Barry Munnik (1866–1942): South African statesman. An ardent Afrikaans nationalist, he played a prominent part in the Boer War, leading a commando raid to the Cape. Afterwards he concentrated on preserving the Afrikaans heritage of his people and founded the Afrikaner Nationalist party. Later, when this was joined by the Labour party, he became prime minister (1924–34) at the head of a coalition government which secured the position of the Afrikaners and restricted the development of Africans and Indians. Having failed to keep South Africa out of World War I, he resigned.

Herzl, Theodor (1860–1904): Hungarian Jew, born in Budapest, who founded modern Zionism (*see* separate entry). In 1896 he published a famous pamphlet *Der Judenstaat*, calling for the preservation of the Jewish race by national reunion, and later proclaimed his hope of "establishing for the Jewish people a publicly and legally assured home in Palestine". His theories were backed by immense personal effort in travel, interviews with various diplomats and powerful written propaganda.

Hesiod (8th century BC): Greek poet. His most famous work (and perhaps the only genuine one to have survived) was *Works and Days,* which contains some personal history and much about the life and labour of the countryside. The poem also includes *The Hawk and the Nightingale*, the earliest known fable in Greek literature.

Hieroglyphics: name for the incised, graphic writing of ancient Egypt, wrought with slow and reverent precision, to immortalise the divinity of Egypt's sacred rulers and their deeds. The meaning was subtly withheld from all aliens, until (AD 1799) the chance discovery of the "Rosetta Stone", now in the British Museum. This small slab of black basalt contains a decree, in honour of Ptolemy V (Epiphanes), dated 198 BC, in three forms: (1) hieroglyphic – sacred; (2) demotic – the writing for the people; (3) Greek. To the scholar Champollion this was the key to interpretation. In ancient Egypt writing with the reed pen, on readily portable papyrus rolls, gradually took simpler and more rapid form. Surviving specimens (like the hieroglyphs) still show a delicate use of mineral colours, perfectly preserved. In the royal "Tombs of the Kings" not far from Luxor (tombs completely sealed for many centuries) we see hieroglyphic mural paintings still brilliant in colour. The influence of Egyptian writing may be seen in Phoenician and in ancient square Hebrew letters. Picture-writing was, and still is, worldwide, e.g. in modern road signs.

¶ HONOUR, ALAN. *The Man Who Could Read Stones: Champollion and the Rosetta Stone.* 1968

See also ALPHABETS; HEBREW LANGUAGE.

Highwaymen: lawbreakers, usually on horseback, who robbed wayfarers. Wherever roads have been bad and police forces scanty, the possibility of meeting some of these "gentlemen of the road" has been an occupational risk of travellers. In the so-called underdeveloped countries they are by no means extinct, while in "developed" countries, such as our own, they have merely updated their tactics. The thugs who ram a car into a van containing pay packets, cosh the driver and make off with the money are only highwaymen, new style.

Dick Turpin clearing Hornsey Gate.

Ned Kelly wearing his home-made armour, as he appeared in The Australian Sketcher *of 1880.*

Time has turned the old highwaymen into figures of romance. Their impudence, even on the scaffold, won them many admirers. Claude Duval (1643–70) was known to dance a graceful *coranto* with the ladies of his victims. Jerry Abershaw (1773?–95) went to execution with a rose between his lips. Dick Turpin (1706–39), the English highwayman, hired mourners to follow the cart which bore him to the gallows. Ned Kelly (1854–80), the bushranger – the Australian word for the species – wore home-made armour made out of ploughshares. Hanged after a career of robbery and murder, he has nevertheless become an Australian folk-hero, immortalised in the paintings of the Australian artist Sidney Nolan (b. 1917). The same curious immortality has been attained in America by the disreputable Jesse Woodson James (1847–82).

¶ PRINGLE, PATRICK. *The Real Book of Highwaymen* 1963

Hill, Sir Rowland (1795–1879): British educationist and postal reformer. Hill's boyhood interest in mathematics later turned to postal systems. In 1837, when charges varying from 2*d* to 1*s* 8*d* severely limited correspondence, he published pamphlet, *Post Office Reform,* advocating a flat rate of 1*d* per half-ounce, whatever the distance. He argued that increased business would quickly overcome any revenue losses. Against Post Office opposition the Government introduced his scheme in 1840. Dismissed from his Treasury post in 1842 when the government changed, Hill was reinstated in 1846 as secretary to the Postmaster-General. Within sixty years his system was copied universally.

J JAMES ALAN. *Sir Rowland Hill and the Post Office.* 1972; STAFF, FRANK. *The Penny Post.* 1964

Himalayas: the main ranges of the great complex of mountains separating the subcontinent of India and Pakistan from the mass of Asia to the north.

The "Great Himalayas", stretching from the Karakoram, north of Kashmir, in the north-west, to Tibet, Nepal and Bhutan in the east, a distance of some 1,500 miles [2414 kilometres], contain many of the highest mountains in the world, such as Everest, Kanchinjunga and Godwin-Austen, and have an average elevation of 20,000 feet [6096 metres]. The western region of these mountains forms the great water-divide between the rivers flowing to India and those to central Asia and China.

The principal political areas are Nepal and the great plateau of Tibet. For centuries their altitude (Tibet averages 18,000 feet [5486 metres]) and inaccessibility made it possible for them to remain largely closed to the outside world, and enormous tracts were virtually unknown. In recent years China has taken over control of Tibet, Nepal has been opened to western influences, and many scientific and mountaineering expeditions have been conducted in the area. But it still contains many hundreds of miles of unmapped country and remains one of the greatest natural political barriers in the world.

Hindenburg, Paul von (1847–1934): German soldier and president of the

The majestic Himalayas rising above the Tolam Bau Glacier on the Tibet/Nepal border.

German Republic. Commissioned in 1865, Hindenburg fought in the Franco-Prussian War, became a member of the General Staff and retired as a general in 1911. He was recalled in 1914, and his brilliant success against the Russians gave him the command of the German field army. He remained a national hero after 1918 and was elected president in 1925, taking his constitutional duties seriously. But the economic and political crises of 1930–33 gradually stripped him of his power, and he was unable to prevent the Nazis taking control of the state in 1933. Winston Churchill wrote of him as "slow-thinking, slow-moving, but sure, steady, faithful, warlike yet benignant, larger than the ordinary run of men".

Hinduism: the social institutions and the religion of the vast majority of Indians, dating from at least 1000 BC. Unlike Christianity or Islam, it is not a personal religion, the individual being regarded as unimportant and always as a part of a greater whole – universe, society, caste or village community – and as a link between an infinite number of lives in the past and in the future. Hindus believe in an all-embracing creative spirit (Brahma), within which are included all the properties and processes of life, evil as well as good. From three main gods – Brahma the Creator, Vishnu the Preserver and Siva the Destroyer (and their wives, lovers and children) – have developed thousands of gods, down to village godlings, who are worshipped with an infinite variety of rites and practices, some of them primitive and barbaric. At its best, however, Hinduism represents a lofty standard of culture and morality, stressing the spiritual as against the material values.

Bronze statue of Síva and his consort Umā, from Madras, 1000 AD.

¶ CROMPTON, YORKE. *Hinduism.* 1971; SHARPE ERIC J. *Thinking about Hinduism.* 1971

Hispaniola: the second largest island in the West Indies, the western third of it belonging to the republic of Haiti (*see* separate entry) and the rest to the Dominican Republic. Originally the whole island was named Haiti, till it was renamed Hispaniola in 1492 by Columbus.

Historians, American: the early histories of America were written by hosts of explorers and settlers who wrote to tell the people in the Old World of their experiences and to attract newcomers and potential investors. Such was the purpose of Thomas Hariot and John Smith in writing the earliest histories of "Virginia" (which in 1600 meant the entire seaboard north to the Maine coast).

The Puritans of New England viewed their coming to America as part of a divine plan: they wrote the story of their migration and with the purpose of recording for later ages God's "wonder-working providence", a concept which dictated the form given to the accounts written by William Bradford, John Winthrop, Cotton Mather and Thomas Prince. Historians who wrote about their 18th-century colonies tended to continue this "promotional" and "providential" style, but following the secession of the Thirteen Colonies (1776) a new form of nationalistic histories became fashionable. These histories were full of patriotic fervour as they told the story of the Revolution. John Marshall and David

Ramsay were the most prominent historians of this era, but their integrity has often been called into question as a result of the way in which they copied other people's writings.

George Bancroft (1800-91) was perhaps the first American historian of any great stature. He wrote an idealistic type of history, which supported the doctrine of America's "manifest destiny" to expand throughout the New World; he also stressed the role of principles and ideas as causes of historical development.

Jared Sparks became in 1839 the first American professor in the writing of history (historiography), when he was appointed to a chair at Harvard. He introduced the first systematic study of the way in which history should be investigated, recorded and written. Towards the end of the 19th century the writing of history in America became a disciplined profession. This process was aided by Charles K. Adams, who pioneered the history seminar (group of advanced students) at Michigan University, and by Justin Winsor. The latter in his capacity as a librarian accumulated source materials and helped to establish contacts with local history societies.

A variety of ideas gradually gave new forms to historical writing. Frederick J. Turner stressed particularly the influence of the Frontier (*see* separate entry). As in Great Britain, history-writing in the United States was dominated by a white Anglo-Saxon Protestant viewpoint, which is today being challenged by American Negroes in their claims for "Black Studies" programmes. The institutional approach was not confined to purely political subjects, and Turner examined the role of sections (the different geographical areas of the USA) in shaping the American character. The sense that the whole life of a people constitutes history (ideas, economy and social form) was central in the work of teaching the "new history" and can be best seen in the work of J. H. Robinson and Charles A. Beard. Arthur Schlesinger Snr and J. B. McMaster were pioneers in the writing of social history in the 1920s and gave prominence to the theory that history should be viewed as the sum total of human activity.

Historians, British: Scholarship should know no frontiers and British historians share the trends and discoveries of a worldwide profession. The British environment has no doubt made a mark on British historians. History can really flourish only in a free society, and freedom came early to Britain. Raphael Holinshed (1515-80?) may have felt it politic to whitewash the Lancastrian kings, and Shakespeare may have written of Macbeth what he felt about Henry IV, but after 1688 historians felt free to tell the truth as they saw it. The comparative moderation with which Englishmen settled religious and civil disputes of the 16th and 17th centuries is reflected in the moderation even of partisan historians. The Catholic John Lingard (1771-1851) wrote with respect of the Protestant martyrs, and the Protestant J. A. Froude (1818-94) wrote similarly of the Catholic martyrs. Lord Acton (1834-1902) preached and practised the principle "never rest till you have made out for your adversary a better case than he could make out for himself".

As British democratic society offered to a large reading public the opportunity of public service, as, e.g., member of parliament, justice of the peace, town councillor, trustee of a church, director of a company, British historians tended to write in a popular style and to regard history as a school of political and social conduct. Lord Macaulay (1800-59) aimed to displace with his history books the latest novels from the tables of young ladies. G. M. Trevelyan (1876-1962) justified his care for the art of graceful narrative on the ground that history, to have any influence, must not just advance the understanding of the expert but form and elevate the opinion of the voting public towards tolerance, foresight and fairness. Sir Walter Ralegh (1552–1618) defined "the end and scope of al Historie" as being "to teach by example of times past, such wisdom as may guide our desires and actions". It is perhaps no coincidence that the greatest flowering of history in Britain came at the time of Britain's greatest need for colonial administrators having to make political decisions on their own and needing the experience history can transmit. As British history has on the whole been one of prosperity and political success, British historians tend to be optimistic, even complacent, about the British people. Thus, S. R. Gardiner (1829–1902) wrote of the 17th century, "It was the glory of England that she had approached more nearly than other nations to the condition of mutual forbearance which renders toleration possible", and W. H. Lecky (1838–1903), historian of the 18th century, wrote, "The English Constitution . . . owed its excellence quite as much to the singular union in the English character of self-reliance, practical good sense, love of compromise, and dislike of theoretical, experimental or organic change, as to any law that can be found in the statute-book".

It would, of course, be a mistake to regard British historians as wholly insular in their outlook and their fields of interest. Edward Gibbon (1737–94) spent twenty years on his *Decline and Fall of the Roman Empire*. Thomas Carlyle (1795–1881) made his reputation with his *History of the French Revolution* and George Grote (1794–1871) with his *History of Greece*.

British historians have not on the whole been academic recluses but men active in society. Lord Clarendon (1609–74) and Winston Churchill were statesmen; Gilbert Burnet (1643–1715) and William Stubbs (1825–1901) were bishops; Sir William Napier (1785–1860) a general and Edward Gibbon a militia officer for eleven years; George Grote a banker; J. R. Green (1837–83) a dockland parson and F. W. Maitland (1850–1906) a lawyer. Ireland is represented by William Lecky and Scotland by David Hume (1711–76), William Robertson (1721–93) and Thomas Carlyle.

Historical novelists: novelists who set their stories in times past, using real or imaginary characters and events, or a mixture of both. Historical novels include some of the greatest works of fiction ever written, as well as some of the worst. Many writers of modest talent have become famous by playing on the romantic element which, rightly or wrongly, many people associate with times gone by. Such novelists – of whom Baroness Orczy (1865–1947), creator of the Scarlet Pimpernel, may serve as an example – wrote, and are still writing, what were, and are, essentially fairy tales in fancy dress. We need not apologise for enjoying such stories. It is pleasant to escape from reality into a world of strange oaths and flashing swords. But a good novel is about believable individuals moving in a society we can accept as real.

The greatest historical novel ever written, if not the greatest of any category, is probably *War and Peace*, the work of Leo Tolstoy (1828–1910). Tolstoy was a Russian aristocrat, a troubled, passionate man of immense vitality and genius. *War and Peace*, which took six years to write, is a novel on a heroic scale, set against the background of Napoleon's invasion of Russia. Its many characters are drawn with a subtlety and insight that have seldom, if ever, been equalled.

If Tolstoy deserves pride of place among

historical novelists on the strength of one book alone, Sir Walter Scott (1771–1832), who wrote no less than twenty-eight historical novels and whose work had an enormous influence throughout Europe, must rank second. Scott, who was born in Edinburgh, began his literary career as a collector of Border ballads and as a narrative poet. His first novel, *Waverley*, published in 1814, was, in a sense, the first historical novel ever written. Earlier works sometimes so described – such as *L'Astrée* by Honore d'Urfé (1567–1625), a nobleman at the Court of Savoy, or *Clélie* by Madeleine de Scudery (1607–1701) – though set by their authors in distant times, show little or no feeling for place, period or human individuality. Only *La Princesse de Clèves* by Madame de La Fayette (1634–93) approaches nearer the modern concept, for its characters have recognisable feelings and emotions. Scott attached more importance to a lively plot than historical accuracy, and, in fact, made it respectable not only to use history in telling a story but to manipulate it, so that the history itself became part of the fiction. Today his novels seem hard to get into; yet a reader who perseveres will find himself rewarded with an exciting tale told with vigour and a deep understanding of human nature.

Robert Louis Stevenson (1850–94), author of *Treasure Island*, was another Scottish poet-novelist. His historical novels, which include *Kidnapped* and *The Master of Ballantrae*, are more elegantly turned than Scott's rugged productions; and accordingly, though they lack the latter's great qualities, they are more acceptable to presentday readers. Stevenson was delicate and tubercular, and it was, perhaps, as a kind of compensation for this that he loved to write about exciting escapes and heroic deeds.

Charles Dickens (1812–70), that larger-than-life genius of Victorian literature, wrote two historical novels – *Barnaby Rudge* and *A Tale of Two Cities* – neither of them among his best work; though the latter, a dramatic story of the French Revolution, has never ceased to hold the reading public.

William Makepeace Thackeray (1811–63), the author of two outstanding historical novels, *Vanity Fair* and *The History of Henry Esmond,* was a kindly man, sociable and humorous; but there was tragedy in his life. His young wife became incurably mad, leaving him with two daughters to bring up. To earn money to provide for their needs, Thackeray was forced to tailor his writings to the prejudices of his middle-class readers. Perhaps for this very reason – getting his own back, as it were – his disreputable characters, such as Becky Sharp, the scheming adventuress of *Vanity Fair*, glow with life, while his priggish heroines fade quickly from the memory.

A novelist whose life had something of the quality of his own romances was Alexandre Dumas (1802–70), the son of a West Indian who became one of Napoleon's generals. Involved in the revolutions of 1830 and 1848, Dumas spent a period in exile, and later, under Garibaldi, fought for Italian independence. He was a man who lived with tremendous gusto, and his novels, of which *The Three Musketeers* and *The Count of Monte Cristo* are the best known, reflect this quality. In many ways carelessly written, they nevertheless survive when better constructed but less exciting novels have been forgotten. His countryman and contemporary, Victor Hugo (1802–85), was also the son of a general and, like Dumas, was forced into exile on account of his political views. But there the resemblance ends. Hugo was one of the greatest poets of modern times, and his best-known historical novel, *Notre-Dame de Paris,* is far better written than anything of Dumas's. Yet it is strangely lifeless; whereas, for all their swashbuckling, Dumas's characters are creatures of flesh and blood.

The United States, in the 19th century a young country still shaping its national identity, nevertheless produced at that time one great novel based on its own past – *The Scarlet Letter* by Nathaniel Hawthorne (1804–54), a strange, solitary New Englander who wrote his masterpiece about the Puritan settlers from whom he himself was descended.

To bring the past alive calls for a quality of poetic imagination, and it is not surprising that many historical novelists have also been poets. Italy's great poet-novelist was Alessandro Manzoni (1785–1873), whose novel *The Betrothed* is still one of his country's favourite books. It is the story of a peasant boy and girl and reflects Manzoni's great concern for the poor and the oppressed.

By contrast, *The Leopard* by Giuseppe di Lampedusa (1896–1957), a superb story of Sicilian life in the second half of the 19th century, is a novel about aristocrats by an aristocrat. Di Lampedusa took many years over its writing and still had not finished it when he died. It was his only literary work, but one to place him high among historical novelists.

Among living historical novelists another poet-novelist – Robert Graves (b. 1895), whose books include *I, Claudius* and *King Jesus* – may be singled out for special mention.

The historical novel having been treated as a product of Western culture, it remains only to point out that, as with so many Western inventions, the Chinese were there before us. The first Chinese historical novel, the anonymously written *San Kuo Chih*, dates from the 13th century.

Some writers have succeeded in producing fine historical novels for younger readers, among modern examples being Leon Garfield, Rosemary Sutcliff and Geoffrey Trease.

Hitler, Adolf (1889–1945): Chancellor and Führer of Germany. Born in Austria, Hitler became leader of the National Socialist (Nazi) Party in 1921, and reorganised it along military lines, determined to exploit the national mood of bitterness and frustration resulting from Germany's defeat in World War I. Through an economic crisis and his own hypnotic oratory he became chancellor in 1933 and instituted a reign of terror whose victims were primarily the Jews but also anyone who by Nazi standards was not a "pure bred" German, or who showed an independent spirit. Hitler's aggressive foreign policy – effective at first – led to Germany's catastrophic defeat in World War II. He committed suicide when Berlin fell to the Russians in 1945.

Neville Chamberlain, British Prime Minister when World War II broke out, wrote of him rather contemptuously: "Altogether he looks entirely undistinguished. You would never notice him in a crowd and would take him for the house painter he once was." Yet he could dominate crowds of hundreds of thousands, indeed a nation; and had he stopped short before his mania for power and his racial intolerance drove his country to disaster, would probably have been hailed as one of the great Germans of history. Many of his theories are expounded in his book *Mein Kampf* (My Struggle) published in 1923.

¶ In KING-HALL, STEPHEN. *Three Dictators: Mussolini, Hitler, Stalin.* 1964.

Adolph Hitler addressing party members at Munich on 8 November 1942.

Hittites: an ancient people who built an empire in Asia Minor and Syria *c.* 2000–1200 BC. Some of their history is contained in the Old Testament and more has been uncovered by archaeologists, the most remarkable find being that of the German Hugo Winckler who, in 1906–07 and 1911–12, dug in the ruins of Boghazkeui, the old capital of the Hittite empire, and brought to light some 10,000 cuneiform tablets (i.e. inscribed with wedge-shaped characters) belonging to the royal archives.

Ho Chi Minh (1890–1969)**:** communist leader and president of North Vietnam from 1954. In 1941 he formed the League for the Independence of Vietnam, made up of nationalist and communist groups, and achieved independence by defeating the French in the war of 1946–54.

Hogarth, William (1697–1764)**:** English artist who painted many fine portraits but who is chiefly remembered as a pictorial satirist who drew the ugly side of contemporary London life with unshrinking realism and who savagely attacked the excesses of high society. After serving as apprentice to a London silver-plate engraver he set up in business for himself and made a modest living engraving coats of arms, billheads for shopkeepers and book illustrations. He became famous as a painter of portraits and of "conversation pieces" – pictures showing groups of people about their ordinary everyday occupations. But his great power was as a satirist, seeking to expose in paint the follies of mankind.

¶ In DALZELL, W. R. *Living Artists of the Eighteenth Century.* 1960

O' The Roast Beef of Old England [Calais Gate] *painted by Hogarth in 1748.*

Hohenstaufen dynasty: ruling German house in the 12th and 13th centuries, deriving its name from a village in Wurtemburg, where Frederick, Count of Buren, built a castle in the 11th century. Frederick supported Henry IV in the Investiture Controversy and was rewarded with the dukedom of Swabia and marriage with Henry's daughter. The Hohenstaufens unsuccessfully attempted to change the office of Holy Roman Emperor from being elective to having hereditary status. In 1138 Conrad of Hohenstaufen became Emperor. The nobles of the Empire began to form two parties, Guelph and Ghibelline, the latter supporting the Hohenstaufens. Their feud was temporarily stopped by the election in 1152 of Frederick of Hohenstaufen, "Barbarossa", whose mother was a Guelph. The feud reopened on the death

of Frederick's son and imperial successor Henry VI. Frederick II (1214–50) regained the imperial title for the Hohenstaufens, succeeded by his son Conrad IV (1250–54), but with the beheading of Conrad's son, Conradin (1268), the male line of the family became extinct.
See also FREDERICK I BARBAROSSA.

Hohenzollern dynasty: German imperial family, which traces its origins back to the 9th century, and which achieved real prominence when the elector Frederick of Brandenburg became king of Prussia in 1701. In the 18th and 19th centuries conflict between the Prussian Hohenzollerns and the Austrian Habsburgs was frequent, and the Austro-Prussian war of 1866 paved the way for a Hohenzollern monarchy in a united Germany. In 1871 Wilhelm of Prussia took the title of German Emperor. The Hohenzollerns seemed to be at the height of their power during the reign of Wilhelm II (emperor 1888–1918); but the military collapse of Germany in 1918 brought about the fall of the dynasty.

Holbein, Hans (1497–1543)**:** German painter and engraver. As a young man he went to Basle, Switzerland, where there was a famous press for which he produced over 300 woodcuts.

Holbein intended to be a religious painter, but the dissensions of the Reformation made it hard to earn a living out of religious pictures – disappointing for Holbein, but posterity's gain, for he became one of the greatest portrait painters the world has ever known. Through him we know what many of the famous people of Tudor times looked like.

Holbein went to England in 1526 and, with one short break, spent the rest of his life there. His sitters included Sir Thomas More and his family, Jane Seymour and, above all, King Henry VIII. His portrait of Anne of Cleves is said to have influenced Henry to choose her for his bride. Even though, when the king saw her in the flesh, he called her a Flanders mare, he seems to have harboured no ill-will against the painter, who continued to enjoy royal patronage until his death.

Holland: a province of the Netherlands, the name of which is often applied to the whole country. The counts of Holland were descendants of Charlemagne. In 1477 Holland passed to the Habsburgs, later replaced by the House of Orange. The province was divided into north and south Holland in 1840.

¶ COHN, ANGELO. *The First Book of the Netherlands* 1963; KING, GERMAINE. *The Land and People of Holland.* 1967
See also NETHERLANDS.

Holy Alliance: the declaration made 26 September 1815 by the rulers of Austria, Prussia and Russia, binding themselves, both in internal and international policies, to govern by Christian principles. The British foreign secretary, Lord Castlereagh, dismissed it as "a piece of sublime mysticism and nonsense"; though the German writer Goethe considered that "nothing greater or more useful for mankind had been invented". It had few lasting results because it was not based on public opinion and ran contrary to much contemporary thought.

Holy Roman Empire: confederation of central European states existing in various forms over a period of about 1,000 years. When the barbarian and mainly Germanic peoples moved into the lands of the western Roman Empire, it was not their wish to destroy the Empire. They had a real respect for it and desired to enjoy its advantages. When it broke up under their crude handling, they were disconcerted. In the dark ages that fol-

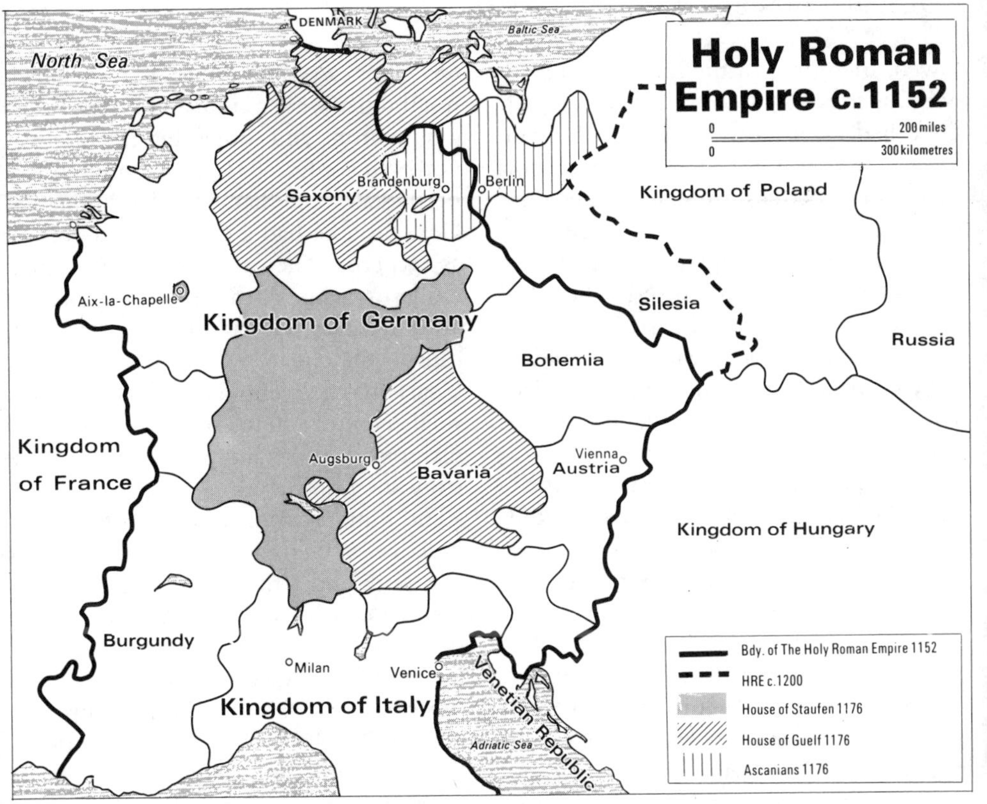

Holy Roman Empire c.1152
0 200 miles
0 300 kilometres
DENMARK
Baltic Sea
North Sea
Saxony
Brandenburg
Berlin
Kingdom of Poland
Aix-la-Chapelle
Kingdom of Germany
Silesia
Russia
Bohemia
Kingdom of France
Augsburg
Bavaria
Vienna
Austria
Kingdom of Hungary
Burgundy
Milan
Venice
Venetian Republic
Kingdom of Italy
Adriatic Sea
Bdy. of The Holy Roman Empire 1152
HRE c.1200
House of Staufen 1176
House of Guelf 1176
Ascanians 1176

SWEDEN
North Sea
DENMARK
Baltic Sea
Prussia
Brandenburg
K. of Poland
Flanders
Saxony
Silesia
Bohemia
Ratisbon
Strasbourg
Bavaria
Vienna
Austria
Lombardy
Milan
Venice
Hungary
Papal States
Rome
Habsburgs
House of Bohemia & Luxembourg
Church Lands
Boundary of HRE
1360

Denmark and Norway
North Sea
Baltic Sea
East Prussia
United Netherlands
Hanover
Berlin
Poland
Saxony
Austrian Netherlands
Aix-la-Chapelle
The Empire
Bohemia
Lorraine
Bavaria
Augsburg
Vienna
Alsace
Austria
Kingdom of Hungary
France
Switz.
Milan
Venetian Rep
Venice
Savoy
Ottoman Empire
Papal States
Kingdom of Sardinia
Tuscany
Adriatic Sea
Rome
Mediterranean Sea
Boundary of HRE
Habsburgs
Brandenburg-Prussia
1790

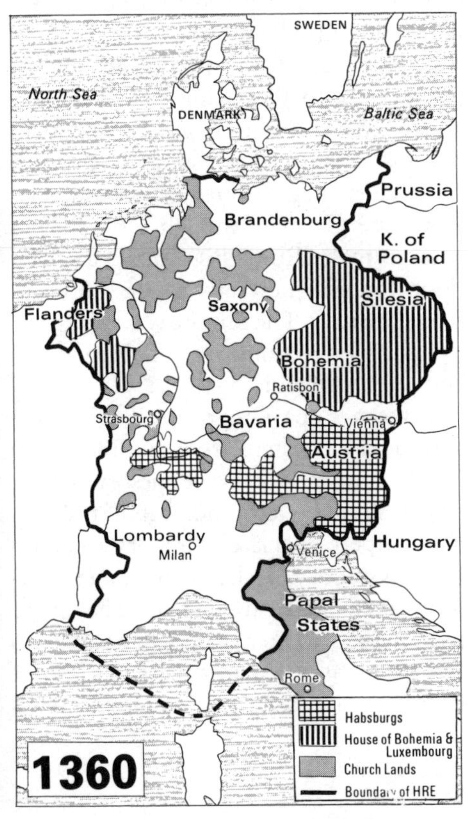

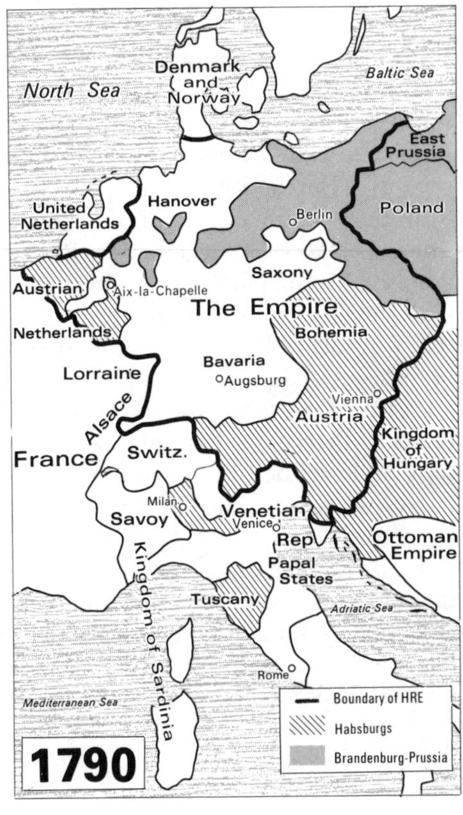

lowed, memories of the Empire mingled with the idea that at some time in the past there had been an ideal form of human society; and all reforms were aimed, not at creating a better future, but at restoring that better past. The Holy Roman Empire, which came into being against this background, was partly an institution but also partly a set of political theories.

By the 8th century nearly all sense of obligation to the eastern Empire had died away in the west, since the Byzantine emperors could no longer maintain a military presence in the west, and their exarch of Ravenna was defeated by the Lombards. The Pope turned to the Frankish king Pepin for protection in 753 and rewarded him, with the title of patrician, which used to be given only by the emperors. In 774 Pepin's son, Charlemagne, defeated the Lombards and gained control of Lombardy. Hadrian I (pope 772–795) tried to maintain his independence and there was produced a spurious document known as the Donation of Constantine which pretended to prove that the Emperor Constantine (306–337) had conferred on Pope Silvester I the imperial insignia and "all the provinces, places and cities of Italy and the western regions". But under Leo III (pope 795–816) these large claims of the papacy suffered collapse. Attacked by the Roman nobility, Leo had to flee for protection to Charlemagne who came to Rome himself. Leo solemnly declared his innocence of charges made against him, and on Christmas Day 800, before a large gatherong at St Peter's, the Pope placed a crown on Charlemagne's head and the Roman nobles acclaimed him as Augustus and Emperor.

The Carolingian rulers continued to hold the title of emperor, sometimes by acclamation, sometimes with a crowning by the Pope, until the deposition of Charles III, known as Charles the Fat, in 887. For a while quite minor Italian notabilities were nominated by the Popes as emperors, and sometimes the title was not even conferred. But the tradition had been established that, if a ruler dominated Germany, he had a claim to recognition as emperor. The first Saxon or Ottonian emperors achieved the title by acclamation after military victory. Otto I (962–73), called "the Great", was in a sense a lesser Charlemagne. Though ruling a much smaller empire, he too supported Christian missionary effort and protected the Pope from the Lombards.

The Empire from now on consisted in practice of Germany and north Italy. It was only under the Saxon emperors that it was usually described as Roman, and the title King of the Romans was adopted for the emperors' successor. It was not yet described as Holy. Some emperors claimed, in the tradition of Constantine, that the emperor was the true Head of Christendom and God's Vicar on earth. Otto I actually deposed two Popes. But from the middle of the 11th century fortune favoured the Popes and not the emperors, and the claims of the Papacy expanded accordingly. As individual nations developed in western Europe, other rulers began to regard the emperor as a mere German, though Otto III had tried to make Rome his capital city. The Pope found a new ally in the Norman rulers of Sicily. The Empire was weakened by the long minority of Henry IV between 1056 and 1065.

Between Pope Gregory VII (1073–85) and Henry IV there arose the Investiture Conflict over whether Popes or secular rulers should elect and install bishops. The emperor declared Gregory to be no Pope. Gregory declared Henry excommunicated and suspended. The Pope proved the stronger, and Henry had to go as a penitent to Gregory at the castle of Canossa, in 1077. But then Henry's

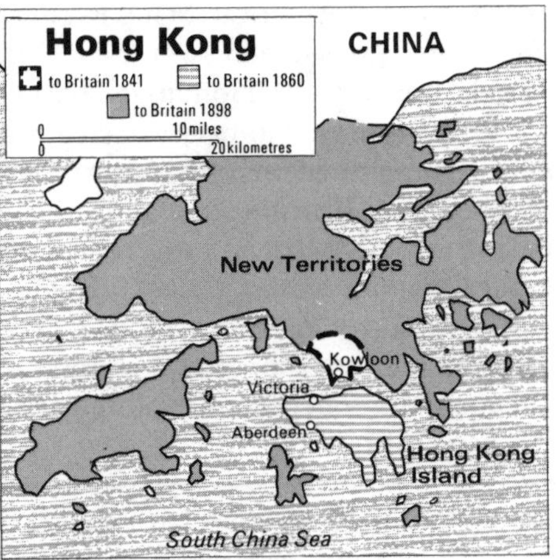

Hoover, Herbert Clark (1874–1964): thirty-first President of the USA. He was born of a Mid-West Quaker family and graduated as a mining engineer from the University of Stanford, California. During and after World War I he achieved prominence directing relief work in Europe, and, after serving as Secretary for Commerce between 1921 and 1928, he was elected as the Republican nominee in the 1928 presidential election. As president he presented his programme, which he had termed in his campaign "the New Day" aimed at developing all the great social and economic power of the American people in an age of developing science. Unfortunately, shortly after taking office his administration was overtaken by a major financial crisis (Wall Street Crash) and a worldwide trade slump; thus his programme did not really make much headway. In the 1932 presidential election Hoover was decisively defeated by Franklin D. Roosevelt (1882–1945), who promised the American people a "New Deal".

Horace (Quintus Horatius Flaccus, 65–8 BC): Roman poet, remembered for his elegant books of odes (*Carmina*), as well as epistles and satires. His father was a freed-man who took his son to Rome where he carefully supervised his education. Horace fought in the Battle of Philippi (42 BC) on the side of Brutus, who was defeated and committed suicide. Horace returned to Rome and, after a period of poverty owing to the confiscation of the family property, established himself in the society of the capital and made a number of influential friends, among them the Emperor Augustus.

Horn-book: early form of reader for the use of children. The earliest type consisted of a sheet of vellum or paper held in a wooden frame with a handle (very similar to the type of hand-mirror found on ladies' dressing-tables) and protected by a thin sheet of transparent horn. Often the text consisted simply of the alphabet in large and small letters. More elaborate examples included the Lord's Prayer and Roman numerals. Early horn-books had their letters arranged in the form of a cross, and afterwards, when they were arranged in lines, the cross was retained at the top. From this – the "Christ cross" – comes the modern term "crisscross".

Left: Embossed leather hornbook, Charles II period. Right: Wooden battledore, black on white with coloured illustration added. Wales, c. 1840.

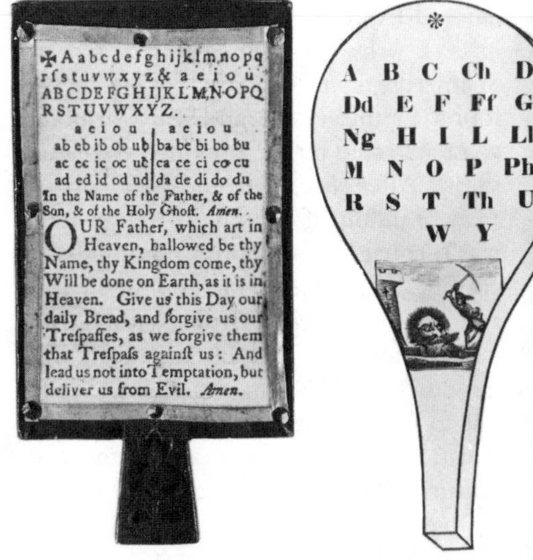

ten years' wandering before he returned home to Ithaca. Both poems were probably composed before 700 BC and show a basic unity; but, although a number of supposed "Lives of Homer" have been written, some of them very early, the details and speculations vary so widely as to make no version especially credible. At least seven different cities are named as his birthplace and six different centuries as the time in which he lived. Most accounts bring Homer from Ionia, and the most popular picture is that of a blind poet, wandering from city to city. What is certain is that the two epics were held in such esteem that they were recited or acted every four years at the Panathenaea – the festivals in Athens featuring the performance of epic poetry and music, accompanied by athletic and equestrian events.

Honan: province of central eastern China, with Chengchow as its capital. Its name means "south of the river", the river Hwang-ho, although, in fact, some of the province lies north of it. Honan was one of the chief centres of early Chinese culture.

Honduras: republic in central America discovered by Columbus in 1502 and entered from Mexico by Hernán Cortés in 1525. It was administered by the Spaniards from Guatemala. Silver was found in the 1570s, and the Caribbean coast attracted pirates preying on treasure ships. After Mexican independence in 1821, a union of central American states was formed but broke up, Honduras becoming an independent republic in 1838 and having much friction with Guatemala, Nicaragua and El Salvador. Military dictatorships alternated with more liberal governments. United States investment became important in the 20th century. The republic joined the Organisation of Central American States in 1951. Population 4,095,000 in 1983.

To the north British Honduras has had a separate history. Timber attracted the British to Belize in the 17th century. The area became a British colony in 1862 and independent as Belize in 1981, remaining in the Commonwealth. Since Guatemala persisted in laying claim to it Britain agreed to station troops in the country to safeguard its independence. Population 154,000 (1983).

Hong Kong: British crown colony on the coast of south-east China. Used as a base by British ships during the Opium War of 1839–42, Hong Kong, a small desolate island, was ceded to Britain in 1841 and became, with the opening up of western trade with China and Japan, the economic expansion of Australia and the cutting of the Suez Canal, a great modern port. It was always in danger from political and military developments on the Chinese mainland. In 1860 Britain, as a means of protection, gained the adjacent mainland peninsula of Kowloon and in 1898 obtained a 99-year lease of the New Territories. Hong Kong fell to the Japanese in 1941 but was freed in 1945. Chinese refugees from the Communist mainland have densely populated Hong Kong. In 1985 Britain and China agreed amicably upon the return of Hong Kong to China in 1997. Population 5,287,800 (1983).

A Kowloon street lined with neon signs in Chinese and English, 1966.

position grew stronger and the conflict went on till it was closed by a compromise in 1122, known as the Concordat of Worms, between Calixtus II and the Emperor Henry V.

The last formidable dynasty of emperors was the House of Hohenstaufen (*see* separate entry). It was Frederick I Barbarossa (1152–90) who, in 1157, added the word Holy to the Emperor's title. The position of the Hohenstaufen was weakened by rivals in Germany, but they had their successes against papal claims, particularly after Henry VI (1191–97) married the heiress of Sicily. But after Henry's early death Pope Innocent III (1198–1216) brought the claims of the Papacy, as previously expressed in the 9th century or under Gregory VII, nearest to realisation. Frederick II (1220–50) lost ground in Italy and was excommunicated and deposed, though he was regaining ground at the time of his death.

After Frederick II came a gap (the Great Interregnum) till, in 1272, Rudolf of Habsburg succeeded as German king; but he was only the head of a federation of princes and was never emperor. The great days of the Holy Roman Empire were over, and it became largely a matter of internal German history, the emperors being elected by the chief German rulers. From 1556 the imperial office was held by the House of Habsburg until it was finally ended by Napoleon in 1806.

See also CHARLEMAGNE; GREGORY VII, etc.

Home Rule: the right to self-government in home affairs within the United Kingdom demanded by many Irishmen in the 19th century. There were 100 Irish MPs in the Westminster Parliament, and most felt that their country was being neglected. In 1873 a kind-hearted lawyer, Isaac Butt (1813–79), formed the Home Rule League to demand a separate Irish parliament. Irish crowds chanted the new slogan and elected fifty-nine Home Rule MPs in 1874. Only when Butt was replaced by the much more ruthless Charles Stewart Parnell (1846–91) did English politicians take Irish demands seriously. Although Gladstone eventually supported them, his two attempts to give Ireland Home Rule (1886, 1893) were unsuccessful, chiefly because of the English mistrust of Parnell (*see* separate entry) and his schemes. Eventually Northern Ireland was given a separate Parliament and limited self-government in 1920 and the rest of the country became the Irish Free State in 1921.

During the 1960s and 1970s there was much pressure from Scottish and Welsh nationalists for home rule within their countries, though adherents are divided in opinion as to the extent that should be demanded for such rule.

See also IRELAND; IRISH REPUBLIC; NORTHERN IRELAND.

Homer: Greek poet, traditionally the author of the great epic poems the *Iliad* and the *Odyssey*; the former relates incidents, chiefly concerning Achilles and Hector, in the Trojan Wars; and the latter the adventures of Odysseus (Ulysses in Latin) after the fall of Troy, during his

Detail of a statue of Homer.

Horses, Famous: the horse has played an important part in the history of mankind from its use in war, transport and work. From early times it was a symbol of kingship, so that it is portrayed on many of the coins of antiquity and appears in countless early mosaics, wall paintings, banners and flags. The white horse was the standard of the Saxons, the rampant white horse the device of the region of Savoy, a galloping white horse the badge of the house of Hanover. Countless hotel and inn signs derive from royal and aristocratic devices of this sort. The horse was also the indispensable symbol of knighthood – "chivalry", "chevalier" and "cavalier" being only a few of the terms derived from words for horse. The Spanish *caballero* and the Italian *cavalliere*, both meaning knight or gentleman, tell the same story.

Horses have sometimes been raised by their owners to the status of public officials or even gods. The Roman emperor Caligula decided that his favourite horse Incitatus ("spurred on") should be made a consul – one of the chief magistrates of the city. The Maya Indians of Yucatan in Central America, who had never seen horses till the arrival of the Spanish conquistadors, made Cortés's charger Morzillo, or its likeness, into a new god, when the horse fell sick and was left with them to be cared for in 1524.

These favourite companions of man through history were domesticated from wild horses in earliest times. As late as the present century bands of these survive in remote places. Some in western Mongolia are descendants of the type described by Marco Polo (*see* separate entry), in his 13th-century travels:

"Their horses are fed on grass alone, and do not require barley, or other grain. The men are habituated to remain on horseback during two days and two nights, without dismounting; sleeping in that situation while their horses graze . . . When one of the great Tartar chiefs proceeds on an expedition, he puts himself at the head of an army of an hundred thousand horses . . . Each man has, on average, eighteen horses and mares, and when that which they ride is fatigued, they change it for another."

A wild Mongolian horse, the first one known to western scientists and natural historians, was presented to a Russian explorer named Prejvalsky in 1879. In 1902 a German, Karl Hagenbeck, led an expedition to find other specimens. His company consisted of 2,000 Kirghiz tribesmen – descendants of the old Mongolian warriors. He returned with about thirty-two foals for breeding purposes, and specimens of these short, compact, immensely tough horses of the type that carried the barbarian hordes can now be seen in many zoological parks and gardens.

They may be contrasted with the fine-limbed thoroughbred modern race-horse. It is a remarkable fact that all pedigree stock in Europe, North and South America, Australia and New Zealand, and many other places in the world, can be traced back to just three horses, brought into England within a period of some forty years. These were the so-called "Byerly Turk", named after a young soldier who captured it from the enemy in Turkey in the 1680s and brought it back to England; the "Darley Arabian", bought in Aleppo, Syria, and shipped home in about 1706; and the "Godolphin Arabian", whose origins are obscure but which was presented to Lord Godolphin in about 1728.

Inevitably, many of the most famous horses of history belonged to military commanders and are always associated with them. The best known example from the period before Christ is Alexander the

(a)

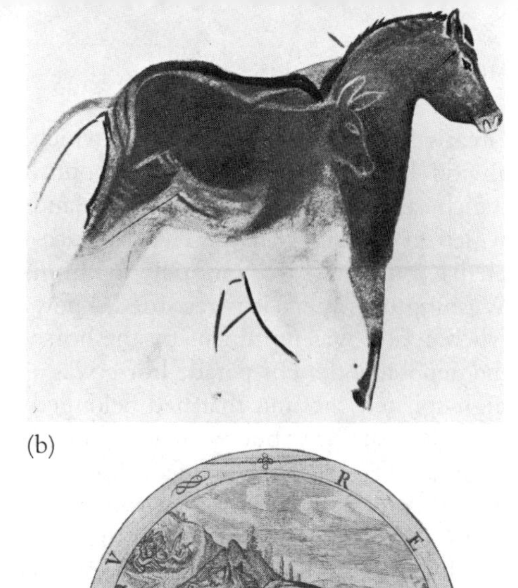

(b)

(d)

(e)

(c)

(f)

(a) The probable appearance of the Hyracothenium, the four-toed ancestor of the horse. (b) Paleolithic painting of a horse in the Altamira caves of Northern Spain. (c) The mythological Pegasus. (d) Bucephalus, Alexander the Great's legendary steed. (e) Warren Hastings' Arabian stallion. (f) Copenhagen, the Duke of Wellington's charger. (g) Marengo, Napoleon's beloved mount. (h) Trigger, Roy Rogers' movie star horse.

;)

(h)

Great's Bucephalus ("Oxhead"), which always knelt for his master to mount, which served him for thirty years and which eventually had the city of Bucephalia built as a memorial to him. Washington's men, it is recorded, knew when action was imminent by the horse the general rode. His parade horse was a high-spirited chestnut that had belonged to the British army; but when he mounted his small sorrel (i.e. a horse of a yellowish-brown colour) the word went round the ranks: "We have business on hand!" The Duke of Wellington had his halfbred chestnut Copenhagen, which, on 17 and 18 June, at Waterloo, he rode for a total of nearly thirty hours. Napoleon had his favourite white Barbary horse, brought over from Egypt, which he named Marengo, after the battle of that name (1800) in which the emperor was carried with impressive sure-footedness and steadiness under fire. In more recent times Field Marshal Earl Roberts, who won fame in India and the Boer War, had his famous Colonel; and in World War I General Jack Seely was inseparable from Warrior, about whom he later wrote a book.

From the long list that could be compiled, the following is a small selection of horses that have helped in the making of history.

Kantanka: the white horse of Buddha (563–483 BC), the Indian founder of the Buddhist religion.

Fadda: the white mule of Mohammed (*c.* 570–632), founder of Islam.

Babieca: (meaning "simpleton") the horse of the famous Castilian hero Rodrigo Diaz de Bivar (1040–99), known as "The Cid" or "Cid Campeador" ("the lord champion").

Black Saladin: the horse of Richard Neville, Earl of Warwick (1428–71), "Warwick the King-maker".

Carman: the horse of one of the most famous knights of history, the Chevalier Bayard (Pierre du Terrail, *c.* 1474–1524), who has come down as the ideal of chivalry, *sans peur et sans reproche* (without fear and without blame).

Morocco: the horse belonging to the Scottish showman Thomas Banks or Bankes (active in the reigns of Elizabeth I and James I of England), who taught it such bewildering tricks that it is mentioned by Shakespeare, Ben Jonson and most of the other great writers of the day.

Sorrel: the horse that William III of England (1650–1702) was riding when it stumbled on a mole-hill and caused a fall from which the King died.

Ronald: the chestnut that carried Lord Cardigan, commander of the light cavalry brigade, through the charge at Balaclava (1854).

See also CAVALRY.

Hospitals: institutions for the care of the sick or wounded. The earliest recorded hospitals were in Egypt, where certain priests were skilled in healing and there were buildings where the sick could be housed attached to the temples of Saturn. In 260 BC many Indians travelled to the hospital at Surat, where the Buddhist priests treated their diseases; this hospital was eventually destroyed by Brahmin invaders.

In Rome the Emperor Hadrian (AD 76–138) had a military hospital built so that wounded soldiers could be looked after. As Christianity spread through the Roman Empire, more and more people began to feel that it was a duty to provide for members of the community who were both ill and poor. In many towns the Christians opened "surgeries", which in some ways resembled the out-patients departments of presentday hospitals. A few people, who were too ill to walk were kept at the centre, but the majority called there daily until they were cured. Women were treated by female practitioners, and patients paid the doctors.

The Emperor Constantine (AD 274–337) established hospitals, known as *Nosocomia,* in various cities of his Empire. At Caesarea and at Constantinople special hospitals for lepers were built, though more with the idea of isolating lepers than of curing them. Fabiola, a wealthy Roman lady, paid for a hospital to be built in the city and gave her country house for the use of convalescent patients, whom she herself helped to nurse.

In the East the Caliph Haroun al-Raschid (AD 763–809) ordered that a medical college be attached to every large mosque, with a hospital adjoining each college. In Baghdad he erected an asylum for the insane and at least two free public hospitals.

Christian hospitals continued to be maintained by the Church, and eventually they became the responsibility of the monastic orders. Most religious houses had an infirmary where the monks or nuns looked after the sick, but in England this system broke down abruptly when Henry VIII closed the monasteries. Sick folk who were homeless now had nowhere to go: they thronged the cities, where they spread infection and frequently died in the streets. To end this state of affairs, a few hospitals were built, but this development was a slow one. Tudor and Stuart England was remarkably indifferent to the sufferings of the poor, and as late as 1710 there were still only two hospitals, St Bartholomew's and St Thomas's, in London, while many other cities had none.

Real concern for public health did not develop until after the Industrial Revolution, when epidemics could spread like wildfire through the insanitary slums of manufacturing towns. Voluntary hospitals, maintained by subscription, were built, where doctors gave their services and poor patients were treated free of charge. Conditions were bad at first: nurses were difficult to recruit, and the majority were ignorant women, quite untrained. The work of Florence Nightingale (*see* separate entry) eventually improved the standards of nursing.

A few of these old hospital buildings are still in use. Twentieth-century ones are far more conveniently planned, with pleasant surroundings and small, light wards. These improvements help patients and ease the work of the medical staff.

A 1927 census showed that there were then nearly 7,000 hospitals in the United States, representing about half the world total. In July 1948 ownership of 2,688 out of 3,040 municipal and voluntary hospitals in England and Wales was vested in the Minister of Health.

Almost all countries have vastly improved their hospital services in recent years, and there has been a strong movement away from the impersonal and institutional atmosphere to a more friendly and architecturally beautiful setting. Norway, Denmark, Sweden and Holland have been among the pioneers in this direction.

¶ EDWARDS-REES, DESIREE. *The Story of Nursing.* 1965

See also HEALTH.

Hostage: a person handed over, or seized by force, as security for the performance of certain conditions or the carrying out of an agreement. Thus, after the French defeat at the battle of Poitiers (1356), King John and a number of nobles were taken to England and held hostage till their ransoms were paid. A modern, and more violent, example was the hijacking in 1970 of three airliners by Palestinian guerrillas and the holding of 234 passengers and crew as hostages in the Jordanian desert as security for the return of captive guerrillas in Britain, Switzerland, West Germany and Israel.

Hottentots: descendants of an African aboriginal race. A dark-skinned people of slight build, once found in the western part of southern Africa, the few survivors today live mostly in South-West Africa. By the early 18th century European diseases and warfare with the Dutch settlers at the Cape over cattle and grazing rights had substantially reduced their numbers.

Hour-glass: early device for measuring time, known also as a sand-glass. It consists of two bulbs of glass connected by a narrow channel through which sand trickles from one half of the instrument to the other for an hour (or any other desired interval of time). Some modern egg-timers are based on the same principle. Hour-glasses were formerly much used in churches and on board ship. A two-minute sand-glass is still used in the British House of Commons to allow time for "division bells" to be rung as a warning to members outside the Chamber that a vote is about to be taken.

An early ship's hour-glass.

Housing: The earliest human beings lived in the open. It was not until the era known as the Ice Age, which brought about a great drop in the temperature of the northern hemisphere, that man felt a need for shelter to protect him from the weather and the attacks of hungry animals. There was no knowledge of building as yet, and the first homes were caves. Not until the ice had receded and men began to keep cattle on the open hillsides did they build dwellings. These early houses often consisted merely of shallow pits, dug in the ground. A low wall of earth was raised around the pit, and in the centre was a post, from which a thatched roof of reeds and bracken, resting on thin branches, reached to ground level. Several family groups would make their pit-dwellings in the same area, and surround them with a stockade. People who lived in marshy districts built houses of similar design, but instead of digging pits they erected a raised floor on wooden piles above the level of the water, and the clay walls and thatched roof rested on this.

The Egyptians adapted themselves to a settled life on the banks of the Nile. The poorer people used mud from the river banks to build themselves small huts which they thatched with reeds. But the priests and the pharaohs had great palaces of stone. Wood was scarce in Egypt, so little of it was used, but there were stone quarries and many slaves to move the blocks of stone. The Babylonians, who had no stone quarries, built their temples and palaces of sun-baked bricks. People used whatever building materials came easily to hand.

The Greeks, who lived in a beautiful climate, spent most of their time out of doors. Their houses were built on a square plan, opening onto a central courtyard without a roof, surrounded by a roofed colonnade where most of the daily life of the household was carried on. Behind the colonnade were small inner rooms, bedrooms and a kitchen. These houses were built of stone and roofed with tiles.

The houses of the Romans were very similar to those of the Greeks, but Roman cities were planned so that the buildings were grouped in an orderly manner, not clustered together haphazardly as were the Greek houses. Rome itself was a very crowded city, and the poor lived in tenements several storeys high. The aristocrats had large houses on the outskirts of the city. Some had two central courtyards, surrounded by many rooms with walls which were brightly painted with murals and floors laid with patterned tiles or covered with mosaic pictures. Wealthy Romans made houses of this type wherever a Roman city was built, so their remains can be seen in many parts of Europe.

For hundreds of years after the fall of Rome, the people of Western Europe led a barbaric existence, fighting other tribes and frequently moving from place to place. They deserted the Roman towns but made no new ones. In the north, the Danes and Norsemen built wooden halls for their chiefs and warriors, oblong in shape and roofed with thatch. There was a fire in the centre of the earth floor and a hole in the roof to allow the smoke to escape. Sometimes there was a separate kitchen, and the women's quarters were partitioned off by a curtain of hides. Humble people lived in small huts built on a framework of curved branches meeting at the top to form an arch. The arches were joined by horizontal beams fixed along their sides, and the whole structure was covered with thatch. Wood was the natural material for these people, because when they settled anywhere they first cleared a space in the forest, then used the timber to build their villages.

From Norman times the countryside in England and elsewhere had been domi-

A MESOPOTAMIAN REED HUT

EGYPTIAN CLAY MODEL

MEDIAEVAL 'BLACK & WHITE'

MANOR HOUSE 1569

MODERN TOWER FLATS RISE BEHIND VICTORIAN HOUSES

COUNTY KERRY HOVEL

nated by massive stone castles built to withstand attacks by marauding bands and the armies of enemy barons. By the end of the Middle Ages these fortresses were giving place to manor houses, many still fortified, but homes rather than bleak garrisons. There was a hall for meals and general use, with a private room called the solar for the owner and his family at one end of it and a large kitchen at the other. Sometimes a dormitory for the servants was built above the kitchen.

Poor people were still living in low huts built over wooden frames, thatched, and walled either with mud or with rubble kept in place by a framework of woven wattles. This type of dwelling is known as a cruck cottage.

In medieval times walled towns grew up where merchants lived together in order to trade. Their houses were built close together because space inside the walls was limited. A wooden framework was first made, and the spaces between the beams filled with plaited laths daubed with plaster. The inside walls were sometimes covered with carved wooden panels; there was a chimney, and the roof was thatched. This method of building on a wooden frame continued to be used up to Tudor times, and many such houses are still occupied today, particularly in the midland and western counties of England. We often call them "black and white" houses, but the beams which we now paint black were originally left in the natural colour of the wood.

By the time of Elizabeth I, people had rediscovered the art of making bricks, forgotten since Roman times. So late Tudor houses were made of brick, although their plan still resembled that of a medieval timber-framed building.

In the early 17th century houses were being built in Italy which imitated the style of the Romans. An architect named Inigo Jones introduced this style into England, but he adapted it slightly. His houses were flat-fronted, made of stone, with square windows symmetrically grouped on either side of a central porch supported on pillars. This rather severe style was described as classical: it was further developed by Sir Christopher Wren, who carried out the rebuilding of London after the Great Fire of 1666. During the reign of Queen Anne, a similar type of house was built using bricks instead of stone. Many of the early settlers in the southern states of America built their homes in the classical style.

The Industrial Revolution of the 18th century brought about many changes in house building. Towns grew up rapidly, and the people who went to work in the new factories were housed as quickly and cheaply as possible. Small, mean brick houses, without gardens, were put up in closely packed rows in order to save valuable ground. In contrast, the newly rich factory owners built great houses for themselves, often ornamented with turrets and gables which gave them a vague resemblance to Bavarian castles.

During the later 19th and 20th centuries, people realised that hideous houses, like those of the Industrial Revolution, ruined the landscape as well as the health of the occupants. Housing estates were planned, with green spaces and gardens. The modern tendency is for houses to have large, flat windows and for all the houses built in one district to look alike. Where building land is scarce, high blocks of flats are made in order to save space. These are a conspicuous feature of many American cities. The tall buildings are made of concrete blocks in a steel framework. Many people can be housed in these flats, but they present problems for elderly people and for young families with babies.

A quick way of putting up a house is by using prefabricated units. The sections

– walls, floors and roof – are made in a factory and brought to the site, where they are assembled on a concrete base. The materials used are wood, steel and aluminium, all of which are strong and light. Such houses are used when it is necessary to accommodate families quickly – for example, at a newly established research centre or a military camp.

¶ DIXON, J. *Houses and Housing*. 1967

See also INTERNATIONAL STYLE.

Houston: largest city and major port of Texas, USA, named after Sam Houston, leader of the Texans against the Mexican army in 1835–36. From being such an insignificant place that, in 1837, the skipper of a paddle-steamer went by without noticing it, Houston now has a population of over 900,000 and supports chemical, food-processing, metallurgical and oil industries.

Howard, John (1726–90): British philanthropist. A grocer's apprentice, he found himself on his father's death rich and decided to travel. Captured by a French privateer while sailing to Portugal, he suffered great hardships in a French gaol. On his release he settled at Cardington, Bedfordshire, built model cottages and a village school and became high sheriff of the County of Bedfordshire in 1773. He then began his life's work on prison reform by an attempt to secure salaries for gaolers instead of fees extorted from their prisoners. His famous book, *The State of the Prisons*, appeared in 1777. He travelled 50,000 miles in Europe, inspecting prison conditions, and died at Kershon, while investigating an epidemic in the Russian army.

Hudson, Henry (d. 1611): English explorer and navigator. In 1607 and 1608 he tried to find a north-east passage to China, and in 1609 explored the American coast from Virginia to the Hudson River. In 1610 he sought a north-west passage round America, entering Hudson Bay and, as the result of mutiny, perished with his young son after being set adrift in an open boat. Though he penetrated further than previous explorers he did not actually discover the bay, strait and river carrying his name. These had been entered or sighted by the Cabots and other adventurers, but not explored.

¶ LAMBERT, R. S. *Mutiny in the Bay: Henry Hudson's Last Voyage*. 1963; SYME, RONALD. *Hudson of the Bay*. 1955

Hudson's Bay Company: trading company founded in London in 1670 to exploit and sell the products of the area of northern Canada called after Henry Hudson, who explored it in 1609–10. Among the Company's founders was Prince Rupert. The French were already engaged in fur trading with the Indians in the same area, and fighting broke out round the Company's forts or "factories" (places where "factors" or traders operated), which became outposts of British jurisdiction and military power as well as of British trade. The fighting was sometimes very bitter, the French, who had been first in the territory, regarding the British as interlopers. Both sides made alliances with the native Indians. The ending of French claims by the Treaty of Utrecht, and the yielding of the Hudson's Bay territories to Britain in 1713, strengthened the Company. Its privileges and territory were confirmed after a parliamentary enquiry in 1749. Conflict with France officially ended in 1763 when all Canada was ceded to Britain, but much unofficial fighting continued. A North-West Fur Company of Montreal was for long a bitter rival, but it was amalgamated with the Hudson's Bay Company in 1821. Extensive trading rights over other areas,

including British Columbia and Oregon (later ceded to USA), were given to the Company. After the Dominion of Canada was set up in 1867, the Company's special jurisdiction ended and most of its fifteen million acres [6 million hectares] of land were bought out for £300,000. It continues its long history today as a prosperous trading company with its own fleet of ships.
See CANADA for map.

Huguenots: the Protestants of France, originating in Switzerland under Calvin and deriving their name from the German *eidgenossen,* men pledged to one another by oath. They became an important force, political as well as religious, in France during the latter part of the 16th century. In 1562 a law was passed giving them freedom to worship as they wished, but the massacre of a group of Huguenots by the troops of the Duc de Guise, the Catholic leader, marked the beginning of a series of Wars of Religion which tore France asunder for many years. During these wars, there was first an attempt to assassinate Coligny, the Huguenot leader, and then the notorious Massacre of Saint Bartholomew (24 August 1572) when great numbers of Protestants all over France met a violent death. Only in 1598, when Henry IV had become established as King of France, did the Edict of Nantes give satisfactory terms and a guarantee of security to the Huguenots. Not only was their freedom of worship assured, but they were allowed to keep their fortified towns (such as Montauban, La Rochelle, La Charité) and to hold assemblies for the discussion of civil and political as well as religious matters. This more satisfactory state of affairs continued until well into the 17th century, but the highly centralised government developed under Louis XIII and Louis XIV did not look favourably on minority groups. Under the influence of Louvois, the king's chief minister, the Edict of Nantes was revoked in 1685. The Huguenots fled from France to Holland and England, taking with them their skills as craftsmen, particularly as silk-workers, and their gifts as scholars and theologians. Not until the Revolution of 1789 did religious liberty become finally established in France.

¶ GRANT, ALISON and MAYO, RONALD. *The Huguenots.*

Hun: member of the nomadic Asian people who invaded Europe in the 4th and 5th centuries and occupied much of the territory now covered by Germany, Poland and European Russia. Their most famous leader was Attila (*see* separate entry). The term is still sometimes used to describe someone barbaric, ruthless and destructive.

¶ SOBOL, DONALD J. *The First Book of the Barbarian Invaders.* 1965

Hunan: mountainous province of south-eastern China with its capital at Changsha. Its economic life through the centuries has been based on the two large river valleys, those of the Siang-kiang and the Yuen-kiang. The province maintains a large agricultural industry and produces coal and metallic ores.

Hundred Days: the period from 20 March 1815, when Napoleon returned to Paris after his escape from Elba, to 28 June 1815, when Louis XVIII was restored to the French throne after the battle of Waterloo.

Hundred Years War: the struggle between England and France, which lasted intermittently from 1337 to 1453, interrupted by many truces and the Treaties of Brétigny (1360) and Paris (1396).

From 1066 English kings had held fiefs in France as vassals of the French kings, and there had been many feudal struggles between them, but Edward III changed the entire situation by laying claim to the French crown. The English export trade in wool to Flanders was suffering because the Count of Flanders (a vassal of the French crown) was hostile. By posing as the rightful king of France, Edward gave the Flemish citizens a legal excuse to disobey their count.

Some details of the English victories at Crécy, Poitiers and Agincourt, followed by the gradual eviction of the English from all of France except Calais, may be found elsewhere, but certain broader aspects are of interest. The war fostered a new national spirit, particularly in France, which produced leaders of genius, first Bertrand du Guesclin, and later Dunois and Joan of Arc. The supremacy of the English longbow, and the growth of bands of professional soldiers raised by Commissions of Array, spelt the end of the mounted knight and the feudal levy, and, after this war ended, these mercenary soldiers were the scourge of England for thirty years during the Wars of the Roses.

See also ARCHERY; GUESCLIN; JOAN OF ARC, etc.

Hungary: a land-locked republic in central Europe. Hungary emerged as a separate state in the 9th century with the arrival of the Magyars. Her history was long dominated by her efforts to throw off Turkish rule – in which she finally succeeded in 1699 – then by her increasingly reluctant membership of the Austrian Empire until the latter's collapse in 1918. Hungary then became a fully independent state. Her geographical position and territorial ambitions brought her under the influence of Hitler, and she joined in Germany's attack on Russia in 1941. This the Hungarians were to regret, for in 1945 the victorious Russians placed them under their control. In 1956 a largely popular revolt directed against both the Hungarian government and its Russian protector was put down only by Russian tanks, troops and aircraft. Since then, the Communist Party leader Janos Kadar (b. 1912) has presided over a gradual rise in his people's prosperity, contact with the West, and personal and national freedom.

See BALKANS for map.

¶ CSICSERY-RONAY, ISTVAN. *The First Book of Hungary*. 1970

Hus, Jan or **Huss, John** (c. 1369–1415): Bohemian religious reformer. As a reformer, Hus is often considered to be a forerunner of the Protestant Reformation. He was a university teacher and a popular preacher in Prague, influenced greatly by the works of John Wyclif. Hus preached vehemently against Church abuses, finding much support amongst the Bohemian people, despite his own excommunication (1410) and the laying of an Interdict upon Prague (1411). The Council of Constance condemned and burned Hus as a heretic (1415). After his death, Hus's followers caused a civil war in Bohemia lasting nearly twenty years. His teaching still survives in the Moravian Church.

¶ In THOMAS, H. and D. L. *Religious Leaders*. 1959

See also REFORMATION and WYCLIF, JOHN.

Huygens, Christiaan (1629–95): Dutch mathematician, astronomer and physicist. He was born at The Hague and spent most of his life there, apart from a visit to France from 1666 to 1681. His improved telescope enabled him, on 28 November 1659, to make the first drawing of Mars, which astronomers have used, together with modern observations, to determine that planet's rotation period to within one-fiftieth of a second. He was the first to discern the true nature of Saturn's Rings, discovered Iapetus, one of

Saturn's satellites, and also the Great Nebula in Orion. He did much to develop the wave theory of light and invented the pendulum clock, which replaced the former type of movement.

Christiaan Huygens' pendulum clock. Above: front face. Below: the inside showing pendulum movement.

Hyder Ali (*c.* 1722–82)**:** ruler of Mysore and the most formidable native opponent the British met in India. A Muslim of humble origin, he rose to power through the Mysore army and displaced the sultan in 1763. In alliance with the Nizam of Hyderabad he attacked the British in the Carnatic in 1767, and in 1769 almost dictated a treaty to the government in Madras. This treaty provided for mutual aid and assistance, which Hyder Ali claimed after his defeat by a Mahratta army. Enraged by their failure to honour the agreement, Hyder Ali bided his time till the British began their struggle to drive the French from India; then, allying himself with the French, invaded the Carnatic with a large army. After considerable initial success he was thrice defeated by Sir Eyre Coote.

Hyderabad: (1) the most important native state of India, occupying a large portion of the Deccan. It became independent in 1724 when Asaf Jah repudiated the control of the Mogul emperor. Under the British, the Nizam (ruler) was normally an ally of the East India Company and remained faithful during the Mutiny. The Nizam was Muslim, the inhabitants Hindu, and when, after partition, the Nizam wished to remain independent, the Indian government forcibly incorporated the state into India.

(2) a powerful fortified city near the River Indus, capital of Sind until after its capture by the British (Battle of Miani, 1843), when the capital was transferred to Karachi.

Hydrogen bomb: the H or fusion bomb, the patent for which was filed in the USA by Doctor John von Neumann, a Hungarian-born mathematician, on 26 May 1946. It releases enormous energy

Hydrogen bomb explosion off Christmas Island in 1958.

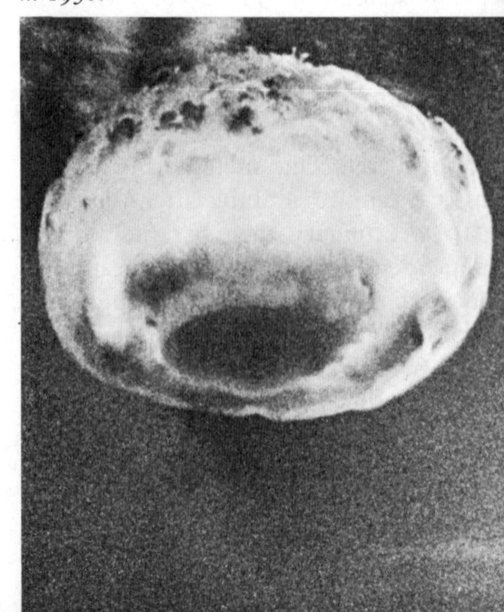

by the fusion of nuclei of isotopes of hydrogen to form helium.

Hyksos: name, meaning "shepherd kings", of the earliest invaders of Egypt. They were Asians who ruled the country from *c.* 1785 to 1570 BC.

Hymns: sacred poems set to music. The word is Greek, and the so-called Homeric Hymns date from the 7th century BC. The "hymn" sung at the Last Supper (Mark 14:26) was probably one of the psalms.

We have hymns dating from the earliest Christian times, but it was not until the Reformation allowed congregations to share in the services that they became important as an element of worship. At first metrical versions of the psalms were much favoured. Thus, the *Old Hundredth* tune is so called because of its association with the hymn *All people that on earth do dwell* derived from the hundredth psalm. Succeeding centuries, and particularly the 19th, have been fertile in the composition of fresh hymns and in the translation of old ones from Greek and Latin. Most hymns are written in rhyme, and many, such as those in *The Christian Year* of John Keble (1792–1866), are primarily poetry, not always easily fitted into the strict tempo of congregational singing. Very few hymn tunes at present in use are of any great antiquity, the medieval plainsong being too difficult for the average layman to appreciate or perform.

Hymns have many fascinating legends connected with them: two only must suffice. St Theodulph (750–821), Bishop of Orleans, is said to have earned his release from prison by writing the Latin original of *All glory, laud and honour,* while there is a tradition that *Rock of Ages* was composed by Augustus Toplady (1740–78) as he sheltered from a storm under a crag in the Mendip Hills.

I

Iberian peninsula: the modern Spain and Portugal. Carthaginians ruled Spain's Mediterranean coast in the 5th century BC, but under the Roman Empire the peninsula was romanised and spoke Latin. The Vandals invaded it in 405, and a Visigothic kingdom was set up. Arab rule extended into it from the 7th century, and Christian resistance to Islam dominated Iberian history. Spain was politically united in 1469, Portugal remaining separate. Spain acquired an empire in America, and Portugal in Brazil and Africa. Both lost most of their imperial role in the 19th century, but their languages and culture dominate Latin America.

See EUROPE for map; *see also* PORTUGAL; SPAIN.

Ibn Saud, Abdul Aziz (*c.* 1880–1953)**:** founder and king of Saudi Arabia. As warrior and, later, administrator, he succeeded in welding diverse elements into a nation and, in the words of one historian, achieved "a position perhaps unparalleled in the annals of Arabian history since the immediate successors of Mohammed himself".

See also SAUDI ARABIA.

Ice Age: the period of geological time when much of the earth's surface was covered by glaciers and icefields. The term is usually applied to the Pleistocene period, which began about one million years ago, but there were at least two earlier glacial periods.

¶ LAUBER, PATRICIA. *All About the Ice Age.* 1965

Iceland: republic in the North Atlantic, 250 miles south-east of Greenland, colonised by Norwegian Vikings from AD 870 after the first settlement on the south coast. Government was an aristocratic republic, with the Althing, the legislative and judicial assembly, established AD 930, exercising control. After Iceland became a Danish dependency in 1380, its powers waned till it was eventually revived and reformed in 1843. In the 19th century, despite increasing national consciousness, Iceland's isolation and poor economy helped to maintain its political backwardness. From 1918, as an independent constitutional monarchy in union with Denmark (who retained control of Iceland's foreign affairs), the country attempted to improve the economy by expanding trade and extending communications. In 1940 the Icelandic government assumed sovereign control, in spite of British and, later, American occupation in 1940–41 for strategic reasons. After a plebiscite in 1944 the union with Denmark was revoked and a republic established, with ministerial responsibility to the Althing, the parliament at Reykjavik.

¶ PECK, HELEN E. *Iceland and Greenland*. 1967

Above: a great jet of steam from the sulphur mountains of Iceland. Below: Icelandic costume. Both from Mackenzie's Travels in Iceland, *1812.*

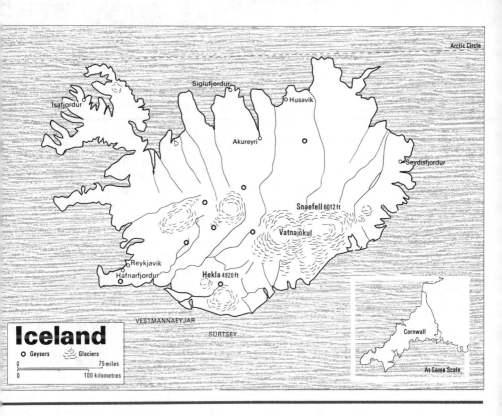

Arctic Circle

Siglufjordur
Isafjordur
Husavik
Akureyri
Seydisfjordur
Snaefell 6012 ft
Vatnajökul
Reykjavik
Hafnarfjordur
Hekla 4920 ft
VESTMANNAEYJAR
SURTSEY

Iceland

Geysers Glaciers

0 75 miles

0 100 kilometres

Cornwall

At Same Scale

Ichthus or **ichthys:** the Greek word for a fish, used in early times as a pictorial symbol for Jesus Christ. It was also used occasionally to symbolise the newly baptised and for the sacrament of the Eucharist. (For such symbolism, *see* ICONOGRAPHY.) The earliest examples date from the 2nd century, but the origin of the idea is obscure. Some would connect it with the fact that the first letters of the Greek words for Jesus Christ, Son of God, Saviour, spell the word Ichthys. Any connection with the use of fish on fast-days must be regarded as speculative.
See also CHRISTIANITY.

The fish symbol from the Catacombs in Rome.

Iconography: the study of the representation by symbols and imagery of the basic teachings of a religion. The term, derived from the Greek word *eikon,* an image, is generally applied to the art of the Christian Church but is not necessarily confined to that field.

The earliest forms of Christian art were largely symbolical; thus Christ was represented by a fish (*see* ICHTHUS) and the Church by a ship, while a peacock portrayed immortality. As the power and influence of Christianity grew, this art developed a greater measure of realism, but the basic purpose of the workers in mosaic, painting, sculpture and stained glass remained didactic, that is to say they tried to teach a lesson to people still largely unable to read the written word. The pictures and symbols tended to follow fixed rules and patterns so that the beholder would be more likely to understand the message. Thus St Laurence might be shown bearing the gridiron on which he was roasted to death; a saint would have a nimbus or halo round his head. The cathedral at Chartres is rich in decoration organised on these lines.

In the Eastern Church, until comparatively recent times, the symbolical painting of *icons* (tablets displayed in church or worn in miniature suspended from a person's neck) was developed to great heights. In the West, by the 14th century, Christian art began to move away from symbolism and appeal more directly and realistically to the emotions of the viewer.

Ignatius Loyola, St (1491 or 92–1556)**:** founder of the Society of Jesus, or Jesuits (*see* separate entry). Born of a noble family at Loyola in north-east Spain, Ignatius began a military career; but a long period of inactivity following a severe wound turned his thoughts towards a life of service as a soldier of Christ. After visits to Rome and Jerusalem and several years of study at universities in Spain and Paris, he again went to Rome and in 1540 obtained from Pope Paul III formal permission to establish his Society, to which he devoted the rest of his life. He was canonised in 1622.

¶ LIVERSIDGE, DOUGLAS. *St Ignatius of Loyola*. 1972

Illuminated books: manuscripts enriched in gold and colour. This art began about the 6th century and continued into the printing era. Block-printed marginal decoration occurs in Caxton's *Fifteen Oes* (1490). Through preserved manuscript books we learn of the beginning of page-design as used today. These books, mainly of a religious category, range in size from small *Books of Hours* to various much larger church service books.

In illumination (implying the use of gold-leaf) there are three elements: (1) Border, using fine, partly imaginative, flower,

In nomine patris et filij et spiritus
sancti.amen ¶ Pater noster/Aue
maria. ¶ Psalmi
Deus in noīe tuo saluū me fac/& c
Deus misereatur nr̄i et bn̄dicat nob
De profūdis clamaui ad te dn̄e/
Uoce mea ad dn̄m clamaui/Uoce
Ad te leuaui oculos meos/qui hitas
Leuaui oculos meos in montes
Beati omnes qui timent dn̄m
¶ Jhus autem transiens per medium
illorum ibat. ¶ Oracō ad patrem
Domine sc̄e pater omnipotens
eterne deus/in illa sc̄a custodia
et memoria in qua comendasti
gloriocissimum spiritū filij tui dn̄i nr̄i
Jhesu cristi/quando misisti eū de celis ad
terram/et in illa sancta custodia et me:
moria in qua respondisti et cōmendasti
gliosā matrē et personā filij tui existēs
in bn̄dicta cruce. quā cōmendasti Johi

leaf, bird and animals forms. By the 16th century it became too realistic and out-of-scale. An over-elaborate border sometimes distracts the eye from the text. (2) The gold-enriched frames of chapter-heading capitals, which contain miniature human figures. These delicate gems were often executed by another hand. This art developed, with the coming of gold-leaf, in the 13th century. (3) Line filling. Often the text leaves a line-end gap, afterwards filled with varied pattern-work, brightened with gold-leaf. The basis, with few exceptions, of this European but locally flavoured art was the Church. Today this art and craft continues, usually in single-leaf form.

Above: Caxton's Fifteen Oes *of 1490. Below: a decorated capital letter from a Latin Vulgate Bible, 9th century.*

Illumination (lighting): artificial means of allowing man to see in the dark. Until recent times – recent, that is, in man's history – the only source of artificial light has been fire, and indeed much modern lighting still relies on the essential essence of fire, combustion. In many parts of the world man has still to depend for lighting on the open flame.

Primitive man relied – and in some parts of the world still relies – on fire for warmth, for protection and for light, especially during the hours of darkness. A burning brand from the fire was obviously the earliest form of portable light, and adaptations of this type of flaming torch continued in use in even the most civilised and urban parts of Europe and America until the introduction of organised oil- and gas-fired street lighting before and just after 1800, respectively.

The earliest lamps, essentially small reservoirs for oil into which a wick was dipped, date from prehistoric times and were made of stone, pottery or metal; some very early lamps appear to have been wickless. By about 500 BC oil lamps with wicks had come into general domestic use in civilised communities, and during Roman times lamps were developed which were not only highly ornamented but also multi-wicked. Most oils used in lamps before this period were derived from animal or vegetable sources, but early in the Christian era reference is made to the use of mineral oils.

There has been a limited use of other natural illuminants, including glow-worms and fireflies, the phosphorescence of dead fish (which was used as late as the 19th century in some English coalmines where there was a danger of explosion). The carcasses of fatty animals or birds have also been used, with a wick through them.

The oil lamp has been gradually improved; a pressurised oil lamp was invented in the 1st century AD, Leonardo da Vinci (1452–1519) introduced considerable modifications, and during the 18th century the best scientific arrangement of a lamp was investigated. The type invented by the Swiss A. Argand in 1784 is still in use. It consisted of a cylindrical wick between two concentric tubes and produced a circular flame which was later improved by the addition of a glass chimney. During the second half of the 19th century the oil lamp was further developed, especially with the introduction of paraffin and of pressurisation. The portable paraffin lamp is still manufactured and finds a ready sale.

The other type of illumination which has been used alongside the lamp has been the candle. Here, a solid fat was required, with a central wick, and various substances have been used over the centuries for both fat and wick. In ordinary houses of civilised countries the use of candles was almost certainly more general than oil lamps until, from the early 19th century onwards, the availability of gas and later of electric lighting began slowly to usurp the position of both these earlier forms of lighting.

Although there had been earlier experiments in the use of natural and coal gases for lighting, the first successful and extensive use of coal gas for this purpose was made by William Murdoch (1754–1839), an engineer employed by Boulton and Watt at their famous Soho works, near Birmingham, England. In 1792 he lit his offices and home with gas and some six or seven years later he introduced a gas apparatus at the works. Its use in mills and factories spread and in 1807 it was first brought into service to light a public place, at Golden Lane, London. This was followed, also in London, by the general introduction of street lighting in the period 1813–20 – an idea soon followed by the United States. During the 19th

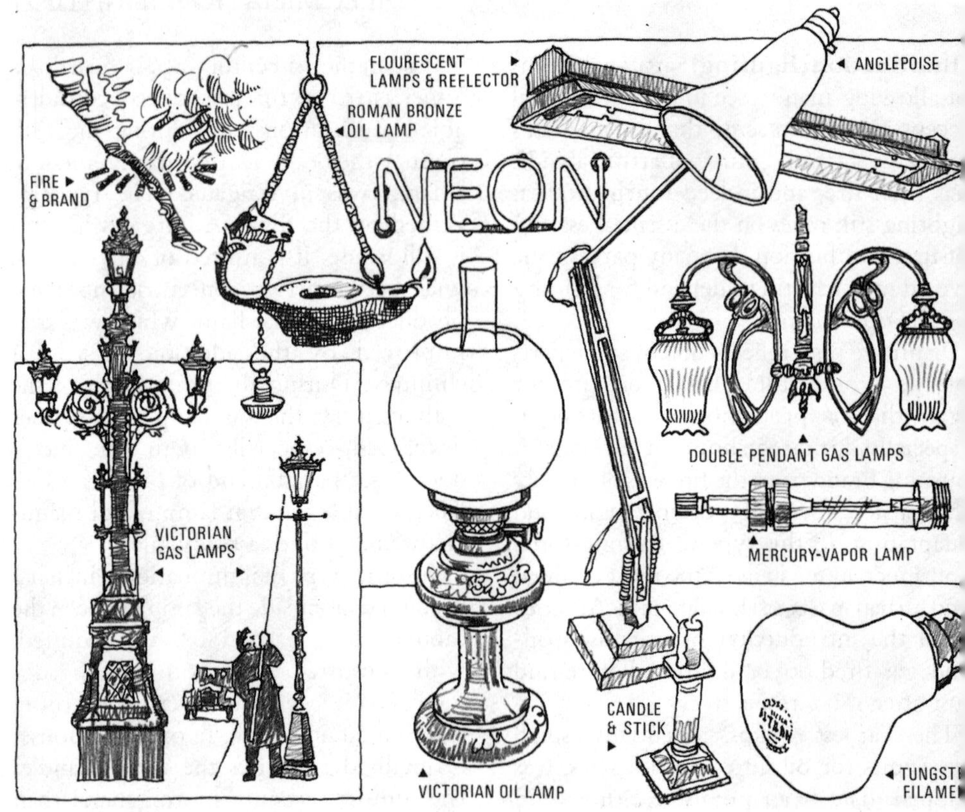

century great improvements were made both in the quality of gas and in the lighting apparatus itself; gas was also used for cooking and heating purposes.

The use of electricity to give light was investigated as far back as the 17th century, but it was not for another two hundred years that a cheap and practicable electric lamp was produced by Joseph Swan in England (1860) and nineteen years later by the American Thomas A. Edison (*see* separate entry).

¶ MITCHELL, RAY. *Study Book of Lamps and Candles.* 1959

See also ELECTRICITY.

Immigration: entering a country of which one is not a native, in order to settle there. The opposite is emigration; leaving one's own country in order to settle in another. Many countries have been compelled to adopt legislation to restrict the number of immigrants from undeveloped, overcrowded or oppressed areas of the world seeking a more secu and prosperous future elsewhere.

Impeachment: in Britain, trial by th House of Lords of a person indicted by th Commons. Dating from 1376 it becam a powerful weapon for the assertion c parliamentary control over the govern ment. Fairly frequent for a time, im peachments were superseded during th Wars of the Roses by bills of attaind but were revived in 1620–21 (Mompes son's Case). The Act of Settlement (1700 following on Danby's Case, provide that a royal pardon could not be used t prevent impeachment. The trial of War ren Hastings lasted for seven years (1788 95) and ended in his acquittal. Th process, though legally still possible, h been unused in Britain since Melville Case (1805). In the USA impeachme (a trial by members of the Senate follow ing charges by the House of Representa ves) is still used against public officials. 'he threat of impeachment proceedings ›llowing the Watergate Scandal hasten-d President Nixon's resignation in 1974. *see also* Andrew Johnson).

mperial Preference: a shortlived rrangement (1931–33), by which mem-er countries of the British Common-ealth gave preference to goods from ne another by imposing lower tariffs an were charged to other countries.

mperialism: belief in the value of olonies, or rule over alien peoples. It has een constantly practised, the nations of oday having resulted from the imperial-m of tribes which admitted their de-ated neighbours to full citizenship. trong and energetic peoples have always een tempted by the possessions and esources of unwarlike neighbours. It has ot always been the advanced peoples ho have conquered the backward; ie cultivators of fertile regions near eserts have often been subdued by the omads, Arabs, Turks or Mongols – hose own harsh environment made iem ferocious and who reduced to aste whole areas of skilfully cultivated nd.

Motives for colonisation vary. Land-unger and the pressure of rising popula-on are the most fundamental and explain ie German colonisation east of the Elbe, ie Portuguese settlement of Madeira and ie Azores and the exodus of Chartists to ustralia. The ambitions of rival generals layed a part in the Roman Empire. The earch for religious freedom drove nglishmen to Massachusetts and Mary-nd. The search for security has been a requent motive: the surest way to pre-ent attack by a neighbour is to rule his erritory instead. Karl Marx, criticising Western powers for softness to Tsarist Russia, warned that the frontier the Russians sought ran from Stettin to Trieste – exactly the present line of Soviet influence. The scramble for Central Africa was hastened by Bismarck who tried to ensure that his possible enemies in Europe quarrelled among themselves. Belief in some sort of divine mission – or a pretence to belief – has often supplied a motive. To the Arabs the holy war against the infidel was an article of faith. The Lawrence brothers (*see* separate entry) in the Punjab, Lugard among the Fulani of Africa, felt that England was entrusted with a civilis-ing mission to "lesser breeds without the law". Slavery, widow-burning, ritual murder were real evils to be suppressed. The Nazis thought they had a destiny as the master-race to dominate the Slavs.

The advancement of trade has always been an important motive and is now the dominant one. It partly explains the Greek colonisation of the Aegean islands and littoral. The British Empire was the creation of the trader and investor rather than of the statesman or soldier. The government intervened in India, Burma and Malaya to regulate the injustices arising from the contact of British mer-chants with peasant societies. Clive and Hastings in the period 1752–82 saw it as a moral duty openly to take responsibility for administering those areas where the activities of English merchants had cor-rupted or undermined native authorities. Statesmen at home did not welcome the cares and embarrassments which the possession of colonies imposed on them; "Africa is the country created to be the sore of the Foreign Office", said Lord Salisbury in the 1880s. Belgium had to take over the Congo to regulate the activities of King Leopold's Central Africa Company.

Imperialism is bound to affect both the whole life of the imperial power and the colonial territory. The flow of cheap colonial produce – coffee, sugar, rubber, calico – enriches the importer and the processor and raises the standard of living of all. The colonial civil service, defence forces, forestry and civil engineering departments offer careers for the adventurous and self-reliant, "a vast system of out-relief for the upper classes" as James Mill rather unfairly put it. The wealth derived from exploited colonies did not always equal the expense of defence and administration and in the case of Spain did much to shatter the home economy. The settlers and colonial merchants could become powerful pressure-groups at home. Macaulay described the "wicked old Nabob, with a tawny complexion, a bad liver and a worse heart", whose lavish spending put up the price of everything "from fresh eggs to rotten boroughs". The traders to the West Indies drove Walpole into the War of Jenkins' Ear. The Algerian settlers led a desperate and dangerous opposition to de Gaulle.

The effects on the subject peoples are more obvious. Their natural resources – oil, copper, timber – may be exploited by foreign companies paying only nominal royalities. The money-lender may flourish under the protection of European judges, the ruling class may degenerate as they draw the revenues but do not accept the proper responsibilities of government, the people lose their self-confidence, even their sense of identity, their tribal organisation collapses and they are confronted with the superior education and techniques of the white settler. They develop what President Kaunda of Zambia called the "bwana complex", always looking over their shoulders for the white man's approval. Later they react and resent the condescension, real or imagined, of the white man.

Chief Sithole wrote: "The logical consequence [of civilising any given people] is that civiliser and civilised become equals or partners." When the civiliser refuses or delays accepting this equality, a fight for freedom develops. Thus, New England fought old England for the English principle of "no taxation without representation". Thus, the peoples of Africa and Asia demand the right of "self-determination", the slogan of the Western statesmen at Versailles in 1919. Thus, the Ibos are forced to belong to the "Nigerian nation" – "Nigeria" a word only coined in 1897 and "nation" a European concept introduced into tribal Africa. Once the demand for nationhood has been kindled in the educated class, no degree of good government will content them. It did not matter that India had "never had such a sweet, just, boyish master" as the district officer who "carried his English weather with him in his heart" from the playing fields of English public schools.

Better communications may eventually end the variations in economic and social development, but until they do there remains a danger of imperialism or "dollar imperialism", the uncontrolled economic penetration, which may be "worse than the ancient wrongs".

¶ LICHTHEIM, GEORGE. *Imperialism*. 1971

Impressionists: name given primarily to a group of French painters of the second half of the 19th century. Outstanding among them were Edouard Manet (1823-83), Claude Monet (1840-1926), Camille Pissarro (1830-1903), Alfred Sisley (1840-99), Georges Seurat (1851–91), Edgar Degas (1834–1917) and Auguste Renoir (1841–1919).

Artists show far too many individual variations for Impressionism to be labelled a school of painting. What all share is a preoccupation with light and colour, a freedom of treatment quite unlike the painstakingly finished work of their academic predecessors and a willingness to sacrifice detail in the interest of the general impression.

The impressionists applied pure colours directly to the canvas, placing them side by side. It is the observer who does their mixing for them. When viewed at a distance, the colours blend together as in nature.

Impressment: the act of recruiting by force for the public service, usually for the army or navy – a device which was often used in the past in times of national need. As an example, the British Navy at the height of the Napoleonic Wars probably needed an annual recruitment of some 40,000 men and could achieve it only by impressment. The best known method was by the press-gang because it has featured in so many plays and novels. But ideas about the extent of the press-gang's activities are often exaggerated. Care should be taken to avoid confusion between two different words that came to be spelt alike. A "prest man" was one who had received a "prest" or "imprest", i.e. a sum of money paid in advance as a means of persuasion to join the service. A "pressed man" was one taken against his will.

Incas: properly speaking, the rulers of Peru from about AD 1200 until the Spanish conquistador, Francisco Pizarro, murdered the last reigning Inca in 1533. The term is often loosely, but less correctly, used for the people ruled by the Incas. These people lived over 10,000 feet high [3050 metres] in the Andes Mountains. Starting from the valley of Cuzco, which became their capital city, the Incas conquered their neighbours, and during the 15th century their most able rulers extended their empire until it reached over 2,000 miles [3219 kilometres] from Quito in the north to the deserts of Chile in the south.

The majority of the people lived in village huts and grew maize, but the

Left: the Inca fort of Sacschuaman, a masterpiece of engineering which took 30,000 workmen 70 years to build. Right: a functional Inca jar of simple design.

major cities had strong fortresses and temples built from massive stone blocks. These cities were linked by a remarkable road system that crossed deep valleys over suspension bridges. Since they used no wheel and the llama was their only beast of burden, their roads were used by men on foot – marching to battle or running with messages for the Inca. They obtained fresh fish from the far coast.

This well-organised civilisation was destroyed after the capture of Atahualpa, the last Inca. He was ransomed for a room full of gold, and it took 13,265 lb [6016.45 kg] of gold to fill it. He was not set free but treacherously executed, and without their divine leader the people of Peru could not drive the Spaniards away. Nevertheless they did resist in remote mountain valleys. Indeed, in many villages their way of life has not really changed much during the last 400 years.

¶ BECK, BARBARA L. *The First Book of the Incas*. 1971; VON HAGEN, VICTOR W. *The Incas*. 1963

Income tax: tax levied on the income of an individual, a business etc. First introduced in Britain by William Pitt in 1799 at a standard rate of two shillings in the pound, it was discontinued in 1816 but reintroduced by Sir Robert Peel in 1842 "for a period of three years" and has never been repealed since, rising to ten shillings in the pound during World War II. Other countries to introduce the tax were: Belgium (1828), Austria (1849), United States (1862), Italy (1864), Germany (1894), France (1914). A surtax on higher incomes was first imposed in Britain in 1909. Income tax provides a widely varying portion of the national income in different countries, ranging from about 78 per cent in the United States to 29 per cent in France and 15 per cent in Italy, though in the latter case the low figure results from an inefficient system of collection, only a small fraction of returns being made by a high working population.

Incunabula: books printed before 1500, from the Latin word for "swaddling clothes", denoting the period of the infancy of the art and craft of printing. The second half of the 15th century may be regarded as a period of transition between manuscript reproduction (with many possible errors) and exact, accurate printing by machine.

The virtues of the compressed medieval script were various. First, to the literate, by lifetime familiarity with those forms of letters, accepted abbreviations and the number of words that could appear on a page, it made for economy of reading time and of material. Again, by reasonable size, it proved legible in what to us today would be termed a poor light. So it came about that no great change was needed, save in more rapid means of production, when the increasing demands of the literate people of Europe made it impossible to produce enough manuscript copies. In Western Europe the final solution, i.e. the invention of movable type, is attributed to Johann Gutenberg, who was of aristocratic lineage, and whose real name was Gensfleisch zur Laden, born *c.* 1398 in Mainz (Mentz). Before his time, it had been a practice to cut separate metal punches for marking, for instance, various articles with the owner's initials. Another earlier practice for producing copies of (often illustrated) texts was that of cutting a whole page upon a wood block. These are now called "block books".

In all incunabula there stands out clearly the centuries-old love of page design, proportion, balance and colour, carried over from the illuminated manuscripts, their forerunners, so patiently devised, corrected, rearranged, and reset. Since, in any form or translation of the Bible,

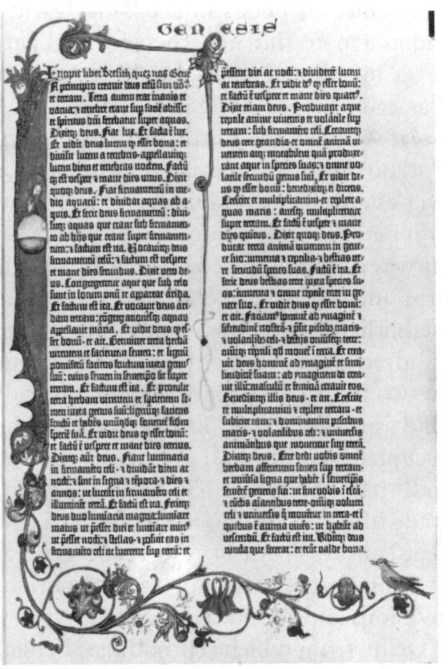

Above: First page of Genesis in the 42-line Bible, c. 1455. Above right: Latin Psalter by Fust and Schoeffer printed in Mainz in 1457. Below right: The Biblia Pauperum of 1463.

neither chapters nor verses received Arabic numbering until the Geneva Bible of 1560, those red and blue versal capitals still played their parts. Brilliant devices appeared for instance in the "Latin Psalter" printed at Mainz in 1457, by Fust and Schoeffer, in which we see chapter initial-capitals printed in blue and red by separately cut and finally conjoined metal blocks.

Among the British Museum incunabula, some printed upon vellum, are: (1) The "42-line" Bible *c.* 1455 known as the "Mazarin" or "Gutenberg" Bible, a beautifully illuminated volume of 641 leaves. (2) The "Biblia Pauperum", a block book of *c.* 1450. (3) The Mainz Psalter of 1457, the first book ever to contain the printer's name. As time passed variously-sized "founts" of type were evolved, e.g. the main text in a central panel, surrounded by beautifully type-filled margins of comment. Folio or page-numbering was devised by two printers in Leipzig *c.* 1489.

See also BOOKS, ILLUMINATED BOOKS; PRINTING, etc.

India: the name historically applied to the whole subcontinent south of the Himalayas, comprising the modern independent states of India, Pakistan, Bangladesh and Nepal.

In the four thousand years of which we have some knowledge, the area has never been ruled, even under the British, as one nation from one centre. Its vast size and history of frequent invasion led to the development of local patriotisms, with marked differences of race, language and culture, which made it difficult for conquerors and conquered to merge. But there did develop a recognisably "Indian" civilisation under the humanising influence of the great religions, Hinduism,

Buddhism and, much later but no less effective, Islam; and during the later part of British rule there grew up the feeling that westernisation, with all its material improvements, represented a move away from the other values which were specifically Indian – retrogression rather than progress.

India contains many racial types, and more than two hundred languages and dialects are spoken. The original inhabitants were a short, dark, snub-nosed people whose descendants are still to be found in southern India. Somewhere around 1500 BC the first waves of Aryan invaders began flooding through the north-western passes, driving back the aborigines into the wilds and the tableland of the Deccan. With the invaders came the remarkable Vedic literature, and in the Punjab there evolved Brahminical Hinduism, with its elaborate system of *castes* – innumerable self-contained groups, debarred from ordinary relations with one another – which has moulded so much of the social development of the country.

Later, from about 500 BC, in the upper Ganges area, Buddhism and Jainism came into existence. The latter never spread extensively; the former, though eventually driven from India, now has 250 million adherents world-wide.

There were other invaders too, Sakas, Kushans, White Huns, some of them Aryan, others, probably coming through the north-eastern passes, Mongolian in character, and their intermarriage with the peoples they found led to further variety of race and language. The result of this early history is that, on the whole, the peoples of the north are Aryan, those of the Deccan pre-Aryan. The tribes of the south, speaking a variety of ancient tongues, are termed "Dravidian".

There have been many empires and kingdoms in Hindustan. From about 500 BC the Indus valley was, for a short period, a province of Persia under King Darius, and in 479 BC Indian archers formed part of an invading Persian army defeated at Plataea in Greece; in 326 BC Alexander the Great subdued the north-western region. But no lasting imperial dominion was ever established by a Hindu government, in spite of several promising attempts.

It was not until the coming of Islam that firm and lasting governments were ever established, and then only after five hundred years of fighting. From about AD 700 the Arabs began their conquest of Sind; in 862 Ghazni in Afghanistan was occupied by Muslim Turks; between 997 and 1026, Mahmud, Sultan of Ghazni, made fifteen raids into northern India and kept Lahore. From 1175 to 1206 a general of Mohammed of Ghor carried out six invasions and founded a Turkish dynasty at Delhi, from which centre Bihar, Bengal and some of the Deccan were acquired. In the following three centuries (1206–1526) there were four dynasties of Muslim kings at Delhi, and ruling Muslim houses established themselves at many points in central and southern India, crystallising into five Deccan kingdoms which carried on almost perpetual war with Vijayanagar, the chief Hindu state of South India.

Then came Babar the Mogul, chief of Farghana in Turkestan; from 1505 he carried out a series of invasions, culminating at the great battle of Panipat, 1526, where he overthrew the last of the kings of Delhi and became the first Mogul emperor. His son was driven back, but his grandson, Akbar (1556–1605), an almost exact contemporary of Elizabeth I of England, extended his empire far to the south, to the line of the River Godavari, and established an efficient administrative system. Akbar's successor, Jahangir (1605–27), a contemporary of James I of England and not unlike him in character, granted the first facilities to the British East India

CHINA
PERSIA
Nepal
Delhi
Oudh
Sind
Calcutta
Diu
Bombay
Goa
Mangalore
Calicut
Madras
Pondicherry
1707
Area under Moguls 1707
British settlements
French settlements
Portuguese influence
Dutch influence
AFGHANS
Kashmir
Battle
CHINA
Punjab
TIBET
NEPAL
Oudh
Sind
Bihar
Plassey 1757
Bengal
Assaye 1805
Hyderabad Nizam's territory
Goa
Mysore
Seringapatam 1803
Canatic
Ceylon
1756-1858
British areas under Clive 1756-67
British control 1805
Acquired by British 1805-58
Dependent States
India
AFGHANISTAN
Khyber Pass
Jammu & Kashmir
Srinagar
CHINA
150 miles
300 kilometres
Tibet
Indus
Lahore
HIMALAYA MOUNTAINS
Punjab
PAKISTAN
Lhasa
Bramaputra
Delhi
NEPAL
Katmandu
SIKKIM
Everest
BHUTAN
Uttar Pradesh
Rajasthan
Assam
Gwalior
Jumna
Ganges
Patna
Karachi
Bihar
Dacca
Gurerat
Madhya Pradesh
Bengal
BURMA
Calcutta
Maharashtra
Orissa
BANGLADESH
Bombay
Arabian Sea
Bay of Bengal
Rangoon
Mysore
ANDAMAN IS.
Madras
Mangalore
Pondicherry
LACCADIVE IS.
Kerala
Madras
after 1858
Acquired by British 1818-1914
Boundary of British India 1937
Boundary of India and Pakistan 1947
Area of conflict after 1947
CEYLON (Independent 1948)
Indian Ocean
MALDIVE IS.
Colombo
NICOBAR IS.

Company, and for three years Sir Thomas Roe lived as ambassador at his court. By this time the Mogul power was firmly established, and general peace was preserved for a century.

The last effective Mogul emperor was Aurangzeb, who died in 1707, and the half century which followed saw the double process of independent rule by the great Mogul viceroys and of the growing intervention of European powers in India. Their rivalry and enmity led to British domination after the wars of the 18th century and, eventually, to the conversion of India into British India.

The first period of the British East India Company's history was that of "simple trade", on principles laid down by Sir Thomas Roe, who had seen the losses incurred by the Portuguese and Dutch through their militant policy. "Let this be received", he wrote, "that if you will profit, seek it at sea and in quiet trade; for . . . it is an error to affect garrisons and land wars in India." This advice was followed until the emergence of French rivalry, with its principle, initiated by Benoît Dumas and developed by Dupleix, of using native alliances to secure advantages. The British Company was then compelled to take political and military action.

The process began, in earnest, with the winning of territory during the Seven Years War and Clive taking over the financial control of Bengal, Bihar and Orissa. This was followed by a period of extortion by the Company's officials which, with financial difficulties of the Company, compelled the British government to take a hand, and led to North's Regulating Act of 1773 and Pitt's India Act of 1784. Cornwallis, Governor General 1786–93, was the first to hold that office without being a servant of the Company; Wellesley, 1798–1805, elder brother of the Duke of Wellington, strove unashamedly for Empire. But with

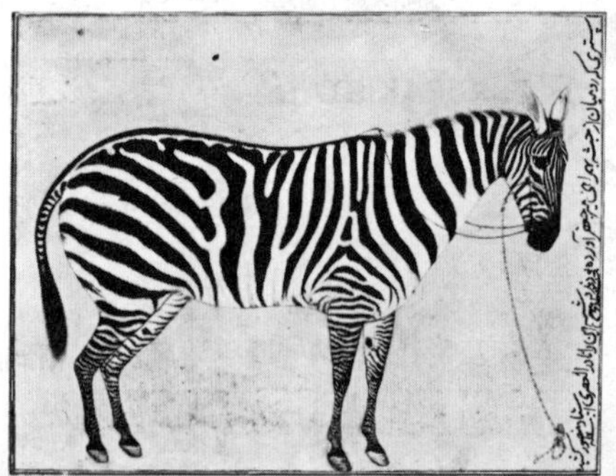

Above: 9th century bronze image of Jina from Western India. Above right: zebra painted by Mansur, Jahangir period, 1621. Below right: Sudāma approaching the Golden City of Krishna, c. 1785.

power there came also a growing awareness of the duty of the governing power to improve the conditions of life for native Indians, and the period of office of Bentinck, 1828–35, saw many social reforms, such as the abolition of *suttee* (by which a widow, with her own consent, was burnt on her husband's funeral pyre) and *thuggee* (murder and robbery by the Thug religious sect), the introduction of an effective penal code, and of education (with teaching in English) – which, because of its liberal character, gave to educated Indians a belief in the value of self-government. Under Dalhousie, 1848–56, improvements in such forms as roads, railways and telegraphs, and the taking over of land, were so violently swift as to alarm Indians and to lead, almost directly, to the Mutiny of 1857. This had two results; the first formal, the dissolution of the Company; the second more fundamental, the rupture of close and confident relations between British and Indians.

Nationalist feelings grew in India during the 19th century, helped by the extension of education and research into ancient Hindu civilisation. Indian National Congress was founded in 1885 by Hume, of the Bengal Civil Service, and was commended by Lord Dufferin as "a useful channel for the expression of Indian public opinion". Its first fruits were local native councils to co-operate with the Indian Civil Service, under the Dufferin Act (1888), and advisory councils with some Indian members under the Lansdowne Act (1892). But the extremist Bal Gangadhar Tilak converted Congress into an assembly encouraging unrest and agitation, and this led to the *Swadeshi* movement for the boycott of British goods. The Morley-Minto reforms of 1909 gave a measure of Indian responsibility but no control over the British executive.

During World War I the Indian contribution was great, but by 1916 Indian members of the Viceroy's council were formulating plans for *Swaraj* (self-rule), and the following year government policy was declared to be steady progress towards administration of India by Indians. The India Act of 1919, following the Montagu-Chelmsford Report of the previous year, set up all-Indian Central and Provincial Legislative Assemblies, but the royal veto and vice-regal powers of legislation remained; unrest continued, culminating in the Amritsar affair, when General Dyer's troops fired on a hostile crowd, a tragedy which converted Gandhi into a total opponent of British rule. Agitation was not confined to Hindus; the Muslim *Khilafat* movement spoke loudly for that minority.

An attempt, after the Simon Report of 1930 and three "Round Table" conferences, to resolve the problem by the India Act of 1935 was never fully tested, as the 1939 outbreak of World War II altered the situation. In 1940 the Indians were asked to frame their own constitution, and a mission under Sir Stafford Cripps in 1942 came near to success. But internal suspicion and rivalry were too acute for a single great state to be preserved after the British departure, and in 1947 partition into India and Pakistan proved the only answer.

The independent republic of India consists of seventeen states and ten centrally administered territories, with their capital at Delhi. The former French territories have been incorporated and the Portuguese possession of Goa annexed (1962). The powerful central government created and led by Jawaharlal Nehru (1947–56) gave the new republic a strong start and did much to combat the enormous problems of over-population and poverty; but not all the story has been of peaceful progress. Frontier disputes with China are an anxiety of long standing; a bitter dispute, not yet resolved, has occurred over the future of Kashmir. When East Pakistan determined to secede from West Pakistan in 1970/71, India fought West Pakistan on its behalf and Bangladesh was born. Indira Gandhi, Nehru's daughter, became prime minister in 1966 and dominated Indian politics until her assassination in 1984.

See also AKBAR; CLIVE; EAST INDIA COMPANY; GANDHI; HASTINGS; INDIAN MUTINY; JAHANGIR; NEHRU; PAKISTAN; SEVEN YEARS WAR; and other separate entries on people, places and events.

Indiaman: a British merchant ship engaged in the India trade. The East Indiamen ranged in size from about 800 to 1,100 tons (812.88 to 1,117.71 tonnes): the West Indiamen were rather smaller. The ships were armed and, if need be, could give a good account of themselves. In 1804 an East India convoy put to flight a strong French battle squadron, including a 74-gun ship. The ships were run on Royal Navy lines, smart and tightly disciplined.

British East Indiamen shown in action against French men-of-war, 1804.

Indian Mutiny: the rebellion (1857–58) of the native Bengal troops against British rule in India. The mutiny spread through central India, resulting in heavy casualties before it was put down with great severity (*see* DELHI; LUCKNOW; LAWRENCE, SIR HENRY; etc.). The most important result of the mutiny was that control of India passed from the East India Company (*see* separate entry) to the British Crown.
¶ CARDWELL, PAMELA. *The Indian Mutiny*. 1972

Indians, North American ("Red Indians"): the original inhabitants of America were the Red Indians, so called from Columbus's mistake in supposing he had reached the Indies. Wherever white explorers landed on the American continent they found these copper-coloured, high-cheek-boned people. Their way of life was very primitive; they practised a simple form of agriculture and made crude pottery. At first the Indians were generally friendly towards the white man and this friendship might have become a lasting association. Instead, the white man's cruelty, greed and treachery towards them turned their first warmth into a deep hate, resulting in endless frontier wars as the newcomers moved ever westwards.

It has been estimated that there were probably over one million Red Indians scattered over North America: their present number is just under 400,000, many of them still living on "reservations". The various tribes can be grouped according to certain main regions and occupations. There were the tribes which hunted the caribou in the northern forests; the peoples of the north-west Pacific coast who lived mainly by fishing; the tribes of the eastern woodlands who lived partly by hunting and partly by cultivation and who were the first to be affected by the arrival of European colonists; the Plains Indians who hunted

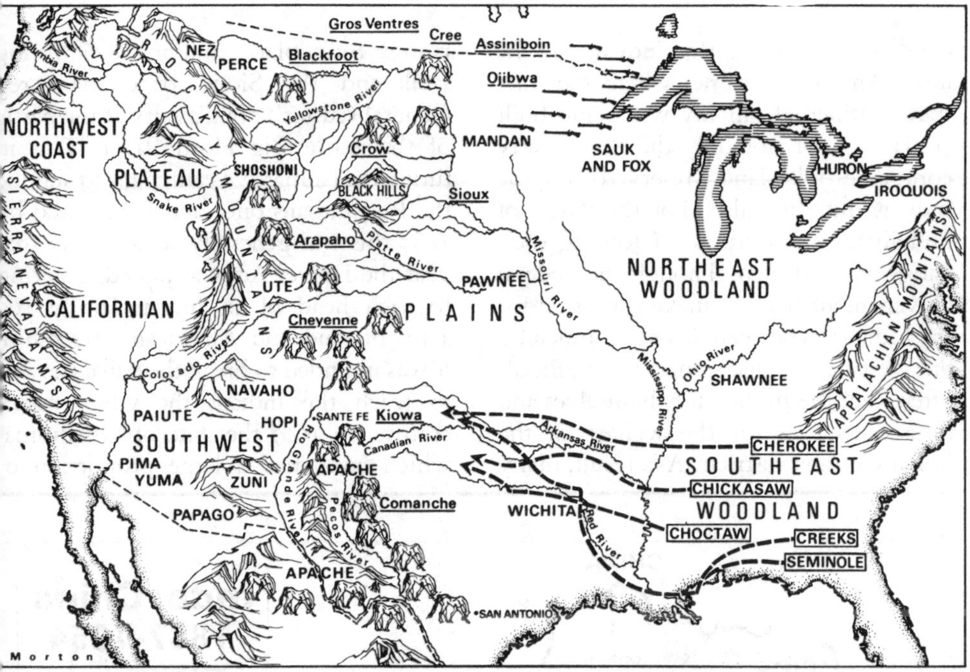

NORTH AMERICAN INDIANS: *important tribes are shown in capital letters, while the roving warriors of the plains are in small letters and underlined. The horse and gun symbols show the routes by which they spread among the tribes and the arrows trace the removal of the eastern tribes on to the prairie.*

the buffalo; and the Pueblo Indians in the south-west who raised sheep and grew maize (Indian corn).

The French and Indian War (1745–63) ended with a general rising by the Eastern Woodlands Indians under the leadership of Pontiac, in which many of the colonies' western outposts were destroyed. The British government secured the friendship of these Red Indians in 1764, when a boundary line was set beyond which no westwards advance would, for the time being, be permitted. But the colonists disregarded the wishes of the government in London and people like Daniel Boone blazed the trails to the West. After the War of American Independence (1775–83) the thirst for new lands became greater. In 1811 a frontier war broke out when the Indians, led by Tecumseh, objected to the surrendering of 50 million acres [20 million hectares] of territory in Indiana. The next major

Tashawah, a Comanche, photographed by Will Soule at Fort Sill in 1869.

conflict between the Red Indians and the new Americans came when the first transcontinental railway was being built (1863–69), for not only did the railway companies take land "reserved" for the Indians but they also shot thousands of buffalo for the purpose of feeding their gangs of workmen. Though the Federal Government tried to make provision for the Indians, who were losing so much by this westwards expansion, corrupt officials often kept the money for themselves and refused to care for the welfare of the Indians in their districts. As a result, many risings took place, and in 1876 Sittin Bull and the Sioux tribe massacre General Custer's 7th Cavalry at the battl of the Little Big Horn River. This i turn led to a massive campaign to subdu the Red Indians once and for all, and b 1887 this was generally achieved. In tha year the Dawes Act was passed, grantin to each head of an Indian family 16 acres of land and American citizenship It was intended to break the tribal ties an to teach the Indians the white man' culture. In 1907 the state of Oklahoma which contained a large proportion o

ndians amongst its population, was admitted to the Union. Today, though many Indians still live on the reservations, the aims of the Dawes Act have been fulfilled and the survivors of this long-oppressed people have taken a fuller place in American society.

¶ BREWSTER, BENJAMIN. *The First Book of Indians.* 1962; MORRIS, RICHARD B. *The First Book of the Indian Wars.* 1959

Indo-China: name applied to the area of south-east Asia which became French colonial territory during the 19th century. It comprised the protectorates of Annam, Tonking and Cambodia, the colony of Cochin-China, part of Laos, and Kwang-Chow Bay.

French influence in the area dates from 1787, when the missionary Pigneau de Behaine, Bishop of Adran, secured the signature of a treaty between the king of Cochin-China and Louis XVI. From this time the French remained active, in 1801 assisting an Annamite prince to regain his throne. There was, however, much anti-European activity, and it was not until 1862, when Admiral Charner captured Saigon, that French rule was established and the three eastern provinces were ceded to France. Continual revolts caused the annexation of the western provinces in 1867. In 1874 Tonking became a protectorate by treaty with the Emperor Tu-Duc who, however, continued to negotiate with China; and in 1883 Annam united with China in war on the French, ending with treaties which defined the frontiers. The first governor-general of the whole area was appointed in 1887.

To administer districts of such diverse race and culture was not easy. The French tried to give native representation on the Council of Government, but it was only partly successful, and resentment against the occupation gave force to organised resistance after the second World War, when the French forces were defeated and the country reverted to the independent states of Tonking, Vietnam, Laos and Cambodia.

¶ POOLE, FREDERICK KING. *Southeast Asia.* 1972

See also CAMBODIA; CHINA; LAOS; VIETNAM; etc.

Indonesia: a republic made up of a large group of islands off south-east Asia. Politically the most important island is Java. Others are Sumatra, Celebes, part of Borneo, Bali, Lombok, Timor and the Moluccas. The cultural background of most of the islands has strong Hindu and Buddhist elements. Conversion to Islam occurred between the 13th and 15th centuries. The Portuguese began trading in the Moluccas in the early 16th century, closely followed by the Spaniards and then, in the following century, by the Dutch and British. The Dutch East Indies Company, founded in 1602, gained territory as well as trading rights. The Dutch made production for export compulsory, forcing the peasant economy of Java and other islands to turn outwards to world markets. Tin and petroleum became important exports. In the 20th century natives were allowed to take some share in government. In World War II Indonesia fell under Japanese occupation. On Japanese withdrawal an Indonesian Republic declared its independence. The Dutch resisted but in 1949 handed over the government to a United States of Indonesia. The Indonesia government ended this union and formed a single republic in 1950. Under Ahmed Sukarno, Indonesia was strongly aligned with communist interests in south-east Asia and combined this with territorial ambitions and military intervention in Malaysia. Communist alignment was ended by a military coup, and in 1967 Sukarno was replaced as president by General Suharto. *See* map p. 456.

Indulgences: defined by the Roman Catholic Church as "the remission of temporal [i.e. earthly] punishment which often remains due to sin after its guilt has been forgiven". Thus, Urban II, when mustering support for the First Crusade (1096–99), said that any who went in a spirit of pure devotion could count the journey "in lieu of all penance". It was the sale of indulgences by the German monk Johann Tetzel that provoked Luther (1517) to nail his defiant theses to the church door at Wittenberg. Indulgences could be *plenary* (full) or *partial* (extending over a stated period of time).

Indus civilisation: When the Indo-Aryans, ancestors of the present inhabitants of northern India, began, around 2000 BC, their invasions of India, they must have found in the Indus valley a civilisation of an advanced kind. Excavations at such sites as Mohenjo-Daro and Harappa have uncovered great cities with brick buildings on a planned grid pattern, and amenities such as good water-supply and drainage, baths and public buildings, as well as powerful fortifications, with a strong citadel at the west of each town.

This appears to have been a city culture in a land still practising primitive agriculture, and its origin remains obscure. Some features of it show traces of Mesopotamian influence, though scholars judge that its quality was superior to that of contemporary Egypt or Sumeria, with

Seal found in a tomb at Mohenjo-Daro, showing pipal tree and the heads of horned animals.

both of which it has affinities. The units of measurement, for instance, very exact, were much the same as those of Egypt. Pottery, jewellery and carvings show trading links with Persia, southern India and possibly further afield, but it has so far proved impossible to decipher the script on seals which have been found. Skeletons uncovered show the inhabitants to have been of a variety of races.

The civilisation flourished for something under a thousand years, in the third and second millennia BC and probably, but not certainly, was destroyed by the invasions of the Indo-Aryans, whose ancient literature speaks of a dark-skinned enemy who were driven back into their fortified towns. *See also* INDIA.

Industrial archaeology: the study of the antiquities of industrialisation. Although the use of the term "industrial archaeology" is of recent introduction, the study of industrial monuments has been the concern of economic and local historians for a far longer period.

The contribution of industrial archaeology to the studies of the economic, social and local historian is difficult to state in any precise manner, except to say that a study of physical remains will often make clear what might be obscure from documentary sources alone; and where documentation is sparse or missing the remains in the field may be the only evidence.

The range of the remains of industrialisation which are within the scope of the industrial archaeologist are – perhaps happily – unlimited: mills of all kinds, factories and workshops, agricultural installations, mines, roads, waterways and railways are obvious objects for study, as is their associated housing; and, extending the field still further, even such facilities as chapels and churches, public houses and clubs, cinemas and Mechanics' Institutes.

The industrial archaeologist must be able to bring together knowledge and skill in a number of subjects usually regarded as separate. This is perhaps the principal contribution to scholarship to be made by industrial archaeology, for the study must ultimately involve the economic historian, the architectural historian, the historian of science and technology, the student of archives and books, the local historian, the excavator, the photographer and the draughtsman. The study of industrial archaeology, however, has up to the present chiefly involved the amateur rather than the professional academic, so that much of the work done locally has been of a somewhat haphazard nature and both unknown and unavailable to other interested persons.

The rate of modern urban development has made the work of the industrial archaeologist of increasing importance, even if his work is only carried to the extent of making full records of buildings and sites, or perhaps of rescue excavations. The techniques of industrial excavation are exactly the same as those used in classical archaeology. Apart from excavation work, the industrial archaeologist is concerned to record surviving buildings or their remains, together with their machinery, the derivation of their architectural style, the technological improvements incorporated in them, the materials of which they were built (and their sources), dates and builders.

In Britain, some few enlightened local authorities have themselves financed the surveying of such remains within their areas, but the majority of such work has been undertaken by local societies, the Workers' Educational Association and the universities, and by individuals. A number of local historical and archaeological societies now also publish articles on industrial archaeology in their journals, and there are a number of periodicals – notably *Industrial Archaeology, Textile*

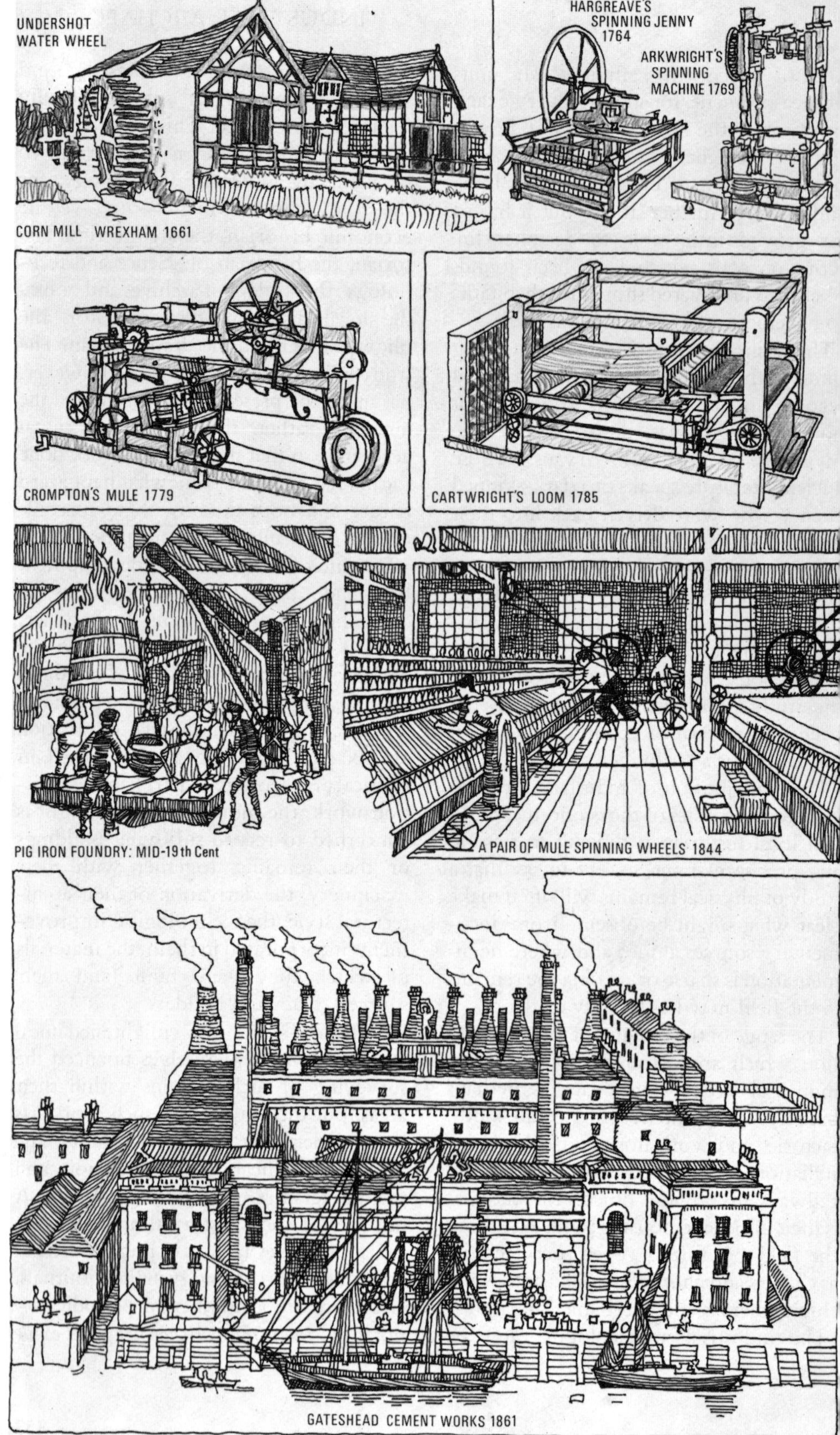
UNDERSHOT WATER WHEEL
CORN MILL WREXHAM 1661
HARGREAVE'S SPINNING JENNY 1764
ARKWRIGHT'S SPINNING MACHINE 1769
CROMPTON'S MULE 1779
CARTWRIGHT'S LOOM 1785
PIG IRON FOUNDRY: MID-19th Cent
A PAIR OF MULE SPINNING WHEELS 1844
GATESHEAD CEMENT WORKS 1861

History, and *Transport History* – which deal very largely with these matters.

A number of museums devoted to the illustration of local industry and social history have been developed within the last few years: they all adopt rather different approaches to these subjects, varying from the general scientific and technological museums of London, Birmingham, Manchester and Newcastle to the regional and hence more specific museums such as that at Helmshore in Lancashire (textiles) and the South Yorkshire Industrial Museum near Doncaster, concerned with industrialisation within a specific area.

¶ VIALLS, CHRISTINE. *Cast Iron*. 1970; VIALLS, CHRISTINE. *Windmills and Watermills*. 1971

Industrial Revolution: the name first made familiar by Arnold Toynbee in the 19th century to describe changes in the economic life of England caused by a remarkable series of inventions during a period from about 1770 to 1815. Though the term has wider applications it is used especially in British history.

Perhaps we can best give some idea of the magnitude of this revolution by first considering England as it was in 1760, when George III came to the throne. The largest towns, after London, were Bristol and Norwich. The characteristic unit was not the town but the country village, still surrounded by its open fields but less purely agricultural than it was later to become: its craftsmen produced most of the necessities of life themselves. Spinning was the special task of the women and children. Weaving was done either by professional weavers, who collected the spun yarn from the cottages, or sometimes as a by-industry by the agricultural labourer himself in the evenings or when field labour was slack. Most roads had no prepared surface, but were pack-horse roads, along which travelled trains of pack-horses, carrying corn, coal, cloth and hardware. The iron industry was centred in the forests of Sussex and Surrey, which provided the charcoal for the smelting.

The process by which this picture was changed to one more familiar to us today has no definite beginning, but one of the first steps was the invention of the flying shuttle by Kay of Bury in 1733. Before this the weaver had passed the shuttle through the threads of the warp from hand to hand, thus limiting the width of the cloth to about three-quarters of a yard [0.69 metres]. Kay's flying shuttle enabled a wider cloth to be woven and more than doubled the rate of working, thus using up yarn faster than the spinners could provide it. The balance was restored by James Hargreaves of Blackburn, who invented the spinning-jenny in 1764, followed by Richard Arkwright, whose water-powered roller spinning frame appeared in 1769. Finally Samuel Crompton's "muslin-wheel", later known as the "mule", was invented in 1779 and made possible the spinning of yarn fine enough for delicate muslin fabrics.

All these machines were at first powered by water, but weaving still remained a manual process till the Rev. Edmund Cartwright patented his power loom in 1785. His first machine was powered by a bull, but by 1789 his Doncaster factory was fitted with a steam-engine. These inventions first had their effect in the cotton industry, but by the last decade of the 18th century Benjamin Gott adapted them for use in the woollen industry. The use of water-power led to the concentration of the spinning and weaving industries in the valleys of Lancashire and Yorkshire, where many of the mills still stand on the banks of the streams which supplied their power before the advent of the steam-engine.

Meanwhile the inventions of Smeaton,

Cort, and three generations of the Darby family revolutionised the iron industry, which now used coal instead of charcoal for smelting, and moved to the North and the Midlands, where coal and iron ore were found together. The increased importance of coal produced steam-engines to help to raise it and canals to distribute it. James Watt vastly improved but did not, as is sometimes said, invent the steam-engine. By 1781 it was said "the people in Manchester are all steam-mill mad". Factories and mills, hitherto on river banks, began to collect in towns where coal was cheap. From 1770 onwards hundreds of miles of canals were completed, anticipating the "railway mania" of the 19th century. Roads, too, were vastly improved as the result of John Loudon Macadam's idea of solidifying them with small hard stones.

With this growth of an industrialised society came many social problems. The employment of child labour in factories and the mushroom growth of new towns, built without regard for health or proper planning, left a host of problems to be dealt with, while the rapid enclosure of the open fields drove more country dwellers into the towns.

Some statistics for the years 1760 and 1815 will emphasise the magnitude of this revolution: exports rose in value from £15 to £59 million; imports from £10 to £33 million.

Thus England became "the workshop of the world", a description used by Disraeli, but the term "Industrial Revolution" may be used in a wider sense, and may be considered to be still in progress. Industrialisation spread to other countries and, in the latter half of the 19th century, was most rapid in Germany and the United States, though here the change depended on the growth of railways, whereas in England it preceded it.

The first quarter of the 20th century saw steam power largely replaced by electricity, which was readily available.

As other nations became more industrialised, England's economic supremacy declined, especially as coal was threatened by the new rivals of oil and nuclear power. Thus England pioneered a change which is still spreading as more and more nations become involved in it, and the search for the raw materials to support this vast activity becomes more widespread.

¶ ADDY, JOHN. *A Coal and Iron Community in the Industrial Revolution.* 1970; LANE, PETER. *The Industrial Revolution.* 1972; POWER, E. G. *A Textile Community in the Industrial Revolution.* 1969

See also COAL; COTTON; ELECTRICITY; RAILWAYS; STEEL; etc.

Infanta: old title of all the daughters, except the eldest, of the kings of Spain and Portugal. Similarly, the title *Infante* was borne by all the sons, except the eldest or the heir apparent. Other titles were carried by the eldest children, e.g. the Spanish heir was *Il principe de Asturias,* prince of Asturias.

See also DAUPHIN; PRINCE OF WALES.

Infantry: part of an army which consists of men who march and fight on foot. In the armies of ancient Greece the infantry carried spears, bows, swords and slings. The Roman foot-soldier, who was disciplined and tough, carried a javelin and sword. The use of cavalry in the 9th century resulted in the infantry being regarded with increasing contempt. Organised foot-soldiers in William the Conqueror's army played an important part in the 1066 invasion, and in the long wars with France the English archer established a special renown for toughness and reliability. A distinction should be made between the unarmed and the armed or semi-armed (in the sense of body armour) infantrymen fighting in close ranks with mobile auxiliaries skirmishing on the flanks.

Highly disciplined formations of massed pikemen, combined with archers, dominated the battlefield for many years. They were in time replaced by the infantryman of the time, armed with musket and, later, the ring bayonet, who usually fought in regular formations such as the "line" or "square". In the late 17th century other types of foot soldier emerged, e.g. grenadiers, who had to get close to the enemy to throw grenades, and light infantry chosen for their marksmanship. When regiments were formed towards the end of the 18th century some British units were trained as marksmen and taught to fight as individuals in open formation. This development was encouraged in the 20th century by the invention of the breech-loading rifle which could be loaded while lying down. Field Marshal Montgomery, the famous British general of World War II, said: "The infantry soldier remains in battle day and night, with little rest and without adequate sleep. He can use very expressive language about the way he has to bear the main burden in battle, but he does it!"

¶ In TREECE, HENRY and OAKESHOTT, EWART. *Fighting Men.* 1963; In TUCKER, ERNEST J. *Soldiers and Armies.* 1967

See also FIRE-ARMS.

Ink: fluid for drawing, writing and printing. Devised long ago in the East, a soluble carbon-and-gum compound is still in use. The Roman architect Vitruvius, writing in the 1st century BC, refers to similar ink-making. Other early writers mention a variety of other ingredients, including the secretion of the cuttle-fish to give "sepia", hawthorn bark and wine. Juan de Yciar (1550) mentions oak-galls and "copperas", i.e. iron sulphate. The last was the ingredient which produced permanent ink and throws light on the original meaning of ink, derived from *incausta*, "burnt in". The British sovereign, on state documents, uses an indestructible black ink.

Inns: houses where, for payment, travellers can obtain meals and accommodation. In many countries, in times past (and as it still is, to some extent, in the Orient) the hospitable reception of strangers was accepted as a religious duty. A traveller had only to knock at the first door along his way to be assured of food and a roof over his head for the night.

As the number of travellers grew, particularly along trade routes and the roads taken by pilgrims journeying to famous shrines, private and amateur goodwill, even eked out by monastic guest-houses, became unequal to the situation. Inns which, in primitive form, had existed from early times, multiplied. The innkeeper, the professional host, came into his own.

The inn at Nottingham quaintly named *The Trip to Jerusalem* is claimed to be the oldest in England. Chaucer (*c.* 1340–1400) in his *Canterbury Tales*, has left us an animated picture of a medieval inn, The Tabard at Southwark, whose landlord was "right a merry man".

Old inns in Southwark, London, 18th–19th century.

When more and better roads were built inns became important way-stations for the changes of horses needed to service mail and stage-coaches. Then came the railways, and it seemed that inns had had their day; but first the bicycle and then the motor-car brought travellers back to the roads. Today inns are busier than ever with a new variety, the motel, added for good measure. If today's inns, mostly owned by large, impersonal companies lack the good fellowship of the past, there was a reverse side to the picture. Many innkeepers were in league with highwaymen, alerting them to the approach of wealthy travellers. Cervantes (1547–1616), the author of *Don Quixote*, indicated a widely held point of view when he made one of his characters declare piously: "Though I am an innkeeper, thank Heaven I am a Christian!"

¶ BATCHELOR, D. *The English Inn*. 1963

Inquest: legal enquiry into the facts of a violent or unexplained death; also, in Britain, enquiry into the discovery of objects which may be declared treasure trove. Inquests are conducted by coroners, officials whose original title, *custos placitorum coronae*, guardian of the pleas of the crown, dates from the 12th century. The early coroners were collectors of fines and forfeitures to the king. Many payments of this kind arose out of a violent death, so the scope of their enquiries broadened to include all the surrounding circumstances. For example, any animal or object which caused a death – a horse which threw its rider, a boat which overturned with fatal consequences – was forfeit to the crown to be applied to charitable uses. These deodands, as they were called, were abolished in 1846 when, it is said, fears arose that a fatal accident on the railways might render an entire train forfeit.

nquisition, The: a special ecclesiastical ·ourt set up to enquire into allegations of ıeresy (*see* separate entry). The inquisiion first came into being in 1232 and vas instituted by the Emperor Frederick I, though Pope Gregory IX immeditely and successfully claimed it as the ›roper province of the Church. Torture, ıs a means of extracting confession, was irst permitted in 1252. This type of :ourt was known in many countries, but he term is especially applied to the Spanish Inquisition, set up with papal ıpproval by Ferdinand and Isabella in 1479, orginally to try Moors and Jews in heir kingdoms, but later confronting Protestants as well. Torquemada (1420–)8) was its first and best known Grand nquisitor. The inquisition was not finally ıbolished in Spain till 1834.

Interdict: decree or sentence by an ecclesiastical body forbidding public worship, some of the sacraments and other rites. It was formerly a device used to punish whole communities and peoples rather than individuals. In 1181 Pope Alexander III placed Scotland under an interdict. France suffered the punishment in 1200 and England in 1209.

International, The: an association of national socialist parties. The first international was founded in 1864 by Karl Marx and Friedrich Engels, but collapsed in 1872. The second international, formed in 1889, looked to the achievement of Socialism by parliamentary means. It was dissolved in 1914 but was revived in 1923 and exists today as the Socialist International. The third international, or Comintern, was founded by Lenin in 1917 and comprised those revolutionary communist groups which had been excluded from the second international. The movement was closely controlled by Russia and was dissolved by Stalin in 1943.

International date-line: imaginary line between the poles, following the 180th meridian except for three deviations, one east to include eastern Siberia, then one west to include the Aleutian Islands with Alaska, and, south of the equator, one east

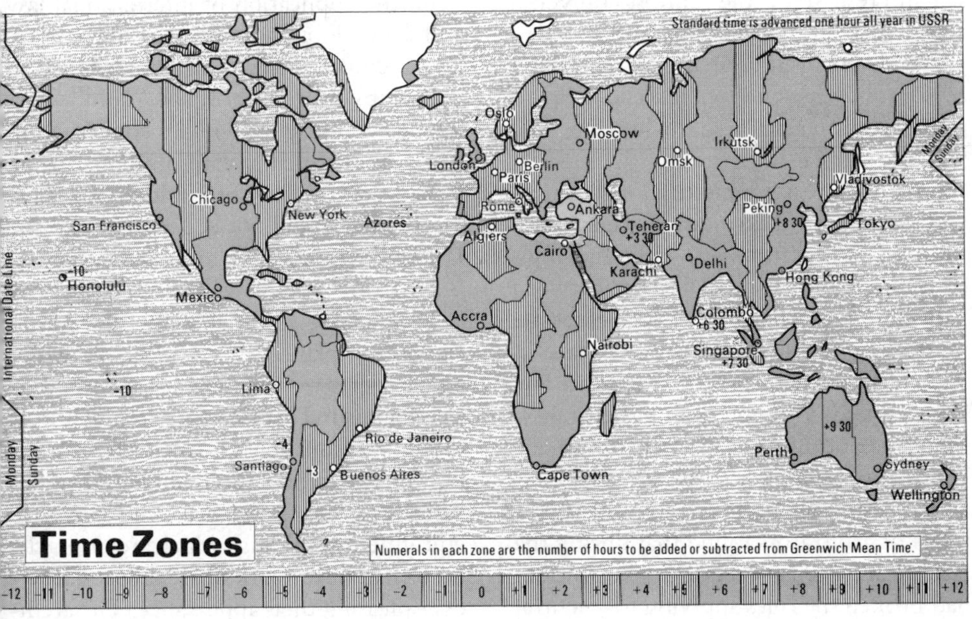

to include certain islands (including Tonga and the Chatham Islands) in the same time zone as New Zealand. When this line is crossed on a westerly course the date is advanced one day; on an easterly course it is put back one day. The line therefore marks the difference in time between East and West.

International law: rules by which sovereign nations agree to be bound. The term was invented by Jeremy Bentham (1748–1832), a man of enormous intellectual output over a vast range of human activity.

Laws regarding the humane treatment of prisoners of war and related matters are given in the Old Testament, but the honour of pursuing the idea in modern times goes to a Dutchman, Hugo Grotius (1583–1645), whose *De Jure Belli et Pacis* (concerning the Law of War and Peace), published in 1625, has had a lasting influence on jurists.

Contacts between nations are regulated by custom, treaties, exchanges of trade, etc., and by co-operation based on mutual self-interest, e.g. the almost universal acceptance of the activities of the Red Cross. Even disinterested goodwill plays a part, as when nations extend help to areas of disaster through earthquake, civil war and similar horrors.

Territorial waters, international waterways, drug traffic, extradition of criminals, immunity of embassies, aircraft, ships, commerce and communication between nations – these are a few of the peacetime matters to which international law is applied. In time of war international law is concerned with questions of neutrality, blockade and even the so-called humane conduct of hostilities.

Two examples are here given. In 1872 a panel of arbitrators found that during the American Civil War (1861–65) Britain had broken the rules applying to a neutral state by supplying the Confederate navy with ships, one of which particularly, the *Alabama*, had wrought havoc among the Yankees. Even though Britain had not actually supplied the guns, she was required to pay an indemnity of $15,500,000 in gold to the US. In 1946 two British destroyers in Corfu Channel struck mines with consequent damage and loss of life. The Albanian government was held to have known of the existence of the mines and to have been under a duty to warn ships in her waters. The compensation payable to the United Kingdom was fixed at nearly £1 million.

Two of the most important steps in the development of a code of international law were the Hague Conferences held in 1899 and 1907, the first being attended by representatives of twenty-six states and the second, forty-four. The 1899 Conference established the International Court of Arbitration at The Hague, the chief town of South Holland, and the Court's headquarters, the Palace of Peace, was dedicated, ironically, the year before World War I broke out.

But the application of international law still depends on the consent of the nations, and decisions under it cannot be enforced except by war – "hot" or "cold". Far-seeing men of goodwill are concerned to bring about such a state of affairs in the world that the Law of Nations shall have a moral basis and not degenerate into the law of the jungle. We are still a very long way from achieving this object, now believed to be essential to the survival of life on this planet.

International style (of architecture)**:** the predominant style of 20th century building. Architecture, unlike painting, sculpture, and music, is for use as well as enjoyment. Buildings which are impractical to live or to work in are failures, however pleasing their appearance. The archiect therefore has a threefold task – to design structures which are not only attractive to the eye but also fit their purpose, and which at the same time correspond to the spiritual needs and aspirations of the society for which they are intended.

We can understand how this works out in practice if we think of the great medieval cathedrals. Strictly speaking, they might be called an appalling waste of labour and resources, since God can be worshipped equally well anywhere. In fact, they filled a deeply felt need. They expressed the religious faith of the age.

The architecture designed in what, for want of a better label, is sometimes called the international style takes its inspiration, not from religion, but from the Industrial Revolution. The label is misleading, since Western architecture has for centuries ignored national boundaries. Allowing for regional variations, Gothic buildings for example, or those in the style of the Italian Renaissance are to be found throughout Europe. What renders the modern international style more of a unity than any style of the past is its use of man-made materials – especially steel, plate-glass and reinforced concrete – which make it independent of a particular locality and pose structural problems that have to be solved in more or less the same way in whatever country the buildings are erected.

Concrete was a material used by the Romans but then neglected for many centuries. Reinforced by having steel bars embedded in it – a technique first developed in France in the mid-19th century – it has become a building material of great strength and versatility. But the first architects to employ concrete acted as if there were something shameful about using it. They did all they could to make it look like stone and added imitation classical ornamentation as a further disguise. One of the first to recognise concrete as a material in its own right was the French architect, Auguste Perret (1874–1954), whose block of flats at 25B Rue Franklin, Paris, built in 1903, is generally accorded the place of honour as the first reinforced concrete building to be erected.

Once the large buildings of a community were its temples, its churches, its castles and palaces. With the growth of population and industry completely new kinds of buildings were called for – factories, railway stations, department stores, blocks of flats. At first, like so much of 19th century architecture, these too were designed in imitation period styles, but gradually a new generation of architects cast off the restraints of outworn tradition and forged a new architecture that, based on new materials and modern technology, was partly engineering. Honesty was their keynote – in design, in materials, in function. Ornament was out, simplicity in. Their buildings revealed their structural framework for all to see.

The pioneers, only a few of whom can be singled out here for special mention, belonged to many countries. In the United States Frank Lloyd Wright (1869–1959) began to design houses with the open-plan interiors and large window spaces that have now become commonplace but were then revolutionary. In Weimar, Germany, at the end of World War I, Walter Gropius (1883–1969) founded the *Bauhaus* (the House of Building), a school which aimed at unifying the arts instead of teaching each in isolation. The *Bauhaus* acquired an international reputation and attracted students from all over the world. In 1930 Mies van der Rohe (b. 1886) became its director.

Nazi Germany was no better a place for freedom in architecture than for freedom in anything else, and the *Bauhaus* did not survive the Hitler regime. In 1938 Mies van der Rohe went to the United States

INTERNATIONAL STYLE: *Above: 25b Rue Franklin, Paris, built by Auguste Perret in 1903. Below: The Bauhaus, Dessau, built by Walter Gropius in 1926.*

(a)

(b)

(c)

Above: (a) The Weissenhof Settlement, Stuttgart. Mies van der Rohe's steel-skeletoned apartment block built in 1927. (b) A house in Wayland, Massachusetts, built by Walter Gropius and Marcel Breuer in 1940. (c) Minerals and Metal Research, University of Chicago, built by Mies van der Rohe in 1943. Below: Aerial view of Brasilia.

Above: the interior of Ronchamp. Below: the interior of Coventry Cathedral.

The Sydney Opera House.

as Director of the Architectural Department of the Illinois Institute of Technology, which he made into a distinguished centre for architectural studies.

Some of these pioneers, in the first flush of their new-found freedom, undoubtedly went too far. Buildings which are stark geometrical shapes, however finely proportioned, may yet lack an essential quality – humanity. In their enthusiasm for the Machine Age some of the architects forgot that architecture is for people.

A great architect who fell into that error less than most was Le Corbusier (1887–1965). Le Corbusier was Swiss, though most of his working life was spent in France. He was a painter, sculptor and author as well as an architect, and perhaps because of this breadth of interest his architectural work, startling as it often is, seems to grow naturally out of the past rather than being consciously opposed to it. The interior of one of his later works, the chapel at Ronchamp, France, has an air of mystery comparable to the churches of the Middle Ages. Designing a church for a secular age poses special problems, and it is interesting to compare the Ronchamp chapel with an English example, Coventry Cathedral, designed by Sir Basil Spence (b. 1907).

There are other welcome signs that the bleakness of the early international style is entering a mellower phase. Despite the unceasing flow of new man-made materials a place is being found increasingly for natural ones. Fantasy, a distinctly human quality, has crept into some of the major architectural projects of recent years – notably in the buildings designed by Oscar Niemeyer (b. 1907) for the astonishing city of Brasilia, carved out of the Brazilian wilderness, and the Sydney, Australia, Opera House, the work of the Danish architect Jørn Utzon (b. 1919) which is poised at the edge of the water like a ship in full sail.

Internationalism: belief in, or movement towards, friendly co-operation between nations; the promotion of a community of interests. The opposite is nationalism which seeks to uphold independence and national unity.

Interregnum: strictly speaking, the period between two reigns, but used also of the interval between two ministries, governments, etc.; in English history, specifically, the interval between the execution of Charles I (30 January 1649) and the restoration of Charles II (8 May 1660).

Investiture question or controversy: the struggle between Church and State for supremacy in medieval Christendom. It arose from the question who had the right to invest bishops with the symbols of their office. Churchmen had gradually been forced to entrust their lands to laymen for protection, and their loyalties were divided between their temporal and spiritual overlords. The main conflict was in the Holy Roman Empire in the 11th century between the Emperor Henry IV and Pope Gregory VII (the former Benedictine monk called Hildebrand), breaking Charlemagne's "bond of perfect charity" between Empire and Papacy, and there were lesser disputes simultaneously in England and France.
See also GREGORY VII.

Ionian civilisation: the qualities and achievements of the Ionian Greeks. Ionia was strictly that part of Asia Minor colonised by Ionian Greeks, but the influence of its civilisation extended to include parts of Aeolis and Caria to north and south. Between the 8th and 5th centuries BC Ionia led Greece in the formation of new ideas. The most striking developments were in literature and natural philosophy or science, but political ideas included a confederacy, and there were religious innovations. In literature Ionia claimed Homer as her own, and other poets of the epic cycle came from such places as Miletus. Lyric poetry flourished in Samos and in the Aeolian island of Lesbos, where Alcaeus and Sappho both lived. In natural philosophy the Ionians were concerned with the origin of the universe. Various ideas were put forward about the constitution of matter by men like Thales, Anaximander and Anaximenes, while Pythagoras and Anaxagoras tried to develop whole philosophic systems. The Ionians were great colonisers, and Miletus especially was in the forefront of the opening of the Black Sea to the Greeks. Not surprisingly they boasted the first western geographer, Hecataeus (fl. *c.* 500 BC). The conquest of the region by the Persians in the first decade of the 5th century may be said to mark the end of an era, but the recovery of Greek influence under Athens and later under Alexander and his successors led to further achievements in Greek thought and Greek art (*see* HELLENISM).

Ionian Islands: the seven small islands of Corfu, Cephalonia, Zante, Cerigo, Santa Maura, Paxos and Ithaca off the west coast of Greece. They figure in the Homeric poems, Ithaca being the birthplace of the hero Ulysses. Corfu, or Corcyra, was colonised by the Corinthians about 734 BC and became a rich and powerful little state. A sea battle between the Corcyrans and the Corinthians in 664 BC, the most ancient recorded sea fight in Greek history, was won by the islanders. Corcyra was drawn into the Peloponnesian War (*see* separate entry), mainly on the Athenian side, and had a chequered history till it fell under Roman rule in 229 BC. The islands were then little heard of for about eight centuries. The Norman rulers of Sicily occupied them

or a while; the Venetians took them over n AD 1401; and the French took them rom the Venetians in 1797. In 1800 they ecame an independent "Septinsular Reublic" under the joint protection of Turkey and Russia. In 1807 they were estored to France. In 1814 the islands vere placed under British protection and dministered by British high commisioners until 1864, when they were ncorporated in the kingdom of Greece.

ran: modern name for Persia. With the verthrow of the Sassanian dynasty in AD 641 by the Arabs and the conversion f the country to Islam, the history of ncient Persia ended. A succession of lynasties battled for control of Iran. Turkish invaders provided the Ghaznavid nd Seljuk dynasties. In 1219 the Mongol Genghis Khan invaded Iran. At first lestructive, the Mongol invasion gave ran a further dynasty of constructive ulers soon well assimilated to Iranian civilisation. The Safavid dynasty made the Shi'i form of Islam the state religion. Conflict with the Turkish Empire was recurrent. Under the Qajar dynasty pressure from Russia, seeking a warm-water port, was countered by British pressure concerned for the safety of India. European influence and capital increasingly entered Iran. A constitution was adopted in 1906 and a parliament established. A coup d'état in 1921 made Reza Khan, a cavalry officer, ruler of Iran, and in 1925 he founded the Pahlavi dynasty and worked for modernisation, westernisation and freedom from foreign interference. In 1941, during World War II, Britain and Russia invaded Iran, fearing German influence. Mohammed Reza continued his father's policies and attempted to westernise the country. A violent reaction forced him into exile in 1979 when Iran came under the domination of the Ayatollah Khomeini and turned back to fundamentalist Islamic principles. Since 1980 Iran has been at war with Iraq. *See map* p. 470.

Iraq: Arab republic of West Asia, with the medieval city of Baghdad as its capital. Formerly consisting of the Mesopotamian provinces of the Turkish Empire, after Turkish defeat in World War I it was internationally agreed that Mesopotamia, which had fallen under British occupation, should form a new self-governing state. Britain accepted in 1920 a League of Nations mandate to give aid and guidance to Iraq till it was ready for complete independence. In 1921 the Amir Faisal was recognised as king. In 1932 Britain's mandate ended in spite of many elements of instability in the country including frontier trouble with Turkey and Saudi Arabia and risings among the strongly nationalist Kurds. Faisal's death in 1933 was followed by

unrest. Ghazi I was succeeded in 1939 by the infant Faisal II. Appeals by extremists for Nazi aid led to British intervention during World War II and until 1947. In 1948 Iraq, with Egypt and other Arab states, invaded Palestine but was forced to withdraw. With her own rising fortunes based on petroleum sales, Iraq was not keen to accept Egyptian dominance of the Arab League, founded in 1945, and entered into the Baghdad Pact of 1955 with Turkey, Britain, Pakistan and Iran. In 1958 the monarchy was overthrown and Iraq became a republic. Her growing oil wealth brought prosperity and allowed rapid development. Iraq adopted a generally radical stance in Arab affairs. In 1980 she went to war with her neighbour Iran.

Ireland: the second largest of the British Isles, just over one-third the size of its richer neighbour, Britain. The mountainous west has rain and gales from the Atlantic, and there is widespread bog and heathland in central Ireland. Most of the people live in the richer east and north. Ireland today is divided between Northern Ireland and the Irish Republic, but a much earlier division was between the five ancient kingdoms of Meath, Ulster, Munster, Leinster and Connacht. Almost everybody speaks English, but the Republic hopes to revive the Irish (Gaelic) language, spoken widely in the west.

Much evidence of Ireland's past can be seen, prehistoric cemeteries, castles, monasteries and peasant homes from other centuries. There are few industries or spreading towns to obliterate them, and

Irishmen take great pride in their heritage.

Remote from most European progress and civilisation, and often dominated by Britain, Ireland has usually been relatively backward. Yet 2,000 years before Christ gold and bronze helped to make Irish chieftains powerful: some of them lie in massive stone tombs under great mounds of earth in the bend of the Boyne River, thirty miles [48.28 kilometres] north of Dublin.

While Romans occupied Britain, there lived in Ireland Celtic warriors whose legendary exploits (like mighty Cuchulainn's single-handed defence of Ulster) were often retold by later Irishmen. Some raided Roman Britain, and in the 5th century they carried off a boy named Patrick. Patrick later escaped but returned to spread Christianity, and thereafter Ireland became a centre of Christian learning. Great stone preaching crosses were set up, carved with vivid biblical scenes. Monastic settlements spread, clustered beehive huts with little churches and tall round bell-towers. Some became famous universities, some produced richly illustrated gospel manuscripts like the famous Book of Kells. Irish monks carried Christianity to Scotland (St Columba), northern Europe (St Columbanus), and even, according to legend, America (St Brendan).

Then the Vikings came to raid, pillage and finally settle, founding cities and ports like Dublin. In 1014 the high king Brian Boru, overlord of all Ireland, broke their power at Clontarf, now a Dublin suburb. But Brian himself was slain, and thereafter Irish chiefs fought each other incessantly. In 1169 a king of Leinster, seeking aid from England, offered the powerful Earl of Pembroke, known as Strongbow, his daughter in marriage and succession to his kingdom. Strongbow's prize brought many Norman-English adventurers in his footsteps to establish lordships of their own; but often their descendants adopted Irish ways, and, though English kings claimed to be Lords of Ireland, only the land around Dublin (the "Pale") was firmly under their rule. Beyond the Pale hundreds of Irish and Anglo-Irish chiefs lived in strong tower-keeps.

The Tudors resolved to end this disorder, especially since most Irishmen remained defiantly Roman Catholic. Irish resistance to Elizabeth centred on Hugh O'Neill, Earl of Tyrone (*c.* 1540–1616), but at length (1601) his army was destroyed near the little south coast port of Kinsale. Thereafter Scots and English were encouraged to settle in "plantations", particularly in Ulster, to develop industry and commerce, spread protestantism, and "civilise" the Irish. Twice Irish Catholics rebelled, but first Cromwell and later William III defeated them, and after the battle of the Boyne (1690) harsh penal laws made it difficult for Catholics to hold land or office. Some, the "wild geese", emigrated to seek better fortune.

Ireland remained unstable, often rebellious. In 1800 the British Government tried a new solution: abolishing the separate Irish parliament, it created a single United Kingdom. Unfortunately this often meant neglect of Ireland's special problems. When the potato crop, on which Irish peasants depended, failed in 1845 and 1846 there followed a Great Famine in which over a million died, and many Irish felt bitterly that a government in Dublin might have averted disaster. Thereafter a swelling stream of emigrants crossed the Atlantic; enterprising Irishmen felt their best chances lay far from their impoverished homeland.

In 1916 Irish nationalists began their final struggle to separate from Britain. They succeeded, partly because world (particularly American) opinion was sympathetic, partly because a recent movement to revive Irish culture and language had caught the imagination of young men, turning them into fiery patriots. Guerrilla warfare dragged on until 1921, when the British agreed to Irish self-government, though without the Protestant north-east. The Free State, later (1937) called Eire or the Irish Republic. It left the Commonwealth in 1949. Ireland enjoyed moderate prosperity during the 1960s and 1970s and joined the EEC in 1973. In recent years her leaders have endeavoured to work with British governments in seeking a solution to the problem of Northern Ireland.

See also the next two entries and GLADSTONE; HOME RULE; NORTHERN IRELAND; O'CONNELL; PARNELL.

Irish Republic: republic in north-west Europe. It includes five-sixths of Ireland's area, though only two-thirds of its population. It has been completely separated politically from Great Britain since 1949. Ninety-five per cent of its people are Roman Catholics.

There were always many Irishmen who wanted their country to be separated from Britain. The Irish, they argued, were a distinct race with their own way of life and language, which ought to be protected and preserved. In 1858 they formed a secret Irish Republican Brotherhood (often called the Fenians, after a band of legendary Irish warriors). Their hopes of starting a rising against the British failed, but their secret organisation remained. It was reinvigorated by Tom Clarke (1857–1916), a Fenian who returned in 1907, after long imprisonment and exile, to a little tobacconist's shop in

A barricade in Great Brunswick Street, Dublin, during the Easter Rising of 1916.

ublin. At Easter 1916 the republicans arted their long-planned armed rising y seizing the General Post Office in ublin; and their Commandant-General, adraic Pearse (1879–1916), a poet and hoolmaster who passionately desired to eate a truly Irish Ireland, announced "... we hereby proclaim the Irish Republic as a Sovereign Independent State".

Only about 2,000 men and women took part in the Easter Rising; It was suppressed, but the prompt execution of the leaders roused much anger and sympathy. Three years later the Sinn Fein (Ourselves) Party, led by Eamon de Valera (b. 1882), set up *Dail Eireann,* an independent Irish parliament. Ultimately Britain had to accept a self-governing Irish Free State (1922), which in 1949 became the Republic. *See also* HOME RULE, etc.

amon De Valera in 1957.

Irish Republican Army (IRA): the illegal force seeking an all-Ireland republic. From 1919 to 1921 it fought a terrorist war against the British; then its leaders, rejecting the agreement partitioning Ireland, made bitter civil war on the Free State. Since 1923 its main activities have been directed against Northern Ireland.

Iron Age: era of iron implements, beginning in Asia Minor about 1400 BC with the discovery of iron-smelting. Compared with bronze, iron tools and weapons could be produced economically. Invasions by Celtic peoples brought iron to southern Europe *c.* 1000 BC and northern Europe some five hundred years later.

The Iron Age is often considered as falling into two separate cultures: the earlier called the Hallstatt, after the Austrian village where discoveries were made that well illustrate the transition from bronze to iron, and the La Tène, from an archaeological site in Switzerland which exemplifies the later Iron Age, with more sophisticated implements and ornaments, agricultural systems, etc. In archaeological terms this ends about the 1st century AD, though in practice the Iron Age is still a reality, despite some attempts at new terms such as the Age of Steel and even of Plastics.

Iroquois: original Red Indian inhabitants of the east coast of the USA. During the colonial period the Iroquois were the native American people of the greatest political importance. The name has been adopted for the group of tribes who spoke a similar language and who lived mainly in the area now known as New York State. These tribes (the Mohawks, Oneidas, Onondagas, Cayugas, Senecas and Tuscaroras) practised maize agriculture and lived in villages, which in time of unrest were palisaded. Warfare against their enemies, the Algonkins and the Hurons, was frequent and ruthless, captives being tortured, enslaved or adopted. According to tradition Hiawatha, a Mohawk, induced the five tribes (the Tuscaroras did not join the confederacy until 1715) to form a league which in 1570 united them in common council for both peaceful and warlike

activities. It came to be known as th League of the Six Nations. From the fir the Iroquois were consistent and bitt enemies of the French. They traded wit and fought for the British settlers, an after the success of the American Revo lution in 1782, they continued the association by migrating in large numbe to the Ontario province of British Canad

---

Isabella I (1451–1504)**:** Queen of Castil Her energy, patriotism and moral influ ence raised the country into becomin "the nursery of virtue and of generou ambition". One example of her insigh was her recognition of the worth Columbus's schemes and her offer t pawn her jewellery to finance them Treasury support was not forthcoming.

Islam: the religion of the 555 millio Muslims who inhabit Asia and Afric today. All these people follow the teach ıgs of Mohammed (AD 570–632), and so lam is the most recent of all the world's ıajor religions. The word Islam means submission" because Muslims submit ıemselves to the will of God. Muslims :e sometimes called Mohammedans, but ıis is not strictly correct because they do ot worship Mohammed. They believe ıat he was an ordinary man but a great ·acher: a prophet who was inspired by iod, like Moses.

Mohammed's teaching, which after his eath was written down in the Koran, is ery simple: all men are brothers, and all 'ho believe in Allah are equal. Muslims ıust respect parents, be generous to the oor, be kind to slaves and animals. They ıust not drink wine or make idols to 'orship. They must pray to Allah regu-ırly every day, and for one month every ear they must fast between sunrise and ınset. They were told that Islam must e spread, if necessary by a holy war. This mple and aggressive faith appealed to ıe Arab peoples, and within thirty years ıey had conquered Persia and Palestine, ıpturing both Babylon and Jerusalem. 'he religion of Islam easily replaced 'hristianity in all of North Africa and arts of Spain, and it also spread East, to 'urkish tribesmen and to many of the eoples of northern India. From India ıissionaries went to Malaya, Java and ıe Philippines.

The many peoples who were combined ı Islam created together a new civilisa-on, with its religious centre at Mecca and s richest city at Baghdad. The knowledge f the Greeks was recorded in Arabic, and ıe study of medicine, mathematics and ;tronomy flourished in many universities om Cordova in Spain to Cairo and 'imbuktu in Africa.

The capture of Constantinople by the urks in 1453 suggested for a time that lam might be able to destroy Christian urope. For a time the expansion of Christian Europe put Islam on the defensive. In the period since the end of Empires there has been a resurgence of militant Islam. Throughout the Middle East a revival, often fundamentalist as in Iran, has become one of the most potent forces of the 1980s.

¶ EL DROUBIE, RIADH. *Islam.* 1970; TAYLOR, JOHN B. *Thinking about Islam.* 1971

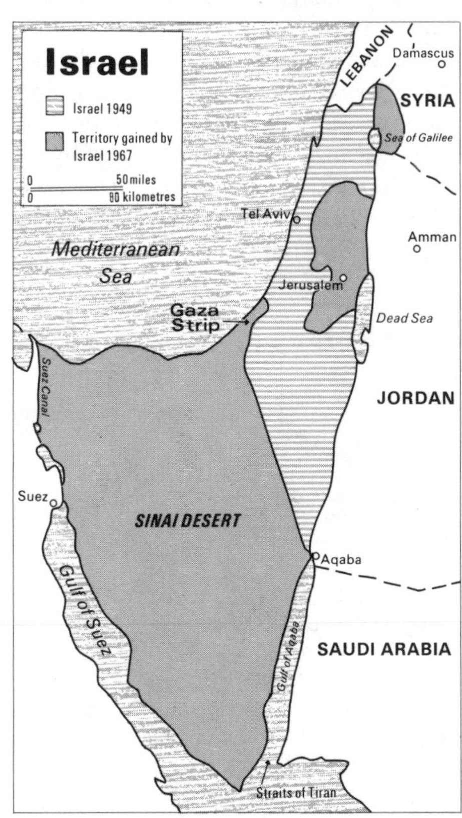

Israel, Republic of: state in south-west Asia. The establishment of the state of Israel was proclaimed on 14 May 1948, on the departure of the British Palestine high commissioner. Chaim Weizmann was first president and David Ben-Gurion first prime minister. The adjacent Arab states of Egypt, Jordan, Iraq, Syria and

Lebanon immediately attacked the new state. There were many more Arabs than Jews in Palestine and they looked on the land as rightly theirs. Jordanian Arabs took over the Jewish quarter in the old city of Jerusalem. A United Nations mediator, Count Folke Bernadotte, obtained a cease-fire, but fighting was resumed by the Arabs, and Bernadotte was assassinated. Armistice agreements were reached in 1949, and Israel was admitted to the United Nations. The new republic organised itself rapidly but in a state of uneasy peace. There was sharp controversy over the status of the divided city of Jerusalem, where the Jewish holy places were in Jordanian Arab hands. Arab feeling against Israel was increased by the existence of a large population of Arab refugees from Israel, who lived and multiplied in camps, mostly on Jordanian territory. In 1956 and 1967 Israel fough wars with her Arab neighbours in bot of which she was clearly victorious. I the Yom Kippur War of 1973 her Ara opponents performed better militaril although Israel held her own with mas sive US assistance. Following Presider Sadat's peace initiative and the Cam David agreement of 1979, Israel restore Sinai to Egypt but kept the Golan heigh and the West Bank. In 1982 Israel occu pied southern Lebanon in a move de signed to force the PLO to abandon i bases in that country.

See also HERZL; JEWS; JORDAN; PALESTIN

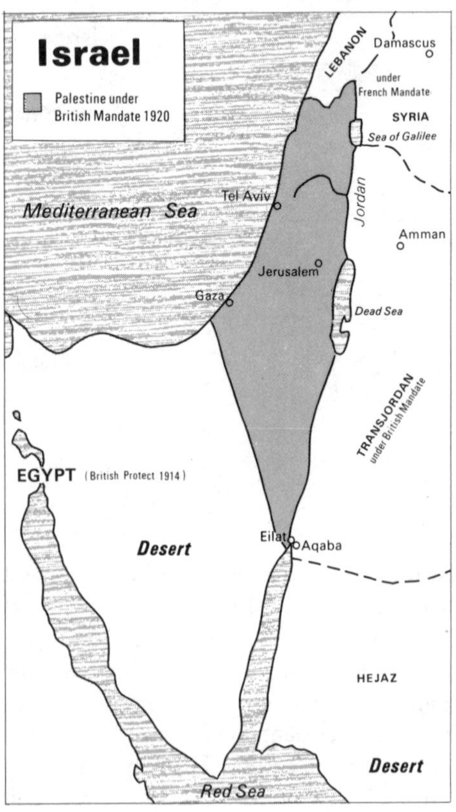

Italy: republic in south-western Europ Italy is a new nation. She was political united, with Rome as her capital, recently as the year 1870, the year whe modern Germany became a nation-stat the unification of both countries followe on the defeat in that year of France b Prussia.

Yet it would be quite wrong to think Italy as a new country. Her capital city the oldest of western Europe, having bee the capital of that mighty empire (*s* ROMAN EMPIRE) that extended over mo of Europe and gave civilisation, unity an justice to the continent during the fir centuries of the Christian era. But durin the 5th century AD this empire was unde mined by the waves of barbarian invade who poured into Europe from the nort and from the east, and it was a barbaria Odoacer, who was proclaimed king Rome in the year 476. But the ancie civilisation lived on longer in Italy than did in the rest of western Europe: it live on in her buildings, in her splendid a and architecture, in her roads, and al in her laws and institutions. It was onl gradually that this civilisation was broke down and replaced by one that we ca recognise as new. Not until the 12t century do we find fully developed th

The medieval walled city of Florence from a fresco by the School of Vasari.

new order of society which we now call the Middle Ages, or medieval civilisation, a civilisation that reached its full flowering in the 13th and 14th centuries and which was more advanced and richer in the cities of northern Italy than in any other part of Europe.

This new medieval civilisation in Italy grew up in independent city-states such as the industrial city republics of Florence and Siena, or the merchant city republics of Genoa and Venice with their enormous overseas trade carried in ships that sailed as far as London or Hamburg or Constantinople. It grew up, too, in cities that were ruled by the Church, especially Rome, where the popes were the rulers, and Ravenna. And it grew likewise in the cities at the foot of the Alps which controlled the passes into northern Europe, cities that grew rich on the overland trade with the rest of the continent. The most powerful of these cities was Milan.

By the 16th century Italy had passed into the period we now know as the Renaissance (the age of the *rebirth* of classical art and thought), and it was then that these Italian cities reached their greatest wealth and splendour, with artists and architects such as Leonardo da Vinci, Raphael, and Michelangelo whose fame has never been surpassed. But, while the peninsula was thus growing wealthy and leading Europe in art and culture, it remained politically divided. Whereas by the 16th century Italy's neighbours to the west, Spain, France and England, had all achieved their political unity, under kings who ruled from their capital cities of Madrid, Paris and London, there was nobody who occupied an all-powerful position of that kind in Italy. The southern part of the peninsula (Naples and Sicily) had fallen into the hands of Spain, much of the central part was ruled by the Pope, and in northern Italy the kings of France, in their efforts to gain control over wealthy Milan, were in constant conflict with the Habsburg family which ruled over Spain and Austria. Venice still remained a proud and independent republic, but she was beginning to lose her dominant position in the world of trade as the discovery of America and of the overseas routes to Asia favoured those countries, like England and Portugal, that bordered on the Atlantic Ocean. Florence, the most advanced city in Italy in knowledge and the arts, was still ruled by the powerful family of the Medici, under whom she had attained her greatest glory in the previous century, but Florence, like Milan, was now becoming subject to French influence and even French control.

Thus the Italians, though they felt they belonged to a "nation", and one with a glorious history, failed to give political unity to their peninsula despite the geographical unity that had been given to it by the sea and by the Alps, and despite their enjoyment of a common language and so many common traditions. Working against that unity were the foreign armies (Spanish in the south, French or Austrian in the north) that ravaged her countryside and plundered her cities, the presence of the States of the Church which, by running across the centre of the peninsula, divided it in half, and the fierce spirit of independence of the many republics and principalities to the north of those states. These factors, which kept Sicily, Naples, Rome, Florence, Venice, Milan, Genoa and her other cities separated, may have favoured the extraordinary cultural vitality those cities showed, but it was not good for the future of the peninsula at a time when the future lay, in Europe, with the large states.

In other countries, and notably in France and England, the 17th and 18th centuries were a time of rapid political and economic progress, but in Italy they were a time of decline and decay, when trade was stifled by the barriers, economic as well as political, between her different states. And these barriers remained until the end of the 18th century when Napoleon (*see* separate entry) invaded the peninsula, destroying the existing governments down as far as Rome, and even creating a shortlived "Kingdom of Italy", subservient to France. But the Napoleonic adventure was brief: by the year 1815 the conqueror was defeated and in exile, and the Congress of Vienna was rearranging the map of Europe and restoring the old ruling families to Italy. Moreover this congress, by placing Venice and Milan, and the rich intervening country of the valley of the river Po, which is known as the plain of Lombardy, under the dominion of Austria, ensured that powerful foreign armies would be watching to prevent any national movements in the peninsula that might end by uniting Italians and depriving Austria of rich and coveted territories.

Napoleon's rearrangement of the peninsula had shown that the many ruling families could be swept away, that the barriers between the states could be broken down, and that Italians could, if they would, give political expression to the feeling that was now growing amongst them that they were truly a nation and should control their own destiny. It was in the year 1831 that a young patriot from Genoa, Giuseppe Mazzini, became leader of a secret society called Young Italy, sworn to win the unity and freedom of the fatherland: he was driven into exile, but from London he carried on ceaseless propaganda. In 1848, when democratic revolutions broke out all over Europe, there were risings promoted by Young Italy in many Italian cities, and although these were quickly suppressed they gave birth at Rome and at Venice to republics that lasted for several months.

The thriving port of Genoa in the 1880s.

Austrian power, however, remained a formidable obstacle, and it was only when Camillo Cavour, a statesman at Turin (the capital of the little Italian kingdom of Savoy, at the foot of the Alps), persuaded the French Emperor Napoleon III to fight the Austrians in 1859 that the foreigner was driven out of Lombardy and it became possible to unite northern Italy. In the following year the hero Giuseppe Garibaldi, with his famous volunteers called the "Thousand", invaded Sicily and destroyed the power of the Neapolitan king in that island and at Naples, after which Garibaldi handed over southern Italy to the new king of the north, Cavour's king, Victor Emmanuel of Savoy. In this way the whole peninsula at last became united save for Venice (still retained by Austria) and Rome (still retained by the Pope) which were gained in the years 1866 and 1870, respectively. By 1870 Victor Emmanuel was ruling at Rome as king of United Italy.

The difficulties faced by the new kingdom were very great. Italy was not rich in those raw materials, coal and iron, which, in the latter part of the 19th century, were very important; nor had she yet developed the hydroelectric and chemical industries which strengthened her economy in the 20th century. In the period between 1870 and World War I (1914–18) Italy was much poorer than the other large European nations. These were the years of imperialism, especially in Africa: to compete with France, England and Germany in Africa, Italy had to spend a great deal of money on armaments, and this she could not afford. Taxation bore very heavily on southern Italy and especially Sicily, where the peasants were (as they remain today) very poor, and the new national government was sometimes harsher than the old government had been. Many Sicilians

The Galleries Vittorio Emanuele in Milan.

and Neapolitans emigrated to Africa or America in search of a better life.

Thus the new political order found little popular support in Italy, and matters became worse when, after allying with France and England in World War I, the country emerged victorious over Austria but with little to show for her victory save heavy casualties, increased poverty and increased subservience to the western nations. Amidst a discontent and a contempt for the existing government a party of "toughs", dressing themselves in black shirts and organised and led by the ex-socialist Benito Mussolini, seized power in October 1922 and established a new national government called fascist because it adopted as its symbol the *fasces* or bundle of rods carried by the lictors who enforced order in ancient Rome.

Mussolini ruled Italy for twenty-one years, satisfying national aspirations by conquering Ethiopia and Albania but rashly defying France and England and allying himself with Adolf Hitler (*see* separate entry) who had won power in a similar way in Germany in 1933. This alliance imperilled Italy by bringing her into ever closer dependence on her more powerful neighbour and finally ruined her by involving her in 1940 on Hitler's side in World War II. Defeated in Africa and invaded from the south by the British and American armies, the country became the scene of fierce fighting between the allies and the retreating Germans till peace came at last in the spring of 1945, and enraged Italian patriots seized and murdered Mussolini. His fall was followed by the setting up, by popular vote, of a republic, and the restoration of parliamentary government at Rome.

Since then Italy, ruled mostly by her Christian Democratic party, has surprised the world by the speed and extent of her recovery, achieving an "economic miracle" that has greatly reduced unemployment and raised the standard of living of a large part of her population while yet leaving much of the south, and especially Sicily, in poverty. Increasingly, in recent years, the political and economic hopes of the country have become centred on closer European unity. Population: 56,345,000 (1983).

¶ EPSTEIN, SAM and BERYL. *The First Book of Italy* 1965

See also FASCISM; FLORENCE; FLORENTINE ART; GARIBALDI; MAZZINI; MUSSOLINI; NAPOLEON; PAPACY; RENAISSANCE; etc.

Ivan: the name of several outstanding Russian rulers. Ivan I, who died in 1341, was grand duke of Vladimir. With the help of his overlord, the Tartar khan of the Golden Horde, Ivan conquered Moscow and moved his headquarters there. Ivan III (1440–1505) broke away from Tartar control, extended his territories, drafted a new code of laws and established diplomatic and trading relations with western countries. He married Sophia

Palaeologus, niece of the last Byzantine emperor. This marriage was later regarded as giving to the Russian Tsars some moral claim to be the successors of the Eastern Roman Emperors. It was Ivan IV (1530–84), known as Ivan the Terrible, who was the first Russian ruler to assume the title of Tsar of Russia. Succeeding as a child, he took over personal rule at the age of fourteen and was proclaimed Tsar of Moscow, or Muscovy. He added Kazan, Astrakhan and western Siberia to his dominions and struggled to reduce the power of the boyars, or nobles. He encouraged trade and was the first Russian ruler to make a treaty with England. In later life he showed violence, cruelty and mental instability and murdered his own son, also called Ivan.

Ivan the Terrible and his dying son, by Pepin.

Ivory: the hard dentine forming the tusks of certain animals. The tusks of elephants or mammoths form true ivory, although the horn of the narwhal, walrus and hippopotamus is frequently included in the term. The substance is strong and suitable for carving.

The earliest ivory carving known, 30,000 years old, is a woman's head, two inches [51 millimetres] high, discovered in Czechoslovakia. Ivory objects have been found in Egyptian and Etruscan

14th-century ivory cover for writing tablets showing a Hawking Party.

tombs, and the Greeks frequently decorated their statues with ivory and gold: such work is termed "chryselephantine".

Ivory is mentioned in the Bible, and in medieval times it was often used in church regalia. The Japanese carved ivory buttons in the form of delightful figurines of men and animals and for *netsuke,* the much-prized ornamental toggles for attaching purses etc. to belts.

Ivory Coast: republic in West Africa and a former French colony. In the 19th century the French gradually established a colony on the Ivory Coast of West Africa which they valued for its palm-oil. Despite repeated risings they held on, and today it is one of the most prosperous of the French-speaking countries of Africa, largely because its conservative, pro-French leadership has attracted a large share of French aid. After leading a nationalist movement against French assimilation, the present President Houphouet-Boigny (b. 1905) decided more could be achieved by working with the government than against it, and until the Ivory Coast became independent in 1960 he served in successive ministries in France.

Jackson, Andrew (1767–1845): seventh president of the USA. He was a Tennessee lawyer who was elected to the Senate in 1797. He withdrew from public life in 1806, partly because of his fiery reputation as a duellist and partly because of a dispute with President Thomas Jefferson (1743–1826). He became a popular hero in 1815 when he repulsed a British landing at New Orleans in the Anglo-American war (1812–14). He was elected president of the USA in 1828, securing re-election in 1832 (when he was nominated by the newly styled "Democratic Party"). Jackson, nicknamed "Old Hickory", won support as a hero of the wild frontier, the image of the new American common man and a vigorous supporter of states' rights against federalism. His administration was marked by wars with the Indians, the expansion in Texas and his attacks on the Bank of the US.

Jackson, Thomas Jonathan (1824–63): American general. Thomas Jonathan Jackson, commonly known as "Stonewall Jackson", was an outstanding Confederate general during the American Civil War (1861–65). He received his military training at West Point Military Academy and was commissioned as a second lieutenant of artillery. After serving with distinction in Mexico he was appointed to a professorship at the Virginia Military Institute. When the Civil War broke out he became the ablest of General Robert E. Lee's generals. In him were combined a deep religious fervour (he was a devout Presbyterian whose men compared him with Oliver Cromwell) and a fiercely aggressive fighting spirit. He was a master of rapid movement and surprise tactics. Jackson's determined resistance to the onslaught of General George B. McClellan at the first battle of Bull Run (July 1861) earned him the nickname "Stonewall". He then led the Confederate troops on a series of successful raids in the vicinity of Washington. He achieved with Lee a major victory at Chancellorsville, but at the moment of victory he was accidentally wounded by his own troops (2 May 1863) and died of his wounds eight days later.

Jacobean style: term applied to English architecture, furniture and interior decoration of the early 17th century. King James I of England reigned 1603–25, and the adjective derives from *Jacobus,* the Latin form of his name. Since, however, architecture and furniture do not change their shapes overnight with the accession of a new monarch, much of what, for convenience, we label Jacobean was produced during Elizabeth's reign, or long after James I had departed the scene.

It was an age when, for the first time, houses were becoming homes – that is, more than a roof over one's head or a fortress against one's enemies. Comfort became a consideration, and so chairs began to be upholstered, tables draped with carpets, and beds covered with draperies.

Oak, strong and well-suited to what were still rude and boisterous times, was the wood most used for the presses, court-cupboards (once not cupboards at all, but two open shelves supported by columns) and tables on carved, bulbous legs. Chairs sprouted baluster and bobbin legs, and barley sugar twist mouldings became popular. There was little elegance but much gusto, a feeling of craftsmen enjoying the work of their hands. In great houses chimney pieces and splendid staircases were adorned with carvings of bursting vitality. Rooms were panelled with plaster friezes, and ceilings decorated with strapwork often picked out in colour.

Outside, many Jacobean buildings were often something of a hotchpotch. The

The Jacobean style in furniture: Above left: an oval dropleaf table with "barley-sugar twist" legs. Below left: stool with bulbous legs. Above: an ornately carved high-backed chair.

architectural ideas of the Renaissance, with their emphasis on classical forms, took time to cross the Channel. It took an architect of genius, Inigo Jones (1573–1652) (*see* separate entry), to evolve a style that, based on the Italian, was yet wholly English.

¶ DONCASTER, ISLAY. *Elizabethan and Jacobean Home Life.*

Jacobins: one of several political clubs formed during the French Revolution. They derived their name from the old convent in Paris where they used to meet and which had previously belonged to a religious order of that name. Originally standing for reasonable constitutional reform, they became the most extreme of the Revolutionaries. Led by Robespierre, they were responsible for the September massacres of 1792, for the guillotining of King Louis XVI in 1793, for the setting up of the Committee of Public Safety, and for the Reign of Terror in 1793–4. In 1794, with the execution of Robespierre himself, the extreme violence of the Revolution was spent, and the Jacobins faded from the scene. The name "Jacobin" subsequently came to signify anyone holding extreme political views.

Jacobites: supporters of the exiled house of Stuart (from Latin *Jacobus,* James). James II of England (1633–1701), a Roman Catholic, was deposed by the Revolution of 1688 which placed Protestant William III (1650–1702) and Mary (1662–94) on the throne. After James II's death, his son James Francis Edward Stuart (1688–1766) became, in the eyes of the Jacobites, the rightful king. To his opponents he was the Pretender (later the Old Pretender, to distinguish him from his son) or, derisively, Old Mr Melancholy.

Most Jacobites were Catholics. A majority were Scots, since the Stuarts originated in Scotland. In 1715 James led an

Bonnie Prince Charlie *by Petrie*.

unsuccessful rising to claim his birthright. In 1745–46 his son, Charles Edward Stuart (1720–88) – Bonnie Prince Charlie or the Young Pretender according to where loyalties lay – met with no better luck. The Jacobite defeat at Culloden was less a battle than a massacre.

Gradually Jacobitism ceased to be a live issue and became a sentimental attachment to a lost cause. Even so, during the 18th and 19th centuries and up to the reign of Edward VII (reigned 1901–10), finger bowls were not used at royal meals for a curious reason. Jacobites liked to drink the health of "the king over the water" (i.e. in exile across the English Channel), and no monarch of the Hanoverian line, apparently, wished to run the risk of having treasonable toasts drunk surreptitiously over the finger bowls on his own dinner table. George III was, however, generous enough to employ the sculptor Canova to erect a monument to James Stuart in St Peter's, Rome.

The present Stuart heir, if he cared to press his claim, is the Duke of Bavaria. Organisations such as the Royal Stuart Society still keep alive a token Jacobitism.

¶ STEVENSON, WILLIAM. *The Jacobite Rising of 1745*. 1968

Jacquerie: the name given in 1358 to an uprising of oppressed peasants against the nobles, near Beauvais, north of Paris. The work is said by some to derive from "Jacques Bonhomme" by which the nobles commonly referred to any peasant, and, by others, from a garment characteristically worn by peasants. The revolt was put down with great ferocity, and the name "jacquerie" subsequently came to signify any uprising suppressed with cruelty and violence.

Jahangir, or **Jehangir** (1569–1627): Mogul emperor. "Jahangir", the title he assumed on his succession, means "conqueror of the world". Though a man of ability and a patron of art and literature, his rule became a dissolute tyranny, with effective government in the hands of his avaricious Persian wife Nur Jahan.

Jainism: a sect which broke away from Hinduism, at about the same time as Buddhism, in the 5th century BC. It is strongest in western India among traders of some wealth, which gives it an importance greater than its numbers (*c.* $1\frac{1}{2}$ million). In its strictest form, however, it objects to any material property.

Jamaica: island and independent sovereign state in the West Indies. It was discovered by Columbus in 1494 and passed under Spanish rule. The native Arawaks were exterminated and negro slaves introduced. The English captured Jamaica in the Cromwellian period, and from 1661 it was ruled by a governor and council. Later a legislative assembly was established. British right to the island was confirmed by Spain in 1670. The island became a major region for piracy, slave trading and smuggling because it was close to Spanish America. French attacks were withstood in 1694 and 1782. In 1807 the slave trade was abolished by

A view of Port Antonia, Jamaica in 1770.

ritain, and all slaves were set free after 833. Coffee, sugar and, in the late 19th entury, bananas, were the main exports.)uring and after the ending of slavery here was much friction between the ocal landowners and the British government, with local threats of secession to the Jnited States of America. There were lso several slave revolts. A period of lirect colonial rule from 1866 brought nany reforms. Representative government was progressively restored from 884. In 1944 universal adult franchise vas introduced. In 1958 Jamaica entered he Federation of the West Indies, but n 1962, when the Federation was dissolved, Jamaica became a separate state nd member of the Commonwealth.

See also CARIBBEAN; WEST INDIES, etc.

---

amestown: first English permanent ettlement in America. In May 1607 about hundred colonists, financed by the London Company of Merchants, landed t Chesapeake Bay, sailed up the river, which they called the James in honour of he ruling monarch of England, and made he first permanent English settlement on the American mainland. The park-like country, with its splendid trees and rich vegetation, gave every prospect of success for the settlers, but the subtropical climate was hotter than that to which they had been accustomed, the diseases more virulent, and the Indians hostile. The settlement barely survived the difficulties of its early years, but the determination of Captain John Smith (1580–1731) and, later, of the newly appointed governor of the colony (called Virginia), Lord De La Warr (1577–1618), saved the settlement from being abandoned. Its success was assured only when tobacco and sugar became the staple crops and slaves were introduced to cultivate them.

¶ GILL, W. J. C. *Captain John Smith and Virginia.* 1968

Jamestown in 1622, fifteen years after the first permanent settlement in America.

Janissaries or **janizaries:** the former military force constituting the standing army of the Ottoman Empire. The original meaning of the word was "new troops". At first a bodyguard composed of forcibly conscripted Christian children, the force gained so many privileges that there was great competition for enrolment. So strong did the janissaries become that they were a constant threat to the security of the sultans and, after an existence of 500 years, were extinguished in 1826 after an armed revolt.

Janissaries in fantastic headgear.

Japan: empire in East Asia; capital Tokyo. Its island location gave Japan an isolated and inward-turned history. Once inhabited by the Ainu, a Caucasian race, Japan was populated by invaders of Mongol origin from Korea and China before the Christian era. Arts and crafts were brought from China and also the first system of writing. The earliest historical writings tell of a mythical divine origin of Japan and of the imperial family. The first mythical emperor of Japan, Jimmu Tenno, was said to have been descended from the sun goddess and to have become emperor in 660 BC. This imperial family remained the factor of continuity on which the history of Japan is threaded. For centuries that history is of the rise and fall of great landed families who competed for control of the emperors. Although the emperors were often

treated badly, imperial approval was necessary to legitimise the acts of any clan that seized power. At the same time there was a development of government round the emperor, much influenced by the bureaucratic practices of China. Shotoku Taishi, regent for the Emperor Suiko, not only introduced Buddhism but made a code of political principles in AD 604.

From the middle of the 7th century to the 11th century the emperors were dominated by the powerful Fujiwara family. Noble families established themselves in the provinces, and from the 12th to the 16th centuries Japan was in a state of constant civil war. This did not prevent progress in the arts of civilisation.

From the 12th century there developed a form of regency called the Shogunate. The Shogun was a military head of the government who acted in the name of the emperor. At first a temporary appointment, from the 12th century the Shogunate was permanent, dominated by a succession of powerful families. A strong warrior class developed that tradition of obedience, endurance and harsh treatment of the defeated which has been called *bushido*. There was much misery in the lower ranks of society.

Mongol invaders tried to gain a foothold in Japan in 1274 and again in 1281 but were repulsed. Unsuccessful Japanese attempts to conquer Korea and China in the late 16th century were exceptional and had no sequel till the 20th century.

In 1600 the Tokugawa family gained the Shogunate and began the policy of excluding all foreigners from Japan. Following the Portuguese, who had discovered Japan in 1542, St Francis Xavier (*see* separate entry) had introduced Christianity, but after some time this religion was banned and its followers virtually exterminated. With the exception of one Dutch trading port, all foreigners were expelled from Japan in 1642 and

Christianity was not tolerated again until 1873, about which time, by one of the miracles of history, it was discovered that small Christian communities had survived for 200 years. Before the exclusion policy there had been some contact with Portuguese, Spanish, Dutch and English traders.

The government was now more strongly centralised, and relative internal peace was maintained. The declining aristocracy of samurai, or warriors, was replaced by a wealthy and influential merchant class. Buddhism declined and Shinto, the cult of the mythical past, expanded.

In 1854 Commodore Perry of the United States Navy secured the acceptance of a United States consul at a Japanese port and western influence returned to Japan. This stimulated modernisation and reorganisation. The long Tokugawa Shogunate came to an end, and the Emperor Meiji was given real power in 1868. His government broke the power of the samurai and replaced them by a state army. A parliament, established in 1890, was little more than a front for autocracy.

Nationalism was now a rising force in Japan. After a small military adventure in Formosa in 1874, war with China in 1894 gave Japan Formosa and the Pescadores. In 1904 war with Russia gave Japan control of Korea, half the island of Sakhalin and extended rights in Manchuria. Intervention with other powers in China gave Japan a chance to make a favourable treaty with Britain. With Japan's military imperialism in the Far East went a vigorous expansion of industry and commerce, in which the great mercantile families of Mitsui and Mitsubishi played a prominent part. This in turn stimulated the idea of a great empire on the Asian mainland. Korea was finally annexed in 1910.

In 1914 Japan entered World War I as Britain's ally against Germany and gained mercantile advantages and an increased control in China. There was a great earthquake in 1923 and an economic slump in 1929. The Japanese army overran Manchuria in 1931. There followed extended Japanese occupation of large areas of China. The Japanese army and public were inspired by an aggressive nationalism.

World War II offered still greater temptations. With the collapse of France and the Netherlands in 1940, French Indo-China and the Netherlands Indies were left vulnerable. In September 1940 Japan made a pact with Germany and Italy. In December 1941 Japan simultaneously attacked the United States base at Pearl Harbour, the British colony at Hong Kong, the Philippines and Malaya. Unlike earlier wars, this Japanese adventure had no limited aim but sought to create a vast Asian and Pacific empire.

Commodore Perry delivering the President's letter to Imperial Commissioners on 8 March 1854.

This folly, though pursued with relentless dertermination and odious atrocities, led to a perilously wide scattering of forces. The first quick victorious overrunning of territory was followed by a long series of defeats and retreats leading, in 1945, to unconditional surrender which was hastened by the dropping of two atomic bombs on Japan. The brief period of Japanese expansion had big effects in south-east and eastern Asia, leading to the establishment of serveral new independent postwar states, particularly Indonesia.

Occupation of Japan, mainly by United States forces, lasted from 1945 to 1952. The emperor issued a rescript rejecting the notion that the emperor is divine. A new constitution was adopted. Recovery gained speed and Japan's industrial growth quickly put the country in an advanced position so that today she ranks third as a world economy after the USA and the USSR.

Over the centuries Japan has made a great contribution to the arts and crafts of civilisation, its most sought after products in the West being paintings and woodcuts, executed with great originality and freshness; its ceramics; its famous samurai swords; and such minor articles as the *netsuke*, made of carved wood or ivory and serving as toggles or buttons.

A busy street scene in Tokyo, 1973.

Java: politically the most important island of the Republic of Indonesia. First influenced by Hindu culture and art, Java turned to Islam in the 15th century. The Portuguese traded with Java in the 16th century. In the 17th century the Dutch established trading posts and were gradually drawn into Javanese affairs and exercised rule over parts of the island. There was a period of British rule during the Napoleonic Wars; then Dutch rule was resumed, with large capital investment much economic development and a rapidly rising population. From 1903 the native Javanese were gradually admitted to a share in political life. A nationalist movement grew. During World War II Java was overrun by the Japanese, and at the end of the war an independent Republic of Indonesia was established. Although this republic includes islands scattered across 3,000 miles [5,000 kilometres] of sea, Java has been its political heart and its most highly developed component.

Jefferson, Thomas (1743–1826): third president of the USA. Born in Virginia, he studied law and later became a delegate to the Continental Congress. He was responsible for the drafting of the Declaration of Independence (1776), for the Land Ordinance (which formed a basis for the later organisation of the new territories) and for the introduction of a decimal system. From 1785 to 1789 he was the American minister (ambassador) in Paris and witnessed the early stages of the French Revolution. He returned to America as the first secretary of state, serving until 1793, when he resigned in protest at the efforts of Alexander Hamilton (1757–1804) to make the central government all-powerful. Later, in 1797, as vice-president under John Adams (1735–1826) he continued advocating a policy of states' rights, even proposing in 1798 that a state had the right to overrule

Monticello, the home of Thomas Jefferson.

federal legislation of which it did not approve. In the presidential election of November 1800 he tied with Aaron Burr, securing office only with the support of Alexander Hamilton. His presidency lasted from 1801 to 1809. Jefferson's administrations were marked by economy at home, by the Louisiana Purchase (April 1803 – the biggest land sale in history, in which the size of the USA was doubled by the purchase from France of the whole of the Mississippi valley up to the Rockies) and by measures to maintain American neutrality during the Napoleonic wars. After his retirement he founded the University of Virginia (1819) and encouraged the spread of neo-classical architecture throughout the southern states.

A graceful tribute to Jefferson's scholarly qualities was paid by President Kennedy when, entertaining American Nobel Prizemen in literature and science, he said that there was more talent and genius gathered in the White House that night than there ever had been "except when Thomas Jefferson dined alone".

Jenkinson, Anthony (d. 1611)**:** English sea captain and traveller, the first Englishman in central Asia. "A man well travelled whom we mind to use in further travelling", he was sent in 1557 as captain-general of a fleet of four vessels fitted out by the Muscovy Company to trade with Russia and explore a possible land route to Cathay. Jenkinson reached the White Sea after a voyage of 2,250 miles [3,600 kilometres] and, after a further expedition by boat and sledge, arrived on 6 December in Moscow, where he was well received by Ivan the Terrible. Jenkinson made several other important journeys as merchant and diplomat and greatly increased geographical knowledge.

Jenkins' Ear, War of (1739–41)**:** war (which merged into the War of the Austrian Succession, 1740–48) arising from public indignation at an act of barbarity by Spanish coastguards who were alleged to have cut off the ear of Robert Jenkins, master of the trading sloop *Rebecca*, when it was boarded in search of contraband. Jenkins carried the ear about wrapped in cotton for display purposes. He is credited with the remark, "I have committed my soul to God, and my cause to my country". The whole story was probably a fabrication, but, in the outcome, Sir Robert Walpole's efforts to preserve peace were overcome by press and public.

Jenner, Edward (1749–1823)**:** English discoverer of vaccination against smallpox. In 1796, after nearly twenty years of study in his native Gloucestershire, he successfully vaccinated an eight-year-old boy, using cowpox matter, and two years later published his discovery to the world. In London, as a result of vaccination, the average yearly death rate from smallpox soon fell from 2,018 to 622. In view of this, it is curious that not till 1853 was vaccination made compulsory in the United Kingdom although many European countries had already done so – Bavaria (1807), Denmark (1810), Sweden (1814), Würtemberg and a number of other German states (1818) and Prussia (1835).

Jenner innoculating against smallpox, a cartoon by Gillray.

In the USA many separate states introduced direct or indirect compulsion, beginning with Massachusetts in 1809.

¶ LEVINE, I. E. *Edward Jenner*. 1962

Jericho: a town in Palestine in the fertile valley of the Jordan fifteen miles [24.14 kilometres] north-east of Jerusalem. It was in this area that the Children of Israel under Joshua first crossed into the Promised Land and destroyed the town in the miraculous manner described in Joshua, Chapter 6. Close to its site a later city was founded by Herod the Great (*c.* 73–4 BC), and this is mentioned in the Gospels, both as being visited by Christ himself and also as the destination of the traveller who was succoured by the Good Samaritan in the parable.

After long obscurity, the place again rose to modest prominence during the period of the British Mandate over Palestine after World War I. In 1949 it came under the Kingdom of Jordan but since the brief war of 1967 has been in Israeli hands.

Jerome, St (Eusebius Hieronymus, 347–420)**:** biblical scholar. Born near Aquileia, in Italy, he spent much of his life in the Middle East and was for over thirty years head of a monastery in Bethlehem, where he died. He is chiefly remembered for accomplishing a fresh translation of the Bible into Latin from the original tongues. The translation is known as the Vulgate and, with some later re-editing, is still the official text of the Roman Catholic church, while its excellence is acknowledged by scholars generally. Pictures of the saint often show him working in his cell with a tame lion dozing at his side.

Jerusalem: an ancient city in Palestine situated, at a height of 2,500 feet [762 metres], some thirty-five miles [56 kilometres] from the Mediterranean Sea.

The site was captured by the Israelites under King David about 1000 BC, and here his son Solomon built the first Temple. After the Captivity in the 6th century the remnant of the nation returned and rebuilt the Temple *c.* 520 BC.

At the time of Christ's crucifixion in Jerusalem the Romans had been in possession for some ninety years, though still permitting the Jews to continue their religious practices. In AD 70, however, in the suppression of a four-year rebellion, the city was besieged and destroyed by Titus, the future emperor.

In the year 135, it was refounded by the Emperor Hadrian as Aelia Capitolina and, with the spread of Christianity, flourished until its capture by the Muslims in 638. The temporary success of the Crusades (*see* separate entry) resulted in the setting up of a Christian kingdom between 1099 and 1187. Over the subsequent centuries, under the rule of the Turks, Christians of various denominations were permitted an increasing freedom of organised worship in their holy places.

In World War I the city was taken in 1917 by British and Australian forces under General Allenby, and thereafter Palestine was placed under a British Manate until 1948. Jerusalem was then most ncomfortably divided between Israel and ordan until, in the war of 1967, it fell vholly into Israel's hands.

SHEPPARD, E. J. *Babylon and Jerusalem.* 1972

esuits: members of the Society of Jesus, ounded in 1540 by St Ignatius (*see* eparate entry). The aim of the Society vas "not only to seek . . . the salvation and erfection of one's soul, but . . . to labour or the salvation and perfection of others". ts head was styled General, and its nembers were expected to show instant nd soldier-like obedience to all comnands. By one of the vagaries of history he third general of the order, the dediated St Francis Borgia (1510–72), was a lescendant of a family notorious for xtravagantly immoral living and dishonesty (*see* BORGIA, FAMILY OF).

From early days the Jesuits won fame for heir missionary work in distant corners of he world. St Francis Xaxier (1506–52) 'the Apostle to the Indies", penetrated as ar as Japan, and his magnificent shrine an still be seen at the old city of Goa in outhern India. It must also be remembered that Jesuits bore the brunt of the perilous missions which kept their faith alive in England during the reign of Queen Elizabeth I (1558–1603).

At the same time, the Roman Church was, in the 16th and 17th centuries, involved in the counter-reformation, the movement for internal reform of certain abuses. In this work, too, the Society played a prominent part and gained the reputation of being shock troops, as it were, at the direct disposal of the Pope himself. This, together with the intellectual subtlety and pre-eminence of many of its members, roused considerable suspicion in certain rulers of Europe and even the envy of other interests within the Roman Church itself. In consequence, Pope Clement XIV was persuaded in 1773 to abolish the Society by the Bull *Dominus ac Redemptor,* and its corporate existence barely survived through a small community in Russia, until Pope Pius VII reestablished it in 1814. Today the Society flourishes and continues to be particularly respected for its influence in education up to the highest university levels.

¶ HOLLIS, CHRISTOPHER. *A History of the Jesuits.* 1968

Jesus Christ (*c.* 6 BC–AD 30)**:** the Jewish religious leader whom Christians worship as the Son of God and the Saviour of mankind.

Neither singularly nor collectively do the four Gospels give a full record of the life of Christ. Scholars in the past 150 years or so have devoted much attention to the problems of their origin and authorship and to the probable existence of earlier written records, now lost, on which they may have been based. It is thought likely that the earliest traditions of the story were, for thirty years or more, transmitted orally. It must also be borne in mind that the essentially local circumstances of the Gospel story make references to outside sources very few indeed.

The details of the early years are, in consequence, particularly the product of oral tradition. The date anciently given for the Nativity, AD 1 – since there is no zero between that and 1 BC – arises from a calculation in the 6th century by Dionysius Exiguus; but we now know that Herod the Great, who was alive at the time, died in 4 BC so that the birth of Jesus must be placed slightly earlier.

It seems probable that Christ's ministry lasted for about a year, though St John's Gospel suggests rather longer. It is customary to place the crucifixion in the spring of the year 30. We know that Pontius Pilate was procurator of Judea 26–36.

¶ CHUTE, MARCHETTA. *Jesus of Israel.* 1962; GRAHAM, ELEANOR. *The Story of Jesus.* 1959

Jewellery: personal ornaments of precious, or imitation, stones and metals. Mankind has, from earliest times, worn jewellery both as an adornment and as a symbol of authority. In Tel-el-Amarna, Egypt, necklaces have been discovered fashioned in rows of flowers, fruit and corn, while an onyx and enamel amulet from the tomb of Tutankhamen was decorated with lotus blooms and a green scarab bettle. These Egyptian jewels are almost 4,000 years old.

In Europe, uncut gems and lumps of gold and silver were worn by tribal chieftains as a mark of distinction and also as a convenient method of carrying their personal fortunes. Not until a tribe ceased to be nomadic and made a permanent settlement were craftsmen able to develop skills in polishing gems and setting them in precious metals. The jewels of a chief were buried with him, as in the burial mound at Sutton Hoo, England.

The most famous of Anglo-Saxon jewels was discovered in AD 1693, at Athelney in Somerset. Consisting of an enamelled head set in gold, it bears the words *Aelfred Mec Heht Gewyrean* – "Alfred had me made". It is thought to have belonged to Alfred the Great (AD 849–901), who hid in the Athelney marshes to escape the Danish invaders.

Much medieval jewellery was made for churches. Jewelled crosses have been discovered and small jewelled boxes, known as reliquaries, were used to hold relics of saints. The most famous of these belonged to Charlemagne. It was reputed to contain a lock of the Virgin Mary's hair, and was buried with him at Aachen, Germany, when he died in AD 814. When his tomb was opened in AD 1000, it was removed to the cathedral treasury until given as a coronation gift to Napoleon's wife, the Empress Josephine, 800 years later. Eventually it passed to the Empress Eugenie, who presented it to the Archbishop of Rheims after the bombardment of his

Above left: chieftain's gold belt buckle from the Sutton Hoo Ship Burial. Middle: the ring of the Anglo-Saxon King Ethelwulf and an 18th century French ring made from Sévres porcelain. Below left: gold and enamel rosary, English, 16th century. Below: a "Suite Set" of French costume jewellery, 18th century.

athedral during World War I. In World War II the reliquary disappeared.

Personal jewels of medieval times, such as rings and brooches, were often believed to have magical properties. English ladies began the fashion of wearing their rosaries as necklaces.

In medieval and Renaissance times, men sometimes outshone women in the wearing of jewellery. When Richard I of England went to meet the emperor of Cyprus, not only was his person a blaze of gold and silver but he rode on a saddle of gold embroidered with silver hearts. Henry VIII had among his jewels "a double collar of rubies, decorated with gold leaves and pearls". His daughter Elizabeth I, however, surpassed him. Many of her trinkets were made by Nicholas Hilliard, artist and jeweller. She had a magnificent collection of watches, including one of crystal adorned with a golden lion. Such watches were worn on necklaces as pendants. She appreciated to the full some of the treasure brought home by Drake, such as "thirty-nine agates, small and great"; "one hundred and eighty-nine small stones, which we esteem to be garnets"; and "one chain of gold esses, with four diamonds and four rubies".

In the 18th century, ladies wore "suite sets", consisting of matching earrings, necklace and brooch. Marie Antoinette, tragic queen of France, owned one of these, made of sapphires, rubies and diamonds.

In the 19th century, the jewels of the Russian royal family were renowned. During the Revolution, when the last Tsar Tsarina were shot with all their family in 1918, pearls and diamonds were discovered sewn into the clothes of the princesses, who had carried them in the hope of escaping.

One of the most celebrated collections of jewellery in the world is the British Crown Jewels, housed in the Tower of London. They include the Black Prince's ruby, given to him by Pedro of Castile in 1367 and worn by Henry V on his helm at Agincourt.

Jews: a widely scattered race of Asiatic origin. Although this nation has a history stretching far back in time, it owes its continued identity more to tradition and religion than to any marked racial purity. Indeed, the repeated process known as the *Diaspora* (dispersion), either through choice or necessity, over the face of the globe, could not fail to introduce the blood of other races. A group of Jews surviving in China within living memory had characteristic Chinese features.

The earliest historical records of the nation are derived from the books of the Old Testament; and, though scholars and archaeologists have somewhat modified the details of the story, and dates must often be approximate or uncertain, the main facts can be accepted. The story begins somewhere between the years 2100 and 2000 BC with the removal of Abraham, the "father" of the race, from Ur in Mesopotamia to the region which was to remain, albeit with long intervals of exile, the homeland of the Jews until today. This is the stretch of country lying at the eastern end of the Mediterranean between roughly the parallels 31°30′ and 33° and stretching back to the Jordan valley or a few miles beyond. It has been successively known as the Promised Land, Canaan, Israel (from which at one point the kingdom of Judah was detached), Judaea, Palestine and, again today, Israel. From its geographical position it has often been the battlefield or passageway for warring armies from the empires to the north or south.

The second generation after Abraham was compelled by famine to move to Egypt, whence, after living peaceably for some time under the Hyksos dynasty, the nation, as it had now become, was forced by the persecution of their successors to set forth, under the leadership of Moses, across the Red Sea into the wilderness of Sinai. From there, after a period of wandering (traditionally for forty years), they crossed again into Canaan, and gradually subdued the native peoples, though their greatest rivals, the Philistines of the south-west, nearly proved too strong for them. In due course, as a result of popular demand, the first king, Saul, was elected. The reigns of his successor David and the latter's son Solomon (died *c.* 933 BC) saw the establishment of the temple and the capital at Jerusalem and a period of great prosperity and influence. Thereafter, however, the division of the nation into two kingdoms, together with pressures from outside, led eventually to the total disappearance of the northe kingdom of Israel and the removal of th people of the southern kingdom, Juda to captivity in Babylon in the 6th centu BC.

For the period after the return fro captivity (*c.* 520 BC) the Old Testame gives us little historical guidance. Th Persian empire was succeeded by that Alexander the Great (d. 323 BC), who reported to have shown favour to th Jewish religion, but the division of h empire among his generals brought fu ther troubles from invaders, until som thing of a national revival was achieve in the heroic times of the Hasmonaea family, generally called the Maccabees, i the 2nd century BC.

But the shadow of Rome's empire w spreading over the Middle East. In 63 B Pompey captured Jerusalem, and, thoug

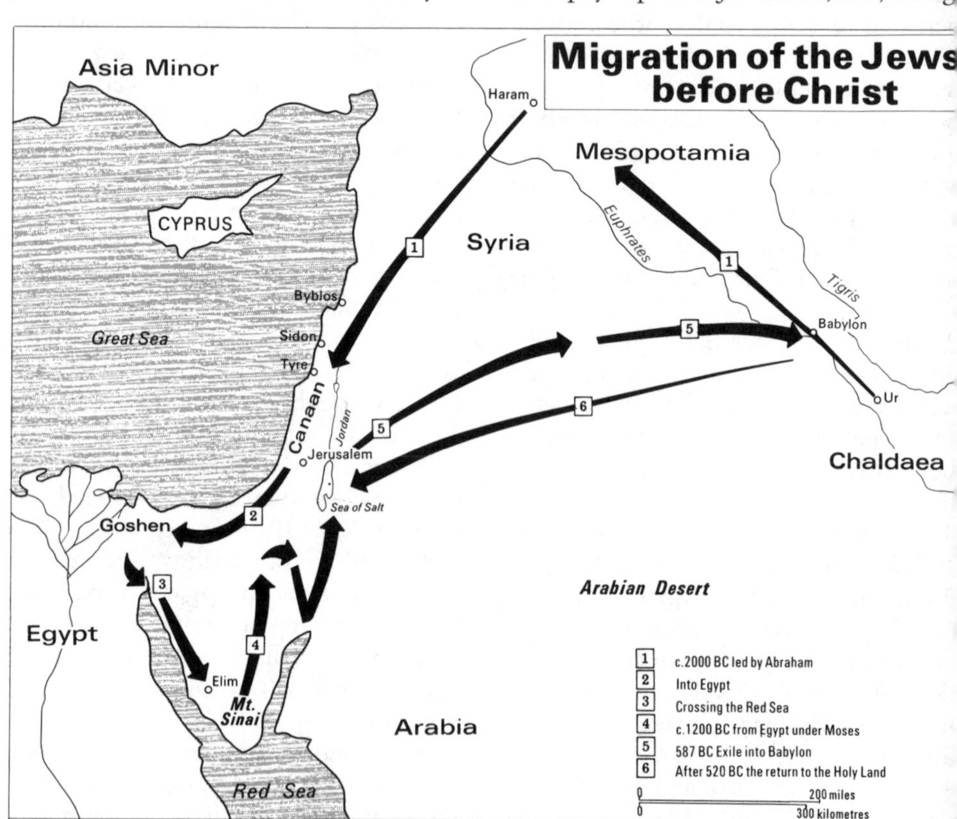

r a time the Romans governed through tive rulers, particularly Herod the reat (73–4 BC), on the death of the tter the most important region, that of daea, was entrusted to Roman pro-rators, such as Pontius Pilate, who was overnor at the time of Christ's cruci-xion. But the insensitive attitude of the omans towards the strong religious elings of the people resulted in a bellion which led to the destruction of rusalem in 70, and after a further up-sing in 135 the Jews were expelled from eir homeland.

They were now widely scattered and eir fortunes varied in different lands d in different centuries. Their charac-ristic skill and diligence in business and e fact that they were prepared to lend oney at interest (nominally prohibited Christians) caused them to be treated times with tolerance, at others with vy and persecution. In 1290, for in-ance, they were banished from England, d from France in 1306. In Spain the quisition (*see* separate entry) pressed eavily on them.

Gradually, however, the Jews began to cover their position in Europe. Thus, uring the Commonwealth (1649–58) liver Cromwell encouraged their return England, though it was not for another 00 years that they gained their full rights citizens. Nevertheless in some countries, articularly in Russia, they still suffered om outbreaks of persecution, though ese were far exceeded by the outrages f Nazi Germany in the present century. ven today in Poland the authorities are id to make the position of Jews very ncomfortable. Applications from Jews leave Russia for Israel have been con-stently refused by the authorities.

Meanwhile the movement known as ionism, aiming at restoring Palestine to e Jews, had been set on foot by Theodor Ierzl (1860–1904), and in 1948 the British Mandate, which had controlled the country since the end of World War I, gave way to the sovereign state of Israel, which, at the moment of writing, has considerably increased its boundaries as a result of the war of 1967 against its neighbours.

There are approximately 14 million Jews worldwide: 3,250,000 in Israel, nearly 6 million in the USA, 800,000 in Canada, 2,200,000 in the USSR, 700,000 in France and 425,000 in Britain.

See also HERZL; ISRAEL; JERICHO; JERUSALEM; JUDAISM; PALESTINE.

Jingoism: advocacy of an aggressive foreign policy. The term came into use during the Russo-Turkish war of 1877–78, when a popular British song proclaimed:

We don't want to fight, but, by jingo,
if we do,
We've got the ships, we've got
the men, we've got the money too.

Jinnah, Mohammed Ali (1876–1948): Pakistani statesman and leader of the Muslim League. He developed that body into an organisation powerful enough to insist, in the face of opposition from Congress and the British government, on the partition of India into Hindu and Muslim countries when independence was granted in 1947. He became the first governor-general of the state of Pakistan.

Joan of Arc, or **Jeanne D'Arc, St** (1412–31): the Maid of Orleans, known in France as Jeanne d'Arc or La Pucelle. She was born of peasant parents at Domrémy in Lorraine, in eastern France. From the age of thirteen she claimed to hear the voices of Saints Margaret, Michael and Catherine commanding her to drive the invading English from France and to have the Dauphin Charles crowned king. In 1429 she succeeded in

From The Life of Joan of Arc *by Antoine Dufour, 1505.*

persuading the authorities to allow her, dressed in armour and riding a white horse, to lead an army to relieve Orleans, then besieged by the English. Subsequently she led Charles to Rheims Cathedral, the traditional place of coronation of French kings. Her phenomenal success aroused much hostility towards her on the part of the Burgundians, the English and high officials of the Church. Regarded by her followers as a saint, her enemies denounced her as a witch, and the Burgundians handed her over to the English, who burnt her at the stake in Rouen market-place in 1431. In 1455 she was rehabilitated by a papal committee, and in 1920 she was canonised.

Much has been written about St Joan by historians and others. Probably George Bernard Shaw's play bearing her name is the work best known to the general English reader.

¶ PAINE, A. B. *The Girl in White Armour: the story of Joan of Arc.* 1969

John, Don, of Austria (*c.* 1545–78): Spanish general and admiral, the son of the emperor Charles V. At first intended for the monastery, he chose instead military career and won a number victories, the most notable of which w the destruction of the Turkish fleet the sea battle of Lepanto (7 October 157 when he commanded the forces of Spai Venice and the Vatican. The Turks lo some 25,000 men, and 15,000 Christi galley slaves were freed. Don John subsequent career, including a period governor-general of the Netherland was less successful.

Johnson, Andrew (1808–75): seve teenth president of the USA. Johnso was prominent in Tennessee state politi between 1835 and 1857. He was electe to the Senate in 1857 and was the onl Southern senator to support Abraha Lincoln (1809–65) during the Civil Wa Lincoln secured Johnson's adoption Union-Republican candidate for vic president in 1864. Upon Lincoln's deat in 1865, Johnson automatically becam President but found it impossible to carr through the policy of peaceful recon struction with the South for whic Lincoln had striven. Northern oppositio to him in Congress grew, and the sought to limit his powers by passing a act preventing presidents from dismissin high officers in the government withou the approval of the Senate. Johnson, in test case, dismissed his secretary of wa (Edwin Stanton), and the House o Representatives used, for the only tim in US history, its constitutional right t impeach the president before the Senate The move failed by only one vote to gai the necessary two-thirds majority, bu Johnson was doomed, for his party re garded him as a traitor, calling him "th dead dog in the White House". In 186 Ulysses S. Grant (1822–85) obtained th Republican nomination in preference t Johnson.

›hnson, Samuel (1709–84): English xicographer and man of letters. His vo-volume *Dictionary of the English inguage* (first edition 1755) was the first stematic study of the English tongue ıd exercised great influence on its use. e was also a considerable poet, critic, sayist and conversationalist, his persoılity and great intellectual powers nerging clearly in James Boswell's *Life Samuel Johnson LL.D.*, the greatest and est known biography in the English nguage. In appearance Johnson was npreposessing, "large and well-formed ıd his countenance of the cast of an ıcient statue; yet . . . rendered strange ıd somewhat uncouth by convulsive amps, by the scars of that distemper hich it was once imagined the royal ›uch could cure, and by a slovenly mode f dress . . . ; when he walked, it was like ıe struggling gait of one in fetters" 3oswell). Macaulay predicted that future enerations would be more interested in ıe man than in his works; but Johnson's ıtellectual and literary achievements enure as among the greatest in literature.

The Banqueting House, Whitehall, by Inigo Jones, built in 1622.

Jones, Inigo (1573–1652): architect, largely responsible for introducing the Palladian style into England. Little is known of his early years, which included extensive travels in Italy. He first attracted notice as a stage designer for the masques presented at the English court and as the introducer of movable scenery. He was over forty before he came to fame as an architect. Perhaps the most perfect of all his works, though others were on a grander scale, was the Banqueting House (1622), still standing in London's Whitehall, from a window of which Charles I stepped out onto the scaffold on 30 January 1649.

¶ In LUTYENS, R. *Six Great Architects*. 1959

Jones, John Paul (1747–92): US naval hero. Jones was born in Scotland and at the age of thirteen became a cabin boy. After sailing in various ships engaged in the Atlantic trade, he became the master of a merchant vessel. In December 1775 he was commissioned as a first lieutenant in the Continental (US) Navy. He achieved instant success in harrying the ships of the British Navy, his most resounding victory being when he led a squadron of five ships against British merchantmen off Flamborough Head (1778). Though his exploits were of slight military value, his tactics and audacity made him a hero in the United States, and he has subsequently been accorded a place in the traditions of the US Navy comparable to that of Nelson in the Royal Navy of Great Britain.

¶ LA CROIX, ROBERT DE. *John Paul Jones*. 1962

Jordan: kingdom in south-western Asia. Formerly known as Trans-Jordan, this area between the River Jordan and the desert had been part of the Syrian province of the Turkish Empire. Its separate political existence arose from the Arab revolt against the Turks during World War I. Britain was given a mandate for the Palestine area, including Trans-Jordan. Abdullah Ibn Hussain became amir in 1921, with British advisers. The country became largely independent but remained under British protection until the close of World War II. In 1946 the amir became king of the Hashemite kingdom of Trans-Jordan. When Britain's Palestine mandate ended in 1948 and the state of Israel was established, the Jordanians joined with Egyptians, Syrians, Lebanese and Iraqis to attack the new Jewish state and were the chief gainers among the Arab states from the war, occupying part of the city of Jerusalem and a large area of Palestine, containing many refugees and displaced persons. Abdullah was assassinated in 1951. His son Talal was deposed the following year and his grandson Hussein, still in his teens, succeeded. In 1956 King Hussein dismissed his British advisers. The Jordanian monarchy survived precariously through a period of Egyptian dominance in the Near East and vigorous pan-Arab movements. Its strongest sup port was from the tribesmen who mad up the Arab Legion. A source of instabilit was a large population of displaced Arab from Palestine and their descendants. I the war with Israel in 1967, Jordan lost i hold on Jerusalem and much fronti territory.

See ISRAEL for map.

Joust: combat between two knights o men-at-arms on horseback, in which the engaged each other with, often, speciall made blunted lances. The joust, or jus unlike some of the other competition where many knights fought each other a one time, gave special opportunity fo showing off individual dexterity wit arms and attracting the general notice. I conduct was rigidly enforced according t the rules of chivalry, and no one under th rank of esquire was allowed to take par A series of points was awarded accordin to the number of lances broken an where hits were scored. The highest poin were given for a hit on the opponent head, encased in a heavy tournamen helm, and to hit an opponent on the leg or "below the belt", was considered foul. Prizes were given to those who wer judged to have given the best perfor mance.

The two combatants rode towards eac other on separate sides of a barrie called a tilt, introduced at the beginnin of the 15th century. Originally made o cloth hung over a rope, after the middl of the 15th century it was replaced by wooden barrier which gave addition protection against the horses from runnin into each other.

The joust was mentioned by William o Malmesbury (1080–1143), and it was sai to have been practised during the reig of King Stephen (1135–54). It continue to be fashionable throughout the perio

Joust at the Eglinton Tournament in 1839.

knightly chivalry, and, latterly, per-anent tilt-yards were established adja-nt to royal castles and palaces.

Many attempts have been made to revive e joust in modern times in England, the SA, Germany, Austria, Denmark, Italy, veden and Malta. A number of meetings ere held in the southern states of merica between 1830 and 1860. The ost ambitious affair in Great Britain as staged at Eglinton Castle, Ayrshire, 1839, when about 100,000 people nverged to watch the contest.

MITCHELL, R. J. *A Medieval Tournament.* 1958

e also TOURNAMENT.

an Fernandez Islands: group of three lands in the south Pacific, belonging to hile. They were first discovered by a panish pilot in 1563 and named after m. The most famous figure in the lands' history is Alexander Selkirk 676–1721), a seaman who was marooned ere by his captain in 1704 and whose lventures almost certainly inspired aniel Defoe's *Life and Strange Surprising dventures of Robinson Crusoe of York, Mariner,* one of the most popular stories world literature.

e PACIFIC OCEAN for map.

udaism: the religious beliefs and prac-tices of the Jewish people (*see* JEWS). Judaism shares with Christianity and Islam (the Mohammedan faith) a common feature in the belief of a universal god conceived as personal in his relationship with men as individuals. The term is derived from the Kingdom of Judah, restored in the 6th century BC after the Captivity, but the roots of the faith go back to the earliest traditions of the Jewish race. No nation has, perhaps, been more faithful to its religion, though scattered in all quarters of the globe and enduring centuries of persecution.

¶ DOMNITZ, MYER. *Judaism.* 1970; DOMNITZ, MYER. *Thinking about Judaism.* 1971

Judge: officer appointed to administer the law in a court of justice. Ideally judges are more than the administrators of justice: they are its custodians. When they are above bribes and independent of the government they are a country's best defence against the loss of its liberties. In the United States of America it is considered more democratic to elect judges – at least of the lower courts – by popular vote.

England's judiciary today is universally considered to be above reproach. It was not always so. In 1289 chief justice Thomas de Weyland (*fl.* 1272–90) was banished for offences which included incitement to murder. In 1351 another chief justice, Sir William de Thorp (*fl.* 1350), was sentenced to death for bribery, a penalty afterwards reduced to losing his possessions. A third, Baron George Jeffreys (1648–89), in what is called the Bloody Assize, savagely sentenced hundreds to death or transportation after the suppression of the Duke of Monmouth's rebellion. He died in the Tower.

Justice was one of the qualities of kingship. The king dispensed it as a privilege – his subjects had no right to demand it. The early judges, usually men in holy orders, served the king, not the people, and could be dismissed if they displeased their master by giving decisions which conflicted with the royal interests.

This state of affairs was ended in England by the Act of Settlement (1700) which followed the Bloodless Revolution (*see* separate entry) when King James II lost his throne. Since then, judges of the superior courts hold office *quamdiu se bene gesserint* ("as long as they are of good behaviour") and cannot be removed except upon an Address of both Houses of Parliament. The lord chancellor, though the head of the legal profession, is the only judge whose term of office is otherwise terminable: he is a member of the government and must resign when it changes. The lord chancellor has the power to remove from office certain inferior judges and magistrates in cases of misconduct.

English judges are appointed by the Crown on the recommendation of the prime minister or the lord chancellor. Thus they represent the Crown and do not stand when the queen is toasted in their presence. In the USA judges in the Federal Court and a few of the state courts (e.g. Minnesota and New Jersey) are appointed by the executive; otherwise they must look to the popular vote.

In the United States and Great Britai and in most countries with long established courts, a judge applies existin rules of law to the case in hand. He bound by statute and precedent: it is nc his function to make new law. Inevitably an obscurely worded Act of Parliamer or of Congress requires his interpretatio and there are cases for which there is n precedent. Only then can a judge be sai to make new law. And, of course, h decision is normally subject to appeal t a higher court. In England, the ultimat Court is the House of Lords.

Jugoslavia or **Yugoslavia:** sociali federal republic of south-east Europe. Th state of Jugoslavia was formed afte World War I from territories of th former Austro-Hungarian empires. Ex tending from central Europe to th Balkans, different parts have been sub jected to various historical, religiou cultural and geographical influences. Eve today there are three official language Serbo-Croat, Slovene and Macedoniar both the Latin and Cyrillic alphabets ar used, and the three main religions ar Catholicism, Orthodox Christianity an Islam.

In ancient times this area was occupie by Illyrians, Thracians and Greeks. Th Romans conquered a large part in the 1s century AD, and by the 7th century ha been ousted by the Slavs. During th Middle Ages small states emerged Croatia, then Serbia and Macedonia Montenegro and Bosnia. For centurie these little states struggled for thei individual existence by fighting amon themselves and against a succession o foreign overlords, usually the Turks.

At the Congress of Berlin (1878), Serbi and Montenegro were given full inde pendence. Croatia and Slovenia and, i 1908, Bosnia-Herzegovina, came unde ustro-Hungarian rule. On 28 June 1914 rchduke Franz Ferdinand, the heir to e Austrian throne, and his wife were ssassinated when visiting Sarajevo, the pital of Bosnia. The resulting Balkan onflict expanded into World War I.

On 18 December 1918 the Kingdom of e Serbs, Croats and Slovenes was rmally proclaimed in Belgrade. In 1920 was renamed the Kingdom of Jugoavia. The new state was harassed by ternal political strife and economic ifficulties which were due to its diverse rigins. From 1929 to 1931 King Alexnder suspended the constitution and uled as an absolute monarch. After his ssassination at Marseilles in 1934 his rother, Prince Paul, ruled as regent for e young king, Peter. From 1936 the ountry was associated with Germany nd Italy, but remained neutral in World Var II until 1941. Following a meeting etween Prince Paul and Hitler, Jugolavia entered the war on Germany's side n 25 March. A popular uprising folowed on 27 March, Paul abdicated and he new government under King Peter eaffirmed Jugoslav neutrality. On 6 April German and Bulgarian forces invaded, nd within a fortnight the country urrendered.

Various underground resistance movenents were quickly formed. The leader f the Communist partisan movement, Marshal Josip Broz Tito, emerged as the trongest political force in Jugoslavia and ed the way in the creation of the Republic f Jugoslavia in 1945. He became its resident in 1953.

Although a Communist state with a ne-party constitution, Jugoslavia under Tito jealously guarded its independence rom the East as well as West, even when Tito's quarrel with Stalin in 1948 made er position precarious. The country has efused economic aid from either Russia r America when she has felt that this might have strings attached. In view of the fact that Jugoslavia suffered enorhindered economic growth. Following Tito's death in 1980 the country has been run by "collective" leadership.

¶ ROTHKOPF, CAROL. *The First Book of Yugoslavia.* 1971

See also AUSTRIA; BALKANS (for map); HUNGARY, etc.

Jung, Carl Gustav (1875–1961)**:** Swiss psychologist and psychiatrist. He studied medicine at Basle and early began to specialise in mental diseases; he worked for eight years in a Zurich hospital and pioneered the study of schizophrenia ("split personality"). He was professor of psychiatry at Zurich university from 1933 to 1941. His most important contribution was his study of the unconscious mind, and he founded a school of psychiatry in which the patient was encouraged to probe his own unconscious – hence Jung's emphasis on dreams and such tools of treatment as art therapy. He ranks with Freud and Adler as a pioneer of psychiatry.

Juries: bodies of men and women put on oath to decide issues of fact in judicial proceedings.

Jurors were part of the primitive legal institutions of many countries. Originally they were themselves witnesses who swore to what they knew. As developed in England under the Normans and later, juries took two forms: the Grand Jury of twenty-four members, which presented (i.e. accused) prisoners for trial, and the Petty Jury of twelve members. Over the centuries the former were superseded by the preliminary investigations of the magistrates. Independent witnesses began to be called to give evidence before the courts, and by the 15th century the petty jurymen had, to all intents and purposes, assumed their modern function to decide the facts.

To be on call for jury service is obligatory in England on men and women between twenty-one and sixty who are ratepayers and British subjects. Doctors and clergymen are exempt from jury duty.

The jury system is traditionally considered to be one of the chief safeguards of the liberty of the individual. Today, its use is in decline. A very large number of offences is now dealt with summarily by magistrates, and only a few indictable offences actually go before a jury.

Justinian I, called **"the Great"** (483–565)**:** Roman emperor of the East from 527. From 531 he tried to reunite the Roman Empire. Under his general Belisarius, his armies launched attacks to recapture first Africa and then Italy by 538. Ravenna was established as the capital of his exarch (or deputy) in Italy, and Justinian figures on the mosaics there. His imperial ideas were coupled with large building projects at Constantinople, especially the completion of the great church of St Sophia, one of the most magnificent buildings in the world. He also ordered his important codification of Roman Law. At home he managed to patch up a religious compromise: far more troublesome were the activities of the Circus, the public horse and chariot racing in which the rival teams were distinguished by different colours. Beginning simply as popular entertainment, the teams sometimes came to be supported by, and identified with, political parties. In Justinian's time the "blues" and "greens" were two such highly quarrelsome organisations.

The Emperor Justinian and his followers from a mosaic in San Vitale, Ravenna, 6th century.

Jutes: members of a Germanic tribe, probably originating from the Jutland peninsula of north-east Europe, who invaded Britain in the 5th century and settled in Kent, the Isle of Wight and Hampshire.

¶ JOLLIFFE, J. E. A. *Pre-Feudal England: the Jutes.* 1962

Jutland, Battle of (31 May 1916)**:** main naval engagement of World War I when, about sixty miles [97 kilometres] west of Jutland, the German High Seas Fleet, under Admiral Reinhard Scheer, were engaged by the British Grand Fleet, commanded by Admiral John Jellicoe. Though the British lost fourteen battleships and other craft against Germany's eleven ships, and over 6,000 men killed compared with Germany's 2,545, the British fleet was left in control of the seas and the German fleet did not leave harbour again.

¶ HOUGH, RICHARD. *The Battle of Jutland.* 1964

K

Kaaba or **Ka'bah:** the shrine of Islam in the Great Mosque at Mecca, containing the religion's most sacred object, the Black Stone, traditionally given by the angel Gabriel to Abraham.

Kabul: capital of Afghanistan, on the Kabul River. At a height of 6,900 feet [2103 metres] and commanding all the important passes from the north and west, it has been a place of great strategic importance for countless centuries. Considerable improvement and modernisation of the ancient narrow and congested city began in 1880 with the accession of the Emir Abdul Rahman (1844–1901), who was subsidised by Britain.

Kaffir: name, usually disparaging, used by white South Africans in referring to black South Africans. It comes from the Arabic word *Kafir* meaning infidel and probably reached Africa from the east coast, where the Portuguese found it used by the Muslim Arabs about the Bantu people they found there.

K'ang Hsi (1654–1722)**:** Chinese emperor of the Manchu dynasty who enlarged the empire by conquering Mongolia and Formosa. In more peaceable pursuits he showed himself a considerable patron of art and literature.

Kashmir: area, one of the most beautiful in the world, of the northern Punjab. After suffering many invasions and passing through Buddhist, Hindu and Muslim phases, it settled down under British control after the first Sikh war (1846) as a largely Muslim state under a Hindu ruler. The decision of the Maharajah, Sir Hari Singh, to join India in 1947 caused an uprising, unofficially supported by Pakistan, leading to undeclared war. A cease-fire was arranged by a United Nations commission in 1948, but a plebiscite was refused by India, and further fighting in 1965 led to continued dangerous tension between India and Pakistan.

Kay, John (1704–*c.* 1778)**:** British inventor. Though he is said to have died a pauper in Paris as a result of law cases to protect his patents, his inventions of the "fly-shuttle" or "flying shuttle" (1733) and a power loom (1745) greatly influenced the course of the Industrial Revolution (*see* separate entry) and brought wealth to the manufacturers who used them.

Kellogg-Briand Pact (27 August 1928)**:** agreement banning war, signed by Frank Billings Kellogg, US Secretary of State, and Aristide Briand, prime minister of France. It was subsequently ratified by more than sixty countries but proved ineffective against the Nazi aggression of the 1930s.

Kennedy, John Fitzgerald (1917–63)**:** thirty-fifth president of the USA. He was born in Brookline, Massachusetts, the second of nine children of the financier Joseph Kennedy (1888–1969). After a distinguished period of war service in the Navy (1941–45) he entered politics as a Democrat, serving in the House of Representatives (1947–53) and in the Senate (1953–60). In 1960 he narrowly defeated Richard Nixon in the presidential election, his victory meaning that for the first time a Roman Catholic had been elected president. Kennedy served less than three years of his elected term, for he was assassinated on 22 November 1963 at Dallas. Being the youngest president ever elected, Kennedy represented the new rather than the traditional in American life. He surrounded himself

John F. Kennedy.

with young advisers recruited from the leading universities, but encountered difficulties in obtaining the support of Congress for many of his policies. He was able to initiate a space programme that ultimately took man to the moon, but was unable to push through a programme of social reform.

¶ REIDY, JOHN P. *John F. Kennedy, the Youngest President.* 1968

Kenya: state in East Africa. Kenya was probably one of the first countries in which man walked the earth (*see* FOSSILS), and there is a scatter of written records of the coast going back to about 45 AD. The Arab coastal settlements, however, had little contact with the interior, which was on the whole a Bantu world of small farming communities until invading pastoralists from neighbouring areas caused widespread movements of populations in the 15th and 16th centuries. By then the Portuguese had begun their rule on the coast which lasted from 1502 to 1699. Britain's interest in Kenya began in the 19th century, when she concerned herself with abolishing slavery.

In 1895 England took over responsibility for the government from a trading company; but men said Kenya was really conquered in 1901, when the Uganda railway was finished with the help of Indian immigrants. European settlers were encouraged to make the railway pay and built up the economy, schools and hospitals were founded, and representative government was introduced.

A strong nationalist movement, which grew after World War II, and the Mau Mau rising (*see* separate entry) led to Kenya becoming independent in 1963. *See* AFRICA for map.

Kepler, Johann (1571–1630): German mathematician. Physically handicapped and a mystic by nature, he worked on the results of Tycho Brahe with enormous perseverance and intellectual integrity to produce a set of navigational tables and his three laws of planetary motion: 1. The planets move in ellipses with the sun at one focus. 2. The radius from a planet to the sun sweeps out equal areas at a constant rate. 3. The cubes of the mean distances of the planets from the sun are a constant ratio of their times of revolution squared. These laws did not describe the type of mathematical perfection he had expected but they provided the vital evidence which led Newton to his law of gravitation.

¶KNIGHT, D. C. *Johannes Kepler and Planetary Motion.* 1965

Keynes, John Maynard, 1st baron (1883–1946): British economist and lecturer in economics at King's College, Cambridge, from 1908 onwards. In 1919 he expressed dissatisfaction with what he regarded as excessive reparation demands on Germany in *The Economic Consequences of the Peace*. His most famous work, *The General Theory of Employment, Interest and* *'oney* (1936) was inspired by the econo-ic depression of the 1930s and greatly fluenced economic policy and govern-ent action all over the world. He was ritain's chief representative at the Bret-n Woods Conference (1944), which sulted in the establishment of the ternational Monetary Fund to stabilise changes.

---

han: title of respect in Mohammedan untries (e.g. the Aga Khan), derived om the word for sovereign used among e Mongols. The title was assumed by enghis when he became ruler, and his ccessors were known as the Great hans, or Chams.

e also GENGHIS KHAN; KUBLAI KHAN; LO, MARCO.

---

hartoum: capital of the Sudan, on the ft bank of the Blue Nile near its con-ience with the White Nile. The city ew out of a permanent camp established

eneral Gordon's last stand at Khartoum, inted by Joy.

by the Egyptians in 1822. The name, meaning "elephant's trunk", was derived from the shape of the promontory at the junction of the two Niles. During the Muslim revolt against Egyptian rule, General Gordon was killed (1885) in defence of the city, which was virtually destroyed. It was recaptured by Lord Kitchener in 1898.

Khmer Republic: formerly Cambodia and now Kampuchea, it has been a centre of violent upheaval for years. The government is supported by Vietnam but the former ruler, Prince Sihanouk, leads a government in exile and there is constant guerrilla opposition to the government.

Khyber Pass: the most important of the passes from Afghanistan into India. Early invaders used easier routes but the British developed the pass into the principal route between Kabul and Peshawar. Three main forts, Jamrud on the east, Ali Masjid – the scene of several sieges – at the summit, and Landi Kotal on the west, guard the pass.

Kibbutz: a collective farm or settlement in modern Israel, derived from the Hebrew *qibbus*, a gathering. The *kibbutzim* (the plural form) represent important experiments in co-operative ownership and organisation.

Kiel: a north German city, in the *Land* of Schleswig-Holstein. It became a city in 1242 and was a member of the Hanseatic League. After 1871 it became the chief naval port of Germany and consolidated this position in 1895 when Kaiser Wilhelm II opened the Kiel Canal, linking the Baltic with the North Sea. A strongly fortified city, Kiel was a prime target of the Allies in World War II and was badly damaged by bombing and shelling.

Several fine old buildings survive, however, including the 13th century castle and the 17th century university building.

Kiev: capital of the Ukrainian republic of the USSR. The princes of Kiev, on the River Dnieper, formed in the late 9th century the first Russian state. In 1240 Kiev was devastated by the Tartars under Batu Khan. Under Lithuanian, Polish and, in 1793, Russian control, Kiev became a centre for the Ukrainian Cossacks. World War II saw it destroyed, but it was soon rebuilt and has become a centre of engineering, chemical and manufacturing industries.

Kimberley: diamond centre in Cape Province, South Africa. In 1871 De Beer sold his farm in South Africa, on which diamonds had been found, for £6,000, and a rush then began to the diamond-rich area where the town of Kimberley grew up round the diggings.

King's Evil: name given to a tubercu swelling of the glands, especially of t neck, that was popularly believed England and France to be curable by t touch of the king or queen. A late examp was that of Doctor Johnson (*see* separ entry) taken to London at the age of thr to be "touched" by Queen Anne a presented with a piece of gold – t "touch-piece" – as a type of talisman.

Kirghizia or **Kirghiz Republic:** public of the USSR north-east of Sov central Asia and bordering on China. T Kirghiz people were of Turkish orig and were tribal and nomadic; but t Russians overran the area and colonis it in the later 19th century. In 1916 t natives rose in a revolt which was savage suppressed. After the Russian Revoluti they were not at first recognised as separate people; but the Kirghiz Repub was finally constituted in 1936. It is mountainous area but has coal and le

Mining and dry-sorting at the Kimberley diamond fields in 1871.

Gold-mining in the Klondike, 1898.

ines and provides agricultural products. frontier with China has given it ategic importance.

ish: a city of ancient Iraq or Mesopo-nia, the ruins of which lie ten miles [16 lometres] east of Babylon. It was a ntre of rule and seat of several dynasties that remarkably advanced civilisation hich developed in Babylonia about 3000 . The city was inhabited until Sassanian nes (the early centuries of the Christian a). The remains that have been excavated e extensive and include an elaborately nstructed Sumerian palace.

e also MESOPOTAMIA; SUMER.

londike: district in Yukon Territory, anada, on the Alaskan frontier. It was e scene (1897–98) of one of the greatest ld rushes of history, a population of ,000 arriving in three or four years. By 10 most of the gold-bearing gravels had been worked out, though other deposits, e.g. the silver-lead ores, afterwards achieved importance.

¶ BERTON, PIERRE. *The Golden Trail.* 1954

Knight: in history an honourable military rank given to a man, usually of gentle birth, who had proved his worth in training or on active service. From about the 11th century this rank was bestowed on men of superior worth, ability and fortune. Later the honour became a special recognition by the sovereign for services rendered to Crown or country. The title of "Sir" is prefixed to the name, but the honour is not hereditary.

Under the feudal system "All persons having ten pounds yearly were obliged to be knighted or pay a fine". There was also a liability to serve the king in time of war. The profession or vocation of knighthood was highly regarded in most of Europe, and the chivalric code required

Ewer in the form of a knight on horseback about 1300, found in the River Tyne, England.

every knight to place his son in the service of another knight to prepare him for promotion to the knightly ranks. These youths were termed pages or varlets, and in addition to training with lance and sword, they performed the most humble functions in the household of their adopted parents. Their moral and religious education taught them respect for women, obedience to their masters and sympathy for a just cause. As esquires, at the age of fourteen, they took part in all assemblies and state ceremonies, concerned themselves with the special etiquette of their masters' households, assisted at the tournament and attended on their lords on the battlefield.

The knighting ceremony could take several forms. The simplest was the blow or touch on neck or shoulder, often on the field of battle, by the king or another knight. The most colourful was the less common ecclesiastical form, where the squire kept vigil in church all night with his weapons laid on the altar.

Whatever the form, the knight was th bound to the code of chivalry for li

¶ OAKESHOTT, R. EWART. *A Knight and His Armo* 1961; OAKESHOTT, R. EWART. *A Knight and I Horse.* 1962; OAKESHOTT, R. EWART. *A Knight a His Weapons.* 1964

See also CHIVALRY.

Knox, John (*c.* 1505–72): Scottish r former and writer. Although original trained for the Roman Catholic pries hood, he became a strict Protestant ar was the founder of Scottish Presbyter anism. Of his attacks on the establish religion his early congregations are r corded as saying: "Others snipped t branches; this man strikes at the roots In June 1547 he was captured when t French fleet attacked St Andrew's ar was thrown into the galleys on the Riv Loire, where for nearly two years remained in irons and frequently suffer the lash. The rest of his life, spent partly exile on the Continent, where he m Calvin (*see* separate entry), was devoted furthering the Reformation in Scotlan where his powers as a preacher and writ made him a predominant influence.

¶ In LANG, T. *Great Men of Scotland.* 1957

.oran or **Qur'ān:** the sacred scripture of lam, regarded as the Word of God :vealed directly to Mohammed. Meanıg "recitation", the Koran consists of 114 *ıtras* (or chapters) of varying length overing every aspect of Muslim life and ıcluding the joys of heaven and the ortures of hell, religious observances, ivil and criminal law.

.orea: peninsula in north-east Asia. :hinese influence reached the peninsula f Korea early, and Chinese colonies were stablished in the north in the first century c. The early history is of the rise and fall nd the conflicts of several kingdoms on ıe peninsula. In the 10th century AD the ingdom of Koryo, or Korea, was estabshed. Chinese Confucianist influences lended there with Buddhism. The :hinese established dominance in the 11th

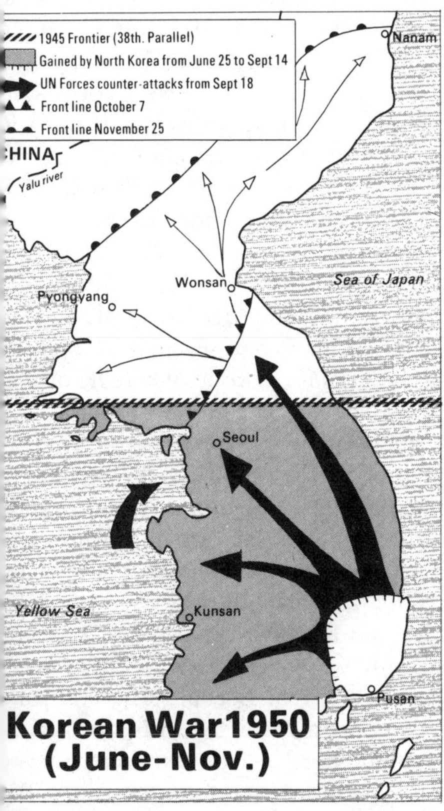

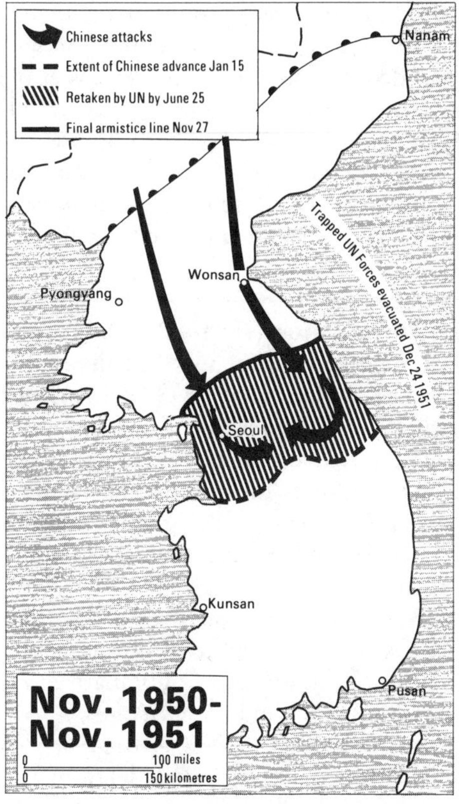

century, and the Mongols invaded Korea in the 13th century, when Kublai Khan used Korea as his base for an attempted invasion of Japan. As Mongol power waned, the native Yi dynasty was established at the end of the 14th century. In 1592 the Japanese invaded Korea but were driven out. From the mid-17th century Manchu power in China extended to Korea, which again became subordinate to China. At the close of the 19th century both Japanese and Chinese troops entered Korea. Later Korea became an issue between Russia and Japan, but, having successively defeated both China and Russia, Japan in 1910 annexed Korea. As Japan collapsed at the end of World War II, Russian troops entered north Korea and the peninsula was divided into Soviet and United States zones at the 38th parallel. North Koreans invaded South

Korea in 1950, and troops from many countries, but mainly the United States, defended the south in the Korean War of 1950–53. No agreement could be reached as to the ideology – communist or western democratic – under which the peninsula could be reunited, and North and South Korea continued as separate republics.

Kossuth, Lajos (1802–94)**:** Hungarian statesman and patriot who led the Hungarian Revolution of 1848, demanding parliamentary government for Hungary. In 1849, virtually dictator, he issued his declaration that "the house of Habsburg-Lorraine, perjured in the sight of God and man, had forfeited the Hungarian throne". His shortlived spell of power ended with the Austrian suppression of the revolution in the same year, and he went into exile, enjoying extraordinary popularity in England, France and the USA.

Kremlin: the fortress or citadel of many Russian cities and towns. The word refers especially to the Moscow Kremlin, a huge collection of palaces, ancient churches and government buildings, erected at various periods and surrounded by a wall nearly a mile and a half in length [2·4 kilometres], built by the Tzar Ivan III (1440–1505). In modern times it has become the headquarters of the government of the USSR, and the name is often used to designate that government. (Other examples of thi trick of speech are the Quai d'Orsay, fo the French Foreign Ministry; Downin Street, for the British government; th White House, for the executive government of the USA.)

Kruger, Stephanus Johannes Paulus usually known as **Paul** (1825–1904) Boer statesman. As President of th Transvaal Republic (1881–1900), he wa strongly opposed to British expansion i South Africa and made several visits t London in an effort to get the annexatio of the Transvaal cancelled. To the *Uitlanders*, or emigrants (usually British) i the Transvaal and Orange Free State h said: "This is my country; these are m laws. Those who do not like to obey m laws can leave my country". His narrow internal policies eventually led to th Boer (or South African) War, durin which, at the age of seventy-five, he lef the country for Europe, where he died a Lake Geneva.

Krupp, Family of: German armament manufacturers. In 1848 Alfred Krup (1812–87) inherited a small iron forge i Essen. By the 1860s he had turned hi attention to making heavy weapons; b 1914 the Krupp firm employed 80,00 men and was supplying weapons of ever type to most of Europe. The compan was now owned by Alfred's granddaughter Bertha, who lent her name t the enormous long-range gun "Bi

The Spasskaya Tower of the Kremlin, Moscow

Kublai Khan carried to the hunt in a litter borne by elephants.

Bertha". Between the wars Krupp's plant was kept intact, producing agricultural and other machinery, but when the Nazis came to power the firm turned once more to producing armaments on an unprecedented scale. At the end of World War II Alfred Felix Krupp (b. 1907) was imprisoned by the Allies until 1951, and his empire was split up.

Alfred Krupp's foundry at Essen.

Kublai Khan (1216–94)**:** Emperor of China. The grandson of the Mongol conqueror, Genghis Khan, Kublai Khan founded the Mongol or Yuan dynasty in China. When he succeeded his brother Mangu in 1259 he had already made conquests in northern China. In twenty years after succeeding to the khanate he had conquered all China, establishing his capital at Peking where he had a court of great magnificence, the fame of which has echoed through history and literature. Keenly interested in what could be learned from other countries, he entertained and employed foreigners, including Europeans. One such was the Venetian traveller Marco Polo. Kublai Khan was sympathetic to ancient Chinese culture. He played with the idea of introducing Christianity and made overtures to the Pope, but finally preferred Buddhism. Several later attempts to extend his empire overseas against Japan and Java and overland against Burma and Vietnam were unsuccessful.

¶ In UNSTEAD, R. J. *Royal Adventurers.* 1963

Ku Klux Klan: American secret society. This was originally founded in 1866 to re-establish white supremacy in the Southern states of the USA after their defeat in the American Civil War (1861–65). Its methods were to terrorise the Negroes and their sympathisers, a burning fiery cross accompanying their acts of violence. General Nathan Bedford Forrest was the first leader of the Klan (his title was "Grand Wizard") and attracted the

Members of the Ku Klux Klan taking an oath at an initiation ceremony in Baltimore in 1923.

support of the poor whites ("rednecks"). The hooded white-sheeted Klansmen whipped, shot and lynched the newly freed Negroes. Disbanded in 1871, the society was refounded in 1915 and became very active in the 1920s, showing hostility towards Negroes, Roman Catholics and Jews. The movement revived in the mid-1950s with the introduction of civil rights programmes to aid Negroes, and workers of that movement were killed by Klansmen even in the late 1960s.

Kuomintang: the Chinese nationalist party which ruled China from 1928 to 1949. A republican movement under the empire, it became a political party in 1912 when the Chinese republic was founded. Under Sun Yat-sen the Kuomintang collaborated with the Communists. When Chiang Kai-shek overcame the provincial warlords in the late 1920s, the Kuomintang became identified with his personal rule. This led to a split with the Communists under Mao Tse-tung and eventually to civil war. When the Communists got control in 1949, Chiang and the traditions of Kuomintang were driven out to Formosa.

Kushan Empire: empire of a centra Asian people who invaded northern Indi from Bactria through the Pamirs an Hindu Kush, establishing a rule whicl extended over Afghanistan and the Pun jab. Their most outstanding ruler wa Kanishka who reigned about AD 120. H extended the empire to include a grea part of northern India as far east as th modern Varanasi, as well as Kashmir Afghanistan and Chinese Turkestan. Th city of Peshawar was his capital. H patronised Buddhism and made tradin contact with the Roman Empire. In th early 3rd century the dynasty declined and the empire broke up.

Kutuzov, Mikhail Ilarionovich Prince of Smolensk (1745–1813) Russian field marshal who forced Napo leon to begin the celebrated retreat fron Moscow (1812) and harried him s successfully that only a remnant of th army regained France. In 1805 he ha counselled against engaging the Emperc at the battle of Austerlitz (*see* separat entry) and is said to have taken so littl interest when his advice was disregarde that he fell asleep during the reading of th battle orders.

Kuwait, Kuweit, or **Koweit:** indepen dent Arab state and port town at the hea of the Gulf, Kuwait came under Britisl protection in 1899. Huge oil resource have made this tiny state one of th richest countries on a per capita basis i the world. The special relationship witl Britain was ended by mutual consent i 1961 when Kuwait became fully inde pendent. She joined the United Nation in 1963. Sandwiched between powerfu neighbours, Kuwait follows a moderat policy in Arab affairs and is a majo source of aid.
See IRAQ for map.

L

ace: open-work fabric incorporating rnamental designs. It can be made of nen, cotton, silk, wool, synthetic fibres r even of gold or silver thread. Lace in iis sense dates from the beginning of the 6th century.

There are three different kinds of hand- iade lace – needlepoint, pillow and rochet. The first, as its name implies, is one with a needle. Pillow lace is really specialised form of weaving. The parch- ient pattern is fastened to a pad or pillow ith pins which prick out the design. he threads – of which there may be ozens – are held by bobbins and are wisted round the pins and interwoven ith each other as the pattern dictates. rochet may have a longer history than ie other two, for it is done with a hook of a kind used from very early times for making netting.

The best of the early laces came from northern Italy, especially Venice, and from Flanders. France and England, by importing Venetian workers, acquired lace-making industries of their own. The first machine for making lace was invented in 1768.

La Fayette, Marie-Joseph, Marquis de (1757–1834): French general who began his career in the French army and was so stirred by the American struggle for independence that he went to Philadelphia and offered his support. At that time a wealthy nineteen-year-old nobleman, he was immediately commissioned by Congress as a major-general. He quickly won the respect and friendship of George Washington and was entrusted with the task of negotiating with France for naval support against the British. His achievement of this task was a great help to the

colonists, and a grateful emerging nation showered praise and rewards upon him. When America entered World War I in 1917 General Pershing visited La Fayette's grave in Paris, removed his cap and said "La Fayette, we are here".

Lake Dwellings: primitive dwellings built over lakes and marshes. During the Neolithic and Bronze Ages in Europe, numbers of these human settlements appear to have been made on wooden platforms either over the waters at the edge of a lake, or over bogland. They were supported on piles, and some settlements, existing over a long period, may at various times have been successively over dry land, over open water and over bogland. The historian Herodotus refers to dwelling platforms erected in the 5th century BC. It would appear from this reference and from physical remains that the communities living in these settlements could be of some size and of some degree o civilisation.

The existence of lake dwellings was firs brought to the attention of the archaeological world in the middle of the 19th century. Noteworthy examples have been identified in Scotland and Ireland and in Swiss and Italian lakes.

Lancaster, House of: line of English kings founded by John of Gaunt (Shakespeare's "time-honoured Lancaster" and third surviving son of Edward III) by his first marriage to Blanche, heiress of the Duchy of Lancaster (1359). Their eldes son, Henry Bolingbroke, was exiled (1398) by his cousin Richard II, who later seized the vast Lancastrian lands on Gaunt's death. Bolingbroke returned to claim his lands but found Richard II so unpopular that he claimed the throne as well, forced his cousin to abdicate and was proclaimed as Henry IV (1399). He

Above: John of Gaunt, Duke of Lancaster, dining with the King of Portugal.

was succeeded by his famous son Henry V (1413–22) and his grandson, the unhappy Henry VI (1422–61), in whose reign the Wars of the Roses broke out.

John of Gaunt also had three sons and a daughter by the mistress he later married; his Beaufort family was afterwards legitimised but debarred from succeeding to the throne. Henry VII, through his mother Lady Margaret Beaufort, was descended from this line.

¶ STOREY, R. L. *The End of the House of Lancaster*. 1966

Land reclamation: the recovery of derelict or submerged land. The reclamation of land for agricultural and other purposes, involving the irrigation of wastes, the draining of marshes and the reclamation of land on the edge of a sea, a lake or a river, has been practised from pre-Christian times. An early example is recorded in an inscription on the tomb of a queen of ancient Egypt: "I constrained the mighty river to flow according to my will and let its waters fertilise lands that had before been barren and without inhabitants."

In Europe, low-lying lands on both sides of the North Sea were reclaimed extensively from the 17th century, the engineers being paid either by the grant of newly reclaimed land or by a salary from a

King Henry V.

body of commissioners. On some of these reclaimed lands, silt-bearing waters were allowed on to the land at certain times of the year, so that its level was both raised and enriched. This process was known in England as warping.

The experience of the Dutch in land reclamation led to their engineers being regarded as the most expert in the world. At home, they carried out increasingly ambitious projects, culminating in the Zuider Zee scheme, by which an area of over half a million acres [203,430 hectares] was recovered from the sea. In the United States of America, irrigation farming proved highly successful in the more barren of the states. Though there were earlier small schemes, the pioneers of modern irrigation methods in the United States were the Mormons, who began their ultimately very extensive irrigation farming in Utah just before the middle of the 19th century. In England, great areas of the East Anglian fens have been successfully drained, including Whittlesey Mere, the largest lake in the country, six miles [9·66 kilometres] long.

Landscape painting: the painting of inland scenery.

In the field of the arts landscape painting

was fairly late in starting. Stone Age paintings depicted wild animals and, occasionally, the men who hunted them, but made no attempt to place either in their natural setting. The first artists to take all nature as their domain were Chinese. Over many centuries they evolved a subtle and lively art, based on brushwork and line. Their landscapes have no perspective in the Western sense, yet the works of the great Chinese landscape artists – notably those of the Sung dynasty (960–1280) – have a realism that transcends exact representation.

Few Greek or Roman paintings have survived the passage of time. So far as we can judge, both the ancient Greeks and the Romans were more interested in the human figure than in landscape. Nevertheless, wall paintings such as those in the villa of Livia, at Prima Porta near Rome, show the existence in the classical world of landscape painters of skill and imagination.

Modern landscape painting, grounded in an interest in nature for its own sake, dates from the 15th century. The Italians, Masaccio (*c.* 1401–28) and Giovanni Bellini (*c.* 1430–1516), and the Flemish painter Jan van Eyck (*c.* 1390–1441), were among the first to practise this new approach. Even so, landscape remained literally in the background. Not until the 17th century were pictures painted in which nature had pride of place, with figures, when any were included, subordinated to it.

There were two great 17th-century schools of landscape painting – the French and the Dutch. The French painters – of whom the best known are Claude Lorraine (1600–82) and Nicolas Poussin (1594–1665) – specialised in picturesque landscapes which existed only in their imaginations. The Dutch, more homely, took nature as they actually found it. The famous painting of the avenue of poplars at Middelharnis by Meindert Hobbema (1638–1709) typifies the best Dutch landscape painting of this period.

In the early 19th century it was England's turn to produce landscape painting of the highest quality. John Constable (1776–1837) and the artists of the Norwich School distilled the essence of the English countryside into pictures which are a balm to the eye and the spirit. John Mallord William Turner (1775–1851) gave us landscapes full of light and movement – paintings which influenced the French Impressionists, that group of late 19th-century artists whose aim it was to capture in a swift impression a fleeting moment of light and shade.

The French painter Paul Cézanne (1839–1906), building on both the freedom of the Impressionists and the discipline of the Old Masters, produced paintings, many of them landscapes, which revolutionised not only painting but the very way we look at the world about us. Since his day, while many painters have continued to paint landscapes representationally, others, such as Henry Matisse (1869–1954), Pablo Picasso (1881–1973) and Georges Braque (1882–1923), have used nature as a point of departure for pictures which make no pretence to photographic accuracy or even recognisability. Others, like the English artist Ben Nicholson (1894–1982), have pared landscape to its barest essentials of colour and form.

¶ CLARK, KENNETH. *Landscape into Art*. 1956

Language: organised system of speech, usually of human beings. Language has been described as "the most wonderful creation of the mind of man".

Noah Webster (1758–1843), the American lexicographer, defined language as "the expression of ideas", adding: "Language, as well as the gift of speech,

bove: View of Hampstead *by John Constable. Below:* Trees at the Jas de Bouffon *by Paul ézanne.*

was the immediate gift of God." Thus, he tried to put his finger on the one thing hidden from us, the origin of language.

Another definition comes from C. K. Ogden (1889–1957), whose *Basic English Dictionary* defines language as "words and their use". Certainly language is the means by which we communicate ideas to each other and in a manner far and away beyond the primitive forms of communication used by other species. Philologists (literally, those who love words) investigate language scientifically and many of them believe that differences of speech may have come about through variations in man's physical structure: primitive people with short upper lips, for example, using consonants such as "f" and "k" rather than "p" which comes more naturally to those with long upper lips. We do not know whether language has a common origin.

It seems likely that speech came before writing and that its invention came about through man's impulse to communicate his wishes and feelings. It is, of course, possible to communicate simple wishes without uttering a syllable, as is done in small communities in which a vow of silence is taken. But life in general as now organised and lived would be impossible without speech and writing.

Among the earliest sounds uttered by man were cries of joy and pain; the war-cries of warriors; the decoy sounds of the huntsmen; and the many noises made in imitation of animals and natural phenomena.

Though by "language" we mean all communication, the very word, derived from French *langue* and Latin *lingua,* meaning "tongue", indicates the greater part played by speech in human communication. But the voice lacked the permanence of writing. We do not know how writing began, but it was probably in the form of crude and simple pictures of objects which served the purpose the time as tokens or symbols of wh men wanted and desired to say. We ca them pictographs, a word made up b putting together a Latin and a Gree word: *pictus*, artistic, and *grapho*, I writ The religious markings on the mon ments and tombs of the ancient Egyptia are called hieroglyphs, another made-u word contrived by putting together tw Greek words: *hieros*, sacred, and *glyph* carving.

The invention of writing, and later i extension by the invention of the alphabe was an enormous step forward in huma communication, making it possible t preserve records and events and to sen messages by a more reliable method tha by speech. Similarly, in modern times, th invention of wire and tape recording o sound has enabled us, by recording con versation, to give a degree of permanenc to the voice. This must appreciably in crease our store of knowledge and affe to an unpredictable extent the speech o generations to come.

It is estimated that more than half th population of the world can be reache by thirteen of the 3,000 living language Of these English is second to Chinese i the number of its speakers, followed b Hindi, Russian, Spanish, Japanese, Ger man, French, Italian, Malay, Bengali an Portuguese. The first recorded languag is Sumerian. The oldest living languag is Chinese.

The problem of communication betwee different nations with different language has long given rise to a desire for a uni versal language – as is said to have existe before the Tower of Babel was built wher according to the Bible story, "the whol earth was of one language and of on speech". This desire runs counter to th pride which nations take in their ow language, a pride which has helped t restore national status previously lost – a ith the Czechs, the Irish and the Jews. ut a compromise idea is gaining ground, nd that is to establish an international cond language which shall be used by l the nations side by side with their tional tongues. C. K. Ogden believed at this international second language ould be English and devised a system, hich he called Basic English, for that urpose. The best known artificial lanuage is Esperanto, invented in 1887 by e Polish linguist Doctor Zamenhof.

BARBER, CHARLES. *The Story of Language*. 1964

ee also ESPERANTO; HANDWRITING; HORTHAND, etc.

aos: republic in south-east Asia enclosed by China on the north, Vietnam on the east, Kampuchea on the south, and Thailand and Burma on the west. Laos s mainly inhabited by Buddhist Thais or peoples closely resembling them. French, Japanese, Chinese, Americans and Russians have influenced the defining of the confused boundaries. Communications within the country are too poor to bind the inhabitants into strong nationhood.

Laos became an independent kingdom in the 14th century. At the end of the 19th century it was incorporated into French Indo-China. Following the end of the Vietnam war (1975) the Pathet Lao (armed forces) took over and made Laos a People's Democratic Republic. The new regime was extremely repressive and required the support of the Communist government in Vietnam. In 1980, however, the government adopted more liberal economic policies, allowing a measure of private enterprise, and the economy has done better as a result. Population 3,993,000 in 1983.

See also VIETNAM, etc.

Lao-Tse or **Lao-Tzu** (*c.* 604–*c.* 531 BC): title given to Li Erh, who worked in the imperial library of the Chow dynasty and founded Taoism, one of the three great religions of China. His teachings were mystical and obscure in meaning, but he believed in the strength of quiet-

Lao-Tse and his disciples.

ness as a way to virtue, *tao* meaning, roughly, "the way". The religion developed in the centuries after his death, with its many gods and its magic, bears little relation to his original teaching, and the system of worship, with its temples and monasteries, was largely borrowed from Buddhism.

Lapland: region, mostly above the Arctic Circle, comprising parts of Norway, Sweden, Finland and Russia (Kola Peninsula). The Swedish name for the inhabitants – Lapps – means nomads. Lapland was still little known as late as the 16th century and the single incursion of its people into European affairs occurred when they were recruited into the armies of Gustavus Adolphus of Sweden (ruled 1611–32). Lapland has been subjected to many masters and its population has now been largely absorbed by neighbouring countries.

La Salle, René Robert Cavelier, Sieu de (1643–87): French explorer who w one of the first Europeans to enter centr North America. Arriving in New Franc (now Quebec Province, Canada) in 166 he established a fur trading post ne Montreal and spent the years betwee 1669 and 1671 exploring the Ohio an Great Lakes region. After the existence c a water highway from the St Lawrenc to the Gulf of Mexico had been estab lished, La Salle determined to exten French power southwards to the Missis sippi delta. Louis XIV of France mad him grants of land and "a patent to buil forts, trade and explore". Between 167 and 1682 he descended the Mississipp River to its mouth and claimed the whol valley for France, naming it Louisiana i honour of the French king. La Salle die in 1687, murdered by his own troop in the territory now known as Texas.

¶ SIBLEY, DAVID. *With La Salle Down the Mississipp* 1965

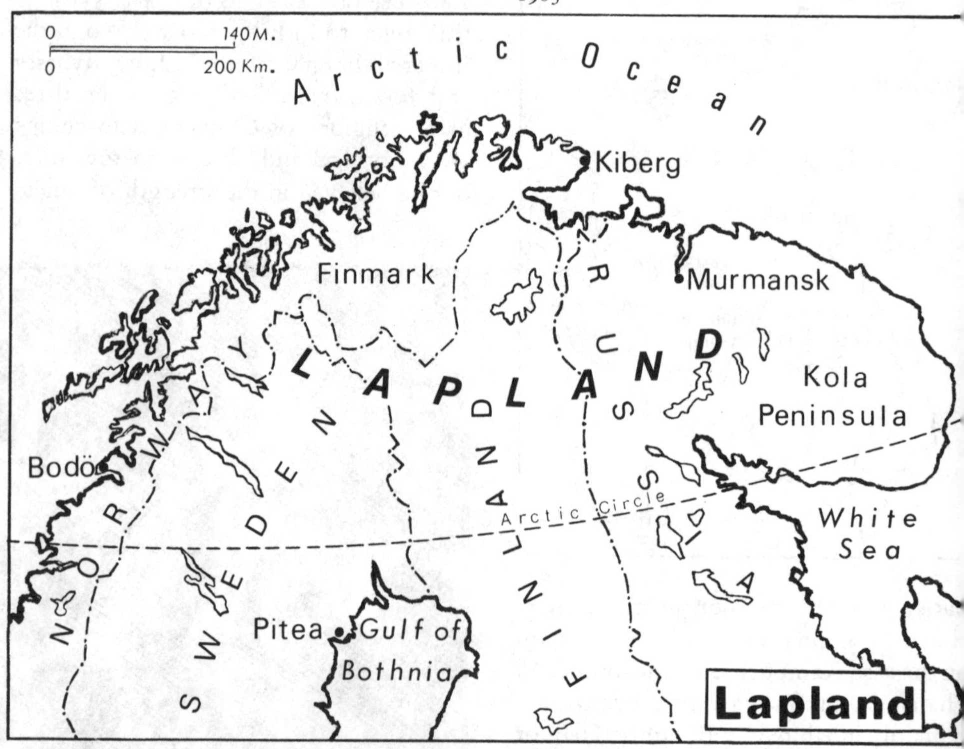

Latin America: the countries of Central and South America where Spanish and Portuguese are the predominant languages spoken. The 372 million people of this area (1982) include many races: native and European, African Negro and Asiatic Indian, and many of mixed origins. Most speak either Spanish or Portuguese, because for 300 years these lands were ruled by Spain and Portugal. At the end of the 18th century new ideas of freedom and equality began to challenge the control of overseas colonies by European monarchies, especially after Napoleon invaded Spain and Portugal. Brazil declared itself independent of Portugal in 1822. All the Spanish territories, except Cuba and Puerto Rico, gained their independence in a series of ferocious wars between 1810 and 1825, and as a result about twenty new republics were formed. Some of the leaders of these revolutions, like Simon Bolívar (1783–1830), had hoped to form a United States of South America. But local rivalries prevented leaders from co-operating, and the geographical obstacles of mountain and jungle hindered easy trade and communications. Unfortunately, quarrels between these twenty new nations began as soon as the wars for independence ended. They have remained divided ever since, and their weakness has often attracted interference from outside, as in 1862 when Napoleon III tried to take over Mexico. The 20th century history of the region has been troubled and today dictatorships (usually military and right wing) are frequently opposed by left wing guerrilla movements. This is especially the case in Central America.

Latin language: originally the tongue of the Romans and the tribes of the surrounding district of Latium. It belongs to one of the groups of Indo-European languages and conveys its meaning to a large extent by inflection (changes in the endings of words).

As the language of the Roman Empire and of the Western Church, it had a powerful influence on many modern European tongues, especially those of the Romance group, which includes French, Italian and Spanish, and has left many traces in our own. Until comparatively recently Latin was the means by which ideas were spread in western Europe, and it is still much used in legal, medical and botanical terms.

Laud, William (1573–1645): archbishop of Canterbury. He was educated at Reading School, being born in that town, and at St John's College, Oxford, of which he later became president. He was bishop successively of St David's, Bath and Wells, and London, which last appointment he combined with the Chancellorship of Oxford University. In 1633 Charles I promoted him to Canterbury.

Laud's support of the Court of Star Chamber (*see* separate entry) and other arbitrary methods of government; his insistence on the forms of worship laid down in the Prayer Book in England – and, with less success, in Scotland; and the people's strong suspicion that the archbishop was, in fact, a papist, roused enmities which even Charles, who supported him, could not resist. He was imprisoned by Parliament in 1641, but not brought to trial until 1644, and executed on a charge of high treason on 10 January 1645.

See also CANTERBURY, ARCHBISHOPS OF.

Lavoisier, Antoine-Laurent (1743–94): French chemist, perhaps best known for his recognition that oxygen is an element and that combustion is the process of combining with oxygen, a discovery that helped lay the foundations of modern chemistry. To provide money for his researches he became one of the government collectors of revenue. For this he was brought to trial during the Revolution and condemned to the guillotine, one of the charges against him being that he had "put water in the tobacco". He appealed in vain for a fortnight's respite to finish some experiments.

¶ In SHEPHERD, WALTER. *Great Pioneers of Science.* 1964

Lawrence, Sir Henry Montgomery (1806–57): soldier and hero of the Indian Mutiny, the fourth of six sons of a colonel in the service of the East India Company. Although he distinguished himself more than once as a soldier, he is chiefly remembered for his ability and devotion in political and administrative matters, particularly in the Punjab. A strong Christian belief was the inspiration of everything he undertook. On the outbreak of the Mutiny in 1857, Lawrence found himself charged with the defence of Lucknow, where he died of wounds soon after the siege began.

¶ In KAMM, JOSEPHINE. *They Served the People.* 1954

Lawrence, John Laird Mair, first **Baron Lawrence** (1811–79): Viceroy of India, the sixth of the brothers mentioned above and the only one to join the Company's service as a civilian. Like his brother, he distinguished himself in the Punjab, though unfortunately they quarrelled over questions of policy; and it was his hold over the area that enabled the British gradually to gain the upper hand in the Mutiny. He was made Viceroy of India (1864–69).

¶ In KAMM, JOSEPHINE. *They Served the People.* 1954

Lawrence, Thomas Edward, known as **"Lawrence of Arabia"** (1888–1935): British archaeologist and soldier. After extensive travels in Syria and Mesopotamia and excavations at Carcemish (1910–14), he helped, during the war, to promote and lead an Arab revolt against Turkey (1916–18) which protected the right flank of the British advance into Syria. He told the story in *The Seven Pillars of Wisdom.* In 1922, disgusted by what he regarded as the betrayal of the Arabs, he changed his name to Ross (later to Shaw), to avoid publicity, and joined the RAF as a mechanic. He was killed in a motor-cycle accident in 1935. Several recent books, plays and films have rekindled interest in a controversial figure, about whose character, motives and achievements there is much division of opinion.

T. E. Lawrence, known as "Lawrence of Arabia".

¶ BARBARY, JAMES. *Lawrence and His Desert Raiders.* 1965; THOMAS, JOHN. *Lawrence of Arabia.* Muller 1973

League of Nations: an international organisation which was born at the end of the first World War and which effectively died at the beginning of the second. Its purpose was "to prevent future wars . . . and to promote co-operation . . . between the nations of the world". Membership was open to all self-governing states. The League's main institutions were: the Assembly, consisting of delegations from all member states; the Council, consisting of permanent and non-permanent representatives; and the Secretariat, which was the administrative body, working under a Secretary-General. In addition, there was set up the Permanent Court of International Justice at the Hague. Under the covenant of the League, member states undertook not to go to war until all possibilities of a peaceful settlement had been exhausted; to register treaties publicly with the League; and to collaborate in promoting action in such fields as labour conditions, public health and colonial and minority problems.

Although the League did much useful work of social and economic reconstruction, it was powerless to prevent war. The military adventures of Japan, Italy and Germany in the 1930s and their withdrawal from the League (the USA never joined) meant that by 1939 it was an irrelevant and broken institution. Statesmen and peoples had expected much from the League, but it was betrayed through the determination of governments to put "vital" national interests above all else, and their failure to grant the League the power to bite as well as to bark.

¶ GIBBONS, S. R. and MORICAN, P. *The League of Nations and UNO.* 1970

Lease-Lend Bill: US legislation approved by President F. D. Roosevelt on 11 March 1941, drawn up primarily to help Britain, and any other country fighting Germany and her allies, to obtain essential war supplies. Lease-Lend enabled any country whose defence the President deemed vital to that of the United States to receive arms and other equipment by sale, transfer, exchange or lease. The total Lease-Lend for World War II amounted to fifty billion dollars.

Lebanon, Republic of: republic in western Asia at the eastern end of the Mediterranean, between Syria to the north and east and Israel to the south. The inhabitants speak Arabic and are mostly of Arab race.

Like other parts of this Levantine coast, Lebanon shared in the sea trade of goods crossing the land bridge between the Persian Gulf and the Mediterranean. Tripoli, Beirut, Byblos (now called Jubail), Sidon and Tyre are very ancient ports where routes through the mountains reach what is still the main highway north and south. Phoenicians, Egyptians, Romans, Venetians and others used these centres of trade, which, situated on peninsulas or on islands just off shore, are protected by the sea on at least three sides.

After long domination by the Ottoman Empire, Lebanon became autonomous in 1861 after a massacre of Christians had brought about intervention by European powers. Following a period under French mandate (1920) and as a republic (1926), Lebanon was occupied by British as well as French troops during World War II. The country became an independent republic in 1944 and joined the Arab League and the United Nations in 1945.

Since the mid-1970s the country has been torn by civil war between its Christian and Moslem communities; and as a base for the PLO came under increasing attack from Israel which invaded the southern part of the country in 1982.

See ISRAEL and SAUDI ARABIA for map.

¶ SALIBI, KAMAL S. *The Modern History of Lebanon.* 1965

Lebensraum: living-space; a slogan of German imperialism which referred in the early 20th century to the need for colonies overseas to solve the (alleged) problem of Germany's over-population; later used by Hitler in *Mein Kampf* (1923) and subsequently to justify the idea of German expansion in Europe, especially towards the east.

Le Corbusier (Charles Eduard Jeanneret-Gris, 1887–1965)**:** French architect of Swiss birth and one of the most influential of modern times, as well as being author, painter and sculptor. Le Corbusier was interested in the total urban environment. He prepared town-planning schemes for many important cities – among them Algiers, Sao Paulo, Rio de Janeiro, Buenos Aires, Barcelona, Geneva, Antwerp. He designed a new capital city for the Punjab at Chandigarh and was one of the consultants employed on the design of the New York headquarters of the United Nations. Two of his best known work are in France – the housing scheme a Marseilles known as the *Unité d'Habitatio* (1947–52) and the chapel at Ronchamp (1955).
See also INTERNATIONAL STYLE.

Right: Unité d'Habitation, *Le Corbusier's housing scheme in Marseilles. Below: Chapelle Notre Dame du Haut at Ronchamp.*

ee, Robert Edward (1807–70): mmander-in-chief of the Confederate rces in the American Civil War. He was mmissioned in the engineers in 1829 it by 1855 had assumed command of valry on the Texas frontier. In 1859 he mmanded the troops which put down hn Brown's raid on the military arsenal Harper's Ferry. At the outbreak of the ivil War he declined field command of e US Army offered by Abraham Linoln, accepting instead that of Virginia's ilitary forces. His brilliant leadership ought many unexpected successes for e South, but his defeat at Gettysburg as the turning point of the war. He rrendered to Grant at the Appomattox ourthouse (9 April 1865) and advised the outh to create a future within the Union.

In WALTON, J. *Makers of the USA*. 1943

ee also AMERICAN CIVIL WAR.

portrait of Thomas Coke of Holkam with the mous breed of sheep which is associated with im.

eicester of Holkham, Thomas Villiam Coke, Earl of (1752–1842): gricultural improver. Popularly known his lifetime and to posterity as Coke of Norfolk, Coke was the son of a Norfolk quire and was for many years a member f parliament for his native county, in the Vhig interest. He was among the leaders f the agricultural revolution of the 18th entury. The poor land which formed his Holkham estate was improved by such measures as the use of fertilisers and the proper rotation of crops, and both the produce of the soil and the quality of his farm livestock were increased to such an extent that his Holkham estate rental is reputed to have risen from £2,200 to over £20,000 a year. In old age, in 1837, he was created Earl of Leicester of Holkham.

See also AGRICULTURAL IMPROVERS.

Lenin (1870–1924): the name adopted by Vladimir Ilyich Ulyanov to hide his identity from the police; Russian revolutionary and founder of the Soviet Republics. An event that considerably influenced him in early years was the execution of his eldest brother for his part in an unsuccessful attempt on the life of Alexander III (1891). Another great influence was Karl Marx (*see* separate entry), whose writings he studied deeply. He began writing and organising himself, and in 1895 founded in St Petersburg (afterwards renamed Leningrad in his honour) an illegal society called "the Union for the Liberation of Working Classes". In a few months he was arrested, and spent the next three years in prison and exile.

One of the landmarks of his career – and of world history – came in 1903 when at a conference of the Russian Social Democrats in London the party split into *Bolsheviki* ("majority men") led by Lenin, and the more moderate, now outvoted *Mensheviki* ("minority men"). Thereafter the Bolsheviks and Mensheviks became bitterly opposed to each other. After a long period abroad Lenin returned to Russia in 1917 and overthrew the government that had been set up by Aleksander Kerenski and for the rest of his life was virtual dictator, putting down all opposition to the Bolsheviks, now renamed the Communist Party, with great ruthlessness. "There is room for other parties," he said,

Lenin with Joseph Stalin.

"only in jail." His exertions laid the foundations of Russia's strength as a great world power.

¶ LIVERSIDGEE, DOUGLAS. *Lenin.* 1970; *Lenin and the Revolution.* 1972

Leningrad: second city of the USSR, founded in 1703 by Peter the Great on swampy land conquered from the Swedes. Named St Petersburg, it became his capital in 1712 and, with only a short interval, remained capital of Russia till 1918. St Petersburg was Russia's outlet to the Baltic and attracted much industry, including shipbuilding. It was the scene of the revolutions of 1917. Renamed Petrograd in 1914, it became Leningrad in 1924. In World War II Leningrad was besieged by the Germans 1941–44, and 900,000 died. Peace brought extensive rebuilding.

¶ MILLER, WRIGHT. *Leningrad.* 1970

Leonardo da Vinci (1452–1519)**:** Italian artist and scientist. Few men in history have displayed such breadth of knowledge, skill and inventiveness, and, with this, great charm of character. He has been called "the Universal Man".

Born in Florence, he was patronised as young man by Lorenzo de' Medici, b later moved to Milan, where he execute one of his most famous pictures, "Th Last Supper". This, now sadly deteric rated, can still be seen on the wall c which it was painted.

From 1499, always in demand, he w moving between Rome, Florence, Venic and Milan, until, in 1518, King Francis persuaded him to settle in France. He die at Amboise, supported, it is said, in th King's arms. He had brought with hi an even more famous picture, his portra of a woman generally known as "Mor Lisa", which is now in the Louvre, Pari

His mathematical and mechanical ski brought him fame as a civil and militar engineer, and evidence for his versatil abilities lies in the volume of annotate drawings with his curious right-to-le writing, now in the Royal Collection a Windsor Castle.

¶ GILLETTE, H. S. *Leonardo da Vinci: pathfinder science.* 1963

See also FIFTEENTH CENTURY; FRESCC RENAISSANCE.

A design by Leonardo da Vinci, for a flyin machine based on the wing of a bird; and co taining an example of his right to left writing.

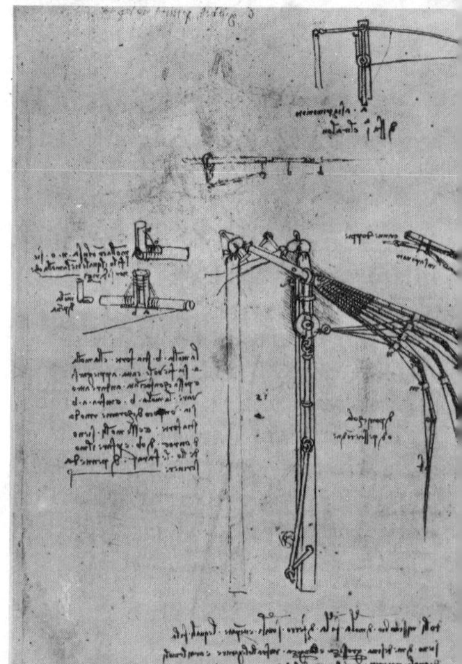

eopold II (1835–1909): King of the elgians 1865–1909; son of Leopold I. s a young man he served in the army and avelled widely in the East and in Africa. 1876 he formed the Association Internationale Africaine and proceeded to xploit the little-known region of the ongo as his personal property. Growing iticism prompted him to set up a commission to inquire into the administration f the area; its report in 1905 revealed rious inefficiency and corruption, and 1908 Leopold handed over the Congo the state. At home his reign was markable only for the domestic scandals which his family was involved.

---

epanto, Battle of (1571): naval victory f the West over the Turks. Ever since the ll of Constantinople (1453) the Turks ad been pressing forward, both by land nd by sea, against the states of Western urope, whose disunity often prevented ffective resistance. At length, however, ne exertions of Pope Pius V brought a ombined fleet of over 300 Spanish and 'enetian galleys and other craft under Don John of Austria face to face with bout the same number of Turkish ships n the narrows of the Corinthian Gulf. At rst the Turks were successful on the right nd left flanks. Then the Christians broke ne centre, capturing the commander-in-hief's galley and smashing his squadron. epanto was the last great battle in history o be fought with oar-driven ships. The 'urks lost an estimated 25,000 men, the Christians 8,000. Some 15,000 Christian laves were set free from the Turkish galleys. G. K. Chesterton gives a striking icture of the battle in his poem 'Lepanto".

---

esseps, Ferdinand Marie, Vicomte de 1805–94): French canal engineer. He was esponsible for the Suez Canal, completed n 1869, which enabled ocean-going ships

Ferdinand de Lesseps (second from right) and his helpers in Alexandria in 1865.

to pass between the Mediterranean and Red Seas. His project for the Panama Canal, between the Atlantic and Pacific Oceans, was not put in hand until after his death and was completed only in 1914.

¶ In CROWTHER, J. G. *Six Great Engineers*. 1959

See also SUEZ CANAL.

Letter of marque: licence or commission granted by a country at war to a private owner, authorising him to use his vessel as a ship of war or privateer. The letter of marque system attracted many captains in hope of rich profits. The Congress of Paris (1856) declared that "privateering is and remains abolished".

Levant: the coastal lands of the eastern Mediterranean, especially Lebanon and Syria. The name derives from French *lever,* to rise, indicating the east and the rising of the sun. In earlier centuries the Far East was known as the High Levant.

Liberia: independent African republic on the west coast of Africa. One hundred and fifty years ago a group in the USA formed the American Colonisation Society to return freed Negro slaves to their homeland. A pioneer settlement was established on the border of Sierra Leone and named Liberia – the free state. The early settlers had a hard struggle, but by 1847 they numbered over 30,000 and felt

sufficiently established for President Joseph Roberts, their first Negro leader, to issue a Declaration of Independence. The new state was recognised by the major European powers which enabled Liberia to escape colonisation during the Scramble for Africa 30 years later. The True Whig Party ruled for a century (1878–1980) but in the latter year a military coup brought Master Sergeant S Doe to Power. The economy depends upon commodities for export – rubber, iron ore, and small deposits of gold and diamonds. Most of the people remain subsistence farmers. Population 2,091,000 (1983).
See AFRICA for map.

Libraries: places set apart to contain books for reading, study, reference or borrowing. There is evidence that from earliest times scholars found places to store the material they required. In the beginning this was not in the form known to 20th century readers. Inscribed tablets, cylinders of baked clay and scrolls of parchment were the forerunners of the printed book. When few could read, these precious documents were kept for scholars' use in temple, colonnade or hall, or in libraries beside the Roman baths.

In the Middle Ages most libraries were found in monasteries. Reading and writing had a special place in the rule of each religious order, especially that of the Benedictines. The number of books was small, but it was increased by the monks' diligent hand-copying. On the dissolution of the monasteries in Britain many libraries were destroyed or their contents dispersed abroad. The manuscripts which survived, often beautifully illuminated, are now treasured in national, cathedral, university and private archives. Books are no longer fastened to reading desks with chains, at first an essential practice but one which was discontinued when, with the invention of printing in the late 15th century, books grew plentiful; a fe examples of chained libraries surviv e.g. in Hereford Cathedral, England.

The Chained Library of Hereford Cathedral.

By the end of the 18th century th collecting of books, which had been th province of the rich, became fashionabl among a wider section of the more literat population. The growth of public an private libraries was fostered by th development of publishing and the succes of the book trade. Compulsory educatio in the late 19th century encourage reading, and the need to provide mor books in universities and schools, as wel as for the use of the general public, wa increasingly recognised. Subscriptio libraries from which books could b borrowed for a fee became popular.

Today the world is full of libraries - public libraries in cities and towns; stat and county libraries providing a wid range of services; libraries attached t institutions of learning, cathedrals, universities, colleges and schools; libraries i ships, hospitals, factories, governmen offices, banks and industrial concerns. It would be difficult to find an organisation which does not have a need for books and ɔes not somehow find the means to ːovide them.

'To every scholar his boke", is a wish hich can now be fulfilled and he need ɔt journey far to find it. In some ɔuntries, under national lending schemes, ːaders can borrow from libraries hunːeds of miles away. Using photographic ːocesses, librarians can also send microlm copies of books and articles wherever ıey are required, even overseas.

From being mere custodians guarding ıeir treasures chained to desks, librarians, beit still curators, have become the ıeans of propagating and exploiting the 'orld's literature. The names of some ave already passed into history and are ːmembered with other benefactors in ıe libraries they founded; e.g. Sir Thomas odley (1543-1616), scholar of Oxford, 'hose library was made available in 1602; ɔhn Rylands of Manchester, a rich man 'hose widow built a library in his ıemory and opened its collection of treasures to the public in 1899; Sir William Osler, whose books on the history of medicine were bequeathed to McGill University, Montreal, Canada, in 1919; Henry Clay Folger (1857-1930), collector of Shakespeareana, who built the Folger Library in Washington, D.C., to house his collection; Henry Huntington, commemorated in the Huntington Library, Los Angeles; and, foremost in the public library service, Sir Andrew Carnegie (1835-1919), whose wealth endowed free libraries in the United States, Canada and Britain.

'he Reading Rooms of two of the world's most ɔmplete libraries. Above: The British Museum ı London. Below: The Library of Congress in Vashington.

History has seen the destruction and recreation of many libraries. The Vikings are known to have pillaged monasteries in England, taking the books for the value of their jewel-encrusted covers. Libraries were considered lawful booty in war; for instance, the *Bibliotheca Palatina* in Heidelberg was removed during the Thirty Years War, and later presented to the Pope. Gustavus Adolphus confiscated several libraries which he sent back to Sweden to enrich the University of Uppsala. The Royal Library in Stockholm was similarly augmented by captured books. In recent wars libraries have played a varied part, sustaining the morale of prisoners of war through libraries in prison camps, lending books to people in air raid shelters and hospitals. Many libraries were, however, bombed and burnt or had their contents scattered or destroyed for other reasons. Sometimes it seemed the damage could never be repaired. But when war ended, the printing presses came to life again, libraries were re-stocked and continued to fulfil their centuries-old rôle.

¶ IRWIN, RAYMOND. *The Origins of the English Library*. 1958

Libya: Socialist republic of North Africa bounded by the Mediterranean, Egypt to the east, Chad and Niger to the south and Algeria and Tunisia to the west. Libya was occupied by a succession of colonisers and conquerors, including Phoenicians, Greeks, Romans, Arabs, and Turks. The country was annexed by Italy after war with Turkey in 1911, the Arabs of the interior being put down with great brutality by Graziani's forces. After the defeat of Italy in World War II, a British military caretaker administration ruled the country until 1951, after which it became independent under the Emir Mohammed Idris al-Senussi as king. A military coup brought the monarchy to an end in 1969 and Colonel Muammar al-Qaddafi to power. From 1970 onwards Libyan policy has been to reduce western influence in the Arab world (British and American base facilities in the country were cancelled) and Qaddafi has become one of the Third World's most controversial figures. Libya has immense oil resources. Population 3,498,000 (1983). *See* AFRICA for map.

Lifeboats: craft, based on shore, designed for rescue work near the sea coast. The lifeboat proper is specially built to seek out and meet conditions that other craft try to avoid.

The first known boat to be specially made or adapted for saving life at sea was the work of an English coach-builder, Lionel Lukin, who converted a small fishing coble into an "unimmergible" (i.e. unsinkable) boat by fitting it with a number of hollow, watertight spaces to give it greater buoyancy and replacing some of the heavy woodwork with cork. This coble was stationed in 1786 at Bamburgh Castle, Northumberland, and saw good service on that storm-swept, rocky coast.

Four years later, in 1790, as the result of a competition organised by a group of English north country gentlemen, the first boat designed and built as a lifeboat was launched on the River Tyne. Christened the *Original*, it was constructe by Henry Greathead of South Shiel from a clay model. In the next fourtee years Greathead built another thirty-or lifeboats, eight of which went abroad t other countries. Greathead used some the ideas of another South Shields ma a singing master named William Woul have, whose memorial in the church South Shields describes him as "Clerk this Church and inventor of that invalu able blessing to mankind, the Lifeboat' Who, then, was the real inventor of th lifeboat? The answer seems to be th Lukin first converted a boat for lif saving purposes; that William Would have designed the first self-righting boa i.e. a craft that, even if it were overturne in rough weather, would immediatel come upright again; and that Greathea was the first successful builder on considerable scale.

Twenty-one years after his first experi ment, Lukin built the first sailing lifeboa a forty-foot craft to serve among the san dunes off the east coast of the Britis Isles. The first powered lifeboat was nc used till 1890 – the fifty-foot steel-buil *Duke of Northumberland,* which lasted ove thirty years.

The year 1834 saw the foundation i England of "The Royal National Lifeboa Institution for the Preservation of Lif from Shipwreck". The man chiefly re sponsible was Sir William Hillary, wh after a distinguished career as a soldier turned his energies to the problems o saving life at sea. He himself shared in th rescue of over 300 lives and was thre times awarded the Gold Medal of th Lifeboat Institution, the highest award i can bestow. A noteworthy feature of hi conception of a lifeboat service was that i must extend to ships of all nations, whethe at peace or war, irrespective of race colour and creed.

The British lifeboat service, despit

he launching of the Shoreham, Sussex, lifeboat.

me periods of financial difficulty, has ways been independent of government ntrol and is supported entirely by luntary contributions. The same is true a number of other countries. A survey ade in 1961 showed that Germany, the etherlands, Sweden and Uruguay were mpletely financed by voluntary sub-riptions. Others had state and municipal bsidies: a third group, among them anada, Denmark, India, the USA and e USSR, were state financed.

The size of lifeboat fleets naturally varies ith such factors as the length of coastline, e volume of shipping using its ports and e money available. Some idea of the ariety may be gathered from a few xamples from the 1961 returns made by feboat societies throughout the world:

ountry	*Strength of fleet*
enmark	24 motor lifeboats
	19 pulling and sailing lifeboats
celand	3 motor lifeboats
	4 patrolling rescue cruisers
	14 pulling surf boats
	1 ambulance aircraft
apan	30 motor lifeboats
	67 pulling lifeboats
ndia	2 motor lifeboats
taly	3 lifeboats
JSA	1,335 motor boats
	1,508 pulling boats
USSR	72 lifeboats and tenders
	14 salvage tugs

The modern tendency, with the development of air rescue services, is to reduce the number of stations in favour of a smaller number equipped with more powerful, longer-ranging craft.

¶ ASHLEY, BERNARD. *The Men and the Boats: Britain's Lifeboat Service*. 1968; UDEN, GRANT. *Life-Boats: a survey of their history and present state of development*. 1962

Lighthouses and lightships: strategically placed beacons on land and sea serving as navigational aids to ships. The original lighthouse or Pharos, built by Ptolemy off Alexandria, Egypt, *c.* 280 BC, was lit by wood fires. Subsequent illuminants were coal fires, tallow candles (as in Eddystone Light, south-west of Plymouth, England, 1756), oil-burning wicks (introduced by Swiss inventor Argand, 1784), vaporised oil and electricity, followed in the 1960s by mercury and high pressure arc lamps.

One of the earliest institutions concerned with lighthouses, Trinity House, London, received its first charter from Henry VIII in 1514. This fraternity organised pilotage and was responsible for erecting and maintaining lighthouses and navigational marks around the British Isles. Today it continues to provide this service together with similar organisations in Scotland and Ireland. Local authorities are responsible for lights within their harbour boundaries.

Lightships are moored in shallow waters to indicate shoals and sandbanks such as the Goodwin Sands area in the English Channel. They are also placed off important harbours to indicate the entrance channel as in the case of the Ambrose lightship off New York and the Bar lightship in Liverpool Bay.

Light Lists published by the governments of most countries give full descriptions of lights in use. For identification

The famous Eddystone Lighthouse built originally in 1698. It stands on a small and dangerous rock near Plymouth, England. It was destroyed many times but always rebuilt and the lighthouse stands today on the same spot.

purposes, either by day or night, the mariner requires to know the height, colour, visibility range, characteristics, e.g. group of three white flashes every ten seconds, and, in poor visibility, details of fog signals. Today most of the strategically placed lights act as radio beacons, and navigation in confined waters can be assisted with the many electronic aids available.

¶ CHADWICK, LEE. *Lighthouses and Lightships.* 1971

Lima: capital city of Peru, situated six miles [9.66 kilometres] from the Pacific coast on the River Rimac. It was founded in 1535 by Francisco Pizarro, the conqueror of the Incas. He personally supervised the lay-out and building of its broad avenues, spacious gardens and massive public buildings, and was himself buried in its magnificent cathedral. The city was rebuilt on its original foundations when destroyed by an earthquake in 1746. From

The Ambrose Offshore Light Structure in Ne York Harbour. It is manned by a resident U coastguard crew.

Lima the Spanish Viceroy ruled over mo of South America, until in 1824 it be came the capital of the new independer republic. The various wars and revolutior that have racked Peru have left thei mark on the capital. When the countr was at war with Chile (1879–94) th Chilean army occupied the city for nearl three years and ruthlessly despoiled i buildings and its collections of literary artistic and scientific treasures. The preser city is a mixture of old and new.

See also PIZARRO, FRANCISCO.

Lincoln, Abraham (1809–65): sixteent president of the USA. Born into a illiterate and wandering frontier family he eventually settled at New Salem Illinois, where he ran a store, served a postmaster and studied law. He wa admitted to the Bar in 1836 and moved t Springfield, where he became an out standing lawyer and served four terms i the state legislature, representing Illinoi as a Whig in Congress from 1847 to 1849

Lincoln joined the Republicans in 1856 and two years later campaigned strongly, though unsuccessfully, for the Senate. He quickly emerged, however, as the leading candidate for the Republican presidential nomination. He became president in 1860, largely because of splits amongst the Democrats. As a result of his election, seven slave states seceded before he assumed office in March 1861. A month later the Civil War broke out. As a war leader he was at first fumbling and indecisive. What caused the change has never been clear; but from July 1862 he suddenly emerged as master of the situation, assuming direct control, appointing and dismissing his own generals, and protecting them from civilian interference. As president his greatest qualities were the skilful handling of his party and his generals, his personal integrity and ability as a speaker, the best example being the famous Gettysburg Address in 1863, in which he urged the nation's dedication to a new freedom and spoke of "government of the people, by the people, and for the people". The historical legend that represents him as fighting to free the slave population is misleading. Even a late as August 1862 he said: "My paramount object is to save the Union, and not to save or destroy slavery". A week after the surrender of the main Confederate army, he was shot by John Wilkes Booth in Ford's Theatre in Washington on Good Friday 1865, dying the next morning (15 April).

Abraham Lincoln photographed by Matthew Brady in February 1861.

¶ LATHAM, FRANK B. *Abraham Lincoln*. 1972
See AMERICAN CIVIL WAR; AMERICAN PRESIDENTS; GETTYSBURG; SLAVERY etc.

Lingua franca: jargon or mixed language used between people of different nations; originally basically Italian with Spanish, French, Greek and Armenian and used as the common speech of the Mediterranean Sea and its ports.

Linnaeus, Carolus (Carl Linné, 1707–78)**:** Swedish botanist who originated the binomial (two-name) classification of plants, i.e. the name of the genus, group or class, and the specific name of the individual plant. The system was widely accepted throughout much of the world and, with considerable modifications, is still in use today. The adjective *Linnaean* derives from the botanist's name, which is the Latin form of the Swedish.

¶ DICKINSON, ALICE. *Linnaeus*. 1970

Lisbon: capital of Portugal and major port at the mouth of the River Tagus, the lower plain of which is so fertile that wheat was said even in medieval times to grow in forty days.

Lisbon became the capital in the mid-13th century and flourished as an entrepôt for spices and other goods from the Levantine coast *en route* to Holland and the Hansa cities, from about AD 1300. When the Turks broke the monopoly of Venice after 1453, Henry the Navigator explored the Cape route to India. This

The ruins of Lisbon after the earthquake of 1755.

brought Mediterranean trade to the Atlantic and greater profit to Lisbon. After a devastating earthquake in 1755 had destroyed half the city, it was replanned in magnificent symmetrical style by the Marquis de Pombal, foreign secretary 1750–77. When Napoleon invaded Portugal and the royal family fled to Brazil (1808) the city began to decline and did not climb to importance again till after 1850. Various revolutions in this century have brought considerabl damage, but Lisbon remains one of th finest cities of Europe.

¶ WRIGHT, CAROL. *Lisbon.* 1971

See also PORTUGAL.

Lister, Joseph, first Baron Lister (1827 1912): English surgeon and pioneer c antiseptic surgery. Anaesthesia had mad the work of surgeons easier, but man patients died because gangrene and bloo poisoning attacked them after an opera tion. Doctors believed that infection wa carried to open wounds by the air, bu Lister studied the researches of Pasteu and was convinced that germs caused it

Lister tried soaking dressings and band ages in dilute carbolic acid to kill germs but the acid often destroyed tissues as well He then insisted on the disinfection of th hands and instruments of the surgeons and sterilised his hospital with a carboli spray. His methods greatly reduced th risk of post-operational infection.

¶ CARTWRIGHT, F. F. *Joseph Lister, the man who mad surgery safe.* 1963

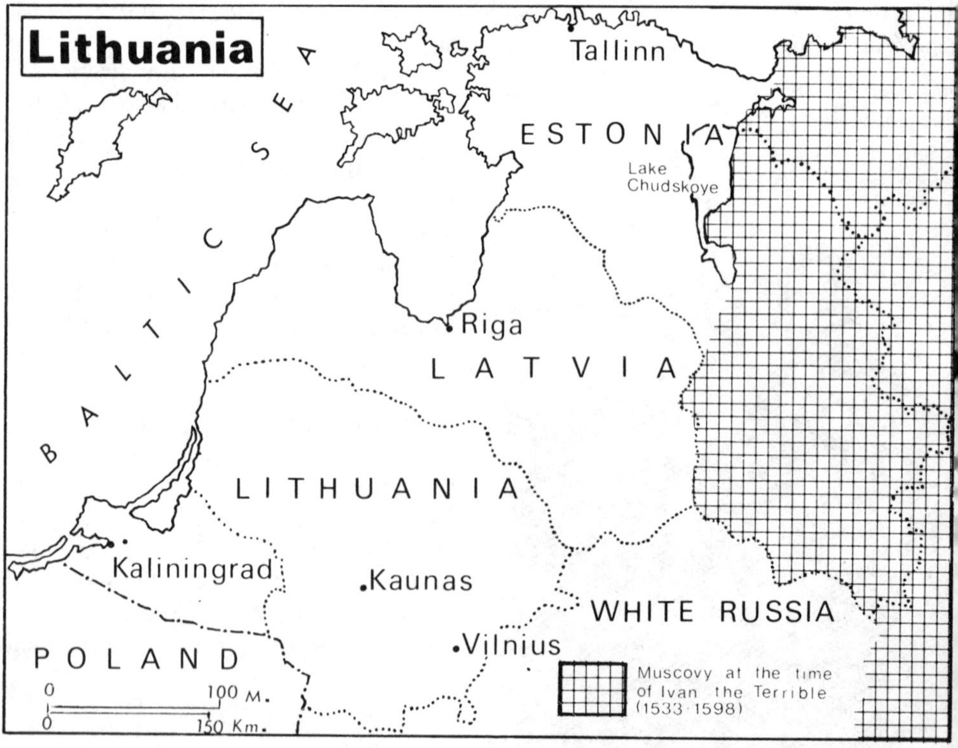

Lithuania: constituent republic of the USSR. The state of Lithuania dates from the 13th century, emerging from Slav tribes settled along the eastern shore of the Baltic Sea. By the 15th century it stretched from the Baltic to the Black Sea, and north to Muscovy. In 1385 Lithuania's Grand Duke, Jagiello, was elected hereditary king of Poland, the two countries being formally united in the Polish Commonwealth in 1569. Russia acquired most of present day Lithuania by the 1795 partition of Poland. Independent from 1919, the state was annexed by Stalin in 1939 and today remains part of the USSR.

Liverpool: second largest port of England, on the estuary of the River Mersey, Lancashire. Settlements existed in the 8th century and trade developed with Ireland, France and Spain. The rise of Lancashire industries greatly increased this trade and extended it to the West Indies and the Americas. Liverpool also profited from slave-trading in the century 1709–1807. In 1618 the Privy Council declared Liverpool to be dependent on Chester, but the volume of water evacuated on the ebb tide scoured the basin by contrast with Chester, which silted up. Engineering work added to these natural advantages and a major dock development occurred in the 18th and 19th centuries. In 1800 the total tonnage of ships entering Liverpool was 450,060. In the next 120 years it rose to over 30 million tons [30,483,000 tonnes] coming from every part of the world, and carrying a great variety of commodities. The trade with America has been the most important, with cotton ranking as the chief import. The port is also an important outlet for the manufactures of Lancashire and the West Riding of Yorkshire.

¶ BORER, MARY CATHCART. *Liverpool.* 1971

Livingstone, David (1813–73): Scottish explorer and missionary; joined London Missionary Society 1838, qualified as medical doctor 1840; posted to Kuruman Mission, N. Cape Colony 1841; married Mary Moffat, daughter of Robert Moffat, founder of the mission in 1844. To his staunch Christianity was added a passion for exploration, and he gloried in blazing the trail for other missionaries. In 1849, with Oswell, he discovered Lake Ngami, and in 1850 followed the Zambesi to its source at Mwinilunga, continuing west to the Atlantic coast at Luanda. In 1855–56 a journey down the Zambesi led to his discovering the Victoria Falls. Later explorations included the discovery of Lakes Nyasa and Shirwa. He died at Ilala 1 May 1873 and, after his body had been carried by natives across Africa to Zanzibar and conveyed thence to England, was buried in Westminster Abbey in 1874.

¶ MATHEWS, B. *Livingstone the Pathfinder.* 1960

Livy (Titus Livius, 59 BC–AD 17)**:** Roman historian. He was born and died at Patavium (Padua) in Lombardy. His *History of Rome*, from the foundation of the city (traditionally 753 BC), is said to have taken forty years to complete and to have amounted to 142 books, of which only thirty-five have survived.

Lloyd George, David, first Earl Lloyd George (1863–1945): British Liberal statesman. The son of a Welsh schoolteacher, he entered Parliament in 1890 and in 1905 joined the Liberal government, becoming Chancellor of the Exchequer in 1908. In 1916 he replaced Asquith as leader of the wartime coalition government, thus splitting and hastening the decline of his own party. After his defeat in the 1922 election he never again held office, becoming an elder statesman of occasionally eccentric opinions. He is most remembered for the social legisla tion, including provision for old-ag pensions and national insurance, which h piloted through parliament in the yea 1908–11 and for his vigorous wartim leadership, as well as for his fiery orator and colourful personal life.

¶ In WHITTLE, J. *Great Prime Ministers.* 1966

Lloyd's of London: an associatio which began in the City of London in th 17th century for the insurance of ships an cargoes. It was named after Edward Lloy (1688–1726) who kept a coffee-hous where the shipowners and merchants me the insurers. In return for a premium th insurers undertook to pay an agreed sun if a ship were lost or damaged. News o the movement of ships was collected fron the docks and published in *Lloyd's New* which still appears and is now known a *Lloyd's List.* The society flourished an today Lloyds of London is a world centr for shipping intelligence and insurance.

¶ GIBB, D. E. W. *Lloyd's of London.* 1957

A busy day in Lloyds Coffee House in Lombar Street; 18th century.

ɔcke, John (1632–1704): English philopher. He was educated at Westminster
hool and Christ Church, Oxford, and
came secretary to the politician who
as later created Earl of Shaftesbury. On
e latter's disgrace, he fled to Holland
d remained there until James II had
uitted the throne.

n all his thought and writing he placed
eat emphasis on reason and reasonable-
ss, with an acknowledgement that, in
atters of religion, some things are by
ture unknowable. As a result he stood
r toleration and broadmindedness. His
ost famous philosophical work is the
say concerning Human Understanding
690).

n THOMAS, H. and THOMAS, D. L. *Great Philoso-
ers.* 1959

ollard: in English history, a follower
John Wyclif (*see* separate entry), the
ligious reformer who, with the help of
s friends, translated the Bible into
nglish. The derivation is doubtful, but
rhaps is from the German *lollen,* to
ng, from their custom of singing hymns,
from the Dutch *lollaert,* a mumbler.
he term is also applied to a 14th-century
utch heretical sect.

ombards: name originating from the
ɔmbardy region of northern Italy, where
e Teutonic people known as Lombards
ttled in the 6th century, but applied in
edieval times particularly to Italian
erchants and bankers. As the Canon
w forbade Christians to lend money on
terest, finance in England was largely
the hands of the Jews until their expul-
on in 1290. They were succeeded by
alian merchants and bankers from Pia-
nza, Siena, Lucca and Florence, all
nown in England as Lombards. They
rst arrived in Henry III's reign, and were
nally banished by Elizabeth I. They
ayed a large part in the state finances of
oth England and France. Edward II repaid his father's debt of £56,000 to the Frescobaldi, and both Edward III and Henry V pledged their jewels to the Lombards to raise money. Lombard Street in the City of London commemorates their residence there.

London: capital of England and the United Kingdom. The Greater London Council (GLC) administers an area of 616 square miles (1595 square kilometres), home of 6,765,100 people (1983). This vast urban sprawl is less a city than a collection of villages which have been sucked into the maw of the metropolis, yet still obstinately retain something of their former character. London abounds in important buildings – the Houses of Parliament, St Paul's Cathedral, the Tower, Westminster Abbey, palaces, concert halls, museums – but despite the efforts of such architects as Nash and Wren little is systematically planned. It grew up haphazardly, and this is a great part of London's charm.

The city's beginning was a remote outpost of the Roman Empire called Londinium, established at that particular spot because it was the lowest point where the Thames could be crossed and was also the tidal limit of the river. Over the centuries, despite sackings by Vikings, plagues, fires and Hitler's blitz, that favourable geographical position across lines of communication by land and water has ensured London's growth into one of the most important trading centres of the world.

The nucleus of its prosperity, the City of London, is a square mile, the boundaries of which have not changed since the 13th century. Here are the Bank of England, the Stock Exchange and commercial and financial institutions on which the economic wellbeing of the country in large measure depends. Half a million workers pour into that square mile daily,

An aerial view of modern London.

but only a few thousand people live there. At night the narrow, winding streets are quiet and the City becomes a village, like all the other component parts of London.

¶ HAYES, JOHN. *London from the Earliest Times to the Present Day*. 1959; HAYES, JOHN. *London: a pictorial history*. 1969

See also BANK OF ENGLAND; CLEOPATRA'S NEEDLES; DOWNING STREET; LLOYD'S OF LONDON; TOWER OF LONDON; WREN, SIR CHRISTOPHER, etc.

London Bridge: bridge over the Thames connecting the City of London wi Southwark and Bermondsey. There ha been many London Bridges, Roma Saxon, English, the most famous built the 14th century with houses, shops an chapel on it. The buildings, much d cayed, were demolished in 1675, and t bridge itself replaced in 1831. This brid (widened 1902–04) was sold to an Ame can oil company which had it re-erect at Lake Havasu, Arizona (*see belou* while London got yet another ne London Bridge.

¶ JACKSON, PETER. *London Bridge*. 1971

ongitude: an arc of the equator con-ined between the prime meridian and ıe meridian passing through a given ɔsition on the earth's surface; or, alter-ıtively, the angle subtended at the pole ɛtween the prime meridian and that ıssing through the position. The prime ·eridian is usually that which passes ırough Greenwich, London, represent-ıg 0° longitude.

Γhe problem of finding an accurate ·ngitude at sea was not resolved until ıe 18th century. Latitude could be found ısily. In the northern hemisphere it was nly a matter of measuring the height of ıe Pole Star above the horizon. The early ıariners could sail north or south until ıe latitude of their destination was con-rmed, then proceed east or west to ·ach their objective.

Finding longitude by "lunar distance" r "timepiece" methods required two ital factors not as yet available, namely ccurate predictions of the moon's posi-on and a ship's clock to keep Greenwich me within seconds. The Board of ongitude, inaugurated in London in 714, offered rewards of up to £20,000 ɔr practical methods of achieving these bjectives.

The award eventually went to John Iarrison, an Englishman who made a ·ries of special timepieces for use in ıips. His Number Four chronometer 'as tested at sea 1761–65 to the satisfaction f the Board. Another Englishman, Lar-ɔm Kendall, produced a copy in 1770 ıd Captain Cook tested its accuracy uring his 1772–75 voyage.

The longitude by timepiece method was ıus established through the ingenuity of ɔhn Harrison. The *Nautical Almanac,* first ublished in 1767, provided the necessary stronomical data for the lunar distance ıethod.

'ee also HARRISON, JOHN; GREENWICH IEAN TIME.

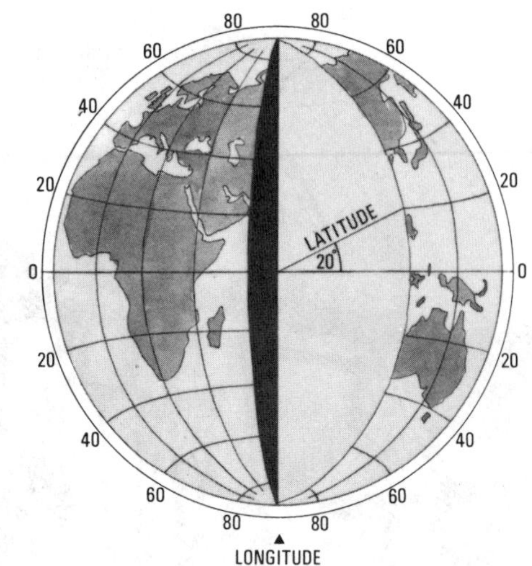

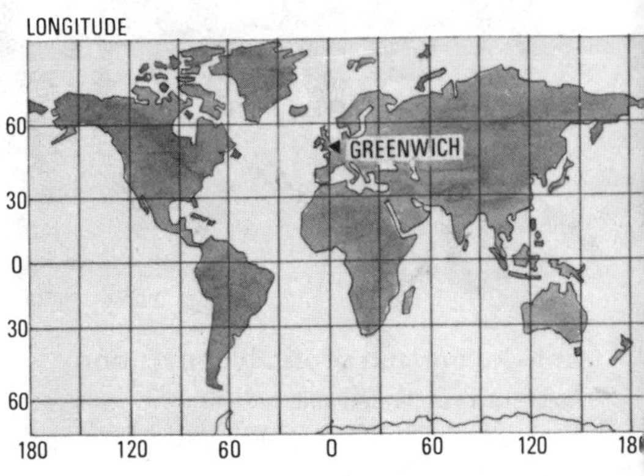

Loom: frame or machine for weaving cloth. Pictures in Egyptian tombs show women working at large looms, consisting of a horizontal beam resting across two upright posts. Long threads – the warps – hung from this beam, kept taut by weights attached to their ends. Thread was fastened to a flat piece of wood or bone – the shuttle – and this was passed under and over the warps, like a threaded darning needle. In this way cloth was woven. All primitive people appear to have used looms, which changed little through the ages, although later looms were flat, resembling bed-frames. The introduction of steam and electric power made the mechanical driven loom a

SYRIAN TREADLE LOOM AND GROUND LOOM FROM PALESTINE
BOTH NOW IN THE BRITISH MUSEUM

time-saving and profitable invention.
¶ ELLACOTT, S. E. *Spinning and Weaving*. 1962
See also COTTON; TEXTILES, etc.

Lorraine: former province of eastern France. Once a duchy of the Holy Roman Empire, it was occupied by France, at first partly, from 1552 till 1766, and then wholly. The Moselle region was annexed in 1871 by Prussia to form Alsace-Lorraine but was officially restored to France in 1918.

Louisiana Purchase (April 1803): the biggest land sale in history, by which the USA bought from France the whole of the Mississippi Valley up to the Rocky Mountains, an area of 828,000 square miles [21,000 hectares]. The price paid was fifteen million dollars. Louisiana had been French until 1762, when it was ceded to Spain; it was return to France in 1800. Napoleon, after rejec ing the idea of a new American empir decided to sell the territories, and Pre dent Thomas Jefferson was anxious acquire them. The treaty was neg tiated in Paris by the American amba sador, Robert R. Livingston, and by t future president, James Monroe. T agreement left the boundaries ill-define While the Gulf of Mexico was fixed the line to the south and the Mississippi that to the east, there was no clear unde standing as to whether the cession i cluded West Florida and Texas. This w to cause further trouble, especially ov Texas. The Senate approved the pu chase treaty on 20 October, and form possession was taken in the last days the year. William Claiborne was install as territorial governor in October 180 In 1812 the state of Louisiana became t rst to be admitted to the Union from ıe new territorial area.

ourdes: famous place of pilgrimage in ›uth-west France, at the foot of the yrenees. In 1858 a peasant girl, later ınonised as St Bernadette, had visions of ıe Virgin in a grotto at this place. At the ıme time a spring of water appeared, to 'hich miraculous healing powers were tributed. Since then pilgrims in millions ave visited Lourdes seeking cures for ıeir ailments, and a magnificent church as been built close to the one which was ected above the grotto. The anniversary f Bernadette's vision is celebrated on ı February.

ouvre: palace in Paris, once the resience of the kings of France. Today it ouses government offices and one of the est art collections in the world. The atue of the Aphrodite of Melos, comıonly called the Venus de Milo, and eonardo da Vinci's portrait of Mona isa are only two of the famous works of rt on view there.

he Venus de Milo, Greek 3rd century BC.

Low Countries, Pays-Bas: collective name for Belgium, the Netherlands and Luxembourg (*see* separate entries).

Lucknow: the old capital of Oudh, India, on the River Gumti, a tributary of the Ganges. It was captured by the British after the battle of Buxar, 1764. During the Mutiny, 1857, its Residency, defended by Sir Henry Lawrence (*see* separate entry), who was killed, withstood a three months' siege, until relieved by Havelock.

Luther, Martin (1483–1546): founder of the reformed Protestant Churches in Western Europe. Son of a Saxon miner, he studied philosophy at Erfurt University before entering the order of Augustinian Brothers and being ordained priest. In 1508 he became a lecturer at the new University of Wittenberg.

Gradually, however, he found himself growing dissatisfied with some of the teaching of the Roman Church and increasingly critical of its abuses, particularly in the offer of *indulgences,* the partial remission of punishment in the next world, to those who, in this instance, contributed to the rebuilding of St Peter's, Rome. In 1517 he nailed to the door of the principal church in Wittenberg a paper containing ninety-five theses (arguments) denouncing this practice. From now on his writing and preaching emboldened others to protest against what they saw wrong in the Church and to band together in furtherance of their ideas. Although Rome took vigorous steps to condemn the unrest and in 1521 summoned its originator before the Diet of Worms, where he refused to recant, the strength of the new movement, to which more than one of the rulers of the German States lent support, saved him from being put on trial for his life.

In 1524 Luther finally renounced his Augustinian vows and next year married a former nun. He spent the rest of his life in promoting the new faith and trying to preserve unity among its followers.

His translation of the Bible had a pro found effect on the development of th German language.

¶ PITTENGER, W. NORMAN. *Martin Luther.* 1972

Luxembourg: Grand Duchy of wester Europe. At various times under the ru of Burgundy (1441–1506), Spain (1506 1714), Austria (1714–95) and Franc (1795–1815), the territory was constitute a Grand Duchy by the Congress c Vienna in 1815 and was recognised as a independent neutral state in 1867. Despit the Duchy's small size (now only 99 square miles [2587 square kilometres], th western part having been incorporate into Belgium), Luxembourg once boaste in its capital (also called Luxembourg) th strongest fortified city in Europe, al though the name Luxembourg *(Lutze burg)* means "little fortress". Opinion differ as to whether it yielded first plac to Gibraltar in impregnability, but i situation on cliffs overhanging a rive gave it a strong claim. The actual fortre was demolished in 1867, with the recog nition of neutrality. *See also* EUROPE.

A 19th century engraving of the fortress of Luxembourg.

M

IcAdam, John Loudon (1756–1836): ›ad maker. His claim to fame rests ıiefly on the improvements he made in ıe smoothness and durability of roads, y constructing them in layers of broken ›ones in graded sizes. The use in more :cent times of tar to bind the surface roduced "tarmacadam" ("tarmac").

In WALTON, J. *Seven Civil Engineers*. 1948

enator Joseph McCarthy.

IcCarthyism: vicious charges against ıdividuals, often without satisfactory vidence, of pro-Communism and un-merican activities. During the years nmediately following World War II valry between America and the USSR ›d to US politicians using the anti-Communist platform as a vote-getting evice. Many Congressmen called for loyalty oaths" from teachers, civil service mployees and government officials. Be-ween 1947 and 1952, such was the ysteria that there were no less than three ongressional committees concentrating ıquiries into Communism in the US and :eking out subversion in unions, schools, hurches, the press and the armed forces.)vershadowing all other investigators was Senator Joseph McCarthy (1909–57), using methods of smear, innuendo and intimidation that many people considered were not in keeping with traditional American liberties. McCarthy and his associates finally overreached themselves, and their methods of investigation became in turn the subject of a Senate inquiry. McCarthy was officially censured, or reproved, by the Senate and lost his influence.

Macedon: ancient kingdom of N.E. Greece, established in about 814 BC by Caranus. Subsequently, under Philip II (ruled 359–336 BC), it rose to dominate Greece and under his son Alexander III (ruled 336–323 BC) defeated the Persian empire. Macedon was annexed by Rome in 146 BC.

See also ALEXANDER III; PHILIP II, etc.

Macedonia: (1) mountainous constituent republic of southern Yugoslavia, lying between Greece, Bulgaria and Albania; (2) mountainous region of the Balkan peninsula, consisting of a part of northern Greece, southern Jugoslavia and south-western Bulgaria. The region became part of the Byzantine Empire in 395 and subsequently passed under Bulgarian, Serbian and Turkish control. After the Balkan Wars of 1912–13 it was divided between Greece, Serbia and Bulgaria.

Machiavelli, Niccolo (1469–1527): Florentine statesman and author, famous for his political philosophy which shaped post-medieval politics and diplomacy. His ideas evolved during his work for the Florentine government, when he was sent on diplomatic missions throughout Europe. The adjective "Machiavellian", when applied to politics, has come to mean "unscrupulous", and it is possible that the infamous Cesare Borgia (*see* BORGIA) was the inspiration for Machiavelli's best known work *Il Principe* (The Prince) which asserted the paramount role of the state and its ruler. It taught that any treachery or cunning on the part of a ruler is justified if it upholds his power and security. Following the seizure of Florence by the Medici in 1512 Machiavelli retired from public life, and devoted himself to writing.

Niccolo Machiavelli.

The magnificent terraces of Imtehuatana Hi near the north of Machu Picchu, the nan means the "place to which the sun was tied".

Machu Picchu: mountain fortress of th Incas, north-west of Cuzco, discovere in 1911. It hangs 1,500 feet [457·20 metre above the Urumbaba River and may hav been built to keep out savages from th Amazon forest. The stone buildings an surrounding terraces for farming hav survived undisturbed as the Incas le them 400 years ago.

McKinley, William (1843–1901) twenty-fifth president of the USA. Bor in Ohio, he served as a major in th Union Army in the Civil War, late becoming an attorney and eventuall Governor of Ohio (1891). In 1896 he wa elected president on the Republican ticke His administration saw the highest tarif in American history and the acquisitio of Hawaii, the Philippines, Puerto Ric and Guam. He was re-elected for a secon term in 1900 but was assassinated o 6 September 1901.

ladeira: name applied to a collection of lands belonging to Portugal, some 360 iles [578 kilometres] west of the African oast. Madeira (the Island of Woods) is so the name of the principal island. ;enoese sailors explored the group before 400. Its rediscovery in 1419 was one of ie first triumphs of Henry the Navigator *ee* separate entry) in his extension of 'ading routes along the west African oast. It was occupied by the British in 801 and from 1807–14. The chief local roducts are Madeira wines, bananas, ıgar, fish and handicrafts.

ladison, James (1751–1836): fourth resident of the USA. He was born in 'irginia and played a prominent part in he politics of the state from 1775 to 1780, vhen he served in the Continental Con-;ress. He was largely responsible for the ontent of the American Constitution. Ie succeeded Jefferson as president in 809 and served for two terms of office. Iis fumbling leadership of the Anglo-American War of 1812–14 lost him much prestige. His second administration saw a move towards more central government control of tariffs and banking.

Madras (originally **Fort St George**): third most populous city of India, on the south-east coast, with a fine artificial harbour, and capital of the large Madras Province. Founded by Francis Day in 1640, it became a presidency of the East India Company in 1653, and one of the largest English trading stations in India. In 1746 Madras was captured by the French and remained in their hands for two years. Recaptured by the English, it resisted other attacks by both French and native forces. Its more peaceable progress was marked by the foundation of a bishopric in 1833 and a university in 1857, with important medical, engineering and veterinary colleges. *See also* INDIA.

Madrid: capital and chief commercial centre of Spain, situated on a high plateau almost in the middle of the country. Madrid is mentioned (as Majerit) by 10th-century Arab scribes. It was captured from the Moors by Alphonso VI in 1083 and rose from being a mere hunting lodge of the Spanish kings to become the capital, in 1560, of Philip II. During the Peninsular War (1808–14) it put up a heroic resistance to the French. Among its notable buildings and institutions are the Prado (1785), housing one of the greatest art collections in the world; the Royal Palace and Armoury, containing magnificent collections of armour, furniture, tapestries, clocks, musical instruments etc.; the 17th-century Gothic cathedral; the America Museum; museums specialising in Spanish naval and military history, etc. A more recent memorial is the Valley of the Fallen, thirty miles [48 kilometres] from Madrid, dedicated to those who fell in the Spanish Civil War (*see* separate entry). *See also* PENINSULAR WAR; SPAIN.

Mafia: worldwide network of secret societies, originating in Sicily. *Mafia* (or *Maffia*) is of uncertain origin but may derive from a Sicilian dialect word meaning swaggering and boastful.

Of all the world's secret societies this probably has the most widespread reputation for intimidation and criminal activities. The organisation began in the lawless period of Sicily's history following Napoleon's invasion of southern Italy. Landowners entrusted the safeguarding of their property to unscrupulous ruffians who intimidated the peasant population and formed a league throughout the island which soon turned against the landowners themselves, the Mafia demanding extortionate sums for the "protection" they gave, controlling the sale of lands and crops and establishing a ruthless control far stronger than that of the official administration.

This combination of forces against law and order did not prevent internal quarrels in the Mafia, leading to bitter feuds and ruthless self-imposed justice. Spasmodic efforts were made to stamp out the organisation, but the chief result was to spread its activities and code of criminal conduct to other countries, especially the United States. In October 1890 the New Orleans chief of police was murdered by the Mafia. At the subsequent trial of eleven *mafiusi* the jury was so terrified by the organisation that most were acquitted.

It is one of the things most to the credit of Mussolini and his fascist government that, when they took control of Italy in 1922, they used the dictatorial powers they possessed to root out and exterminate this vicious organisation. Tried in large batches, with the witnesses against them having adequate police protection, many *mafiusi* received life sentences. Nevertheless, such organised evil and the fear it inspires die hard. There is no evidence that the Mafia has been finally extermi-

Part of a cache of rifles and ammunition di covered by police after a raid on a Mafia hideo in Southern Italy, 1969.

nated. The American branch, the *Cos Nostra,* is still very active, especially i the bribery of city officials. Its own un breakable traditions that no membe victimised by the Mafia shall ever appl for help to the police or give the leas assistance in bringing a fellow-membe to book, whatever the crime committed encircles the society with such protectio that only great courage and determinatio can break it. New anti-Mafia legislatio was passed in Italy in 1982 and at a majo trial in 1983 in Palermo, 59 of 75 defend ants were found guilty. Palermo's chie investigating magistrate, Rocco Chin nici,, was killed by a Mafia-planted bom in retaliation.

Magellan, Ferdinand (*c.* 1480–1521) Portuguese soldier and navigator wh served in the East Indies 1505–12 an Morocco 1513–14. Falling into disfavou with King Manuel of Portugal, he re nounced his Portuguese nationality an ansferred his allegiance to Spain. Charles put him in command of five ships to ·ek a westward route to the Moluccas. fter steering his fleet for thirty-eight ays through the strait named after him, lagellan entered the "Great South Sea" he Pacific) seen by Balboa in 1513, and ɔntinued for another ninety-eight days ll he made landfall, probably at Guam, the Ladrones. In the Philippines he llied himself with the ruler of Cebu gainst the neighbouring island of Mactan, nd was killed there by the islanders in 521. Of his ships, only the *Vittoria* reurned home, the first ship to sail round ne world. The chief source for the story f the circumnavigation is the account f Antonio Pigafetta, who was on the oyage and who refers to Magellan as so great a captain", though he was only small man and lame from wounds eceived in Africa.

HONOLKA, KURT. *Magellan*. 1962

Magna Carta, or **The Great Charter** 1215): feudal charter, now regarded as a oundation of English liberties. Barons in pposition to John (ruled 1199–1216) orced him to put his great seal to this harter on 15 June 1215 at Runnymede, ear Windsor. Many of its sixty-three lauses dealt with the barons' grievances ut some were of wider importance, e.g. o freeman was to be punished without a rial and the king could not demand taxes vithout the Great Council's consent. So mportant was it that copies, of which our survive, were sent into every shire. Though John repudiated it, the charter vas confirmed by later kings.

JONES, J. A. P. *King John and Magna Carta*. 1972; HOLT, J. C. *Magna Carta*. 1961

Magyars: the dominant racial group in Hungary, who settled there in the 10th century and, under the Hunyadi dynasty n the 15th, became a bastion against the Turks, who frequently occupied much of the country. From the 16th century until 1919 the Austrian emperor was their king, but they retained self-government, and Magyar as their official language.

Maharaja (**Maharajah**): the title of chiefs of high rank in some of the greater states of India, often of those which never came under direct British rule, *maha* meaning "great" and *raja(h)* "ruler"; e.g. the Maharaja of Gwalior, or the Sikh Ranjit Singh, Maharaja of Lahore.

The Old Palace, Gwalior.

Mahrattas, Marathas: a mixed people of central India, welded into a fighting power by Sivaji Bhonsla (1627–80) but splitting during the 18th century into the five states of Baroda, Gwalior, Indore, Nagpur and "the Peshwa's Dominions" (Poona). Generals Lake and Wellesley, in the third Mahratta War (1803–05), were mainly responsible for subduing them.

Maillart, Robert (1872–1940): Swiss engineer who added a new elegance to buildings and bridges in reinforced concrete by integrating the supporting and the supported parts of a structure into a unified whole. The bridge over the Rhine at Tavanasa, Switzerland, where roadway and arch are designed as a

Maillart's bridge over the Rhine at Tavanasa, Switzerland.

single unit, is a typical example of his work.

Mainz: West German city, on the left bank of the Rhine. The site of Celtic and Roman settlement, it became an important medieval city. Gutenberg set up his printing press there in the 15th century. In more recent history Mainz's border position has made it a prime sufferer from Franco-German conflict.

Malagasy Republic, formerly **Madagascar:** island republic in the Indian Ocean about 300 miles [482 kilometres] off the east coast of Africa. The early inhabitants were Indonesians and Indians from the east, mixed with African Muslims from the west. Several countries, including England, attempted to gain a footing but only the French were able to establish themselves, in 1750. Pirates found it a convenient base in the 18th century. It was seized from the Vichy French during World War II to preven the Japanese occupying it. After its retur to France, local uprising led to its indepen dence in 1960.

See MAURITIUS for map.

Malaria: infectious, chiefly tropica disease. The word means "bad air", an the disease was at its worst in marsh areas; hence, it was also termed "mars fever". In Italy medieval overlords buil their castles on the foothills of th Apennines to raise them above the sourc of infection, which Hippocrates believe to be the vapours from the marsh. Thi theory persisted until a French doctor Laverin, discovered malaria "parasites' in 1880, and Italian scientists studied thei action in human blood. In 1895 an Englis scientist, Ronald Ross, found that thes parasites developed in certain mosquitoe which bred in the marshes and that thei bites infected humans. Malaria is now controlled by spraying the breeding grounds of mosquitoes.

¶ KAMM, JOSEPHINE. *Malaria Ross.* 1955

alawi (formerly **Nyasaland**): republic central Africa. In 1859, when Living-one (1813–73) first saw Lake Nyasa, the rtile land around had been turned into a ilderness by the Arab slave trade which as destroying African tribal society. aves were captured to make the long aul of ivory overland. Steamers on the ke would make this unnecessary. Living-one's reports led to the establishment of ission stations, two of which were amed after him; and the African Lakes ompany was set up to put down the ave trade and develop peaceful trade. inally, in 1891, the British government eluctantly took over responsibility for Iyasaland. It remained an agricultural ountry, many of whose people sought ork in the Rhodesias and South Africa. ommunications were a big problem, nd in order to provide an outlet for Iyasaland's exports a railway was com-leted in 1915 from Port Herald to Chindi on the north bank of the Zambesi. Seven years later another was opened, from Beira to the south bank of the river.

In 1953 Nyasaland was federated with the Rhodesias, despite African opposition. Six years later the situation became so serious that a state of emergency was declared. Agitation continued, and in 1963 the Central African Federation broke up. Nyasaland, now called Malawi, became independent under the leadership of Dr Hastings Banda (b. 1905) and, in 1966, a republic within the Common-wealth. *See* AFRICA for map.

¶ ROTBERG, ROBERT. *The Rise of Nationalism in Central Africa: the Making of Malawi and Zambia 1873–1964*. 1966

Malaysia: a federation formed in 1963 to consist of Malaya, Singapore, Sarawak and Sabah, Britain's former colonial territories in the area (except Brunei). The

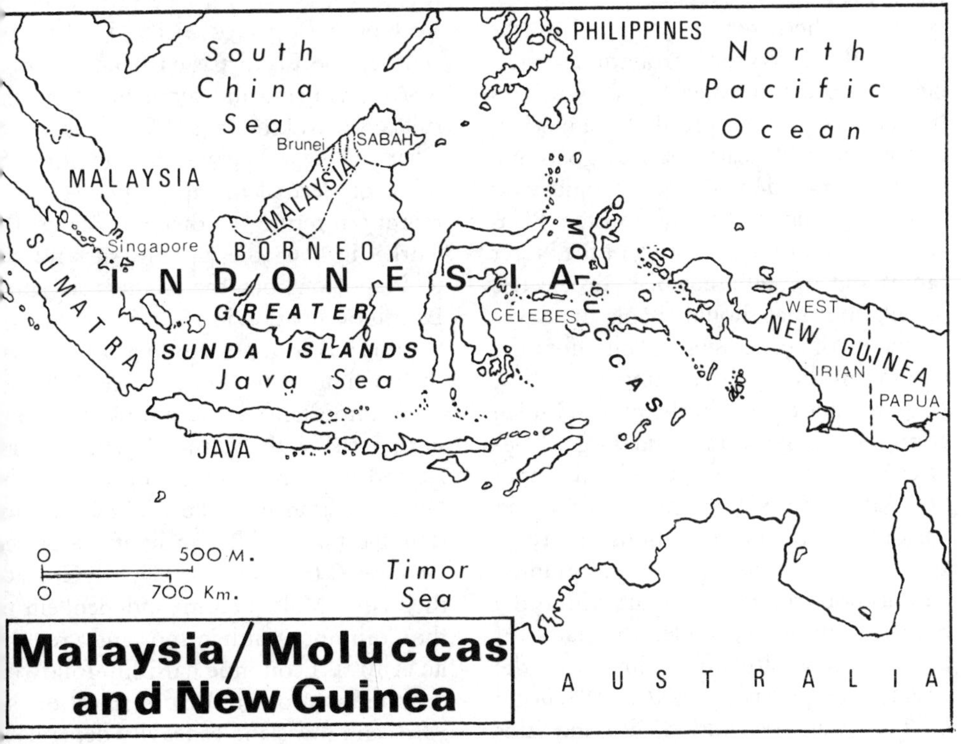

Malaysia/Moluccas and New Guinea

federation's principal problem was always to find a balance between the main ethnic groups – Malay, Chinese, Indian and (in eastern Malaysia) Dayak. In 1965 Singapore with its predominantly Chinese community left the federation to become a republic within the Commonwealth. Even so the federation is one of the richest countries in Asia with tin and rubber its main products. Britain established trading posts on Penang Island in 1786 and Singapore in 1819 but only achieved control of the whole Malay peninsula by 1930. Britain granted independence to Malaya in 1957 when it was clear the long struggle against the communist guerrillas had been won.

See also SARAWAK; SINGAPORE.

Mali (formerly **French Sudan**): West African republic bounded in the north by Algeria; east by Niger; south by Upper Volta, the Ivory Coast and Guinea; and in the west by Senegal and Mauritania. In the southern region, irrigated by the upper Niger, cotton, groundnuts, rice, beans, maize and millet are grown. Fish from the Niger find a ready local market, and in the north cattle, sheep, goats and camels are raised by nomadic people, who move on as the grazing is exhausted. Plans are in hand for the damming of the Niger rapids and the building of hydroelectric installations that should enable the development of processing plants for the natural products of the country.

The former colony of the French Sudan comprised Senegambia and Niger. Between 1904 and 1920 it was called Upper Senegal and Niger: then, following various boundary alterations in 1933, 1948 and 1954, the country was granted autonomous republican status within the French community under the name of the Sudanese Republic. In 1959 the country temporarily joined with Senegal in the Mali Federation, leaving this partnership the following year on bei granted full independence as the M Republic. *See* AFRICA for map.

Malplaquet, Battle of (11 Septemb 1709): the last and most fiercely contest of Marlborough's victories in the War the Spanish Succession. In this battle, wi the help of Prince Eugène, he defeat the French under Villars, who were tryi to relieve the siege of Mons.

Malta: island and independent state the western Mediterranean. Known ancient times as Melita, Malta has alwa been of considerable importance. It w colonised by the Phoenicians, the Gree and the Carthaginians before comi under Roman rule in 201 BC. In AD St Paul was supposedly shipwrecked o the Maltese coast. The island's prosperi declined through successive barbari invasions, but from 870 to 1090 the Ara fortified it as a naval base until expell by Count Roger of Sicily. In the 13t century the island passed from Norm to Angevin rule and subsequently to t rulers of Aragon and Castile. In 153 Charles V gave Malta to the Knights of John of Jerusalem in perpetual sov reignty in return for their aid against th Turks. In 1798 the Knights surrender to Napoleon, but the Maltese accepte British occupation in 1802, and the isla became a British possession in 1814. Wit the opening of the Suez Canal Malta be came important as a coaling station, an during the 20th century a vital Britis air and naval base. In World War II th heroic resistance of the Maltese to co stant German and Italian air attack cause George VI to award the George Cross t the island. Malta became independent i the Commonwealth in 1964 and a repub lic in 1974. Economic hardship followe the rundown of the British naval dock yards and the island is heavily dependen ɔon aid. It follows a non-aligned policy.

e MEDITERRANEAN for map.

BLOUET, BRIAN. *The Story of Malta*. 1972

lammoths: enormous elephants, now xtinct. They resembled the Indian elelant in shape, but their skins were shaggy ıd their tusks were nine or ten feet long. ·048 metres]. Mammoths appear to have ınged through northern and central urope and North America until the end f the Ice Age and were contemporary ith early man. The hunters of southern rance drew pictures of them on the walls f their caves. In Siberia, USSR, quantis of mammoth ivory have been found.)ccasionally, in a warm season, the ice ıelts to expose a complete mammoth, lmost perfectly preserved – and still, pparently, edible.

VEVERS, GWYNNE. *Elephants and Mammoths*. 1968

Ianchester: city in Lancashire, England. Manchester grew rapidly in size and mportance with the development of the cotton industry in the 19th century. It is ıow a great commercial centre for the nany towns in the area engaged in texiles, chemicals, engineering and atomic nergy. Although it is thirty-five miles 56 kilometres] from the sea, the Manchester Ship Canal, which connects the city with the Mersey estuary, makes

The Manchester Ship Canal, Chester to Warrington Section.

Manchester the third largest seaport in Britain. Manchester Airport is the most important in Britain after London. Manchester has a university and some famous libraries.

¶ FRANGOPULO, N. J., editor. *Rich Inheritance: a guide to the history of Manchester*. 1962

Manchuria: historical region of northeastern China. The area had gradually been brought under Chinese rule, but the Mongol invasions of the 13th and 14th centuries partly reversed this process. The Manchus finally conquered China and gave it the imperial dynasty which ruled from 1644 to 1912, joining Manchuria to China until 1932. A frontier with Russia was fixed at the Amur River in 1689. In 1860 China conceded more Manchurian territory to Russia. In 1898, after the Sino-Japanese War of 1894–5, Russia obtained a long lease of the tip of the Liaotung Peninsula, with Port Arthur and Dairen, together with extensive railway rights, administration of territory and substantial trading concessions. With

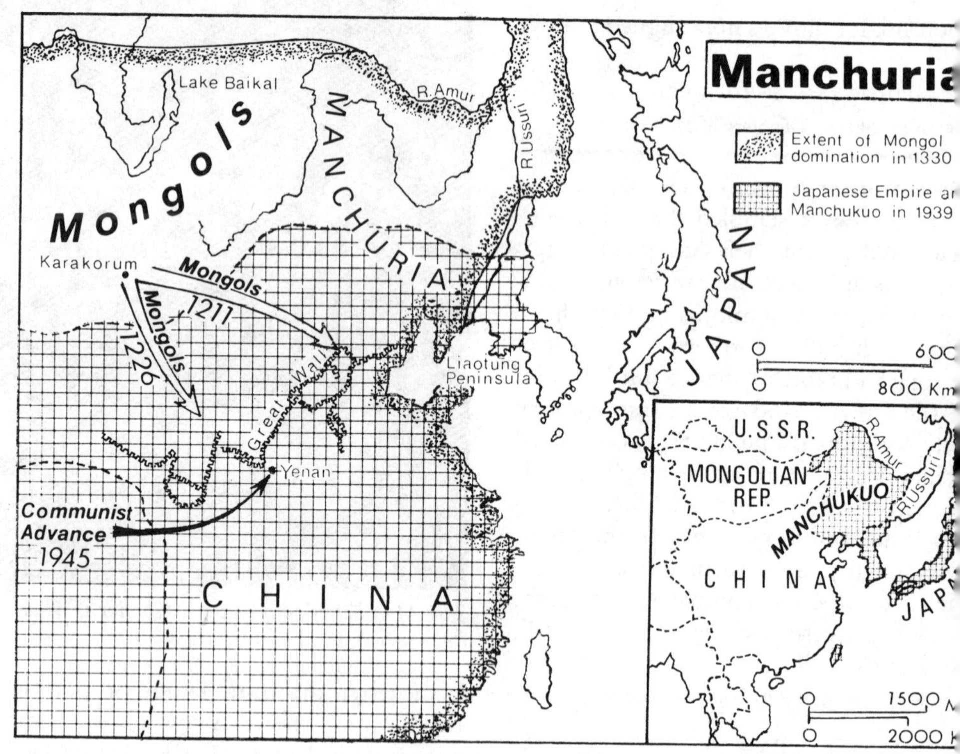

the close of the Russo-Japanese War in 1905, Russian rights in southern Manchuria were transformed to Japan, which now replaced Russia as the power most dangerous to China. In the disorganisation following the Chinese revolution of 1911, authority in Manchuria was successfully exercised by Chang Tso-lin, a former bandit chief, murdered in 1928. In 1931 Japan occupied Manchuria, setting up in 1932 a new state called Manchukuo, including Jehol and part of Mongolia. This collapsed with the Japanese surrender in 1945 at the close of World War II. Russia regained control of Manchuria, letting it pass, however, to the Chinese People's Republic by the Sino-Russian treaty of 1950 and withdrawing all troops by 1955. In 1969 there were clashes between Russians and Chinese on the Ussuri and Amur frontier rivers, followed by negotiations.
See also CHINA.

Mandarin: name once given by th Portuguese to all public officials of th Chinese empire. The mandarins were a exclusive class selected by severe com petitive examination. The word *mandari* was also applied to the educated Pekin dialect of Chinese used for official purpos through the empire.

Mandates: the settlement agreed a Versailles, 1919, and operated unde Article 22 of the League of Nation Covenant, of colonial territories take from Germany and Turkey. Each territor was entrusted to a "Mandatory Power" responsible for developing it in th interests of its native population.

Mandates were of three types (Man datory Powers in brackets): Class A - Turkish territories, Iraq and Palestin (Great Britain); Syria (France); recognised as provisionally independent, but stil requiring assistance.

Class B – German Central African lonies, Tanganyika (Great Britain); ameroons and Togoland (Great Britian ıd France); Ruanda (Belgium); manıtaries responsible for administration.

Class C – S.W. Africa (South Africa); ımoa (New Zealand); New Guinea ıustralia); W. Pacific Islands north of e equator (Japan and Great Britain); ıder direct rule.

Iandeville, Sir John (14th century): ıysterious author of *Travels* which exıted Europeans with tales of the Great han of Cathay, the Dog-faced People, ıe Gold-digging Ants and other wonders. cholars have questioned his existence. A iège chronicler, Jean d'Outremeuse, ported that Jean de Bourgogne on his eathbed in 1372 revealed himself as Iandeville. The claim of St Albans, ngland, to his burial place is poorly ıpported. The *Travels*, concocted from Villian de Boldensele, Odoric, and Albert f Aix's history of the Third Crusade ımong others, remain a delightful colection of preposterous adventures. The arliest known manuscript, in Paris, is ated 1371.

DENNY, NORMAN and FILMER-SANKEY, JOSEPHINE. *he Travels of Sir John Mandeville.* 1973

Ianila: capital of the Philippines in the vestern Pacific and principal port, induscrial and cultural centre of these islands, nore than 7,000 in number.

The Spaniards settled at Manila in 1571 nd strong Catholic influences were stablished. Struggles with the Dutch, vho also had settlements in the East ndies, spread over the 17th century. The city was captured by the British in 1762 ınd held for two years, after which it was eturned to Spain by treaty.

The Pacific directly links Manila with he USA as it had linked the city with Spain's Mexican possessions. When the USA defeated Spain in 1898 as a result of their quarrel over Cuba, the Philippines were transferred to the victors, becoming a republic in 1946. In 1980 greater Manila had a population of 5,925,900.

See also PHILIPPINES.

Mantua: Italian city in the valley of the River Po, about seventy-five miles [120 kilometres] from the Adriatic Sea. Its impressive ducal palaces and castles contain fine tapestries and frescoes, some by Andrea Mantegna (1431–1506), who is buried in the Church of St Andrea. The Roman poet Virgil (70–19 BC) was born at Andes, a village in the neighbourhood. Mantua is also the name of the province.

The Castello di San Giorgio, Mantua.

Maori: member of the aboriginal Polynesian race of New Zealand. Europeans who landed after Captain Cook found an advanced Neolithic civilisation, whose members were much given to warfare. Though in 1839 Gibbon Wakefield organised the New Zealand Company for trade and land purchase, the 1840 Treaty of Waitangi guaranteed Maori rights under British rule. The granting of electoral rights and representation in the legislature after the wars of 1860 and 1871 has helped to preserve Maori numbers, skills, customs and traditions. They number about seven per cent of the population of New Zealand and are mainly confined to North Island.

¶ PEARCE, G. L. *The Story of the Maori People*. 1969

A celebration in honour of Mao's re-election as Chairman of the Chinese Communist Party in 1969.

Mao Tse-tung (Zedong) (1893–1976): Chinese statesman and one of the chief founders of the Chinese Communist Party. He was greatly influenced by the ideals of Sun Yat-sen (*see* separate entry), and showed a rare combination of qualities as poet, scholar, political philosopher and guerrilla leader. He organised peasant and industrial unions (1921—26), raised a people's army probably superior to any in China's long history, led the great march from Kiangsi to Yenan (1934–35), and became Chairman of the Central Committee of the Communist Party in 1936. In 1949 he came to virtually supreme power as Chairman of the People's Republic of China when the Kuomintang (or Nationalist Party) under Chiang Kai-shek (*see* separate entry) were driven from the mainland. Although he relinquished the office of Chairman in 1958 he remained the supreme figure in the Republic, not only because of his political stature but through the extraordinary influence of his writings and "thoughts".

In 1966 he launched the Cultural Rev lution, which captured the loyalties Chinese youth, spread Mao's teaching kept alive revolutionary fervour a helped the emergence of a new Chi which according to an experienced Eur pean observer, boasted that every chi learns to read and write, and everyone h sufficient to eat. His death in 1976 end an era of China's history.

Map: from the Latin *mappa*, a tableclo or napkin; a representation, generally c a plane surface, of the political and phys cal features of the earth's surface, or pa of it, on a greatly reduced scale. Topo graphical maps show both the artifici and natural features of an area, e.g. road railways, telegraphs, canals and towns well as forests, rivers, highlands an valleys. The one-inch Ordnance Surve maps of the British Isles are excelle examples of the topographical map in tended to guide travellers. The so-calle cadastral map (from Latin *capistratum*, register for taxation purposes) is on larger scale, shows greater details, and used for management, legal and admin strative purposes, since it shows size c fields, boundaries and the like. Man cadastral maps were produced to eas assessments of taxation and were ver important in countries like Egypt wher the annual Nile floods could easily wip out boundaries. The general or atlas ma has the smallest scale of all. The nam "atlas" for a book of maps is supposedl taken from the frontispiece, showin Atlas supporting the earth, of *Atlas: or Geographical Description of the World* b Gerard Mercator and John Hondt, 163 A chart is a specialised form of map, of th coast and surrounding areas, showin buoys, soundings, wrecks and light houses; or of the ocean.

The oldest existing map is a sketch ma

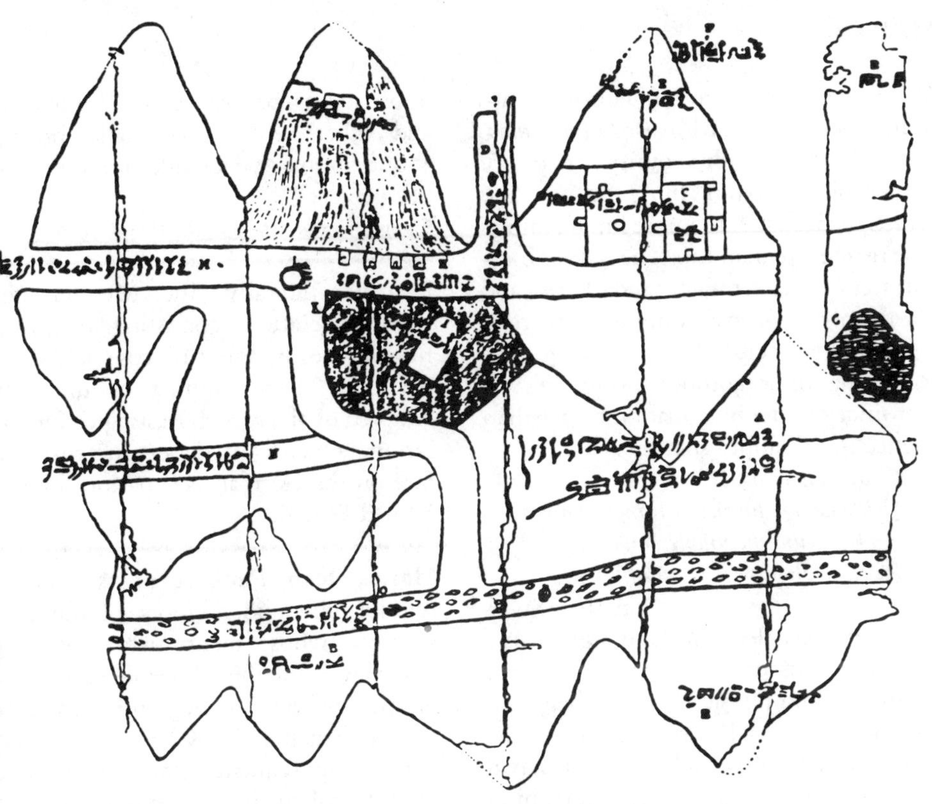

Map of Egyptian gold mine, 1320 BC, the world's oldest existing map.

f access roads to an Egyptian gold mine bout 1300 BC. Maps such as those used y Rameses II enabled Eratosthenes (276–94 BC) to measure the distance from lexandria to Syene by which he estiiated the circumference of the earth. 'he *Geographia* of Claudius Ptolemy, AD 160, fixed the arrangements of arallels and meridians which form the asis of all map projection. Medieval rtists produced maps of biblical, especilly Old Testament, stories or ancient nyths. Two notable examples are the vorld map of Mohammed al Idrisi at 'alermo, *c.* AD 1150, and the *mappa nundi* of Richard of Haldingham at Iereford, *c.* AD 1300. The monk and hronicler Matthew Paris produced one f the best English maps in about 1250. After 1500 editors of Ptolemy's *Geographia* ncluded up-to-date maps of European ountries. Martin Behaim constructed the irst modern globe at Nuremberg in 1492. Excited by stories of the voyages of Amerigo Vespucci, Martin Waldseemüller of Alsace first used the name America on a map in 1507. John Schoner showed many of the new discoveries on paper-covered wooden spheres between 1515 and 1533, and Diego Ribeiro's world map of 1529 gave a reasonably accurate picture of the shape and proportions of the Pacific. Italian publishers, masters of line engraving, dominated map-making to 1570, as the instruments produced at Nuremberg advanced the science of surveying. Flemish craftsmanship and the reputation of Mercator helped to shift the centre of cartography to the Low Countries, and Abraham Ortelius at Antwerp produced the first atlas since Ptolemy, *Theatrum Orbis Terrarum*. The Dutch in turn replaced the Flemings. A map of Asia of 1632 by J. Blaeu is surprisingly accurate, except for the proportions of China, and beautifully illustrated, as are more conventional maps of India in Terry's *A Voyage to East India,* 1655. The English county maps of Christopher Saxton (fl. 1570–96) and John Speed (1552?–1629) are fine examples of artistic craftsmanship. The royal observatories at Greenwich and Paris and Harrison's work on chronometers were of tremendous help in improving the reckoning of longitude, though it was customary to use imagination rather than science to fill empty spaces.

Geographers in Afric maps
With savage pictures fill their gaps
And o'er uninhabitable downs
Place elephants for want of towns

Jonathan Swift

Conventional lettering and signs came generally into use in the 18th century, and towns and physical features began to appear in plan rather than picture. The 18th century, a period of great naval activity, saw a number of mapping achievements, including those of Joseph Desbarres (1722–1824), who published charts of the Atlantic and North American coasts; Thomas Jefferys, whose West Indian and American atlases were published in 1774 and 1778; and James Rennell (1742–1830), the surveyor-general of Bengal, who produced his Bengal Atlas in 1779. With the founding of the English Ordnance Survey towards the end of the 18th century Britain became the best mapped country in the world. During the 19th century almost every other European country completed small-scale maps for their territories.

In 1891 Professor Penck put forward a plan for an International Map of the World (Carte du Monde au Millionème) on a uniform scale – that of one-millionth of nature. The idea made slow progress at first but took a great step forward at the 1908 Geneva Geographical Congress, when the US delegation proposed fixed rules for the production of the map. Subsequent conferences in Rome, Pa[ris] and other centres eventually broug[ht] about almost worldwide agreement [o]n this project.

¶ RAISZ, ERWIN. *Mapping the World.* 1956

Maquis: literally, the Mediterrane[an] coast vegetation, consisting mainly [of] myrtle, heath, arbutus, rose laurel an[d] oak, but more familiar as the nam[e] adopted by the French Resistance Organi[-]sation, which carried out guerrilla war[-]fare on the German occupation forces [in] World War II.

Marat, Jean Paul (1743–93): Frenc[h] revolutionist and member of the Con[-]vention, whose inflammatory writing[s] helped to incite the wholesale massacre [of] political prisoners in September 1792. H[e] was assassinated by Charlotte Corday[,] who was subsequently guillotined. Mara[t] was described by a contemporary a[s] having "the burning haggard eye of [a] hyena"

The Death of Marat *painted by Jacques Lou[is] David.*

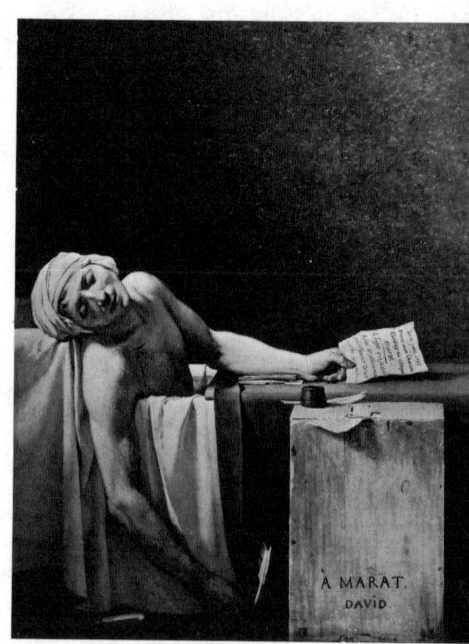

arathon: district in Attica some twenty les [32 kilometres] north-east of Athens, iere the Greeks defeated the Persian vaders in 490 BC. Meanwhile Pheidip-les had set out on his 150-mile [240-ometre] run to summon aid from arta, which he accomplished in two ys: from this the term "Marathon ice" is derived. *See also* PERSIAN WARS.

arconi, Guglielmo (1874–1937): ilian pioneer of radio communication. orn in Bologna, the son of an Italian ther and an Irish mother, he was ucated in Bologna and Florence, later idying physics under Vincenzo Rosa at ghorn. He began his experiments in ily but in 1896 came to London, where e chief engineer of the Post Office gave m facilities for his work. In December 01 he succeeded in transmitting signals ross the Atlantic from Poldhu in Corn-all to St John's, Newfoundland, and, in ptember 1918, sent the first wireless essage from England to Australia. He as a Nobel prize-winner in 1906.

READE, L. *Marconi and the Discovery of Wireless.* 63

larengo, Battle of (14 June 1800): efeat of the Austrians by the French nder Napoleon Bonaparte in the course f his campaign in northern Italy. apoleon's white charger which fre-uently carried him in his later campaigns as named after this important success in is early career.

laria Theresa (1717–80): Empress of ustria. Despite her importance in the urope of her time, Maria Theresa seems have been overshadowed by her arch-nemy Frederick the Great of Prussia. o maintain her position in face of the ostility of, among others, Prussia and rance, she fought the War of Austrian uccession, losing Silesia to Prussia. Maria heresa gained by participating in the 1772 partition of Poland, and allied Austria with France, marrying her daughter Marie-Antoinette to the future Louis XVI. In overhauling the government of her Empire, she carried out what one historian calls "a political, constitutional and administrative revolution".

Marie-Antoinette (1755–93): queen of France and wife of Louis XVI. A woman of "elevated manner, lofty demeanour and graces of deportment", rather than the physical beauty with which she is often credited, she became intensely unpopular as the centre of reactionary opinion at the French court and of intrigue with foreign powers in an effort to suppress the Revolution. She was imprisoned in 1792 and executed soon after her husband. Though the remark "*Qu'ils mangent la brioche*" ("Let them eat cake") is usually attributed to her when she was told that her people were without bread, the saying is at least 700 years older.

Marie Feodorovna (1847–1928): Empress of Russia 1881–94. The daughter of

Christian IX of Denmark, she was happily married to Tsar Alexander III. The Tsarina played no part in politics, other than attempting to warn her son Nicholas II against the influence of Rasputin. She endeared herself to the Russian people by her active interest in philanthropy and education. Visiting England in 1914 (her sister Alexandra married Edward VII) she returned to Russia at the outbreak of war and worked for the Red Cross. The Bolsheviks allowed her to live under close guard in the Crimea, where she remained throughout the German occupation, not choosing to leave Russia until the Armistice of 1918.

See also NICHOLAS II; RASPUTIN.

Marines: soldiers trained for fighting at sea as well as on land. In Great Britain, an Order in Council dated 16 October 1664 authorised 1,200 soldiers to be raised and formed into one regiment for sea service. In 1684 the third regiment of the line was called the Marine Regiment. In 1698 two further marine regiments were raised, and from then onwards the "sea soldie became an integral part of the Ro Navy. In 1704 a detachment was land from Admiral Rooke's ships and play a prominent part in the capture Gibraltar.

In 1755 the sweeping reforms of Admi Lord Anson brought the marines und the direct control of the Admiralty, a they were grouped into three divisions Chatham, Portsmouth and Devonpc for training purposes. While afloat th performed the same duties as the seame but in action their specialised trainii adapted them for small arms fighting ai landing on enemy shores.

In 1802 the prefix "Royal" was grant in recognition of their fidelity during tl naval mutinies. In 1855 they were divid into light infantry and artillery sectio and remained as such until 1923, wh they became a single force.

In the 20th century the Royal Marin continue to serve ashore and afloat b during World War II and subsequentl their primary functions have included tl provision of commando units, landin craft crews, special boat sections (frog men) and detachments for amphibio operations. The corps also provides ban for HM ships and shore establishments.

The United States Marine Corps w founded in 1795, when it consisted of tw battalions to assist in the defence of th colonies. Its original organisation an training were modelled on that of Britai and it has remained an integral part of th US naval service, with its headquarte in Washington, where the commandant house dates from 1805 and captured flag from various battles are on permane display. Its defined function is "to suppor the fleet or any part thereof in th accomplishment of its mission"; and i fulfilment of this role the Marine Corp has played a vital part in every war i which the United States has been involve d has also participated in the peacetime cupation of foreign countries, as well providing routine guards for naval tallations, US legations abroad, etc. ome twenty other countries maintain nilar marine organisations.

arionettes: puppets controlled by ings. The name may come from an lian word, *morio,* meaning "fool" or uffoon" or from the French *Mariolettes,* nall figures of the Virgin Mary. The rmer derivation is more likely, because e Italians have always loved both arionettes and puppets.

There is a difference. Puppets are manipu- ted from below, either by the operator's ngers as glove puppets or by means of ds which can be pushed and pulled to ove the figure. Punch and Judy are ppets. Marionettes, on the other hand, e made to move by means of strings or ires attached to the jointed limbs of the olls, which may be made from wood,

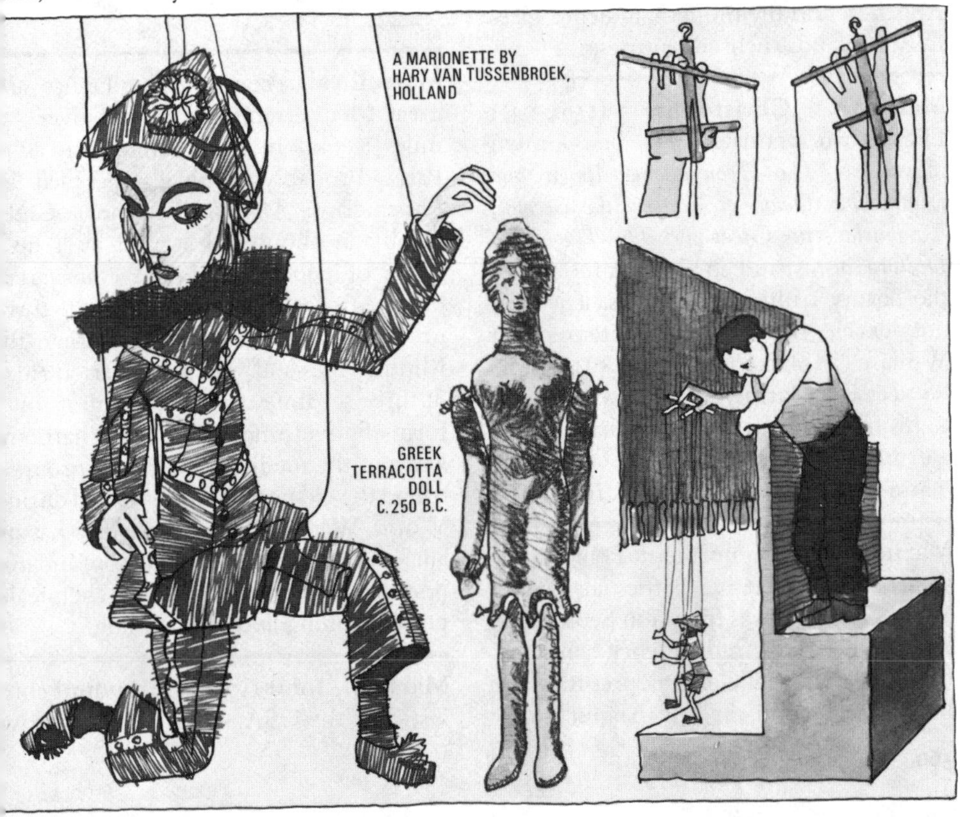

Above: Marionette theatre featuring the favourite characters of the Italian Comedie del'Arte. Below: the strings are pulled by the puppeteer standing behind and above the puppet stage.

A MARIONETTE BY
HARY VAN TUSSENBROEK,
HOLLAND

GREEK
TERRACOTTA
DOLL
C.250 B.C.

wax or plaster. The wires are fastened to thin slats, by moving which the operator can make the marionettes nod, walk or dance.

Marionettes have been found in Egyptian tombs. Greek children played with them. In India and China their shadows, enlarged on to a screen, entertained audiences for generations.

In 16th century England marionette plays of biblical stories were popular. In 1667 Samuel Pepys mentioned a performance of "a puppet play of Patient Grizel", but his puppets were really marionettes, and so was the familiar Pinocchio, who sings "There are no strings on me".

Sicilians still love marionettes. In Palermo there is a marionette theatre where traditional stories from the life of Charlemagne are performed. The figures are quite large – about two feet high [5·08 centimetres] – and heavy. The favourite characters are Roland, Oliver, Turpin and Angelica, and the modern audience gleefully applauds their adventures.

Marlowe, Christopher (1564–93): Elizabethan dramatist. His best known plays are *The Troublesome Reign and Lamentable Death of Edward the Second*, *Tamburlane the Great* and *The Tragedy of Doctor Faustus*; and, in his finest moments, the beauty of his verse equals, if it does not excel, that of his contemporary William Shakespeare (1564–1616). "Sweet Kit Marlowe", as he was known to his friends, died young, as the result of a drunken quarrel.

¶ HENDERSON, P. *Christopher Marlow*. 1952

Marne: river of northern France, the scene of two decisive battles in World War I. The first was fought in September 1914, when an Anglo-French counter-offensive relieved German pressures on Paris; the second, in July-August 1918, saw the final German attempt to bre[ak] through on the western front defeated [by] the Allies.

Marrakesh or **Marrakech:** one of t[he] four chief towns of Morocco on t[he] north-west side of the High Atlas mou[n]tains, and at one time capital of t[he] Moorish Empire. It lies 158 miles [2..] kilometres] south-south-west of Ca[sa]blanca, present capital of Moroc[co]. Founded in the year 1062, Marrake[sh] reached its heyday in the 14th centur[y]. Though much of the ancient town is [in] decay, modern buildings are rising in a[nd] around it, and there are important carp[et], textile, leather and food-produci[ng] industries.

Marseillaise: the French nation[al] anthem, introduced during the Fren[ch] Revolution. It was composed in 1792 b[y] Rouget de Lisle, an army officer, an[d] brought to Paris by soldiers fro[m] Marseilles.

Marseilles: second city of France an[d] great Mediterranean port, just over 53[..] miles [853 kilometres] south-south-east [of] Paris. Probably originally peopled b[y] Phoenicians, *Massalia* became a Gree[k] colony in about 600 BC and built up [a] chain of dependencies and commerci[al] links. After a period of decline, the tow[n] grew in importance again during th[e] Middle Ages and was at one period rule[d] in three separate units, each with its ow[n] form of government and its own harbou[r]. Most of the medieval buildings, groupe[d] round the old port, were destroyed durin[g] World War II. The present city has a[n] ancient university (founded 1409) and im[portant] portant industries, including chemical[s], petrol refining and shipbuilding.

Marshall, John (1755–1835): third chie[f] justice of the USA. After taking an activ[e] rt in the American revolution, he ended law lectures at William and ary College and was admitted to the r in 1783. Marshall was a delegate to e state convention which ratified the deral Constitution. He declined the sition of Attorney General when it was fered to him by George Washington in '95, but was appointed the chief justice the US Supreme Court in 1801. His irty-four years on the bench built up the estige and power of the court, and he tablished much important legal pre-dent by his interpretations of the nstitution.

arshall Plan: name given to the ogramme launched by US Secretary of ate George C. Marshall on 5 June 1947 an address at Harvard University in hich he declared that US policy was irected "not against any country or octrine but against hunger, poverty, esperation and chaos. Its purpose should e the revival of a working economy in e world so as to permit the emergence f political and social conditions in which ee institutions can exist." The plan was rimarily designed, by the provision of oney and materials, to help the recovery f Europe after the ravages of World Var II, but the USSR and the other embers of the Eastern Bloc refused to articipate.

artinique: French possession in the Vindward Islands group of the West dies. Its most spectacular feature is Aont Pelée, which erupted in 1902 illing 30,000 people.

Columbus discovered the island in 1502, ut settlement by Europeans did not occur ntil 1637 when the French took it. Martinique figured in the piratical activi-ies of English, Dutch and French during he 17th century but became recognised n 1814 as a possession of France, on whom the island depends for some foods, on and textiles in exchange for sugar, cotton and fruits. Slavery was abolished in 1848.

Martinique became one of the French overseas departments in 1946.

See CARIBBEAN for map.

Martyrs: those who die for their faith. The term is chiefly used of Christian martyrs and is derived from a Greek word meaning "witness".

The early years of the Church, before it won recognition from the rulers of the Roman Empire, saw the great period of martyrdom. St Stephen was stoned to death very shortly after Jesus had left the earth, and St Peter and St Paul, though not chiefly remembered as martyrs, both suffered death for their faith. The first British martyr was St Alban, who perished during the reign (284–305) of the Emperor Diocletian, which was marked by particularly intense persecutions, though mass martyrdoms occur through history, an instance being the crucifixion of twenty-six Japanese converts of the Jesuits at Nagasaki in 1597.

Section from a medieval panel showing the Martyrdom of Saints.

The Roman Catholic Church continues to this day to bestow sainthood upon its martyrs, though these are not of course its only saints; and the process, known as canonisation, in the case of those who died for their faith in England in the 16th and early 17th centuries is now nearly completed.

The Church of England has never adopted the practice of canonisation, but it holds in reverence those who died for the Reformed Faith in the reign (1553–8) of Queen Mary I, while for many years the Prayer Book made provision for commemorating King Charles the Martyr on the anniversary of his execution (30 January 1649), and there are five churches in England dedicated to him.

Marx, Karl (1818–83): the founder of communism. Born of a German-Jewish family, Marx took up the ideas of revolutionary socialism as a young man, and in collaboration with Engels he set these out in the so-called *Communist Manifesto*, published in 1848. In 1849 he went as a political exile to London, where he spent the rest of his life in near-pover relying largely on Engels's support. H most important work was *Das Kapital* study of English capitalist society, whi with his other works constitutes t "bible" of communism in the 20 century.

Karl Marx.

Marx interpreted history in terms economics and the constant struggle the working classes to secure a bett future in the face of capitalist oppressic which he saw as doomed to be ove thrown. It was the duty of the workers hasten this overthrow by every means their power, especially the strike. H most famous cry, from the *Manifesto* 1848 was: "The workers have nothing lose in this world but their chai Workers of the world, unite!"

¶ KETTLE, A. *Karl Marx*. 1963

Masaryk, Jan Garrigue (1886–1948 Czechoslovak statesman, son of Czech slovakia's first president. In 1940, aft varied diplomatic experience, he becan foreign secretary of the Czechoslov government-in-exile in London, an through frequent broadcasts to h German-occupied country he was popular choice as foreign secretary aft the liberation. Communist pressure mad his job increasingly difficult, though h did not resign immediately when th Communists seized power, with Russia support, on 25 February 1948. But o 10 March his body was found under th window of his room at the foreign offic suicide being alleged.

¶ In LARSEN, EGON. *Men Who Fought for Freedo* 1958

Mason-Dixon Line: boundary lin between Pennsylvania and Marylan USA. In the early days of the establish ment of British colonies there wer frequent boundary disputes. Perhaps th most contentious of these concerned th boundary between the colonies of Mary

HE **Mason-Dixon** LINE

ıd and Pennsylvania. It ended in 1767, hen the English astronomers Charles ason and Jeremiah Dixon carried out a rvey and plotted the boundary between e two colonies. Later this line took on a rger significance as the boundary :tween the free states of the North and e slave-owning states of the South.

Mathematical instruments: early mathematical instruments arose from the practical needs of building and surveying. Simple dividers for dividing lines and angles, and compasses for drawing circles, were of very early origin. On the tomb of a Roman surveyor we find represented the isosceles triangle with a plumb line from the vertex, a square resembling the ordinary carpenter's square, and an object resembling the set square of angles 30, 60 and 90 degrees. With such simple tools the glories of Gothic architecture were achieved.

Perhaps the best known of all early instruments was the astrolabe (*see* separate entry). Although the name is Greek (meaning the taking of the stars), it is thought that the Greeks derived their knowledge of the instrument from the Near East, whence it also spread to China and India. It has been described as the oldest scientific instrument in the world.

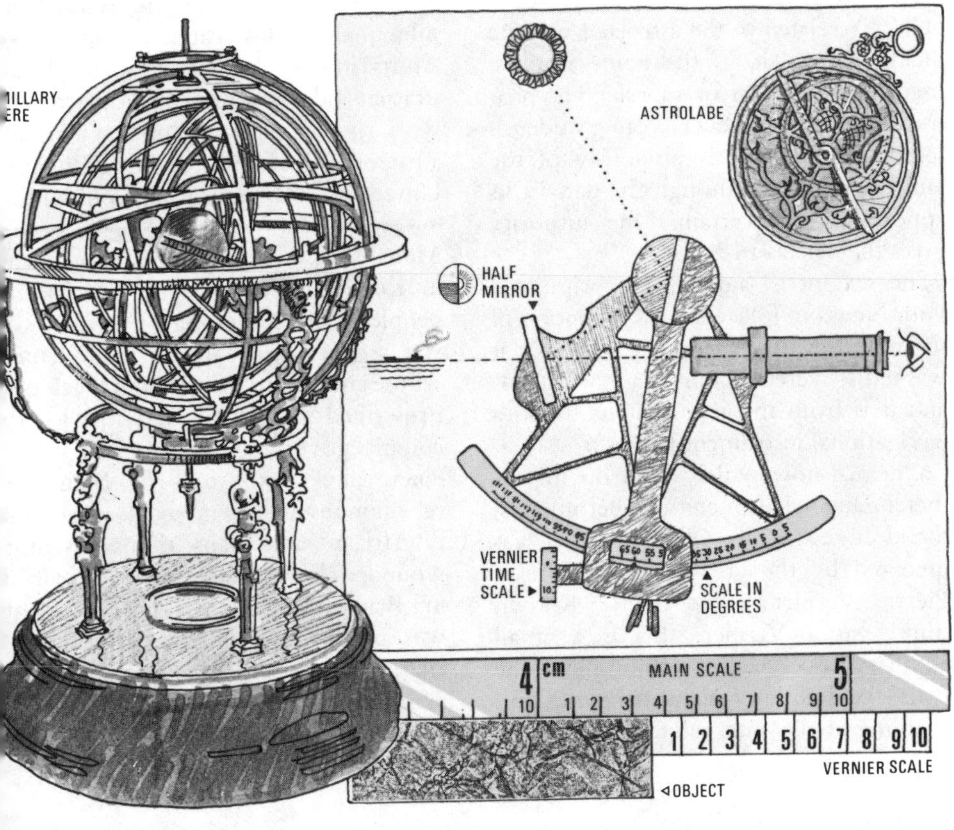

It was used in various ways for measuring angles, although its most important applications were in astronomy and also in navigation. There were several types, of which the simplest was the planisphere. This consisted of a circular disc, the circumference of which was marked off in degrees. Attached to the centre of the disc were two movable arms, which could be sighted on distant objects. Another form was the armillary sphere, a three-dimensional version. This got its name from the armillae, or rings, which were arranged concentrically but at right angles to each other. There were usually two, but sometimes three, such circular rings. One ring corresponded with the plane of the equator and the other with the plane of the meridian. The ancient astronomer Ptolemy describes this instrument. Chaucer also wrote a treatise on its use, and a magnificent astrolabe, now to be seen in the British Museum, may have been used by him.

Closely related to the astrolabe was the quadrant, which, as the name implies, used only a quarter of a circle. The protractor, now part of every young student's set of instruments, is obviously of the same derivation, although the date of its appearance is uncertain. One authority gives the date as 1658.

The sextant is said to have originated with Newton, following his invention of the reflecting microscope in 1672, but it was rediscovered by John Hadley in 1731, and it is from this date that its use as a navigational instrument begins.

A device now widely used on micrometer gauges, barometers, cathetometers, theodolites, sextants, telescopes, etc., was invented by the French mathematician Pierre Vernier (1580–1637). Known simply as a Vernier, this is a small auxiliary scale made to slide along the main fixed scale of an instrument, thus enabling smaller intervals to be measured.

A whole range of new mathemati instruments began in 1814 when the fi planimeter, a device for measuring area bounded by an irregular curve, w invented. An instrument much used engineers is the slide-rule, which, using the logarithmic scales sliding alon side each other, enables multiplicatic division and other mathematical pr cesses to be carried out very quickly.
See also NEWTON, SIR ISAAC; PTOLEMY.

Matthias I Hunyadi or **Matthi Corvinus** (*c.* 1440–90)**:** King of Hunga 1458–90 and of Bohemia 1478–90. M: thias was not crowned King of Hunga until 1464, following a long struggle wi the Turks, Bohemia, the Empire ar dissenting Hungarian factions. Almc perpetually at war, he was a fine milita leader and strategist. In 1468 he conquer Moldavia and Wallachia. In 1478 he ma peace with Bohemia, gaining Moravi Silesia and Lusatia. He captured Vienn subsequently his capital, and Low Austria in 1485. A great diplomat, admin strator and legislator, his capacity f work rivalled that of Napoleon I. He w a patron of learning, founding Budape University and bequeathing a library.

Mau Mau: a secret society which aro in Kenya, mainly among the Kikuy people at the beginning of the 1950s. was a nationalist terrorist moveme whose aim was to bring about black rul Proscribed in 1952, its activities led th colonial government to impose a state (emergency (1952–59). The Mau Ma rebellion resulted in 13,500 deaths (mai ly African) and many thousands mo wounded. It was a vital factor in persuac ing Britain to decolonise. Jomo Kenyat was imprisoned by the British on charge (which he always denied) of man aging Mau Mau. Later he became the fir president of independent Kenya.

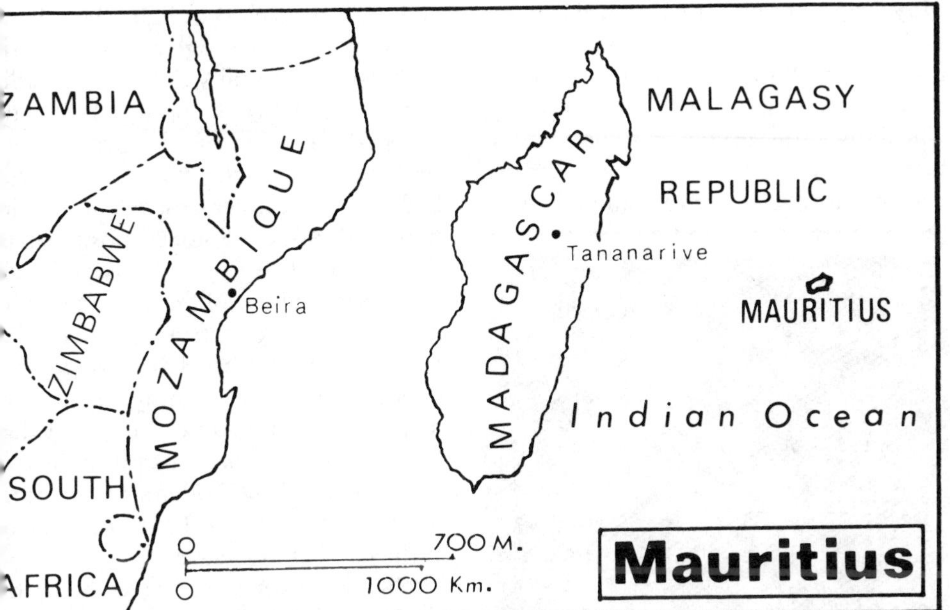

lauritius: independent island in the ıdian Ocean forming part of the ommonwealth and occupied mainly by ›rmer Indian immigrants, with African, uropean and Chinese minorities. It may ·ell have been visited by Arab traders in ıe Middle Ages and by Portuguese later, ut it became a French possession under ıe name "Ile de France" in 1715 and still artly maintains the French language and ·aditions. Being on the route to India the land became a bone of contention etween Britain and France until the ›rmer seized it in 1810. Cholera, malaria nd other epidemics, and cyclones, have aused periods of devastation. Permanent rosperity has been supplied mainly by ıgar export.

---

laximilian I (1459–1519): King of ;ermany 1486–1519, Holy Roman ;mperor 1493–1519. Attempting to re-·ive the old glories of the medieval ;mpire, Maximilian caused considerable lisorder. However, he carried out military eforms, established the *Reichskammer-ericht* (Imperial Court of Justice) and patronised the arts. By the marriages arranged for his family the Habsburgs gained vast possessions. Maximilian married Mary, heiress of Burgundy; Philip, their son, married the heiress of Spain; Ferdinand, Maximilian's grandson, married the heiress of Hungary and Bohemia. All these territories were ultimately ruled by Maximilian's grandson Charles V (*see* separate entry).

Maximilian (1832–67): Emperor of Mexico. He was the son of Archduke Charles and brother of Francis Joseph (1830–1916), Emperor of Austria. In the early 1860s Mexico was torn by civil wars, one side being supported by the northern states of USA, the other by the southern states and by Napoleon III, Emperor of France (*see* separate entry). The latter in 1864 persuaded Maximilian to accept the throne of Mexico; but, despite the backing of French troops, later withdrawn, his attempts ended in failure. He was captured and executed by the republicans. His widow became insane but lived until 1927.

May Day: ancient spring festival held on 1 May when people decorated their houses with flowers, danced around the maypole and crowned the May Queen. The festival still survives in some country districts. In most countries of Europe 1 May is now celebrated as Labour Day.

A Mayan carving showing a penitent kneeling before a priest, approximately 709 AD.

Mayan civilisation: an early but advanced civilisation of Central America. The first great cities were on the plains of northern Guatemala, but these were abruptly abandoned during the 6th century BC, the population moving to Yucatan and the highlands of southern Mexico and Guatemala. By AD 1100 a stable civilisation was established under three princely houses, Itza, Xia and Cocom, who dominated the area for two centuries. Thereafter there were three centuries of intermittent civil war, and when the Spaniards arrived they found complete political disorder.

In its earliest known period the Mayan culture had reached a high level. The was writing in a hieroglyphic script and calendar. Great skill was shown in arch tecture, stone carving, pottery and texti work. But iron was not known, nor w the principle of the wheel. The gre buildings were constructed from u mortared blocks of stone, mostly sma though in a few cases very large bloc were used, and one of the *stelae* (column is a single block measuring twenty-fiv feet [7.62 metres] from the ground. Th builders used stone implements f quarrying, facing and carving, and the were ignorant of the principle of the tru arch. Many of the buildings were pyr mids, not tombs as in Egypt but servin as the bases of high altars.

Religion appears to have been th worship of the forces of nature, with superior creator god, Quetzalcoatl, whos early emblem was a feathered serpen which later became a man with serpe and bird characteristics. Human sacrific probably did not occur in early times bu was introduced later from the Aztecs.

¶ GALLENKAMP, CHARLES. *Finding out about t Maya.* 1963

"Mayflower": ship that carried th English Puritans or Pilgrim Fathers t establish a settlement in North America i 1620. Few details are known of th original *Mayflower* but the vessel i assumed to have been a small merchant man of about 180 tons [183 tonnes] an 90 feet [27·4 metres]. The three mast carried square sails on the fore and mai and a lateen sail on the mizzen. Steerin was by whipstaff. Captain Christophe

A modern replica of the Mayflower *prepares sail from Plymouth to America.*

nes sailed *Mayflower* from Southamp-n, but bad weather forced him into artmouth and Plymouth. He finally eared Plymouth on 16 September 1620 ith 102 souls on board. Landfall was ade near Plymouth, Massachusetts, on November. *Mayflower* returned to ngland in 1621.

azarin, Jules (Giulio Mazarini, 1602–): Italian-born French statesman and rdinal. His enemy Cardinal de Retz id, "his strength was to listen. . . . He d brains, an insinuating manner, cheer-lness, style, but his shabby mind spoilt all." Others commented on his lack of nity and his immense capacity for work. e became chief minister of France in 642, extended France's territorial limits d created a powerful central admini-ration, though his policies considerably epleted the royal finances of Louis XIII d XIV.

Iazzini, Giuseppi (1805–72): Italian atriot. Born in Genoa, he founded in 831 "Young Italy", a revolutionary novement dedicated to the achievement f a united Italian republic. Exiled to Iarseilles, then to London, he continued is campaign, returning to Italy in 1848. He helped to set up the short-lived Roman Republic, but with the defeat of the revolutionaries was again exiled. While Cavour and Garibaldi worked to establish the kingdom of Italy, Mazzini remained a strong republican. He was undoubtedly the prophet of a free Italy, as well as an inspiration, through his writings, to liberals in Europe and America.
See also GARIBALDI; ITALY, etc.

Measurement: the science known more academically as metrology. Before we begin to measure anything we must first fix a suitable unit of measurement. Measures of length in early times were largely derived from the human body. Perhaps the most familiar of these, the cubit, was the length of the ulna, or forearm; hence we obtain the English ell and the French *aune*. The cubit was used in ancient Egypt and Babylonia and occurs frequently in the Old Testament. The foot was originally, of course, the length of the human foot. This varied widely from place to place, ranging from the Italian foot of about 275 millimetres to the Olympic foot of 320 millimetres. We read in an early manuscript that the English foot was obtained by selecting "a mickle man, a muckle man and a middling man" and taking the average length of their feet. Both Greeks and Romans used the fingerbreadth and the palm (four fingerbreadths). The fathom was the length of the extended arms, the mile (from *mille*) a thousand double paces. In ancient India the finger was also used but was subdivided into eight breadths of a *yava* or barleycorn. The word "yard" is said to be derived from the Anglo-Saxon *gyrd* (a rod or stick). Its origin can be seen in the method still used for a rough measurement of a length of material, by holding it at arm's length and taking the length from there to the ear as one yard;

hence the "cloth yard shaft" of the English archers. An old chronicle tells us of Henry I "that there might be no abuse in measures, he ordained a measure made by the length of his own arm, which is called a yard". The daily routine of the countryman provided the furlong (the furrow long), the distance the oxen could plough, before they were given a rest, and turned round for the return journey. The acre is thought to have been derived from a morning's ploughing, the cattle being put out to pasture in the afternoon. The continental *morgen* is similarly derived, although in Holland this was about two acres [0·8 hectares], while in Prussia, Norway and Denmark it was about two-thirds of an acre [0·3 hectares].

The origin of the gallon as a unit of volume is obscure. The present British gallon of 277·42 cubic inches was adopted in 1824, replacing two different units, the ale gallon of 282 cubic inches and the wine gallon of 231 cubic inches. The quart is merely the quarter of a gallo The gill was also a wine measure, deriv from the French *gille* or *gelle*.

Another fundamental process measurement, weighing, is very old. Th first weights so far discovered date fro about 3400 BC in Egypt, and the w pictures of the temples show simp balances, usually held in the hand. Th shekel (about a quarter of an ounce) w an ancient unit of weight of the Babylo nians, and of the Phoenicians and th Hebrews. It was also a silver coin of th weight, and in Exodus we read: "Th they shall give, every one that passet among them that are numbered, half shekel after the shekel of the sanctuary . an half shekel shall be the offering of th Lord." This quotation is also interestin in that it shows that the standard shek was kept in the Temple.

In ancient Rome the pound was the un of weight. This was divided into twelv parts (*unciae*); hence the derivation of th

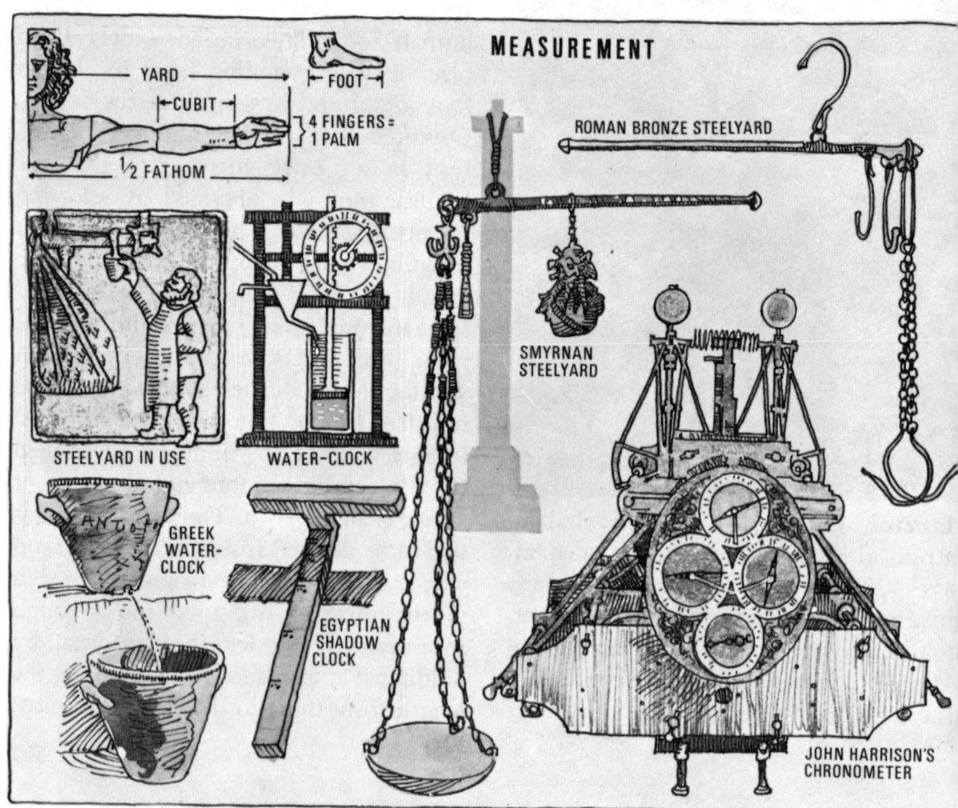

rd "ounce". In Troy weight there are twelve ounces in the pound. This tem came from the French town of oyes and is thought to have been roduced by foreign merchants who ended the fairs which played such a ominent part in the commercial life of Middle Ages. It was probably introced into England soon after 1250. Troy ight was ultimately replaced by Avoirpois for most purposes, Troy weight ing restricted to the trade of the Golditns. Avoirdupois seems to have been Spanish origin and to have reached gland about 1300. By Elizabeth I's ne we are told that "Haberdepoyse is more usual weight".

When the British Houses of Parliament ere destroyed by fire in 1834 the stanrd pound and the standard yard were t, and this led to a more scientific definin of them. The new standard yard was anufactured in 1845. The Weights and easures Act of 1878 defines it as the stance at 62° Fahrenheit between two es engraved on gold studs embedded in bronze bar. The pound is defined as the eight *in vacuo* of a cylinder of pure atinum about 1·15 inches [43 millietres] in diameter and 1·35 inches [50 illimetres] high.

All the units of measurement so far entioned are of a purely arbitrary nature, it during the 18th century the idea of a natural" unit became popular. What we ow know as the metric system originated om a report made to the French ational Assembly by the Paris Academy Sciences in 1791. As early as 1670 abriel Mouton, the vicar of St Paul's hurch, Lyons, had proposed as the basic nit of length the length of one second of c along a great circle of the earth. The nit now decided upon was the metre, hich was to be one ten-millionth part of quarter of a meridian. For this purpose a areful survey was made of the meridian from Dunkirk to Barcelona, and a platinum bar, the standard metre, was constructed. As it turned out, the measurement was not quite accurate owing to an error in finding the latitude of Barcelona, but the standard as first constructed was not altered. The metre, therefore, is in fact just as arbitrary as the other units we have mentioned. The unit of mass was the gramme, defined as the mass of one cubic centimetre of pure water at the temperature of 4° Centigrade, the temperature at which water attains its maximum density. This new system only gradually replaced the old one and was not made compulsory in France until 1840.

In 1875 the International Bureau of Weights and Measures was established at Sèvres, on land ceded by the French government and declared by them to be international territory. The first task of the Bureau was to construct new standards for the metre and the kilogram and to distribute them to the nations supporting the work. In 1960 an International Conference in Paris adopted a new definition of the metre in terms of the wave length of light. The metric system is now the most widely used system of units.

It is perhaps difficult in these days of standardisation and careful inspection of weights and measures to realise the wide diversity and inaccuracy which once prevailed. To quote only one example, in France, before the introduction of the metric system, there were nearly four hundred different ways of measuring land.

Finally, a brief mention must be made of the measurement of time. Ancient peoples usually divided the day and the night each into twelve equal parts, so that what we should call the hour varied in length from season to season. The earliest method of measuring time was the sundial. This seems to have been first used in Egypt, and Herodotus tells us that it was introduced into Greece from Babylon. It is also thought that the circular rows of stones set up by the Druids were used to mark the sun's path, and to indicate the times and seasons. The need to tell the time at night or when the sun was obscured by clouds gave rise to various other devices, such as the hourglass and the clepsydra (or water clock), while King Alfred is said to have used wax candles enclosed in a horn lantern. Clocks appear to have been introduced in Europe during the 13th century. Salisbury Cathedral has one dating from 1386 and Wells Cathedral one dating from 1392. These were not originally pendulum clocks. The pendulum clock was the invention of Huygens in 1657. Reliable clocks and watches also played a large part in the determination of the longitude of a ship at sea, and in 1714 John Harrison (*see* separate entry) devised a chronometer which won him a prize of £20,000 from the British government. The most modern development in accurate time measurement is the quartz crystal clock, in which a quartz crystal, kept in a state of electrical vibration, replaces the pendulum.

¶ HOGBEN, LANCELOT. *The Wonderful World of Mathematics*. 1968

Mecca: the birthplace of Mohammed (*c*. AD 570) and the most sacred city of Islam. It lies in Arabia about forty-five miles [72 kilometres] from the port of Jidda on the Red Sea and is visited by more than one million pilgrims each year. Non-Moslems may not enter Mecca.

In the central courtyard of the great mosque Mecca, stands the Sacred Black Stone believed have been built by the patriarch Abraham and son Ishmael.

Medici, Family of: as a personal na properly written in the Italian form, Medici. The family was centred Florence, but wielded a significant fluence over Italian and European hist for over three centuries.

It is first found about the year 1 engaged in the business of banking, which its fortunes were founded. I said that the three golden balls wh used to hang over the doors of pav brokers' shops were taken from Medici coat-of-arms. Another tradit of the family was that of combin personal wealth and power with sy pathy for the cause of the common peo

The greatest days of the family were the times of Cosimo the Elder (13 1464), his son Piero (1416–69) and latter's son Lorenzo the Magnific (1449–92). Not that these were untroub years in an age of plottings and jealous especially on the part of those opposed the popular cause. Piero is remarkable having forgiven those who conspired take his life; but the vengeance of people on those responsible for murder of Giuliano, Lorenzo's brilli brother, was so savage that Sixtus (Pope 1471–84), who was thought some to have had knowledge of the pl put Florence for a time under an interdi During all this period the Medici we virtually lords of Florence, though th rejected any grandiose or formal titl They introduced a number of enlighten reforms and were generous patrons scholars and artists, among the latter t painter Botticelli (1444–1570).

The years that followed the death Lorenzo were a troubled time for Floren and the other states of Italy, but the peri saw two of the family become Pope first Giovanni de' Medici (1475–152 the second son of Lorenzo, elected Po in 1513 as Leo X, and second Giulio (147 1534), the son of Lorenzo's murder

THE MEDICI FAMILY: *Top row from left to right, Cosimo I, Piero, Lorenzo, called the Magnificent. Left Giuliano, and right Giulio who became Pope Clement VII. Bottom row left to right, Alessandro, Marie and Catherine de Medici.*

:other, who became Pope as Clement II in 1523 and was a patron of Michel-ıgelo and other artists.

Meanwhile, towards the end of this eriod, Alessandro de' Medici (1511–37), bastard son of the family, whose ırentage is debated, became Duke of lorence in 1532, and with his death the eadship of the line passed to another ranch of the Medici, which brought bout a revival of the power and influence f Florence and in 1569 earned from Pope ius V the enhanced title of Grand Duke f Tuscany for the head of the family. In omewhat reduced prestige the last grand uke died in 1737, and his sister soon fterwards bequeathed all the Medici easures to Florence.

It remains to mention two ladies of the ımily who became queens – and, for a me, regents – of France, where the name usually spelt de Médicis: Catherine (1519–89), who married Henri II, and Marie (1573–1642), wife of Henri IV and mother of Henrietta Maria, the queen of Charles I of England.

¶ ALLEN, E. *The Story of Lorenzo the Magnificent.* 1961; CHAMBERLIN, E. R. *Florence in the Time of the Medici.* 1972

Medicine: The Egyptians, Greeks and Romans held practitioners of medicine in great respect. In Egypt, Imhotep was said to be the "father of medicine" and was worshipped as a god. Egyptian doctors were priests, and so also were many of the Greek doctors. There was an early link between medicine and religion, and both were revered by ordinary people as mysteries not fully understood by the layman.

In about 400 BC Hippocrates, a Greek physician, founded a school of medicine. He and other doctors exchanged ideas and examined theories of treatment in a scientific manner. Hippocrates taught his pupils the importance of observing and recording the symptoms of disease, and he held that it was impossible to treat one part of the body without some understanding of the functioning of all the other parts. Presentday graduates in medicine still take the oath ascribed to Hippocrates (*see* separate entry), known as the Hippocratic Oath, which regulates medical ethics.

Roman doctors worked in a similar way, and many gained considerable experience while serving as army surgeons with the legions. Some could even supply artificial limbs of wood or ivory to soldiers who had lost an arm or a leg in battle. In the later days of the Roman Empire the city of Rome became greatly overcrowded, and epidemics of typhus and other diseases swept the poorer districts. When Christianity became the official religion of the Empire, public doctors were paid by the state to attend the poor.

The knowledge of medicine declined in Europe after the fall of Rome, although it still flourished in the eastern Empire, kept alive by the Arabs, who trained skilful doctors. In the centuries of warfare and tribal movement which followed the collapse of Roman rule, formal medical training disappeared in Europe, and attempts to cure disease became a matter of charms, spells and magic. In this the Church did little to help, often looking upon illness as being the will of God, inflicted as a punishment for wrongdoing or as a test of faith. Moreover, interest in the body was held by many to be sinful, so that anatomical study was discouraged. In these circumstances, curative medicine became a hit-or-miss affair, usually practised by unskilled persons having a little knowledge of the use of herbs. It is possible that the medieval practice of smearing open wounds with cobwebs and decaying matter could have been the forerunner of penicillin.

One result of the Crusades was t infiltration into Europe of Arabic medi knowledge. Early in the 13th century medical school was established at Saler in Italy, where a student had to study five years and then serve for a peri under a recognised physician before could claim the degree of doctor. B even these men, though they we scholars, remained very ignorant of t internal structure of the human body. was impossible, for obvious reasons, study a living body, and the Chur forbade the dissection of a dead one, in t belief that it would be rejected at t Resurrection.

It was not until the Renaissance that a serious anatomical study began, initiat by Italian artists who felt that they need a complete understanding of what th were drawing. Doctors seized this oppo tunity to make anatomical dissectio and the knowledge thus gained increas their competence. An Italian surgeo Andreas Vesalius of Padua, was the tr founder of modern medicine. He pu lished a book entitled *The Fabric of t Human Body*, which he illustrated wi woodcuts full of anatomical deta Students flocked to his lectures; h audience at the University of Pisa was great that on one occasion the special built operating theatre collapsed.

In England and France, although Ves lius's book was studied, there was litt development in medical research un the 17th century. Physicians belonged a trade guild, surgeons were also barber and scientific research was of interest any cultured gentleman. In Novemb 1666 Samuel Pepys mentioned in h diary that he witnessed an experime when the blood of one dog was let in the body of another, and the followin year he saw a "frantic man" who ha been calmed by a transfusion of bloo from a sheep.

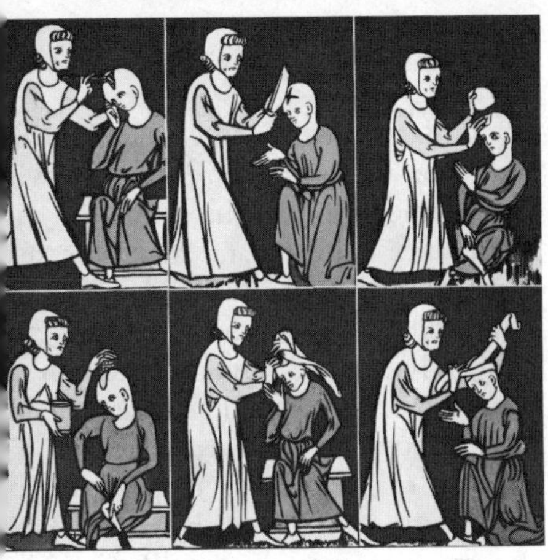

bove: an operation for trepanning in the 13th ntury, using the ancient Egyptian method. elow: an apothecary's shop in the 15th century.

Above: blood transfusions as practised in the 17th century. Below: a surgical operation in the early days of antiseptic surgery, mid-19th century.

elow: 16th century method of "cauterisation" sealing a wound with a hot iron).

Below: modern germ-free surgery takes place in a vinyl tent filled with sterilized air.

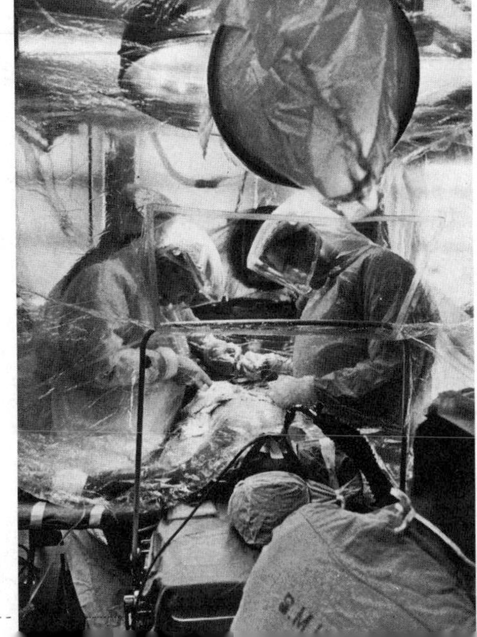

In 18th century England the world of medicine was dominated by the physicians. Their underlings were the apothecaries and the surgeons. The latter, struggling to break with the Barbers' Guild, were considered too lowly to be awarded any degree. That is why an English physician is addressed as "Doctor", while a surgeon still clings defiantly to the title of "Mister".

But the great British medical schools were established during this century – in Edinburgh by the Munro brothers and Dr Knox, in London by John and William Hunter. In France, too, the Academie de Medicine encouraged medical research. Soon students from America were coming to Europe to train, and taking back their new knowledge to their own country.

Medical science now advanced rapidly in many fields. To name some major contributions, at the end of the 18th century an English country doctor, Edward Jenner, discovered the secret of inoculation against smallpox. At about the same time a revolution began in the sadly ignorant and barbaric treatment of the mentally sick. In a single week the French physician Philippe Pinel (1745–1826) had the chains struck from fifty pitiful creatures who were brought into air and sunlight. His fight for treatment by greater kindness and freedom from harsh restraint was taken up and extended by, among others, William Tuke (1732–1822) and John Conolly (1794–1866) in England, and by Dorothea Dix (1802–87) in the U.S.A.

The use of anaesthetic gases to reduce the pain of operations was pioneered in English by the chemist Humphry Davy (1778–1829) and the physicist Michael Faraday (1791–1867). In America nitrous oxide was successfully used for a tooth extraction in 1842 and, in the same year, ether for a surgical operation. A Scottish physician, James Young Simpson (1811–70) used chloroform to ease childbirth a method that became respectable wh Queen Victoria made use of it.

In France the husband and wife tea Pierre (1859–1906) and Marie (186 1934) Curie made the researches in radioactivity that have resulted in t wide use of the metallic element radiu in various medical treatments. T scourge of malaria in tropical regio was partly conquered by two Briti experts on tropical diseases, Patrick Ma son (1844–1922) and Ronald Ross (185 1932), who identified the mosquito as t agent transmitting the disease to huma beings. Insulin, one of the most effectiv ways of dealing with diabetes, was di covered by the Canadian Frederick Ba ting and his associates in 1921. Such me as Louis Pasteur (1822–95) had achieve important work in the prevention infectious disease, but only comparative recently have there been great advanc in the use of antibiotics (Greek *ant* against and *bios* life). Alexander Flemin (1881–1955) discovered penicillin almo by accident in 1928 and experimente with its uses for some twelve years, h work being furthered by the Australia Howard Florey and the Russo-Germa Ernst Chain. Streptromycin, another im portant antibiotic, was discovered by th Russian Selman Waksman, working i the USA. All the last four men name received the Nobel Prize for medicine.

Another group of scientific and medica investigators, known as psychologists psychiatrists and psychoanalysts, hav worked on the problems of huma behaviour and the links between mind an physical illness. Though the approache and objectives may differ the use of th Greek word *psuche* (psyche), meaning th soul or mind, both conscious and un conscious, indicates that much commo ground is shared by workers in these field of medicine. Among the most importan ames are those of Sigmund Freud (1856–939), Carl Jung (1875–1961) and Alfred dler (1870–1937).

Finally, mention should be made of the ıbject of transplants – the substitution of healthy organ for a diseased one in the uman body. Some work in this field, .g. in the treatment of kidney trouble, ad passed virtually unnoticed. But in 967 a South African doctor, Christian 3arnard, gained worldwide publicity by ransplanting a human heart. Many ımilar operations, most with little sucess, have since been performed in various ountries; but violent controversy has een aroused, not only on medical but thical grounds – and not only from the eneral public but within the medical rofession itself.

DELGADO, ALAN. *A Hundred Years of Medical Care.* 1970; TAYLOR, BOSWELL. *Medicine.* 1962

See also ALCHEMY; ANAESTHESIA; BARBER-URGEONS; DENTISTRY; HARVEY, WILLIAM; IIPPOCRATES; HOSPITALS; INOCULATION; ENNER, EDWARD; KING'S EVIL; NIGHTIN-GALE, FLORENCE; PARACELSUS; PASTEUR, OUIS; PENICILLIN; PLAGUES; VACCINA-TION; X-RAY.

Medieval (Mediaeval): pertaining to the Middle Ages, itself a term popularised by 7th century historians for the period etween the fall of Rome and the Renaissance. The adjective, coined in the 9th century, dates from a time when nany artists and writers looked back to what seemed to them, a romantic and colourful era. The general use of the term n historical writing now is devoid of hese overtones.

Medina, Arabic **Al-Madina:** town in Arabia, 250 miles [402 kilometres] north of Mecca. The Islamic calendar is reckoned from AD 622, the date of Mohammed's flight (Hegira) from Mecca to Medina. Hejaz railway from Damascus to Medina (completed in 1908) was for use by pilgrims. Its destruction in World War I was closely connected with the exploits of Lawrence of Arabia.

Mediterranean Sea: sea, 1,145,000 square miles [2,965,500 kilometres] in area, enclosed by the land masses of three continents, Europe, Asia and Africa, with access to the Atlantic by the Strait of Gibraltar. Although it includes several smaller seas – the Aegean, Adriatic, Ionian and Tyrrhenian – it is itself only the small remnant of a vast ocean which in geological times encircled half the globe.

Its name, from Latin *medius*, middle, and *terra*, land, indicates not only its geographical position but its importance as a centre of the ancient world, carrying a vast burden of trade and providing a highway to the East before the discovery of the Cape of Good Hope route. Being almost tideless, it encouraged early seafaring; known currents and the daily alternation of land and sea breezes made coastwise navigation easy; and voyagers from, for example, the Egyptian Delta, could confidently make the round trip via the Syrian coast, south Asia Minor and Crete, and count on the wind from the north to bring them home to the Libyan coast and the mouth of the Nile. This is not to say that seafaring in the Mediterranean was without its hazards, especially out of season. Hesiod, writing *c.* 700 BC, recommended as the best periods for sailing either the spring or "fifty days after the solstice, when the burdensome days of summer come to an end" and counselled "do not wait for the time of the new wine and the terrible blasts of the North Wind which accompany the heavy autumnal rain". There is confirmation of the perils of winter sailing in the Mediterranean in the graphic story of St Paul's shipwreck, *c.* AD 60, as told in the Acts of

Al. Albania
Bul. Bulgaria
Gr. Greece
Isr. Israel
Leb. Lebanon
Lib. Liberia
Min. Minorca
Mon. Monaco
Mo. Montenegro
FRANCE
Mon.
YUGOSLAVIA
Bul.
Black Sea
U.S.S.R.
Adriatic Sea
Mo.
ITALY
Corsica
Alb.
Gr.
Aegean Sea
TURKEY
Sardinia
Min.
Tyrrhenian Sea
PORTUGAL
SPAIN
MEDITERRANEAN SEA
Ionian Sea
Sicily
Crete
SYRIA
Cyprus
Leb.
Malta
Gibraltar
TUNISIA
Isr.
JORDAN
Atlantic Ocean
MOROCCO
ALGERIA
LIBYA
EGYPT
Red Sea
SAHARA ARAB DEMOCRATIC REPUBLIC
(claimed by MOROCCO)
AFRICA
MAURETANIA
MALI
NIGER
CHAD
SUDAN
NIGERIA
700 M.
750 Km.
Lib.
Mediterranean

ıe Apostles, 27: 27. The north-western ırt of the sea is especially liable to rocious winter storms.

Throughout the centuries the Mediterınean has been the scene of great sea attles. The year 480 BC saw the decisive efeat of the Persians by the Greeks at alamis. Two thousand years later Don ›hn of Austria, leading the fleets of pain and Venice, broke the might of)ttoman seapower at Lepanto (*see* separate entry). In World War II the Allied eets of steel battleships and aircraft arriers, descendants of the war galleys f the ancient world, fought in the seas f Crete and Sicily and up the coasts of taly.

The Mediterranean, in fact, despite the pread of the map east, west, north and outh, to cover a greater world than the arly civilisations dreamt of, has never lost ts "middle land" strategic importance. If t has known long periods of political tagnation it has also witnessed sudden brupt upheavals in the pattern of nations, ıs in the years 1910–27 when the long tranglehold of Ottoman power was ›roken and the new states of Egypt, Yugoslavia, Albania and (so changed as o be virtually new also) Greece and Turkey emerged; with, alongside them, new colonies and mandated territories attached to the Great Powers.

¶ PACK, S. W. C. *Sea Power in the Mediterranean: a history from the seventeenth century to the present day*. 1971

Melanchthon (Philipp Schwarzerd, 1497–1560): German scholar and religious reformer. He was largely responsible for putting the Protestant doctrines of Martin Luther (*see* separate entry) into systematic order. The name Melanchthon is the Greek form of his native name, a practice common among scholars of the period.

Memphis: former city of northern Egypt on the west bank of the River Nile, the centre of the worship of Ptah, creator of the world and all living things. Its founder, Menes, was the first Pharaoh. The bull of Apis was housed there, and Memphis was a centre of priestly training. The city lost its importance with the rise of new religions and the foundation by Alexander of Alexandria as his capital. The city of Memphis in Tennessee, USA, was so named because of the supposed similarity of its location.

Mendel, Gregor Johann (1822–84): Austrian monk and botanist who, as the result of his experiments in the garden of the Augustinian monastery at Brünn (Brno), worked out a number of important laws of heredity (the transmission of characteristics and qualities from parent to offspring) in plants and (as was later proved) in animals and human beings. The discoveries that have resulted from his original work are of particular importance in the study of certain hereditary human diseases and abnormalities, such as haemophilia (excessive and too-ready bleeding) which is normally found only in boys and is handed down by their mothers; and colour blindness which, again, is handed down by women but is manifested only in men.

Mendel published his findings in an obscure natural history journal, where they remained largely unknown for sixteen years, when they were rediscovered by other investigators in the same field. Medical scientists afterwards pronounced Mendel's discoveries as the most important in the whole science of life.

¶ SOOTIN, HARRY. *Gregor Mendel*. 1961

Mensheviks: the moderate wing of the Russian Social Democrat Party. At a Party Congress in 1903 the moderates were outvoted and were labelled *Mensheviki* (minority) to distinguish them from the extremists, who were the majority (*Bolsheviki*) on that occasion. Their leader was Martov, a former colleague of Lenin, and Trotsky was associated with them for a short time.

Merchant Adventurers: an organisation of English merchants, with trading factories in Holland and later Hamburg and other German cities. A Merchant Adventurers Company began to operate from England in the reign of Edward III. The earliest charter dates from 1407, though the company was not incorporated until 1553, at a time when Sebastian Cabot (1476–1557) was a governor. The Merchant Adventurers formed a private company to export manufactured articles, mainly cloth, to Europe. Its members were English, unlike the Staplers, who included foreigners in their organisation and traded in unfinished goods, particularly wool. The Merchant Adventurers may have developed from the medieval trading guilds, and it has been suggested that freemen of the Mercers Company of London formed the nucleus of the company. New trading companies formed in the 16th and 17th centuries, such as the East India Companies, were no doubt modelled on the Merchant Adventurers.

From the start the company found itself in competition with the Hansa, a German group which had previously monopolised trade in the North Sea ports and throughout Europe. The 1545 edict of the Emperor Charles V seriously interrupted English trade with the Netherlands and temporarily re-established the Hansa's monopoly in carrying English cloth to Antwerp. Yet commerce with the Low Countries expanded throughout the 16th century. Countermeasures reduced and finally ended the Hansa's special privileges, and in 1598 Elizabeth I of England closed the Steelyard, where the Hansa had its headquarters in London from 1232. The Merchant Adventurers company is thought to have employed up to 50,000 people in the Low Countries at its most prosperous period. The trade in woollen cloths had rapidly overtaken the export of wool in the later Middle Ages. In two centuries, from the middle of the 14th exported cloths had risen from 500 bales to 100,000, while wool exports had fallen from 30,000 bales to 4,000, to the distress of the Staplers and the merchants of Calais. Inland towns like Colchester, the main entrepôt (i.e. centre for importing and re-exporting), prospered through the activities of the Merchant Adventurers as did such towns as Braintree, Coggeshall Norwich and Halstead. The ports through which cloths were shipped, especially London, throve equally on the trade. The annual turnover of Dutch and German trade in the reign of James I has been estimated at one million pounds sterling. Yet the Adventurers clearly encouraged other activities. The Pilgrim Fathers sailed to found the Plymouth Colony under the aegis of the Merchant Adventurers. They differed from the later joint stock companies (e.g. the East India and Hudson's Bay Companies) in that each Merchant Adventurer traded on his own capital in accordance with the company's rules. The joint stock companies traded as a whole, and any profits or losses were distributed among the shareholders.

By the 18th century the Merchant Adventurers had become known as the Hamburg Company, since Hamburg was the central depot for the trade, embracing other German ports. Here the company remained until 1808 when Napoleon's "continental system" and a hostile Europe brought about its dissolution.

¶ LEWENHAK, SHEILA. editor. *The Merchant Adventurers* (Jackdaw). 1967

See also HANSEATIC LEAGUE.

Merchant Navy (Britain); **Merchant Marine** (USA): From a very early period en have engaged in trade and this has volved transport by sea in ships. Because wars and piracy these "merchant" ships ve always had to fight on occasions, and e very distinct division between war-ips and others is of comparatively odern origin. A primary function of the arship has always been the protection of ade.

ulius Caesar invaded Britain because of e help given by the Britons to his emies in Gaul, and there was trade ross the Channel long before this, deed as long as the islands had been opulated. The Vikings, who invaded ritain after the Romans had left, were een traders by sea in ships which they iled and rowed. In the Middle Ages the rger round ships, with a single mast and square sail, visited Iceland for cod and pain for wine. Dried and salted cod rmed a staple preserved food in the days hen the refrigerator was unknown. The me type of ship was used for the export f wool to Flanders. The Hanseatic eague was a powerful international ombine of merchants which directed his kind of trade in northern waters. rom the Mediterranean and such ports s Venice and Genoa great merchant rading galleys brought the spices of the ast to Britain and northern Europe.

Fighting fleets or military transports vere usually formed by temporarily aking over merchant ships. The Cinque orts on the south coast of Britain under-ook to meet the requirements of the king or a number of ships in this way, in eturn for special trading privileges.

The 15th and 16th century voyages of liscovery by Portuguese and Spanish raders encouraged English merchants to eek distant markets and to fight for pecial benefits. But in time of war trade vas stopped by embargoes, and many nerchant seamen were impressed by the tate to man its warships.

In time of peace commerce flourished. Merchant companies, such as the English Muscovy Company and the East India Company, were formed and traded in new commodities in the newly discovered regions of the world. Certain ships were designed for particular trades. The colliers from Newcastle, the whalers from Hull and the stately Indiamen out of London are cases in point. The richer trades encouraged the building of finer ships; the East Indiaman of 1,000 tons [1,016 tonnes] laden with spices was larger than the West Indiaman of 500 tons [508 tonnes] bringing home the sugar. Otherwise ships differed little in appearance except in size, and the warship was very like the merchant ship, distinguished only by the many more guns and men carried. Trade rivalry was the cause of many wars, and the big merchant trading companies such as the East India Companies of England, Holland, France and Portugal had their own fighting fleets to settle local rivalries.

The seaman was a breed apart, used to being cooped up in ships, familiar with other parts of the world, able to mix with foreigners and jealous of his freedom when faced with the discipline of a warship. He suffered from old salt meat and sour beer on long voyages, but found compensation on his travels over the oceans of the world and did not envy his fellows tied to the land, farm, smallholding or town office.

In the 19th century ships grew larger; steam power and iron replaced sail and wood. The glamorous days of the Anglo-American rivalry in the tea trade, with tea clippers racing home with the first crops of tea, lasted only some twenty years, 1850–70.

Before the 1860s ship owners were often small groups of persons, perhaps owning one ship divided into sixty-four shares. One of the owners might well be a seaman

The Clipper ship Nightingale.

and the master in command. This system was replaced in the latter half of the 19th century by shipping companies, which often proved more remote from ships and men. The ship master was now the servant of the company. Regulations, such as the British Merchant Shipping Acts, from 1851 onwards laid down conditions for the construction of vessels, the provision of navigation lights and the training of men, but the sailor's lot was nevertheless often far from easy. In the 1870s Samuel Plimsoll waged a campaign in the British Parliament which led to the successful establishment of a load line for ships (*see* PLIMSOLL LINE).

In the United States the merchant marine grew rapidly in the 18th century. Not only was there flourishing trade with Europe, the Mediterranean and Spanish America but in 1784 the merchantman *Empress of China* reached the Far East and forged commercial links with the Orient. By the beginning of the 19th century there were over one million tons [1,016,050 tonnes] of American shipping on the trading routes of the world, operating from Boston, New York City, Philadelphia and many smaller ports. From about 1803 onwards New Orleans and Baltimore came into prominence as centres of thriving trade with the Latin American countries.

As in Britain, the seaman suffered fro severe exploitation, and legislation be came necessary to protect him. One of th most effective measures was the Seaman Act of 1915, sponsored by Robert L Follette, which ensured better workin conditions, freedom from oppressive con tracts and more life-saving equipment.

In 1983 the total world merchant flee came to 422·6 million gross registere tons (grt). The top eight national flee in order, were: Liberia, Japan, Greece Panama, the USSR, the USA, Norwa and Britain. Between them these eigh accounted for 261·9 grt. Many ship especially tankers, have been laid up o sold for scrap over recent years as a resul of world recession and lower transpor demands. The huge fleets of Liberia an Panama are mainly "flag of conveni ence" ships.

See also EAST INDIA COMPANY, etc.

The Liverpool Bay, *a modern container ship o the Merchant Navy.*

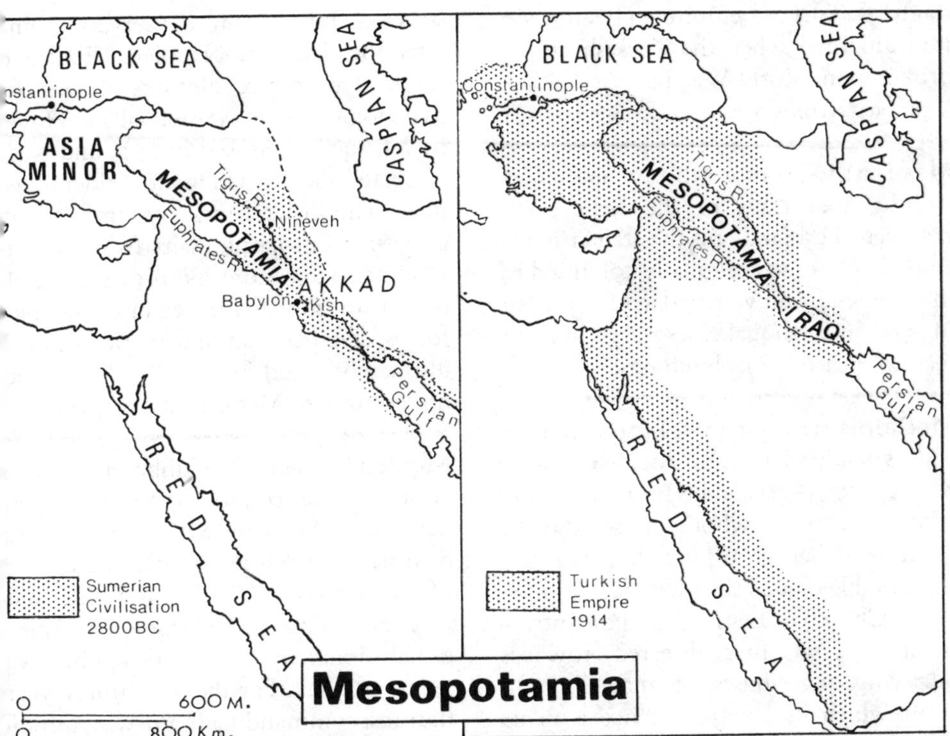

Mesopotamia

ſerovingian: pertaining to the line of rankish kings whose territories included ıost of what is now modern France and ·ho ruled from 448 to 751. The most nportant members of the dynasty were :lovis (ruled 481–511) and Dagobert ·uled 628–639). The Merovingians were ›llowed by the Carolingians.

ſesopotamia: the land "between ivers", i.e. the Tigris and Euphrates. rom here come mankind's oldest written istorical records. The fifth millennium c was a time of much migration of eoples, and the establishment of villages nd primitive agriculture. By the 28th entury BC the Sumerians were established ı walled cities with satellite towns on the ɔwer Euphrates. Further north, by the nd of the third millennium, the Akkad ivilisation was established, based on the ity of Kish. Sargon (*c.* 2300 BC) moved the apital to Akkad. The Akkadian language was Semitic, and cuneiform writing was used in the administration of the Akkadian Empire, superseding the Sumerian language and pictograph writing. Then a new Semitic people, the Amorites, founded an empire based on Babylon. Hammurabi (*c.* 1792–50 BC) won control of all Mesopotamia. From the 14th century BC there arose an Assyrian empire, beginning with the city of Ashur and later based on Nineveh. The Assyrian empire expanded over much of the Middle East. Nineveh fell in 612 BC to the Medes, rulers of Iran, but the southern part of Mesopotamia fell under the rule of Babylon and is known as Chaldaea. Cyrus, the Persian, captured Babylon in 539 BC. Greek influence came with the conquests of Alexander the Great in the 4th century BC. Muslim conquest began in AD 633. The Mongol invaders in 1258 looted Babylon, destroying its irrigation canals. In 1534 Mesopotamia became part of the stagnant Turkish empire. The modern Iraq emerged when the Turkish empire broke up in World War I.

¶ COTTRELL, LEONARD. *Land of the Two Rivers*. 1963

Messina: town in north-east Sicily controlling the straits of the same name between the island and the Italian mainland. The site was originally colonised by the Greeks. Its university dates from 1549. In 1908 an earthquake destroyed in a few seconds nearly all its buildings.

Methodism: a system of Protestant faith and worship. Its originators were John Wesley (1703–91) and his brother Charles (1707–88), with whom must also be mentioned George Whitefield (1714–70). It is notable that all these were clergymen of the Church of England, and the movement was at first directed towards purifying the abuses of that Church, from which its chief difference is in its system of government.

In 1983 the World Methodist Council comprised 64 member churches operating in 90 countries with a world-wide membership of 23,696,476 (1981). Controversy has been aroused by the political activities of some branches of the Church in the USA, Britain, Australia and South Africa where its support (real or alleged) for radical causes has come in for criticism.

Methuen Treaty (1703)**:** negotiated between Portugal and Britain by Sir John Methuen, the English Ambassador. Duties on Portuguese wines and English wool were reduced reciprocally. From this period is said to date the English fondness for port wine.

Metternich, Clemens Werzel Lothar, Prince von (1773–1859)**:** foreign minister and chancellor of Austria. This brilliant diplomat was the architect of the Vienna settlement (1815) which reconstructed Europe on conservative lin[es] after the defeat of Napoleon. Exiled t[o] England by the revolutions of 1848 (h[e] lived for a time in a seaside villa in Hove) he returned to Austria in 1849 and was [a] respected and often influential elder states[-]man. The "Metternich System", whic[h] governed European affairs from 1815 t[o] 1848, tried to restore and preserve the ol[d] power of monarchies against the nev[w] forces of Liberalism and Nationalism. [It] ultimately – and inevitably – failed, bu[t] not entirely to Metternich's surprise.

Mexico: federal republic of Nort[h] America. The country secured indepen[-]dence from Spain in 1821 when Augusti[n] de Iturbide (1783–1824), with the suppor[t] of the Catholic Church and the land[-]owners, proclaimed Mexico a constitu[-]tional monarchy. A federal republic wa[s] set up in 1824. For the next thirty year[s] the most commanding figure was Antoni[o] de Santa Anna (1797–1876), who tried t[o] centralise the government but was continually faced by internal rebellions an[d] American intrigues. Numerous frontie[r] incidents between 1836 and 1846, and th[e] occupation of Texas in 1845 by the USA, led to the Mexican War of 1846–48 President James K. Polk (1795–1849) sent American troops into a disputed area along the frontier and, when they were attacked, accused Mexico of "shedding American blood on American soil". Monterey and Mexico City were captured, and the war ended in September 1846. By the treaty of Guadeloupe Hidalgo (February 1848) Mexico renounced claims to Texas, recognised the Rio Grande frontier and, in return for fifteen million dollars, ceded New Mexico and California. In 1855 a liberal movement drove out Santa Anna but the country soon became involved in civil war and in the French attempts to set up a Catholic Empire under the Archduke ıximilian of Austria, who was the minee of Napoleon III of France. From 53 to 1867 Maximilian ruled Mexico th the help of French troops but, when ey were withdrawn, was overthrown Benito Juarez (1806–72). Thereafter, exico made considerable economic pro- ess, especially under Porfirio Diaz 330–1915). In 1917 a new constitution came the basis for great social reforms. recent years Mexico has made great ides in industrialisation, financed in rt by revenues from its large oil and tural gas deposits. In the 1970s the untry's annual rate of growth was 7 per nt but her population increased at 3 per nt a year. By the 1980s she ranked cond only to Brazil as a debtor nation. exico maintains a non-aligned policy spite heavy dependence upon Ameri- n investment for development. Popu- ion 73 million in 1982.

e AMERICA for map, *also* AZTECS, MAYAN VILISATION, etc.

---

ichael Feodorovitch (1596–1645): ar of Russia 1613–45, founder of the omanov dynasty. Born of an old and ble Moscow family of Prussian origin, was chosen as Tsar by a national sembly. He was content to reign by aving government largely in the hands his advisers.

---

ichael VIII Palaeologus (1224–82): mperor of the Eastern Roman Empire. 1261 he drove out of Constantinople e Western usurpers who had occupied e city in 1204, and established the st line of Eastern emperors which ded when Constantine IX Palaeologus rished in the storming of Constan- nople by the Turks in 1453.

The family name still survives. In ngland there is a 17th century tomb of a laeologus at Landulph, Cornwall, and nother fought at the battle of Edgehill (1642); while, as late as World War I, the French ambassador to Russia was a Paléologue.

ght: Michelangelo's Madonna and Child *in e Cathedral at Bruges, Belgium.*

Michelangelo (Michelangelo Buona-rotti, 1475–1564): Florentine artist. His skill as a painter came mainly from his deep knowledge of sculpture, which he always preferred. The disturbed state of Florence after the death of his patron Lorenzo de' Medici (*see* MEDICI FAMILY) in 1492 and personal anxieties gave Michelangelo a distrust of his fellow men which showed itself in his jealousy of Leonardo da Vinci (*see* separate entry) and pursued him through his long life.

After a few years in Rome, where he made the figure of Cupid, now in the Victoria and Albert Museum, London, he returned to Florence and produced his famous statue of David; but in 1508 Pope Julius II induced him to undertake the painting of the ceiling of the Sistine

Chapel in the Vatican, Rome, a task which occupied four-and-a-half years and left the artist permanently crippled through having to work on a high scaffold with his head thrown back. His panel showing the Creation of Man is one of the most sublime paintings of all time.

His later years took him back to Florence to work as designer and sculptor in the Medici Chapel and again to Rome (1534) for a further five years of painting, this time on a vertical surface, in the Sistine Chapel. As he approached the age of seventy he turned architect and designed the vast dome which crowns St Peter's today. He continued to work as a sculptor to within a week of his death.

¶ ALLEN, AGNES. *The Story of Michelangelo*. 1953
See also FLORENTINE ART.

Microscope: optical instrument by which objects are so magnified that details invisible to the naked eye can clearly seen. The simple microscope merely a magnifying glass, usually double convex lens. To remedy t colour fringes which occur in the ou parts of the field of view, a modifi form, known as the Coddington le has been devised.

Of much more importance is the co pound microscope. This consists of t objective, which is a lens system of sh focal length creating a real image of t object inspected, and the eyepie through which this real image is viewe

The first compound microscope appe to have been invented in 1590 by Zach rias Jansen. He used a convex objecti and a concave eyepiece, but its field view was very limited. This was followe about 1628, by what is known as Keple microscope, although not made by hi This used convex lenses for both objecti and eyepiece. In 1684 Christiaan Hu gens (*see* separate entry) improved th

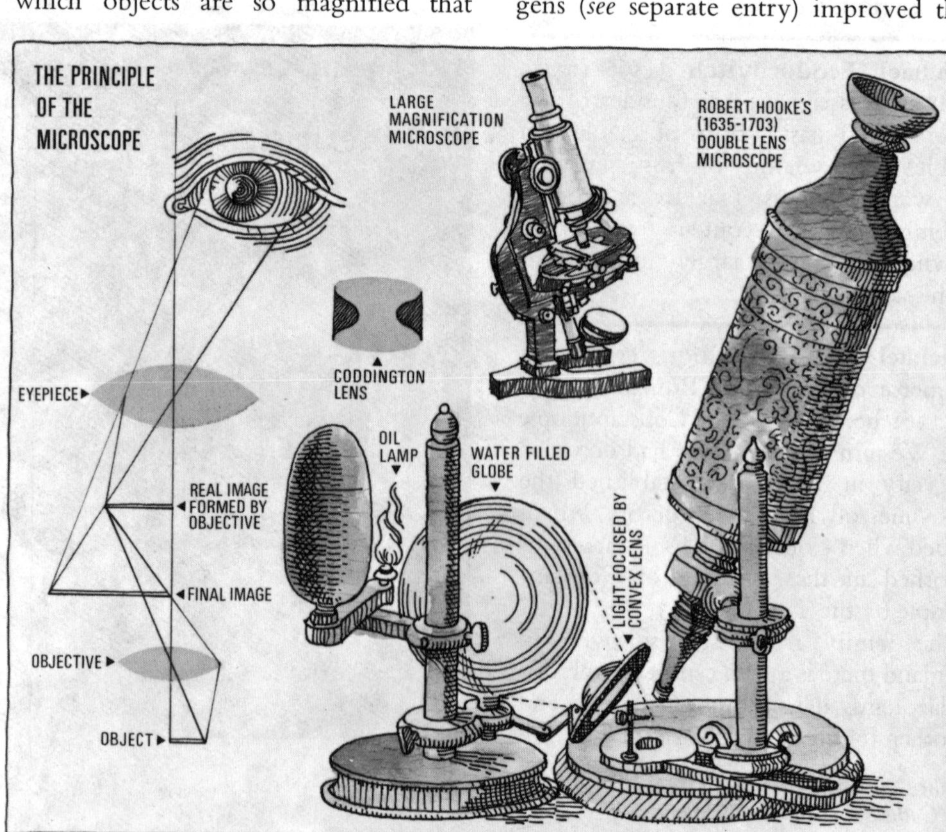

system by devising an eyepiece using two lenses. It was not, however, until the early years of the 19th century that the microscope became a widely used instrument, by which time improved grinding and design of lenses had done much to remove the colours and distortions to which early models were subject.

The electron microscope was first devised by Knoll and Ruska in 1932 and by 1945 this had become a widely used instrument.

Middle Ages: an imprecise term covering the thousand years of western European history from the middle of the 5th century to the middle of the 15th century. Old history books often give 476, the year when Romulus Augustulus, the last Roman emperor in the West, was deposed, as the date when the Middle Ages began and the fall of Constantinople in 1453 as marking the moment they ended. But history is not a slab of cake which divides up into neat slices. Ancient Rome did not fall, any more than the Renaissance began, on any one day. We must guard against viewing the Middle Ages as if they were, so to speak, a walled city in an old tapestry, its inhabitants frozen for all time in quaint and picturesque attitudes. On the contrary, they are part of the stream of history, just as medieval churches and cathedrals are part of contemporary villages and towns.

The first 400 years of the Middle Ages are sometimes further differentiated as the "Dark Ages". As the western Roman Empire crumbled from internal weaknesses and from the pressure of the barbarian hordes surging west and south towards the rich lands beyond the Rhine and the Danube, western Europe did indeed, for a period, go down into darkness. Roman culture was largely submerged, pagan tribes overran wide areas, and out of the East came a new threat, the rise of Islam.

Most of the barbarian tribes, fortunately, were not savages. Leaving out such exceptions as the Huns and the Vandals, whose names have remained bywords for cruelty and destruction, they were vigorous and adaptable people. Though they destroyed much of the old classical world, they were willing to learn what they could from it.

Heralds of better times were the Frankish kings, Clovis and Charlemagne. Clovis (*c.* 466–511), who became a Christian in 496, by uniting the Frankish tribes under one rule may be called the creator of modern France. Charlemagne (*c.* 742–814) carved out an empire stretching from Spain to the Danube. He encouraged learning and the arts and saw himself as the champion of Christendom. On Christmas Day 800, in St Peter's, Rome, Pope Leo III crowned him Emperor of the Romans. While Charlemagne's territorial empire did not survive its founder, the Holy Roman Empire, idea of an earthly counterpart to the spiritual authority of the Pope, lasted – if for long periods little more than a name – for a thousand years. The reign of Alfred (849–?901), King of the West Saxons, warrior, lawgiver, encourager of learning and himself the author of many works, was another milestone on the long road back to ordered government.

For ordinary people, most of them poor peasants, life in those troubled times was precarious in the extreme. Their only hope of security lay in putting themselves, for a price, under the protection of a powerful landowner. The price, according to the time and the circumstances, might consist of military service, agricultural labour, goods or money. Such, reduced to its simplest terms, was the feudal system, the system of land tenure which for hundreds of years shaped

In the Middle Ages, called the Age of Faith, the Church was at the centre of all aspects of life. *Above*: The Crusades; Christian Crusaders fight the Saracens at Damietta in 1218. *Below*: carving of a hawker in a tree by the great stonemason Peter Wynwode from the stalls of Winchester Cathedral, 1307.

Superstition and belief in the Devil were also powerful forces in this religious age. Above: an old woman struggles with a Devil. Below: pilgrimages combined piety with sociability and here weary pilgrims stop to refresh themselves on their journey.

edieval society (*see* FEUDAL SYSTEM). The stem was, as it were, a great pyramid, th the king, who held the kingdom om God, at the top; and at the base, well low the tenants-in-chief and various eholders, the poor villeins. For the ter it was a harsh and meagre existence, ade tolerable, perhaps, by its relative curity and by the Church's promise of wards in the world to come.

At a time when national states were in eir infancy the Church was the great ifying influence of western Europe. ie Pope, as Christ's representative on rth, commanded the spiritual allegiance all Christendom. The Middle Ages are metimes called the Age of Faith. One s only to go into one of the great edieval cathedrals to appreciate some- ing of the tremendous spiritual con- ction which could bring into being such quisite and technically sophisticated uctures in an age when so much else as crude and rudimentary.

The Church intervened in almost every ld of human activity. The monasteries, hich had preserved what remained of e learning of the ancient world, were, r the poor and oppressed, the sole liable sources of charity and compassion. hey served as hospitals and schools. nder the direction of the monks, forests ere cleared and marshes drained. When e Church called for volunteers to join crusade to free the Holy Land from the Iohammedans, men in their thousands rsook their daily occupations to "take e cross".

The Crusades, not one of which attained s object other than temporarily, in many ays illustrate the Middle Ages and what, us, appear its strange contradictions. Iany who went on them did so out of ligious faith, yet they were bloodstained xpeditions, disfigured by treachery and ts of cruelty hard to reconcile with ther Christianity or the medieval code of chivalry, which was intended to humanise the conduct of war. Not only Turks and Jews were slaughtered by the Crusaders – that, in the context of the time, was to be expected – but fellow-Christians as well.

The Crusades had the unlooked-for result of greatly increasing western Europe's trade with the East. Missionaries and merchants pushed ever deeper into Asia, returning with new trade goods, new knowledge and new ideas. The closed medieval world was opening out.

The growing merchant class and the expanding towns were outside the old system of bartering land for services. For trade, money was the key. In 1348 the bubonic plague, known as the Black Death, which wrought dreadful havoc across Europe, further undermined the old order. With labour in short supply, labourers, for the first time, found themselves in a favourable bargaining position.

As time passed, even the Church found itself challenged. Reformers like John Wyclif (*c.* 1320–84) tried to bring it back to its ancient simplicity. In Prague in 1415 Jan Hus (*c.* 1373–1415) died at the stake in the same cause (*see* separate entries under both these names).

Men, in fact, had begun to question their place in the universe. They were no longer content to accept the Church's teaching that life was nothing more than a preparation for heaven. Painters like Giotto (*c.* 1266–1337) began to paint figures which seemed to be made of flesh and blood instead of being merely decorative motifs; sculptors like Donatello (1386–1466) turned away from the elongated saints of the medieval cathedrals to the realistic sculpture of ancient Rome, itself Hellenistic in origin and tradition. Chaucer (*c.* 1340–1400) wrote poems full of an affectionate and humorous regard for human frailty.

Once such men had begun to demonstrate that human life had its own dignity and worth, the days of the Middle Ages were numbered.

¶ ROWLING, MARJORIE. *Everyday Life in Medieval Times.* 1967; SOBOL, DONALD J. *The First Book of Medieval Britain.* 1970

Middle Atlantic States, USA: region situated in roughly the middle of the eastern coastline of the United States and comprising the states of Delaware, Pennsylvania, Maryland, New York and New Jersey. Although the Appalachian and Adirondack Mountains are to be found in this region, it also possesses broad fertile plains supporting large-scale agriculture. Among the many rivers in the area the most important are the Hudson River in New York and the Susquehanna River, which runs primarily in Pennsylvania.

During the early colonial period, this area was settled by colonists from a variety of European nations – Swiss, Finns, Dutch, as well as the English. New York City, for example, was founded by the Dutch West Indies Company in the 1620s and remained in Dutch hands until 1664. However, the region soon became an integral part of the English colonies, and by the time of the American Revolution was a major source of supply of provisions, especially for the colonies further south. It was at Philadelphia, Pennsylvania, that the American Constitution was written, and New York City and Philadelphia served as the first capitals for the new nation. The area has, moreover, grown in significance since the early days of the republic. Although much "truck farming" is to be found in New Jersey, and though there are dairy farms and other agricultural production in the rest of this region, the Middle Atlantic states are especially noted for urbanisation and manufacturing. Thus, Pittsburgh, Pennsylvania, is a major centre for steel production; Rochester, New York, is tl site of much manufacturing of electric goods; and many other cities and tow play vital roles in the industrial life of tl United States. Overshadowing them a however, is New York City, the hub the region, and one of the major cities the world. Here are concentrated tl main offices of most of the major firms the financial, commercial and commun cations industries. Here are also to b found such cultural centres as the Linco Centre for the Performing Arts, tl Metropolitan Museum of Art and tl Museum of Modern Art. New York also the home of such distinguishe foundations as Columbia University an New York University, the latter bein among the largest private universities the world. This region is thus in man ways central to the economy and cultur of the nation.

See AMERICA for map.

Middle West, USA: area of the US beginning at the margin of the Alleghen Plateau, stretching westwards across th Plains of the USA and ending in the dr grasslands and the "blown" areas of th Dakotas, Nebraska and Kansas. The fir settlers came in the later years of the 18t century. They included many adheren of small religious sects, including th Mennonites, the Amish and the Latte Day Saints. Subsequent immigrants t the area, especially from northern Europ reinforced this traditionally Protestan character, so much so that it is known a the "Bible Belt". The Middle We contains about a quarter of the populatio of the USA, and its chief cities are Chicag the "home" of isolationism, Cincinnat St Louis, Minneapolis and St. Paul. Th region yields the greater part of the wheat corn, cattle and dairy produce in th USA, and also a considerable share of it manufactures. In the Civil War, true t traditions, it sided with the North ainst slavery. The Mid-West has always d great political importance in the untry, and six out of the last eleven esidents have been Middle-Westerners. e AMERICA for map.

idway, Battle of: decisive sea and air ttle between US and Japanese forces, 6 June 1942. After the surprise attack by panese aircraft on the US naval base at arl Harbour (Hawaii) on 7 December 41, the forces of Japan swept all before em in the Pacific and Far East. But the val and air battle at Midway in the ntral Pacific resulted in their first major feat. The attempted seizure by Japan of idway Island ended in failure, with the ss of four Japanese aircraft carriers and 5 planes. This action restored American orale, checked the advance of the panese across the central Pacific, elimi-ted the threat to Hawaii and restored e balance of naval power.

BARKER, ARTHUR J. *Midway*. 1971

ligration: the process of leaving one ountry or area for another, for either mporary or permanent settlement. The iftings of peoples have been a major ctor throughout human history, from rehistoric wanderings in search of food more organised movements for eligious and political motives such as, or example, the Mormon settlement in Jtah, USA, or the Great Trek (1835–36) f Boer farmers from Cape Colony to scape British rule. In the 19th century nillions of Europeans migrated to the JSA to seek a new start. In recent times he EEC has attracted worker migrants rom countries like Turkey as have the ich oil states of the Gulf. During the 950s and 1960s many Commonwealth itizens from the West Indies and Paki-tan in particular migrated to Britain in earch of new opportunities.

Milan Cathedral.

Milan: north Italian city, dating from Roman times, on the Lombardy Plain where routes through Alpine passes meet. Its cathedral (begun 1386) is one of many fine churches, one of which contains Leonardo's "The Last Supper". Milan became a duchy in 1395 and was a great Renaissance centre under the Sforza family. It was later attached successively to the crowns of Spain (1535–1713) and Austria (1713–96 and 1815–59) before being incorporated into Italy in 1861.

Miletus: Greek city on the coast of Caria in Asia Minor. It was known in Homeric times and was later seized by colonists from Athens. In its turn Miletus founded many colonies chiefly round the Black Sea, including Odessa. The birthplace of Thales and other early philosophers, it later declined into insignificance.

Mill: building for grinding grain. The word comes from Latin *molere*, to crush or grind. It was originally applied to the building in which the crushing apparatus was housed. The handmill used for grinding corn was called a quern, and consisted of two circular stones, placed one above the other. The grain was put between them and the upper one – the millstone – was rotated until the grain was crushed to form flour.

This laborious manual process survived

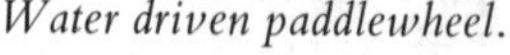

Water driven paddlewheel.

Windmill.

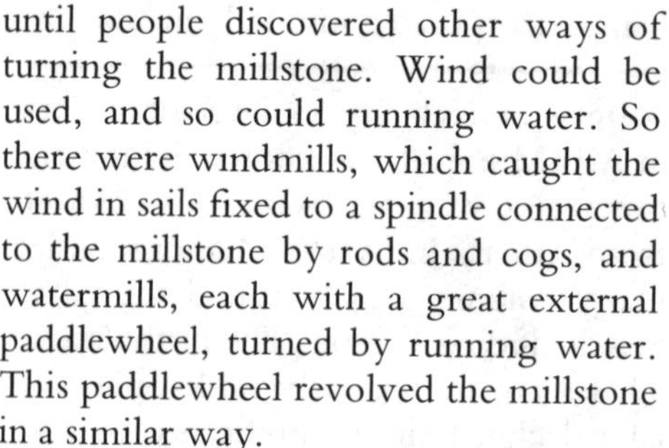

until people discovered other ways of turning the millstone. Wind could be used, and so could running water. So there were windmills, which caught the wind in sails fixed to a spindle connected to the millstone by rods and cogs, and watermills, each with a great external paddlewheel, turned by running water. This paddlewheel revolved the millstone in a similar way.

In medieval times milling was a profitable occupation and the miller a man of substance. The local mill was often owned by the lord of the manor or the abbot of a monastery, who charged the villagers a sum of money for its use. Sometimes ancient charters mention the right of citizens to establish a mill.

Eventually, any form of rotary processing became known as "milling", and many industrial buildings were called mills (e.g. cotton mills). In 1561 a Dutchman, Eloye Mestrel, introduced into England the milling, or scoring, of th edges of coins. This prevented unscrupu lous persons from clipping silver or gol from the coins for their own use.

Milton, John (1608–74): English po and political writer. Born in Londo Milton was a precocious student. "M appetite for knowledge", he wrote, "wa so voracious that from twelve years c age I hardly ever left my studies or wen to bed before midnight." It was all part c his conscious preparation for becoming great poet, and there can be no doubt tha his belief in his own genius was justified His best-known work, *Paradise Lost*, i considered one of the great epic poems o the world. He became blind in 1651, an his *Samson Agonistes*, with the blinde Samson as hero, has therefore a particula poignancy.

A supporter of Oliver Cromwell, Milto became Latin Secretary to the Counci

ing the Commonwealth. His prose itings, while often impractical and oured by prejudice, include the *Areo-itica*, an appeal for freedom of thought ahead of its time.

UIR, K. *John Milton*. 1955

ng: word meaning "bright", the ne adopted by the dynasty which ed China 1368–1643. It was a period ween great invasions, the Mongol l the Manchu, and a time when China iberately chose to cut herself off, so far possible, from the rest of the world. ch inward-looking ages are not the st favourable for artistic creation. ough many beautiful paintings, fine ttery and bronzes date from this period, y do not reach the standard of work ecuted under the Sung dynasty (960–80), which preceded the Mongols. ng works of art are outstanding for ir exquisite simplicity. Ming artists and ftsmen tended to overdo the orna-ntation. In so doing they lost the nderful purity of line which distin-ishes Chinese art at its best.

e also CHINA; POTTERY AND PORCELAIN.

th century Ming ewer, decorated and with a e underglaze.

Mining: the extraction of various natural mineral products from below the surface of the earth. This has been undertaken from at least the Neolithic period, when extensive flint mines were opened, the flints being used to make a wide variety of domestic tools. The extraction of metals and other mineral products followed. The earliest metals which were used by primitive man were obviously those which occurred at or very close to the surface. Lead and copper were mined in Britain during Roman times, and coal was used by the Romans, where it occurred close to the surface, for heating, iron working, pottery, brick and tile making, and for cremations. We do not know much about the actual mining methods used by the Romans, although a few underground galleries still exist which could be of Roman date. The Romans probably used at different periods direct slave labour and private capitalists to work such mines.

Mining continued in the centuries following the collapse of the Roman Empire, though on a smaller scale. In medieval times the mining techniques of western Europe, especially those of the Germanic states, were the most technically advanced in the world. An excellent pictorial account of the most modern usages in mining is given in Georgius Agricola's *De re metallica*, published in 1556. German miners were brought to England in Elizabethan times to open up large copper mines in the Lake District, and continental mining techniques gradually spread throughout the various branches of the English mining industry. Many of the problems which had to be faced by the miner were, of course, common to all types of mining, although the risk of an underground explosion resulting from fiery gases emerging from the mineral itself was confined to coal mining.

Mining is always carried out below the

Above: modern ore mining. Right: ancient methods of sifting ore from the De Re Metallica of Georgius Agricola: A. workman carrying broken rock in a barrow. B. First Chute. C. First Box. D. Its Handles. E. Its Bales. F. Rope. G. Beam. H. Post. I. Second Chute. K. Second Box. L. Third Chute. M. Third Box. N. First Table. O. First Sleeve. P. First Tub. Q. Second Table. R. Second Sieve. S. Second Tub. T. Third Table. V. Third Sieve. X. Third Tub. Y. Plugs.

surface, and the mineral, according to its particular physical form, is worked by opencast working (i.e. the removal of overlying strata), by shafts sunk from the surface, and by workings then extended within the mineral itself, or by inclined galleries following the line of the mineral underground. Underground water has always been a difficulty to miners. At first pumps were worked by man and beast and by various devices using wind and water. Then, in the 1710–20 period, came the first application of steam power for mining purposes.

The use of power-driven machinery for mining underground dates from the 19th century when such machines as mechanical coal cutters were invented. That century also saw the introduction of compressed air, and beginnings of the use of electricity, as motive power for mining machinery, though the pony and man's strong right arm continued as sources of power into very recent times.

The relatively small-scale mine deposits of western Europe were rivalle particularly from the early 19th centur by the discovery of much larger depos in more distant parts of the world; e. the mineral deposits of South Ameri were exploited on a large scale from tl period. The size of these deposits, and t ease with which they were worked, ove came the disadvantage of greater distan from the manufacturing centres of wes ern Europe. In fact, the smaller miner deposits of many of the old-establish industrial countries of western Euro ceased to be worked during the 19 century, though some countri specialised in producing certain mineral Britain, for example, produced immen quantities of coal, which were used n only in that country but also in Europ The North American continent foun itself able to produce within its ow itories most of the minerals required large-scale industrialisation and thus ; able to build its vast prosperity.

recent years coal has been losing its ition as the most important fuel, with and other forms of domestic heating h as electricity and gas taking its ce. But mining will remain a major rld industry into the foreseeable future. e vast gold-field of the Witwatersrand l the diamond pits of Kimberley, ıth Africa; the iron deposits of Russia l Brazil; the copper of Chile; the silver l zinc of British Columbia, Canada; lead of Broken Hill, Australia; the ıgsten, mercury and antimony of ina; and the manganese, barite and lmium of Japan, are only a few ımples of the vast mining activity ɜded to support the modern world in r and peace.

inoan and Mycenaean civilisations: : Bronze Age civilisations of Crete and eece, respectively named after the ;endary king Minos and the leading y in Greece, Mycenae. The chronologi- . problems of their histories are still solved and the relationship between the ·o is far from clear. The Minoan ·ilisation, for example at Knossos, lasted ›m about 2800 to 1200 BC, while places e Mycenae and Tiryns flourished for out 400 years from 1600 BC. Knossos d Mycenae are unforgettably con- cted with the archaeological work of r Arthur Evans and Heinrich hliemann respectively.

:rete in its heyday about 1600 BC was a aceful place. Great palaces like those at nossos and Phaestus were undefended. ıe social system was based on control · government officials. The Cretans ere also seafarers, as legend states, for ere is obvious evidence of extensive im- ·rts. The language they spoke has still to discovered, but it was not Greek. By 1600 they had refined an older pictorial script to write down this language, and in this so-called "Linear A" each symbol presumably stood for a syllable. The palaces dominated life, and most of the typically Minoan works of art naturally come from them. That at Knossos will serve as an example. Covering an area of over five acres [2 hectares] it has few large rooms but a mass of storage space, and a variety of state apartments lavishly decorated with murals. Utensils and other objects in daily use were often beautifully made. The Minoans excelled in miniature art, the work on the small seals being exquisite. About 1400 BC some vast upheaval brought the golden age to an end. Possibly an earthquake or tidal wave destroyed or weakened the palaces and laid them open to Greek-speaking peoples. But the old sites were not abandoned, and the invaders adopted the Cretan writing system for their own language.

Who these Greeks were and where they came from is still a mystery. At various sites – Mycenae, Tiryns, Argos, Thebes – fortress cities seem suddenly to have sprung up. Later they were even more heavily defended, but their usual position on a hill or rock outcrop suggests a much less stable situation than in Crete. For some time these cities were artistically dependent on Crete, whatever their political position, but the rich finds at Mycenae indicate a people of a very different character. There is less fun, less dancing, more need for swords and helmets. The artistic skill was great, famous examples being the gold death-masks and inlaid dagger blades. Shortly after 1200 all these cities suddenly collapsed. Perhaps the invasion of the Dorians hastened their end, or they may have been caught up in a greater conflict over the whole of the Near East.

Minorca: one of the Balearic Islands, a

detached portion of the Sierra Nevada, lying between southern France and Algeria. Because of its controlling position in the Mediterranean and its fine harbour, it was seized by the British Navy in 1708. The island was lost in 1756 owing to weakness of the British fleet, for which the nation blamed the government. The government in turn blamed the commander, Admiral John Byng, who was shot *"pour encourager les autres"*, as Voltaire said. Britain regained Minorca from the French by the Peace of Paris, 1763, but it was given to Spain under the Treaty of Amiens in 1802.

See MEDITERRANEAN for map.

Mir: the ancient village assembly or commune in old Russia. After the emancipation of the serfs in 1861, the *mir* distributed a good deal of the land and helped the poorer peasants. The *mir* formed a useful basis for the establishment of collective farms after 1917.

Mirrors: reflecting surfaces of polish
metal or glass. The earliest known mirro
apart from wet pieces of slate, were
obsidian, black volcanic glass, in u
c. 6000 BC in Anatolia. The first met
mirrors, *c.* 3000 BC, were Egyptian – fi
of copper, then bronze.

Mirrors must have been regarded as
great value in the ancient world, as th
were often buried with such precious o
jects as swords, jewellery and fine potter
Not only was possessing a mirror a ma
of distinction, it also held some religio
significance. Egyptian ritual mirrors we
decorated with religious scenes and i
scriptions. The Greeks, Etruscans a
Romans all devoted their talents to t
manufacture of mirrors.

Women did not get much satisfacti
from their reflections in the metal
mirrors, but in the Middle Ages t
method of backing glass with thin shee
of metal was tried out extensively.
guild of glass mirror makers was

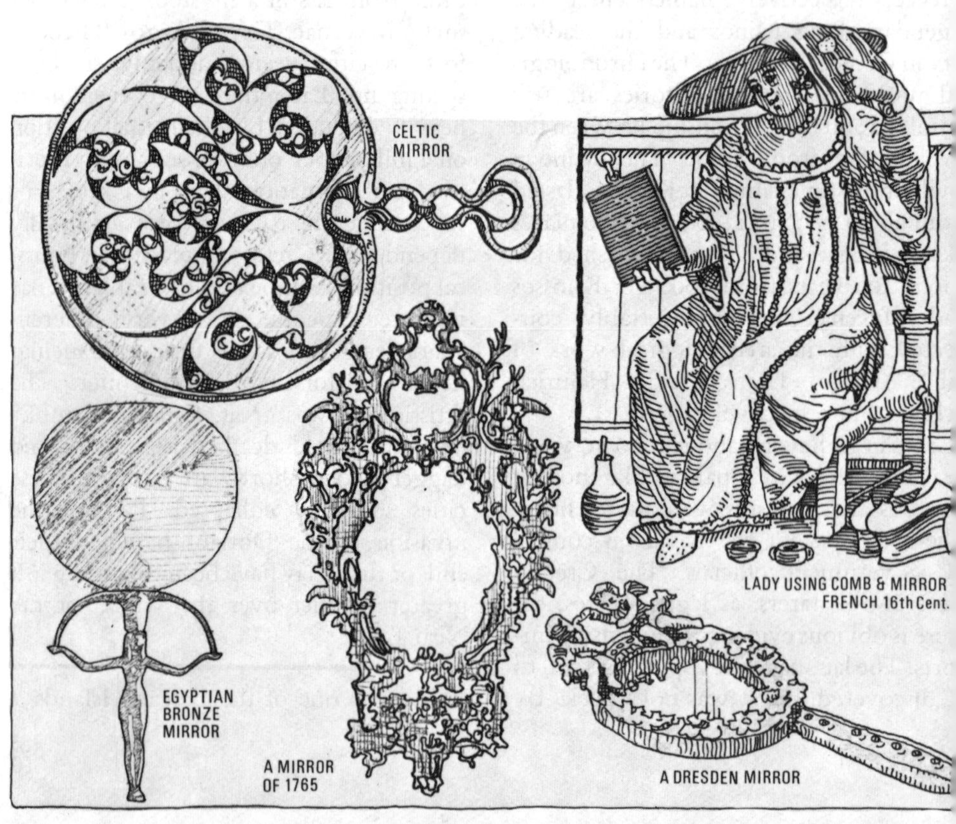

ıstence at Nuremberg, Germany, in 73. Glass mirrors remained expensive, ›ecially those made of Venetian glass at ırano. The Venetian method of backing .ss with an amalgam of tin and mercury ıs introduced into England in the 17th ıtury and was in use for over a hundred ars. The chemical process of coating ıss with metallic silver, known as lvering", was discovered by Justus von ːbig in 1835.

ıst as important as the reflecting power the mirrors was the style, shape and coration of the frames. They show me of the finest skills and artistic alities of individual civilisations. ındles and frames of Indian mirrors ːre of carved ivory, Chinese mirrors had corative settings of bronze, inlaid with ›ld, silver, turquoise and jade. Frames ːre also to become part of the decoration a room and reflected the changing ideas art, architecture and interior decorating ʼles. In Louis XIV's France, for example, irrors were enormous, with richly rved gilt frames, and completely lined e room. One only has to think of ersailles to picture the splendour such irrors could produce, especially at night. .eading architects were designing irrors for their clients in 18th century ıgland, but this was the high peak in eir design. Frames then fell out of shion. Tomorrow's archaeologists, rning up mirrors of 20th century origin, ill find them quite plain but of a brilliant flecting power.

ıissionaries: people sent abroad to read a religious faith. The Apostles were e first missionaries, of whom St Paul as the most famous. When Christianity ːcame established, the early Church sent ıissionaries to convert the heathen of ırope: Augustine to England, Patrick › Ireland and Denys to France.

The Jesuits, founded by Ignatius Loyola, became the great missionaries of Roman Catholicism. Jesuits went out to Spanish South America and also accompanied the Armada in the hope of bringing the English back from Protestantism.

See also JESUITS; LIVINGSTONE, DAVID, etc.

Missouri Compromise: group of measures passed in the USA, 1820–21. For the first twenty years of the 19th century a precarious political balance was maintained between Northern and Southern interests by admitting "slave" and "free" territories alternately to statehood. This balance was endangered by the creation of new states out of the Louisiana Purchase (*see* separate entry) where, under the Spaniards and the French, slavery had been permitted even in the northernmost regions. In March 1820, after a bitter conflict between the Senate and the House of Representatives, Congress admitted Missouri as a slave state to be counterbalanced by Maine as a free state; but, at the same time, prohibited slavery in those regions of the Louisiana Purchase north of the line 36° 30′. This settlement was known as the Missouri Compromise and was regarded by Southerners as being contrary to the Constitution. The Supreme Court eventually decided against the Compromise in the Dred Scott Case of 1857 (*see* separate entry).

Mogul: the Persian and Arabic form of *Mongol* (*see* separate entry), applicable to the Muslim inhabitants of west and northwest India, but used more commonly of the emperors ("Great Moguls") of the dynasty founded by Babar after the battle of Panipat, 1526, of whom Akbar (1556–1605) was the greatest. The Great Moguls held effective control of their empire continuously from Akbar's time until 1707, when Aurangzeb died. Thereafter they became puppets of native princes until the capture of Delhi by the British,

1803. The last, Bahadur Shah, was banished to Burma after the Mutiny, 1857.

Mohammed, Turkish, **Mahomet** (*c.* 570–632)**:** the founder of Islam, the Muslim faith. Brought up in Mecca, he first worked with trading caravans to Syria and southern Arabia but abandoned this after his marriage (595). He became leader of a sect, at first secret, aiming at restoring the purity of the faith of Abraham. He claimed to receive, while in a trance, messages from the angel Gabriel; these were written down by his followers and formed the basis of the Koran. Preaching in public first in about 616, he offended many Meccans and was forced, in 622, to flee to Medina. From this flight, the *Hegira*, the Muslims date their calendar. Here Mohammed became dictator, broke with Judaism and declared Mecca, not Jerusalem, the holy city.

Successful attacks on Meccan caravans brought him revenue, one such ventu leading to the battle of Badr (624), whe his victory enabled him to spread h influence over a wide area. In spite of defeat in 625 at Mount Uhud, his followe increased, and in 628 Mecca surrendere to him. It now became the religio capital, and the Muslim faith compulso for all Mohammed's followers.

The Ascent of Mohammed to heaven mounted on his horse Al-burak from a Persian Ms of 1502.

Though he claimed that Islam was t confirmation of both the Jewish and t Christian scriptures, he broke with bo and offered to all who came under h dominion the alternatives of conversio destruction or tribute; the acceptance the last provided the bulk of his revenu Before his death (7 June 632) he was control of the whole of Arabia, had sun moned Persia and the Eastern Emperor accept his faith and was preparing for w with Syria.

¶ WARREN, RUTH. *Muhammad, Prophet of Isla* 1971

See also ISLAM.

Moluccas: group of islands in the Pacif between Celebes and New Guinea. T inhabitants are a mixture of Papua Malayan, Javanese, other races of t region and some European blood. The are extremely primitive elements, b Christianity, Islam and a higher cultu generally are found where contact wi other peoples has occurred, e.g. in coast areas. The islands were a source of spic as far back as Roman times, and the grou was long known as the Spice Islands.

Portuguese, Spanish and Dutch rival eventually resulted in Dutch contr until 1942. After a period of occupatio by the Japanese (1942–45) they becan part of Indonesia in 1949.

Monaco: small principality on the easte flank of southern France, bordering t Mediterranean. Monaco is also the nan of its chief town occupying a peninsu which, with two other connected towns

Condamine and Monte Carlo sur-
unding the habour – is governed by a
ince but under the protection of France.
ne headland once bore a temple used
different times by Greeks and Phoeni-
ans. Monaco has belonged to private
milies, to France, Spain, Sardinia and
stly to the family of Prince Rainier
ho, in 1956, married the American film
ar Grace Kelly. She died as a result of a
agic car crash in 1982.

onastery: building housing a comunity of monks. Because they were
signed for religious communities, mon-
teries tended to follow a similar general
an. The most important building was
e church. On its south side was a square
rth or garden surrounded by an arched
oister, in the sunniest side of which the
onks could study and copy manuscripts,
ch man working in a little alcove known
a *carrel*. In another part of the cloister
ne novices were instructed, and some
ctions were used as offices by the
llarer, who was responsible for the
onastery's domestic arrangements.

The *refectory* adjoined the cloister, and a
ashing-room, with running water, was
tached to it, as the monks were obliged
wash before and after meals. The
itchen, conveniently near to the refec-
ory, also had a water supply. Monasteries
vere always situated beside a stream
ecause of this insistence on cleanliness
nd good drainage.

In the *warming-room* a fire was kept
urning during cold weather. Above
ither this room or the refectory was the
ormitory, usually approached by two
ights of stairs, the day-stair leading from
he monastic buildings and the night-stair
y which the monks could go directly
nto the church for night services.

The *chapter house*, where daily meetings
vere held, stood close to the church. At a
ittle distance from the main buildings was the *infirmary*, where aged and sick monks were cared for. The abbot's house and the monastery guest-house were beside the main gateway, where stood also a small office used by the almoner to distribute food and clothing to the poor.

¶ UNSTEAD, R. J. *Monasteries.* 1970

See also ABBEYS *for* illustration; ORDERS, MILITARY; ORDERS, RELIGIOUS.

Money: medium of exchange for goods and services. R. G. Hawtrey wrote that 'Money is one of those concepts, which, like a teaspoon or an umbrella, . . . are definable primarily by the use or purpose which they serve'. Its primary function is to be the medium of exchange. Thus we receive money for the work we do or the goods we produce, and we use this to pay for the goods and services we require. This replaces a system of barter, in which goods are exchanged for other goods. Secondly, money is a unit of account. It enables us to evaluate goods, services, wages, rents, insurance contracts, etc. Thirdly, money provides a reserve of purchasing power.

All kinds of strange commodities have been used as money in different parts of the world at various times. Pastoral peoples have used cattle, and the word "pecuniary" is derived from the Latin word *pecus*, cattle. In the early days of New South Wales, rum was the medium of exchange, and cigarettes served this purpose in the black markets of Europe after World War II, while in Borneo human skulls were used as the standard of value, and pigs and palm nuts were used for the actual process of exchange. In the Western system gold is the standard of value and paper money the medium of exchange.

In highly developed countries over 90 per cent of the total value of money transactions is settled by cheque, while small transactions are usually paid for in cash. Thus the bank deposits serve as money; the cheques are merely instructions to the banks about the handling of these deposits.

¶ QUIGGIN, A. H. *The Story of Money*. 1956

Mongolia: the Mongolian People's Republic lying between China and the USSR, and Inner Mongolia, stretching along the Republic's southern border. The Living Buddha of Urga was Mongolia's titular head, with a government dominated by a local aristocracy who broke away from China after the 1911 revolution. With Russian aid a revolutionary government was set up in 1921, Urga the capital becoming Ulan Bator. Part of inner Mongolia fell under Japanese rule during Japan's Manchurian adventure in the 1930s. The revolutionary socialist leader, Choibalsan, headed the Mongolian government 1939–52. After a plebiscite in 1945 independence was recognised by China. Mongolia became a member of the United Nations in 1961.
See CHINA for map.

Mongols: group of nomadic tribes in east-central Asia, who raided for over 2,000 years the more settled peoples,

The Mongols lay siege to a Chinese city, killing, burning, cutting down forests and overthrowing fortresses, from a manuscript in the Bibliotheque Nationale, Paris.

particularly the Chinese. They we united into a single people by Gengl Khan in the early 13th century. The er pire which he established came to inclu nearly all Asia and Russia, omitting Inc and Arabia. It split up within a centu but gave dynasties to China, India ar Persia and contributed indirectly to tl emergence of a Russian state. Though tl first impact of the Mongol invasion w wholly destructive, the later Mong rulers were in many cases enlighten administrators.
See also GENGHIS KHAN; MOGUL, etc.

Monopoly: literally, "single selling". one person has the sole right to sell particular article, he can charge what likes. From Norman times onwards tl English kings used the granting of mon polies to obtain money from merchan who were then able to make huge profi In modern times monopoly is broug about by companies engaged in the san business joining together to make or great firm. In England this is now con trolled by the government through tl Monopolies Commission. Some of tl greatest industries, such as coal, ga electricity and the railways, have bee "nationalised", i.e. they have becom government monopolies operated for tl benefit of all.

In the USA the more familiar term "Trust". Most famous of the early virtu monopolies were the Standard Oil c John D. Rockefeller and the United State Steel Corporation (1902). There wer also Whiskey, Lead and Sugar Trusts, an other industrialists built empires i mining, railways and tobacco. Despit such measures as the Sherman Anti-Trus Act of 1890, there was little effectiv control. A more important landmark wa the Clayton Anti-Trust Act of 1914 which greatly strengthened the earlie measure.

Ionroe Doctrine: declaration con-
ained in the annual message to Congress
f President James Monroe (1758–1831), rompted by the threat of European owers to suppress the revolt of the panish-American colonies. The doctrine naintained that the American continent vas no territory for future European olonisation, that there was an essentially ifferent political system in the Americas om Europe, that the USA would regard ny attempt by European powers to ex- end their influence in the Americas as angerous to its peace and security, and nat the USA would not interfere with xisting European colonies, nor partici- ate in purely European wars.

Iontcalm, Louis, Marquis de (1712– 9): French general. A soldier all his life, e distinguished himself in the wars of olish and of Austrian Succession and in 756 was given command of the French roops in Canada. Here he was at first utstandingly successful, capturing Forts Oswego (1756) and William Henry (1757) nd defeating Abercromby's attack at iconderoga (1758). He did not, however, xploit his success and fell back to defend Quebec against Wolfe. For two months e repulsed all attacks but was outflanked by the British scaling the Heights of Abraham. In the battle which followed, after behaving with conspicuous gallantry, he was mortally wounded.

Iontcalm congratulates his victorious troops fter the Battle of Carellon, 1758.

Monte Cassino: ancient monastery on a mountain massif about fifty miles [80 kilometres] north of Naples. The monastery was founded by St Benedict of Nursia in 529 on the site of a temple of Apollo. Fourteen hundred years later the Germans took advantage of its almost impregnable position guarding the road northwards to delay the Allied advance in 1943. It was almost destroyed as a result but has since been rebuilt. As the first house of the Benedictine Order, Monte Cassino was the prototype of such institutions in Western Europe.

¶ MAJDALANY, FRED. *Cassino*. 1957

Montenegro: Balkan country formerly independent, incorporated in Yugoslavia after World War I. It rises from the eastern shore of the Adriatic Sea to a rocky plateau, from which it took its name meaning "Black Mountain". This difficult terrain helped its people against the Turks in the 14th and 15th centuries and against the Germans in 1941.

The seal of Simon de Montfort.

Montfort, Simon de, Earl of Leicester (*c.* 1208–65): baronial leader in England. Born in France, Simon inherited the earldom of Leicester through his English grandmother. Provoked by favouritism to foreigners and heavy papal taxes, he led the opposition to Henry III (1216–72), whose sister he had married, and secured the concessions known as the Provisions of Oxford, which set out methods for the reorganisation and reform of the country's affairs. When Henry broke his agreement to these measures, Simon defeated him at Lewes (1264) and summoned a parliament containing town representatives for the first time. He was defeated and killed at Evesham (1265).

¶ LUCKOCK, ELIZABETH and GRUNDY, CAROLINE. *Simon de Montfort: reformer and rebel.* 1970

Montreal: Canadian city situated 1,000 miles [1,600 kilometres] up the St Lawrence river. Jacques Cartier first reconnoitred the site in the 1530s, and Catholic missionaries settled there permanently in 1642. Extensive fortifications in 1722 marked its growing defensive, trading and manufacturing importance. In 1760 de Vaudreuil effectively ceded Canada to Great Britain by surrendering Montreal. American colonists occupied the city in 1776–77. After the Lachine canal construction in 1825 it displaced Quebec a the chief port. A centre of culture and in dustry it is the second largest Frenc speaking city in the world (after Pari with a population in 1982 of 2,850,900. vies with Toronto for first place in Can ada. The words of an early settler tha they were planting "a grain of mustar seed destined to overshadow the Land proved prophetic.
See CANADA for map.

Moors (Spanish *moros*, dark): a race c people now spread widely through coun tries of North Africa from Egypt t Morocco, to which they give their name and descended from the ancient Mau with admixture of blood contributed b the various conquerors of the land: Arab Numidians, Phoenicians and Roman plus some Spanish acquired through thei own domination of Spain during th Saracen occupation of the peninsula be tween AD 710 and 1238. In the latter hal of the 8th century the Moors restore the ancient Roman university of Cordov which became their main centre c learning, and excelled in science, mathe matics and philosophy. Being largel Muslims they were threatened by th upsurge of Christianity in Spain in th 11th century, but King Yusuf of th Almoravids in North Africa came t their aid and seized the whole of Anda lusia, which led to the Moors' regainin control of the peninsula, with the kin of Morocco as their ruler. In the first hal of the 13th century, however, th Christians conquered the Muslims, wh were driven into Granada, where the settled. In 1568 Philip II of Spain ordere the suppression of Moorish ways and Christian education for all children. Th Moors of Granada rebelled and man fled to Africa, the last remnants of th Muslim Moors being expelled in 1609.

oral Rearmament: a 20th-century igious movement. Its founder, Frank chman, was a Lutheran minister in the A who, inspired by a conference in gland in 1908, returned home to devote nself to fostering, at first especially ong university students, a life lived re closely under God's guidance, by ct following of moral principles and mutual help and encouragement in ritual matters. The movement spread twards and reached England in 1926, ere it flourished particularly in Oxford, hough the name "Oxford Group" was parently first applied later in South rica. It met some opposition and was cused of Fascist sympathies; but it is w firmly established, though no longer nspicuously spreading, with head-arters in Los Angeles and, for Western rope, at Caux in Switzerland.

UCKMAN, FRANK. *Remaking the World: Moral -Armament*. 1961; THORNTON-DUESBERY, J. *The en Secret of Moral Re-Armament*. 1964

ore, Sir Thomas (1478–1535): English olar and statesman and Roman Catholic artyr. After studying law, he entered rliament in 1504, and in due course his lents attracted the notice of King enry VIII, who advanced his career until in 1529 he was appointed Lord Chancellor to succeed the fallen Wolsey. His home at Chelsea was notable both for the calm and happiness of his family life and also for the scholars and writers who were welcomed there. Of More's own writings, the *Utopia*, a description of an imaginary ideal human community, is the most famous. His strong religious principles compelled him to oppose Henry in his efforts to divorce Queen Catherine and in the king's break with the Pope, and he was executed on a charge of high treason. In 1886 the Roman Catholic Church conferred on him the title of Blessed and in 1935 that of Saint.

¶ STANLEY-WRENCH, MARGARET. *The Story of Sir Thomas More*. 1961

Morganatic: term applied to the marriage of a man or woman of royal, or occasionally of noble, birth to someone of inferior social status. This is of little account today, but in the past it could prevent the offspring of the marriage from succeeding to the nobler partner's titles or possessions. It is incorrect to apply the term to the marriage of a reigning sovereign.

Moriscos or the **Little Moors:** Spanish Muslims who accepted baptism, and their descendants, many being of the same race as the Christians but descended from converts to Islam. They were hard workers and therefore valued by the community; but, following the suppression of all Moorish ways in 1568 and the resulting rebellion, they were expelled from Spain, some of them becoming pirates on the Barbary coast and others conspiring against Spain with various enemies, especially France. It is said that the English Morris Dance is based on a dance of the Moriscos.

Mormons: religious sect, now number-

Joseph Smith preaching in the wilderness.

ing over two million followers, also known as the Latter Day Saints, owing its origins to the publication in 1830 of the *Book of Mormon*, based on a revelation claimed by Joseph Smith (1805–44; *see* separate entry). The new Church, first established at Fayette in New York State, aroused much opposition on social and religious grounds. Nevertheless, the movement spread to centres in Ohio, Missouri and Illinois, growing in numbers and influence. Violence often followed the settlers, culminating in the lynching of Smith in the jail at Carthage. The leadership of the Mormons passed to Brigham Young (1801–77; *see* separate entry), who led mass migrations to the valley of the Great Salt Lake in Utah and from 1850–57 was the governor of the new territory. The Mormon religion countenanced marriage to more than one wife at the same time (polygamy), and not till this was abolished, in 1896, was Utah admitted into the Union as the 49th State.

Temple Square, Salt Lake City, during a conference.

Morocco: the westernmost of the thı Maghreb states with Atlantic and Me terranean coastlines and containing t most spectacular part of the huge At Mountain chain. The area came unc Carthage and Rome, the Vandals a then the Arabs. Morocco became French protectorate in 1912 and inc pendent in 1956. A traditionalist Mosle society, it is one of the few monarchies Africa politically right wing and pr West. Its claim to former Spanish Saha has involved it in warfare and confl with the OAU ever since 1975.

See MEDITERRANEAN for map.

¶ CAVANNA, BETTY. *Morocco*. 1972

Morris, William (1834–96)**:** poet, artis craftsman and social reformer. He held strong belief that mechanical process were destroying the beauty of craftsma ship, particularly in the making of hous hold objects and the production of fi books. Some of his wallpapers may sti be found in domestic use. Morris was member of the group of artists known the Pre-Raphaelites, formed in Londo in 1840.

¶ In WARREN, C. H. *Great Men*. Vol. 5, 1956

A mosaic in the Apse of the Basilica of S. Apollinare in Classe, Ravenna.

osaic: pictures and patterns made of ıy pieces of stone, glass or other subs- ınces set closely together. The word ımes, not from Moses, but from the nine ter-goddesses of the arts, the Muses. .osaic was known in ancient Meso- ɔtamia, Greece and Rome. It was used ·st for floors, and later on walls and ilings as well. It was an art which ached great heights under the Byzantine npire, and the mosaics to be seen in the ıurches of Ravenna, Italy, and in St ɫark's, Venice, were executed in the yzantine tradition.

The Mayas and Aztecs of Central merica used mosaic on ceremonial ıasks and shields and fashioned wonder- ıl mantles out of mosaic made with athers.

ROSSI, FERNANDO. *Mosaics: a survey of their story and techniques.*

ɫoscow: with its administrative strong- ɔld of the Kremlin, the capital city of the USSR. The 800th anniversary of its founding was celebrated in 1947. It was a centre of resistance to Mongols and Tartars and became, in the early 14th century, the chosen base of Ivan I, grand duke of Vladimir. Ivan III (1440–1505) made it the capital of his Russian kingdom. In 1712 St Petersburg (Leningrad) replaced it as capital. Napoleon occupied Moscow for five weeks in 1812. It again became the seat of government in 1918 after the Revolution. The Germans approached within twenty miles [32 kilometres] in 1941. Population 8,398,000 in 1983.

See also KREMLIN. *See* USSR for map.

Motion (moving) pictures also known as **movies, films, cinema pictures,** etc.: film sequence, with or without soundtrack. Properly speaking, there is no such thing as a moving picture. A great industry and art form which has had an incalculable effect on the social history of the 20th century depends ultimately on an optical illusion.

Scientists call this "persistence of vision", by which they mean the way the retina, that part of the eyeball which registers images of things seen, actually retains that image for the merest fraction of time after it has, in fact, passed from view. If, that is to say, a series of still pictures – for example, of a child running, each picture showing a slightly later development of the action than the one preceding – is viewed fast enough, the eye, by means of overlapping images, supplies the illusion of continuous movement. A reel of film consists of just such a series of still pictures. If there *is* any such thing as a moving picture it is the human eye that is its prime inventor. What the so-called inventors provided was the apparatus – the cameras, projectors, roll-film and so on – which made it possible to exploit this fact of physiology.

The development of the "movie" occurred almost simultaneously in three countries – the USA, Great Britain and France. Which deserves the chief credit is still a matter of polite patriotic contention.

In 1889 Thomas Alva Edison (1847–1931) (*see* separate entry), invented a motion picture machine which he called the Kinetoscope, a slot machine containing a film 50 feet [15.24 metres] long. Marketed commercially in 1894, it proved so popular that soon Kinetoscope Parlors were to be found all over the United States. In the same year Woodville Latham invented a rudimentary projector, the Panoptikon, which projected moving pictures on to a large screen for mass viewing. In England in 1889 William Friese-Greene patented the first of a series of motion picture cameras. Working along broadly similar lines in France were the brothers Auguste and Louis Lumière. On 23 November 1897 Queen Victoria set the seal of royal approval on the ne craze when, at Windsor Castle, s watched a film of her Diamond Jubi procession, shot in the preceding June.

In their early days films were part of t entertainment offered at music hal That is why the length of a reel of fil was – and has remained ever since – fix at 1,000 feet [304.8 metres], a length th took about as long to run as the avera variety turn.

The film industry grew and prospere When World War I (1914–18) broke o the United States, far removed from t battlefields, was able to draw ahead of h European competitors. Hollywood California became the film capital of t world. The "star" system develope Charlie Chaplin (1889–1977), Bust Keaton (1895–1966) and Mary Pickfo (1893–1980) were examples of actors an actresses whose names became househo words.

Colour and sound, as applied to cinem tography, interested the inventors fro the very beginning. Coloured fil originally coloured by hand, has gradua been improved to a point where, if it h a fault, it is that of being almost too go to be true. In 1927, with the phenomen success of a film called *The Jazz Sing* which was part "talkie", the moti picture industry entered a new phase.

Since then, the film industry has look for further refinements, in particular t stereoscopic or three-dimensional imag The three-dimensional film aims at pr senting moving images with a measurab dimension of depth, thus re-creating t solid world seen by binocular (two-eye human beings. This effect has not be achieved with complete success, althou films do appear containing 3-D sequenc and several full-length 3-D films we produced in the 1950s.

Television has brought far reachi changes. An enormous proportion of t

ove left: Charlie Chaplin as he was in the ·s of his famous silent films. Middle: Buster aton in Paris with his pet monkey. Right: ary Pickford, "America's Sweetheart" and st famous filmstar of the twenties. Right: odern film techniques used in filming The ast Must Die *in 1971.*

ms made every year are now produced r television. The development of simple me video-tape machines (these record und and vision very much in the same ay as an ordinary tape recorder records und) means that people can record their vourite television programmes, and see em again whenever they wish. It is also ssible to hire other taped programmes om video-tape libraries. From the iddle 1970s, there has been a pheno-enal growth in the home video indus-y and before long most homes will be le to use video cassette recorders at will. ociologists are still trying to decide hether, on balance, this is good or bad. ertainly, for millions of people nowa-ays, moving pictures wield more in-uence than the printed word.

ROBINSON, DAVID. *World Cinema: a short history.* 73

lotor car, car, automobile: self-opelled passenger vehicle for use on roads. The word "automobile", more used in America than in Britain, is a hybrid of Greek and Latin. This article confines itself to the motor car, but it has, of course, much in common with the van, the coach, the omnibus and the truck in its mechanical features and in the history of its development.

Apart from wind-propulsion, the earliest motive power applied by man to a moving vehicle was steam; and indeed a steam driven car was placed on the road by Joseph Cugnot in France in 1769, some thirty-six years before the first steam locomotive ran on rails. Technical difficulties, such as the weight of the vehicle on the roads of the time and the limited range of operation, prevented its general adoption, though the steam motor car, in its later development, had reached by the 1920s quite a high level of performance, which was, however, outstripped by that of the contemporary petrol driven car. Nevertheless it still has some support, particularly in the USA, and may yet prove one of the answers to the problem of the pollution of the atmosphere by exhaust gases from petrol engines.

The first electric car was produced in 1888, and this means of propulsion has enjoyed some success, particularly for its silence and absence of exhaust, but further experiment is needed to make it suitable for general motoring use.

The motor car as we know it today is propelled by internal combustion, that is to say by the explosion of gases in the cylinders of the engine, which sets up a motion that is transmitted mechanically to the road wheels. The explosion is generally produced by an electric spark igniting vaporised petrol; the alternative of using diesel oil, exploded by compression, is less suited to motor cars than to larger commercial vehicles.

It is not easy to pinpoint the date of the appearance of the first petrol driven car, and the line between the earliest motor cars and motor tricycles is seldom clear. An experimental vehicle was exhibited in Vienna in 1873, but the honour of being responsible for the first commercially produced vehicles, in the years 1885–86, appears to lie between Carl Benz and Gottlieb Daimler.

Paul and Gottlieb Daimler in the world's first car, the 1886 Daimler.

The early motoring enthusiasts wer very much shackled by legal restriction at a time when most people travelled th roads on or behind horses: indeed th earliest cars were often called "horsele carriages". In England, it was not unt November 1896 that the last requiremen were repealed of the Acts of Parliament c 1865 and 1878, that a man should walk i front of any mechanically propelle vehicle on public roads, though fro 1878 he no longer had to carry a red fla The speed limit, however, on all roa remained very low, and even after Worl War I it was still 20 m.p.h. for some year The annual London to Brighton run c veteran cars commemorates the "liber tion" of 1896.

The main technical problems whic faced the early motorists were the mea of exploding the gases in the engi cylinders and the manufacture of reliab pneumatic tyres, with which the name c John Boyd Dunlop (1840–1921) is assoc ated. Subsequent progress in developme and design can be broadly described improvements and refinements of th original concept, such as electric lightin four-wheel brakes, independent suspe sion and automatic transmission.

On the manufacturing side, the ear handmade cars were, in due cours superseded by mass-produced vehicl put together on a production line. Hen Ford (1863–1947) (*see* separate entry) the USA was a pioneer of this develo ment with his famous "Model T".

¶ ELLACOTT, S. E. *Wheels on the Road.* 195 ROLT, L. T. C. *Motor Cars.* 1957; THOMAS, DAV ST. J. *The Motor Revolution.* 1961

Mountain states, The, USA: inla western region of the United States, ma up of the states of Arizona, Colorad Idaho, Montana, Nevada, New Mexic Utah and Wyoming. In the southe reaches the dominant feature is the Gre merican Desert. Although rising in the est to the Rocky Mountains, the tallest nge in the United States, the land is very y. The major rivers in the area are the issouri and Colorado.

ettlement came late to this entire region. hough many settlers passed through the sert and mountains on their way to the cific coast, the region remained basic-y in the hands of scattered tribes of merican Indians until the last thirty ars of the 19th century. Even after a ries of Indian wars led to the opening of e area for settlement, population grew owly. Arizona and New Mexico did not, fact, become states until 1912, and the gion remains by far the most sparsely ttled part of the continental United ates.

Aining, grazing and tourism provide ost of the income for the region. In the rth, sheep are grazed in the plains and ateaux, while in the south herds of ttle are maintained on vast areas of near-sert. In the various mountain ranges of e region, such vital minerals as molyb-num, lead, silver, copper and oil are all tracted. Tourism also is crucial. The most untouched mountains and valleys the north, organised into such areas as ellowstone National Park, draw thou-nds of campers and sightseers each year. Nevada the lure of legalised gambling d elaborate stage shows have made Las egas an entertainment centre and pro-de the basic force in Nevada's economy. ut this is primarily a land of wide, thinly opulated areas – the least tamed of all the nd area in the continental United States. e AMERICA for map.

lozambique: mainly lowland stretch-g for 1500 miles along the southeast astline of Africa. Vasco da Gama nded on this coast in 1498 and Portu-ese colonisation followed. The coun-y became independent in 1975 after ten years of bitter fighting against Portugal. One of the poorest countries in Africa, Mozambique has faced many political problems since independence including attempts to destabilise its Marxist gov-ernment by neighbouring South Africa. Its President, Samora Machel, provided bases for the ZANU forces of Robert Mugabe in the final phase of the struggle which ended white rule in neighbouring Rhodesia. Capital: Maputo. Population 12,615,200 (1982).

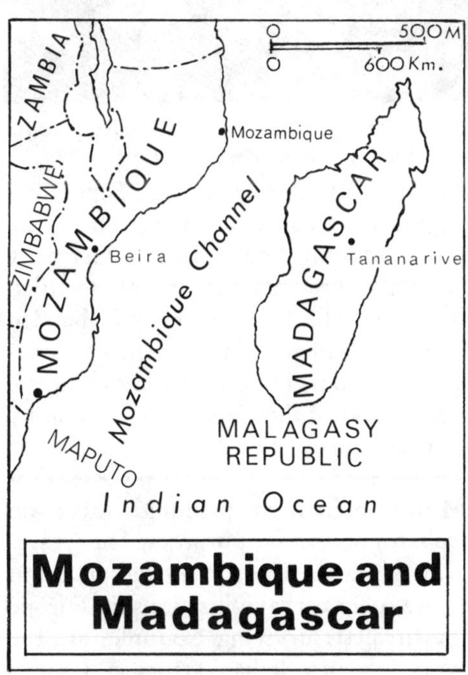

Mozambique and Madagascar

Munich: German city, capital of the *Land* of Bavaria. It originated as a Benedictine settlement (*Munichen* – home of the monks). From the 13th century until 1918 it was the home of the Wittels-bach rulers of Bavaria and grew in size and prosperity, its commercial expansion being checked only by the Thirty Years War (1618–48). The nineteenth century brought renewed and rapid expansion and it became an important centre for international exhibitions and congresses.

In the 1920s the city was the breeding-ground for extremist political groups – notably the Nazi Party – and Hitler's first mass meetings were held there.

Prime Minister Neville Chamberlain returns with the Munich Agreement of 1938.

Munich Agreement (29 September 1938)**:** a settlement of the Czechoslovak crisis reached by France, Britain, Germany and Italy, by which the strongly fortified district of the Sudetenland was handed over to Germany. The agreement, virtually dictated by Hitler, led to the complete destruction of the Czechoslovak state by Germany in 1939.

Mural painting: painting direct on walls for decorative purposes. The art was widely practised in ancient Egypt and in many other early civilizations. In Europe the greatest surviving examples are the work of such Italian artists as Giotto, Masaccio, Fra Angelico, Andrea del Sarto and Raphael (*see* FLORENTINE ART). Among more recent examples, one of the best known in England is the Painted Hall at Greenwich, south-east London, executed by Sir James Thornhill (*c.* 1676–1734) in what is now the Royal Naval College.

¶ MERRIFIELD, MARY. *The Art of Fresco Painting*, edited by A. C. Sewter. 1952

Muscovite: from Moskva or Moscow. The people of that area, and their rulers, formed the nucleus of a Russian state. Ivan III (1440–1505), grand duke of Muscov made himself independent of Tar control; and Ivan IV (1530–84) was t first proclaimed Tsar of Muscovy and, effect, the first Tsar of Russia.

Museums: buildings where natural a man-made objects from different perio of time all over the world are stored a displayed.

The word "museum" was originally t name given by the ancient Greeks temples devoted to the Muses, the ni sister goddesses of the arts and scienc The famous Museum of Alexandri founded *c.* 280 BC and destroyed in 48 B was more like a university than a museu There is little evidence that things we deliberately preserved for posterity duri the earlier civilisations, but, with t coming of the Renaissance to Weste Europe, interest in the past was awaken and people began to hunt for classic relics. Royal and noble families form collections of antiquities and artist treasures which were added to by succee ing generations; but they were prompt only by personal interest or pride possession, and little attempt was ma to gather objects for the benefit of othe Nevertheless the acquisitive habits princes gave rise to many of the gre European museums. These rich colle tions, often still housed in the pala homes of their former owners, gradual passed into state ownership as a result social or political upheaval: treasur accumulated by the Medici family can b admired today in the palaces of Florenc the famous Hermitage in Leningrad is called because it was the retreat to whic Catherine the Great invited her frien to admire the collection she started 1765, while the Louvre, housing roy treasures, became public property duri the French revolutionary period.

The 16th and 17th centuries were perio

exploration and discovery: learned men quired curios brought back by travels from foreign parts, hoarding them : investigation. One such scholar col-tor was the naturalist John Tradescant 10, with his son, built up the "Museum adescantianum" in London. In 1659 e younger Tradescant gave this collec-n to Elias Ashmole, who in turn pre-nted it, with his own collection of coins d curios, to Oxford University. Sir nristopher Wren was commissioned to sign a building to house the gifts, and e Ashmolean Museum was opened in 83 as what seems to have been the first ublic museum". The collection out-ew its first home, replaced by the esent Ashmolean in 1841–8. The orig-al building now houses a collection of ientific instruments.

So far, the collections which were to rm the basis of modern museums had en miscellaneous affairs depending on e enthusiasms of their originators. uring the 18th century, collecting be-me much more methodical and one of e foremost collectors of this period was 1 English doctor, Sir Hans Sloane, who athered natural history specimens during is travels. On his death his collections ere purchased by the government as the undation of the British Museum, opened 1 1759 – the first instance of public ioney being used to found a museum.

The Industrial Revolution contributed a rapid development of museums in the estern hemisphere, especially during ie 19th century. The progress of scientific ivestigation and the development of echnology brought in its train a thirst for nowledge and a desire for popular ducation. The Great Exhibition of 1851 ave impetus to museums in Britain, and he South Kensington group of national nuseums were constructed to house the bjects of natural interest, applied and nechanical art, arranged for public exhibition at the instigation of the Prince Consort.

In the New World the first museums were established towards the end of the 18th century, and from then on nearly all of them were deliberately planned as part of the educational system. Resources were greater than in other parts of the world, and before long the USA was leading the world in the richness of collections, buildings designed to house them, the techniques applied to their preservation and display and the means adopted to make them attractively useful to the whole community. One of the most complex and exciting is the Guggenheim Museum in New York.

The Guggenheim Museum, New York, designed by Frank Lloyd Wright in 1943–46.

Modern developments have included open air museums, pioneered in Sweden, consisting of complete homes, farms, streets, etc., restored or re-erected to illustrate life in a particular region or period. In recent years increasing attention has been paid to industrial collections, representing the working lives of people and their artifacts, as well as their artistic and cultural achievements.

Today, museums are actively engaged in the life of the communities they serve, organising services for schools and children, concerts and film shows and local expeditions. They are growing closer to the original meaning of the word as homes for the muses – for history, art, music and all the branches of science which have developed since the days of Aristotle.

See also INDIVIDUAL ENTRIES.

Musical instruments: devices, made variously of metal, wood and other vegetable, mineral and animal substances, for sending out sound waves which can be received and translated by the receptive ear. While anyone can bang on a piano or twang a guitar and produce a noise, the function of musical instruments is to serve as vehicles for producing those patterns of organised sound to which we give the name of music.

The beginning of musical instruments is lost in antiquity. Probably the earliest were *percussion instruments*, those from which sound is produced by striking. The simplest of these instruments – the tom-tom of tribal Africa, the Chinese gong, the Spanish castanet, the cymbal, triangle and tambourine – can produce no melodies, no harmonics, even in the hands of the most accomplished performer. How, then, are they musical instruments at all? The answer lies in that basic ingredient of all music – rhythm.

Percussion instruments can produce rhythmic patterns of long and short beats of great dramatic quality. The beat of drums, repeated over and over again in a pattern of steadily increasing intensity, can have an almost hypnotic effect, rousing its hearers to a warlike frenzy or religious ecstasy.

Stringed instruments, from which sound is produced by vibrating a string, can be subdivided into three categories. In son the vibration is achieved simply plucking the string. The lyre, so oft shown in representations of Apollo, t Greek god of music, is an example of ancient stringed instrument of this ty Others are the harp (*see* separate entr the lute and the guitar.

In a second group of stringed instr ments, sound is produced by drawing bow across strings. The bow was oriental invention which the W adopted and greatly improved upon. long ago as the 8th century BC the Persia possessed a boat-shaped, bowed string instrument called a *rubab* or *rebab*, adapt tions of which are still to be found in pa of the East. From it was derived t European rebec, a stringed instrume which, in medieval religious painting may be seen as a component of many a angelic orchestra.

An important part of the mode orchestra is made up of the bowe stringed instruments which form th violin family: the violin, viola, violor cello (more often nowadays abbreviate to cello) and double-bass. The ancesto of all four were six-stringed viols, whic were far inferior to the instruments whic superseded them. Violins made by th great Italian makers of the 17th and 18 centuries, notably Antonio Stradiva (1644–1737) and Nicolo Amati (1596 1684), both of them members of famo families of violin makers, have never bee surpassed.

Strictly speaking, the third subdivisio of stringed instruments, that of stringe *keyboard instruments*, requires a certai qualification. All such instruments a played by striking the keys of a keyboar and to this extent utilise an element o percussion. In the pianoforte and clavi chord, one of the piano's forerunner percussion plays a larger part. When clavichord key is pressed down it raises

nall, wedge-shaped piece of brass (called "tangent") which strikes the corres-onding string, setting it vibrating. In the ıano, tiny hammers take the place of the ngents.

With the virginals, the spinet and the arpsichord, all three of them members of ıe keyboard family, we are, at one emove, back to plucking strings. Striking ıe keys of their keyboards activates little ieces of wood called "jacks". Quills alled *plectra* – singular, *plectrum*), which re attached to the jacks, pluck the strings.

Among stringed keyboard instruments ıe piano is the outstanding solo musical ıstrument of the Western world and ne for which many composers have reated some of their best works. The man vho made the first instrument to which ıe name of pianoforte could properly be pplied deserves a greater fame than osterity has accorded him. He was Bartolommeo Cristofori (1655–1731), a harpsichord maker of Padua in Italy, who made the first piano in 1709, while in the service of Prince Ferdinand de' Medici.

Not all keyboard instruments are stringed. The carillon, a complete set of bells capable of being rung by one man, and the organ, a wind instrument, both possess keyboards.

Man must have found out very early in his history that a hollow reed or stalk, or an animal's horn, plus the power of his own lungs, could produce a sound. Once he had acquired that basic knowledge the evolution of *wind instruments* was bound to follow. All wind instruments, however apparently sophisticated, are extensions of that simple pipe, that natural horn.

Among wood-winds – which, as the name implies, are wind instruments made of wood – are the flute and its smaller brothers the piccolo and the fife. The recorder, a simple wind instrument dating back to the Middle Ages and for a long time almost forgotten, has had a return to popularity in recent years. The oboe, a development of the 18th century hautbois ("high-wood") is, well played, an instrument of entrancing purity of tone. The bassoon, with its lower register, and the versatile clarinet are other wood-winds indispensable to a well-balanced orchestra.

Brass instruments were originally made of brass and are still so called even though they may be made of some different metal (just as, to make things easy, saxophones, which are made of metal, are classed as wood-winds because they have reed mouthpieces). They include horns, bugles, trumpets, tubas, trombones, cornets, saxhorns and flugelhorns.

A wind instrument of ancient pedigree is the bagpipe. Although we associate it particularly with Scotland, it arrived there only towards the close of the Middle Ages. Centuries earlier the bagpipe was known in ancient Persia, in India and China. A bronze figure, found at Richborough in Kent, of a Roman soldier playing a bagpipe suggests that the Romans may have brought the instrument to Britain.

Muslims: name given to the followers of Islam, the religion founded by Mohammed, who accept the *Koran* and undertake the five obligatory duties of reciting their creed, daily prayers, payment of alms, fasting, and pilgrimage to Mecca. There are several divisions, holding different beliefs as to who is the true successor to Mohammed as head of the whole Muslim community. The largest group are the *Sunni,* who cling to tradition and the mystical character of religion; among others are the *Shia*, who expect the return of the twelfth Imam, Mohammed al-Muntazar, who disappeared in 878, and the *Ismailis*, led by the Aga Khan. Oil wealth and consequent modernisation in the Islamic countries of the Middle East have in some cases produced a violent backlash and demands for a return t strict fundamentalist principles. Islam ha gained many converts in Africa in the er since independence and is at present th world's fastest growing religion with a estimated 555 million members world wide in 1983.

Muslim League: founded in 1906 t encourage educational and politica advance among the Muslims of India, i became the principal agent in the struggl against the domination of the Hind majority. In 1909 it secured separat Muslim constituencies under the Morley Minto reforms. From 1916 until his deat in 1947, Mahommed Ali Jinnah was it President. Though he welcomed the 193 India Act, his fear of an India dominate by the Hindu Congress Party made him from 1940, proclaim partition as th Muslim policy, and, more than any othe influence, the League was responsible fo the creation of the Muslim state o Pakistan (*see* separate entry).

Mussolini, Benito (1881–1945): Prim Minister and Dictator of Italy, frequentl called *Il Duce*, the leader. The son of blacksmith with revolutionary opinions he early developed an insubordinat spirit, organising trade unions, promotin strikes, being sent to prison and watche by the police as a trouble-maker. Widel read and a skilful journalist, he became powerful force in the Italian Socialis party, editing the *Avanti*, its official news paper and, later, founding his ow journal, *Il Popolo d'Italia,* which greatl influenced the workers and the younge generation.

After World War I, in which he wa seriously wounded, he broke away fron the Socialists and founded the Fascis political movement (*see* FASCISM). Usin the symbol of authority in ancient Rom (the *fasces*), the Roman military salute o

the outstretched arm, and parading in black shirts, the party staged an appeal which won them thirty-six seats in the government (1921) and culminated the next year in the dramatic Fascist march on Rome, organised by Mussolini but not led by him (until the final stage, undramatically, in a motor-car). Awed by this show of force the king (Victor Emmanuel III, ruled 1900–46) and the government gave way and Mussolini, though theoretically remaining a monarchist, became undisputed dictator, pursuing rapid reconstruction and economic expansion at home and an aggressive foreign policy abroad. The latter made him first the ally, then the subordinate, of Hitler, and eventually brought Italy to disastrous involvement in World War II on the side of Germany. The would-be Roman emperor was executed by his own countrymen in 1945.

Mutiny: the refusal of orders from, or revolt against, constituted authority, especially of men in armed forces. Though it may be revolutionary in character or the first stage in a revolutionary movement, mutiny differs from revolution in being a rising not against government but against officers, within confined limits – ship, fleet, regiment or army.

The mutinies which have most caught public imagination have been those at sea. Perhaps the best known of all was that led by Fletcher Christian, mate of HMS *Bounty*, against Captain Bligh in 1789, when Bligh and eighteen others were cast off in an open boat in mid-Pacific and made a remarkable 4,000-mile voyage to Timor, while the mutineers established the little community on Pitcairn Island.

Two mutinies in the British Navy in 1797 are interesting in their different character. That at Spithead, led (almost certainly) by Valentine Joyce, resembled a well managed strike against intolerable conditions. Winning the sympathy of landsmen, it was fully successful, the loyalty of the mutineers never being in question, and it ended without any punishments. That at the Nore was much more bitter: "United Irishmen" and French sympathisers were among the crews, and it ended with the hanging of the ringleaders, Parker and others.

Three naval mutinies which had far-reaching effects were those of the Russian Navy at Kronstadt in 1917 – one of the early moves of the revolution – and of the Austrian Navy at Cattaro and the German at Kiel in 1918, which marked the collapse of the Central Powers in World War I.

Some mutinies on land illustrate the varied reasons prompting them. That of Dumbarton's Scottish Regiment in 1688 was a protest against the appointment of a foreign commander. The six regiments of the Pennsylvania Line who rose against General Anthony Wayne in 1781, and who might, if successful, have lost the war for the Americans, were protesting against appalling winter conditions. The very grave mutiny in the French armies in 1917, when over a million men refused orders, was due to the enormous casualties at Verdun (1916), the failure of

Nivelle's disastrous offensive, and perhaps partly to the Russian example; only Pétain's prestige and drive restored discipline in time to resist the later German offensives. The mutiny in China in 1936, when troops kidnapped General Chiang Kai-Shek and held him for several days, broke out because they wanted him to stop fighting Communists and concentrate on the Japanese in Manchuria.

For British people "The Mutiny" means the Indian rising of 1857–58. This certainly began as an army mutiny, prompted by motives which were partly social, partly religious and only indirectly political. Indian writers claim that, in spite of its limitations, it was a national movement aimed at driving foreigners out of India; and undoubtedly large numbers of civilians joined the rising, and some of the leaders wished to promote a general revolution.

Formerly the penalty for mutiny was always death. This was why escaped mutineers so often took to piracy or banditry. There was no place for them in settled society.

¶ CARDWELL, PAMELA. *The Indian Mutiny*. 1973

Mysore: state of southern India, enlarged 1953–55 to cover roughly the area in which Kanarese is spoken. Coming under the sway of the South Indian state of Vijayanagar in the 14th century, Mysore superseded that power in the 16th and, seizing Seringapatam and other territory, became prosperous under a series of able *Wadiyars* (rulers). But in the 18th century misgovernment made possible a takeover of power by Hyder Ali, whose hostility, and that of his son Tipu Sultan, towards the British led to the conquest of Mysore by Britain (1799). Responsibility for government was restored to the dynasty in 1883, and, with Indian independence in 1947, the Maharaja became Governor. *See also* INDIA.

N

Nagasaki: city on Kyushu Island and th oldest open port in Japan. In the 16t century it saw the first establishment of Christian community in Japan. It re mained open to foreign trade throug two centuries of Japan's total exclusion c foreigners. Nagasaki received in 1945 th second and more powerful atomic bom dropped on Japan. Thirty-five thousan people died, but destruction was limite by the hills which give this city i beautiful setting, damage proving le than at Hiroshima. Quickly recovering Nagasaki soon led the world in ship building output and also has steel, arma ments, electrical equipment and pea industries.

Nanking: a former capital of China, o the south bank of the Yangtze River an capital of Kiangsu province. The nam means "southern capital". When th Ming emperor Chu Yüan-chang over threw the Yüan (Mongol) dynasty i 1372, he established his capital there building the city walls, though late Peking became the capital. Nanking wa captured by the British in 1842, thu opening China to western trade. Su Yat-sen here became president of th Chinese Republic, and in 1927 it was mad the capital once more. In 1937 th Japanese captured it, surrendering it i 1945. From 1949 Peking has been China' capital.

Nansen, Fridtjof (1861–1930): Norwegian arctic explorer. Oceanographic anc arctic studies led to his daring and successful venture in 1888 to cross unknowr Greenland. In 1893 he sailed in the *Fram* and in three years drifted across the Arctic Ocean to Spitzbergen, whence, with one mpanion, he crossed the ice along ° 74′ N to Franz Josef Island. His work repatriating war prisoners won him e Nobel Peace Prize in 1922. Refugee oblems and Russian famine relief cupied his later years.

NOEL-BAKER, F. *Fridtjof Nansen*. 1958

---

antes, Edict of (1598): the order by enry IV of France granting freedom of orship to the Protestants. Its later revo- tion (1685) drove many Huguenots rench Protestants) into exile, with nportant economic consequences both r France and for the countries that ceived them.

Iaples: south Italian city and port. robably founded as Neapolis ("new own") by Greek colonists *c.* 600 BC, it as captured in 328 BC by the Romans, ho eagerly patronised it as a university f Greek culture (Nero's first public stage ppearance was at Naples). After the fall f Rome the city changed hands many mes and, having been a Habsburg posses- on from 1503 to 1734, became the apital of an independent Kingdom of icily. Thus it remained, with an interval uring the Napoleonic Wars, until 1860, hen it became part of the new Kingdom f Italy. Today the trade of the city ourishes but the overcrowding and overty of many of its inhabitants is a roblem yet to be solved.

Napoleon I, Napoleon Bonaparte 1769–1821): Emperor of the French 804–15. Born in Corsica, he entered the rmy as an artillery officer in 1785 and vas acknowledged a great general after is victories against the Austrians in orthern Italy in 1796. He failed in his ttempt to cut British trade routes by aking Egypt, but on his return to France n 1799 he overthrew the Directory and ecame First Consul. He was made Consul for life in 1802 and crowned himself Emperor in 1804. Undoubtedly an autocrat, Napoleon was also a brilliant administrator, and reforms such as his legal code (*Code Napoléon*) enshrined as state policy many ideas of the French Revolution. By 1808 a series of remarkable victories, including Austerlitz (1805), Jena (1806), Friedland (1807) and Wagram (1809) had given him control of much of Europe, but his ravenous appetite for further military conquest led to the ruinous Russian campaign (1812), in which the long winter retreat from Moscow virtually destroyed his army. Thereafter he conducted a desperate rearguard action against a circle of enemies and was forced to abdicate in 1814, when the Allies granted him the right to rule the Mediterranean island of Elba. In February 1815 he escaped, landed near Cannes, and again ruled France for the "Hundred Days", which ended in his final defeat by the British and Prussians on 18 June at Waterloo and his exile to St Helena, where he died in 1821.

¶ CAMMIADE, AUDREY. *Napoleon*. 1957
See also NAPOLEONIC WARS.

Napoleon and his Army during the disastrous retreat from Moscow in 1812.

Napoleon III (1808–73)**:** Emperor of France 1852–70. Bonaparte (see previous article) was his paternal uncle. After years spent in prison or in exile, partly in England, he returned to France in 1848 on the expulsion of King Louis Philippe and was elected president of the new Republic. This he overthrew and in 1852 became emperor. His reign, known as the Second Empire, brought increased prosperity to France and saw energetic planning development in Paris; but a somewhat chequered foreign policy ended in a crushing defeat by Prussia in 1870. After a short term of imprisonment he went into exile in England, where his widow Eugénie (d. 1920) long survived him.

¶ SMITH, W. H. C. *Napoleon III*. 1972

Napoleonic Wars (1803–15)**:** wars at the beginning of the 19th century when Napoleon I and the French armies fought two coalitions of European powers. Very few wars have been named after their leaders, and it is a measure of Napoleon Bonaparte's dominant genius that history has so labelled these struggles, just as the adjective "napoleonic" is accepted to describe someone with his qualities.

After the French Revolutionary Wars (*see* separate entry) the Peace of Amiens (1802) produced only a temporary and uneasy lull. The next year Britain declared war on France and the air was full of the threat of invasion as Napoleon massed a vast flotilla at Boulogne to cross the Channel, his overall plan involving the union of three fleets, from Toulon, Rochefort and Brest, further strengthened by the Spanish squadrons, to command the narrow intervening stretch of water. It was as near as Britain had come to successful invasion by a foreign power since the Conquest by William of Normandy more than seven centuries before.

Pitt had returned to office in 1804 and immediately set about forming a coalition to resist Napoleon. This consisted Russia, Austria and, later, Prussia. T next five years saw the collapse a virtual annihilation of this coalitio Austria went down at Ulm and Austerli ("Roll up that map," said Pitt of Euro when he heard of the latter defeat. "It w not be wanted these ten years.") Russi too, was smashed at Austerlitz and, late at Eylau and Friedland. Prussia w crushed at Jena in 1806, followed b Sweden the next year. Austria tried aga and succumbed at Wagram in 180 Everywhere Europe lay in ruins befo the apparently irresistible French co queror. It was more than symbolic tha after 844 years, the Holy Roman Empi was officially dissolved by his decree.

Only slowly was Napoleon proved t be less than invincible. At sea, the Batt of Trafalgar (1805) finally destroyed h dream of an invasion of England, just a in 1798, the Battle of the Nile had pre vented his conquest of the East. The stor ran on, if not always with such dramati quality, with a series of other reverses fo him, the retaking of the Cape of Goo Hope, the surrender of the Danish fle at Copenhagen, the capture of Marti nique, Guadeloupe, Mauritius, the forcin of the Dardanelles and the capture of th Dutch East Indies, to name but a fev chapters. And in the Peninsular Wa (1808–14) Wellington conducted at firs a defensive and then an offensive war tha pinned down 200,000 French troops i Spain and finally drove them from th peninsula.

Another major reverse had alread occurred in Russia when, in 1812, out o half-a-million French troops sent on th Moscow campaign only 60,000 half starved, half-frozen and dispirited sur vivors straggled back over the frontie after the horrific retreat from the blazing city. In 1813 a new coalition, of Britain Prussia, Russia, Sweden and Austria mmoned heart to defeat Napoleon at ›ipzig in the Battle of the Nations (1813), d the Emperor was exiled to Elba.

The story of his escape after a few onths and his last rally of the French mies to march to final defeat at Waterloo 815) provides the last sombre scene of ughter of the Napoleonic Wars, with › to 30,000 French troops left dead on e battlefield and the Iron Duke Vellington) showing less than iron when › wrote: "My heart is broken . . . nothing ‹cept a battle lost can be half so melan-ıoly as a battle won."

LACHOUQUE, HENRY. *Napoleon's Battles: a history his campaigns.* 1966; MORRIS, THOMAS. *The apoleonic Wars*, edited by John Selby. 1967

asmyth, James (1808–90): British ›ientist and engineer. Although he is ıiefly remembered as the inventor (1839) f the steam hammer, which revolu-onised a number of processes in the roduction of iron and steel, he was also ›sponsible for other inventions in the ıdustry, including a planing machine, a eam pile-driver and hydraulic mac-inery, and made notable contributions › astronomy in his studies of the surface f the sun and moon.

Nassau: German duchy, now part of the tate of Hesse in West Germany. The ›ounts of Nassau adopted the title in 1160. In 1292 Adolf I of Nassau was elected King of Germany. Nassau was created a duchy in 1806. A younger branch of the family inherited the principality of Orange in 1544 and became princes of Orange-Nassau. They included the Netherlands leaders William the Silent (1533–84), Maurice of Nassau (1567–1625) and William III (1650–1702) who became king of England in 1688. Descendants still form the Netherlands royal house and the grand-ducal house of Luxembourg.

Nasser, Colonel Gamal Abdel (1918–70): Egyptian statesman and leader in the Arab world. With Mohammed Neguib, he organised the military coup which overthrew Farouk, the last king of Egypt, in 1952 and became, first, premier (1954–56) and then president. In July 1956, without warning, he nationalised the Suez Canal Company, in which Britain was a principal shareholder, and thus gained control over the passage of ships through it. His name will also be permanently linked with building (backed by Russian finance) the Aswan High Dam, and the bitter Middle East struggle with Israel. *See also* ISRAEL.

Natal: province of South Africa. In the early 19th century the area was controlled by the Zulus under Chaka (1787–1828), a great military leader. He was succeeded by Dingaan, and in 1837 a party of Boer trekkers asked permission to settle in his land. This was given, but Dingaan later became alarmed, invited the leaders to a war dance and killed them. In 1838 they were revenged by a Boer victory at the Battle of Blood River; meanwhile the British Governor of the Cape tried to arrange peace terms. The weakness of Natal and internal unrest in South Africa, however, led England to annex Natal in 1840. It became a separate colony in 1856 and, after annexing Zululand and parts of the Transvaal, joined the Union of South Africa in 1910.

National Aeronautics and Space Administration (NASA): the controlling organisation in the USA for manned and unmanned space flights. Recently NASA has sought the co-operation of other countries, chiefly through various European ministers of technology and science, in planning future space programmes.

National Debt: the amount of money owed by a national government. Kings of England from early times had borrowed money for immediate use, to be repaid as taxes were collected, but, in 1694, a group of financiers undertook to raise £1,200,000 to lend to the government at eight per cent interest, the capital not being returnable. For this service, they became incorporated as the Bank of England, and certain government taxes were assigned to the Bank to ensure the payment of the interest, which was to be a permanent charge on the government. From this time onwards the National Debt has risen rapidly in time of war, sometimes followed by a slight reduction during the ensuing peace, and in 1974 stood at £35,839,000,000. Most nations now have a National Debt.

National Socialist German Worke Party: German political party motivat by policies of armed aggression, an semitism and belief in a master race Caucasian stock with no Jewish taint. came into being after World War increased its influence in the econom crisis of 1929–30, and proved a rea vehicle for the rise of Hitler, who broug it to totalitarian power from 1933 o wards. The party disintegrated with t collapse of the Third Reich in 1945 b has since shown signs of revival.
See also HITLER, ADOLF; NAZI.

Nations, Battle of the (16–19 Octob 1813): also called the Battle of Leipzi in Saxony. Encouraged by Napoleo Bonaparte's disastrous invasion of Russ (1812), the nations of Europe faced hi with growing confidence and eventuall defeated him with heavy losses in th battle, which, with Wellington's suc cesses, led to the Emperor's abdication i the following year.

NATO (North Atlantic Treat Organisation): organisation, headed b a Council of Foreign Ministers, constituted by the twelve signatories of th North Atlantic Treaty (1949) – Belgiun Canada, Denmark, France, Great Britai Iceland, Italy, Luxembourg, the Netherlands, Norway, Portugal and the US Greece and Turkey joined in 1952, an West Germany in 1955. The formation o NATO was promoted by Presiden Truman of the USA as part of his polic to stop the spread of Communism b giving economic aid to underdevelope countries. The parties to the Treaty agree that an attack upon any one membe should be considered an attack upon all NATO forces operate under an integrate command, Supreme Headquarters o Allied Powers in Europe (SHAPE), bu all retain their national identities. SHAP as located in Paris until the late 1960s, hen General Charles de Gaulle adopted independent policy and withdrew his untry from the Organisation. Spain ined NATO in 1983. Amongst the nerals who have commanded this hield of the West" against the USSR d her allies were General Dwight D. senhower (1950–52) and General Louis orstad (1956–62). Each year NATO ounts a defence exercise as well as its rmal observation and patrol work.

aval Gunnery: the art and science of ing the gun in a ship of war. Since the vention by the Frenchman Descharges . 1500) of the porthole, warships were ecially built to carry guns mounted in heeled carriages within their hulls. The uzzle-loading gun to fire cast iron nnon balls was the main armament of e sailing man-of-war from the 16th to e early 19th century. The propellant as a gunpowder cartridge ignited by atch through the touch-hole. Extreme nge was about one-and-a-half miles. ·41 kilometres]. Guns were designated cording to weight of shot, i.e. 6, 9, 12, 8, 24, 32 and 42 pounders. The heaviest uns were carried on the lowest gun deck. he carronade, a more powerful short nge gun, was introduced into ships in 779. The principal guns could be fired nly in a fixed direction, hence the objecve in naval battles was to so manoeuvre ; to be able to fire a broadside.

Naval gunnery underwent great changes 1 the 19th century. The shell gun, firing missile that exploded on impact, was ntroduced by the French, *c.* 1825; in 1859 e French wooden warship *La Gloire* vas fitted with armour plating to withtand the new destructive shell. In 1860 he British ironclad *Warrior* was fitted vith the new Armstrong rifled gun with n experimental breech opening. The argest was a 7-inch 110 pounder. Guns were now referred to by calibre (i.e. the diameter of the bore) instead of weight of shot.

In 1862 the US *Monitor* had an experimental revolving gun turret. This had far-reaching effects on future naval gunnery. In 1868 the British *Monarch* had two turrets. The year 1881 saw a satisfactory method of breech loading established.

The British *Dreadnought* of 1906 had five twin 12-inch guns in turrets. During World War I "director" control was introduced, firing all guns simultaneously and allowing for target speed, wind, roll of ship, etc. Before the end of World War II self-propelled guided missiles were introduced and are now carried in all major war vessels.

Navarino, Battle of (1827)**:** naval engagement off south-west coast of Greece. The Turks had called on their vassal, the Pasha of Egypt, for help in resisting the Greeks' successful struggle for independence. A combined English, French and Russian fleet, under Sir Edward Codrington, was watching events, but became engaged with the Turco-Egyptian fleet and destroyed it.

Navarre: former European kingdom bordering the Bay of Biscay, now partly in French and partly in Spanish territory on either side of the Pyrenees. The kingdom was first established by the Basques in the 9th century and reached its highest power under Sancho Garcia (*c.* 905) and his immediate successors, including Sancho III (*c.* 1020) called "the Great". After 1234 the kingdom passed by marriage to a succession of French kings till, in 1516, Spanish Navarre was annexed by Ferdinand of Spain. French Navarre survived as a small separate kingdom till it was united to the French throne by Henry IV of France (reigned 1598–1610), familiarly known as Henry of Navarre.

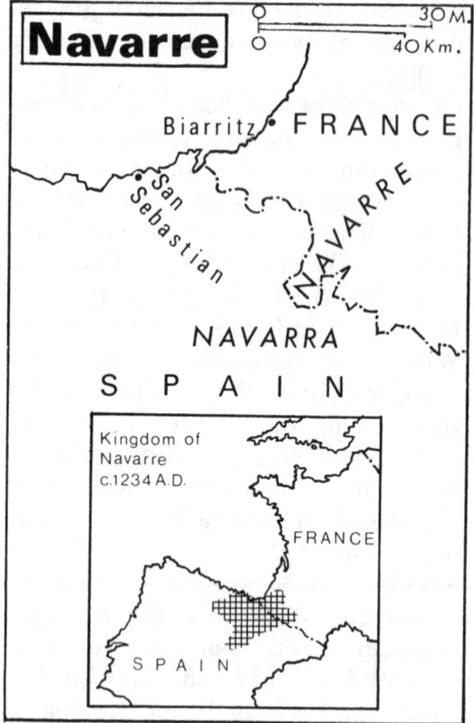

Joan (or Joanna) of Navarre was married to Henry IV of England in 1401.

Nazareth: village in Palestine where Jesus spent his early years before setting out on his ministry (*see* JESUS CHRIST). It was the home of his parents, although, at the time of his birth they had to go to Bethlehem to take part in a census. It lies about sixty miles [96·56 kilometres] north of Jerusalem, overlooking the valley of Esdraelon, and is today a notable place of pilgrimage.

Nazi: member of the *nationalsozialiet* (national socialist) party in Germany (*see* NATIONAL SOCIALIST GERMAN WORKERS' PARTY). The term became synonymous under the Hitler regime with brutal aggression, anti-Semitism and the theory of the master Nordic race. The party's symbol was the swastika.

¶ BROWNE, H. *Hitler and the Rise of Nazism*. 1969

Neanderthal man: palaeolithic ty which because extinct some 50,000 ye ago. The first discovery of the bones this flint-using man were made in 18 in the Neanderthal valley, western G many, and remains have since been fou in a number of European and Medit ranean countries. Neanderthal man h thick and curved thigh bones. The sk was large but low, with a shallow fo head and a receding chin, the whole set a thick neck. He lived in the mid Palaeolithic period (*see* GEOLOGIC PERIODS).

¶ QUENNELL, MARJORIE and QUENNELL, C. H. *Everyday Life in Prehistoric Times*. 1959; DICK SON, ALICE. *The First Book of Stone Age Man*. 19

Nehru, Jawaharlal (1889–1964)**:** India nationalist leader, educated in England Harrow and Cambridge. In 1920 h joined Mahatma Gandhi's nationali movement and in the next seven yea was imprisoned eight times for his leader ɪip of resistance to British rule. The son f a president of Congress (Motilal Nehru), he became president himself in 929 and, in 1947, the first prime minister f independent India. Though a resolute ghter for independence second only to Gandhi in prestige and influence, his esistance was directed against political omination by Britain. On the economic ront, however, his early years in England nade him understand the need for western ndustrial development to improve the eneral standards of Indian life, which vere considerably raised under his leadership. In world affairs his policy was one of trict neutrality.

LENGYEL, EMIL. *Jawaharlal Nehru*. 1970

Nelson, Horatio, Viscount Nelson (1758–1805): British admiral and national hero. Born at Burnham Thorpe, Norfolk, on 29 September 1758, he went to sea at he age of twelve as midshipman in the *Raisonnable* under his uncle, Captain Suckling. After varied experience he was given command of the *Hinchinbroke* at the age of twenty, and was noted for being "first in every service". In 1787 he married Mrs Frances Nisbet, a widow, at Nevis in he West Indies. In *Agamemnon* in 1793 he ost an eye at Calvi. Jervis's victory off Cape St Vincent (February 1797) owed nost to Nelson when, without waiting for orders, he left the British line of battle and engaged seven Spanish ships (one of hem, the *Santissima Trinidad*, the largest and strongest in the world) and captured wo. Knighted and promoted, Nelson ost an arm at Santa Cruz the same year. In 1798, sent to the Mediterranean to counter Napoleon's ambitions, he was elevated to the peerage after the total victory at the Battle of the Nile.

Vice-admiral under Hyde Parker at Copenhagen in 1801, and exercising his "right to be blind sometimes", he disregarded the signal to break off and

continued close action till ships and shore batteries surrendered. In 1805, after chasing the French admiral Villeneuve to the West Indies, he came ashore in England, then, after Admiral Sir Robert Calder's indecisive engagement off Finisterre, took command for the last time. "This maimed and battered little man" embarked in HMS *Victory* and won one of the most decisive battles in history over the combined fleets of France and Spain off Cape Trafalgar, 21 October 1805, falling mortally wounded about an hour and a quarter after the action had begun.

¶ BRYANT, ARTHUR. *Nelson*. 1970

See also TRAFALGAR.

Neo-Gothic: architecture and art in the revived Gothic style (*see* GOTHIC ART AND ARCHITECTURE). This revival flourished chiefly in the 19th century and particularly in the building of churches, as a reaction from the classical styles, but the line from the old to the new Gothic was never completely broken.

Neolithic (from Greek *neos*, new, and *lithos*, stone): belonging to the period of neoliths, or polished stone implements – the last period of the Stone Age. The establishment of settled communities, cultivating wheat, barley and (probably) sheep, which marked the opening of the Neolithic Age in Europe, was brought about by itinerant farmers from south-west Asia. By about 3000 BC there were large settled Neolithic communities, presumably descended from the earlier local Mesolithic (middle Stone Age) hunters and fishers. The settlements became trading centres, which in their turn enabled the arts and products of the already highly developed civilisations of Asia to become widely known among these people.

¶ QUENNELL, MARJORIE and QUENNELL, C. H. B. *Everyday Life in Prehistoric Times.* 1959; DICKINSON, ALICE. *The First Book of Stone Age Man.* 1963

Nepal: independent kingdom on the slopes of the Great Himalayas north of India. Its modern history begins with its conquest in 1768 by the Gurkha Prithvi Narayan and expansion under his successors. After war against the British, 1814–16, the present boundaries were fixed, a British envoy was accepted at Katmandu and, later, Gurkha troops served with the British Indian army.

From 1847 the country was controlled, under the king, by a hereditary prime minister, an office ending with the 1951 revolution, which attempted to introduce democratic government. The king, Mahendra, suspended the constitution in 1960, and in 1963 an indirectly elected national assembly was formed.

Nero Claudius Caesar (AD 37–68): Roman Emperor 54–68. He was the son of a Roman senator and his wife Agrippina, who later married the Emperor Claudius and persuaded him to adopt Nero. His reign was marked by violence and brutality: he caused his mother and his first wife to be murdered and was insanely jealous of any rivalry, especially in the world of music and poetry, where he delighted in performing in public. He was said to have "fiddled while Rome burned" and tried to blame the ea Christians for the fire. Faced with revo he committed suicide.

Netherlands: kingdom of weste Europe on the North Sea. The Rhi delta formed part of Charlemagn empire (AD 800). A Duchy of Hollan later including Zeeland, was governed b dukes from 922 to 1417. Other importa magnates were the dukes of Guelder a the bishops of Utrecht. Flanders and t south made progress in trade and cultur but the northern provinces were bac ward until the 13th and 14th centuri when they developed fishing and carri goods to the British Isles and the Balti and reclaimed land for agriculture.

The Netherlands passed to the dukes Burgundy with the death of the last duk of Holland, and then to the Habsburg The Emperor Charles V (1500–58) w actually born in Ghent; but his son Phili II (1527–98) was born and lived in Spa and left Margaret, duchess of Parma, regent in the Netherlands. The Protesta Reformation had made progress in th northern Netherlands, and religiou antagonism was added to resentme against Spanish troops under the duke Alva and against the Spanish rulers, wh ignored the States General, representin the councils of the seventeen Netherland provinces, and persecuted the Protestant The execution in 1568 of counts Egmon and Horn, who had resisted the severity o Spanish rule, started a war of independenc led by William the Silent, Prince of Orang (1533–84). Don John of Austria persuade the southern provinces to uphold Catholi orthodoxy, but the northerners, by th Declaration of Utrecht (1579), decided t fight for religious freedom and declare their independence in 1581.

William the Silent was murdered i 1584 and was succeeded as leader of Netherlands Union by his son Maurice

ykes, canals and windmills, the famous symbols the Netherlands.

adholder or governor of five of the seven ovinces of Holland, Zeeland, Utrecht, elderland, Overijssel, Groningen and iesland. The defeat of the Spanish rmada in 1588 and successes by the nion on land led finally to a truce in 509. After further war, the independent nited Netherlands were recognised by e Peace of Westphalia in 1648.

The new republic was already a major uropean power with a growing overseas mpire in the East Indies and elsewhere. fought a series of wars, first with England, then against France. In 1688 William I, stadholder of the Netherlands, became lso king of England. It was an age of reat commercial and cultural activity or the Netherlands, with the Dutch East ndia Company successful overseas, and e Dutch school of painting at its height the work of such painters as Rembrandt nd Frans Hals (*see* separate entries). After e death of William III (1702) there was decline, but the further wars of the panish Succession (1702–13) and the ustrian Succession (1741–48) strengthned loyalty to the house of Orange.

Following the French Revolution the Netherlands were overrun by the French, nd in 1815 the great powers united the Netherlands, Belgium and Luxembourg n one kingdom under William I. This asted only fifteen years. Belgium revolted n 1830 and Luxembourg also became Independent, leaving eleven provinces. In World War II the Germans occupied the Netherlands from 1940 to 1945. The Netherlands Indies achieved complete independence in 1949. In 1948 the Netherlands joined in an economic union with Belgium and Luxembourg (Benelux) and later became a founder member of the European Economic Community.

Neutrality: the state or condition of remaining aloof from a war or controversy and assisting neither side. Thus, the federal republic of Switzerland remained neutral in both world wars, 1914–18 and 1939–45, this being one reason why the country has gained importance as the headquarters of various international organisations, including the Red Cross and the League of Nations (1920–46). It was the invasion of Belgium, whose neutrality had been guaranteed by the Great Powers, that led to Britain's declaration of war on Germany in 1914. Both world wars saw America trying to maintain a state of neutrality, till Germany's unrestricted submarine warfare forced a change of policy in 1917 and the Japanese attack on Pearl Harbour brought the same result in 1941.

New Deal: phrase used to describe the social and economic reforms of Franklin D. Roosevelt (1882–1945) between 1933 and 1939. The First New Deal (1933–35) aimed at relief and recovery from financial depression and unemployment. The Second New Deal (1935–39) was especially concerned with social security for the working population and price guarantees for small farmers.

New England: region lying to the east of the Hudson River and to the north-east of New York City. It includes the present states of Maine, New Hampshire, Vermont, Massachusetts, Rhode Island and Connecticut. It was presumably named by Captain John Smith (on his map of 1616), who discovered the rich cod fisheries off Maine. Permanent settlements began with those of the Pilgrims at Plymouth (1620), followed by the larger influx of Puritans into the Massachusetts Bay area (1630). The threat of Dutch expansion and Indian raids led to the New England Confederation (1643–84), which unified the colonists. Because New England had more extensive foreign commerce than other colonies, it was more adversely affected by the English Navigation Acts (1651–96). It was the centre of the events leading to the American Revolution, especially after 1765, and the scene of the opening engagements of the War of Independence (1775). From New England stemmed the great migration to the Northwest Territory, and prior to the Civil War the section furnished leaders for most of the social and humanitarian movements in America. It was also the leading literary and educational centre of the nation, with its well-known universities such as Harvard and Yale. In the 19th century vast numbers of immigrants from Europe changed the character of the region. The southern Irish settled in Boston and still dominate the politics of the city and its suburbs. New England remains something of a byword for social exclusiveness and moral and religious intolerance.

Newfoundland: Canadian province and former British colony, situated to the north-east of the Gulf of St Lawrence in 48° North and 52° West. It is usually said that John Cabot discovered Newfoundland in 1497, though evidence of Norse settlement antedates Cabot by 500 years. Gaspar de Cortoreal's visit in 1500 quickly brought French and Portuguese to the fisheries. Sir Humphrey Gilbert in 1583 formally annexed Newfoundland Queen Elizabeth of England. The Tre of Utrecht, 1713, confirmed Englan sovereignty. But the French claimed t fisheries on the western and southe shores and the Labrador coast, recognis as part of the colony, even after 17 when the Treaty of Paris ended the Sev Years War.

Newfoundland had a representative sembly in 1832 and responsible gover ment in 1855. Entry to the Canadi Confederation was unsuccessfully ca vassed before the British North Ameri Act of 1867. The economy's continui dependence on the fisheries was the chi factor in a financial crisis in 1894. Aid by Canadian finance, the colony ther after diversified her products into pape timber and pulp, iron and other minera A referendum in 1948 resulted in Nev foundland and Labrador joining Cana as its tenth province.

New Guinea: large East Indian isla north of Australia and only 100 mil [161 kilometres] from Cape York, fir seen by a Portuguese sailor in 1512 an settled by several European nations late The early inhabitants were a mixture races, including negroid types on the we and Melanesians, resembling south-se islanders, on the east. The Dutch colonise the west until 1963, when this territor became part of Indonesia (Irian Barat The eastern portion is now the indepe dent territory of Papua New Guinea.

New South Wales: oldest Australia colony, so named by Captain Cook i 1770. Sydney, the capital city, w founded on Port Jackson from the convi settlement and from free settlers. Trans portation of convicts ceased in 1840. Th Australian Colonies Act 1850, gave Ne South Wales self-government, thoug "squatter" sheep-farmers predominated ırgraves discovered gold in 1851, conbuting to a population increase from ,793 in 1837 to 503,981 in 1871. The 55 Constitution prefaced thirty years political, agrarian and educational adnce. Despite setbacks such as a financial sis in 1893, which forced ten banks to ɔse, and a severe drought in 1902, the lony continued to make progress and the period 1901–15 the area of land ıder cultivation was almost doubled.

ewspaper: printed publication, usually ıblished daily or weekly, giving current ·ws and opinion. The Romans had a nd of newspaper which was started by lius Caesar. During the first three nturies AD orders, official notices, births, arriages and deaths and other items of terest were written on a whitewashed ɔard and put up in a public place in ome. These were called the *Acta Diurna* 'happenings of the day"). In the Middle ges the great trading city of Venice had milar announcements posted up. These ere called *Gazettas* after the name of the ɔin charged for reading them.

Modern newspapers have their origins the handwritten newsletters sent to ıbscribers by professional news gatherers various capitals such as Vienna, Augsurg, Ratisbon and Nuremberg. This was slow process and it was not till the ıvention of printing that a real newsaper became possible. With a printing ress, many copies could be produced in fairly short time. The first English newsaper proper is generally considered to e *The Weekly Newes* issued in 1622. The

The 23. of May.

VV E E K E L Y

Nevves from Italy,

GERMANIE, HVNGARIA,

BOHEMIA, the PALATINATE,

France, and the Low Countries.

Tranſlated out of the Low Dutch Copie.

Numb.

The Daily Courant.

Wedneſday, March 11. 1702.

From the Harlem Courant, Dated March 18. N. S.

Naples, Feb. 22.

ON Wedneſday laſt, our New Viceroy, the Duke of Eſcalona, arriv'd here with a Squadron of the Galleys of Sicily. He made his Entrance dreſt in a French habit; and to give us the greater Hopes of the King's coming hither, went to Lodge in one of the little Palaces, leaving the Royal one for his Majeſty. The Marquis of Grigni is alſo arriv'd here with a Regiment of French.

Rome, Feb. 25. In a Military Congregation of State that was held here, it was Reſolv'd to draw a Line from Aſcoli to the Borders of the Eccleſiaſtical State, thereby to hinder the Incurſions of the Tranſalpine Troops. Orders are ſent to Civita Vecchia to fit out the Galleys, and to ſtrengthen the Garriſon of that Place. Signior Caſali is made Governor of Perugia. The Marquis del Vaſto, and the Prince de Caſerta continue ſtill in the Imperial Embaſſador's Palace; where his Excellency has a Guard of 50 Men every Night in Arms. The King of Portugal has deſir'd the Arch-Biſhoprick of Lisbon, vacant by the Death of Cardinal Souſa, for the Infante his ſecond Son, who is about 11 Years old.

Flanders under the Duke of Burgundy; and Duke of Maine is to Command upon the Rhine.

From the Amſterdam Courant, Dated Mar. 18

Rome, Feb. 25. We are taking here all poſſible cautions for the Security of the Eccleſiaſtical S in this preſent Conjuncture, and have deſir'd to 3000 Men in the Cantons of Switzerland. The P has appointed the Duke of Berwick to be his Li tenant-General, and he is to Command 6000 on the Frontiers of Naples: He has alſo ſettled on him a Penſion of 6000 Crowns a year during

From the Paris Gazette, Dated Mar. 18. 1702

Naples, Febr. 17. 600 French Soldiers are arri here, and are expected to be follow'd by 3400 m A Courier that came hither on the 14th. has brou Letters by which we are aſſur'd that the King Spain deſigns to be here towards the end of Mar and accordingly Orders are given to make the ceſſary Preparations againſt his Arrival. The Troops of Horſe that were Commanded to the bruzzo are poſted at Peſcara with a Body of Spa Foot, and others in the Fort of Montorio.

British government became alarmed at political and religious questions being discussed in newspapers, pamphlets and books and tried by various means to control all printing. There was great argument about "the freedom of the press", and by the time of Queen Anne (1665–1714) there were many newspapers in which politics and religion were discussed by such writers as Addison, Steele, Swift and Daniel Defoe. The first British daily newspaper the *Daily Courant* (*above*) was published in 1702. By the end of the 18th cent. news of parliament was printed in the *Morning Chronicle*, the *Morning Herald*, the *Sun* and other papers, and politicians and even the monarchy were freely criticised. During the 19th century foreign news and other new features were included and *The Times* began using steam machinery in place of printing by hand. An important factor in a vastly increased newspaper reading public was the growth of state education.

The modern newspaper contains very much more than political news. It attracts its readers by articles on sport, amusements and fashions, by cartoons and crossword puzzles, by photographs, and by advertisements. Some newspapers give away a weekly colour supplement. Producing a newspaper is now very costly indeed, and much of the cost has to come from what is paid for advertisements.

A very important part is played by provincial papers, which are able to concentrate upon the interests of particular localities much more than the great dailies. The first example in England was the *Worcester Postman*, which appeared in 1690, closely followed by the *Lincoln, Rutland and Stamford Mercury* in 1695.

The newspaper in the USA has followed much the same lines of development as in Great Britain. As early as 1619 John Pory, secretary of the Virginia Colony, was sending newsletters home to his "good and gracious lord" in London. John Campbell, postmaster at Boston, sent fairly regular news bulletins to various colonial governors in New England. These developed into the first American newspaper – *The Boston News-Letter*, which Campbell printed for the first time in April 1704. The first daily newspaper was *The Pennsylvania Packet and General Advertiser*, published in September 1784. The papers with the longest unbroken history are *The Hartford Courant*, which began life as *The Connecticut Courant* in 1764, and *The New York Evening Post*, the name of which has remained unchanged since 1801.

¶ SMITH, GEOFFREY. *News and Newspapers: the story of the British Press.* 1962; WIKERSON, MARJORIE. *News and Newspapers.* 1970

Newton, Sir Isaac (1642–1727)**:** English mathematician and man of science. Born at Woolsthorpe, Lincolnshire, he was

educated at Grantham School and Trini College, Cambridge, becoming Lucasi Professor of Mathematics at Cambrid (1669), Fellow of the Royal Society (167 MP for Cambridge University (168 Warden of the Mint (1696) and Master the Mint (1699). He was knighted Queen Anne (1705).

One of the greatest mathematicians, h chief discoveries were the Binomi Theorem; his Law of Gravitation, whi laid the foundation of modern Dynamic and his method of "fluxions". This la which we now call the Differential an Integral Calculus, was almost simu taneously discovered by Leibnitz but wi a better notation than Newton's. Th first edition of Newton's immense influential book *Principia mathematica* w published in 1687. His contributions optics and the theory of light are als notable. *See also* GRAVITATION.

¶ KNIGHT, DAVID C. *Isaac Newton, mastermind modern science.* 1963

New World: name used until the earl years of the 16th century to describe th Americas. In the early years of the 16t century a mapmaker, Waldseemulle was at work compiling a new map of th known world. He had heard of the recen voyages westwards across the Atlanti and of lands newly discovered on the fa side. The New World had first bee "discovered" in 1492–1504 by Christophe Columbus and his reports of inhabitan and products emphasised the contrast wit the "Old World" of Spain and Portugal Waldseemuller, however, based his ma in part upon the narrative of Amerig Vespucci, who, following Columbus, ha explored much of its coast. As the Nev World lacked a name, Waldseemulle named it "America" after Amerigo. Th New World made as great an impressio on the 16th-century European mind a outer space does today with us.

Jew York: chief city in the United tates and the centre of the most conested metropolitan area in the Western Iemisphere. Situated at the mouth of the Iudson River, New York comprises the ve boroughs of Manhattan, the Bronx, Brooklyn, Staten Island and Queens. As Jew Amsterdam, on the tip of the island f Manhattan, in 1626 it was the capital of ne Dutch colony of New Netherland nd so it remained until the British seized nd renamed it (after James, Duke of 'ork, subsequently James II) in 1664. The ity developed as a major commercial and nipping centre during the first half of the 8th century, and after the War of ndependence it was, briefly (1789–90), ne first capital of the emergent nation. 'he construction of the Erie Canal in 825 enlarged New York's hinterland and became the financial, commercial and nipping capital of the United States. The inancing of vast railway networks inreased the significance and power of Vall Street, where New York's bankers ongregated. Before the Civil War, imnigrants poured into the city from Europe, creating vast slum areas on the ower East Side. After the Civil War, nigration from the South made the opulation of Harlem predominantly Jegro. In the 20th century New York ecame the mecca of those seeking careers n trade, finance and the arts. The city has ong been a centre of musical activity and the headquarters of American drama Broadway). Today the city still retains s predominance in the political and ultural life of the nation, and its experince in attempting to make city life olerable in the 20th century is being tudied by all major conurbations. New 'ork is also the name of a state (nickamed the "Empire State"), touching Canada in the north and the Atlantic in ne south, with Albany as its capital.

See AMERICA for map.

New Zealand: since 1907 a self-governing dominion of the British Commonwealth, comprising two large and numerous small islands in the Pacific. Though Tasman sighted the South Island mountains in 1642, our only knowledge of "Ao-te-roa", the "Long White Cloud", derives from Maori story until Cook's voyage of 1769–70. Missionaries landed in 1814, with Samuel Marsden from New South Wales (*see* separate entry), who, during a visit to London in 1807, had been presented by George III with five Spanish sheep that were the ancestors of many of the great Australian flocks. Marsden favoured the appointment of an officer to supervise the colony, but the first, James Busby, who was subordinate to New South Wales, failed to unite the Maori tribes. Edward Gibbon Wakefield (1796–1862) in 1839 organised the New Zealand Company for land purchase and settlement, stressing the danger of French annexation. The government, questioning the legality of such purchases from the chiefs and fearing Maori risings, annexed New Zealand to New South Wales in 1840. The Treaty of Waitangi, 1840, guaranteed the possession of their lands to the Maoris, with a Crown right to purchase. Wakefield's systematic settlement against official opposition encouraged colonisation, and Maori dissatisfaction smouldered until, under the governorship of Robert Fitzroy (1805–65), who had commanded the *Beagle* on Darwin's famous voyage, it broke out into the native war of 1845–48. From 1845 to 1853 a strong governor, Captain George Grey, worked for peace, held a fair balance between the races and brought about a measure of prosperity, permitting settlement in the least populated areas. In 1848 Presbyterian Scots settled at Dunedin in Otago district, and in 1850 Anglicans founded Canterbury and Christchurch. Grey gave the colony

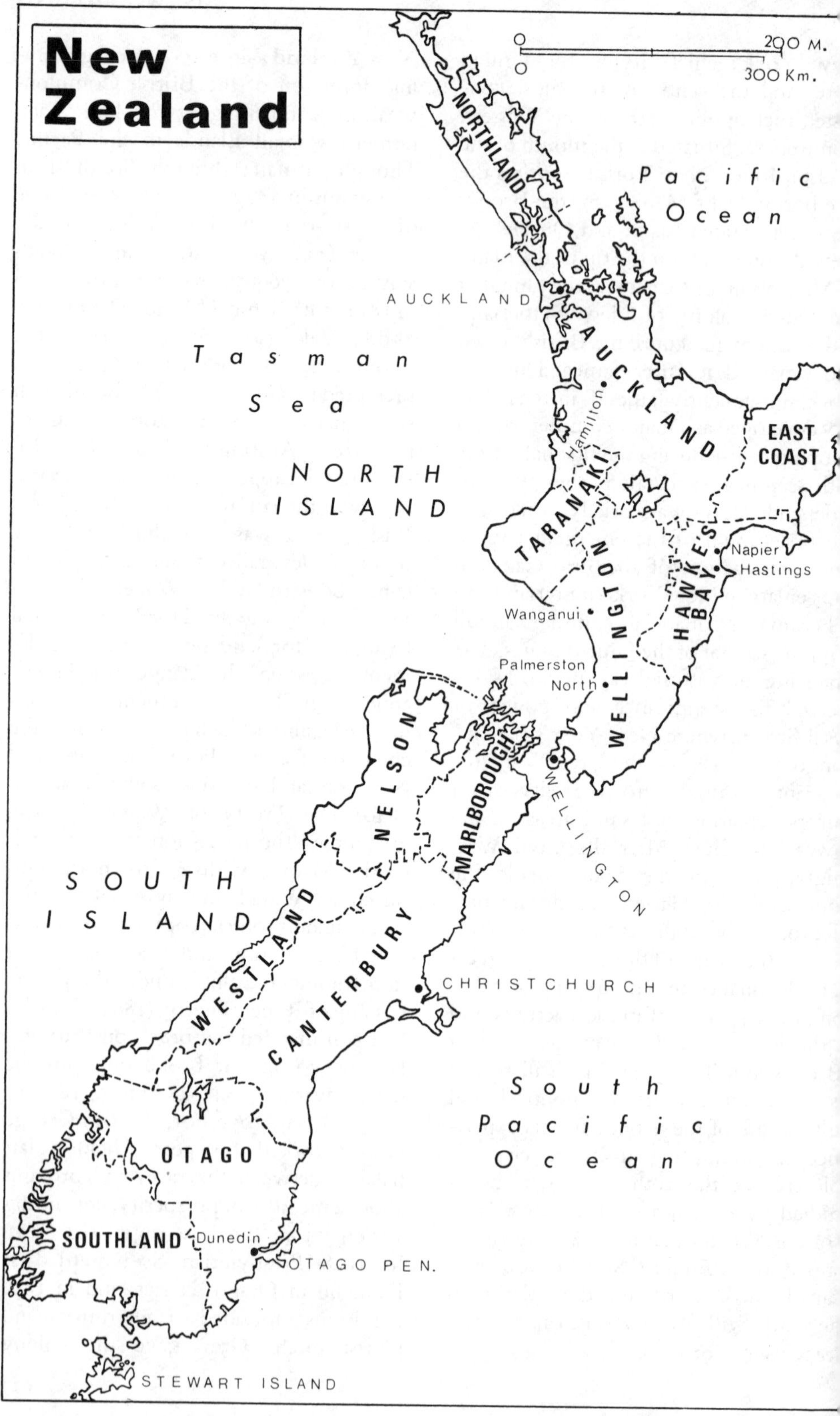

New Zealand

0 200 M.
0 300 Km.

NORTHLAND
Pacific Ocean
AUCKLAND
AUCKLAND
Tasman Sea
Hamilton
EAST COAST
NORTH ISLAND
TARANAKI
HAWKE'S BAY
Napier
Hastings
WELLINGTON
Wanganui
Palmerston North
NELSON
MARLBOROUGH
WELLINGTON
SOUTH ISLAND
WESTLAND
CANTERBURY
CHRISTCHURCH
South Pacific Ocean
OTAGO
SOUTHLAND
Dunedin
OTAGO PEN.
STEWART ISLAND

ponsible government by the New aland Constitution Act of 1852, with ovincial parliaments.

hough government purchase of land d replaced Company activities, the aoris still felt threatened. The sending t again of Grey, the "Good Gover-r", for a further term of office could t prevent bitter warfare between 1860 d 1870. After the war, the Colonial Act olished provincial parliaments and ve representation to the Maoris in the ower House. The Native Schools Act rther fostered racial partnership.

Despite the discovery of gold at Otago 1861, New Zealand retained its sentially agricultural economy, though e Budget of 1870 encouraged rail-ay construction and new industries. ew Zealand supported Britain in both orld Wars and has maintained tradi-onal ties with her since. At the same me she has become increasingly involv-d in Asian affairs: she sent forces to orea, joined ANZUS (with Australia d the USA) and concentrates her aid pon countries in the region. Her policy rbidding nuclear-armed ships to enter er ports led to a row with her ANZUS artner, the USA, in 1985.

---

icholas I (1796–1855): Tsar of Russia 325–55. Third son of Paul I, he succeeded is brother Alexander I in 1825. In ontrast with Alexander, who was vaguely beral and had played with schemes of lf-government and constitutional rule Poland and Finland, Nicholas was a ncerely convinced autocrat. He helped suppressing popular risings in the ustrian Empire as well as in his own ominions. He extended Russian territory nd power in Asia and hoped to benefit rom a break-up of the Turkish Empire nd to obtain Constantinople. His policy d to the Crimean War.

ee also CRIMEAN WAR.

Nicholas II (1868–1918): Tsar of Russia 1894–1917. Born in 1868 he succeeded in 1894. In 1898 he issued an appeal for international peace, resulting in the first Hague peace conference of 1899. He conceded parliamentary institutions to Russia but also arbitrarily retracted con-cessions. His armies fought the disastrous Russo-Japanese war of 1904–05 and suf-fered heavy defeats in World War I. He was forced to abdicate in March 1917 and was murdered with his family in July 1918. He was the last Tsar of Russia.

Nigeria: republic of West Africa named after the Niger, one of the four great rivers of Africa. Among its many peoples the three main groups are the Hausas in the north, the Yorubas in the south-west, and the Ibos in the south-east but al-together there are about 250 ethnic or tribal groups. It is the most populous country in Africa with an estimated 90 million people in 1982.

One of the earliest known African civilisations, the Nok culture, flourished on the Jos Plateau from 900 BC to 200 AD. And from the region of Nigeria great migrations spread across Africa – east-wards to the lakes and then south, or south through the tropical forests of Zaire – beginning about 500 BC and only ending in modern times. The Kanem-Bornu Empire (centred upon Lake Chad) arose about 800 and by the 13th century stretched as far as Kano. In the south the Yoruba kingdom of Oyo and the Ebo kingdom of Benin reached considerable heights of culture and organisation be-tween the 12th and 16th centuries. From the 16th century onwards the coast was much affected by the slave trade. After 1815 the British became the dominant power on the coast. Britain annexed Lagos Island in 1861 and by 1885 had proclaimed her rule over most of the coastal regions. Britain then extended her control over the interior and by 1914 had become master of the whole country whose separate protectorates she merged that year to form Nigeria. The first governor-general was Lord Lugard, whose name became linked with the idea of indirect rule (through the emirs) which he pioneered in the north. In the period between the wars colonial government was firmly established.

Nigeria became independent in 1960 but deep rivalries between the three main ethnic groups produced tensions which led the Ibos to attempt secession in 1967 when they proclaimed the state of Biafra. The Nigerian Civil War lasted for 30 months; at its conclusion (January 1970) parts of the former eastern region were ravaged and starving. The decade of the 1970s saw the rehabilitation of the defeated Ibos, huge development as a result of the country's new oil wealth, and the emergence of Nigeria as leading spokesman for Black Africa. In 1979 the military who had ruled the country since 1966 returned power to the civilians but four years later (at the end of 1983) the army again resumed political control.

¶ WATSON, JANE WERNER. *Nigeria: republic of a hundred kings*. 1970

Nightingale, Florence (1820–1910): reformer of hospital nursing. After considerable study of hospitals and nursing discipline both in England and abroad, she first came into prominence in 1854 when she was invited to the Crimea to organise the nursing of the British sick and wounded sent back from the battle front. At Scutari, on the eastern shore of Bosporus, and elsewhere, she succeeded, in spite of much opposition from the military authorities, in transforming the hospitals, often working for twenty hours at a stretch, and bringing the death rate down from 42 per cent 2 per cent in a few months. She w known as "The Lady of the Lamp". May 1855 she visited Balaklava, wh she caught Crimean fever and was d perately ill for twelve days.

She returned to England in 1856 and f more than forty years, despite frailty body, continued her work for nursi and hospitals, her greatest achieveme being the development of adequate trai ing for nurses. Nurses trained at Thomas's Hospital, where she found her first establishment, are still nic named "Nightingales".

¶ HARMELINK, BARBARA. *Florence Nighting Founder of Modern Nursing*. 1972

See also CRIMEAN WAR; NURSING.

Nile: the world's longest river. It rises Lake Victoria 3,900 feet [1188 metre above sea level, and runs through La Kioga and Lake Albert, then on Khartoum as the White Nile, bein joined there by the Blue Nile, after whic it is simply the Nile, finally entering t Mediterranean by a many-branched delt Its length from the source of the Whi Nile is 4,053 miles [6522 kilometres].

¶ MOOREHEAD, ALAN. *The Blue Nile*. 1965; MOOR HEAD, ALAN. *The White Nile*. 1966

Nile, Battle of the, sometimes calle the **Battle of Aboukir Bay,** (1 Augu 1798): British naval victory by whic Nelson destroyed the French fleet and c off Napoleon's army in Egypt, ensurin the failure of the French expedition.

Nineteenth Century: 1801–1900. Th military dictatorship established in Franc by Napoleon Bonaparte (1769–1821) w an unforeseen outcome of the Frenc Revolution. His Grand Army passed ove Europe, sweeping feudal and ecclesiastic privilege away. At the same time, peop the conquered countries, resenting ·ir subjection to France, first awoke a sense of their own national identity. It .s a realisation which was to remake : map of Europe. In 1815, after poleon's final defeat at the Battle of aterloo, the great powers tried in vain restore the old order.

he industrial revolution, in which itain led the way, turned her in the th century into the wealthiest industrial tion in the world. New processes were covered, factories were built, roads, lways and steamships were developed; : middle classes increased in numbers, wer and wealth. The other side of the in was to be found in the overcrowded ıms where workers lived and their long urs of work for pitiful pay in often palling conditions. Gradually, through e work of social reformers such as Lord aftesbury (1801–85), a series of Factory cts and Mines Acts remedied some of e worst abuses. Workers began to ganise themselves into trade unions. eform Acts brought parliamentary mocracy nearer reality, and in 1870 the st Education Act was passed.

ndustries can only expand if raw aterials are available, as well as customers whom the finished products can be ld: hence the importance to Britain of Empire which could supply both. But ritain did not have all her own way. ther nations which were developing eir industries entered the competition r colonial lands and markets. Some of em – Belgium, Italy, Germany – were olitical creations of the 19th century. he rivalry which developed among the uropean powers for the one remaining nexploited continent has been aptly lled "the scramble for Africa".

In the scramble the French spread out ong the North African coast and southard into the Sahara. Belgium took the ongo, Italy and Germany other parts of Africa. Britain, as the major shareholder in the Suez Canal (opened 1869), controlled Egypt. She also occupied large areas in the southern half of the continent, where her differences with the Boers, settlers of Dutch origin, eventually led to the Boer War (1899–1902).

The greed for land and markets sowed the seeds of many wars. China was forced at gunpoint to grant trade and territorial concessions to the western powers. In 1853 a squadron of the US Navy anchored off Uraga, in Japan. The sight of western battleships brought Japan out of its medieval isolation into the modern world. Having decided to imitate western ways Japan became itself an aggressive imperial power, strong enough by 1904 to defeat Tsarist Russia.

Russia in the 19th century was a country where a small privileged class enjoyed a high level of culture while the great majority of the population consisted of peasants living in a state of serfdom. In 1861 Tsar Alexander II (1818–81) freed the serfs, but their material condition did not greatly improve. All reforms came to an abrupt halt in 1881 when the Tsar was assassinated. Thereafter liberal movements, however moderate, were driven underground, a state of affairs which ensured that when change came at last to Russia, as it did in 1917, it would be a violent explosion.

It is odd to reflect that the bible of the Russian Communist revolution, *Das Kapital*, was largely written in the British Museum Reading Room. It was the work of an exiled German socialist, Karl Marx (1818–83). The widespread and continuing influence of Marx's political theories makes him one of the most significant personalities of the 19th century.

Another was Charles Darwin (1809–82) whose theory of Evolution, expounded in his book *On the Origin of Species by Means of Natural Selection* (1859), shook the religious beliefs of the century. Darwin himself, as it happened, was a religious man; but people who took the Bible for literal truth attacked him.

It was during the 19th century that the United States of America emerged as a great power. Settlers poured in from Europe, some impelled by hunger, some by religious or political persecution, and others by ambition and love of adventure. Thousands of Irish people emigrated to the USA following the great Potato Famine of 1846, in which a million of their countrymen died of hunger. Towards the end of the century there occurred many brutal massacres (called *pogroms*, a Russian word meaning "destruction") of Jews living in Russia and parts of Poland. As a result Jews left Eastern Europe in large numbers, the majority going to the United States.

Ironically, the United States, the goal of the poor and oppressed, had its own problem of poverty and oppression. In the Southern states Negroes were still kept in slavery, a condition it took a civil war (1861–65) to put right. Unfortunately, Abraham Lincoln (1809–65), the American president, was assassinated soon after the close of the war, and the removal of his wise and moderating influence at a crucial time left the country with many unsolved problems.

(Era Histories 8). 1967; HART, ROGER. *English Life in the Nineteenth Century*. 1971

See also AMERICAN CIVIL WAR; BOER WAR; FRENCH REVOLUTION; INDUSTRIAL REVOLUTION; LINCOLN, ABRAHAM; NAPOLEON I.

Nineveh: ancient city on the River Tigris, about 500 miles [805 kilometres] from the head of the Persian Gulf and near the modern town of Mosul. It was the capital of the Assyrian Empire and was destroyed in 612 BC. The ruins were uncovered by Sir Austen Henry Layard (1817–94).

Nobel Prize Medal.

Nobel, Alfred Bernhard (1833–96 Swedish chemist and inventor. Nob was especially interested in explosives ar in 1867 he discovered the powerf explosive mixture, dynamite. From th and other inventions he became a ve rich man. When he died he left most his great fortune to provide five priz every year for outstanding work in phy sics, chemistry, medicine, literature an for services in the cause of world peac Each prize is worth about $192,000, an all prizes are open to men and wome in all countries of the world. Since th awards began, many famous people (an many not so well known to the gener public) of various nationalities hav received a Nobel prize. The first winner in 1901, were: W. E. Röntgen (Germa for physics; J. H. van't Hoff (Dutch) fo his work in stereochemistry; E. A. Vo Behring (German) for his work o tetanus and diphtheria; R. F. A. Sully Prudhomme (French) for poetry; an the peace prize was shared between H Durant (Swiss), the founder of the Re Cross, and F. passy (French). Seven priz were awarded in 1983.

Nomads: members of tribes that lead wandering life seeking pasture for the flocks. Much early history is the story the coming of such wandering folk int led communities, sometimes of a erent culture. Some areas of the world demand a nomadic way of life, e.g. land, where the inhabitants support mselves by herding reindeer.

rdenskiöld, Baron Nils Adolf Eric 32–1901): Swedish explorer and geo-pher. After expeditions to the Arctic l Spitzbergen, he was the first to navi-e the North-east Passage in 1878–79 in steamship *Vega*. The results of this loration, published 1882–87, and his ok *Periplus*, 1897, contributed greatly geographic and scientific research.

rman Kings: the four rulers of gland, 1066–1154.

William I (1066–87), the bastard son of bert III, Duke of Normandy, and lette, a tanner's daughter, was born at laise in 1027. Edward the Confessor omised him the English throne, but rold, Earl of Wessex, became king in uary 1066, and William therefore vaded England, winning the Battle of stings (14 October 1066). He ruthlessly ushed all rebellions, strengthened the udal system, built strong castles, e.g. the White Tower of London, and had the support of the Church under Archbishop Lanfranc. The Domesday Book (1086) was made largely for taxation purposes.

2. William II (1087–1100), the second son of William I, succeeded as king of England, and his elder brother Robert became Duke of Normandy, according to their father's wish. An unscrupulous, bad-tempered bully, he forced Archbishop Anselm into exile, but he was a powerful and able ruler. He was killed by an arrow in the New Forest.

3. Henry I (1100–35), the youngest and ablest of William I's sons, defeated Robert and secured Normandy. The chroniclers praised him warmly – "good man was he and there was great awe of him" – and nicknamed him the Lion of Justice.

4. Stephen (1135–54), son of William I's daughter Adela, "a mild good man", was preferred as ruler to Matilda, Henry I's daughter. "Nineteen long winters" of civil war followed, ended by the Treaty of Winchester (1153) making Matilda's son Henry successor to Stephen.

¶ DOREY, ALAN and LEON, A. *The Norman Kings*. 1964

e four Norman Kings: William I, William fus, Henry I and Stephen.

Normandy: province of France bordering the English Channel. It took its name from the Vikings or Northmen who raided it in the 9th century. This ancestry gave the Normans a hardihood and enterprise which marked much of their history. Normandy became closely linked with the fortunes of England after Duke William conquered England in 1066. For nearly 150 years it remained intermittently in English hands and was torn by the Hundred Years War. Normandy was finally secured by France in 1450. Its unfortunate role as one of the most battle-scarred areas of Europe was revived in both world wars. The final defeat of Germany began with landings in Normandy under Eisenhower (6 June 1944).

North America: the northern part of the land mass comprising the Americas of the western hemisphere, which includes continental United States and Canada, Mexico and the countries and islands of the Caribbean area. As thus defined it is the third largest continent, occupying slightly above sixteen per cent of the earth's land area, with a population approaching 300 million. Tremendous cultural differences exist between the two major components of the continent. Canada and the United States have both experienced the colonising effects of Great Britain, and many examples of their common heritage are evident, including a common language, similar political and legal institutions, and many everyday customs. The rest of the continent received its cultural institutions from Spain and Portugal and, like the countries of South America, is primarily Latin in its culture.

The first Europeans to discover America were the Northmen, part of a population movement that took Scandinavians to Normandy, Scotland, England, Ireland and the islands to the west and north between AD 700 and 1100. They were pirates, plunderers, traders, and settlers attracted by coastal waters teeming with fish, or driven by population pressures, or by the wrath of rivals or rulers at home. The Northmen sailed by way of Iceland and Greenland and made settlements on the coast between Labrador and New England. These settlements were temporary and it was not until the nations of the Atlantic seaboard of Europe entered into an age of geographical discovery in the 15th century that attempts at permanent colonisation were made. The rise to eminence of the national states of Portugal, Spain, France, England and the United Netherlands coincided with this age of discovery.

In the tradition of militant Christianity, Europe wished to convert the non-Christians of the world. With the con of the Reformation in the early century, religious differences sharp national rivalries as Protestants trie outstrip the Roman Catholic Spanish Portuguese, whose kings had divided newly discovered areas of the world papal approval in the Treaty of Torde in 1494.

By the middle of the 16th century m of southern and north-eastern N America was known to Europeans. Sa passed along the Atlantic coast an main features were being accura represented on the maps of the per Though few penetrated inland, ex perhaps up some of the great river favourable picture was given of coastal lands from Cape Cod to Flor Settlers were attracted by the beauty riches of this land, but some were ru disillusioned by disease, Indian attack severe winters.

Towards the end of the 16th cent three areas along the Atlantic seabo came to be settled by people of Europ stock. The French settled in the valley the St Lawrence River, from the sea u Montreal. Grain crops were grown cattle reared, but fishing and trapping wild, fur-bearing animals offered a me of livelihood no less important. French also settled in the valleys of Ohio and Mississippi Rivers, this a being known as Louisiana. The other t main settlements were by the Briti the essentially Puritan colonies of N England and those of the "gentlem adventurers (and the slaves they impor from West Africa) in the tobacco grow plantation settlements of Maryland Virginia. There was also limited Span settlement in Florida and New Spain.

In the mid-18th century the total num of settlers was small. In the whole of French-settled areas there were proba no more than 20,000 white people. T

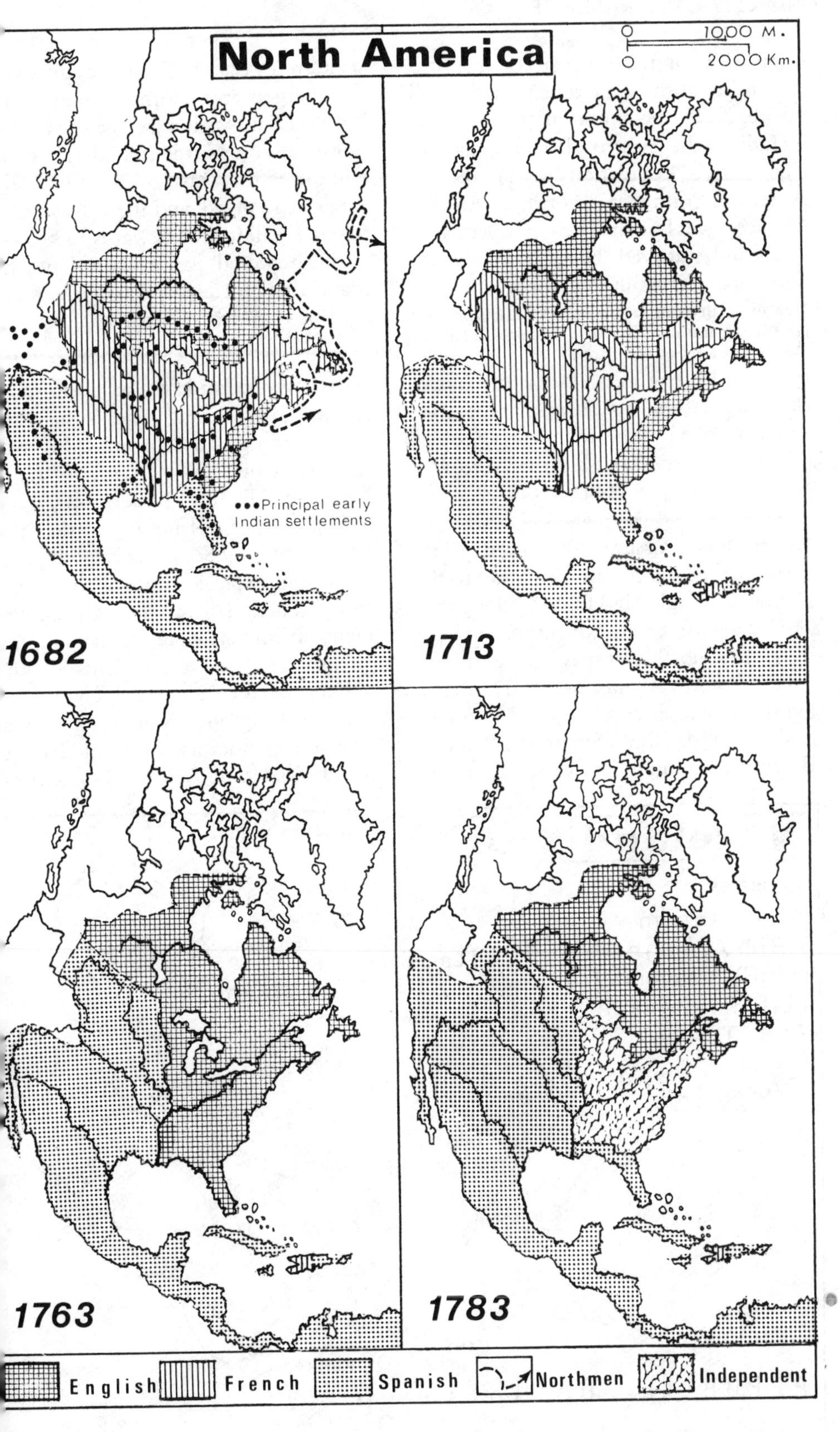
North America
0 1000 M.
0 2000 Km.
•••Principal early Indian settlements
1682
1713
1763
1783
English
French
Spanish
Northmen
Independent

population of the English colonies was larger, but at the same time probably did not exceed one-and-a-quarter million, including the Negro slave population. The native population of the North American continent – north, at least, of Mexico – was Indian. Their numbers were small and scattered, being probably not more than two million in total.

¶ BROWN, GEORGE W., HARMAN, ELEANOR and JEANNERET, MARSH. *The American Colonies: Canada and the USA before 1800.* 1962

For later history *see* AMERICA, DISCOVERY OF; AMERICAN COLONIES; CANADA; MEXICO; etc. For some of the early peoples of America *see* AZTECS; INDIANS, NORTH AMERICAN; MAYAN CIVILISATION.

North-East Passage: the eastern route from Europe via the Arctic Ocean to the Pacific. Though Sir Hugh Willoughby, sent by the Merchant Adventurers in 1553 to seek a north-east passage, perished, Chancellor's overland journey to Moscow led to the Muscovy Company's foundation. In 1594 the Dutchman William Barentz explored Novaya Zemlya's western coasts. In 1596 he discove Spitzbergen and Bjornaya, wintered Novaya Zemlya, but died before reach home. Baron Nordenskiöld was firs complete the passage to the Ber Strait in 1878–79, and the Russian Co mander Vilkitski westwards in 1913- Atom-powered ice-breakers have n made the North-east Passage a feasi sea lane to northern Siberia.

Northern Ireland: the six north-east counties of Ireland, which had th own provincial government at Storm (Belfast) while still part of the Uni Kingdom. Eastern Ulster, one of richest parts of Ireland, was settled in 17th century by Scots and English prot tants who expelled most of the cath Irish. When, late in the 19th centu many Irishmen were demanding se government, the descendants of th settlers feared rule by relatively poor a backward catholics. Some English Co servative politicians, resenting Irish d mands for Home Rule, encouraged pr

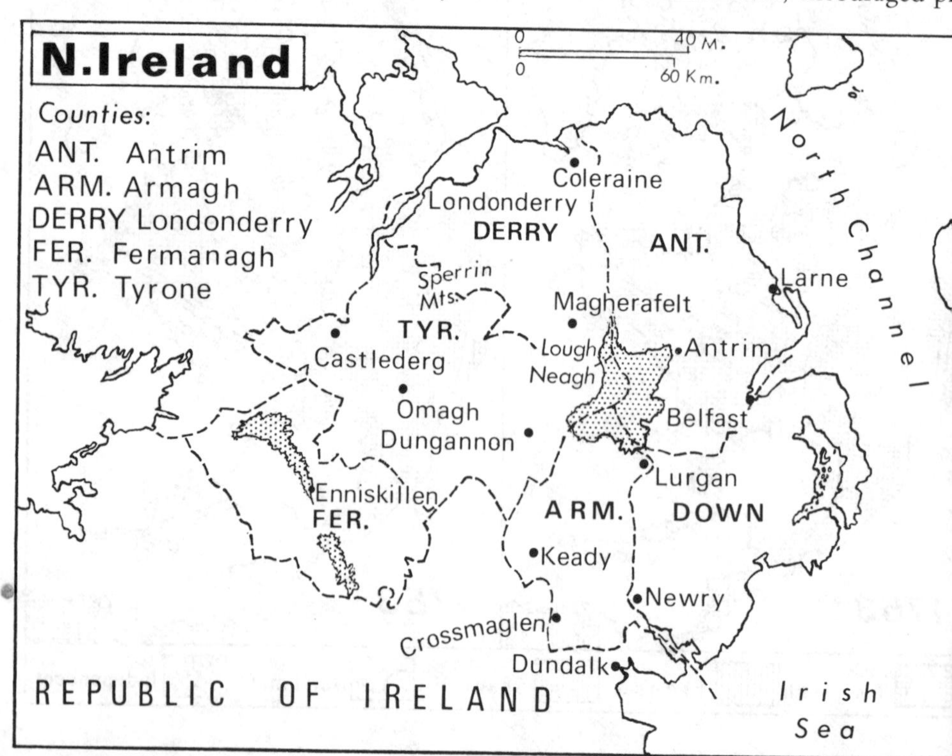

tant fears. In 1886 Lord Randolph ıurchill coined the slogan "Ulster will right". When Irish self-government emed imminent in 1912, many Ulster-en joined in a Covenant to "defeat the esent conspiracy to set up a Home Rule rliament" and preserve their United ingdom citizenship. The leader of these nionists was Sir Edward Carson (1854–35), a forceful Conservative statesman Irish protestant origin; and they cruited an armed Volunteer Force for e fray. So determined were they never accept catholic rule that in 1920 the ritish Government established a separate arliament for the six counties, where ıost of the protestants lived. Northern eland has resisted all attempts at reunion ith Ireland.

After disturbances in Belfast and Lon-onderry in August 1969, responsibility or security was given to the British Army. April 1972, direct rule was imposed fter the breakdown of talks between the ritish Prime Minister (Mr Edward Ieath) and the Prime Minister of Nor-ıern Ireland (Mr Brian Faulkner, leader f the Unionist Party). The political situ-tion was to remain troubled throughout he 1970s and into the 1980s with vio-ence by extremists on both sides, IRA omb outrages and periodic meetings etween British and Irish Prime Minis-ers to find a solution. By 1985, at least acitly, it had been accepted in London hat Dublin could not be ignored if any ong-term solution (none was then in ight) was to work.

North-West Frontier (Province)**:** the "tribal areas" of mountainous country on he north-west of western Pakistan, a eparate province from 1901–55 and evived in 1970. It lies on the "pass routes" Khyber, Malakand, etc.) to Afghanistan nd neighbouring areas. The district has een, historically, in the hands of Persians, Greeks, Sakas, Parthians, Arabs, and Turks; the last established Muslim ascendancy, though rule from Afghanistan was not effective. Sikh invasions began in 1818, and in 1849 the British annexed the area. In 1947 a referendum favoured joining Pakistan. The Afghans carried out two incursions (in 1960–61) aiming at a separate *Pathanistan*, but since 1963 they seem to have accepted the settlement.

North-West Passage: navigable route to Asia round North America. Martin Frobisher (1535?–94), sponsored by English merchants, in 1576 sailed to the Bay named after him and Baffin Island, and twice returned to the search. John Davis (1550?–1605) in 1585, 1586 and 1587 explored the Greenland coast and sailed into Baffin Bay. In 1607 Henry Hudson (d. 1611), commissioned by the Muscovy Company to find a passage via the Pole, reached the eightieth parallel. In the next decades the Dane, Jens Munk, and others sought a passage via the bay Hudson entered in 1610. In 1616 William Baffin (*c.* 1584–1622), exploring the bay named after him, discovered Lancaster Sound. The Hudson's Bay Company (1670) fostered both trade and exploration until, in the early 19th century, governments became interested. The disastrous 1845 expedition of Sir John Franklin (*see* separate entry) inspired numerous combined exploration and rescue operations. In 1850 Robert McClure (1807–73), sailing eastwards in *Investigator*, completed the passage, though largely overland, after having to abandon his ship. In 1859 Francis McClintock charted a route which the Norwegian Roald Amundsen (1872–1928) followed in navigating the passage in 1903–04. In the 1940s Larsen made the return voyage from Vancouver to Nova Scotia. In 1957 a deeper channel via Bellot Strait was discovered.

¶ NEATBY, LESLIE H. *In Quest of the North-West Passage*. 1958

Norway: kingdom in north-west Europe, with a long Atlantic seaboard. Though human life there can be traced back to 12,000 BC, Norway entered European history only when pressure of population and the rise of kings caused restless *jarls* to seek an outlet overseas. Harold Fairhair (AD 850–933) made his jarls feel the weight of his royal power, and the *vikings*, men of the *viks*, or creeks, raided abroad and presently made settlements in the Orkneys, Shetlands and Hebrides, Scotland, Ireland, Wales, northern England and the Isle of Man, and colonised Greenland, Iceland and the Faroes. At the beginning of the 11th century Norwegian vikings discovered North America.

Christianity was adopted in Norway under Olav Tryggvesson, who ruled 995–1000. In the 11th century Norway passed under the rule of Canute the Great of Denmark (*c.* 994–1035) (*see* separate entry) who invaded England and was its sole ruler from 1016 until his death. In 1066 the Norwegian king Harold Hardrada tried to conquer England. The 12th century saw civil war and much bloodshed in Norway, and the 13th century witnessed the last period of true Norwegian independence for some five hundred years. Trade and town life developed, particularly at Bergen, by intercourse with the German Hanseatic ports.

By the Union of Kalmar, 1397, Norway, Denmark and Sweden were brought under the one king; but the Swedes broke away and the union ended finally in 1523. Norway existed in obscurity under Danish domination. Through Bergen the German Reformation entered Norway and gave it a Lutheran national church.

Wars between Denmark and Sweden brought to the latter some Norwegian provinces. Royal absolutism in Denmark from 1660 gave Norway stability, and culture and literature developed. The wars of Charles XII of Sweden (1700–2[illegible] affected Norway little; and Norway was not involved in Sweden's disasters and dismemberment in 1808–09. But when the Swedes joined the last coalition against Napoleon, they obtained a transfer of Norway to Swedish rule to compensate for Sweden's loss of Finland. Norway was ceded to Sweden by the Treaty of Kiel in 1814. Norwegians objected, formed their own constitution and elected a king, but had to capitulate and accept an act of union. Under the Swedish crown Norway retained its own constitution and later even had its own flag. In 1905 the Norwegian Storting voted in favour of dissolution of the union. Sweden conceded this, and Prince Carl of Denmark was chosen king as Haakon VII.

Norway adopted women's suffrage in 1913. The country developed a large merchant shipping industry and wood pulp industries, making great use of hydroelectric power. Labour governments have often been in office since 1935 and a welfare state began to develop with old age pensions in 1936.

In April 1940 Germany invaded Norway. Haakon VII and his cabinet escaped to London. Norway regained her freedom in 1945 and was a founder member of NATO in 1949. Norway has free trade with Sweden, Denmark, Finland and Iceland. In 1960 she became a member of the EFTA but in a referendum of 1971 rejected membership of the EEC. Her long-term economic prospects have been transformed by oil and gas finds in the North Sea.

Nova Scotia: Canadian province lying between 43° and 47° N and 59°40′ and 66° 25′ W. In 1605 it was occupied by French colonists and named Acadia, but Sir William Alexander, who was given jurisdiction over the territory by James I of England, changed the name in 1621.

he Treaty of St Germain-en-Laye, 1632, stored rench suzerainty. Cromwell nt occupying forces in 1654, but by the reaty of Breda, 1677, the French re- urned. Nova Scotia finally became ritish in 1713, and in 1755 most French habitants withdrew. The colonists had presentative government from 1758, ully responsible legislative powers in 848, and Canadian provincial status in 867. The capital, Halifax, was vital to tlantic strategy in both world wars.

Nuclear power: power derived from tomic energy. The atom consists of a entral nucleus surrounded by a number f negatively charged particles called lectrons. The nucleus consists of posi- ively charged particles (protons) and articles without charge (neutrons). Hydrogen, in its ordinary form, has one lectron and a nucleus of one proton, and his structure becomes more and more omplex as we proceed to the heavier lements, such as uranium.

Ordinary chemical reactions are associ- ted with the outer electron structure, vhile atomic energy is derived from the ucleus. Energy can be released from the ucleus in two ways: (1) by fission (split- ing) of the nucleus of a heavy element nto two different lighter elements, or (2) by fusion of the nuclei of lighter elements. The first is the principle of the first tomic bomb, the second that of the vastly more powerful hydrogen bomb.

For producing industrial power these processes must be slowed down. This has been achieved in the fission process, and nuclear power stations use Uranium 235, subjected to a controlled bombardment of neutrons; but so far a controlled reaction of the second type has not been devised.

It has been estimated that the energy from the fission process is about 100 times that of existing coal and oil reserves; moreover, the fusion process might yield as much as 100 million times that of those reserves.

Numerals: symbols by which numbers are represented. These came long after people had learned to count. It has been suggested that an early method of counting beyond ten was to employ two men; the first held up one finger to represent one unit and when all ten were used up the second man held up one finger to represent ten. The Mayan civilisation of Yucatan used a scale of twenty, representing numbers by a combination of dots and dashes, the dot representing one and the dash five. In the Near East vertical strokes were used (e.g. IIII for four); in the Far East they were usually horizontal, and it is possible that 2 and 3 are the result of writing cursively = and ≡. All these symbols probably represented fingers, and we still use the word digit in two senses. In the same way the Roman V represented the open hand, and the X

two Vs combined. C stood for *centum* and M for *mille*.

The Greeks used the first nine letters of the alphabet for 1 to 9, the next nine letters for tens from 10 to 90, and the next nine for hundreds from 100 to 900. As their alphabet contained only twenty-four letters they reinserted two obsolete letters (*digamma* and *koppa*) and a third symbol from the Phoenician alphabet.

Our own familiar numerals seem to have developed from the Devangari numerals used in India in the 8th century, modified by the Eastern Arabs and again by the Western Arabs or Moors. The oldest known European manuscript containing our modern numerals was written in Spain in AD 976.

Nuremberg: leading manufacturing town of northern Bavaria, West Germany, medieval centre of commerce and of the German Renaissance. Among its later and less enviable claims to fame, it gave its name to the vicious Nazi anti-Semitic laws (1935) and was the setting for the trials of the leading Nazi war criminals (1945–46).

Nursing: tending the sick and injured. In ancient civilisations, nursing was done at home, by the women of the family, and was regarded as part of their duty. The word "nurse" comes from a Latin word, *nutrire*, meaning to nourish or to cherish, and has been applied to the care of the very old and the very young, as well as to the sick. Invalids were sometimes brought to temples to be healed, but there the nursing was done by male priests and slaves.

The early Christian communities appointed *deaconesses* whose principal duty was to tend the sick. After the establishment of monastic orders, their work was continued by nuns. Patients were taken to the infirmary of a religious house to be looked after, and certain orders of nuns became especially skilled in nursin The Augustinian Sisters of the *Hotel-Di* Paris, are the oldest nursing order in t world. A nun always wore a veil; this why a modern nurse wears a white ca A nun was addressed as "sister" – so is senior nurse.

During the Crusades an order of knigh was founded whose duty was to prote and nurse the wounded. They worked the Hospital of St John at Jerusalem an were known as Knights Hospitallers Knights of St John. When the Tur captured Jerusalem in 1187 the Knights St John fled to Malta, where they built large infirmary. Women were admitte to the order as nurses. Its badge was th Maltese cross worn today by members the St John's Ambulance Service.

When Henry VIII closed monasteri and convents in England, some hospita were established because homeless sic people had nowhere to go. In Franc Vincent de Paul, a priest, together wit Mademoiselle de Gras, a wealthy Parisia lady, recruited a band of young country women and taught them the art nursing. They were known as Sisters Charity, whose communities are no found all over the world.

In 1836 a German pastor, Theodc Fliedner, and his wife established nea Dusseldorf a hospital where "women c good character" could be properly traine in nursing. Frau Fliedner's notes on thei training became the first nursing tex book. It was read with great interest b Elizabeth Fry, who visited the Fliedners hospital. Florence Nightingale (*see* separate entry) was another visitor to th Fliedners, and was influenced by th Sisters of Charity. Through her influence nursing in England became a real profession, with its own council, examination and rules.

¶ EDWARDS-REES, DESIREE. *The Story of Nursing* 1965

O

ak: common name for trees belonging
genus *Quercus*, distributed over much
the world. To Britons and Germans
e oak means strength. It is also a symbol
age. Pliny mentioned oaks in Rome
der than the city itself, and there are a
w trees in England probably seen by the
ıxon kings. Oak timber is hard and rots
owly. For this reason it was a favourite
ipbuilding timber. The Coronation
hair, made of oak by Master Walter
Durham in 1300 is still used for the
ronation of every English monarch.
mong oak trees famous in history are
e Boscobel or Royal Oak in which
harles II of England hid after the battle
Worcester (1651), and the Charter Oak,
Hartford, Connecticut, USA, its site
ow marked by a memorial. In 1687 the
nglish governor Andros came to take
way the royal charter originally granted
the colony of Connecticut, since it
ave the colonists too much independence.
t his meeting with the officials the
ndles were suddenly extinguished. By
e time they had been rekindled the
harter had been removed from the con-
rence table and hidden in the oak tree.

he Coronation Chair in Westminster Abbey.

Oakum: old shredded rope, usually tarred, driven into the seams (or spaces between planks) of ships by mallet and chisel to make them watertight. "Picking oakum" (i.e. untwisting old ropes) was formerly a common occupation in prisons and workhouses. The process of stopping the seams is known as caulking.

Prisoners picking oakum at Clerkenwell, 1874.

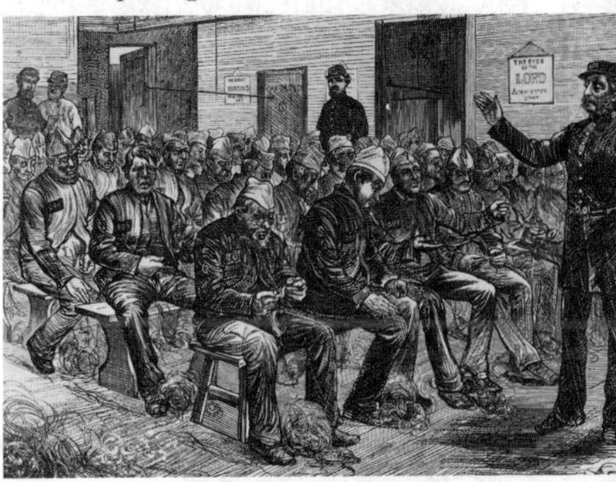

Obelisk: Egyptian stone pillar, four-sided, tapering to a pyramidal point. The Egyptians made their huge obelisks at the quarry, cutting them out on three sides and then drilling holes along the line of the fourth, into which they inserted wooden pegs. These, when made wet, swelled and split the stone. The finished obelisks were covered with hieroglyphs (*see* separate entry) and erected in temples and in towns to celebrate special events. They were also connected with sun worship. Their use spread to other early peoples, including the Canaanites, Phoenicians and Assyrians. The British Museum's "Black Obelisk" of Shalmanesar the Third shows the submission of King Jehu of Israel in the 9th century BC. A 3,000-year-old obelisk from Luxor now stands in the Place de la Concorde, Paris; in the 19th century the Egyptian government presented examples to Britain and America (*see* illustration p. 642, *and* CLEOPATRA'S NEEDLES).

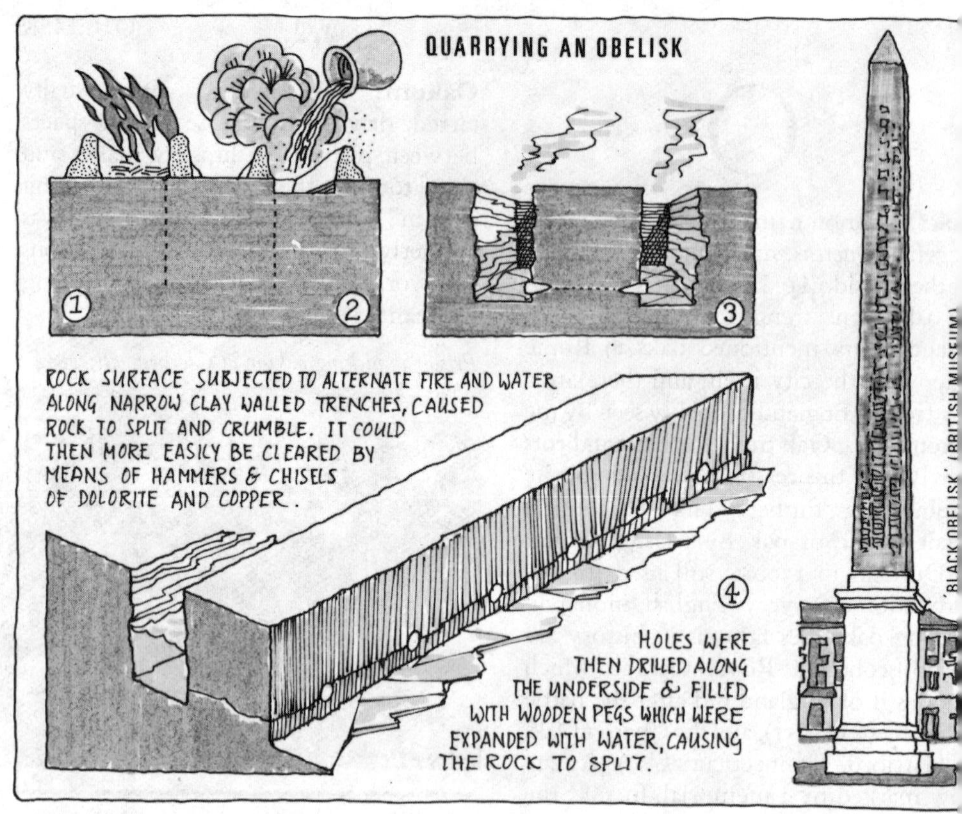

QUARRYING AN OBELISK
1
2
3
ROCK SURFACE SUBJECTED TO ALTERNATE FIRE AND WATER ALONG NARROW CLAY WALLED TRENCHES, CAUSED ROCK TO SPLIT AND CRUMBLE. IT COULD THEN MORE EASILY BE CLEARED BY MEANS OF HAMMERS & CHISELS OF DOLORITE AND COPPER.
4
HOLES WERE THEN DRILLED ALONG THE UNDERSIDE & FILLED WITH WOODEN PEGS WHICH WERE EXPANDED WITH WATER, CAUSING THE ROCK TO SPLIT.
'BLACK OBELISK' (BRITISH MUSEUM)

Oberammergau: village in Bavaria famous for its religious play. In 1633 the villagers, in gratitude for deliverance from a plague, vowed to enact every ten years the Passion and Death of Christ, appointing the cast of some 700 actors from their own members. From 1680 the basis of the ten-year interval was changed and has since been maintained, the only omissions being in 1870, 1920 and 1940 by reason of war, though a postponed performance was staged in 1922 and a 300th anniversary in 1934. The play takes eight hours and is repeated many times throughout the summer. Despite the crowds that nowadays resort to Oberammergau, the play remains a moving and unique experience.

¶ SATTELMAIR, RICHARD. *Oberammergau: its environment and tradition.* 1970

Observatory: an institution where the positions, movements and physical nature of astronomical phenomena such as th sun, moon, stars and planets are observe and recorded scientifically. An essenti part of this work is the accurate and regul publication of such records.

The earliest observatories, often ten porary arrangements, had only rudimer tary instruments. Established in templ in Mesopotamia and Egypt at the dawn c civilisation, they were principally cor cerned with astrological forecasts an with the computation of a calendar fc religious festivals and for sowing an harvesting crops. The development c Greek mathematics, particularly gec metry, from the 5th century BC and c simple angular measuring instrument such as the quadrant led to the refinemer of observations and scientific astronomy In China, government observatories wer established as early as the 7th or 8th cen turies BC for the regulation of the calendar Chinese observations between the 5th an

›th centuries BC are the most reliable ›ailable for the period.

In the 7th century AD the Arab peoples ›nquered the Near East, inherited the ›ork of the Greek astronomers and ›unded observatories at Damascus and aghdad. In the 8th century their know-dge was transmitted to Europe as a ›sult of the conquest of Spain in 711. Ionastic and, later, university obser-atories were established in Europe but ke their predecessors they were transi-›ry. Ulugh-Beg, son of Tamerlane (*see* IMUR), founded a great observatory at amarkand about 1420, where he com-uted astronomical tables used by the rst English Astronomer Royal, John lamsteed, at Greenwich three centuries ıter.

National observatories were founded ı Europe in the 17th century, in Paris by ouis XIV (1667) and in England by ›harles II (1675).

Today there are great observatories throughout the world, supported by governments, universities and scientific institutions. To mention a few, Great Britain has those at Herstmonceux, Sussex, and Jodrell Bank, Cheshire, the latter housing the first steerable radio telescope. Among the most important in the USA are the Yerkes Observatory, Wisconsin, operated by the University of Chicago and using the world's largest refracting telescope; the National Radio Astronomy Observatory, Green Bank, Virginia, with its 300-foot [91·44 metres] diameter dish-type radio telescope; and the Kitt Peake National Observatory, Tucson, Arizona, which has a 480-foot [146·30 metres] long solar telescope.

Among the chief Russian observatories are those at Zelenchchukskaya in the Caucasus Mountains and Chuguyev, in the Ukraine; the first has the world's largest operational telescope and the second the largest radio telescope. Other great observatories are located at Puerto

›elow, the Old Royal Observatory, Greenwich. ›ight, the radio-telescope at Jodrell Bank, ›heshire, England. Below right, moonlit view › the 200-inch Hale telescope dome with shutter ›pen, at Mount Palomar, USA.

Rico, West Indies; in the Effelsberger Valley, West Germany; and in Owens Valley, California.

See also PLANETARIUM; RADIO ASTRONOMY; TELESCOPE.

Occident: the west, as distinct from the east (the Orient). The term, formerly applied to Europe, to distinguish it from Asia, is now extended to cover other parts of the world inhabited by people of European descent, including America. The word derives from Latin *occidere* (setting), referring to the sun.

Oceania: geographical area embracing the islands of the South Seas. Racially, the inhabitants fall into several distinct groups, three of them being Polynesian, Micronesian and Melanesian. Archaeological remains include the great stone figures of Easter Island (*see* separate entry), totem poles and other survivals of ancestor worship.

Oceanography: the scientific study of the oceans. Four main sciences are involved – physical, biological, chemical and geological. Man has been concerned with physical oceanography ever since he first learnt to sail the seas. He found that the course of his ship was affected by ocean currents and tidal streams. He had, however, to wait until the 19th century before scientific data concerning these ocean movements became available. The valuable scientific observations made by the British navigator Captain Cook between 1768 and 1779 proved of enormous value in determining the extent of the oceans. In 1847 the American Commander M. F. Maury published his wind and current charts. The mariner was now able to plan his ocean routes taking into account the data in Maury's charts.

The first purely oceanographic expedition was carried out by the British HMS *Challenger* 1872–76. Under the directi of the Scottish naturalist Sir Wyvi Thomson, the *Challenger* carried out search in every known branch of mari science and brought back samples bottom sediments and marine life a many thousands of deep sea soundin This information enabled the ocea ographers to establish the nature a shape of much of the ocean bed. Anoth pioneer was Prince Albert of Monac who organised deep-sea expeditions b tween 1885 and 1915 and established t first oceanographical museum at Monac

In the 20th century the submarine wor is explored by deep-sea submersibles. O of these, the bathyscaphe, invented Swiss scientist Professor Auguste Picca (1884–1962), reached the greatest know depth of seven miles in the Challeng Deep, Pacific Ocean. (*See* PICCAR AUGUSTE and UNDERWATER EXPLORATION

Professor Piccard's bathyscaphe Trieste.

The enormous potential of the biologica chemical and geological aspects of ocean graphy can be summed up by quoting t words of Professor Piccard's son, D Jacques Piccard, in his introduction *Down to the Sea: a century of oceanograph* by J. R. Dean. "Fifty thousand millio million tons of natural chemical produc (sufficient to fill a goods train long enoug to girdle the earth 1,000 million times consisting of 2,000 million million tons magnesium, nearly 800,000 million to aluminium, 30,000 million tons of iron l 15,000 million tons of copper, nearly ,000 million tons of gold, hundreds of ›usands of millions of tons of nitrates, osphates and potassium, to say nothing strontium, radium and uranium, and ıctically all the other elements too. ındreds of thousands of square miles of or literally carpeted with nodules of ınganese and other useful metallic ores: ›usands of millions of tons of plankton, ntinually produced and with a possible ntent of up to 50 per cent and more of ;h-quality proteins – enough to provide undant food for many times the present pulation of the world. Lastly, in the rm of currents, waves, tides and differces in temperature, enough calories, ot-pounds and kilowatt-hours to supply full measure all the energy needed by ın, as well as another far from unportant item: over one million million illion cubic metres of water. Such is the reditament of the sea."

›AUGHERTY, CHARLES MICHAEL. *Searchers of the ı: pioneers in oceanography*. 1963; STEWART, RRIS B., JR. *Deep Challenge*. 1966

'Connell, Daniel (1775–1847)**:** Irish ıtesman known as "the Liberator". 'Connell was deeply concerned at the ndition of the Irish people, particularly ith the subservience of the Catholic asses. He united the Irish Catholics and ccessfully campaigned to improve their t. He failed, however, in the other cause which he was a lifelong champion, the peal of the Act of Union with Britain.

October Revolution: the second Russian revolution of 1917. Military defeat, armies and fleet near mutiny, industrial workers in revolt and an irresolute government all created a situation in Petrograd (now Leningrad) which Lenin saw as ripe for revolutionary action. The need to forestall a congress of soviets (revolutionary committees) to be held on 7 November, at which his Bolshevik party might not have had a majority, settled the date for Lenin. On the night of 6 November (24 October by the Russian calendar) infiltration of government buildings by his supporters and the absence of effective resistance put the government into the hands of Lenin, Trotsky and their followers.

¶ HINGLEY, RONALD. *The Russian Revolution*, 1970; MACK, DONALD W. *Lenin and the Russian Revolution*. 1970

Trotsky (left) and Lenin (centre) in 1917.

Octobrists: members of a moderate and constitutional political party in Russia, brought into existence to defend and secure the fulfilment of the manifesto issued by Tsar Nicholas II on 30 October 1905 granting civil rights to all and promising a *Duma* or parliament with full legislative powers.

Oder-Neisse Line: the frontier between East Germany and Poland since World War II. It follows the River Oder, then its

tributary the Neisse, southwards from Szczecin to the Czech border. By the establishment of this frontier in 1945 Germany lost one-fifth of its prewar area, including a prosperous source of wheat and potatoes. It was intended as a temporary boundary until a freely elected government in Poland could make a permanent agreement. However, the Communists took control in both Poland and East Germany, and in 1950 they accepted the Line as a permanent frontier.

Odyssey, The: Greek narrative poem describing the adventures of Odysseus, whom we often call Ulysses from the Latin *Ulixes*. To say that the poem was composed by Homer is to repeat a tradition that ignores modern controversy over the date and authorship of the work (*see* HOMER). Like its companion Homeric poem, the *Iliad*, the *Odyssey* is divided into twenty-four books and describes the ten years' wanderings of Odysseus and his companions on his way home from the siege of Troy to the island of Ithaca, where his faithful wife Penelope awaited him.

¶ HOMER. *The Odyssey*, trans. E. V. Rieu. 1970

Oecumenical or **ecumenical:** from the Greek, an adjective meaning "embracing all the inhabitants of the earth". The word is chiefly used to describe the great councils of the Church. The earlier of these, such as the first Council of Nicaea (AD 32[illegible]), truly brought together representatives of the whole Church. After the split between the Eastern and Western Churches in 10[illegible] the term was confined to the gatherings of the Roman Church, for instance, the Council of Trent, which lasted from 15[illegible] to 1563. In modern times an Oecumenical Movement is gathering force with the object of bringing all Christendom back into one fold.

Oersted, Hans Christian (1777–1851): Danish physicist and chemist. Oersted laid the foundation for the science of electromagnetism. In 1820 he noticed the needle of a compass wavered whenever he put it near a wire carrying an electric current. In this way he discovered the connection between magnetism and electricity which was later put to use by Faraday through his invention of the dynamo (*see* ELECTRICITY). Oersted is also credited with producing the first aluminium in 1825.

OGPU: initials of the Russian for "General Political Administration of the State"; one of the names given to the secret police of the USSR, who used espionage, arrest without trial and torture to achieve aims. Founded in 1918 (*see* CHEKA) to send opposers of Communist Party rule to labour camps, it was later used by Stalin to get rid of personal rivals

Higgins, Bernardo (1776–1842): lean revolutionary leader. Son of ıbrosio O'Higgins, Irish-born viceroy Chile and Peru, Bernardo was educated England. He became a leader in the lean struggle for independence from nish rule and was the new republic's president. A Chilean province was ned after him.

---

fields: areas with subterranean sup-s of oil capable of being extracted for nmercial use. Seepages of petroleum, ether with bitumen and salt, were put ıse in prehistoric times. The Chinese, example, several centuries BC, drilled oil, using bamboo piping. But oilfields ered modern history when Colonel win Drake struck oil in 1859 after ling at Titusville, Pennsylvania, USA. 1861 the first cargo of American oil ssed the Atlantic to London in barrels. ıundred years later, in the 1960s, fuels m the world's oilfields provided half world's total supply of energy. A usand million gallons were being used h day, and the products of oilfields had come the most important single class of rchandise in world trade. The chief ıse of this economic revolution was the ention of the internal combustion gine. A significant development was application of compression ignition to ger engines in 1897 by Rudolph Diesel. the USA John D. Rockefeller, through Standard Oil Company, founded in 70, created a virtual oil monopoly by tting control of refineries, pipelines and nsport. The Anglo-American Oil mpany, Standard's overseas subsidiary, ıs organised in 1888 and soon possessed world's largest oil fleet. In 1911, how-er, anti-trust legislation broke Standard l into more than thirty companies.

ussian petroleum output was even gger than that of the USA, the great ku oilfield being developed from 1874. In the Far East drilling was begun by the Dutch in Sumatra in 1884. In Europe Rumanian oil was developed by the Germans, and in South America a big oil-field in Venezuela was opened up in 1914. Drilling was begun in Persia in 1908 by the Anglo-Persian Oil Company, which in 1914 won a long-term contract to supply the British Navy.

Oilfields had thus acquired major str-tegic importance to the great powers. They also had brought wealth and political importance to parts of the world which had previously been backward and little known.

After World War I there were big oil strikes at Kirkuk in Iraq and pipelines were laid to Tripoli and Haifa. This was fol-lowed by discoveries of oil in Bahrain, Saudi Arabia and Kuwait, bringing about great social and political changes in those areas of the Near East.

Governments of countries with oilfields began to contest the right of American, British, French and other foreign oil firms to make large profits from their territories. In 1938 Mexico expropriated foreign oil

Oil pipe-lines in the Agha Jari area, Iran.

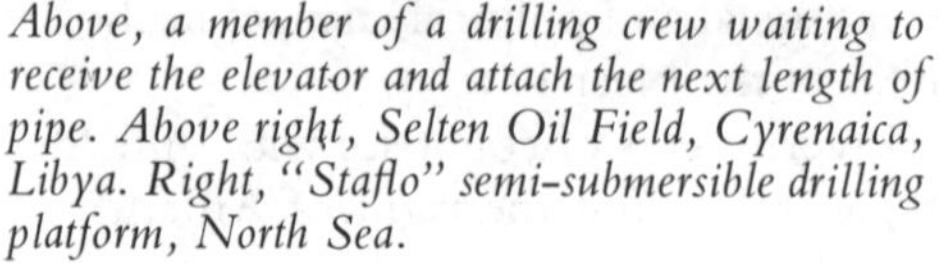

Above, a member of a drilling crew waiting to receive the elevator and attach the next length of pipe. Above right, Selten Oil Field, Cyrenaica, Libya. Right, "Staflo" semi-submersible drilling platform, North Sea.

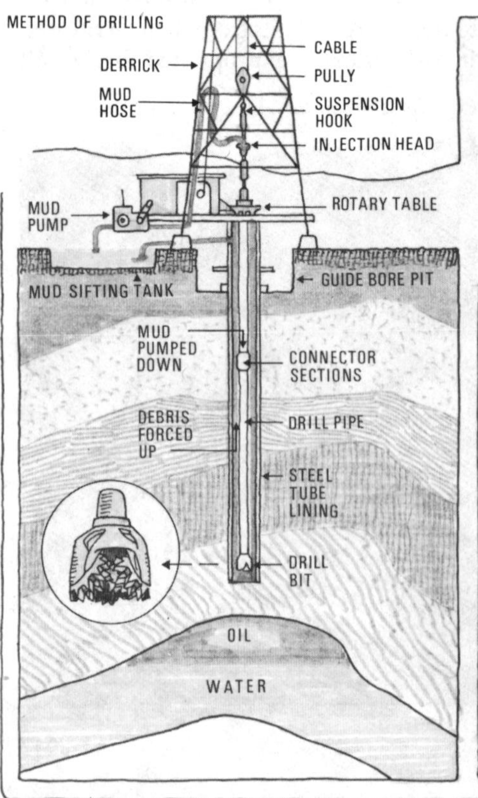

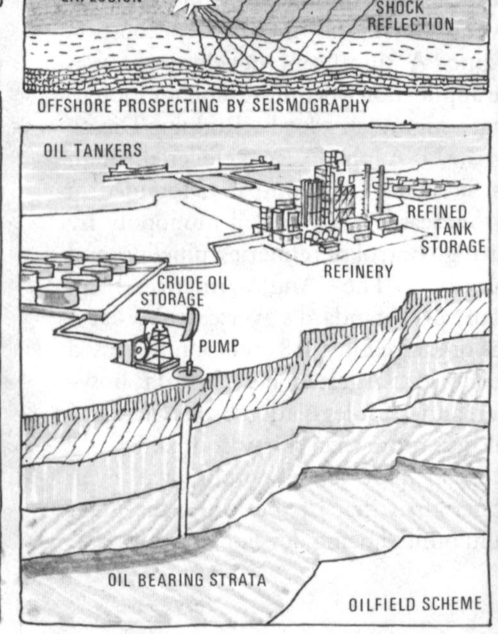

-ms. In Iran, Venezuela, Saudi Arabia, uwait, Iraq, Bahrain and Qatar a system as adopted by which the governments ot a much larger share of the profits from e oilfields in their territories.

As American and Russian petroleum as increasingly used inside those counies, and as petroleum supplies from both ear East and Far East were put in hazard times by political disturbance, oilfields ere increasingly sought elsewhere. There ere new strikes of oil in North Africa, articularly in Libya in 1959, and in Nigeria. Offshore drilling for under-sea ilfields was pursued off North America, the Persian Gulf and in the North Sea, here both oil and natural gas have been ound. A big oilfield was found in Alberta, Canada, and vast new sources in Alaska.

O K (Okay): expression now common mong all English-speaking peoples, neaning "I agree", "all right" or "satisactory". It is thought it originated from political organisation (the O K Club) ormed to support Martin Van Buren President of the USA 1837–41) in his nsuccessful campaign for re-election. O K stood for his birthplace, Old Kinderhook, New York.

Okinawa: one of the Ryukyu Islands in he Philippine Sea, approximately 900 miles [1,448 kilometres] south-west of Tokyo.

Following the crushing defeat of the Japanese navy at Leyte (23–26 October 1944) the US land and sea forces were in a position to drive north directly toward Japan itself. On 1 April 1944 the US Marine Corps and Army units landed on Okinawa. Desperate *kamikaze* (suicide plane) attacks failed to dislodge the supporting fleet, which sustained 5,000 fatalities, 368 damaged ships and 36 minor vessels lost. Using Okinawa as one of its chief bases the US mounted extensive air raids and fleet bombardments of the Japanese mainland, inflicting heavy blows at industrial targets and war plant. Preparations for the invasion of Japan, using Okinawa as the springboard for the operation, were being made when the atomic attacks on Hiroshima and Nagasaki ended the war. The Ryukyu group remained under US military control till, in 1953, the northernmost islands were returned to Japan and, in 1972, Okinawa itself.

¶ BENIS, FRANK. *Okinawa*. 1970

Olaf I (*c.* 969–1000)**:** Norwegian king. Once a relentless Viking raider of Britain, Olaf was converted to Christianity by a hermit in the Scilly Isles. Thereafter, he ceased his marauding and attempted to convert Norway. He died fighting the Swedes and Danes and became a legendary hero to his people.

Olaf II (*c.* 995–1030)**:** Norwegian king and patron saint. A Christian himself, he completed the conversion of Norway begun by Olaf I. His reforms provoked dissension, and he was defeated and killed by a rebel army. He became the symbol of national independence and a saint, centre of many legends.

Old Bailey: name by which the Central Criminal Court, London area, is known, from the name of the street in which the Court is situated. It is presided over by a High Court Judge and Jury. Appeals from its decisions are to the Criminal Division of the Court of Appeal and from that court to the House of Lords.

Old Guard: the crack troops of Napoleon's Imperial Guard, when this became enlarged after 1806. Service in the Guard was an honour, as only the finest troops were selected. For the Old Guard there was the added qualification of experience: at least five years service and two cam-

A Grenadier, one of Napoleon's Old Guard.

paigns. Napoleon deliberately limited its use in battle, keeping it in reserve for emergencies.

Today the term Old Guard is used for any section of an organisation (such as a political party) that does not want to see any change, preferring to cling to the old ways and opposing what younger members call progress.

Old master: general term covering any one of the great painters of earlier centuries, especially the European artists of the 15th to 17th centuries. It is also applied to a painting by such an artist.

Old North-west, The: the north-central region of the USA, bordering on the Great Lakes between the United States and Canada, and including the states of Illinois, Indiana, Ohio, Michigan and Wisconsin. The states furthest south – Illinois, Indiana and Ohio – are primarily rolling plains. Michigan and Wisconsin, although also possessing wide plains, include as well many lakes, small islan and extensive forests. The region also h some sizable rivers, especially the Ohi which was a major factor in the growth population and commerce.

These states, as their name implies, wer formed out of the territories ceded t Britain by the French in 1763 and, afte the War of Independence, acquired (1783 by the new American nation. They wer organised into the Northwest Territor by legislation in 1786. Many peopl settled in the territory in the 1820s an 1830s. Of special importance in this movement was the development of canals to make it easier to send farm produce to the east coast. The most notable of these were the Erie Canal in New York State and the Ohio Canal system in Ohio. These, together with the Great Lakes, made settlement potentially profitable, and spurred the growth in the region. During the Civil War period, this area was a "free soil" centre (i.e. where slavery was disapproved of), and provided much of the manpower with which the Confederacy was forced back into the Union.

Agriculture is still of great importance in the region. Indiana and Illinois are leading producers of corn, wheat and soybeans; Michigan and Wisconsin specialise in dairy products; while Ohio produces large numbers of livestock. However, the region is also a major industrial area. Detroit in Michigan is the centre of the massive automobile industry; Gary, Indiana, is a major steel town; while the production of paper products is based on the forest resources of Wisconsin. Beer, iron ore and bauxite are also produced in this region. *See* AMERICA for map.

Old South, The: the south-eastern section of the United States, comprising the states of Alabama, Florida, Georgia, Mississippi and South Carolina. This region borders on both the Atlantic cean and the Gulf of Mexico and is imarily an area of low plains and flat astlands, with wide areas of swamps in eorgia and Florida. It has numerous vers, most of them small, and, with the ception of some hills in the Appalachian nge in northern Georgia, is virtually ithout mountains.

Although the Spanish established a umber of missions in Florida, notably e settlement at St Augustine, most of the opulation in this region stemmed from e English settlers in South Carolina and eorgia, and from later population movements into Alabama and Georgia after the Jnited States had become independent. ettlement in these latter two states dated om the early 1800s, when high cotton rices and the deterioration of soils in the outhern states along the coast led to the xpansion of the plantation system and otton production into the fertile lands f these territories. During the period eading to the American Civil War the ntire region was the centre of agitation gainst the Republican Party, and in avour of the protection and expansion of lavery in the United States. When secession came, it was again these states that led he way. The first capital of the Confederacy was established in Montgomery, Alabama, and much of the rhetoric and ustification for the rebel cause was drawn rom the writings of John Calhoun, the Senator for South Carolina.

Although efforts are being made to increase manufacturing in the region, and while there are some important cities – notably Birmingham in Alabama and Atlanta in Georgia – this is primarily a rural, agricultural region. Cotton lint, peanuts, tobacco, livestock and fruits are of primary importance. Also of growing significance is the tourist business, especially in Florida, where the mild climate and fine beaches have made a centre for recreation for retired people.

Old Testament, The: the books of the Bible covering the period before the coming of Christ, at which point the Old Testament is succeeded by the New. Books accorded a place in the Christian Bible are termed canonical, and the original canon of the Old Testament corresponds closely with that of the Jewish religion (*see* JUDAISM). After the Reformation (*see* separate entry) some Churches relegated certain books from the canon to what is called the *Apocrypha*.

The researches of modern scholarship have modified many previous ideas of dates and authorship. To the Jews the customary division of the books in question is threefold: (1) the five Books of the Law (*Pentateuch*), containing also the narrative of the early period of Jewish history, (2) the Prophets, including books of later history, and (3) the *Hagiographa* (sacred writings), such as the Psalms, which do not fit into either of the other two categories.

A translation from the original Hebrew into Greek was made at Alexandria as early as the 3rd or 2nd century BC. It is known as the *Septuagint*.

¶ GRISEWOOD, JOHN. *The Book of the Bible.* 1972
See also BIBLE; INCUNABULA.

Old Three Hundred: the original 300 American families settled in Texas in 1823 by Stephen Austin, under formal authority from the Mexican government. Stipulations were that they should be virtuous and willing to accept the Roman Catholic faith.

Old World: the Eastern Hemisphere, especially the continent of Europe, as distinct from the New World or Western Hemisphere.

Oléron, Laws of: one of the various codes of maritime law developed in the Middle Ages. The *Consolato del Mare* was used by Mediterranean ports, the Laws of Oléron by Normandy and Brittany, the Laws of the Hanse Towns by Germany, and the Laws of Wisby by ports further north. England appears to have adopted the Laws of Oléron at an early date, as they were cited in a court case in 1349 and are found in the early customs records of London, Southampton and Bristol. They deal with the duties of the Master and crew of a vessel and of the lodeman (steersman), liabilities arising between merchants and the Master, and such matters as freightage and jettison (throwing goods overboard to lighten the ship).

Oligarchy: political term meaning the rule of the few, as contrasted with aristocracy, the rule of the nobles, democracy, the rule of the people, or monarchy, the rule of a king: all display the same slight variation of the original words in Greek. In British history it is usual to speak of the Whig Oligarchy to describe the years between 1714 and 1770, when the first two Hanoverian kings, George I and II (and George III for the first ten years of his reign), allowed themselves to be dominated by parliaments managed, both at elections and in session, by a closely knit group of county families representing the Whig faction.
See also DEMOCRACY; WHIG; etc.

Olivares, Gaspar de Guzmán (1587–1645): chief minister of Philip IV of Spain. For twenty-two years (1621–43) he was responsible for controlling a vast world empire. He was blamed for Spain's repeated diplomatic failures and military defeats at the hands of the Dutch, French and Portuguese and died in disgrace.

Olympia: sanctuary in ancient Greece dedicated to the worship of Zeus and scene of the Olympic Games (*see* separate entry), held every four years in his

The Gymnasium, Olympia, as it is today.

honour. The site is in the north-we[st] corner of the Peloponnese, and excava[-]tions have produced some outstandin[g] relics of ancient art from its sacred build[-]ings, as well as revealing the outlines o[f] the stadium.

The large hall in Kensington, London[,] where indoor horse-shows, militar[y] tournaments, trade exhibitions and othe[r] large displays are staged, is named afte[r] ancient Olympia.

Olympiad: period of four years betwee[n] successive celebrations of the Olympi[c] Games (*see* next article). It was also use[d] in ancient times for dating historica[l] events, the first Olympiad starting i[n] 776 BC and the 293rd and last in AD 393. The interval is still observed with the revived Olympic Games.

Olympic Games: athletic festival originating in ancient Greece. In the modern

sion a white-clad youth, the last of a es of torchbearers who have brought flame all the way from Greece, enters stadium. Holding his torch on high watched by the silent crowd, he unts the rostrum and touches his ne to the brazier. It flares into life, and Olympic Games have begun.

is a solemn and impressive ceremony, alling the great Pan-Hellenic festival d every four years at Olympia in thern Greece. This was primarily a igious festival in honour of Zeus, the preme god. In the enclosures where the mes were held stood temples. Sacrifice, ayer and hymn were the background ainst which the festivals were set.

'o the Greeks religion implied art; and beauty of form and athletic prowess man ranked as high as his intellect and irit. Poets and sculptors followed the rtunes of the Games, proclaiming to the orld and posterity, in words and stone, e exploits of their heroes. The prize was mbolic – a crown of wild olive. The al triumph of the victor was the ode in hich his praise was sung.

The list of Olympic victors begins in 6 BC. The great popular spectacle lasted ve days. The first was taken up by camination of the competitors, all of hom were men and youths, since omen were totally excluded from the ames. Then competitors and judges ere sworn in to obey the rules. The orning of the second was set aside for e chariot race and other events of the ippodrome and the rest of the day for the entathlon, a competition in the five vents of running, jumping, discus and velin throwing and wrestling. The orning of the third was devoted to the reat sacrifice to Zeus. In the afternoon he contests for boys took place. The ourth day was for a programme of men's vents, and the fifth was given over to easting and celebration.

A young German athlete rehearses the lighting of the Olympic flame.

The Olympic Games reached their zenith in the 5th century BC, when victory in a major event conferred the highest distinction on the city of the victor. Later on, professionalism entered the contests, and a process of deterioration set in which led to their final suppression in the 4th century AD.

The Olympic Games of modern times resulted from the enthusiasm of Baron Pierre de Coubertin, no athlete, but a scholar who believed that Greece owed her Golden Age in part to her emphasis on physical culture. He hoped too that, on the friendly fields of amateur sport, national rivalries and political and religious differences would be forgotten. To Athens went the honour of staging the Olympic revival in 1896, with competitors from eight countries. Following the four-year cycle, the second Games were held in Paris in 1900.

Supreme control rests with the International Olympic Committee, who have ruled that every competitor must be an amateur, that women can compete, and that the highest standards of sportsmanship must be observed.

Recent Games have been staged in Rome (1960), Tokyo (1964), Mexico City (1968) and Munich (1972).

¶ GIRARDI, WOLFGANG. *Olympic Games*. 1972

Omar Khayyam (full name, Ghiath Uddin Abdul Fath Omar Ibn Ibrahim Al-Khayyam, *c.* AD 1050–1123): Persian mathematician, astronomer, philosopher and poet, born near Nishapur and employed by the Seljuk Sultan Malikshah to reform the calendar. The Persians, who judged poetry by form rather than content, regarded him as a fourth-rate poet and remembered him chiefly as an unhappy atheist and materialist and champion of Greek learning (i.e. philosophy). He is valued as a poet in England because of the free translation of his quatrains (*Rubaiyat*) published by Edward Fitzgerald (1809–83). *Rubaiyat* were epigrams designed to be read independently and were arranged alphabetically in Persian collections, but Fitzgerald arranged them to read as a coherent poem. Khayyam means "tentmaker", possibly the trade of Omar's father. Mathematicians also remember him as the author of a treatise on algebra.

¶ OMAR KHAYYAM. *Rubaiyat*, trans. Edward Fitzgerald, edited W. A. Wright. 1958

Ombudsman: name (taken from Sw ish) describing a kind of public watch called a Parliamentary Commissio appointed in Britain by the Parliament Commissioner Act, 1966, which gi greater powers of investigating citiz complaints against bureaucratic wro doing than is possible by questions letters to Ministers. So far, the jurisdict of the Ombudsman extends only ove strictly limited field.

Omnibus: vehicle with seats for a nu ber of passengers. The word is a Latin o meaning "for all" and is now commo shortened to "bus". Although we spe of an airport bus, hotel bus, etc., the te is normally applied to a public serv vehicle plying on a fixed route. T modern motor bus may be either a doub decker or a single-decker.

Although hackney carriages for perso hire were used in some cities of weste Europe from the 17th century, the fi omnibus appeared in 1825, when an En lishman, George Shillibeer (1797–186

GREYHOUND 'SUPER SCENICRUISER' USA

oduced these single-decker covered icles, drawn by pairs of horses, on the ets of Paris and, four years later, of ıdon also. The venture failed, but some rs later the omnibus became a familiar ure of many cities. In London the bus ver and his conductor were famous for ir wit and repartee in the traffic jams ich occurred even then. In due course covered seats were added on the roof he vehicle, reached by a steep stairway, ere passengers sat back to back, which e rise to the name "knifeboard". arly in the 20th century the petrol gine began to replace the horse, though he 1920s some of Tilling's steam-buses re still operating in London. Later velopments included covered top decks d the use of diesel engines, while, in ne places, trolley-buses were introced to make use of the overhead wires obsolete tramways.

part from urban services the bus has also ade great changes in the habits of life in e country – habits which the increasing vnership of private cars is again altering. ower costs have caused many people to efer coach to train for long-distance urneys, and travel organisations now fer "package tours" by which, e.g., uch of Europe can be covered by coach. teresting comparisons can be made over period of less than a century. In England was reckoned a great feat when, in 1888, stage-coach was driven from London to righton and back, a distance of 108 miles 73·8 kilometres] at an average speed of ·79 m.p.h. [22·19 kilometres per hour] nd involving 14 changes of horse-team. the US today, the Super Golden Eagles f the Dallas Continental Trailways, each -foot [18·29 metres] long and carrying ore than 60 passengers, can travel at m.p.h. over long distances.

KAYE, DAVID. *Pocket Encyclopedia of Buses and rolleybuses 1919–45*. 1970; *Pocket Encyclopedia of uses and Trolleybuses since 1945*. 1968

Ontario: chief industrial and agricultural province of Canada (capital, Toronto). Following the explorations of Samuel de Champlain (1613–15), the territory was settled by French and English traders, and Jesuit missions were established to work among the Indians (*see* JESUITS). One of the saddest chapters in Jesuit history was the massacre of Fathers Brebeuf, Lalement and their companions when the Huron Indians, among whom a mission had been founded, were wiped out by the Iroquois in 1649. Apart from isolated areas, Ontario was still largely untrodden wilderness till the 19th century, when the end of the French Revolutionary and Napoleonic Wars brought opportunity for wide development. The territory had become British in 1763 and part of the province of Quebec in 1774. It achieved independence within the Dominion of Canada in 1867, when it received its present name. Ontario now dominates the international nickel market, producing half the world supply and, as well as its agricultural products, has rich resources of timber, hydroelectric power, gold, silver, copper and uranium to support its many industries.

See CANADA for map.

Open fields: arable fields without hedges. The German tribes described by Caesar and Tacitus had no permanent arable fields. A piece of land would be ploughed one year and deserted the next, while a fresh piece would be ploughed. This was "extensive" as opposed to "intensive" cultivation, where the same land was used each year. At the time of the Domesday survey (1086–87) the three-field system was in general use in England. The village was surrounded by three large fields, temporarily fenced while crops were growing but open at other times so that cattle could graze on the stubble. A three-year rotation of crops was used, one field yielding spring crops, the second winter crops, while the third lay fallow and was ploughed twice during the year. Each field was subdivided into acre or half-acre strips, and each man's holding consisted of a number of these strips scattered throughout the fields, so that the best land did not all go to one person. It has been suggested that this scattering was the result of communal ploughing.

Open shop: factory, firm or workshop where workers who are not members of a trade union are employed alongside those that are. The opposite is a closed shop, which admits only trade union members.

Opera: drama with musical setting. Opera began in Italy with the Renaissance, when Florentine aristocrats wanted to restore the Greek presentation of drama. They used mythological subjects in dramatic or poetic form with musical settings Solo voices using natural speech were accompanied by supporting chords. Sh choruses were interspersed, moving, like the madrigal as an interweaving melodies, but straightforwardly in blo of chords. Orchestras, at first, were ti only five instruments perhaps.

The earliest opera still surviving is *Eu dice*, by Peri, 1600. Another great la mark was *Orpheus*, 1607, by Monteve who developed the style further, usin larger orchestra and establishing Italian Aria. This led to the triumph of solo singer with a high standard of vo tone and musical agility.

Other great names in the early histo of opera are those of Jean-Baptiste Lu (*c.* 1632–87), who wrote thirteen wo based largely on classical themes and ma ing considerable use of ballet; and, England, Henry Purcell (1658?–95), wh still only in his thirties when he died, ga opera, in such works as *Dido and Aene* a dramatic life it had not achieved befo

The greatest figure in 18th century ope (and for many the greatest in all opera history) is that of Wolfgang Amade Mozart (1756–91), the Austrian compos who had a natural feeling for the sta and was able to convey to a remarkab degree the intense emotions of real li men and women. Two of his maste pieces are *Le Nozze di Figaro* (*The Ma riage of Figaro*) and *Die Zauberflöte* (*T Magic Flute*). Another Austrian, Fra Joseph Haydn (1732–1805), though bett known for other forms of compositio wrote at least fifteen operas which hav recently been receiving greater attentio Beethoven's only opera was *Fidelio*, th moving story of Leonora, wife of Fe

La Scala in Milan, Italy, is one of the world most famous and distinguished opera house Above left, a scene from Rossini's highly colou ful opera The Italian Girl in Algiers. *Belo left,* Aida *written by Guiseppi Verdi in 1871. is one of his later, more strongly dramatic work*

ado Florestan who, when her husband s a state prisoner, took the name of elio and dressed as a man in order to ve as a jailer in the same prison.

he 19th century saw the cheerful, light-rted works of the Italian Gioacchino tonio Rossini (1792–1868), best known *Il Barbiere di Siviglia* (*The Barber of ville*) and, in more serious vein, *Guil-ne Tell* (*William Tell*). Equally popu-today are the works of Giuseppe Verdi 13–1901), a peasant who became Italy's t-loved composer through such operas *Rigoletto*, *Trovatore*, *La Traviata* and *llo*. In Germany, Richard Wagner 13–83) broke away from previous eratic conventions by seeing opera as ringing together of all the arts – music, rature and painting – and in such tre-ndous works as *Tannhäuser*, *Lohengrin*, *e Ring of the Nibelungs* and *Die Meister-ger* put himself among the immortals.

he 20th century has seen a complex and erse picture, which includes the tuneful wing melodies of Giacomo Puccini 58–1924) and his compatriots Leon-vallo and Mascagni; works achieved der political pressure, such as Sergey okofiev's *War and Peace*, the satirical eras of Kurt Weill, the advanced experi-ntal exercises of Paul Hindemith and, in England, the achievements of Sir Benjamin Britten and Sir Michael Tippett, to name only a few.

performance of Die Miestersinger Von rnberg *(1862–7), one of Wagner's most ular works.*

¶ WECHSBERG, JOSEPH. *The Opera*. 1973

Opinion polls: efforts to forecast, e.g. election results, by sampling public opinion. They date from about 1935 in the United States and were associated with the names of George H. Gallup (Institute of Public Opinion), Archibald Crossley (Crossley Poll), and Elmo Roper and Paul Cherington (Fortune Survey). Conflicting results of different polls taken at the same time have cast doubt on their reliability, and they are subject to error at each stage, i.e. the selection of those interviewed, the selection of the questions, and in the recording and analysis of the answers. The first of these stages is achieved either by quota sampling, which attempts to make the small sample a copy of the entire nation according to the frequencies of age, sex, occupation, economic status, etc., or by random sampling, in which, for example, every fifth or tenth person is interviewed in a selected area.

Opium War (1839–42): a discreditable episode in 19th-century British overseas expansion. Chinese imperial authorities had protested against the import of opium into China by British traders. In 1839 a large quantity of opium was seized and destroyed. Sharp disagreement over this incident gave a pretext for hostilities from which the British gained extensive trading privileges in China. The Chinese Empire was ill equipped for resistance. The island of Chusan was captured by the British Indian fleet, along with Hong Kong and Amoy. By the treaty of Nanking, Hong Kong was thrown open to European trade, together with Amoy, Fuchow, Nanking, Canton and Ningpo. The Chinese government paid an indemnity.

Oporto: second city of Portugal, near the mouth of the River Douro. It was already a flourishing trading centre when the Romans, who called it Portus Cale, occupied it. For five centuries, from its capture by the Visigoths in 540 till its occupation by Christian forces in 1092, it suffered frequent invasion and partial destruction. Its later prosperity, though it has not been uninterrupted by European wars and internal rebellions, has been founded on the port wine trade. It also manufactures textiles, leather, pottery and various luxury goods. Among its most interesting buildings are the cathedral and the church of Sao Martinho de Cedo Feita, the latter built by the Visigoth King Theodemir to receive the relics of St Martin of Tours.

Oppenheimer, Robert (1904–67): American physicist, from 1943 to 1945 director of the Los Alamos Laboratory, New Mexico, which produced the atomic bomb used in the destruction of the Japanese cities of Hiroshima and Nagasaki (6 and 9 August 1945).

From 1946–52 he acted as Chairman of the General Advisory Committee to the US Atomic Energy Commission. In 1954, though the investigating committee declared him a "loyal citizen", and though the move was strongly opposed by many leading scientists, it was decided his communist sympathies were too strong and his government security clearance was withdrawn, thus denying him access to all secret material.

¶ In PRINGLE, PATRICK. *Great Discoverers in Modern Science*. 1955

Oracle (from Latin *orare*, to speak, to pray)**:** the place where a deity or specially inspired priest could be consulted about the future; or the god or human agency itself. The most famous example in the ancient world was the oracle at Delphi on Mount Parnassus, Greece, consulted by, among others, Croesus and Phili[p of] Macedon. The pronouncements of [the] oracle were frequently enigmatic [and] capable of at least two interpretations. *See also* CROESUS; DELPHI; PHILIP II.

Orange Free State: province of So[uth] Africa with a population (1980) [of] 1,931,860 of whom a fifth were wh[ite]. Originally thinly populated by Bushm[en], Bechuanas and Zulus, it had known o[nly] a few European hunters and missiona[ries] till groups of Dutch farmers from C[ape] Colony, ranging in search of past[ure], settled with their flocks in 1834, to [be] quickly followed by others who t[ook] part in the Great Trek of 1835–36 [(see] separate entry). The territory was anne[xed] in 1848 by Britain but six years later [be]came independent as the Orange F[ree] State. A further annexation took plac[e in] 1900 as a result of the Boer War [(see] separate entry), the name being alte[red] to Orange River Colony, and over f[ive] million pounds was spent by the Bri[tish] government in repairing the ravages [of] war. The country was finally incorpora[ted] in the Union of South Africa in 1910.

Orange, House of: the ruling house [of] Holland and the founders of Du[tch] independence. The house takes its na[me] from the small independent principal[ity] of Orange, now part of the department [of] Vaucluse, south-eastern France. Willi[am] the Silent (1533–84), Prince of Oran[ge] and Stadtholder (chief magistrate) [of] Holland, Zeeland and Utrecht, like [his] ancestors, served the Habsburgs u[ntil] Spanish tyranny drove him to resistan[ce]. He held his countrymen together in [de]feat, cutting the dykes to drive back t[he] Spaniards. His son Maurice of Nass[au] (1567–1625) led the Netherlands forces [to] victory, and their successors furth[er] strengthened the Republic under su[c]cessive Stadtholders. Marriage broug[ht]

'illiam I,
e Silent.

William III.

lliam IV.

William I,
King of the
Netherlands
(1815).

ie connections with England, and in 9 William III (1650–1702), leader of resistance to Louis XIV, and his wife ry (1662–95) became joint rulers of gland after the flight of James II. After death of William III there were eral rival claimants to the title of nce of Orange. Eventually John lliam Firsco of Nassau-Dietz sucded to the principality as William IV. 1815 his son William VI became lliam I, King of the Netherlands.

---

angeman: member of an organisation, ned after William III of England, nce of Orange, formed in 1795 to upld Protestantism in Ireland. Subsequent ents have tended to concentrate the ganisation's energies in the province of ster; but it is active throughout orthern Ireland and groups of Orangeen may also be found in many other glish-speaking countries.

Orators: public speakers, particularly those who, by their eloquence and concentrated feeling, hold the attention of, move and influence their audiences.

In ancient Greece and Rome oratory was taught as a subject, much as history or mathematics is taught today. It was treated as a branch of *rhetoric*, which, in turn, may be defined as the art of using language to influence people. Budding orators were required not only to learn how to marshal their thoughts in logical order but to master an elaborate set of rules governing the grammatical construction, the rhythms and the figures of speech permissible in their orations.

The greatest orator of ancient Greece was Demosthenes (*c.* 383–322 BC), who, in a series of famous speeches known as *Philippics*, warned Athens of the threat represented by Philip of Macedon (383–336 BC) to the Athenian way of life. Stories are told of how Demosthenes, struggling to overcome a speech defect, would go down to the seashore where he would fill his mouth with pebbles and, thus handicapped, try to make himself heard above the noise of the waves. The outstanding Roman orator was Marcus Tullius Cicero (106–43 BC), who lived in the turbulent years which saw the end of the Roman Republic and was himself the victim of political murder.

In the Middle Ages many universities appointed Orators who acted as their special envoys. Oxford and Cambridge retain this ancient office in the person of Public Orators whose task it is to make speeches in the name of the university on such special occasions as the conferring of honorary degrees.

Oratory in the modern sense is not something which takes place in a vacuum. Great orations are fashioned out of great occasions, and great oratory is, therefore, a by-product of leadership, since great leaders owe much of their power to their ability to sway large numbers of people to follow their lead.

Thus, it is not surprising to find that many great orators are associated with periods of war, violence and revolution. Examples include Girolama Savonarola (1452–98), the friar who, though he did not himself preach violence, was instrumental in expelling, for a time, the ruling Medici family from Florence; Georges Jacques Danton (1759–94) and Maximilien de Robespierre (1758–94), two leading figures of the French Revolution; Charles de Gaulle (1890–1970), whose voice rallied defeated France at a later period; and Adolf Hitler (1889–1945), who exactly illustrates the point where the orator deteriorates into the demagogue, or rabble-rouser. Hitler's speeches were illogical and full of lies, but his personal magnetism led the German Reich into the horrors of World War II.

The English parliamentary system has produced many statesmen who v notable orators: Charles James Fox (1 1806), Edmund Burke (1729–97), D Lloyd George (1863–1945) and Sir W ston Churchill (1874–1965) may specially mentioned. In American hist few could match Daniel Webster (17 1852), the lawyer and statesman wh "clear, massive, gorgeous, overwhe ing eloquence carried juries with hin well as parliaments". Religion, too, had its orators. Savonarola has alre been mentioned. A religious orator different kind was Peter the Hermit (c 1115), the French monk who persua some 20,000 people to embark on disastrous First Crusade, from which returned to tell the tale. John We (1703–91), founder of the Metho Church, preached more than 40, sermons and initiated a great religi revival. Among the 19th-century pu orators the English preacher Cha Haddon Spurgeon (1834–92) had enormous following; and in our own the phenomenal evangelistic campai of the American Billy Graham show t this type of eloquence can still comm a vast audience in an age when polit oratory is largely a thing of the past. *See also* individual entries.

Ordeal, Trial by: method of try accused persons by seeking a miracul decision or judgment from God rat than man. The ordeal is very ancient origin and continues today among so primitive peoples. Among its many for have been the ordeal by boiling wat when the accused immersed his hand a arm and was adjudged innocent if scalds had healed within a stated peri of time. In Europe the ordeal by "swi ming" was well known, the accused bei thrown bound into water which reject him (i.e. allowed him to rise to the surfa if guilty. If innocent he sank and v

ial by boiling.

uled out again. Ordeal by fire could ke the form of passing through flames, rrying red-hot iron, or walking bare- ot over glowing ploughshares. One ueen of England, Emma, mother of dward the Confessor, is said to have survived such an ordeal unscathed, walk ing on nine red-hot shares and afterwards presenting in commemoration nine manors to the Church of Winchester.

Orders of architecture: name given primarily to the three main styles of classic Greek architecture: the Doric, Ionic and Corinthian. The Romans added two further Orders, the Tuscan and the Composite, to the list. Technically, an Order, in this sense, consists of the up-right column with its base and capital, together with those horizontal parts of the building – the architrave (lower part), frieze (middle part) and cornice (upper part) — which the columns support.

The Doric, the earliest to be developed, while understandably the simplest, has an unsurpassed strength and grandeur. A Doric column, which has no ornamental base, has a simple fluted shaft of, usually, twenty shallow flutes, and terminates at its upper end in a plain square slab called an abacus. The Ionic Order, with its scroll capitals, which perhaps derived from the ancient Egyptian lotus motif, is more elegant than the Doric, while the last of the Greek Orders, the Corinthian, with its stylised decoration based on the leaves and calyx of the acanthus, is altogether more florid and ornate.

The Romans, who appropriated so much that was Greek, were fonder of the Corinthian style than the Greeks themselves. The Romans were imitators rather than innovators, and their Tuscan Order was based on the massive unfluted columns which were a characteristic of the architecture of the Etruscans, early inhabitants of central Italy. The Composite Order, very ornate and reserved largely for triumphal arches, combined Corinthian and Ionic decoration.

See also ATHENS; GREEK ART.

Orders, Military: organisations of knights living under various forms of monastic rule. These originated during the Crusades, when groups of knights banded together in companies having both religious and military aims. Three are especially famous.

In AD 1113 the Pope recognised the order of the Knights Hospitallers, later known as the Knights of St John. Their aims were to protect pilgrims travelling to Jerusalem and to care for the wounded. The order still survives in many countries, where its primary function is the care of the sick. In England the head of the St John's Ambulance Brigade still keeps the old title of "Grand Master".

The Knights Templar, a similar order, had a primary duty to defend holy places against the Turks. Their purpose was to be "first to attack and last to retreat", and this often led them into foolhardy situations. During the 14th century the Templars' preoccupation with worldly goods brought upon them the antagonism of King Philip IV of France and Pope Clement V, who in 1312 disbanded t order.

The Teutonic Knights were similar pledged to assist Crusaders and pilgrin Later they undertook to defend Centr Europe against the heathen. Their pow declined during the 14th and 15th ce turies. The order now survives as a sm body of Dutch Protestant noblem whose badge is a black cross edged wi white. *See also* CRUSADES.

Orders, Religious: organisations of m and women living according to rule religious communities.

When the Roman Empire adopt Christianity as its official religion, son Christians felt that life rapidly becan too easy and that only by suffering an hardship could true faith be kept aliv Such men often went to live in t desert, frequently to be near some wel known religious leader. They share food and prayed together. The first tru monastic group was formed in Egy during the 4th century AD, by the fo lowers of St Anthony, a hermit wh lived for twenty years in a tomb. Anoth group, at Cappadocia, in Asia Mino lived in caves in very uncomfortab conditions.

Members of these early religious com munities had two aims – to live a life c prayer and to do without comfort of an kind, since they thought that bodily eas interfered with their devotion to Go Many neglected themselves to the poi of illness and starvation.

Towards the end of the 5th centur Benedict of Nursia founded a monaster on Monte Cassino, in Italy, which be came a model for all monastic com munities. His monks' lives were ordere by a code of conduct known as the Ru of St Benedict. It had to be kept by every one, from the abbot to the humbles novice. The rule made it plain that onk's first duty was prayer and the worip of God, but since a man could not ay wholeheartedly if he were underd or ill Benedictines were allowed an lequate amount of food and rest. They ore black robes and sandals; in winter ey were given woollen underclothing id fur boots.

A Benedictine's day was carefully ornised. It began at midnight, when rvices called Lauds and Matins were eld in church. He then returned to bed ntil seven o'clock, when he attended nother service, Prime, followed by Mass. fter breakfast, the monks met in the apter house to discuss the day's business; this meeting, any brother was permitted voice his opinion. High Mass, the rincipal service, was celebrated at ten, nd afterwards the monks dined in the efectory. From noon until five they vorked, then attended Vespers, after hich they were allowed to talk and rex. At half-past six they ate supper, returning to church at seven for Compline. They then went to bed until summoned to Lauds at midnight.

During the 500 years after Benedict's death monasteries became wealthy and many monks grew lazy and fond of luxury. Reformers tried to bring back the old ideals, and new orders developed as a result of their work.

In 1084 a monk named Bruno decided to relinquish comfort for a life of hardship. With six companions he settled at a desolate place in the French mountains, named Chartreuse. Here the monks lived in deliberate austerity, doing all their own work, cultivating crops and rearing livestock. They refused to own more land and cattle than they needed, worked in silence and spent their leisure time alone. They wore plain white habits over hair shirts, and were known as Carthusians. A few branch communities were formed, but there were never many members because of the unusual strictness of this order.

ife has changed very little from the traditional pattern for these Benedictine Monks in a monastery on e Isle of Lerin, France.

Fourteen years later, twenty monks settled at Cîteaux, a swampy area near Dijon. Believing that a monastic community ought to be self-supporting, they drained the land, built their house, grew crops and reared sheep and cattle. These Cistercians were the farmers of monastic life, even shortening their services in order to attend to agriculture.

In Italy, Francis of Assisi formed an order of Friars (Brothers), who did not live in monasteries but worked amongst people. After his death his successor, Elias, reorganised the Franciscans on lines resembling a Benedictine community, although the majority still travelled about. In 1216 a friar named Dominic gathered about him in Toulouse a number of men who were prepared to explain the Bible to the ignorant. His followers were known as Dominicans. They wore white habits under black cloaks; many scholars were attracted to this order because of their interest in biblical studies, and Dominicans frequently taught in universities.

In the 12th century a Crusader named Berthold had settled on Mount Carmel with twelve others who devoted their time to prayer. The community grew, but eventually had to flee from the Saracens, reaching Europe in 1240. The majority came to England, and elected an Englishman, Simon Stock, as their General. He adopted the way of the Franciscan Friars, but the Carmelites always wore distinctive white mantles over their brown habits.

Women were admitted to this order in the 15th century. St Teresa, who was trained at the Carmelite convent of Avila, in Spain, reformed their rule, bringing back the devout self-denial of the original hermits.

See also ABBEYS; BENEDICT OF NURSIA; FRANCIS OF ASSISI; FRIARS; JESUITS; MONASTERIES; ORDERS, MILITARY; TERESA OF AVILA, etc.

Ordnance: (1) general term for hea guns, cannon and artillery; (2) gover ment department concerned with t maintenance of stores of weapons, m nitions and other military equipment.

Ordnance Survey: government surv of Great Britain and Northern Irelar As a result of difficulties experienced English troops during the Jacobite reb lion of 1745, the Master-General of t Ordnance was ordered to make a surv of northern Scotland, so that accura maps could be prepared. During the ne hundred years civilian surveyors and t Royal Engineers extended this survey the whole of the British Isles. An impo tant feature was the preparation of detail maps which have since been regularly r vised and improved.

Oregon Question: the dispute over t western boundary between the USA a Canada, left undetermined in 1818 b cause the mountain chain of the area h not been explored. The British were i terested in the area because of its val to the fur trade, while the America claimed it because their explorers h opened it up. An agreement was sign between Britain and the USA on 15 Ju 1846, by which the Americans acquire all the territory now comprising the stat of Washington, Oregon and Idaho, whi Britain obtained Vancouver Island.

Oregon Trail: the 2,000 mile [3,2 kilometres] overland route from the Mi souri to the Columbia. In 1842–43 Jo C. Fremont (1830–90), known as "t Pathfinder", made a scientific invest gation of the Oregon trail which stim lated interest in the Far West. This in tu led to a great migration to the Oreg country as "Oregon fever" sprea throughout the Mid West, and result in an influx of settlers from Missou o and Kentucky. The trail, which had viously been used only by fur traders explorers, extended from Independe-ce (Missouri) to Astoria at the mouth he Columbia River and became the n route for emigrants to the Far West.

RKMAN, FRANCIS W. *The Oregon Trail.* 1931

ganisation of African Unity AU): organisation with headquarters Addis Ababa, set up in 1963 and com-sing all independent African states (ex-t South Africa) to promote African erests and maintain solidarity. Mem-ship reached 50 in 1980 when newly ependent Zimbabwe joined.

ganisation of American States AS): organisation, with headquarters Washington, set up in 1948 to encourage l co-ordinate social, technical and nomic co-operation among the states the Americas, more than twenty of ich are members.

ganisation of Central American ates: union, formed in 1951, of Costa a, Guatemala, Honduras, El Salvador l Nicaragua, to promote and protect economic, social and cultural interests member states.

ganisation for Economic Co-eration and Development (OECD): 1948 sixteen European nations formed association to co-ordinate their trad-g and economic activities and to help minister the Marshall Plan (*see* separate try). This was the Organisation for ropean Economic Co-operation EEC). It was replaced in 1961 by the rganisation for Economic Co-operation d Development, with wider scope and embership. This includes not only some enty European countries as either full associate members, but also Canada, the USA and Japan. Its aims are basically the same as those of the earlier organisation – the economic development of member countries, the expansion of world trade and aid to underdeveloped countries. Its headquarters are in Paris.

Organisation of Petroleum Exporting Countries (OPEC): formed in 1960 it only rose to prominence as an international cartel after the 1973 Arab-Israeli war. Its co-ordinated price rises during the 1970s transformed the world economic situation and gave OPEC great influence. It has 13 members.

Oriflamme: the ancient banner of France, meaning "gold" and "flame", carried before the king and, in time of peace, kept in the Abbey of Saint Denis. Originally plain red, the banner was later embroidered with golden flames or stars.

The Oriflamme, top left, at the Battle of Nancy.

Orléans: city on the River Loire and strategic key to central France. In AD 451 the Roman Aëtius united Romans, Gauls and Germanic tribes to repulse Attila's Huns. In October 1428 the Duke of Bedford besieged it till it was relieved by the army of the Bastard of Orléans, encouraged and guided by Joan of Arc (*see* separate entry), whose "voices" dictated the plans. She entered the city on 29 April and broke the English threat by taking the southern approaches to the bridge on 7 May. The victory was not followed up but was sufficient to encourage the crowning of Charles VII at Rheims. Orléans was a Huguenot headquarters in the Wars of Religion and was the pivot of the second phase of the Franco-Prussian War of 1870.

Orléans, Houses of: younger sons of French kings, and their descendants. Louis, Duke of Orléans, 1372–1407, was younger brother of Charles VII and governed in his name when he was insane. He was murdered by the Burgundian faction. He married Valentina Visconti and thus gave his descendants, Louis XII (1462–1515) and Francis I (1494–1547), a claim to Milan. His son, Charles of Orléans (1391–1465), was wounded and captured at Agincourt, and was a famous writer of the type of verses known as rondeaux. The family device was a porcupine. The title was revived in 1626 for Gaston, second son of Henry IV and Marie de Medici, the figurehead of the plots against Cardinal Richelieu. It was revived again for Philip (1640–1701) the younger brother of Louis XIV. His descendants were suspected of ambitions to supplant the Kings of France. Ph (1674–1723) became Regent of Fra 1715–22. Louis Philippe (1747–93) knc as Philippe Egalité had encouraged s of the revolutionary orators, but peris in the Terror; Louis Philippe (1773–1 became the Citizen-King of the Fre 1830–48.

The assassination of the Duke of Orléans.

Orsini: family of Roman nobility of Guelph faction, their device a bear re ling their founder, Ursus, their war- "Orsini for the Pope" opposed to "Col na for the People", the cry of t Ghibelline rivals. Over many centu they produced popes, cardinals, gene and a few poets. Celestine III (pope 11 98) was an Orsini, so was Nicholas (pope 1277–80) who distributed to kinsmen principalities and castles in Campagna from which they repeate threatened the citizens of Rome and l popes. On his death, two Orsini cardi were kidnapped while their collea elected a new pope. In 1303 the Or rescued Boniface VIII from the Colon but kept him prisoner themselves unti died. The clan was ruthlessly reduced sword and poison of the Borgia in 15 The last Orsini pope was Benedict X (pope 1724–30). Count Felice Or (1819–58) was guillotined for a bo attack on Napoleon III in the cause Italian independence.
See also GUELPHS AND GHIBELLINES.

Orthodox: (from a Greek word mean "right in opinion") in line with tra tional and accepted views, especially faith and religion. The opposite is u orthodox, unconventional, heretical independent.

Orthodox Eastern Church: Christ Church of eastern Europe and the la round the eastern end of the Medit ranean. The early Christians gradua lved an organisation of groups of munities presided over by Patriarchs took their titles from Alexandria, ioch, Constantinople, Jerusalem and ne, where the style was later changed Pope. All enjoyed equal status, but nstantinople gained prestige as the seat he Eastern Empire, and Rome's claim pre-eminence through St Peter was r reinforced by Charlemagne assum- the title of Holy Roman Emperor. se rivalries were aggravated by dis- es over doctrine, and the final split ween Rome and Constantinople came 054, the other three patriarchates be- for the time, submerged in Moham- lan conquests. Attempts at reconci- on in the 13th and 15th centuries were uccessful.

the later history of the Orthodox urch, the most significant event was the blishment of the Russian patriarchate 589, while Constantinople itself was agan hands: this Church still survives he USSR though sadly harassed by state. In the following centuries, as the Turks were driven back or became more accommodating, the old patriarchates were revived, and a number of new and smaller ones, self-governing but generally headed by archbishops, were created. The tiny patriarchate of Sinai comprises less than 150 souls.

Orthodox Cathedral of St Basil, Moscow.

The Oecumenical Patriarch of Constantinople is still given this traditional title as head of the general body; but this does not take away the individual independence of the other patriarchates, which is the chief bar to any reconciliation between the Eastern and Roman Churches. On the other hand, relations between the Orthodox Church and the Anglican Church are increasingly close.

¶ MEYENDORFF, J. *The Orthodox Church: its past and its role in the world today.* 1965

See also CHARLEMAGNE; OECUMENICAL; PATRIARCH; PROTESTANT; REFORMATION.

Osaka: second city of Japan, with an important trade in textiles, shipbuilding, tea, iron, glass, chemicals and sugar-refining. Its rise began in the late 15th century with the building of a temple. In 1909 a third of the city was destroyed by fire. Among its recent notable buildings is its university (1931).

Oslo: capital city of Norway. The old city was founded by the Viking, Harold Hardrada, in the 11th century, but was totally destroyed by fire in 1624. It was rebuilt on a grand scale, and its excellent harbour, landscape and Viking Museum have attracted much trade and tourism.

Ostend: Belgian sea port on the North Sea, handling considerable traffic with England and the continent of Europe. It is also the headquarters of the Belgian fishing fleet and maintains an important school of navigation. In the Middle Ages it was strongly fortified and withstood a number of sieges.

Ostia: the port of Rome, some sixteen miles [25·8 km] to the south-west, at the mouth of the River Tiber, which is not navigable to vessels of any size. Originally a naval base, its importance grew when, in the 1st century AD, it became increasingly necessary to import grain to feed the city's multitudes. The original harbour was then silting up, and a new one was built three miles to the north. The old town, however, flourished for many years and has in recent times yielded rich archaeological remains.

Ostracism: originally a system of banishment for political reasons practised in ancient Athens. The term is derived from the Greek word for the broken pieces of pottery on which the citizens scratched the name of the man whom they wished to send into exile: Many such fragments have been dug up. Ostracism was not designed as a punishment for crimes against the state, but as a kind of safety valve for relieving political pressure. A few other Greek states had similar procedures.

In modern times, we use the word to denote a community shunning (or, in Britain "sending to Coventry") persons of whose behaviour or sentiments it disapproves.

Otis, James (1725–83): Boston lawyer who was one of the early leaders of the American Revolutionary movement. In 1762 he published a pamphlet *A vindication of the conduct of the House of Representatives* which affirmed the privileges of the colonies under the British Constitution. In 1764, as a result of the Sugar Act, he published his best known writing *The rights of the British Colonies asserted* in which he raised the argument of no taxation without representation. In 1772 he became chairman of the Boston Committee of Correspondence which represented the views of the people of Bos on the question of colonial rule to the of the Thirteen Colonies and to the World. It was this committee that instrumental in calling the First C tinental Congress of 1774.

Ottawa: city selected by Queen Vict as the capital of Canada (1858). Its orig name was Chaudière, from the Ind *Asticou*, or "boiler", a reference, m tioned by Samuel de Champlain (16 to the Ottawa river cataract with eddying basin and its thunderous n that could be heard "for more than t leagues". The first permanent settlem in the neighbourhood was not till 18 and the present heart of Ottawa once farmland, cleared in 1820. It n supports major industries in lumberi sawmills, hydroelectricity, paper-m ing, and many light manufactures. I portant buildings include the Univers (1866), the Parliament Buildings (191 cathedrals, museums, and the Domin Observatory.

See CANADA for map.

Otto I, called "the Great" (AD 912–7 Holy Roman Emperor (962–73) a German king (936–73). He was not o the greatest political and military lea of his time but encouraged the spread Christianity (if only as a political inst ment) and, unlettered himself, was patron of scholarship.

Ottoman Empire: Turkish state crea by Othman, a leader of ghazis – dev Muslims dedicated to Holy War a plunder. Othman's father, Ertughrul, v leader of a band of nomad refugees fr Mongol-dominated Central Asia. T Seljuk Sultan gave him land near Bru the last Byzantine territory in Asia Min He could, therefore, offer hopes plunder and conquest. Othman attrac

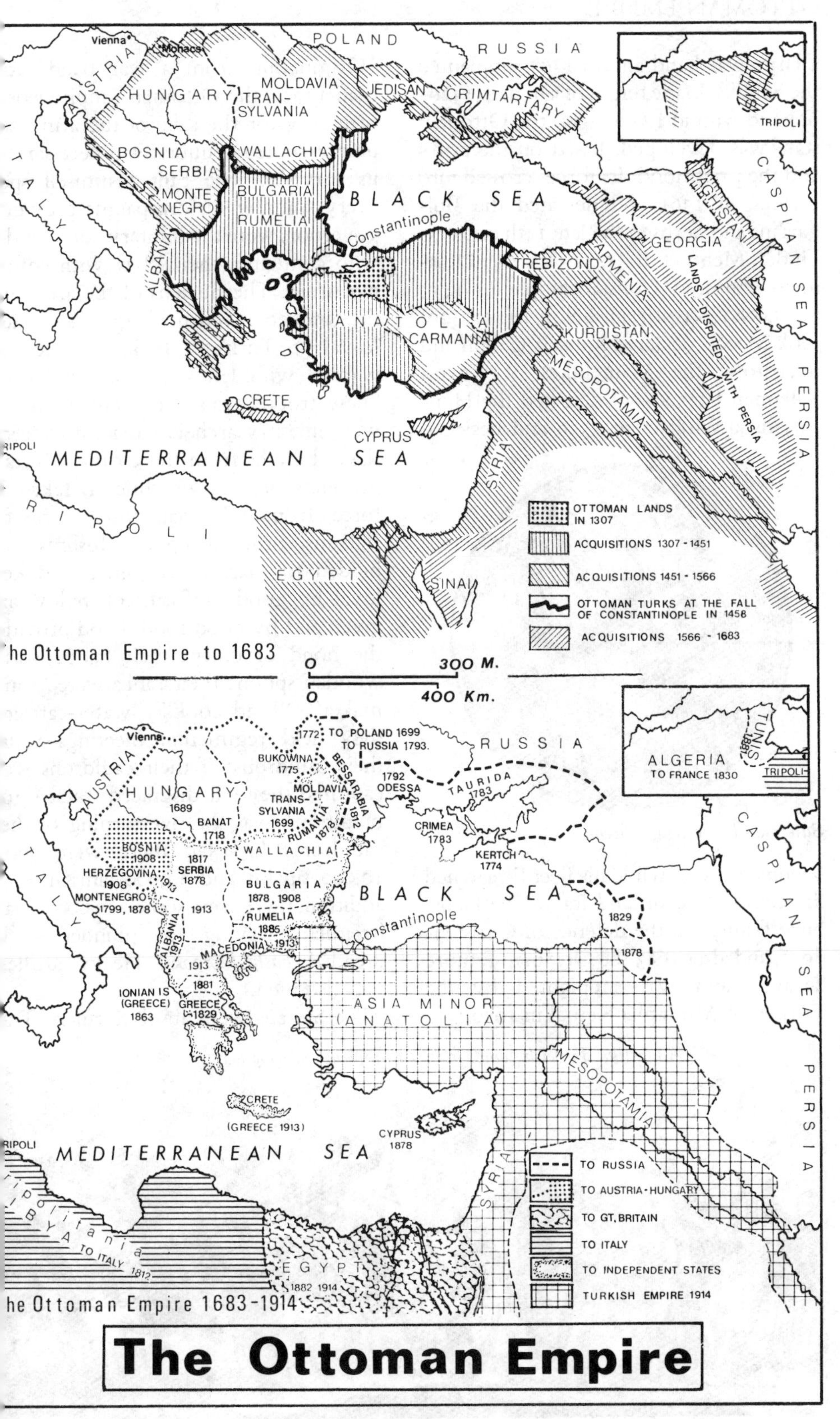

The Ottoman Empire

a large war band and in 1307 supplanted the Seljuks. In the reigns of Orchan (1326–62) and Murad I (1362–89) the Ottoman state was developed, based on the army and the priesthood. Its forces crossed into Europe in 1361 and defeated the Bulgarians and Serbs in the late 14th century. Under Mehmet II (1451–81) the Ottomans captured Constantinople in 1453 (*see* CONSTANTINOPLE). Selim I (1512–20) took Mecca, declared himself Caliph and overthrew the Mamelukes of Egypt. Suleiman I (1520–66) defeated the Hungarians at Mohacs in 1526 and besieged

Suleiman I, the Magnificent.

Vienna in 1529, while his fleet threatened the coasts of Spain and Italy. The Habsburg family led the defence of Christendom, and after 1683 the Ottoman Empire decayed and was supplanted by the Turkey of Mustapha Kemal in 1920.

Originating from a war band rat
than a race, the Ottoman Empire exis
primarily for the sake of the army, a
uninterrupted conquest was necessary
its survival. The Sultan himself sp
every summer on campaign; provinc
governors were the military command
who contented themselves with enfo
ing order. The nucleus of the army v
the trained, well-paid guards: sipa
(cavalry), Turks or Balkan subjects
warded with lands, and janissaries, t
"new troops" raised in 1330. Janissar
were infantry archers (later musketeer
slaves bought from the Crimean Tata
prisoners of war, or children taken
force from Christian villages in t
Balkans, brought up as Muslims, fo
bidden to marry, disciplined and ke
loyal by good uniforms of yellow a
green and by good food. Food provid
the bond of unity; their badge was
wooden spoon; their ranks were "sou
maker", "head cook", "water-carrier
they held regimental meetings rou
their cauldrons; if their cauldrons we
captured they felt disgraced; their sign
of mutiny was the overturning of the
cauldrons. In 1520 there were abo
10,000 sipahis and 12,000 janissaries.
addition, there were some 250,000 unpa
irregulars serving for plunder – t
dreaded *bashi-bazooks*. Heavy artille
was also used.

The Sultans were absolute rulers. Th

A warlike Turkish game, from a European encyclopaedia, c. 1830.

estalled rebellion by murdering their others and chose their successors from sons of their slave wives. They selected eir household servants and officials m Christian slaves reared in the Palace hool.

his harsh regime was tempered by the *ma*, Muslim priests and jurists who aintained the law courts, schools and spitals. They were chosen by the ltan and acted as his watchdogs, being ached as religious advisers to the guilds confraternities into which the soldiers, lors, merchants and craftsmen were ganised.

he Christian subjects were left in ace if they paid their tribute of money d children, and were allowed to practise eir religion. But the Turks contributed thing to civilisation themselves, though ey used the talents of those they conered – Persian architecture, Arabic ripts, Byzantine administrations. They mained nomads at heart, the houses en of the rich containing nothing that uld not be loaded in a caravan and rried into the desert.

VUCINICH, WAYNE S. *The Ottoman Empire: Its cord and Legancy*. 1965

---

udenarde, Battle of (1708)**:** victory tained by the allied forces of Marlborough and Prince Eugène over the ench during the War of the Spanish ccession (*see* separate entry). The French tended to seize Oudenarde, but, coverg fifty miles [80 kilometres] in sixty-five ours and attacking before his army had nished crossing the river, Marlborough rprised and scattered their forces.

---

uter Space Treaty: treaty (January 967) inspired by the United Nations, tempting to define the aspirations and nduct of space exploration and stating at astronauts are to be looked on as envoys of mankind". The treaty has some eighty signatories, the chief exceptions being France and Communist China. An extension of the treaty (July 1968) provides for the safety of astronauts who land in the territory of a foreign state.

Outlander: generally, a foreigner or an alien settler; particularly (*uitlander*) a British settler in the Transvaal and Orange Free State in the pre-Boer War period.

Outlawry: a primitive punishment putting an offender outside the protection of the law. In its most savage form it reduced a man to the status of a wild animal. Every man's hand was against him, and he could be killed with impunity. Later, the outlaw might be killed only if he refused to surrender or tried to escape. Otherwise the king alone had power of life and death over him.

Depending on the gravity of his offence an outlaw forfeited his goods, his lands, his civil rights, or all three. Gradually the offence, in England, lost its extreme seriousness, becoming, rather, a means of forcing accused persons to stand trial. It was used as a punishment for debt and for contempt of court. Already long obsolete, it was formally abolished in 1879.

Outlawry has gone by other names. When Lucius Cornelius Sulla (138–78 BC) was dictator of Rome he issued *proscriptions* – lists of political enemies whose property was confiscated and who were declared outlaws in the fullest sense of the term. The ancient Athenians practised *ostracism* (*see* separate entry), a relatively civilised form of outlawry by which people deemed politically dangerous might be exiled for ten (or, at a later period, five) years.

In fact, from the time when David took refuge from King Saul in the cave of Adullam, gathering about him a band of followers just as Robin Hood, the English folk-hero, did many centuries later, outlaws have often been people whose differences with authority have been political rather than criminal. Today's outlaw may be tomorrow's king.

Outremer: literally, "overseas"; the general name for the territories fought over during the Crusades, including Palestine, Cyprus, Cilicia and the Nile Delta.

Outwork: defensive structure outside the main fortifications, e.g. curtain wall, moat, ditch, earth bank.

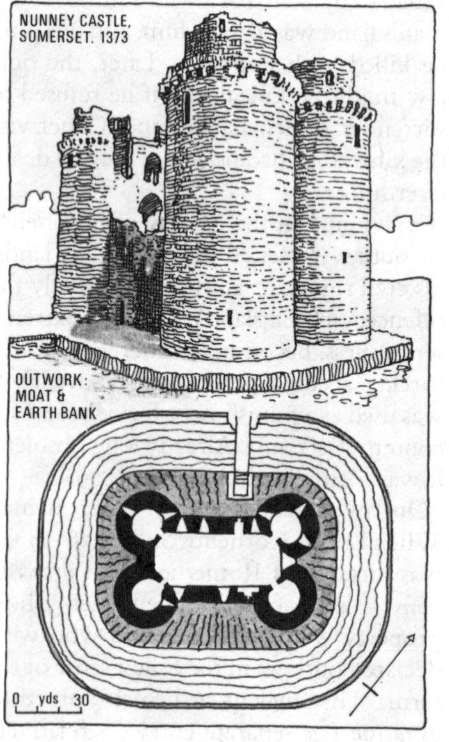

Ovid (Publius Ovidius Naso, 43 BC–AD 17): Roman poet. He was born at Sulmo near Rome and educated for the law, but, having private resources, devoted himself to poetry. His works, which are of outstanding quality, can be divided into three categories: (1) myths and legends of gods and men; (2) poems

on the art of love and the remedies for its tortures, which incurred the displeasure of the emperor and resulted in his banishment to Tomis (less correctly, Tomi) on the Black Sea; (3) laments over his punishment and prayers for recall, which were of no avail, for he died in exile.

Owen, Robert (1771–1858): early socialist and founder of the co-operative movement in Britain. Born in humble circumstances, he prospered as a cotton manufacturer, married his employer's daughter and used his wealth for the betterment of working conditions. Visitors from all Europe came to his model settlement at New Lanark in Scotland where working hours were limited and workers had good houses and an infants' school where the children included singing and dancing among their activities. Other ventures,

Quadrille lessons at Robert Owen's Institution, New Lanark.

nned community, New Harmony, in ıerica and the Grand National Con-dated Trades Union, whose members re to control industry through a system co-operative production, were short-ːd.

. UNSTEAD, R. J. *Great Leaders*. 1966

fam: British relief organisation, start- in 1942 as the Oxford Committee for nine Relief and being renamed Oxfam 1965. It depends on voluntary con-ɔutions and the profits from its shops many of the larger towns. One of the ɔst successful British non-government agencies, Oxfam now covers a wide ıge of development activities. It also ses funds which it distributes to other ganisations working overseas.

ford, England: university and indus-al city on the upper reaches of the ıames, north-west of London. The be-nnings of the university date from the e 12th century, but it was not until 1266 ıt the first college, Merton, was founded. ost of the rest had come into being by ː early 17th century, though there have en later additions, particularly the ɔmen's colleges. During the Civil War ː city was the Royalist headquarters 542–46). In modern times the motor dustry and others have considerably ered the character of Oxford through such developments as the growth of suburbs to house workers, the building of trunk roads, and greatly increased traffic congestion.

Oxford Movement: period of unrest within the Church of England, to which approximate dates 1838–50 may be assigned. It originated with a body of clergymen, chiefly Oxford graduates, who stood against the movement away from the Anglican ideals of the 17th century (*see* PROTESTANT) both by Parliament and by some sections of the Church itself. Since it was a recall to earlier ways, some of its members in due course felt compelled to return to the Roman Church, the most notable being John Henry Newman (1801–90) who eventually became a cardinal. Henry Edward Manning (1808–92), although not prominent in the movement, was another Anglican clergyman who became a cardinal and also Archbishop of Westminster. Two other leaders, however, John Keble (1792–1866), the hymn writer, and Edward Bouverie Pusey (1800–82), an Oxford professor, remained with the English Church.

Cardinal Newman.

The Oxford Movement should not be confused with the Oxford Group (*see* MORAL REARMAMENT).

P

Pacifism: a belief in the abolition of violence and war. In peacetime most people agree with this ideal, and support efforts of organisations like UNO to achieve it. Many sympathise with individuals like Gandhi and Luther King who spoke out for non-violence. But most people would resist if attacked and fight in a conflict they thought just. Pacifists oppose all war on moral grounds and refuse normal military service. Called conscientious objectors, in Britain and the USA they must prove by argument their sincerity, or be imprisoned. Some flee abroad to avoid conscription (e.g. Americans, to escape Vietnam).

Pacific Ocean: world's largest ocean, 10,625 miles [17,000 kms] wide, covering one-third of the area of the globe. Its size, remoteness from Europe, the broad belt of equatorial calms, typhoons, the storms of Cape Horn and the reefs of the western approaches delayed its exploitation by Europeans. Chinese and Arab seamen, though well able to make ocean passages, were content with coastal trade, and the colonisation of the Pacific islands was left to peoples who never, except in Easter Island, developed a written language. The Melanesians, of Negroid type, settled the fertile volcanic islands from New Guinea to the Solomons, New Hebrides and New Caledonia. The Micronesians, of Mongoloid stock, settled the coral atolls from the Philippines – Carolines, Marshalls, Marianas. The Polynesians, of Caucasian stock, were the greatest ocean pathfinders, sailing their outriggers and double canoes 2,000 years ago to the remotest islands. Their friendliness and courteous manners endeared them to European settlers.

Europeans reached the Pacific after 15
Antonio d'Abreu visited New Gui
from the Portuguese East Indies in 15
Balboa saw the Pacific from a peak
Darien in 1513, and Magellan's circu
navigation (1519–22) started the Span
search for a route to the East Indi
Miguel de Legaspi began the Span
settlement of the Philippines in 1559, a
Andres de Urdaneta, by finding t
counter-trade winds back to Ameri
made the regular Manila to Acapul
voyages possible. Spain gave half-heart
support to seekers of the Southern Con
nent – Terra Australis – Mendana a
Torres. The discoveries of the Solomo
and Torres Straits were not exploited
Spain or revealed to the world. Nor d
the Dutch exploit the discoveries
Tasman or Roggeveen, who found East
Island in 1722. British exploration, un
the 1760s, was confined to the search f
the North-West Passage, raids on t
Isthmus of Panama and the plunderi
voyages of Drake, Cavendish and Anso
At the end of the Seven Years War bo
France and England sent frigates to pro
the South Pacific, commanded b
Bougainville, Byron, Carteret and Wall
James Cook in Whitby colliers survey
the central Pacific from the Bering Strai
to the Antarctic Circle and exploded t
myth of Terra Australis.

European powers were for long relu
tant to annex the scattered islands of t
South Pacific, and in the early 19th ce
tury the islands were exposed to the rai
of ruthless whale hunters, sandalwoo
cutters and "blackbirders" who ki
napped islanders for slave labour i
Queensland, Mexico or Peru. The
aroused in the islanders a suspicion
white men that led to the murder of man
of the first missionaries. The missionar
societies persevered and converted th
islanders from cannibalism to a Christ
anity which is still vigorous in many area

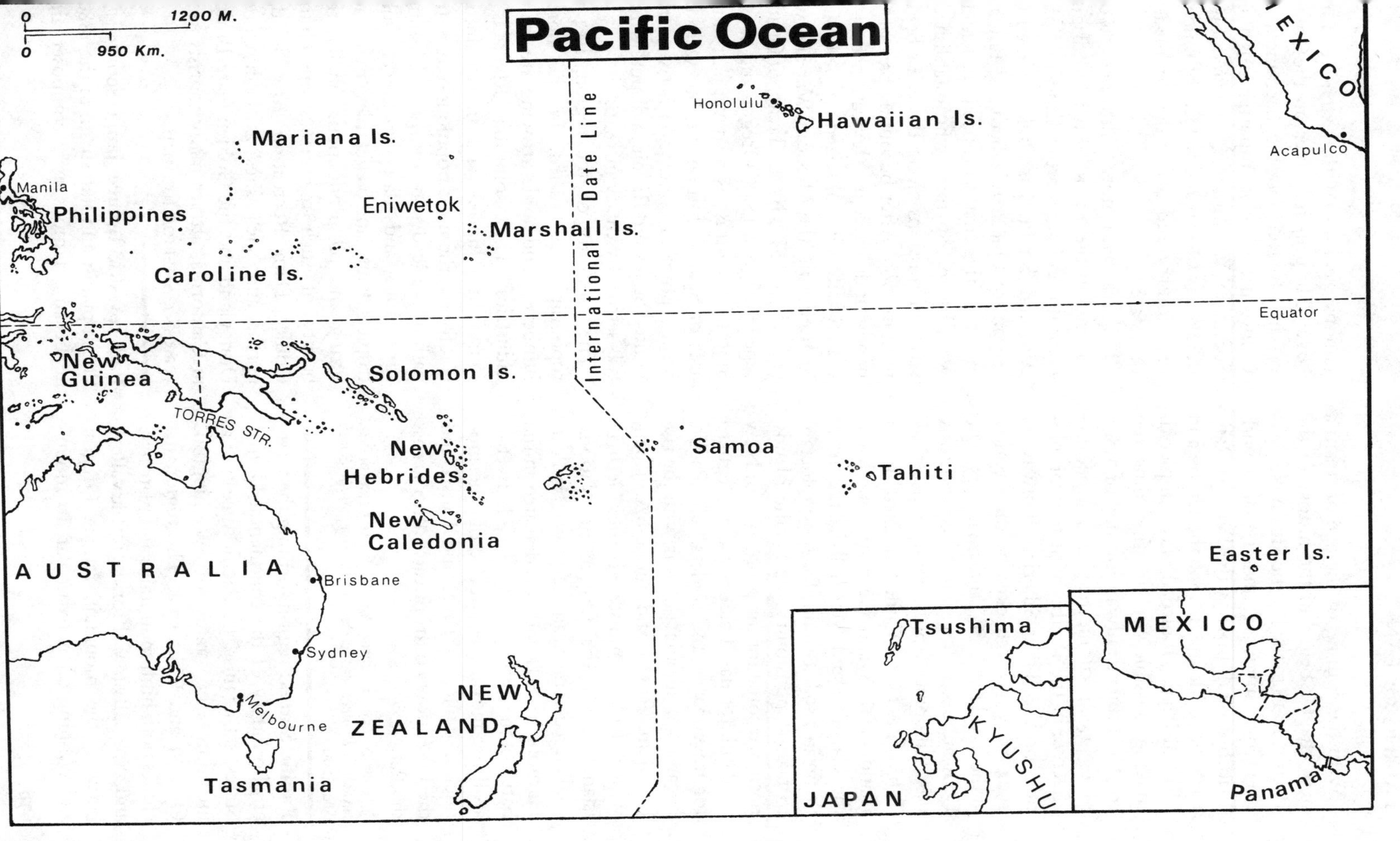
Pacific Ocean
0 1200 M.
0 950 Km.
EXICO
Honolulu
Hawaiian Is.
Acapulco
Mariana Is.
Manila
Philippines
Eniwetok
Marshall Is.
International Date Line
Caroline Is.
Equator
New Guinea
Solomon Is.
TORRES STR.
Samoa
Tahiti
New Hebrides
New Caledonia
Easter Is.
AUSTRALIA
Brisbane
Sydney
Melbourne
NEW ZEALAND
Tasmania
Tsushima
KYUSHU
JAPAN
MEXICO
Panama

With the coming of the age of steam a new chapter began in the history of the Pacific. In 1840 the Pacific Steam Navigation Company was founded, mainly with British capital. In 1855 the Panama Railroad was built and in 1869 the Union and Central Pacific Railroad was completed, making possible for the first time the trans-continent railway journey of 1,848 miles [2,974 kilometres]. Russia became effective in the Pacific with the completion of the Trans-Siberian Railway in 1904, only to be checked by the Japanese at the naval battle of Tsushima, 1905. The USA annexed Hawaii in 1898, and took the Philippines from Spain. France took Tahiti in 1880, Chile annexed Easter Island in 1888 and Germany purchased the Caroline and Marshall Islands from Spain in 1898. Britain, for long reluctant to take responsibility for Pacific islands, occupied some for the protection of New Zealand, for naval bases or as a safeguard for missionaries and traders. The Pacific became a main arena of war with the rise of Japan, Russia and the USA. Japan, which had administered the German islands under the League of Nations, challenged American sea power at Pearl Harbour in 1941 and was defeated in the battle of the Philippines in 1944. Eniwetok atoll became the scene of tests of a thermonuclear device in 1952, and Russia and the USA now confront each other across the Pacific.

¶ HOBLEY, L. R. *Exploring the Pacific.* 1957; RABLING, HAROLD. *Pioneers of the Pacific: the story of the South Seas.* 1967

Pacific States: region forming the western boundary of the continental United States, set against the Pacific Ocean and including the states of Washington, Oregon and California. The region includes both high mountains and plateaux, and, especially in California, fertile valleys between the mountain ranges. Oregon and Washington, in particular, are mountainous regions with extensive for cover. The principal rivers are the Colu bia in Oregon and the Sacramento California. Also of importance is Pu Sound in Washington, an extension the Pacific Ocean and the site of much the industry and urban development that state.

The area that is now California was d covered in the 1540s by Juan Rodrigu Cabrillo, sailing for the King of Spa Although Sir Francis Drake claimed t region for Queen Elizabeth I of Engla in 1579, the first European settleme were by the Spanish, who established series of missions along the coast begi ning in 1769. After becoming part of t newly independent Mexican nation 1822, California was seized by the Unit States during the Mexican War and w ceded by Mexico by the Treaty of Guad lupe Hidalgo in 1848. Oregon and Was ington, in contrast, were never part of t area of Spanish settlement, but were i stead a point of contention between t United States and Britain, a dispute whi was settled by treaty in 1846.

The economy of the region, like topography, is varied. In the nort lumbering and apple growing are maj industries. The Columbia River is source of Chinook and silver salmo California, the most populous state in t nation, is a leader in commercial fishin agriculture and dairy products, su tropical fruits and vegetables, manufa turing and oil production. Finally, t beauty of such regions as the Gra Coulee Dam Recreation Area in t north, and such sites as Hollywoo Disneyland and the Golden Gate Brid in California, attract many tourists ea year. *See* AMERICA for map.

Paderewski, Ignace Jan (1860–1941 Polish pianist and statesman. In the 188 he became famous as a composer an

n early photograph of Paderewski.

fted pianist. He toured Europe and the SA for ten years, and his composition *olish Fantasia* was very popular. He itterly resented Russian control of oland, and in World War I he turned om music to politics. At the 1919 Peace Conference he presented Polish claims for dependence and became the country's rst Prime Minister. He was respected for is moderation, although many of his ountrymen thought he should have emanded more territory. In the 1920s he eturned to the concert stage.

In CANNING, JOHN, editor. *100 Great Modern ives*. 1965

Padua: Italian city near the River Brenta n Venetia, 22 miles [35·40 kilometres] vest of Venice. Founded in 89 BC as Pataium by the Romans, it became second in vealth only to Rome. It was sacked by Alaric but revived in the 8th century and ecame a free commune in 1164. Its position in the plain of Lombardy exposed it o conquest by a series of tyrants: the ruel Ezzelino de Romano, 1225–50; the della Scala, 1338; the Visconti, 1388. Venice tried to control it by installing the native Carrara family, but when they proved treacherous Venice absorbed Padua into her Empire in 1406 and held it until 1797. Padua University, founded in 1222, flourished as Venice protected it from Papal intolerance and gave it contact with Greek scholars. It was famous for the study of law, mathematics and medicine. Vesalius and Galileo taught there, and Thomas Linacre and William Harvey (*see* separate entry) were students. The Botanic Garden was established in 1545, perhaps the first in Italy. From 1814–66 the city was ruled by Austria and then became part of United Italy.

Pakistan: former independent federal republic in southern Asia, consisting (1947–71) of West Pakistan (capital Lahore), East Pakistan (capital Dacca) and the Federated Territory of Karachi. The two main areas are separated by the territory of Northern India.

The republic was formed in 1947 as the result of the campaign of the Muslim League, led by Mohammed Ali Jinnah (1876–1948), to secure an independent Muslim state. The partition caused bitter riots in which thousands were killed and a vast cross-traffic of Hindu and Muslim refugees seeking what they felt to be their true home country.

The subsequent history has been no happier. Pakistan was at war with India from 1947–49 over the still-disputed region of Kashmir. The United Nations imposed a cease-fire, but the problem remains. In 1958 there was a military take-over of the government and Ayub Khan took the presidency, only to be ousted in 1969 by General Yahya Khan. All this internal and external turmoil took place against a background of constant food shortages and other economic difficulties. In 1970 a cyclone devastated large areas of East Pakistan, causing a catastrophic loss of life and property. This natural disaster was soon followed by another, man-made and of even worse proportions. Shaikh Mujibur Rachman of East Pakistan headed a movement to found an independent new state called Bangla Desh (*see* separate entry). Yahya Khan sent in troops and put this attempt down with ruthless severity. Several million refugees crossed the border into India to add yet another problem to that country's burden.

In 1971 India invaded Pakistan, forced Yahya Khan to resign and recognised the new independent state of Bangla Desh, a move soon followed by other nations. In 1977 General Zia al-Huq led a coup which ousted Bhutto (later hanged) and imposed authoritarian (strict Islamic) government. Since 1980, following the Soviet invasion of Afghanistan, Pakistan has had to cope with up to 3 million Afghan refugees.

Palatinate: either of the two regions of Germany which, from the 14th century, formed an electorate (or princedom) of the Holy Roman Empire. There were originally six Electors who chose the Holy Roman Emperor. The Palatinate of the Rhine achieved supreme importance because of its strategic position controlling the trade and army routes through the middle Rhine, and because of its university at Heidelberg. In 1356 its Count Palatine, already a leading imperial adviser, became one of the electoral princes.

Commercial wealth and the electoral right involved the Palatinate in two important struggles in the 17th century. Its protestant ruler Frederick accepted the Bohemian crown in 1619 and this led to the Catholic-Protestant struggle of the Thirty Years War (*see* separate entry). Later, in 1685, France claimed the Palatinate when the ruling house died out. T area was devastated by French tro when the Emperor refused and this co flict developed into the War of the Gra Alliance (*see* separate entry). After this Palatinate declined in importance, a was gradually divided up between ot German states.

Palermo: Panormus in classical tim seaport on the north coast of Sic developed by Phoenicians and Cart ginians in a capacious bay sheltered fro westerlies. It fell to Rome in 254 BC, the Vandals in AD 440 and to Byzantiu in 535. The Arabs made it capital of Sic in 831. It reached its zenith under t Normans and Hohenstaufens betwe 1072 and 1266, when it was, after Co stantinople, the largest and richest ci of Christendom. Its cathedral of Mo reale and its Palace Chapel show t fusion of Romanesque, Byzantine ar Saracenic design. It was torn by the rival of Angevins and Aragonese and declin under Spanish domination. It was libe ated by Garibaldi's patriots in 1860 and 1946 became the seat of a parliame when Sicily was granted home rule.

Palestine: region of Asia Minor at th eastern end of the Mediterranean approx mately 150 miles [240 kilometres] fro north to south, between the paralle 31°30′ and 33°, and stretching back fro the sea, to an average depth of eight miles [128·75 kilometres], as far as the ari eastern scarp of the Jordan valley. Th famous river, rising in Mount Hermo away to the north, flows down to th Dead Sea, 1,240 feet [377·95 metre below sea level, where, in one of th hottest and driest places in the world, i waters evaporate.

The name Palestine, said to be derive from the Philistines, is first found in th 2nd century AD and was in general use a time of the Crusades, which were ected thither by the fact that the land s the ancient home of the Jews and ntained the holy city of Jerusalem and ner places dear to Christians. Now, as modern state of Israel, it is once more home of the Jewish race.

'he area, with the inhospitable desert etching along its eastern side, is a tural corridor through which the mies of the great empires of the cient world would march or in which ey would clash, a process which can read as a background to the biblical count of Jewish history. In the Chrisn era, the Romans and their successors, e eastern emperors of Constantinople, led over the land until in 636 the lohammedan conquerors took their ace and, with the 200-year interlude of e "Latin" kingdom of the Crusaders, mained in possession until the collapse Turkey at the end of World War I. he country was then entrusted to Great Britain under a mandate and the name Palestine formally revived. In 1948 it was handed over partly to the new state of Israel and partly to that of Jordan, but since then the former has occupied nearly the whole of the area.

See also ISRAEL; JERUSALEM; JORDAN; PHILISTINES.

Palestrina, Giovanni Pierluigi da (*c.* 1518–94): Italian composer of the great age of counterpoint. In counterpoint independent voice-parts, sung simultaneously, are combined to produce the kind of tonal texture later supplied by musical instruments. Palestrina's compositions are among the finest 16th-century works of this kind.

Palladio, Andrea or **Andrea di Pietro** (1508–80): Italian architect who modelled his designs, though with a freedom of invention all his own, on the buildings of ancient Rome. He designed churches and

hiswick House, London, modelled by Lord Burlington on Palladio's Villa Rotonda, near icenza, Italy.

palaces and, especially, magnificent country villas which greatly influenced the work of such famous 18th-century English architects as Inigo Jones (1573-1652) and Sir John Vanbrugh (1664-1726). He gave his name to the architectural style now known as "Palladian".

Palmerston, Henry John Temple, third Viscount (1784-1865): British Foreign Secretary for fourteen years and Prime Minister for ten. Intolerant of foreigners, "Pam" typified the attitudes of his time: distrust of Russia and France, sympathy for Liberal causes (e.g. in Belgium and Italy), patriotism and determination to uphold all Englishmen.

Palmyra: Solomon's Tadmor, or "city of palms", an oasis of sulphur springs at the junction of caravan routes to the Euphrates, Damascus and Petra. By 2000 BC it had been developed by Babylonians and Aramaeans and reached its zenith when Rome and Parthia confronted each other across the Syrian desert. Rome s[...] ported the local king Odenathus and [...] daughter Zenobia. Under them Palm[...] became the greatest caravan city, [...] 30,000 inhabitants, a banking capital w[...] agents on the Tigris and Danube, [...] Egypt, Gaul and Spain. The Palmyre[...] spoke Aramaean or Greek, took th[...] house design from Babylon, furnishi[...] from Persia and philosophy from Gree[...] Their mounted archers served Rome [...] far away as Hadrian's Wall. Palmyra w[...] sacked by the Emperor Aurelian in AD 2[...] after which it never recovered its form[...] importance. Its ruins – the temple of [...] and the great colonnaded way – survi[...] and were revealed to scholars by Rob[...] Wood's *Ruins of Palmyra*, 1753.

Pan-: prefix (deriving from a Gre[...] word meaning "all" or "completely[...] often applied to countries, moveme[...] and organisations aiming at unity or co[...] pleteness. The following four entries a[...] typical examples. Others are the nou[...] Pan-Arabism, Pan-Germanism, and t[...]

The Ruins of Palmyra, *1753 by Robert Wood.*

ectives Pan-Hellenic, Pan-Christian, n-Islamic, etc. Similarly, a *pandemic* is epidemic affecting a whole country or wide area of the world, e.g. the Black eath of 1347–51, which is estimated to ve caused 75 million deaths. A *pan-nonium* (a word coined by Milton), or te of confused uproar, means literally e abode of all demons.

n-Africanism: movements, especi-y in the 20th century, designed to pro-ote African unity and establish black premacy in Africa (*see*, e.g., ORGANISA-ON OF AFRICAN UNITY).

an-American Highway: the great ad system running from Fairbanks, laska, to Buenos Aires, Argentina, with anches to all Central and South Ameri-n countries. It is the longest motorable ad in the world and will eventually retch 13,859 miles [22,300 kilometres] om Alaska to southern Chile. There is present a 450-mile [725-kilometre] gap he "Darien Gap") across the border of nama and Colombia.

an-Americanism: movement to pro-ote full co-operation among all the ates of the Americas (*see* ORGANISATION F AMERICAN STATES). Pan-American Day celebrated on 14 April. The Pan-Ameri-n Union has its headquarters in Wash-gton, DC, an organisation maintained y more than twenty North and South merican countries to encourage friendly lationships.

an-Slavism: movement aimed at pro-oting the unity and independence of lav peoples, i.e. the group of Eastern uropean races which includes the chief thnic groups of the USSR, Ukrainians, oles, Czechs, Slovaks, Serbs, Croats, ulgars, etc. Though at its best encour-ging cultural and political co-operation, it has often been a vehicle for securing territorial expansion (e.g. by Russia) and has led to a number of wars.

Panama: republic in Central America. It covers the isthmus of the same name joining the two American continents, being some 350 miles [565 kilometres] long with an average breadth of approximately 60 miles [95 kilometres]. It is not always realised that this larger axis lies from west to east and that the Panama Canal (*see* next entry) actually runs in a south-easterly direction from the Atlantic to the Pacific Oceans.

The first contacts with Europe came when the Spaniards found the isthmus an essential link between their colonies on the two oceans, shipping their treasure from Peru to Panama and transporting it across the part of the isthmus known as Darien to Porto Bello. After the revolutions of the early 19th century, Panama was for nearly 100 years part of the state of Colombia, its neighbour to the south; but in 1902 the USA, anxious to revive the Canal project, helped to secure the independence of the Republic of Panama, in return for control of the Canal Zone, now the subject of much national emotion. The political history of the new state has been, and remains, unsteady and violent.

¶ HOWARTH, DAVID. *The Golden Isthmus*. 1966

The Panama Canal under construction.

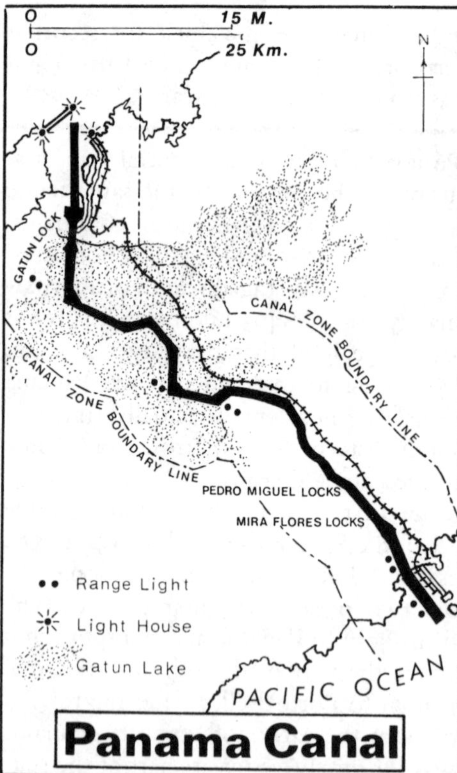

Panama Canal: passage for ocean-going vessels through the isthmus of Panama, saving the long journey round Cape Horn. The distance between deep water at either end is fifty miles [80·47 kilometres], and six massive pairs of locks are needed for crossing the central ridge. The first attempt at making a canal, by the Frenchman De Lesseps (*see* separate entry) of Suez Canal fame, ended in scandal and failure in 1889; but a fresh undertaking with the backing of the USA was successfully completed after ten years work in 1914. A project is now being examined to use atomic force to blast a fresh passage through the isthmus at sea level throughout its course.

¶ CAMERON, IAN. *Impossible Dream: the building of the Panama Canal.* 1971

Pankhurst, Emmeline (1858–1928): British suffragette leader. She worked with her husband for the passage of the Married Women's Property Act, a with her daughters Christabel and Syl founded the Women's Social and Politi Union (1898). Their methods includ interruption of political meetings, vi lence and hunger strikes. Several tim imprisoned, once for attempting to f Lloyd George's house, she was releas in 1914 and supported the war effo Once a Liberal, then a member of t Independent Labour Party, in 1926 s became a Conservative candidate f Parliament. She died a month befo women of twenty-one obtained the vot

¶ KAMM, JOSEPHINE. *The Story of Mrs. Pankhu* 1963; SNELLGROVE, L. E. *Suffragettes and Votes Women.* 1964

See also EMANCIPATION OF WOMEN.

Pantomime: a traditional stage ente tainment which includes dancing, mus and spectacle devised round the core a fairy story or folk tale. According to th particular plot, the cast includes certa characters, usually broadly comic, suc as the Ugly Sisters and the Broker Men in *Cinderella*, which have becom hallowed by time.

Ancient Greek and Roman pantomim were dumb shows. Their stylised pos

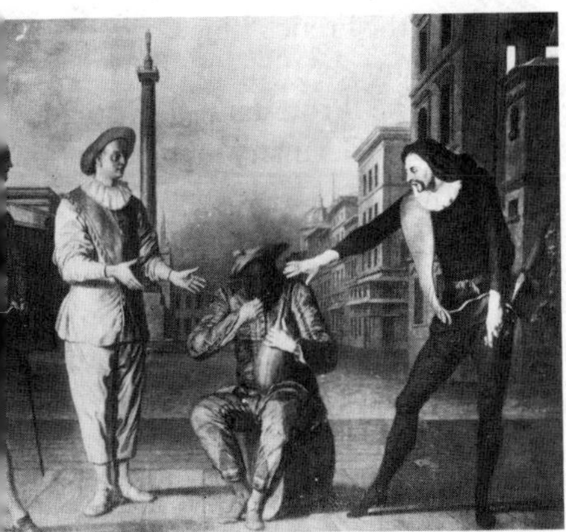

scene from the Commedia Dell' arte, by Gillot, ŀth century.

ıd gesticulations had more in common ith ballet than with drama.

Towards the end of the 16th century a ›mic entertainment originating in Italy ıd known as the *commedia dell' arte* be- .me popular in many European ›untries. France had a low-comedy ıtertainment of its own, popular at fairs, ıown as *vaudeville*. English pantomime we know it today may be said to have ɜveloped from a combination of these vo elements, with a spice of Victorian ıusic-hall thrown in for good measure.

---

aoli, Pasquale (1725–1807)**:** Corsican atriot. Sharing his father's exile, he ained as a cavalryman in the army of laples. In 1755 he successfully led a ;orsican rising against Genoa, and intro- uced reforms based on his study of ;ousseau. When Genoa sold Corsica to rance in 1768, he resisted French attacks ut was beaten at Ponte Nuovo in 1769 nd fled to London, where he was wel- omed by Dr Johnson's circle. The French ⁊evolution allowed him to resume power ı Corsica in 1791, but he thwarted the 3onaparte family, was denounced by hem and accepted British protection. 3ritain preferred to govern through ›ozzo di Borgo, and Paoli retired to ,ondon, where he died.

Papacy, The: the name given to the office held by the popes, in the same way that "the monarchy" is the name given to the office held by kings and queens. The word "pope" means father, deriving from late Latin *papa*: in earlier centuries all Christians regarded the pope as father of the Christian family, and he is still regarded in that way by Roman Catholics. The position of the pope rests on the belief that Jesus Christ came on earth to found his Church, and that before he ascended into heaven he entrusted that Church to Peter and the other disciples, but to Peter especially because he evidently took the lead amongst the disciples of Jesus and to him Jesus said, "Thou art Peter, and upon this rock I will build my church." (The name Peter comes from the Latin *petrus*, a rock.) Peter went to Rome, where he suffered martyrdom; so his successors as bishops of Rome were, from the 1st century, generally regarded as heads of the Christian Church, and they still enjoy a certain precedence among the bishops of the world, although their authority today extends only over the Roman Catholic Church. St Peter's Cathedral, at Rome, was built over the tomb of her first bishop.

In the days of the ancient Roman Empire the popes were subject, like other Christians, to persecution and martyrdom until the reign of the first Christian Emperor, Constantine (AD 307–337). But this same Constantine moved the imperial capital from Rome to the eastern city named after him, Constantinople, which left Rome subject to many centuries of war and revolutions, and the papacy itself was often in great danger. Later, in the 8th century, the Frankish kings, whose rule extended over much of what today we call France, and who had been converted to Christianity, protected the popes by giving them political rule over some territory around Rome to serve for their defence: in this way there first appeared the Papal States (*see* separate entry) over which the pope ruled as a "temporal" or *political* ruler, in contrast to his *spiritual* rule over the Christian Church as a whole; but today the pope is *political* ruler only over the city state of the Vatican at Rome.

In the Middle Ages, at least until the 13th century, the position of the popes tended to grow stronger; they settled disputes about religious doctrine, insisted on the rights of the Church against emperors and kings, or sent out missionaries to convert heathen lands, as Pope Gregory I sent Augustine to convert England in the year 597. It was in the 13th century, under Pope Innocent III, that the papacy of the Middle Ages attained to its greatest spiritual and political influence; men came to speak of the "two swords" by which they meant the "sword" of the spiritual and the "sword" of the political authority, the former wielded by the popes and the other bishops and the latter by emperors and kings; and of these two swords the more effective was often the spiritual. The pope, indeed, was often strong enough to compel even emperors and kings to obey him. Yet already the authority of the papacy was challenged. The Church centred on Constantinople (later known as the Orthodox Eastern Church) repudiated the pope's authority in the 11th century, and in the 14th century the disturbances at Rome became so serious that for a time the popes moved to Avignon in France to be under the protection of the French kings, who natur took advantage of their position as p tectors. The Protestant Reformation England and Germany in the 16th cent was largely a revolt against the pa authority, while later on, in the 1 century, even the Catholic rulers Europe often defied the pope on matt of church discipline and dogma. T great French Revolution of 1789– which was partly a revolt against Catholic Church, saw the fortunes of papacy at their lowest ebb. The rul pope, Pius VI, was dragged into Fra as a prisoner and it seemed that the life the papacy itself was at an end.

But a new revival now took place, a the 19th and 20th centuries saw the off of the papacy renewed in strength. W the disappearance, in the 19th century, the pope's political rule over the Pa States in central Italy, the religious au ority of the popes grew stronger, playi an important part in the general religic revival which took place in that centu and in the great expansion in missiona activity all over the world. In the ye 1870, at a General Council of the bisho of the Catholic Church, and now know as the First Vatican Council, it was d creed that, on the (very rare) occasio when the pope defines a dogma co cerning a matter of faith or a matter morals, he speaks infallibly, that is say he cannot be mistaken because he w be guided by the Holy Spirit. This called the "papal infallibility", som thing that belongs to the office of po rather than to a particular person, an something in which the Catholic Chur has generally believed in past centuri although it only came to be defined in th 19th century.

The Vatican made history in 1978 wh the cardinals elected Cardinal Kar Wojtyla as Pope John Paul II. He was th first Pole and the first non-Italian in 4

The Palace of the Popes, Avignon.

ırs to hold the post. He succeeded Pope ın Paul I who only lived two months the office. Pope John Paul II has velled more widely than any Pope in tory and imposed an authoritarian :hodoxy in matters of dogma.

e also AUGUSTINE, ST; CONSTANTINE; THODOX EASTERN CHURCH.

ıpal States: parts of Italy at one time led by the pope. The pope, though .hop of Rome and spiritual head of the ıtholic Church throughout the world, ed also to be the political ruler of central .ly: this was called his "temporal" as ntrasted with his "spiritual" power and meant that he provided the ordinary vernment in that region. When he first quired these states, in the 8th century, ey extended for only a few miles around ɔme: later they came to cover the whole central Italy, including the city of Bologna, which is some 200 miles [320 kilometres] north of Rome. And, whereas at first they provided a useful protection for the papacy, they later brought so many political problems for the popes that they became a distraction and a spiritual danger. In the wars of 1860–70, by which the kingdom of Italy was united, Pope Pius IX was deprived of these states. In protest he shut himself up in the palace of the Vatican and for a time was known as "the prisoner in the Vatican"; but in 1929, by the Lateran treaty with the kingdom of Italy, Pope Pius XI recognised the new kingdom, and the king of Italy, in exchange, recognised the independence of the pope's Vatican city state, a small territory around the Vatican palace at Rome, which serves today to ensure that the pope is not the subject of any government.

¶ DEEDY, JOHN. *The Vatican.* 1970

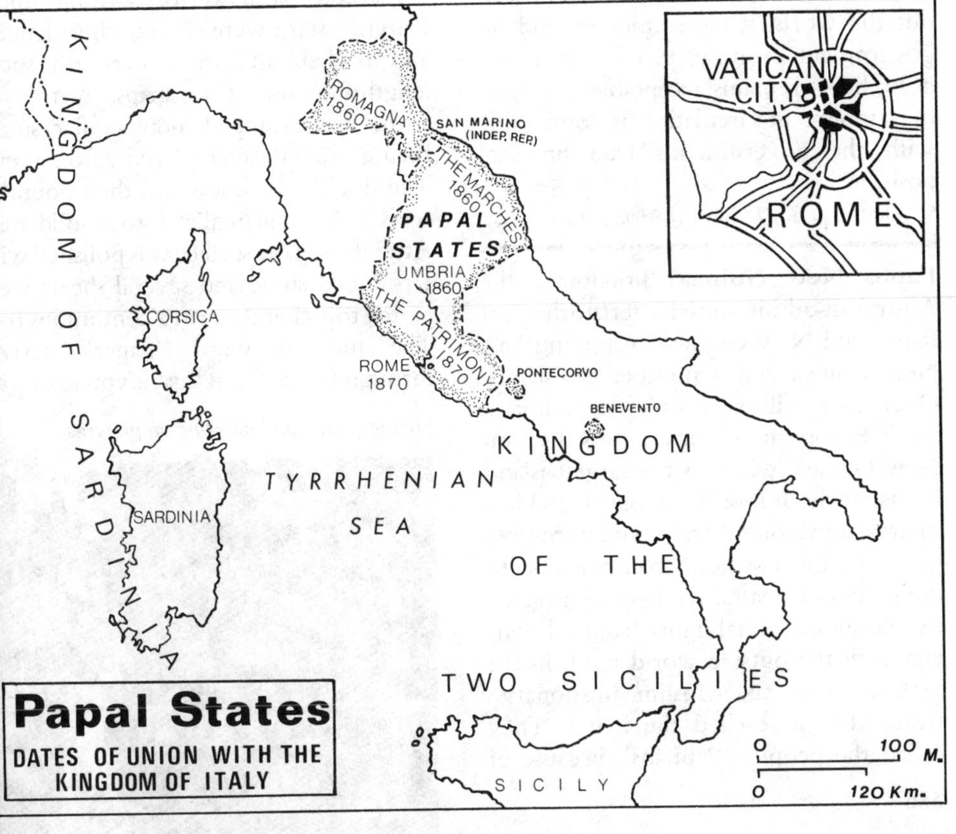

Paper money: printed documents issued by a government to serve as currency. In England, the Bank Charter Act of 1844 laid down that almost the whole issue of Bank of England notes must be backed by gold. The sovereign and half-sovereign were replaced during the war of 1914–18 by Treasury notes, and the issue of these was transferred to the Bank of England in 1928. In September 1931 Great Britain abandoned the Gold Standard, and Bank of England notes became inconvertible (i.e. could not be exchanged for gold). In the USA non-convertible bank notes, the famous "greenbacks", were issued during the Civil War to the extent of $450 million. When Rutherford Hayes (president 1877–81) took office there were still about $350 million in circulation and he consented to an act of Congress (1878) making them a permanent part of the currency.

At the present time most money throughout the world is paper money, and no government promises to convert it into gold, but it remains acceptable as long as the amount in circulation is compatible with the government's true financial position.

¶ QUIGGIN, A. H. *The Story of Money*. 1956

Papua New Guinea: previously the Australian-administered territories of Papua and New Guinea, occupying East New Guinea and a number of islands. Over two million people, including a small European minority, now live on New Guinea, which is the largest island in the world. It is only 80 miles [130 kilometres] north of Australia, and its remote geographical position, combined with difficulties of coastal navigation, isolated its Melanesian inhabitants from all contact with the outside world until, in the 15th century AD, Muslim missionaries from Malaya reached the island. They called the people "Papuans" because of their curly black hair (Malay *pepu* frizzled).

The Portuguese named the island "N Guinea" when they discovered it in 15 The Dutch came in the 17th century a kept control of the western half (n called West Irian) until driven out Indonesian troops in 1962. The easte half had been partitioned between Brit and Germany in 1884, but after 19 Britain claimed it all for Australia. Du ing World War II the whole island w ruled by the Japanese. Papua New Guin achieved independence in 1974.

Papyrus: aquatic plant originating the Nile valley. The papyrus reed c grow up to 10 feet [3 metres] tall, with thick stem crowned by a feathery gre top. As early as 3,000 BC the Egyptia knew how to make from the reeds fabric which they used for sails, ropes ar sandals, as well as for writing upo Papyrus stems were cut into short lengt and peeled, and the inner pith slic lengthwise into thin strips. A row strips was arranged along a flat ston then a second layer placed across ther The double thickness was then pound with a wooden mallet into a solid ma After drying, its surface was polished wi a rounded stone and several sheets we pasted together to form a continuous ro The modern word "paper" deriv through Greek from this Egyptian origi

Hieroglyphics and painting on papyrus.

racelsus, Philippus Aureolus (1493–41): Swiss physician and chemist. This ntroversial figure attacked the foundons of ancient medicine and some of theories foreshadowed modern medipractice. He introduced mineral baths his treatments and added such inedients as opium, mercury, iron, arsenic d copper sulphate to his medicines. He o wrote a book on mental diseases.

rachute: umbrella-shaped contrivance r dropping men or supplies from a ight, the fall being slowed by resistance the air gathered in the fabric cover durg the descent. The first practical demonration, made as a useful means of escaping om fire, was from the tower of Montllier Observatory in 1783 by Sebastian normand. J. P. Blanchard (1753–1809) iginated the idea of parachute drops om balloons, the possibilities being rther demonstrated by André Jacques arnerin (1770–1823), who made fre-

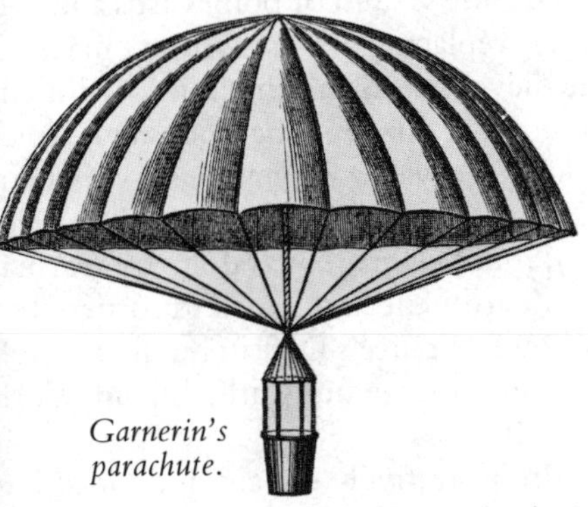

Garnerin's parachute.

uent descents from balloons both in rance and in England. In 1797, at Monceau Park, Paris, he dropped from a eight of 2,236 feet [681·53 metres]. The rst parachute descent from an aeroplane vas made in 1912 by Captain Albert Berry of the US Air Force. The greatest ltitude (and the longest delayed parahute opening) was recorded by another JS airman, Captain Joseph Kittinger, vho in 1960 dropped 102,200 feet [31,151 metres], the first 84,700 [25,816] being a "free fall". The total descent was over 19 miles [30·57 kilometres], made in 13 minutes 45 seconds.

¶ DWIGGINS, DON. *Bailout: the story of parachuting and skydiving.* 1969

Paraguay: republic of central South America, between the rivers Paraguay and Parana, now inhabited by some three million people. The first Spanish settlement was made at Asunción in 1537, and this became the centre for Spanish exploration and conquest of the surrounding forests and grasslands. Here the Jesuits (see separate entry) set up forty-eight remarkable mission settlements, from which they directed the life, work and worship of thousands of natives and, by hard work and good organisation, produced cotton, tobacco and hides. Fields and cattle were common property. Unfortunately slave traders from Brazil destroyed more than half these missions, and when the King of Spain expelled all Jesuits from his empire in 1767 these prosperous communities broke up. Paraguay declared itself independent of Spain in 1811, but an attempt to extend its territory in 1865 led to a war against Argentina, Brazil and Uruguay which drastically reduced its population. Its boundaries were not finally settled until 1938 after another war (1932–35), with Bolivia. Political unrest has made steady economic progress difficult and communications remain poor. Considerable mineral resources, among them copper, iron and manganese, are largely unexploited. Exports include timber, cotton, tobacco, hides and meat.

See ENDPAPERS for map.

¶ WARREN, H. G. *Paraguay: an informal history.* 1949

Parchment: skin of calves, sheep, goats, etc., prepared for writing, or a paper made to imitate it. In former times many

documents testifying to competence in various professions were written on it, so that to "receive one's parchment" was a common expression. The name originated from the city of Pergamum (modern Bergama) in north-west Asia Minor. Since parchment was an expensive commodity it was frequently re-used in early centuries, after the original inscription had been scraped off. Such a document is termed a *palimpsest*, from Greek words for "again" and "scrape".
See also ILLUMINATED BOOKS.

Paris: capital of France, one of the most visited cities in the world, and a centuries-old leader in European art and culture.

The city's growth from what was, in the 1st century BC, a fishing village on an island in the Seine, may be attributed partly to its position at the intersection of important natural highways and trade routes, and partly to its choice by Clovis, early in the 6th century, as the capital from which he could administer his newly won territories of southern France. The present-day map shows Paris like the hub of an immense wheel with roads, railways and air routes converging on it from every point of the compass.

Among its great buildings are the Cathedral of Notre Dame, built on the site where the Romans had a temple of Jupiter; the Basilica of Saint Denis, where a succession of sixty-three abbots ruled for more than a thousand years, where the ancient banner of France was kept in time of peace and where twelve centuries of royalty were brought to rest; and the Louvre, formerly a royal palace and now the national art gallery and museum of France. More modern structures include the Eiffel Tower and the Arc de Triomphe (which Napoleon planned to celebrate the victories of his legions, but which he never saw completed). A legacy of his namesake, Napoleon III's reign, is the

Looking towards the Arc de Triomphe, Place l'Etoile, Paris.

handsome system of boulevards and ave-nues replacing the twisting maze c medieval streets in which it was difficu to control a mob. The wide new stree allowed cavalry to charge down them During the Franco-Prussian War (1870–71), much damage was done by Germa bombardment and in the disorders tha followed France's Defeat; but fortunatel the city emerged unscathed from Worl War II.

Administratively the city is divided int twenty *arrondisements* (wards or districts) each made up of four *quartiers* (quarters) Less official, but even better known, ar such popular terms as "Left Bank" fo the area containing the famous Universit (or Latin) quarter and most of the surviv-ing medieval buildings; and "Righ Bank", which is the financial and com-mercial nerve-centre. It must not be for-gotten that, although it is over 100 mile [160 kilometres] from the sea, Paris is on the greatest ports of France and that it responsible for about a fifth of the untry's total production.

e also BASTILLE; FRANCE; FRANCO-USSIAN WAR; LOUVRE; ST DENIS; VER-ILLES.

aris, Treaty of (1763): treaty signed ter four months of negotiation to end e conflict of Britain with France and ain in the Seven Years War (*see* separate try). France gave up to Britain all anada and lands east of the River Mis-sippi, four West Indian islands, and cepted the domination of the British ast India Company in trade; to Spain, ance gave Louisiana and control of the ississippi mouth. The French had lost dly and their colonial power was virtu-ly ended. But some Englishmen thought e treaty was not glorious enough; only fficulty in raising taxes to continue the ar prevented England from demanding erner terms.

arliament: chief law-making body of any countries. The *Anglo-Saxon Chron-le* tells us that William the Conqueror eld "very deep speech with his Witan", d the French name for this discussion or arley was *parlement*, although this name as not actually used for meetings of the reat council of England until the Statue f Westminster in 1275. The Model arliament of 1295 set the pattern of ture developments. By this time, what ad begun as a feudal assembly of tenants-1-chief had become an assembly of the ree estates of the realm, clergy, barons, nd commons. The third estate consisted f the knights of the shire and the bur-esses. We first find mention of the former 1 a summons to a council at Oxford in 213, which directed the sheriffs to bring vith them "*quatuor discretos milites . . . ad oquendum nobiscum de negotiis regni nostri*" four wise knights to discuss with us the business of our realm), while representa-tives of the boroughs were summoned for the first time in 1265 at the instigation of Simon de Montfort. On this occasion the towns received their summons directly from the Crown, and not, as in 1295, through the sheriffs of their shires. We do not know exactly when Lords and Com-mons began to sit as two separate houses. The historian William Stubbs thought that they did so from the Model Parlia-ment onwards, but Frederick Maitland, professor of the laws of England at Cam-bridge, favoured the middle of the 14th century. The Commons sat in the Abbey Chapter House, while the Lords gathered in the painted Parliament Chamber at the south end of the palace of Westminster.

The Parliament at Westminster has been called "the mother of Parliaments", as this system has been copied in many countries. In this connection it is impor-tant to remember that the English Con-stitution is largely unwritten and flexible, whereas its imitators throughout the world have generally tried to base their system on a written and more rigid con-stitution. The constitutional struggles of the 17th century were an attempt to pre-vent the officers of government acting independently of Parliament and also interference by the Crown with its rights as a law-making body. The Bill of Rights 1689, and the Act of Settlement 1701, en-sured the supremacy of Parliament, the responsibility of Ministers to Parliament, and the independence of judges. This type of arrangement is often referred to as The Separation of Powers; i.e. the separation of the legislative body (who make the laws) from the executive (the officials who seek to administer and enforce the laws) and the judiciary (the judges and other law officers who interpret the laws in the courts, when they have been broken or are in dispute). This was of great im-portance, as it inspired the French Decla-

Above, seating plan for the opening of Parliament at Blackfriars, 1525, drawn by Garter King at Arms. Above right, The House of Commons, 1793. Below right, moving to address the Crown, 1833.

ration of the Rights of Man (1789) and the Constitution of the United States. Nevertheless, separation of powers does not exist in this country to the extent that it exists in the United States. The House of Lords is a part of the supreme legislature, but it is also the final Court of Appeal; the Cabinet forms the Executive, but its members are also members of either the House of Commons or House of Lords. Judges have no power to declare a statute void, although they do protect the rights of individuals against Parliament in anything less than statute. Further, a government could not remain in office without the command of a majority in the House of Commons, whereas an American President may find himself faced by a representative assembly dominated by the opposition party. This happened to President Truman in 1946 and to President Eisenhower in 1956.

Further difficulties arise in the application of parliamentary government federal states. Two different solutions a possible, as exemplified by the constit tions set up in Canada and Australia wh they achieved Dominion status within t British Commonwealth. Australia is genuine federation in that the states ha handed over some forty topics for t consideration of the federal legislatur retaining all other powers themselve while in Canada the reverse is the cas the provinces having definite powers legislation on sixteen allotted subject while the residue of power lies with th central legislature. In the United Stat also the residuary power lies in the stat and not with the central legislature.

Parliamentary government has met wit varying success in different countries. O authority suggests that it has proved mo successful in Belgium, Holland and th Scandinavian countries, where the u written conventions on which it depen supported by "a basis of beliefs and litions comparable to those that pre- in England" and by monarchies dedi- ed to constitutional rule. Parliamentary vernment in France which developed ing the 19th century was intended to ow the British model, but results were appointing, chiefly because election by portional representation led to the ation of a large number of small parties, h incapable of forming a government itself. Hence a government was formed a coalition of parties, and this tended be unstable and of short duration, and apable of reaching a final decision on al problems. This was seen when the tem collapsed on being confronted by Algerian problem. The arrangement er adopted (1958) was a blend of itish and American elements. Similarly, system adopted in Germany after the r of 1914–18 was on the French model, d this also collapsed and was replaced the Nazi dictatorship. Following orld War II, Germany adopted a new nstitution in May 1949 which provides r parliamentary government of the itish type, adapted to federalism. The esident is elected for a five-year term, e Lower House is elected by universal ffrage for four years, while the Upper ouse consists of delegates of the *Länder* ne States of the Federation) with no ed term of office.

t remains to discuss the power of a rliament to amend the constitution. In e United Kingdom there are no funda- ental constitutional statutes, and Magna arta or the Bill of Rights could be re- ealed by Parliament in the same way as ny other piece of legislation, although is of course is unlikely to happen. With written constitution, amendments to e constitution require a different legis- tive procedure from that used for her purposes. Thus, in the United tates, the constitution can be changed only on the motion of two-thirds of each House of Congress, ratified by the legislatures of three-quarters of the states, while in Eire and Australia a referendum is used for this purpose.

¶ ALLEN, AGNES. *The Story of Our Parliament.* 1971; PRENTICE, D. M. *Your Book of Parliament.* 1967; MACKENZIE, K. R. *Parliament.* 1962

See also CONSTITUTION (AMERICAN); CONSTITUTION (BRITISH) *etc.*

Parnell, Charles Stewart (1846–91): Irish Nationalist leader. Known as the uncrowned king of Ireland, Parnell nearly obtained Irish self-government, but domestic scandal ruined his career. As an MP and head of the Home Rule Party, he used the balance of power between Liberals and Conservatives to secure land reforms for Ireland.

Pascal, Blaise (1623–62): French mathematician, scientist and religious philosopher. A precocious genius, at the age of sixteen Pascal interested Descartes in his book on geometry. Centuries ahead of his time, he worked on the problems of the vacuum, equilibrium of liquids, atmospheric pressure and the theory of probability. He also invented the first calculating machine. Because of a religious experience, he turned overnight from his former life to become a Jansenist monk. His *Provincial Letters* are literary classics that replied to Jesuit condemnation of Jansenism. *Pensées* presented his belief that only faith can free men from their tragic situation.

Pasteur, Louis (1822–95): French scientist. Pasteur discovered that bacteria spread diseases and can live almost everywhere, but can be controlled. He showed how to preserve milk, beer and foodstuffs by means of controlled heat (pasteurisation), which killed germs. In his method of vaccination, he first weakened microbes

Louis Pasteur in his laboratory.

in the laboratory, then placed them in an animal's body. The animal afterwards developed immunity to the microbe. Another great discovery was the successful treatment of rabies, for which there had previously been no remedy.

The Pasteur Institute in Paris was founded in 1888 as a world centre for the study, prevention and treatment of diseases. Here Pasteur is buried in the place where he worked on bacteriology to benefit humanity.

¶ BURTON, M. J. *Louis Pasteur: founder of microbiology.* 1964

Patagonia: region of southern Argentina. Magellan named this land "Patagonia" because he found "large footsteps" on the coast in 1520. These were made by the clumsy moccasins worn by Indians, whose descendants, though a tiny remnant, still inhabit the rocky and windswept territory which extends from 40° South latitude to the islands of Tierra del Fuego. The Spaniard Pedro Sarmiento started a settlement on the Straits of Magellan, but it was attacked by English sailors and renamed "Port Famine". Welshmen who settled on the Chabut River in 1865 s[urvived] vived with Indian help, and the sett[le]ment exists today. In 1881 Patagonia w[as] partitioned between Chile and Argenti[na], the boundary being the Andes.

See ENDPAPERS for map.

Pathan: generic name given to warri[or] Muslim tribes – Yusufzais, Khatta[ks], Mohmands, Afridis, Wazirs, Mashuds on and beyond the North-West Fronti[er] of Pakistan (formerly India). Their risi[ng] against British control in 1897 was p[ut] down by the Malakand Field Force a[nd] the Tirah expedition, both campaig[ns] brilliantly described by Winston Church[ill] who accompanied them.

Patriarch: in general, the tradition[al] founder of a tribe or family. The wor[d], however, has a special meaning in [its] application to the founders of the hum[an] race up to the time of the Flood as na[r]rated in the Old Testament. It is also t[he] title of certain holders of the highest offic[es] in the Orthodox Eastern Church (*s*[ee] separate entry).

Patrician: in general, an adjective deno[t]ing membership of an aristocratic [or] privileged class. In particular, the word [is] applied to a feature of the political syste[m] of Rome during the republican e[ra] (roughly five centuries from 519 BC) when the patrician class filled by righ[t] most of the chief positions in public life.

See also PLEBEIAN.

Patrick, St (*c.* 385–461)**:** patron saint [of] Ireland. Facts can be separated fro[m] legends about the apostle only by usin[g] his own writings. Reputedly born i[n] Wales, son of a Romano-British deacon he was captured in his youth by pirate[s] and taken to Ireland as a slave. Afte[r] escaping to France, he entered a mona[s]stery at Lérins. He was trained for th[e] esthood at Auxerre and consecrated hop. Then he returned to Ireland which, ough no longer pagan, was not fully nverted, particularly in the remoter gions. First Patrick tackled the princes Tara and then went on to convert the ople, in the face of stern opposition om the Druids. He established numerous urches and religious communities and unded the Cathedral Church of magh, thenceforth the centre of Irish ristianity. Croagh Patrick in Country ayo became a pilgrim centre, and the lt of St Patrick began after his death.

UFFY, JOSEPH. *St. Patrick in His Own Words.* 72; HANSON, R. P. C. *Saint Patrick.* 1968

aul III (Alessandro Farnese, 1468–1549): ope 1534. He became pope by promisg to call a General Council, which he id not do for over ten years. He promoted the Counter-Reformation (removal of imperfections within the Roman Church) appointing a number of saintly ardinals, encouraging missions and new eligious orders (Theatines, Jesuits), and n 1537 setting up a commission to recommend reforms. After several frustrations e called together the Council of Trent which met in 1545 and dragged on till 563. Cautious and persistent, he saw the eed for reform, and promoted it without ever himself becoming fired by its arnest sincerity. Brought up at the court of Lorenzo da Medici, he enjoyed the luxury of his villa at Bolsena, made Michelangelo papal architect, consulted astrologers before any decision and made two unworthy grandsons cardinals.

Paul VI (Giovanni Battista Montini, (1897—1978): pope elected 1963. He found the burden of Infallibility heavy when faced with demands by Catholics for a married clergy (when there is a shortage of priests) and for birth control (when the world faces overpopulation). From his father, lawyer, politician and newspaper owner, and his mother, an active social worker, and he was sympathetic to the worker-priest movement. He proved an able administrator in the Papal Secretariat, but apart from a chaplaincy to students held no pastoral charge until made Bishop of Milan in 1954. There he sold Church lands to build new churches, and was a tireless visitor of mines and factories. The first pope to travel to all continents, he narrowly escaped assassination in Manila in 1970. He was represented at the enthronement of the new Archbishop of Canterbury, Dr Coggan, in 1975.

¶ MACGREGOR-HASTIE, ROY. *Pope Paul VI.* 1966

Paul, St (d. *c.* AD 64 or 67): the "Apostle of the Gentiles", a Jew, born at Tarsus and in his early years called Saul. He was not one of the original band of apostles and, indeed, persecuted the early Church until, on the road to Damascus, a sudden vision changed his whole life. Thereafter he laboured unceasingly to spread the Christian message, particularly among the Gentiles – that is to say the non-Jews – of Greece and Asia Minor. His missionary journeys are recorded in the Acts of the Apostles, and we also learn much about him from the Epistles (letters) which he wrote to the early Christian communities and in which he developed many of the ideas which guide the Church today. In due course he was arrested by the authorities in Jerusalem; but, since he happened to enjoy Roman citizenship, he claimed his right to appeal to the emperor. Brought to Rome, after shipwreck on the voyage, he remained in captivity for two years and was then beheaded, traditionally on the same day as that on which St Peter (*see* separate entry) also suffered martyrdom in a different way.

¶ LUCE, H. K. *St. Paul.* 1957

Pearl Harbour: main US naval base in Hawaii. Although there had been no declaration of war, Japanese aircraft attacked Pearl Harbour on 7 December 1941. In an action lasting only two hours the Japanese sank or disabled nineteen ships, destroyed 120 aircraft, and killed 2,400 people. Such a treacherous act, carried out while diplomatic negotiations were still proceeding, led to the entry of the USA into World War II. Congress declared war on Japan on 8 December: Germany and Italy, Japan's allies, declared war on America on 11 December. The immediate effect of this attack on Pearl Harbour was, as a result of American naval losses, to give an initial advantage

The USS West Virginia *on fire after t Japanese attack, Pearl Harbour, 1941.*

to Japanese sea power in the Pacif Ocean.

¶ BARKER, ARTHUR J. *Pearl Harbour.* 1970

Peasants' Revolt: name given to rebellion which took place in England i 1381. The Black Death, which in the 14t century killed off a third of the populatio upset the economy of the country, an led to great unrest among the peasant an labouring classes. The war with Franc (the Hundred Years War) put an ad ditional strain on the nation's resource In 1381 an unjust poll tax brought dis content to a head. Rioting, which wa widespread, in Kent assumed the characte of rebellion.

Under the leadership of Wat Tyler (tha is, Wat the tiler) the rebels seized Canter bury and marched on London, burnin and pillaging on the way. Sympathiser let them into the city, where the destroyed palaces and prisons. Kin Richard II (1367–1400), a boy of fourteen bravely rode out to confer with them a Mile End, outside the city walls, and - having no other choice — agreed to thei demands, which amounted to the abo lition of the feudal system.

While the necessary documents wer being prepared, Tyler and a party o

›els entered the Tower and murdered non of Sudbury, the Archbishop of nterbury, and Sir Robert Hales, the yal treasurer. For two days London was ven over to mob violence, the rebels ereby forfeiting much popular sym-thy. Richard again went to meet them, s time at Smithfield. Tyler's demands ere now much more sweeping, his anner so threatening that the Lord ayor and one of the King's squires led him. Richard averted a perilous uation by courageously spurring his rse forward, shouting to the rebels: irs, will you shoot your king? I will be ur chief and captain, you shall have m me all that you seek."

he King did not keep his word. With yler's death the rebellion collapsed, and e lot of the English peasant remained uch as before.

LINDSAY, JACK. *Nine Days' Hero: Wat Tyler.* 64

eel, Sir Robert (1788–1850)**:** British litician and prime minister. When eel died from a fall from his horse, orking people wept, remembering that e had sacrificed his career and his party's interest for their welfare. He had removed the duty on imported corn, which kept up the price of bread, in opposition to his Conservative colleagues, who favoured protection. Peel was a great administrator. As Home Secretary, he had reformed the harsh penal code and created the first police force – "bobbies" and "peelers" as they were affectionately known from their founder's names. He met economic depression and a national deficit by redesigning the tariff system and reintroducing income tax.

¶ In WHITTLE, J. *Great Prime Ministers.* 1966

bove, Sir Robert Peel. Right, a political artoon showing Peel as a baker selling cheaper read.

Peking: Chinese city of ancient origin, serving as a provincial capital under several early dynasties. Destroyed in 1215 by Genghis Khan, it was rebuilt by Kublai Khan. As Peiping it became in 1421 the capital of the Ming emperor Yung Lo who made the ground plan of the present city. Called Peking, it remained capital of the Chinese Empire. In 1900 troops of eight western nations intervened there to rescue besieged foreign nationals. Peking was capital of the Chinese Republic until

PEEL'S CHEAP BREAD SHOP,
OPENED JANUARY 22, 1846.

The Forbidden City, Peking.

1928. Under occupation by Japan from 1927–45, it became in 1949 the capital of the Communist Chinese People's Republic. The popular Pekingese dog is an ancient breed imported from China.

Peloponnesian War (431–404 B struggle between Athens and her riv for predominance in Greece. These riv were the two leading states of Peloponnese, the southern part of Gre joined to the northern by the narr isthmus which took its name fr Corinth, a commercial city anxious her seaborne trade, while Sparta, h ally, was motivated chiefly by the f that a powerful enemy might encoura her slave population (*see* HELOTS) revolt.

On land the Peloponnesians had t advantage, and for some time an invasi of Attica, the territory of the Athenia who took refuge inside their Long Wa (*see* PIRAEUS), was almost an annual eve At sea Athens was the more successf but in 415 she rashly sent an expediti against certain Greek cities in Sici which were allied to her enemies, a this ended two years later in the disast at Syracuse (movingly described by t

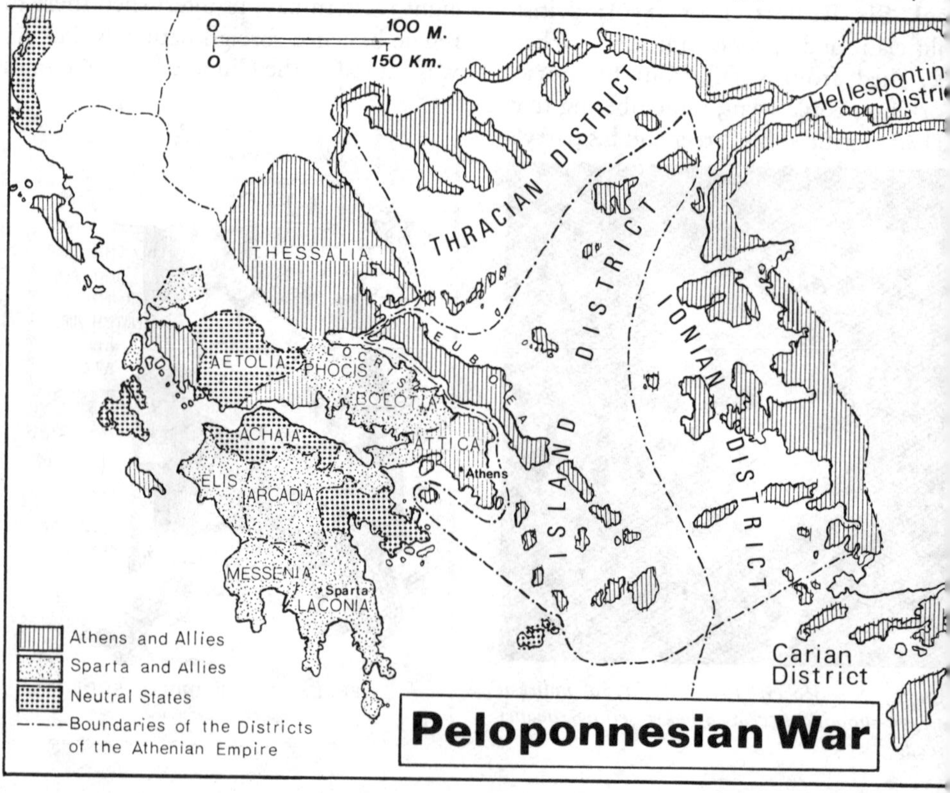

Peloponnesian War

Athens and Allies
Sparta and Allies
Neutral States
Boundaries of the Districts of the Athenian Empire

torian Thucydides) when the Athenian
t was shattered in two naval battles and
army cut to pieces on land. The war,
wever, dragged on for a further seven
rs before Athens capitulated, and her
ng Walls were destroyed.

HUCYDIDES. *The History of the Peloponnesian r*, trans. Rex Warner. 1962

---

nang: state of Malaysia, including nang Island and, on the mainland, ovince Wellesley. The island, off the st coast of the Malay Peninsula, was nost uninhabited when it became in 86, under the British East India Comny, the first British Malayan settlent, then called Prince of Wales Island. e Sultan of Kedah finally ceded it by aty, adding Province Wellesley on the inland in 1800. Singapore outstripped nang in trading activity; but with the owing demand for rubber production nang increased in population and imrtance. In 1948 the island with its inland extension became the member te of Penang in the Federation of laya, later Malaysia.

---

nicillin: substance capable of destroy; bacteria in an infected part of the body thout damaging the tissues. In this it fers from antiseptics, which can cause ious injury to living matter. Penicillin s discovered by the British bacteriolot Sir Alexander Fleming (1881–1955), o was awarded the Nobel prize for dicine in 1945.

---

ninsular War: war fought 1808–14 the Iberian peninsula by Britain, Spain d Portugal against France, beginning a defensive action and changing to an ensive which drove the French from peninsula. It is one of the best exples in history of guerrilla tactics. The r was a permanent drain on Napoleon's ources, occupying 360,000 men in 1810 and 230,000 in 1812. In 1807 Napoleon sent Junot to occupy Portugal when her regent refused to join the Continental Blockade. In 1808 a Spanish rising against the crowning of Joseph Bonaparte allowed the Portuguese to rebel, and Sir Arthur Wellesley (later Duke of Wellington) was sent with 13,500 British and beat Junot at Vimiero. In 1809 Sir John Moore was killed extricating his force from Corunna after a raid on French communications, saving the Spaniards in the south. In 1809 Wellesley did not win at Talavera decisively enough to save Spain (only Cadiz held out) and learnt not to trust Spanish generals. In 1810 he "blooded" his Portuguese contingents in a favourable position at Busaco and preserved his Lisbon base by retiring to the Lines of Torres Vedras. In 1811 he secured the gateways into Spain by his victories at Ciudad Rodrigo and Badajoz and drove the French from Madrid by defeating Marmont at Salamanca. In 1813 he broke the French at Vittoria and drove them from the Peninsula by a series of bold outflanking marches, supplied from the Biscayan coast. The British were effectively supplied by sea, whereas the French had to live off the land. Wellington's custom, when on the defensive, of hiding his troops on the reverse side of a hill hindered the French artillery, and in the open he showed great individuality among the commanders of his day in using line regiments (i.e. men marching abreast) against the conventional columns. This gave full play to the English musketry and the redoubtable "Brown Bess" (*see* FLINTLOCK). The French, trying to subsist by plundering the peasants in a barren plateau, brought on themselves bitter reprisals from *guerilleros*. *See* map p. 698, *also* CONTINENTAL BLOCKADE; GUERRILLAS; TORRES VEDRAS, etc.

¶ LACEY, ROBERT, editor. *The Peninsular War (Jackdaw)*. 1970

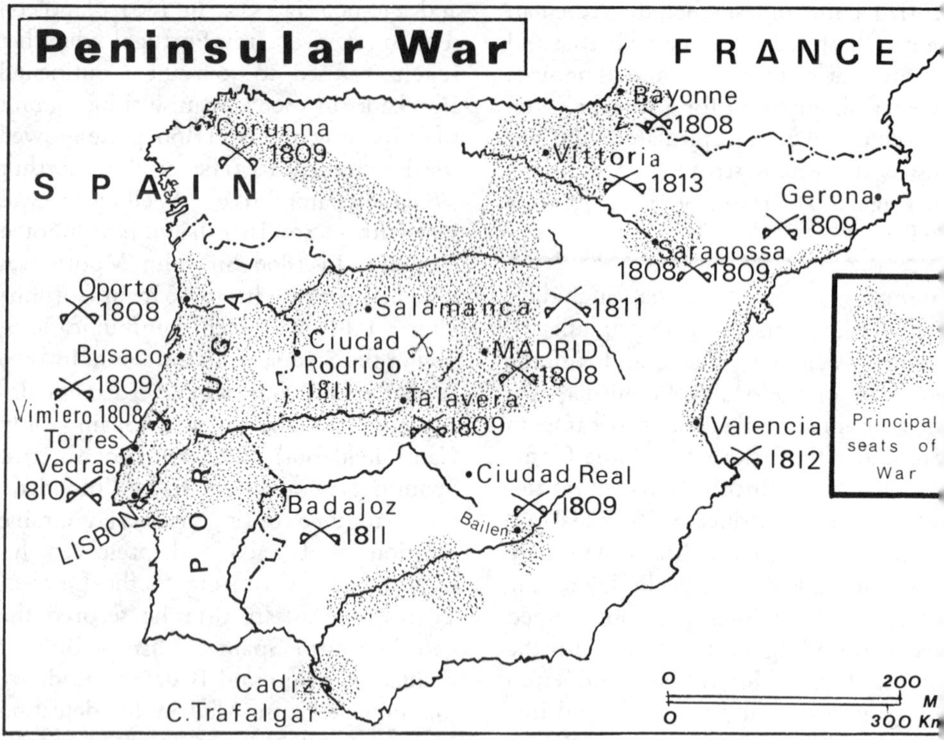

Peninsular War

Penn, William (1644–1718): English Quaker and founder of Pennsylvania. Early in life William Penn learnt the meaning of intolerance – he was sent down from Oxford for his religious views. Later, he was imprisoned three times for similar reasons. Quakers were persecuted by Anglicans and Puritans alike: in fact, Penn decided he would get more sympathy from Roman Catholics.

Penn's father had influence with the Duke of York, later James II, and was owed money by the Crown. Penn asked that, instead of repayment, he himself should be allotted a territory west of the Delaware, America. Having received a grant from Charles II, in 1681, of a tract of land about 300 miles by 160 [483 kilometres by 257], Penn founded a new settlement, known as Pennsylvania (Penn's Woods), which attracted English, Welsh, Dutch, Scandinavians and Germans as a haven for all persecuted se particularly Quakers.

Penn was the governor and drew up constitution, which embodied much his own idealism and greatly influen later charters, even the Constitution the United States.

¶ In GILLETT, N. *Men against War.* 1965

nsions: (1) a stated allowance to a son for past services performed by nself or by some relative, or (2) a payment made to a person retired from vice because of age or illness.

uring the latter half of the 17th century throughout the 18th century perual pensions were granted as rewards political or military services. Thus, in tain, the Duke of Marlborough reved £4,000 and Lord Nelson £5,000 annum. Towards the end of the 19th tury there was much criticism of such petual pensions, and a select commit- of the House of Commons was apnted to examine the question. As a ılt, most of these pensions were exguished by commutation, the cost in case of the Marlborough pension ng £107,000. The Nelson pension nained until 1951, when it ceased as a ılt of the Trafalgar Estates Act, 1947. er the war of 1914–18 capital sums re voted to Lord Haig and others, but petual pensions were not created.

he second class is of much wider incice and greater importance. Such nsions may be contributory or nonntributory, i.e. the person ultimately receive the pension may or may not vide part of the cost by deductions m his wages during his working life. ther, such pensions may be provided individual employers or as part of a ional pensions scheme. Pension emes of the first kind differ widely in ir details, and they may be financed ough an insurance company or from specially allocated trust fund, into ich the contributions of employer l employee are paid. Such a trust fund nvested in really reliable securities, and income derived from it is used to pay pensions as they fall due. A common ision of cost between employer and ployee is for the former to pay tword and the latter one-third of each payment into the fund. This type of private pension scheme began on a small scale in the early years of this century, but is now widespread. In the United States, it was estimated that by 1960 about fourteen million employees of private industry were covered by about 20,000 different pension schemes.

In 1889 the German Reichstag passed a "Law of Insurance against Old Age and Infirmity", and this led to agitation in Great Britain for some form of state pension. But it was not until the Budget of 1908 that Lloyd George introduced a non-contributory pension of five shillings a week for those over the age of seventy with an income not exceeding ten shillings a week. This was replaced by a contributory scheme in the National Insurance Act of 1911, which introduced the now familiar collection of contributions from employer and employee by stamped cards. From this small beginning has arisen the present massive structure of "social security". Following the Beveridge Report (*see* separate entry), the National Insurance Act of 1946 extended the scope of compulsory insurance to cover almost everyone over school-leaving age and under pensionable age.

In the United States, President Roosevelt in 1934 called for "legislation to safeguard men, women and children against misfortune", and this led to the Social Security Act in the following year. This provided for a federal old age insurance system. In the Scandinavian countries state pensions are mainly financed by taxation. In most countries, as in Great Britain, a change in the rates of payment of pensions can be brought about only by legislation, but in a few countries (e.g. Holland) these are automatically geared to the cost of living.

Pepys, Samuel (1633–1703): English naval administrator and diarist. His diary of personal and national affairs covers the period January 1660 to May 1669. He sailed with the fleet bringing Charles II home at the Restoration, lived through the Plague of London (1665), when grass grew "all up and down Whitehall . . . and nobody but poor wretches in the street", saw the Great Fire in the next year, and heard the Dutch guns when their fleet sailed up the River Medway. Failing sight made him abandon his diary, but not before he had left an invaluable record of life and domestic incident in the 17th century. As Secretary to the Admiralty he played an important part in reforming the administration of the navy. He was also President of the Royal Society, 1684–6.

¶ In THOMAS, M. W. *Makers of Britain*. Bk. 2. 1963; MURPHY, E. *Samuel Pepys in London*. 1958

Samuel Pepys.

Pericles (*c.* 495–429 BC): leading Athenian statesman at the time of the city's greatest prosperity. Not only did he direct the external and internal affairs of the state, but he was responsible for the erection of many fine buildings, in particular the Parthenon.

¶ In ROBINSON, C., editor. *Plutarch: Ten Famous Lives*. 1963

Perry, Matthew Calbraith (179
1858): American naval officer sent Japan in 1853 to negotiate better tre ment for American nationals and open trade facilities. His gifts of a telegraph and a miniature railroad convinced Emperor and his officials of the bene of Western civilisation, and the Treaty Kanagawa (31 March 1854) effectiv ended Japan's isolation and opened up ports.

Persia: the ancient name of Iran (separate entry) and still an official alter tive name. The history of the Irani plateau begins with the coming of vaders who spoke an Aryan langua The first wave of invaders from cent Asia came about 1500 BC, many passi on into India. A second wave of th Indo-Iranians came soon after 1000 Many of these Iranian tribes remain nomadic; but two of them, the Me and Persians, adopted a more settled li the Medes in the north in the area south the Caspian, and the Persians south them, towards the Persian Gulf, in t area which came to be called Persis.

The Medes, inhabiting a more fert country, were at first dominant. In 612 their king Cyaxares (625–585 BC) ma an alliance with Babylon, destroyed t power of Assyria and established an e pire which stretched from central A Minor almost to the Indus. But the Pe sians, a hardy shepherd people, revolt under their own Achaemenid dynast and in 553 BC Cyrus the Great unit Medes and Persians under his rule. In 5 Cyrus occupied Babylonia, and his s Cambyses conquered Egypt.

The history of Persia comes down to as a history of kings. Of these, Dari who reigned 521–485 BC, was the greate His empire stretched into north-w India, reached the Caucasus and includ Thrace, the modern Bulgaria. He al

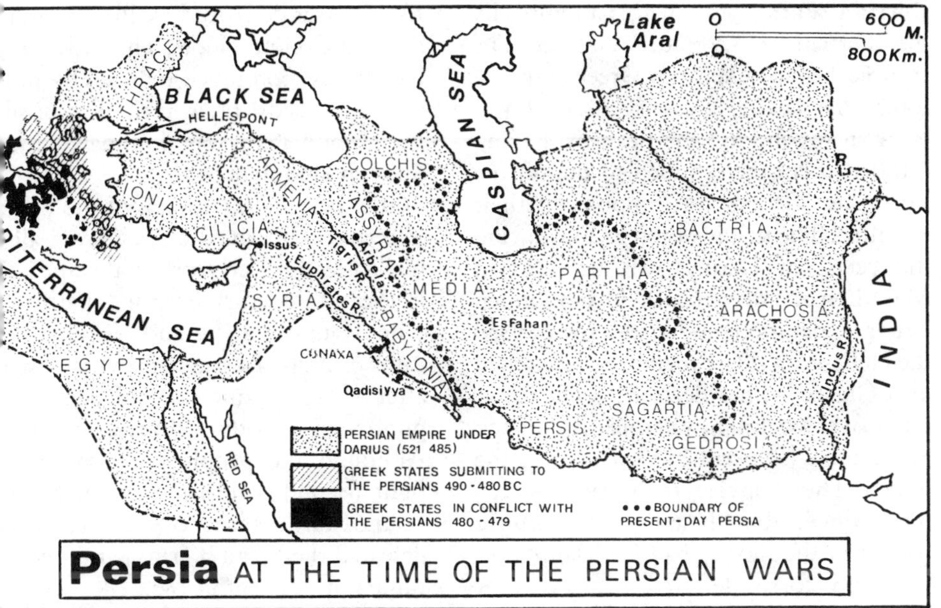

Persia AT THE TIME OF THE PERSIAN WARS

ne into collision with the Greeks, who resented a new European kind of ilisation. Revolts of Ionian Greek onies along the coast of Asia Minor re aided by the cities of their Greek meland. Darius crushed the Ionian onists but his large army was disas-usly defeated, 490 BC, at Marathon by mall Athenian army. His son Xerxes, h another expedition, captured Athens : had to withdraw after a severe naval eat at Salamis, 480 BC.

a struggle for the Persian throne, a unger Cyrus hired an army of Greeks fight Artaxerxes II. At Cunaxa on the phrates, Cyrus was killed (401 BC) but Greeks elected new generals and ught their way back home. The Greek torian Xenophon (*see* separate entry) ompanied this expedition.

ollowing the tradition of Greek superi-ty over Persians, Alexander the Great 6–323 BC) of Macedonia (*see* separate ries) landed on the Asiatic mainland in 4, defeated the huge armies of Darius at Issus (333) and Arbela (331). Before died, aged thirty-two, he had conquered the Persian Empire and entered the Punjab. After his death Persia was ruled by the Seleucid dynasty, descended from one of Alexander's generals. The Parthian ruler Arsaces I (ruled 247–246 BC) rebelled, and in 141 BC Mithridates I established the Parthian dynasty. From the time of Phraates III (70–37 BC), Persia suffered three centuries of warfare with the Roman Empire.

A new dynasty, the Sassanids, was established by Ardashir (reigned AD 224–241). His son Shapur I captured the Roman Emperor Valerian at Edessa, AD 260, with 70,000 prisoners, including engineers and architects whom he put to good use. Chosroes II (reigned 589–628) almost destroyed the Byzantine Empire but was defeated at Nineveh in 627 by the Emperor Heraclius.

In 636 Yezdegerd III was defeated by Islamic forces at Qadisiyya and in 641 at Nihawand. With Yezdegerd's assassination in 651 the story of ancient Persia ends.

¶ WATSON, JANE WERNER. *Iran: Crossroads of Caravans.* 1968

Persian Wars (499–449 BC): attempts by the Persians to conquer Greece. The trouble began when the Greek cities of Ionia, the coastal areas of Asia Minor, were in revolt, and the Persians, having crushed them, determined to punish the European Greeks for supporting their kinsmen. The first invasion in 490, during the reign of Darius, was defeated at Marathon and driven back. In 480 a much larger expedition under Xerxes crossed the Hellespont (Dardanelles) and marched into Greece with a fleet on its left flank. After overwhelming a heroic force of 300 Spartans, who perished to a man in the pass of Thermopylae, the invaders occupied Athens; but their fleet was utterly routed in the nearby bay of Salamis and the land force defeated next year at Plataea.

In the next thirty years desultory fighting eventually restored nearly all that the Greeks had lost in Ionia, and in the following century the Greeks, in their turn, overran Persia under Alexander the Great.

See also ALEXANDER; DARDANELLES; DARIUS; MARATHON; THERMOPYLAE.

Peru: republic of western South America with a population (1982 estimate) of 17,400,600, of whom 46 per cent were Indians.

It is surprising that any people can live in the high mountains, infertile desert and inhospitable jungle of Peru; yet the republic supports this high population, and it once was the home of the remarkable Inca civilisation.

Two thousand years before the Incas came to Peru other Indian peoples learned the skills of farming and building, weaving and pottery, in the valleys of the Andes and on the coast of the Pacific. The Inca way of life was based on the knowledge of these earlier people, and the final conquests of the Incas were made in AD 1525, only a few years before the whole
Empire was destroyed by Pizarro and
Spanish Conquistadors. The native pop
lation was soon much reduced by dise
and by forced labour in the Potosi sil
mines, and Peru was dominated by
Spanish landowners.

Lima became the capital of the Span
Viceroy, who ruled at first over all
territories formerly under the Inca. E
in the 18th century Peru was partition
when Quito, La Paz and Valparaiso b
came capitals of separate provinces whi
after 1810, became the independent
publics of Ecuador, Bolivia and Chi
Although the people of Peru did n
fight for independence like their neig
bours, Bolivar's army of volunteers fina
defeated the Spanish army, and Peru b
came independent in 1824.

The modern republic of Peru is the
fore much smaller than the Inca Emp
had been, and many of the native peop
are poorer today than their ancestors we
500 years ago.

¶ PENDLE, GEORGE. *Land and People of Peru.* Bla
1966; PRESCOTT, W. H. *History of the Conquest*
Peru, edited J. F. Kirk. 1959

See also BOLIVAR; INCAS; etc.

Perugia: fortified city on a hilltop co
manding the corn lands of Umbria a
the Tiber valley. It was an Etruscan stron
hold, which in 310 BC was taken by Rom
in Byzantine times it was one of a ser
of forts linking Rome and the Adriat
In the 13th century it declared for t
Guelph party and asked the help of Po
Innocent III to resist the Emperor, ther
by giving later popes the pretext f
claiming it. From 1350 to 1540 it mai
tained its independence and prospered
spite of violent internal feuds under
succession of condottieri (*see* separa
entry), notably of the Baglione famil
Raphael studied painting there und
Pietro Perugino (1445–1523). Its unive
sity was established in 1308.

See also GUELPHS AND GHIBELLINES.

shawar: principal city of the north-st frontier of Pakistan, eleven miles ·7 kilometres] from the eastern end of Khyber Pass. Its earlier inhabitants re Indian and, at one time, under the ne of Gandhara, it was a centre of ddhism. In the 15th century it became Afghan province and the area acquired athan population (*see* PATHAN). It was vourite residence for the Afghan rulers. vas captured by the Sikh Ranjit Singh 1834, came under British rule in 1849 l in 1901 became capital of the North-st Frontier Province.

stalozzi, Johann Heinrich (1746-27): Swiss educationalist. Pestalozzi ght be lightly dubbed a glorious failure. .ny of his enterprises failed because of l management. Yet his ideas and thods produced the revolutionary con-t that even the poorest child deserved ication. Education, he taught, should based on the natural development of child, who should learn by observa-n and discover things for himself. At institute, Yverdon, in Switzerland, the curriculum included drawing, singing, physical exercises, modelling, making collections, map reading, and field studies. The centre, which housed a teacher training department, attracted educationalists, such as Froebel, from all over the world.

Pétain, Henri Philippe (1856-1951): French soldier-statesman. During World War I he won praise for his resistance to incessant German attacks at Verdun in 1916 and gained rapid promotion to lead the French army in the closing battles of 1918. He entered politics after the war and in May 1940 became Vice-Premier. This time he was convinced Germany would win and arranged an armistice. Bitterly hated for this capitulation and for his leadership of Vichy France, he was found guilty of treason in 1945 and was imprisoned for the rest of his life.

Peter I, called "the Great" (1672-1725): Tsar of Russia from 1696. Although he upheld the traditional autocratic rule which lasted in Russia, with minor con-

Peter the Great (right) and his son.

cessions, until the Revolution of 1917, Peter succeeded in many ways in bringing his country out of medievalism into the modern era. He was enormously tall and strong; simple, though sometimes coarse, in his tastes, but intelligent and firm-minded. Being interested in the way of life of Western Europe, he sent his young nobles there to study and himself spent the years 1697–98 in Holland and England, where he gave particular attention to naval architecture, himself working as a shipwright in the yard at Deptford, Kent. For this purpose he rented the nearby home of John Evelyn, the diarist, where his revels somewhat damaged the property.

He made many internal reforms and innovations, including the founding of St Petersburg (*see* LENINGRAD). At the end of his reign the Russian Empire had b increased by his conquests to stretch fr the White Sea to the Caspian. He diec the result of a chill caught when he p sonally took part in rescuing some sail from shipwreck.

¶ In UNSTEAD, R. J. *Some Kings and Queens.* 19

Peter Claver, St (*c.* 1581–1654): cal "the Apostle of the Negroes". He was Spanish birth and entered the Jes Order (*see* JESUITS). While studying his life's work, he was inspired to conv the heathen in the New World, to wh already slaves were being shipped fr Africa under unspeakable conditions. F long years he laboured among them a is said to have won some 300,000 Negr to Christianity. He was canonised in 18

¶ ROSS, ANN. *Peter Claver: Saint among Slaves.* 1

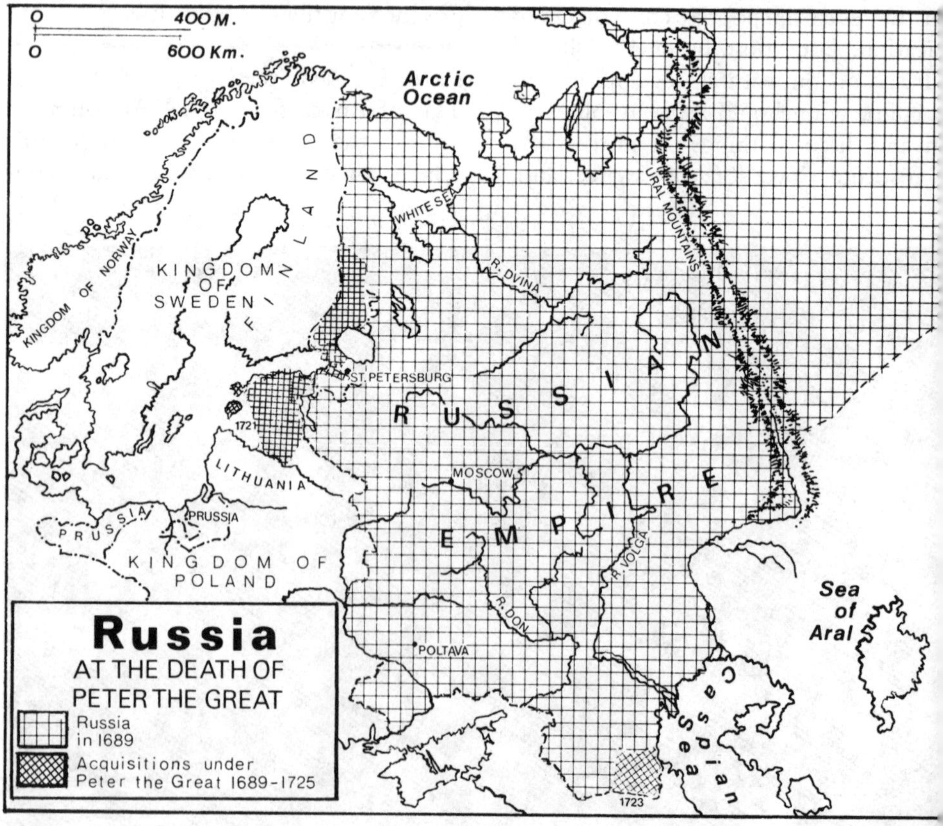

Russia
AT THE DEATH OF PETER THE GREAT

Russia in 1689

Acquisitions under Peter the Great 1689–1725

er the Hermit (*c.* 1050–1115): one of most forceful preachers of the First ısade (*see* CRUSADES). He addressed ıself chiefly to the common folk of his ive France and led a band of them as as Asia Minor, where they perished, ugh Peter himself escaped and eventu- reached Jerusalem with the main body.

ter, St (d. *c.* AD 64 or 67): the "Prince :he Apostles" and brother of Andrew,) one of the earliest to answer the call follow Jesus. From the first he was ir leader and spokesman and at times s inclined to be rash and hasty. He ›wed momentary cowardice when ıs was arrested before his crucifixion; :, when their master had left the earth, proved himself a fearless and resolute der of the apostolic band. There is a ɔng tradition that in due course he ne to Rome, where he met the death a martyr under the Emperor Nero. He ;aid to have asked to be crucified head wnwards, as unworthy to suffer in the ne posture as his master. His tomb is l shown in the great church that bears name.

is through St Peter, whom Jesus called ıe rock on which I will build my ırch", that the papal claim to the dership of Christendom is principally rived.

e also PAPACY.

tition of Right (1628): presented by rliament to Charles I (King of England 25–49), in an attempt to prevent taxa- ›n without the consent of parliament, mpulsory billeting of soldiers, marital v and arbitrary imprisonment. The king fused to allow his prerogative to be rtailed by law but could not afford to ssolve parliament. He attempted vague swers but finally consented in tradi- ›nal style "*Soit droit fait comme est siré*" (let it be done as you wish), adding later: "I have granted no new but only confirmed the ancient liberties of my subjects." Although the immediate effects were little felt he had, in fact, suffered a constitutional defeat.

Petrarch (Francesco de Petrarca, 1304–74): Italian poet and humanist. Petrarch's love poetry, especially that in praise of Laura (whose identity remains obscure), reveals him as one of the great poets of all time and master of the Italian sonnet. His style set the pattern for poetry in Europe for 250 years.

¶ WILKINS, E. H. *Life of Petrarch.* 1961

Petrie, Sir William Matthew Flinders (1853–1942): British archaeologist and Egyptologist. When Petrie arrived on the archaeological scene, he found excavating methods haphazard. Treasure hunting was the main object, finds unknown to the excavator were discarded, relative positions unnoted. Petrie's scientific system involved careful sifting, exact dating using pottery, and study of everyday objects to reveal the life of the people of the period. Thus he laid down rules followed by modern archaeologists. Petrie was first professor in Egyptology at University College, London, founded the British School of Archaeology in Egypt, and brought to light an unknown period of Egyptian civilisation.

¶ In CANNING, JOHN, editor. *100 Great Modern Lives.* 1965

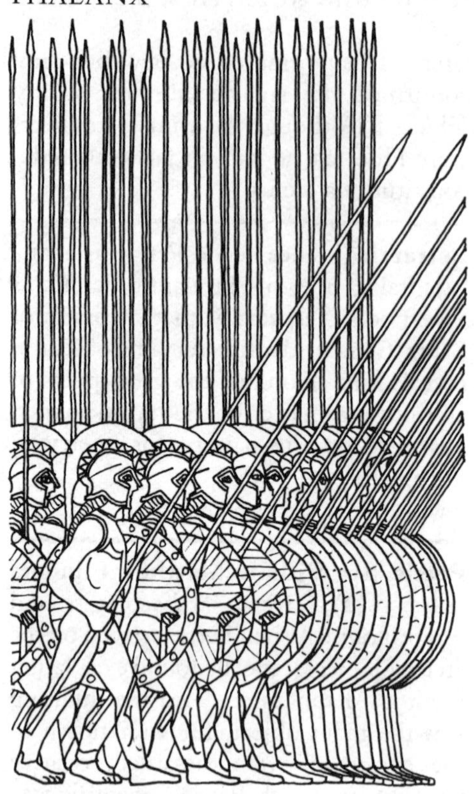

Phalanx: tactical formation of Greek heavy-armed infantry. Though the word was used in earlier times, it is generally applied to the Macedonian infantry to whom Philip II (382–336 BC) and his son Alexander the Great (356–323 BC) owed much of their success in battle. In spite of being armed with pikes 13 feet [3·96 metres] long and marshalled sixteen deep, the phalanx remained comparatively mobile because of its high standard of training. Later efforts to increase its depth and to arm it with even longer weapons destroyed its effectiveness, as was proved when it confronted the Roman legion in the early 2nd century BC.
See also ALEXANDER III; PHILIP II.

Pharaoh: old title of the rulers of Egypt, just as Roman emperors were *Caesars* and Russian emperors *Tsars*. The word pharaoh means "Great House".

Egypt consisted originally of two kingdoms, Upper and Lower Egypt, wh were united by Narmer, the first phara approximately 3,000 years before birth of Christ. Narmer's successors w the Double Crown, which consisted the tall, white linen crown of Up Egypt, encircled by the red crown Lower Egypt. The pharaoh also carri on ceremonial occasions, a crook, show that he was the shepherd of people, and a flail, with which to pun evil-doers. A woman could be phara Queen Hatshepsut ruled in her own ri for twenty years and even led her ar into battle. The exact number of pharaohs is not known, but histori divide them into family groups kno as dynasties. There were probably thir one dynasties, beginning with Narn and ending with Cleopatra, who kil herself in 30 BC.

The pharaohs of the early dynast were worshipped as gods, and their su jects credited them with divine powe

Amenhotep III enthroned. Tomb of Khaemh

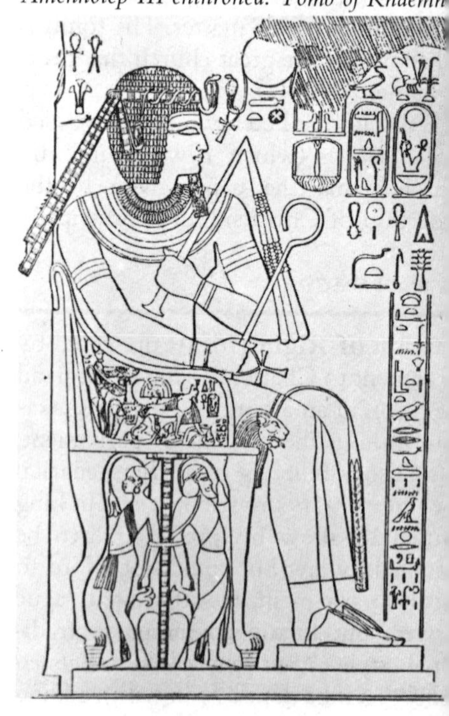

ause of this they could command
›lute obedience, which was also given
he priests and visiers to whom they
egated authority. When a pharaoh
d, he was buried with great splendour,
everything he could possibly need
his after-life was placed in his tomb,
ich was furnished like a palace. Little
his wealth remains today; it has been
en long ago by tomb robbers. An
eptional discovery was that made in
2 of the tomb of Tutankhamen (*see*
arate entry) of the 15th dynasty.

AYNE, ELISABETH. *All about the Pharaohs.* 1966

---

aros, The: white marble lighthouse
he entrance to the harbour at Alexan-
a, Egypt. Erected in the 3rd century
it has since disappeared. It stood on an
nd of the same name, which was linked
a stone causeway to the mainland, and
s accounted one of the Seven Wonders
the Ancient World. The French word
are (lighthouse) is derived from it.
also ALEXANDRIA; SEVEN WONDERS OF
E ANCIENT WORLD.

---

idias (*c.* 431–417 BC): Athenian
lptor of the 5th century BC. His work-
g life coincided with the period in which
ricles (*see* separate entry) adorned Athens
th building and statuary. No work from
e hand of Phidias now exists: he him-
f worked in bronze, but he is known to
ve made the models (probably in clay
plaster) for the marble sculptures of the
rthenon, which have partially survived.

---

hiladelphia: "the City of Brotherly
ove", established in 1682 by William
enn, the Quaker founder of the Comonwealth of Pennsylvania. It is situated
n the north-western bank of the Dela-
are River, approximately 90 miles [145
lometres] from the Atlantic Ocean.
rom the first the site of Philadelphia was favourable for ocean commerce; its immediate hinterland was in early days more populous and more productive than tha of New York. At the time of the War o of American Independence, Philadelphia, with a population of 42,000, became the capital of the Union and remained so until the foundation of the city of Washington in 1800. The city was the setting for the first Continental Congress (1774) which met in the Carpenter's Hall and later issued the Declaration of Independence (1776). It was also in this city that the Convention met in 1787 to draft the American Constitution. The 20th century has seen a great increase in population and vast industrial expansion, which proved a major factor in America's effort in both world wars. The Philadelphia Orchestra is one of the most renowned in the world. Population 4,716,818 (1980).

Philip II (382–336 BC): King of Macedon from 359. To the general reader of history he is greatly overshadowed by his brilliant son Alexander the Great (*see* separate entry). The latter's achievements, however, were made possible only by the fact that his father (1) unified Macedon, a state on the northern fringes of the Greek world, (2) built up the Macedonian army as a formidable fighting force (*see* PHALANX) and (3) brought the rest of Greece under Macedonian rule. Had his base not been thus secured behind him, Alexander could never have ventured into Asia. The leader of Greek resistance to Philip was Athens, where the orator Demosthenes (384–322) denounced him in speeches that are among the treasures of classical literature (*see* ORATORS).

Philip II (1527–98): King of Spain and the Two Sicilies, 1556–98. Spain under Philip was the most formidable power in the world. His empire included the

Netherlands, Portugal, parts of Italy and of the Americas as then known. One of his three marriages was to Mary, Queen of England. He was handicapped by the sheer size of his problems and his refusal to delegate responsibility. He was in conflict with France, England, the Netherlands, and, as the chief Catholic monarch, with Protestantism. Nevertheless, he had moderate success against France, won the sea battle of Lepanto (*see* separate entry) and annexed Portugal (1580). But his Armada failed against the English, and he could not tame the rebel Dutch.

¶ CUBITT, H. *Spain and the Empire of Philip II.* 1975
See also SPAIN.

Philippines, Republic of the: group of islands in the Far East which were ceded to the USA by Spain after the Spanish-American War of 1898. The Filipinos, led by Emilio Aguinaldo, conducted a guerrilla war against the Americans and in favour of independence from February 1899 to April 1902. It was ironic that the man whom the Americans aided in leading the struggle against the Spaniards in Manila should then turn against them. In 1902 the Philippines were given a representative assembly, but demands for full independence continued, and successive American administrations prepared various plans to give more statutory autonomy to the Filipinos. During World War II the Japanese invaded the Philippines and captured Manila in January 1942. In 1943 President Roosevelt announced that the USA would grant independence to the Filipinos as soon as the Japanese had been ejected. The Republic of the Philippines was established on 4 July 1946.
See PACIFIC OCEAN for map.

¶ AGONCILLO, TEODORO A. *A Short History of the Philippines.* 1970

Philistines: ancient race inhabiting the south-western area of what is now called Palestine, the most serious rivals enco tered by the Jews (*see* separate entry) their conquest of the Promised La Their principal city was Gaza, which retains its name.

The term "philistine" is today appl to one who lacks appreciation of literature and music.

Philosophers: those who love and p sue wisdom, from Greek *philos*, lovi and *sophos*, wisdom or a wise man. Th are people who study the most diffic subject of all – the nature of man's ex ence and experience in the universe.

The philosopher accepts nothing wi out question. His aim is to examine appearance of things and enquire how this corresponds to reality. Some phi sophers, aware that everything exists relation to everything else, try to unco these relationships, to discover a patt in the universe. This branch of philosop is known as Metaphysics, a word deriv from the Greek *metaphusica* (Latin, *me physica*) meaning after physics, or follo ing on from the study of natural scien This is because in the works of the gr Greek philosoper Aristotle (384–322 the philosophical writings followed lectures on physics. Another bran ethics (from the Greek for character disposition), concentrates on the idea right, wrong, justice and so on – on whi we found our scale of moral values. further branch of philosophy deals wi political theory – the nature and tr functions of the state and of governmer and yet another with aesthetics – t appreciation of the beautiful in nature a art. Philosophers have profoundly i fluenced world thought and, cons quently, history.

Phoenicians: a maritime nation of t ancient world. To the geographers antiquity Phoenicia was a land at t stern end of the Mediterranean, its undaries corresponding broadly with ose of the modern state of Lebanon; it the trading and colonising enterprise the Phoenicians carried them into ery corner of that sea as well as into the ormier waters of the Atlantic and dian Oceans. They voyaged far along e eastern and western coasts of Africa d probably also came to Britain in arch of tin from Cornwall and the illy Isles, though in this case they may ve travelled overland. They do not pear to have penetrated the Black Sea. Their early home is unknown, but excavations have shown them occupying the ty of Byblos in the Lebanon as early as 000 BC, and they are known to have been ading with Egypt about 1250. Later the hoenicians of Sidon supplied some of e best ships for the invasion of Greece 480 (*see* PERSIAN WARS).

In due course their settlements stretched long the southern shores of the Mediterranean, particularly to Carthage, traditionally founded by Queen Dido, though evidence suggests a date in the 8th century BC. It was from Carthage that the second stage of Phoenician colonisation originated, penetrating into Spain (Cadiz), southern France (Marseilles) – though these settlements are but two examples among many – and Sicily. The Phoenicians have left few remains.

¶ PHILIPS-BIRT, D. *Finding out about the Phoenicians.* 1964

Photography: science and art of producing pictures by the action of light on chemically prepared materials. The word is derived from the Greek for "light" and "writing".

Nowadays, it is necessary to keep still for only a fraction of a second to have a photograph taken, but in the mid-19th century sitters were required to remain motionless for twenty minutes, with the head clamped in position by a device with

Stone carving of a Phoenician merchant ship.

three adjustable points. Nevertheless, people in Europe and America flocked to undergo this mild form of torture.

The desire in man to represent on a flat surface the three-dimensional scenes around him began early, as we know from such prehistoric cave paintings as those at Lascaux, south-west France. Ten thousand years ago the Chaldeans and Egyptians, resting in their dark tents, were fascinated to see that sunlit objects outside, in line with a small hole in the tent's wall, formed a replica, upside down, on the opposite wall. The ancient science of optics (the formation of images by pinholes) was mentioned by Aristotle about 350 BC, and fifty years later Euclid published a treatise on optics that contained the first known construction of an image by geometric means. Neither, apparently, appreciated the full significance of this phenomenon. Nor did Leonardo da Vinci see any practical use for the *camera obscura* he described in an account, complete with drawings, published in the early 16th century.

It was Professor Barbaro in 1568 who saw in the apparatus an aid to the understanding of perspective for an artist. The *camera obscura* consisted of a darkened box or room, with a lens at one end and a flat surface at the other. If the *camera obscura* was so small that the image must be viewed from outside, a translucent screen such as ground glass was used, but if the apparatus was large enough to enter, the image was thrown, upside down, on to a white reflecting surface. An improved version of the *camera obscura*, with a complicated arrangement of lenses and mirror and, in the case of the *camera lucida*, a prism, was used by artists, famous and amateur, to secure accuracy in drawing. This apparatus was similar in principle and essentials to the modern photographic camera, but it was nearly 300 years before an effort was made to make the optical image permanent.

To reproduce an optical image by usi light energy, a substance has to be us which undergoes some chemical chan when subjected to light action. Durir the 18th century it was recognised th salts of the metal silver are very sensiti to light. Both the German J. H. Schulz c. 1727, and the Swedish chemist Ka Scheele experimented fifty years later i this field. In 1802 Thomas Wedgwoc described his process of making pictur on paper impregnated with silver nitra and using a painting on glass as a negativ He could not, however, keep his imag from darkening. John Herschel had mor success in achieving permanency in print by his use of sodium thiosulpha (hypo). He was the first to use the term "photograph" and "photography".

All this time, experiments along differen lines were being made in various countrie all with the same purpose – to "fix" th photograph permanently. In France Niépce obtained a record of a view fron his bedroom, using asphaltum coated o to metal or stone, with a full day's exposure. For a while he and the artis Daguerre were in partnership. Afte Niépce's death, Daguerre reverted t the use of silver salts and in 1839 announced the Daguerreotype process o making a positive image directly upon metallic silver plate. This process becam extremely popular for a few years.

It is to the Englishman Fox Talbo (1810–77) that the title "inventor o modern photography" is given. Working with a *camera obscura* and "negative" material, consisting of paper impregnated with silver chloride, he produced a number of views of Lacock Abbey. His calotype process, with subsequent improvements, has evolved into modern photographic practice.

Another experimenter, Scott Archer, invented the wet collodion plate, which

A

B

C

D

E

A. *Daguerreotype photograph, 1857.* B. *Daguerre.* C. *William Henry Fox Talbot.* D. *Photograph by Fox Talbot using his Colotype process, 1844.* E. *Camera Obscura used by Sir Joshua Reynolds.* F. *Wounded Union soldiers after the Battle of Fredericksburg, photographed by Matthew Brady with a stereoscopic camera, in 1863.*

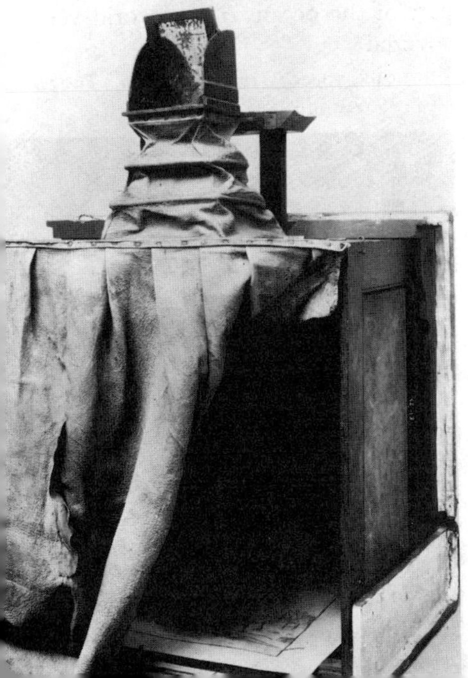

F

was used by the famous photographer Matthew Brady in his portable darkroom wagon on the battlefields of the American Civil War.

At least one woman can claim eminence in the early days of photography – Julia Margaret Cameron (1815–74), who was born in Calcutta and came to England in 1848. About 1865 she took up photography and had among her sitters Charles Darwin, Robert Browning and Lord Tennyson. Another enthusiastic early photographer was Charles Dodgson ("Lewis Carroll") the author of *Alice in Wonderland*.

George Eastman, founder of the Kodak Company of America, was responsible for the great popularity of photography as a hobby today. He marketed the first roll film, and from 1895 the home photographer could load his own film and afterwards get it developed and printed at his local chemist.

Modern developments such as high-speed shutters and automatic focusing have removed many of the difficulties of the processes of photography. Probably the camera's achievements are at their most impressive in the cinema and television studio where, rather than the carefully posed solitary sitter, vast crowds and panoramic scenes can be brought within the compass of a small screen.

¶ GERNSHEIM, HELMUT and GERNSHEIM, ALISON. *The History of Photography*. 1969

Picardy: former province of Northern France. Its chief towns are Amiens (the early capital, with a magnificent Gothic cathedral), the Channel port of Boulogne, and Abbeville, where important Palaeolithic and Bronze Age archaeological discoveries have been made.

Picasso, Pablo Ruiz (1881–1973): Spanish, one of the most influential artists of the 20th century. Most famous as a painter, he also sought expression [in] stone, pottery, the graphic arts a[nd] costumes for ballet. His early work [is] sometimes classified according to the pr[e]dominating colour he used at vario[us] times, e.g. the "blue period" (1901–[4]) and the "rose period" (1905–7). He w[as] one of the founders of the school [of] cubism, which saw familiar objects in fl[at] geometric terms and permitted vario[us] aspects of the object to be seen simu[l]taneously. Much of his work was dom[i]nated by horror of war and the celebr[a]tion of the process of physical creation.

¶ RIPLEY, E. *Picasso*. 1959

Piccard, Auguste (1884–1962): Swi[ss] physicist who made balloon ascents int[o] the stratosphere and developed the bathy[s]caphe for deep underwater exploratio[n]. In a succession of these spherical vessels h[e] and his son Jacques progressively estab[lished] new depth records from 10,335 fee[t] [3150 metres] in September 1953 to 35,80[0] feet [10,912 metres] in January 1960 when with Lieutenant D. Walsh of the U[S] Navy, Dr Jacques Piccard took the bathyscaphe *Trieste* down into the Mariana Trench in the Pacific Ocean, the deepes[t] part of the oceans of the world yet discovered.

¶ HONOUR, ALAN. *Ten Miles High, Two Mile[s] Deep*. 1959

dmont: "foot of the mountains", ile plain of northern Italy enclosed on ee sides by alpine ranges. Ligurian lts settled astride the mountains and re subdued by the Romans (225 BC), ded by Saracens, and overrun by mbards and Franks. As guardian of the ses from France to Italy, Piedmont was eatedly threatened by greater powers retained its independence. This was to the wariness and vigour of the use of Savoy, Burgundians from the per Rhone. By marriage and by aining titles of Imperial Vicar (12th tury) and Duke (1416), by moving ir capital from Chambéry to Turin 62) and by exchanging transalpine ssessions for lands in Italy, they built dmont into a compact state. By en- ing Habsburg aid against France they vived attacks by Francis I and, later, uis XIV. They persecuted or tolerated Waldensian heretics as policy dictated d maintained efficient defences. tween 1859 and 1870 Piedmont was an ective instrument in building Italian ity.

e ITALY for map.

---

ero della Francesca (*c.* 1415–92): lian painter from Umbria whose works clude altar pieces, frescoes and portraits. s considerable gifts as a mathematician ve him a mastery of perspective, to nich he added subtleties of space, light d atmosphere which mark him out as e of the greatest of Renaissance painters.

---

late, Pontius: Roman governor (pro- rator) of Judaea (AD 26–36), who dered the crucifixion of Jesus under essure from the leaders of the Jews.

ittle else is known for certain about his reer, but several legends have gathered und his name.

e also JESUS CHRIST.

Pilgrimage: journey undertaken from religious motives to some place reputedly sacred. During the Middle Ages a familiar figure was the wayfarer dressed in a rough grey cloak emblazoned with a red cross, wearing a broad-brimmed hat and carrying a staff, sack and gourd. He would be immediately recognisable as a pilgrim to the Holy Land, or one of the centres of pilgrimage in Europe. Possibly he would be wearing the badges of the shrines he had visited, palm leaves from Jerusalem in his hat, a cockle shell emblem from St James of Compostella in Spain, the crossed keys of St Peter from Rome, or a tiny flask from Canterbury, England, reputed to contain a drop of St Thomas Becket's blood.

Pilgrimages to a place considered sanctified by the Deity, or a holy person, are part of the cult of most religions. Every Muslim is required to visit Mecca at least once in his lifetime; devout Hindus frequently make the journey to Benares and bathe in the River Ganges; places associated with the birth, teaching and death of Buddha are the goal of Buddhists. Pilgrimages to places connected with Christ and his saints began early in Christian history. Around AD 325 the Emperor Constantine and his mother Helena erected memorial churches on the holy sites in Palestine, ushering in a great period of pilgrimages to the East. In the West, the veneration of the martyrs provided the impetus, Rome becoming the great attraction for its association with Peter and Paul. These long and often dangerous journeys were undertaken in the hope that pardon would be obtained for sins, and diseases cured. Miracles were hoped for and sometimes appeared to happen.

The medieval Church was increasingly convinced that the miraculous power of the Deity attended the bodies of saints and their relics. Santiago in Spain, Tours, Le

Puy and Chartres in France, Canterbury and Glastonbury in England, Cologne and Aix la Chapelle in southern Germany, all drew their pilgrims by the thousands. The great attraction became the acquisition of relics – objects connected with the hallowed corpse, such as wax dropped from a taper or a little dust from the grave. Soon, however, this was not enough, and the desire arose to acquire portions of the actual body, by fair means or by trickery.

Because people in the Middle Ages were acutely conscious of sin, these journeys were increasingly undertaken as expiation: in fact, a priest would often order a penitent to undertake a pilgrimage for a major sin. This led to the development of indulgences, which consisted of the remission of part of the penance, because, perhaps, the penitent returned with a relic.

In order to accommodate the increasing number of pilgrims, hospices were built along the routes, particularly on the great Alpine passes. The oldest, the Septimer, dates from 800, the Great Bernard from the 10th century, t Simplon from the 13th century and t St Gotthard from the 14th century. Th were similar refuges in the Mediterrane towns and in Jerusalem.

The hospices were run by the hospi fraternities, lay organisations worki for the Church. From the most importa of these, the Hospitale Hierosolymitanu founded around 1065, arose the order St John, earliest of the great orders knighthood. Associations were form to help pilgrims bound for the Ea Protection was very necessary once t Holy Land was no longer held by Christian power but had been conquer by Islam. In fact, ultimately this led to t Crusades, which in many ways we armed pilgrimages. The journey to Pal stine was expensive in the 12th century well as hazardous. Pilgrims formed then selves into unions with an elected maste Their travelling arrangements were oft made through the Knights of St John ar

The blessing of the sick in Rosary Square, Lourdes.

grims on their way to Canterbury.

: Knights Templar. There were even vel books – the most famous, *The ok of the Ways to Jerusalem* by John de aundeville (*c.* 1336), was translated into eral languages.

ocially the pilgrimages were important. ey improved communications, in-ased opportunities to travel, spread as in art and architecture. For instance, me of France's Romanesque churches rived from St James of Compostella, ain. In literature, they produced the *ansons de Geste* and Chaucer's *Canter-ry Tales.*

'he movement was checked by the formation, particularly in England, but the 16th century and again in the 19th ntury big revivals took place. The dication of the church at Lourdes, ance, took place in 1876, in the pre-ice of 3,000 priests and 100,000 pilgrims.

ROWLING, MARJORIE. *Everyday Life of Medieval avellers.* 1971; THOMSON, GLADYS SCOTT. *edieval Pilgrimages.* 1962

ilgrim Fathers: the Puritan refugees ho sailed from England in the *Mayflower* 620). In 1608 a congregation of radical ritans fled to Leyden in Holland to cape religious persecution. They came om the area in England where York-shire, Lincolnshire and Nottinghamshire meet, from towns such as Gainsborough and villages such as Scrooby. Though this was the beginning of the Pilgrim Fathers' journey to freedom, it was their second attempt to leave England. On the first occasion they were betrayed by the captain of the ship they had chartered, and were imprisoned in the Guildhall, Boston, in Lincolnshire. When later they reached Holland, they were extremely dissatisfied with the local people, whom they judged to be too frivolous and lacking in respect for the Puritan way of life. After long negotiations with King James I, they obtained permission to settle on English-owned land in North America. The Puritans were joined by more sympathisers – as well as by a number of adventurers – and set sail from Southampton in two ships, the *Mayflower* and the *Speedwell.* The *Speedwell* sprang a leak and had to be abandoned. The *Mayflower* put into Plymouth where the citizens who sympathised with the Pilgrims' religious views gave them a warm welcome. As they afterwards wrote, they were "courteously used by divers friends there dwelling". The Pilgrims finally sailed from Plymouth on 6 September 1620.

The Pilgrim Fathers leaving for America.

It took the *Mayflower* more than three months to cross the Atlantic, and in December 1620 the Pilgrim Fathers (as they later became known) landed at a spot which by a strange coincidence had, six years earlier, been named Plymouth by Captain John Smith. Before landing, the Pilgrims signed a simple worded Compact, which became the cornerstone of the American democratic tradition. The little colony had a very chequered career and struggled with great courage against crop failures and attacks by Red Indians. In 1691 the Plymouth colony was absorbed by the neighbouring colony at Massachusetts Bay. This new Puritan economy thrived and expanded rapidly during the next ten years, during which time another 15,000 immigrants arrived to join it. Its large numbers kept it safe against Indian attack and enabled it to absorb the smaller settlements around it. Eventually there was established a representative form of government which superseded the direct democracy of the early settlement, the population of which had barely exceeded 100 people.

¶ COWIE, LEONARD W. *The Pilgrim Fathers.* 1970; GILL, W. J. C. *The Pilgrim Fathers.* 1964

See also MAYFLOWER.

Pilsudski, Jozef (1867–1935)**:** statesman and, with Paderewski (*see* separate entry), founder of modern Poland, in 1919. A vigorous nationalist, he led a Polish army against Russia in World War I. Afterwards, whilst trying to enlarge the new Poland into a Polish-Ukrainian Union, he was defeated by the Red Army. He believed in strong rule, and later seized power as prime minister for a time.

Piraeus, The: port of Athens, Greece, about four miles [6·5 kilometres] south-west of the city. At the height of Athenian prosperity in the 5th century BC the Piraeus was joined to Athens by two long parallel walls some 200 yards [180 metr apart, within which the people from countryside could take refuge from vasion (*see* PELOPONNESIAN WAR). Mu enlarged, the Piraeus is still busy a prosperous.

Pirates: sea robbers. In films and fictic pirates are often pictured as roman figures – swarthy, black-bearded adve turers or even elegant gentlemen, w gold earrings, rapier in hand and a bra of pistols in their belts. In fact, they we more often desperate, drunken ruffia tattered and unwashed, who had turn to piracy because of oppressive co ditions at home or on board their me chant ship. They preferred a dangero life with the chance of fabulous riches a steady job with low pay. An und ciplined lot, they often lost their mon and ships. Pirates of any nationali usually received short shrift at the han of their captors.

Since ancient times pirates have harass merchant ships on all the oceans of th world. Early records cite the Phoenician there are references to sea rovers in th Odyssey, Greek pirates were mention in Assyrian documents of the 8th centu BC. The pirates of Cilicia destroyed Roman fleet at Ostia, and not until th time of Augustus was the Adriatic final cleared of marauders.

The Vikings continuously raided th coasts of Britain, Ireland and France. North Africa the corsairs established th Barbary States: from Algiers and Tripo they sailed out to plunder passing ship or landed on the Spanish coast and ca ried away Christians to sell as slaves. N until the 19th century were they final suppressed.

In Tudor times piracy flourished roun the British Isles, particularly in souther Ireland, where there were safe retreats an willing receivers to buy the stolen good

Left, the notorious pirate, Captain Henry Morgan laying siege to Port-au-Prince, 1680. Right, Ann Bonny, one of the few women pirates, convicted of piracy in Jamaica, 1720.

ıd grow rich on the profits. As life beıme more difficult in home waters, the irates moved further afield – to the West ıdies, New England, the Red Sea and ladagascar, which swarmed with pirates reying on the sea routes from Europe to ıdia and the Indies. There, in the 1600s, ıey set up their own communistic state f Libertatia.

Spanish America, forbidden by Spain › trade with foreigners, eagerly bought muggled goods at low prices from the uccaneers. As a result, the most powerful irate fleet of all time flourished in the Caribbean. Pirate crews were reinforced y privateers (armed merchant ships icensed to attack enemy shipping in warime) and by unemployed naval seamen, eady to take any job going, for no wages ut a share of the booty. First task of a ıewly created pirate crew was to draw ıp ship's articles, and choose their flag, ısually the "skull and crossbones" – the "Jolly Roger". The commander was chosen by vote. If he was a strong character, like the famous Bartholomew Roberts, a strict disciplinarian and teetotaller, who would allow neither women nor gambling on board, then success was assured.

Piracy flourished in the Caribbean and North Africa until wiped out by the concerted efforts of British and American navies in the 1830s, but pirates were still common among the Greek islands in the 1850s, and the Chinese pirates of Taya Bay, north of Hong Kong, were active until World War II.

¶ EPSTEIN, SAMUEL and WILLIAMS, BERYL. *The Real Book of Pirates.* 1962

See also BUCCANEERS; PRIVATEERS.

Pisa: Italian port on the River Arno; one of the earliest free communes (AD 1081). It prospered greatly in the 11th and 12th centuries when its seamen with the help of the Genoese drove the Saracens

from Sardinia, Corsica and Majorca. It sent ships on the First Crusade and established factories at Acre and Constantinople. It declined in the 13th and 14th centuries because it attempted simultaneously to fight the Genoese for control of Corsica and supported the Ghibelline cause against Guelph Florence. By sacking Lucca in 1314 it drove silk weavers to Florence, by demanding tolls in 1356 it drove Florentine exporters to use Leghorn. Its trade declined, its harbour silted up. It fell to the Milanese and then in 1405 to Florentine overlordship. The Medici partially revived its trade and founded its university. Among its buildings is the famous "leaning tower" (*below*), begun in AD 1174, which is about 16 feet [4·88 metres] off the perpendicular. Modern industries include cotton and silk.
See ITALY for map.

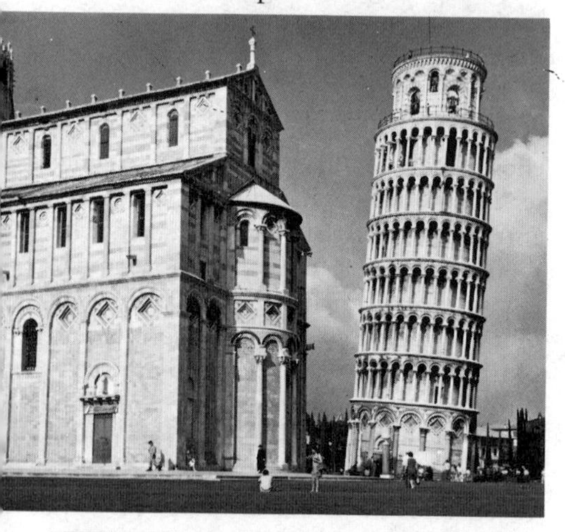

Pitcairn Islands: British colony in the central South Pacific, administered by the governor of Fiji and consisting of the islands of Pitcairn, Henderson, Ducie and Oeno, only the first of which is inhabited (1965 population, 186). Pitcairn's place in history dates from 1789 when mutineers from HMS *Bounty*, led by Fletcher Christian, took refuge there. Most of the present inhabitants are descended from the mutineers. The *Bounty*, commanded [by] Captain William Bligh, was a small ves[sel] of 215 tons purchased by the Brit[ish] Admiralty to carry breadfruit from t[he] Pacific to the West Indies.
See PACIFIC OCEAN for map.

Pitt, William, first Earl of Chatha[m], known as "Pitt the Elder" (1708–78) British statesman and prime minist[er]. He entered parliament in 1735. When [in] 1756 he took office as secretary of stat[e] government was ineffectual, showi[ng] vagueness and indecision in the face [of] worldwide French aggression. Pi[tt] breathed a new spirit into his countryme[n]. "I know that I can save England, and [I] know no other man can" expressed h[is] unswerving confidence in himself an[d] England's destiny. A great orator an[d] strategist, he could inspire generals an[d] arouse the people. His genius as w[ar] minister in the Seven Years War wit[h] France brought a succession of victori[es] in Europe, India and Canada. His backing of Frederick the Great of Pruss[ia] against France paid dividends, leavin[g] him free to grasp the mastery of the sea[s]. As a result, Britain became an imperi[al] power with worldwide commitment[s]. Frederick the Great said of him: "Englan[d] has been in labour a long time . . . but [at] last she has given birth to a man."

¶ PLUMB, J. H. *Chatham*. 1965

t, William, known as "Pitt the
unger" (1759–1806): British statesman
prime minister, second son of Pitt
Elder. Where Chatham's genius lay
war, his son's talents were best suited
peace. The second Pitt, at twenty-four
youngest prime minister in British
tory, took office when England's for-
ies were at their lowest ebb (1783).
r American colonies were lost, and she
od alone in Europe. Parliament was
rupt and swayed by George III's
litical manoeuvres. Pitt was patriotic,
h principled and popular with the
ople. He tackled the problem of parlia-
ntary reform, gave India good govern-
nt and Ireland the Act of Union. In
ance he showed his genius. Though
vate wealth was rapidly increasing
m industry and trade, the national
bt was mounting after the French and
nerican wars. Through his budgets he
ablished a better balance, introducing
income tax for the first time. He strug-
ed to keep England from war with
ance and did much to save her when,
evitably, it came.

DERRY, J. *William Pitt.* 1962

Villiam Pitt the Younger, by Gillray.

Pittsburgh: port and industrial centre of Pennsylvania, USA. Situated at the point where the Allegheny and Monagahela Rivers form the Ohio, Pittsburgh was laid out in 1764 as a trading post and fort by John Campbell and grew rapidly until in 1816 it was one of America's largest cities. The same strategic situation that had made it the logical point for a fort to control the Upper Mississippi Valley also made it the entrepot for waves of migration to the West. Pittsburgh became a major industrial centre for the production of iron, steel and glass, and played a major role in supplying the Union armies with cannon and armour plate in the Civil War.

Pius V, St (Michele Ghisliere, 1504–72): Pope. Born of poor parents near Alessandria, he became a Dominican friar, inquisitor-general in 1551 and Pope in 1566. He combined uprightness of character and strictness of living with bigotry and harsh persecution. Rising at dawn and taking little rest, he laboured to root out heresy, repel the Turk and reform the Papal Court. He applauded Alva's executions of Flemish protestants and urged Charles IX to take no prisoners in the war against the Huguenots. He inspired the defeat of the Turkish fleet at Lepanto in 1571 (*see* separate entry). He halved the personnel and expenditure of the Papal Court. He was canonised in 1712.

Pius IX (Eugenio Mastai-Ferretti, 1792–1878): Pope, often referred to as "Pio Nono". Born at Sinigaglia, he became Bishop of Imola and, from 1846, pope for thirty-two years – the longest rule in the history of the Papacy. A man of simple piety, "warm hearted, but weak in intellect" (Metternich), he weakened his authority by relaxing censorship and freeing political prisoners, and was in 1848 cast for the role of president of a free, federal Italy. But he shrank from war with Austria and became a bitter opponent of Piedmontese attempts to absorb the Papal States. He reacted against liberalism and condemned democracy and much of modern science. To the despair of liberal Catholics he urged the declaration of Papal Infallibility by the Vatican Council, 1870.

Pius XII (Eugenio Pacelli, 1876–1958): Pope 1939–58. Of Roman family, after serving as cardinal secretary of state for ten years he was elected Pope in the critical year 1939, which saw the outbreak of World War II. He won respect by his ministry to the wounded in the Allied bombing of Rome, but has been criticised for failure to condemn Nazi persecution of the Jews. He was preoccupied with fear of Communism and was unwilling to imperil the Church in Germany. He became more conservative after 1950, when he proclaimed the dogma of the Bodily Assumption of [the] Virgin Mary into heaven, condemn[ed] the theory of evolution (*see* DARW[IN,] CHARLES) and dissolved the worker-pri[est] movement in France. He deepened t[he] gulf between Catholic and non-Cathol[ic]

Pope Pius XII.

Death of the Inca Atahualpa.

Pizarro, Francisco (*c.* 1475–1541[)]: Spanish general. Pizarro was one of t[he] most successful of the Conquistadors (s[ee] separate entry). In Spain he began life [as] an illegitimate and illiterate swineher[d,] yet his determination drove his followe[rs] to discover and to destroy the Inca Empi[re] of Peru. He went to America o[n] Columbus's second voyage in 1493 an[d] learned much from Balboa and Corte[s.] He began to search for a rich souther[n] empire in 1515, but it took seventee[n] years before his final expedition of 18[0] men with twenty-five horses was read[y] to climb the Andes to Cajamarca, whe[re] the Inca Atahualpa was ambushed, ran[-]somed for a roomful of gold, then kille[d.] After the capture of Cuzco Pizarro bega[n] to build a new capital city at Lim[a.] Unfortunately the Spaniards quarrelle[d] among themselves. Pizarro executed [his] former partner, Almagro, but he wa[s] assassinated in 1541, and a new Governo[r] was sent from Spain to rule Peru.

Place-names: Place-names are a cod[e] from the past which, deciphered, tells u[s] about people who lived long ago an[d] ɔut physical features which time may ve altered out of all recognition. They :ord man's hopes and fears, successes d defeats; his love of beauty and his struction of it to serve his own ends. ıere was an ancient belief that every ıce possessed its own attendant spirit, *genius loci*. A place-name enshrines the en and women who, by the magical act naming, separated the human comunity from the anonymous wilderness. :nglish place-names are a roll-call of the fferent waves of invaders which, until 66, swept over the country. Even if we d not know from other sources that the ɔmans held Britain in military subjection r nearly 400 years, we could deduce as uch from their legacy of place-names corporating *-cester, -chester* or *-caster* ;loucester, Worcester, Lancaster, hester and so on) all derived from the ıtin *castrum*, a fort, or from *castra*, the ural form of the same word, meaning fortified camp. These place-names were ldom entirely Roman. *Castrum* or *castra* as often added to a Celtic (i.e. early ritish) place-name already in existence. hus Worcester, for example, means "the oman fort of the tribe called Weogoran".

In the 5th and 6th centuries the Angles ıd the Saxons turned Britain into ngland. Except in the west, the British nguage was quite submerged in that of ıe conquerors. Even so, some Celtic lace-names survive in the eastern half of ıe country, particularly the names of vers, for which the British had a special eling, regarding many of them as ıcred. It may be that the newcomers, out f superstitious awe, forbore to tamper vith these ancient names of power. Thus, ɔr example, the Darenth (Kent) comes rom a Celtic word meaning "river where he oaks are plentiful". The Thames is nother river whose name, meaning, ɔrobably, and today most appropriately, 'dark water", goes back to the Celts.

Some Anglo-Saxon names, like *North Folk* and *South Folk* (today's Norfolk and Suffolk), are straightforward tribal designations. The many names ending in *-ingas* and *-ingaham* (modern *-ing* and *-ingham*) denoted smaller groupings. Hameringham (Lincolnshire), for example, means "village of the dwellers on the hill".

The Anglo-Saxons became Christians during the early 7th century, but many place-names attest to their former paganism: for example, Wednesbury (Kent) from the god Woden; Tuesley (Surrey) from Tyr, the war-god; and Thundesley (Essex) from Thunor, god of thunder. Other place-names – such as Stokenchurch (Berkshire) "the church built of timber", and Halstow (Devonshire) "holy place" – advertise their conversion.

In the 9th century the Danes and other Scandinavian races began to make inroads into England. Many of them settled permanently. Place-names tell us exactly where. Those which end in *-by*, *-thorp(e)*, *-beck*, *-dale*, *-car*, *-thwaite*, *-fell*, *-gill* and *-holme* are all of Scandinavian origin.

Last of the successful invaders were the Normans. They must have enjoyed their new possession, judging from the number of places they called *beau-* or *bel-*, "beautiful". Beaulieu (Hampshire), Bewley (one in Durham and one in Westmorland), and Bewdley (Worcestershire) all mean "beautiful place". Perhaps tastes differed in those days, since the Normans re-named Fulepet (Essex) which meant "filthy pit, or hollow", Beaumont – "beautiful hill".

The invention of English place-names did not come to an end in 1066. It still goes on, whenever a new street, new housing development or new town needs a card of identity. The Industrial Revolution spawned such names as Coalville (Leicestershire) and Ironville (Derbyshire). Another 19th-century *-ville*, Waterlooville (Hampshire), took its name from a nearby inn called *The Heroes of Waterloo*.

One of the richest treasuries of place-names is to be found in the USA. Over the centuries people have come to it from many countries, in war and peace, and – like the early English settlers who, perhaps homesick, called their new homes Boston, Cambridge, London, and so on – have re-used the names of the towns and villages they left behind in the Old World. In addition, a great many Indian place-names were taken over, with the land itself, from the original inhabitants of the American continent: names like Mississippi, "the great water", and Oklahoma, "land of the red people". Americans named many towns after their national heroes, such as Washington and Lincoln; a practice followed by the Russians when, for example, they changed Petrograd (previously St Petersburg) to Leningrad, and Nizhni Novgorod to Gorki. (With Stalingrad, named in honour of the former ruler of the USSR, the process was reversed. Today the city is called Volgograd. Thus place-names chronicle history in a nutshell.)

Other American place-names reflect the naïve optimism of the immigrants – there are sixteen places called Athens, to say nothing of Rome, Carthage, Sparta, Nineveh and Troy – and their simple religious faith. There are nine Canaans in the US and eleven Jordans. There are even two places called Sodom.

In conclusion, a few place-names from all over the world, selected at random: Peking means "the northern court"; Bolivia takes its name from the South American revolutionary leader Simon Bolívar (1783–1830); Barcelona, Spain, derives from the Carthaginian general Hamilcar Barca (*c.* 270–228 BC) who is thought to have founded the city; Hong-Kong is a contraction of Hiang-Kiang, "the place of sweet lagoons".

Plagues: pestilences, extremely infectic
diseases. Throughout history, at vario
times, a great many people have di
from plagues and they have often be
regarded as divine punishments for mai
wickedness.

The plagues recorded in the Book
Exodus in the Bible are in a class by ther
selves. The frogs, lice, boils, etc., and t
killing of the firstborn were, rather, aim
at bringing home to Pharaoh the power
the Israelites' God, so that he would,
Moses demanded, "let my people go".

At a time when medical knowledge w
rudimentary, almost any infectious i
ness of swift and high mortality might
labelled plague. Today, in medical term
nology, the word is generally restrict
to a bacterial disease carried, in the fir
instance, by the bite of a flea which mak
its home on rats. People who have co
tracted the disease may spread it by the
coughs and sneezes or other infecti
discharges. Plague may take one of thr
forms, attacking the lungs, poisoning t
bloodstream, or breaking out in glandul
swellings known as buboes. This las
known as bubonic plague, is actually le
lethal than the first two, but since th
spectacular swellings make it instant
recognisable, it is the one with the be
documented history.

The first historical reference to plagu
dates from the time of the Roman Emperc
Trajan (AD 53–117), when it was recorde
as being rife in Syria, Libya and Egypt.
was from Egypt that, some 400 years late
it spread into Europe, via Constantinopl
where it is said to have killed 10,00
people in a single day. In Italy so man
people succumbed to it that, when Ger
manic invaders, the Lombards, swep
down from the north, they met with litt
opposition and were able to establish
kingdom which lasted for over 200 year

The terrible 14th-century visitatio
known as the Black Death, which kille

'ring out your dead", the cry of the corpse lectors in London, 1665.

f perhaps half the population of Europe, d irreversible consequences. The bells at tolled the passing of so many souls lled also the end of the Middle Ages. ıe feudal system could not long survive e wholesale slaughter of the human aterial on which it depended.

ingling out the peak plague years does ɔt mean that the intervening ones were ague-free. For centuries the plague was ıe of the facts of life, though by the 17th ntury its virulence had much declined. Nevertheless in 1665–6 London suffered a last dreadful outbreak in which robably at least 100,000 people died.

The Great Fire of London (1666) unoubtedly destroyed many squalid tenements where the flea-carrying rats had ound congenial homes. But in fact the lague bacillus was weakening everyhere. Gradually European outbreaks eased altogether and those in the East ecreased to much smaller proportions. Modern hygiene and drainage have peeded that decline, to say nothing of ıch modern medicaments as sulpha rugs and streptomycin. But in exceponal conditions, when modern amenies fail, plague can still strike, as in the isaster area of East Pakistan after the yclone havoc of November 1970.

NOHL, JOHANNES. *The Black Death: a chronicle of e Plague compiled from contemporary sources.* 1961

Plains States, The (USA)**:** In the north central region "the Great Plains" area includes the states of Iowa, Kansas, Minnesota, Missouri, Nebraska, North Dakota and South Dakota. Although actually not flat, since the plains rise from about 800 feet [244 metres] above sea level to about 4,000 feet [1219 metres] on the west among the foothills of the Rockies, this is indeed a large, uninterrupted plain. It is an area of grasslands and large farms, with no major rivers or other breaks in the landscape. Described by its first settlers as a vast "sea", its rolling hills and plains do suggest the undulating surface of the oceans.

Though parts of the region were explored by the Spanish, especially by Coronado in the 1540s, and though settlement in Minnesota began under the leadership of the American Fur Company during the 1810s, much of the region remained virtually uninhabited until the decades just before the American Civil War. In the middle of the century, the entire area, but especially Missouri, was considered the "Gateway to the West", as it was from this region that settlers venturing to California bought final provisions for their trek across the desert. Recently a gigantic arch has been erected in St Louis, Missouri, to commemorate this period in the history of the region.

This is, above all, an agricultural region. On these plains settlers, mostly from German, Irish and Scandinavian stock, established large farms devoted to the production of grains, grass and livestock. Though some coal, lead and oil are extracted, and some transport equipment is manufactured, the main feature of life in this region is the relative isolation of existence on the large farms of the plains.

Planetarium: an instrument for demonstrating the positions, relationships and movements of the sun, moon, planets, stars and other astronomical phenomena. Early planetaria had trains of gear wheels and were manually operated models of the solar system. Archimedes of Syracuse (287–212 BC), the mathematician, is recorded as having devised and used a water driven example. Later, with the invention of clockwork in medieval times, a mechanical drive could be provided.

The orrery, a table instrument, was developed in the early 18th century and named after Charles Boyle, fourth Earl of Orrery (1676–1731), for whom the first English example was devised.

The projector, London Planetarium.

The modern instrument, which projects a representation of the heavens on to a semicircular ceiling, was invented by the German Dr Bauersfeld of the Zeiss works at Jena in 1913. The instrument operates by means of a powerful light source, electric motors, lenses and mirrors. In this way the positions and movements of heavenly bodies, not only in the present day but in the past and future, and as observed from different latitudes, can be demonstrated. The watcher can thus explore the heavens from the comfort of a chair in a warm room. Problems connected with mathematics, survey work and navigation can be resolved a demonstrated simply.

Planetaria are used widely for ed cational and cultural purposes in the U and Germany. In England the use planetaria for educational purposes increasing and public performances given in the City Museum, Liverpo and in London at The Planetariu Baker Street, and at the National Ma time Museum, Greenwich. The worl largest planetarium, built at a cost $1,500,000, is at Dangerfield Island on t Potomac, Washington, DC, USA.

See also OBSERVATORY.

Plantagenet, House of (1154–1399 line of English kings, here named wi their dates of succession only.

The first was Henry II, son of Willia the Conqueror's daughter Matilda by h second marriage to Geoffrey of Anjo called Plantagenet from his habit of wea ing a sprig of broom (*planta genista*) in h cap. He succeeded Stephen in 1154 ar is chiefly remembered for his strong ru and for his quarrel with Becket (s separate entry). To remark that his co cern was as much with his lands in Franc as with the realm of England is t emphasise a feature, albeit with varyin fortunes, of all the reigns in this line. H was succeeded in turn by two of his son Richard I (1189), a romantic militar figure who spent very little time i England, and John (1199), one of th traditionally "bad" English kings, fro whom the barons wrung Magna Cart

Henry III succeeded his father John a the age of nine, and his reign was a lon one, but he was not a satisfactory rule That of his son Edward I (1272) saw revival of the prestige of the throne an the early growth of our parliamentar system. Edward II (1307) failed sadly t follow his father's path, but his so Edward III (1327) was a strong king wh

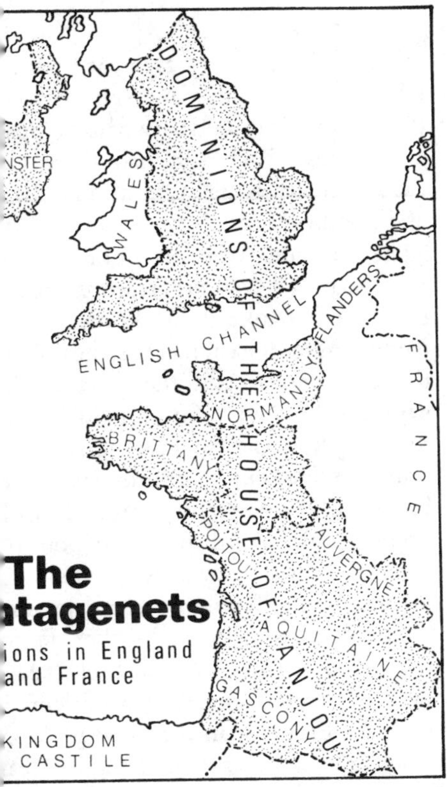

ımpaigned successfully in France (*see* ᴇᴄʏ; ᴘᴏɪᴛɪᴇʀs), though he sank into a rdid old age. He was a great lover of ivalric display and founded the Order the Garter. The last of the line was his andson Richard II (1377), son of the ack Prince, a headstrong king, unable control his nobles. In 1399 one of these, enry of Bolingbroke, later Henry IV ıd also a grandson of Edward III, overırew him, and he was done to death.

The succession then became a matter of ıspute between the houses of Lancaster ıd York (*see* WARS OF THE ROSES).

The last legitimate male Plantagenet ad perished by 1499, but it is interesting find the badge of the house still rememered in the reign of Elizabeth I, who had dress embroidered with the device.

HARVEY, JOHN. *The Plantagenets.* 1963

ee also LANCASTER, HOUSE OF; YORK, OUSE OF.

Plassey, Battle of (1757): fought near a village of that name on the Hooghly river in Bengal. Here Clive, with an army of 3,200, defeated the 50,000 of the Nawab Siraj-ud-Daula, establishing thereby the dominance of the British in Bengal. Clive had previously entered into a plot to dethrone the Nawab with Mir Jafar who commanded a large section of Siraj-ud-Daula's army. Though Mir Jafar did not openly declare himself until the issue was decided, he held back the troops under his command, thus undermining the spirit of the Indians, and it was a rout rather than a battle, Clive losing 23 killed and 49 wounded, and fewer than 500 being killed in the Nawab's huge army.

¶ EDWARDS, MICHAEL. *Plassey: The Founding of an Empire.* 1969

Plastics: materials which can be made to change shape under pressure or heat. Nature abounds in such materials, some of which, such as clays and waxes, have been used from time immemorial. Today, however, when we use the term, we generally mean the tremendous range of man-made materials (usually by-products of coal or oil) which have become all but indispensable to our industrialised society.

Plastics of this kind fall into two main categories: thermoplastic and thermosetting. Thermoplastic resins become soft and malleable under heat (i.e. they can be shaped without being broken), but undergo no permanent change. Thermosetting resins undergo a chemical change when heated and cannot be remoulded.

Some of the first plastics to be made were produced from a combination of phenol and formaldehyde. Bakelite (named after Dr Leo Baekeland, a pioneer in this field) is an example of this kind of plastic. Other plastics resins are polyvinyl chloride (PVC), polythene, polystyrene, and various forms of cellulose.

Plato (*c*. 427–348 BC): philosopher of ancient Greece, a man of aristocratic family and the disciple of Socrates, the great philosopher who was condemned to death on the accusations of the many enemies he made in his fearless pursuit of truth. Plato founded a school in the grove of Academus, just outside Athens, where mathematics, astronomy, science and philosophy were taught and ideas spread which (sometimes in distorted form) have greatly influenced Western thought. Plato's philosophy is based on two convictions – the possibility of human improvement and the supremacy of the intellect. His best-known works are in dialogue form, with his old master Socrates as the central figure. The most famous is the *Republic*, his version of an ideal state ruled by an aristocracy of intellect.

¶ In THOMAS, H. and D. L. *Great Philosophers*. 1959
See also SOCRATES.

Playing cards: cards used for indoor games and providing a history lesson in themselves, so much have they been affected by events. For six hundred years they have been known in Europe, for centuries longer in India and China. They have been used for divination, conjuring and education, as well as for gaming.

The cards, usually oblong or square, have been made in a variety of materials, but mostly of pasteboard and, nowadays, of plastic. The faces of the early European cards were hand painted, engraved or lithographed, putting them beyond any but a nobleman's purse, but after 1423 stencilling or wood block printing made them cheaper.

The earliest European pack, the *tarots*, first appeared in Italy in the early 14th century. It consisted of seventy-eight cards, including King, Queen, Knight and Varlet, together with twenty-one *atouts*, which also had pictures and titles.

Later came the fifty-two card pack know today, with four suits, two (Hearts and Diamonds), two black (Spa and Clubs). Each suit had three co cards, usually King, Queen and Kna and ten spot cards.

The four suits were common to all European packs, and represented the fo estates of mankind, as known in Middle Ages: the ruling class, the milita the commercial and the peasants. T symbols, however, varied from count to country – the Spanish signs, for i stance, were cups, swords, coins a batons. Our own cards derived from t French, a great card making nation fro the 15th century onwards.

Court cards down the centuries sho pictures of royalty and other famo figures, sometimes, as in the French car with the names inscribed. Charlemag was also Emperor in the tarot pack, a from 1480 he became the King of Hea in the French pack. For the other King the French chose David to head t Spades, Julius Caesar Diamonds, a Alexander Clubs.

During the French Revolution the em blems of royalty disappeared, the Kin became Sages, Dames (French title for t Queens) Liberties, Valets, Braves. B with the crowning of Napoleon, ba came the royal insignia.

Similar republican trends were found the American Civil War, when the pac were headed by army officers. Agai when South Africa left the Commo wealth, Kommandant, Vrou and Bo replaced the usual court cards.

The course of history can be traced such packs as the 18th-century Englis "Imperial Royal Cards", with Henr VIII shown as King of Spades, Ann Boleyn as his Queen, and Cardin Wolsey as Knave. A topical pack of 181 portrays the Duke of Wellington as Kin of Spades, while the other Kings a ıcher, Schwarzenberg and Kutusov. eir respective Queens are England, ıssia, Austria and Russia, while the .aves represent the private soldiers of four nations.

ı World War II, a variety of pack was culated in the Resistance Movement, th the Kings disguised as Churchill, osevelt, De Gaulle and Stalin.

uring the 19th century the French and glish packs became standardised with uble-headed court cards, but individual odern cards of historic interest can still found, with ancient Greek heroes ap- aring on Greek court cards and Biblical ;ures on those of Israel.

---

ebeian: adjective denoting member- ıp of the lower classes. The word is rived from the Latin *plebs*, the common lk of the city of Rome, whose political ;hts, particularly during the republican a (*see* PATRICIAN), were strictly limited law.

---

lebiscite: a vote of all the electors of a ecific area or country to decide some ıportant issue. The plebiscite was used the French Republic and Napoleon to ve their foreign conquests and annex- ions the semblance of the approval of ıe subjected populations. Perhaps the ɜst known plebiscite of this century was ɜld in the Saar in 1935, when its inhabi- nts voted to be reunited with Germany, ıus bringing to an end the administration f this area by the League of Nations.

ee also REFERENDUM.

FREEBOARD MARKING FOR SHIPS:
A diagram of the modern markings placed on the side of merchant ships to show the levels of loading for different seasons and conditions.

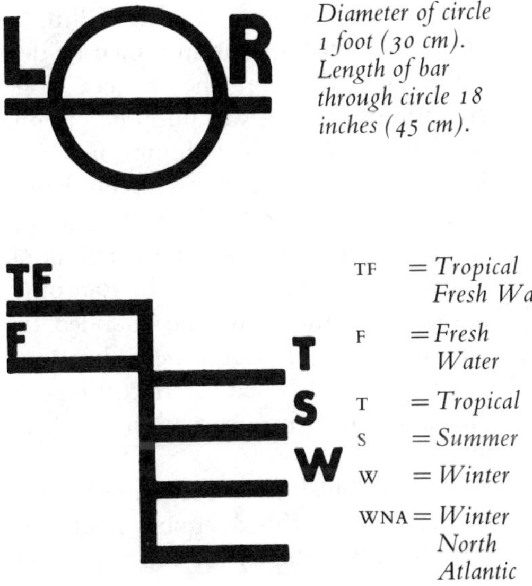

limsoll line: horizontal line painted on ıe side of a merchant ship denoting the mit to which it may be legally loaded. is named after the English radical parlia- ıentarian Samuel Plimsoll (1824–98).

The frequent losses of ships at sea caused y overloading by unscrupulous owners led Plimsoll to campaign for the introduction of a compulsory load line. After much opposition he succeeded, and the British Merchant Shipping Act of 1876 was passed bringing in the necessary legislation. In 1930 the matter was further pursued by a convention signed in London by forty nations defining the limits to which ships on international voyages may be loaded.

Plough: agricultural implement drawn by horses, oxen or tractor.

Food is the basis of life, crops are grown for food, the soil is cultivated for crops, and the plough is used for cultivation. A pointed stick can be used to scratch the soil to make a seed-bed, but such a digging-stick is not a plough. A plough pushes the soil aside as well as disturbing it. The part that does the pushing is the *breast* or *mouldboard*. This was at first a flat board; but experiments proved that a curved breast did better work, and that the shape of the curve influenced the way in which the soil was pushed to one side and turned over.

In Britain the Agricultural Improvers (*see* separate entry) were much concerned with plough design. Walter Blith, in 1641, published a book in which he described his ideas on the subject. John Arbuthnot's design was published in one of Arthur Young's volumes in 1771. James Small, calling himself "Husbandman and Artificer" (as we would say, farmer and mechanic), published his book *The Plough* in 1784. James E. Ransome, grandson of the man who founded the famous firm of Ransome, Sims and Jefferies, is recorded as lecturing on ploughs at the Royal Agricultural College in 1865.

These are but four of the many farmers and craftsmen who designed, made and used ploughs until, by the end of the 19th

Harfordshire wheeld plough
Pag 199
Single wheeld Plough
Pag 194
Pag 203
Pag 110 Plaine Ploug
The Double Plough ploughing two Furrows at one time
The Pure Dutch Share
English Share

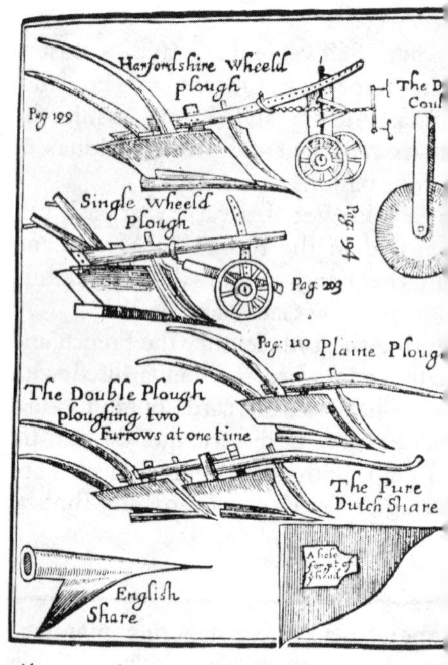

Above, 17th-century ploughs from Walter Blit English Improver Improved, *1652. Belo 19th- and 20th-century ploughs.*

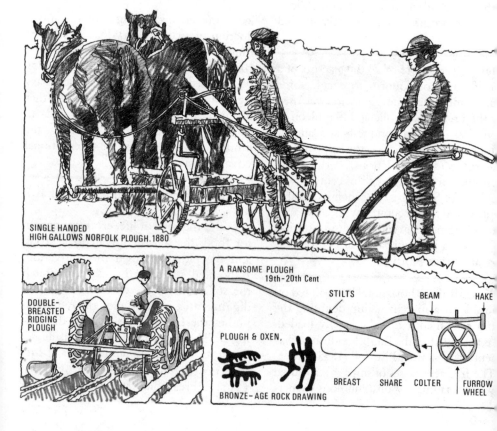

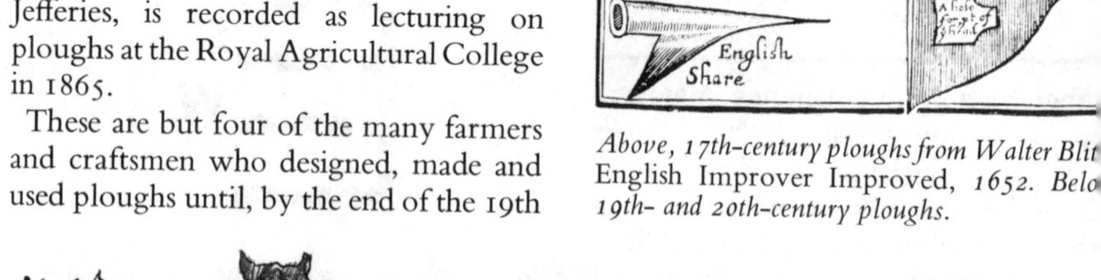

SINGLE HANDED
HIGH GALLOWS NORFOLK PLOUGH. 1880

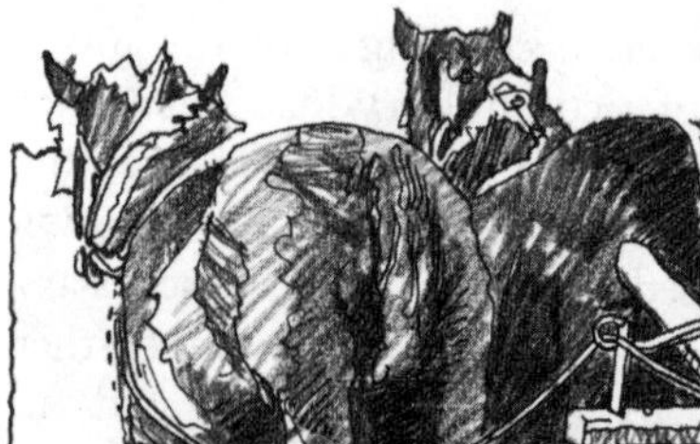

DOUBLE-BREASTED RIDGING PLOUGH

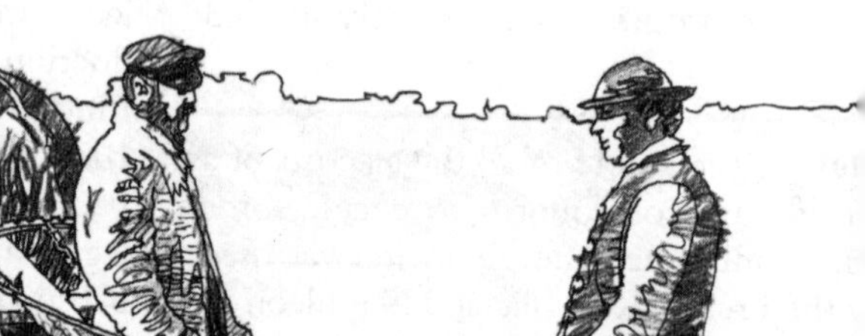

A RANSOME PLOUGH
19th-20th Cent
STILTS
BEAM
HAKE
BREAST
SHARE
COLTER
FURROW WHEEL
PLOUGH & OXEN,
BRONZE-AGE ROCK DRAWING

tury, most ploughs were being made ıctories. Local requirements and manu- ure resulted in a great variety of gn and name, famous ones being the ·tfordshire plough, the Kent plough the Suffolk plough, amongst others. plough with a single breast turns the :ow over (moves the soil aside) either :he ploughman's right or to his left, ording to how the breast is fitted. If it be changed so that when going in one :ction up the field it turns it to his right, when coming back it turns it to his , it is called a one-way plough. Such ughs, in the beginning, needed adjust- nt whenever they turned on the head- d at the end of the field.

·mouth (England): seaport between Tamar and Plym estuaries, south- st Devonshire, in a capacious harbour osed only to southerly winds. It de- oped on Sutton Pool in the Bronze Age Roman times and expanded in the h century. Expeditions for Gascony :mbled there under Edward I, wine s imported, and tin, lead, fish, hides l wool were exported. There was also usy traffic in conveying pilgrims to the ine of St James of Compostella in ain. In 1254 Henry II granted a market utton to the Prior of Plympton, and in ,o, after repeated French attacks showed need for fortification, Plymouth re- ved a charter. With the loss of Gascony 1451 the wine trade decayed and ·mouth turned to piracy. Under zabeth the town flourished as the base privateers – Huguenots, Sea-Beggars l the native Hawkins family – preying Spanish commerce. It is also imperish- y associated with the name of Sir ıncis Drake and with the sailing of the grim Fathers to New England. The val dockyard of Devonport developed er 1690, John Rennie's breakwater was ilt 1812–48, the Great Western Railway linked Plymouth with London in 1849.

Plymouth is also the name of at least ten places in the USA, the most celebrated being Plymouth, Massachusetts, the landing place of the Pilgrim Fathers (1620) and the first permanent settlement by Europeans in New England.

¶ BRACKEN, C. W. *History of Plymouth and Her Neighbours.* 1970

See also INDIVIDUAL ENTRIES.

Pocahontas or **Matoaka** (1595–1617): daughter of an American-Indian chief, Powhattan. According to the not entirely trustworthy account of Captain John Smith (*see* separate entry), leader of the Virginian colonists, she saved him from execution. She subsequently became a Christian and married John Rolfe, a settler, who in 1616 brought her to England where she dressed in Stuart fashion and was received at Court. She died at Gravesend, apparently on the eve of returning to America. Among her descendants through her son was the wife of President Woodrow Wilson.

¶ BINDER, P. and GOELL, K. *Pocahontas.* 1964

Pocket battleship: a powerful modern warship combining features of a "battleship" and a "cruiser". Battleships were designed to be the finest ships in a navy, with the most powerful guns and best armoured protection, but their high cost and international attempts to limit the power of navies led to the increased importance of the cruiser, normally of 10,000 tons standard weight and with

The Admiral Graf Spee *at the Fleet review, 1937.*

8-inch guns. Germany, however, in order to meet the Treaty of Versailles specifications, which limited size, in 1929 developed the Pocket Battleship, which was really a cruiser of 10,000 tons but with 11-inch guns and armour-plated sides and decks. In 1939 she had three, of which the commerce-raiders *Admiral Scheer* and *Graf Spee* were to become famous.

Poison gas: gas used in chemical warfare. Gas was first used effectively on 22 April 1915 by the Germans against the British and French at Ypres. It was employed throughout World War I, and in the 1930s by Italians in Abyssinia and Japanese in China.

The gas first used was chlorine, cylinders of which were opened on the German side, and the greenish-yellow cloud drifted in the breeze over allied positions. It smelt like bleach and caused a violent irritation in the lungs. Another "choking" gas, phosgene, was later fired in shells.

Mustard gas was used at Ypres in 1917. This is a pungent-smelling "blister" gas, droplets of which burn the skin after five hours. Breathing it causes bronchitis after twenty-four hours.

Nerve gas, developed in World War II, was never used for fear of retaliation. Odourless and colourless, it causes headaches, vomiting and convulsions. A droplet on the skin left untreated can kill in fifteen minutes. A less harmful but temporarily effective type, much used in quelling civil disturbances and dispersing crowds, is "tear gas", so named because of its effects as an eye irritant.

Poitiers: town on rocky promontory commanding the route from Gascony to the Loire. There Clovis and his Franks defeated the Goths in AD 507, and Charles Martel defeated the Moors in 732, the shield-wall of the Franks standing "like a rampart of ice". On 19 September 1356 John of France, with 16,000 men, o manoeuvred the Black Prince, with 6,5 The Prince, refusing to abandon his pl der, fought off pursuit at Maupert south-east of Poitiers. His men-at-ar withstood waves of French attack while English archers and Gascon knig attacked their flanks. King John was tak prisoner, his heir fled, but his fourth s Philip fought at his side and was rewar with the Duchy of Burgundy, whence and his successors plagued future Fre kings. Today Poitiers is a town of so 62,000 population, with important che cal and metal working industries.

Poland: republic of central Euro bounded by the Baltic Sea, Germa Czechoslovakia and Russia. A great i perial Polish state (Rzeczpospolita) exis in late medieval times, stretching acr the central European plain from Prus into today's Soviet Union. Through trading city of Danzig it grew rich on export of grain to the cities of west Europe. But the country's wealth v concentrated in the hands of the lar owners. The peasants were serfs, worki up to six days a week on the lord's la For the common people life was lit more than a miserable existence.

Poland's decline began in the 17th ce tury. In a struggle for domination north-eastern Europe Poland lost Sweden. For over a century the tv countries fought each other. Swedish s diers brought great destruction to cent Poland: grain mills were destroyed, far left empty. A third of Poland's pop lation fled or were killed. The strain war weakened the government, and t introduction of the *liberum veto* (i.e. t power to veto or prevent) made matt worse. By this laws had to be voted u animously by members of the D (Polish parliament). The result was th few laws were passed, let alone enforce

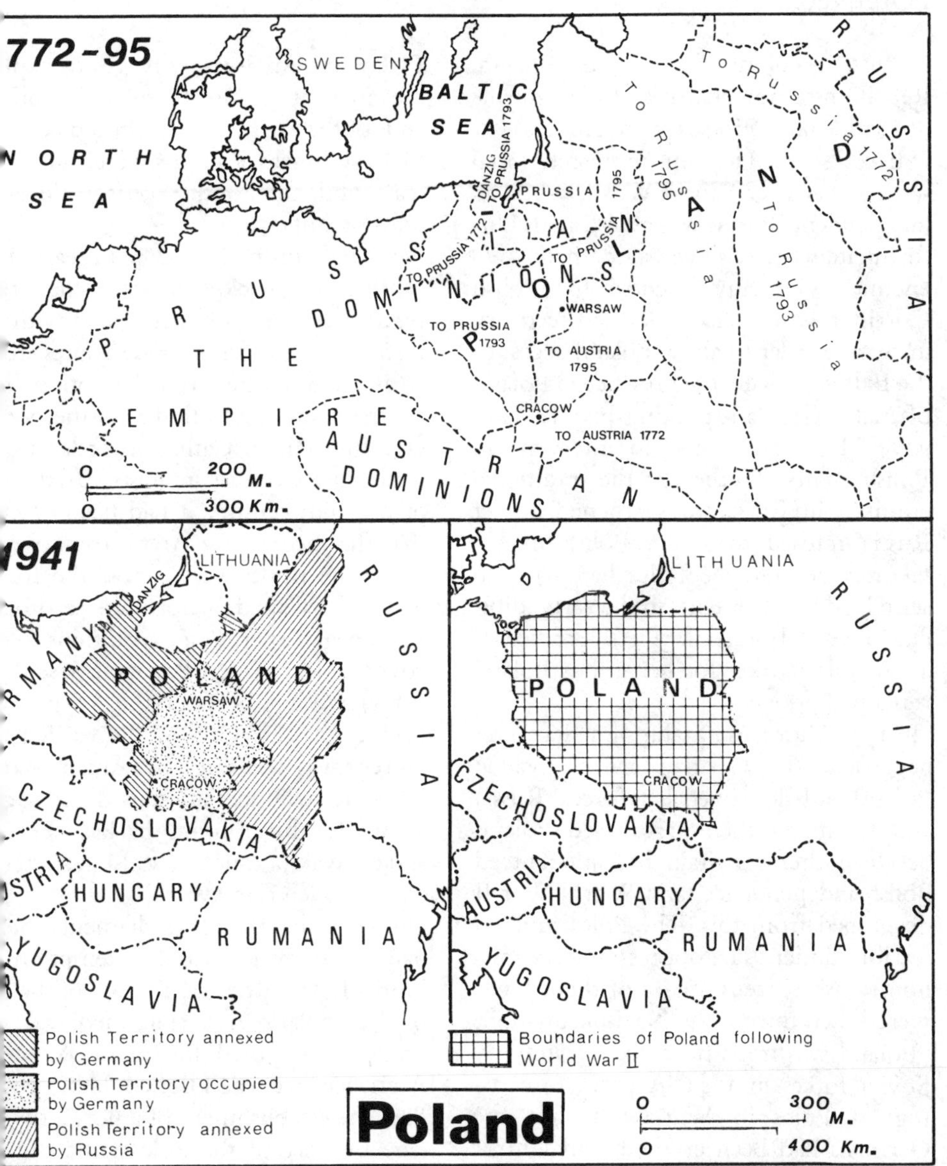

Poland

the central government. Real power in the provinces with the landowners their vast estates in eastern Poland. ey were proud, quarrelsome and re-ted any interference in their local rule. lthough Sweden was defeated by ssia at Poltava in 1709, Poland was now rrounded by other hostile powers: ssia to the east, Turkey to the south, andenburg-Prussia and Austria to the st. Poland had no natural frontiers such as rivers or mountains. So, without an efficient central government and lacking proper defences against ambitious neighbours, the country was seized and partitioned by Russia, Austria and Prussia in three stages: 1772, 1793 and 1795.

Attempts by the Poles to resist or change this situation had little success. A revolt led by Kosciuszko in 1794 was crushed by the Russians. In 1815 a small Kingdom of Poland was re-created, but it was more of a Russian colony than a free Poland. Rebellions against harsh and foreign rule in 1830, 1846 and 1863 were failures.

Success seemed to come in the territorial settlements after World War I, when an independent Poland was established. Unfortunately the new state had two enemies. Germany resented the Polish Corridor which sliced German territory in two in order to allow Poland access to the Baltic. As well, the presence in Poland of many German-speaking peoples later gave Hitler an excuse to intervene in Polish affairs. To the east the traditional enmity with Russia was sharpened. Soviet Russia refused to accept Polish manufactures because the Poles had tried to seize land towards Kiev in the early, difficult days of Bolshevik rule. Deprived of a valuable market for her goods Poland remained poor.

In 1939 Hitler and Stalin signed a secret pact, and the German army invaded Poland and destroyed her forces. Russia and Germany then partitioned Poland between them. Britain had guaranteed Polish independence, and World War II developed from this. The Poles suffered terribly under Nazi oppression. Six million Polish citizens, many of them Jews, were killed during the Nazi occupation.

Poland was freed from this tyranny by Soviet forces in 1944. A premature rising of Poles in Warsaw against the Germans had been crushed, and with it was destroyed the future leadership of an independent Poland. Instead Poland came under Soviet influence. A communist government has ruled the country ever since. The rise of the union-based "Solidarity" movement at the end of the 1970s faced the government with growing demands for a relaxation of its rigid communist doctrines. Its founder, Lech Walesa, received the Nobel Prize for Peace in 1983.

Polar expeditions: voyages to expl the areas at the northern and south ends of the earth's axis. It should be no that the North Pole is situated in fro seas, while the South Pole is in the la mass of Antarctica.

North Pole. From the 16th to the early 1 centuries Polar expeditions in the Ar regions were mainly concerned with discovery of possible trade routes. K rivalry existed between the countries northern Europe to find a northerly p sage through to Cathay in order to pand their overseas interests. By the e of the 16th century it had become cl that the most likely Arctic route wo be to the north-west, across the fro wastes of Canada's northern territor Thus began a series of expeditions to d cover a North-West Passage (*see* separ entry) as a link between the Atlantic a Pacific Oceans. One of the earliest plorers was the English seaman Mar Frobisher who in 1576 caused a sensati in London by bringing back an Eski and a kayak (a canoe of sealskin stretch on a wooden framework).

In 1821 the British parliament offe handsome rewards for an attempt on t North Pole. Little was known of the i mediate polar regions since medieval g graphers supposed the existence of Arctic ice-free sea. If this could be prov then the establishment of a northern p sage by way of the Pole was a disti possibility. In 1827 Sir Edward Pa sailed in HMS *Hecla* to a base in nor west Spitzbergen. Ice prevented furt progress by sea. Parry then started off the Pole hauling the two ship's boats sledges. He got to within 435 miles [7 kilometres] but was forced to retire fatigue. This was the first of many dir attempts on the North Pole by men many nations. The North Magnetic P was discovered by the Englishman James Clark Ross in 1831. A name

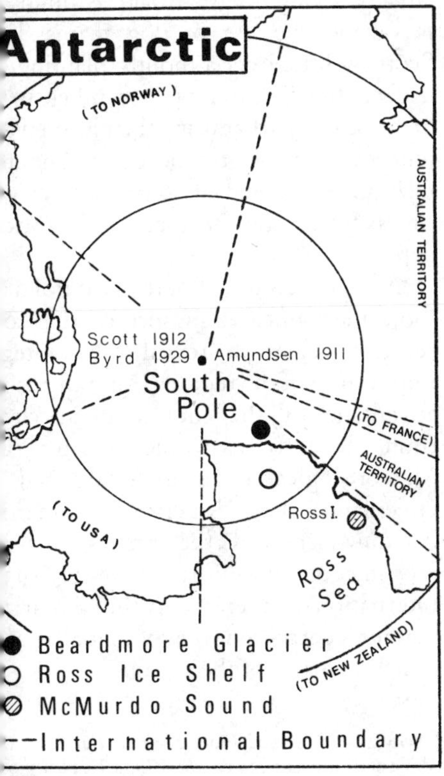

delibly written into the history of the North-West Passage is that of the English explorer Sir John Franklin. With his ships HMS *Erebus* and *Terror* he was trapped in the ice 1847–8. Many relief expeditions were organised but only relics were found. It was during one of these in 1850 that Captain Robert McClure in HMS *Investigator* proved the existence of the North-West Passage by sailing through the Prince of Wales Strait into Melville Sound.

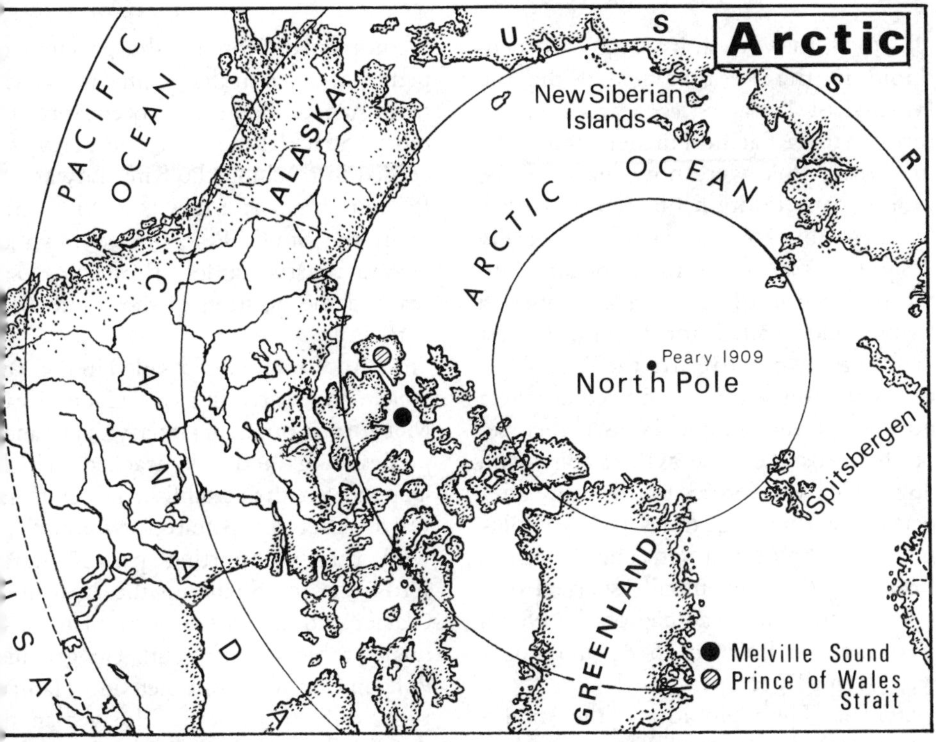

By the 1850s the independent private explorer was making his appearance. The first American Arctic expeditions were sponsored by Henry Grinnell of New York. Their aim was to combine a search for Sir John Franklin with attempts to reach the Pole. The Americans Elisha Kane, Isaac Hayes and Charles Hall all made northerly discoveries in the Ellesmere Island direction. The British Arctic Expedition of 1875–6 under Sir George Nares went still further north.

In 1878 the Swedish A. E. Nordenskiöld in the *Vega* navigated the old North-East Passage (*see* separate entry) through to the Pacific. Further attempts on the North Pole were now made by the Norwegians Fridtjof Nansen and Otto Sverdrup. In 1893 Nansen in the specially designed *Fram* drove his ship hard into the pack ice north of the New Siberian Islands and waited for the north-west drift to carry him towards the Pole. After two years this was not achieved despite a north-west movement. Nansen then set off towards the Pole with sledges and dogs. He was forced to give up after getting within 224 miles [360.50 kilometres] – the nearest yet. The American Robert E. Peary eventually succeeded in planting the American flag on the North Geographical Pole on 16 April 1909. It was his third attempt.

South Pole. The exploration of the Antarctic presented a very different problem from that of the Arctic. The popular belief till at least the end of the 17th century was that a great fertile southern continent existed. Scientific observations made by the English navigator Captain James Cook did much to disprove this. He found no trace of the continent during his voyages in southern latitudes in the 1770s.

Early in the 19th century considerable interest in the Antarctic was aroused. British, French, German, American and Russian expeditions made important discoveries. By the end of the century the Royal Geographical Society, London, under its energetic president Sir Clements Markham, planned an expedition in which Captain Robert Falcon Scott was to explore the Ross Sea area. In 1902 Scott sailed in the *Discovery*. From Ross Island, where he wintered, sledge teams set out to explore the Ross Ice Shelf and mountainous land eastward.

In 1907 Sir Ernest Shackleton, who had accompanied Scott on the previous e pedition, sailed in the *Nimrod* to carry from where Scott had been forced retire. Shackleton, with one party, su ceeded in reaching the King Edward V Plateau some 97 miles [156 kilometr from the South Pole in 1909, while second party under Professor Da reached the position of the South Ma netic Pole.

In 1910 Captain Scott sailed in the *Te Nova* and, arriving at Cape Eva McMurdo Sound, in January 1911, land ponies, dogs and two tracked vehicl Depots were then established to the sout ward. After the Antarctic winter Sco with three supporting parties, start across the Ice Shelf, up the Beardmo Glacier and across the polar plateau. I finally achieved the South Geographi Pole on foot with four men on 17 Janua 1912, only to find the Norwegian fl already flying there. Roald Amundse favouring the use of dog teams, be Scott by little over a month, planting h flag on the Pole on 14 December 191 Scott and his party during their homewa journey were overcome by fatigue a died in a snowed-up tent only elev miles from one of their well-stock depots.

Since the attainment of the two Poles o foot, mechanical transport of the 20 century began to reveal the strateg importance of the regions. Aircraft takin advantage of the shorter great circ route now fly over the North Po Meteorological bases are established Greenland. The American submarin *Nautilus* achieved the first submarin crossing of the North Pole in 195 International interest in the Antarct mainly centres on the potentially ri mineral wealth of the region.

¶ BOWMAN, GERALD. *From Scott to Fuchs*. Cad edn. 1960; KIRWAN, L. P. *The White Road*. 1959

lice: that department of the civil ninistration entrusted with the en- cement of law and order.

s the social units into which human ngs organise themselves have become ger and more complicated, some more nplex law-enforcing agency has be- ne necessary. In Egypt, under the olemies (the Macedonian kings who ed from 304–30 BC), the police force s organised along the same lines as the ny, with mounted desert patrols and achments stationed in each of the rty-six territorial divisions into which country was divided. The ancient eek city-states employed men to patrol streets at night. Others were set the k of catching brigands. The Romans, pert organisers in many other ways, re surprisingly slow at developing a lice system, a deficiency which may plain the many riots of the Roman mob. e Emperor Augustus (63 BC – AD 14) ated three *cohortes urbanae* (city troops) order to control the unruly element.

nglo-Saxon communities were en- uraged to police themselves. In Britain, izens of each Hundred (an admini- ative unit, part of the shire) were held ntly responsible for a crime committed thin its boundaries, unless the actual ongdoer could be produced. This, in ect, turned everyone into an honorary liceman for, if the criminal were not thcoming, the Hundred as a whole was nalised with a collective fine.

'he London police force may be said to ve had its beginning in 1285 when a tute of Watch and Ward (i.e. watch by ght, ward by day) appointed watch- en to keep the peace in the City of ondon. Further Acts for this purpose llowed in 1585, 1737 and 1777; yet ll, at the end of the 18th century, gland was a country infested with iminals of every kind.

great step forward was taken in 1753 when Henry Fielding (1707–54), the famous novelist who was also a magistrate at the Bow Street police court in London, organised what was virtually the first English detective force, a small group of constables known familiarly as "Bow Street Runners" or "Robin Redbreasts" (from their scarlet waistcoats). The Bow Street Patrols, set up in 1782, were charged particularly with combating highway robbery.

Credit for the foundation of the modern British police force goes to Sir Robert Peel (1788–1850) who, as Home Secretary in 1829, persuaded parliament to agree to the formation of the Metropolitan Police. Six years later the Municipal Corporations Act set up police forces in the provinces.

In the United States, development of a police organisation followed much the same pattern as in England. The office of constable was created by many townships in the early Colonies and night-watchmen were established in the larger communities. Just as in England, the distinction appeared between "watch" by night and "ward" by day, the two forces often being of poor calibre, independently controlled and not working harmoniously together. In 1844 came a major step forward with the passing of a law in the New York State legislature for a unified "day and night police". With this lead, similar organisations soon followed in Boston, Chicago, New Orleans, Baltimore and other important cities.

Despotic or totalitarian governments use their police as tools of policy, as spies and as tormentors of their political opponents. Indeed, we have come to call such regimes "police states". Dictators, by declaring democratic opposition a crime, force it underground and turn honest men into conspirators. Louis XIV (1638–1715) established the Paris police force and used it in this way; and so, a century later, did Napoleon Bonaparte (1769–

1821), especially under the dreaded Joseph Fouché who, as minister of police, established a vast spy system. The Russian Tsars and various Communist régimes have had their Tcheka, Ogpu, NKVD, MVD – successive names for the same thing, a political police force. The Nazis' equivalents were the Gestapo and the SS.

¶ ASHLEY, BRIAN. *Law and Order*. 1971; SPEED, P. F. *Police and Prisons*. 1968

See also INDIVIDUAL ENTRIES.

Political parties (general): A political party is a group of people who have certain ideas and interests in common. It seeks power in a community to make decisions which will then become the laws of the country.

The common interests of a political party can develop from many things. A group may wish to protect its religious belief or its language from being swept away by rivals. Townspeople will find that their wish for cheap food conflicts with the countryman's desire for a high price for his produce. Those who make their living from rents paid on their property will wish for different priorities in law from those who work at a trade or profession for their living.

When one party has gained power, it may then get rid of its opponents by killing, imprisonment or exile. This has often taken place in dictatorships or one-party states. Senior army officers may use their control of military power to seize the government, but they are not properly called a political party. A fascist party argues that a regular choice of party programmes is inefficient; so it offers state-organised prosperity in exchange for a people's liberty of choice. The communist parties in soviet states refuse to allow other parties to form: they argue that these give opportunities to rivals who might be enemies of the working classes.

The fairest system would allow each group with a particular interest to ha its own political party, and for all th to be represented in proportion to votes given in an election. There wo of course be many groups, and in th multi-party states politicians can disc a problem with all opinions given a voi But with all the talking it is very diffic to get quick decisions. Also, as one pa rarely has an overall majority (that more than 50 per cent of the seats) it to work with other parties to form coalition. This easily breaks up when important, controversial issue is disc sed. So, instead of a country getting a f government, it often gets poor, sho lived governments. Italy has had as ma as seventy-three officially registe parties at one time.

In many countries a workable comp mise has developed: the two-party s tem. Although different states give th own names to their parties, they can roughly divided into political parties the "right" wing and political parties the "left" wing. Those of the right conservatives who wish to preserve particular society or at least allow o slow change; whilst the left are t radicals who want more or less ra changes in support of their intere These parties also have different ideas how the wealth of a state should be pr duced and distributed. Those of the rig support competition in commerce, a encourage the enterprise and judgme of individuals in the production of goo If some people are more successful a wealthy than others, then this is the ward for their efforts. Parties of the l argue that modern economies are t complicated for individuals to contr and stress the importance of co-operati and planning by public authorities (su as nationalised industries). Any wea produced should be shared out mo equally; for instance, the highly succe should be taxed heavily in order to ›vide welfare services for anyone in :cial need.

'hus parties of the right tend to attract ›perty-owners, industrialists and those jobs with great security. Parties of the t tend to attract the less well-off in a mmunity, those skilled and unskilled ınual workers whose jobs are not always :ure.

›litical parties, Britain: When there an election for Parliament almost all ndidates claim to belong to a political .rty: Conservative, Labour, Liberal or ıore recently) Social Democrat Party DP). This has not always been so. In the rly days of parliament there were no rties. In the 13th century, when the king anted money, he called representatives ` the Church, the counties and the ›roughs to meet him. Such meetings of ırliament were held simply to carry out e king's wishes. As time passed, the ›werful barons did not always agree ith the king and by the time of Henry III (reigned 1509–47) there were differences about money, religion and other atters. Later, when Charles I (reigned ›25–49) claimed divine right and tried › exact taxes without the approval of ırliament at all, the members took des for or against the king. After ıe Revolution of 1688, there were two ıain groups, or *parties*: the Tories, ho supported the king to be controlled y Parliament (*see* TORY and WHIG). But ıe Whigs and the Tories in the 18th :ntury were not political parties as we now them. Both groups represented the ch and powerful: the great mass of the eople had no "party" at all.

)uring the 19th century changes were :ought about in both parties by two :eat statesmen: William Ewart Gladone (1809–98) and Benjamin Disraeli (1804–81). Gladstone, who began his political life as a Tory, later became a Whig and, as its leader, changed that party into what later became known as the Liberal Party. Under Disraeli's leadership, the Tory Party became known as the Conservative Party. The Conservatives wanted to keep things as they were, while the Liberals aimed at improving the life of the mass of the people.

During the 19th century, as more people won the right to vote, they thought of themselves as either Conservatives or Liberals. When there was an election, the party with most Members of Parliament formed the government, either Conservative or Liberal. Then in 1900 a meeting was held in London of men who believed that there should be working men in parliament to speak for all working people, the largest class in the country. This was the beginning of a new party, the Labour Party. In the general election of 1906 the Liberals won a huge majority over the Conservatives, but twenty-nine Labour candidates were also elected. Although the Liberal government passed laws to improve the housing, health and education of the people and to relieve poverty and sickness in old age, it gradually lost the support of the mass of voters. Meanwhile, the Labour Party won more seats in parliament, until it took the place of the Liberal Party as the official opposition to the Conservatives. In 1924 the Labour Party, only twenty-four years old, won the general election, and its leader Ramsay MacDonald became prime minister for a short period. Since then the government has been either Conservative or Labour. During the 1970s there were signs that the two party system Britain had come to accept was in danger of fragmentation. The greatest threat to the existing party line-up comes from the new Social Democrat Party (SDP).

The pattern of government by the strongest party numerically has occasionally been broken in times of crisis by the formation of coalitions designed to use the best abilities of all parties.

Political parties, USA: Loosely organised political parties existed in the American colonies from the latter part of the 17th century onwards. Chief among them were the Tories and Whigs, who with the coming of the American Revolution came to be known respectively as Loyalists and Patriots. Later the controversy over the Federal Constitution produced two parties, one in favour of, the other opposed to, the adoption of the Constitution. It should, however, be stressed that they were scarcely organised and disciplined in the modern sense. During this time, and for much of the early national period, real political organisations existed only in the states, and even these tended to be little more than factions springing up around some forceful and colourful personality.

National parties may be said to have come into being when Jefferson, finding himself in disagreement with the policies of George Washington's administration, resigned from the Cabinet in order to build up an organisation which would support his own ambitions for the presidency. Thus perished the hope of the Founding Fathers that all shades of opinion should be represented within the administration itself. Henceforth, competition for the presidency, as well as for other elective offices, tended to centre not on individuals but on candidates supported by rival organisations, representing the consensus of their membership. After 1832 candidates were selected by conventions of the parties. The multiplication of Federal offices (jobs) and the practice of distributing them as rewards to the party faithful – a practice which grew up during the democratic rev of the Jacksonian period – immeasural increased the importance of parties. T "spoils system", indeed, gave the pa system its enduring vitality. From 17 to 1824 the Federalists, who in ma cases were the original champions of t Constitution, opposed the Republica (Jeffersonians), who were the heirs, terms of ideas, of those who had o posed it. The Federalist party was su ported principally by commercial a industrial elements, the Republicans the agricultural elements.

Following Jefferson's election in 18 the Federalists went downhill steadil in 1820 they made no nomination for t Presidency. Shunning at first the ti "democratic" as smacking of the Fren Revolution, the party of Jefferson ca to be known later as the Democrati Republican party. Toward the end of t period during the so-called "era of go feeling", which was really an era of i tense personal politics, voters genera accepted the Republican label but f lowed various leaders: Adams, Clay, a Calhoun; Crawford, Clinton and Jackso From 1842 to 1860 the two princip parties were the Whigs, who accepted t Federalist tradition and were support by the same classes plus the rising man facturing element then chiefly centred New England, and the Democratic el ments, no longer fearful of being call by that name. Fused by Jackson, the were powerfully reinforced by Weste settlers and newly enfranchised laboure in the older parts of the country. Min political groups, some of them confin to one or a few states, made their presen felt during this period, among them t Anti-Masons, Barnburners, Hunke Cotton Whigs, and the Know Nothi Party. By far the most successful of the were the Liberal party and its successo the Free Soil party, out of which gre modern Republican party – this was fact the only instance in American tory where a third party emerged to come one of the two major contenders power. With the rise of the slavery ie, party lines were shattered; by 1856, cause of this issue, the Whig party was ished and the Democratic party hope-sly split. From 1862 to the present day two great political parties have been Republicans and the Democrats.

etween 1860 and 1876 the major politi- controversies concerned war and onstruction; subsequently issues of pute have been mainly economic in aracter, though during the 1960s Civil ghts and American military involve-ent in South-East Asia have loomed ge. Since 1862 there have been numer-s "third parties". Prohibitionists nomi-ted their first presidential candidate in 72; Greenbackers gave expression to rarian discontent, and they were suc-eded by the Populists in the 1890s. The rest amongst industrial workers led to formation of the Union-Labour, cialist Labour, Social Democratic, cialist and Communist parties. Twice ring this period the Republicans suf-ed heavy defections. In 1912 Theodore osevelt resigned his membership and rmed the Progressive Party. And in 24 Robert LaFollette led an agrarian volt of Independent Progressives. In cent times the only major "third party" ndidacies to attract a significant number votes have been those of Strom Thur-ond campaigning for "states rights" and overnor George Wallace on a "white premacy" platform.

oll tax: tax per head of population. Its st appearance in England was in 1377, hen a groat per head was levied on ergy and laity. The poll tax of 1380 was direct cause of Wat Tyler's rebellion in e following year. The device was inter-mittently used until the 18th century. Perhaps its most controversial use was in the Southern States of America, from approximately 1890 to 1920, as a means of excluding the Negro elector by requir-ing payment of such a tax before a vote was allowed. This device was declared illegal in both federal and state elections in 1964 and 1966.

Polo, Marco (1254–1324): Venetian traveller and author. When Marco Polo returned to Venice with his father and uncle, after twenty-five years of adven-turous journeys in the mysterious East, their relatives failed to recognise the travel-stained wanderers in their out-landish garb. They laughed at Marco's wonderful stories of million-peopled cities, innumerable jewels and vast treasures, dubbing him "Messer Marco Milione". The Polos invited the doubters to a sumptuous banquet. When their guests were seated, they entered dressed in robes of crimson satin. During the meal they discarded these for crimson damask, then for velvet. Finally, Marco ripped open their old Tartar jackets and showered the guests with jewels.

Marco Polo sets out on his travels from Venice.

One of Marco's journeys, occupying four years, brought him to the court of Kublai Khan in China, where he was given an official appointment. His duties took him to Tibet, Burma, Laos, Java, Japan, even Siberia. He dictated an invaluable record of his travels and impressions to a scribe in about 1299. The original manuscript of this "Book of Marco Polo", written in rough French, is probably the one in the National Library of Paris, though more than eighty other manuscripts are known.

¶ BRETT, BERNARD. *The Travels of Marco Polo*. 1971
See also KUBLAI KHAN.

Polynesia: eastern division of Oceania (*see* separate entry). The Polynesians now inhabit the easternmost of the Pacific islands, such as Samoa and Hawaii. They were already a civilised people when they left their original homes on the Indo-Chinese coast of Asia. In the 6th century AD, using outrigger canoes and navigating by the stars, they spread rapidly east across the Pacific and south to New Zealand.

Their islands were visited by the Spanish sailor Pedro Fernandez de Quiros in the 17th century and explored thoroughly by Captain Cook in the 18th century. In 1797 the first missionaries arrived and not only converted the Polynesians to Christianity but also taught some of them to read. *See* PACIFIC OCEAN for map.

Pompeii: town in Italy on the Bay of Naples, destroyed in an eruption of Mount Vesuvius in AD 79. The same disaster overtook Herculaneum (*see* separate entry); but, whereas the latter town had retained much of the character of its Greek origin, Pompeii had been largely rebuilt by the Romans after an earthquake sixteen years before, and its remains, which have been intermittently explored since 1748, teach us much about a Roman provincial town. It served a market for the produce of its fert countryside, a port for Mediterrane trade and a centre for certain specialis industries. All this was buried under t lava for nearly seventeen centuries.

The letter-writer Pliny the Younger 61–*c.* 114) has left us an account of t eruption, in which his uncle Pliny t Elder perished as the result of his ov scientific curiosity.

¶ BRION, M. *Pompeii and Herculaneum*. 19
TAYLOR, DUNCAN. *Pompeii and Vesuvius*. 1969

Pompey (Gnaeus Pompeius Magnu 106–48 BC): Roman politician and ge eral. He was born of a family of midd rank, to which the highest offices state were normally denied; but t turbulent years of the 1st century B when the republican constitution was its final decline, enabled him to use h military successes, particularly in t East, to play a dominant part in politi at home. But a rival was at hand in t person of Gaius Julius Caesar (*see* sep rate entry), with whom he at first co laborated. Later, however, civil war brok out between them, resulting in the defe of Pompey (9 August 48) at Pharsalus northern Greece. He fled to Egypt ar was stabbed to death as he stepped ashor

---

Pondicherry: town, seaport and distri on the west coast of India south Madras, formerly the principal Frenc settlement in southern India. Founded b François Martin in 1674, it was tak by the Dutch in 1693, to be returne with much improved fortifications, 1699. It was captured by the Englis general Sir Eyre Coote in 1761, an given back with fortifications destroye and a limit imposed on the size of i armed forces, in 1763. Thereafter it w occupied by the British at the outbrea each war with France, in 1778, 1793 l 1803, to be restored on each occasion the return of peace. Pondicherry was ited with India in 1954.

'oor whites": people at the bottom of iite society in the southern USA. A atively small group, they lived in apidated huts and were plagued by okworm, pellagra, malaria and tuber-losis. The women bore the brunt of rning a livelihood while their menfolk ifed around chewing home-grown bacco and drinking locally distilled t-gut ("moonshine"). The poor whites, ainly illiterate, were reluctant to work r their subsistence as they thought that would reduce them to the level of the egroes, whom they despised. Their ccessors survive in diminishing num-rs, but the term is not found very ceptable in modern America.

ort-of-Spain: capital of Trinidad and obago. One of the finest towns in the 'est Indies, it has two cathedrals, impres-ve public buildings and a safe, sheltered rbour that has made it the state's chief mmercial centre.

ortrait painting: the art of painting eople, especially their faces and from life. ortrait painting has always presented eculiar difficulties for the artist. On the ie hand, a portrait must be a likeness, a ue record of the person portrayed. On ie other, when, as often happens, the ortrait is specially commissioned, the itended subject wishes, not unnaturally, be shown in the most flattering light. Only a truly great artist can reconcile iese two conflicting elements with a iird – the demands of his own genius. great portrait is something more than a iccessful representation of a human be-ig, whether glorified or shown, as Oliver Cromwell demanded of the painter Lely, "warts and all".

The first portrait painter known history was Polygnotus (*c.* 475–447 BC), a Greek who introduced portraits into his murals on public buildings. Unfortunately none of his work, nor that of any other ancient Greek painter known to us by name, survives. Apelles (4th century BC), by reputation the greatest of them, was portrait painter to Alexander the Great (356–323 BC). By royal edict no one else was allowed to paint the great man. We can only guess, from a description that has come down to us of a portrait of Alexander holding a thunderbolt as if he were Zeus himself, that Apelles, like many court painters since, had to make concessions to his clients' vanity.

Modern portrait painting dates from the Renaissance. Medieval Christian man was taught to despise his body as a receptacle of sin, doomed to decay. Not until the 13th century did this joyless attitude begin to change. By the 15th century painters like Domenico Ghirlandaio (1449–94) in Florence, and Hugo van der Goes (*c.* 1440–82) in Flanders, were introducing into religious pictures portraits of the men who had commissioned them. Ghirlandaio went further, including portraits of well-known Florentines in many of his large-scale compositions.

Portrait painting proper soon came into its own. These early Renaissance portraits are among the best ever painted, full of the most delicate observation of character and, above all, honest. If anything, some of the Flemish and German painters of the period, in their search for truth, tended to go to the other extreme: their sitters cannot all have been so ugly.

Among the great Italian portrait painters may be mentioned Giovanni Bellini (*c.* 1430–1516), Giovanni Moroni (1520–78) and, greatest of all, Tiziano Vecelli, known as Titian (*c.* 1489–1576). During his long life Titian painted popes, doges, kings, dukes and duchesses with a splendid enjoyment. His portraits, while in the grand manner, are full of humanity.

To the greatest of the German portrait painters of the time, Hans Holbein (1497–1543), we owe our conception of what Henry VIII and his court looked like, reminding us that portrait painters are – or were, before photography – pictorial historians. We see the past through their eyes.

Sometimes we have to make corrections. Thus, we know from other sources that King Charles I, for all his undoubted good qualities, was not the impeccably noble monarch so often painted by Anthony Van Dyck (1594–1641). This Flemish painter settled in England and was knighted for his service.

The Spanish royal family was apparently less eager for flattery or more conscious of the deference due to genius. Diego Velasquez (1599–1660) painted the court as if it consisted of men and women no different from the common run of humanity; while, more than a hundred years later, another great Spanish painter, Francisco de Goya (1746–1828), depicted the royal family of his day almost as a collection of nincompoops.

Rembrandt van Rijn (1606–69), the Dutch painter, had, fortunately for his art if not his pocket, no such royal patronage. His incomparable portraits, full of humour, wisdom and the wounds of experience, have been called "a continous self-portrait".

England for centuries favoured foreign above native artists. Not until the 18th century did a distinctive English school of painting develop. In Thomas Gainsborough (1727–88) and Sir Joshua Reynolds (1723–92) it included two portrait painters of superb quality.

The invention of photography has undoubtedly narrowed the field for portrait painters: yet there will always be ro
for a view of humanity filtered throu
the eye and mind rather than a cam
lens. Perhaps it is due to the camera tak
over the task of literal presentation t
for many modern artists – for examp
Pablo Picasso (1881–1973) and Fran
Bacon (b. 1910) – a portrait has beco
more a point of departure than an end

See also INDIVIDUAL ENTRIES.

Port Royal: careening place on a san
spit enclosing Kingston Harbour, Jamai
(Careening was the tilting of a ship
that her bottom could be scraped clean
barnacles, etc.) It was developed by t
British after 1655, fortified in 1656 a
used by buccaneers and traders. It w
partly submerged in an earthquake
1692, survivors moving to Kingston.
was rebuilt as a dockyard in 1735 and w
the base for the English Admiral Verno
squadron, 1739–42. The harbour w
capacious, but its approaches were d
ficult. Boats had to go seven miles [
kilometres] for provisions and twel
[19 kilometres] for water, it was co
manded from windward by the Fren
in Hispaniola, and it was periodica
scourged by hurricanes, notably in 174

Portugal: nation-state on the Atlan
coast of the Iberian peninsula, 350 mi
[563 kilometres] from north to south a
between 70 and 136 [112 and 218 kil
metres] from east to west, with mou
tains in the north and a sandy plain in t
south. Until the 12th century the histo
of Portugal and Spain cannot be separate
The first settlers were probably Afric
in origin. Phoenicians, Greeks and Carth
ginians came by sea to trade; Celts can
by land to settle in fortified hill-village
The Romans occupied Portugal from 2
BC to AD 409, and left roads, cities a
their language. Other invaders broug

: heavy wheeled plough, a law code d a form of Christianity. The Muslims vaded from Africa in 693 and, though me Visigoths held out in the northern ountains, the majority accepted oorish rule and gained from them owledge of seafaring, rotation of crops, afting of fruit trees and irrigation by ater-wheel.

he first step in reconquest from the oors was taken by Alfonso of Castile-on (1072–1109), who gave the County Portugal as dowry with his daughter Henry of Burgundy. Their son Alfonso enriques took the title of King in 1139 d was recognised as independent in 43. By 1267 Portugal had driven out e Moors and attained her present ontiers. To encourage settlers on re-nquered lands the kings granted *fueros*, charters, to those who would establish alled towns, and any freeman could aim unoccupied land "with trumpet d royal flag". The military Order of viz and the Cistercian monks both ayed a large part in the reconquest and ere granted large estates. A later king, lfonso II (1211–23), was excommunicated for trying to recover part of these estates. King Denis (1279–1325) earned the nickname "the Farmer" for his efforts to develop his kingdom. He drained swamps, developed a fleet and a system of marine insurance, founded Lisbon University (moved to Coimbra in 1537), and formed the military Order of Christ out of the disbanded Knights Templar. His French wife Isabel scattered an apronful of pine cones from Provence on the windswept dunes and started the royal forests.

Portuguese independence was repeatedly threatened by the growing power of Castile. In 1385 John of Castile claimed Portugal on his marriage to Beatrice, heiress of Portugal. Clergy and nobles supported him, but the merchants supported the Master of Avis, an illegitimate prince who, as John I, founded the dynasty which built the overseas empire. English archers helped him win the battle of Aljubarrota against the Castilian party. Portuguese independence was again saved when, in 1469, Isabella of Castile married Ferdinand of Aragon rather than the

Portugal: left, the Praia da Rocha, in the Algarve. Right, the Tower of Belem on the River Tagus.

elderly King of Portugal. Castile triumphed when Sebastian, King of Portugal, leading an ill-advised crusade in Morocco in 1578, lost 8,000 men and was killed himself. Philip II of Spain became King of Portugal, and from 1580 to 1640 Portugal was ruled by Spanish kings. Her empire was exposed to Dutch attacks, until the house of Braganza re-established an independent Portuguese kingdom.

The Portuguese empire in Africa, the East Indies and Brazil, built up between 1420 and 1510 with the help of Jewish and German mapmakers and Italian navigators, brought little good to Portugal. It enriched the king and freed him from dependence on the *Cortes* (parliament), but it lured the Portuguese away from agriculture into plunder of the Indies and concealed from them, for a time, the consequences of expelling the Jews. Portugal thus began the decline which has left her with the lowest standard of living in western Europe.

Links with Flanders and England had been forged as early as the 12th century and, in the struggles against Louis XIV, Napoleon and the Kaiser over a period of nearly 300 years, Portugal remained true to the English alliance. She lost her eastern empire to the Dutch in the 17th century, but the discovery of gold in Brazil sustained her until Brazil became independent in 1825. In 1926 a military dictatorship was established and from 1932 Dr Oliviera Salazar controlled the country until his death in 1970. By then Portugal was fighting three wars – in Angola, Mozambique and Guinea–Bissau – in a vain effort to retain control of her African empire. A military coup overthrew Dr Caetano (Salazar's successor) in 1974 and a year later all Portugal's African possessions had become independent. Portugal's entry to the EEC in 1985 holds promise of a new economic era for the country.
See SPAIN for map.

Postal history: the first mention o postal services in Europe is attributed t the Venetians in the 10th century. Earl in the 14th century in Venice, wel organised postal services were operate which eventually extended throughou the Venetian Empire, to Constantinopl and to the Balkans. About this time, too Omodeo Tasso from the Lombardy cit of Bergamo "couriered" mails through out Italy and into neighbouring countries The family of Tasso became genera superintendents of the posts of the Hol Roman Empire under the German em peror and, having been ennobled, adde the surname of Torre to their name Moving to Germany the family change its name to Thurn and Taxis. This famou postal family controlled and organise the posts in nearly all of Europe for si centuries until 1867.

Postal services in Great Britain develope in a gradual and haphazard way. In orde to send a letter in the 15th century it wa necessary to find someone who could b trusted, usually one's own servant or friend. Often the common carrier wh went from town to town with goods sometimes a traveller, or maybe a soldie going in the right direction, could b relied on to deliver a letter. Royal letter and letters of state were carried by th Royal Messengers who rode to all parts o the kingdom. Innkeepers along the mai routes were compelled to keep ready change of horses so that the messenger had no delay. Sir Brian Tuke in the reig of King Henry VIII was in charge of thi service, with the title of Master of th Posts.

In 1635 the first attempt to establish postal service for ordinary people wa made by Thomas Witherings when "running post", i.e. a postman on foot was organised between cities and towns and for the first time a system of posta rates was tabled, based on mileage. Th tman carried a horn to announce his val. On the longer journeys he rode on seback. In 1657 the Post Office was blished by an Act of Parliament, and onfirmed on the Restoration in 1660. s important Act is known as the Post ice charter. Date stamps were first oduced in 1661 by the Postmaster neral, Henry Bishopp. Private enterse in the postal services, although forden, continued in many ways. The st famous of all was the venture by lliam Dockwra and Robert Murray, o organised the London Penny Post 1680. This splendid service operated th hourly collections and deliveries thin and around the cities of London d Westminster. Triangular shaped rks denoting ONE PENNY PAID were mped on the letters - the first paid mps. The government took over this vate post in 1682 and maintained it on ich the same lines, but less efficiently, til the end of the 18th century.

ı 1711, by an Act of Queen Anne, the neral Post Office established post offices British Dominions and possessions erseas, with rates of postage tabled to d from London. Benjamin Franklin, e former postmaster of Philadelphia, as made a Deputy Postmaster General the American Post Office - a branch of e GPO. Postal services were eventually ganised and extended throughout all e North American colonies, Canada d the British West Indies. Subsequently ail services by government-subsidised cket boats and the East India Company ere arranged to most places in the world, ıt privately owned merchant ships also ayed a big part in the carriage of mail verseas.

An important development was the rriage of mail by coach. The first mail ach carrying passengers and mail, tended by an armed guard, set out from ristol to London on 2 August 1784. This

The Bristol, Bath and London coach collecting mail without halting.

was the start of a romantic period in British Post Office history, with the mail coach playing a vital part. Because of the able administration of Sir Francis Freeling, Secretary of the Post Office from 1798–1836, greatly improved postal services were now maintained throughout the kingdom. By the 1820s Penny Post Offices were functioning in nearly every city, town and village throughout the entire United Kingdom. This wonderful service enabled letters to be sent for one penny within a prescribed distance. At the same time, however, general postal rates between places were greatly increased, making it sometimes impossible for those of limited means to send a letter. Robert Wallace, MP for Greenock, attacked the Post Office in 1833 for the excessively high postage rates. His complaints and argument were followed through by a former schoolmaster, Rowland Hill, who proved that a letter could be profitably carried anywhere in the United Kingdom for less than a penny. Organised agitation and petitions for postal reforms took place during 1837–39 which ultimately resulted in a uniform postal rate of one penny per half-ounce letter coming into force on 10 January 1840. The man responsible for the clever propaganda and for much of the organisation for these postal reforms was Henry Cole, an ardent supporter of Rowland Hill's plan. On 6 May 1840 the world's first adhesive postage stamps, the famous Penny Black and Twopenny Blue stamps – as well as pre-paid pictorial envelopes

An envelope bearing the famous "Penny Black" stamp.

and covers designed by William Mulready, RA – were available to the public.

One other reform of importance abolished the centuries-old privilege of "franking", whereby the letters of members of parliament as well as others of high rank were carried free of postage. The person's signature on the envelope or outside of the letter served as the frank (or free) mark.

With the introduction of uniform penny postage, envelopes were now popularly used for the first time; previously only those with the privilege of franking were able to use them freely, for their use automatically incurred a higher rate of postage.

Because of the new penny post, people who previously could not afford the expense of sending a letter were now able to do so. As well, greetings cards, especially Valentines, were now sent in huge quantities; in later years the Post Office had to cope with this annual flood of mail by employing extra staff.

In the same year, 1840, on 4 July Samuel Cunard started a regular line of mail steamers between Liverpool, England, and Boston, USA. This wonderful service was responsible in later years for co petition with other maritime natio particularly the USA, for using relia and fast steamships to carry the mail l tween Europe and North America. A consequence of this, the coveted "Bl Riband" of the Atlantic came about.

The momentous postal reform giving uniform penny post made Britain the en of the world, so that other countr attempted to follow her example, thou not all were able to offer such improv services with such greatly reduced pos rates. In the USA, where a postal syste based on the British pattern had been i herited since the War of Independen great agitation took place for pos reforms during the 1840s and 185 Reductions in rates came about slowl and it was not until 1 October 1883 tha uniform two cent rate (the equivalent a penny) was established. Certain loo holes in the US Postal Laws, howev allowed many private posts to be orga ised. These usually occurred where t government itself maintained no servi or facilities for the carriage of ma Consequently, in the far West many the express companies contracted to car the US Mail, a very well-known o being that of Wells, Fargo.

The American Overland Mail attacked l Indians on its way across the prairies, 1860.

1846 a series of events brought to ɡland an American philanthropist, ıu Burritt, known as the "learned ıcksmith" because of his humble up-nging and self-acquired education in town of New Britain, Connecticut. is remarkable man organised a number international movements from his ıces in London and was concerned with ıiversal Peace, the Brotherhood of ın, and with a campaign for a cheap ıan postage which he started in 1847. s ideas for an ocean penny postage were cussed by the governments of the

ondon Letter Box No. 2.

Jnited States and Great Britain. His cam-aign led to a reduction in the overseas ostage rates and paved the way for the ounding of the International Postal Union n 1 July 1875. By this Union, a uniform ate of postage was settled for all member ations. This is still in force today and is ne of the most important international rganisations of our time.

On 1 October 1869 the world's first post-card for a short written message was intro-duced by the Austrian Post Office. Great Britain followed a year later, on 1 October 1870, with a postcard rated at a halfpenny postage.

In December 1898 an Imperial Penny Post was introduced for certain countries within the British Empire. A few years later, with the collaboration of the Ameri-can Postmaster General, the Hon. John Wanamaker, a Penny Post between Great Britain and the United States came about on 8 October 1908. This agreement re-mained in force (as the domestic rate be-tween the two countries) until the 1950s, when it was abolished.

Experimental airmail services for special events took place in several countries during the few years before 1912, but it was not until after World War I that regular airmail services were inaugurated.

¶ JAMES, ALAN. *The Post.* 1970; MARTIN, NANCY. *The Post Office: from carrier pigeon to confravision.* 1969; ZILLIACUS, LAURIN. *From Pillar to Post.* 1956

Potemkin, Grigori Aleksandrovich (1739–91): Russian prince and statesman, adviser to Tsarina Catherine the Great. For twenty years he influenced Cath-erine's policies, especially in expanding the southern frontiers of Russia. Militarily he distinguished himself in wars with Turkey for control of the Crimea; as an administrator he used his great energies to improve Russian naval power (Sebastopol harbour is largely his creation); and he planned a gigantic colonisation of the south Russian steppes. He was ruthless, yet attracted many followers. In the long term his activities were too costly for the 18th-century Russian state to continue them.

Potomac, River: river draining the western slopes of the central Allegheny Mountains into the Chesapeake Bay. A freshwater river for about 300 miles [482·8 kilometres] the Potomac below Washington, DC, is a tidal estuary 125 miles [201·1 kilometres] in length and from 2 to 8 miles [3 to 12 kilometres] wide. After the founding of Maryland in 1634 the Potomac was the early passageway of the area. In the following decades this was gradually settled by Virginian colonists, and later the German and Scotch-Irish migrants crossed the Potomac and settled in the Shenandoah valley. The Potomac valley became the main pathway to the Ohio valley and was of great strategic importance in the Civil War. An Army of the Potomac was formed to protect Washington, DC, after the disastrous shattering of the North at the first battle of Bull Run. Under General George McLellan this army evolved into the best force supporting the cause of the Union.

Potsdam: East German city, 17 miles [27 kilometres] south-west of Berlin. It used to be the capital of Brandenburg and was founded by Frederick William "the Great Elector" in the late 17th century. It gradually gained a reputation as the centre of Prussian military tradition, and Frederick the Great built his palace of Sans Souci there in 1747.

Potsdam Conference: conference in July–August 1945 between Russia, the USA and Britain to decide on Germany's future after her surrender in May. The ideas and practice of Nazism were to be destroyed, and German industry was not to be used for making war weapons. To do this Germany was split into four zones, controlled by the French, British, US and Soviet armies. Stalin claimed heavy reparations from Germany to pay for the enormous war damage in Russia. This was hotly disputed, but Russia was allowed to take away industrial machinery from her zone.

Pottery: objects made of clay, rende hard and durable by being subjected fire. In some countries, in the past, pott has been left to harden in the sun's he but pottery of this type does not last lc and has been made only by races wh have not yet learned the uses of fire hardening their clay utensils. Porcelai a fine, translucent form of pottery.

Pottery-making is one of the oldest man's skills. Clay, a product of the natu decomposition of rocks, possesses, so as pottery making is concerned, two i portant qualities. First, it is plastic: wh moistened it can be easily kneaded moulded. Second, as already mention firing will transform the malleable cl into a hard and durable article. Potte while easy to break, is hard to destroy. a consequence, archaeologists find it i valuable. A bucketful of potsherds (pc tery fragments) excavated from a "di can tell the expert a surprising amou about the people who lived on the s many centuries ago.

The most important invention in t history of pottery making was the potte wheel. No one person invented it, a more than one person invented t vehicular wheel. Gradually, it was fou that a lump of clay, placed on a disc ke constantly rotating, could be stretch and shaped symmetrically by the potte hands working against the centrifug force which, unimpeded, would cau the clay to fly off the wheel.

ove, a potter operating his wheel by foot-
idle. Below left, a potter at work, showing the
e being shaped on the revolving wheel. Porce-
figure by Bustelli, c. 1770.

further discovery was how to make ttery smooth and waterproof. This was ne by means of a *glaze*, a thin coating glass applied to the fired clay and then ade permanent by a further firing. Some the most beautiful glazed pottery ever ade comes from Egypt, its glowing lours scarcely dimmed by time. Ancient eek pottery, unsurpassed for purity of rm, was varnished or polished instead of azed, and often decorated with painted ezes of animals and human beings.

The earliest makers of porcelain were e Chinese – indeed, *china* is the name by hich we now commonly call it. From *neware*, which is a very hard pottery it lacks delicacy and translucence, they adually evolved a porcelain which, first iown outside China in the 12th century, came the admiration of the Western orld. After several earlier attempts at nitation the first successful European orcelain was produced at Meissen, near resden in Germany, in about 1710.

Thereafter factories for the production f porcelain were established in many ountries, notably France, at Sèvres – here, at first, a porcelain known as *pâte ndre* (soft paste), a fragile, glassy material, was used – and England, where the Bow, Chelsea, Worcester and Derby factories acquired great reputations. The English factories developed *bone china*, which incorporates burnt and ground animal bone with the china clay, and can be fired at a lower heat. Almost all English porcelain made today is of the bone china type.

¶ HAGGAR, R. G. *Pottery through the Ages*. 1959
See also INDIVIDUAL ENTRIES.

Power politics: a government's policy of expanding the nation's frontiers or influence, often at the expense of smaller countries and by using threats or force; or, since important nations are often referred to as "powers", the give-and-take of international manoeuvring of a less unscrupulous sort.

Pragmatic sanction: in general, a royal decree with the force of law; in particular, the settlement (1713) laid down by Charles VI, emperor of Austria (1711–40), when he tried to safeguard the succession of his daughter Maria Theresa (empress 1740–80) to all his hereditary lands. Although upheld initially by most other European rulers, it was generally repudiated after his death.

Prague or **Praha:** capital of Czechoslovakia, on the River Vltava. Industrially important for its heavy and precision engineering, its medieval architecture and extensive Stromovka Park attract many visitors. By the 14th century Prague, then capital of Bohemia, had a university with students from all over the continent, and its position at the crossroads of east–west, north–south trade routes made it a prosperous place for craftsmen and merchants. The city has seen much controversy and fighting. Religious opponents quarrelled when Jan Hus was an heretical figure at the university, and later when Catholic fought Protestant at the Battle of the White Mountain early in the Thirty Years War. Prague was occupied many times in the next three centuries, for it lay in path of rival Austrian, Prussian a French armies. Czech nationalism always been a powerful feature of Pragu history. The Nazi leader, Heydrich, assassinated there in 1942; and in 19 opposition to a domineering form of co munism was crushed by Russian tanks

Prehistoric: belonging or relating to time in man's history before writ records began.

Prehistoric animals: animals that liv before the age of recorded history. D covering how ancient animals looked a behaved requires detective work. T clues are the fossils dug from the ear petrified bones, shells, casts, even m impressions in rock, coupled with t knowledge of living animals. Palaeontol gists know that life existed 2,700 milli years ago, but fossils found before t Cambrian period, about 600 milli

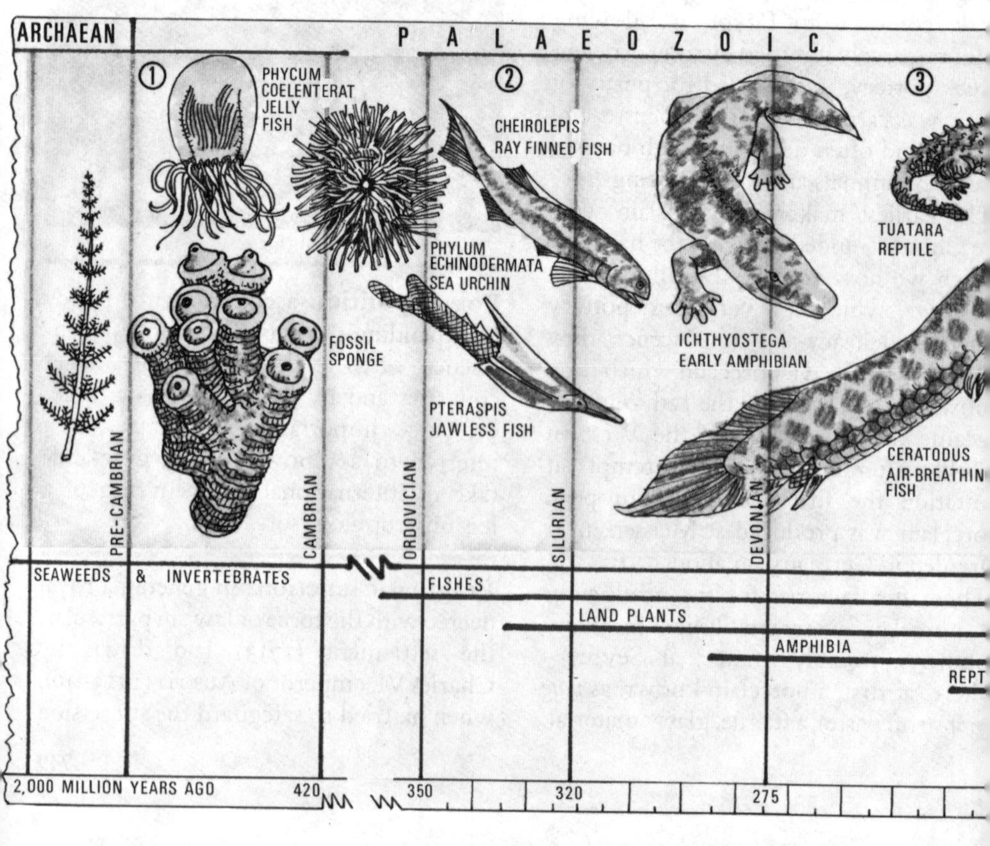

rs ago, are mostly algae, simple plants. ncient animals ranged in size from tiny -celled protozoa to huge awkward osaurs. Some looked like animals today, others completely different. As earth changed, animals had to change . If they did not adapt fast enough to new conditions they died out.

fe, it is believed, began in the ancient s. The oldest known animal fossils, ing from the Cambrian period, were atures without backbones, the inverte- tes – trilobites, jellyfish, sponges, etc. e development of the backbone in mals, about 450 million years ago, was najor advance. The oldest of the verte- tes, the ostracoderms, resembled fish thout jaws, had tiny mouths and athed through gills. Gradually they veloped jaws and, by the Devonian riod, could eat other animals. Vast anges took place in the earth's structure, rthquakes shook the continents, land nges were thrown up. One kind of fish developed lungs, so that it could breathe when the water drained away and survive in swamps. Some of these creatures grew fins resembling limbs, so that when a river dried up in a drought the fish could walk on land breathing through its lungs.

Meanwhile, land plants, mosses and ferns, had appeared, food for the newly arrived amphibians, ancestors of the present day salamanders, frogs and toads, with legs and feet instead of fins. They lived along the shores of the steaming swamps. Within the next 200 million years, all the big backboned animals, the reptiles, birds and mammals had put in an appearance. The reptiles had scaly skins that protected their bodies from drying out, so that they could live in dry places. Their eggs had shells and could therefore be safely laid on land. They grew huge and powerful, rulers of the land. The age of the dinosaurs, most spectacular of land animals, began 200 million years ago and lasted for the next 140 million years.

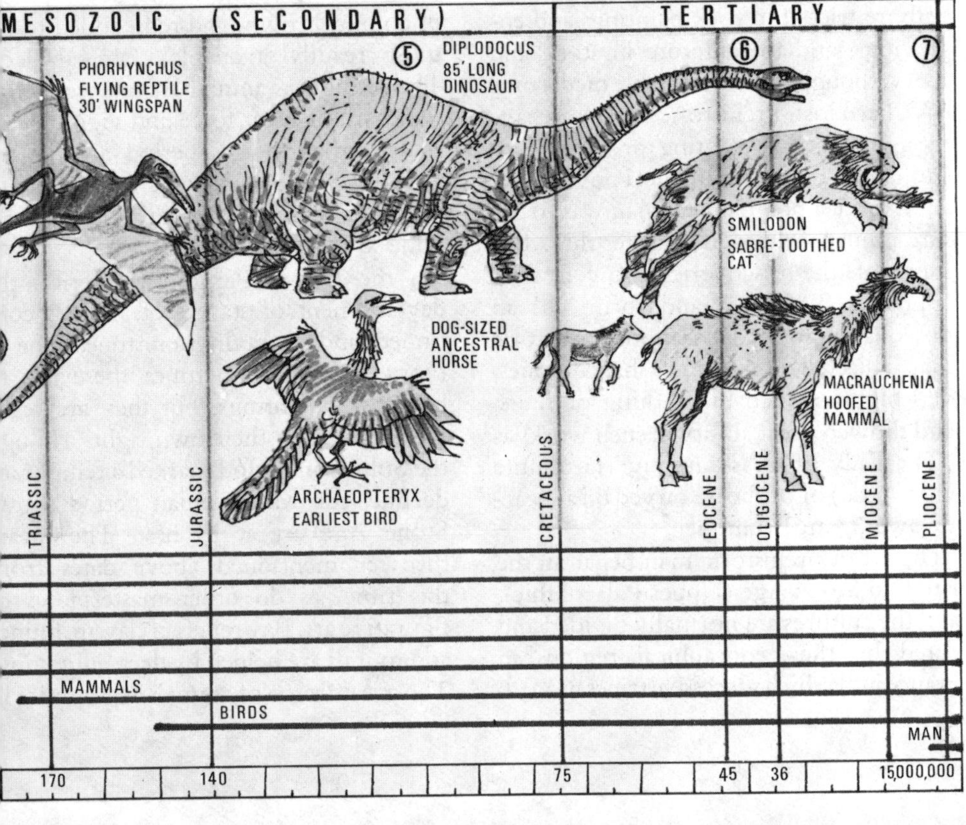

The age of mammals, the Tertiary era, began about 65 million years ago. The surface of the earth changed considerably, mountain ranges rose, shallow oceans drained away, swamps dried up, and the climate grew colder and drier. Most reptiles could not adapt and died out, but mammals, ancestors of the modern horse, camel, cat and dog families, mice, etc., could adjust to the new conditions. Twenty million years ago, mountains began to wear down and grasslands appeared. Pigs, rhinoceros and deer roamed the plains. During the Ice Age, the Pleistocene period, prehistoric man appeared on the scene. From his drawings in caves we know he hunted bison, giant bear, long-haired mammoths, driven south by the cold.

¶ PETERSEN, KAI. *Prehistoric Life on Earth.* 1963

Prehistoric art: the art of man before he adopted a settled civilisation. That of some modern primitive tribes often shows marked similarities. Prehistoric art is essentially restricted to rock paintings and engravings, and to sculpture in stone and ivory, though more perishable media may have been lost. Prehistoric man may have thought that by painting or carving an animal he could gain magical power over it; to carve a pregnant woman was to ensure human or agricultural fertility. But some of the discoveries show a clear appreciation of line and form and an obvious delight in decoration. Prehistoric man collected interestingly shaped stones, was highly skilled in working of flints, and showed great ability in such works as "The Lady of Brassempouy" (a minute ivory head) or the horse carved on a spear-thrower from Bruniquel.

The art of prehistoric man began in the late Old Stone Age (Upper Palaeolithic), and the cultures are normally divided and dated by the geographical regions in France into which successive tribes moved. So the Aurignacian period precedes, order, the Upper Perigordian, the So trean, and the Magdalenian. These ar were all in central or south-weste France, and the combined period th covered spanned a time from rough 25,000 BC to 10,000 BC. Another gr centre at this time was in northern Spa and the whole of this general culture last until a change of climate altered the livi patterns of the tribes. Eastern and sout ern Spain and the Saharan region pr duced a vast amount of art in the Mes lithic Age, certainly by 6000 BC, and the is a clear but unexplained link betwe the centres. South African prehistoric a is of about the same date, while the Au tralian Stone Age began about 3000 B

The Aurignacian period is the time the great series of murals at Lascau south-western France, but the number paintings discovered elsewhere has be considerable. At first men drew hands abstract lines, and this led on to the gre naturalistic paintings. The developme of colour, browns and reds, added to th most readily available charcoal-blac The result was animal art of a very hig standard, of great force and vigour. Als associated with this period are the s called Venuses, extremely fat femal figurines which have been found over wide area of southern Europe.

In the Upper Perigordian period th development of statues of animals co tinued, and engravings on stone, bone c ivory appear. Sometimes these are t help rock paintings, but they are ofte works of art in their own right. Thoug the Solutrean period marked a temporar decline, the Magdalenian period show Stone Age art at its best. The spear thrower mentioned above dates from this time, as do other masterpieces o figurative art. Bas-reliefs in clay are found and murals are helped by deep engraving The great fresco of animals at Altamira i

Pyrenees belongs to this period.
ıe Mesolithic Age in eastern Spain ws a change to the painting of small-.e human scenes. Pictures of humans he previous age had been very rare in k paintings, and very rudimentary as ll. In many ways these new, much re dramatic pictures resemble the con-ıporary works from the Sahara. There paintings of running huntsmen ainly in pin-man form) are joined by uralistic and animated engravings of mals. Closely related to these are the uth African murals, especially fine ng a series of lifelike giraffes.
ustralian Stone Age paintings are most eresting. Clearly magic had great in-ence here, as seen in the extraordinary ndjina figures which were thought to tect the inhabitants against tropical ns.

IARCUS, REBECCA B. *Prehistoric Cave Paintings.* 70

e also CAVE ART.

emier: from Latin *primarius*, through ench *premier*, meaning first; hence, used a noun, chief or prime minister in Great itain and a number of other countries. ıe longest premiership to date was that Antonio de Oliveira Salazar, who held fice in Portugal from 1932–70. Used as adjective, e.g. premier duke or baron, means the holder of the oldest title of at rank. In Britain the premier duke is orfolk (created 1483), the premier earl Shrewsbury (created 1442) and the emier baron is De Ros (created 1264).

resident: the elected head of govern-ent in many republics (e.g. USA, ance and the Irish Republic) and of any educational institutions, commer-al organisations, etc. Its literal meaning, om Latin *praesidere*, is one who sits over before others.
ee also AMERICAN PRESIDENTS.

Prester John: Presbyter John or John the Priest, a legendary medieval character. He was reputed to be a Christian ruler in the unknown East, located by earlier tales in central Asia, later in Ethiopia.

Pretenders: a pretender is a claimant to a throne occupied by someone else. The term is a loaded one. If you consider the claim to be well-founded, the person concerned, in your opinion, will not be a pretender at all, but the rightful ruler, deprived of his inheritance by a usurper.
Thus, James Francis Edward Stuart (1688–1766), son of the deposed King James II of England, is often called the Old Pretender, and his son, Charles Edward Stuart (1720–89), the Young Pretender. However, according to the Jacobites (who are still not extinct), their proper titles are King James III and King Charles III, respectively, since, in the view of the upholders of the Stuart dynasty, the House of Hanover had no right to the English throne. The mystery surrounding the fate of the Dauphin (1785–?95) during the French Revolution led some forty pretenders to claim to be Louis XVII, rightful King of France.

Priestley, Joseph (1733–1804)**:** British scientist and theologian. The unusual variety of his gifts and achievements may be judged by the facts that he mastered, among other languages, Chaldee, Syriac, Arabic, French, German and Italian; became a nonconformist minister and had one of his theological works burnt by the common hangman at Dort; discovered oxygen and identified many other gases, though he had had no scientific education, and invented soda-water. In 1794 the unpopularity of his revolutionary political opinions led him to emigrate to America, where he settled in Pennsylvania.

¶ In SHEPHERD, WALTER. *Great Pioneers of Science.* 1964

Prince of Wales: Edward VII (left) was created Prince of Wales in 1841 at the age of one mont and remained so for sixty years; The Duke of Windsor was a very popular Prince of Wales befor his accession and abdication in 1936; and the present Prince of Wales, HRH Prince Charles.

Primitive: belonging to, or having the characteristics of, the earliest periods of civilisation (*see* e.g. ABORIGINES). Applied to a piece of art it can mean either dating from the time just before the Renaissance or a modern attempt to work in a crude or unsophisticated style.

Prince Edward Island: island in the St Lawrence River forming one of the provinces of Canada. Sighted by Cartier in 1534 and colonised by the French, it was called Isle St Jean until, after having been ceded to England in 1763, it was renamed after Edward Duke of Kent in 1808. After just over a century it joined the Canadian Confederation [1873].

Prince of Wales: title of the English heir apparent. The first native (i.e. Welsh) Prince of Wales was also the last. Llywelyn ap Gruffydd assumed the title in 1258, rallying the Welsh against the English. He was killed in battle in 1282. Two years later, Queen Eleanor, wife of Edward I, bore a son at Caernarvon. The King's heir, later Edward II, was created Prince of Wales by his father. Since then, the male heir apparent of England has almost invariably been created Prince of Wales: the title is not inherited. Since the reign of Edward II the monarch's eldest son has always been Duke of Cornwall at birth, and draws his income from the Duchy and not from the Principality of Wales. The present Prince of Wales, Prin Charles, son of Elizabeth II, was invest at Caernarvon in 1969.

Princeton University: private unive sity, Princeton, USA, founded in 174 as the College of New Jersey, the four college founded in the British coloni of North America. It was inspired by t "Great Awakening" (a series of religio revivals that swept over the colonies the early decades of the 18th centur and six of the seven original truste were leaders of the "New Light" fa tion of the Presbyterian Church. In 17 a building, known as Nassau Hall, w erected with funds raised in England a Scotland. Princeton College (as it the was) played a distinguished role in t American Revolution. One in six mem bers of the Constitution Committee w a Princeton graduate, and James Madiso of the class of 1771 was the first Princeto man to become President of the Unite States (1809–17). A graduate school w founded in 1877 and enhanced Prince ton's academic prestige. In 1896 the Co lege was renamed Princeton Universit and in 1902 Woodrow Wilson (Preside of the United States 1913–21) becam president of the University. Toda Princeton, though relatively small, mai tains its place of importance amongst th so-called "Ivy League" universities.

nting: the reproduction of letters or igns upon paper or other substances means of pressure upon the inked sur- of types, blocks, or plate. By provid- written information on a large scale, nting has been a major factor in the elopment of the modern world.

he earliest printing (originating in a, almost certainly China) was done h wood blocks. Ink was applied to racters or designs carved out of a flat ck of wood. By pressing paper or th against the inked block the design s transferred. This method of repro- ction was first used for making numer- s copies of prayers, charms, and religious tures. Examples of such printing sur- e from the 8th century, but the method y well have been in use as much as two nturies earlier. Book-printing by this thod, each page in its entirety having st to be carved by hand, was, compared th our modern printing presses, a very w process.

Movable type – whereby, instead of a hole page having to be carved and inted as a single unit, component letters designs are made separately and can erefore be used over and over again in rying combinations – was first made in y, in China in the 11th century. Under e Ming dynasty (1368–1644) movable pe was made, successively, of wood, pper, and lead.

The West discovered printing indepen- ntly. The first European books were inted from wood blocks. Credit for the ropean invention of movable metal pe is generally given to Johann Guten- rg (*c.* 1398–1468) of Mainz, Germany, ough some experts believe this honour ghtly belongs to Lourens Janszoon oster, or Koster (*c.* 1405–84) of Haarlem, the Netherlands (*see* GUTENBERG BIBLE).

The first English printer learnt his craft road. He was William Caxton (*c.* 1422– 1), a native of Kent who became a suc- cessful silk merchant in Bruges, in Low Countries, where he lived for th three years. Caxton was himself a ma some literary parts. In 1469 he began make an English translation of a popular French romance of the time, and in 1474 or 1475, having set up a press in Bruges, he printed it, under the title *The Recuyell of the Historyes of Troye*. This, so far as we know, was the first printed book in English.

Caxton returned to England in 1476, setting up a press in the almonry of West- minster Abbey. There he published the first book actually to be printed in England. It was called *The Dictes or Sayengis of the philosophres* (1477). There- after, until his death in 1491, Caxton was indefatigable, as writer and translator as well as printer. In all he published some ninety-six works or editions of works, books ranging from the first French phrase book for the use of English visitors to France to Chaucer's *Canterbury Tales* and Malory's *Morte d'Arthur*.

For centuries afterwards Caxton books continued to be printed in much the same way as in his time. Many of these early books, employing beautifully designed typefaces, are works of art in themselves. Among printers who have left behind books of outstanding beauty may be mentioned Johann Froben (d. 1527) of Basel, Switzerland, Jean de Tournes (1504–64) of Lyons; Henri Estienne (*c.* 1470–1520) of Paris, his son Robert (1503–59), and other members of the Estienne family. Apart from certain im- provements in the construction of print- ing presses – made, notably, by the Dutch- man Willem Jansoon Blaeu (1571–1638) and by Charles, 3rd Earl of Stanhope (1753–1816) – printing, even with movable type, remained a slow process until the beginning of the 19th century.

The first practicable modern printing machine was invented by a German,

Friedrich König (1774-1833). In 1814 *The Times* newspaper installed two of his machines, powered by steam, and was able to print at the hitherto unheard-of rate of 1,100 sheets per hour.

Before long this achievement in turn was left far behind. A new era was at hand, improvements in printing techniques going forward with comparable improvements in the production of paper. In 1806 Henri Fourdrinier (1766-1854), a Frenchman, took out the first patent for making paper in a continuous roll. Today, newspapers are printed on continuous strips of paper more than five miles long.

Rotary presses, in which the type, first clamped, later curved, round a large cylinder, is pressed against the paper as the cylinder rotates, made their first appearance in the 1840s. Among inventors who played a significant part in the development of this type of press, which made possible a printing rate of 10,000 sheets an hour, an Englishman, Augustus Applegarth (1789-1871), and Rich Hoe (1812-86), an American, may specially mentioned. In 1865 anot American, William Bullock (1813-(of Philadelphia, invented the first press print from a continuous roll of paper. T machine, after teething troubles, wa great success. Its inventor came to a end, killed by being caught in the drivi belt of one of his machines.

The foregoing inventions were all i provements affecting only one side printing: the actual transference of inked pattern, whether of words, illust tions, or designs, on to paper. The otl essential part of the printing process, t "setting" or "composing" of the ty was mechanised much later. Althou machines to do the job mechanically we invented in the second half of the 19 century, hand typesetting persisted w into the present century.

The two principal inventions in tl field were American, the Linotype a

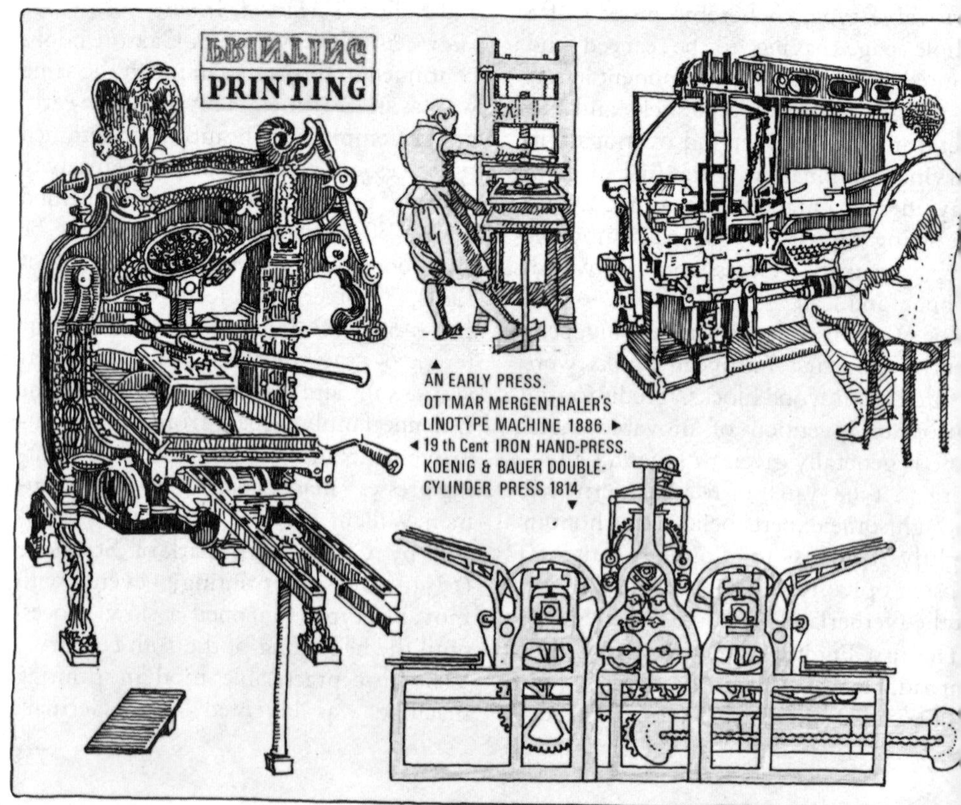

▲ AN EARLY PRESS.
OTTMAR MERGENTHALER'S LINOTYPE MACHINE 1886. ▶
◀ 19 th Cent IRON HAND-PRESS.
KOENIG & BAUER DOUBLE-CYLINDER PRESS 1814 ▼

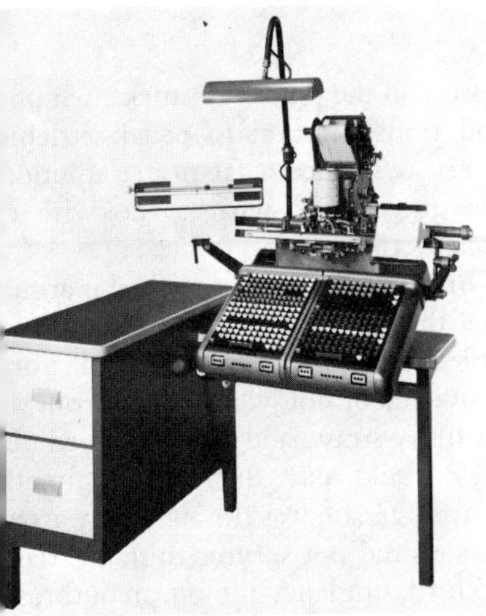

notype keyboard.

Monotype, the first invented in 1886 Ottmar Mergenthaler (1854–99), the ond patented by Tolbert Lanston 344–1913) in 1885. Both machines in-rporate keyboards, rather like type-iters. When a linotype key is pressed a ould of the letter required falls into a k. When a whole line is completed in s way, molten metal is forced into the oulds, forming a line of type which idifies within seconds. Monotype keys nch, in a strip of paper, holes which nd for letters of the alphabet. This strip paper is then passed through a casting achine which "reads" the holes and oves its moulds so that each presents elf in the correct order for the recep-n of the molten metal.

Vith the development of *offset litho-aphy* the actual type no longer requires be a three-dimensional piece of metal d this has led to the introduction of msetting where type is produced as an age on film for platemaking.

This book has been set on a Monophoto lmsetter which is a later development the Monotype Caster and presents lines filmset characters in place of lines of hot etal type. Again it is controlled through Keyboard, producing a punched tape hich in turn activates a movable matrix case containing film negatives of the characters required. As each character is centred over a light source a photograph is made onto a roll of film within the filmsetter. After being read these "galleys" of film are made up into pages by hand.

More recently, the demand for faster typesetting, especially for newspaper and periodical work, has resulted in the development of various systems of electronic, computer assisted filmsetters. These work at much higher speeds and are operated by paper or magnetic tapes bearing coded instructions for the composing units. Page make-up instructions and corrections are punched on a separate tape and the two merged to produce a final page of film ready for printing down onto a metal printing plate.

An important development in high-speed modern printing was the introduction of *stereotyping*, a process known from the 18th century but not used to any extent until after 1850. Stereotyping is a method of copying a page of type by pressing papier-mâché against it so that the latter becomes indented with the shape of the type. If molten metal is then poured over the papier-mâché a new printing surface is formed in a fraction of the time taken if, for every duplicate required, the page in question had to be set anew. The development of a curved stereotype, which enabled rotary presses, for the first time, to print simultaneously on both sides of a strip of paper, in effect brought into being today's newspapers.

Photographic processes have further extended printing technology, making possible today's large and low-priced editions. The computer, too, has been pressed into service – as when, for example, entries in a catalogue, fed into a computer at random, have been sorted and indexed in their proper alphabetical sequence.

¶ HARLEY, E. S. and HAMPDEN, J. *Books: From Papyrus to Paperback.* 1964

Priory: religious house governed by a prior or prioress. Some large monastic houses had an abbot and a prior, the prior being the official next in seniority to the abbot. Abbeys frequently sent members of the community to found another branch of their order elsewhere; the daughter-house was known as a priory and its head as the prior. The abbot of the parent foundation made periodic visits to the priory and supervised its organisation until it became fully established.

¶ WRIGHT, GEOFFREY N. *Abbeys and Priories.* 1969
See also ABBEYS; MONASTERIES.

Prisons: places of detention. Originally they were not primarily places of punishment. Their principal function was to provide places where arrested persons could be kept in custody until trial and, if convicted, pending the carrying out of sentence. They also served as a means of persuasion for the payment of debts and fines.

To early governments the idea of keeping malefactors in prolonged confinement at the expense of the state would have made no sense whatever. From their point of view the death penalty, exposure in the pillory or stocks, whippi and transportation to penal settlem overseas seemed a far neater solution the question of what to do with c victed criminals.

Dire as such penalties were, it is argu that they were to be preferred to the rible squalor of the early prisons. Prison convicted or not, were kept in irons, s on filthy straw, and all but starved un they could pay their jailers for th board. Disease was rife and many arres persons did not survive to stand trial. Oxford, England, in 1577, an outbreak jail fever, as it was called, killed off people, including the judge.

In western Europe, in the 16th centu the decay of the feudal system and enclosure of agricultural land for past left many people homeless. In count affected by the Reformation the solution of the monasteries which h provided many poor people with fo and shelter added to the general mise Governments found it hard to distingu between such homeless wanderers a confirmed rogues and vagabonds.

Above, the inside of Newgate in the 18th century. Above right, the treadmill at Brixton, erected 1817. Right, the centre section of Wakefield Prison. The clock tower surmounts the main entrance.

gland, Holland and Germany Houses Correction were set up where beggars l vagrants were not only deprived of ir freedom but set to some useful work. these Houses of Correction may be n the seeds of the modern prison. A at name in the work of humanising prisonment is that of John Howard 26–90). He inspected prisons in Britain l abroad and what he saw, summarised *The State of Prisons* (1777), makes hor-c reading. Slowly, improvements be-n to be made. The prison system set up the Quakers of Pennsylvania, in nerica, made a deep impression on eral opinion. The Quakers aimed at orming criminals rather than merely nishing them. They tried to preserve human dignity of the inmates of their isons instead of degrading it. Another uaker, Elizabeth Fry (1780–1845), an nglishwoman, also did much to im-ove the lot of prisoners, especially omen.

Britain's loss of the American colonies osed an outlet which, in its time, had ken some 50,000 of her convicts. Be-veen 1787 and 1867 160,000 more were ansported to Australia. France, during e 19th century, established penal settle-ents in the Pacific and on Devil's Island ff the coast of French Guiana), a alaria-ridden hell-hole which deserved name. The last of the French penal olonies closed down in 1950. After the ss of the American colonies some British onvicts were housed, in dreadful con-tions, in old warships turned into make-ift prisons. An escape from one of these ulks, as they were called, forms the nub f the plot of Charles Dickens's novel *Great Expectations*.

Many large prisons were built in the 19th entury. A prison like Pentonville, ondon (opened 1842), which today ems so grim and forbidding, was in its me a great step forward. In 1878 prisons were transferred to state ownership under a Board of Prison Commissioners. In 1902 the first English institution designed specifically for young offenders was opened in Kent, at Borstal (from which all such institutions have subsequently taken their name). Wakefield, Yorkshire, the first "prison without bars", was opened in 1936. The 20th-century em-phasis has been on a relaxation of severe restraints and on the rehabilitation of convicted persons. But the great rise in crime during recent years, coupled with some sensational escapes, has forced the prison authorities to reassess their prio-rities. The criminal must be deterred, restrained, and, if possible, rehabilitated; but at the same time the law-abiding community must be safeguarded.

In the USA the late 18th century and early 19th produced two very different schools of thought on prison discipline. The so-called Pennsylvanian system re-lied on keeping prisoners in solitary confinement in the hope that reflection and lack of contact with other vicious types would bring about reform. The Auburn system, originating in New York, preferred separate confinement at night but allowed the congregating of pris-oners in the workshops and at meal-times. They were not however, allowed to talk, so that this was known as the "silent" system as contrasted with the "solitary" system. A combination of the two systems is now very common in a number of countries, with "solitary" reserved as a special punishment. Of US prisons none has attracted more notoriety than Alca-traz on a 20 acre [8 hectare] island ("Peli-can" island) in San Francisco Bay. In the period 1934–62, of twenty-three men who tried to escape twelve were recap-tured and eleven shot or drowned.

In addition to prisons, some countries have experimented with penal camp systems. The largest of these, in Russia, have held up to 1,500,000 prisoners at a time. It is reckoned that China has had 10 million in prison camps at some periods.

¶ SPEED, P. F. *Police and Prisons.* 1968

Privateers: armed vessels privately owned and commissioned by governments to commit hostile acts against enemy ships (*see* LETTER OF MARQUE).

Up to the 19th century privateers of many nations figured in sea warfare. Ship to ship duels were frequent, and prize money could be claimed if a captured vessel was officially condemned by a competent court. Some privateers were built on warship lines but more often they were merchantmen converted for fighting purposes. They carried no cargo and were thus able to ship large crews – necessary for sending prizes into port.

The Declaration of Paris, 1856, signed by most nations with the exception of America, Spain, Mexico and Venezuela, finally abolished privateering.

Privy Council: body which, in Britain, advises the sovereign and through which the sovereign exercises power. It has its own independent statutory duties. Until the 18th century the chief source of executive power in the state, it was gradually supplanted by the system of cabinet government and its power largely transferred to the cabinet as an inner Committee of the Privy Council. Newly created government departments have taken over much of the work of the original committees. The number of its members is usually about 300, chosen (for life) by the sovereign from eminent public men in the Commonwealth on the recommendation of the prime minister. When the sovereign is ill or abroad it is presided over by councillors of state. Usually at least four privy councillors attend, although three make a quorum; but the whole Council meets when sovereign announces an intention marry, or dies.

The Privy Seal.

Privy Seal: in British history, a seal the Crown, intermediate between t Privy Signet and the Great Seal, a employed chiefly as an authority affix the Great Seal. The Privy Seal w abolished in 1884. The Privy Signet is o of the sovereign's seals, used in seali private letters. The Great Seal, introduc by Edward the Confessor, is the emble of sovereignty.

The post of Lord Privy Seal is still r tained in Britain but involves only tho duties which the prime minister of t day may assign to the member of t government he has nominated to fill it.

Prohibition: the ratification of the 18 Amendment to the Constitution in 192 which ended a long campaign in t United States against the liquor traffi The failure of brewers and distillers curb the excessive use of intoxicants, t wild behaviours in bars and saloons a the judicious political tactics of the Ant Saloon League (1893) led to a concert effort to control "the demon drink Many different motives influenced t voters as they went to the polls in t various states of the Union. The arde reformers argued strongly that the liqu interests represented a demoralising for

American politics, that as industry ıme more and more mechanised ›loyees must be sober to be safe, and it was the taxpayer who really paid bills for an industry which was filling poorhouses and prisons with its ims. The amendment, originally ved by Senator Morris Sheppard of :as, prohibited the manufacture, sale :ransportation of intoxicating liquors beverage purpose. Opponents of hibition attacked the efforts of govern- ıtal agencies to enforce the law. They roved the banishment of the saloon, insisted that it had been replaced by gal "speakeasies" and night clubs. The it traffic in intoxicants was breeding ›otleggers", racketeers and gangsters, l, under such conditions, corruption ırished in the police forces and other orcement agencies. Popular disgust w over the failure of enforcement, and Democratic National Convention of 2 demanded the repeal of the legis- on. Following the Democratic land- le election victory of November 1932 ngress accepted a further amendment the Constitution (21st) which repealed anti-liquor laws (22 March 1933).

---

oletariat: the lowest class in modern lustrial society. According to Marxist :ory these are the workers who own no ›perty and possess no capital and live the sale of their labour to their ıployers.

---

onunciamento: from a Spanish word :aning, originally, a pronouncement, ›clamation or manifesto. In effect, it is Spanish equivalent of the French *ıp d'état*. In the turbulent history both Spain and her colonies of South ıerica, proclamations stating the aims the insurgents frequently preceded risings or revolutions, and the term ne to be applied to the uprising itself.

Propaganda: information, often of a biased or prejudiced nature, spread in support of a cause or school of thought. The Sacred Congregation *de Propaganda Fide* (for the propagation of the faith) was founded in Rome for the education of missionary priests (1622), and the English word is taken from the Latin.

Propaganda and, to a lesser extent, advertising, are in a special class of communication because of the underlying motives. Advertisers try to arouse our longing to the point where we are willing to part with our money in order to possess the products they sell. Legislation tries to protect us from misleading advertisement for the sale of goods or services, but there is no such protection from the excesses of propaganda which deals with prejudices and emotions and is intended to incite to action. Propaganda – such, for example, as campaigns to prevent accident or disease – can be socially useful. When, however, it consists of half-truths and outright lies it is dangerous and destructive. In totalitarian countries where all the media of communication are in the hands of the state, propaganda of this kind is dinned into the population until the victims cannot distinguish false from true.

Protectorate: (1) in general, a form of government over a territory which has not been formally annexed but which, by custom, grant or treaty, is under the jurisdiction of another power; (2) particularly, the period in English history (1653–59) when the country was ruled by Oliver Cromwell and briefly by his son Richard.

Protestant: one who protests, though the term is generally applied as an adjective to the system of Christian belief and worship which had its rise in the Reformation of the early 16th century.

The originating spirit of the Reformation was Martin Luther (1483–1546) and among the contemporaries who caught his spirit were Ulrich Zwingli (1484–1531) and John Calvin (1509–64). Although simplification can only too often be misleading, the main points of their teaching may be summarised as (1) accepting the Bible as the only source of revealed truth and more important than the pronouncements of the Church (*dogma*), which in the Roman view were equally valid; (2) insisting that faith alone (*sola fides*) could secure for a Christian the hope of salvation in the world to come, though, in Calvin's view, this could be no more than hope, the ultimate decision resting in the inscrutable will of God. From this second principle it followed that salvation could not depend on the performance of good works, even if these involved stern self-denial and sustained religious exercises. Such works were, indeed, thought to have value in shaping human character (though Rome had permitted some abuses to creep in); but faith was the watchword of the Protestant creed. This had the result that sermons and teaching were regarded as more important than ceremony and ritual, some of which were held to be superfluous or even superstitious.

From these beginnings stemmed the Protestant Churches as we find them today, the Lutherans of Germany and Scandinavia, the Calvinist French Church, to which the Huguenots belonged, various other Protestant Churches in Europe and the Protestant Episcopal Church of the USA, with a membership of over 3,500,000. In the British Isles the term Protestant has never formally been accepted by the Church of England. Indeed, such is the breadth of views held within it that, while the Anglican or "High" Church (which moved less far from Rome in the first instance) would not accep the "Low" Churchman would be pr to do so. To the Methodists and c "dissenting" churches the title is welc *See also* HUGUENOTS; HUS; LUTHER; CLIF, etc.

Protocol: a word in the languag law and diplomacy meaning an orig draft or record of proceedings in ecclesiastical cause or, in internati law, a record of preliminary negotiati The word is also used to describe rules of conduct and ceremony in di matic relationships: how dignit should be addressed, who precedes wh in a procession, and so on.

Provence: former province of Fra occupying part of the fertile Rh valley and the southern slopes of Maritime Alps. The ancient capital Avignon, famous for its bridge da from 1177–85, the fortified papal pa where the exiled popes lived (1309- and the anti-popes (1378–1417), and 13th-century cathedral of Notre D des Doms.

Prussia: former north German state, largest in Germany. Its area varied c siderably from the 10th century. Pr began as a frontier land stretching ac a forested and marshy plain from River Elbe eastwards. In it feudal bar fought to keep their estates from Slav tribes of Russia. Germanic colo moved in from the west, but the soil poor and standard of living low. Hohenzollern rulers of Prussia had t ruthless in fighting ambitious neighbo

Two events of the 17th century chan Prussian fortunes. In 1618 Brandenb was joined to Prussia to form a lar state. In 1640 Frederick William, " Great Elector", became ruler. A mar great energy, he laid the foundations ndenberg-Prussian power by building he army and an efficient civil service. 1740 Frederick the Great used this s to add to Prussia the rich province ilesia, and later to seize large areas of and, thus linking together some of his tered lands. But this led to a century of er conflict with Austria: both were ls for supremacy in the German-king states of the old Holy Roman pire. The Prussian statesman Bis-ck was determined in the 1860s to this rivalry. With a highly efficient machine Prussia defeated Austria in en weeks. In 1871 all the German states ept Austria joined Prussia to form the man Empire. Led by the Prussian g and chancellor, the new empire erited Prussia's military tradition and trained soldiers, and made it a power-new force in international affairs.

ter the collapse of the Third Reich in 5 Prussia was divided between West many, East Germany, Poland and the SR. *See* GERMANY for map.

ARRIOTT, *Sir* J. A. R. and ROBINSON, *Sir* C. G. *Evolution of Prussia.* 1946

also INDIVIDUAL ENTRIES.

---

lemy (Claudius Ptolemaeus, 2nd tury BC): mathematician and geo-pher. Born in Egypt, then part of the nan empire, near Alexandria, where spent his life, he wrote a number of ntific works, some of which survive whole or in part. The most notable was Geography, in eight books with an s of maps, which, for all its errors rected by later discoveries, was for turies a standard work of reference.

---

lemy I (d. 283 BC): general of xander the Great (*see* separate entry) founder of a dynasty of kings, nbering fourteen in all and known as Ptolemies, who ruled in Egypt from -30 BC. Ptolemy I, called "Soter" (saviour) built the great library of Alex-andria (*see* separate entry) and wrote a reliable history of his former emperor.

Puerto Rico: fourth largest of the Carib-bean islands. It was occupied by the Spaniards in 1510, and, although the natives were friendly at first, they were treated so harshly that the entire popu-lation died out, and was replaced by Negro slaves as labourers.

The island was attacked by the English in the 16th century, by the Dutch in the 17th century and by the English again in 1797, but it remained under Spanish rule until it was occupied in 1898 by the army of the USA during the Spanish-American War. Puerto Rico has remained US territory ever since.

Pulitzer, Joseph (1847–1911): American newspaper publisher. Born in Hungary, he arrived penniless in St Louis in 1865, after serving for a year in the 1st New York Lincoln Cavalry. Having worked as a reporter and qualified as a lawyer, he became a newspaper proprietor and built up an immense fortune which he used liberally in the endowment of a number of Pulitzer prizes and scholarships, awarded annually in the fields of drama, music, letters and journalism.

Punic Wars: struggle in the 3rd and 2nd centuries BC between the Romans and the Carthaginians of North Africa, whom they called *Poeni* as descendants of the Phoenicians. The clash of interests first arose in Sicily, where the Carthaginians had established themselves.

The first war (264–241 BC) saw the rise of Hamilcar as a Punic leader and a success-ful attempt by Rome to engage in naval warfare, where her adversary had pre-viously excelled. It ended in the loss of Sicily and the payment by Carthage of a heavy indemnity.

After an interval in which Rome seized Corsica and Sardinia and the Carthaginians retaliated by successes in Spain, the second war (218–201 BC) saw the invasion of Italy by Hannibal and the rout of the Roman armies in several battles on their own soil. In time, however, the tide turned, and Hannibal was finally defeated at Zama in Africa by Scipio.

Carthage was no longer a great power, but certain Romans, such as Cato, continued to call for her destruction (*delenda est Carthago*). A quarrel with Massinissa, one of Rome's chief African allies, was made the pretext for the third war (149–146 BC), which resulted in Carthage being razed to the ground.

See also INDIVIDUAL ENTRIES.

Punjab: the land of the "Five Rivers" (tributaries of the Indus), and home of the Sikhs, a sect founded in the 16th century and developed into a warrior nation by Govind Singh (1675–1708). After a period of anarchy in the 18th century, the country was united by Ranjit Singh (1780–1839), who made an alliance with the British. Power later passed to the army of a military sect, the *Khalsa*, who from 1845 conducted wars against the British but were defeated notably at Sobraon (1846) and Chilianwala (1849), after which the Punjab was annexed to Britain. It was brilliantly pacified by Henry and John Lawrence (*see* separate entries). The Sikhs later formed some of the finest units of the British Indian army and did not mutiny.

The Province was diminished by the separation of the Delhi Territory (1859) and the North-West Frontier Province (1901), and in 1947 it was divided between India and Pakistan.

Puritan: a word describing all those who, in the 16th and 17th centuries, wanted to purify the Church, attacking the use of vestments and ceremonies and, finally, church government. Puritans dre simply, often called their children biblical names and shunned wor pleasure and self-indulgence.

Pyongyang: ancient city of north- Asia, now the capital of North Ko forty miles up the Taedong River. main settlement was founded in the e 12th century AD, but some remains d from BC. The modern city's indust include mining, mechanical engineeri textiles, chemicals, sugar and cement.

Pyramid: masonry structure with squ base and triangular sides meeting at top. Pyramidal buildings are found number of early civilisations. (For so examples *see* AZTECS and MAYAN CIV SATIONS.) Probably the best known, h ever, are the royal burial places of anc Egypt. During the earlier Egyptian nasties the Pharaohs were buried in th huge tombs, the most famous of wh stand near the Nile delta, at Gizeh. these, the largest is the colossal pyran of Khufu, which was completed ab 2600 BC. It took approximately twe years to erect, contains over two mill stone blocks each weighing over t tons [two tonnes], and its square b covers thirteen acres [five hectares].

Modern Egyptologists think that builders were not slaves but freeb workmen, who came to do an ann period of labour on the king's tomb. Th used very primitive tools: wooden mal and bronze knives, neither strong enou to hew granite out of the stone quarr So they chipped shallow channels i the rock, and filled these with wo This was soaked with water until it panded, causing lumps of granite to br away. These were shaped into rou blocks which gangs of men hauled tree-trunk rollers to the Nile, wh barges carried the stone to the site.

› make the right-angled corners of base, men worked in threes, using a ›e twelve cubits long, each cubit rked with a knot. A man stood at the ner, holding one end of the rope, ile the second man walked to a point ee knots away and knelt there. Then third man proceeded to a distance of ≥ knots from him, knelt, and threw the t of the rope to the first man, who led it tight, making a triangle. The nt at which he stood was always the ner of a right angle.

fter the square was pegged out it had be levelled. The level was checked by ›ans of a network of clay water-trenches ilt around the base and across it. These nches were of equal depth, so the face of the water they contained lay the same height if the base were level. e level was tested by using a cord tened to two short sticks, stretched ›m trench to trench like a gardener's e. Then the ground was built up until easuring rods, standing vertically be-ath the line, showed an even height. it the architects at Khufu made a small or, so one corner of the pyramid is lf-an-inch [13 millimetres] higher than ≥ other three.

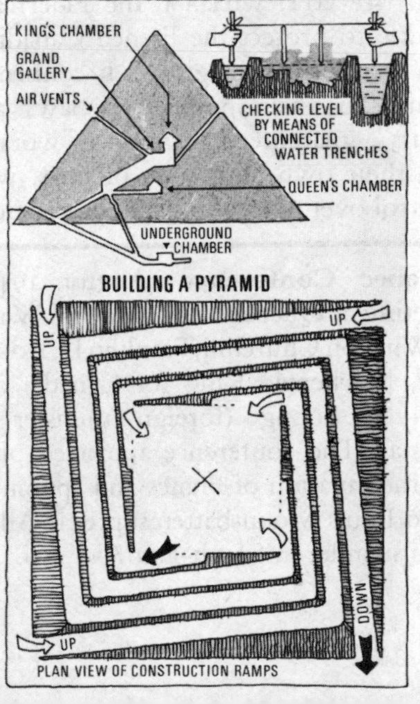

The granite blocks were dragged into position and hauled up ramps made to encircle the structure. Masons cut the sides smooth. The capstone is 481 feet [147 metres] above the base, and the pyramid is solid apart from the burial chambers and the galleries leading to them.

¶ EDWARDS, I. E. S. *The Pyramids of Egypt.* 1970

Pyramids, Battle of the (July 1798): victory over the Mameluke rulers of Egypt which gave Napoleon temporary control of the country. This was brought to nothing a few weeks later when Nelson's defeat of the French fleet at the Battle of the Nile isolated the Emperor's army and forced its withdrawal.

Pyrenees: the 250-mile [402 kilometres] range of mountains in south-western Europe separating France from the Iberian peninsula. Its passes have seen much of human history, the most celebrated incident being the defeat of Charlemagne at Roncesvalles in AD 778 when, returning from Spain, his rearguard was annihilated by the Moors. The tale, with Count Roland as its hero, was so enriched by minstrels and troubadours that it became the most famous story of the Middle Ages.

Pythagoras (*c.* 580–*c.* 500 BC): Greek mathematician and philosopher. Probably born at Samos, he seems to have travelled widely in Egypt and Asia

Minor. He eventually settled in Crotona, on the south-east coast of Italy, where he founded a fraternity having all things in common and dedicated to secrecy, self-discipline, temperance, purity, and obedience. Their system was a curious blend of morality, philosophy, and mysticism, built on a mathematical foundation. Thus their studies were numbers absolute (arithmetic), numbers applied (music), magnitudes at rest (geometry), and in motion (astronomy), these forming the *Quadrivium* of the Middle Ages. According to Plutarch, they related virtues to numbers, and believed that earth, fire, air, and water were derived respectively from hexahedron, pyramid, octahedron and icosahedron. Attributed to his school is the so-called Pythagoras's Theorem, which proves that the square on the hypotenuse (the longest side) of a right-angled triangle is equal to the sum of the squares on the other two sides.

¶ In PRINGLE, PATRICK. *101 Great Lives*. 1964

Quai d'Orsay: street in Paris from which the French Ministry of Foreign Affairs takes its name, just as the British Government is identified with Whitehall.

Quakers: members of the Society of Friends (*see* FOX, GEORGE and FRIENDS, RELIGIOUS SOCIETY OF). The name Quakers is one of a number of epithets in history given originally in mockery but later adopted as an honourable name. In this case George Fox records that "Justice Bennet, of Derby, was the first to call us Quakers, because I bade him quake and tremble at the word of the Lord" (*Journal*, 1694).

Quebec: fortress commanding the upper St Lawrence, where an expedition broke the French encirclement of the English colonies in America. Louisburg, at the entrance to the St Lawrence, was taken in 1758, but the French were able reinforce Quebec when the ice thawed 1759. James Cook (1728–79) piloted expedition up-river. The campaign v successful because land and sea forces operated willingly. The general, t moody and brilliant James Wolfe (172 59), and the admiral, the reserved a stolid Charles Saunder (1713–75), learn to trust each other on the voyage o This trust survived the repulse of Wolf first assault on the Beauport shore, wh the landing craft grounded. The passa of frigates and sloops under Char Holmes (1711–61) into the upper riv gave Wolfe the chance of making surprise night landing above the tow Quebec surrendered on 18 Septemb five days after the English won t decisive engagement on the Heights Abraham with one controlled musk volley. Wolfe and his opponent, Mor calm (1712–59), were both killed. Briti command of the Atlantic ensured that was British ships which reached the star ing garrison when the ice thawed in 176

Quebec Act (1774): British Act Parliament, sponsored by Lord Nor despite the powerful opposition of Cha ham (*see* PITT, WILLIAM, the Elder) a Burke, to protect the French Canadia and secure their allegiance. It confirm them "in their possessions, laws ar rights", guaranteed freedom of worsh and their own civil code of laws, wi control over everything except taxatio

---

Quebec Conference (August 1943 meeting at Quebec during World War of Winston Churchill, Franklin D. Roos velt, Mackenzie King (of Canada) a Tse-ven Soong (foreign minister China). The conference approved pla for the invasion of France and appoint Lord Louis Mountbatten supreme Alli Commander in South-East Asia.

ıeen Anne style: style of English :hitecture, furniture design, etc., as- :iated with the early 18th century. It ›duced houses of simple elegance, ıally of brick, decorated in a pleasantly trained classical manner. The furniture characterised by the generous use of ılnut wood, cabriole legs, marquetry ›rk and graceful proportions.

ıeen Anne's War: the American me for the War of the Spanish Suc- ssion, 1701–14, terminated by the Treaty Utrecht. The American colonies sided th Britain against France and Spain.
e SPANISH SUCCESSION, WAR OF.

---

ueensland: north-eastern and second 'gest state of the Australian Common- ealth, with Brisbane as its capital. The ıtch reached Cape Keerweer in 1606, ›el Tasman the gulf of Carpentaria in 44 and James Cook Bustard Bay in 1770. hn Oxley discovered and surveyed the isbane River in 1823. The convict :tlement established at Moreton Bay in 24, on Oxley's recommendation, closed ›wn in 1842, but aboriginal opposition nded to inhibit free settlement. Dr ›ichhardt's notable discoveries, parti- ılarly of the Mackenzie and Dawson vers in 1844–6, and Thomas Mitchell's plorations of the Warrego and Maranoa territories encouraged colonisation. The first immigrant ship direct from England to Moreton Bay arrived in 1848. Separatist ideas gained ground until in 1859 the whole north-east of New South Wales became the new colony of Queensland. The state, predominantly pastoral, prospered also through gold discoveries in 1848 and exports from her cotton plantations during the American Civil War. Queensland, the only Australian state unrepresented at the 1897 colonial conference, played her full part when Commonwealth replaced colonies. She retains her position as the leading cattle state, supported by dairying, mining, forestry and fisheries, though manufactures now account for two-fifths of her economy.

Quetta, locally **Shal Kot:** chief town of Baluchistan, India, standing at a height of 5,000 feet [1,524 metres] 20 miles [32 kilometres] north-west of the Bolan pass to Afghanistan. It was rented by the British from the Khan of Kalat in 1876, and became a garrison town and the southern point of the line of fortresses guarding the north-west frontier of India. On 31 May 1935 it was completely detroyed by an earthquake which killed some 20,000 people, but has been largely rebuilt and today holds the Staff College of Pakistan. It is a centre for trade with Afghanistan, Persia and much of central Asia.
See INDIA for map.

Quiberon Bay, Battle of (1759)**:** fought near the mouth of the Loire and the crowning victory of Pitt's "Wonderful Year", 1759, where the English admiral Edward Hawke (1705–81) defeated a French squadron under Admiral Conflans in a gale on a lee shore. This vindicated the policy of close blockade by the Western Squadron. Since May, Hawke had kept his ships watching Brest, though this service was unpopular with captains and exhausting for men. By issuing fresh vegetables and sending vessels in relays to clean ship and to refresh their men in Torbay, Hawke kept his fleet fit. Conflans left Brest when a gale had driven Hawke to Torbay, but he was overtaken on 20 November at Quiberon and lost five capital ships. With Boscawen's defeat of the Toulon squadron off Lagos in August, this victory saved England from invasion and freed her navy to support the conquests of Canada and India.

Quintain: device used in the Middle Ages for knightly training. A dummy figure on a pivot was charged with lance or spear. Sometimes a weighted sandbag was attached which would swing round and strike the rider who was too slow in getting away after scoring a hit on the dummy. Such figures may still be seen in use in some annual re-enactments of medieval pageantry and pastimes, e.g. in Italy.

Vidkun Quisling.

Quisling: collaborator with an ene power. Vidkun Quisling (1887–1945 Norwegian, founded in Norway in 19 the Nasjonal Samling (National Uni party in imitation of the Nazi (Natio Socialist) party in Germany. At the o break of World War II he invited Germans to occupy Norway and, in 19 proclaimed himself head of the N wegian government. From February 19 he became the willing puppet of the G mans with whose armed support he ru his implacably hostile countrymen w when the Germans were defeat arrested, tried and sentenced him death. He was shot on 27 October 19 The word Quisling is now a univer term of contempt for one who betrays people into the power of a foreign desp

---

Quito: capital city of Ecuador, situat over 9,000 feet [2,743 metres] high in t Andes of South America, and because its height enjoying a mild climate ev though it lies virtually on the Equat The earliest town on this site was built Indians who were later conquered by t Incas.

When Pizarro (*see* separate entry) ca tured Cuzco he ensured that Quito mained part of his territory, forestalli an expedition from Guatemala, and grad ally Quito became a Spanish city witl vast cathedral and an impressive Jes college, both of which survived the eart quakes of 1797 and 1859.

R

ıcism: fashionable contraction of *ialism*; a pernicious doctrine which lds that some races are inherently su-rior to others, thereby encouraging tred of, and discrimination against, nority elements of a different racial gin from the bulk of the population. any conquerors, from time immemor-, have enslaved those they have de-ıted or have treated them as second-ss citizens. In its modern context :ism goes further. It covers an objection the presence of members of an alien :e and, in its most virulent form – as in : Nazis' attempt to wipe out the Jews – objection to their very existence.

ɴʏᴅᴇʀ, ʟ. ʟ. *The Idea of Racialism.* 1963

---

adio: transmission and reception of essages by electromagnetic waves. An ernating current is one in which the w of electricity starts at zero, builds to peak in one direction and then subsides zero; it then rises to a maximum flow the opposite direction, after which the ırrent again returns to zero, only to ırt the process all over again. One com-ete excursion as described is called a cle, while the number of cycles per-rmed in a second of time is termed the equency. A unit of one cycle per second a "Hertz" (Hz), named after the German ıysicist Heinrich Hertz (1837–94).

n 1865 a great Scottish physicist, James lerk Maxwell (1831–79), suggested that ght and heat were electromagnetic aves of incredibly high frequency which, ıstead of flowing along a wire conductor, ere radiating through space. This was ıbsequently proved to be true. (To give ɔme idea of the tremendous frequencies ıvolved, the sensation we call heat is ıused by electromagnetic oscillations at frequencies between one billion and 100 billion Hz; light wave frequencies are higher still.)

Maxwell also predicted the existence of other waves at frequencies above and below those of light and heat. We now know that above the light frequencies there are invisible waves called (in order of ascending frequency) ultraviolet rays, X-rays and gamma-rays. Those frequencies which lie below the heat waves, down to 10,000 Hz, are termed radio waves.

The existence of radio waves was confirmed by Heinrich Hertz in 1888, but no practical use was found for them until 1895–96 when the Italian Guglielmo Marconi (*see* separate entry) found that by connecting Hertz's apparatus between an elevated aerial wire and an earth connection the invisible waves would radiate for considerable distances through space. By interrupting them by means of a Morse key Marconi was able to send coded messages over several miles. This process, known as wireless telegraphy, was the earliest form of radio communication. Today, improved out of all recognition, it is still widely used and signals can be sent all over the world.

In the early 1900s various people tried to transmit speech and music by radio waves, but without much success because no means then existed of generating radio-frequency oscillations which were sufficiently pure. It was not until 1913, when it was discovered that a triode radio valve could generate oscillations of a suitable character, that radio telephony became a really practicable proposition.

Although a radio telephony system can be very complex, the basic principles are simple enough. First, a microphone is used to convert the pressure waves (sound waves) from a voice or musical instrument into electrical waves of exactly the same frequencies. The human ear can detect sounds which range in frequency from about fifteen cycles per second to about 20,000 cycles per second, so the electrical frequencies produced by the microphone are also within this range. These oscillations are fed into valve or transistor amplifiers which enlarge the signals considerably.

For various technical reasons it is not practicable to radiate these signals directly, so in another part of the transmitter special types of valves or transistors are used to generate oscillations of a much higher frequency – ones which will radiate from an aerial system. The relatively low (audio) frequencies from the microphone circuits are then superimposed in one of various possible ways on to the radio frequency waves and are in this manner carried pickaback-fashion to the aerial system and radiated as electromagnetic waves into space.

At the receiver the combined waves are picked up by an aerial system, amplified and then separated back into their original forms. The radio frequencies, having done their pickaback job, are discarded, while the audio frequency microphone signals, after further amplification, are fed to headphones or a loudspeaker. These devices re-convert the electrical oscillations into pressure waves in the air, which are interpreted by our ears as copies of the original sounds.

Although entertainment broadcasting is the most familiar form of radio, this is only one aspect of the matter. Radio telephony is very widely used in other ways. The police, for example, find it invaluable to keep their officers and squad cars in continuous touch with headquarters. Taxi drivers are directed to pick up fares by the same means, and there are a hundred and one other uses for the "walkie-talkie" type of equipment. The armed services rely heavily on radio communication. Post Office authorities throughout the world maintain huge radio stations in addition to their landline and cable s vices, so that it is possible to pick up telephone receiver and speak to people almost any land over a radio link. Su messages are not usually sent broadc (that is, radiated in all directions) but a beamed towards their destination, a sy tem developed by G. Marconi and C. Franklin in the 1920s. Again, in ma countries in which the natural conditio are unsuitable for pole-and-wire com munication, radio links are used instea The signals are beamed from point point and many simultaneous priva telephone conversations can be carried a single beam. The world's shipping an aircraft also make extensive use of rad telephony.

The most recent development is satelli communication. In this, the signals a transmitted from an earth station (such a in Great Britain, the Post Office station Goonhilly, Cornwall) to a satellite whic has been put in orbit at just the rig height (about 22,000 miles – 35,400 kil metres) for it to maintain a stationar position relative to the ground station. I the satellite a receiver picks up the groun station's transmission, amplifies it an passes it to a transmitter (also in the sate lite). This re-radiates it earthward t another ground station which may b thousands of miles from the first. Pro vided an optical path exists between eac of the ground stations and the satellite transmission and reception can be effected The equipment is duplicated so tha signals can pass simultaneously in both directions, thus enabling normal tele phone conversations to take place.

Various workers in the 19th centur tried to produce television pictures bu failed, largely because they lacked suitabl photocells and means of amplifying sig nals. John Logie Baird was the first t demonstrate television pictures having movement (1926) but others soon fol ved. All these pioneers, however, used chanical means of scanning (see below). 1911 A. A. Campbell Swinton sugges- the use of an all-electronic scanning tem, and in the late 1920s and early 30s such systems were developed by vorykin (USA) and Shoenberg and his m in Britain.

1936 the Baird system using mechan- l scanning was publicly demonstrated ainst the Marconi-EMI all-electronic stem, and the latter was chosen to carry world's first public high-definition evision service which began in Novem- r 1936 from the BBC station at exandra Palace, London.

DE VRIES, LEONARD. *The Book of Telecommuni- ion.* 1962; GIBSON, D. *Radio.* 1968

e also TELEVISION.

---

adio astronomy: branch of astronomy hich records and interprets by means of dio apparatus electro-magnetic signals om outer space.

n 1931 Karl G. Jansky, an American ectronics engineer, while working on dio communication problems, found at his radio receiver was picking up ssing and spluttering noises from outer ace. It was discovered that these radi- ions were coming from various stars d galaxies, and from these small begin- ings emerged a new branch of science lled radio astronomy. The instruments sed consist of specially designed aerials nd highly sensitive radio receivers, the e apparatus being collectively known s a radio telescope. That at Jodrell Bank a well-known example.

The radio signals are not generated by ny form of intelligent life; they are natu- al radiations which occur at various vavelengths. Some of the radiations are airly constant in strength while others, or reasons not yet properly understood, luctuate at regular intervals. These are alled "pulsars".

By careful analysis of the signals scientists have been able to discover much about the composition of stars and galaxies that could not be found by using optical telescopes, and this has enabled new theories about the origin of the universe to be formed. The radio telescope does not make the optical telescope obsolete. Each helps the other in the quest for scientific knowledge.

¶ CROWTHER, J. G. *Radioastronomy and Radar.* 1958; HYDE, F. W. *Radio Astronomy.* 1962

See also OBSERVATORY.

Railways or **railroads:** systems of pairs of steel rails laid at a fixed distance apart on a prepared road-bed, along which trains of vehicles are hauled by a locomotive. It seems to have been the iron-miners of Germany who, in the 16th century, discovered that a loaded wagon would run more easily and require less effort to draw and to guide it if the wheels ran on smooth rails rather than on a normal road surface. In these early systems, worked by humans or horses, the rails were made of wood, and when iron was first substituted (to be followed much later by steel) the cross-section of the rail assumed many different shapes. In England the term platelayer is still used for the man who looks after the track (or permanent way), thus recalling the flat metal plates with a low flange to steady the wheels, which were often used, though this made the provision of points (switches) difficult.

It was in Britain that the earliest development of modern railways took place, though the USA (where the term railroads is generally used) did not lag far behind. On Tyneside, in north-east England, the wagon-ways which conveyed coal from the pits to the quays were the scene of early experiments in haulage by steam locomotives, in which George Stephenson (1781–1848 *see* separate entry) took a leading part. These

Trevithick's Railroad, Euston Square, 1809.

trains, however, moved at little more than a walking pace. From these beginnings sprang the earliest public locomotive railway in the world, the Stockton and Darlington in Co. Durham, opened in 1825. Although it conveyed passengers, its chief purpose was the carriage of coal: indeed, anyone who was willing to pay a toll could put a horse-drawn wagon on the line, which did not lead to easy operation. The true forerunner of the modern railway was the Liverpool and Manchester, thirty miles long and opened in 1830. Here the proprietors (the railway company) had complete control of the working of their line, which carried passengers and assorted goods. In both these early railways George Stephenson was again the moving spirit.

The engineers of this period had to experiment as they went along. It took a little time to realise that the smooth iron tyre on the driving wheel of a locomotive would grip the surface on the rail, even when drawing a load up a gradient. In consequence many early lines were laid out to be as level as possible, and cable-hauled inclines were introduced as thought necessary. The stiff climb out of Euston Station (London) and the even stiffer one out of Queen Street (Glasgow) were originally tackled by this means.

As already remarked, the earliest railroads in the USA appeared almost as soon as those in England; and here, in d course, once the eastern mountains h been crossed progress across the plai could be rapid, as the rails were push forward through undeveloped territor In the older countries, by contrast, t surveyor had to find a path for his li against the resistance, sometimes amoun ing to physical violence, of landowne and the proprietors of canals and turnpik roads. Space does not permit a detaile account of the development of railwa in different parts of the world. In Euro it gathered momentum from about 184 onwards, often with English contracto and engineers engaged on the work. O of the early locomotive engineers i France had the good English west countr name of William Buddicom.

A problem soon arose over the questio of gauge (the distance between the rails 4 feet 8½ inches [1·4 metres], chosen fro that in use on Tyneside. For the Gre Western Railway, however, Brunel (*se* separate entry) chose 7 feet [2·1 metres and, though the company was soo compelled to use the standard gaug or a mixed one for most of its lines, it co tinued to run "broad gauge" expresses t the west country until 1892. It was als unique in laying this line with the rails o longitudinal balks of timber, in contra to the almost universal practice of usin transverse sleepers (or, as the America call them, ties). In Ireland, for no ver apparent reason, 5 feet 3 inches [1· metres] was adopted. In much of Europ the gauge is close enough to our own t permit the same vehicles to run on bot systems, but Spain and Portugal have feet 6 inches [1·68 metres] and USS 5 feet [1·5 metres]. In difficult country, o when traffic is light, a narrower gauge often used, 3 feet 6 inches [1·07 metres metre, 3 feet [0·9 metres], or even les indeed in much of Africa some very fin locomotives work on the 3 feet 6 inch

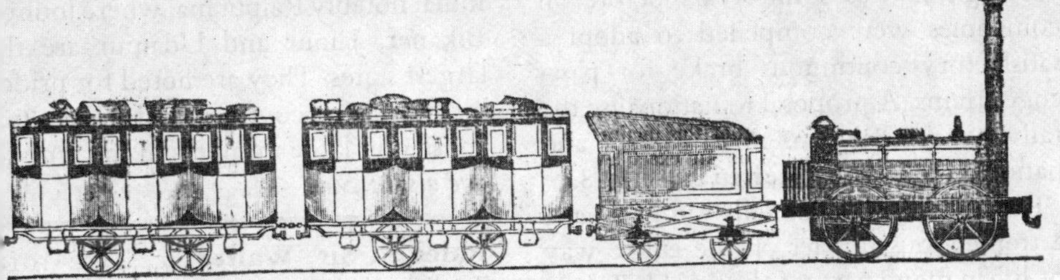

Above, opening of Stockton and Darlington Railway, 27 September 1825. Below, locomotive race at Rainhill near Liverpool won by Stephenson's Rocket, *1829.*

The Planet, *one of the first inside cylindered locomotives, 1833.*

Above left, shooting buffalos on the track of the Kansas–Pacific Railroad, USA, in 1871. Below left, driving in the Golden Spike in 1869 joining the Union Pacific and Central Pacific Railroads. Above right, Liverpool Station in 1831. Below right, super modern electric commuter trains now on trial for British Rail.

[1·07 metres] lines. Australia provides a sad example of failure to foresee the time when separate systems would be linked up, there being no less than three different gauges to cause annoyance and delay.

From early days many countries kept their railways to some degree under state control. In England parliament claimed the right to decide whether or not projected lines should be approved and to enforce regulations to promote safety: although it was some years before all companies were compelled to adopt a satisfactory continuous brake for passenger trains. A proposal to nationalise the railways in 1844 was not pursued, and nationalisation was deferred until 1948.

The development of railways has made a tremendous impact on the entire way of life in many parts of the world. Whole continents, as in North America, were opened up, trade and commerce revolutionised, social habits changed. Even in warfare, as those who have studied the American Civil War (*see* separate entry) will know, strategy had to be completely revised. Nevertheless railways are now giving way to other forms of land transport which have the advantage of operating in smaller units and can convey goods and passengers more nearly "from door to door". Again, air travel can reach a far higher speed than that obtainable on the ground, though for a short journey, as between London and Manchester, accelerated rail services are bringing passenger traffic back.

In the more highly developed countries there has been, in the last few years, a large number of closures of secondary lines, but on the main routes the introduction of diesel and electric locomotives has led to notably higher speed in regular service schedules. In this, the French and Japanese have, since the end of World War II (*see* separate entry), been conspicuous pioneers, particularly where electric haulage is concerned. The fut of the Railway, which in less than years has played such a vital part in lives of a large proportion of human ki is now somewhat doubtful.

¶ FERNEYHOUGH, FRANK. *Railways.* 1970; IN BRIAN. *The Saga of the Railways.* 1973

Rajput: Indian warrior class, rank second in the caste system after Brahmin priests. Their home is north India, notably Rajputana, where Jodhp Bikaner, Jaipur and Udaipur are th largest states. They are noted for pride birth and for courage, and have alw enlisted in large numbers in the army. *See also* INDIA.

Ralegh, Sir Walter (*c.* 1552–161 English adventurer, poet and prose writ The story, dating from the mid-17 century, that he spread his cloak over puddle for Queen Elizabeth to walk may well be true, as it accords so perfect with Ralegh's personality. Dashing a quick-witted, for several years he was t Queen's favourite. In 1595 he sailed f South America, vainly seeking the legen ary kingdom of El Dorado.

Ralegh was a man who made mar enemies, largely because of his pride a arrogance. (John Aubrey tells us "he w damnable proud".) After Elizabeth death he found the new king, James among them; was accused of treason ar sentenced to death. Reprieved, he spe thirteen years in prison, obtaining h freedom by offering to return to Dorado and bring back at least half a to of gold. James warned that if the exped tion came into conflict with the Spanis colonists his life would be forfeit. No gol was found and, while Ralegh lay ill wit fever, his lieutenant burned a Spanis settlement. Ralegh returned home to di with great courage, on the scaffold. H fortitude moved even his enemies t

Walter Ralegh and his son.

miration. Of one spectator who wit- ssed his trial it was reported that vhereas when he saw Ralegh first he was moved with the common hatred that : would have gone a hundred miles to e him hanged, he would, ere he parted, ive gone a thousand to save his life".

TREASE, GEOFFREY. *Fortune My Foe.* 1949

---

amakrishna (1836–86): Hindu mystic whose philosophy all religions were ually valuable as an approach to the ernal. Unlike some Hindus, he believed active concern for others rather than ithdrawal from the concerns of life.

---

amillies, Battle of (23 May 1706): the cond of the Duke of Marlborough's ajor victories in the War of the Spanish uccession (*see* separate entry), fought between Namur and Louvain in south-western Belgium. Marlborough, commanding the allied British, Dutch and Danish forces, defeated the French under Villeroi and as a result was able to occupy most of the Netherlands.

Ramses II (*c.* 1304–*c.* 1223 BC): Egyptian Pharaoh, warrior and builder. He defeated the Hittites at the Battle of Kadesh and drove them out of Egypt. He erected many monuments and obelisks, including the temples of Abu Simbel, recently raised by the engineers above the level of the new Nile dam. Ramses was the "Ozymandias" of Shelley's poem.

Rangoon: capital and great port of Burma, near the mouth of the Irrawaddy. Rebuilt by Alompra, founder of the Burmese monarchy, 1753, it contained a British "factory" by 1790 and was annexed by the British in 1852 (Second Burmese War). It contains the 368 foot [112 metres] Shwe Dagôn Pagoda, covered with pure gold from base to summit.

¶ PEARN, B. R. *History of Rangoon.* 1972

See also BURMA.

Ranjit Singh (1780–1839): "The Lion of the Punjab", chief of the Sukarchakia Sikhs, whose ambition was to weld the whole of the Punjab into one Sikh empire. Seizing Lahore (1799), Amritsar (1802) and Multan (1810), by 1820 he controlled all territory between the Sutlej and the Indus. He disputed the British claim to Punjab lands south of the Sutlej, but in 1809 gave way at the Amritsar treaty. His army, trained by European officers, provided stiff opposition to the British in later Sikh wars. In 1833, when Shah Shujah of Afghanistan took refuge with him, he seized from him the Koh-i-noor diamond, now among the British crown jewels.

Ransom: to redeem someone from captivity, or recover possession of something which has been unlawfully detained, by paying the price demanded: also, the actual price paid or demanded.

Richard I (1157–99), King of England, on his way home from a Crusade (*see* CRUSADES), fell into the hands of the German Emperor Henry VI (reigned 1190–97), who demanded 150,000 marks as his price for the King's freedom. The ransom was paid and Richard was released after two years' imprisonment. The great Spanish author, Cervantes (1547–1616; *see* separate entry) was captured by Moorish pirates who took him to Algiers where he served in the galleys for four years until he was ransomed.

The 1970s have seen old practices put to criminal uses. In many South American countries guerrilla groups (*see* GUERRILLAS) opposed to the ruling governments have kidnapped foreign diplomats and held them to ransom against the release of political prisoners. In some cases a bargain has been struck. In others, the unfortunate captives have been murdered or else remain in captivity. In 1970 the FLQ, a French-Canadian separatist organisation, kidnapped Pierre Laporte, a member of the Quebec government, and James Cross, a British diplomat, the price demanded being the release of FLQ members held in prison. M. Laporte was found murdered: Mr Cross was eventually recovered unharmed. No prisoners were handed over, but Mr Cross's captors were allowed to leave the country.

In 1970 too, Palestine guerrillas hijacl three civil airliners and held them in Jordanian desert, with their crews a passengers as hostages for the release their comrades held for crimes in countries to which the planes or the p sengers belonged. The planes were blo up, but all the passengers were not fr until the countries concerned yielded the guerrillas' demands and freed t prisoners.

Raphael (Raffaello-Sanzio, 1483–152 Italian painter, called by his contemp aries *il divino pittore*, "the divine painte His work is characterised by grace, gent ness and exceptional skill. Among most famous paintings are a number frescoes in the Papal Signature Room the Vatican (*see* separate entry) and, the Pope's private chapel, the Sisti Madonna.

¶ RIPLEY, E. *Raphael.* 1961

Rasputin, Grigori Yefimovich (187 1916): Russian religious leader of di reputable character. He won the favour the Empress Alexandra, wife of Nichol II (*see* separate entry), by his hypnot success in checking the grave illness of h son, the heir to the throne. Rasputin use his position to influence church, govern ment and military appointments, and be came virtual ruler of the country despit the opposition of many members of th royal family and court, a group of whom conspired to assassinate him in 1916.

Hijacked airline passengers held in the Jordania desert, 1970.

he Church of St Francis, Ravenna.

avenna: city of northern Italy, situated n a marshy plain six miles [9·656 kilo-etres] from the Adriatic coast. A thriv-g industrial centre, it is famous as a easure-house of Byzantine art. Ravenna as the last capital of the Western Roman mpire and, later, the chief city of Theo-oric, King of the Ostrogoths (454–526), ho, despite a savage three-year-long ege to gain possession of it, brought it to peak of splendour. It was from early hristian times the seat of an archbishop. t is due to this admixture of political and ligious importance that Ravenna pos-sses more than a dozen churches built etween the 5th and 8th centuries when hristian art, in the opinion of many, was its freshest and most spiritual. The many osaics to be found in Ravenna, with eir stylised, elongated figures, radiate a nique combination of stillness, strength, nd deep religious devotion.

ee also MOSAIC for illustration, *and* separ-te entry for BYZANTIUM; GOTHS.

Red Cross, International: worldwide rganisation for the relief and prevention f human suffering. In June 1859 a young wiss businessman, Jean Henri Dunant, eeking an interview with Napoleon III f France, entered the little Italian town of olferino. The surrounding area had just een the scene of a battle between the ustrians, the French and the Sardinians, during the struggle for Italian independence. The town was full of wounded soldiers, and no one was doing much about them. Dunant, horrified, began to organise help. He coaxed the women of the town to nurse and to supply bandages, the children to carry water, and anyone else who happened to be there to help the wounded. After five weeks the situation improved, but Dunant left Solferino convinced that, if this were the usual aftermath of a battle, some organisation was needed to give help to all casualties, irrespective of nationality.

He published a book, *A Memory of Solferino*, recording his experience. It made a great impression in Europe. A lawyer from Geneva, Gustave Moynier, together with Dunant, established in 1863 a Permanent International Committee, the forerunner of the International Committee of the Red Cross. It was a neutral body composed of Swiss, because Switzerland was invariably a neutral country. Its aim was to assist people who became casualties of war.

In 1864 an international meeting known as the *Convention of Geneva* agreed that its member nations would allow Dunant's organisation to help all wounded soldiers. It adopted as its badge a red cross on a white ground and became known as the *Red Cross Society*. Some Islamic (*see* ISLAM) nations wished to join it: instead of a red cross, they took a red crescent as their badge, while Persia used a red lion, but their aims were identical. A war casualty was no longer an enemy, but a fellow man needing help.

As years passed more nations became members of the Geneva Convention. During two world wars the Red Cross helped the wounded, established hospitals, hospital ships and hospital trains, delivered parcels of food and clothing to prisoners of war and – most important – let their families know what had happened

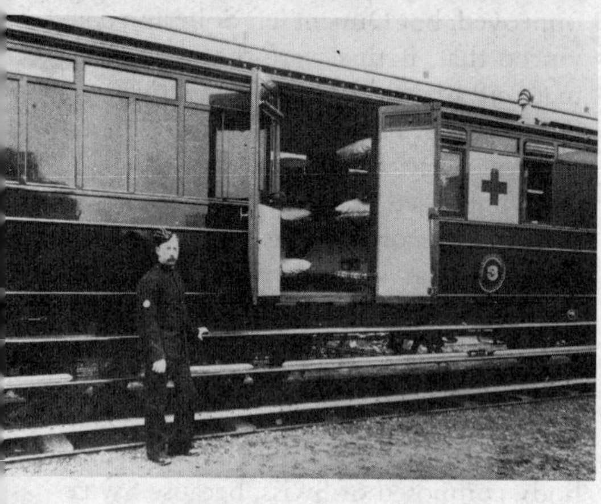

Above left, the hospital launch Queen Victori[a] *with medical staff and accommodation for twenty two patients, 1884. Below left, Red Cros[s] hospital trains in Boer War, 1899. Above, Firs[t] Aid Yeomanry at work in camp, 1909.*

to them. After World War II (*see* separate entry) the Red Cross looked after refugees and helped to reunite families.

During peacetime Red Cross and Red Crescent Societies undertake relief work. The Canadian and Finnish Red Cross send medical help to Eskimo communities in the Arctic Circle. The Persian Red Lion Society specialises in mother and child welfare. Wherever disasters such as flood, hurricane or earthquake strike, Red Cross helpers are immediately at the scene. The expenses of the League of Red Cross Societies are largely met by voluntary contributions of member societies, by special grants from other international organisations and, from time to time, individual governments.

¶ PEACEY, BELINDA. *The Story of the Red Cross.* 1969; ROTHKOPF, CAROL. *Jean Henri Dunant: Father of the Red Cross.* 1971

Reformation, The: term given by historians to a period of strife and change in western Christendom which came to [a] head in the 16th century. It arose from [a] growing desire among thoughtful men t[o] reform or remove certain beliefs an[d] practices in the Roman Catholic Churc[h] which they felt were contrary to th[e] truths of early Christianity. Such criticisms had been made before; but the 14t[h] century had witnessed the scandal of th[e] popes driven from Rome and living a[t] Avignon in Provence (1309–77) unde[r] French protection, and this was followe[d] by a period of forty years when riva[l] popes held office simultaneously. Th[e] lowered reputation of the papacy was no[t] improved by the greed and worldliness o[f] some 15th-century popes, so that more than one of the rulers of Europe grew restless under papal claims to regulate the religious affairs of their domains. At the same time there were questionings of matters of belief, as in the teaching of John Wyclif (*c.* 1320–84) in England and Jan Hus (*c.* 1369–1415) in Bohemia.

t was, however, from Martin Luther 483–1546) that the movement gathered ll impetus. The son of a Saxon miner, uther began by serving the Roman atholic Church as friar, priest and uniersity lecturer. His first protest was gainst "indulgences", whereby remison of punishment after death for sins ommitted in this life was purchased by fts of money to the Church. Soon, hower, he was challenging some of the asic principles of Catholic teaching, as hen he asserted that by Faith alone could an attain salvation and not, as the hurch maintained, by the practice of ood works. He also denounced the papal ower, with the result that some of the ilers of the German states, together with e Kings of Denmark and Sweden, reormed their Churches on his principles, ius founding the Lutheran Church which xists today.

Iartin Luther.

Meanwhile, a Swiss priest, Ulrich wingli (1484–1531), had also left the oman Church and was preaching reorm in Zurich. He gained a considerable ollowing but was killed in a skirmish vith those who opposed him.

The third great figure of the Reforormation was John Calvin (1509–64). hough born in France, he exercised his reatest influence in Geneva. He does not

John Calvin.

appear to have had direct contact with Luther, and, although he too made Faith the central theme of his message, his teaching was less humane and his conclusions were far more severe than those of the German reformer. Nevertheless, it was the doctrines of Calvin, however modified in the course of years, that had the widest influence among the Churches that sprang from the Reformation in many parts of western Europe.

In Scotland the movement, under the leadership of John Knox, who was deeply influenced by Calvinistic teaching, followed in many ways the same pattern as elsewhere. In England the course of events was different. It is true that there already existed a national tradition of resistance to the claims of the papacy, but Henry VIII's quarrel with the pope was originally on personal grounds, namely the King's desire to be divorced from Catherine of Aragon. Although he came

John Knox.

to claim the supreme headship of the English Church, dissolved the monasteries, and persecuted those of his Catholic subjects who opposed him, his own attitude to the old faith remained at his death very close to the spirit in which he had written the attack on Luther which earned him the title of *Fidei Defensor* (Defender of the Faith) twenty-six

Golden Bulla of Pope Clement VII, affixed to the Papal Bull which confirmed Henry VIII as Defender of the Faith.

years before. But reformers from the continent were already receiving a sympathetic hearing in England, especially at Cambridge University, and the reign of the boy king Edward VI that followed saw the issue of a royally approved prayer-book in the English language, largely translated from the Latin service books formerly in use. Certain Romish doctrines were at the same time formally renounced, and the removal of many church ornaments, regarded as objects of superstition, was required. But the government of the Church through archbishops and bishops was retained, and, on this and other grounds, many men in England felt that the reform of the established Church had not gone far enough. Such men formed the nucleus of the Puritans who were a divisive element in the religion and politics of the country up to the end the next century.

¶ COWIE, LEONARD. *The Reformation.* 1968; COW LEONARD. *The Reformation of the Sixteenth Centu* 1970

See also individual entries.

Reformed Church: term applied to body of Churches springing from tl Reformation (*see* previous article). Whi it is sometimes used in a wider sense embrace all Churches of such origin, it more accurately applied to those who beliefs and practices are founded on tl teaching of John Calvin, as distinct, e pecially, from those which trace the history back to Martin Luther (*see* se arate entry) direct and are called Luthera This is due to the fact that, even as early the end of the 16th century, the Calvini tic Churches were already claiming f themselves the Latin title of *ecclesi reformatae*.

Reformers, Religious: people wh have tried to purify religion and religio institutions in accordance with what the believed to be the will of God. For ce turies few people in Western Euro challenged the authority of the Church Rome. When the Roman Empire w overrun by barbarians, the Church su vived to represent civilisation, law an order, education, learning and cultur Anybody who questioned the beliefs an doctrines of the Church was accused heresy and severely punished.

During the Middle Ages many thinkin people realised the need for reforn Geoffrey Chaucer (*c.* 1340–1400) an William Langland (*c.* 1330–1400) wer both critical in their writings of id clerics who neglected their duties, c cheated people with false relics, or sol "pardons come from Rome al hoot" John Wyclif (*c.* 1320–84) believed th people should be able to read the Bib r themselves and form their own judgents, and he inspired "poor preachs", who went about preaching and aching the scriptures in English. His herents became known as Lollards, and eir movement was one of the forces hich paved the way to the Reformation.

'yclif's ideas influenced Jan Hus (John uss, *c.* 1369–1415), the great Bohemian former and national hero, who witssed fearlessly in his writings and his achings for the reform of the Church id was condemned by the Council of onstance and burnt at the stake for resy. Wyclif's ideas were also conmned by the Council of Constance: in 15 it was ordered that his writings ould be destroyed and his bones dug up id scattered, an edict which was carried it in 1428.

ome religious reformers have wished reform the Church from within: for stance, a little group of 16th-century hristian Humanists, amongst them John olet (1466?–1519), who taught at xford and later became Dean of St aul's; St Thomas More (1478–1535), enry VIII's personal friend, who was ppointed Lord Chancellor in 1529, and esiderius Erasmus (*c.* 1465–1536), a utch scholar who lived in England for me years and was appointed Professor f Greek and Theology at Cambridge. ll these men were friends and scholars, nd all believed that the Church could be formed by a return to the ideals and the iscipline of primitive Christianity. John olet studied Greek in Italy as a young ıan, and, after reading the New Testaıent in the original, his lectures on St aul's Epistles threw a flood of light on ıe life of the Early Church. He founded t Paul's School in London and encourged the boys to learn Greek as well as the ustomary Latin. St Thomas More was a ıost lovable and charming man: he rested Henry VIII's determination to reform the Church to serve his own ends, and so died a martyr on the scaffold. Erasmus spent the latter part of his life in Switzerland; a man of peace, he was appalled by the violence of the Reformation which he himself had helped to create. When it was suggested to him that he had laid the egg from which the Reformation was hatched, he shook his head sadly and accused Martin Luther of hatching out "a fighting cock".

The great Protestant Reformation was brought about, not by the men of peace who had paved the way for it, but by men of iron will and determination. Even so, Martin Luther (1483–1546), the great architect of the German Reformation, did not set out deliberately to destroy the unity of the Church: he protested against the flagrant abuses which were the scandal of his time and so incurred the enmity of the authorities and the wrath of the Pope himself. The day on which he nailed his famous ninety-five theses (*see* INDULGENCES) to the door of the church at Wittenberg – 31 October 1517 – has been described as the birthday of the Protestant Reformation. His teachings were condemned by the Pope, who ordered his writings to be burnt, but Luther replied by publicly burning the "Bull", or papal message, which had announced the Pope's displeasure. Summoned to be tried before the Emperor at Worms, he refused to go into hiding: "I will go, though every tile in the city were a devil!" he said. At the trial he steadfastly refused to recant, though in peril of his life. "Here stand I," he declared. "I can do no other. So help me, God."

Martin Luther's courageous lead was taken up by other religious thinkers of his day: Ulrich Zwingli (1484–1531), the great Swiss reformer and admirer of Erasmus; Philip Melanchthon (1497–1560), friend of Luther but of a gentler spirit; John Calvin (1509–64), the great

French thinker and theologian, who set up a Protestant regime in Geneva which became a rigid dictatorship, but which offered shelter to Protestant refugees from other parts of Europe, including England; and John Knox (*c.* 1513–72), who shaped the Reformation in Scotland and became the bitter enemy of Mary Queen of Scots. The men who led the Reformation were as intolerant as they were sincere; Calvin punished those who disagreed with him, and burnt "heretics" at the stake – for instance, Michael Servetus (1511–53), who differed from other Protestants in his beliefs.

The English reformers had different problems to face. Henry VIII's seizure of power over the Church for his own ends freed England at a stroke from the power of Rome and put an end to the whole monastic system, but on the other hand it gave little indication as to what kind of Church was to survive. The great English reformers, amongst them Hugh Latimer (*c.* 1485–1555), Thomas Cranmer (1489–1556) and Nicholas Ridley (*c.* 1500–55), attacked old ways and customs and instituted new ones, only to fall from power and go courageously to their deaths at the stake when Mary Tudor restored the Roman Catholic Church during her short reign. With the establishment of her sister Elizabeth on the throne came the compromise of a "middle way" which flowered gloriously in the Anglican Church. The Catholic right wing and the Puritan or reforming "left wing" continued, and suffered persecution, until men slowly learned to tolerate one another in matters of religion.

See also REFORMATION and many of the names mentioned in this article.

Reformers, Social: people who have worked constructively to remedy social evils and injustices. Few great social reforms have occurred spontaneously. They have generally been the result of slc pioneering work which has brou about a change of ideas and attitudes, a resulted finally in a struggle – sometir bitter – between enlightened and reactic ary forces. Sometimes the early work are forgotten. For instance, the cause the "climbing boys" is for ever link with the great Earl of Shaftesbury (18c 85), but its first champion was Jo Hanway (1712–86), better remembe as the first Englishman to use an umbre

In 1773 Jonas Hanway made the fi protest against the use of climbing boys sweep chimneys. At that time, mas sweeps would buy unwanted childr harden their limbs with brine, and tr them brutally to climb up chimne Many died of suffocation: others cc tracted diseases or were stunted or maim The protest spread slowly. In 1788 a again in 1794 Blake expressed it in ver in 1837, after the first Acts restricting t practice had been passed and ignor Dickens exposed the situation in *Oli Twist.* Lord Shaftesbury took up t cause in 1840, and other Acts were pass in succession and again ignored. In 18 Charles Kingsley published *The Wa Babies*, and public indignation began mount, but it took ten more years campaigning by Lord Shaftesbury befo in 1875, a Bill was introduced which p an end to the scandal, over a hundr years after the first protest had been mac

Lord Shaftesbury also championed t child workers in the factories and t mines, continuing the protest made such outspoken men as Richard Oast (1789–1861) and Michael Sadler (178 1835). The cotton spinners vowed th their industry would be ruined if restri tions were introduced, though Robe Owen (1771–1858) had demonstrated New Lanark that it was possible to make fortune out of cotton spinning witho employing a single child under ten.

'chael Sadler.

'he work of social reformers is often mpered by unimaginative people who nnot recognise the victims of social ustice as human beings like themselves. r example, Jonas Fielding described a adle who drove some climbing boys t of church, with the comment: "What siness have chimney-sweeping boys in urch?" And another social reformer, sephine Butler (1828–1905), encoun-red the same attitude in her work for ostitutes. "Now look at Jesus," she rote. "He . . . never judged people as a ss. He always took the man, the woman, the child as a *person*."

t would be difficult to exaggerate the rt played by men and women of letters social reform. Dickens attacked not ly the employment of climbing boys it bad housing, bad sanitation, bad hools, bad prisons, bad political and gal customs, and a bad poor law. izabeth Gaskell and Benjamin Disraeli posed the social inequalities of their day certain of their novels; Elizabeth arrett Browning and Thomas Hood, some of their poems; and Mrs Stowe's mous *Uncle Tom's Cabin* roused the nscience of the world against slavery. pton Sinclair's novel, *The Jungle*, ompted an investigation by Roosevelt which resulted in the Pure-Food Legislation of 1906 and eventually swept away the scandal of the Chicago stockyards. John Galsworthy's play *Justice* was acknowledged by Winston Churchill (then Home Secretary) to have played a considerable part in the campaign for penal reform, and Brand Whitlock's novel *Turn of the Balance* (1907) influenced the same cause in the United States.

Early workers for penal reform were John Howard (1726–90) and Elizabeth Fry (1780–1845), and, in America, Dorothea Dix (1802–87), who also campaigned for the humane treatment of the insane, another reform which took generations to achieve. First in the field were the Philadelphia Quakers, who opened a hospital for the insane in 1757, and William Tuke of York (1732–1822), who founded The Retreat in 1796. Again a popular author struck a blow for reform: Wilkie Collins in *The Woman in White* (1860) and Charles Reade, in *Hard Cash* (1863), revealed the scandalous conditions in private asylums.

At one time women had no more rights than lunatics, with whom they were bracketed as persons unfit to vote. A husband might promise: "With all my

Elizabeth Fry.

worldly goods I thee endow", but in practice all his wife's property passed into his control. Mrs Millicent Garrett Fawcett (1847–1929) recorded that when her purse was stolen it was described on the charge sheet as being her husband's property. This strengthened her resolution to campaign for the right of a married woman to control her own property – from her purse to her fortune – which resulted in the Married Women's Property Act of 1870. Millicent Fawcett also worked for the Higher Education of Women and for Women's Suffrage. The cause of Women's Rights in the United States is said to have received its first impetus from the World's Anti-Slavery Convention in London in 1840, when women delegates were refused admission except as observers. Elizabeth Cady Stanton (1815–1902) and Lucretia Mott (1793–1880) resolved that "the Woman Question" must be tackled forthwith, and so followed the historic Women's Rights Convention at Seneca Falls in 1848 which launched the cause of their emancipation in the United States.

Dr Barnardo with some of his "Village" girls, Barkingside, 1890's.

Many social reformers have tack social evils directly, by practical measur In Britain, Doctor Thomas John Barnar (1845–1905) founded homes for destitu children and, it is estimated, help 250,000 during his lifetime. Octavia H (1838–1912), appalled by the housi conditions of the poor, and encourag and sponsored by Ruskin, started an e periment in housing management in 18 which proved revolutionary: she a campaigned for open spaces, and t preservation of common land, and th was to lead directly to her friendship wi Canon Rawnsley and to the establishme of the National Trust in 1895. Oth social reformers have tackled housi conditions indirectly, by demonstrati the possibility of creating a new kind town – for example, Ebenezer Howa (1850–1928), who introduced the idea a "garden city". Again, others ha founded settlements in slum areas – Toy bee Hall in Whitechapel, Kingsley H in Bow, Hull House in Chicago (found by Jane Addams, winner of the Nob Peace Prize) – to serve as growing poin for education and social reform. Son have influenced social reform by the revolutionary theories; for instanc William Morris (1834–96), whose cr sade against ugliness in all its forms faile to check industrial development b nevertheless resulted in a revival of goo craftsmanship and a more widely share apprehension and appreciation of beaut in everyday life.

See also EMANCIPATION OF WOMEN; NEGR PRISONS; SLAVERY; and separate entries f HOWARD; OWEN; QUAKERS; SHAFTESBUR EARL OF.

Refrigeration: process of produci low temperatures for long storage pu poses. A mammoth found preserved the frozen Siberian tundra had flesh goo enough to feed to dogs, though it ha en in cold storage for 15,000 years. fter the Battle of Edgehill (1642), during e Civil War in England, the body of Sir ervase Scroop, with sixteen severe ounds and stripped naked by plunrers, was preserved through cold and osty weather from about 3 o'clock on unday afternoon till the evening of the llowing Tuesday, when he was disvered still alive by his son. Here, reigeration was accidental. However, ound 1000 BC the Chinese were cutting d storing ice. Until the 19th century, e and cold cellars were the only means preserving food. In 1831 a British iceaking process using air compression as invented: and, later, an American ie using expansion of volatile fluids. he USA made the first cold air refrigering plant: Australia developed refrigerion further in factories, ships and dustrial plants.

Regency: period when, the king being under age or incapacitated, a kingdom is ruled by an administrator or a council. An example of a regency during the king's minority is that of Philip, Duke of Orleans, from 1715–23, during the childhood of Louis XV.

In 1811 King George III of Britain was judged insane. The Prince of Wales was appointed Regent, succeeding his father in 1820 as George IV. In consequence, the word is also used as an adjective to denote a style of architecture, furniture and decoration characteristic of the 1810–30 period. The Regency style flourished, though coarsening, until the first years of Victoria's reign (1837–1901). Its prime characteristic was an elegant simplicity deriving from classical forms, often softened with a touch of fantasy. John Nash's (1752–1835) terraces at Regent's Park, London, show Regency architecture at

Cumberland Terrace, Regent's Park, built by John Nash in the early 19th century.

its elegant best, while the Pavilion at Brighton (also Nash's work) shows Regency fantasy carried to an astonishing but delightful extreme.

Regicide: the killing of a king, or one responsible for such a killing; in England, the eighty-four men named in 1660 as responsible for the execution of Charles I (1649), among them Cromwell (*see* separate entry), Ireton, Bradshaw and Harrison; in France, men like Robespierre and Danton who had a hand in the death of Louis XVI (1793).

Regnal years: the years of a reign, dating from the king's or queen's accession. Thus, the 1st regnal year of Elizabeth I of England is from 17 November 1558 to 16 November 1559 and her 33rd regnal year is from 17 November 1590 to 16 November 1591. For historians this system is of great importance since, e.g. in English history, for many centuries no other method of dating is used in public documents, so that a mistake of one day in calculation can mean an error of a whole year in establishing a date.

Reichstag: former name of German parliament, in which in medieval times chosen members met to advise Holy Roman emperors. Bismarck re-established it as an elected group in 1867, but Catholic and socialist opponents protested that he allowed them very limited power.

First session of the new Reichstag, 27 May 1924.

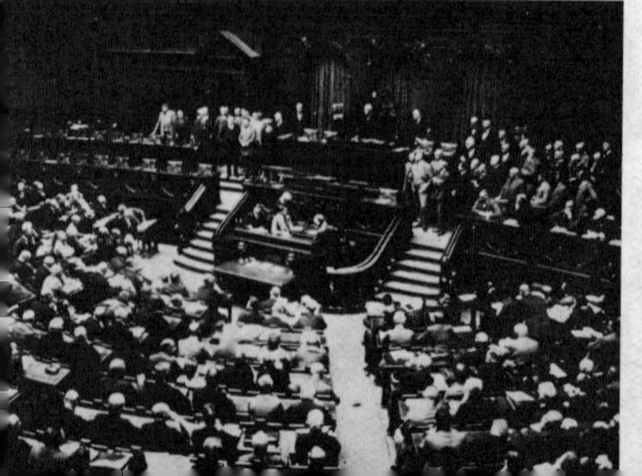

After the defeat of Germany in Wo
War I the Reichstag became the supre
law-making assembly of the Wein
Republic. Subsequently the Nazi Pa
gradually increased its membership of t
Reichstag, and when Hitler became Cha
cellor in 1933 opposition to him in it w
eliminated.
See also BISMARCK; HITLER; NAZIS; WOR
WARS I and II.

Reign of Terror or **The Terror:** na
given to the period of the French Rev
ution from June 1793 to July 1794. In 17
a ruthless political group, the Jacobi
headed by Robespierre (*see* separate entr

Robespierre being shot in the face by a gendarn
during his arrest, June 1794.

seized power and took over the Con
mittee of Public Safety. Ruling France
a dictatorship they strove to rouse nation
resistance and save France from invasio
Threats by foreign armies and civil war i
the west were met by a vast military co
scription scheme. Food was scarce an
traders who overcharged were punishe
Representatives sought out thousands
royalist sympathisers, priests and o
ponents of Jacobin rule, who were trie
before a Revolutionary Tribunal, thos
found guilty being publicly guillotine
Though these harsh actions preserved th
revolutionary spirit in France, within
year serious quarrels split the Committe

Public Safety, and Robespierre him-
˜ was overthrown and executed. In the
·vious six weeks some 1,285 victims of
Terror had been guillotined.

·ims, Rheims: city in northern France a tributary of the Aisne, called after the llic tribe who lived in the district in ·man times. It was the seat of a bishop- as early as the 3rd century, and Clovis : Frank was baptised there in 496 by St migius with oil, according to the ;end, from a Holy Phial brought from aven by a dove. In 972 the scholar ·rbert (Pope Sylvester II) was drawn to ims, where he founded a great school logic, music and astronomy, and intro- ced the abacus into northern Europe. 1080 Bruno of Cologne developed ere his ideas for the Carthusian Order monks. Reims Cathedral, rebuilt after ire in 1210, was the place of coronation French kings. The sculptures there by ucher (worked 1247–55), graceful and gorous, were imitated in Germany, ly and Spain. Towards the end of the apoleonic Wars it was captured and re- ptured several times, and during the Franco-Prussian War of 1870-71 was made the headquarters of a German governor-general. In World War I the city suffered heavy damage from enemy bombardment, the cathedral itself being severely hit. Modern industries include champagne, textiles and mechanical engineering.

See also FRANCO-PRUSSIAN, NAPOLEONIC, and WORLD WARS.

ie west front of Reims Cathedral, France.

Religion, Wars of: struggles arising from attempts to impose beliefs by force and often ending by corrupting and discrediting the religions they are meant to protect. Because religious belief – unlike nationality – is a matter of choice or tradition, treachery and changing sides are hard to prevent, and therefore religious wars tend to be more bitter than dynastic wars. They are attended by massacre and assassination, and followed by exile or oppression of the defeated.

In Europe, wars of religion followed the Reformation (*see* separate entry), beginning with the war between Zurich and the Forest Cantons (1528–31) and ending with the Thirty Years War (1618–48). The term is often specifically applied to the series of Huguenot struggles for freedom of worship in France, 1562–98.

Wars of this nature may be between rival religions (Muslim and Christian) or between orthodox and reformers in the same religion (Sunni and Shia in Islam, Catholic and Protestant in Christendom). *See also* individual entries.

Rembrandt Harmenszoon van Rijn (1606–69): Dutch painter with an incomparable insight into human nature. His portraits, self-portraits, and groups such as *The Sortie of the Banning Cocq Company* (popularly known as *The Night Watch*) are among the greatest pictures ever painted. As a young man Rembrandt built a high reputation but, too original,

Old man with flowing beard *by Rembrandt.*

too uncomfortably truthful for the general taste, he outlived his popularity. In 1656 he was declared bankrupt. In contrast, in 1961 his *Aristotle Contemplating the Bust of Homer* was sold for $2,300,000, then about £821,428.

¶ RIPLEY, E. *Rembrandt.* 1956
See also ETCHING; PORTRAIT PAINTING.

Renaissance: rebirth; the name given in 1845 to the surge of intellectual and artistic activity which arose after 1400 in Italy and which spread in the late 16th and early 17th centuries to northern Europe after the Italian movement had been extinguished by the Inquisition. The traditional view was that a spontaneous outburst of intellectual energy revived the study of the Classics – long neglected in the Middle Ages – and led to a spirit of bold enquiry, of confidence in man's power to improve his condition by deliberate action, of frank enjoyment of worldly pleasures – conversation, physical exercise, the arts, family life. Anyo who had excelled in art or thought Cimabue in painting, Petrarch in letter was lifted out of the Middle Ages a explained as a "precursor" of the Rena sance. Reacting against this view, lat students showed that medieval schol grounded their physics in Aristotle (38 322 BC), their astronomy in Ptolemy, a that Gothic was more advanced th Renaissance architecture. Yet 15th-ce tury Italians were conscious of belongi to a pioneer movement. Vasari spoke Giotto "restoring the art of design", a Marsilio Ficino wrote: "This is an age gold which has brought back to life t almost extinguished liberal disciplines poetry, eloquence, painting, architectu sculpture, music." In the other parts Europe where arts were flourishing – t Flemish towns, South Germany, Spain artists did not show the same dissatisfa tion with the Gothic style. In the cit states of Italy there had emerged a class wealthy merchants, educated in secul schools, well-informed by the practice commerce, practised in public affairs their guilds and civic councils, forced b party strife and the struggles of pop against emperors to take thought f their own survival and to regard no aut ority – priest or prince – as beyond attac The ideals of the Greek city-states seeme more relevant to these men than those knights or monks. Individually or members of city councils, they becam lavish and discerning patrons of the art A host of manuscript hunters, teachers c Greek, travelling lecturers on classic authors, satisfied their thirst for the work of Greece and Rome. Sculptors burie their own works and dug them up a antique discoveries. Many Renaissanc scholars were devout Christians – Floren tine biblical scholarship started the move ment which culminated in Erasmus's Nev Testament and Luther's Bible – but som rew off Christian morality and provoked the reaction towards rigid orthodoxy which stifled the Renaissance in Italy after 1540. "Cicero is driving out Christ", Erasmus wrote of the Renaissance preoccupation with style. In the long run, this preoccupation killed Latin as the working language of scholars and may have diverted men from the study of science.

¶ BULL, GEORGE. *The Renaissance.* 1968; BURKE, PETER. *The Renaissance.* 1964; HALE, J. R. *The Renaissance.* 1967
See also individual entries.

Reparations: money, or the equivalent in services, paid by a defeated nation in recompense for the damage and loss it has inflicted. This term first appeared after World War I, though, before then, a nation victorious in war had often levied a substantial punitive "indemnity" from its enemy.

The term has also been used for such payments as those by West Germany to Israel for Hitler's crimes against the Jews, and Israel's obligations to Arab refugees. *See* separate entries for HITLER; JEWS; WORLD WAR I.

Restoration: reinstatement to a former state or condition. Someone who has fainted may be *restored* to consciousness; a damaged oil painting may be *restored* to its original condition. Kings who have lost their thrones have sometimes, after an interval, been restored to them: e.g. Haile Selassie, Emperor of Abyssinia (Ethiopia), forced from his throne in 1936 by an Italian invasion but restored in 1941. In France in 1814 the Bourbon dynasty was restored following the enforced abdication of Napoleon I.

In English history the term Restoration specifically refers to the return in 1660 of the Stuart royal family, in the person of Charles II (1630–85), after an eleven-year interregnum in the course of which Oliver Cromwell (1599–1658), and later, for a brief spell, his son Richard (1626–1712), assumed the title of Lord Protector. The term is also used descriptively of the years following Charles's return, e.g. in such terms as the Restoration dramatists.

¶ BRYANT, SIR ARTHUR. *Restoration England.* 1960
See also individual entries.

Revere, Paul (1735–1818): American hero of a night ride from Charleston to Lexington (18–19 April 1775) to warn the Massachusetts colonists of the coming of British troops at the outbreak of the War of American Independence (*see* separate entry). Of Huguenot descent, Revere became well known as a worker in metals and as a bell founder. Many of his bells still hang in New England churches.

¶ In *Great Lives, Great Deeds.* 1965

Rhine: chief river of western Europe, a third of its 824 miles [1,326 kilometres] being navigable. With its two tributaries, the Moselle and the Ruhr, the Rhine basin has carried much of western Europe's trade for centuries. The Romans used it as a frontier against the barbarians. Danton in 1793 proclaimed the Rhine as France's natural frontier, but German hostility has made this impossible.

¶ REES, GORONWY. *The Rhine.* 1967

Rhineland: area of West Germany, lying on both banks of the middle Rhine. Much of it is forested and hilly, but its valleys are fertile, producing famous wines. Other parts are heavily industrialised. Germany and France have fought for centuries for the control of its valuable land and river routes.

Rhodes: mountainous Greek island, the most easterly of the Aegean Sea. Archaeological remains (*see* ARCHAEOLOGY) suggest settlement as early as 2000 BC, and by the Christian era the island had reached a great height of naval and commercial prosperity, with a maritime code and standard of coinage widely recognised in the Mediterranean. One of the Seven Wonders of the World (*see* separate entry) was the statue of Helios which stood at the entrance to the harbour of Rhodes. From the 1st century BC the island experienced the rule, or misrule, of a variet
of conquerors and raiders, includin
Romans, Saracens, Italian adventurer
Turks, Crusaders and Ottoman sultan
From 1912–47 it was controlled by Ital
after which it was ceded to Greece.

Rhodes, Cecil John (1853–1902)
British statesman. Following a severe il
ness in 1869, he went out from England t
Natal, South Africa, to recuperate, re
turning four years later to Oxford Uni
versity. Illness again interrupted his edu
cation, but, after another spell in Sout
Africa during which he invested in som
diamond diggings in Kimberley, he even
tually graduated in 1881. He then joine
Barney Barnato and several other diamon
diggers to form De Beers, the grea
diamond producers who now virtuall
control the market. In 1889 he was instru
mental in forming the British South Afric
Company, which until 1922 wielde
enormous influence in the whole o
southern Africa, especially Northern an
Southern Rhodesia, to which he gave hi
name. In 1890 he became Prime Ministe
of Cape Colony, holding the post unti
the ill-fated Jameson Raid precipitate
the Boer War (*see* separate entry). He die
on 26 March 1902 and is buried in th
Matopo Hills near Bulawayo in Zimbabwe. His Cape Town house, Groote
Schuur, is now the South African Prime
Minister's residence. He endowed a large
number of Rhodes Scholarships at Oxford for the benefit of students from the
Empire, the USA and Germany. He
advocated British imperial expansion in
Africa "from the Cape to Cairo". In
power he was impatient of control and
opposition, and for this reason failed to
build up a strong team of co-workers in
the worthy causes for which he laboured.
But he was in many ways an enlightened
administrator and is justly regarded as a
principal maker of the British Empire.

:hodesia (now **Zimbabwe**)**:** the coun-
y's name was changed to Zimbabwe in .pril 1980 on the attainment of indepen-ence under African majority rule. Pre-iously known as Southern Rhodesia, the :rritory had been taken over by White :ttlers from the Cape in 1890. They)ught two wars against the Ndebele efore establishing full control over the ountry which (along with Northern .hodesia, now Zambia) was named after :ecil Rhodes. From 1898 to 1923 the ountry was ruled in theory by the Brit-h High Commissioner in South Africa, 1 practice by the British South Africa :ompany (BSA) and the settlers on the pot. In 1923 it was granted internal self-,overnment by Britain which only re-

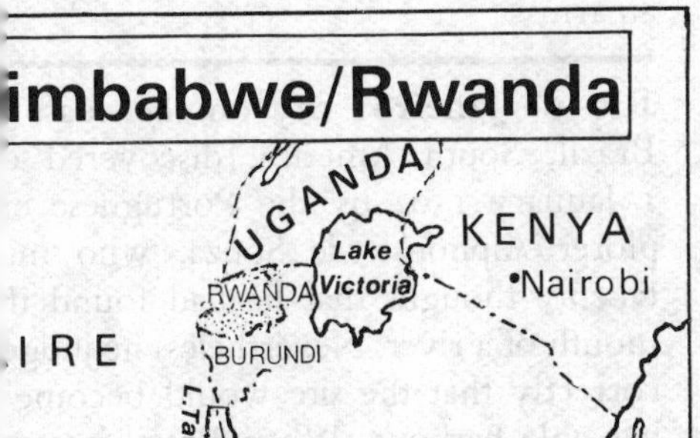

imbabwe/Rwanda

ained control over foreign affairs and he right to safeguard native interests, a ight Britain never exercised. In 1953 Britain formed the Central African Federation (CAF) consisting of Southern Rhodesia, Northern Rhodesia and Nyasaland despite the opposition of the African majorities in each territory. Ten years later, following mounting African opposition, Britain dissolved the Federation (31 December 1963) and in the following year Nyasaland became independent as Malawi and Northern Rhodesia as Zambia.

The white minority in Southern Rhodesia immediately demanded independence but without a one-man-one-vote constitution so as to perpetuate white control. This was refused by Britain and on 11 November 1965 the cabinet of the White Rhodesia Front Party under Ian Smith made a unilateral declaration of independence (UDI). For the following 15 years white Rhodesia was isolated by the world community, condemned by the UN (which imposed sanctions) and increasingly under strain as it fought what became a losing war against the black guerrillas or freedom fighters, principally in the northeast of the country. Finally after many abortive attempts to find a solution it was agreed at the 1979 Commonwealth heads of government meeting in Lusaka to hold talks in London (at Lancaster House) at the end of that year.

The guerrilla war had cost 30,000 dead and many thousands more wounded or maimed. Following elections held in March 1980 the new state of Zimbabwe was born on 18 April 1980 with Robert Mugabe as the country's first prime minister. Zimbabwe is rich in mineral resources, is normally self-sufficient in agricultural production with foodstuffs for export. It has one of the best developed infrastructures on the African continent. The two main ethnic groups are the Ndebele and the Shona.

Richelieu, Armand-Jean du Plessis de (1585–1642)**:** cardinal, and chief minister

of Louis XIII. The third son of a Poitevin noble, he was trained for the army but accepted the family bishopric of Luçon when his brother became a monk. He worked tirelessly for the unity of France under royal authority and against the disruptive privileges of the nobles. He broke the military power of the Huguenots but preserved their freedom of worship and employed many in high office. He did not shrink from alliance with Protestant Sweden and Holland to contain the Habsburgs (*see* separate entry). He built up the French navy and mercantile marine. Frail and moody, he "lay awake at night that others might sleep in the shadow of his watching".

¶ In CANNING, JOHN, editor. *100 Great Lives.* 1953

Richmond: the name of many places in the world, two of them being the municipal borough in Surrey, England, which grew up round the royal manor and palace of Richmond, the scene of many episodes in English history; and the cap tal of Virginia, USA, first settled in 16 by Captain Francis West and famous bo for its part in the War of Independen and as the Confederate capital during t Civil War.

Rights, Bill of (1689): Act giving stat tory force to the terms on which Willia III and Mary II were accepted on t throne of England. It excluded Rom Catholics from the throne, insisted th parliament should meet frequently an enjoy freedom of speech, and limited t use of arbitrary royal power, exercised b previous kings, e.g. in suspending an dispensing with laws, levying taxes wit out parliament's consent, and in raisin an army.

Rio de Janeiro: city on the coast Brazil, South America, discovered o 1 January 1502 by the Portuguese ex plorer Alphonso de Souza, who mi takenly thought that he had found th mouth of a river. Nevertheless he judge correctly that the site would become valuable harbour. When Brazil becam free of Portuguese control in 1822 Ri naturally became the capital city, but was replaced in 1960 by a new capita Brasilia.

Sugar Loaf Mountain, Rio de Janeiro.

r Emmanuel and Garibaldi meet at Teana,

orgimento: Italian word meaning urrection". In the 19th century edu-d Italians bitterly resented the harsh-and inefficiency of the foreign govern-ts, especially the Austrian, that ruled them. "Risorgimento" became a ring-cry to encourage all Italians in a onal revival that would lead to uni-ion and prosperity. In particular, the e is applied to the movements led by zini, Garibaldi and Cavour, 1815–70.

OOLF, S. J. *The Italian Risorgimento.* 1969

---

ads: strips of land expressly designed the passage of men, livestock and cles. It is not an accident that the test road builders in the past have 1 the military powers – the Romans, French under Napoleon, and, in the century, Germany and Italy under er and Mussolini. To move troops their equipment across country kly it is essential to have wide, straight, l-surfaced roads, with strong founda-s requiring minimum maintenance.

ong central government over a wide , with power to command labour and loy technical experts, has always been l for a good road system. Small or k states rarely could afford adequate ls. Seafaring nations, like the Egypt-, the Carthaginians and the Greeks, ld do with a minimum. Even Britain ld manage for centuries to transport the bulk of her goods using coastal shipping and inland waterways.

The first roads probably followed trails and paths made by animals, leading from feeding grounds to watering places, and those of men, searching for food, fuel and water. As trade developed between towns and villages, early roads were built in the Near East, *c.* 3500 BC, soon after the invention of the wheel. The first known example of an empire large enough for a road system was that of the Akkadian ruler, Sargon, *c.* 2600 BC, who held sway from Babylonia to the Mediterranean. Assyria, *c.* 800 BC, also had roads, built on low embankments in the valleys, with the gradients on hills eased with cuttings.

Around 500 BC two great roads connected the Mediterranean with the top of the Persian gulf. One, beginning at Sardis, crossing the Euphrates and the Tigris, and ending at Susa, was travelled by Herodotus. After his conquest of Babylonia in 539 BC, Cyrus built a road connecting Babylon with Egypt. China exported silks, jade, etc., as far as Rome and pre-Christian Europe along caravan routes crossing Turkestan, India and Persia.

The Romans were the first great road builders: 50,000 miles [80,500 kilometres] of roads, some of them still in use, stretched across their Empire in southern and western Europe, North Africa and the Middle East. In the main these were military routes, designed to move the Roman legions and carts directly and easily. Generally the roads ran in straight lines, passing over hills rather than round them; where there were bends they were of a large radius and widened for passing. The road bed was of great strength, made by layers of broken stone bonded together with mortar. On top was a gravelled layer covered with cobbles or paving – the overall thickness varying between two and five feet [0·6 and 1·5 metres]. It is a curious fact that the British

Remains of the Roman road near Blakeney Hill, Gloucestershire, England.

had better roads under the Romans than under the Stuarts 1,200 years later, and that no one in Britain made any new hard roads till the 18th century. After the collapse of the Roman Empire, the chaotic conditions caused by the barbarian invasions led to the ruins of these fine roads. Nevertheless, some still endure; and the historian G. M. Trevelyan was able to write: "Stretches of them have been repaired and modernised, and the motor-car now shoots along the path of the legions."

Inevitably the centuries of small European kingdoms, without adequate resources and with their recurring wars, made it difficult to maintain an efficient road system. During the 12th and 13th centuries pilgrims making for the famous shrines sometimes had their routes slightly improved by feudal barons, who levied tolls and spent some of the money on the upkeep of the roads. Bishops encouraged people to give their labour to the improvement of roads as an act of piety.

By the end of the Middle Ages (*see* separate entry), despite the rise in trade and the real need for better roads, the technique of road building had greatly deteriorated. Under the medieval system in Britain it was the duty of each parish to maintain the roads within its boundaries; but, as more people travelled, trade increased, and wheeled traffic grew, the state of the highways became deplc and stood in the way of economic gress. Only on the other side of the v was there an adequate road system d this period – in South America, w between 1200 and 1500, the Inca In built a network of 10,000 miles [1 kilometres] of roads to connect their c

Although Continental roads impr during the following centuries, in B it was a case of summer travel only the late 18th century. After the aut tarian government of Oliver Cron (*see* separate entry), the English tend resist any interference in local affairs central authority. The provision maintenance of roads was one of dubious privileges of local author dignitaries and landowners, with th evitable result that the main routes sisted of local roads of widely var standards of construction and repair. obligation on parishioners to give days' annual labour to the roads constantly shirked, roads often be impassable for wheeled traffic in wi and goods had to be carried by animals between the new indu centres. When the Emperor Charle visited England in 1703, his fifty-mil kilometres] journey from London to worth took three days, the imperial c overturned a dozen times, and it ne constant help from Sussex peasant heave it out of the mud. Private en prise, in the shape of the Turnpike C panies, which took over sections of rc putting up gates and exacting tolls, siderably improved the situation at end of the 18th century, as did the techniques in road building of J McAdam (1756–1836) a century l. (*See* TURNPIKES and MCADAM.)

French roads were generally in b state than those in the rest of Eur Strong central government, first u Louis XIV, imposed forced labour

building. The Corps des Ponts et
ıssées was instituted, also a college
·oad engineers. Their studies bore
not only in France, but all over
pe. Standards were laid down for
construction, coach services started,
oads opened – in fact, a new interest
ad communication began. Napoleon
·ted a great series of military roads
ting from Paris and others across
Alps.

)ugh from the 1840s railways began
vert attention from other land com-
ications, the invention of the motor
efocused it on roads. The provision of
major highway systems has become
:occupation of many countries.

ne examples are the modern inter-
road system of Belgium; the German
·bahnen, completely repaired since the
ıstation of World War II; the Italian
:trade, bidding fair to link the whole
nsula by one great highway; the
ly completed Yugoslavian network,
ıding the beautiful road running the
th of the Adriatic coast; the master-
es of highway engineering in Switz-
ıd; the highway from Vienna to
burg in Austria and the *felbertauern*
·ugh the Alps; and Holland's fine
em, covering the whole country. As
ht be expected, the USA has the great-
system in the world, with about 4
ion miles [6 million km.] of graded
ls. The longest motorable highway
ıe world will stretch, when completed,
n Alaska to southern Chile, a distance
·ver 14,000 miles [22,500 kilometres].

DEY, HUGH. *Roads.* 1971; RUSH, PHILIP. *How ls Have developed.* 1960

·erleaf complex near New York, USA.

Robespierre, Maximilien François Marie-Isidore de (1758–94)**:** French revolutionary and leader in the "Reign of Terror" (*see* separate entry). As a lawyer in Arras in the 1780s he had gained respect for his hard work, virtuous behaviour and sympathy for the poor. During the Revolution he entered politics, becoming a powerful orator and a member of the Committee of Public Safety which saved France from defeat and civil war in 1793. His nickname "the Incorruptible", bestowed on him by his friends, is some indication of his ruthless sincerity of purpose and honesty of life; but his enemies in the Convention overthrew him in 1794 and brought him to the guillotine to which he had been instrumental in sending so many hundreds of his fellows.

Rockefeller, John Davison (1839–1937)**:** American industrialist who, after boyhood and youth on a small farm in New York State, built up a near-monopoly of oil-refining in the USA. Reputedly a dollar "billionaire" (a billion dollars now being worth something over £400 million), he gave away some 750 million dollars in his lifetime to various medical, scientific, educational and religious funds and institutions.

Rockets: cylindrical cases of paper or metal containing an inflammable composition. They are propelled into the air by recoil action due to the high speed expulsion of gases generated by the combustion of the contents.

The origin of rockets is not known. The Chinese, Persians, Arabians and Greeks are known to have used them before the Christian era. The Chinese developed a mixture of saltpetre, sulphur and charcoal for pyrotechnic (firework) purposes and later used it for propelling arrows. By the 13th century Europe was using rockets for military purposes but with the introduction of gunpowder their use was mainly limited to display.

Early in the 19th century a new type of military rocket was introduced by the English inventor Sir William Congreve (1772–1828). Ships were specially fitted with angled firing ramps from which the Congreve rockets were fired. The 20th-century rocket was to develop into extremely formidable weapons such as the giant V1 and V2 rocket-propelled missiles used by Germany in 1944. Exceptionally powerful rocket motors have since been developed to propel ballistic missiles and moon capsules.

Pyrotechnic rockets are part of the emergency equipment carried by sea-going vessels. When a ship or boat is in distress and requires immediate assistance a rocket throwing coloured stars is fired in order to attract the attention of nearby ships or coastguards. Rockets are also used by coastal life-saving teams to fire lines to a stranded vessel and thus provide an eventual means of rescuing the crew.

The most spectacular development in rocket propulsion has taken place with the USA and USSR space programmes (*see* SPACE TRAVEL). Though the principles had been established much earlier, the first rocket launched by liquid fuel was at the hands of US inventor Robert Hutchings Goddard (1882–1945) in March 1926, when his missile travelled a distance of 184 feet [56 metres] and reached an altitude of just over 340 feet [104 metres].

V2 Rocket taking off in New Mexico, USA.

Russia's first effort came three years l
From these modest beginnings cam
less than fifty years, the mighty roc
used in space probes and moon landi
Though precise figures have not
revealed, it is estimated that the ro
which launched the Russian Proton s
lites in 1966 had a thrust of at least 4 mil
lb [1,814,400 kilogrammes]. Saturn V
one used for the Apollo lunar expedi
of 1968 was powered by five Rocketc
F-1 engines, each giving a 1,500,00
[680,400 kilogrammes] thrust. Anc
five engines, with a total thrust
1,150,000 lb [521,640 kilogrammes]
Stage II on its way, and Stage III nee
an eleventh engine with a 200,00
[90,720 kilogrammes] thrust. The
horsepower generated was 173,800,
the fuels used being various combinat
of liquid oxygen, liquid hydrogen
kerosene. More powerful rockets
since been developed and experiment
being made with other propellents,
as caesium vapour and ion discharges

¶ BRAUN, WERNER VON. *History of Rocketr Space Travel.* 1967

Rodrigo or **Ruy Diaz de Bivar** (1
99): Castilian hero known as "the C
or "Cid Campeador", meaning "the
champion". He won glory figh
against the Moors but, as with many m
eval heroes, such a body of legend
gathered round his name that it is
almost impossible to distinguish betw
truth and fiction.

¶ GOLDSTON, R. C. *The Legend of the Cid.* 196

Roman Catholic Church: larges
the Christian Churches, with membe
every land, numbering some 621 mill
or about a half of all Christians. It is ca
Roman because its members accept
authority of the Bishop of Rome, or P

see PAPACY), and Catholic – a Greek word neaning "universal" – because it claims o be the original Church founded by Christ and continued by His disciples and heir successors (the bishops) for the salation of all mankind.

For the first thousand years of Christian istory the unity of Christendom was reserved by means of General Councils f the Catholic Church (meetings of ishops and others) and the decisions of opes. But from the 11th century onvards various revolts against the authrity of the popes produced a number of ifferent churches, many of them claimng to speak and teach with the same uthority as had hitherto been enjoyed by he Catholic Church. Thus, in the year 054 a schism (separation) between the astern Church, centred on Constannople, and Rome, led to the appearance f the Orthodox Churches of eastern urope, with services, sacraments and eaching very similar to those of the Roman Catholic Church, but which deied the authority of the pope. In the 16th entury, under the influence of teachers ke Luther and Calvin, the Protestant hurches were formed in Europe, some f them, like the Church of England, nder the guidance and with the support f national governments, others, like the Baptists or Quakers, as independent sects. n the end several hundred independent Churches emerged in this way; but, lthough they differed greatly from each ther, they were all called Protestant ecause they protested against the authrity of the popes at Rome and the teachngs of the Roman Catholic Church. They onsidered that the popes had grown orrupt, and were too fond of easy living nd magnificent display; and they proested against elaborate ceremonies and superstitions". Luther, in particular, laimed that faith alone was needed for lvation, and not the sacraments of the Roman Catholic Church. To these religious objections were added political objections; thus, the English kings and parliament considered that the pope had favoured the French, and the German princes claimed that he had favoured the Holy Roman Emperor, from whom they were trying to free themselves. So it came about that objections against Rome, some of them religious, some of them political, gave rise to the growth of many independent Churches, and since it was supposed that a country must have one religion only, lest its unity should be destroyed, religious toleration was seldom adopted, and the 16th and 17th centuries saw hideous and brutal religious wars that devastated most of Germany, France and the Netherlands. When at last, in the 18th century, men of different religions had learnt to live together more peacefully, and religious toleration had been widely adopted, Europe had become divided between the Roman Catholic Church and a number of Protestant Churches. Thus, the countries bordering on the Mediterranean sea – Italy, France, Spain and Portugal – were predominantly Catholic, as were also some of the countries of northern and central Europe – Poland, Hungary, Austria, southern Germany, the Rhineland, Belgium and Ireland – while the rest of Europe was mainly Protestant. The overseas dependencies of European countries followed the religion of the parent country; so that South America was Catholic and the English colonies in North America were Protestant.

There has been little change in the relative extent of the Roman Catholic Church and the Protestant Churches in the last two centuries. Excluded from most of Asia, the Roman Catholic Church, like the Protestant Churches, has spread rapidly in much of Africa and in Australia. She has also reformed herself since the days of Luther and the Reformation, first at the Council of Trent (1545–63), which dealt particularly with the abuses complained of by the reformers and set up a more rigorous system for training priests; later at the two Councils of the Vatican (1869–70 and 1962–65). But it cannot be said that the relations between the Roman Catholic Church and other Churches have been friendly, until recent years. The Roman Catholic claim to be the only true Church, founded by Christ, and the Catholic teaching that the pope, when defining matters of faith or morals, speaks infallibly, have been resented by other Christians, while the Catholic belief that the bread and wine, at Mass, become the body and blood of Christ, has been regarded by many as superstition. But since the Second Vatican Council (1962–65), summoned by Pope John XXIII, whose concern was for all mankind, there has been a marked change. That Council showed a new respect for other Christian Churches and a willingness to share with them the blame for the quarrels and persecutions of the past. It also, for the first time, encouraged *oecumenism*, which means the drawing together of all Christians in the love of their Founder and an effort to break down the barriers that still separate the Churches from each other.

¶ HOARE, ROBERT J. and HEUSER, ADOLF. *Christ through the Ages, vols 1 and 2.* 1966; HUGHES, PHILIP. *A Short History of the Catholic Church.* 1967

See also individual entries.

Romanesque: European style of art and architecture of the 11th and 12th centuries, corresponding to Norman in England. It developed from a study of Roman ruins, though the 11th-century builders had not the skill of the ancient Romans and had to modify their plans accordingly. Nevertheless, Rome was the inspiration: hence the name.

Romanesque architecture is characterised by the semicircular arch. Churches with their great square towers and massive pillars give an impression of strength, fortresses of God. Sculpture, save on the west doorways of some cathedrals, was simple and formalised. Wall paintings and stained glass decorated the interiors.

Romania, Roumania, or **Rumania** republic in south-eastern Europe. Excavations by archaeologists of many ruined towns enable Romanians to trace their history back to Roman times, when their land was the prosperous province of Dacia. After the fall of Rome the noble landowners on the northern bank and near to the mouth of the Danube river faced a thousand-year battle for survival. To the north the Poles and to the west the Magyars of Hungary tried many times to seize the territory. Out of these struggles two provinces were forged, Moldavia and Wallachia, but both had to submit to the powerful Turkish Empire of the 17th century.

With the decline of Turkey, and the

ıllowing Crimean War (*see* separate ıtry), the two provinces gained partial ıdependence, and at the Congress of erlin (1878: *see* BERLIN, CONGRESS OF) ıternational recognition was given to ıe combined country of Romania. It has .ways been an important agricultural and mber-producing land, but in the 20th entury the discovery of oil attracted the ttention of Germany. In the 1930s Nazi ·erman influence (*see* NAZIS) grew rapidly ırough the Iron Guard (a kind of .omanian SS). In 1940 the Romanian .ing, Carol II, was forced to abdicate vhen the Guard helped Antonescu to ·ize power as a dictator. But Romania ıffered heavily, first in supporting Iitler's invasion of Russia, and later when ıe great Ploesti oilfields were severely amaged by American bombing.

After 1945 Soviet Russian influence re- laced German. In 1947 a Communist 'eople's Republican government took ·ver. In the 1960s Romania broke away rom close Soviet control and under 'resident Nicole Ceausescu has striven or maximum independence; it has a ·referential trade link with the EEC and a rade agreement with the USA.

Romanov: name of the last Russian uling dynasty. Michael Romanov (1596–645), a nobleman of Prussian descent, vas elected Tsar of Russia in 1613. The Romanov male line ended in 1730 with he death of Peter II, grandson of Peter he Great (1672–1725 *see* separate entry) vho had been the greatest of the Rom- novs; the dynasty continued by female lescent or marriage. From 1762 until the bdication of Nicholas II (*see* separate ·ntry) in 1917, the Romanov rulers of Russia were descendants of Anne, daugh- er of Peter the Great.

Rome: capital city of Italy, on the River Tiber, about half-way down the western side of the peninsula and twelve miles [19 km.] from the sea. Few cities in the world have a longer history.

Its situation among low hills at the last ford over the river attracted early human settlement, but its story begins with the fable of the founding of Rome by Romulus, a descendant of Aeneas, who had escaped from the fall of Troy (in the 16th century it was fashionable to claim Trojan origin for the Britons likewise), and the traditional date for this was 753 BC, the Romans subsequently reckoning each year as the . . .th from the founding of the city. For a time the Etruscans, a neighbouring and rival tribe from the north of the Tiber, imposed a line of kings upon the city, but these were driven out at the end of the 6th century, and the period of the Republic followed, to last for the next 450 years.

The control of affairs was, to begin with, entirely in the hands of the patricians, the upper class who monopolised the senate and elected annually two chief magistrates, called consuls, one of their main duties being to command the citizen-armies in war. Over the years the plebeians, the lower classes, gradually gained some influence, so that it became at least possible for a man of humble origins but unusual ability to make his way to responsible public positions.

Meanwhile Rome was gradually extending her influence and her boundaries – often by aggressive means – throughout the rest of Italy, and this eventually brought her into conflict with other Mediterranean nations. Her struggle against the Carthaginians in the Punic Wars resulted in Spain becoming a Roman province in 201 BC and Africa in 146 BC. Over the same period she became involved in the affairs of Greece and Asia Minor, where the break-up of the empire of Alexander the Great (d. 323 BC) had in due course produced much strife and confusion: in these regions, too, new provinces were established.

By the opening of the 1st century BC Rome was almost encircling the Mediterranean (Egypt was not annexed for another seventy years), but the extent of her territories raised problems and strains with which the existing machinery of government could not cope, and political life was more and more controlled by military commanders who, with their troops behind them, could defy the authorities. The last of these, Gaius Julius Caesar (100–44 BC) had virtually made himself dictator when he was assassinated. From the civil wars which followed, his nephew Octavian (63 BC – AD 14) emerged in the year 27 BC as the first of the Roman emperors, with the title of Augustus.

The historian Edward Gibbon in his famous work *The Decline and Fall of the Roman Empire* starts his first chapter by fixing the death of the Emperor Marcus Aurelius (AD 180) as the point at which this vast organisation began, albeit with more than one period of recovery, its long period of decay. It is difficult to assign all the reasons for this. The accusations of luxury and idleness made against the Romans themselves can all too easily be exaggerated. The overriding causes seem to be that the Empire was too vast to be controlled from one centre, even by a race with a marked genius for orderly administration, and that the frontiers, which had been pushed further forward as a definite measure (the conquest of Britain from AD 43 is an example of this), could not be held against the pressures exerted on them at a time when the tribes and nations outside them were in a state of movement and restlessness. In the end these barbarians, as they were called, broke into Italy: in 410 Rome was sacked, not for the first or last time, and in 475 Romulus Augustulus, the last emperor of the west (who ironically derived his name from the founder of Rome and the founder of the Empire) was deposed by th Gothic leader Odoacer.

In this rapid summary of the events o many centuries, Rome has been treate as the centre of wide territories, rathe than as a city in itself; but the same centuries saw its development from a primitive township to one of the proudest citie in the ancient world. Only some of i main features can be mentioned here: th Capitol, which was the sacred hill at th centre, like the Acropolis at Athens, th Palatine Hill where the houses of th rulers stood (hence the word palace) an the marsh drained to establish the Forum originally the market-place, round whic the official buildings were located. T these must be added the public baths, th bridges over the Tiber, the city walls an the public water supplies. It was said o Augustus that he found Rome a city o brick and left it a city of marble, and certainly the finest of the many remains o ancient buildings which survive date from the years of the Empire, some having bee ruthlessly pillaged for materials in late centuries. The Castel Sant' Angelo, originally built by the Emperor Hadrian (c AD 138) as a mausoleum (tomb) for himself and adapted in the Middle Ages as fortress in which popes and others at time took refuge, is still intact, while th Colosseum and the Baths of Caracalla ar impressive even in their massive ruins.

From the time of the barbarian invasion until the middle of the 19th century Rom ceased to be a capital city and, as tim went on, developed into one of the city states, like Florence, Milan or Venice which, over a long period, are a feature o Italian history. In one respect, however there was an important difference: th growing power of the Church, which th barbarians on the whole treated with respect, and the leadership claimed by th popes, who had their dwelling in the city

The Colosseum, Rome.

ave it a particular distinction, while in ourse of time the surrounding territories ;ere claimed by or given to the papacy ; its own domains. Though Charlemagne ;as crowned in St Peter's, Rome, in the ear 800, the city was never the true capi-ıl of his empire, and in the Middle Ages · had its full share of the unrest and viol-nce that plagued the whole of Italy. 'here was a time when a local family ontrolled elections to the papacy and in 55 chose a boy of seventeen, noted for is evil ways, as John XII. In 1089 the city ;as sacked by the Normans, and it was requently torn by internal quarrels, as ;hen Arnold of Brescia (d. 1155) and ıter Cola di Rienzi (d. 1354) led popular isings against the upper class rulers. 'inally things came to such a pass that the ·ope fled to Avignon in southern France, vhere he and his successors remained for nuch of the 14th century, and, when a eturn was made in 1377, there followed a further forty years of strife and rivalries within the Church. As a result of all this, the city was by now in a sorry state of ruin and desolation: an English traveller records that he saw wolves fighting with stray dogs in the shadow of St Peter's.

The situation, however, had a brighter side. By the 15th century the Renaissance, with its delight in art and architecture, was in its early vigour, and the popes of the period, worldly and selfish as some of them were, took a leading part in encouraging the long process of restoring the city in the new styles. The rebuilding of St Peter's was taken in hand by Bramante (1444–1514) and continued by others, including Michelangelo (1475–1564), many other ancient churches were restored and new *palazzi* erected for noble families. Despite the setback of one of the most savage of all the sackings of Rome by the Emperor Charles V in 1527, the process continued. The Sistine Chapel in the Vatican was started by Sixtus V (pope 1585–90), and the restrained classical styles of the Renaissance were gradually succeeded by the Baroque, seen in the later *palazzi* and in the many fountains designed by Bernini (1597–1680) and others which still adorn the city.

During the 17th and 18th centuri Rome was comparatively peaceful a was much visited by wealthy travell from England and other European cou tries; but the reign of Napoleon (En peror of France 1804–14) saw Pope Pi VII a prisoner at Fontainebleau, nea Paris, and Rome itself under French rule. On Napoleon's fall the popes regained their territories in central Italy, but lost the larger part of them, the States of the Church, in 1860 when Italy was in process of becoming one nation. Only Rome itself and the Papal State immediately surrounding it remained protected by a French garrison sent by Napoleon III which was recalled in 1870, as a result of the Franco-Prussian War. The city then became the capital of Italy, and the popes withdrew as "prisoners" inside the Vatican. In 1929 the Vatican City was declared an independent state with an area of 108 acres [44 hectares], its own postal services and its own railway station.

Rome today has a number of fine modern buildings to complement the architectural treasures of over 2,000 years.

¶ JOYCE, P. W. *Concise History of Rome.* 1960
See also individual entries.

Theodore Roosevelt.

Roosevelt, Franklin Delano (1882–1945): 32nd president of the USA (1933–45), the first American to be elected for more than two terms of office. By a coincidence, he came to power at the same time as Adolf Hitler, the German leader whom Roosevelt's measures were to do much to defeat. The most noteworthy features of Roosevelt's presidency were his strong lead away from isolationism his "good neighbour" policy toward Latin America, his "New Deal" programme at home, his "Lease-Lend" support for countries fighting the Axi powers, in World War II and, eventually his leadership of America at war after the Japanese attack on Pearl Harbour. He died a month before Germany's unconditional surrender. His wife Eleanor (1884–1962) won a great reputation in her own right as a worker for humanity and served as Chairman of the United Nations Human Rights Commission.

¶ HIEBERT, ROSELYN and ELDON, RAY. *Franklin Delano Roosevelt.* 1972
See also LEASE-LEND; NEW DEAL; etc.

Franklin Roosevelt.

Roosevelt, Theodore (1858–1919): 6th president of the USA (1901–09). He ame into the public eye as a dashing avalry leader in Cuba during the Spanish-American War (1898), was elected Re-ublican vice-president in 1900 and suc-eeded to the White House after President McKinley's assassination. At home he ttacked the power of the great business rusts and did a great deal to safeguard the ountry's natural resources. Abroad, he nediated successfully in the Russo-Japan-se War and gained the Nobel Peace Prize in 1906.

In *Canning, John*, editor. *100 Great Modern Lives.* 965

See also individual entries.

Roses, Wars of the: wars in England arried on intermittently from 1455 to 485, and deriving their name from the ed and white emblems of the rival houses of Lancaster and York. One historian lescribes this period under the heading: "The Suicide of the Feudal Baronage". That there is some truth in this description nay be seen from the fact that only 29 lay peers were summoned to Henry VII's irst Parliament in 1485, compared with .g. the 65 earls and barons called to Edward I's Parliament of 1295. Although orming a dynastic struggle between Lancaster and York, the Wars were largely he result of the termination in 1453 of the Hundred Years War (*see* separate entry), which had led to the formation of bands of mercenary soldiers who now found hemselves unemployed, and, as Trevel-yan says, "fit for any mischief".

Three periods may be discerned in these wars. Before 1459, opposition to Henry VI's advisers, notably the unpopular Duke of Somerset, was the keynote; the years 1459 to 1461 saw the struggle be-come a dynastic one. In 1460 Richard Duke of York (1411–60) proclaimed him-self king, but two months afterwards his

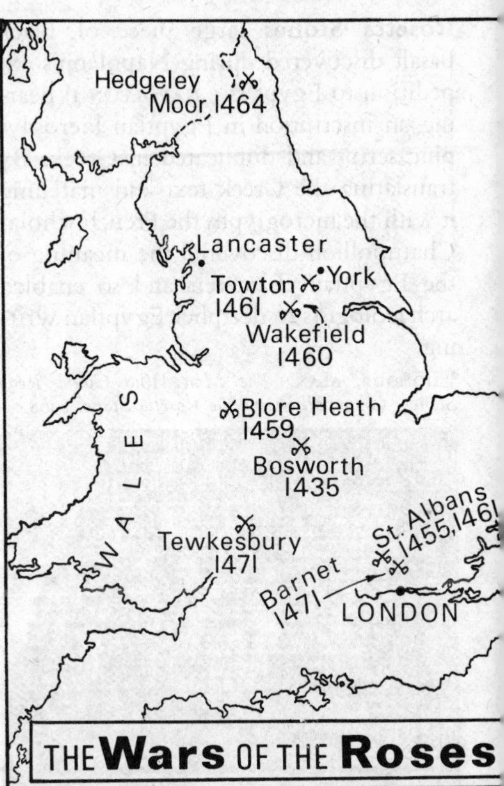

severed head, adorned with a paper crown, appeared on the walls of York. His son Edward (later Edward IV, ruled 1461–83) made good his claim to the Crown after the destruction of his enemies at Towton in 1461. Thereafter the House of York retained the throne, although Edward's position was not really secure until he defeated the Earl of Warwick (Warwick "the Kingmaker", 1428–71) and his forces at Barnet, and followed this up by a vic-tory over Margaret of Anjou, queen of Henry VI, at Tewkesbury in 1471. There-after, apart from sporadic local outbursts, England had peace for fourteen years, until the final battle was fought at Bos-worth Field (1485), where Richard III was slain and Henry VII, head of the house of Lancaster, won the throne and later united the warring factions by marrying Eliza-beth of York.

¶ ALLEN, KENNETH. *The Wars of the Roses.* 1973

Rosetta Stone: large piece of black basalt discovered during Napoleon's expedition to Egypt (*see* NAPOLEON I) bearing an inscription in Egyptian hieroglyphic script and duplicated in Greek. By translating the Greek text and matching it with the hieroglyphs the French scholar Champollion discovered the meaning of the Egyptian characters and so enabled archaeologists to decipher Egyptian writing.

¶ HONOUR, ALAN. *The Man Who Could Read Stones: Champollion and the Rosetta Stone.* 1968

A detail of the Rosetta Stone, showing the Hieroglyphic, Demotic and Greek scripts.

Rothschild, Meyer Anselm (1743–1812)**:** German-Jewish financier, born at Frankfurt-on-Main. Starting life as a bank clerk, he set up in business for himself and, displaying great talent in money matters, founded the great family of international bankers who dominated 19th-century European finance. Other prominent members were his son Nathan Meyer (1777–1836), who had charge of the London house, and Nathan's son Lionel (1808–79), who became the first Jewish member of the British House of Commons.

Rotterdam: second city and greatest port of the Netherlands. It rose in the 13th

century as a fishing port and place o transhipment between sea and river craf of Rhine and Meuse, beside a dam an sluice on the Rotte river, and was built o piles in drained ground. In 1572 it wa one of the first towns to defy the Spaniard but was treacherously taken, and 400 o its citizens were massacred. As ships be came larger and the colonial trade devel oped, it surpassed Dordrecht and Amsterdam as a port and became the centre o sugar refining. The German bombing o 14 May 1940 – after Holland had aske for an armistice – destroyed 30,000 homes Reconstruction work was begun fou days after the bombing and complete with vision and determination. The city' shopping centre, the Lijnbaan, with pedestrian ways, fountains, flowerbeds an sculpture, is greatly admired by tow planners.

Rouen: city of northern France, on th River Seine. Today a busy manufacturing town, it was the ancient capital o Normandy. William the Conqueror die there in 1087. It was held by the English until 1204 and again between 1419 an 1449. In 1431 Joan of Arc (*see* separat entry) was burnt as a heretic in the cathedral square. The Cathedral, a magnificent structure built between the 13th and 16th centuries, was badly damaged in World War II. Its southern tower is called the Tour de Beurre (Butter Tower) because the people who contributed the money for its building were, in return, allowed to eat butter during Lent.

ısseau, Jean-Jacques (1712–78): osopher and writer, usually described 'rench though born at Geneva. He ·lled against many of the accepted s of his time and came to the con- ion that man in his primitive state was ırally good but had been corrupted by progress of civilisation and by the cture of society that had developed. It , therefore, desirable to return to the of simplicity. These views he put for- d in his main work *The Social Con-* , which had great influence on the ıocratic ideas which inspired the ıch Revolution (*see* separate entry).

yal Society, The: leading scientific iety in Great Britain. An association of ıilosophers" meeting weekly at Gre- m College, London, from 1645, was nted a charter by Charles II in 1662. ce then the Society has encouraged l financed experiment, research and olication in every field of science and thematics, and frequently advises the vernment. Among its presidents have en Sir Christopher Wren, Samuel pys and Sir Isaac Newton (*see* separate ries). The Society's published records its activities date from 1665.

NDRADE, E. N. DA C. *A Brief History of the Royal iety.* 1960

Rubber: elastic substance formed from the juice of certain tropical trees and shrubs. Natural rubber grows in South America, Mexico and Malaya. Little is known of the early use of the product, but in AD 1500 it was mentioned by a Spanish historian. It seems possible that Columbus (*see* separate entry), on his second voyage to the West Indies, saw natives bouncing a rubber ball. In 1736 samples of rubber were sent to Europe from Peru, but no one appears to have considered it a useful commodity: it was regarded as a curiosity.

The earliest record of the export of rubber was in a Brazilian trade account of 1825. It could be made into soles for shoes, waterproof clothing and buffers to soften the impact of heavy articles, but it was not a popular material because of its tendency to become jelly-like during hot weather. A London businessman, James Hancock, set up a small factory for the manufacture of rubber articles in 1820, but it did not prosper.

An American, Charles Goodyear, was impressed by the possibilities of rubber, which was so pliable that it could be moulded into any shape. He worked at experiments to make it durable and eventually discovered the process known as *vulcanisation*. This involved mixing sulphur with raw rubber, then heating the mixture. When cooled it remained unaffected by climatic conditions.

After this the demand for rubber grew. In 1876 Sir Henry Wickham, an English biologist, brought rubber seeds from the Amazon to the Royal Botanic Gardens at Kew (London), where they were germinated in the glasshouses. The saplings, exported first to Ceylon, formed the basis of extensive plantations in Malaya and Burma. In recent years there have been considerable advances in the manufacture of synthetic rubber. Two particularly important branches of the rubber

In Ceylon rubber is still collected by tapping the rubber tree.

industry are those concerned with various types of footwear and the production of tyres for automobiles and cycles.

¶ SCHIDROWITZ, P. and DAWSON, T. R. editors. *History of the Rubber Industry.* 1953

Rubens, Sir Peter Paul (1577–1640): Flemish painter on the grand scale. Although assisted by pupils, only an artist of prodigious genius and vitality could accomplish so many enormous altar-pieces, cover so many palace walls and ceilings with fluent paintings glowing with life and colour. Rubens was also a diplomat. Sent to England, he was knighted by Charles I, who commissioned him to decorate the Banqueting Hall in Whitehall. Two of his greatest masterpieces are *The Raising of the Cross* and *The Descent from the Cross*, both in Antwerp Cathedral.

¶ RIPLEY, E. *Rubens.* 1958

Ruhr: important industrial area in \ Germany, with huge engineering, che cal, coal and steel production. In peak years before 1939, 150 million [152,400,000 tonnes] of coal and 16 lion tons [16,300,000 tonnes] of steel v produced annually. By 1914 Boch Dortmund and Essen had developed the north bank of the Ruhr river, Dusseldorf was growing just up rive the Rhine. Essen's growth was spectac when it became the home of Al Krupp, whose firm soon dominated German armament industry. A Fre and Belgian invasion of the Ruhr in 19 to compel Germany to pay war rep tions, met with passive resistance from workers whose production would h helped the army of occupation. Tho this resistance hindered the invader also caused the collapse of the Gern economy and destroyed the value of currency. The Ruhr was a major tar for Allied aircraft in World War II separate entry) when, from 1943 onwa 1000-bomber raids smashed much of industrial heart of Germany. After war the process of recovery was am ingly rapid and the area became ag the greatest industrial concentration Europe.

Rupert, Prince (1619–82): son of Fr erick V, Elector Palatine, and Elizabe daughter of James I of England. Com to England in 1642, he was appoin General of the King's Horse by his unc Charles I, and proved a brilliant leader a strategist, the cavalry being undefea until Marston Moor, 1644. After Nase he was for a time estranged from Char I, but later (1647) commanded a roya navy until driven from the seas by Bla In 1660 he again became Admiral a played a brilliant part in the later Dut wars. He was the first President of t Hudson's Bay Company (*see* separ

[..]ry). He had scientific and artistic in[..]sts and was an early expert at mezzo[..] engraving.

[..]IGHT, FRANK. *Prince of Cavaliers*. 1967

[..]ssia: former country of eastern Europe [..] Asia. For post-1918 history, *see* UNION [..] SOVIET SOCIALIST REPUBLICS.

[..]r some 800 years, from 400 BC to AD [..], Greek cities flourished on the shores [..]the Black Sea and did much to civilise [..] Scythian tribes of the interior of what [..] now call Russia; but the westward [..]vements of Avars, Goths and Huns [..]ped out these cities. Later, a few primi[..] Slav communities established their [..]vns on the great rivers. Menaced by [..]rkish tribes and by each other, they [..]ight the aid of the Scandinavians. In [..] 862 Ruric led his Norsemen into [..]ssia from the Baltic. They established [..]ding cities at Novgorod and Kiev, [..]cended the Dnieper and even attacked [..]nstantinople. The name Russ, which [..]plied to the energetic Scandinavians, [..]s given to the land they now ruled.

[..]ladimir (980–1015), ruler of Kiev, [..]opted Christianity in its eastern Greek [..]m and married a sister of the Byzantine [..]nperor Basil II. Religion in Russia was thus closely united with the state as in the Byzantine Empire. Kiev was destroyed in 1169 in the wars fought for the title and powers of Grand Prince. The town of Vladimir became the new Russ capital. In the 13th century Russia was overrun by the Mongolian invaders and became part of the empire of Genghis Khan. Though this empire quickly broke up, the people of the Islamic Tatar "Golden Horde" established themselves for two centuries on the lower Volga and in the south-eastern steppes. The small Russian cities and princedoms survived, provided they paid tribute.

The Grand Princes of Moscow gained power by becoming the agents and tax gatherers of the Tatar Khans. The economic foundation of Moscow was agricultural rather than trading. It became the political and religious capital. From the west the Lithuanians and Poles pressed hard upon the Russians. In 1380, however, Dmitri Donskoi defeated the Tatars at Koulikovo. The Golden Horde also came under attack from Timur in the east. The Grand Princes of Moscow emerged as the heirs alike of the fallen Byzantine Emperors and of the fallen Tatar Khanate. Ivan the Great (1462–1505) took the title of Tsar or Caesar, married Sophia Palaeologos, a Byzantine princess, and adopted the imperial double eagle as his symbol.

Rus Vikings.

Russia
1054 - 1914
North Sea
NORWAY
SWEDEN
GERMANY
Baltic Sea
FINLAND
Poland
White Sea
Barents Sea
ARCTIC OCEAN
Kara Sea
Bering Sea
Sea of Okhotsk
Sakhalin Island
MANCHURIA
SINKIANG
AFGHANISTAN
CASPIAN SEA
1.
KINGDOM OF THE VOLGA BULGARS
R. Volga
RUSSIA
EMPIRE OF THE KHAZARS
Black Sea
L. Aral
Caspian Sea
2.
RUSSIA
Moscow
Kiev
BULGARS
KHANATE OF THE GOLDEN HORDE
Black Sea
L. Aral
3.
RUSSIA
Moscow
Kiev
KHANATE OF SIBIR
KHANATE OF KAZAN
KHANATE OF ASTRAKAN
Black Sea
L. Aral
4.
FINLAND
RUSSIA
Moscow
Ufa
Kiev
Black Sea
L. Aral
5.
RUSSIA
Moscow
Ufa
Kiev
Black Sea
L. Aral
0 400 M.
0 500 Km.
1. Early Russia in the KIEVAN PERIOD c.1054
2 Russia during the TATAR INVASIONS c.1237
3.Russia at the time of IVAN THE TERRIBLE (1533–98)
Russia in 1533
Acquisitions under Ivan the Terrible
4.Russia at the death of Peter the Great, 1725
Russia in 1598
Acquisitions 1598–1725
5.Russia at the Accession of Alexander I, 1801
Russia in 1725
Acquisitions 1725–1762

Under the first Tsars, Russia remained ackward and isolated from western urope. In the early 17th century Russia's urvival was in desperate peril, Poles and wedes having made vast inroads. But a ational army was raised, Michael omanov was elected Tsar in 1613 by a ational assembly, and the Russians ultinately drove back the Poles. Peter the reat became Tsar in 1689. He imported vestern methods and advisers, founded he city of St Petersburg as his capital and ave Russia military security against wedes and Poles. His successors continied to employ German generals and ninisters who carried on Peter's policy, xtended Russian territory to the Black ea, into Poland and into Asia, and mainained an alliance with Austria.

By the end of the 18th century the ussian Empire was well established as ne of the great European powers, and nder Alexander I (1801–25) played a reat part in the defeat of the French rmies of Napoleon, who invaded Russia n 1812, and in shaping the settlement of urope after Napoleon's final defeat.

In the 19th century eastern Europe was listurbed by two developments – the reak-up of the Turkish Empire and the mergence of nationalism among the nany peoples of the Austrian and Turkish mpires. Russia supported Austria in uppressing nationalist revolutionary novements in 1848 and had also joined with Austria and Prussia in dividing all Poland among them. Russian governments were also eager to annex large portions of the Turkish Empire, including Constantinople, an aim which other powers, including France and Britain, wished to frustrate. From this arose the Crimean War (1854–56). Russia also expanded into Asia and caused Britain some concern for the safety of India.

Although serfdom was abolished in Russia in 1861 and many reforms were made, the government of Russia was narrowly autocratic. Dissatisfied liberals, land-hungry peasants, discontented town workers, minority communities, irresponsible landowners and an inefficient administration, all in different ways threatened the structure of empire. It was further weakened by a disastrous war with Japan in 1904, by popular revolts and a shifting and irresolute policy towards experiments in parliamentary government. At last the strains of World War I broke the Russian Empire. The last Tsar, Nicholas II, abdicated in March 1917 and was later shot with his family. In November a further revolution placed power in the resolute hands of Lenin and the communists.

Workers protest demonstration against provisional Government in Moscow, 1917.

¶ CLARKSON, J. D. *A History of Russia from the Ninth Century.* 1965; PARES, B. *History of Russia.* 1955

See also BYZANTIUM; CRIMEAN WAR; GENGHIS KHAN; ISLAM; IVAN; LENIN; MONGOLS; MOSCOW; NICHOLAS I; NICHOLAS II; PETER I; RUSSO-JAPANESE WAR; TATAR; TSAR.

Russian authors, painters and composers: Russia has a splendid heritage of peasant songs and tales of heroes and giants, spread, centuries ago, by wandering minstrels. There is also a religious literature going back to the 11th century. Russian literature as an integral part of modern European culture dates back no further than the early 18th century, to Peter the Great (1672–1725), that most unliterary ruler who nevertheless broke down Russia's isolation from Western thought and influences.

Mikhail Lomonosov (1711–65) may be called the father of modern Russian literature, in that he was the first to use the vernacular, the everyday language of ordinary people, in his writings. Alexander Pushkin (1799–1837) is Russia's greatest poet. He was a romantic figure who died as the result of a duel at the age of thirty-seven. Mikhail Lermontov (1814–41) was another poet of great lyric gifts.

Nikolai Gogol (1809–52) ushered in the golden age of the Russian novel. Fyodor Dostoevsky (1812–81) and Leo Tolstoy (1828–1910) are among the world's greatest novelists, just as Anton Chekhov (1860–1904) is among its outstanding dramatists and short story writers.

Leo Tolstoy, 1903.

To fulfil his function a writer must have freedom of thought and expression. This was never easy under the repressive regime of the Tsars – Lermontov and Dostoevsky, for example, were both sent into exile – and it is no easier today in the USSR. Some of Russia's greatest writers since the Revolution – for example Boris Pasternak (1890–1960) and Alexander Solzhenitsyn (b. 1918) – having had their works suppressed in the USSR, are better known in the West than in their native land.

Echoes of Russia's folk music are found in virtually all her famous composers. Prominent among 19th-century composers are Mikhail Glinka (1804–57), Alexander Dargomijsky (1813–69), Alexander Borodin (1833–87), Modeste Moussorgsky (1839–81) and Nikolai Rimsky-Korsakov (1844–1908). Peter Ilich Tchaikovsky's (1840–93) music is among the most popular classical music of the Western world.

Like the writers, Russian composers have not always found life easy. Serge Rachmaninov (1873–1943) left Russia for good in 1918. Serge Prokofiev (1891–1953) spent the years 1918–36 in France, and after his return to the Soviet Union had disagreements with the authorities. Igor Stravinsky (1881–1971), one of the great modernist composers, became first a French then, in 1945, a US citizen. Another composer in the modern idiom who has stayed in Russia, Dmitri Shostakovich (1906–75), was in disgrace for a time because one of his compositions displeased Stalin.

Christianity spread to Russia from Constantinople, the capital of the Byzantine Empire. It is therefore Byzantine influences which are paramount in early Russian art, an art concerned entirely with religion. Icons – devotional pictures painted on wooden panels or sometimes hammered out of copper or silver – were produced in large numbers. Many of

These icons are exquisite, deeply moving works of art. Experts in this field distinguish between many schools within the prevailing Byzantine idiom, each with its own characteristics.

Peter the Great brought many Western European artists to Russia: but Russian painting in modern times has not risen above the mediocre. The outstanding Russian artist, Marc Chagall (1889–1985), left Russia as a young man.

See also BYZANTIUM; CHRISTIANITY; PETER I.

Russian Orthodox Church: patriarchate within the Orthodox Eastern Church (*see* separate entry). Although Christianity (*see* separate entry) had been established in Russia in the 9th century and had survived the Mongol invasions (*see* MONGOLS) it was not until 1589 that the separate self-governing Russian Church was proclaimed. It still survives despite discouragement by the rulers of the USSR.

Russo-Japanese War: war of 1904–05 between Russia and Japan, caused by conflicting commercial and territorial ambitions in the Far East. With the trans-Siberian railway inefficient and incomplete, Russia was defeated in battles at the Yalu River, Nanshan, Liao-yang, Sha-ho and Mukden. The Japanese captured Port Arthur, destroyed a Russian fleet at Tsushima and overran Sakhalin. A peace very favourable to Japan was made by the Treaty of Portsmouth in 1905. This war showed grave weaknesses in Russian government and organisation, and strengthened the forces making for reform and, ultimately, for revolution. It also marked Japan's emergence as a world power.

¶ MARTIN, CHRISTOPHER. *The Russo-Japanese War.* 1967

Ruyter, Michael Adriaanszoon de (1607–76): Dutch admiral who distinguished himself in the naval wars against England during the Commonwealth (*see* separate entry), his most noteworthy feat being to bring his fleet up the River Thames and to burn a number of ships (1667). A vivid account of him was written by Gerard Brandt, who knew him and who records that, though he was naturally healthy, "in his youth he had once been accidentally poisoned through eating bad fish" and that "this had resulted in a slight trembling in all his limbs, which lasted to the end of his life". He not only showed great skill and bravery against England, but also captured several Turkish vessels in the Mediterranean, defeated the Algerine pirates and fought for Denmark against Sweden. He was killed in a battle off Messina, Sicily, helping the Spaniards against the French. A magnificent monument to him was erected in Amsterdam.

Rwanda: central African territory, formerly part of Ruanda-Urundi, annexed by Germany in 1884 and then added to German East Africa. In 1919, after World War I (*see* separate entry), it became a Belgian Trust Territory, being administered by the Belgian Congo until 1962 when the two territories broke off and split into Ruanda and Burundi. Ruanda then became the Republic of Rwanda, with Uganda to the north, Tanzania to the east, Burundi to the south and Congo (Kinshasa) to the west.

See RHODESIA (now ZIMBABWE) for map.

Ryswick, Peace of (1697): treaty which ended the French wars against the League of Augsburg (1686) and England (1688). France was exhausted and needed to recuperate before facing the problem of the Spanish succession. Louis XIV therefore surrendered all that he had gained since the Treaty of Nimwegen (1678), with the exception of Strasbourg, and recognised William III as king of England.

S

Saar: industrial region of Saarland, West Germany, between the Rhine and Moselle river valleys. It is rich in coal and iron. Formed in 1919 from Bavarian and Prussian territories, Saarland was administered by the League of Nations (*see* separate entry) from 1919 to 1935, when it reverted to Germany. After World War II (*see* separate entry) it formed part of the French zone and was attached to France economically, but was reunited with the German Federal Republic in 1957.

Saarinen, Eero (1910–61): Finnish-American architect, son of Eliel Saarinen, well known Finnish architect who emigrated to the United States with his family in 1923. Eero Saarinen came to the forefront of his profession with his design for the General Motors Technical Centre at Warren, Michigan (1951–55). He designed many college buildings in the USA, and also the US embassies in Oslo and London. His chapel at the Massachusetts Institute of Technology has a thin-skinned concrete dome which is of great interest to both architects and to engineers. In his best designs, such as that for the TWA (Transworld Airlines) Airport Terminal, New York, he handled concrete with an amazing lightness of touch.

Interior of the TWA terminal at Kennedy Airport, designed by Eero Saarinen.

Sabotage: malicious damage to prop
erty, installations, etc. Originally, a
action by workmen, such as the destru
tion of machinery, which somehow hir
dered their employer, today the term h
been extended to include large-scal
destruction of communications and build
ings by "underground" opponents of
government, and especially during a wa
against an army of occupation.

Saga: ancient Norse or Icelandic pros
narrative. The word derives from *segj*
"to say". Long before sagas were writte
down they were recited by professiona
story tellers. As written prose com
positions they date from the Middl
Ages (*see* separate entry). Some are his
torical, while others are a fascinatin
mixture of local tradition and myth
Among the most famous are the *Land*
námábok, which reached its final form i
about 1220 and which contains, amon
other material, lives of the early kings o
Norway and pedigrees of the first settlers
and, romantic rather than historical, th
Njalssaga, the great story of Njál, a figur
embodying law and justice in early Scandinavian history.

Sahara: largest desert in the world
covering approximately 3,500,000 s
miles [8,750,000 sq km] extending in th
east to the Nile valley, with Chad, Nige
and Mali to the south and the Atlanti
coastline in the north-west. The greate
part of its population consists of Arab and
Berber nomads.

See AFRICA for map.

¶ WELLARD, JAMES. *The Great Sahara*. 1964

St Denis: originally a Benedictine abbey
north of Paris, founded *c.* 625 and containing the shrine of the patron saint o
France, of the same name, who suffered
martyrdom some 350 years earlier. Many
French kings are buried there.

Helena: a remote, mountainous, canic island in the South Atlantic. Its ital and only town is Jamestown. It s discovered in 1502 by the Portuguese l after various changes of ownership ne finally under the British Crown in 4. The island is chiefly known as the ce of the exile and death of Napoleon I separate entry). Today the farmhouse ere he lived is a museum containing a lection of Napoleonic mementoes.

James's Palace: London palace built Henry VIII (1491–1547). After the ace of Whitehall was burnt down in 7 the royal household moved to St nes's. In 1809 most of the latter, too, s destroyed by fire. George III (1738–20) moved to Buckingham House ter Buckingham Palace). Foreign dip-nats, nevertheless, are still accredited to Court of St James, which remains the icial name of the Royal Court.

iew of St James's Palace before the Great Fire London in 1666.

Kitts, St Christopher: island in the eward group of the Lesser Antilles and e oldest British West Indian settlement 523). French claims dated from 1624, t the Treaty of Utrecht ceded St Kitts Britain. In 1782 Admiral Hood, though able to prevent the island's capture by de Grasse, ejected the French. St Kitts was again ceded to Britain in 1783. The abolition of slavery in 1834 produced little social change. The 1956 Leeward Islands Act united St Kitts, Nevis and Anguilla, with an elected council and responsible ministers. In 1969 Anguilla broke away and claimed independence. St Kitts-Nevis became fully independent in the Commonwealth in 1983; Anguilla remains a British dependency.

St Lawrence River: North American river flowing from Lake Ontario 700 miles [1120 kilometres] north-eastwards to the Atlantic. Jacques Cartier discovered the St Lawrence Gulf in 1534, explored the river beyond Quebec and Montreal (Mount Royal) in 1535 and 1536, and indicated the route for later explorers and traders, Chauvin (1599), Champlain at Quebec (1608), de la Salle and Duluth (1679). Louisbourg's fall in 1758, during the Seven Years War (*see* separate entry), opened the St Lawrence to British forces, thus making possible Wolfe's victory at Quebec and the seizure of Canada by Great Britain. The Great Lakes – St Lawrence – Welland Canal system, improved continuously from the 1840s, became in 1958 the St Lawrence Seaway, a combined Canadian-USA enterprise (114 miles: 184 km long) which bypassed the rapids and shoals between Lake Ontario and Montreal and opened the St Lawrence to oceangoing ships.

St Peter's, Rome: principal basilica of the Roman Church. The title "major basilica" is restricted to the four great churches of the city, among which St John Lateran is, in fact, styled "the mother church of the city and the world". St Peter's, however, being in the Vatican

St Peter's Basilica, Rome.

City (*see* separate entry), is the scene and setting of the great ceremonies of the Church. The first basilica was erected by Constantine (*see* separate entry) in the early 4th century on the traditional site of St Peter's martyrdom: the present one was begun in 1506 and finished in 1614. Several architects were involved, of whom Bramante (*c.* 1444–1514) played the largest part, while Michelangelo (1475–1564; *see* separate entry) designed the dome. The basilica is 619 feet (188 m) long, the largest church in Christendom. Over 130 popes are buried there, and St Peter lies under the High Altar.

¶ LETAROUILLY, P. *Basilica of St Peter.* 1953

Saladin (Salāh-al-Din or Salāh ad-Din Yusuf, "Honour of the Faith", 1138–93): sultan of Egypt and Syria and the last and greatest of three Muslim rulers who completely altered the balance of power in the Near East in a period of fifty years. Zanghi of Mosul conquered Aleppo and Edessa, and his son Noureddin conquered Damascus and Egypt. In 1174 Saladin succeeded Noureddin, under whom he had served as a soldier. He captured Jerusalem in 1187, thus giving rise to the Third Crusade (*see* CRUSADES), organised by Frederick Barbarossa of Germany (*see* separate entry), Philip Augustus of France and Richard Coeur-de-Lion of England. This resulted only in the capture of Acre and a truce with Saladin, giving Christian pilgrims free access to the Holy Sepul[chre] at Jerusalem; Saladin died the follow[ing] year. He was slight in stature, modest [and] scholarly, but a formidable leader. I[n an] age of rough justice he is noteworthy [as a] chivalrous opponent and a gener[ous] conqueror.

¶ WALKER, KATHRINE SORLEY. *Saladin: Sulta[n of] the Holy Sword.* 1971

Salamis, Battle of (480 BC): n[aval] victory of the Greeks over the Persi[ans]. In face of the overwhelming number[s of] the invading Persian land army, [the] Athenians abandoned their city, [but] through the strategy of the Athen[ian] leader Themistocles the Persian fleet [was] tricked into fighting in the narrow wa[ters] of the Bay of Salamis, where its va[stly] superior numbers could not be used [to] proper advantage. The dramatist Aesc[hy]lus, who probably fought in the bat[tle], later described the Persian king Xer[xes] as watching from a high cliff at the s[ea's] edge and rending his clothes in despai[r as] the Greeks tore the enemy fleet ap[art], destroying about 200 ships before the[y] retreated in disorder.

¶ In ALLEN, KENNETH. *Sailors in Battle.* 1966

See also AESCHYLUS; PERSIAN WA[RS]; THEMISTOCLES; XERXES.

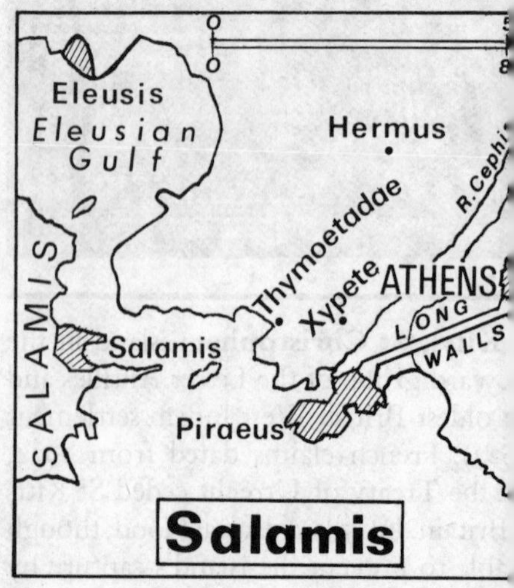

c Law: ancient penal code, originating with the Salian Franks though much nded and added to by such rulers as rlemagne (*see* separate entry). The : was mainly concerned with fines for ous offences; but there were some l law enactments (i.e. concerned with rights of private individuals rather 1 with criminals). The most famous of e excluded succession to land by or ough females. In the 19th century it ught about the separation of Hanover n Britain when Queen Victoria came he throne in 1837.

isbury, Robert Arthur Talbot scoyne-Cecil, third Marquis of (1830 03): leading Conservative statesman three times Prime Minister of England ween 1886 and 1902. Like the present rquis, he was directly descended from abeth I's minister, William Cecil (*see* rate entry), whose son Robert built field House, still the family home. His ign policy was described in 1896 as of "splendid isolation", a peaceful erialism based on the strength of the ish Empire rather than on alliances in ope.

t: name of the naturally occurring npound sodium chloride. Nowadays, is a cheap common commodity, but e it was so rare and valuable that it was d as money. Caesar's soldiers received t of their pay (*salarium*) in salt.

hen ancient man started farming, salt ame essential – meat contains a high content, cereals little. People living r the sea, or possessing salt mines, exted salt. Trade routes devoted to salt eloped: salt from Palmyra was carried ween Syria and the Persian Gulf; the Salaria was built from the salt works Ostia to Rome.

lt had a religious significance to early ples. It was associated with sacrificial offerings, and the Hebrews rubbed salt on newborn babies to ensure good health.

Salt became symbolic of a binding agreement, not only because of its preservative qualities but because covenants and pacts were often made over a meal containing salt. To eat a man's salt was reckoned a bar to treachery or betrayal.

¶ TELFER, DOROTHY. *About Salt.* 1967

Salvation Army: international Christian organisation, originating in London in 1865 for missionary and social work, particularly among the very poor. Its founder was William Booth (1824–1912), and members of his family were prominent among its early leaders. The title, which was adopted in 1878, indicates a disciplined body organised to fight against poverty and ignorance: members wear uniform, and pride is taken in the musical proficiency of its bands. Booth himself was styled "General", and his son succeeded him, but the office became elective in 1931. Subordinate officers also have military titles, as those acquainted with Bernard Shaw's play *Major Barbara* will know. The movement flourishes in England, the USA and elsewhere in the English-speaking world.

Whitechapel Salvation Army Hostel, Britain's first Labour Exchange.

Salzburg: Austrian province and picturesque capital city beautifully sited on the banks of the River Salzach. As the birthplace of the composer Wolfgang Amadeus Mozart (1756–91) and the centre of an annual musical festival, Salzburg attracts visitors from all over the world.

Samarkand: city in the fertile loess valley of Transoxiana, West Uzbekistan, USSR; from ancient times a great trading centre on the caravan route between China and the Near East. As Maracanda, it was taken by Alexander (*see* separate entry) in 328 BC and harshly treated after his troops were twice ambushed by Sogdian tribes. It revived and was taken by the Arabs in the 8th century AD. They learnt paper-making there and transmitted it to Spain. In 1369 Timur (Tamerlane) made Samarkand his capital, enriching it with booty and captive craftsmen and scholars from India, Persia and Syria. The turquoise tiled domes of his tomb and of the great madrassehs (Muslim colleges) flank the cobbled Registan, "the noblest public square in the world". Turki princes succeeded the Timurids. The railway reached Samarkand in 1888, two years after the Russians annexed the city. Today, while not holding its former dominant position, it remains an important commercial centre, with food-processing, textile and engineering industries.
See RUSSIA for map.
See also TIMUR.

The Shir-Dor Madrasah, Samarkand.

Samoa: archipelago of volcanic isla[nds] 2,700 miles [4,345 kilometres] east [of] Australia, visited by Roggeveen in 17[..], de Bougainville, Lapérouse and Edwa[rds] before 1800 and von Kotzebue in 18[..]. Commerce soon followed the missi[on]aries of 1830. In 1899 Britain withdr[ew], US interests east of 171° W were rec[og]nised, and German interests in West[ern] Samoa. The latter, mandated to N[ew] Zealand in 1920 and a trusteeship territ[ory] from 1947, achieved independence [in] 1962. American Samoa has since 1[9..] attained universal suffrage and par[lia]mentary institutions.

Samurai: "one who serves", a mem[ber] of the class of professional warriors wh[o] rose in Japan in the 10th and 11th centu[ries] AD when the emperors delegated po[wer] to great clan leaders. The samurai follov[wed] "the way of the horse and the bow'[', a] code which stressed pride in pedigree [and] loyalty to a lord who rewarded his w[ar]riors with the lands of the defeated. [In] defeat, they preferred suicide to tort[ure] and dishonour. Their bows requi[red] great strength to string, and their swo[rds] were the keenest and most finely balan[ced] ever produced. When Japan's volunt[ary] isolation deprived them of warfare, t[hey] elaborated their chivalric code of *bush[ido]* (literally, the doctrine of the warri[or]). When, after 1870, Japan began to co[m]pete with Western powers, the samu[rai] lost their social privileges, but were [the] mainspring of Japanese militarism [in] World War II (*see* separate entry). Th[eir] swords are still greatly prized by collect[ors] all over the world and command hi[gh] prices in the salerooms. Such is the uni[que] craft of the Japanese swordsmiths t[hat] these prized blades are still sent back [to] Japan for cleaning and repolishing.
¶ GIBSON, MICHAEL. *The Samurai of Japan.* 197[.]
See also JAPAN.

ı **Francisco:** city of California, chief
t and commercial centre of western
A. It has one of the largest natural
bours (456 square miles: 1,140 square
›metres) in the world, with its en-
ıce spanned by the famous Golden
:e Bridge (completed 1937, 4,200 feet:
:80 metres]). The main history of this
t centre is crammed into little more
n a hundred years, from the time in
.1 when thirty families in the village of
:ba Buene, near the end of the penin-
ı now occupied by the city, formed
entire population.

hough the peninsula had been dis-
'ered a little earlier, the first ship to
er the Bay from the Pacific was the
ınish packet *San Carlos* in 1775. The
'nt that transformed the small settlent was the discovery of gold at Colma,
lifornia (1849). By 1860, when the
d rush was over, San Francisco was
ll on the way to becoming the main
:t on the Pacific coast.

he havoc brought about by a number
fires and earthquakes (*see* EARTHQUAKES)
been overcome by the remarkable
ırage and energy of its people. The
y has housed several conferences that
ve shaped the modern world, including
t which established the United Nations
ganisation (*see* separate entry) and the
ernational Court of Justice (1945). The
ıce treaty between the Allies and Japan
s signed there in 1951.

· AMERICA for map.

---

n Stefano, Treaty of (1878): treaty
ıich ended the Russo-Turkish War of
77–78 after the defeat of Turkey. The
ms were specially favourable to Russia
l included territorial gains in the
ucasus and the creation of a large
lgaria with an Aegean Sea outlet. Fear
increased Russian power led to this
aty being severely altered at the Con-
ess of Berlin (*see* separate entry).

Santa Fé Trail: the overland trail from western Missouri to Santa Fé in New Mexico, an important trade route till the coming of the railway in the 1880s. One writer has said: "It was about eight hundred miles from Independence, Missouri, to Santa Fé, across prairie, river, creek, mountain and desert; and to travel it in fifty days was considered fast moving."

Santiago de Compostela: city of Galicia, north-west Spain. Its cathedral, dating mainly from 1078–1188, contains the shrine of St James the Greater and was one of the greatest places of pilgrimage in the Middle Ages. The special badge worn by the Compostela pilgrims was the scallop shell, mention of which occurs often in medieval pictures and literature. The road to Compostela from the Pyrenees is one of the most historic in Europe and features in the earliest guidebook for travellers known to us.

Santo Domingo: the early name of Hispaniola from 1496 when Bartholomew Columbus founded the city first called Santiago de Guzman. The western parts, occupied by the French from 1625, were called Santo Domingo (Saint Dominique after the Treaty of Ryswick, 1697; *see* separate entry) until 1804, when the Haitian Republic was established. The Dominican Republic, founded in 1844, covers the eastern half of the island. The name still exists in its capital, the oldest European town in the Americas, rebuilt as a modern city after hurricane devastation in 1931 and known as Ciudad Trujillo from 1936 to 1961 in honour of the dictator.

See also individual entries.

Saracen: name used by the later Greeks and Romans for the nomadic peoples of the Syro-Arabian desert, from whom their eastern frontiers had to be defended. During the Crusades (*see* separate entry) the word described any of the Mohammedan enemies engaged by the Christians. Later still, in the 16th century, the word was used to denote any infidel or non-Christian.

Saratoga, Battle of (1777)**:** the first major American victory in the War of Independence when the British general Burgoyne, with about 3,500 men and near-famine conditions in his ranks, surrendered to General Gates, commanding about 16,000. The victory not only greatly heartened the rebels but had worldwide repercussions, France at once acknowledging "the Independent United States of America", closely followed by Spain and Holland.
See also AMERICAN WAR OF INDEPENDENCE.

Sarawak: a state of north-west Borneo, Indonesia, which for a century was ruled by white English Rajahs. In 1841 the Sultan of Brunei ceded it to James Brooke (1803–68) who had supported the Dayaks against an oppressive l ruler. Brooke ruled independently u 1868, when he was succeeded by nephew, Charles Johnson Brooke, ing whose reign, 1868–1917, much ther territory was added. The cour became a British protectorate in 18 The third Rajah, Sir Charles Vy Brooke, ruled until 1946 when country became a British colony. Dur the Brooke dynasty much developm was undertaken and there was no pu debt. In 1963 it became part of the r Federation of Malaysia.

Saskatchewan: Canadian province fr 1905, after responsible government fr 1897, lying between Manitoba Alberta and formed from the Nor West Territories. Henry Kelsey of Hudson's Bay Company (*see* sepa entry) explored the Carrot River in 16 and the French later built forts on Saskatchewan River. In 1774 the old settlement, Cumberland House, was tablished, and in the 1790s Pond Thompson explored the territory. Set

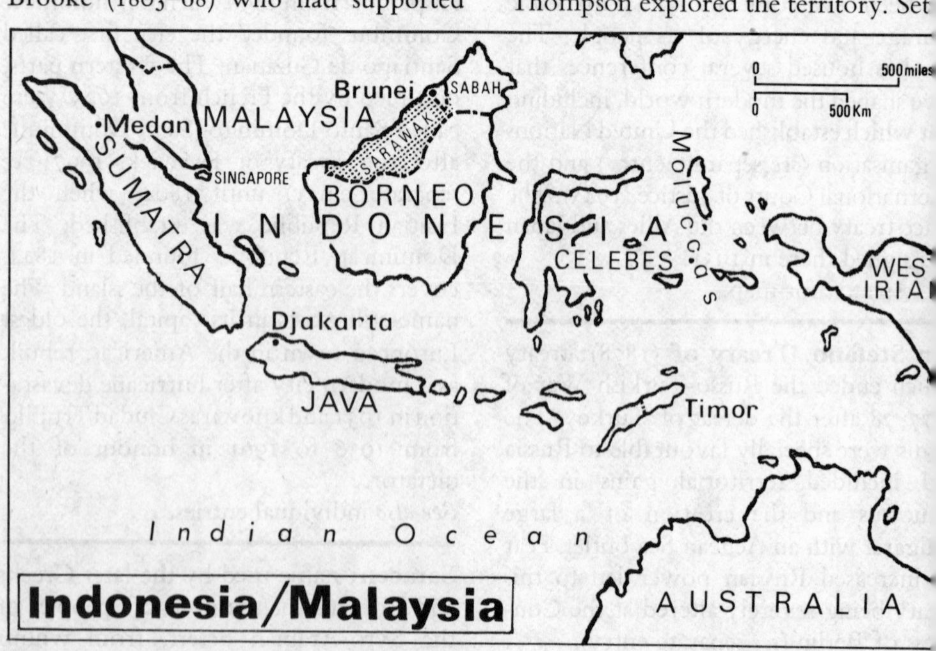

Indonesia/Malaysia

t was sporadic until Canada acquired Company's territories, established r by means of the North-West inted Police and encouraged railway struction. A rebellion of the Métis f-breeds) under Louis Riel (1844–85) shortlived, but his trial and execution treason led to an outburst of racial ng in Quebec and Ontario which ost brought down the government. r 1900 European settlers came into territory in large numbers.

Saudi Arabia: kingdom formed by the on of the sultanate of Nejd with the gdom of Hejaz under Ibn Saud in tember 1932. The kingdom occupies greater part of the Arabian peninsula, inded by Jordan, Iraq and Kuwait to north, by the Gulf, the United Arab irates and Oman to the north-east, by ith Yemen to the south, and by the Red Sea to the south-west. The capital, Riyadh, is also the capital of Nejd, situated on the central plateau, whilst Mecca is the capital of the Hejaz. Other important towns are Anaida, Buraida, Medina and Taif. The population of Nejd is largely nomadic: consequently, there is little agriculture, and before the discovery of oil at Dammam the main trade was in camels and sheep; but oil in Nejd has revolutionised the whole economy of Saudi Arabia.

The Hejaz is the site of many historic events. Medina, "City of Light", is the burial place of Mohammed, who died there on 7 June AD 632. Mecca, his birthplace, contains the mosque in which is placed the sacred shrine of Islam – the Kaaba, or black stone, which Abraham is said to have received from Gabriel.

See separate entries for ISLAM; MECCA; MEDINA; MOHAMMED.

Savonarola, Girolamo (1452–98): Dominican friar who preached reform in Florence. He denounced the evils which he saw in the life of the city and of its clergy; but the severity of his language and his claim that divine inspiration placed him above human control brought

Savonarola being burned at the stake in Florence.

him into conflict with Lorenzo the Magnificent (*see* MEDICI) and Pope Alexander VI. The people of Florence turned against him, and he was hung from a cross and burned.

Saxe-Coburg-Gotha: small German duchy near Saxony in the old Holy Roman Empire (*see* separate entry). Its family gained prominence in the 19th century when Albert, the younger brother of the ruling duke, married Queen Victoria and became Prince Consort. Saxe-Coburg-Gotha became the name of the British royal house until it was changed to Windsor in 1917.

Saxon: member of a north-central German race, originally living near the mouth of the River Elbe. The first mention of the Saxons occurs about the middle of the 2nd century, when Ptolemy's *Geography* places them on the Cimbric peninsula, which is now Holstein. From AD 286 [onwards Roman historians frequently re]fer to them as pirates infesting the North [Sea] and a naval force was maintained in [the] Channel and fortifications erected to p[ro]tect the coasts of Gaul and Britain fr[om] their raids. In Britain the command [was] in the hands of an officer with the t[itle] *Comes Litoris Saxonici*, Count of [the] Saxon Shore. With the decline of Ro[man] power under Honorius the Saxons [not] only raided the coasts of Britain but be[gan] to settle there.

Bede (*see* separate entry) says "from [the] Saxones . . . came the East Saxons, So[uth] Saxons and West Saxons", thus plac[ing] them in the modern Essex, Sussex a[nd] Wessex, and sharply differentiating th[em] from the Jutes of the Isle of Wight a[nd] Kent and the Angles of East Anglia, [the] Midlands and the North, but recent h[is]torians have taken the view that t[his] account overemphasises the differen[ces]

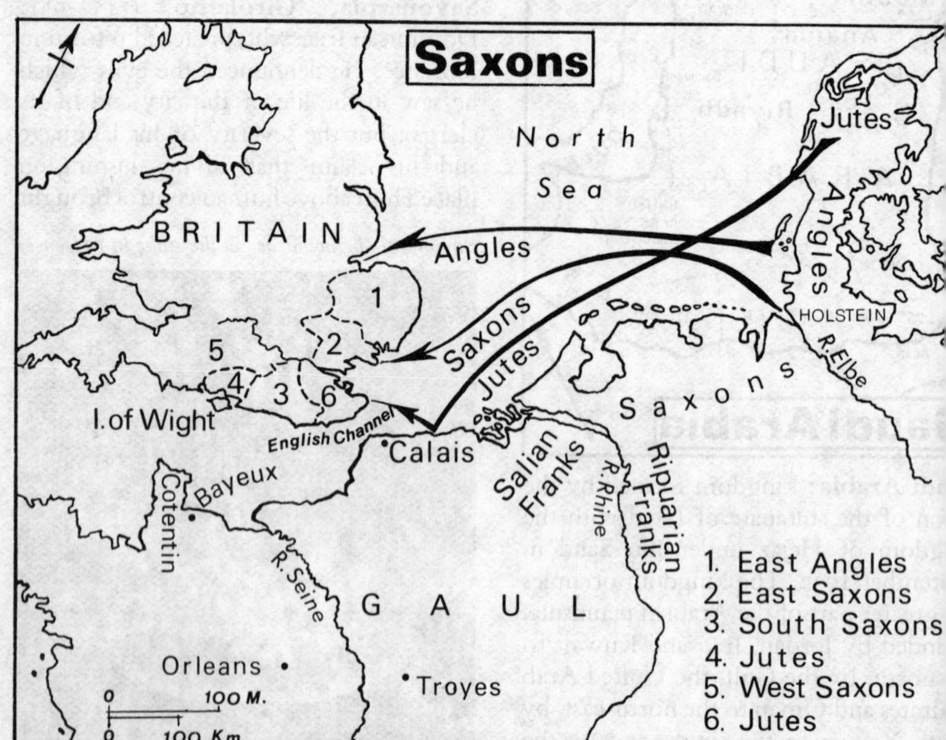

etween the various Germanic invaders. Their settlements in Gaul had a less ermanent effect than in Britain. They eized part of the north coast between the Cotentin peninsula and the mouth of the Seine, with Bayeux as its focal point, and probably an area around Calais, but they vere ultimately subdued by the Franks, nd at least one authority suggests that his diverted the stream of Saxon invaders rom Gaul to Britain.

PAGE, R. I. *Life in Anglo-Saxon England.* 1970; ELLMAN, R. R. *The Anglo-Saxons.* 1959

Scandinavia: name given to the peninula in north-western Europe which is livided between Norway and Sweden; out a loose reference to "the Scandinavian ountries" is often assumed to include Denmark as well, and sometimes Finland nd Iceland. All five countries have hisoric and cultural links.

PROCTOR, G. L. *Ancient Scandinavia.* 1965

Schools: places where people gather in large or small groups for education and instruction. Although this article confines itself to the teaching of young persons, the word is frequently also used in an adult context, as when military authorities establish a School of Artillery, or a famous artist has a "school" of other artists who base their work on his style. Curiously enough a group of marine mammals is also called a "school", e.g. of whales or porpoises. Readers may be surprised to know that *scholé* is a Greek word meaning "leisure", while the Latin word for a school, *ludus*, means "play".

Evidence for the existence of schools goes back to very ancient times, but, in following the subject, two points must be observed: the first, that, for most of the period of past history, education was the privilege of the upper or, at best, the middle layers of society, although children of ability could often make their way upward from below, sometimes even from the slave classes, many of the famous, or infamous, civil servants of the Roman Empire rising from such origins: the second point to remember is that much of the education of boys, and particularly of girls, was given at home or, in medieval times, in the households of patrons or relatives.

To go no further back than Greece of the 5th century BC, we lack the evidence to form a comprehensive picture of the schools themselves (which were almost exclusively for boys), but, except in Sparta (*see* separate entry), the ideal was a balanced education of mind and body and the development of an inner harmony in which music played an important part. We know, however, something about the schools attended by Roman boys, to which they went escorted by slaves to look after them in the streets and carry the wax tablets on which they wrote their lessons. These slaves were called by the Greek term *pedagogues*, which we now sometimes apply, jocularly but incorrectly, to schoolmasters. The poet Horace recalls for us the name of one such master, Orbilius, who was noted for the severity with which he flogged his pupils. The Roman schools placed great emphasis on the skills of speaking and self-expression.

The barbarian invasions of the western world brought confusion and disarray to the cause of learning, and it fell to the Church to maintain and foster what could be preserved. Bede (*c.* 673–753) in his monastery at Jarrow, in north-eastern England, was among the early upholders of the cause of learning, and the Emperor Charlemagne (742–814) urged the clergy of his dominions to improve their knowledge of Latin and encouraged the foundation of schools. He was assisted in his aims by Alcuin (753–804), an Englishman who had been headmaster of the cathedral school at York where he himself had been educated. Latin, as the language of the Church and of international diplomacy was, from the pupils' early age, almost the exclusive study of the schools. Greek underwent an almost complete eclipse in the West until it shone forth again with the Renaissance.

Meanwhile, the growth of the feudal system saw the rise of a warrior class whose education lay in a different direction, physical prowess and the various arts of war. It is probably wrong to draw too wide and easy a distinction between such men of action and the *clerics*, as men of education, whether priests or not, came to be called. At the beginning of the period, the English king Alfred (849–899), a great patron of learning, is said to have taught himself to read when he was already a grown man, while King Henry I (1068–1135) was called "Beauclerk" because of his academic attainments. It is probable that the medieval knight, even when he lacked the elementary skills of the schoolroom, was often a ready speaker and familiar with music and poetry. Nevertheless, it was to the schools that the western nations looked for their churchmen and administrators, the functions being frequently combined in one person.

Such schools were often attached to monasteries, but the masters were generally secular priests (not members of an order) or laymen. Even before the Reformation, a movement had started to found schools by private benefaction: in England the most famous is Eton College, founded by King Henry VI in 1440. At the same time, there were certainly schools of a sort for younger children, where they made their first contact with the alphabet and other simple skills; but it is difficult to form a picture of their nature or the extent to which they existed. Another question is how far learning penetrated down the social scale. There were, of

a

b

c

d

a. Boys school from a Greek Kylix. b. 12th century scholars form a ring round their teachers, from the Canterbury Psalter. c. Flemish Village School *painted by Jan Steen in the 17th century. d. Quaker school under John Bunyan's Meeting House, 18th century. e. Boys striking against corporal punishment, 1889. f. Primary school gymnastic lesson, 1973.*

e

f

course, wide differences from century to century and country to country, but it probably went deeper than is commonly supposed.

During the Reformation the monastic schools disappeared in many countries, but those which took their place were often strongly influenced, if not directly controlled, by the various Protestant churches. In England these took the form of so-called grammar schools, some of which developed into the curiously named "public schools", the distinctive system of fee-paying schools for the middle and upper classes, often confined to resident scholars only, which still exist for boys and, of more recent origin, for girls. (The equivalent schools in the USA are more accurately called "private schools".) It was only gradually that other subjects were allowed to take their place in the curriculum beside Latin and Greek ("the classics") and mathematics. A classical education was regarded as the hallmark of an educated man until quite recent times. In 1865 John Wilkes Booth, the assassin of Abraham Lincoln, proclaimed his defiance after the deed with the words *sic semper tyrannis* ("such is ever the fate of tyrants"), and, even in the earlier part of the present century, the studies of some of the English public schools were predominantly classical.

It is from the 19th century onwards that the greatest changes in the scholastic scene have occurred. In the first place, education in an increasing number of countries has become compulsory for all children and has been more and more frequently provided at public cost, though parents are sometimes left free to patronise private schools at their own expense. Secondly, there has been a tremendous upsurge and change in the pattern of theories of education, often carrying forward the ideas of earlier pioneers such as Vittorino da Feltre (1378–1446), Comenius (1592–1670), Rousseau (1712–78) and Pestalozzi (1746–1827). One of the greatest educational thinkers of modern times was the American, John Dewey (1859–1952), the champion of learning through experience rather than through formal instruction.

¶ DURES, ALAN. *Schools.* 1971; MEYER, ADOLPHE E. *An Educational History of the Western World.* 196[illegible]

See separate entries for ALCUIN; ALFRED; BEDE; CHARLEMAGNE; LINCOLN, ABRAHAM; PESTALOZZI; PROTESTANT; REFORMATION; ROUSSEAU, etc.

Scotland: country occupying the north of Great Britain. It is, in fact, sometimes described as North Britain but, though the description is geographically correct, to those who belong by birth and ancestry the country means much more than that, since it is distinctive in structure, vegetation, climate and in the character of its inhabitants. Highlander and islander, lowlander and borderer are recognisably different even in the 20th century. Five races had settlements in the first centuries AD – Picts, Britons, Angles, Scotti and Norwegians, each with their own language and all warlike, but having to find a common allegiance. They found it in a royal line. Wars with England and the leadership of such men as Sir William Wallace and Robert the Bruce (*see* separate entries) helped to make the people one, but a spirit of individualism and independence prevailed, "for it is not Glory, it is not Riches, neither is it Honour but it is Liberty alone that we fight and contend for, which no Honest Man will lose but with his life". Such was the Declaration of Arbroath, 1320, given in a letter from the nobility, barons and commons of Scotland to Pope John XXII asking him to exhort the King of England "to suffer us to live at peace in that narrow spot of Scotland beyond which we have

habitation". Such battles as Bannock-
·n (1314), when the Bruce's ragged
le army broke the might of Edward
chivalry, and Flodden Field (1514),
en James IV of Scotland, less successful
equally gallant, died with about 12,000
ots, were but two expressions of the
ional spirit.

his love of liberty, which made the
ottish nation, carried her people even-
lly far beyond "the narrow spot", to
y a leading part in the colonisation of
rth America, India, Australia and New
aland, and to be conspicuous in world
tory as warriors, traders, adminis-
ors, teachers and missionaries.

otland in her turn owes much to con-
ental influence. The Court in the 11th
tury was "filled with southern
eigners". Norman influence was
ong, and for long the royal house was
ench in race and manner of life, in
ech and in culture". The execution of
Roman Catholic Mary Queen of Scots (1587) and the triumph of Protestantism ended this "Auld Alliance". Links with England were then to be forged, and the Union of the Crowns in the person of James VI of Scotland, I of England, was achieved in 1603. The Act of Union, 1707, uniting the two kingdoms under the name Great Britain and guaranteeing the Hanoverian succession, ended years of strife. Clan risings in 1715 and 1745 on behalf of the exiled Stewarts were crushed and were followed by harsh laws which contributed to the depopulation of the Highlands. Crofts once fertile were left to the rabbit and the deer. The 18th century, however, also saw much road, canal and bridge building in Scotland, together with commercial development and the ending of the almost slavelike conditions in the coalmines and saltpits. The Reform Act of 1832 brought about much-needed voting reforms and increased the Scottish

ert the Bruce's victory over the forces of vard II at Bannockburn in 1314.

ht, The March of the King's Forces, under Earl of Mar, into Perth in August 1715.

representation in parliament. Today the Scottish Development Board aims at re-creating Highland industry and tourism is encouraged. Aberdeen, the granite city, has now become the capital of Britain's North Sea oil industry, Glasgow is Britain's third city, St Andrews, paradise of golfers, Dundee, famous for jute, marmalade and cake, Edinburgh (*see* separate entry), seat of learning, law and government, all cities with universities, give Scotland its character, *multum in parvo*, and the roll call of its great men and women in theology, medicine, exploration, engineering, literature and the arts would be difficult to parallel in any country of comparable size.

See GREAT BRITAIN for map.

¶ BROWN, P. HUME. *History of Scotland.* 1955; MACKIE, ROBERT L. *Short History of Scotland.* 1962

See also BRUCE; CARNEGIE; COVENANTERS; EDINBURGH; HADRIAN'S WALL; JACOBITES; KNOX; LIVINGSTONE; MCADAM; NASMYTH, SCOTT, SIR WALTER; SIMPSON; STEPHENSON; STUART, HOUSE OF; TELFORD; WALLACE; WATT, etc.

Scott, Robert Falcon (1868–1912): British naval officer and Antarctic explorer. He led the expedition of 1901–04 to explore the region of South Victoria Land and during a second expedition reached the South Pole, 18 January 1912. He had, however, been forestalled by one month by the Norwegian Roald Amundsen (*see* separate entry). Held back by terrible blizzards and weak from sickness and insufficient food, Scott and four companions all perished on the return journey. Scott's tent, with his records and diaries intact, was found in November 1912, only eleven miles [17 kilometres] from a food depot which might have saved him.

¶ BRIGGS, P. *Man of Antarctica.* 1959; SCOTT, CAPTAIN R. F. *Scott's Last Expedition.* Foreword by Peter Scott. 1964

See also POLAR EXPLORATION.

Scott by Sir Edwin Lands

Scott, Sir Walter (1771–1832): Scott historical novelist and man of letters. T titles of some of the many biograph written of him, *The Wizard of the No The Great Unknown, The Laird of Abb ford*, epitomise his character, life a work. For long he remained anonym and preferred to be so. His *Minstrelsy the Scottish Border* and the series of *Wav ley Novels* placed him in the forefront writers of the Romantic Movement home and abroad. Fired by his imag ation, German, French and Italian lite ture of the period reflected his influen and the whole world of letters was fore enriched. Among his most famous boo a number of them brought to the cine and television screen, are *Ivanhoe, Ke worth, Rob Roy, The Talisman, Sir N* and *Quentin Durward.*

¶ In THOMAS, H. and D. L. *Famous Novelists.* 19

Seals: stamps used to authenticate do ments. The term can mean either device which makes an impression or impression itself. Sigillography, the stu of seals, is one of the oldest hobbies in world. It became a craze in ancient Ro and Julius Caesar was a collector.

The art of seal engraving began arou 4000 BC. A ruler could best establish authorisation to a document in the motest regions of his country by affixi personal seal, without fear of forgery. ople of standing had private seals for same purpose and to mark their own operty.

merian "temptation" seal c. 2300 B.C.

umerians and Babylonians possessed em and used them for business transions. Jars and documents were sealed th stamp or cylinder seals, made of ne and engraved with simple designs or nes of everyday life showing the cosnes, social customs and religious rites the period. The Egyptians made scarab

yptian pottery seal from tomb, 18th–26th nasties.

d button seals of pottery, the Cretans graved scenes such as the bull sports on ndant or bracelet seals. Chinese seals re beautifully carved on semiprecious nes, metal, wood or soapstone, the perial examples being large, five inches seven, others miniature, an eighth of inch square. The Greeks engraved eirs on ivory or stone, the Persians on ms. From Roman times, the seal was en used for security, to fasten documents or chests and doors, to show they had not been illegally tampered with.

When the impression made by the die is on metal, it is called a bull. This method was used by the Eastern emperors from Justinian onwards and was later adopted by the popes. Hence, papal documents were often known as "bulls".

In England, Saxon royalty had its seals, consisting of an effigy and the inscription, Edward the Confessor originating the double seal. After the Norman Conquest, with the frequent transfer of landed property and because so few of the laity could write, the custom of sealing documents became general. At first, seals bore just an inscription identifying the owner, but, with the rise of heraldry, the upper classes used a coat of arms as well. Because forgery of a seal was more difficult than of a signature, the use of seals continued long after writing became general. King John could write, but he sealed, not signed, the Magna Carta. Where large numbers of people were parties to an agreement, dense clusters of seals are sometimes found. One early 13th-century example in the Public Record Office, London, has no less than fifty.

13th century English seal from the Public Record Office. It is in the "vesical" shape.

Signet rings were made by engraving the design on gems or metal – gold, silver, latten, brass or steel. Shapes for the clergy and for ladies were often oval or "vesical", i.e. of a shape made by two arcs of a circle, giving a point at each end. Most others were round. The impressions were formed in coloured wax, normally natural dark yellow, red or green, and applied directly on the face of the document, or appended to the deed by a parchment label or silk cord. As an added protection, counter-sealing became common, with two dies, each with its own device.

15th century Royal seal of Elizabeth I of England.

The design of the Royal Seals of England has changed with every sovereign. Monarchs and other people of rank possessed both private and official seals, which they used for different purposes. Until 1884 the Privy Seal authorised the issue of money from the Treasury. The office of Lord Privy Seal still exists in Britain.

After 1520 the combination of seal and signature became universal practice, though not until 1677 were signatures alone made legally necessary on deeds. With increased knowledge of handwriting sealing gradually came to be a mere formality, though in Britain it is still statutory on certain documents.

See also BABYLON; JUSTINIAN; NORMAN KINGS; SAXON; SUMER.

Secession: withdrawal from an allian federation, political or religious organ ation, etc. Two instances may clarify t definition. In 1733 a number of persc deserted the Established Church of Sc land and set up a rival body known as t Secessionist Church. This remained existence until 1847, when it becan merged in the United Presbyteri Church. Perhaps the best known examp gave rise to the American Civil War (separate entry). In 1860–61 the Southe States individually followed South Car ina's example and seceded from the Unic following Abraham Lincoln's election the Presidency (*see* LINCOLN, A.), a formed themselves into the Confeder States. Attempted secession has often to bitter warfare. Recent examples ha been the attempt (1967) of Biafra establish a state independent of Niger and the move of East Pakistan to form t government of Bangladesh, a breakaw from the federal republic of Pakist (1971).

See also BANGLADESH

Security Council: part of the structu of the United Nations Organisation (separate entry). Originally it had elev members: five permanent (China, Fran Russia, Great Britain and USA) and elected by the General Assembly for tw year terms. Since 1965 the number non-permanent members has been creased to ten.

The duty of the Council was to m frequently to deal with emergenc which threatened world peace. But ability to veto any decision of the Coun a power which each of the perman members possesses, has been used ove hundred times by Russia to protect co munist interests. With one exception, Council has acted only in places wh the Great Powers were not directly volved, as in the Congo or Cyprus. T eption was Korea in 1950, when a ıporary Russian "walk-out" from the uncil after a dispute enabled the United tions to send a force against a communist invasion of South Korea.

ecause of these difficulties, since 1950 most important decisions of UNO e been made in the General Assembly, in the Security Council.

lition: commotion and unrest in a e, likely to lead to organised rebellion, stopping short of treason, which ally involves working with the enemy.

gregation: literally, a separation from flock, and hence the separation of a s of persons from the general body.

n early example of this is seen in the ablishment of *ghettos*, in which Jews re compelled to live. In medieval times ncentrated Jewish communities (Jewry, eria, etc; *see* JEWS) were found in many es, though these were not always ause of legal requirements. Later, wever, the segregation was enforced. A etto was established in Rome in 1556, l this precedent was ultimately followed almost all Italian cities. They were also nd in Germany, where they were own as *Judengasse*. The ghettos were losed by walls and gates, which were ked at night. They gradually disbeared during the 19th century with growth of more liberal opinions, ugh they reappeared to some extent the time of World War II.

the United States, following the Civil ar, Washington DC and seventeen thern states established segregated ool systems, under which white and ck children were educated in separate ools. Transport systems were similarly regated. Such restrictions have been ich attacked since the end of World ar II (*see* separate entry). In 1954 the preme Court ruled that segregation in schools was a denial of equality and therefore prohibited by the Fourteenth Amendment. Following this, moves towards integration met with resistance, an example being the Little Rock disturbances from 1957 to 1959. In 1955 a Negro boycott of buses in Montgomery, Alabama, was organised by Martin Luther King as a protest against segregation on buses; this was followed by a Court Order prohibiting such segregation.

In South Africa the word segregation is replaced by apartheid (*see* separate entry), but the basic idea is the same. This again involves separation of the races in public transport, banks, etc., as well as the establishment of native reserves for separate development, such as the Bantustans which were established in the 1960s.

Semitic: adjective denoting a group of languages found among ancient peoples of Western Asia, some of which, in a derived form, continue to this day. The word is sometimes transferred to people speaking such a language, e.g. the Jews (*see* separate entry). It comes from Shem, one of the sons of Noah.

Senate: name given to certain governing and law-making bodies, albeit differing in scope and origin. The term originates in Rome and is derived from a word meaning "elders". The Senate of the Republican era (roughly the last five centuries BC) was, despite certain political checks on its authority, effectively the power which governed the state. Although qualification for membership was earned by holding certain public offices, it was largely an aristocratic and hereditary body, which in the end lost its effectiveness when military leaders began to challenge its authority.

In more recent times, when systems of democratic government gained acceptance in the western world, and where the constitution provided for two houses of representatives, the term "senate" was sometimes given to the upper house, the members of which (senators) generally enjoyed more security of office than those of the lower house. This is the case, for instance, in France and the USA.

The word has also been adopted to denote the governing bodies of certain universities, for instance those of Cambridge and London, and is commonly so used in the USA.

Senegal: republic on the west coast of Africa between Mauritania and Guinea. Formerly a French colony, it elected in November 1958 to remain within the French Community and in 1960 attained independence as a socialist republic under President Léopold Senghor. The capital, Dakar, is a sophisticated city containing a large part of the European population of West Africa. It is an important industrial and trade centre and a focus of educational and research institutions. A railway runs from Dakar to Bamako on the River Niger in Mali, with branches to St Louis and Linguere. The port offers modern facilities for bunker fuelling and the export of groundnuts and phosph ore. At the end of 1980 Senghor reti to be replaced by Abdou Diouf.

Serbia: part of present day Yugosla Its peoples, the Serbs, joined with ot neighbouring Slavs (e.g. Croats and S venes) to form the state of Yugoslavi 1918. The capital of Yugoslavia, Belgra was also the chief city of old Serbia.

A united kingdom of Serbia existed early medieval times, but at a great ba on the Field of Blackbirds in 1389 Turks destroyed its independence. Ea in the 19th century a movement dev oped to free Serbs from the harsh rule the Turks. Two rival Serbian fami began a bitter contest for supremacy. first the Karadjordjevići, who looked Russia for support, gained the up hand; but in 1878, when Serbian indep dence was once again recognised, th opponent, an Obrenovići, became first king, with Austrian support. T rivalry became murderous when the popular Alexander Obrenović and family were assassinated in 1903. Un the new dynasty Serbian ambitions r rapidly. The cry of "Greater Serb

:atened Austria, who still had many bs in her empire, and in 1914 Austria d to use the Sarajevo assassinations to :roy Serbia, thus precipitating World r I (*see* separate entry).

tlement, Act of (1701): English establishing the Hanoverian succes- to the throne. William III had no r, and the death (1700) of the Duke of ucester, last surviving child of Princess ne, left the succession open. Parliament refore passed this Act, settling the suc- ion on Sophia of Hanover (1630–1714) her heirs. Sophia was the grand- ghter of James I of England and the rest Protestant heir. The Act also ex- ded foreigners from all offices and ured judges from arbitrary dismissal.

astopol, Sebastopol: Russian Black port and naval base in the Crimea, with one of the finest anchorages in Europe. In the Crimean War (*see* separate entry) it was evacuated by the Russians after an eleven-month siege which destroyed the fortifications and damaged much of the city. In World War II (*see* separate entry) it withstood another long siege (1941–2) before being taken by the Nazis. It was recaptured by the Russians in 1944.

Workers making mines in an underground factory during siege of 1942.

Seven Wonders of the World: monuments of the ancient world considered unique for their size, beauty or splendour. They have been variously listed, but, according to tradition, were described in the reign of Alexander the Great (*see* separate entry) by two Greek travellers, Antipater of Sidon and Philo of Byzantium. Only the *Pyramids of Egypt* remain today. The other Wonders were:

The Hanging Gardens of Babylon, thought to have been terraced gardens watered by an artificial irrigation system which enabled trees and flowering plants to grow in an arid country. Legend says that Nebuchadnezzar had the gardens made for his Queen.

The Mausoleum, a magnificent tomb erected for King Mausolus by his widow. Designed by Greek architects and sculptors, it stood at Halicarnassus, in Asia Minor.

The Colossus of Rhodes, a gigantic figure dedicated to the sun god Apollo, which

The vanished Wonders of the World, imagined by artists of later generations.

a. Hanging Gardens of Babylon.

b. Mausoleum at Halicarnassus.

c. Temple of Diana at Ephesus.

d. Colossus of Rhodes.

e. Statue of Zeus at Olympia.

f. Pharos at Alexandria.

·od at the entrance to the harbour of
odes, possibly bestriding it. After fifty ars it fell in an earthquake.

e Temple of Diana at Ephesus, the city ıich saw the riot of silversmiths so vidly described in the Acts of the ostles. The building was destroyed by Goths in the 4th century AD.

e statue of Zeus at Olympia, site of the ympic Games. The statue was of gold d ivory and was created by the Greek ılptor Phidias.

e Pharos at Alexandria, the first light-use. It was a stepped tower 440 feet [134 etres] high, on top of which burned a acon which could be seen far out to sea, brightness intensified by a mirror. The aros survived for over 1,000 years and s finally destroyed in the 14th century ring an earthquake. An alternative is *Palace of Cyrus*, overlaid with gold. n attempted list of Seven Wonders of Middle Ages gives the Colosseum of me, the Catacombs of Alexandria, the eat Wall of China, Stonehenge, the aning Tower of Pisa, the Porcelain wer of Nankin and the Mosque of St phia at Constantinople.

e also EPHESUS; OLYMPIA; PYRAMID, etc.

---

ven Years War (1756–63): war in ıich Prussia and Great Britain fought ıstria, France and later Russia. Causes re the determination of Austria to re-in, and Prussia to keep, Silesia, and ıglo-French colonial and mercantile alry. In spite of some reverses, Frederick of Prussia (*see* separate entry) defended country brilliantly (with victories at ssbach and Leuthen, 1757, Zorndorf, 58, Leignitz and Torgau, 1760), and at Peace of Hubertsburg with Austria, 63, Prussia emerged as a first class wer. The British contribution, apart m victory at Minden, 1759, was mainly val and colonial (battles of Lagos and ıiberon and capture of Quebec, 1759, Wandewash, 1760), and Britain emerged by the Peace of Paris, 1763, as the principal colonial power.

¶ PARKMAN, F. *The Seven Years War*. 1968

Seventeenth century: the years 1601–1700. Perhaps the most remarkable feature of the 17th century, because it was world-wide, was the establishment of the modern states system, with more or less permanent boundaries. This occurred not only in Europe, where the treaties of Westphalia, 1648, and the Pyrenees, 1659, established national frontiers which, with comparatively minor alterations, lasted until the 20th century (though certain debatable lands changed hands from time to time); but also in the Far East where China under the Manchu dynasty, starting with Li Tzu Ch'eng in 1644, became a centralised and firmly ruled Empire, and where in Japan of the Tokugawa period, from about 1600, arbitrary centralised government under a "Shogun" was developed and the expulsion first of Christianity, after the Shimabara revolt, 1637, and then of all foreigners, left Japan a closed country.

With the establishment of boundaries came also the distinctive character and importance of various states. Brandenburg-Prussia emerged from the Thirty Years War as the most powerful state of northern Germany and moved, under the Great Elector, Frederick William I (1640–88), towards that parity with Austria

Thirty Years War: The Surrender of Breda *painted by Velasquez.*

achieved by Frederick the Great; the Austrian Habsburgs, though still powerful as Archdukes of Austria, were Holy Roman Emperors little more than in name. France, emerging from the welter of her religious wars, became, under the guidance of Henry IV, the two great Cardinals, Richelieu and Mazarin, and Louis XIV, the most powerful nation in Europe, eclipsing Spain which entered a long period of decline; the Turks, although the reforms of the Kiuprili "dynasty" of Grand Viziers from 1656 made them for a time formidable, suffered a long series of incompetent Sultans who brought about a shrinking empire; Russia, under the successors of the first Romanov, Michael (1612), gradually established itself as a European power, winning territory under Peter the Great from the Turks at the Treaty of Carlowitz, 1699, and Baltic lands from the Swedes at Nystadt, 1720. Sweden, after a period of expansion (which she had not the economic resources to support) under the Vasa kings, culminating in Gustavus Adolphus, declined from the position of a first class power, in spite of the meteoric campaigns of Charles XII (1697–1718).

The century saw also the establishment in most countries of a despotic form of government, and the decline, except in Great Britain and Holland, of representative institutions. In the East government had always been despotic, but the Manchus in China, the Shoguns in Japan and the Great Moguls in India made despotism really effective. The same can be said of the Bourbons in France where, after 1614, the States General did not meet for 175 years. And although, in Germany, the Emperor's attempt to regain effective control was finally defeated in the Thirty Years War, every one of the hundreds of individual states which made up "the Empire" was despotically ruled. Administrative reforms in Prussia and Russia only
left the central authority more effectiv
despotic, and in countries where this v
not so, such as Poland, there was anarc
The attempt of the Stuarts to operat
despotic system in England was defeat
perhaps fundamentally because Brita
insular position had meant that kings l
never needed to keep a standing army

During the 17th century religion v
displaced by economics and politics as
motive force in national and internatio
policy. Though Spain continued duri
the first half of the century to supp
Roman Catholicism wherever it seen
to be threatened, in other countries d
velopments which appeared to be religi
in character often had fundamentally d
ferent motives. The Whigs who resis
the Catholic policy of James II were rea
resisting his attack on the political pov
they had become accustomed to, a
which was the condition of their econor
prosperity: they merely used the rallyi
cry of "No Popery!" to gain popular su
port. And though Louis XIV was perso
ally a Roman Catholic he quarrelled w
the Pope, and his revocation of the Ed
of Nantes (1685) was as much to emph
sise his personal power as to serve
religion. The Thirty Years War (1618–4
appeared to have a religious charact
but, though the Emperor was backed
counter-Reformation forces, his main ai
was to re-establish his imperial authorit
and the treaties of Westphalia which end
the wars acknowledged the existence
Calvinism as well as Lutheranism, and
some states a practical toleration did d
velop. Gustavus Adolphus, "the knigh
errant of Protestantism", was probal
moved as much by Swedish ambition
by religion; and modern research h
shown that even the stern puritans of t
English revolution had an often unrealis
economic motive for their resistance
the Crown.

It was a century of expanding Europe

stavius Adolphus "the knight-errant of protes-tism" in 1632.

lonisation and trade, with consequent ernational friction which led some-nes to war, as between English and utch. The English and Dutch East India ompanies were founded at the begin-ng of the century, the French somewhat er. The first permanent English colony the North American continent, Vir-nia, was settled in 1607, and there were even more by 1700. Champlain first sited Canada and explored the St wrence in 1603: he was followed by a ccession of French explorers, and, after 32, the struggling "New France" be-me firmly established, backed by Riche-u. European traders were active all over e world, introducing new commodities ch as tea and tobacco to their home untries, and beginning the "western-ation" of foreign lands which has so ofoundly influenced their development. ast, but not least important, this was e century of the "Scientific Revolution", hen the freedom of thought promoted the Renaissance began to bear fruit; hen men like Galileo and Harvey, ewton and Descartes upset the centuries-d systems of thought and belief, and odies like the English Royal Society and e French *Académie des Sciences* were in-estigating every branch of science and athematics, astronomy and medicine, nd were developing new systems of philosophy. In politics, economics, science, religion and philosophy, the 17th century foreshadowed the development of the modern world.

¶ CLARK, SIR GEORGE. *The Seventeenth Century.* 1947; PENNINGTON, D. H. *Seventeenth Century Europe.* 1970

See also individual entries.

Seward, William Henry (1801–72): American statesman and colleague of Abraham Lincoln (*see* separate entry). After a distinguished career as a lawyer he entered politics. In his various appointments he showed himself a humane and tolerant administrator and was one of the most powerful political opponents of slavery. Twice an unsuccessful candidate for the presidency himself, he was appointed Secretary of State by Lincoln in 1860. In Lincoln's early days, Seward, as the much more experienced public figure, strove to impose his will on the cabinet; then, coming to recognise Lincoln's personality and qualities, served him loyally and gave great service to the nation, not the least of his achievements being the purchase of Alaska from Russia in 1867.

Shackleton, Sir Ernest Henry (1874–1922): British Antarctic explorer. In 1908–09, in the *Nimrod*, he commanded an expedition that reached a point about 97 miles [156 kilometres] from the South Pole. During an attempt to cross the Antarctic continent, 1914–16, Shackleton's ship *Endurance* was crushed in the ice and abandoned. He reached uninhabited Elephant Island using boats and sledges. Shackleton, with five companions, then made an epic 800-mile [1,280 kilometres] open boat voyage to South Georgia to obtain help. He died during a fourth Antarctic expedition.

¶ ALBERT, M. H. *The Long White Road.* 1960; LANSING, ALFRED. *Shackleton's Valiant Voyage.* 1963

See also POLAR EXPLORATION.

Shadow Cabinet: term invented by the British Press after the parliamentary election of 1929 to describe a body of advisers selected by a Leader of the Opposition. At first there was no precise allocation of duties to its members, but the Labour Opposition between 1951 and 1964 appointed shadow Ministers, and this example has been followed by subsequent Oppositions.

Shaftesbury, Anthony Ashley Cooper, seventh Earl of (1801–85): British social reformer and philanthropist. Lord Shaftesbury was horrified at the desperate conditions in which homeless children lived in the London slums of the early 19th century. He influenced Parliament to pass laws which improved their lot and with his money founded *Shaftesbury Homes* where orphans could be trained to earn a living. He was also active in the causes of lunatics, chimney sweeps, juvenile offenders and the housing of the poor. Of particular importance were the laws he was successful in forcing through parliament limiting the hours women and children might work in factories.

¶ FANCOURT, M. ST J. *The People's Earl.* 1962

Lord Shaftesbury.

Shah Jahan, Jehan (*c.* 1592–1666): t fifth Mogul Emperor. Ruling from 16 to 1658, when he was imprisoned by his son, he brought Mogul power to greatest point, exerting control even ov the Deccan princes. A great patron Indian architecture, he was responsil for the Taj Mahal and the Pearl Mosq at Agra.

See also MOGUL.

Shakespeare, William (1564–1616 England's, and the world's, greatest pc and dramatist. Despite his pre-eminenc little is known for certain about hi There are even groups of people wl declare that "Shakespeare's" works we written by a different person altogeth the two most popular candidates bei Francis Bacon (1561–1626; *see* separa entry) and the seventeenth Earl of Oxfo (1550–1604).

Leaving such controversies aside, it c be stated that Shakespeare, the son of glover, was born at Stratford-on-Avon, Warwickshire town which has become shrine to his memory. In 1582 Shakespea married Anne Hathaway, of Shotter by whom he had three children. After h rriage he went to London where he :ame an actor and achieved fame as :t and dramatist. He earned enough to y a fine house at Stratford, New Place, which he eventually retired. He is ried in Stratford Church. His birth-ce, Anne Hathaway's Cottage and w Place are among the buildings ociated with him that have survived. nakespeare's plays fall into three main oups: the Histories (e.g. *King John, hard II, Henry V*); the Comedies (e.g. *ich Ado About Nothing, A Midsummer ght's Dream, The Taming of the Shrew*); d the Tragedies (e.g. *Macbeth*, *Hamlet*, *ng Lear*). They were written over the riod approximately 1590–1613. Shake-:are also wrote several long poems and 4 sonnets. The plays were first pub-ied together in 1623 in a volume gen-

ally known as the First Folio. It is one of e most valuable books in the world and a the rare occasions when one is offered r sale it makes many thousands of ounds. Most copies are in the USA, the eatest collection being the Folger nakespeare Library, Washington, DC.

BURTON, H. M. *Shakespeare and His Plays.* 1958; AINES, CHARLES. *William Shakespeare and His 'ays.* 1971

Shanghai: China's greatest seaport, near the mouth of the Yangtze River, with an estimated population of 11,859,700 in 1982. It was little more than a small fishing town until the 1840s when, as one of the five "Treaty Ports", it was opened to foreign trade by the treaty of Nanking (1842). International settlements were established in Shanghai by Britain, France and the USA, the British and American settlements being merged in 1863 as the International Settlement, In 1896 Japan gained a concession in Shanghai, which was a scene of Sino-Japanese conflict in 1932 and 1937 (*see* separate entry). In 1943 Britain and USA restored the International Settlement to Chinese rule. Under Communist rule (*see* COMMUNISM) from 1949, foreigners were excluded but the port has remained busy and important.

Shaw, **George Bernard** (1856–1950): critic, novelist and playwright. Born in Dublin, he lived there until he was twenty, when he went to London to earn his living as a writer. He made little mark with his early novels but became known for his brilliant public speaking on socialism and for his criticisms of art, music and drama. When, after some years, his first plays were acted it became clear that a new and original playwright had arrived. In the course of a long life, he wrote over

fifty plays, of which perhaps *St Joan*, *Major Barbara* (*see* SALVATION ARMY), *Man and Superman*, *Back to Methuselah* and *Heartbreak House* are the best known. In all his plays he used the stage to expound his views on politics, religion, war, economics and other subjects. He was awarded the Nobel prize for literature in 1925.

¶ WARD, A. C. *Bernard Shaw*. 1951

Sheridan, **Philip Henry** (1831–88): American soldier and Union general in the American Civil War (*see* separate entry). His ability and daring were recognised by General Grant (*see* separate entry), who, when he was appointed lieutenant-general of the Union forces in 1864, placed Sheridan in charge of the cavalry, in which capacity he showed himself probably the best leader on the Union side. In a series of subsequent high commands he carried out a number of successful campaigns in which he showed courage combined with great tactical ability and a rare quality of leadership which made him a popular figure with his troops. One of his exploits was "Sheridan's Ride" – a 20-mile [32 kilometres] dash to meet his troops fleeing from the Confederate General Early at Cedar Creek, ending with his rallying cry, "We must face the other way!" and turning defeat into victory. It was Sheridan's decisive turning of Lee's flank in April 1865 that forced the latter's retreat to Appomattox, Virginia, where he surrendered to General Grant.

Sheriff: literally, shire reeve, the chief administrative officer of a district or county. According to the British legal historian Maitland the whole history of English justice and police might be brought under the single heading of "The Decline and Fall of the Sheriff".

For a comparatively brief period after the Norman Conquest in England the sheriff became virtual ruler of the count He was chief accountant to the Ro Exchequer, the leader of the *posse comi tus* (a force raised to suppress riots, et and the chief police, military and exe tive officer. The king could by writ "Justicies" direct him to hear any p except one relating to land. From t position of power he has descended importance in England until today position is a somewhat expensive a empty honour, most of the survivi legal duties being performed by an und sheriff.

Criminal justice was largely taken out his hands by the Assizes of Clarend (1166) and Northampton (1196), a passed into the hands of the royal justic Magna Carta (1215; *see* separate entr and the rise of Justices of the Peace furth reduced his power. His civil jurisdicti declined following the Statute of Glou ester, 1278. With the appointment Lords Lieutenant in Mary's reign h military powers ceased, while his fisc (financial) powers had long since declin with the growth of forms of taxation which he had no part, and his attendan at the Exchequer was no longer necessar

In Scotland the office of sheriff still r tains administrative and judicial function The country is divided into fifteen sheri doms. The sheriff acts as returning offic in parliamentary elections within his are he also is one of the judges of the Sheriff Court, which has a wide local jurisdictio both civil and criminal.

In the United States the office of sheri is in most cases elective. In rural area acting as an agent of the state, he is th law enforcement officer, with a wid jurisdiction over most crimes and mis demeanours, but his importance is declin ing as law enforcement tends to becom more the concern of the state or Feder authority. The formation of the sheriff posse, so familiar in "western" films an ries, is an interesting linguistic survival the English medieval *posse comitatus*.

erman, William Tecumseh (1820–): American soldier and Union general the American Civil War (*see* separate try). In his early years he combined ldiering with banking and the study of w. In the Civil War he rose to command rst the army of Tennessee, then the ilitary division of the Mississippi, numering in all 100,000 men. With this force carried out the invasion of Georgia, cluding the famous "March to the Sea", om Atlanta to Savannah. As a result of e campaign, a large section of the onfederate forces surrendered.

hinto: ancient native religion of Japan, om Chinese *chin tao*, the way of the ods. Its chief features are the worship of ature, national heroes and family ancesors. It also involved belief in the divinity f the emperor, a claim renounced by the present ruler Hirohito (b. 1901) in 1946. Unlike most religions, it claims no historical founder.

hinto shrine at Nikko, Japan.

Ship of the line: ship sturdy and well armed enough to take her place in a line of battle. The broadside of heavy guns, first used in the battle off Shoreham, England, in 1545, was seen by 1665 to require a line-ahead formation. Such ships ruled the sea until the days of mine and torpedo. Three-deckers of 100 guns served as flagships, but the main ships of the line were the Third Rates carrying 74 guns on two decks. They cost some £60,000, displaced 1,400 tons [1,422 tonnes] and carried 650 men. The last of them, HMS *Defiance*, 1861, was little larger than the *Sovereign of the Seas* built for the Ship-money fleet in 1637. Though the ships were traditionally built of English oak, the shortage of home-grown timber eventually brought about a much more cosmopolitan product. In the words of R. G. Albion (*Forests and Sea Power*), "her mainmast came from the forests of Maine, her topmast from the Ukraine, her small spars from the mountains of Norway, her planking was floated down the Vistula to Dantzig, and her curved frames came from the hedgerows of Sussex".

HMS Canopus, *1796, of 80 guns.*

Shipbuilding: the science of shipbuilding, though of immense age, is barely documented before the 16th century. The functional shape of the ship and its general outline have been known since the earliest times. The basic tools of the shipbuilder in wood, the saw, adze, chisel and drill, have been found in Egyptian tombs dating from about 2000 BC. The Viking burial ships and remains of trading vessels excavated in northern Europe provide information on ship construction of the early centuries AD. Though they had appeared earlier, towards the end of the 15th century larger vessels carrying three masts such as the Flemish carracks were becoming common. Fortunately the Renaissance artists were able to portray these vessels with considerable accuracy including details of their construction.

Shipbuilding in the 14th century.

Early in the 16th century Henry VIII (1491–1547), king of England 1509–47, built permanent dockyards at Deptford and Woolwich on the River Thames for the construction and repair of his ships. He brought in skilled craftsmen from the shipyards of Genoa and Venice and these, together with the British shipwrights, formed a technical corps well equipped to build the largest type of vessel.

One of the earliest attempts to set down on paper the form of a ship is found in *Fragments of Ancient English Shipwrightry* – preserved at the Pepysian Library, Cam-

Sovereign of the Seas.

bridge, England. It is probably the wo of Mathew Baker, master shipwrigl and written about 1585. The manuscri contains plans, elevations and sections o number of ships. One of the earlie names associated with English shipbuil ing is that of Pett. Phineas Pett, born 1570, designed Charles I's great ship t *Sovereign of the Seas*, 1,522 tons [1,5 tonnes], carrying 100 guns. His son Pet supervised the building at Woolwi dockyard and launched the ship there 1637. In America the early settlers in Ne England launched their first ship in 163 By the 18th century more than a third British merchant ships were being built American yards.

Comprehensive textbooks on the buil ing of ships began to appear at the end the 17th century, and the practice making scale models of important vesse was introduced. Draughts or plans ships were produced by the master ship

Shipbuilding in the 17th century.

ights before building. The British lmiralty collection of draughts has sur- ved almost intact from about 1700 and ·ms a unique record of the shape and velopment of warships.

)uring the 18th century the heavy mand for ships both for trade and war rposes led to a considerable expansion the shipbuilding industry both in itain and in the USA. In addition to the vernment dockyards, private shipyards ge and small were established in rivers, uaries and seaports. The three main quirements were a sheltered position, ficient water for launching and easy cess to the forests for timber. Some of smaller shipyards were merely a aring in the forest with one or more pways running down to the water. ude scaffolding was set up. Saw pits, ns for steaming timbers, small furnaces r iron work, sheds for keeping the tools, ch, tar, oakum, etc., were set up nearby. is not surprising that, as a result of this pansion of the industry, supplies of oak nber were becoming rapidly depleted. n example of the amount of timber re- uired to build a 74-gun ship in 1781 is ven by Henry Adams, shipbuilder, at ickler's Hard on the Beaulieu River, ampshire, England. His estimate was ooo oaks and this would deplete an area about forty acres [sixteen hectares].

Before building, the shipwright and his sistants would go into the forest and lect suitable trees for felling. These ould have to include a considerable nount of naturally curved "grown" or ompass" timber from which the knees, os or frames could be shaped. The nber was roughly cut in the forest and ansported to the shipyard. The keel was d, usually of English elm, and the stem d sternposts scarphed (rejointed) on rward and aft. Next the floor timbers ere laid across the keel and the keelson aced on top and bolted through. The frames were then set up and the ship was allowed to season "in frame" if time permitted. After this the planking was laid using oak pegs or "treenails" as fastenings. Deck beams supported by heavy wooden knees were next fitted across the ship and the decks laid and caulked. The underwater portion of the hull was "graved" with a mixture of tallow, pitch, tar and resin and the ship was ready for launching.

The effects of the Industrial Revolution soon became apparent in the shipbuilding industry. Steam paddle engines were being fitted in ships in 1812 and the screw propeller in 1838. The desperate problem of finding sufficient timber for ships was considerably resolved when iron came into general use as a substitute about 1830. The first large iron passenger vessel driven by a screw propeller was I. K. Brunel's *Great Britain* launched at Bristol, England, in 1843 and now preserved at that port.

With the added strength of iron the designers were able to increase considerably the size of ships. As a result many new shipyards sprang up on rivers and estuaries where there was access to coal and iron. In Britain the greatest concentrations were in the north of England and the lowlands of Scotland. The River Thames was an iron shipbuilding river during the 19th century but declined soon after 1900 owing to its distance from essential mineral supplies. Shipbuilding in iron required the use of heavy machinery, and large steam hammers, rolling mills, drilling and punching machines were installed in the new yards. A new and more varied labour force including platers, riveters, drillers, etc., was also required.

The substitution of steel for iron after about 1875 may be said to have abolished the limiting factor in the size of ships. As a result many shipyards adapted themselves to build vessels of the greater ton-

ROMAN ROUND SHIP
GALLEON
LONG SHIP
CARAVEL
SLOOP
MERCHANT CLIPPER
CARRACK
FRIGATE
SHIP OF THE LINE
GALLEY
CORVETTE
DESTROYER
ATOMIC SUBMARINE

ge. The period 1890–1914 saw an ormous expansion in the world's merntile and naval fleets. Between 1892 and '94 shipyards in Great Britain produced .8 per cent of the total gross tonnage of e world's merchant ships, but competiɔn from shipyards in Germany, Japan, olland and Italy soon began to be lt.

The shipbuilding industry of the 20th ntury is a highly competitive one. The -called big ship era between the two 'orld Wars produced many large passnger liners, culminating in the *Queen 'izabeth*, formerly 83,673 [85,015] and ɔw, as a result of much modification, ,998 tons [84,330 tonnes], and launched ı the Scottish river Clyde in 1938. In ly 1969 she was sold at Fort Lauderdale, orida, with the intention of converting r to a floating hotel and convention ntre. Liners have not exceeded this tonıge but oil tankers are by far the largest ips of modern times.

HARDY, A. C. and TYRRELL, E. *Shipbuilding: backɔund to a great industry*. 1964

e also individual entries.

---

hips, Types of: the word "ship" in its roadest sense can be used to refer to any pe of seagoing vessel propelled by sails mechanical means. The specific defiition "a three or more masted vessel ith bowsprit, square rigged on all masts" applicable only to the sailing ship.

Long ships and round ships. The countries f the Mediterranean supply us with the ırliest known information about ships. he people of Crete by about 2000 BC had essels which fell into two distinct catgories. Their "long ships" with fine nes and ram bow were the fighting ıips propelled by oars, while the "round ıips" were the heavier type of craft uilt mainly for sailing. This marked ifference in the fighting and trading essels, though not apparent in Egyptian ships, can be traced through Greek and Roman vessels almost to the end of the wooden ship era. Two fine examples of long ships are the 9th-century Viking ships (*see* VIKINGS) preserved at Oslo, Norway. These are the Gokstad and Oseberg ships with their long, open, clinker-built hulls. They were double ended with high stem and stern posts and propelled by oars but a large square sail was carried in addition.

2. *Caravel*. A small vessel usually three-masted with lateen sails, the largest forward, originating in Portugal in the 15th century. One of Columbus's ships the *Nina* was a caravel, though square sails were fitted during the 1492 voyage. The *Santa Maria*, often erroneously referred to as a caravel, was a three-masted square rigged ship.

3. *Carrack*. The large 15th-century three-masted sailing vessel with a forecastle projecting far over the stem. Originating in the Mediterranean as a trading vessel it soon became known over most of Europe. The carrack usually carried large square sails on the fore and main masts and a lateen sail on the mizzen. This was to be the basic pattern for the full rigged sailing ship that was to remain the same in many essentials for nearly 400 years.

4. *Galley*. Originally a seagoing vessel propelled by oars. The descendants of the great war galleys of the Greeks and Romans with their many tiers of oars continued in the Mediterranean until the end of the 18th century. By the 15th century the biremes and triremes, etc., gave way to single decked vessels using sails in addition to oars. They were usually manned by slaves or criminals. They could be highly manoeuvrable when under oars and were the standing fighting vessels of the Mediterranean. In the Battle of Lepanto (*see* separate entry and *colour section*) in 1571 more than 200 galleys were engaged on both sides. Fighting was mainly hand to hand but in the 16th century guns began to be carried.

5. *Galleon*. This was usually a four-masted vessel built to some extent on the lines of the galley but higher out of the water and with a long beakhead extending forward. The galleon was a true man-of-war with cannon carried on decks within the ship. Spain is usually associated with the galleon but by the mid-16th century this type was to be found in most European countries. The Spaniards used their large galleons of the 17th and 18th centuries for trading with their colonies in America.

6. *Galleass*. A combination of the galleon and galley, this 16th-century war vessel was usually three- or four-masted but carried a large number of oars in addition to sails. The galleass was extensively used by Mediterranean peoples, particularly the Venetians, but it disappeared from northern Europe after about 1600.

7. *Ship of the line*. This term was applied to the larger class of sailing warship carrying not less than fifty guns. From the mid-17th century onwards the great fleets of Europe were mainly organised in line ahead for fighting purposes and only the more heavily armed ships could take their place in the "line". The modern counterpart is the all big gun battleship. (*See* separate entry.)

8. *Frigate*. The origin of the term is u certain but it was used in the 17th centu to describe a wide variety of craft fro small Mediterranean oared vessels to t great English three decker *Naseby*. It possible that the word was original applied to the shape rather than to a ty or class of ship. The familiar frigate of t 18th century was a small, fast, thre masted vessel of twenty-four to thirt two guns. It had two decks but guns we carried only on the upper deck. Previous the small two decker had a few guns c the lower deck but these were quite us less in rough weather. Most navies carri a number of frigates. They were used f reconnaissance work and maintained vit

signal links with the commander-ir chief afloat. They were virtually th "eyes" of the fleet and as such were greatl in demand during wartime. They wer also extensively used for convoy escor work. The name still applied to such ves sels until well into the steam era bu lapsed during the 1880s when a ver much larger version was reclassified as "cruiser". The term was reintroduced i 1943 to describe the convoy escort vesse specifically armed against the U-boat Frigates in large numbers are now in ser vice in the navies of the world arme with all the sophisticated equipment fo defence and attack in the nuclear age.

Sloop. There are two meanings to this ɔrd. One applies to the rig of a small ıgle-masted vessel. The other is con- rned with a class of small ship rating xt below the frigate. The 18th-century ɔop-of-war was a single-decked vessel rrying about eighteen guns. It was :her three-masted and known as a ship- ɔop or two-masted and known as a ig-sloop. Escorting convoys was one of e functions of these little vessels, which ɔntinued into the steam age as paddle ıd screw sloops respectively. During the vo world wars convoy protection was ;ain the main task. After 1945 the sloop as reclassified as a frigate.

). *Cruiser*. The *Gentleman's Dictionary* of 705 states "Cruisers are small men-of- ar made use of, to and fro, in the hannel and elsewhere to secure our Ierchant Ships from the enemy's small igates and privateers. They are generally ıose that sail well and are therefore ɔmmonly well manned." The word ·uiser, certainly used as early as the 17th :ntury, was derived from the verb "to :uise". Any small craft, from cutters to ıree-masted sloops, could be termed ruisers. The modern vessel substantively assified as a cruiser appeared during the 880s. This can be described as a self- ıfficient heavily armed fighting ship of igh speed and able to cruise the oceans ɔr considerable distances without refuel- ng. Its main wartime function is to patrol ıe ocean trade routes, giving protection ɔ the Merchant Navies.

11. *Corvette*. This was originally a French term for a small ship with upper deck armaments similar to the British ship-rigged sloop of the 18th century. Very few sailing corvettes were included in the British navy, but during the 1860s and 1870s many of the steam variety were built and the term was extended to include vessels with main deck guns. These were small-to-medium sized warships but they never figured in any fleet action. The term lapsed with the introduction of the cruiser in the 1880s. At the beginning of World War II a new type of corvette was introduced into the British navy for convoy escort work. This was the famous Flower class based on the design of a whale catcher. Numbers of these seaworthy little craft were turned out to give anti-submarine protection to convoys. They eventually proved too small for their tasks and were superseded by the frigate.

12. *Destroyer*, originally termed torpedo-boat-destroyer. The menace of the fast torpedo carrying craft of the 1890s necessitated the building of vessels larger, faster and more powerfully armed than the craft they were to destroy. The recently invented steam turbine gave them the necessary high speed and, with their slim lines, they became the highly manoeuvrable vessel turned out in large numbers for the navies of the world. Today they are armed with guns, torpedoes and guided missiles, and can take offensive action as well as acting as main fleet and convoy escorts.

13. *Submarine*. This is a submersible warship armed with torpedoes, capable of navigating under water. Although invented towards the end of the 19th century the submarine is essentially a 20th-century vessel and now ranks as the world's most formidable warship, atomic powered and armed with Polaris missiles. (*See* separate entry.)

14. *Merchant ship*. The merchant ship, designed for cargo and passenger-carrying purposes, developed on much the same lines as the warship until the 19th century. By about 1840 the need for speed brought about a change and a much finer type of hull was designed. This was the birth of the clipper ship (*see* separate entry). The introduction of steam power at about the same time saw the evolution of the screw-propelled merchant ship.

15. *Aircraft carrier*. With the greatly increased use of aircraft in modern warfare has come the development of warships with specially constructed decks to carry them for operational purposes. In 1914 the British Government fitted a tramp steamer, renamed the *Ark Royal*, with a flying-off deck and two cranes to hoist seaplanes on board. From such small beginnings have come such giants as the atomic powered USS *Enterprise*, of 85,350 tons [86,720 tonnes] and a complement of 100 aircraft using a 4½ acre [1·82 hectare] flight deck; and the even larger USS *Eisenhower* approved in the 1969–70 Defence budget.

¶ LANDSTROM, BJORN. *The Ship*. 1961

Shorthand: method of speedy writing by substituting contractions or arbitrary signs for letters, words, syllables and sounds. It is also known as stenography.

The ancient Greeks appear to have had a shorthand system as early as the 4th century BC, but the first one of which we have accurate knowledge is that devised by Marcus Tullius Tiro, a friend of Cicero (*c*. 60 BC). Plutarch tells us that the speeches made in the Roman Senate at the time of the Cataline conspiracy were recorded verbatim by various *notarii* using this system.

Modern shorthand originated in England with the publication in 1588 of Bright's *Characterie: an Arte of Shorte, Swifte and Secrete Writing by Character*. This was followed in 1602 by *The Arte of Sten graphie* by John Willis. This had a cor plete alphabet, but also used dots plac near the consonants to represent vowe Thomas Shelton some thirty years lat used signs to denote two or more co sonants, such as ng, sh, th. Perhaps t best claim to fame of Shelton's system that it was used by Samuel Pepys (s separate entry) in his *Diary* (1659–6 which remained undeciphered until 182

These systems were orthographic alphabetic. The idea of a phonetic syste came later, in the second half of the 18 century. One of the best known systen appeared in 1837, when Isaac Pitm (1813–97) published his *Stenograph Sound Hand*. This uses straight lines ar simple curves to represent consonant while vowels are represented by a dot or dash, the position of which indicates t particular vowel. On this system, not a strokes are of even thickness, as oppose to "light-line" systems, where no shadin or thickening of the characters is use Perhaps the best known of these is th Gregg system, widely used in the Unite States.

See also HANDWRITING.

Siberia: part of the USSR east of th Urals and north of the central Asia republics. Once the Tatar Khanate Sibir, it passed gradually under Russia rule from the 16th century. Military civil and penal settlements were made i the 18th and 19th centuries. A trans Siberian railway was constructed 1891 1900. Siberia was the scene of fightin after World War I, anti-Soviet Russia forces under Admiral Kolchak bein supported by a Czechoslovak Legion an by an American, British, French an Japanese expeditionary force in Easter Siberia. Kolchak was defeated and sho in 1920 and his allies withdrew. Thoug its resources are not yet fully known o

'he main street of Salikhard, Siberia, centre of indeer breeding.

eveloped Siberia plays an important art in the economy of the USSR and is ch in coal, iron and other minerals, with ie western lowlands producing oil and as.

icily: island off south-western Italy, ow an autonomous area of Italy. Settle-ient is recorded before 1000 BC, and the land afterwards became a prosperous ireek colony (9th – 5th centuries BC) vith Syracuse as the most important own. Its subsequent troubled history in-luded occupation by Carthaginians, Romans (for whom it was a main source f corn supplies), Vandals, Saracens and Normans. In 1282, following the islanders' evolt (known as the Sicilian Vespers) gainst Charles Duke of Anjou, a French-nan who was their ruler at the time, icily was temporarily joined to Aragon vhose king, Pedro III, had come to its ielp. After a later long period of domi-ation by Spain, a more settled time began n 1860 when Garibaldi (*see* separate ntry) united Sicily to the kingdom of taly. The complexity of Sicilian history s increased by the existence for a long eriod of the Kingdom of the Two Sicilies, a state made up of the island and he southern portion of Italy.

See ITALY for map.

See also MAFIA.

Sidney, Sir Philip (1554–86): English poet, diplomat and soldier, remembered above all as the soul of honour and chivalry. His best known works are *Astrophel and Stella*, the *Defence of Poesie*, and *Arcadia*. In 1586 he joined an expedition sent to help the Netherlands in their fight against Spain. In an attack on Zutphen Sidney who, recklessly but characteristically, had taken off his leg-armour so as to put himself on equal terms with a friend who wore none, was wounded in the leg. Offered some water, he handed it instead to a dying soldier with the famous words: "Thy necessity is yet greater than mine." Sidney died of his wounds twenty-six days later.

¶ In UNSTEAD, R. J. *Discoverers and Adventurers.* 1965

Sieges: operations, often protracted, to reduce fortified positions by starvation and bombardment. They began as soon as man fortified his settlements. The very early siege of Troy showed many characteristics of siege warfare – the failure to take the city by storm at the start; the besiegers wearying and falling out; the defenders sallying to the Greeks' ships; the attempt to terrorise the citizens by dragging the body of Hector before the walls; the final capture of the city by stratagem (the wooden horse). The great sieges have been of positions so vital that they must be held at all costs: capital cities – Constantinople in 1453, Vienna in 1683; river-crossings – Orleans in 1428; naval bases – Gibraltar in 1782, Sebastopol in 1854–55, Port Arthur in 1904. Often sieges, not battles, have been the decisive events: Charles V abdicated partly because he failed to take Metz in 1553; the Dutch revolt might have collapsed had Leyden fallen in 1574; "Peace lies within the walls of Maastricht", said Marshal de Saxe and, when he took it, France gained their terms at Aix-la-Chapelle in 1748.

When fortifications are stronger than missile weapons, or when generals are reluctant to risk battle, sieges dominate warfare. In the First Crusade, the great events were the capture of Antioch by the help of a traitor in 1098, and of Jerusalem, by siege-towers, in 1099. By 1400 artillery was dominating fortification, notably the guns of the Bureau brothers who blasted the English out of France; but by 1520 engineers had developed improved fortresses with guns mounted in bastions to cover every wall-face, and with water-filled ditches proof against mining. The Dutch revolt of 1572–1647 was decided by sieges: towns secure behind water defences commanded the water routes by which alone siege guns could be moved, and neither the Duke of Alva nor Maurice of Nassau liked open warfare. The greater generals of Louis XIV's time, Turenne and Marlborough, preferred open warfare but could rarely find an opponent prepared to meet them. More typical of the age w
Sebastian de Vauban, the greatest exp
nent of siege warfare both in attack an
defence. In the 18th century roads an
guns improved, and the great genera
avoided sieges: Frederick the Great wou
not defend even his capital and relied o
keeping his field army intact; Napoleo
struck at his enemies' field armies; Ts
Alexander refused to be trapped
Moscow. Since 1860 artillery has grow
in destructive power, and the bomber an
missile have appeared, but some areas ar
so vital that they must still be defende

Sieges make great demands on th
morale of attacker and defender. Mont
of watching and digging test the deter
mination of the attacker: Richelieu at
Rochelle in 1628 and Wolfe at Quebec i
1759 stood this test. Troops who too
walls by storm expected the reward o
pillage, and the laws of war allowed i
Defenders, encumbered by women an
children, eating rats and boiled harnes

Roman assault towers being rolled into position.

hreatened by epidemic or massacre, need rm leadership, and great leaders have merged under siege. La Valette inspired he knights of Malta to repel the Turks in 565; Adrian van der Werff shamed the itizens of Leyden by offering his right rm for their sustenance; Baden-Powell nobilised the boys of Mafeking (in the Boer War) to bear a part in its defence.

BELFIELD, E. M. G. *Sieges.* 1967; JEFFREYS, STEVEN. *Medieval Siege.* 1973

ee also CONSTANTINOPLE; CHARLES V; CRUSADES; FREDERICK THE GREAT; NAPOLEON I; RICHELIEU.

---

iege weapons: devices for breaking own the defences of besieged towns and ortresses. Siege weapons of great variety nd ingenuity were in use in warfare from arly times for demolishing walls and for hrowing heavy stones, flaming projectes and other missiles into enemy strongolds. The earliest and simplest was the attering ram, either manhandled or lung from a heavy protective framework. Siege engines dating from Roman and Greek times included the catapult, balista, rebuchet and spring engine, each with ndividual mechanical principles. The atapult for throwing small stones developed into the perrier or petrary, which onsisted of a heavy beam, one end being ecured in a huge skein of twisted horseair or sinew which acted as a powerful inge when the beam was pulled backvards. On release a stone weighing forty o sixty pounds [18 to 27 kilogrammes] vas projected from a cup at its extremity.

The balista was really a large cross-bow nounted on a massive wheeled frame. ts mechanism was set by a windlass and it projected four- to six-foot javelins [1.2 to 1.8 metres] a distance of about 450 yards 410 metres]. A variation of this was the rcubalista which incorporated two separate arms fixed in two wound-up skeins of hair or sinew.

The trebuchet was invented in the 12th century, its principal component being an arm up to 50 feet [15m] in length with a sling at one end pivoted about an axis and having a heavy counterpoise at the other end. This could project stones weighing up to 300 pounds [136kg] a distance of 300 yards [274m].

The spring engine, which was probably the least effective of these machines, had a flexible arm so arranged as to strike a bolt or javelin forwards with great violence. Medieval armies were accompanied by special siege trains, bringing along most of the necessary equipment. Some, however, such as scaling ladders and movable wooden towers, were often knocked up on the spot from whatever timber was available. With the development of artillery (*see* separate entry) the use of these primitive devices declined.

Siena: hilltop walled city commanding the road from Tuscany to Rome. Founded by the Etruscans (*see* ETRURIA) in the 13th century it vied with Florence and Pisa as a trading centre for cloth, spices and banking. It was ruled by a bishop until 1186 when Frederick Barbarossa (*see* separate entry) granted municipal rights. It supported the Ghibelline faction, and in 1261 it defeated the Florentines at Montaperto after the protecting shadow of the Virgin Mary had been seen on its walls. Painting in Byzantine style and Gothic architecture flourished there. St Catherine of Siena

The Market Square, Siena.

(1347–80) nursed victims of the Black Death and persuaded the popes to return to Rome in 1377. Weakened by feuds of nobles and townsmen, it surrendered to Charles V in 1555 and was ceded by Spain to the Medici Dukes of Tuscany in 1557 (*see* MEDICI, FAMILY OF). The Palio, the traditional barebacked horse race between the ten wards of the city, is still held annually for the honour of gaining the silk banner.

Sierra Leone: independent state on west African coast, bounded to the north-west to north-east by Guinea, to the south-east by Liberia and to the south-west by its Atlantic coastline. Sierra Leone was so called by the Portuguese navigator Pedro de Sintra (1462) either because the background mountains bore a rough resemblance in shape to a lion or because of the menacing roar of thunder-storms along the mountain ridge. At the time of de Sintra's exploration the area was inhabited by African peoples such as the Temne. The first settlements from outside, apart from early trading posts, were designed by philanthropists seeking to provide a home for runaway slaves and Negroes discharged from the US army and navy after the American War of Independence (*see* separate entry). In 1792 1,100 Negroes were brought from Nova Scotia, and the population was further increased when slavery was declared illegal by the British parliament. Frequent changes in governorship (17 changes in 22 years) made steady development difficult, but ultimately an industrious and self-reliant community was built out of the poor material dumped by outside agencies. Freetown, the present capital, provides the best harbour on the west coast of Africa, and exports include iron ore, diamonds, bauxite, palm kernels, coffee and cocoa. In 1961 Sierra Leone became an independent state within the Commonwealth and the one-hundredth memb of UNO.

See AFRICA for map.

Signalling: the sending of orders intelligence by prearranged signs – visu or aural – quickly and over long distance It is so vital in warfare that it is of gre antiquity. It probably developed first the clear air and wide plains of Asia. shield flashing in the sun told the Persia at Marathon (490 BC) that Athens w empty of troops. Aeschylus wrote th the news of the fall of Troy reache Greece by fire signal, but this story ma originate from the line of signal statio across the Aegean built by the Persia Mardonius in 479 BC. When Alexand sent a patrol to scale the Sogdian Roc (328 BC) with rope and tent-peg, he lear of their success by the waving of whi flags. In Roman times Polybius (204–12 BC) described a method of signalling b flag or torch which could transmit a alphabetical code. In Britain Hadrian Wall was linked to York by a line signal stations, and remains of six roun bases at one of these suggest that an elabor ate code with six columns of smoke w used. Trajan's column shows a sign tower with haycocks and bundles of fag gots at hand.

Europeans were very slow to develo signalling systems: they were outclasse by the Africans with their tom-toms an the Red Indians with their smoke signal

Semaphore arms are suggested b Vegetius (4th century AD). It was not ti the 17th century that they were demon strated to the Royal Society by Rober Hooke (1635–1703), and it was 1799 be fore a line of frames with six shutter relayed messages from Portsmouth an the Nore to the Admiralty. The tactica use of signals in land battles develope even more slowly. Dust or gunsmok made visual signals unreliable, and the di

muel F. B. Morse.

battle drowned the drum and, at times, ?en the trumpet. Most commanders greed with Wellington: "I was always 1 the spot. I saw everything, and did ?erything myself." Verbal messages carried by galloper were used, though their breathless messages were often misunderstood. The Mongols, operating in small mobile detachments, used bells and gongs to communicate, but among Europeans no effective land communications were established until the introduction of telegraphy. Invented by Samuel Morse (1791–1872) it was used in the Crimea and the Indian Mutiny, when the mutineers cursed it as "the wire that strangled us". Visual signals by Morse Code were used by the British in Abyssinia in 1867. By 1904 the Admiralty could send messages by wireless to Gibraltar.

Signalling has played a bigger part in sea warfare. Distances and visibility are greater, despatch vessels less reliable than gallopers, the ships' masts are a ready-made signal frame and there is greater scope for concerted manoeuvre after

he International Code of Signalling, adopted · general use in 1934, and used by all nations sea.

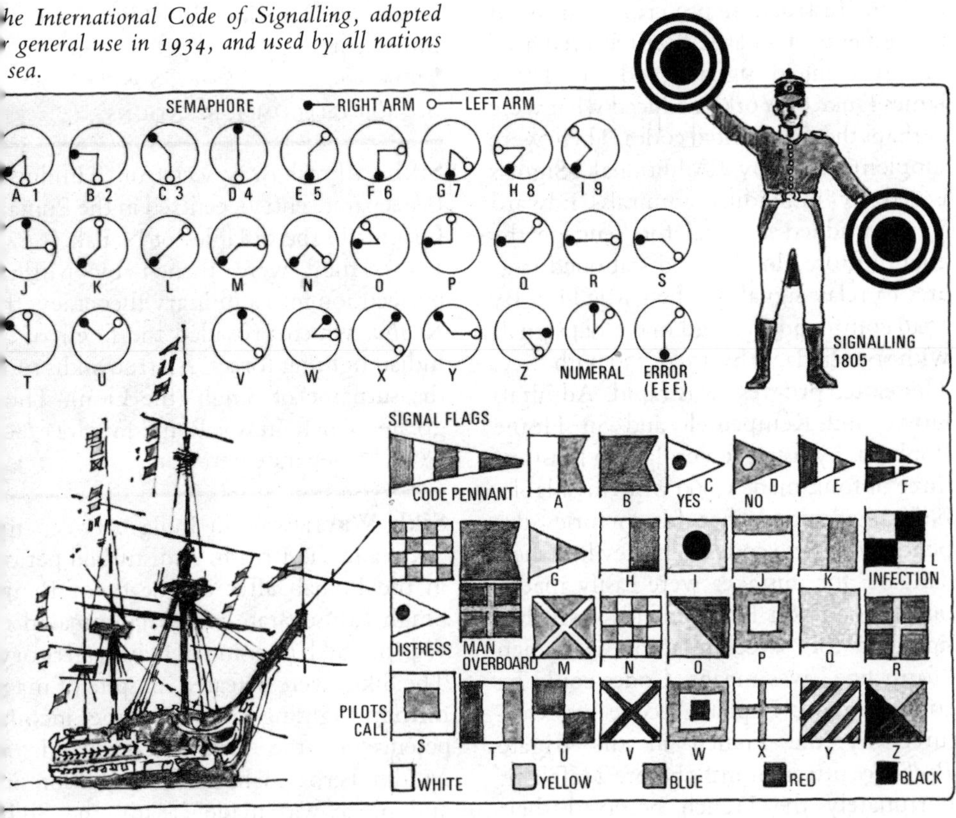

SEMAPHORE — RIGHT ARM — LEFT ARM

A 1, B 2, C 3, D 4, E 5, F 6, G 7, H 8, I 9, J, K, L, M, N, O, P, Q, R, S, T, U, V, W, X, Y, Z, NUMERAL, ERROR (EEE)

SIGNALLING 1805

SIGNAL FLAGS

CODE PENNANT, A, B, YES C, NO D, E, F, G, H, I, J, K, INFECTION L, DISTRESS, MAN OVERBOARD, M, N, O, P, Q, R, PILOTS CALL S, T, U, V, W, X, Y, Z

WHITE, YELLOW, BLUE, RED, BLACK

battle is joined. At Salamis (480 BC) a red cloak on an oar signalled the wheel and advance of the Greek fleet on the Persians. The Byzantine Emperor Leo VI (AD 866–912) wrote that an admiral should use a banner or streamer in a conspicuous position to convey his orders and that all officers should be practised in interpreting the signals. In England King John first demanded the salute at sea in 1201, and the Black Book of Admiralty (1378) listed two signals – for sighting an enemy and for summoning captains to a Council. The Spanish developed a slightly more elaborate code in 1430, using flags by day and lights by night, but there was little progress till the late 17th century, when large professional navies developed. In the Anglo-Dutch wars Robert Blake devised twenty-five signals based on five prominent parts of a ship's rigging. Fighting Instructions prescribing the main movements of a battle fleet required a set of prearranged signals, and in 1172–3 James Duke of York produced what were perhaps the first printed codes. These were supplemented by Additional Signals issued by individual admirals. Edward Vernon added a signal for "engage the enemy more closely" and stationed frigates to relay signals to the battle line. By 1746 commanders could make 144 signals with sixteen flags; by 1780, 330 with fifty. Thereafter progress was rapid, Admirals Howe and Kempenfelt and Sir Home Popham, by using fewer flags in hoists of three or four, made 1,000 words available. Nelson admitted that his victories depended on these codes, but they had their dangers, for mistakes were easily made: on one occasion Kempenfelt's own ship signalled for "weekly accounts" when "form line" was meant. Codes could be compromised: Popham's code was captured by the French in the frigate *Redbridge* fifteen months before Trafalgar. Fortunately the French betrayed their knowledge of it by using it to lure a sh into Toulon. Thereafter code books we bound in lead for easy sinking. T development of wireless made co munications at sea easy, but wirel silence is still needed to elude the enem and the Admiralty is sometimes tempt to radio tactical decisions which would better taken on the spot.

Reference was made at the beginning this article to a shield flashing in the su This could be reckoned an early examp of the heliograph, an apparatus design to send signals by reflecting sunlight fro a movable mirror. Its invention is att buted to Sir Henry Christopher Man (1840–1926), who developed it during h work with the Persian Gulf Telegra department of the Indian Governme As recently as World War II the equi ment was issued to some British troo when an invasion by Hitler seem imminent.

¶ DOWNING, J. G. *The Story of Signalling*. 1967
See also TELECOMMUNICATIONS.

Sikh: a breakaway sect from Hinduis (*see* separate entry), centred in the Punja Originally the disciples of Nanak (146 1538), they were turned by Musli persecution into a military theocracy, th *Khalsa*, which provided the finest of a Indian fighting forces. All true Sikhs too the surname of Singh (the Lion). The greatest chieftain was Ranjit Singh (1780 1839; *see* separate entry).

Sikh Wars: wars in India between th Sikhs and the British. A disturbed perio in the Punjab after the death of Ranj Singh (*see* separate entry) culminated i 1845 in a Sikh invasion of British territory The Sikhs were defeated, in spite of mag nificent fighting and of some incom petence in the British command, a Mudki, Ferozeshah, Aliwal and Sobraon and peace was made (1846), the Sikh

sing Kashmir and territory east of the ıtlej, and accepting a British Resident d garrison at Lahore. In spite of en- ghtened control by Henry Lawrence, rest flared again into fighting in 1848. ord Gough fought a costly action at hilianwala, and finally won a decisive ctory at Gujrat (1849), after which the khs surrendered. The Governor Gen- al, Dalhousie, then annexed the Punjab, hich was settled under Henry and John ıwrence (*see* separate entries).
e INDIA for map.

ilver: precious metal capable of being aped and drawn out without breaking. ancient times silver was associated with e moon goddess because of its pale eam. In the Acts of the Apostles a lively count is given of a riot of the silver- niths of Ephesus, who, since they sold lver images to travellers visiting the mple of Diana, feared that they would se their livelihood if Christianity spread.
Silver ornaments were made long before Paul's day: the metal has been found in mbs dating back to 4000 BC, and the ode of Menes, reputedly the first haraoh, 3500 BC, laid down that "one easure of gold equals in value two-and- -half measures of silver". Silver was nown in Crete, where inlaid silver aggers have been found and one silver ıp almost 4,000 years old. The Egyp- ans knew how to do silver inlay work, nd silver vases have been discovered in truscan tombs in northern Italy. Phoeni- ian traders sometimes carried silver owls. The Greeks had mines at Laurium 1000 BC, and Greek silversmiths were ıuch employed by the Romans, though ıe latter imported most of their supplies f the metal from Spain. The early Christians used silver for making church essels, a tradition still widely followed in ltar furnishings and communion plate. The discovery of America brought vast new sources of supply. It has been calculated that between the years 1493 and 1520 the average annual world production of silver was 1,511,000 ounces [42,836,000 grammes] of fine silver. By 1545–60 this figure had risen to 10,018,000 ounces [284,005,290 grammes].

The addition of lead made silver easier to work, but this gave dishonest smiths an opportunity to add too much of the baser metal, so silver articles were examined by officials who marked them to certify their value. In England these marks, known as assay or hallmarks, were first used in Edward I's reign. They are invaluable in establishing the dates of silver. Early silver articles, especially by famous makers, command prices far in excess of the value of the metal. In 1965, £45,000 was paid in London for a soup tureen, cover and stand made in 1758 for the Empress of Russia. In 1968, also in London, a pair of 1686 silver tankards was sold for £56,000.

In 1982 the world's leading silver producers were Peru, Mexico, the USSR, Canada, the USA and Australia.

¶ TAYLOR, GERALD. *Silver through the Ages.* 1964
See also CHRISTIANITY; PHARAOH; PHOENICIANS.

Simpson, Sir James Young (1811–70): Scottish physician. Simpson was certain that chloroform, first prepared by German chemists in 1831, would prove a successful anaesthetic, but he did not know how much of it could safely be given to a patient. To find out, he administered it to himself in varying quantities and in 1847 published the result of his experiments, which greatly aided the development of painless surgery. He also made important contributions to the knowledge of obstetrics (childbirth).

Singapore: independent republic on a small island at the tip of the Malay Peninsula. Sir Stamford Raffles chose and

annexed it in 1819 as the site of a new British stronghold under the East India Company. In 1826 Singapore was joined with Penang and Malacca to form the Straits Settlements and became, in 1832, their seat of government. In 1867 the Straits Settlements became a crown colony. Trade rapidly expanded in rubber and tin from Malaya and with the Netherlands Indies. In 1922 Singapore became the main British defence base in the Far East. It fell to the Japanese in 1942 but was liberated in 1945. It became independent in 1957, and joined the Federation of Malaysia in 1963. This did not prove successful for Singapore which left the Federation in 1965 though remaining a member of the Commonwealth.
See SARAWAK for map.

Sinn Féin: name (meaning "we ourselves" or "ourselves alone") of an Irish political movement established in 1905. It asserted the right to complete political and economic independence, to be brought about by self-initiated action and not by legislation or negotiation in Britain. After an unsuccessful rising in 1916, Sinn Féin candidates were overwhelmingly successful in southern Ireland in the 1918 general election and met in Dublin as *Dáil Éireann* to form the nucleus of an independent Irish government, which came into effect in 1921, with the six counties of Northern Ireland remaining outside the new Free State. Today the movement survives as a comparatively small extremist group which represents politically the outlawed Irish Republican Army (*see* separate entry).

Sino-Japanese Wars: The first major conflict between Japan and China occurred in 1894–95 and was a battle for supremacy in Korea. By the treaty of Shimonoseki (1895) China acknowledged Korean independence and ceded territory to Japan together with an indemnity an large commercial concessions. China incapacity in this war encouraged tl movements of revolt which ended tl Manchu empire in 1912. In the 192 further conflicts occurred in Manchuri In 1931 Japan seized Mukden and in 19 established the new state of Manchuku Open war began in 1937. Rapid Japane advances captured most ports and cities far west as Hankow, but after the fir two years there was stalemate till 194 and the onset of Japanese defeat in Worl War II. Meanwhile guerrillas had take over wide territories behind the Japane lines and Communists took control of th government of China in 1948.

Sixteenth century: the years 1501 1600. Though it would be absurd t confine the historical development of th 16th century within exact dates, it has flavour and character of its own, particu larly in Europe. Here it was the era whic saw the abandonment of the mediev ideal of a united Christendom and th creation of completely independen sovereign states, not all practising th same brand of Christianity. Spain wa dominant; the work of Ferdinand c Aragon (1479–1516) and his wife Isabell of Castile (1474–1504) in creating a natio from at least five independent states, an the magnificent army trained by "th Great Captain", Gonsalvo de Cordoba led to a climax of Spanish power unde Charles I (1516–56), who became Hol Roman Emperor Charles V in 1519; an signs of decline were not evident unti towards the end of Philip II's reig (1556–98). France fought its first recog nisably national war when Charles VII (1483–98) led his troops into Italy in 1494 In England, after a long period of civi disturbances, Henry VII founded a lastin dynasty in 1485, and Henry VIII em phasised national sovereignty by takin ntrol of the Church (and its finances) d by sweeping Wales into the national stem of administration.

ı Germany and Italy, certainly, moves wards national cohesiveness were either feated, as was Charles V's attempt to ert imperial control, or non-existent, in Italy, which formed the battle ground the great powers, Spain, France and e Empire. But the general feature was e development of strong monarchies d recognisably national states, such as at created by the Vasa dynasty in veden. Portugal, with largely extra-ıropean interests, although she was ab-rbed by Spain in 1580, followed the me course under the remarkable line of vis kings, of whom the most powerful as John III (1521–57). The whole ocess is typified by four young mon-chs who came to the throne early in the ntury: Charles I of Spain (1516–56) mperor from 1519), Francis I of France 515–47), Henry VIII of England (1509-7) and Suleiman I, "the Magnificent", f Turkey (1520–66), under whom the ttoman Empire reached its greatest oint. Further east, though conditions ere different, there are indications of the me kind of movement, with the tablishment of the Mogul dynasty in ıdia by Babar (1526–30) and Akbar 556–1605), and with the work of the ling dynasty in China, which prepared e ground for the centralisation of the lanchus in the next century.

In the West it was the century of the eformation and of religious discord. uther's revolt in 1517, followed by those f Zwingli at Zurich and Calvin at Geneva, caused a final rupture in the ıbric of western Christendom. The doption of the new doctrines by half the rinces of Europe, for political and conomic as well as for religious reasons, nd the attempt of "Counter Reforma-ion" forces to win them back to Roman Catholicism, led to a long period of religious struggles, both within individual states – as in France for most of the second half of the century – and internationally. Charles V failed to recapture Germany as a whole for the old faith, largely, perhaps, because his political enemies, notably Francis I and his ally (from 1530) Suleiman, never allowed him uninterrupted time to do so; Philip II's attack on Elizabeth of England had the nature of a crusade, and its failure helped to confirm the peculiarly national form of Protestantism in the Church of England; and, although the revolt of the Netherlands against Spain, lasting roughly from 1567 to 1609, was prompted by political and economic grievances, before its end it had the character of a struggle between Catholics and Calvinists. There grew out of the religious struggle also a radical reform of the Roman Catholic Church, the creation of new Orders, notably the Jesuits, and the final definition of Catholic doctrine at the Council of Trent (the Tridentine Decrees, 1563). The religious turmoil led also to a remarkable period of theological scholarship, of which Luther's vernacular Bible (which almost standardised the German language), Erasmus's Greek New Testament, and the Spanish Polyglot Bible were the first fruits.

The century witnessed the first great period of European expansion. In 1487 Bartholomew Diaz had rounded the Cape of Good Hope and ten years later Vasco da Gama reached India by that route: Columbus, in an attempt to find a westward route to Cathay, had discovered new lands across the Atlantic in 1492. Eastwards, the Portuguese were the first in the field by the new route, ousting the Arabs from their monopoly of trade in the Indian Ocean and, with remarkable speed, establishing trading stations in India, Malacca, China and Japan. West-

The Spaniards subduing Mexico.

wards, the Spaniards took the lead, Cortés discovering and subduing Mexico, Pizarro, with a ridiculously small but ruthlessly efficient company, conquering the Incas of Peru. Following the Treaty of Tordesillas (*see* separate entry) both Spaniards and Portuguese claimed a monopoly of the areas in which they operated. The objective of the Spaniards was at first the Far East, but the three ships which crossed the Pacific in 1527 found the Portuguese too strongly entrenched there, and Spain was comforted by the discovery in her central American colonies of immensely rich silver and gold deposits, which were to play a powerful part in the price rise which began to afflict Europe. In the second half of the century the Spanish monopoly was challenged by English seamen, notably John Hawkins, who opened the slave trade from Africa, and Francis Drake, and the mounting Anglo-Spanish friction which resulted was one cause of the war in the latter part of the century. Cathay and the Spice Islands (Moluccas) remained a powerful lure and were responsible f the many attempts to find a north-west a north-east passage to the Far East, ar for the century's most notable geo graphical discoveries. The Far East ex perienced the coming not only of trade but of missionaries too. The Jesui reached China and Japan, Xavier landin in the latter in 1549, and they were fo some time in charge of the Chines Bureau of Astronomy, though they wer expelled from Japan in 1587.

The outward-looking adventurousne of the century was reflected in a vigorou literature, served and encouraged by th new art of printing.

¶ HILLERBRAND, H. J. *Men and Ideas in the Sixteen Century*. 1969; KOENIGSBERGER, H. G. and MOS GEORGE. *Europe in the Sixteenth Century*. 1968

See also individual entries.

Skyscraper: any very tall narrow build ing, usually with many storeys, a tern originating in the USA which pioneere this form of architecture. The term wa used in the sailing navy to describe topmost sails, above the fore, main mizzen royals. Among the best wn skyscrapers are the Chrysler lding, New York (1929–30, 1,046 [318 metres]), and the Empire State lding, New York (1929–30, 1,250 [381 metres]). The Port of New York hority's World Trade Centre (1966– is a twin-towered building of 110 eys, 1,353 ft [412 metres] high. Other es – Chicago, Montreal, Toronto – have well-known skyscrapers.

New York skyline.

very: a condition involving the en- subjection of one set of human beings another. A slave belongs to his master, ns no wages and has no rights as a zen.

avery dates back to very early times. mitive warriors killed their captives, t, as the first civilisations grew up, nquered people were enslaved. Many the great civilisations of the past pended on slavery. Slaves could be ptives from a conquered nation, or people who had been born into slavery, or debtors unable to pay their debts, or children sold into slavery by their parents or other relations (the story of Joseph and his Brethren in the Old Testament is an example of this) or the victims of pirates or slave-raiders. St Patrick, for instance, first went to Ireland as the victim of pirates who sold him for a slave.

The last trace of slavery, in its modified form of serfdom (attachment to the land of an overlord), disappeared from England during the 16th century. Englishmen could, however, still be sold into slavery overseas by their own countrymen – e.g. Royalist prisoners by Cromwell and West-Countrymen after the Monmouth rebellion. Scottish and Irish prisoners suffered a similar fate after the Jacobite risings. African slaves introduced into England by travellers were at first regarded as the property of their masters, but in 1772 the Lord Chief Justice decreed that slavery did not exist in the British Isles and that as soon as a slave set foot on British soil he was free. This judgment was given in a case supported by Granville Sharp (1735–1832), an indefatigable campaigner against slavery.

The iniquitous slave trade across the Atlantic was begun by Spain and Portugal. One of the first Englishmen to pursue this traffic was Sir John Hawkins (1532–95), in 1562. In 1620 a Dutch ship offered African slaves for sale to the tobacco planters of Jamestown, Virginia, and thus slavery was introduced into the English colonies on the mainland of America. In the ensuing years millions of Africans (for instance, 2,130,000 between 1680 and 1786 alone) were transported to the West Indies and the mainland in hideous and inhuman conditions, many of them dying on the way. The trade became firmly entrenched and prosperous. In England the principal ports involved were London, Bristol, Liverpool

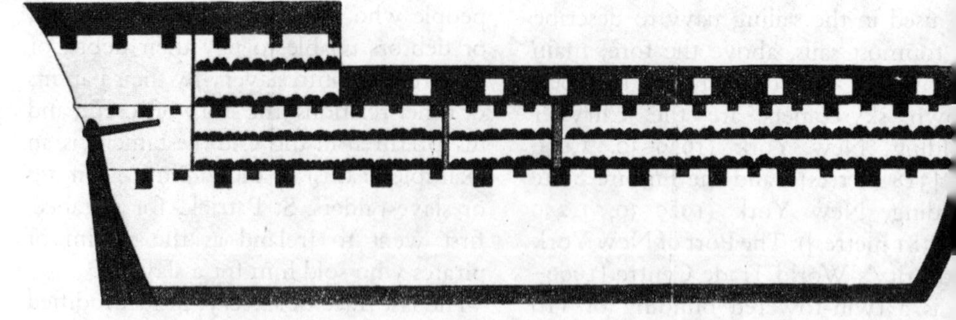

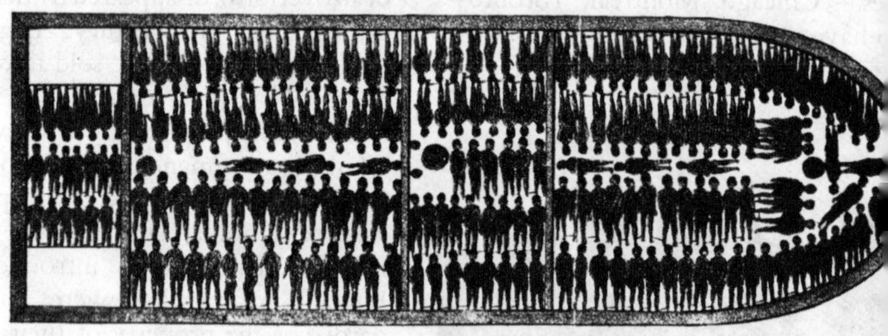

Diagrammatic print by Ackermann, showing how slaves were packed into a slave ship.

and Lancaster; between them they were responsible for over 50 per cent of this infamous traffic. Subsidiary industries grew up, giving many people a vested interest in the trade: shackles, handcuffs and chains were manufactured and sold, and the farmers round Bristol found a new and profitable crop in horse-beans, which provided a diet sufficient to keep a slave alive.

The first organised protest against slavery was that of the Germantown (Pennsylvania) Quakers in 1688. This protest was continued by many of their coreligionists, notably by John Woolman (1720–72) and Anthony Benezet (1713–84). The writings of Anthony Benezet inspired Thomas Clarkson (1760–1846), the great English leader in the early campaign against slavery, to devote his life to the cause: he in his turn inspired William Wilberforce (1759–1833), member of parliament for Yorkshire and friend of William Pitt. When, eventually, Wilberforce, for reasons of health, had to pla less active part in the fight against slave he looked "for some member of par ment who . . . would be an eligible lea in this holy enterprise" and enlis Thomas Fowell Buxton (1786–184 later to be known as "Buxton Liberator".

Denmark was the first European coun to prohibit the slave trade. Shortly aft wards, in 1807, it was abolished throug out Great Britain and her dominions Act of Parliament, largely owing to untiring efforts of the Society for Abolition of the Slave Trade, formed 1787 under the chairmanship of Granv Sharp.

The campaign to abolish slavery it was continued by the British and Forei Anti-Slavery Society, founded in 18 In 1833 a Bill was introduced to free slaves and compensate their owners. T dying Wilberforce said: "Thank God t I have lived to witness a day wh gland is willing to give twenty million ling for the abolition of slavery." The ancipation of the slaves throughout the tish Empire took place at midnight on July 1834. A scheme for an interim iod of Negro apprenticeship was so lly misused by the planters in the West ies that it was brought to an end summarily, largely owing to the work of eph Sturge (1793–1859) who himself nt out to the West Indies to collect the essary evidence.

avery seemed firmly entrenched in the thern states of the United States of ıerica, in spite of the declared views of ny leading American statesmen. "I nble for my country when I reflect t God is just", wrote Thomas Jefferson 43–1825). The earlier efforts of the akers had cleared their Society of e-owning. Some of them, including poet Whittier (1807–92), played an ive part in the vigorous anti-slavery vement, led by William Lloyd Garri- (1805–79), but others favoured a more dual approach. Women were active in campaign, including Lucretia Mott 93–1880) and Harriet Beecher Stowe 11–96), author of *Uncle Tom's Cabin.* e abolitionists met with unreasoning tility from those who did not share ir views: their meetings were mobbed l their homes threatened, and in Philadelphia their newly built centre, the Pennsylvania Hall, was set on fire and destroyed. The British abolitionists rallied to the support of their American colleagues, and in 1840 a World's Anti-Slavery Convention was held in London.

ve auction at Charleston, South Carolina, in 6.

The feeling between the Northern states and the great slave-owning states of the South on this issue became so acute that the anti-slavery movement was held to be one of the main causes of the American Civil War, which broke out in 1860 when the Southern states attempted to secede. The Northern victory in 1865 preserved the Union, and the emancipation of the slaves immediately followed.

Slavery has now been abolished in nearly all parts of the world, and where it still lingers, openly or in a disguised form, it continues to be the active concern of the still-existing Anti-Slavery Society and of the United Nations.

¶ GRATUS, JACK. *The Great White Lie.* 1973; LANGDON-DAVIES, JOHN, editor. *The Slave Trade and its Abolition* (Jackdaw). 1965; WHITE, JOHN and WILLETT, RALPH. *Slavery in the American South.* 1970

See also AMERICAN CIVIL WAR; CROMWELL; HAWKINS; JEFFERSON; PITT, WILLIAM, the Younger; QUAKERS; TOUSSAINT L'OUVERTURE; WILBERFORCE.

Slave state: in the USA, any one of the fifteen states south of the Mason-Dixon line (i.e. the boundary line between Maryland and Pennsylvania) in which slavery was legal before the American Civil War (*see* separate entry). They formed the bulk of the Confederated States which broke away from the Union.

Slovakia: an area of central Europe inhabited by Slovaks, a Slav people. It is mostly mountainous, but part of it lies in the fertile Danube valley. It has never formed a separate country. After its peasant peoples were overrun by the Magyars in the 10th century, it formed part of Hungary and, later, the Austro-Hungarian Empire. In 1919, after the collapse of this empire in World War I (*see* separate entry), Slovakia became the eastern section of the new state of Czechoslovakia. Some Slovak leaders have resented being governed from Prague in the west but have never succeeded in breaking away to form a separate state. *See* SERBIA for map.

Smith, Adam (1723–90): Scottish political economist. He is best remembered for his book *The Wealth of Nations* (1776), which condemned monopolies and too much state control, and supported free trade, competition and private enterprise. His work exercised great influence both in Great Britain and the USA, and laid the foundations of the modern science of political economy.

Smith, Ian Douglas (b. 1919): Rhodesian political leader. Educated at Selukwe School, the Chaplin School, Gwelo, and Rhodes University, Grahamstown, South Africa, he served with distinction in the RAF 1941–46; then, while farming, he became interested in politics, being elected to the Southern Rhodesia legislative assembly in 1948 and serving as an MP in the Federal Parliament from 1953 to 1961, when he resigned from the United Federal Party to assist in founding the so-called Rhodesian Front which proved successful in the 1962 elections. In 1964 he was appointed Premier, and minister for external affairs and defence. On 11 November 1965, he made a unilateral declaration of independence (UDI) and was to remain Prime Minister of the illegal Rhodesia government until independence in 1980.
See also RHODESIA.

Smith, Captain John (1580–1631): soldier and colonist, the effective founder of Virginia, where he voyaged in 1
as one of a company of 120 settlers. T
truth of the most famous story about h
that he was taken prisoner by Indians
rescued by the princess Pocahontas
separate entry), has never been satis
torily proved. Smith was president
the new colony in 1608–09 and aft
wards published the first account of i
A True Relation of such Occurrences
Accidents of Note as hath happened
Virginia since the first planting of
Colony (1608). Smith's 1612 map
Virginia was so accurate that it was
in use in the 19th century.

¶ GILL, W. J. C. *Captain John Smith and Virg*
1968; SYME, RONALD. *John Smith of Virginia.* 1

Smith, Joseph (1805–44): Ameri
founder of the Mormons (*see* separ
entry), or the Church of Jesus Christ
Latter-Day Saints. Smith claimed to h
found, in 1827, guided by a vision, a se
of golden plates, covered with hie
glyphics of Egyptian character, which
translated and issued in 1830 as *The B*
of Mormon (the name of the mythi
author of the original writings) which
accepted by Mormons as one of
scriptures, divinely inspired, long w
the Old and New Testaments.
See also MORMONS.

Smuts, Jan Christiaan (1870–195
South African soldier and statesm
After graduating at Stellenbosch U
versity, he came to England and gaine
double first in law at Cambridge a
afterwards practised as a lawyer in
home country. During the Anglo-B
War (1899–1902) he served as a Boer co
mando leader but later, as Color
Secretary in the Transvaal, worked w
the British to heal the rift between the t
countries. In World War I he comman
the Allied forces in East Africa, and
World War II, despite opposition in

ı Christiaan Smuts.

›uth African Parliament, led his country co the struggle against Germany and as promoted Field-Marshal. A dedicated ternationalist, he helped to start the :ague of Nations, supported the devel- ›ment of the British Commonwealth .d, in 1945, assisted in drafting the UNO harter and himself led the South African legation. In 1948 he was defeated by the ationalist Party under Doctor Malan. e was a keen botanist and President of e British Association in 1931.

in GILLETT, N. *Men Against War*. 1965

e also BRITISH COMMONWEALTH; LEAGUE NATIONS; WORLD WARS I AND II.

›cialism: political theory which teaches at land, business, industry, transport and e means of production should not be wned by individual people or groups of :ople but by all the people of a country. ›cialism is different from communism, ith which it is often confused, in that it ms to bring about the change by demo- atic methods and not by revolution.

The idea of common ownership was 1own to the ancient Greeks, the Romans ıd to the early Christians. There have ways been those who asked, why are ıe few rich and the many poor? For many hundreds of years it was believed by most people that there was no answer to this question. There had always been rich and poor and there always would be. In the 19th century a number of writers, of whom the most famous is Karl Marx (1818–83), explained that the poor were poor because they did not own any land or other property and had to sell their labour in order to live. They sold their labour to those who did own the property, or "capital". If all capital was owned by all of the people, there need not be any more rich and poor, it was thought. Communists said that the only way to do this was by revolution: socialists thought it could be done through parliament when a majority of the people voted for a socialist party.

Socialism spread rapidly through many countries of Europe in the 20th century but made very little headway in the USA. In Great Britain, many workers' organisations such as the trade unions, co-operative societies and the Christian Socialists supported the Labour Party which was formed at the beginning of the century. By 1924 the Labour Party had most seats in parliament and formed a government which remained in office for a short time. After World War II the Labour Party won a great victory in the general election of 1945. It then began the move towards socialism by taking the great industries of coal mining and the railways from their private owners and making them the property of the nation. This was called nationalisation. The owners received compensation, and the change was brought about by peaceful means. Since that time, the British Labour Party has provided the alternative government to the Conservatives, ruling from 1964 to 1970 and 1974 to 1979. The Conservative Party is opposed to socialism and therefore to nationalisation, and when it is in power it puts a brake on what the Labour

Party has tried to do to bring about common ownership.

As in England, socialism spread after World War I in Belgium, France, Germany and Scandinavia, where the Social Democratic parties have been particularly successful. The Labour Party has held power in Australia and New Zealand for long spells but Canada, like her neighbour USA, has developed no strong socialist party.

¶ MACKENZIE, NORMAN. *Socialism*. 1966

See also CAPITALISM; COMMUNISM; CO-OPERATIVE SOCIETIES; DEMOCRACY; MARX, KARL; TRADE UNIONS; WORLD WARS I AND II.

Social security: the provision of a minimum income for a family when its normal sources of income are cut off or reduced, health services, retirement benefits, etc. In 1935 the United States passed the Social Security Act as part of the New Deal (see separate entry). This measure, financed mainly from a tax upon employers of eight or more persons, provided for unemployment and old age. In England the term first became familiar following the Beveridge Report, which was followed by the enactment of the National Insurance Act 1946, the National Health Service Act 1946, and the National Assistance Act 1948.

See also PENSIONS.

Societies, Secret: organisations whose rules, ritual and, sometimes, purposes are communicated only to their members who, on invitation, take vows never to disclose the organisation's secrets. Many primitive communities have secret societies restricted to the adult males in the community. At puberty a boy is introduced into the confraternity in a ritual which usually includes some test or ordeal. In the Poro, a secret society found among tribal groups in West Africa, the initiate is scarred and circumcised and acts out ritual which symbolises his death as child and rebirth as an adult who mu share responsibility for the tribe's we being. Secret societies of this kind are t repositories of tribal wisdom, morals a religion. Myth and magic, the two wa in which primitive peoples try to expla and control the forces of nature, are important part of the secrets which mu be guarded under threat of dire penalty the oath be broken.

In ancient civilisations there were man secret religious cults, or "mysteries", they were called, whose members, b following the prescribed ritual, felt them selves assured of immortality. At Eleusi in Greece, Demeter, the "corn mother was the presiding deity. Ancient Egyp had its secret cults of Serapis – a combin tion of god and sacred bull – and th goddess Isis. From Persia came the cult the sun god Mithras, who was suppose to have a sacred bull from whose flank sprang corn and vines. Initiates we bathed in the blood of a dying bull, an then sat down to a sacred feast of brea and wine.

Many secret societies had purposes bo religious and political. The Assassin members of a dissident Muslim sec settled in the mountain fortress of Alamu in Persia, and terrorised the surroundin lands, using secret murder as a weapon policy. The young men selected to do th murders were first drugged with hashis (hence the word *assassin*). The power the Assassins was broken in 1256 whe the Mongols captured Alamut.

The Thugs, or Phansigars, an India secret society, combined religion wi murder and robbery. Before being rob bed, travellers were strangled with twisted waistcloth as sacrifices to Ka the Hindu goddess of destruction. Th Rosicrucians, the Brotherhood of th Rosy Cross, founded in Germany in th th century, were members of a mystical :ret society which appears to have com- ned elements of alchemy, the Hebrew ystical book the *Cabala*, and the Her- etic Books (actually written in the 3rd ntury AD but believed by the Rosicru- ıns to contain the key to the ancient ;yptian mastery of the spiritual and ıysical universe). Interest in the Rosicru- ıns revived in the 19th century. In 1915 Spencer Lewis, a New York advertis- g man, founded the Ancient Mystical rder Rosae Crucis. Its headquarters are California. Another secret society of merican origin is the Church of Scien- logy, founded by L. Ron Hubbard. Its ethods, which involve a certain mental d psychological "processing" (its own ord) of its initiates, have evoked much verse criticism in countries as far apart Australia and Great Britain.

Though there are between five and six illion Freemasons the society still en- deavours to remain secret. There are passwords and ceremonials and oaths of secrecy. The movement, which makes great use of words and symbols associated with building (God is the "Great Architect"), may have grown out of the medieval stone-masons' guilds. The earliest Freemasons' lodge was founded in London in 1717. The aims of freemasonry are wholly benevolent – to help fellow masons and their dependents, to dispense charity, to encourage brotherhood generally. Freemasons are required to believe in God, to be loyal to the state and never to discuss either religion or politics at their meetings.

Many secret societies grew out of political oppression. At the end of the 18th century some 20,000 Irish Catholics joined the United Irishmen, a secret society which, in 1798, unsuccessfully attempted a rebellion against their English rulers. The Fenian Brotherhood was

he symbols of 18th century Freemasons' lodges rround the portrait of their founder, Sir Richard teele.

founded in 1848, after the miseries of the Potato Famine. In 1916 a third Irish group, The Citizen Army, dedicated to driving the English out of Ireland failed in its Easter rebellion in Dublin. Other politically motivated secret societies include the Boxers or *I Ho Chuan* ("Fists of Righteousness"), directed against foreign aggression in China; the Carbonari (the "charcoal burners"), prominent in the struggle for Italian national unity; and the anarchists or nihilists (Latin *nihil*, "nothing") who held that *all* national states should be overthrown. Like the Assassins of old they made rulers their target, killing, among others, the Russian Czar Alexander II (1881) and King Umberto of Italy (1900).

The notorious secret society called the Mafia (Arabic, "place of refuge") also began as a movement against injustice. Romans, Arabs, Normans, Spaniards successively oppressed the Sicilians, many of whom took to the hills rather than become the serfs of an invader. The modern Mafia, while enjoining great loyalty and brotherliness between members, frequently perpetrates murder and barbarous acts of revenge on outsiders and on members who transgress its code. Today it, rather than the legal government, is the real ruler of Sicily. Between 1922 and 1928 the Fascists did much to suppress the society. Ironically, it was the Allies who put the Mafia back in charge when, in 1943, during World War II, they accepted Mafia help during the landings in Sicily. Sicilian immigrants took the Mafia to America, where it has become a criminal conspiracy with international ramifications. Nowadays the vast profits from illicit activities are often channelled into legal enterprises, and former *mafiosi* become, at least outwardly, respectable business men.

The Ku-Klux Klan, a secret society founded out of a sense of grievance, became a vicious instrument of racial big-

A member of the Ku Klux Klan holds a burni cross, 1923.

otry. After the American Civil W (1861–64) the North did not treat t defeated Southern States gently, and t Klan first operated as a guerrilla mov ment against the corrupt Northerne who were profiting from their humili tion. Then, with its white hoods a sheets it began to terrorise Negroes, stop them from exercising their new acquired right to vote. The Klan's histo is a hateful record of whippings, tarrin and-featherings and murders. Its ignorar bigoted members were against Rom Catholics and Jews as well as Negro Officially, the Klan disbanded in 1947; b that its influence still casts a baleful shado over the South is shown by the murder Civil Rights workers and of the Neg leader Martin Luther King (1929–68).

¶ DARAUL, A. *Secret Societies.* 1966

See also AMERICAN CIVIL WAR; ASSASSINA TIONS; FENIANS; KU-KLUX KLAN; JEW MAFIA; MONGOLS; MUSLIMS.

ocrates (469–399 BC): Athenian philopher, of whose personal life little is nown. For his philosophical teaching we e wholly indebted to the writings of ato (*see* separate entry), who shows that s method of seeking the truth was rough questions and answers among nall groups of friends, in which he ually took the lead. When he was eventlly accused of spreading harmful ideas nong the youth of Athens, he declined go into exile and drank the poison fered to him, as described in Plato's *aedo*.

---

olomon (*c.* 986–*c.* 932 BC): king of the raelites, succeeding his father David 972. He built the national Temple (*see* parate entry) and was renowned for his fluence over the neighbouring kingoms, and for his wealth and his wisdom, hich, we are told, caused the legendary ueen of Sheba to pay him a visit.

---

olomon Islands: Melanesian archielago in the western Pacific, named by Mendana in 1568, but not rediscovered ntil 1767 by Carteret. The Solomons, a ritish sphere of influence from 1886 and protectorate by treaty with Germany 1893, were mandated to Australia in 20, becoming trusteeship territories in 47 and fully independent in the Comonwealth in 1978.

---

omalia or **Somali Republic:** republic cupying the coastline of the north-east rn of Africa, from the Gulf of Aden st Cape Gardafui to the Kenyan border. he Somali are a proud and turbulent ce of Hamitic origin, traditionally omads tending herds of cattle, ponies, eep and camels and owing no allegiance their Arab neighbours in the hinterland f Aden. The rockbound coast was unviting to traders or explorers, and European contact came only late in the 19th century when Britain, France and Italy established protectorates. The small French protectorate of the Afars and Issas become independent as Djibouti in 1977.

The British Somaliland Protectorate, administered since 1905 by the Colonial Office, and the former Italian Colony, latterly a United Nations Trust Territory (*see* separate entry for UN), merged on 1 July 1960 in an independent Somali Democratic Republic with its capital at Mogadishu (Mogadiscio). In 1969 power passed to a Revolutionary Council with General Mohammed Siyad as Chairman.

In 1977 Somalia invaded and occupied most of the Ogaden Province of Ethiopia but when faced with massive Cuban reinforcements (backed by Soviet aid) the Somalis withdrew in 1978. A result of the war was an influx of about one million refugees into the country. Somalia remains one of the poorest countries of Africa.

See AFRICA for map.

Sorbonne: part of the University of Paris, a college founded by a priest, Robert de Sorbon (1201–74). It became a famous theological centre and attained a European reputation. In 1792 it was suppressed as an independent foundation, and in 1808 was formally made part of the university. It now houses the faculties of letters and science. In 1968 it was the scene of serious riots, led by militants who openly proclaimed their intention of using the universities as bases from which to overthrow the capitalist system.

Soto, Hernando de (1496–1542): Spanish soldier and explorer. He accompanied Pizarro (*see* separate entry) when in 1532 he led the Spanish expedition to conquer the Incas of Peru. De Soto afterwards returned to Mexico and was created Governor of Florida, but his own search for the fabulous cities of Cibola failed, and he died in 1542 on the banks of the River Mississippi.

South Africa, Republic of: republic occupying the southern part of the continent of Africa, with the Atlantic washing its south-western shores, and the Indian Ocean to the south and south-east. Namibia, former German South-West Africa which South Africa controls in defiance of the United Nations, lies to the north-west; Botswana to the north; Zimbabwe, Mozambique and Swaziland to the north-east with Lesotho, a small mountainous enclave lying on the western side of the massive Drakensberg range. South Africa consists of four provinces: Cape of Good Hope (or Cape Province), Transvaal, Orange Free State (OFS) and Natal. The administrative capital is Pretoria, Transvaal; the legislative capital, Cape Town, Cape Province.

The country has great natural wealth in minerals, its principal exports being gold, diamonds, copper, tin, silver, asbestos, wool, wines and spirits, fresh and canned fruit, and canned fish.

The Cape of Good Hope was first reported by Bartholomew Diaz in 1487, and in 1652 Jan van Riebeeck established a "Tavern of the Seas" at Cape Town as a staging post for the Dutch East India Company. At that time the only inhabitants of what is now South Africa appeared to be the nomadic Bushmen and Hottentots. It was in the 18th century, when the venturesome Dutch Voortrekkers were pushing northwards, that equally adventurous Bantu tribes were moving south from central and east Africa, and inevitable clashes followed, during which the indigenous nomads were squeezed out, fleeing to the Kalahari regions. There was an influx of French Huguenots in 1688, following the revoking of the Edict of Nantes, and these brought new skills and arts to the country.

The British occupied the Cape in 179 staying for eight years before returni control to the Batavian republic. In 18 five thousand British settlers landed a settled in what later became the easte Cape and south Natal. This followed t cession of the Cape to Britain by t Dutch in 1814 and began a period of d satisfaction on the part of the Boers whi led to the Great Trek of 1835, when son 10,000 of them trekked north in a gre convoy of covered wagons, each drav by the traditional span of sixteen oxen, order to escape from the hated Briti rule and to found the new republics the Orange Free State and Transvaal. F courage and hardihood this epic exod was on a parallel with the opening of the Wild West in America. Clash with the Bantu became frequent, and 1838 there was a massacre of the Boers the Zulus at Weenen which was aveng on 16 December that same year at t battle of Blood River, where the Zul were heavily defeated, and the Boe finally won control of the country.

While the Boers were establishi themselves on the farms of South Afric the British settlers were developing t mining resources of the country, its bu nesses and communications. In 1871 Ca Colony was granted self-government, a the Transvaal republic was proclaimed 1880, arranging a sort of union with t Orange Free State in 1897. The Anglo Boer War (1899–1902) was the culmin tion of years of Boer resentment encroaching British power. The di covery first of diamonds (1869) and the gold (1886) on the Rand brought a hug influx of businessmen and adventurer many British, whom the Boers calle *uitlanders* (foreigners) and to whom the would not grant citizenship rights. Th Boers were defeated and following th Peace of Vereeniging (May 1902) th

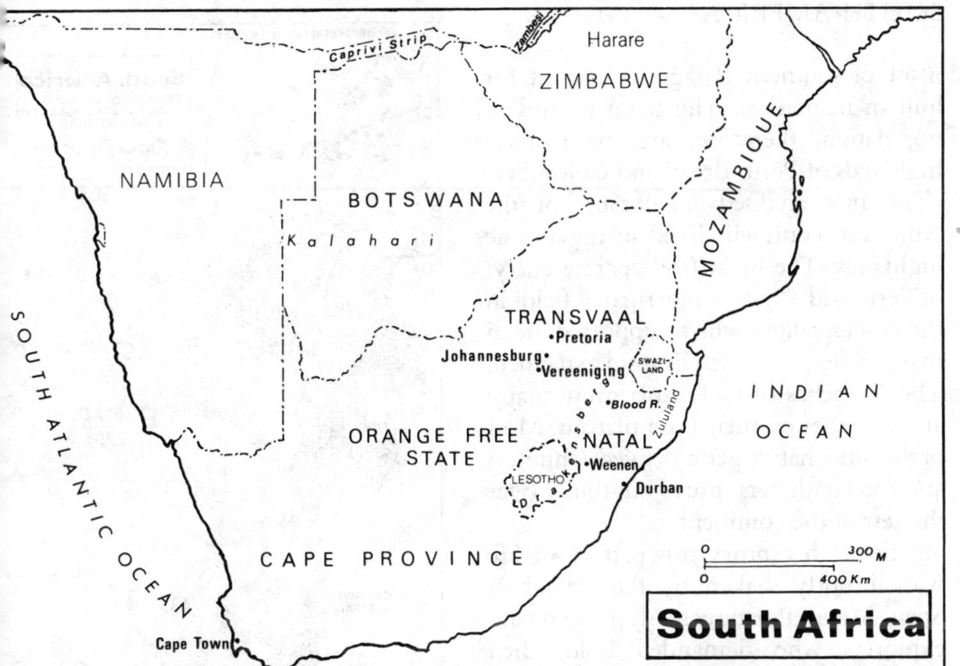

ɪrange Free State and Transvaal were ınexed to the Empire. In 1909 Britain ıssed the Act of Union which brought ·gether the four territories (the Cape rovince, Natal, the Orange Free State ıd the Transvaal) in a single Dominion, ıe Union of South Africa.

Though some South African leaders, pecially General Smuts, worked for nderstanding between Briton and Boer, ıere was bitter Boer opposition to enter-ıg World War II on Britain's side in 1939 though Smuts did succeed in btaining a majority for war. In 1948 the frikaner Nationalist Party under Dr lalan won the elections and began to galise racial separation under the apar-ıeid laws. In 1961 South Africa's whites oted to become a republic and opposi-on from the new Asian and African embers of the Commonwealth led outh Africa to leave the association on ı May 1961.

ee also APARTHEID; BOERS; CAPE OF GOOD IOPE; GREAT TREK; HERTZOG; ORANGE REE STATE; SMUTS, J. C.; TRANSVAAL; ORSTER; ZULU, etc.

South America: fourth largest continent, constituting nearly one-sixth of the total land surface of our planet. It is so remote from most historical centres of population that its people have always been on the edge of events in world history, and have not yet played a full part in the affairs of the world. In the 20th century the ten republics of South America were little affected by the world wars which so devastated other parts of the globe.

South America had a population of 244 million in 1982. Although some parts of the continent have fertile soil for farming, and parts of Chile and Venezuela are rich in mineral resources, most of the people are very poor. The tropical forests of the Amazon and the mountain blocks of the Andes and the Brazilian Highlands have made trade or travel very difficult. As an English historian wrote 100 years ago: "The mountains are too high to scale, the rivers are too wide to bridge. The progress of agriculture is stopped by impassable forests, and the harvests are destroyed by innumerable insects." Much of the Pacific coast is barren desert, while most of southern Patagonia is unfit for human habitation. The main centres of population, therefore, are the tropical highlands of Peru, Brazil and Colombia.

The first civilised inhabitants of the American continent lived in these same highlands. The Incas (*see* separate entry) of Peru used a system of irrigated fields in the Andes valleys which supported life in many cities as the Inca Empire expanded. The Chibchas of Colombia grew maize and potatoes on their high plateau. Most of the other native peoples lived as hunters and food gatherers spread out thinly over the rest of the continent.

In the 16th century this pattern of life was abruptly shaken by the arrival of Spanish and Portuguese ships, carrying explorers who demanded gold, then bringing soldiers with horses and muskets, followed by settlers with sheep and cattle. The old empires were destroyed and a new way of life developed.

Different types of people came to live in South America. The Spaniards in the 16th and 17th centuries intermarried with the natives to produce a large "Mestizo" population, while at the same time the native population was cut by European diseases to half its previous size. The Spanish government passed laws in 1542 to prevent the natives from being treated as slave labour, but many died working in the Spanish silver mines at Potosi. Meanwhile the Portuguese brought Negro slaves from Africa to cultivate a new crop, sugar cane. Other Negroes were employed as household servants, and in Brazil a population of mixed race also developed. By 1600 there were in South America many new cities with fine cathedrals and universities. Ports grew on the Atlantic and Pacific coasts. Precious shipments of silver went regularly to Spain, while the "Manila Galleon" sailed annually across the Pacific Ocean to Acapulco. The Spanish language was used

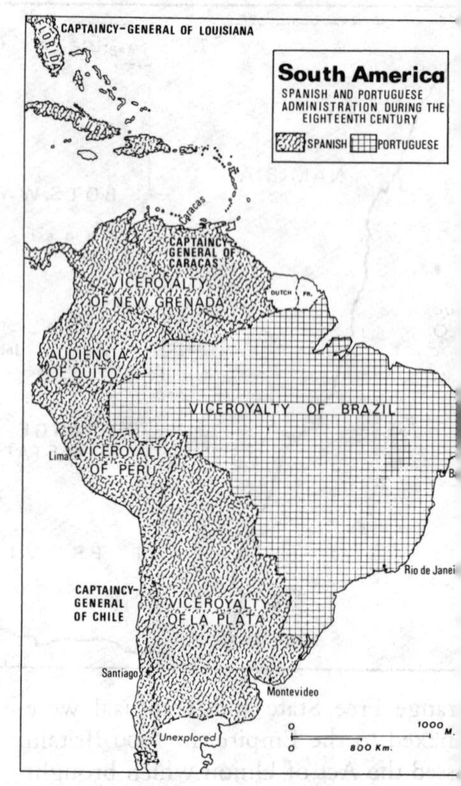

everywhere, except in Brazil, and th Catholic faith was practised by nativ and settlers alike.

In fact life had not changed so complete as may appear. The Spaniards did n create one united empire, but left th continent to be administered in provinc or even smaller units. The cities did not a flourish: the ports were often sleepy co lections of wooden huts. Not all nativ were easily subdued: the Araucanian of Chile refused to surrender to th Spaniards, and warfare was prolonge The Spaniards abandoned their fir settlement on the Rio de la Plata when (i spite of its name) it failed to produ gold. The horses they left behind the were tamed and ridden by the nativ gauchos of the pampas. The Inca peopl were not completely subdued either. The continued to fight from mountain retrea for the next 200 years.

The Spaniards and Portuguese were n the only Europeans to be drawn to Sout ıerica. French sailors were among the t to explore the coast of Brazil and to lect the red-coloured dyewood which ve Brazil its name. The English were ticularly attracted to the forests surınding the Orinoco, where they hoped find the kingdom of the fabulous lorado. Sir Walter Ralegh (*see* separate ry) explored this coast in 1595, noting th interest Trinidad's lakes of pitch. The ıtch, during their 17th-century conflict th Spain, captured many of the Brazil- coastal sugar plantations, but these re regained by Portugal after 1644. The ıtch then concentrated on developing de with all peoples in North and South nerica, disregarding any colonial rules ıich forbade such commerce. The ıtch also began settlements on the same ast of Guiana which had attracted legh. The British and the French, too, imed territory there.

Nevertheless Spain and Portugal together dominated South America for 300 ars. At the end of the 18th century itish colonies in North America fought obtain independence, and the French volution began to spread ideas of uality as well as those of freedom. So hen Spain was invaded by Napoleon *e* NAPOLEON I), American leaders like olivar (*see* separate entry) and San artin began to liberate South America, cisively defeating the Spanish forces in 24. The result was not a United States South America, but a continent divided to ten republics, often hostile to each her and still bound to sell their cash ops to Europe. The years since 1945, owever, have seen rapid economic de- elopment with Argentina, Brazil and enezuela in particular making great lvances. Brazil, with vast resources and population of 124 million in 1982 is, spite great differences of wealth and overty, likely one day to be an econoıic super power. Venezuela and Ecuador are members of OPEC. In 1983 Argentina returned to democratic rule (after the disastrous Falklands adventure) and in 1985 so did Brazil after twenty years of military rule. But the politics of the area remain volatile.

See also ENDPAPERS for map.

Southampton: port and county borough in Hampshire, with one of the finest harbours in Britain, 79 miles [127 kilometres] south-west of London. Remains of Saxon (*see* separate entry) and Roman settlements are plentiful, and it was a royal borough before 1086. It has a long history as a flourishing port and in the 13th century was the second wine port in the country. Though there was later some decline, prosperity returned in the 19th century with the opening of the rail link to London and the provision of extensive pier and harbour facilities.

South Arabia, Federation of: British-protected federation situated at the southern end of the Arabian peninsula, with Saudi Arabia and the Yemen to the north. The federation, which co-ordinated education, defence, medical services and the exploitation of natural resources, was formed in 1959 by the states of Audhali, Aulagi, Baihan, Dhala, Fadhli and Yafa, which were joined in 1963 by Aden and several other small emirates. The federation, a British attempt to counter more radical pressures for independence, was not a success and its constitution was suspended in 1965. Then its territories became part of the new People's Republic of South Yemen which achieved independence from Britain in 1967.

See SAUDI ARABIA for map.

South Australia: state in south-central Australia, with Adelaide the capital. The coast, surveyed by Tasman (*see* separate entry) in 1644, was charted by Flinders in

1802. Following explorations of the Murray River after 1828, an English colony was proposed, and was founded in 1836 with Adelaide as the capital. Poor resources, difficulties between governors and commissioners and shortage of settlers resulted in South Australia becoming a crown colony in 1842. Copper discoveries in the 1840s helped the economy, but gold strikes in the state of Victoria in 1851 affected trade and drew away population. In 1856 responsible government was achieved, and from 1863 the colony took over responsibility for the Northern Territory. In the 1860s drought and the inability of many squatters to purchase their holdings caused much land to be abandoned. Oversettlement in the 1870s exhausted the soil and competition from Queensland made farming hazardous. Iron deposits on the Spencer Gulf assisted manufactures, though agriculture, mainly wheat-growing, still lagged behind the economy generally. In 1901 it became one of the states forming the Commonwealth of Australia and conditions gradually improved. Since World War I (*see* separate entry) moderate labour and liberal country party governments have done much to stabilise the economy.
See also AUSTRALIA, and for map.

South Central, USA: region, including the states of Arkansas, Louisiana, Oklahoma and Texas, bordering on the Gulf of Mexico, Mexico, the Old South and the Old Northwest. It is really two regions, separated by the Mississippi River. To the east of the river are Arkansas and Louisiana, to the west Oklahoma and Texas. Arkansas is a land of low, rugged hills, picturesque valleys and substantial forests of hardwood and pine trees. Louisiana has some low hills in the north, but its southern areas, bordering on the Gulf of Mexico, are mainly coastal marshes, creeks and tributaries. Especially important in southern Louisiana is t Mississippi River Delta, formed by s carried down by the river. The Del ever growing, is at present one-third the total area of the state. On the weste side of the river, Oklahoma and Tex are part of a relatively flat rolling pla and are largely given over to grassland

Much of this region was explored by t Spanish and the French in the 16th a 17th centuries. Spanish settlements we concentrated to the west of the Mississip while a large French colony grew up the Louisiana Territory. Picturesq streets, houses, and other survivals fro this period can still be found in parts New Orleans, the major city of Louisian The territory east of the river, as well parts of Oklahoma, were bought by t United States in 1803 as part of the Loui ana Purchase (*see* separate entry). Tex remained part of first the Spanish Empi and then of Mexico until 1836, when rebellion, led by Americans who h settled in the region, succeeded in esta lishing an independent Texas natio This was in turn annexed to the Unit States in 1845. During the American Civ War (*see* separate entry), this entire regic joined the Old South in secession.

South-East Asia Treaty Organisatio (SEATO): established by the Mani Pact of 1954 as a collective security devi in that area and as a Pacific version NATO (*see* separate entry). Not strongly constituted as NATO, it pro vided for no joint force or comman Member states were to act together if an one of them should be attacked. Th Organisation's council consisted of th foreign ministers of the member countrie Australia, France, New Zealand, Pakista the Philippines, Thailand, United King dom and USA. Its role largely disappear ed with the emergence of the Associatio of Southeast Asian Nations (ASEAN).

uthern Pacific Railroad: part of the ;t transcontinental railway link be- een the Atlantic and Pacific seaboards the USA. This was achieved in 1869, ıen the Union Pacific, pushing west m Omaha, Nebraska, met the Central cific, later incorporated into the larger tem of the Southern Pacific, coming t eastward from Somerset, California.

uth West Africa (Namibia): terri- ry, administered as part of South rica, facing the Atlantic Ocean be- een Angola, Botswana and the Cape ovince of the Republic of South rica. It was a German colony from 84 until World War I (*see* separate try), and from 1920 was administered South Africa under a League of ations mandate. In 1945 the United ations (*see* separate entry) established a usteeship Council with the duty of couraging the economic, social and ucational development of all the rmer mandated territories.

outh Africa has consistently refused to cognise UN jurisdiction over the terri- ry in which it applied its apartheid licies. African nationalists formed the uth West African People's Organisa- on (SWAPO) which has waged a guer- lla war against South Africans since 1966. In 1968 the United Nations changed the name of the country to Namibia and in 1971 South Africa's presence in Namibia was declared to be illegal by the International Court of Justice. Efforts to make South Africa relinquish control of the territory have so far failed.

Although one of the driest lands on earth, Namibia has great potential wealth. About 12 per cent of the population are European, the rest come from some eight ethnic groups and altogether numbered just over one million in 1985. *See* AFRICA for map.

semi-permanent bushman's hut.

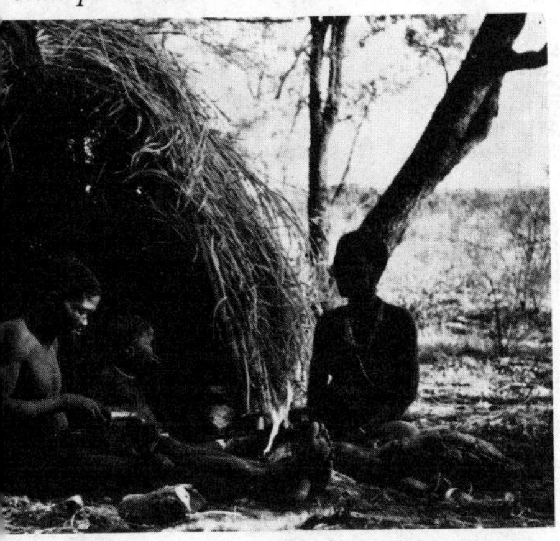

Space travel: travel in the regions outside the earth's atmosphere. For years men have dreamt of travelling through space, but have known that in order to do so the pull of earth's gravity must be overcome by the development of propulsion units of immense speed and power. For years, too, rockets have been considered the only possible source of such power and in 1944, when the German Wernher von Braun (b. 1912) developed the V2, capable of rising to a height of 60 miles [96 kilometres], post-war space research became a reality. It was then realised that a space vehicle composed of several stages, each falling away in due course in order to increase the speed of the nose capsule, was within the bounds of possibility.

Although von Braun was recruited by the USA after the war, it was the Russians who launched the first satellites in orbit: *Sputnik 1* in October 1957 and *Sputnik 2* in November, with a dog aboard. The American *Explorer 1* and *Vanguard 1* were launched early in 1958, and later that year the National Aeronautics and Space Agency (NASA) was organised. The Russians still led, and in April 1961 Yuri Gagarin (1934–68) became the first man to orbit the earth. A month later America's first space man Alan Shephard (b. 1923) made a fifteen-minute sub-orbital flight to a height of sixteen miles [25 km]. In August 1961 Major Titov (b. 1935) became the second man in orbit and in February 1962 the American John Glenn (b. 1921) became the third, orbiting the earth three times in *Friendship 7*.

Space travel has not been confined solely to moon probes, and in March 1962 an orbiting solar observatory was launched by the Americans followed by *Ariel 1*, an international satellite designed to collect data about the upper atmosphere, and in July 1962 by *Telstar*, a communications satellite. In December 1962, after a sixteen-week journey, *Mariner 2* sent back scientific data from a distance of only 21,594 miles [34,751 km] away from the planet Venus, and in November 1964 *Mariner 4* was launched towards Mars. In April 1965 *Early Bird*, the world's first commercial communications satellite, was launched into service above the Atlan
Meanwhile, manned space flight had be
taken a stage further by Gordon Coope
(b. 1927) thirty-four-hour 22 orbit flig
in May 1963 and the following month
Russia's Valentina Tereskhova (b. 193
the first and, so far, only woman in spa
who orbited the earth forty-eight tin
in *Vostock 6*.

In October 1964 the Soviet *Voskhod* to
three men into space – the first mul
seater space craft – and another "first" w
Leonov's (b. 1934) first walk in spa
lasting ten minutes, in March 1965, t
same month that two American astr
nauts became the first men to steer th
craft from one orbital path to another.
June 1964 Edward White (b. 1930) walk
for twenty-two minutes in space and
December two *Gemini* space craft mad
rendezvous, coming to within a foot [
centimetres] of each other.

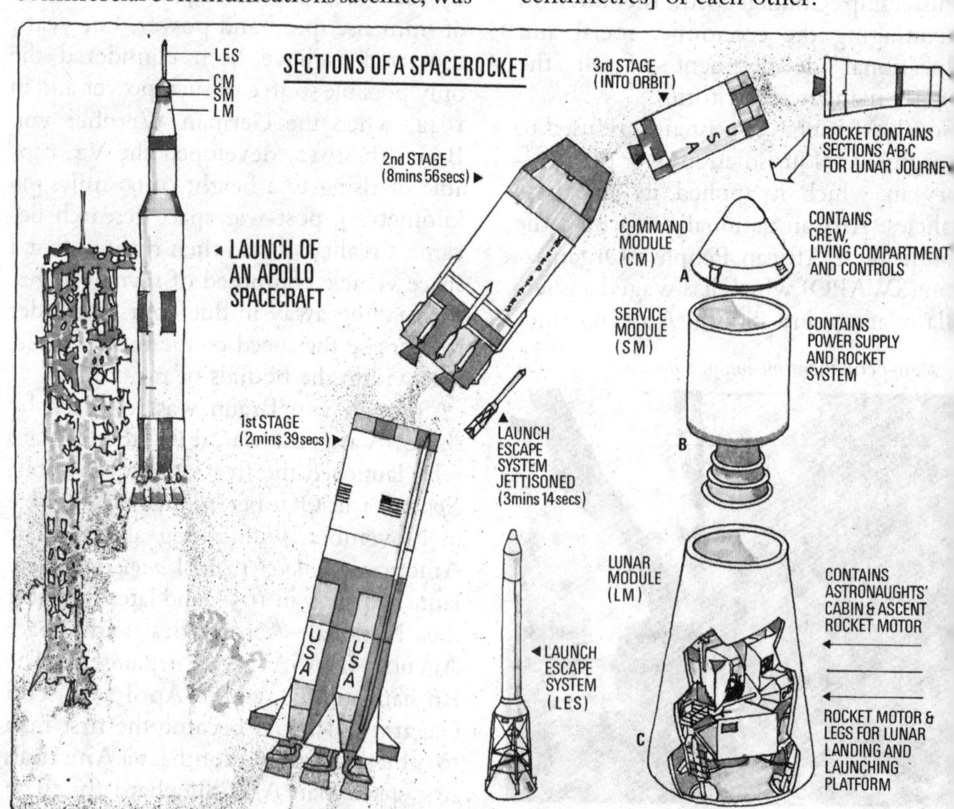

e first Soviet sputnik, 1957.*

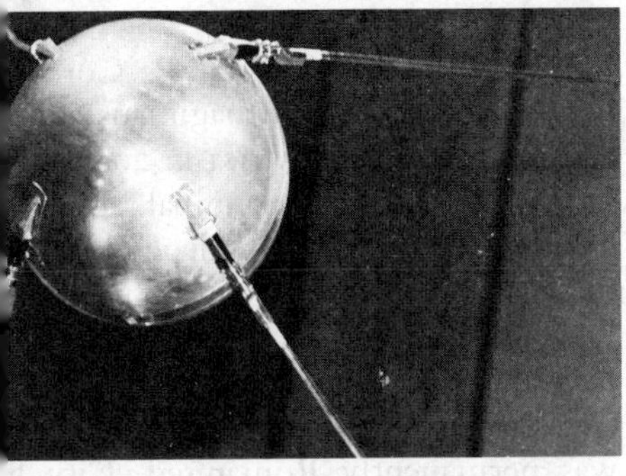

uri Gagarin became the first man to orbit the rth in 1961.

The first landing on the moon had been iade in July 1964 by the American *anger 7* with a planned crash landing after ending back valuable photographs; and ie first soft landing was made by the ussian *Lunar 9* in February 1966. In 1966 ie Russians put an artificial satellite, the rst of five, into orbit around the moon, nd the American *Surveyor 1* soft landed, ending back TV pictures of the surface. In January 1967 occurred the first known pace tragedy when three American astro-auts were killed by fire on the launching ad at Cape Kennedy, followed three ionths later by Vladimir Komarov's eath when the braking parachute on *oyuz 1* failed to open.

The first unmanned space link was in)ctober 1967 when two Soviet satellites inked and separated automatically. In eptember 1968 the Soviet *Zond 5* was he first craft to go round the moon and

Apollo 8 blasts off from Cape Kennedy on 21 December, 1968.

US astronaut, Edwin Aldrin, walks on the moon, 16 July, 1969.

return to earth. Meanwhile the Americans were testing out new space craft designed to take men to the moon, and *Apollo 7* made a ten-day space journey in October 1968. Then in December 1968 came a great leap forward into the unknown when Borman (b. 1928), Lovell (b. 1928) and Anders (b. 1933) made the first manned flight to leave the influence of earth's gravity, when they flew ten orbits round the moon, each lasting two hours, in their *Apollo 8* space craft powered by the giant *Saturn 5* rocket. For the first time ever, human beings came under the gravitational influence of another planet and for the listeners in the control room at Houston, Texas, there were tense moments when the astronauts were out of radio communication as they passed round the far side of the moon.

For the first time men saw the moon's surface at close range, including the rear part which never faces the earth; and short range photographs were obtained.

The dress rehearsal for a moon landing came in May 1969 when *Apollo 10* orbited the moon thirty-one times and the command module, detached from the main space craft, descended to within nine miles [14 kilometres] of the moon's surface. Then on Sunday, 20 July 1969, at 9.17 p.m. (BST) the lunar module *Eagle* of *Apollo 11* touched down on the moon's surface whilst the command vehicle *Columbia* continued in orbit under Collins (b. 1930). For the final descent Aldrin (b. 1930) had to take over manual control of the module in order to avoid the enormous boulders littering the Sea of Tranquillity. The next morning at 3.52 a.m. Armstrong (b. 1930) took man's first step on the moon whilst his colleague televised him. Both men gathered rock samples from the surface and left mementos of their visit, including a plaque inscribed "Here man from the planet Earth first set foot upon the Moon, July 1969 AD. We came in peace for all mankind."

Steady progress has been made and knowledge gained ever since. In 1983 the American Pioneer 10 crossed the orbit of Neptune to become earth's first space vehicle to leave the solar system. It was powered by atomic battery. Also that year the American space shuttle made its first earth landing in darkness.

Spain: constitutional monarchy (the monarchy was restored following the death of Franco in 1975) of south-western Europe. The country entered history in the 3rd century BC as part of the empire of Carthage, conquered and organised by Hamilcar Barca, father of Hannibal. The Romans also had interests in Spain. While Hannibal campaigned in Italy, the Roman general P. Corneli Scipio drove the Carthaginians out Spain, crossed into Africa in 204 BC ar decisively defeated Hannibal at Zam From that time the independent ar turbulent people of Spain came und Roman rule. They were not rapidly co quered, but by the first century of tl Christian era a great part of the peninsu was permanently Romanised. City li was well established and the languag fashions and culture of Rome prevaile The agriculture, minerals and manufa tures of Spain contributed to the eco omic stability of the Roman Empire. Tw of the early Roman emperors, Traja (98–117) and his successor Hadrian (117 138), though not related, were both Spanish birth.

With the Empire's decline, Spain suffere severely. When the Rhine frontier brok in 405, the Sueves, Alans and Vanda pillaged Gaul for three years and the entered Spain. Later Spain was ruled b the Visigoths. Efforts by the easter Emperor Justinian (483–565) failed t restore more than the seacoast to Roma rule. A Visigothic Christian kingdor lasted in Spain till the early 8th century Then the militant expansion of Islam i North Africa reached the Straits of Gib raltar, and in 711 the Muslim army c Tariq won a decisive victory over th Visigoths on the Guadalete. By 713 a Spain, except the country of the Basque and a few other small northern areas, wa under Muslim rule.

The history of Spain during several cen turies was thus largely concerned wit war to the death between the proud an fanatical representatives of two riva civilisations, the Christian and the Islamic Islam was too divided by theological an dynastic issues to endure as an empire, an Spain, under the highly civilised Umayyad Chalifate of Cordova, was largel cut off from the eastern sources of Muslin

c.409-460 A.D.
Gallaecia
West Goths 413
Vandals 409
Vandals 420
S P A I N
TARRACONENSIS (SARAGOSSA)
West Goths 419
West Goths 417
TARRACO (TARRAGONA)
BARCINO (BARCELONA)
HISPALIS (SEVILLE)
CARTHAGE NOVA (CARTAGENA)
Vandals 460
c.800 A.D.
AQUITAINE
KINGDOM OF GALICIA AND ASTURIAS
GASCONY
SPANISH MARCH
UMAYYAD CALIPHATE OF CORDOVA
CORDOVA
Mediterranean Sea
c.1097 A.D.
LEON
FRANCE
COUNTY OF PORTUGAL
NAVARRE
ARAGON
CATALAN COUNTIES
CASTILE
EMIRATE OF SARAGOSSA
Toledo
DOMINIONS OF THE ALMORAVIDS
DOM. OF THE CID
c.1212 A.D.
LEON
FRANCE
NAVARRE
PORTUGAL
CASTILE
ARAGON
Toledo
Cordova
GRANADA
NORTH AMERICA
SPAIN and PORTUGAL
1501
LINE LAID DOWN BY TREATY OF TORDESILLAS 1494
1497-98
1492
NEW SPAIN
JUANA (CUBA)
1493-96
1497-98
1502-04
AFRICA
1498
1499
CAPE VERDE ISLANDS
1499-1500
1519-21
1500
PERU
SOUTH AMERICA
BRAZIL
0 2000 miles
0 3200 Km
Principal Voyages of Discovery to America
Spanish
Portuguese

Spain

power. Small Christian states kept alive in the north. While the Umayyad dominions broke into many small states, the Christians co-operated rather more. Alfonso VI (1073–1109) united Castile and Leon and conquered Toledo in 1085. This advance from the north continued until the battle of Las Novas de Tolosa in 1212 confined Islamic rule to Granada. Then for two centuries the Spanish Christian kingdoms competed with one another and were torn apart by turbulent nobles. Castile alone had a frontier with Granada. Unity came only after Ferdinand, the heir of Aragon, married Isabella, the heiress of Castile, in 1569. Granada had been conquered in 1492. War with France gave Ferdinand the opportunity to seize all Navarre south of the Pyrenees. Portugal still preserved its separate existence. The Spanish Inquisition harshly imposed religious uniformity upon Jews, Muslims or any others out of step with Catholic orthodoxy.

Thus united, Spain, at the close of the 15th century, was on the threshold of a great imperial destiny. The notion was already in circulation that the wealth of the Indies might be reached by sailing west instead of using the eastern land routes. In 1492 the Pope Alexander VI, himself a Spaniard, issued bulls awarding to Spain and Portugal all lands and islands already discovered or hereafter to be discovered "in the west, towards the Indies or the Ocean seas". With the voyage of Christopher Colombus in that year, the new world was opened to European conquest. The Pope's ruling of 1492 was quickly followed by the Treaty of Tordesillas in 1494 which assigned to Portugal everything east of a line drawn down the Atlantic 370 miles [595 kilometres] west of the Cape Verde Islands and everything west of it to Spain. This enabled the Portuguese to claim Brazil; but the rest of the new world, the extent of which was still unknown, was thrown open to explor tion and exploitation by Spain. In t years that followed Spanish *conquistador* with tiny forces but superior arms ar tactics, added vast territories to a gre Spanish American empire, Cortés i Mexico, Pizarro in Peru, and many mor Fleets carried gold and the produce "the Indies" to Spain. This brought Spai into sharp competition with other nav powers omitted from the Pope's awar

In Europe, also, Spain went throug great change. Not only did Spanish co quests extend to Sicily, Naples and par of Italy, but several dynastic marriag united the Spanish crown with the rule ship of other European lands, includin the huge Habsburg dominions. Charles (Holy Roman Emperor 1519–58) becam the ruler of Spain, Austria, Hungar Bohemia, parts of Germany, the Nethe lands, Milan, Naples, Sicily, Sardini Mexico, Central America, Venezuel Peru, Bolivia, western Chile, Argenti and Paraguay, and his empire was exten ing into California and Florida. The was at the same time a notable flowerin of literature and art in Spain.

The peak of power reached unde Charles V was not wholly maintaine under Philip II (reigned 1556–98) and steady decline set in. Though Philip di not succeed to the whole of the Habsbur dominions, his empire, still huge an cumbersome, invited hostility in to many quarters and came into collisio with formidable opponents in Englan France and, particularly, the Netherlan on which Spain tried to impose its reli gious orthodoxy. Concentration solely o military and administrative tasks an dependence on gold from overseas and o colonial slavery caused decline of produ tivity and economic life in Spain.

Spain remained a major European pow through the 17th and 18th centuries, but declining and unfortunate one. By th

›se of the 18th century the overseas ıpire was breaking up, and Spain itself came a battleground for France and itain in the Napoleonic War of the rly 19th century. The Spanish American ıds achieved their independence.

pain was not involved in either of the orld Wars of the 20th century. A mocratic republic was established in 31 but was overthrown by an army utiny led by General Francisco Franco, ho, after a savage civil war (1936–39), tablished a dictatorship. On his death 975) Juan Carlos became head of state d King as already arranged and pre-led over a successful return to demo-acy. In 1982 Spain joined NATO and in 85 the EEC.

VILAR, P. *Spain: A Brief History*. 1967

panish-American War (1898): war ught by the USA and Cuban revolu-onaries to free Cuba from Spanish ntrol. Spain was quickly defeated (in e four months of the war America lost ıly twenty men) and by the Treaty of ıris Spain gave up the Philippines, Guam d Porto Rico to the USA, and Cuba me under temporary military occupa-on by US forces.

panish Civil War (1936–39): struggle etween Fascist and republican forces in pain. The policies of a right-wing overnment (1933–35) precipitated revolt Catalonia and Asturias. In February 936 a left-wing government came into ower with a strong majority. In July eneral Francisco Franco (*see* separate ıtry) led a mutiny of the army, moving to Spain from Morocco. A savage civil ar followed, in which Germans and alians participated on the rebel side and ussia and Mexico aided the government. n ill-equipped and largely untrained nti-Fascist International Brigade was ormed of foreign volunteers. In June 1937 Bilbao fell to the rebels, Barcelona in January 1939 and Madrid in March 1939, after a siege of twenty-eight months. It was a struggle that embittered Spanish life for years after the war had ended; and one that led to the passionate involvement of many people from other countries who saw the clash for what it was, a cynical curtain-raiser by powerful aggressor nations for the conflict that followed.

¶ PURCELL, HUGH. *The Spanish Civil War*. 1973

Spanish Succession, War of (1701–14): war between England, the Netherlands and certain German states against Spain, France, Portugal and other allies. It arose because Louis XIV of France accepted the will of the last Spanish Habsburg, Charles II (1661–1700; *see* HABSBURG, HOUSE OF), and broke the Partition Treaty by which interested powers had agreed on the fate of Spain. Charles left the Spanish Empire to Louis's grandson, Philip, and, if he refused it, to the Austrian Archduke Charles. Louis made war inevitable by moving French troops into the Spanish Netherlands and into the Dutch forts there. The Grand Alliance of Austria, England and Holland, formed in 1701 by William III, was sustained by the victories of Marlborough and Eugène in Flanders and Italy, and of Peterborough in Spain. The terms of the Peace of Utrecht, 1713, confirmed Louis's remark that the war was about trade. Though Holland gained nothing after exhausting efforts, England gained Gibraltar, Minorca, Newfound-land and Nova Scotia, the Asiento (*see* separate entry) allowing trade with the Spanish Indies, and trading rights in Portugal. Philip retained Spain, but Austria was compensated with the Spanish Netherlands and Naples. Savoy and Prussia were expanded as checks on French power. The Catalans, who had assisted the allies against Philip, were abandoned to his vengeance.

Sparta: state in the centre of the Peloponnese, the southern peninsula of Greece. Sparta was also the name of the capital and the whole territory was often called Lacedaemon. The Spartans came as invaders from the north, and, though they subdued the people whom they found in possession, they were always on guard against internal revolt and attack from surrounding states. This resulted in a highly organised society, with military efficiency and physical endurance as primary aims. The rigorous training to which boys – and girls too – were subjected has become proverbial, and the word Spartan is applied to any situation of austerity or discomfort.

The armies of Sparta were held in awe by the rest of Greece, where Athens was her traditional enemy. By the early 1st century BC Sparta was absorbed into the Roman Empire.

¶ FORREST, W. G. *A History of Sparta 950–192*. 1968
See also ATHENS; HELOT; PELOPONNESIAN WAR; THERMOPYLAE.

Sphinx: type of monument originating in Egypt and spreading, in a variety of forms, throughout the ancient world. In Egypt, the leonine body represented the sun god, while the human head was a likeness of the Pharaoh. The great Sphinx of Giza was erected by Chepheren, builder of the second pyramid. Its huge head was battered by Turkish artillery, and until 1816 most of its body lay under drifted sand. When this was cleared away a ruined temple was discovered between the paws, and an inscription relating how, centuries before, Tuthmosis IV had also caused the sand to be removed, having been told to do so in a dream.

In Greek mythology the Sphinx was a female monster who inhabited a rock near Thebes and hurled from its top all passers-by who could not answer the riddle: "What walks on four legs in the

The Great Sphinx of Giza.

morning, on two at noon, and on three the evening?" Oedipus (whose story used by the dramatist Sophocles), son Laius, king of Thebes, solved the ridd as describing man in infancy, in his prin and in old age.

Spies: or secret agents, people paid l others, usually to secure informatio especially naval, military, aeronautic and scientific from other countries. The have also been employed internally l governments against their political o ponents. Thus, in the 16th century agen were used extensively, especially by Lor Burleigh and Sir Francis Walsinghan ministers of Elizabeth I of England. Wa singham at one time had thirteen agen in France, seven in the Low Countrie five in Italy, six in Spain, nine in German and three in Turkey; such men we usually business agents reporting on th state of the markets as well as being i government service.

Modern times have seen a tremendou increase in the scale of internation espionage, both in war and peace, and th activities of secret agents have been greatl helped by the clever inventions th science has brought to their aid in th shape of special cameras, a wide range o ingenious microphones and other "bugg ing" devices, telephone tapping tech niques, etc.

ince 1945, when World War II ended, ere have been a number of notorious es. In 1950 Karl Fuchs, a brilliant rman-born nuclear physicist working Harwell, England, believed that all entific information should be shared ernationally and passed vital atomic crets to the Soviet Union. In 1951 Guy rgess, who had worked for British telligence, and Donald Maclean, of the reign Office, were about to be arrested acting as Russian agents when they caped to the Soviet Union after being arned by the so-called "third man", arold Philby, who had been a Communist since 1934 and a Soviet agent since 56. Philby also was given political ylum in Russia. In 1961 George Blake as given the heaviest sentence ever passed Britain, of 42 years imprisonment, for pionage on behalf of the Soviet Union, ough he escaped after five years. In 1962 leg Penovsky, a Russian senior military telligence officer who had passed vital formation to the Western powers, was rested and shot; and Greville Wynne, s contact with British Intelligence, was dnapped in Budapest and imprisoned in ussia. He has since been released.

n 1969 Russia had about 250,000 secret gents – more than the number employed all the Western powers together. The nancial estimate for maintaining the ritish Secret Service in the same year as £10·5 million.

n the USA the main responsibility for pionage and counter-intelligence work in the hands of the Central Intelligence gency. There, too, the post-1945 period d the long "cold war" with the Soviet Jnion, has produced a number of espioage cases that made headlines all over e world. Shortly after the Fuchs affair Britain had created such disquiet, five mericans were arrested and put on trial r acting as Soviet agents in the United tates. All were found guilty and two, Julius and Ethel Rosenberg, were executed. In 1950 Alger Hiss, a high official in the Department of State, was sentenced to five years' imprisonment for conveying secret documents to a Russian courier as far back as 1937 and 1938. Another sensational case was that of Francis Gary Powers, an airman in the employ of the Central Intelligence Agency who was shot down while taking high altitude photographs over Russia in 1960. He was sentenced to ten years' imprisonment but was later exchanged for a Soviet spy captured in the United States.

Spoils system: system ("to the victor belong the spoils") by which the offices and privileges formerly belonging to a defeated political party are taken over by its victorious opponents when they come to power. While such a system is, within varying limits, an inevitable part of changing political fortunes, it is particularly associated with the USA where, e.g., not only politicians but also trusted government servants have been stripped of office.

Sports and athletics: Although there is evidence of organised sports and athletics in very early times, such as wrestling among the Sumerians (*see* SUMER) in Mesopotamia 5,000 years ago, it is among the ancient Greeks that athletics seem first to have become a major part of social life. The word itself comes from Greek *athlon*, a prize.

Certain basic forms of sport have developed in widely separated parts of the world. Contests between man and man, or between teams, have been organised in many forms, but basically as a kind of fight, with or without weapons. The imposition of rules also came very early, to prevent sporting contests from leading to real fighting. The rules were not always such as we have now. The ancient Greek athlete who, realising that he could not himself win the race, tripped up another runner in order to ensure that his friend would win, was praised and admired.

In Homer's *Iliad* there is an account of games being held as part of the ceremonies at a funeral. The religious and social importance of games was particularly expressed in the Olympic games (*see* separate entry), established in 776 BC and held every four years. The ancient Greeks also looked for all-round accomplishment and not only for specialisation in one sport. A characteristic institution among them was the *pentathlon* or fivefold contest in ability in running, long jumping, throwing the javelin, throwing the discus and wrestling.

Women were excluded from the Olympic games even as spectators, but athletic ability was not regarded as unwomanly. Girls engaged in athletics, particularly among the Spartans, and there still exists an attractive statue of a mini-skirted Spartan girl running. At Argos women held their own games in honour of Hera, who was peculiarly the goddess of complete and fulfilled womanhood.

The word gymnastics also comes from Greek, from *gymnos* meaning naked. From 720 BC no clothing at all was worn at the Olympic games by competitors; but Greek girls normally wore some clothing at their games.

It may be noted that the Olympic games of 624 BC included horse-racing, a sport at least 3,000 years old. The earliest known horse race in Britain was held in about AD 210, during the Roman occupation.

As early as the 5th century BC the distinction between amateurs and professionals began to emerge, the ancient Greek professionals being slaves. This led on to the practices of Roman times, when gladiators (Latin *gladius*, a sword) fought for the entertainment of spectators. Gladiatorial shows were an institution borrowed by the Romans from the Etruscans, an old Italian civilisation. The first record Roman gladiatorial event was at fune games held in 264 BC.

Generally the Romans were interest in games as a spectacle rather than as e pressions of healthy living. At Ro itself they were largely professional pe formances provided by the state, appe ing increasingly to a brutal and degradi interest in scenes of violence, cruelty a slaughter. Gladiators fought to the deat with each other and with animals. B fighting was a Roman practice which st survives in Spain and elsewhere. Y there was as well much display ordinary athletic speed and skill at t Roman public games, races, particular with horses and chariots, being popula The Roman games also had political well as social importance, for they pr vided an occasion when a large crow could show approval or disapproval t wards its rulers.

After the decline of the Roman Empi and through the Middle Ages of Europe history (*see* separate entry), war and t struggle for existence occupied so muc of human life that sport and athletics we not separated from training for war from hunting. From archery practice contests with staves among the humbl people to the jousting and similar exe cises of their knightly masters and ruler nearly every exercise of skill or stami seemed to be directed to training f attack or defence.

Yet the human impulse to pursue spo for enjoyment and for healthy exerci kept emerging. In 1365 Edward III England felt it necessary to prohibit t playing of football because it interfere with military training.

More civilised, stable and leisurely way of life produced an increasing readine among the wealthy and aristocratic class to pursue sport and athletics as a re

ORTS: *Above, Roman gladiatorial combat. ove right, tennis as played in the 17th century. ght, cricket in the 18th century. Below, ctorian ladies archery tournament held in gent's Park, 1894.*

ow jumping.

Skiing.

reational outlet. In addition, the renaissance of classical learning in the 15th and 16th centuries encouraged imitation of the ancient Greeks in many fields, including their cultivation of athletics. Various ball games were popular. Henry VIII of England was fond of tennis, then a form of handball played against a wall, which had indeed been popular from the 14th century; and Mary Queen of Scots took an interest in golf, a game which was being played at St Andrews about 1552.

From the middle of the 18th century various sports were taken up at English public schools. Football began to take its modern form; and at Rugby in 1823 the game took on its alternative form, which allowed the ball to be carried as well as kicked.

For track running, the first meeting on modern lines in Britain was held in 1817.

In many European countries in the 19th century, athletic meetings were held in association with nationalist political movements. This occurred in Germany and among the Czechs and Magyars and to some extent in Ireland.

In the later decades of the 19th century a golden age of sport and athletics began. Settled life and increasing prosperity and leisure in the more technically and politically advanced countries gave opportunity for far wider participation in sports. Improved travel facilities and communications caused the forms of sport which were once confined to particular countries to become known throughout the world.

From now on sports were adopted by people living far away from the physical or social conditions which had given rise to them. Mountaineering and winter sports were taken up by people living in countries where there was little or no natural ice or snow and possibly no mountains, but travelling abroad to pursue these interests. Japanese forms of wrestling, e.g. *jujitsu* and *judo*, were tak up by people in countries far from Jap French Canadians adapted an Indian ga and called it lacrosse because the nett stick used in playing it resembled bishop's crozier. In athletics, forms skill previously confined to particu places became more general. Pole vau ing achieved status as a recognised for of athletics. Above all, nearly every sp that had hitherto been confined to m was now pursued also by women. Und the stimulation of variety, new forms old games were invented, lawn ten coming into being in 1873, while hockey was invented in 1875.

The wider interest in athletics led the setting up of organisations to sta dardise the rules of various games, regulate matches and competitions a to encourage interest in them. An Engli Amateur Athletic Association w founded in 1880, and similar associatio were established in many other countri To enable these associations to wo together, adopting similar standards a holding international track meetings a competitions, an International Amate Athletic Federation was set up in Swed in 1913. Already, in 1896, the Olymp games had been restored in modern for Similar national and international bodi were established to organise and regula a wide variety of games and sports, su as football, swimming, skating, cyclin horse riding, lawn tennis, boxing, etc.

An acute problem facing some of the bodies was that of defining amateur a professional status. The paid player cou give his whole time to training and pra tice and could treat his sport as a full-tin occupation, gaining thus a great adva tage over amateurs, who pursued t sport as a spare time amusement. B with growing competition, bigger priz and the growth of national and instit tional support for various sports, ma

-called amateurs came to be in reality id professionals, though they managed gain their financial support in ways hich were not strictly direct payments r competing in sport. Scholarships or ecially created employments in which work had to be done, and similar vices, enabled supposed amateurs to be id to give their whole time to competitive sport.

'he greater organisation and stanrdisation of sport by the many national d international associations did not move all the varieties simultaneously isting in the various games. Thus, for ample, in football the two main types mained – those played with feet only, controlled in Britain by the Football ssociation and familiarly known as occer", and those in which the ball is ndled – and there remained also much riety inside the two types (*see* FOOTBALL).

n the late 19th century, and more parcularly in the 20th, technology entered ort. This vastly changed the older inruments of sport, making them better lapted to their purpose, and it also introiced new ones like the modern trampoie in gymnastics. Footballers in older mes kicked a ball filled by the inflated adder of an animal; today they kick a ghly sophisticated industrial product; id so it is in many other forms of sport, here there are better rackets, better hulls id rigging for yachts, and so on. Techological advance also brought into being mpletely new types of sport involving owered machines, such as motor cycles r speed boats for racing, or activities such water skiing behind power boats or iotor-paced pedal cycling. Technology so created the airborne sports such as iding and parachuting, and the underater forms of sport and recreation.

Technology transformed sport in another way, through scientific study of the uman body, giving an entirely new understanding of what is required in the training of an athlete, while a wide variety of devices, from the stop watch to the electrocardiograph, have made it possible to measure much more accurately both the performance of the athlete and the physical resources on which he or she can venture to make demands. At the close of the 1920s the Finnish long-distance runner, Paavo Nurmi, made history by measuring his performance, not by what the other competitors were doing, but by calculations based on reading a stop watch which he carried in his hand. Calculations and research into what is physiologically possible produced performances which would at one time have been thought impossible. The early 1960s saw a hundred yards [91 metres] run in ten seconds and a mile [1·6 kilometres] in four minutes.

By the 1980s it had become almost automatic for old records to be broken and new ones established at almost every international sports meeting. In most countries sport is now regarded as a major aspect of educational and social life.

Sri Lanka: formerly Ceylon, an island off the southern tip of India, producing tea, rubber and rice. A republican constitution was adopted in 1972. Sri Lanka continues to be in the Commonwealth. Population in 1982: 15,189,000.

Stalin, Joseph (Joseph Vissarionovich Dzhugashvili, 1879–1953): Russian dictator whose adopted name means "man of steel". After studying for the priesthood and being expelled from his seminary, he joined the Bolshevik wing of the Communists, organising a bank robbery in Tiflis in 1907, and over 1,000 other raids, to provide funds for the party. In 1922 he became powerful as general secretary of the Communist party and

after Lenin's death in 1924 became virtual ruler of the USSR. In 1928 he inaugurated the first five year plan for industrialisation and collective farming. The "second revolution" in Russia was achieved by ruthless "re-education" of the people, involving forced labour, the seizure of land, the corruption of the law courts, the extermination of all rivals, the suppression of free opinion in the arts and literature and all the other machinery of the police state. Graphic pictures of the terror of life under Stalin may be found in such books as Arthur Koestler's *Darkness at Noon*, Alexander Solzhenitsyn's *One Day in the Life of Denisovitch* and Boris Pasternak's *Dr Zhivago*.

In August 1939, though he and Hitler were completely opposed on many points, Stalin signed the Russo-German pact. If this was a drastic shock to the Western powers, so, in June 1941, was the German onslaught on Russia to Stalin. Thereafter it may be considered that Stalin showed at his best, as a patriotic war leader, uniting his vast country, ordering that "the enemy must not be left . . . a single pound of grain or gallon of fuel". They must be "hounded and annihilated at every step". He subsequently took p in the Allied Conferences at Teh (1943), Yalta (1945) and Potsdam (194

Three years after his death in 1953 methods, particularly the "personal cult" which demanded pictures a statues of himself all over Russia, w officially condemned by his successo History will be slow to pronounce a fi valid verdict on the leader who, "cap cious, irritable and brutal" (in Khrus chev's words) achieved great things Russia at such a price of human life a happiness.

¶ LIVERSIDGE, DOUGLAS. *Joseph Stalin.* 19 ROBERTS, ELIZABETH MAUCHLINE. *Stalin, Man Steel.* 1968

Stalingrad, now **Volgograd:** Russi city on the lower Volga, once call Tsaritsyn, on the River Tsaritsa. Jose Stalin (*see* separate entry) took a leadi part in its defence in the revolution 1917, and in 1925 it was renamed Stali grad in his honour. It saw rapid and exte sive industrial development under Sov rule. In World War II (*see* separate entr the Germans tried to cut the River Vol here (August 1942–February 1943), b Stalingrad was stubbornly defended a the Germans were driven out in Janua 1943 with losses estimated at 330,000. T city was rebuilt and, in 1961, renam Volgograd.

¶ JUKES, G. *Stalingrad.* 1969; SAMMIS, E. R. *L Stand at Stalingrad.* 1966

Stamp Act (1765)**:** British Act of Parli ment that was one of the immedia causes of the War of American I dependence. By it, customs duties we charged on imports into the colonies, a it forecast "certain stamp duties" as a ba for further legislation. The act aroused t famous cry, echoed by Pitt in Britai "No taxation without representation and the Stamp Act was repealed in Mar

66, along with some of the most ob-
:tionable customs duties.

ɔICKINSON, ALICE. *The Stamp Act.* 1971

e also AMERICAN WAR OF INDEPENDENCE;
ᴛT, WILLIAM, THE ELDER.

:andish, Miles (1584–1656): one of the iginal Pilgrim Fathers who sailed from :yden to America in the *Mayflower* 620, *see* separate entries). He settled at ew Plymouth and became military cap-in of the colony, largely contributing to ; success by his skilful exploits against e Indians. Standish House, built by the n of Miles Standish in 1666, still stands Duxbury, Massachusetts.

tanley in Africa, 1878.

tanley, Sir Henry Morton (1841–904): British explorer. He was born in Jorth Wales but moved to New Orleans ı 1856. After travelling widely in the Vest Indies, Spain and Italy during 863–64, in 1867 he joined the staff of the *Jew York Herald*, continuing his travels s a special correspondent. He achieved vorld fame by seeking and finding the nissing Scottish explorer David Living-tone (*see* separate entry) at Ujiji on Lake 'anganyika in 1871.

HALL-QUEST, O. *With Stanley in Africa.* 1962

tar Chamber: building in Westminster, ngland, used for meetings of the King's Council from Edward III's time, and developing into a court of royal justice dealing with riots, maintenance, libel, etc. Strengthened by Henry VII, it dealt effectively with overpowerful subjects. Used by the Stuarts to support arbitrary royal power, it became hated and was abolished by the Long Parliament in 1640. The court was so called because of the building's ceiling, decorated with golden stars.

Stars and Bars: the original flag of the Confederate States (*see* separate entry) of the USA. It consisted of three wide bars, red, white and red, with, in the upper left-hand corner, seven stars on a blue field, representing the seven states (South Carolina, Mississippi, Florida, Alabama, Louisiana, Georgia and Texas) that broke away from the Union in 1861.

Stars and Stripes: the national flag of the USA, consisting of thirteen alternating red and white stripes (*see* THIRTEEN COLONIES) and, in the top left-hand corner, fifty white stars on a blue field – one star for every state. The flag (with the crosses of St George and St Andrew instead of the stars) was first raised by George Washington (*see* separate entry) in 1776.

Star-spangled Banner, The: poetical name for the USA flag, from the famous poem, officially adopted in 1931 as the national anthem, written in 1814 by Francis Scott Key (1779–1843). The original manuscript is in the possession of the Maryland Historical Society, Baltimore. The refrain (with slight variation from verse to verse) runs:

> And the star-spangled banner in
>   triumph shall wave
> O'er the land of the free and the
>   home of the brave.

Statue of Liberty: the bronze figure of a woman lifting a torch on Liberty Island, New York Harbour, the proper name being "Liberty Enlightening the World". Designed by F. A. Bartholdi, the statue was the gift of the French people and was dedicated in 1886. The statue itself weighs 225 tons [240 tonnos] and is 151 feet [46 metres] high, though, on its pedestal, from sea level to the tip of the torch is 330 feet [100 metres].

The Statue of Liberty in New York Harbour.

Steam: vapour produced by raisi water to boiling point. In civilisation has a number of uses, but this article confined to considering steam as a sour of mechanical energy, which will be di cussed from a historical rather than technical standpoint.

Steam engines as we know them tod (and the term includes many types besid railway engines, which are properly call locomotives) work on principles deriv from the power of steam to expand. T earliest engines of the Industrial Revol tion, however, worked by the condensi of steam in a cylinder, causing a vacuu and producing a power stroke. This ty of engine was developed by Thom Newcomen (1663–1729) and greatly in proved by James Watt (1736–1819, s separate entry). These engines worke slowly and had limited application, bein largely used for draining mines.

It seems that Watt appreciated t possibilities of using a cylinder or cyli ders into which steam was admitte alternately at either end to act directly o a piston; but he was probably discourage by the extremely low steam pressure considerably less than ten pounds p square inch (p.s.i.) [0·7 kilogrammes pe square centimetre] which was all th the boilers of his time could safel produce. It is difficult to trace clearly th first stages of the development of th non-condensing high pressure engine the name of the Cornishman Richar Trevithick (1771–1833) and in Americ Oliver Evans (1755–1819) may be men tioned, but records are scanty. From thes beginnings, however, was derived th steam engine which revolutionised in dustry – and indeed life itself – in almo every part of the world during the 19t century. It provided power for factorie it changed the railways from local horse drawn affairs to a vast network in man countries and a thin lifeline in others, an

The Watt double-acting steam engine.

enabled ships of increasing tonnage to ross the oceans in a fraction of the time equired under sail.

The action of steam on a piston in a ylinder remained the basic principle of ll types until the turbine was developed ı the 1880s by Charles Parsons (1854–931). Here motion is produced by steam cting on a number of vanes arranged ound a shaft. Turbines, which are capable f a high rate of revolution, are particuırly suitable for ships' engines and for riving electric generators.

The first necessity for any type of steam ngine is a suitable and sufficient supply of team. As the 19th century advanced im-rovements in the art of boiler-making, specially after the use of steel was dopted, enabled increasingly higher ressures to be used. For the locomotive rials at Rainhill, Liverpool (1829), a ressure of 50 p.s.i. [3·5 kg p.s.cm] was pecified (and a leaking boiler on one of he competitors was plugged with oat-neal until the feed-pump was clogged vith porridge); but, by the middle of the century, although in the meanwhile boiler explosions were fairly frequent, 150 p.s.i. [10·5 kg p.s.cm] was being used. Except for occasional experiments, locomotive boilers have never exceeded 250 p.s.i. [17·6 kg p.s.cm], though steamships have used up to twice this pressure, while in industry a lower one has generaly sufficed.

Steam, however, has its drawbacks. It is "inefficient" in the sense that a considerable proportion of the energy produced in the form of heat by the burning of fuel (coal or oil) to raise steam is lost in the process of converting this into motive power. Moreover, a locomotive or a ship has to carry its fuel with it: a locomotive also carries water to replenish its boiler, while a ship needs space for apparatus to make sea-water usable. Lastly, the maintenance of boilers, particularly those burning coal, requires the frequent clearance of ash and clinker from tubes and fireboxes. For this purpose the fire must be allowed to die, and it takes some time to raise steam again. In contrast, a diesel or electric engine can stand idle for a long time and then be started merely by pressing a switch. For these reasons, steam as a source of mechanical energy is in many fields being abandoned in favour of internal combustion or electric power.

¶ HART, I. B. *James Watt and the History of Steam Power*. 1961

Steel: any one of numerous alloys of iron and carbon (the latter in the general range of 0·1 to 1·5 per cent), often combined with other metals, such as nickel, chromium and manganese, according to the special physical properties required for the job in hand. As compared with iron, steel has a higher tensile strength, with consequent saving in weight, and greater hardness.

In ancient times, long after iron was in general use, bronze or brass was often preferred for armour or weapons, but in the Middle Ages steel came into favour, the sword blades produced at Damascus (Syria) and Toledo (Spain) being especially prized.

As long as wood remained the fuel for smelting, even though a primitive blast-furnace was invented, little technical progress was made, until, in the early 18th century, the use of coke was introduced and higher temperatures could be applied. In 1740 Benjamin Huntsman (1704–76) discovered a process of making cast steel which revolutionised the cutlery industry and showed the way to the development of machine tools.

In 1856 Sir Henry Bessemer (1813–9 *see* separate entry) invented the "co verter": this blew hot air through t molten metal to remove impurities a produced a "mild" steel, which in mediately had many engineering applic tions throughout the world. On railway for instance, the use of steel instead of ir for rails and wheel-tyres led to great safety and economy: boilers of all sor could be made to withstand higher stea pressures: ships' hulls could be made steel and warships armoured. The Fort Bridge, Scotland (1889), was the fir large bridge to be built of this materia

An event of domestic importance w the development of "stainless steel" f cutlery, etc., following the discovery 1912 that steel containing 12 per ce chromium is virtually rustless. Anoth important modern discovery was that tungsten, a particularly hard element no much used for tipping cutting tools a for electric lamp filaments. The tech nique known as "continuous casting has recently speeded up steel-making b cutting out some of the chief steps in th long-established conventional processe

¶ FISHER, DOUGLAS. *Steel: From the Iron Age to th Space Age*. 1968

Stephenson, George (1781–1848) an **Robert** (1803–59): father and son, earl British railway engineers. George rightly regarded as the "Father of Rail ways". A self-educated man fro Northumberland, he used his early ex perience of transport in the coalfield t lay out and construct the Stockton an Darlington Railway (opened 1825) an the Liverpool and Manchester (1830) continuing thereafter to assist the development of railways and of the coal and iro industries in Derbyshire. Robert, thoug perhaps less famous in common estimation, became, thanks to his early co-operation with his father and a bette

The Bessemer "converter", 1856.

ucation, an engineer of wider scope d impressive achievements both in gland and abroad.

ROLT, L. T. C. *George and Robert Stephenson.* 1935; LLIAMSON, J. A. *George and Robert Stephenson.* 58

---

ockholm: capital, chief port and in-strial centre of Sweden. Sometimes lled "the Queen of the Baltic" or "the nice of the North" from the beauty of setting, it began as a fortress and a ding post in the 13th century on an and linking Lake Mälaren with the ltic. Stockholm spread till it occupied large cluster of islands and peninsulas d became the capital in the 17th cen-ry. It supports a variety of industries luding iron and steel, engineering, tiles, chemicals, petrol refining and nting. There are also highly important ucational and medical foundations.

---

one Age: period in all human cultures en man used stone tools. Stone survives ough humans become dust, so pre-torians learn about early man from his ol-making techniques. The Stone Age gan when man first used flint chopping ols, about 700,000 years ago, and ended en he discovered how to make bronze. he Palaeolithic (Greek *palaios*, ancient, d *lithos*, stone) period roughly cor-ponds to the Ice Age, finishing about 00 BC. People lived nomadic lives, ltering in caves, the men hunting and ning, the women gathering wild fruits d vegetables. They learnt how to make s, to flake blades from flints for har-ons and spears. Ritual, centred on nting magic and fertility cults, was ved by artistic schools producing ani-l paintings, engravings and carvings. hen the ice retreated, forest replaced dra, and the great herds, man's food, appeared. Mesolithic (i.e. Middle Stone

Stone Age pierced axes found in Germany.

Age) man had to change his way of life and devise new tools. He set tiny flints in shafts as arrows for the hunt. While women collected shellfish, he went fishing and fowling in canoes, which he made with his new wood cutting tools, and built huts for shelter.

The Neolithic (New Stone Age; *see* separate entry) period was revolutionary. The foundations of civilisation were laid in lands from the Nile Valley to the Indus. Animals were domesticated, crops planted, food stored, wealth accumu-lated. People stopped wandering, lived in settlements and built houses of brick or stone. They ground and polished their tools and began potting and weaving. Religion centred on agricultural life, good crops depending on weather, so that earth, rain and sun were thought of as gods.

¶ DICKINSON, ALICE. *First Book of Stone Age Man.* 1965; QUENNELL, MARJORIE and C. H. B. *Everyday Life in Prehistoric Times.* 1959

Stonehenge: remains of a very ancient arrangement of large stones, set in con-centric circles, on Salisbury Plain, Eng-land, probably erected between 1800 and 1400 BC. It seems to have been a place of great religious significance and was prob-ably an observatory. Some of the stones appear to have been brought from South Wales, and despite a variety of attempted

Stonehenge, on Salisbury Plain.

explanations, it is a mystery how the men of the time could handle such massive weights.

¶ ATKINSON, J. R. C. *What is Stonehenge?* 1962; BRANLEY, FRANKLYN. *The Mystery of Stonehenge.* 1972

See also AVEBURY.

Stowe, Harriet Elizabeth Beecher (1811–96): popular American writer. Her best known book *Uncle Tom's Cabin* made her world-famous and powerfully influenced public opinion against slavery. Translated into many languages, it is still read, though considered out of tune with modern thought on race relations. Mrs Stowe was honoured by Queen Victoria and admired by many famous writers of her day, including Tolstoy and Dickens.

Strasbourg: main city of Alsace, eastern France, situated on a tributary of the Rhine. Originating as a Celtic settlement, it became the headquarters of the Roman eighth legion against the barbarians to the east. It became part of the German kingdom in the 10th century and was given the status of a free imperial city. It was annexed by Louis XIV in 1681. Among its notable buildings is the magnificent cathedral with a famous astronomical clock built in 1574 and restarted after a considerable overhaul in 1843. Another claim to fame was the city's association with the work of the printer Gutenberg (*see* GUTENBERG BIBLE; PRINTING). In 1949 Strasbourg was chosen as the offi meeting place for the Council of Euro

Strategy: literally, the art of the gen or commander-in-chief, though strate decisions can be taken by a group, e.g council of war. In contrast, tactics concerned with the actual manoeuvr of troops or ships in contact with enemy and are therefore the job subordinate commanders.

Strikes: the refusal of workers, act together, to go on working unless employer grants them some impro ment such as more pay or shorter ho When this happens, both sides suffer. T workers get no pay from their emplo while they are on strike, and the emplo himself has no goods to sell and so lo his profits. Sooner or later, one side or other gives in. Sometimes there is agreement in which both sides yiel little with the workers accepting less th they asked for and the employer granti more than he wanted to. The opposite a strike is a lock-out, that is, the emplo offers no work to his workers unless th accept new terms. When a strike ordered by the trade union concern it is called "official": other strikes, supported by the trade union, or defiance of it, are called "unofficial".

Millions of working days are lost ev year through strikes. In 1926 coal min in Britain struck against the coal own demand for them to take lower wages a to work longer hours. The position of miners grew desperate, and the Tra Union Congress (*see* TRADE UNIO called a General Strike in sympathy. trade unionists in the great industr struck, and a very serious situation aro Over three million workers were strike, and the major public services, su as the railways, came to a halt. There w no newspapers, but the governm

Strikers in the streets of London during the 1926 General Strike.

ıed a special paper called *The British* *zette* and took control of the radio. :er ten days of great anxiety, the neral Strike collapsed after a loss of 500,000 working days. The workers nt back to work, and the miners were to continue their strike alone.

he British government was so alarmed the General Strike that in 1927 it made ew law, the Trades Disputes and Trade ıions Act, which made sympathetic kes illegal, but this was repealed by the oour government in 1946. In recent ırs there have been many strikes, both icial and unofficial, and the concern of TUC and of the government has been bring both sides in a dispute together a settlement. Not much progress has :n made. In 1970 over 12 million ›rking days were lost through strikes. ıe weapon of the strike is now recog-ed by professional workers such as chers and doctors as well as by most lustrial workers. Legislation affecting conduct of strikes was introduced by the Conservative government in 1971.

Strikes are not confined to Great Britain: they happen in most advanced industrial democratic countries where "the right to strike" is recognised. In totalitarian states the trade unions are controlled by the government, and strikes are not permitted.

Organised strikes became fairly common in the USA in the 1830s and 1840s, and in 1834 President Jackson (*see* separate entry) used the army to break a strike of Irish labourers building a canal in Maryland. Massive strikes, sometimes involving the use of federal troops and state militia and serious loss of life, have occurred on the railroads, and in the steel, automobile and mining industries. In 1947 the Taft-Hartley Act introduced important new strike legislation, prohibiting the "closed shop" and providing a "cooling off" period of sixty days.

In 1984–85 a year long strike by Britain's coalminers which generated much bitterness was a reminder that the strike is still very much a part of industrial life.

Stuart, Stewart, or **Steuart, House of:** the royal dynasty which ruled Scotland 1371–1603 and, from 1603–88, Scotland and England combined. The ancestors of the Stuarts came from Brittany. King David I (reigned 1124–53) made one of the family, Walter, seneschal, or steward, of Scotland; and from this hereditary office came the family name. Another Walter married Marjory, daughter of Robert the Bruce. In 1371 their son, as Robert II, became the first Stuart king of Scotland. For centuries England and Scotland were enemies. In one of the few peaceful intervals James IV of Scotland (reigned 1488–1513) married Margaret, daughter of Henry VII. It was this marriage which gave the Stuarts a claim to the English throne. When, in 1603, Queen Elizabeth of England died unmarried, James VI, son of the ill-fated Mary Queen of Scots, became, in addition, King James I of England.

Stuart rule was interrupted from 164 60. Disputes with Parliament led to ci war, the beheading of the King, Charle in 1649 and the establishment of a Co monwealth under Oliver Cromwell. 1660 the Stuarts were restored, but 1688 the dynasty came to an end wh James II, who had become converted Roman Catholicism (*see* separate entr was forced to abdicate.

Two rebellions, in 1715 and 1745 spectively, the first led by James II's s James, the second by the latter's s Charles Edward (Bonnie Prince Charli were equally unsuccessful. Stuart su porters, called Jacobites, are still n extinct – though few would go so far to wish to see the Duke of Bavaria, prese head of the House of Stuart, on the thro of England.

See also COMMONWEALTH; CROMWE JACOBITES.

THE HOUSE OF STUART: *Above (left to right), Mary Queen of Scots, James I, Charles I. Below (left to right), Charles II, James II, James Francis Edward, the Pretender.*

ıbmarines: vessels so designed that ey can be submerged and navigated hen under water. As an instrument of ar they can be traced back to the 18th ntury. Manually operated submersibles ere produced by the Americans David ushnell (1742–1824) and Robert Fulton 766–1815). The *Nautilus*, built by Fulton 1800, was designed to blow up enemy

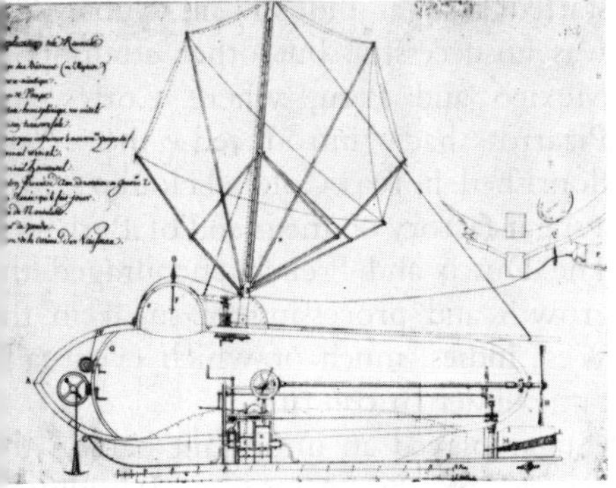

ction of Fulton's submarine Nautilus, *1798.*

ıips at anchor by planting bombs under eir hulls. In 1863 the American Conderate Navy built the *Davids*, semiıbmersibles with long projecting spars ı which torpedoes were attached. They so produced a "torpedo diving boat" :iven with a steam engine in 1865.

The USA's *Holland* of 1898 marked the :ginning of the modern submarine era. rmed with guns and torpedoes the aft was driven on the surface by a petrol ıgine and, when submerged, by an elecic motor powered from a battery. orizontal rudders, or hydroplanes, and allast tanks served by compressed air, ontrolled the diving and surfacing.

The first submarine circumnavigation as achieved in 1960 (24 February–25 pril) by the US nuclear submarine *Triton* Captain Edward Latimer Beach). Fitting- enough, the voyage was named "Operion Magellan", in tribute to the first ırface sea voyage round the world made y Ferdinand Magellan in his flagship *ittoria* four and a half centuries before.

Sudan: republic in north-east Afric having 400 miles [644 kilometres] of Red Sea coastline in the north-east, common boundaries with Ethiopia in the east, Kenya, Uganda and Congo Republic in the south, with the Central African Republic and Chad in the west, Libya north-west and Egypt to the north. Formerly it formed the eastern section of an enormous indeterminate belt known as the Belad es Sudan of Negritia, extending across Africa south of the Sahara, now split up by various agreements and treaties between the Sudan, Chad, Niger, Mali and Senegal and other West African states. The capital is Khartoum, at the confluence of the Blue and White Niles. There is extensive cultivation of the area between the White Nile and Atbara lying to the south-east of Khartoum, thanks to dams and irrigation schemes. The main products are cotton, which is the chief export, millet (the staple food), gum arabic, ebony, papyrus, groundnuts and dates. It is the largest country on the African continent.

Between 1500 and 1200 BC North Sudan, or Kush, was part of the Egyptian empire but existed as an independent kingdom from 750 BC to AD 350. Between 350 and the 7th century the history of Kush is obscure, though some time in the 7th century Muslim invaders replaced Christianity by the Islamic faith. South Sudan, cut off from the north by extensive marshlands, remained primitive until the 19th century, when Mohamet Ali conquered the Sudan in 1801, beginning a period of misrule which General Gordon, as governor-general, tried to put right on his appointment in 1877; but the revolt of the Mahdi led in 1885 to the fall of Khartoum and the death of Gordon, and the Mahdi's successor, the Khalifa, proved to be an even more ruthless ruler. In 1896 General (later Earl) Kitchener started military moves designed to end the regime, which was finally destroyed by the battles of Atbara and Omdurman, and the death at Gedid of the Khalifa.

In 1899 Britain and Egypt began a condominium (joint) form of rule of the Sudan, the country being known as the Anglo-Egyptian Sudan until 1956, when it became an independent state. The country's history since then has been troubled, especially by conflict between the Moslem north and the Christian/Pagan south.

See separate entries for CHRISTIANITY; GORDON; ISLAM; MUSLIMS.

Suez Canal: waterway joining the Mediterranean with the Red Sea and thus allowing oceangoing vessels to reach the East without sailing round Africa. From Port Said, at the Mediterranean end, the canal runs for 101 miles [163 kilometres] through Egyptian territory. The construction of the canal was undertaken by the Frenchman de Lesseps (*see* separate entry), work starting in 1859 and being completed ten years later. In 1875 the major share in the capital of the canal company was purchased by Britain from the bankrupt Khedive (viceroy) of Egypt. In 1956 the Egyptians nationalised the canal, and in 1967 it was put out of action by the war with Israel. The Canal was reopened to international shipping in 1975. Plans to deepen and widen it further exist.

¶ HIRSCHFELD, B. *The Vital Link: the Story of the Suez Canal*. 1968

Sugar: sweet crystalline substance extracted from a variety of plants, especially sugar cane and beet. Sugar cane originated in New Guinea, India and China. Honey was for centuries the only sweetener known in Europe, but in 325 BC Alexander the Great's (*see* separate entry) soldiers ate, in India, "honey not made by bees", and this was the boiled juice of the sugar cane, known in modern India as *jaggery*

By AD 500 there was a flourishing sug industry in the Tigris-Euphrates valle Arab traders carried the sugar to Europ where the trade was continued by Venetia merchants.

In 1420 the Portuguese colonise Madeira and established sugar plantatio there. In 1516 the Spanish governme started a sugar industry in Cuba. Th was unsuccessful, but other attempts i Mexico and Peru, where Cortés an Pizarro had introduced the can flourished. In 1641 Colonel Holdip starte a sugar factory on the island of Barbado The Dutch and French encouraged th growth and processing of sugar in th West Indies, much of which eventuall came under British rule.

Sugar played an important part in th origins of the American Revolutio against Britain. The Sugar Act of 176 instigated by British West Indies sug planters with influence in London, strov to prevent the colonists buying molass (a treacle obtained during sugar refining from French, Spanish and other foreig islands by imposing an import tax threepence per gallon. The loss of Frenc and Spanish currency was a strong fact in the "no taxation without representa tion" cry.

Sugar can also be made from sugar bee a root vegetable which was eaten i Roman times. In 1912 a beet processin factory was established in Norfolk England, but people did not like bee sugar, although it was used widely i Holland. During the economic difficulti of the 1930s housewives started to buy because it was cheaper than cane suga Its use increased during World War I when shipping space was scarce. Nowa days, about one-third of the sugar used i Britain, which is one of the highest con sumers in the world per head of popula tion, is beet sugar.

[Su]leiman I, called **"the Magnificent"** ([1]494–1566): Ottoman Sultan who suc[c]eded to the throne in 1520. He attacked [th]e Christian states, capturing Belgrade [in] 1521 and driving the Knights of St [Jo]hn from Rhodes in 1522. Defeating the [Hu]ngarians at Mohacs, 1526, he was [ch]ecked only outside Vienna in 1532. [H]is fleets ruled the Mediterranean Sea. [Fo]r his period he was an enlightened [ru]ler, drafting many new laws, encourag[in]g the arts and planning fine buildings.
[Se]e also OTTOMAN EMPIRE.

[Su]lly, Maximilien de Béthune, Duc [de] (1560–1641): French statesman. His [de]voted service assisted Henry of Navarre [(H]enry IV) to the French throne in 1594. [A]s superintendent of finance, he reformed [th]e fiscal system and became in effect sole [m]inister of France. After Henry's as[sa]ssination in 1610, Sully surrendered [m]any offices, but was appointed a marshal [of] France in 1634. His *Mémoires* provide [a] valuable picture of the times.

[Su]matra: Indonesian island south-west [of] Malaya and west of Borneo, a Hindu [ki]ngdom from AD 600 to the 11th century, [af]ter which Islamic influences predomi[na]ted. The Portuguese traded in spices [fr]om 1509 but were expelled by the [D]utch before 1600. Except during the [N]apoleonic Wars and the Japanese oc[cu]pation in World War II, the Dutch [E]ast India Company and the Dutch Indies [G]overnment ruled until 1950, when [Su]matra became three provinces of the [I]ndonesian Republic.
[Se]e INDONESIA, MALAYA for map.

[S]umer: ancient region of southern [M]esopotamia. The farmers of Sumer [li]ved on the fertile soil of the Euphrates [v]alley and used the river water to irrigate [th]eir crops. Ur was their most famous [ci]ty, dating from about 4000 BC, and the later Babylonian civilisation (*see* BABYLON) adopted the Sumerian religion and their "cuneiform" system of writing on clay tablets.

¶ CARRINGTON, R. *Ancient Sumer.* 1960
See also ALPHABETS.

Sumter, Fort: fort on an artificial island in Charleston harbour, South Carolina, where Confederate troops fired the first shots of the American Civil War (12 April 1861 *see* separate entry) when provisions were being brought to the Federal force which had occupied the fort.

Sun Yat-sen (1866–1925): Chinese republican leader, more familiarly known in China as Sun Wen. A medical doctor by training (he was the first graduate of the new medical school at Hongkong), he turned to politics in 1893 and soon became involved in revolutionary plots against the Manchu regime. As a result he spent some years in exile, where he worked to bring about revolution and the establishment of a democratic government in China based on the three principles of nationalism, democracy and social welfare. When the revolution took place, ending 2000 years of Imperial rule, Dr Sun Yat-sen returned in 1912 to head the new government, a position which he soon resigned in favour of the younger Yuan Shih K'ai. He held various other offices but was always more effective as a propagandist and theorist than as an administrator.

As organiser of the Kuomintang (*see* separate entry) and inspirer of the revolution, he has fairly been called the Father of the Chinese Republic.

¶ BUCK, PEARL. *The Man Who Changed China.* 1955

Supreme Soviet: the highest legislative authority in the USSR. It has two chambers with equal legislative rights, elected for four years – the Soviet of the Union, consisting of one deputy for every 300,000 citizens of the USSR, and the Soviet of the Nationalities, elected on a regional basis from the various component republics and other areas. Each has over 750 members. The Supreme Soviet elects the Presidium, the supreme authority while the Soviet is not sitting. "Soviet" is the Russian word for "council".

Surinam: formerly Dutch Guiana, on the north coast of South America, an overseas part of the Netherlands since 1922. The first permanent settlement was made by the Englishman Lord Willoughby of Parham in 1650. In 1667 Surinam was exchanged for New Amsterdam, now New York, though twice again, 1799–1802 and 1804–15, it came into British hands. Slave rebellions were common in the 18th century. In the late 1800s Indian and Japanese labourers were imported to ease plantation problems.

Sutton Hoo: site of East Anglian ship burial. This Suffolk (England) burial mound contained a large boat and burial deposit of great richness, belonging to a 7th-century East Anglian king. The custom of ship burial shows links with Sweden, as does the workmanship on the gold buckle, clasps, purse frame, etc.

¶ BRUCE-MITFORD, R. L. S. *The Sutton Hoo Ship Burial.* 1968; GREEN, CHARLES. *Sutton Hoo: the excavation of a royal ship burial.* 1969

Hinged gold clasp decorated with garnets, glass and filligree, from the Sutton Hoo Treasure.

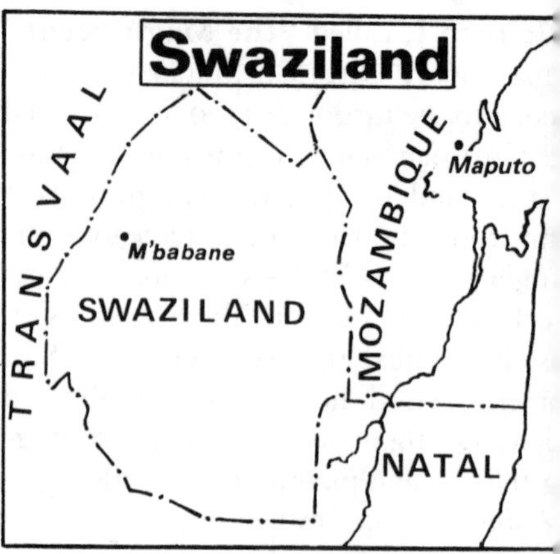

Swaziland: a former British color which became an independent memb of the Commonwealth in 1968. It is monarchy and traditionalist society. tiny landlocked country between Sou Africa and Mozambique, Swaziland nonetheless one of the most prosperou states in Africa, exporting sugar, citr fruits and wood products.

Sweden: kingdom of north-weste Europe, forming the larger part of tl Scandinavian peninsula. It is difficult establish accurately the early story of tl country, because of the absence of reliab written records. The only evidence com trom surviving runes, legends and saga and from many archaeological excava tions. It is clear that the Swedish Vikin moved eastwards to the rivers of Russi and as far as Byzantium. Although the were warlike, they established tradir routes. Christianity spread very slowl among the pagan Swedes, who were tl scourge of northern Christendom unt the 12th century.

After the decline of Viking powe Sweden was rather an isolated countr one of the marchlands on the edge northern Europe. Its kings were weal and real power lay with a highly priv leged aristocracy of nobles and bishop In an effort to regain past glories the

ited with Norway and Denmark by e Union of Kalmar in 1397. But this tempt to make a powerful, single nation Scandinavia failed. A Danish king who ed to curb the importance of the bility stirred up a revolt. Led by ıstavus Vasa, a two-year struggle ended Swedish independence in 1523 and a w royal house of Vasa. At the same ne a quarrel with the Papacy led to the ceptance in Sweden of Protestantism. in England, the monasteries were undered and their lands sold to the bility.

On these foundations Sweden became a eat European nation with a northern ipire. In the 17th century Gustavus dolphus, "the Lion of the North", uilt up his power against the Catholic nperor of Austria by spectacular miliry leadership. Gustavus's intelligence, urage and statesmanship made him one the great figures of modern history. He as killed at the battle of Lützen in 1632. weden failed to hold its empire against e increasing power of Prussia and ıssia. It had neither the money nor the pulation to stand the strain of long arfare with ambitious neighbours. nough reduced in military status the vedes looked for and found a new role play, gaining an international reputaon in the arts. August Strindberg (1849–12) was a genius of literature and the eatre. In the new art form, the cinema m, Ingmar Bergman (b. 1918) has tablished an international reputation and e country has produced a number of mous film stars. In the social field, too, e world found Sweden in the forefront progress. Since 1842 education has been mpulsory and free, and early in the 20th ntury her housing schemes became odels for other European countries. ne millionaire Alfred Nobel increased veden's reputation abroad when he tablished the various Nobel Prizes.

Politically also Sweden has adopted a new role, that of neutrality, preserving it through both World Wars, though much relief work was undertaken in the devastated countries. As a member of UNO Sweden's troops became vital in disputes in which they had no political interest. The country gave the United Nations one of its greatest Directors-General, Dag Hammarskjöld.

¶ MERRICK, HELEN HYNSON. *First Book of Sweden.* 1971

See also BYZANTIUM; CHRISTIANITY; HAMMARSKJÖLD, DAG; NOBEL, ALFRED; PROTESTANTS; VIKINGS.

Switzerland: republic of west central Europe, formed by a confederation of twenty-two cantons (or administrative areas). The Swiss people are descendants of Teutonic tribes which moved westward as the Roman Empire declined, though they did not at first form any kind of united area. First they came under the dominion of Charlemagne. Later the western section became part of the Kingdom of Burgundy, whilst the rest split into small areas with their own rulers. In the 13th century the House of Habsburg extended its control over part of the east.

Because of the dominance of foreigners the Swiss within their various valley regions spoke French, Italian or German. But in spite of this multiplicity of languages there was a general wish for self-rule, preferably in their own localities. For 200 years a struggle for power took place. From small beginnings, in which three forest cantons defeated the Austrians (1315), a combination of most of the Swiss groups developed. In 1499 this Confederation at last achieved independence when it defeated Charles the Bold of Burgundy and the Emperor Maximilian I.

Over the years the Swiss created a tradition of local self-government. Each

Switzerland

canton had its own laws and it was not until 1942 that a national criminal code was drawn up. Even today some parts have "open-air democracy" in which, once a year, the men of an area meet to make some particular laws. Again, only since 1970 have women been allowed to vote. When Napoleon conquered Switzerland and tried to impose a single central government, he failed. In 1815 Switzerland not only regained its independence, but also had its neutrality permanently guaranteed by the big powers of the day. Keeping this independence and neutrality has been both a rewarding and a difficult task. In the 1920s Geneva became the headquarters of the League of Nations with its peace-keeping and humanitarian work; in World War II she found her neutrality extremely hazardous, being surrounded by the German and Italian Axis governments.

Internally one of Switzerland's most serious problems has been religion. Since the Reformation different cantons have been Catholic and Protestant rivals. In the 16th century the country became the centre of international Protestantism. John Calvin established his Church in Geneva and created a model which was followed by groups throughout the world, including Presbyterians in Scotland a the Huguenots in France. Catholic o position was bitter, and a series of sava conflicts as late as the 19th centu showed how prolonged the struggle w

Switzerland has only a small populati and few natural resources. It has relied f its prosperity on the tourist industry a on the specialist talents of a wide varie of people. To the centuries-old craftsma ship of clock- and watch-making th have added optical instruments, banki facilities, medical centres, Pestalo schools and the Nestlé milk industry.

¶ EPSTEIN, SAM and BERYL. *First Book of Switz land.* 1965

See also LEAGUE OF NATIONS; MAXIMILI I; NAPOLEON I; ROMAN CATHOLIC CHURC WORLD WAR II.

Sydney: capital city of New Sou Wales, Australia. Cook sighted the ha bour in 1770. In 1788 Captain Phil established a penal colony, named aft Thomas Townshend, first Viscou Sydney, the Home Secretary, on Sydn Cove in preference to Botany Bay, t first choice. The cessation of the tra portation of convicts from Britain in 18 encouraged free settlement. Sydney h developed into the commercial and i dustrial capital of Australia, with population increasing from 3,000 in 18 to three-and-a-half million in the metr politan area today. Outstanding featu are the magnificent single-span arch P Jackson Bridge (1932), the universities Sydney (1850) and New South Wa (1949), the famous cricket ground, t scene of many notable England v. Au tralia Test Matches and the spectacul futuristic opera house.

¶ KENNEDY, BRIAN. *Sydney.* 1970

Syria: republic of western Asia, stretc ing along the eastern shore of the Medite ranean and to the River Euphrates. Rul ıccessively by Egyptians, Babylonians, littites, Assyrians and Persians, Syria was eeply influenced by Greek civilisation. fell under Roman influence in the 1st entury BC and was under Roman and yzantine domination until, by AD 640, had passed permanently under Muslim ıle. Damascus until 750 was the capital f the Umayyad dynasty (and indeed of ıe Muslim world) but declined with the se of Baghdad. A cultural and literary owering in the 10th and early 11th cenıries ended with conquest by the Seljuk urks.

The Christian Crusaders introduced hristian communities into some towns, ut Damascus remained Muslim, and the rusaders lost Acre in 1291, their last ronghold. Already in the 1250s the longol invasions had ruined Syria. Ruled or a century by the Mamelukes, the rovince then spent four centuries under ıe rule of the Ottoman empire.

During the 18th and 19th centuries, rance became the patron of Catholic hristians in Syria, and Russia of the)rthodox. With the break-up of the 'urkish empire, Syria came under the ontrol of France, who acquired a manate in 1930. Full Syrian independence ras conceded only in 1945, after World Var II.

An active member of the Arab League, yria suffered a setback with the estabshment of Israel. The Syrian Baath arty combined socialism with the ideal f Arab unity. In 1958 Syria joined with gypt to form the United Arab Republic ut withdrew from it in 1961. The ountry remains implacably hostile to srael and is deeply involved in the affairs f its unhappy neighbour, Lebanon.

e SAUDI ARABIA for map.

ee also BYZANTINE EMPIRE; CRUSADES; ONGOLS; MUSLIMS; OTTOMAN EMPIRE; ORLD WARS I and II.

T

Tacitus, Publius Cornelius (*c.* AD 55–*c.* 118): Roman historian. His major works, of which portions are now lost, give an account of the times of the early Roman emperors. Among his shorter books is a life of his father-in-law Agricola (*see* separate entry), describing his military successes in Britain.

Tactics: the art of manoeuvring armed forces in contact with the enemy; the army corporal studies minor tactics, the formation commander and his staff decide major tactics. Tactics depend on thorough training, quick information about enemy movements, an eye for ground, an understanding of the role of each weapon. There is usually a timelag between the introduction of a new weapon by one or two farseeing enthusiasts and the development of suitable tactics. Liddell-Hart wrote that the early battles of World War II were "lost on the steps of the Cavalry Club". He turned to history – the infiltration tactics of the Mongols (*see* separate entry) – to work out the implications of the tank and the lorry.

See also STRATEGY.

Taft, William Howard (1857–1930: 27th president (1909–13) of the USA and chief justice of the Supreme Court (1921–30). He continued the policy of Theodore Roosevelt (*see* separate entry) in promoting his country's financial and commercial interests in Latin America and successfully enforced the laws against the great oil and tobacco trusts, which were broken up.

Taft-Hartley Act (1947): law passed by the US Congress (*see* separate entry) in an effort to control industrial strikes. Among its other provisions, it required sixty days' notice to be given of the ending of a wages contract, and enabled the government to obtain from the courts a legal injunction delaying for eighty days any strike which could be considered harmful to the country's wellbeing or security.

Tagore, Sir Rabindranath (1861–1941): Indian poet, novelist, educationist, social reformer, preacher and mystic, who won the Nobel Prize for literature in 1913. In over 150 books, on immensely varied subjects, he stressed spiritual as against material values. He founded the unconventional Santiniketan School (where weather dictated the daily timetable) in 1900, and Viswabharati University in 1921.

Taiping Rebellion (1850–65): a major rising against the Manchu dynasty in China, begun in 1850 among a Christian sect in Kwangsi and Kwangtung provinces. Its leader was Hung Hsiu-ch'uan, who tried to impose a sort of puritanical Christian socialism. Advancing northwards and down the Yangtze, the rebels captured Nanking in 1853, but their fortunes fluctuated with a changing leadership. When their army approached Shanghai, they were opposed by European and Chinese forces and began to lose ground, Nanking finally falling in 1864. The Chinese emperor was assiste in his military recovery by the Britis General Gordon (*see* separate entry).

Taj Mahal: built at Agra, 1632–50, b the Indian Emperor Shah Jehan as a tom for his favourite wife Mumtaz-i-Maha Designed by Ustad Isa, of white marb with a dome rising to 210 feet [64 metres it is the finest example of Mogul architec ture and one of the most beautif buildings in the world.

Talking machines: devices which re cord and play back the human voice an other sounds. The first step towards suc a device was taken in 1857, when Leo Scott constructed his "phonautograph" which recorded on the smoked surface c a rotating cylinder the movements of vibrating diaphragm. This, however, wa not capable of reproducing the sound recorded. In 1877 Thomas Edison in vented the "phonograph", which wa capable of playing back a record forme on a surface of tinfoil wrapped round cylinder. The familiar disc record wa invented by Emile Berliner, who starte to manufacture his "gramophone" i 1894. This was further developed b Eldridge Johnson, who devised a spring driven motor. The variations in th record track were lateral, not vertical as i the case of the "hill-and-dale" indenta tions of the Edison cylinder. Johnson an Berliner formed the Victor Talkin Machine Company in 1901. Thus far a development had been in the Unite States, but, in England, the Gramophon Company was formed in 1898, an adopted the familiar "His Master's Voice trade mark in the following year. In th late 1940s the American Columbia Com pany produced what was called th Microgroove recording, now familiarl known as LP or long-playing. This wa made possible by speed reduction, fine ooves on the disc and a much finer ylus. In the 1950s further advances came th stereo (stereophonic) recordings hich diffuse the concentrated sound oduced by a single loudspeaker.

The tape recorder, in its modern form, peared in the 1920s. An early form, vented by Valdemar Poulsen of Denark, using a wire of magnetised steel, as shown at the Paris Exhibition of 1900. The application of these ideas to the quirements of a modern business office s led to a variety of dictating machines, ing wax cylinders, plastic discs, wire d coated tape, the earliest of these being lison's Ediphone.

t only remains to mention the teleone, invented and patented in the nited States by Alexander Graham Bell e separate entry) in 1876. His original ectromagnetic transmitter served also as eceiver, the instrument being presented ernately to the mouth and the ear. This as improved by Edison's invention of e variable-contact carbon transmitter. England the first telephone exchange as opened in London in 1879 with only ght subscribers. By 1982 eleven counies had a ratio of more than 50 teleones for every 100 population. They ere in order: Sweden (82·8), the USA 8·7), Denmark (68), Canada (64·7), ixembourg (62·6), New Zealand, etherlands, Australia, Finland, Japan d Britain.

e also TELECOMMUNICATIONS.

alleyrand-Perigord, Charles Mauce de (1754–1838): French diplomat, ually known as Talleyrand. He was an istocrat and a man of extraordinary aptability. Under Louis XVI he was shop of Autun, but the French Revoluon (*see* separate entry) saw him president the National Assembly and later foreign minister, an office which he continued to hold under Napoleon, who made him a prince. On the latter's fall, Talleyrand took a leading part in the recall of the Bourbon king and showed brilliant skill in the negotiations over the reconstruction of Europe. When the Bourbons gave way (1830) to Louis Philippe, he was appointed French ambassador in London.

Tallies, talley sticks: wooden sticks for recording hours of work, payments, etc. In the more complicated examples, notches of increasing width to represent units, tens, hundreds, etc., were cut. The stick was then cut down the middle and the two parties to a monetary transaction each kept one half as evidence of the account, matching them together again when necessary. Tallies were probably introduced into England by the foreign merchants attending fairs and markets, and were recognised by the Law Merchant, while still disapproved by the Common Law. In 1292 we read of a barrister's disgusted remark: "We do not think he ought to be answered on a bit of wood like that, without writing."

Once established, they became the recognised form of receipt for payments into the Royal Treasury until 1826. In 1834 nearly all the ancient tallies were burned in the furnaces which heated the House of Lords. The usual tally was about 9 inches [22·8 cm] long, but the Bank of

13th century exchequer tallies, showing the names of those who had paid and the nature of the account. The notches represent the sums paid, with pounds above and pence below.

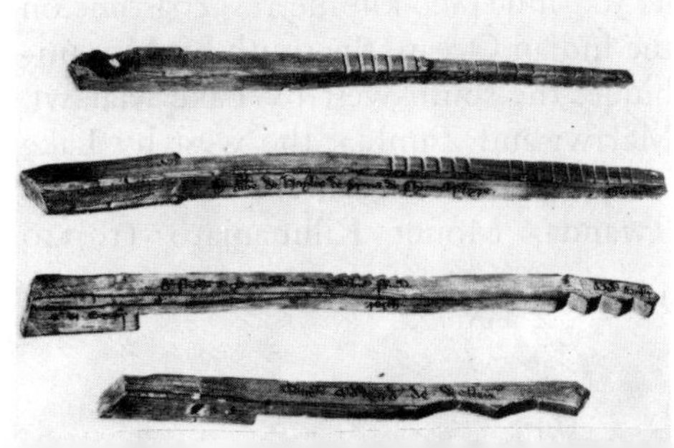

England (*see* separate entry) still preserves a giant specimen over 8 feet [*c.* 2·5 metres] long. Tallies, from the French *taille*, notch, were also put to simpler uses such as keeping the score (itself a Saxon word for notch) in the game of cricket. A free-scoring batsman is still sometimes described as being "in good nick".

Talmud: Jewish religious book (compiled in Babylonia and put into writing from the 2nd to 6th century of the Christian era) giving guidance on the conduct of spiritual life. It embodies the teaching of many centuries and has from time to time been revised.

¶ COHEN, A. *Everyman's Talmud.* 1949

See also JEWS.

Tammany, Tammany Hall: political organisation founded in New York after the War of American Independence and named after an Indian chief noted for his wisdom and love of liberty. At first Tammany represented the interests of the middle classes against the land-owning aristocrats. Later it became a corrupt organisation, with great influence over the Democratic party, organising gangs in furtherance of its political ends and dishonestly acquiring funds, sometimes for private gain for its members. It regained a measure of respectability but since 1930 has declined in power. Its old headquarters, Tammany Hall on 14th Street, occupied since 1868, was sold in 1927 and a new building erected.

Tanganyika: now major part of United Republic of Tanzania, bounded in the north by Kenya and Uganda, the east by its 500-mile [800 kilometres] coastline on the Indian Ocean, the south by Mozambique, the south-west by Lake Malawi, Malawi and Zambia, the west by Lake Tanganyika and Zaire, Burundi and Rwanda. Mount Kilimanjaro (19,340 feet: 5,894 metres – the highest point Africa) and Mount Meru (14,970 fe 4,562 metres) rise from the Tanganyi section of the central African plate whilst the famous Serengeti Natio Game Park covers 6,000 square mi [15,500 square kilometres] of the Arus Mara and Mwanza districts.

Arab traders probably arrived in Ta ganyika in the 16th century and la opened up a slave route from Ujiji Lake Tanganyika to the Indian Oce coast. British exploration began wi Burton's expedition in 1856, he bei followed by Speke, Livingstone a Stanley; but in 1884 Karl Peters esta lished a German protectorate by signi treaties with local chiefs. Revolts whi occurred in 1889 and 1905 were ruthless crushed. Following World War I Ta ganyika was placed by the League Nations under British mandate, and legislative council was set up in 19 After World War II Tanganyika becar a United Nations trusteeship territor still under Britain's wing, then in 19 was granted independence within t Commonwealth, with Dr Julius Nyere as its first president. In 1964 it united wi Zanzibar to form what is now Tanzan

See also BRITISH COMMONWEALTH; LEAG OF NATIONS; LIVINGSTONE, D.; STANLE H. M.; UNITED NATIONS; WORLD WARS and II.

Tannenberg (Grunwald), **Battle** (1410): climax of a struggle for control an area between the rivers Vistula ar Nemen in eastern Europe. The Order Teutonic Knights (*see* ORDERS, MILITAR had been extending its power eastwar and setting up small German settlement This so alarmed two of the strong states the area, Poland and Lithuania, that the sent a joint army under Jagiello again the Order. The Knights attacked b failed to break the ranks of the Poles, wh

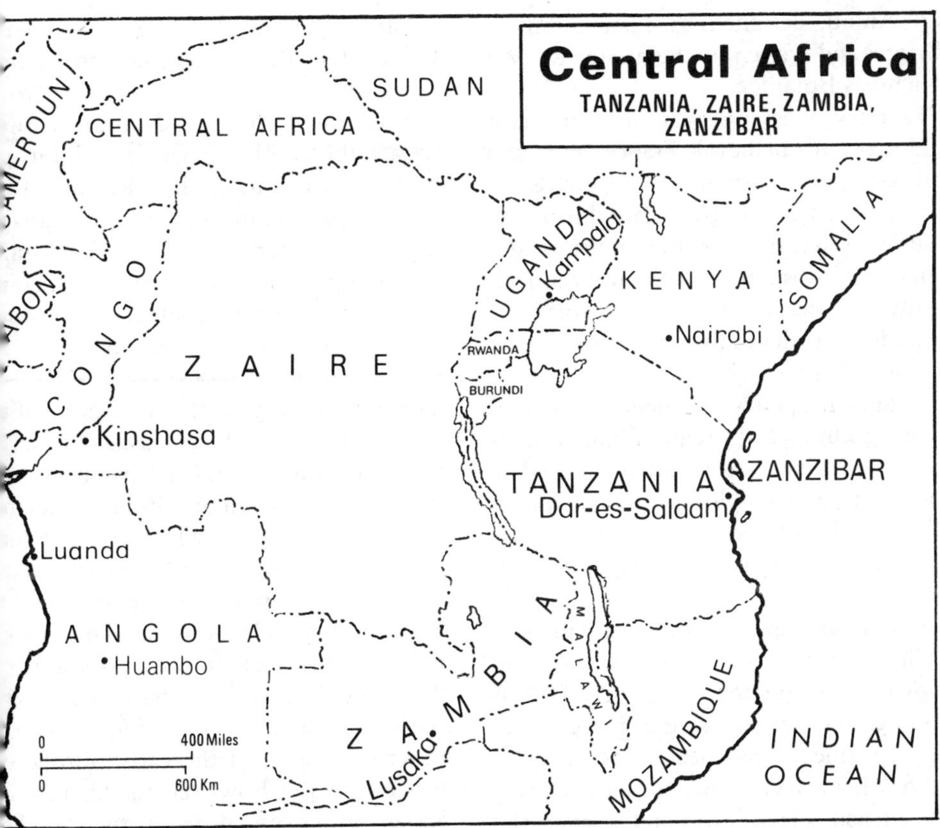

on an overwhelming victory. From this feat the Teutonic Knights never recovered, whereas Poland emerged as a eat power.

anzania, United Republic of: East frican republic composed of Tanganyika and Zanzibar, which became nited in April 1964. For the next 20 ears under the presidency of Julius yerere the country played a remarkable le in African affairs. The Arusha Declaration of 1967 was a classic statement of e problems of development. Experiments in socialism and *ujamaa* (collective) illage life were unique in Africa while anzania played a leading part as a "front-ne state" in the confrontation of Black frica with the white minority regimes the southern part of the continent.

ee also TANGANYIKA.

Tapestry: cloth woven with patterns or pictures; in late medieval and early renaissance times it was used in great houses as a wall covering to give colour and warmth. The earliest known examples are Egyptian, dating from the 2nd century BC.

From the 15th to the 17th century Arras, in the Netherlands (*see* separate entry), was the chief centre for tapestry making – indeed, tapestry was frequently referred to as *arras*. Two people played an important part in its manufacture, the artist and the weaver. The weaver worked from the artist's design copied on to the warp threads of his loom. He filled it in with different colours, using many bobbins; sometimes gold and silver threads highlighted the design. One such tapestry may be seen in Angers castle, western France. It was made in 1377 for the Duke

Of Anjou, designed by Hannequin de Bruges and woven by the master weaver Nicholas Botaille.

Tapestry weaving was an important industry in medieval France and was protected by the many trade guilds involved in its manufacture. But during the Hundred Years War the industry declined and was not revived until the 17th century, when the Gobelins factory was founded in order to produce tapestries for Louis XIV's palaces.

Not much tapestry was made in England. During Elizabeth I's reign William Sheldon, a Warwickshire man, started a factory to give employment to people in his neighbourhood. His chief weaver, Richard Hyckes, went to the Netherlands to learn the art.

A fine example of modern tapestry, "Christ in Glory", hangs in the new Coventry Cathedral, England. This is among the largest single pieces ever woven, measuring nearly 75 feet by 38 feet [22·8 × 11·5 metres]. It preserves the ancient roles of artist and weaver, the designer being the well-known painter Graham Sutherland (b. 1903) and the weavers Pinton Frères of Felletin, France.

See also TEXTILES; WEAVING.

Tartars, Tatars: Turkish-speaking Bulgar tribes, which spread out from the Sea of Azov area in the 7th and 8th centuries. In the 13th century they formed the spearhead of the Mongol conquest of Russia; with other tribes they made up the Golden Horde, dominating southern Russia for two centuries. The Kipchak princedom or khanate of Kazan fell under Russian rule in 1552. Other tribes had broken away to form the Mishars and the Kazimov Tartars, settling on the River Oka. The Tartars continued to be a distinct people through Russian history, speaking their own Turkic language and mostly following the religion of Islai Under the Russian empire the nan Tartar was applied rather loosely to variety of Turkic or Muslim peop within the empire. There are about 4 million Tartars in modern Russia. "Ta tar" has passed into the English langua to describe a person of particularly dif cult temper; and to "catch a Tarta means to come into conflict with som one who is more than one's match.

Tartary, Tatary: early name applied a large area of southern Russia, former ruled by the Mongols (*see* separate entry Previously occupied by a Bulgar khanat it was the area in which Batu Kha founded the Golden Horde, the barbaria who overran eastern Europe in the mic 13th century. This was the khanate c Kipchak, the westernmost extension c the Mongol empire, which for nearly tw centuries had an important influence o eastern Europe and the early history c Russia. In 1430, however, the khanate c Kazan broke away from the Golde Horde and was finally broken up by Iva the Terrible in 1552. Tartaria is now a autonomous state of the USSR.

¶ PARKER, E. H. *A Thousand Years of the Tartar* 1969

Tasman, Abel Janszoon (*c.* 1603–59) Dutch navigator, sent in 1634 by th Dutch East India Company (*see* separat entry) to explore in the Pacific. In 1639 in search of certain "islands of gold an silver", he penetrated to the north-east o Japan and, between 1642 and 1644 discovered Van Diemen's Land (Tasmania), New Zealand, Tonga and Fiji and explored the Gulf of Carpentaria.

¶ SHARP, ANDREW. *The Voyages of Abel Janzoo Tasman.* 1968

Tasmania: formerly Van Diemen' Land, discovered by Abel Tasman ir

›42, the smallest Australian state, lying ı latitude 42° S and longitude 146° E, to e south of the mainland, with Hobart e capital. Du Fresne visited it in 1772, ırneaux in 1773, Cook in 1777. Captain ligh called on his way to Pitcairn, and ass and Flinders charted its coasts in 798. Governor King of New South /ales (*see* separate entry) sent the earliest ttlers, convicts, in 1803. Progress, es- ecially under Governor William Sorrell ter 1817, came with the establishment f sheep-breeding with merino rams in 320, and of the Bank of Van Diemen's and in 1823. The Aborigines (*see* separ- e entry), settled in reservations on linders Island in 1840, are now extinct. /hen the transportation of convicts from ritain to Australia generally ceased, 'asmania continued to receive "recidi- ists" (re-convicted criminals) till 1853. The island, a separate colony from 1825, chieved self-government in 1856. Frozen uit was first shipped to England in 1877. Discoveries of tin, copper and gold in the 870s and 1880s, and the construction of ailways, assisted the economy, though e Bank of Van Diemen's Land failed in 891. Tasmania became part of the Commonwealth of Australia in 1901, and t times since then has needed consider- ble economic help from Canberra.

WEST, JOHN. *History of Tasmania.* 1972

ee AUSTRALIA for map.

'axation: compulsory contributions to e support of local or central govern- ıent. Under the feudal system the lord ved on the proceeds of his own demesne nd the dues exacted from his tenants. The ing, as the apex of the system, likewise erived his income from the feudal dues xacted from his tenants-in-chief. In ngland it was not until the 12th century hat a new expedient was tried, when a ax of a fractional part of the value of every man's movables (i.e. goods, furniture, etc.) was granted for a crusade (*see* CRUSADES). This was known as the Saladin Tithe (1188). Later this was applied to secular purposes, the fraction ultimately becoming fixed as a fifteenth for counties and a tenth for towns. We learn of the early means of assessing this tax as follows: "If anyone in the opinion of his neighbours give less than he ought, let four or six lawful men be chosen from the parish to state on oath the amount which he ought to have stated, and then he must make good the deficit." From about 1334 onwards the grant of a fifteenth and tenth seems to have meant a grant of about £39,000, and, if more than this was required, parliament would grant several fifteenths and tenths.

The poll tax (tax payable per "poll" or head of population) introduced under Richard II proved unpopular, though it was resorted to intermittently until the 18th century.

Indirect taxation was derived from customs duties, and a London merchant of Charles I's reign complained that "in no part of the world are traders so screwed and wrung as in England". A calculation made in 1756 estimated that the average artisan paid £1 5*s* 1*d*, and the average labourer 15*s* 10*d* in taxes each year, and the taxable items included beer, salt, sugar, leather, soap, candles, drugs, tobacco, and windows. In England there are many reminders of the last imposition in the shape of windows filled in or left blind to avoid payment of the tax.

Income tax (*see* separate entry), now a major source of revenue for modern states, was a 19th-century development. Recent examples of new types of taxation in Britain are a *capital gains* tax, levied on the profit made on an asset between its purchase and sale, and a *value added* tax levied as a percentage of value added at each stage of production.

Adam Smith (*see* separate entry) in his *Wealth of Nations* (1776) laid down four guiding rules for taxation. These were: (1) equality – subjects should support the state according to their ability; (2) certainty, not arbitrariness; (3) convenience of payment; (4) economy of collection. Since then, at least three different schools of thought have emerged. These may be summarised as follows: that taxation should be designed purely to raise the revenue required by the expenditure to be met; that it should be used as an instrument to promote social justice; and that it should be used as a part of general economic policy to promote stability. In practice, much of modern taxation arises from a combination of these principles.

Resistance to taxation has been a powerful motive for many great events. A few examples must suffice. Magna Carta (1215) and the Bill of Rights (1689), although now rightly regarded as landmarks in England's constitutional history, were much more the result of a dislike for arbitrary taxation than of any lofty constitutional principles. Again, in the 18th century, the principle of "no taxation without representation" played a large part in the events which led up to the War of American Independence. The French Revolution was also to a large extent caused by a chaotic and inequitable system of taxation.

See separate entries for AMERICAN INDEPENDENCE, WAR OF; BILL OF RIGHTS; FRENCH REVOLUTION; MAGNA CARTA.

Taxi, Cab: car carrying passengers for a fee, either agreed upon beforehand or measured by a taximeter fitted inside. The origin of the word is uncertain, but one interesting suggestion connects it with the ancient German family of Thurn und Taxis who won from the Emperor Maximilian I the right to carry imperial messages.

Tea: dried and processed leaves of shrub used for making a beverage, or tl beverage itself. Tea-drinking appears have been a general custom in China i the 7th century AD. Tea was introduce into Europe by the Dutch East Ind Company and at the beginning of the 17t century could be bought in England £10 a pound. In 1660 Pepys mentione in his diary that he "did send for a cup tee, a China drink, of which I had nev drunk before".

A London merchant, Thomas Garra way, sold tea, and in 1668 the British Ea India Company sent one hundred pounc of it to London. Charles II's Queen Catherine of Braganza, enjoyed it, and s tea became popular in court circles. continued to be expensive, however, an smugglers frequently brought it into th country. In 1777 Parson Woodforde pai 10*s* 6*d* to a smuggler for a pound of tea.

In Victorian times a cheaper tea wa imported from India which, althoug cultivation began there as late as 1836, now the largest producer in the world The principal tea producing countrie today are India, Pakistan, Sri Lanka China, Japan, Indonesia and Kenya.

¶ BRAMAH, EDWARD. *Tea and Coffee: Thre Hundred Years of Tradition.* 1972; JONES, TREVOR *Tea.* 1958

See also EAST INDIA COMPANIES.

Technocracy: government by technicians. The word first appeared in th United States in 1932 to denote the view of certain engineers, scientists and sociologists, who held that economic control o the social system should be vested in scientists and engineers rather than in politicians, whom they thought to be incapable of understanding modern conditions.

Tehran Conference (1943): four-day November meeting in Persia at which oosevelt and Churchill, representing 'SA and Britain, and Stalin, the Soviet ader, were present. They discussed the /orld War II situation and worked out etailed plans to defeat Germany and aly. The scale and timing of carefully)-ordinated attacks from the south, east ıd west were agreed.

'el Aviv: largest town in Israel, on the Aediterranean coast, north of and adjoinıg Jaffa which, by Tel Aviv's phenomnal growth since its founding by Zionists *see* ZIONISM) in 1909 as the first alllewish community, has now been aborbed into the larger town. It is Israel's nain business centre and also boasts utstanding cultural developments – uniersities, museums, art galleries, theatres nd orchestras. *See* ISRAEL for map.

KALIR, M. *et al*, editors. *Tel Aviv's Fifty Years.* 967

Telecommunications: the sending of signals or messages over a long distance (Greek *tele* = far off) by telegraph, telephone etc.

We shall probably never know who first thought of an electric telegraph. Someone who signed himself "C.M." wrote to the *Scots Magazine* in 1756, suggesting that pith balls, attracted or repelled by electric charges, might be used for remote signalling purposes, but the idea does not seem to have been pursued at the time.

Ten years later the invention of the electric battery made it possible to generate a steady current of electricity, and this in turn made possible a really practical electric telegraph. Thereafter many systems were tried, but proved too expensive because twenty-six wires were required between points – one for each letter of the alphabet. At last, however, the English-

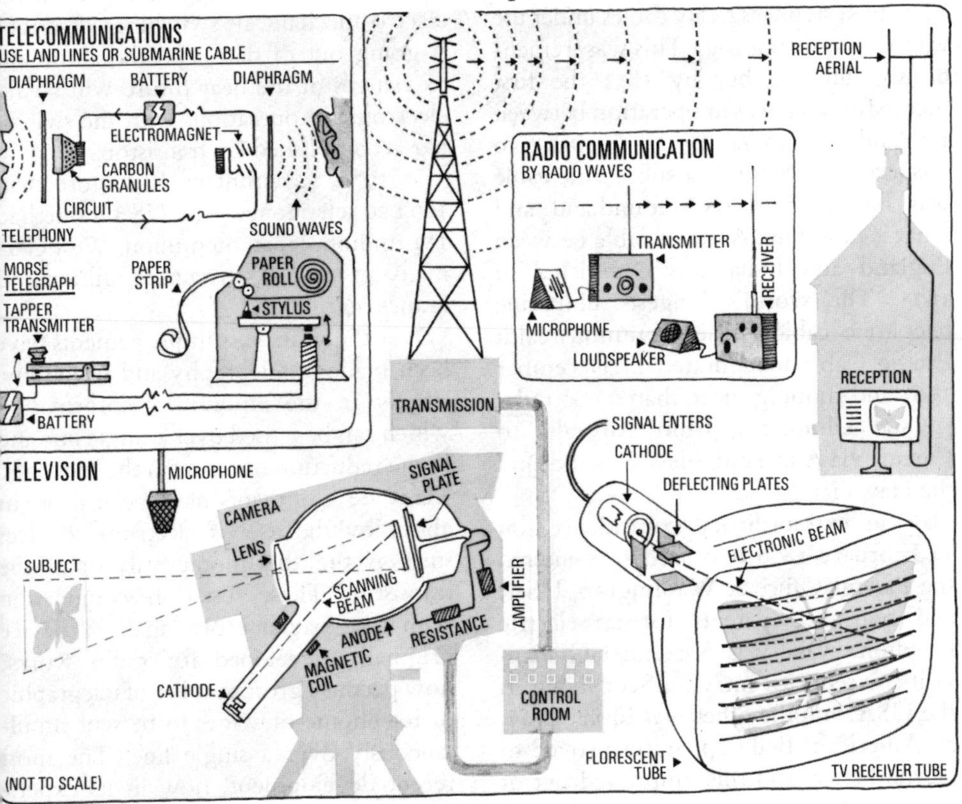

men William Fothergill Cooke and Charles Wheatstone managed in 1837 to reduce the number of wires to five, and later both they and Samuel Morse in the USA found means of telegraphing messages over a single wire. The electric telegraph had arrived. In 1845 a Telegraph Company was formed in England and the use of the new telegraphic system spread from city to city and ultimately even to the smallest village. In the USA Samuel Morse, after failing to sell his system to the Government for $10,000 (the Postmaster General having been "uncertain that the revenues could be made equal to the expenditures"), found private backers, and in 1844 a scheme was launched to erect a telegraph line between New York, Baltimore and Washington. Within little more than six years fifty other companies were using Morse's patents in the US.

The next step was to lay cables under the sea to foreign countries. This was tremendously difficult, but by 1851 the first successful cable was in operation between England and France. By 1866, after two unsuccessful attempts, a submarine cable was laid between Newfoundland and what is now Eire. A direct cable between England and India was completed in 1873. The world's longest submarine telephone cable is the Commonwealth Pacific Cable inaugurated in December 1963 and running more than 9,000 miles [14,500 kilometres] from Australia to Canada via Auckland, New Zealand, and the Hawaiian Islands.

By an extraordinary coincidence, on 14 February 1876 two inventors entered the Patents Office at Washington, USA, and registered patents for an electric telephone. One was Alexander Graham Bell (*see* separate entry), a Scot living in the USA, and the other was Elisha Gray, an American. Bell's apparatus proved to be the better, and this, improved out of all recognition, is still in use today. T Bell Telephone Company (to which t inventor gave his name) is now the large in the world.

The first telephone exchange in Lond was installed in 1879 and served eig subscribers. As more and more peop began to use the telephone, exchang grew in size and employed large numbe of operators whose task it was to conne one subscriber to another. Over t years, however, the Post Office has intr duced automatic exchanges, whereby t action of selecting numbers on the dial the home telephone activates electr mechanical switches at the exchange an connects the caller's telephone to the o he has dialled. At first it was possible t dial only local numbers but now the ST (Subscriber Trunk Dialling) system pe mits a great number of places througho the world to be dialled direct. Even th electro-mechanical switching describe is going out of date, and the automati exchanges of the near future will be al electronic in operation, with the switching accomplished by transistors.

By 1982, 72 countries had more tha 100,000 telephones. The USA alone ha 181 million, Japan 60 million, West Germany 30 million, Britain 28 million an France 26 million.

Over the years vast improvements hav been made in telegraphy and telephony largely in the amount of informatio which can be passed over a single line an in the reduction of errors in the messages Many developments have been brough about by the use of electronic device such as the thermionic valve and th transistor. These, used in conjunctio with the coaxial cable (again, a devic originally developed for radio work) now permit a great number of telegraphi or telephonic messages to be sent simultaneously over a single line. The mos recent development, now in its experi-

ꞏntal stage, is to enclose a radio type of ꞏve in a hollow pipe called a waveguide d to superimpose the signals on this. ꞏ such means it is anticipated that imately about 200,000 (or possibly ɔre) simultaneous two-way telephone nversations may be carried in one ꞏgle pipe. Even more complex systems, ꞏng special forms of light wave trapped a pipe, are being considered, and eoretically these could carry far more essages. It is certainly a far cry from the ys when twenty-six wires were needed convey one telegraphic message, or en from the first Bell telephone, when ꞏly one conversation could be effected ꞏ a single line.

ꞏor a number of other methods of ꞏmmunication *see* SIGNALLING.

ɔE VRIES, LEONARD. *The Book of Telecommunica-ꞏns.* 1962

ꞏe *also* RADIO; TELEVISION.

ꞏel-el-Amarna: site of the capital city f Akhnaten, the "heretic" pharaoh, and ꞏow a small village on the right bank of ꞏe River Nile. When he established the ꞏorship of Aten, the power of the sun, ꞏkhnaten determined to build a new city ꞏee from the influence of the ancient gods f Egypt. He named it *Akhetaten*, meaning Aten is satisfied", and encouraged archi-ꞏects, painters and sculptors to make it as beautiful as possible, in honour of the god.

After Akhnaten's death the priests of the old gods regained their power. The court returned to Thebes and the new city was deserted.

See also AKHNATEN; PHARAOHS.

Telescope: optical device for studying distant objects. This instrument seems to have originated in Holland about 1608. At least three different persons have been credited with its invention, but the traditional story is that Hans Lippershey, a spectacle maker, while holding two lenses, one at a short distance behind the other, happened to direct them towards the steeple of a neighbouring church and was astonished to find that the steeple appeared to be nearer. He afterwards fitted the lenses at opposite ends of a tube and thus constructed the first telescope. He does not appear to have thought of using it as an astronomical instrument, but in 1609 news of it reached Galileo, who constructed several telescopes having a convex objective and a concave eyepiece. This form is still found in the modern opera glass, as it gives an erect image. The largest of his telescopes was little more than an inch [26 mm] in diameter, but the astronomical discoveries he made with it included the mountains of the Moon, the phases of Venus, the satellites of Jupiter, the starry background of the Milky Way and the shapes of spots on the Sun.

In 1611, in his *Dioptrice*, Kepler recommended the use of a convex eyepiece, and the development of this, which is the modern type of refracting telescope, is due to Christiaan Huyghens, who, on 28 November 1659, used it to make the first drawing of Mars.

The reflecting telescope was invented by Newton, who presented one to the Royal Society in London in 1671. In this type the eyepiece is situated in the curved wall of the tube. In 1672 Cassegrain invented a reflecting telescope in which the eyepiece is at the end of the tube. Early instruments had their reflectors wrongly shaped. The shape which gives the best results is a paraboloid or revolution, and this was introduced by Hadley in 1723. Towards the end of the 18th century William Herschel began to make really large instruments of this type. In 1781 he discovered the planet Uranus, using a reflector of aperture 6½ inches [166 mm]. In 1789 he completed an instrument of aperture 4 feet [1·2 m]. Modern instruments of this type include those at Mount Wilson and Mount Palomar, California, of diameters 100 and 200 inches [2,560 and 5,120 mm], respectively. Early reflectors were made of a copper-tin alloy, which soon tarnished and required repolishing, but were later made of glass coated with a thin film of silver. About 1930 a process was devised for making reflectors of glass covered with aluminium; mirrors of this type may last up to ten years without renewal.

Newton developed the reflecting telescope because in the early refracting types the image became distorted as the light passed through the lens, causing a chaotic mixture of colours. This defect was put right by an Englishman, Chester Moor Hall, who constructed the first achromatic telescope in 1733. This was further developed by John Dolland. The object glass of such an instrument is made of two different kinds of glass, a convex lens of crown glass combined with a concave lens of flint glass. Refracting telescopes have so far been made with apertures up to 40 inches [1,020 mm], including the 62-foot [19 metres] long example at the Yerkes Observatory, USA, the largest of this type in the world.

An important recent development has been the radio telescope for studying radio signals of cosmic origin (*see* RADIO ASTRONOMY). The largest in the world is at Chuguyev, USSR, covering an area just over 37 acres [15 hectares].

¶ KING, H. C. *History of the Telescope*. 1955

See also GALILEO; HUYGHENS; KEPL[ER]; NEWTON; ROYAL SOCIETY.

Television: transmission and recepti[on] of visual images by electromagne[tic] waves. The "eye" of a television cam[era] is a device called a camera tube. In o[ne] type of tube the image of a scene [is] focused on a flat plate which consists o[f a] mosaic composed of millions of lit[tle] specks of a photo-electric substance – th[at] is, material which alters its electri[cal] characteristics in accordance with t[he] amount of light falling on it. The effect [of] the image falling on this mosaic is [to] produce a pattern of electric charges or [a] glass target plate which is mounted clo[se] to it. This pattern is an electrical image [of] the scene being televised.

From the far end of the tube an electr[on] beam is made to sweep or scan the targ[et] methodically in a series of lines, one belo[w] the other, so that the beam makes conta[ct] with each charged point in turn. Th[is] neutralises the charge at that point and [in] doing so decreases the number of electro[ns] in that portion of the beam. Thus a whi[te] part of the scene will cause a relative[ly] large charge on the target plate which i[n] turn will, in being neutralised, rob th[e] beam of a considerable number of ele[c]trons at that instant.

The electron beam is made to boun[ce] back from the target plate, but, where[as] before impact with the target there w[as a] constant density of electrons in the bea[m] the return beam shows a variation [of] electron numbers along its length; i[n] other words, a variation in current. Thi[s] after passing through a special amplifi[er] in the camera tube, emerges as a train [of] electrical signals, each variation in whic[h] represents the amount of light reflecte[d] from one point of the televised scen[e] ıese video signals, as they are called, are ıplified still more and then super- .posed on to a radio frequency carrier ıve for radiation throughout the service ;a of the station.

ı the home receiver the picture is ;played on a cathode ray tube. The ıss screen is the end wall of the tube and coated on its inner surface with ıosphors which have the property of ıitting white light when bombarded ıth electrons. The greater the bombard- ent, the brighter the light.

At the back of the tube an electron gun is ounted. This shoots a beam of electrons ward the phosphor coating, which oduces a bright spot at its point of ıpact. The beam, however, is caused to an rapidly to and fro across the screen in ;actly the same way as the target plate is vept in the camera tube and precisely in ep with it. (Special signals are trans- ıitted to keep the receiver scanning in ep with that occurring in the camera ıbe.)

In the receiver, the video signals are parated from the carrier and after nplification are used to control the rength of the cathode ray tube electron eam. When a white point on the studio ;ene is being transmitted, the video gnal will be correspondingly strong and) the receiver's electron beam will also be rong, producing a brilliant white spot n the screen. A black point will produce o video signal and consequently the ;ceiver's electron beam will be cut off, roducing no glow in the phosphor. All ariations of light between the maximum nd minimum reflected from the studio ;cene will be reproduced in terms of lack-and-white on the receiver screen.

Although only one spot at a time is eing illuminated on the receiver screen, he electron beam traverses the screen at uch a fast rate that the eye is deceived into eeing the rapid sequence of spots as a complete picture. When one complete scan is completed the whole process begins again and another picture is built up. Again, the eye is deceived, because the pictures follow one another so rapidly that we get the illusion of seeing one picture which has movement in it.

Colour television makes use of the fact that three coloured lights (usually red, green and blue) can be combined in suitable proportions to produce most other colours, including white. The colour camera contains three camera tubes (sometimes four) one of which is masked by a red filter, one by a green and one by a blue. Thus the video signals from these tubes represent, respectively, the red, green and blue content of the televised scene as three separate signals. A very complex process is used to super-impose these signals on to a radio frequency carrier for transmission to the home receiver.

At the receiver the cathode ray tube contains three electron guns, one for dealing with each colour signal. This time the screen is composed of millions of phosphor dots in groups of three. On impact by an electron beam, one dot emits red light, another green and a third blue.

As before, the video signals, on arrival at the receiver, are separated from the carrier. Each is fed to its appropriate gun and is used to control the strength of its beam. It is so arranged that each gun can illuminate only those phosphor dots which correspond to its colour control signal – that is, the red signal gun can only illuminate red phosphor dots, and so on. Thus, as with the black-and-white pro-cess, a strong video signal from a red part of the transmitted picture will cause a bright red spot to appear on the receiver screen at the right point, and similarly with green and blue portions. As the phosphor dots are microscopic and extremely close together, the eye blends the colours to form pinks, browns, yellows and so on, according to the proportions of brightness of the red, green and blue dots.

By 1983 there were an estimated 434 million television sets world-wide of which approximately 40 per cent were in the USA. After the USA (in order) came the USSR, Japan, West Germany, Britain, France, Brazil, Italy and Canada each of which had more than 10 million sets. There are about 8000 television stations in the world.

¶ ROBERTS, FREDERICK. *Television.* 1964
See also RADIO; TELECOMMUNICATIONS.

Telford, Thomas (1757–1834): civil engineer of Scottish birth. At a time when the Industrial Revolution was demanding better transport for its raw materials and finished products, he was responsible for the improvement of many roads and harbours, particularly in Scotland, and the development of canals in Great Britain, railways being still in the future. He constructed the Caledonian canal from sea to sea through the highlands of Scotland to take sea-going ships of the size then in general use, and the similar Gotha canal from the Baltic to the North Sea for the Swedes. The suspension bridge carrying the road over the Menai Straits, between the Isle of Anglesey and the Welsh mainland, is another monument to his skill. He was also responsible

for the Conway Bridge, for the Ponte sulte aqueduct near Llangollen (one the finest examples of the canal age) a for St Katherine's Docks, London.

¶ MEYNELL, LAURENCE. *Thomas Telford.* 1957

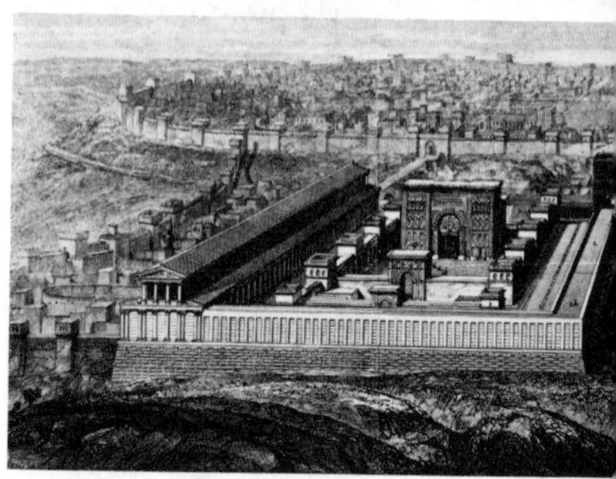

The temple as it appeared in 33 AD.

Temple of Jerusalem: for 1,000 yea the religious centre of the Jews. The fir Temple was built by King Solomo (ruled *c.* 970–*c.* 933 BC) and destroyed b the Babylonians in 586. The second wa started in 520 and was enlarged an beautified by Herod the Great (rule 37–4 BC). This was the Temple known t Jesus, who foretold its total destructior which took place in AD 70, when the cit was reduced to ruins by the Romans. A Muslim shrine now occupies the site.
See also BABYLON; HEROD; JESUS CHRIST MUSLIMS; SOLOMON.

Tène, La: Iron Age (*see* separate entry culture flourishing in Europe from th 5th to the 1st century BC. La Tène cultur took its name from a settlement on Lak Neuchâtel, Switzerland, containing many iron weapons decorated with tendri ornamentation. The same motif, the S shape, producing continuous waves an spirals, was found in Celtic art, and helpe in identifying the far-ranging movements of Celtic tribes over Germany France, Switzerland, Hungary, Britain and Ireland.

Left: La Tène carving on iron showing s-shaped motif. Above: Pierced metal work chariot piece from the Somme-Bionne Burial, France.

.a Tène culture was first developed by e Celtic peoples in the Middle Rhine gion and the Marne area of France, here a wine-drinking warrior aristo- acy traded with the Mediterranean ine regions, especially Greece and Etru- a (*see* separate entry). This led to the troduction of the Etruscan two-wheel ıariot, and the flowering of a magnifi- nt decorative art. In the rich Celtic rrows were found gold and silver ware, ields, jewellery, mirrors and pottery, namented with the flowering arabesques the new style.

ennessee Valley Authority: founded 1933 as part of F. D. Roosevelt's (*see* parate entry) New Deal economic pro- ramme; a central agency of the US overnment for controlling and develop- g the resources of the Tennessee valley ates – Tennessee, Alabama, Georgia, entucky, Mississippi, North Carolina d Virginia. Its responsibilities include ood control, electric power, afforesta- on, navigation and fisheries. The ven- re has been called "the greatest develop- ent in large-scale social planning in the United States" and over a period raised the income level of the inhabitants by 75 per cent compared with a general increase in the country of 56 per cent.

Teresa of Avila, St (1515–82)**:** Spanish nun and reformer. Teresa became a Carmelite nun at the age of twenty-one. The Order had originally been very austere, but the rule had become more lax. She determined to restore its strictness and began her reforms while Prioress of the convent of St Joseph, Avila.

Her ideas were unpopular, but she was a woman whose strong personality and great intelligence attracted likeminded nuns. She was witty and lively and wrote several books. Much of her correspondence has been preserved.

Teutonic: adjective associated with north German peoples. Originally they were Teutons, a tribe who migrated from the North Sea coast to central Europe before being defeated by the Romans. Later the name was given to all Germans, and particularly to a famous group of Knights formed during the Crusades.

Textiles: woven fabrics or fibres suitable for weaving. Primitive man used hides for clothing and warmth, but animal skins were stiff, hot and uncomfortable to wear. It was found that natural fibres – silk, wool, linen and cotton – could be spun into thread and woven into cloth on a wooden frame known as a loom. The spinning and weaving processes did not involve physical strength so in tribal communities were usually done by the women.

The Chinese are thought to have woven silk cloth as early as the second millennium BC. Linen was used in Egypt 5,000 years before the Christian era, cotton in India and Persia about 3000 BC and woollen cloth in Scandinavia and Switzerland during the Bronze Age. In South America cloth woven from llama wool was worn in the year AD 1000 and probably earlier.

The first woven cloths were made very simply, by darning thread wound on a shuttle under and over other threads stretched on the loom. Some looms stood upright, others were horizontal. The finished cloth was usually left in its original colour, although sometimes people tinted it with vegetable dyes.

About 200 BC the Chinese invented a method of weaving patterns into silk, and patterned material dating from the 4th century AD has been found in Egypt tombs. Patterned silk from Byzantiu and Damascus (*see* separate entry) v introduced into Europe in the 7th centu when it was carried by caravans traders across Asia to Constantinop For the first time Europeans began consider silkworm rearing and the man facture of silk; the Norman conquer of Sicily established silk workshops the Silk was also made in southern France.

Northern Europe was more concern with woollen cloth. Wool from Engla was exported to the Netherlands to made up into cloth by the skilful Flemi weavers. Later, English weavers learn to make cloth. Many of the medie guilds were connected with spinning a weaving, and women usually did t spinning – hence the term "spinster".

In the 16th century there was a gre vogue for Persian silks woven with li like pictures of flowers, birds and anima These were copied in Italy and used wall hangings. The Netherlands we famed for woven table linen and spec sets were designed for wealthy buye Henry VIII possessed tablecloths made his order by Belgian weavers.

Cotton was introduced to Europe fro India during the 17th century. Englan France and Holland had all establish

Persian brocade in coloured silk on yellow satin ground, 16th century.

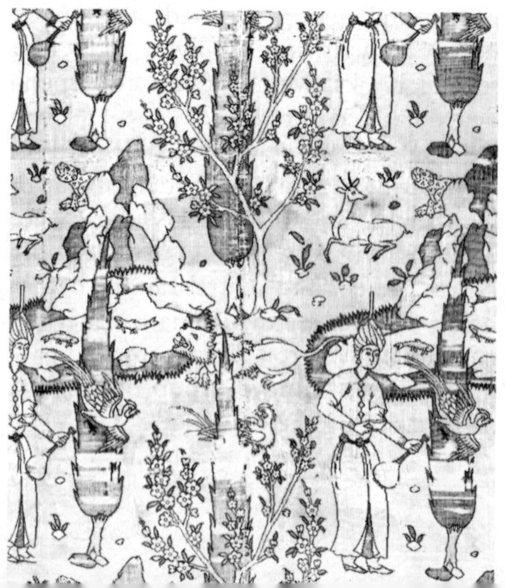

American roller-printed cotton, 1835–40.

ding companies in India and many tures and varieties of cotton were ıong their exports. By 1710 colonists in : southern part of North America had covered that the climate was suitable the cultivation of the cotton plant. e soft, fluffy heads – cotton wool – re picked by slaves, baled and sent oss the Atlantic to be spun and woven o cloth, just as English wool had been pped to the Netherlands 600 years fore. In England this spinning and aving was done in the homes of vilgers, frequently in Lancashire.

ome silk cloth was made in England, t it was very expensive. For years there s been a flourishing silk industry in ance. During the religious wars of the th century many of the weavers fled d some settled in Spitalfields, London, nich became the centre of a small silk dustry.

he 18th century in England saw that enomenon known as the Industrial volution (*see* separate entry). Once it

Spinning 100 denier nylon in Courtaulds modern factory.

was discovered that machinery could be worked by water power, or later by steam, far more efficiently than by manpower, all kinds of inventions appeared, some more successful than others. Many

mmediately after spinning, viscose rayon yarn is strengthened by a process of stretching it while mmersed in hot water.

affected textiles. Kay's *flying shuttle*, Arkwright's (*see* separate entry) *spinning jenny* and Crompton's *mule* all made it possible to produce large quantities of cloth in factories far more quickly and cheaply than by a hand loom at home. These inventions could also be applied to wool, and northern England became a centre for cheap cloth, cotton in Lancashire and wool in Yorkshire. There was also a considerable textile industry in Derbyshire, Nottinghamshire and Leicestershire. Factory owners made fortunes, and until the end of World War I (*see* separate entry) England was the world centre for the manufacture of cotton and woollen goods, a position later rivalled by Japan.

It was cheaper to print patterns on to cloth than to weave the design into the fabric. The Egyptians had known how to do this in very early times, but the process was not introduced into Europe until the 1[illegible]th century AD. In the 17th century the Italians began to print patterns on cotton imported from India, and the idea spread. A large block was made, usually from wood, and a design cut into it. This was impregnated with dye and stamped by hand on to a roll of material, forming a repeating pattern. The great disadvantage was that when the fabric was washed the colours blurred, but chemists discovered ways of fixing them.

Colour printing by hand was a slow process. In 1783 Thomas Bell, an Englishman, invented a method by which the design could be engraved on rollers and the length of cotton passed mechanically between them. By 1820 *roller printing* was in general use in Lancashire. In 1856 a chemist named Perkins experimented with *aniline dyes*. The colours were harsher than those of vegetable dyes, but, because they were more durable, manufacturers used them. By the close of the 19th century Lancashire mills were turning out quantities of cotton cloth in coarse colours. William Morris (*see* separa
entry), an artist and writer, tried to im
prove standards, urging a return to han
printing textiles with vegetable dyes.

Man-made fibres are of two kin
regenerated types such as rayon, ma
from natural fibrous materials dissolv
and then forced through fine holes befo
solidifying; and *synthetic* types produc
by submitting chemical compounds
polymerisation, i.e. a chemical reacti
in which two or more molecules react
form larger molecules until a long cha
of identical units results.

During World War I *artificial silk* w
invented – a fibre made by a chemic
process. It was cheap to produce but h
many disadvantages. Garments ma
from it tended to lose their shape easil
But scientists continued to experime
with man-made fibres and in 1935 t
first *nylon* of serious commercial intere
was produced. The world's first facto
began production in 1940 in the US
Nylon fabrics are more successful th
artificial silk, but they lack the warm
and flexibility of cloth made from natur
fibres. The term "nylon" covers a who
range of fibres.

¶ PAGE, C. E. *Textiles*. 1965; *Textiles* (Macdonal
Junior Reference Library). 1969

See also COTTON; DYEING; LOOM; TA
ESTRY; WEAVING; WOOL.

Thailand, Siam: kingdom in south-ea
Asia. The earliest kingdom of Siam w
set up in the 13th century, with its capit
at Ayutthaya. The Siamese expanded an
several times occupied Angkor, capital
Cambodia. Hindu influence becan
strong and the king of Siam was hailed
divine. The Portuguese, Dutch, Englis
and French made some contacts with Sia
in the 16th and early 17th centurie
Ayutthaya was destroyed by the Burme
in 1767 and Bangkok presently becam
the capital. Rama IV (reigned 1851–6

stablished diplomatic relations with the estern powers and he and his successor ntroduced many western innovations. iam's security depended on a balance etween Britain and France. The period 893–1909 was one of lengthy negotiaons (involving various boundary revions, ceding of territories, treaties, etc.) etween Siam, France and England, ventually resulting in greater stability or Siam and freedom to concentrate on nternal reforms and trade expansion. In ne 1930s Japan took over some of rance's influence. From 1935 the domiant figure in Siam was Field Marshal ibul Songgram, at first defence minister nd then prime minister (1938–44), nrough World War II and a period of apanese dominance. In power again from 947, Pibul Songgram experimented with everal forms of constitution. Finally out f office in 1957, he was succeeded by ther army chiefs. The name of the kingom became Thailand in 1949. It joined he United Nations in 1946 and SEATO n 1954. Though there have been various ttempts at civilian rule Thailand has een largely run by the military since 945. A member of ASEAN Thailand is specially concerned with conditions in er troubled neighbour, Kampuchea.

See ENDPAPERS for map.

WATSON, JANE WERNER. *Thailand: Rice Bowl of Asia.* 1968

See also SEATO; UNITED NATIONS.

Thanksgiving Day: the last Thursday n November, set aside annually in the JSA for commemorating the good harest of the Pilgrim Fathers (1621; *see* eparate entry) and as a general thanksgiving for God's mercies. Thanksgiving lays were celebrated in the 17th century n a number of the early colonies and the ractice continued spasmodically till President Lincoln (*see* separate entry), in 864, appointed the last Thursday in November, each president since following the example by annual proclamation.

Thebes: ancient city of Upper Egypt, on the River Nile. During the 18th dynasty of pharaohs, and for a brief period of two centuries before them, Thebes was the chief city of Egypt.

Ahmose I, who drove out the Hyksos (*see* separate entry) about 1,500 years before the Christian era, came from Thebes, so he and his descendants made it their capital. They attributed their rise to power to *Amon*, the local deity, and caused him to be ranked with the greatest gods of Egypt. Eventually the Theban priests became so powerful that they virtually ruled the kingdom.

Thebes was the religious as well as the secular capital of the country. The government was carried on from there, great temples were built to honour Amon, and in Western Thebes the pharaohs were buried in concealed rock tombs in the Valley of Kings. Later, the countryside round Thebes was the scene of the earliest experiments in Christian monasticism. The city itself was destroyed by an earthquake in 27 BC. The ancient site is now occupied by the villages of Luxor and Karnak.

The great temple at Karnak, itself a ruin, stands on the site of the ancient city of Thebes.

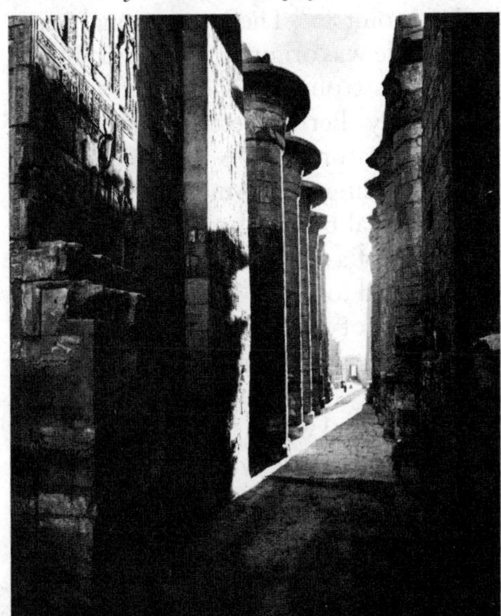

Thebes (now Thiva) was also the name of the chief city of Boeotia, which for a time in the 4th century BC occupied a leading position among the states of Greece.

Themistocles (*c.* 525–*c.* 460 BC): Athenian statesman. He laid the foundations of the naval power of Athens, which crushed the Persian fleet at Salamis in 480 and which later secured her supremacy in Greek waters for many years. After Salamis, however, his intense suspicion of Sparta led him to intrigue with the Persians of Ionia, and he died in exile.

¶ In *Plutarch. Ten Famous Lives*, edited C. ROBINSON. 1963

See also SALAMIS, etc.

Thermometer: instrument for measuring temperature. The familiar type of thermometer, using alcohol as the liquid, seems to have been brought into use by the Grand Duke Ferdinand II of Tuscany as early as 1654. The liquid is inserted in a tube with a very small bore and expands or contracts with variations in temperature. In 1714 Fahrenheit (*see* separate entry) invented the mercury-in-glass thermometer and his scale of temperature. In 1730 the French physicist de Réaumur invented a scale of temperature in which the freezing point of water is 0° and boiling point 80°. The international centigrade scale was originally proposed by the Swedish astronomer Celsius (1701–44). A mercury thermometer cannot be used for temperatures below −40°C, because of the freezing of the mercury. Mercury has a normal boiling point of 357°C, but the range of a mercury thermometer can be increased to about 570°C by filling the upper part of the stem with an inert gas. Alcohol thermometers can be used down to about −110°C and are useful for meteorological work. In order to measure higher temperatures various forms of gas thermometer were evolved in the 19 century.

Thermopylae: name of a narrow pass north-western Greece between the mountains and the sea. Here, in 480 BC, the invading Persian army was held up b Leonidas with a small force of 30 Spartans. The enemy, using a mountai path, surrounded them, and they we annihilated. *See also* PERSIAN WARS.

Third Reich (1933–45): official nam which the Nazi Party gave to its rule i Germany from January 1933. Reich mea "empire". The first had been the Hol Roman Empire, the second Bismarck Empire (*see* BISMARCK, OTTO) which co lapsed in 1918. The term "Third Reich appeared in Germany in the mid-192 and was quickly accepted by politician who looked back with regret at forme glories. The Third Reich, officially pro claimed early in 1934, ended with Ger many's defeat in 1945.

See also NAZI; WORLD WAR II.

Thirteen Colonies, The: the earl American colonies which afterwar formed the United States of Americ These may be considered in three group those of Virginia, New York and Ne England.

The *Virginia* group owes its name to Si Walter Ralegh, who named an unsuccess ful settlement, abandoned in 1586, afte Elizabeth I of England, the "Virgi Queen". The first permanent Englis settlement came on the James River i 1607, when the three ships *Sarah Constan Godspeed* and *Discovery* arrived with company of 105 colonists. *Marylan* originally a part of Virginia, was name after Charles I's queen, Henrietta Maria It became a separate colony under roya charter in 1632. *North* and *South Carolin* originated in the Carolinas, named b ench settlers in honour of Charles IX 'France. The name was bestowed afresh / Charles II of England, who granted ie settlements to eight different groups : proprietors. The arrangement proved ıworkable and the colonists reorganised ıemselves into two governments. *'eorgia*, originally part of the Carolinas, 'as founded in 1732 by Colonel James 'glethorpe as a refuge for debtors and rotestant dissenters from English prisons. New England colonies were first named y Captain John Smith, who made one of vo unsuccessful attempts to establish a ·ttlement in the area. In 1620 the Pilgrim athers founded a permanent colony and ew settlements developed at *New Hamp-ıire* (1622), *Massachusetts* (1628), *Rhode 'land* (1631) and *Connecticut* (1633).

The New York group consisted of *New 'ork, New Jersey, Pennsylvania* and *Dela-ıare*. New Amsterdam, which began as trading station of the Dutch West India :ompany, was granted to James, Duke of 'ork, by Charles II of England in 1664 nd renamed New York, and the district etween the Hudson and Delaware Rivers ecame New Jersey. Pennsylvania (named fter William Penn, though he was rongly opposed to the idea) was pur-hased by Penn from Charles II and ounded as a Quaker colony in 1682.)elaware, also ceded to Penn and origin-lly attached to Pennsylvania, became a eparate state in 1776, having the distinc-ion of being the first state of the USA.

In chronological order of becoming tates of the Union, from 1787 to 1790, he list is Delaware, Pennsylvania, New ersey, Georgia, Connecticut, Massachu-etts, Maryland, South Carolina, New Hampshire, Virginia, New York, North Carolina and Rhode Island.

| BROWN, GEORGE W., HARMAN, ELEANOR and EANNERET, MARSH. *The American Colonies: Canada ınd the U.S.A. before 1800*. 1962

;ee also INDIVIDUAL ENTRIES.

Thirteenth century: the years 1201–1300. One historian says that "as we cross the threshold of the 13th century the dream of world dominion, which had died with an Emperor, springs to life again in the policy of a Pope". This refers to Innocent III, who became Pope in 1198 at the early age of thirty-seven. His reign marks the summit of the temporal power of the Papacy. He excommunicated the Emperor Otto IV, placed England and France under an interdict, secured from the rulers of England, Aragon and Portugal the surrender of their countries as fiefs of the Holy See, and imposed the rule of the Western Church on Constantinople. All this was done in only eighteen years.

This century saw the age of eastern imperialism, with the ruthless Mongol hordes of Genghis Khan sweeping over North China and vast territories in Asia and Asia Minor and threatening, as Attila the Hun had previously threatened, to flood over Europe and submerge western civilisation. The West was so preoccupied with its internal quarrels that it did not appreciate its peril until it was almost too late. In fact, it was an accident of history rather than any dramatic concerted policy by its ill-organised opponents that the overwhelming threat from the East receded, not to return, a pale imitation, till the "Yellow Peril" movement of the 19th century.

In Europe one of the outstanding figures was the Holy Roman Emperor, Frederick II (1194–1250), "the World's Wonder", a complex and brilliant ruler whose achievements included the leadership of the Sixth Crusade, in the course of which he set the crown of Jerusalem on his head, and the establishment of a Court at Palermo where Christian, Jewish and Muslim scholars rubbed shoulders in academic harmony.

As in every century, institutions, dynasties, modes and movements changed, died, were born. The Latin Empire, set up after the Fourth Crusade and based on Constantinople, fell to pieces after a brief and inglorious existence of half a century. The Hohenstaufen line of kings and emperors, which had included Frederick I ("Barbarossa") and Frederick II, ended with the decapitation of Conrad IV in 1268.

This period saw also the foundation of the Franciscan and Dominican orders of friars in 1208 and 1215, respectively. During the century their influence spread all over Europe, and even beyond it, bringing with it a religious revival. Mention should be made, too, of ecclesiastical architecture, in which notable progress was made during the century. There was a movement away from the heavy building of the Norman period to a lighter style, typified in England by the Angel Choir of Lincoln, and the Cathedrals of Salisbury and Wells, while in France t same style was executed on an ev grander scale, of which Amiens Cathedr is a good example. In the field of educ tion, the earliest European universit Naples, was founded in 1224, and England University College and Mertc College at Oxford and Peterhouse Co lege at Cambridge had their foundation

In England the century is one of va importance for its constitutional develo ments – developments which were t prove of incalculable significance in late world history. In 1215 we have Magr Carta, about which many differe opinions have been expressed, rangin from those which regard it as "the pall dium of English liberties" to the view it as nothing more than an attempt feudal reaction by a few barons actin with entirely selfish motives. The leg historian Maitland says of Edward

239–1307): "In Edward's day, all be-mes definite – there is the Parliament the three estates, there is the King's ›uncil, there are the well-known Courts law." By this time the *Curia Regis* (the ng's Court) had definitely split up into ›arate parts of clearly differentiated nctions. The Exchequer had appeared the previous century, but we now have o the Court of King's Bench, which llowed the king on his travels, and the ›urt of Common Pleas, which decided its between subject and subject not iounting to a breach of the peace; agna Carta established that it should eet "in some certain place", i.e. at 'estminster. By the time of the Model rliament of 1295 the foundations of the odern Parliament had been laid, that Mother of Parliaments", in John Bright's licitous phrase, that in after centuries as to nurture so many offspring all over e world.

›UGGAN, ALFRED. *Growing Up in the Thirteenth ntury*. 1962; POWICKE, SIR M. *The Thirteenth ntury, 1216–1307*. 1962

e also INDIVIDUAL ENTRIES.

---

hirty Years War: political and re-gious struggle over the years 1618–48. he struggle, consisting really of a series wars, was caused fundamentally by the :owth of Calvinism (the strictly Pro-stant religion which spread throughout ance and Switzerland during the six-enth century and which was unrecog-ised by the Religious Peace of Augsburg, 555), by continuing Protestant seizure Church property, by the increasing rength of the Counter-Reformation, id by the crystallisation of the opposing rces into the Calvinist Union, under hristian of Anhalt, and the Catholic eague, under Maximilian of Bavaria. he occasion was the revolt of Bohemian obles against their elected king, Fer-inand of Styria, and his replacement by the Calvinist Frederick, Elector Palatine, which seriously unbalanced the body of Electors, to Catholic disadvantage. (For Calvinism, *see* REFORMATION.)

The first (Bohemian) war, 1618–24, saw Mansfeld, a soldier of fortune leading a Protestant army, defeated in the Palatinate, Christian defeated at White Hill, outside Prague, and the departure of Frederick (the "Winter King"), now dispossessed of all his lands, to the Netherlands.

Protestant fears roused by this Catholic success brought about an alliance of the Northern Protestant Union with Denmark and England, an apparently formidable league which fought imperial forces, led by the Holy Roman Emperor Ferdinand III, in the second (Danish) war, 1625–29. The Emperor was saved by the army created by Wallenstein, which defeated Mansfeld at Dessau and the Danes at Lutter, and was not checked until the siege of Stralsund, after which peace was made at Lübeck.

The victorious Emperor then issued the Edict of Restitution, ordering the return of all Church lands "secularised" since 1552. This offended Wallenstein, who was dismissed and disbanded his army, leaving the Emperor militarily weak just as the Swedish King, Gustavus Adolphus (*see* separate entry), began his incursion into Germany, supported later (1631, Treaty of Barwalde) by France. The third (Swedish) war which followed saw the terrible sack of Magdeburg by Imperial troops (1629), Gustavus's victories at Breitenfeld and Lechfeld and his victorious march to the Rhineland and then to Bavaria. The Emperor then recalled Wallenstein, who met Gustavus on the field of Lützen where, though the Swedes had the advantage, their king was killed (1632). The war continued but the Swedes were overwhelmingly defeated at Nordlingen, 1634, and peace was made the following year at Prague.

It was to France's interest to continue the war, though first results were poor. The tide really turned with the defeat of the Spaniards by the brilliant young Duc d'Enghien (later "the great Condé") at Rocroi, 1643. The Spanish general the Count of Fuentes, over eighty years old and crippled with gout, calmly and gallantly met his end in the chair from which he had been directing the battle in the midst of his choicest troops. Later campaigns wore down the Emperor, and peace was at last made (Treaties of Westphalia) granting recognition to Calvinism, substantial territorial gains to France, Sweden and Brandenburg, and independence to Holland and Switzerland.

¶ STEINBERG, S. H. *The Thirty Years War*. 1966; WEDGWOOD, C. V. *The Thirty Years War*. 1938

See also SEVENTEENTH CENTURY.

Thomas Aquinas, St (*c*. 1225–74): teacher whose writings have profoundly influenced the Church. He was born in southern Italy of noble family and became a Dominican. He pursued his early studies chiefly at the university of Paris, with an interlude at Cologne, but his last years brought him back to Italy, though his body rests at Toulouse (France). One theme of his message, in his *Summa Theologica*, the most famous of his many works, was an attempt to reconcile the principles of Christian belief with a philosophical explanation of the operations of the human intellect, and for this purpose he drew largely on the teaching of the Greek philosopher Aristotle (384–322 BC). His friends called him "The Angelic Doctor": his enemies, "The Dumb Ox of Cologne".

¶ PITTINGER, NORMAN. *St. Thomas Aquinas: the Angelic Doctor*. 1969

Tibet: a country of high tableland and mountains, bordered by China, Pakistan, India and Nepal. Its considerable milita power up to the 10th century was alter to spiritual influence with the develo ment of government by Buddhist pries headed by the Dalai Lama (supposed reincarnated after each death since 149

In the 18th century the Chinese esta lished control and closed the country Europeans for over a century. But 1903–04 a British expedition under Francis Younghusband forced a treaty the Tibetans, and in 1911 the revoluti in China enabled Tibet to throw t Chinese out. Thereafter relations wi Britain improved, Tibet even offeri 1,000 troops to fight in World War I (s separate entry), inviting a British repr sentative to Lhasa in 1920 and allowi expeditions to climb Mount Everest (s separate entry).

Tibetan independence was again d stroyed in 1950 by a Chinese invasi which drove out the Dalai Lama a imposed complete military and admini trative control.

See ENDPAPERS for map.

¶ RICHARDSON, H. E. *Tibet and Its History*. 1962

Tigris, River: river of Mesopotami flowing south-east for more than 1,0 miles [1,600 kilometres] from Turk until it joins the River Euphrates. Tw great cities have been built on the Tigri Nineveh, the capital of the Assyrians, w destroyed in 612 BC, but Baghdad becar a centre of Arab and Persian culture aft AD 762, and is now capital of Iraq. *S* MESOPOTAMIA for map.

¶ MEADE, G. E. *Tigris and Euphrates*. 1963

See also BAGHDAD; EUPHRATES; MESOP TAMIA; NINEVEH.

Timbuktu, Timbuctoo: isolated tow in Mali, West Africa, on the fringe of t Sahara, 9 miles [14·5 kilometres] north a navigable stretch of the River Niger Kabara. In the Middle Ages (*see* separa try) it was an important junction of ravan trade routes from Algeria and orocco to the south and from the 14th the 16th century was a centre of Islamic ade and culture (*see* ISLAM). Captured by e French in 1895 and fortified, it was militarised in 1923 but remained under ench rule until 1960 when Mali became independent state.

e AFRICA for map.

---

imur, Tamerlane (*c.* 1336–1405): rtar conqueror who was born near markand and threw himself into tribal litics. By 1369 he had made himself the le ruler of Turkestan and set out on a ries of conquests. His forces reached the aspian Sea, subdued most of Persia and feated the Golden Horde (*see* TARTARS). 1398 he invaded India and sacked elhi, defeated the Turks in 1402 and, hen he died in 1405, was preparing to vade China. Though his immense ergy and resounding victories created legend and shook every country bordering on Turkestan, he did not found a sting empire.

---

ithe: tax, originally a tenth of agriltural produce, etc., almost universal in e ancient world from Greece to China. amuel warned the children of Israel, who anted a king, "he will take the tenth of our seed and your oliveyards . . . the nth of your sheep". The term later ecame attached exclusively to religious ues, and the laws of Charlemagne (*see* parate entry) made tithes compulsory r the maintenance of the clergy.

in England payment in early days was in oods and livestock. The historian G. M. revelyan says "the tenth sucking-pig ent to the parson's table; the tenth sheaf as carried off to his tithe barn".

The Tithe Commutation Act, 1836, ibstituted a tithe rent charge for payment in kind: an Act of 1891 made the landowner, not the occupier, responsible for its payment; and in 1936 an Act was passed for the extinction of tithes.

Titian, Tiziano Vecelli (*c.* 1480–1576): Venetian painter. A superb colourist, for luminosity, subtle gradations of tone, and richness of texture Titian achieved paintings that are unsurpassed. A man of the world, his paintings are sensuous rather than spiritual. He lived a long, successful life, the friend of popes and princes. He was one of the earliest painters to recognise landscape as a subject for painting in its own right, not a mere background detail.

Tito, Josip Broz (1892–1980): Yugoslav marshal and statesman, president of the federal people's republic of Yugoslavia from 1953 to 1980. He emerged as leader of the guerilla resistance against German occupation forces 1941–45 and, with liberation, became head of state. He established a communist republic but showed remarkable individuality and courage in successfully resisting domination by the USSR, preferring to maintain a neutral foreign policy. Since Tito's death Yugoslavia has been run by a presidential collective.

Tobacco: dried and cured leaves of a plant of American origin (probably from Spanish *tobaco*, the native name for a pipe). The North American Indians smoked tobacco both in pipes and rolled into cigars. It was introduced into Europe by Spanish explorers, one of whom presented tobacco plants to Philip II (*see* separate entry) in 1558. Jean Nicot, a Frenchman, gave some tobacco to Catherine de' Medici, who is said to have enjoyed it. The word "nicotine" comes from Nicot's surname. Tobacco was known in England in Elizabeth I's reign, when Ralegh (*see* separate entry) probably popularised its use at court. James I detested it and attacked it in *A Counter Blaste to Tobacco*, published in 1604. Portuguese sailors took tobacco to Africa. When Livingstone (*see* separate entry) explored central Africa he found that the natives smoked and that a warrior's pipe was often buried with him.

In modern times the most popular form of smoking has become the cigarette (or "paper cigar"), reputedly first smoked in Britain by the artist George Richmond (1809–96), the oldest actual example being one made *c.* 1885 and preserved in a New York collection. It was calculated that in 1967 528,000 million cigarettes were smoked in the USA alone. The 1968 figure for the United Kingdom was 2,980 cigarettes for each adult. Recently very considerable evidence has been produced to show a direct connection between cigarette-smoking and certain respiratory diseases, including lung cancer, and intensive advertising and instructional anti-smoking campaigns have been conducted, with unfortunately small results.

Togo: republic lying between Ghana and Dahomey in West Africa, with a seaboard of thirty-five miles [56·3 kilometres] on the Gulf of Guinea. It was part of the German Colony of Togoland from 1884 until World War I (*see* separate entry) and from 1920 was administered by France under a League of Nations mandate.

It became an independent republic within the French Community in November 1958 and attained full independence in 1960. The economy is mainly agricultural, the principal exports being cocoa, coffee, copra, cotton and palm kernels. Phosphates account for 75 per cent of exports; Chromite, bauxite and limestone are also important.

See AFRICA for map.

Tokyo: capital of Japan, the world's most populous city, passing the ten million mark in 1962 – the first urban a in history to do so. In 1590 the village Edo was made a provincial capital a grew into a substantial city. In 1868 E became the imperial capital of Japan a its name was altered to Tokyo. Eart quake and fires destroyed the city in 19 but it was resolutely rebuilt. Hea bombing during World War II (separate entry) again destroyed much the city, but a new influx of populati from lost overseas territories, industrial ation and a high birthrate has caused acu problems of urban organisation a planning.

See JAPAN for map.

¶ KIRKUP, J. *Tokyo*. 1966

Toledo: city on rock in a bend of t Tagus, Spain. In AD 453 it became capi of the Visigoths. Betrayed to the Mo in 712, it became a centre of swor making and weaving. Its recapture Alfonzo VI of Castile in 1085 was the fi success in the Christian reconquest Spain. It then became the meeting pla of Muslim, Jewish and Christian schola where Gerard of Cremona (1114–8 translated Arabic texts of Greek medic and geographical works. It early becan an important Church centre, and, another sphere of activity, geographe used it as their prime meridian. In 1519 was the centre of the Castilian risi against Charles V (*see* separate entry). 1936 a small garrison of Falangists (mem bers of the Spanish fascist moveme which triumphed during the Spani Civil War) survived a bitter siege seventy days in the Alcazar, its citadel.

See also SPAIN.

Tolpuddle Martyrs: name given to t six agricultural labourers of the village Tolpuddle in Dorset, England, wh in 1834 were tried and convicted

vast public demonstration in April 1834, in ›test against the deportation of the Tolpuddle artyrs.

.ministering an unlawful oath in the ›urse of setting up a Friendly Society ˈAgricultural Workers. They were tried Dorchester and sent for seven years' ansportation. In 1836, in response to ıblic outcry, they were given a free ırdon and in 1838 returned to England. ıe sum of £1,300 had been collected provide them with farms and five ttled in Essex, whilst one remained at olpuddle.

The threat of this type of legal action scouraged the formation of all trade ıions for some time.

In LARSEN, EGON. *Men Who Fought for Freedom.* 58

e also TRADE UNIONS.

---

onga: autonomous kingdom in the estern Pacific, formed of a group of ands discovered by Tasman in 1643, ough earlier sighted by Le Maire and :houten. Wallis visited Tonga in 1767 ıd later Cook, who named them the iendly Islands. Wesleyan missionaries *ee* WESLEY, JOHN) landed in 1826. This :riod saw continuing dynastic and civil rife until in 1845 Taufa'ahua Tupou :feated rival claimants. Converted to hristianity in 1831, he and his wife took ıe names of George and Salote (Charitte). By the time of his death in 1893 onga had been transformed from a :oup of cannibal islands – in 1806 only ıe sailor from a British ship survived the cooking pots – into a Christian state with a postal system, legal code, constitution and developing parliamentary government. In 1900 Tonga became by treaty, revised in 1958, a British protected state. George II was succeeded in 1918 by Salote, who reigned for forty-seven years, the world's tallest queen of the world's smallest kingdom, and who, during her visit to England for Queen Elizabeth II's coronation, became a popular figure with the British public. (Independent 1970.) *See* PACIFIC OCEAN for map.

Tordesillas, Treaty of (1494): treaty implementing a ruling given by Pope Alexander VI as to the territorial rights of Spain and Portugal in the New World, of which little was then known. Everything east of a line drawn down the Atlantic 370 miles west of the Cape Verde Islands was assigned to Portugal, the rest to Spain.

This enabled Portugal in due course to claim Brazil. The settlement was quite unacceptable to other maritime powers such as France and England and, later, the Netherlands, who were not participants. Religious bitterness entered the situation when Protestant England and the Netherlands became Spain's main competitors.

Toronto: city chosen in 1793 by Lord Dorchester as the capital of Upper Canada. It suffered greatly at the hands of American troops who captured it in 1813. Self-governing from 1817, York achieved city status in 1834 as Toronto, the Huron Indian word for "meeting place", important for Indians, French, Americans and British alike. Ontario, again separated from Quebec in 1867, took Toronto as its capital. The University was founded in 1827 and the Medical School houses the Banting and Best Institute, named after the discoverers of insulin. Canada's largest city, Toronto had a population of 3,029,300 in 1982.

Torpedo: self-propelled submarine missile carrying an explosive head which is detonated on impact, capable of emitting electric shocks.

Original torpedoes were submarine mines towed or carried into action by small craft or submarines. The prototype of the modern self-propelled torpedo was invented by the Austrian, Captain Luppis. He and an English engineer, Robert Whitehead, produced the cigar-shaped Whitehead torpedo at Fiume on the

A blunt-nosed torpedo being hauled aboard ship during a training exercise.

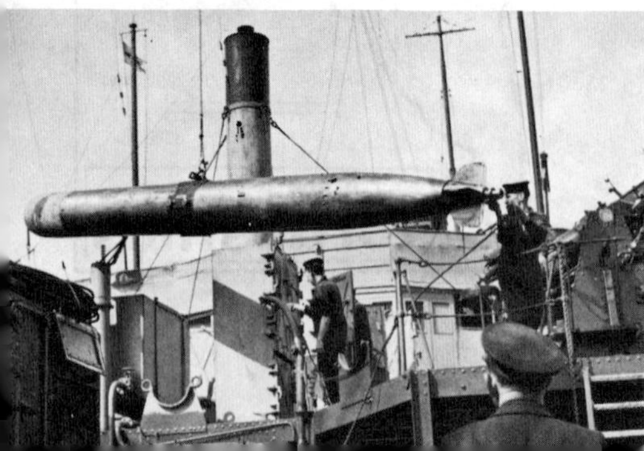

Adriatic in 1864. By 1875 special torpe[do] boats were being built to carry this ne[w] weapon, and by 1900 it was fitted in mo[st] major war vessels.

The early torpedoes had a propell[er] driven by a compressed air engin[e]. Horizontal rudders controlled the dep[th] and a gyroscope held it to its course. Th[e] warhead containing dynamite had a pist[ol] detonator in the nose. The modern ve[r]sion is blunt nosed, is powered b[y] heated gases and can be "homed" on [to] its target.

Torquemada, Tomás de (1420–98[)]: Spanish inquisitor. A Dominican, h[e] became confessor to Queen Isabella an[d] her husband Ferdinand. Obsessed with a[n] urge to suppress heresy, Torquemad[a] persuaded Ferdinand and Isabella to re[-]store the Inquisition in Spain in 1478 an[d] to pursue the conquest of Mooris[h] Granada, completed in 1492. He becam[e] sole Inquisitor General in the Spanis[h] dominions in 1483 and with fanatical ze[al] pursued a reign of terror against Jew[s], Moors, or Christians who deviated fro[m] orthodoxy in any form. Over 2,000 of h[is] victims were condemned to death b[y] burning and thousands more were ex[-]pelled from the country.
See also INQUISITION.

Torres Vedras: two parallel lines o[f] defence, built by Wellington (*see* separa[te] entry) across the Lisbon peninsula 1809[–]10 (*see* PENINSULAR WAR). Dams, ditch[es] and stone walls were constructed to joi[n] natural barriers, such as steep hillsides an[d] rivers. The land in front was levelled fo[r] miles. Behind these lines British troop[s] were supplied by sea, thus preventing th[e] French from gaining total control o[f] Portugal.

Tory: word of Irish origin, originall[y] applied about 1680 to the English politic rty which stood for loyalty to the rone and devotion to the Anglican hurch. The party was thus thrown into me confusion when James II tried to store the Roman Catholic religion (*see* parate entry) in England and so had no rt in the invitation sent by the Whigs – e rival party (*see* separate entry) – to 'illiam III. The name has survived in ritish politics and is still applied to the onservative party.

KEBBEL, T. E. *History of Toryism: from the accession Mr. Pitt to power in 1783 to the death of Lord aconsfield in 1881.* 1972

---

oussaint L'Ouverture, Pierre Dom-ique (1743–1803): Negro guerilla ader and liberator of Haiti. Born a ave, he taught himself to read and made mself leader of the slave revolt against e French. From 1791 he displayed out-anding skill in defeating attempts to ush the rebellion, and became ruler of aiti in 1801. Finally, Napoleon (*see* parate entry), incensed by Toussaint's sumption of governing powers, sent a rench expeditionary force which effec-vely compelled his surrender. He died prison in France the year before Haiti hieved independence.

BENTLEY, J. D. *Touissant l'Ouverture of the West dies.* 1969

ee also HAITI.

---

ower of London: complex of his-rical buildings in the City of London, n the north bank of the Thames. Today is a combined museum and barracks. In s time it has been fortress, palace and rison. The chief building, the White ower, or Keep, is Norman. The Crown wels are kept in the Wakefield Tower. Many famous people were executed in e Tower, a number of them buried in e Tower chapel of St Peter ad Vincula. ueen Anne Boleyn (1507–36) and mes, Duke of Monmouth (1649–85) are both buried there.

The Tower is looked after by the Yeomen Warders of the Guard, popularly called Beefeaters, who wear Tudor dress. A long-established legend has it that when the ravens leave the Tower of London the British royal line will come to an end.

¶ DOBBING, DOUGLAS S. *Tower of London.* 1970; SHUTTLESWORTH, DOROTHY. *The Tower of London.* 1972

Townshend, Charles, 2nd Viscount, "Turnip Townshend" (1674–1738): politician and agricultural improver. Although brought up in the Tory tradition, he attached himself to the Whigs (*see* separate entry) and married a sister of Robert Walpole. But he was of too independent a spirit to succeed in party politics and eventually quarrelled with his brother-in-law, who said, "The firm must be Walpole and Townshend, not Townshend and Walpole". In 1830 he retired to his Norfolk estates, where he demonstrated that the fertility of his land was improved by applying marl and made notable advances in the cultivation of root crops, particularly turnips.

See also AGRICULTURAL IMPROVERS; WALPOLE, SIR ROBERT.

Townshend, Charles, second son of 3rd Viscount (1725–67): British statesman, responsible for the Townshend Acts (1767) which, through their imposition of taxes on such commodities as glass, lead, paper and tea, aroused the bitter opposition from the American colonists that formed a prime cause of the War of American Independence (*see* separate entry). Townshend was a distinguished orator but his career was marred by lack of judgment and principle.

Trade marks: distinctive marks or names, affixed to articles, indicating the

TWO 18th Cent TRADE CUTS BY BEWICK

ARMOURER'S MARK

ASSOCIATED ADHESIVES

MOTHERCARE

McKELLAR WATT (sausages)

CRAFTOR SHOE REPAIRS

SWAN GARAGES

OSMOND TURNER

6 RED CUBES
OXO
For BEEF and all red meats

SOME FAMILIAR TRADE MARKS

anufacturer or owner of the commercial rights. The practice of trade arking has been traced among Syrian ass manufacturers in the 1st century BC. ımian ware, made in Etruscan factories ee ETRURIA) in the 1st century AD, was ›mmonly stamped with the pottery wner's name. Bronze domestic articles ere frequently marked in similar fashion. round 1285 Italian sheet paper makers :gan to use watermarks. Then in 14th-ntury England it was ruled that wherver possible manufacturers should have ıeir name imprinted on an article proıced, as a safeguard against fraud, to ıaintain high standards of quality and to ıforce guild monopolies. In Germany ıd Austria, hammersmiths had to stamp ıeir marks on armour, swords and ıtlery, and similar regulations were ıade for goldsmiths and silversmiths in ngland, France and Italy. During the liddle Ages these were proprietary ıther than trade marks, and enabled ıthorities, especially guilds, to control ade.

Trade marks, in the sense that every ıaker had an individual stamp, began in ıe 18th century. They had publicity alue and helped the retailer to identify ıe object for re-ordering. Laws to pro-ct the rights of the trade mark owner ere developed during the 18th century, ıd by the first years of the 19th century aders were being restrained from audulently passing off their goods as ıose of another, thus laying the foundaon on which later law could be built. As ade became increasingly competitive in ıe second half of the 19th century, usinessmen demanded more legislative :tion, statutes were enacted, and far ıore branded goods became registered. .t present, in Britain, registered trade ıarks hold good for seven years and are ıereafter renewable indefinitely for eriods of fourteen years.

Trade routes: established ways followed by merchants and traders. The Middle East provides the earliest history of goods transported by land and water, between the civilisations of the Tigris-Euphrates and the Nile, eastwards to Southern Arabia, between Egypt and Crete, from Ophir up the Red Sea, and by Phoenicians island-hopping along the African coast to Spain. Carthage, Cadiz, Marseilles, originally trading posts, became independent city-states, as did Greek Tarentum and Syracuse. Trading expansion eastwards followed Alexander's conquests.

Though the Romans are not considered a commercial people, the *pax Romana* (Roman peace) provided the security essential for trade. Roman traders ranged from Britain to the Hellespont, and outside the confines of empire beyond the Rhine, Danube and North Africa. Perfumes, spices, gems, silks from India, Arabia and China arrived through Mediterranean ports and Red Sea depots, whence hundreds of ships sailed annually with wares in exchange. After the fall of Rome and the rise of Islam the Ottoman kingdoms controlled the caravan routes, with Bagdad, Damascus, Cairo and North African and Spanish cities the important entrepôts (i.e. centres importing and re-exporting commodities). After AD 1000 European trade generally revived, and the Crusades intensified the process. Venice and Genoa established factories on the Black Sea. In the mid-13th century Capuchin friars followed the trade routes through Central Asia taken later by Marco Polo. Genghis Khan (d. 1227) and Kublai Khan (1259–94) encouraged foreigners to establish trading posts. By the 14th century routes ran from China via Turkestan, the Caspian and the Volga to Novgorod, or via Azov to the Crimea, through Persia and the Black Sea to Constantinople, and from Mesopotamia to Syria. India had outlets by the Red Sea to Egypt, by the

Persian Gulf to Aleppo and Syria, or over the Khyber Pass to Persia. Mediterranean routes led to northern Italian cities, to Spain through Barcelona, into France through Marseilles and the Rhone, and over the Alps to Germany. Great trading associations, the Hanseatic, Swabian and Rhenish Leagues, distributed commodities to northern Europe and Russia through a network of markets, with reciprocal trade in local products.

The demand for new trade routes was one of the reasons for the work of Prince Henry the Navigator from 1418. Turkish intrusions into Europe, even before the capture of Constantinople (1453) and Egypt (1517), threatened the old routes. Columbus strongly believed in a shorter westward route and Vasco da Gama's voyage proved the practicability of a sea route to India. Thereafter shippers preferred the direct Cape of Good Hope route which, though perilous, was less subject to raids from pirates and avoided the inconvenience of transhipment (the transfer of goods from one vessel to another). The Portuguese regularly despatched trading fleets from 1501 and the capture of Malacca by their forces (1511) finally assured their freedom of action. By 1580, starting from Mozambique, routes ran via Socotra to Ormuz, via Goa, Bombay, northwards to Bassein, eastwards to Colombo, Sumatra, Java and the Moluccas, and from Malacca to Macao. With respective spheres of influence decided, Spain could organise its routes from the Philippines to Acapulco and from the Americas home. Consequently Mediterranean ports declined in importance, though Spanish gold and silver stimulated European trade generally. The Portuguese lost much of their trade to the Dutch in the 1600s, and the Spaniards endured growing English competition. The Treaty of Utrecht, 1713, opened Spanish colonies to Britain and established her as the chief slave-trading nation.

All trade routes shared one commo feature, their attraction for pirates. I ancient Rome Pompey was honoured fc suppressing African pirates: in the 14t century Simone Bocanegra, Doge c Venice, restored her prosperity in the sam way. Barbary corsairs from North Afric were a threat throughout the centurie attacking Mediterranean commerce, an even entering the English Channel. Late Chinese pirate junks and Arab dhows wer equally troublesome. Spain suffered mor than most from piracy, both the Englis and the Dutch on several occasions capturing her treasure fleets. Drake's circumnavigation (1578–80) and Anson's (1740 44) combined privateering with attackin Spain's colonies and commerce. Wes Indian pirates from Jamaica and Tortug were attracted only by prospects of loot.

The Seven Years War confirme Britain's commercial ascendancy, whic continued even after the American Wa of Independence, with ever expandin traffic in textiles, slaves, tobacco, suga and machinery, until British traders wer found on all the world's routes. After th coming of steam, the sailing ship, especially the clipper, was still employed bringing tea and wool from China and Australia. After the Suez Canal opened in 1869 these fine ships declined but continued fo a time sailing the Cape Horn and Africa routes. By the 1880s refrigeration ship were sailing from New Zealand, an steam had ousted sail on passenger route The Suez Canal reduced the voyage fron London to Bombay to eighteen days The Panama Canal, opened to shippin in 1914, shortened the Liverpool to Sa Francisco voyage by 5,666 miles [9,11 kilometres] and brought the latter 7,87 miles [12,608 kilometres] nearer Nev York. The interwar years were the heyday of the passenger liner, with American British, French and Italians competing fo e Atlantic Blue Riband, and regular ilings of luxury liners the world over. Simultaneously, trans-Atlantic, trans-acific and transcontinental air routes ere developing, though economic diffi-ılties limited expansion. Since World Var II almost every country has its air nes, and trade routes have been greatly ffected, both favourably and adversely. 957 saw North Atlantic air passengers as umerous as those by ship. Bulk carriers nd supertankers still sail the oceans, but y 1971 only the liners *La France* and *ueen Elizabeth II* were operating weekly rvices and winter schedules were drasti-ally reduced. In 1982 about 130 million assengers were carried annually on the vorld's international air routes. On land ations construct vast motorway net-vorks. Russian and American ventures nto space bring ever nearer the possi-ility of interstellar flights from space latforms, and, for future generations, he establishment of interplanetary trade outes, pioneered by men as hardy and dventurous in spirit as those whose ack-horses and caravans threaded their vay through the mountains and deserts f Europe and Asia in the Middle ges.

ee ENDPAPERS for map.

DUCHE, J. *The Great Trade Routes*. 1969

ee also INDIVIDUAL ENTRIES.

---

rade unions: organisations of workers ormed mainly to bargain with employers n wages and conditions of work. The nodern trade union does many other hings for its members, but wages, or the rice they can get for their work, are still s chief concern. In Britain in the 18th entury craftsmen began to band together o resist the attempts of their masters to uy their skills for as little as possible. The ndustrial Revolution (*see* separate entry) rought vast numbers of workers together n great factories, and unions grew quickly in many trades. The employers called these early unions "combinations" and did all they could to stop them. A number of Acts of Parliament were passed to prevent such combinations. Some union leaders were imprisoned, and their unions broke up, but new ones were formed in their place. At last, in 1824, the Combination Acts were repealed and the right of workers to form unions was recognised. But other ways were found of making it difficult to form unions. In 1834 six labourers were charged with "administering unlawful oaths" when starting a union. They were found guilty and were transported to Australia with other convicts. This was the famous case of the "Tolpuddle Martyrs" (*see* separate entry). It caused such anger that after two years the men were pardoned.

In spite of all difficulties the trade unions continued to grow in strength. In addition to their main concern with pay and hours of work the unions offered help in times of unemployment and sickness and built up funds from their members' contributions to help them with strike pay when their wages were cut off. There were many ups and downs for the unions as trade was good or bad. When it was good, there was plenty of work and the unions prospered: when it was bad, there was much unemployment, members fell away and the unions were weakened. By the end of World War I (1918) the number of trade unionists in Britain had doubled, but in the slump that followed the war they had a severe setback. The General Strike of 1926 (*see* STRIKES) was a failure, and as a result fresh restrictions were put upon the unions by an Act of Parliament which was not repealed until 1946.

Unions for workers in skilled trades and crafts were followed by general unions, mainly for unskilled workers of many different industries. Such unions as the Transport and General Workers Union

Above left: One of the first trade union card that of the Power Loom Female Weave Society. Below left: The card of the Cor wainers Union, established in 1844. Above: trade union demonstration at Manchester in 187 Below: Members of the Match Girls Union wh struck at Bryant and May, match manufacturer in 1888.

and the National Union of General and Municipal Workers are today among the largest. More recently unions have been formed among professional workers such as doctors, teachers and civil servants, and among entertainers such as actors and professional footballers.

As unions grew during the 19th century, trades councils were formed in most industrial areas. The trades council was made up of representatives from the branches of the different unions in the area. From these local bodies of trade unionists came the idea of a national body, the *Trades Union Congress* which was formed in 1868. The TUC is made up of delegates from all the trade unions affiliated to it who meet for four days every year. A General Council is elected to deal with day-to-day affairs.

Nearly all trade unionists in Britain ar now represented at the TUC which ha grown from about one million member in 1874 to about 9 million in 1970. Toda the TUC has great influence as repre senting the great majority of organise workers of the nation and its Genera Secretary is a national figure. When ther is a dispute between unions, the Genera Council may be asked to give a ruling Although every union is independent, th advice of the General Council is ofte accepted. When there is a dispute betwee a union and the employers, the Genera Council tries to bring about a settlemen and to avoid strike action if possible. Th General Council has regular meeting with the national body representing employers, the Confederation of British Industry, and it keeps in touch with certai vernment departments.

'he TUC links up with trade unionists road through the International Con-deration of Free Trade Unions. It is also member of the International Labour rganisation to which over one hundred untries belong. The ILO is specially ncerned with social justice and peace nong nations. In countries which have me form of dictatorship the trade ions are not independent: they are con-olled by the state and have no "right to ike".

n the United States of America, the st attempts by workers to form unions ere fiercely resisted by the employers, in Britain. After the Civil War (1861–; *see* separate entry) when industry de-loped rapidly, trade unions were formed the major industries, and, in spite of en more violent opposition from the nployers, the unions came together on national basis in the *American Federation Labor*. This happened in 1886, only ghteen years after the foundation of the UC in England. The early years of the FL were marked by violent clashes be-veen unions and employers, who were ten backed by the government. Two ilway strikes, in 1877 and 1886, were th ended by the government using the my against the strikers. As American dustry prospered, both the AFL and the nployers made a move towards settling sputes on a national basis by agreement d arbitration. One of the most active en in the AFL was the leader of the nited Mine Workers, John L. Lewis. fter World War I he grew dissatisfied ith the AFL because it favoured skilled orkers. The rapid development of mass oduction had led to the employment of any unskilled and semiskilled workers. ewis said that the AFL should include workers, both skilled and unskilled. In 35 he left the AFL and organised the *ongress of Industrial Organisations*. This was made up of his own union, the United Mine Workers, and a number of other unions in steel, glass, rubber and car manufacture. The CIO became a very powerful body and, for the next twenty years, the AFL and the CIO existed side by side. Even in 1955, when the two came together again, a number of unions stayed outside the Federation as independent unions. Thus, trade unions in the USA have grown in a different way from the English unions. They have also had more restrictions placed on them by govern-ment action, e.g. by the Taft-Hartley Act of 1947.

See also INDIVIDUAL ENTRIES.

Trafalgar, Battle of: naval battle fought on 21 October 1805 off Cadiz, Spain, between Nelson's fleet of 27 British ships of the line and Villeneuve's 33 French and Spanish. It ended the three-year blockade of French squadrons – in Brest by Corn-wallis, in Toulon by Nelson. Napoleon ordered these squadrons to escape and concentrate with Spanish ships in the West Indies, then to clear the Channel for his *Grande Armée* to invade England. On 30 March Villeneuve eluded Nelson's open blockade of Toulon and reached the West Indies, but, when the Brest squadron failed to break out, he sailed to Cadiz. On 1 September Napoleon struck his camp at Boulogne, marched to the Danube and ordered Villeneuve to carry troops to Naples. When Villeneuve sailed, Nelson's watchful frigates kept contact and warned the main fleet. The battle, fought in light airs and a swell, was won by British sea-manship and gunnery, perfected in the months of blockading. It was bloody and decisive, in contrast to the 18th-century actions fought by the book of Fighting Instructions. A lieutenant wrote, "We scrambled into action as best we could, each man to catch his bird" – a fair resumé of "the Nelson touch", which was to strike at the enemy centre and rear before their van could turn and engage, and to trust each captain to engage closely without orders. Nelson was killed by musket shot, but 19 enemy ships were taken, all but four being lost in the gale which followed the battle.

¶ LANGDON-DAVIES, JOHN. *The Battle of Trafalgar* (Jackdaw). 1963; WARNER, OLIVER. *Trafalgar*. 1959

See also NAPOLEON I; NELSON.

Tramways: systems of public transport by means of cars (trams), sometimes with one or two trailers attached, running on rails laid in the streets. The term "tramway", however, is sometimes applied to minor railways, while the origin of the word "tram" is obscure. Moreover, many tramways, especially in the USA and Europe, run or formerly ran for part of their route on their own tracks across open country. In the USA the word for tram was "street-car", but this is one of the parts of the world from which this form of transport has almost disappeared. In England, where many urban corporations once had their tramway system, that at Blackpool (Lancashire) was the first, as it is now the last, to operate and seems likely to do so for some time. There is a tramway museum at Crich in Derbyshire. In Western Europe, however, as also in India and elsewhere, tramways are still extensively used.

Horse-drawn tram c. 1900.

The earliest trams, drawn by hors were introduced in New York in 1832, Paris in 1853 and in London in 1861. the 1880s a system of cable operation w widely adopted, but by 1900 the use electricity became general, current beir supplied to the vehicles by means of ove head wires. In the early years of tl century trams were to be found in mar parts of the world, including such remo countries as China and the Sudan.

The disadvantage which has since led the widespread disappearance of mar tramway systems is the lack of manoeuv

Traffic jam at the Elephant and Castle, Londo in 1922.

ability of the vehicles in narrow stree with heavy traffic. In some cases tramca have been superseded by trolley-buse running on rubber-tyred wheels ar steered by the driver, but deriving electr power from the existing overhead systen suitably modified. These, though mo manoeuvrable, still have their drawbacl and, as they become worn out, are seldo replaced.

¶ JOYCE, J. *Tramway Heyday*. 1964; JOYCE, *Tramways of the World*. 1965

Transkei: on 26 October 1976, Sout Africa declared that the Republic of tl Transkei was independent. No membe of the international community h recognised the Transkei whose indeper dence has been seen as a device whereb

›uth Africa hoped to gain international cognition for her Bantustan (or separ- e development) policy. Lying between ›sotho and the Indian Ocean most of the rritory consists of poor agricultural ıd. In area 15,831 sqare miles [41,002 km] it has to support about 1·75 illion Xhosa people. Three other Bantu omelands – Bophuthatswana (1977), iskei (1981) and Venda (1979) – were oclaimed as independent but like the anskei have not received recognition.

---

ransport: the carrying of people, uipment and goods. From ancient nes to the 19th century, transport over- ıd was based on the strength of human animal muscles and on road conditions. a transport depended on the oarsman d the vagaries of the wind. Man himself as the first beast of burden, sometimes ith a light yoke slung across his shoulders carry his belongings. He was able to ake life easier by such devices as placing s load on a framework of boughs which dragged behind him. Around 6000 BC learnt to tame animals. In warm untries oxen, donkeys and camels were ıined to pull or carry his loads: in the rth, dogs, in south-west Asia, horses.

'he sledge was the earliest vehicle, made st of hide or tree bark and then, in ımerian times, of wood with a boxlike ntraption on top – ancestor of the four- heel wagon. The slide car was another means of transport in ancient times. Two poles were tied to one or two animals at one end, with the other end, carrying the load, dragging behind. This type, known as a "travois", was formerly much in use among the North American Indians.

ıe "travois", used by the Sioux Indians.

The wheel was one of man's greatest inventions, made around 3000 BC. The first wheels evolved from logs used as rollers to move heavily laden sledges. Rough discs of wood were cut from tree trunks and fastened to each end of a small roller. It is believed that the Sumerians were the first to use wheeled vehicles, and that the nomads of the Central Asiatic steppes were first in putting on roof covers.

Assyrian chariot.

Around 2000 BC the Egyptians were using chariots with spoked wheels. Assyrians, Babylonians and Greeks all used chariots to speed a messenger or launch an attack; so did the Celts (*see* separate entry), the most skilful cartwrights of ancient times. Roman emperors travelled their splendid roads with great pomp. Though they were probably exceptional in their craze for display, Heliogabalus is recorded as journeying in a gem-studded carriage, Nero with a thousand vehicles. One imperial carriage, ancestor of the motor car, is said to have had slaves hidden in its structure, propelling the vehicle with their hands and feet.

Logs were man's first water transport – first just one to ferry him across a stream, then several lashed together for a raft. Using a stone axe he hollowed out a log for a canoe which he could paddle against the current. Later, for a lighter craft, he stretched bark over a wooden frame. At the same time as the invention of the wheel, boats and ships developed, propelled by oars and sails. Fifty centuries ago the Egyptians were sailing on the River Nile in a craft made of planks fastened to a wooden frame.

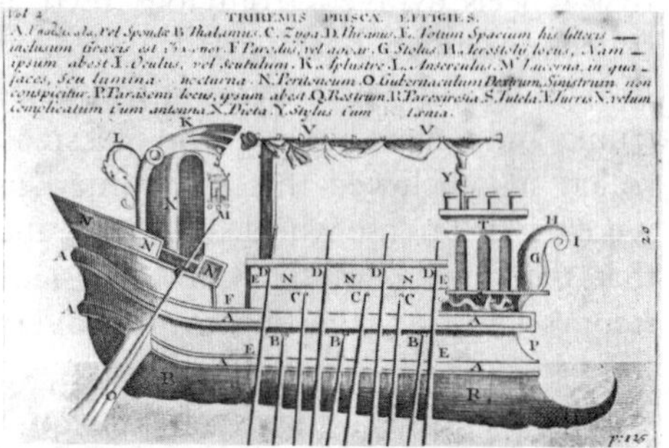

Plan of a Greek trireme.

Soon ships were venturing out into the sea in search of trade. The Phoenicians (*see* separate entry) sailed along the Mediterranean shores using galleys with rows of oars. Their sturdy trading ships began to sail further westward, to Malta and Spain, planting trading stations as they explored. Greater speed was wanted for warships, so boat builders produced first the light bireme, then the heavier trireme, with three rows of oars requiring as many as two hundred slaves, a single sail suspended from the mast and an iron-shod ram at the prow. Greeks and Romans used them for war and the establishment and maintenance of their colonies. Even larger vessels were developed, from quadriremes (four banks of oars) and quinqueremes (five banks) up to a reputed fifteen-banked ship. Roman merchantmen, 180 feet long [64·9 m] and carrying up to 700 passengers, transported armies and equipment to Carthage and Gaul.

After the fall of the Roman Empire the road systems in Europe deteriorated badly. Wagons and carts were still used

A medieval cart pulled by horses wearing ho collars. Cart wheels and horses' shoes were spi because of the mud.

but were so uncomfortable that only t poor used them. The noblemen and we to-do, even women, preferred to go horseback or by litter. Packhorses we used to transport goods. During the ea Middle Ages (*see* separate entry), mode harnessing methods, long known China, enabled the horse to draw heavi loads, and as a result more freight a passenger transport went by road, thou in addition to dust, mud and potho there was the danger from bandits.

The first carriage with suspension of body by chains and ropes appeared Europe during the 15th century, f royalty and the aristocracy; later, t stage coach, suspended on iron or wood supports, came into general use.

Queen Elizabeth I's coach, from a drawing do in 1572.

The main transport developments of t Middle Ages were on water. The ma netic compass, long known by Chine and Mediterranean navigators, came in general use, while ships became larger a more seaworthy. Although we hear of three-masted Saracen ship being sunk Richard I as early as 1191, the earlie known dated portrayal of such a vessel ı a seal of 1466. It was certainly not till ıe 15th century that the three-master ecame common in European waters and, ith its greater wind-power and man-uvrability, made longer voyages pos-ble. Columbus voyaged to America 492), other explorers sailed around frica and across to India. In 1522 lagellan (*see* separate entry) completed ıe first voyage round the world.

The 18th century saw the development f the steam engine, but its first applica-ons were to pumps and industrial ıachinery. It was some time before it was dapted to the propulsion of locomotives nd ships. John Fitch of America con-ructed a steamboat in 1787, with the eam engine operating a set of paddles on ither side of the boat, and in 1839 John ricsson, a Swedish engineer, invented he screw propeller, more efficient than addle wheels.

Although steam locomotives had been ı use on mineral railways since soon fter the turn of the century, the first ublic railway in Britain using this form f traction for some of its traffic was pened in 1825. This was the Stockton and Darlington Railway, but the Liver-pool and Manchester (1830) was in a truer sense the forerunner of the modern railway systems since from the first it used only locomotive power. At much the same time as the latter the first railway in the USA began operation. Steam rail-ways made it possible to open up vast areas of the continents, with a cheap, fast and powerful means of transport. In recent years diesel and electric loco-motives have almost entirely replaced those driven by steam.

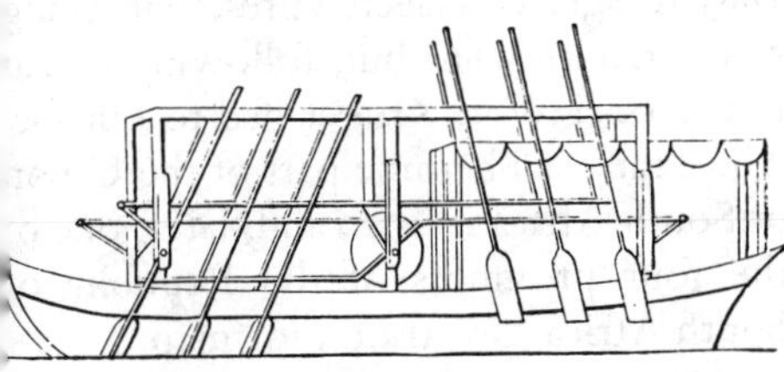

Above: Outline of Fitch's first paddleboat.
Below: Fitch's second steamboat.

Travelling by motor car in 1908.

For local transport the tram or street-car, at first drawn by horses or by cable, but later driven by electricity, enjoyed con-siderable popularity during the later 19th and early 20th century, but it has now given way to the motor bus and this in its turn is threatened by the private motor car (*see* separate entry), which gives a man and his family their own personal means of transport. Tremendous strides have been made in air travel since the Wright Brothers in 1903 made their historic flight. The comparatively new word "aeronaut" (literally, one who sails in the air) is already giving place to "astronaut" (one who sails to the stars).

¶ RIDLEY, ANTHONY. *An Illustrated History of Transport.* 1969

See also AVIATION; RAILWAYS; ROADS; SHIPS; SPACE TRAVEL; STEAM; TRAMWAYS.

Transportation: removal of convicts to penal settlements abroad. James I of England despatched "dissolute persons" to Virginia and his grandson Charles II commuted the death penalty to transportation. Legalised in 1719, transportation flourished after Australia was annexed. The visits of the reformer Elizabeth Fry (1780–1845) to 106 ships carrying 12,000 convicts indicate its scale. New South Wales (Botany Bay; *see* separate entry) took convicts from 1788, including the "Tolpuddle Martyrs" (*see* separate entry). In 1840 Tasmania expanded existing settlements to take in hardened criminals from the mainland. Transportation from Britain ended by 1868. France used Guinea from 1763, and New Caledonia, Guiana and Devil's Island until 1950. In a less familiar sense, transportation may be held to include the removal of political "undesirables". The salt mines of Siberia have served the rulers of modern Russia in the same way as they did the imperial Tsars.

Trans-Siberian Railway: constructed by Russia (1891–1900) to link her own European system with her possessions in the Far East. The length from Chelyabinsk in the Urals to Vladivostok in the Pacific was 4,627 miles [7,446 kilometres]. It was a single line with passing places, and Lake Baikal was crossed by a train-ferry equipped as an ice-breaker. It proved quite inadequate for the military requirements of the Russo-Japanese war of 1904–05 (*see* separate entry). Under Soviet rule the line has been largely doubled (i.e. double-tracked), the lake has been bypassed, and electrification is in progress.

Transvaal: province of the Republic of South Africa. The capital is Pretoria, other main towns being Johannesburg, Germiston, Springs and Benoni, which are situated on the Witwatersrand, where most of the older gold mines are located and where 50 per cent of the Republic's engineering and metal industries are concentrated. The mineral wealth is great and varied. Platinum, chrome, manganese, asbestos, magnetite, diamonds, corundum, beryl, antimony and vermiculite are produced in addition to gold, and granite and marble are quarried. A new opencast copper mine which is now being developed is likely to become the biggest in the world. In the low veld of the East Transvaal and the Magaliesberg district citrus and other subtropical fruits are grown in considerable quantities.

The republic was first established by the Boers who crossed the River Vaal in the course of the Great Trek (*see* separate entry) and in 1836–38 defeated the Matabele tribes, who had earlier driven out the Bantu, Hottentots and Bushmen.

In 1852, after the Sand River Convention had declared the Transvaal an independent republic, the situation became so confused by disputes, in which Marthinus Pretorius and Paul Kruger (*see* separate entry) figured prominently, that in 1877 the Transvaal was annexed by Britain. In 1883 Kruger was elected president, being re-elected in 1886; but, following defeat in the Boer War, Kruger fled to Europe. The Transvaal became part of the Union of South Africa in 1910 and, later, one of the four provinces of the Republic of South Africa. *See* AFRICA for map.

Trieste: port in the north-eastern corner of the Adriatic, sheltered by the peninsula of Istria. The victim of disputes between the patriarchs of Aquilaea and Venice, jealous of its seaport, it accepted the protection of Duke Leopold of Austria in 1382. In 1719 Austria attempted to develop it as an Imperial Free Port and base of her Levant Company. Napoleon annexed it in 1809, but Austria recovered it in 1815, and it became the terminal of e Austrian Lloyd service to the Levant om 1840 to 1860, and later of the Lloyd riestino Line. Italy demanded and obtained it in 1919 as the price of her joining ritain and France in 1915. In 1945 ugoslavia hoped to gain it, but the estern powers occupied it, and it was warded to Italy in 1954, though the ugoslav frontier runs close to it.

---

rinidad and Tobago: West Indian lands off Venezuela, originally inhabited by Arawak and Carib Indians. olumbus (*see* separate entry) discovered rinidad in 1498, but established no ettlement. Despite Spanish searches for old and occasional Dutch and French isits, progress in this Spanish colony was ight. Cocoa was cultivated before 1700, ut the economy revived only with the dmission of Catholic foreigners in 1783 nd French emigrés from Haiti and Domingo during the Revolution. Finally eded to Britain by the Treaty of Amiens, 802, Trinidad became a crown colony vith legislative and executive councils. Amalgamation with Tobago came in 888. Elective government from 1924, dult suffrage in 1946, and responsible elf-government in 1950, led to independence, with membership of the Commonwealth and United Nations in 1962, after Trinidad's withdrawal from the West Indian Federation. Government is hrough a legislature, with Prime Minister, Senate and House of Representatives. The economy, formerly dependent on ugar and cocoa, now includes asphalt, um, fertilisers, oil and coffee.

See ENDPAPERS for map.

Triple Alliances: agreements made by three states for mutual support against their enemies. Of those known to historians by this title, the following are the most important: (1) the pact made in 1668 between England, Holland and Sweden to check French aggression in the Spanish Netherlands which was, however, made largely ineffective by the secret dealings of Charles II with the French king; (2) the alliance between Great Britain, France and Holland made in 1717 to uphold the terms of the Treaty of Utrecht, which next year became quadruple when Austria joined in; (3) the inclusion of Italy (1882) in the existing alliance between Austria and Germany against the possibility of war with France or Russia. By the eve of World War I (*see* separate entry) this was confronted by the Triple Entente, as it was called, between England, France and Russia. Italy eventually entered the war on the latter side.

Trojan War: struggle between Greece and Troy, lasting for ten years and ending in the capture and destruction of Troy. The legend of the war was told by the Greek poets, especially Homer, and the later Greeks believed absolutely in the historical truth of the story. Helen, the wife of the Spartan king, had been

The legendary Trojan Horse.

abducted by Paris, son of the king of Troy. To regain her, a Greek fleet under Agamemnon attacked Troy and eventually took it by means of a wooden horse concealed in which some Greeks were able to get inside the walls and open the gates. The poets recounted many isolated episodes, like the arrival of the Amazons, or the death of Patroclus and the vengeance of Achilles.

For many centuries these stories were regarded as myths, but the German archaeologist (*see* ARCHAEOLOGY) Heinrich Schliemann in 1871 excavated Hissarlik, the traditional site of Troy, and discovered a complex series of remains. He and others have been able to distinguish nine or ten different cities on the same spot, and one of them bears clear evidence of destruction by fire. This city, known as Troy VIIa, appears to date from the early 12th century BC, which tallies well with the traditional date for the fall of Troy in 1184. So Troy, we may assume, existed and was destroyed. Evidence is still lacking about the historical truth of the details told in the story. A reasonable guess is that Troy, situated a short distance from the entrance to the Hellespont (Dardanelles) on the Asian side, imposed a control on those straits and that the Greeks fought to remove it.

¶ HOMER. *Iliad*, translated by E. V. RIEU. 1969

Tromp, Maarten Harpertszoon (1597–1653)**:** lieutenant-admiral of Holland in the First Dutch War between England and Holland. Born at Brielle, he went to sea at the age of eight, was present at a Dutch victory over the Spanish in Gibraltar Bay, saw his father killed by an English privateer, and survived capture by her and, later, by Tangier pirates. He was dismissed his ship in 1629 for criticising the decay of the Dutch fleet, but, recalled in 1639, he destroyed a great Spanish fleet at the Downs under the eyes of the English fleet. His brush with Blake's fle in 1652 started the First Dutch War. Bible-reading Calvinist (*see* REFORMA TION), painstaking and level-headed, l developed signalling, gunnery and t tactics of the line. With inferior ships ar equipment, he protected Dutch convo up and down the Channel. He was kille off Scheveningen in July 1653 breakin the English blockade. He was "the onl admiral under whom all others were co tent to serve – the adored of the seamen" His second son, Cornelius, also became distinguished naval commander.

See also BLAKE, ROBERT.

Trotsky, Leon, Lev Davidovic Bronstein (1879–1940)**:** Russian revol utionary. He joined the Bolsheviks onl in 1917 but took a prominent part in th Russian revolution, becoming people' commissar for foreign affairs. As com missar for war he showed enormou energy and brilliant organising capacity building up the Red Army and ensurin victory in the civil war. An advocate o world revolution rather than of socialism in any one country, he was ousted b Stalin from positions of power afte Lenin's death, forced into exile in 193 and murdered in Mexico in 1940. He wa the founder of a worldwide tradition an philosophy of communist activism.

See also BOLSHEVIKS; LENIN; etc.

Troubadours: minstrel poets of Provence, in the south of France, in the 12th–14th centuries. The name come from a word in the old Provença language (the *langue d'oc*) meaning "to find" or "to invent". The troubadours, many of whom were of noble birth, travelled from castle to castle. Their poems, sometimes recited to a musical accompaniment, were most often about some aspect of love. Another group of minstrel-poets, known as *trouvères*,

ɔurished in northern France. In Germany group known as *minnesingers* (literally ove singers") flourished *c.* 1150–1350.

---

roy: ancient city in modern Turkey, a .ort distance from the entrance to the ardanelles. *See* TROJAN WAR.

---

rucial States, Trucial Coast: seven dependent Arab sheikhdoms on the uth coast of the Gulf, between Cape Iasandam and Qatar, with Saudi Arabia the south. In 1885 Britain renewed and ktended an earlier anti-slavery and anti-iracy treaty by concluding the "Per-etual Maritime Truce" with the seven ates. Oil is the main source of revenue. ı 1971 as Britain withdrew from her mi-colonial role in the Gulf the seven rucial States joined together in the deration of the United Arab Emirates JAE).

Truman, Harry S. (1884–1973): 33rd president of the USA (1945–53). A Democrat and vice-president to Franklin Roosevelt, he came to the White House on the latter's death in 1945, "a farm boy from Missouri . . . too small for Roosevelt's shoes". Against all expectation and prediction, he was elected to a second term in 1948, his simplicity and moral courage appealing to a great mass of American citizens. He took the decision to drop the first atomic bomb on Japan (1945), produced the Truman Doctrine for aiding foreign countries to resist the spread of Communism and introduced the domestic programme of reform known as the Fair Deal. He was also a promoter of the North Atlantic Treaty Organisation (NATO).

See also AMERICAN PRESIDENTS; ATOMIC BOMB; ROOSEVELT, F. D.; NATO.

Tsar, Tzar, Czar: title of the former emperors of Russia, deriving from Latin *Caesar* and sharing its origin with the German and Austrian title *Kaiser*. The last of the Tsars was Nicholas II (*see* separate entry), murdered with his family at Ekaterinburg by his revolutionary captors on 16 July 1918.

See also IVAN; NICHOLAS I and II; PETER I; RUSSIA etc.

Tudor, House of: dynasty ruling in England from 1485 to 1603. Welsh genealogists trace the Tudor line to Ednyfed Vychan, a 13th-century steward of Prince Llewellyn, but it was Owen Tudor who, two centuries later, introduced royal blood into the family. In about 1428 he won the favour of the dowager Queen Catherine, widow of Henry V; and, whether or not they were married, they produced five children. Their son Edmund, Earl of Richmond, added another royal, if questionably legitimate, strain when he married Margaret Beaufort in 1455, and it is not surprising that their son Henry, when he assumed the crown after his victory over Richard III at Bosworth, did not stress his claim as hereditary. He made it real by his victory, by parliamentary sanction, by uniting Yorkist with Lancastrian claims when he married Elizabeth of York, and by his success in defeating all pretenders.

As king (1485–1509), Henry VII established a secure dynasty. Dealing firmly with over-mighty subjects, encouraging trade, avoiding expensive foreign commitments and husbanding his resources with great financial skill, he was able to leave to his son an uncontested title and a considerable sum in the treasury.

There are few periods of history from which the personalities of rulers emerge so sharply (if not always accurately) defined and so firmly impressed on the fickle memory of posterity.

Probably the rising art of the portrait painter has much to do with this. Mic
Sittow's portrait of Henry VII in t
National Gallery, London, shows, in t
words of a former director, "a fascinati
face but not a sympathetic one; the th
lips in a line that borders on the smirk, t
almost sharp nose and the bead-brig
eyes calculating under the utterly u
trustworthy angle of the eyelids. He h
the air, in his little niche, with the Gold
Fleece round his neck, of a far too word
saint, a mean St Money-Bags." T
legend of the shrewd, skinflint king h
endured almost unchallenged; but t
documentary records show that, thou
he was certainly a careful housekeeper,
was often a lavish spender, not only
personal adornment and gifts to h
family, but on his table, on sports a
festivities, on the encouragement a
patronage of scholars.

Henry VIII, his son and successor, h
come down to us as a personality chief

The Tudors: Above: Henry VII and Edward VI. Below: Henry VIII, Mary I, and Elizabeth I

ough the master-brush of Holbein (*see* ›arate entry), "one hand on hip, one nd on the dagger, the shoulders wide, : legs straddled like those of Atlas, but bear his own weight, his own Church, own kingdom" (David Piper: *The glish Face*). It is said that, long after :nry was dead, people still shivered ıen they saw that picture, doubtless nembering the slow corroding transi- •n from the auburn-haired, athletic ince described in the despatches of the :netian ambassador, to the ruthless rant of later years, his rotting legs able to support his vast bulk.

ucceeding to the throne at nine years of e and living only another six years, the •y-king Edward VI passes as a pathetic adow, though he was an accomplished ıguist and scholar as well as musician.

'o his half-sister, Mary, history has been :s than just. Nature did not endow her nerously. She was small of stature, in and shortsighted; though another enetian ambassador reported that "her 'es are so piercing as to command not ıly respect but awe from those on whom e casts them". There is plenty of 'idence that she was spirited and cour- ;eous. Humble children were appren- :ed and educated at her expense and she sited the poor in their homes that she ıight learn how they lived. She was not 'ithout mercy, forgiving conspiracies ;ainst her and freeing political prisoners. ut in religion she was narrow and stead- st to the point of bigotry, and she was ısensible to the tide of national feeling ıat steadily turned against her. It is robably true that she was the only one of ıe Tudors who executed from principle nd not because it was expedient. But the res of Smithfield dimmed all else; and :harles Dickens unfortunately spoke :uly when he said: "As Bloody Queen ſary she will ever be remembered with orror and detestation."

It was left to the last of the Tudors, Elizabeth I, to attain a stature that probably no monarch in English history has been accorded before or since. She was shrewish, vain, vacillating and of no marked beauty, especially in her later years. She could swear at her courtiers, lecture an arrogant ambassador in Latin and aim a kick at another. She could reprimand the Dean of St Paul's in the middle of a sermon. But she could smile, too. Her godson Sir John Harington recorded that "when she smiled it was pure sunshine, that everyone did choose to bask in if they could: but anon came a storm from a sudden gathering of clouds, and the thunder fell in wondrous manner on all alike". Therein lay much of her strength and her power of command – the pure sunshine, the sudden intimidating gathering of clouds. Add to that the mastery of the English tongue that could rise to the heights of the speech at Tilbury and the last "Golden Speech" to her parliament in 1601. "Though God hath raised me high, yet this I account the glory of my crown, that I have reigned with your loves." That this was true was the greatest accomplishment of the greatest of the Tudors.

¶ WINCHESTER, B. *Tudor Family Portrait.* 1955

Tuileries: former palace in Paris on the banks of the Seine, incorporated in the 17th century into the nearby palace of the Louvre by joining the two with a long building called the Grande Galerie. In 1871, in riots following France's defeat in the Franco-Prussian War (*see* separate entry), the Tuileries were burnt down and never rebuilt.

Tull, Jethro (1674–1741): English farmer and agricultural writer who, out of his own practical experience, invented implements, notably seed drills, which brought about a great advance in agricultural methods. His *Horse-hoeing Husbandry, or an Essay on the Principles of Tillage and Vegetation* was published in 1733. *See also* AGRICULTURAL IMPROVERS.

Tunisia: republic of North Africa, with a Mediterranean coastline between Algeria and Libya. The people are mainly Arabs and Berbers. The capital is Tunis. Other towns (some of which figured prominently in the North African campaigns of World War II; *see* separate entry) are Sfax, Bizerta, Sousse, Gabes and Kairouan. The main exports are olive oil, phosphates, grain and wine. Crude oil now accounts for about 30 per cent of export earnings.

In the 2nd century BC Tunisia became the original part of the Roman province of Africa, but fell to the Vandals (*see* separate entry) in AD 439, and was later absorbed into the Byzantine empire in 533, conquered by the Arabs in 698 after a fifty years war of attrition, and converted to Islam (*see* separate entry). Nine hundred stormy years followed with Berber rule predominating in spite of Bedouin and Norman attempts to gain control. In 1575 the North African empire of Turkey spread to Tunisia, and in the 17th century a Turkish Bey founded a dynasty that persisted for three centuries. In the 19th century Britain, France and Italy competed for influence, but Britain dropped out, and the French, by force of arms, obtained the Bey's recognition of Tunisia as a French Protectorate in 1883, the territory achieving independence again in 1956 and becoming a republic on 25 July 1957. President Habib Bourgiba was confirmed as head of state by subsequent elections in 1959, 1964 and 1969. *See* MEDITERRANEAN for map.

¶ SYLVESTER, A. *Tunisia*. 1969

Tunnels: man-made passages beneath the surface of the earth. This article does not include natural caverns or mine-workings or the tunnel-tombs of ancie kings.

A tunnel several thousand years o beneath the River Euphrates, has be discovered in Mesopotamia. In the 6 century BC one nearly a mile [1·6 km] lo was constructed to provide a water supp in the Greek island of Samos. T Romans drove one of 3·5 miles [5·6 kil metres], and 400 feet [122 metres] dov at its deepest point, to drain Lake Fuci in Italy. Early methods of tunnelling we slow and laborious. A short tunnel cor pleted in 1681 to carry the Canal du Mi in southern France for 500 feet [152 r underground was regarded as a notab achievement. Later and longer can tunnels in England were generally ma low and narrow, so that the bargem could lie on the deck on each side a "leg" the vessel along.

It was with the coming of railways th the problems of tunnelling were real faced. To penetrate rock, the pick wield by hand gave way in due course blasting and to the compressed-air dri In soft ground the difficulty was prevent the collapse of the roof, and mo tunnels had to be bricklined as the wo went forward. This delicate operatic was made easier by the use of a "shield" a ring of iron, or later steel, at the workin face. This was first used in England making the short but costly Wappin Tunnel for pedestrians under the Thame completed by Marc Isambard Brunel (*s* separate entry) in 1843. The shield had

Railway through the Thames Tunnel Wapping shown in 1870.

er development in the construction of derground railways in London and ewhere, when a continuous metal tube as built up behind it, thus producing, in ect, the longest railway tunnels in the orld. One of the "tube" railways under ndon is over 17 miles [27 km] long. A zard often met by engineers was the suspected presence of underground ater, as in the Severn Tunnel (1873–86) d earlier in that at Kilsby in Northampnshire (1838). Two further problems, in e days of steam locomotives, were ntilation (usually met by vertical shafts ading up to the surface) and surveying hich was brought to such perfection at the workings of a long tunnel started om both ends could meet with dead curacy deep below the earth).

Only a few of the many long railway nnels in the world can here be menoned. Those beneath the Alps are among e most famous, that under Mont Cenis 871) being the earliest and the Simplon 2·3 miles [19·7 km]) the longest.

Road tunnels of any length are products the motoring age and face the problem ventilation in an acute form. In spite of is, an Alpine tunnel under Mont Blanc ·3 miles [11·7 km]) was opened in 1965. nder water the solution is more difficult; e first Mersey Tunnel, Liverpool (2·6 iles [4·2 km]), has ventilators at the ends ly, and any traffic hold-up means that l engines must be switched off: a second nnel has recently been completed. For e proposed Channel Tunnel (approxiately 25 miles [40 km]) intermediate entilator shafts would endanger shiping, and it seems that it would be ecessary to carry motor vehicles through n the trucks of an electric railway. The ort, double-decked Yerba Buena Island unnel at San Francisco, USA, is remarkble for its great width (76 feet [23 m]) and eight (58 feet [17·7 m]). It is used by 5 million vehicles a year.

Tunnels to convey water present considerably less difficulty – the Delaware Tunnel in the USA (1945) is 85 miles [137 km] long – but the ease with which the natural course of streams and rivers can be diverted in mountainous country is being increasingly recognised.

¶ JAMES, ALAN. *Tunnels.* 1972; WYNYARD, J. *Tunnels and Bridges.* 1964

Turin: city and industrial centre of Piedmont, northern Italy, with extensive trade in mechanical engineering, chemicals, textiles, food processing, leather, etc. Its history goes back to pre-Roman times, and from 1861–65 it was the capital of Italy. Its notable buildings and institutions include its university (1404), cathedral (15th-century), fine palaces, libraries, and several museums internationally famous for Renaissance Art and Egyptian collections.

Turkestan: a name formerly applied to a large area of central Asia. We now speak of Russian Turkestan, Afghan Turkestan and Chinese Turkestan. This area was once peopled by speakers of an Iranian language with trading cities such as Samarkand. It was influenced by the Greeks in the 4th century BC and by the Chinese from the 1st century AD, and was overrun from the 6th century by Turkic tribes who adopted Islam (*see* separate entry), introduced in the 8th century. A Mongol population (*see* MONGOLS) was added in the 13th century. The three modern states divided the area effectively from the later 19th century onwards.

Turkey: republic in western Asia and south-eastern Europe. The ancient Asia Minor was peopled by Hittites in the second millennium BC. It later saw Phrygian invasions, a kingdom of Lydia, settlements of Greeks and the rise and fall of Homer's Troy. The Persians conquered it during the 6th and 5th centuries BC and Alexander the Great in 334 BC. It later became part of the Roman and Byzantine empires. The Seljuk Turks arrived from the deserts of Turkestan in the 10th century AD, and by 1050 had conquered Afghanistan and central Persia. In the 11th century they increasingly controlled Asia Minor. In 1071 the Byzantines were defeated and a Seljuk Sultañate of Rum or Rome was established. Appeals from the Byzantine empire brought in the Crusaders who set up the empire of Trebizond (1204–1461). In the 13th century the Mongol invasion broke the Turks into many small states, but Osman (1259–1326) drew them together, and by the end of the 14th century the Ottoman empire extended from the Euphrates to the plain of Hungary. Constantinople was taken in 1453. The Ottoman empire reached its peak in mid-16th century under Suleiman I (1520–66). Decline set in, with two centuries of ineffective rulers. In 1740 the French won privileges within the Turkish empire and the Russians also gained ground. Outlying provinces in the Balkans and elsewhere became independent in the 19th century. The empire ended 1908 and a republic was establish Turkey was westernised under Ken Ataturk (1880–1938). Neutral in Wo War II, Turkey subsequently became t eastern anchor of NATO.

¶ PRICE, M. P. *History of Turkey*. 1961

See also ATATURK, KEMAL; BALKAN BYZANTINE EMPIRE; CONSTANTINOPL CRUSADES; MONGOLS; OTTOMAN EMPIRE

Turnpikes: barriers preventing entry roads and bridges until a toll is paid. To gates were much the same thing. Fro being the name of a type of gate, the ter "turnpike" soon became applied to t road itself.

Under the late Stuarts, the state British roads was holding back com mercial expansion, as well as being national disgrace. Previously, an unfa burden of road repair had been laid, n on the actual users of the roads, but on t parishes, whose labourers had to giv several days' unpaid labour each year t their maintenance. In Queen Anne reign, the system of turnpike roads w introduced to provide for the great ir

ase in wheeled traffic. First the management of the turnpikes was given to local tices of peace; later special Turnpike usts were established by parliament.

he trusts were composed of local landners and dignitaries, noblemen and mers. They were empowered to conuct and maintain certain stretches of ad, erecting gates and collecting tolls m particular classes of traffic. The tolls ere adjusted on sliding scales, taking count of weight (the principal roads had eighing machines), number of horses d width of wheels. Animals "on the of" and even flocks of geese and rkeys paid toll, though foot passengers ere exempt.

he first turnpike gates had tapered unterbalanced bars, and swung across e road on upright posts. At each one ood a toll house. Rights for toll collectg were farmed out and much defrauding the trusts went on, so profits were not rge. By 1840 there were 22,000 miles 5,200 kilometres] of good roads in ritain. There are still a few survivals of e turnpike or toll-gate system in Britain, it most have now disappeared.

The establishment of turnpikes also ayed an important part in the rise of land urban centres in the USA. Maryland and Virginia were pioneers in this ethod of financing road development. he 62-mile [100 km] stretch of road etween Philadelphia and Lancaster, laid own as a stone highway covered with ravel (1792–94), is still known as the ancaster Pike.

---

utankhamun (ruled 1352–43 BC): gyptian king of the 18th dynasty. This haraoh succeeded his father-in-law, khnaten, "the heretic" (*see* separate ntry) and, after a short reign, died when nly about 19 years of age. His tomb in he Valley of Kings was discovered by the rchaeologist Howard Carter in 1922, almost untouched by tomb robbers. The treasure which it contained demonstrate the splendour of a pharaoh's burial.

¶ STREATFEILD, NOEL. *The Boy Pharaoh, Tutankhamen.* 1972

See also JEWELLERY; PHARAOH.

Twelfth century: the years 1101–1200. So far as England is concerned, the hundred years which began with the accession of Henry I to the throne are of great importance in that they saw the growth of a nation. A writer of the early 12th century describes William the Conqueror as "Rex Norm-Anglorum" (king of the Anglo-Normans), and the English kings for much of the period address their subjects in their writs as "French and English". But, shortly after the close of the century, Magna Carta described John simply as "Rex Angliae" (king of the English). This development is inseparably linked with the foundation of strong central government. The *Curia Regis* (King's Court) began to appear as the supreme central court whose business was the government of the country in all its branches. The *Dialogus de Scaccario* (1117) gives an interesting account of the Exchequer side of its work. In the administration of justice the Assize system was developed, and visitations by itinerant justices, only occasional under Henry I (reigned 1100–35), became regular under Henry II (reigned 1154–89), who first divided the country into circuits.

In the rest of Europe as a whole the picture is very different. In France the monarchy was relatively weak since, though Henry II of England was theoretically a vassal of Louis VII in respect of his French possessions, the English king, through his acquisitions from his parents and his wife, controlled a much greater area of France than Louis himself. In some areas, as in Italy, towns and city-states,

The building of a church in the 12th century, based on a manuscript in the Bibliothéque Nationale, Pa

unrestrained by strong central government, were often at war with one another. H. A. L. Fisher wrote: "If Florence took one side in a quarrel, it was sufficient for Pisa, Siena and Genoa to take the other; if Milan entered into an alliance with other cities, it would not at least be with Cremona and Pavia."

Much of the century was taken up by a prolonged struggle between the Empire and the Papacy, the air being thick with quarrels, renunciations, repudiations, interdicts and all the weapons of Church and State in conflict, including the setting up of half-a-dozen anti-popes. The century saw, incidentally, the election of the only Englishman in the long history of the Papacy – Adrian IV (Nicholas Breakspear) in 1154.

In some other directions, religion enjoyed a more constructive period. The century witnessed the early years of the Cistercian Order, which was to grow to greatness under St Bernard and St Stephen Harding. The Abbey of Clairvaux w founded in 1115. The Carmelites we established in 1150, and Gilbert of Sen pringham, the only Englishman to foun an Order (the Gilbertines received h abbot's staff from St Bernard. Soon aft 1180 Francesco Bernadone was born Assisi (Francis of Assisi), later to renoun riches and found the Franciscan Order.

There were more militant foundation though a number of these, too, we vowed to the service of religion. Th Knights Templars, who adopted the ru of the Benedictines, were established f the protection of pilgrims and the defen of the Holy Sepulchre. The Knights St John of Jerusalem (the Hospitallers c Knights Hospitallers) fulfilled the sam function. It is recorded in 1112 that the monastery or Hospital could accommo date 2,000 guests as well as caring for th sick. In 1190, at the siege of Acre, wa founded the third great religious-militar Order – that of the Teutonic Knights o

ıights of the Virgin Mary, who took
 vow of poverty, chastity and obedi-
ce and concerned themselves especially
ith German pilgrims.

'he Second and Third Crusades folwed their courses, achieving much
ıpty glory but slight success. The
cond (1147–49), led by Conrad III of
ermany and Louis VII of France, proıced an ineffective siege of Damascus.
ıe Third (1189–93), renowned in history
r its two chief protagonists, Richard I
England and Saladin (Salah-al-Din),
sulted only in the capture of Acre and a
ıce with the Saracens.

The Norman invasion of England in the
th century has always demanded and
ceived much textbook space. Less well
ıown, but in its different way equally
markable, was the Norman conquest of
uthern Italy and, in 1130, the establish-
ent of the kingdom of Sicily. There was
is great difference: in England Norman
ower was built on union with the
nquered people, whereas in Sicily it
ught to preserve a sharp distinction
tween rulers and ruled. This was a
atter of shrewd policy dictated by
rcumstances. In England, as we have
en, the English were becoming one
ation. In Sicily and Italy the Normans
ıled many different peoples, and could
st hold them in peace and prosperity by
lying themselves exclusively with none.

The 11th century had seen a partial break
p of the Byzantine Empire with the loss
f most of Asia Minor and the revolt of
arious tribes. Under the Comnenus
ynasty, which ruled 1057–59 and 1081–
185, some recovery was made. But the
ıd was in sight for the vast political and
onomic structure that since 395 had
ood as a bastion between western
urope and the barbarians and had pre-
rved so much of Roman and Greek
ılture. Within a few years of the close of
ıe 12th century Constantinople was sacked by the Crusaders and the Empire gradually broke up into independent states. It was to stage another partial and temporary recovery, but the old prestige and power were not to be regained.

Farther east, in China, one of the country's greatest periods of culture and artistic achievement, under the Sung dynasty, was also approaching its end. The borders of the empire were being threatened or occupied by outlying tribes and the mighty shadow of Genghis Khan, born in about 1162, was soon to fall over the empire.

To return to Europe and to the pursuits of peace, the century is remarkable for the growth of towns all over the continent and, with the towns, the development of organised trade and commerce. A notable factor in this development were the various craft guilds, formed not only to watch over the interests of their members but to insist on proper standards of craftsmanship. Towns began to join together, if only in loose federations, to protect their common trading interests – a movement especially prominent in Germany and the Baltic. The most important group was soon to develop into the Hanseatic League whose headquarters, Lubeck, was founded in 1143, and which, at the height of its power, included over seventy towns which stretched, in the words of Professor Day of Harvard, "from Thorn and Krakow on the east to the towns of Zuider Zee on the west, and from Wisby and Reval in the north to Gottingen in the south."

On the sea, too, with the ever-growing number of merchant ships going about their business, it became necessary to organise and control codes of conduct. From the end of the 12th century (though they are probably based on even earlier codes) have survived the famous Judgments or Laws of Oléron, named after a small island off the coast of France, which was a centre of the wine trade and a rendezvous for shipping.

Finally, the century witnessed a revival of learning in Europe. The University of Bologna became renowned as a Law School, while Peter Abelard made Paris famous as a centre of thought, although the University of Paris itself dates from some time between 1150 and 1170, some years after Abelard's death in 1142. It was from Paris that the University of Oxford is traditionally said to have received its earliest scholars. In 1133 the theologian Robert Pullen came from Paris to lecture there, by the mid-1160s it was apparently a fully equipped university, and a hundred years later was second only to Paris. Thus the scene was set for men who were soon to dominate and change the thought of Europe, among them Roger Bacon (*c.* 1215–94) and John Wyclif (*c.* 1320–84).

¶ BROOKE, C. *The Twelfth Century Renaissance.* 1970

See also INDIVIDUAL ENTRIES.

Twentieth century: the years from 1901 onwards. The century has been one of major warfare, with the maintenance of peace by the old method of a balance of power between rival nations demonstrated as a precarious and outmoded device.

In most countries at the beginning of the century small ruling classes controlled the power and wealth of the community. They seemed mainly interested in seeking international prestige. It was a European-dominated world, and Great Britain with her vast empire, her industrial wealth and sea power had enjoyed an impressive lead for many years. In the rest of the world few countries other than the USA and Japan had the qualities of a world power.

Slowly this pattern changed. Tension over colonies, national boundaries, trade and prestige resulted in World War I. Old and powerful monarchies, among them the German and Austrian empires, co lapsed in defeat. The Tsarist regime Russia disintegrated, and the crumbli Turkish empire was finally destroye New forces appeared. Lenin and t Bolsheviks seized and kept power Russia with ruthless efficiency. Dictato with histrionic appeal to the masses, su as Mussolini and Hitler, came to pow The Japanese set out to become masters Eastern Asia. Hopes that 1914–18 was t "war to end all wars" faded with the r newed tension which culminated in 19 in the outbreak of World War II. Duri this period it became increasingly cle that requirements for world power stat had changed. Now huge manpower a natural resources had to be combin with high technical skill. By 1945 on two countries, the USA and Sovi Russia, possessed these in sufficiently va quantities.

They differed widely in their ideas politics (control by the Communist Par in Russia compared with free speech a elections in the USA) and economi (Soviet state control of production a distribution compared with Americ insistence on the advantages of free ente prise and the incentive of profit). The differences generated an atmosphere yet more fear and tension, nicknamed t Cold War. Hostile alliances like NAT and the Warsaw Pact were created, and third world war has nearly resulted fro a series of crises as far apart as Berlin a Korea, Cuba and Suez.

Apart from China, in whose spectacul modernisation since the Communist vi tory of 1949 both the USA and Russ see future danger, no individual natic can rival these two super-powers. How ever, two groups of countries are wor considering for other reasons. The Con monwealth which consists of 50 indepe dent states (former British colonies) h against many predictions to the contrar

veloped as a multiracial association hich is also a microcosm of the world's ain problems and on occasions shows a markable ability to bridge the North–uth gap that appears to divide our orld. Second, the European Economic ommunity (EEC) which was formed in 57. Beginning as the Six (France, West ermany, Italy and the Benelux coun-es) it was joined by Britain, Denmark d Ireland in 1973; Greece became a full ember in 1981 and Portugal and Spain ere admitted in 1985. The EEC has ormous potential – both economic and litical – but is bedevilled by rival tionalisms. A truly united EEC would rtainly possess the capacity to rival ther of the super-powers.

Although there has been so much war d threat of war, disarmament con-rences have had little success; yet two orld organisations have made an effort negotiate over difficulties rather than ght. The League of Nations, created in 19, was the great hope of the post-World War I generation, but it failed rough the absence of the USA and viet Russia and its lack of a "police" rce. The United Nations Organisation 1945 has been more efficient, both in social work against poverty and disease d in its efforts to prevent crises in aces like the Congo and Suez develop-g into wider conflicts. But UN meet-gs at its New York headquarters have ten been used by the USA and Russia propaganda platforms in seeking sup-ort from the uncommitted nations of the Third World".

This Third World of underdeveloped ations has grown rapidly since the 1940s, more and more colonial territories have ined independence. These have pro-ded one of the biggest problems of the th century, particularly because of overty and the gulf between the rich and poor peoples of the world. While the North American continent, Japan and Europe have become wealthier, many countries of South America, Africa and southern Asia have faced the tremendous difficulties of low food production, little money for industry and, worst of all, a high population growth. Religious teaching and a long tradition of large families prevent many people from accepting modern ideas of birth control.

Scientific developments of the century have given the wealthier nations a great advantage. The "second industrial revolution" in oil and steel, electricity and chemicals, was well under way in 1901; but since World War II yet a third industrial revolution could be said to have developed. Nuclear power offers enormous possibilities, though its peacetime uses have been overshadowed by the fear created since the first atom bomb exploded at Hiroshima. Computers are showing important calculating and information storage possibilities. The space exploration programmes of the USA and Russia have extended the frontier of man's knowledge far beyond the earth, as well as providing superb practical results like worldwide satellite television. Associated with these developments have been some significant changes in the scale of agricultural and industrial organisation. High crop yields and huge numbers of machines and manufactures have resulted from the adoption of mass production techniques.

The century has seen dramatic progress in the conquest of disease: cholera and plague disappeared from Europe as the principles of immunisation became known, whilst antibiotics like penicillin have largely conquered tuberculosis. Ideas on diet, and particularly the discovery of the importance of vitamins, have had a great effect on diseases like rickets and scurvy which spring from not eating the right kind of food. The effects have not all been beneficial. Control of diseases like malaria have cut the death rate so quickly that the resulting population explosion raises serious doubt whether all peoples in future can be properly fed, housed and employed. The world population in 1901 numbered 1,600 million; by 1960 it had almost doubled. By 1982 the world population had risen to an estimated 4,700 million and is expected to reach 6·1 billion in 2000.

Achievements in communication have been revolutionary. The internal combustion engine was already known in 1901, but since then the car has grown to be the most important means of personal transport in industrialised countries. The Wright brothers' first controlled, heavier-than-air flight in 1903 began a development that enabled distant parts of the globe to be reached with ease and speed. Marconi's and Baird's successes with radio and television introduced millions to a powerful medium of information, propaganda and entertainment.

Ease of communication has shown people how others live, and given an impetus to the worldwide desire for equal rights. Throughout the century this has been seen in many ways. First, socialists have demanded voting rights and state welfare schemes for everyone in an effort to improve the way ordinary people live and work. Secondly, possession of material things such as cars and radios has become an important demand by the peoples of the Third World. Thirdly, there have been universal and powerful movements to end discrimination on grounds of religion, race and sex. Jews have fought for and won a new state, Israel, where victims of persecution in Russia, Germany and elsewhere could find safety; black peoples have conducted a long and bitter struggle for civil rights in the USA and against the apartheid ideas of Sou African governments; in many countr women have won the right to vote and compete freely in many professions hithe to regarded as the special province of me

The provision of educational opportu ties for large numbers of children inste of the select few has led to a tremendo rise in world literacy. Books for the m of ordinary people as well as the high educated are sold in millions, and t "paperback" revolution in publishing spreading across the continents. Hu sales of books for leisure reading, as w as for acquiring information, are r corded. New forms of entertainment, to have been directed at the mass marke The century has seen the decline of t western theatre and music hall in favo of filmed tragedy and comedy, which c be seen on large cinema screens throug out the world, or on the small televisic set in a home.

Personal achievement has always been feature of man's life. The 20th century contribution in this field has been varie Everest has been climbed, the Pol reached, and innumerable height, dept and speed records surpassed. Many thou sands choose sport in striving for distin tion. "Barriers" such as the four-minu mile have been broken, while the peak amateur sporting attainment has becom a gold medal in the Olympic Games. Bu the real appeal in terms of mass suppo is exercised by professional "stars" football and baseball teams. Here exce lence can be highly paid as well, and oth sports such as tennis and golf have o ganised themselves similarly.

From these achievements it would see that the main characteristic of the 20t century has been a rapid rise in the stan ards of living for the common man. Th has certainly been so in countries wher the speed of technological change h given people many extra hours of leisur d the money to enjoy life, rather than end it in the drudgery which was the t of the masses in previous centuries.

But this progress, though impressive, nnot conceal the problems facing the xt generations. Poverty still exists on a assive scale. Poor countries have few ctors and teachers to improve their ndards of health and education. Disasrs such as the great San Francisco and kyo earthquakes of 1906 and 1923, and e Bengal floods of 1970, show that man s not yet succeeded in forecasting and apting to nature's behaviour. Even the h countries have created new problems: e loneliness of people living in big ies; the rising pollution menace that reatens the sea, the air and the landscape; e increasing scarcity of certain resources; e destruction of valuable agricultural nd by the relentless growth of towns d industries; a traffic casualty rate of ousands a day on the world's highays.

REASE, GEOFFREY. *This Is Your Century*. 1965; STEAD, R. J. *Britain in the Twentieth Century*. 1966

e also INDIVIDUAL ENTRIES.

---

ypewriter: machine with a keyboard d inked ribbon for producing printed aracters in substitution for handwriting. he typewriter seems to have been first ought of by an English engineer, Henry ill, who, in 1714, took out a patent for n Artificial Machine . . . whereby all riting whatever may be Engrossed in per or Parchment so Neat and Exact not to be distinguished from Print", but details of its construction are known. 1829 William Austin Burt of Detroit ok out a patent for his "typographer", t unlike a modern toy typewriter, with the type mounted on one semicircular ame, which was turned by hand till the quired letter was in position, then essed on to the paper by a lever.

The first typewriter to be produced on a commercial scale came on the market in the United States in 1874, and Mark Twain is said to have been the first author ever to submit a typescript to a publisher. Early typewriters printed in capital letters only, but the familiar shift key mechanism appeared on the Remington Model 2 in 1878. This was followed, a few years later, by the first machine to provide visible typing. The early machines printed on the underside of the cylinder, which had to be raised in order to see what had been printed. These were followed by models which printed downwards on top of the cylinder, and later by those of the modern type which print on the front of the cylinder.

Early typewriters were large and heavy, but portable models began to appear about 1909. The latest development is the electric typewriter, which made its appearance about 1920.

Tyranny: Greek word meaning absolute rule, not necessarily by a single man. Athens, for a brief period, endured Thirty Tyrants. Many of these tyrants were enlightened rulers and patrons of art and literature; but others displayed harshness and brutality, characteristics which are generally attached to the idea of tyranny.

Tyre: city and seaport of the Phoenicians at the eastern end of the Mediterranean. In ancient times it carried on a prosperous maritime trade, as did its neighbour Sidon. In the mountains behind the coast grew the famous Cedars of Lebanon, which were used in the building of the Temple of Jerusalem (*see* separate entry): very few of these trees survive today in their former habitat. Jesus visited the area in the course of His ministry. Tyre was a stronghold of the Crusaders (1124–1291; *see* CRUSADES). The city survives today as Sur, one of the smaller ports of the republic of Lebanon.

U

Uganda: former British protectorate in East Africa adjoining Sudan in the north, Kenya in the east, with Tanzania and Lake Victoria in the south and Rwanda in the south-west. The eastern halves of Lakes Albert and Edward form part of its western boundary with Zaire. The main exports are coffee, cotton, copper and tea. Physical features include high mountains, with the peaks of the Ruwenzori range (the "Mountains of the Moon") rising over 16,700 feet [5,089 m], great lakes, and vast forests infinitely diverse in character. There is a great variety of flora and fauna.

At a very early period, probably three to four thousand years ago, the inhabitants came under the influence of Egyptian civilisation, manifested in such crafts as pottery and metalwork and brought in by Hamitic invaders. Afterwards powerful Negro kingdoms grew up, Bunyoro, Busoga, Ankole and, especially, Buganda. The first European to enter the territory was the British explorer John Speke, in 1862, and Anglican missionaries followed in the 1870s. Britain proclaimed a protectorate over Uganda, 1894–96, and British administration continued until the country was given independence within the Commonwealth in October 1962, becoming a republic five years later, with Dr A. Milton Obote as president. In 1971 General Amin seized power through a coup; his rule was remarkable for its open and vicious tyranny. He was ousted in 1979 and after three short-term presidents, Obote returned to power from exile.

See AFRICA for map.

Ukraine: eastern European constituent republic of the USSR. From Neolithic times Ukrainian people dwelt in the Dnieper and Dniester valleys. There the city of Kiev arose. The Mongol invasi in the 13th century destroyed Ukrain cohesion. A shortlived Ukrainian C sack state emerged in 1648 under Russ protection, while from 1690 weste Ukraine was under Poland and la Austria. In 1917 a Ukrainian republic v formed but passed under Russian rule became a battleground in World War After the war Galicia, the weste Ukraine, was reunited to Russian Ukrai and the country became a member of t United Nations in 1945.

See USSR for map.

See also COSSACKS; MONGOLS; NEOLITH UNITED NATIONS; WORLD WAR II.

Ulster: northern province of Irelan After the Ice Age (*see* separate entry) was through Ulster that man entered I land about 6000 BC, and the province rich in remains of prehistoric peoples. the beginning of the Christian era a kin dom of Ulster extended as far south a west as the Boyne and Shannon but so shrank. Christianity spread through I land from Ulster in the 5th century. T rugged coastline and impenetrable terr repelled invaders, and Ulster was n finally brought under English rule the early 17th century. An English a Scottish Protestant population was intr duced. Heavily industrialised in the 19 and 20th centuries, Ulster resisted Ir secession from the United Kingdom an in 1921, six Ulster counties were give subordinate government within t United Kingdom as Northern Irelan with Belfast as capital. Ulster is no generally used as another name f Northern Ireland. The mixture of re gions and the activities of revolutiona and republican elements have combin to make the province a centre of freque unrest that has not stopped short of bloo ed, terrorist bombing and sectarian ssassinations. So acute did this near-archy become that in 1972 the British overnment applied direct rule to Ulster. o solution was in sight in the mid-80s.

e also IRELAND; IRISH REPUBLICAN ARMY; ORTHERN IRELAND; PROTESTANT.

---

nderwater exploration: the study of recks, submerged towns and harbours d other offshore sites. The archaeolost on land has learned to familiarise himlf with every kind of environment, but nfronted with the world beneath the a he is a comparative newcomer. Nevereless, underwater exploration with the d of modern diving techniques is a fast veloping science.

he examination of offshore sites is ually carried out after a diver has anced to bring up something of interest. The Mediterranean, for instance, has certain points off the coast where the seabed is littered with pottery, anchors and other forms of ancient debris. The number and nature of such objects would indicate that the site was once an anchorage for vessels seeking shelter. The excavation of submerged harbours is basically an extension of land archaeology and requires teams of professional draughtsmen, photographers, etc., in addition to the divers.

The ancient wreck is perhaps the most challenging of all tasks facing the underwater explorer. Probably the first archaeological venture in this field was started in the 15th century. Two large Roman pleasure barges were traditionally thought to have been sunk in Lake Nemi, southeast of Rome. In 1446 the wrecks were located. A raft built of barrels was moored over one of them and ropes were taken down by swimmers and

ivers photographed 50 feet below the surface of the Mediterranean, plotting the position of the wreck a Greek trading ship, sunk near Syracuse in Sicily about 800 BC.

fastened to the wreck. Efforts to float it and pull it ashore failed. In 1535 an early form of diving suit was tried. It had a wooden helmet with a crystal plate in the front which enabled the diver to observe the wrecks. Measurements were taken and samples of the wood brought to the surface. In 1827 a diving bell was submerged close by the wrecks and many fine fragments of marble, mosaics, etc., were recovered. At the same time a barge was constructed, but elaborate equipment to raise one of the wrecks failed once again. In 1895 an amateur diver brought up bronze lion and wolf heads and many more pieces of mosaics, etc. Finally, in 1928–29, the lake was drained and exposed two giant barges of 234 feet [71 metres] and 239 feet [72 metres], respectively, both richly decorated. The hulls were well preserved and proved an invaluable guide to Roman ship construction methods. Unfortunately both barges were burnt during the German occupation in 1944. The long story of the Nemi ships, with the exception of the last unhappy chapter, serves to illustrate some of the attempts at raising and preserving ships and underwater objects over a period of 500 years.

Another successful operation in rescuing ancient ships by the drainage method was carried out in Denmark. In 1962 the remains of five 900-year-old Viking ships (*see* VIKINGS) were discovered in Roskilde Fiord. The water was shallow enough for a large sheet steel cofferdam to be built to enclose the entire site. The water was then pumped out, and the remains of the boats were revealed. The timbers were then cleaned, carefully recorded, photographed and finally removed. A chemical hardening process followed, and the boats were then reconstructed and put on display in a museum nearby.

The seabed of the Mediterranean provides almost unlimited scope for the underwater explorer. The remains
hundreds of ancient Greek and Rom
trading vessels together with their cargo
lie submerged close by the coasts a
reefs. In 1900 sponge-divers off Antik
thera, on the south coast of Gree
accidentally located a considerable qua
tity of partially buried bronze and marb
figures. These were subsequently fou
to be part of the cargo of a Roman tradi
vessel of the 1st century BC. A salva
expedition was organised and spong
divers wearing diving suits and helm
succeeded in bringing up a considerab
number of valuable treasures. In 19
another Roman vessel of about the sa
age was discovered by sponge-divers
Mahdia, Tunisia. This was carrying pric
less Greek works of art. Similar metho
were employed in bringing up much
this cargo. In both the above instanc
the divers, wearing cumbersome equi
ment, had a difficult and dangerous tas
Their periods under water were severe
limited: there were no attempts to e
cavate the hulls and no photograph
drawings or records were made. The tw
discoveries were, however, regarded
marking the beginning of modern unde
water archaeology in the Mediterranea

Little more of note happened in t
Mediterranean until about 1948. T
wartime inventions of the aqualung a
swimfins now made it possible for t
amateur as well as the professional div
to explore the seabed with a freedo
hitherto unknown. The French Co
mander Cousteau and his associates we
soon to popularise this new form of "fr
diving". Many new wrecks were locate
mostly dating from the 1st and 2
centuries BC. In all cases they were tradi
vessels carrying cargoes of liquids co
tained in amphorae. With the new equi
ment now available divers were able
salvage these in great numbers. Th
were also able to carry out detailed studi

Wasa: *Above: Grinning lion heads which* *rated the gun port lids of the warship* Wasa. *w: The* Wasa *raised out of the water on a* *rete pontoon and held in an aluminium* *e". Above right: The lower gun deck after* *vation. Below right: Coins being sifted.*

the remains of the ships, and photo-phs were taken with underwater neras. With the resulting information ers were able to make scale drawings.

unting for sunken treasure is mainly fined to the Caribbean area. Between 16th and early 18th centuries the great nish treasure fleets carrying precious tals for the monetary systems of ope made regular sailings from South nerica to Spain. The hazards of the sea, l to a lesser extent enemy action, were ponsible for a number of sinkings in Caribbean and off the coast of Florida. entieth-century divers have located ny of these and have reaped a rich vest of treasure.

northern European waters some of sunken ships of the 1588 Spanish mada (*see* ARMADA) have been found. e so-called treasure galleon sunk off bermory, Isle of Mull, Scotland, has so yielded little of its riches, but divers e recovered some of the iron cannon.

Owing to the absence of the destructive teredo worm in the Baltic some remarkably well preserved wrecks have been found in Scandinavian waters. Most famous is the great Swedish sixty-four-gun ship *Wasa*, sunk in Stockholm harbour in 1628. Her hull was raised in 1961 and is now being chemically treated and dried so that restoration may be carried out.

¶ COGGINS, JACK. *Hydrospace: Frontier beneath the Sea.* 1967; COOK, J. GORDON. *Exploring under the Sea.* 1964

See also ARCHAEOLOGY.

UNESCO (United Nations Educational, Scientific and Cultural Organisation): a specialised agency of UNO (*see* UNITED NATIONS ORGANISATION) with headquarters in Paris. It came into operation late in 1946 to help peace by supporting close co-operation between nations in education, the arts and science. It works through project committees which investigate problems such as the use of drugs, the effect of television on children, and women's rights; through publications which try to reduce racial hatred and ignorance; and through money grants for travel and study.

¶ LAVES, WALTER H. C. and THOMSON, C. A. *Unesco: Purpose, Progress, Prospects.* 1958

Union Jack: national flag of the United Kingdom. In 1606 the English national flag was combined with the Scottish flag. The red cross of St George on a white ground, device of the king of England at least as early as the 13th century, and the diagonal white St Andrew's cross on a blue ground, recorded in the 14th century, formed the Union flag.

After the union of England and Scotland, difficulties arose over the bearing of the national flags at sea, and in 1606 King James I ordered the use of the new flag instead, the two crosses to be "joined together according to a form made by our Heralds". The details of the design have not survived; but we know it was not popular with the Scots, who rarely used it till the Act of Union in 1707. In 1800 the union with Ireland took place and the red saltire cross which was the badge of the Order of St Patrick was combined with the Union flag of England and Scotland.

A jack is any flag flown from the jack staff in the bows of a warship. Strictly speaking, this is the correct usage of the term Union jack, though the term is now used indiscriminately for the national flag, wherever displayed.

Union of Soviet Socialist Republics (USSR): federal republic in eastern Europe and northern and central Asia. By 1917 the Russian empire was disintegrating. Its armies were breaking up on World War I fighting fronts. The Tsar had been forced to abdicate. The old ruling class was incapacitated by war casualties and disunity. Food and all commodities were short. Administration was breaking down un the provisional government of Alexan Kerensky. The Bolshevik wing of revolutionary movement, led by Le gained control in Petrograd thro workers' soviets and on 7 November 1 the government was seized by Bolsheviks.

To stop German invasion, the treaty Brest-Litovsk was signed by Russia the Central Powers on 3 March 1918 priving Russia of 62 million people quarter of its territory, a third of its fo producing land and half of its industr There followed a desperate struggle existence against foreign intervention counter-revolutionary forces. The n Red Army finally triumphed and rulers of Russia had to face the proble of a ruined land and a starving people

Lenin died in 1924, to be succeeded so by Stalin, who gained an autocratic co trol over Russia. He set about econo reorganisation, introducing the first fi year plan in 1928. The aims were development of heavy industry, mobilisation of all resources and establishment of collective farms. St reorganised rural and industrial soci without regard to the human materia used, meeting resistance with slaugh Russian life in the 1930s was bleak dangerous, as Stalin sought to strengt his personal position by "purges" mass executions. The country was ganised in separate republics but dominated by the one central policy.

In 1939 a Russo-German pact embod Stalin's hope that Germany and western powers would ruin one anot in war, while the USSR remained a sp tator. In 1941, however, Germany vaded the USSR. Victory over Germa cost over 20 million lives, but the tre of Brest-Litovsk was avenged, and Russian style of revolution spread int wide area of eastern Europe.

U.S.S.R.
0
800 Miles
0
1000 Km
ARCTIC OCEAN
BARENTS SEA
Novaya Zemblya
New Siberian Is.
Arctic Circle
NORWAY
SWEDEN
FINLAND
Okhotsk
UNION OF SOVIET
SOCIALIST REPUBLICS
Leningrad
POLAND
MOSCOW
Gor'kiy
Kazan'
Brest Litovsk
Ufa
ROMANIA
Chelyabinsk
Omsk
Novosibirsk
Irkutsk
Nikolayevsk
Vladivostok
Black Sea
TURKEY
Caspian Sea
MONGOLIA
JAPAN
CHINA

After World War II the USA was regarded as the chief rival of the USSR, and a "cold war" developed between the two, emerging in many episodes, including the Korean War. Russia quickly followed the USA in developing fission and fusion bombs and sophisticated rocket devices, putting the first space traveller into earth orbit in 1957. NATO was confronted by the Warsaw Pact.

Stalin died in 1953, lifting a cloud of fear, and at the twentieth communist party congress in 1956 his record of personal rule and terrorism was condemned. Among his successors, Nikita Khrushchev (1958–64) did something to reduce the "cold war" atmosphere. The identification of communism with Russian interests led to clashes with communists in other countries, including Warsaw Pact governments and China. In 1985 the relatively young Mikhail Gorbachov succeeded to the leadership.

¶ ARAGON, L. *History of USSR*. 1964

See also BOLSHEVIKS; LENIN; NATO; RUSSIA; STALIN; WARSAW PACT; WORLD WARS I and II.

United Kingdom Atomic Energy Authority (UKAEA): body responsible for atomic research and development in the United Kingdom. At the end of World War II (*see* separate entry) it became clear that the possibilities of atomic energy must be explored, and the British government established research centres at Harwell, Berkshire, and Risley, Lancashire. In 1953 a start was made on the construction of a nuclear reactor at Calder Hall, Cumberland. In 1954 the Atomic Energy Authority Act established UKAEA, which took over atomic research and development on 1 August 1954.

The Research Group at Harwell conducts fundamental research into nuclear physics, and its equipment includes a million-volt electron microscope for search into radiation damage, while vestigation into radioactive isotope carried on at Wantage. The Weap Group at Aldermaston is responsible the further development of ato weapons.

The groups responsible for Producti Development and Engineering have t headquarters at Risley. These prov specialist advice to electricity boards overseas customers anxious to build re tors and are also responsible for UKAE own atomic power plants at Calder H Chapel Cross, Dumfriesshire; Windsc Cumberland; Winfrith, Dorset; Dounreay, Caithness. These produce el tricity, which is sold to the electric boards and fed into the national grid, their primary purpose is research i atomic fuel and reactor systems. By 19 for example, Britain had 32 nucl power stations, a further 10 under co struction and another one planned.

The Radiochemical Centre at Am sham prepares radioactive isotopes other substances produced by the react for medical and scientific use.

United Nations Organisation (UN(international organisation of independ states founded at the end of World Wa (*see* separate entry) as successor to League of Nations (*see* separate ent A conference of the "United Natio (the Allies who fought the Axis Pow during the war) met in San Francisco signed the Charter in June 1945. T aimed to maintain peace and to supp human rights throughout the world. do this an organisation was set up w headquarters in New York, where debating chamber, the General Assemb meets annually, and in which each mem has one vote. The Organisation has ot ncils and agencies, such as the Food and riculture Organisation, the International Atomic Energy Agency, the International Civil Aviation Organisation and International Monetary Fund. Its chief icial body is the International Court of tice.

AVAGE, KATHERINE. *The Story of the United ions.* 1969

also INTERNATIONAL LAW; HAGUE, E; YALTA CONFERENCE.

---

ited Provinces: name given to the en northern provinces of the Netherds (Holland, Zeeland, Utrecht, Gelderd, Overijssel, Groningen and Friesd) who declared their independence in 81.

---

ited States of America: federal reblic in North America. Much of the tory of the USA is distributed through s work in nearly a hundred separate tries, as well as in biographies and other icles where the country's story is interoven with other events and destinies. way of introduction, there are at least ree considerations that are sufficiently vious to citizens of the US but are t so well understood outside it.

he first, and major, point is the comrative shortness of the period into hich the history of the USA is packed. e most significant part of the history of orth America is crammed into a period less than 500 years. The historian . F. Strong has written: "In the 1940s it came possible to fly across the Atlantic ten hours. Christopher Columbus first ossed that ocean 450 years before, and it ok him ten weeks to do it. What hapned on the other side of the Atlantic tween those two dates constitutes one the most romantic and exciting stories the history of the world."

The second consideration is that, while ere are citizens of America, there is no American race: even the original Indians only now enjoy full citizenship. In 1790 the total population was about three million, of whom more than 2,700,000 were British. It has been estimated that in the period 1820–1967 the USA received over 44 million immigrants, so that, today, "the Americans . . . are not merely a people of many races: they are proud of it".

The third, and least important, is that films and television programmes, in giving a portrait of America to the rest of the world, have exercised an influence out of all proportion and have provided a completely unbalanced one. Thus, to a great many people, the USA is almost entirely peopled with gangsters, corrupt politicians, tough cops, cowboys, strident musicians and of course glamorous film stars. The truth is otherwise.

Below are suggested some of the main divisions into which the story falls and some of the entries through which the theme may be pursued. There is rarely, of course, any sharp division. For example, the settlement of the various states was still proceeding in the 19th century, long after the War of Independence, and the 49th and 50th states, Alaska and Hawaii, were not added till 1959.

The first obvious historical phase is that of discovery, the first occasions when, confronting the eyes of Scandinavian, Spanish, French, Dutch, Italian, English seamen, the vast continent of North America loomed out of the haze, stretching – although they did not imagine its magnitude – some 2,800 miles [4,506 km] from the Atlantic to the Pacific and nearly 1,600 miles [2,575 km] from north to south, a size possible to grasp only in terms of comparisons, i.e. that the present state of Texas is three times the size of Great Britain; and that the smallest state, Rhode Island, is nearly 130 times bigger than England's largest county, Yorkshire.

Next came the long struggle for permanent settlement, the early failures and disappointments; the first harvest of the Pilgrim Fathers, still celebrated in Thanksgiving Day; the grants of vast tracts of land to private individuals and companies; the struggle with the Indians, the Dutch and the French and the beginnings of the long, ugly story of slavery.

A rising sense of nationhood, combined with a lack of understanding and foresight on the part of the British government, led, first to argument and friction, then, when no other choice seemed open to the colonists, to the War of Independence. Many leading colonists, George Washington among them, did not visualise and did not want independence of the Crown. But once the train of events had been set firmly in motion there was no turning back. The final phase came, not with the Treaty of Paris in 1783 but thirty years later in the needless and shortlived War of 1812, after which America finally turned her eyes away from Europe. "It is our true policy to steer clear of permanent alliance with any portion of the foreign world," George Washington wrote in 1796 in his "Farewell Address to the People of the United States"; and five years later Thomas Jefferson expressed the same sentiment: "Peace, commerce, and honest friendship with all nations – entangling alliances with none." The 1812 war turned this theory into hard fact and a practice that was to continue for over a century.

When Jefferson, in two of his 1787 letters to friends, said "a little rebellion now and then is a good thing" and "the tree of liberty must be refreshed from time to time with the blood of patriots", he could have visualised nothing so tragic and wasteful as the events of 1861–65, when North and South were locked in a civil war which left the country poorer by 620,000 men out of three million engaged in fighting – a higher proportion thar World Wars I and II (*see* separate entri

Interrupted by these periods of strife, all the time continuing, and accelerat in times of peace, was a vast build-up commerce and industry, the foundati of great business empires, the opening of the interior, the driving of roads a railways, the growth of cities, a wealth invention and educational progress.

Finally, a picture might emerge of USA, its policies, vicissitudes and achiev ments in the 20th century including massive development of the automob industry and, in another element, t aeroplane; the reluctant emergence frc the isolationism proclaimed by Washin ton and Jefferson; the vast scale of h given to new and emerging countries; the one hand work for peace and securi and, on the other, conflict at home a abroad both social and military; an capturing above all else public imagin tion and interest throughout the worl man's first steps in space.

See AMERICA entries for map.

¶ HILL, C. P. *History of the United States.* 19(
SOMERVELL, D. C. *History of the United States.* 19

See also INDIVIDUAL ENTRIES.

Universities: communities of teach and students to which the followi features normally apply: (1) the universi is a corporate body governed by charter or constitution granted by t state, or in earlier times by the Church; (the students are seeking to graduate, that to say, to be awarded degrees; (3) there a a number of faculties in which differe subjects are studied; (4) selected studen who have graduated may pursue furth studies leading to higher degrees, whi the teachers themselves often give part their time to research. Entry to a unive sity normally depends on a candida having reached a certain education standard, and competition is often sever earlier times this was not always the e: John Donne (1573–1621), later Dean St Paul's, was admitted to Oxford at : age of eleven.

Roman times, while there were no iversities in the modern sense, young n used to resort to Athens, Rhodes and exandria to study philosophy and toric (the art of speaking). The pattern, wever, which we know today, and iich is followed in most parts of the orld, gradually developed in western rope during the Middle Ages. It follows m this that the Church, for long the e upholder and protector of learning, ok a leading part. The seeds were ually first sown when a small band of dents gathered in a town or city to end the lectures of some teacher, and is attracted other similar groups to the ne place. In time the community thus rmed would achieve enough stability d reputation to apply, often to the local shop, sometimes to higher authority, for charter. One of the chief objects of this as to gain protection from townspeople, ho often regarded the newcomers with spicion and jealousy. The word univer-y itself was originally applied to a guild company of students banded together r welfare and safety. At Vercelli, an ilian community which had a brief istence in the 13th century, there were ur universities for young men who me from England, Germany, Italy and rovence.

The earliest chartered university was at lerno in southern Italy, already famed r many years before its formal incor-oration in the first half of the 12th cen-ry as a centre of medical studies. It was llowed not long after by Bologna, 300 iles [483 km] to the north, where civil id canon (Church) law were particu-rly studied. The most renowned of all, owever, was the University of Paris, the rigins of which can be traced to the early 12th century, though its incorporation was by a "brief" of Pope Innocent III dated 1211. It was probably here that degrees were first instituted, that of Master of Arts regarded as a licence to teach, that of Bachelor of Arts being, as it were, a stage in apprenticeship.

From this point there was a steady growth of fresh foundations throughout western Europe: Seville (1242) in Spain, which helped to bring the learning of Christendom into contact with that of the Arabic world, Heidelberg (1386) in Germany, where in later centuries so many universities sprang up, the Polish Cracow (1364) in the east, the Swedish Uppsala (1477) in the north.

In England, Oxford is said to have been started about 1133 by a migration from Paris, but the choice of this particular place suggests that a nucleus may have existed there already. Here, too, strife with the inhabitants was bitter, and a particularly violent riot in 1209 drove the students away, some of them, it is said, going off to form the early beginnings of Cambridge. Five years later, however, Oxford received the protection of papal recognition. In these first two English universities there soon grew up the feature of a number of separate colleges, each to a large extent controlling its own affairs, but preparing its students for degrees con-ferred by the central body. Merton College (1274) was the earliest of such colleges at Oxford, Peterhouse (1284) at Cambridge. Though Oliver Cromwell (*see* separate entry) proposed a northern university at Durham, this was not achieved until 1832. London (1835) was the first to admit students who did not belong to the Church of England, a requirement abolished in the older universities from 1854 onwards. Scotland's three oldest foundations, St Andrews, Glasgow and Aberdeen, date from the 15th century and Edinburgh from 1582. Trinity College, Dublin

(1591), a protestant stronghold in a Catholic country, was for over 300 years the only university in Ireland. From the middle of the 19th century there have been in England, Scotland, Wales and Ireland over twenty additions to the list, nearly half of them since World War II.

In the USA the old foundations of Harvard (1636, reputedly the wealthiest university in the world), William and Mary (1693) and Yale (1701) enjoy a very high reputation. Other famous universities include Princeton, New Jersey (1746), called by President Woodrow Wilson 'a seminary of statesmen'; Columbia, New York City (1754), another very wealthy institution; and Chicago (1890), which is especially well known for its work in education, social sciences and atomic physics. The first separate college of high standing and adequate endowment for women in the US was Vassar, New York (1865), though degrees were being granted to women thirty years earlier. Some of the greatest libraries in the world are housed in American universities, a good example being the collections at Texas.

Universities are now a feature of nearly every country in the world. Great universities established in the British Commonwealth include McGill, Toronto and Laval in Canada; Sydney and Melbourne in Australia; and others in South Africa and India. The largest purpose-built university structure is probably the MV. Lomonosov State University, south of Moscow, 32 storeys high and containing 40,000 rooms.

Returning to Great Britain, another significant development should be mentioned. In 1969 a new type of university received its charter – the Open University or 'University of the Air', providing degree courses largely through the medium of radio and television programmes. *See also* INDIVIDUAL ENTRIES.

Upanishads: a series of prose cc mentaries on the Vedic hymns, the earl dating probably from about 500 which form one of the most remarka sections of ancient Sanskrit literatu They had much influence in develop Hindu beliefs (*see* HINDUISM), particula in *Brahman*, the all-embracing spi *Karma*, the importance of "works" *Yoga*, personal discipline.

Uruguay: republic on the south-e coast of South America. The territo contains rich grasslands which are gc for cattle, so that possession has frequen been a matter of dispute. It was coloni first by the Portuguese, coming so from Brazil in 1680; but in the early 1 century the Spaniards of Argent founded a rival centre at Montevideo, a in 1777 this became the capital city o Spanish Uruguay.

Uruguay, like all the other Span territories in South America, became free republic early in the 19th centu (1814), but it was too small to defe itself easily from the rival claims of Bra and Argentina, and there was confl over its boundaries until 1853, wher treaty was made. With a total populati of about three million, Uruguay is s the smallest of all the South Americ republics.
See also SOUTH AMERICA.

Utopia: an ideal but impracticable soc or political system; originally, an imag native work published in 1516 by Thomas More (*see* separate entry). T title, from the Greek, means "Nowhere and the book describes an ideal com munity living according to the laws nature. This gave scope for impli criticism of the abuses of the tim Samuel Butler (1835–1902) in his *Erewh* and *Erewhon Revisited* presents a fanta on similar lines.

V

Vaccination: inoculation with a virus to secure immunity from smallpox or other disease. Edward Jenner (1749–1823), a doctor in Gloucestershire, England (*see* separate entry), studied smallpox and reached the conclusion that no one had it twice and that people whose work brought them into contact with cattle were never infected, although they frequently suffered from a similar, milder illness known as "cowpox". Certain that cowpox protected the body from smallpox, Jenner deliberately infected patients with it, then exposed them to smallpox. They remained immune. Jenner's method of infection by cowpox was termed vaccination, from the Latin *vacca*, a cow.

Vagrancy: wandering, with no fixed home and often no work. In order to live vagrants may do odd jobs but sometimes beg or steal. Because of this, vagrancy in many parts of the world is an offence against the law.

In the Middle Ages (*see* separate entry) vagrants in England often found food and a night's shelter at one of the many monasteries throughout the country. After the monasteries were destroyed in the time of Henry VIII (1491–1547) this help was not available, and the growing numbers of vagrants became a serious problem, with a great increase in begging and robbery. Towns and villages were besieged by large numbers of these "rogues and vagabonds". From the time of Queen Elizabeth I (1533–1603) many laws were passed to control vagrancy but the problem was not solved. Between the various wars, disbanded soldiers with no trade took to the roads, and, as the army of vagrants grew, the punishments became more severe and hanging was frequent.

Today, in countries with a well developed welfare organisation, vagrancy is no longer a serious problem. In less advanced communities the difficulties remain and, indeed, there are still places where vagrancy is an accepted profession rather than an economic misfortune.

Valletta, Valetta: capital and chief port of the island of Malta on the north-east coast, with a fine strongly fortified harbour. In the 16th century it was the headquarters of the Knights of Malta (formerly the Knights Hospitallers or Knights of St John of Jerusalem) and many evidences of their occupation survive, including the lodging of the grand master, armour, and tapestries. Under British occupation, Valletta became an important naval and military base. Malta became fully independent in the Commonwealth in 1974 and since then has pursued a non-aligned policy.
See also MALTA.

Valois, House of: French dynasty of kings (1328–1589). Valois is part of France, just south of Paris, formerly owned by a younger branch of the powerful medieval Capetian kings. The Valois first became the ruling house in the person of Philip VI (ruled 1328–50). Some later rulers, such as Francis I, were very able, but many were weak monarchs who lost France much prestige during the Hundred Years War and the Wars of Religion. The House died out with Henry III (ruled 1574–89), to be succeeded by the Bourbon Henry IV.
See also INDIVIDUAL ENTRIES.

Valparaiso: South American city (named by the Spaniard Juan de Saavedra after his birthplace in Spain) founded in 1536 on a fine sheltered bay on the Pacific coast. In spite of two disastrous earthquakes, its inhabitants have made it the commercial capital of Chile. Many Scots, Irish, French and Germans live there, attracted by its pleasant climate. Its greatest hero is Bernardo O'Higgins (*see* separate entry).

Vandals: an east Germanic people who invaded Gaul with other peoples in AD 406, passed on into Spain in 409, and then, in 429, into North Africa. Establishing a kingdom with capital at Carthage, they cut Rome off from vital grain supplies. Unlike other Germanic peoples they were implacably hostile to Rome and, having built a navy, sacked the city in 455. They occupied Sicily and Sardinia. Few in numbers, their kingdom lasted only a century, until North Africa was reconquered by the Byzantine Empire. Their destructive energy gave "vandal" and "vandalism", as words of sinister meaning, to the language of later nations.

Varanasi, Banaras, Benares: important commercial centre in north-eastern India, on the River Ganges. The City of Benares (Kasi) was once a Buddhist centre (*see* BUDDHA), containing in the 7th century at least thirty Buddhist monasteries. Now the most sacred city of Hinduism, it has over 1,500 Hindu temples, of which the "Golden Temple" is the most sacred. The Moslem Mosque of Aurangzeb is spectacular. The city attracts annually a million pilgrims who carry out ceremonial bathing in the Ganges.

Vatican and **Vatican City:** The palace of the Vatican, at Rome, is the residence of the popes, or bishops of Rome, the supreme heads of the Roman Catholic Church (*see* separate entry) throughout the world; it also contains one of the finest collections of pictures and manuscripts in the world. The palace, and its grounds, are situated within a part of Rome that is called the Vatican City. Although this city is not much more than a hundred acres [40 hectares] in size an has little more than a thousand inhabitan it is an independent state, in its own righ and not a part of Italy. An independe papal state has existed since the 8t century, and at one time extended rigl across central Italy. But when the Italia peninsula was unified in the 19th centur and the modern Italian state was forme the Pope's lands were taken from hir (1860–70). It was only in 1929 that treaty was made between Italy and th Vatican setting up the Vatican City Stat The importance of this state to the Pop is that, as head of the World Church, h should not be subjected to pressure fro any particular country, and he should b free to receive the ambassadors of a foreign powers. The value of this in dependence to the Pope was made especi ally clear in World War II (*see* separat entry), when Italy was overrun first b the Germans and then by the Wester Allies, but the neutrality of the Vatica City was respected by both sides.

Vedas: collections of hymns and rituals developed in the upper Indus region which form the earliest scriptures of the Aryans in India. The most important, possibly the earliest, work in any Indo-European language, is the *Rig-Veda*, compiled between *c.* 2000 and 1000 BC. The hymns are addressed to the chief Vedic deities, such as Agni the fire god and the divine warrior Indra.

Velasquez, Diego Rodriguez de Silva y (1599–1660): Spanish painter. Born in Seville, Velasquez became court painter to Philip IV of Spain, but he was no mere flatterer of royalty. High-born or lowly, his subjects were painted with equal honesty and unrivalled realism. Visits to Italy, particularly Venice, where he could study the works of the Venetian painters

·e next entry), tempered his early, rather stere, style with colour and warmth. Yet is not really correct to speak of Velasquez influenced by the Italian painters. He ade his own rules and remained in a ass by himself. In 1970 his portrait of his rvant Juan de Pareja changed hands for ‚2,310,000 at auction in London and is ›w in the USA.

In THOMAS, H. and D. L. *Great Painters*. 1959

'enetian art: the school of painting, :ulpture and architecture associated with ıe city and republic of Venice. Splendour ıd colour, warmth and a sensuous delight ı the beauties of the material world – ıese, the prime characteristics of Venetian rt, are what might be expected of the rtists of a city whose face, as it were, was ırned to the East rather than to the rest of :aly; a city into whose busy harbour came he rich fabrics of the Orient, carpets and :welled metalwork, perfumes and spices. 3y a miraculous chance Venice produced succession of painters of genius who, in heir works, captured the spirit of this nimitable city.

Not that the Venetian artists were with-›ut spiritual values: closely linked cul-urally with the Byzantine Empire (*see* eparate entry), the works of its earlier ›ainters, notably Giovanni Bellini (*c.* 1430–1516), are full of that noble and noving religious feeling which is so much ›art of Byzantine art. Bellini, however, ›ne of the earliest great painters to use oils, moved far beyond the static decorative-ness of Byzantine art. His figures are full of movement, his landscapes luminously alive. Giorgione (1477–1501), one of the greatest painters of all time, who may have been Bellini's pupil, allowed the land-scape, in a sense, to take over the picture instead of being mere background. In Titian (Tiziano Vecelli, *c.* 1480–1576) Venice found an artist who in the course of his long life produced a number of magnificent works which sum up the civilisation of his native city-state. Tin-toretto (Jacopo Robusti, 1518–94), a follower of Titian, was a vigorous painter and splendid colourist, though not the equal of his master. Paul Veronese (Paolo Caliari, 1528–88), born in Verona as his nickname indicates, did his best work in Venice and is usually classed with the Venetian School. He painted many very large paintings which, if they lack deep feeling or insight into human nature, give a wonderful impression of magnificence. Jacopo Sansovino (Tatti, 1477–1579) was a second-rate sculptor but a first-rate architect who enriched Venice with many splendid buildings, richly carved and decorated. Andrea Palladio (1518–80), an architect of more austere taste, looked for his inspiration in ancient Roman models. His *I quattro libri dell' architettura*, The Four Books of Architecture (1570), an English translation of which was published by the architect Inigo Jones (1573–1652), had a great influence on English architecture.

In decay, her glories fading, Venice in the 18th century still could boast three great artists. Giovanni Battista Tiepolo (1692–1769) was a decorative painter of tremen-dous facility. Antonio Canale, or Cana-letto, (1697–1768) painted sparkling views of his native city (and of London, which he visited). The works of Canaletto's pupil Francesco Guardi (1712–93), while often very like those of his master, are more impressionistic, sometimes self-consciously picturesque.

Paintings by the great Venetian masters are to be found in the major art galleries of the world. But much of their work – altarpieces, murals, painted ceilings – remains in the Venetian churches and buildings for which it was originally designed, making Venice one of the treasure houses of the world.

See also PALLADIO; TITIAN; VENICE.

Venezuela: republic of northern South America, in the tropical region of South America that lies north of the Amazon basin. The native peoples of the mountains, the Sierra Nevada de Merida, are tough and have always dominated the low-landers on the coastal plain and on the delta of the River Orinoco.

This coast was discovered by Columbus in 1498. A year later Ojeda, accompanied by Amerigo Vespucci, named the land Venezuela, meaning "little Venice". Pearl fishing from the Margarita Islands provided some quick profits, but few Spaniards settled in the small towns which were created along the coast. In the 17th century English and Dutch sailors raided the coastal towns, but Venezuela remained a Spanish province until in 1811 Simon Bolívar began the rebellions which eventually freed all of South America.

Like most republics in South America, Venezuela has suffered from prolonged boundary disputes with all her neighbours and from repeated internal disorder. Over fifty revolutions were attempted in the 19th century, ten of them successful. The exploitation of the vast oil reserves near Lake Maracaibo has brought revenue to the government since 1920 and today Venezuela has one of the most advanced economies in South America.

See also BOLIVAR; COLUMBUS; SOUTH AMERICA; VESPUCCI.

Venice: Italian city built on a number of small islands – little more than mudbanks – within a lagoon at the head of the Adriatic Sea. It would be hard, on the face of it, to choose a less suitable location for a city. Traditionally, it was founded (*c.* 452 AD) as a refuge by families fleeing from Attila, the "Scourge of God", and his terrible Huns.

Despite the fact that its "streets" were waterways and that its buildings had to be raised on piles for want of firm foundations, the city grew, and grew rich, fo Venice lay on important trade routes b land and sea. It became an independen city-state, famous for its magnificenc The Church of St Mark, its principa sacred building, is one of the most richl decorated edifices in the world. Venetia traders travelling to the East were re quired, by law, to bring back somethin beautiful for its adornment.

A "street" in Venice.

Recognising that the city owed it prosperity to the sea, every Ascensio Day the *Doge*, the head of state, went ou in a ship and threw a valuable ring into th Adriatic, to symbolise the "marriage" o Venice and the sea. With the discovery o America, however, and of routes roun the Cape of Good Hope, the pattern o trade shifted and the fortunes of Venic declined. In 1797 it was occupied by Napoleon I (*see* separate entry) and, on his downfall, handed over to Austria. In 1866 it became part of the kingdom of Italy.

Today it is one of the greatest tourist magnets in the world. Its centuries-old glassworks are still famous and there is heavy industry on the mainland. Built on mud, Venice is gradually sinking into the sea. Plans are afoot to construct a system of locks and dams to preserve this unique island city.

See also DOGES OF VENICE; VENETIAN ART.

Verona: fortified city of north-eastern Italy, on the River Adige. Its long history begins with settlement by a variety of

:ly peoples, including the Ligurians, ıuls (*see* GAUL) and Etruscans (*see* RURIA) and later development as a ›man colony. Its notable buildings :lude a Roman amphitheatre, second ly to the Coliseum in size; a 7th-century urch, renowned for its fine vestry and oir; a Romanesque cathedral (12th–16th nturies); and the ancient fortress of ıstelvecchio now housing a famous art llection. To the sentimental tourist with ıakespeare's tragedy of *Romeo and Juliet* mind, the house and tomb of Juliet are a ajor attraction. Among its industries are per manufacture, food processing and rtilisers.

ersailles: French town near Paris, mous as the site of one of the largest and ost ornate palaces in the world, a emorial to the vanity and ambition of ing Louis XIV (reigned 1643–1715), ho ordered its building. The palace is so ıst, so ornamented with sculpture, paint-gs and gilded furnishings, that it is hard conceive of anyone actually living ere; and indeed, the letters and journals Louis's courtiers are full of references the discomforts of life at court. The ırdens, planned by André le Nôtre (1613 1700), are, with their statuary, orna-ental urns and fountains, beautiful in a :ry formal way. The town has given its ıme to a number of treaties, most cently the Treaty of Versailles (28 June ›19) at the end of World War I.

ersailles, Treaty of (28 June 1919): eaty usually considered as securing the ttlement of Europe at the end of World Var I (*see* separate entry), because its pening sections proposed the formation f the League of Nations (*see* separate ıtry). But as other treaties were signed ter with defeated powers, the Treaty of ersailles should properly be named for the German settlement only. The terms were imposed on Germany despite protests that they should have been negotiated on the basis of President Wilson's Fourteen Points (*see* separate entry).

Germany surrendered all her colonies and some territories on her frontier, such as Alsace-Lorraine to France and Schlesvig to Denmark; also, by giving part of eastern Prussia to Poland, Germany was partitioned by the Polish Corridor. Controversial areas such as Danzig and the Saar were to be placed under the League of Nations, and the Rhineland was demilitarised. German military forces were severely limited. She was forced to accept responsibility for the war, the cost of which was to be worked out later by a Reparations committee.

Versailles also gave its name to the Peace of Versailles (3 September 1783) which recognised the independence of the United States.

Vespucci, Amerigo (1454–1512): Italian merchant and navigator who made three voyages to the New World 1497–1512, in the service of Spain and Portugal. It seems likely that he explored the north-east coast of South America, but his own accounts of his expeditions are conflicting and unreliable. A German cartographer, Martin Waldseemüller, first suggested in 1507 that the newly discovered continent should be called America "because Americus discovered it", but the consensus of opinion is that Vespucci has little claim as the pioneer discoverer.

¶ POHL, F. J. *Amerigo Vespucci, Pilot Major.* 1967

Vesuvius: Italian volcano, 5 miles [8 km] south-east of Naples. Early man saw Vesuvius erupt and Roman legends attribute the disturbances to warring amongst the gods. Dormant for hundreds of years, Vesuvius erupted in AD 79, destroying Pompeii and Herculaneum and, incident-

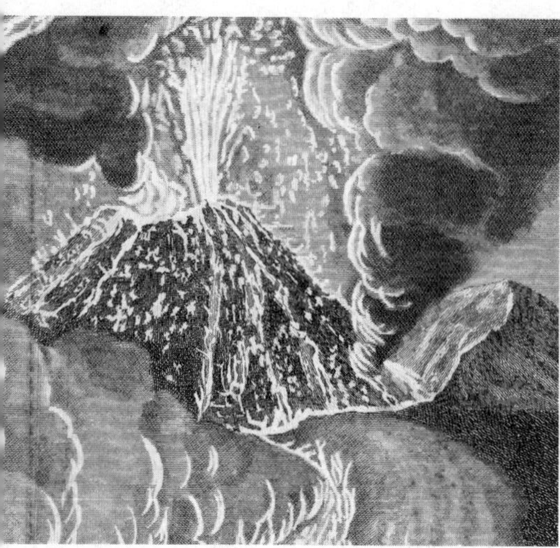

Vesuvius erupting in 1767.

ally, causing the death of the Roman writer Pliny the Elder, whose scientific curiosity was greater than his prudence. In 472, ashes were blown as far as Constantinople. In 1631 18,000 people in surrounding villages were killed by lava and boiling water.
See also VOLCANO.

Victoria: state of the Australian Commonwealth in the south-east of the continent. Though originally part of New South Wales (*see* separate entry), no serious attempts at penal settlement were made. Small-scale free settlement began at Port Phillip in 1814. Edward Henty's party from Tasmania established a station at Portland Bay in 1834 for farming and whaling, in unpromising conditions, but other parties in 1835 founded what was to become the capital city, Melbourne. Reports on this area by Major Thomas Mitchell (later knighted) and settlement schemes attracted immigrants from Britain and farmers from New South Wales, and the population increased rapidly. Hume's explorations, 1824–25, and Mitchell's more extensive researches, 1831–46, opened up districts suitable for further settlement and farming, whic flourished with English demands for woo In 1847 Melbourne, named after th British prime minister (just as the sta was named after the British Queen), w raised to the status of a city. In 185 Victoria separated from New Sout Wales and formed another colony, wit a lieutenant-governor. Responsible con stitutional government was achieved i 1855. Victoria early introduced adu voting rights, and equal elective righ for women in 1908.

Gold was discovered at Ballarat in th 1850s. Agriculture, primarily grazing, ha extended to dairying, fruit and wine. Th chief industries are food processing, tex tiles, chemicals, farm machinery, iron an steel. The 1937 Kiewa project provide readily available hydroelectric power.

Vienna: capital of Austria on the Rive Danube, and until 1916 the hub of the grea Austrian empire. Vienna was founded b the Celts in pre-Roman times. In th Middle Ages its importance as a tradin centre grew slowly, but after 1278 th population increased rapidly because o the city's selection by the Habsbur family (*see* separate entry) as the Imperia capital. Since then Vienna's history ha been largely the history of central Europe It was the focal point of resistance to th Turks and was twice unsuccessfully be sieged by them (1529 and 1683). Habsbur leadership of the Catholic cause for thre centuries made Vienna a symbolic centr and many churches were constructe in the Baroque style. Its art museum hold collections of the great masters, an strong musical and cultural traditions built up in the 18th and 19th centuries continue. Of great popular appeal is th *Spanische Reitschule*, the only school o horsemanship in the world to maintai the methods and traditions of the Classi Riding School. As well as giving regula

assic horsemanship displayed by one of the hite Horses of Vienna.

splays for most of the year, the White orses of Vienna are famous in many her countries.

---

ienna, Congress of: conference of ıropean powers, 2 October 1814 – 23 ıarch 1815. The fall of Napoleon left the sposition of his empire to the principal lies, Russia, Prussia, Austria and Great ritain, and the Congress was held, in an mosphere of gaiety and magnificence, ainly to ratify the decisions of these four. owever, owing to the ineffectiveness of rtain of the delegates and the astuteness the French minister, Talleyrand, animosity arose almost immediately between e allies. Talleyrand's admittance to the ounsels of the "four" and the diplomacy the British delegate, Castlereagh, and the Austrian chairman of the Congress, letternich, secured temporary harmony espite the rival claims of the different ountries, and a settlement was concluded June 1815. Among its results, involving uch give and take among the powers, rance was deprived of all her imperial conquests and Britain gained many colonies, including Cape Colony and Malta. *See* separate entries for METTERNICH; NAPOLEON I; TALLEYRAND-PERIGORD.

Vietnam: region along the southern and eastern coasts of Indo-China. The territory was inhabited by Indonesian tribes which mingled with Thai people who arrived about the 6th century BC and with Mongol people (*see* separate entry) between the 5th and 3rd centuries BC. By the 10th century AD a new distinctive people had come into being on the Red River delta. Ruled first by China, Vietnam, consisting of Tonkin and north Annam, gained independence in the 10th century and expanded southwards, at last reaching Cochin China and the Mekong delta. From the 17th century trading posts were established by western powers. In the 19th century the French became the predominant power and undertook the conquest of Vietnam, establishing the colony of Cochin China in 1867 and protectorates over Annam and Tonkin by 1884. Economic development in French Indo-China was pursued intensively only from the close of the 19th century, rice, rubber and anthracite being main exports. Under French rule a new Vietnamese middle class emerged. After World War I (*see* separate entry) national Vietnamese resistance to French rule increased. Following harsh suppression of uprisings in 1930, nationalist leadership passed to the communists, led by Ho Chi Minh (*see* separate entry). Under Japanese rule (1941–45) during World War II (*see* separate entry), a league of independence, Vietminh, dominated by communists, was formed and, on Japanese withdrawal, proclaimed an independent republic. Chinese forces occupied North Vietnam, and British forces were in the south. France tried to negotiate with the Vietminh for a "free state within the French Union". In Hanoi the Vietminh attacked

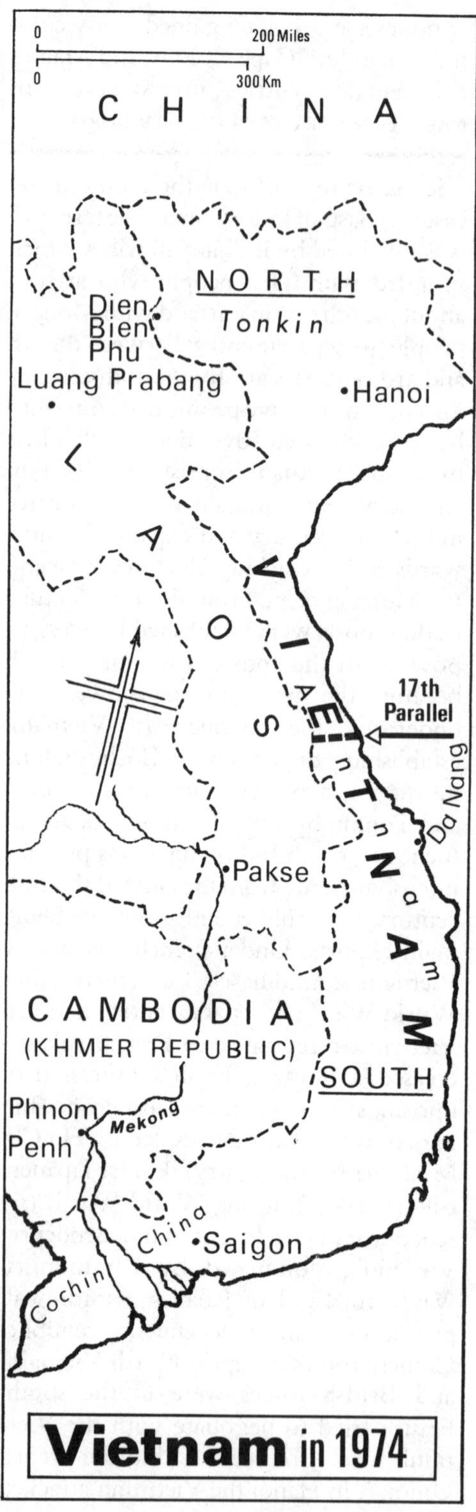

the French (1946). France tried to r southern nationalists against Vietmi but years of struggle led to French disa at Dien Bien Phu. An internatic Geneva convention on Indo-China 1954 arranged an armistice and partitio Vietnam at the seventeenth parallel latitude.

Vietnam, Socialist Republic thirty years of armed struggle and involvement of major outside pow made the Vietnam War one of the m dangerous of modern times. It was als struggle of extreme bitterness and fe city. After the partition of Vietnam 1954 a communist government was fi to consolidate its position in the no with Hanoi as its capital and Ho C Minh (*see* separate entry) as its lead Sweeping agrarian and other econon reforms won widespread popular su port and enthusiastic aid was provid by other communist countries. Nor Vietnam then proceeded to give acti support to the guerrilla forces in Sou Vietnam which were inspired by pr found economic discontents. The res was an escalating war in the south wh government in Saigon was supported the USA which felt the need to repla the French presence in the area in t hope of checking Communism. By 19 there was full-scale war and the US commenced bombing the north. Neg tiations in Paris (1968–73) eventually l to the withdrawal of US forces. The however, the North launched an atta upon the South in aid of the Viet Co guerrillas and in April 1975 the Sou fell. The two Vietnams were reunit after nationwide elections in 1976 as t Socialist Republic of Vietnam. Saig became Ho Chi Minh City. Followi the reunification, however, Vietna faced many problems. The South was n easily merged with the North. Ma hinese and other hill people fled into hina and many thousands fled by sea – e "boat people" of Vietnam. In 1978 ietnam invaded neighbouring Kampu- ea to oust the Pol Pot regime and in- all a government sympathetic to Hanoi. he continuing presence of Vietnamese oops in Kampuchea has caused fears and order incidents with Thailand. There ave been border clashes with a deeply ntagonistic China to the north (seen in lanoi as the country's number one nemy). Vietnam continues to be heavily ependent upon the USSR for aid.

ikings: Scandinavian warriors and sea- aiders who ravaged the coasts of Europe n the 8th–10th centuries and penetrated o Iceland, Greenland, the Baltic and onstantinople. They sacked Paris in 845 nd 860 and, as the Northmen or Norsemen, gave their name to Normandy. In England they were known as Danes (i.e. men from Denmark), eventually occupying the throne and establishing an empire under Canute or Cnut. It seems probable that expeditions also reached the coasts of North America about the year 1000. Fierce fighters and magnificent sailors, they were among the most remarkable of early voyagers and colonisers. Though ruthless and with a reputation for faithlessness, their courage was supreme and, given the opportunity, they showed talent for peaceful government.

See map, page 284.

¶ GIBSON, MICHAEL. *The Vikings*. 1972; HENRY, BERNARD. *Vikings and Norsemen*. 1971

See also CANUTE; ERIC THE RED; LEIF ERICSON; SHIPBUILDING; etc.

Virgil, Vergil, Publius Vergilius Maro (70–19 BC): Roman poet born near Mantua. His fame rests on three works, all written in the hexameter metre, or lines

of six metrical feet: (1) the *Ecologues* or rustic idylls, (2) the *Georgics*, four books dealing with the farmer's life and occupations, and (3) the supreme achievement of the *Aeneid*, describing the adventures of Aeneas, fleeing with his companions from Troy and founding in Italy the future Roman nation.

¶ In CANNING, JOHN, editor. *100 Great Lives*. 1953

VJ Day: day of popular celebrations by the allied peoples of the United Nations to mark the Victory of their forces over Japanese imperialism in 1945. The Japanese government surrendered officially on 14 August, and worldwide festivities over the next twenty-four hours signified the end of World War II (*see* separate entry).

Vladivostok: large seaport in the far east of the USSR, on the Sea of Japan, founded in 1860. It was occupied by the Japanese 1918–22 and, during the first two years of this period, was the base of the anti-Soviet leader Admiral Kolchak. It is the eastern terminus of the trans-Siberian railway and the air line from Moscow, and has major shipbuilding, food-processing and oil-refining industries.
See also DOCKS; USSR.

Volcano: rift in earth's crust through which subterranean material is ejected. The word derives from the name of the island of Vulcanus, near Sicily, so called by the Romans, because they believed it to be the forge of Vulcan, their god of fire and blacksmith of the gods. The mountain seemed to be burning inside like a blacksmith's forge. Vulcanus, or Vulcano as it is called today, has been built, like all volcanoes, of molten material from the inside of the earth, pushed up through cracks in a weak part of the earth's crust. Sometimes, on reaching the earth's surface, it has spilt over as lava and tremendous explosions of gases have flung ou cinders and ash.

Probably no part of the earth's surfac has not been at some time the site c volcanic activity. Regions such as th British Isles, not thought of as volcanic have, in the distant past, experience violent and prolonged activity. Crate Lake, Oregon, USA, was created 6,00 years ago by a tremendous eruption Mount Ararat, where the Bible relate that Noah's Ark came to rest, is a extinct volcano. Some archaeologist believe that the great civilisation o Minoan Crete was destroyed as a result o the Bronze Age eruption of Thera seventy-five miles away, accompanied b devastating tidal waves and ash fall-out.

The eruption of Etna in Sicily, in 47 BC, was described by Pindar and Aeschylu – one of many in historic times, thougl

Mont Pelée's great plug of hardened lava.

ıe most catastrophic was in 1669, when ıe nearby city of Catania was practically estroyed. Although Strabo, the Greek eographer, had recognised Vesuvius as olcanic, the mountain had been quiescent or a long period before its destruction of ompeii in AD 79. There was a lake at its entre when rebellious gladiators took efuge there 150 years before.

A fifth of the population was killed vhen Skaptarjökul, Iceland, erupted in 783. More violent still was the Krakatoa ruption in 1883, when two-thirds of the land in the Sunda Strait was blown away. 'idal waves caused the deaths of 36,000 n the coasts of Java and Sumatra, atmos-heric waves travelled three times round ıe earth, a blanket of ash shrouded hipping a thousand miles away, and a all of darkness spread for 150 miles round. For three years the dust from the ruption produced wonderful sunsets, articularly in Great Britain.

Mont Pelée, in Martinique, one of the slands of the West Indies, though long lormant, erupted again in 1902. An valanche of red-hot lava and clouds of ıot gas swept down the mountain on to he inhabitants of St Pierre, only one of vhom, a prisoner in the jail, escaped.

Although there have been thousands of volcanoes in the world, only about five ıundred have been active in recorded ıistory. Most are situated in the "Ring of Fire", round the edges of the Pacific Ocean – the Philippines contain ninety-eight, Japan thirty-three, Alaska thirty-five. Other areas are the Andes, West Indies, and the Mediterranean. Most are near the coast, and it is possible that eruptions are caused by seeping water contacting subterranean molten matter near a weakness in the earth's crust.

¶ HIRST, W. *Volcanoes.* 1971; FURNEAUX, RUPERT. *Volcano.* 1974

See also VESUVIUS.

Voltaire, François-Marie Arouet de (1694–1778): French philosopher, historian and man of letters. Voltaire was a great mocker, merciless in exposing prejudice, pretentiousness and superstition: as a result he made many enemies. During an enforced stay in England (1726–29) its relative freedom compared with that of France greatly impressed him. In 1833 his *Lettres philosophiques sur les Anglais*, praising England, was burnt by the French authorities, and Voltaire was forced to leave Paris again to avoid arrest.

A strangely contradictory personality – greedy and generous, unscrupulous towards his enemies while hating injustice – Voltaire was a puller-down rather than a builder-up. He proffered no blueprint for a new society. Yet in such masterly satires as *Candide* his witty pen, probing the weaknesses of a corrupt system, helped to pave the way for the French Revolution.

See also EIGHTEENTH CENTURY; FRENCH REVOLUTION.

Vorster, Balthazar Johannes (1915–83): South African prime minister. Elected Nationalist MP for Nigel in 1953, he became deputy minister of education in 1958, minister of justice in 1961 and prime minister in 1966 after the assassination of Dr Verwoerd, a position he retained until 1978. He then became President of South Africa but resigned in 1979 following the "Muldergate" affair with revelations of corruption in the government he had led.

See also SOUTH AFRICA, REPUBLIC OF.

Vulgate: Latin version of the Bible (*editio vulgata*) compiled in the 4th century by St Jerome. There had been earlier versions, but the Vulgate has been the most widely used in the Western Church for nearly 1,600 years.

W

Wagner Act (1935): law passed by the US Congress (*see* CONGRESS, AMERICAN) giving employees the right to organise trade unions and to make collective bargains, i.e. agreements affecting all the workers in one union or group of unions. The Act also set up the National Labour Relations Board (NLRB) to investigate labour disputes, prevent unfair practices and protect the rights given to employees.

Waitangi, Treaty of (6 February 1840): treaty between Britain and Maori chiefs of New Zealand. Gibbon Wakefield in 1839 organised the New Zealand Company for land purchase and settlement. The government, questioning the legality of such purchases from the Maori chiefs, sent a naval officer, Captain Hobson, to negotiate and in 1840 annexed New Zealand to New South Wales (*see* separate entry). The chiefs acknowledged British sovereignty, without perhaps fully understanding its implications. The tribes were guaranteed possession of their lands, subject to crown right of purchase. The Treaty did not prove the hoped-for "happy solution of the coloured-race difficulty". Continuing settlement in new areas and expropriations drove the Maoris to rebellion in 1845–48 and 1860–72. They proved themselves skilful and extremely courageous guerrilla fighters, but were eventually worn down and conciliated by such measures as special representation in Parliament.

See also GUERRILLAS; MAORI.

Wales: principality, situated in the south-west of Great Britain and flanked on three sides by the sea. Its land boundary with England runs from the estuary of the River Dee to the Bristol Channel. Wales is a rugged country with more than 60 pe[r] cent of its total acreage over 500 feet [15[2] m] above sea level. The highest mountai[n] is Snowdon, 3,560 feet [1,084 m].

The Cambrian Mountains form th[e] heartland of Wales. Further south are th[e] Brecon Beacons, the Black Mountain[s] and the Carmarthenshire Fans. Roun[d] this rocky core is a lowland area o[f] varying width which is the most produc[-]tive part of the country. Here, and in th[e] deeply grooved river valleys, lives th[e] majority of the Welsh people.

Wales has a damp mild climate. As muc[h] as 150 inches [3,810 mm] of rain a yea[r] falls on the higher mountains, and mos[t] of Wales gets at least 40 inches [1,020 mm[]] annually. There are, however, no grea[t] extremes of temperature.

Much of the land is infertile – bare rock or moorland good only for rough grazing[.] Some oats and barley are grown on th[e] coastal plain and along the river valley[s] but most of the land available for agri[-]culture is grassland, used for raising cattl[e] and for dairy-farming. Where th[e] countryside is not scarred by industria[l] development it is among the most beautiful in the British Isles.

The wealth of Wales comes not from it[s] soil but from the minerals that lie beneath

Some of the most beautiful of Welsh scenery, looking east towards Mt. Snowdon.

– tin, ironstone, lead, copper, slate, a ttle gold (plans are afoot to prospect new for this) and, above all, coal. The reat coalfields of Glamorgan and Monnouthshire produce nearly all Britain's nthracite coal and much of its steam coal. The steel industry of this area, of which Rhondda and Merthyr Tydfil are the wo largest towns, produces most of Britain's tin plate and much of its sheet teel though by the 1980s the industry vas in decline. During the depression years of the late 1920s and 1930s Wales uffered from unemployment. Great efforts have since been made to diversify the country's industrial output, thus making it less vulnerable to recessions. Factories have been established for the manufacture of many types of goods, including plastics, clothing, synthetic fibres, and electronic equipment. The chief cities of Wales are its ports: Cardiff, Swansea and Newport.

Though Wales was conquered by King Edward I (reigned 1271–1307) in 1283, and united with England by Act of Parliament in 1536, the Welsh have retained a strong sense of national identity. The descendants of early Celtic settlers, forced back into the mountains of the west by successive waves of Roman, Saxon and Norman invaders, they still display many Celtic characteristics both of physique and temperament – on the short side, stocky, dark-haired and long skulled; more emotional than the phlegmatic English and with a great love of music. The Welsh language, spoken by some 26 per cent of the population, is taught in all Welsh schools.

Wallace, Sir William (*c.* 1272–1305): Scottish patriot. Although only a knight of low degree, he won renown for the part he played in fighting for his country's independence. Victory over the English at Stirling Bridge in 1297 gave him authority, but a second invasion brought crushing defeat for the Scots at the Battle of Falkirk followed by the subjugation of Scotland and Wallace's capture and execution. Standing trial in Westminster Hall, accused of treachery, Wallace declared: "To Edward of England I cannot be a traitor, for he never was my Sovereign, he never received my homage, and while life remains within this frame he never shall."

¶ In GRICE, F. *Rebels and Fugitives*. 1963

Walpole, Sir Robert, 1st Earl of Orford (1674–1745): English Whig politician. He entered parliament in 1700 and first held office in 1708. When the Tories (*see* TORY) gained power in 1712, his enemies drove him from parliament and, for a time, secured his imprisonment. In 1714, however, on the succession of George I, he returned to public life and soon became first lord of the treasury and chancellor. He resigned in 1717 but was recalled in 1720 as the only man who could save the situation after the financial disaster of the South Sea Bubble. He held office for the next twenty-one years and helped to ensure both peace and prosperity for the country. Although the position of prime minister was not yet recognised, his leadership foreshadowed the cabinet system (*see* separate entry).

Walsingham, Sir Francis (*c.* 1530–90): English secretary of state from 1573. A supporter of the policy of alliance with France, he urged the necessity of war against Spain and active help for Protestants abroad. As ambassador to France 1570–73, he was responsible for the

Treaty of Blois (1572). Expert at counter-espionage, he raised the English intelligence service to a high pitch of efficiency and was responsible for disclosing many plots, notably Babington's, which led to the execution of Mary Queen of Scots.

War of 1812: war between America and Britain caused mainly by disputes on the high seas, the blockading of American ports, and the alleged support by Britain of the Indians in their struggle for survival. Congress declared war in June 1812 and fought what has been called a second War of Independence, and one conducted with great bitterness. The war marked the beginning of a new era in American history, with the American people finally turning away from Europe and setting out to shape their own destiny. One visible legacy today is the White House (*see* separate entry). In 1814 the British burned the President's official residence, and it was painted white to cover the marks of the fire.

Warsaw, Warszawa: capital of Poland since 1596. In 1795, at the third partition of Poland, Warsaw fell to Prussia, but in 1807 Napoleon created a separate independent Grand Duchy of Warsaw. Under Russian rule this independence was partly preserved but ended in revolt in 1830–31. After World War I, Warsaw became capital of a new Poland. Under German occupation in World War II the Jews of Warsaw were "liquidated", their "ghetto" (or special quarter) being virtually destroyed. In 1944 there was a rising in which, given no aid by the Russians, Warsaw and its patriots were destroyed by the Germans and 600,000 people perished. After 1945 the city was rebuilt and repopulated.

See WORLD WAR I for map.

See also JEWS; NAPOLEON I; WORLD WARS I and II.

Warsaw Pact: a defence pact establishe by the Warsaw Treaty of 14 May 195 by the USSR with Albania, Bulgari Czechoslovakia, East Germany, Hungar Poland and Romania, as a counterweigh to NATO (*see* separate entry). Warsa Pact forces intervened to influence even in Poland and Hungary in 1956 an Czechoslovakia in 1968.

Washington: (1) state of the extrem north-west of the USA, washed by th Pacific; capital Olympia, chief city Seattle (2) capital of the USA, on the other side o the continent, over 2,000 miles [3,218 km distant. It occupies almost all the seventy square miles [180 sq km] of the District o Columbia and is designated Washingto DC, distinguishing it from the Pacifi state, abbreviated Wash.

The original plan of the capital wa drawn up by Major Pierre L'Enfant, under the supervision of George Washingto himself (*see* next entry), and has bee largely preserved, the Government making a praiseworthy effort, in the early 1900s, to clear away some of the 19th-century excrescences that had obscured the fine vistas and viewpoints. The most impressive stretch is the Mall, running from the Lincoln Memorial on the Potomac River north-east to Capitol Hill. The Mall forms the axis around or near which are found most of the great public buildings including the Capitol (modelled on St Peter's, Rome), where the Senate and House of Representatives meet, the Supreme Court buildings, the Library of Congress and the White House (*see* separate entry).

Washington, George (1732–99): first president of the USA (1789–97). Coming from a land- and slave-owning family in Virginia, his early education came more from outdoor occupations and practical pursuits than from books, though he ught himself a good deal of mathemat-s and became an expert surveyor. In 753 he was commissioned in the army ıd spent several years fighting against ıe French and Indians. After his marriage ı 1759 he gave up his military career and evoted himself to his estates. As one of ıe wealthiest tobacco planters, he showed imself a very efficient and hardworking mployer, caring for his slaves and em-loying a doctor for the sick. He was one f the chief leaders of the opposition to British colonial policy and, when the War of American Independence broke ut, became commander in chief of the o-called Continental army. With only mall forces at his disposal, he had to rely n patience, devotion and courage, rather han any dramatic display of military genius, which he probably never pos-essed. Even after he took the supreme command, he did not anticipate, and did not want, independence of Britain. It was nly when he realised that there was no onger any choice that he changed his mind and, after the struggle was over, accepted the presidency.

As president he showed himself cau-tious and methodical, trying to stand aloof from party politics. In the words of Professor Nevins "he believed the head of the nation should be no man's guest. He returned no calls and shook hands with no one, acknowledging salutations by a formal bow." He strove to strengthen the central government and, in the wider affairs of the world, to preserve a strict neutrality.

He resisted pressure to serve for a third term and retired in 1797 to his estates at Mount Vernon (named after the British admiral Edward Vernon). When he died in December 1799, a resolution in the House of Representatives described him as "first in war, first in peace, and first in the hearts of his countrymen". When the news reached Europe, the armies of Napoleon I (*see* separate entry) and the British fleet both paid him tribute.

¶ COY, HAROLD. *Real Book of George Wash* 1963

See also AMERICAN PRESIDENTS.

Waterloo, Battle of (18 June 1815): scene of the final defeat of Napoleon I, near the Belgian village of Waterloo, by the Fourth Coalition forces under Wellington and Blücher. Faced with continued opposition to his rule in France after his escape from Elba, Napoleon moved his army quickly. He crossed the Belgian frontier intending to strike the Prussians at Ligny and the British at Quatre Bras, before they could link up and before help came from Russia and Austria in the east.

Napoleon had the advantage of mobility and numbers (about 72,000 against 68,000), but he made several miscalculations. He relied on Marshal Ney to defeat the British, but Ney moved too slowly, allowing Wellington to retreat and choose a good defensive position at Waterloo. Napoleon's own defeat of the Prussians at Ligny was not followed up properly, and they later regrouped to move in decisively on the crucial battle being fought at Waterloo between Napoleon and Wellington. Repeated French cavalry charges broke against well-trained British infantry "squares". After eight hours heavy fighting Wellington, now supported by the Prussians, moved against the tired and dispirited French army, which disintegrated, leaving up to 40,000 casualties. It is reckoned one of the decisive battles of history and is the source of many anecdotes and quotations, not least Wellington's words in a letter written almost immediately after his return from the field: "Believe me, nothing except a battle lost can be half so melancholy as a battle won."

See also INDIVIDUAL ENTRIES.

Watermarks: identifying marks in sheets of paper. Although the Chinese were the first paper-makers, they did not use watermarks. Paper manufacturing methods from the East reached Europe in the mid-12th century, and around 1285 emblems and designs began to be pressed into paper during its manufacture in Italy.

Early watermarks were simple in design, consisting mainly of maker's initials, stars, crosses and circles; then heraldic devices appeared and ecclesiastical or biblical symbols, such as the paschal lamb, the Holy Grail and the cardinal's hat. The more complicated designs served at first to identify products of individual mills, but later they often became technical terms to describe various types and sizes of paper. Thus the "post horn" watermark, the origins of which can be traced back to the horn that Roland blew in the pass of Roncesvalles, gave its name to post paper; and foolscap came fro[m] the watermark of a jester with cap an[d] bells, used by an Elizabethan paper-mak[er] in England. In the late 17th century man[y] marks bearing royal arms or arms of citi[es] occurred in England and Germany.

Paper was made by placing rag pulp i[n] shallow trays with a base of interwove[n] wires. The long wires, set close together were the "wire lines". The cross-wire[s] were more widely spaced and known a[s] "chain lines". Their impressions are visibl[e] in all hand-made paper when held up t[o] the light and are in themselves a form o[f] watermark. The special devices describe[d] above were additional wire designs interwoven with the rest in the bottom of th[e] tray. Watermarked paper is often used fo[r] documents, bank-notes, etc., to preven[t] counterfeiting. The occurrence of watermarks is characteristic of hand-made paper. In the machine-made product, a

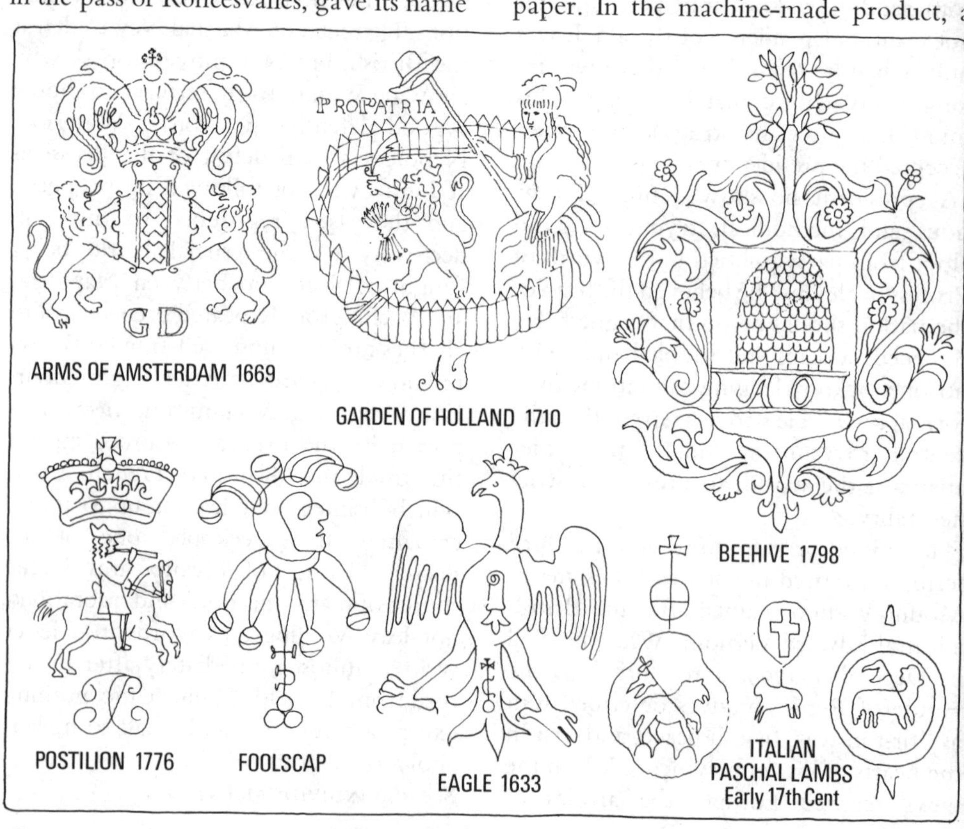

ARMS OF AMSTERDAM 1669

GARDEN OF HOLLAND 1710

BEEHIVE 1798

POSTILION 1776

FOOLSCAP

EAGLE 1633

ITALIAN PASCHAL LAMBS Early 17th Cent

cular rubber form can be used to roll nbols over the surface of the wet paper, t these do not have the clarity and auty of the other type.

att, James (1736–1819): developer of the steam engine, born at Greenock, otland. The engines of his time worked the principle developed by Thomas ewcomen (1663–1729), whereby steam as admitted into a vertical cylinder and en condensed, the resulting vacuum rcing a piston down the cylinder and oducing a power-stroke. In operation ey were very wasteful of steam, and eir use was largely confined to pumping ater from mines. By applying scientific inciples Watt used a separate condenser, hich greatly improved performance. partnership with Matthew Boulton 728–1809; *see* separate entry) at the oho factory, Birmingham, and enjoyg the protection of a patent, he produced rge numbers of his type of engine, evising detailed improvements and new ethods of transmitting motion which ade them adaptable for many uses.

WEBB, ROBERT N. *James Watt.* 1972

ee also STEAM.

Vayne, Anthony (1745–96): American eneral. He distinguished himself in the Var of American Independence, combining military skill, stubbornness and reat personal daring. His exploit in ersonally leading the charge over the alls of the British fort at Stony Point, New York, (July 1779) earned him the opular nickname of "Mad Anthony".

ee also AMERICAN WAR OF INDEPENDENCE.

Weaving: process of interlacing threads o make a fabric. Strands are stretched ongitudinally on a simple frame and other hreads passed in and out of them. The rame is called a *loom*, the threads stretched on it the *warp* and the transverse ones the *weft*. The earliest looms were probably two separate rods between which the warp threads were stretched: the weft thread was wound on a shuttle and the weaving was pushed up into position with a flat piece of wood.

Prehistoric people are likely to have made textiles by weaving grasses, but once a method was discovered of spinning wool, flax or silk into thread, the woven material would be more useful and durable. Egyptian and Greek weavers seem to have made long, narrow strips of cloth on small looms. Later people discovered how to make wider material. Large, strong looms were made of wood, and on these the finished cloth could be pulled back and rolled as it was completed. The warp threads were passed through a perforated strip of wood – the *heddle* – which could be lifted up and down, making it easier to pass the shuttle carrying the weft from side to side. A pattern could be woven into the fabric by using coloured threads.

Civilised man required many different textures of cloth. In cold climates wool was used for weaving, in hot lands linen and cotton. The Chinese appear to have been the first people to weave on a large scale. They used silk and, although their looms were big, they were light because the threads were so fine. Chinese merchants traded in silk, and it is on record

Chinese loosely-woven silk, 6–8th century AD.

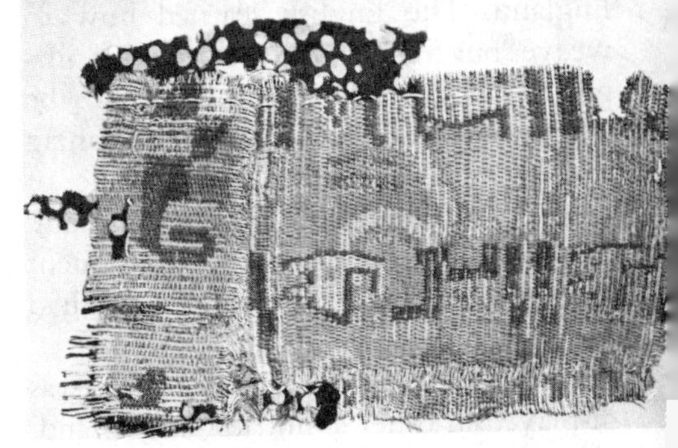

Weavers using handlooms in the Netherlands, 17th century.

that a party of them set out in AD 97 to sell silk in Rome. When they reached the eastern Mediterranean they turned back because they thought they could never cross the sea. The Romans wove both wool and linen. In AD 369 an Imperial decree restricted weaving with gold and silver threads to specialist workshops.

In western Europe people made woollen cloth on heavy handlooms. The people of the Netherlands were particularly skilled weavers and imported wool from England. The English learned how to weave, but for many years preferred imported cloth. The first loom to be mechanically driven was set up in Danzig in 1661. It was said to be capable of weaving cloth without human aid. The authorities, afraid of unemployment among the weavers, destroyed it and had the inventor put to death.

The same fear of unemployment was displayed in other countries. In England, when Dr Cartwright invented a powe loom which he established at Doncaste in 1786, rioters damaged the machiner and burned the factory; but eventually i was realised that mechanical weavin would result in more trade, so that powe looms came to be accepted.

By 1825 there were about 75,000 powe looms in Britain in addition to 250,00 hand looms.

In France an important type known a the Jacquard loom, fitted with a devic for weaving figured fabrics, was invente by Joseph-Marie Jacquard (1752–1834) In 1860 an electric loom was set up i London, devised by Bonelli of Turin The invention of automatic processes ha made it possible for hundreds of looms tc be supervised by one weaver. However the fundamental principle of weaving i the same as it was many thousands o years ago.

See also LOOM; TEXTILES.

[W]ebster, Daniel (1782–1852): American [st]atesman. He combined the practice of [la]w and politics and was elected, first to [th]e House of Representatives, then to the [Se]nate (1827), becoming secretary of [st]ate in 1841. His chief fame was as a [su]perb orator. The English clergyman [an]d wit Sydney Smith described him as [a] steam engine in trousers"; and, after [o]ne of his speeches in Congress (*see* [se]parate entry), another member said: [“]Mr Webster, I think you had better die [n]ow, and rest your fame on that speech."

[W]ebster, Noah (1758–1843): American [di]ctionary maker. His *Compendious Dic[ti]onary of the English Language* (1806) and *[A]merican Dictionary of the English Language* [(1]828) are comparable to Doctor John[so]n's achievement in England (1755) and [h]ave far exceeded it in the number of later [r]evisions and reprints.
[S]ee also DICTIONARIES.

[W]edgwood, Josiah (1730–95): English [p]ottery manufacturer. Born in Burslem, [J]osiah Wedgwood established a pottery in [1]759. He copied Greek designs and in [1]769 opened a new pottery which he [n]amed *Etruria*, after the district of Italy, [n]ow called Tuscany, where a remarkable [t]ype of native pottery, possibly derived [f]rom Greek models, had been produced [i]n ancient times. The Etruria pottery [p]roduced black basalt vases, decorated [p]laques like cameos, and a wide range of [d]omestic ware with a new standard of [a]rtistic merit.

[¶] ARCHER, STUART M. *Josiah Wedgwood and the [P]otteries*. 1974

[S]ee also ETRURIA.

Wellington, Arthur Wellesley, 1st Duke of (1769–1852): British soldier and politician, popularly known as the "Iron Duke". The fourth son of an Irish peer, he entered the British army in 1785. His service in India (1796–1803) first showed his great military qualities, but his outstanding achievement was the successful conduct of the Peninsular War (1809–14) in Spain and Portugal which drove the French out of the Iberian peninsula. For this he was created a duke. When in 1815 Napoleon made a bid to restore his fortunes, it was Wellington who withstood him at Waterloo and, when the Prussians came up, drove him from the field.

Many years of political life now awaited him. He was prime minister 1828–30, and for some time his resistance to change brought him unpopularity; but this was soon forgotten by the nation in its affectionate recognition of one of the greatest men in British history.

¶ WARD, S. G. P. *Wellington*. 1963
See also INDIVIDUAL ENTRIES.

Wesley, John (1703–91): English divine and founder of Methodism, the fifteenth child of Samuel Wesley, rector of Epworth in Lincolnshire. For a time he followed an orthodox university and Church career, being ordained an Anglican priest, preaching in many churches round Oxford and periodically acting as his father's curate. In his early years he enjoyed company, dancing, walking and field sports and was a good swimmer. Around him and his brother Charles in Oxford gathered a small group of serious minded students known as the "Holy Club" who began to follow a stricter rule of life and received the nickname of "Methodists".

In 1735 John and Charles went on a missionary journey to Georgia and founded a religious society at Savannah. His dictatorial methods made him many enemies in America and he left Georgia in 1737. Back in England he appointed lay preachers, founded Methodist chapels (the first at Bristol in 1739) and established a great reputation as a field preacher, riding the length and breadth of the country on yearly journeys which have been called "the most amazing record of human exertion ever penned by man". He regularly travelled some 5,000 miles a year, preaching fifteen sermons a week, often to hostile audiences, his rule being always to look a mob in the face. As a social reformer he was far in advance of his time and, apart from his preaching, his twenty-three collections of hymns and his prose works continued to exercise a powerful influence long after his death. *See also* METHODISM.

Western Australia: largest Australian state, all the territory west of 129° East longitude, with Perth the capital. A plaque in the Amsterdam Museum records the visit in 1616 of Dirk Hartog. Tasman navigated the north-west coast in 1644, William Dampier visited King Sound in 1688, Vancouver took possession of the south-west in 1791, and King explored the north coast 1818–22. Convicts from New South Wales (*see* separate entries) in 1827 settled on King George's Sound under Captain Stirling. In 1829 Captain Fremantle (later knighted) founded the west coast Swan River settlement, the real beginnings of colonisation. In 1850 the colony, in order to secure more settlers and workers, sought the admission of convicts, and transportation continued until 1868, when the protests of other colonies could no longer be disregarded. Between the 1830s and the 1890s Grey, Gregory, the Forrests, Giles, Warburton and Lindsay explored the interior. Western Australia achieved responsible government in 1890. In the 1880s and 1890s gold discoveries at Kimberley and Kalgoorlie made mining the main industry. The state still produces seven-tenths of Australian gold, and is rich in minerals, among them tin, asbestos and silver. After World War I (*see* separate entry) wheat production expande[d] with stock-raising and dairying in t[he] south-west. Programmes of educati[on] and welfare have assisted the survival [of] the Aborigines (*see* separate entry), wh[o] chiefly follow pastoral and domest[ic] occupations.
See AUSTRALIA for map.

West Indies, Federation of the: co[n]federation of certain Caribbean islan[ds] within the British Commonwealth (195[8]–62). In the years after World War II (*s[ee]* separate entry) serious consideration w[as] given to the best method of leadin[g] colonial peoples towards self-governme[nt] and independence. In the West Indies th[e] Caribbean Commission, created durin[g] World War II by the United State[s,] France, the Netherlands and Great Britai[n,] advised on political and other problem[s.] Previously British West Indian island[s] had shown little interest in each other['s] political affairs. Cricket appeared the onl[y] common point of contact. The war ende[d,] Britain cultivated the idea of federation o[f] her West Indian colonies as the way o[f] advancement towards independence. Th[e] Colonial Development and Welfare Ac[t] of 1940 was doing something to ease th[e] widespread distresses of prewar years an[d] to promote the social and economi[c] development of the West Indies; bu[t] economic and population difficulties persisted. The physical nature of the Wes[t] Indies, an archipelago stretching in [a] curve north-westwards from the coast o[f] Venezuela to Florida, was itself daunting[.] Constitutional progress for so man[y] separated units seemed impossible, an[d] federation became official British policy[.] Numerous conferences resulted i[n] agreement in 1956 to establish the Federation of the West Indies. The Order in Council was signed on 31 July 1957, Lord Hailes, first Governor-General, arrived in Trinidad in January 1958, and incess Margaret inaugurated the first rliament of the West Indies at Red ouse, Port of Spain, on 23 April.

ollowing serious differences of opinion nong the members of the Federation on ch matters as economic control and presentation in the federal parliament, maica left the Federation, to be followed on after by Trinidad and Tobago. The deration of the West Indies ended on e date planned for Independence Day, May 1962.

e also INDIVIDUAL ENTRIES.

---

estminster Abbey: great church, in estminster, London, dedicated to St eter. Built on what was once a marshy et, it stands on a site where, traditionally, a church has stood since the 2nd ntury. In 1085 Edward the Confessor unded a new church and in 1245 enry III began a vast rebuilding which as the beginning of the Abbey as we now it today, and developed later into ne of the finest examples of Perpendicular style of Gothic to be found in the ountry. Over the centuries additions and terations took place: cloisters and onastic buildings were erected for the enedictine monks (1300–1400); the nave nd aisles were rebuilt (1340–1483); in 502 Henry VII laid the first stone of the xquisite chapel which bears his name.

Except for Edward V every English onarch since William I (reigned 1066–7) has been crowned in Westminster bbey. Some of them are buried there, s well as many of the nation's greatest nen and the Unknown Warrior, symbol f the nation's dead of World Wars I and I (*see* separate entries). The building must ot be confused with Westminster Cathedral, built 1895–1910, the seat of he Roman Catholic Archbishop of Westminster.

LOXTON, HOWARD, editor. *Westminster Abbey* Jackdaw). 1967

Whaling: the pursuit and killing of whales, immense marine mammals, of which there are many species, measuring up to 120 feet [36 m] and weighing as much as 200 tons [200 tonnes].

Whales were being caught by Norwegians as early as AD 890. The Basques from northern Spain established a whaling industry during the 11th century. The two main commodities obtainable from the whale – oil for lighting and making candles, and baleen (whalebone) – were much in demand. Other byproducts are ambergris, used in the manufacture of perfume, and spermaceti, an ingredient in a number of cosmetics and textile finishes. The Arctic whaling industry was started by the English and Dutch in 1611 and 1614, respectively, and the Germans, Danes and French followed in the next century. The enormous slaughter of the Greenland whale resulted in its near-extinction by about 1860.

In 1712 the Americans from New Bedford started hunting the sperm whale in the Atlantic. This creature, which frequents the warmer waters, is the toothed variety and has no baleen. It yields large quantities of sperm oil, so well suited as a lamp oil. The whaler *Amelia* was the first British ship to hunt the sperm whale in the Pacific, in 1789.

The early whalemen hunted in open boats. The whales were captured by the hand harpoon and finally killed with a spear. Flensing (the stripping away of the skin or blubber) was carried out at the

shore establishments or alongside the mother ship. In 1868 the Norwegian Svend Foyn perfected the gun harpoon with explosive head. This led to an expansion of the industry in which the Norwegians played a leading part.

The 20th-century whale factory ship with fast catcher ships to hunt the rorqual whale in the Antarctic has established the present industry. Whale oil is processed for margarine and soap and the flesh and bones for fertiliser. An International Whaling Commission was founded in 1946 to save the whale from extinction.

¶ REINFELD, FRED. *Real Book of Whales and Whaling*. 1963

Whig: political term in Britain, of Scottish origin and applied from about 1680 to a member of the country party, which, in opposition to the Tories (*see* TORY), stood for the moneyed and trading interest and mistrusted the policies of the Crown. The Whigs were responsible for inviting William III to England in 1688. They continued as a recognised political party until about 1850, when the term Liberals began to be applied to those who inherited their traditions.

White House, The: the official residence of the president of the USA, in Washington, DC. It is the oldest public building in Washington, designed in 1792 by James Hoban, and is esteemed for its architectural simplicity and purity of line, as well as for its many historical associations. (For its name, *see* WAR OF 1812.) As with Downing Street in Britain (*see* separate entry), the term White House is often used to mean the government itself.

Whitney, Eli (1765–1825): American inventor. In 1783 he invented a machine for separating cotton lint from its seeds. Many law suits followed when Whitney tried to protect his invention by taking out a patent, or sole right to manufactu He turned his attention to the manufa ture of fire-arms and obtained ma government contracts.

Whittle, Sir Frank (b. 1907): Brit engineer and inventor of the modern aircraft engine. Until 1948 he served wi the Royal Air Force as apprentice, cad flying officer, instructor, test pilot, et reaching the rank of Air Commodo The first flight of a Gloucester je propelled aeroplane with a Whittle e gine took place in May 1941. Numero international awards and decorations ha been bestowed on the inventor.

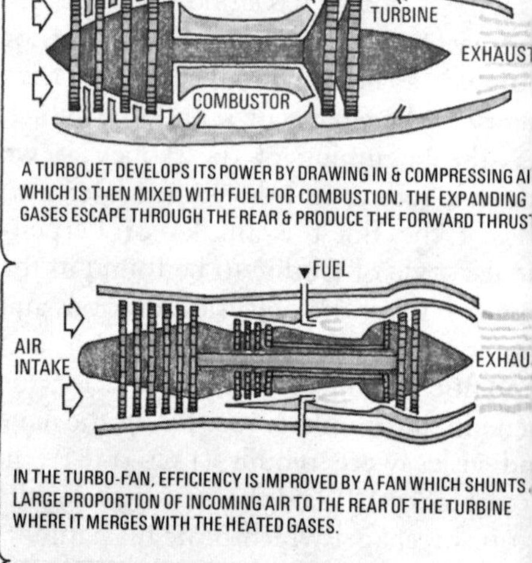

A TURBOJET DEVELOPS ITS POWER BY DRAWING IN & COMPRESSING AI WHICH IS THEN MIXED WITH FUEL FOR COMBUSTION. THE EXPANDING GASES ESCAPE THROUGH THE REAR & PRODUCE THE FORWARD THRUS

IN THE TURBO-FAN, EFFICIENCY IS IMPROVED BY A FAN WHICH SHUNTS LARGE PROPORTION OF INCOMING AIR TO THE REAR OF THE TURBINE WHERE IT MERGES WITH THE HEATED GASES.

THE RAM-JET, SIMPLEST YET MOST ADVANCED, HAS NO MOVING PARTS. INFLOW OF AIR IS NATURALLY COMPRESSED ON ENTERING THE SPECIALL DESIGNED INTAKE, THUS ELIMINATING THE NEED FOR COMPRESSOR OR TURBINE.

¶ In EVANS, I. O. *Inventors of the World*. 1962

Wilberforce, William (1759–1833) leader of the anti-slavery movement i Britain. Born of an old Yorkshire famil he became Member of Parliament fo

ıll at the age of twenty-one. With the ›pport of the younger Pitt he more than ce persuaded the House of Commons pass resolutions against the slave trade *e* SLAVERY), but he had to wait until 07 to see an Act passed prohibiting the ıde as far as British subjects and British ritories were concerned. He continued untiring labours in the cause, the nancipation Act, freeing all slaves in itish possessions, becoming law in the ar of his death.

AWSON, A. and D. *The Man Who Freed the ıves*. 1962

'ilhelm I (1797–1888): king of Prussia ›m 1861 and emperor of the newly rmed German Empire from 1871. He lieved in strong government and the istence of a large Prussian army. He ›pointed Bismarck (*see* separate entry) his minister-president in 1862 and in m found a man of character and ability hose ideas were similar to his own.

'ilhelm II, known as **"The Kaiser"** 859–1941): emperor of Germany from 388 to 1918. He believed in vigorous rsonal direction of government to in-'ease Germany's world prestige. But he ıd little political skill and antagonised ıany European states. Though not en-rely to blame for starting World War I *ee* separate entry), he fled into exile in Iolland in 1918 rather than stand trial on ıe charge of so doing.

Wilkes, Charles (1798–1877): American explorer who, in 1840, first reported the existence of an Antarctic continent. As a US naval officer during the American Civil War (1861–64; *see* separate entry) he stopped a British ship, the *Trent*, and removed two Confederate envoys who were aboard. This violation of neutrality nearly led to war with England.

Wilkes, John (1727–97): English politician, champion of parliamentary reform. In the course of a turbulent career he was imprisoned in the Tower, expelled from the House of Commons, and declared an outlaw. He was four times returned as member for Middlesex, but the elections were disallowed, leading to great popular agitation under the banner, "Wilkes and Liberty!" In 1782 Wilkes was allowed to take his seat in parliament.

Wilson, Thomas Woodrow (1856–1924): 28th president of the USA (1913–21). After endeavouring to pursue a policy of neutrality in World War I, he reluctantly agreed to the declaration of war on Germany in 1917. In January 1918 he enunciated the famous "Fourteen Points" (*see* separate entry), as a basis for a peace settlement, helped to set up the League of Nations, and was awarded the Nobel Peace Prize in 1920.

¶ In CANNING, JOHN, editor. *100 Great Modern Lives*. 1965

Winchester: cathedral city 64 miles [103 km] west-south-west of London on the River Itchen. The Roman invaders of AD 43 found the site occupied by the Belgae, a tribe which had come over from Gaul about a century earlier. Under the name of *Venta Belgarum*, it was one of the most flourishing towns of Roman Britain. Later the kings of Wessex, the Anglo-Saxon kingdom in south and west England, including Alfred the Great, made it their capital: caskets said to contain the bones of several of them can still be seen in the cathedral. During Norman times the city continued to prosper, and the royal treasury was located there. There also grew up a considerable Jewish settlement still commemorated in the name Jewry Street. From the 12th century decline set in, and later recovery never restored Winchester to its former importance.

The present cathedral dates from the 11th century and is the longest in England. Among medieval buildings still in use are the College, founded by William of Wykeham in 1378, and the hospital (almshouse) of St Cross. Among the important events witnessed by the city were the marriage of Mary I of England and Philip of Spain (1554) and the trial of Sir Walter Ralegh (1603), the court having been convened there because of an outbreak of plague in London.

See separate entries for ALFRED THE GREAT; JEWS; PHILIP OF SPAIN; RALEGH, SIR WALTER.

Windsor, House of: English royal house. King George V, second son of Edward VII, came to the throne in 1910. He was a grandson of Queen Victoria, whose husband, Prince Albert, had been a member of the German family of Saxe-Coburg-Gotha. Many German princes were related to this family, so that in 1917, during World War I, King George was advised to change his name and by royal proclamation took the surname of Windsor for himself and his descendants.

George V became an extremely popular monarch. Because he and Queen Mary travelled extensively both at home and abroad, they were known to their subjects in a way that Queen Victoria and King Edward VII had never been.

When George V died in 1936, his eldest son became king. Edward VIII reigned for less than a year and was never crowned. He had been a popular Prince of Wal but, not prepared to conform to the w of his ministers in some matters, bro with them completely over the questi of his proposed marriage to Mrs Wal Simpson, a twice-divorced America He abdicated, married Mrs Simpson a was given the title of Duke of Winds being succeeded by his brother, Geor VI, who was king during World War and the troubled years that followed His daughter, Elizabeth II, became Que after his sudden death in 1952. She a her husband, Prince Philip, have fo children, the eldest of whom is Charl Prince of Wales.

Witchcraft: the practice of magic, us ally understood to be "black" (i.e. malev lent) as distinct from the "white" beneficent variety. Magic, in world hi tory, occupies a unique place, somewhe between science and religion. Primiti peoples, unable to comprehend the natur forces governing the universe, looked f an explanation elsewhere; in gods an goddesses, each charged with dominio over some particular aspect of natur and in certain human beings who, by in voking supernatural powers, were them selves enabled to exercise control ov nature and events.

In developing civilisations witchcra was early seen as a kind of heresy, a thre to organised religion. The Book Exodus (22:18) enjoins "Thou shalt n suffer a witch to live". Educated peop in ancient Greece deplored the use magic. Nevertheless, there are man references to it in Greek myths. Mede the witch who helped the hero Jaso obtain the Golden Fleece, later restore Jason's father to youth by boiling him in stew of magic herbs. The goddess Hecat was the protectress of all witches.

The ancient Romans passed laws punish ing witches. The idea of witchcraft whic ıerged in Europe in the Middle Ages ›e separate entries) was a combination of yth, folk-beliefs, and the early Christian :lief in the power of Satan and his devils. he typical witch was seen as a woman vhile male witches, or warlocks, were ought to exist, the profession was con-lered primarily a female preserve) who ›uld assume animal form, had a familiar a demon in animal guise who was her :lper and guide – and could fly through ıe air, with or without a broomstick. By ›ells, waxen images and the evil eye she ›uld bring harm and death; she ate little ıildren, called up storms, and raised the ead, she celebrated obscene witches' ıbbaths with the Devil, when a travesty f the Christian mass was performed.

From the 13th century on, with the stablishment of the Inquisition (*see* :parate entry), the ecclesiastical tribunal oncerned with the rooting out of heresy, ıe persecution of witches greatly in-reased. In 1484 Pope Innocent III issued a bull against witchcraft, as a result of which thousands of so-called witches were put to death. Between 1580 and 1595 900 died in Lorraine alone. The persecution was by no means an exclusively Roman Catholic activity. Many witches were persecuted in the American colonies, the trials at Salem, New England, being particularly notorious. In England between 1645 and 1647 Matthew Hopkins (d. 1647), known as the Witch-Finder, procured the hanging of some hundred persons in East Anglia.

¶ HART, ROGER. *Witchcraft*. 1971

Iatthew Hopkins, Witch Finder Generall, urrounded by the symbols of his trade.

Witte, Count Sergei Yulievich (1849–1915): Russian statesman, responsible as minister of communications for a rapid expansion of Russian railways (especially the Trans-Siberian), and as finance minister for doubling imperial revenues. He was plenipotentiary at the Portsmouth (USA) treaty which ended the Russo-Japanese war (1905; *see* separate entry), and largely responsible for the constitutional reforms introduced into Russia at that time.

Wolsey, Thomas (*c.* 1475–1530): English statesman. As Cardinal, Lord Chancellor to Henry VIII, Archbishop of York, holder of many other benefices and papal legate, he was virtual ruler of England 1511–29. He strengthened the monarchy by concentrating justice under the Crown, but his expensive foreign policy, successful until 1518, failed after his alliance (1521) with Charles V (*see* separate entry) in a bid for the papacy. He joined with France in 1528, hoping to free the Pope from imperial control and secure papal sanction for Henry's divorce from Catherine of Aragon; but his policy collapsed with France's defeat in 1529. Wolsey was dismissed and died at Leicester on his way to answer charges of high treason.

Wool: fine soft hair forming the fleece of many animals, particularly the sheep. Woollen fibres are easy to spin and weave, and in cold climates woollen cloth is warm and comfortable to wear. In Britain, sheep were reared long before the Roman occupation and cloth was made from their wool. The Romans established a centre for making woollen cloth to keep their soldiers in Britain supplied with clothing.

The climate and low grassy hills made Britain an excellent place for sheep to flourish, and the quality of British wool was renowned. Although the Saxons (*see* separate entry) encouraged their womenfolk to spin, very little weaving was done in Britain. Raw wool and spun thread were exported to the Netherlands for weaving and the finished cloth shipped back to Britain. But William the Conqueror encouraged Flemish weavers to come to Britain, and by the end of the 11th century there were settlements of them at Carlisle and in Pembrokeshire. Henry II encouraged weaving by giving official patronage to a fair, held annually in St Bartholomew's churchyard in London, for the sale of woollen cloth.

The woollen merchants of London were granted the sole right to export raw wool. Edward III forbade this, insisting that all the wool produced in Britain must be woven by British cloth-weavers. This led to wool smuggling on a large scale, and the act proved impossible to enforce. The unrestricted export of wool was not permitted until Elizabeth I's reign. Evidence of the wealth of the wool merchants can be seen in the magnificent churches built and paid for by money made from the sale of wool. Later efforts were again made to control the sale of wool, and it was not until the cotton industry of Lancashire became so profitable after the Industrial Revolution that all restrictions on the sale of raw wool were finally lifted.

There was a woollen industry in Spain, where the Moors had introduced Meri sheep with their fine, silky hair. Meri sheep were later introduced into Austral and cloth made from their wool w manufactured at Botany Bay – hence t name "botany" for light woollen fabri With the growth of the trade in froz meat other breeds of sheep were intr duced into Australia and New Zealan They were sometimes crossed with mer nos and produced a heavier wool. Nov adays, little weaving is done in Austral or New Zealand, but a great deal of ra wool is exported.

See also WEAVING.

World War I (1914–18): Simply know as the "Great War" at the time, the ter "world war" was given only after th Armistice. The spark was the assassinatio on 28 June 1914 at Sarajevo of the heir t the Austrian throne by a Serb – a membe of the "Black Hand" secret society whos aim was the unification of all Slav people of south-eastern Europe under their ow government. Austria and Serbia wer quarrelling over power in the Balkan and a month later Austrian troops in vaded Serbia. The conflict might hav been restricted to that area had it no been for twenty-five years of rising inter national tension.

Germany had ambitions of becoming world power, and this caused mistrust i

1914, Archduke Franz Ferdinand and his wi at Sarajevo shortly before the assassination.

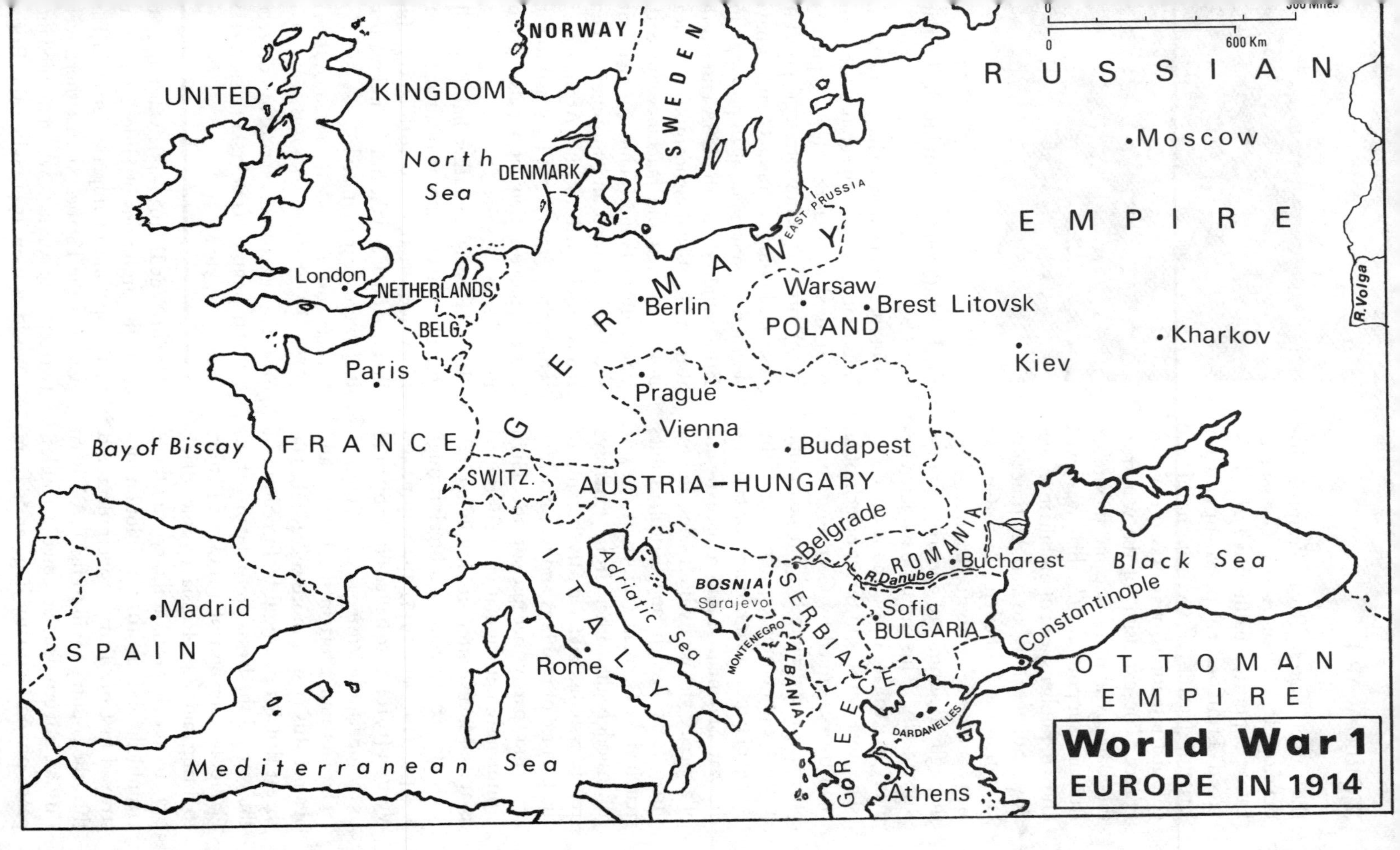
World War 1
EUROPE IN 1914
0 600 Km
RUSSIAN EMPIRE
Moscow
Kharkov
Kiev
Brest Litovsk
Warsaw
POLAND
EAST PRUSSIA
R.Volga
NORWAY
SWEDEN
DENMARK
UNITED KINGDOM
North Sea
London
NETHERLANDS
BELG.
Paris
FRANCE
Bay of Biscay
GERMANY
Berlin
Prague
Vienna
Budapest
SWITZ.
AUSTRIA-HUNGARY
Belgrade
ROMANIA
Bucharest
R.Danube
Black Sea
Constantinople
Sofia
BULGARIA
BOSNIA
Sarajevo
SERBIA
MONTENEGRO
ALBANIA
GREECE
DARDANELLES
Athens
OTTOMAN EMPIRE
Adriatic Sea
ITALY
Rome
Madrid
SPAIN
Mediterranean Sea

the other states. Rival "camps" had developed: a close Austro-German alliance, supported halfheartedly by Italy, faced Franco-Russian co-operation. Britain, fearful of German naval and colonial intentions, was drawn closer to France. The extension of the war from the Balkans in 1914 became inevitable. Russian support for Serbia was well known, but her speed of mobilisation was slow. So, working to a tight timetable known as the Schlieffen Plan, a German army aimed a swift hammer-blow through Belgium to destroy France, Russia's ally. This should have left Germany free to face Russia in the east.

The invasion was in direct breach of an 1839 treaty, signed by Germany among others, guaranteeing Belgian neutrality. It was the contemptuous ignoring of this "scrap of paper" that brought Britain into the war. Stalemate was to replace dreams of a speedy victory by both sides, and for three years French and British armies matched the Germans. Efforts by one side to dislodge the other from extensive trench systems failed, partly because of the balance of numbers and war machinery, and partly because of the High Commands' unimaginative use of frontal assaults. Massive attempts, involving millions of men, to achieve a breakthrough at Ypres (1915 and 1917), the Somme and Verdun (1916) were halted either by mud or by superior defensive machine guns.

The German effort in the Balkans and against Russia was more successful. The threat that Russia might be forced out of the war led the British into the disastrous Gallipoli campaign of 1915, in an effort to bring aid into Russia by the Black Sea route. Russian military resistance crumbled, and in 1917 revolution destroyed first the Tsarist government and then the country's will to fight. A Soviet Russian government accepted a ruthless peace giving Germany huge areas from

Soldiers in the trenches at the Somme, 1916.

the Baltic through Poland to the Ukrair and Caucasus.

But these gains were to have little lastin importance. The appearance of tank (first used by the British in Septembe 1916) introduced new strategic possibili ties. Following a rash German nava decision to sink neutral ships supplyin Britain and France, the USA entered th war and in 1918 the enormous America power in men and machines ended th stalemate in France. This, coupled wit shortages of food and mutinies in Ger many itself, led to the Armistice, i which the Germans not only had to sub mit to a peace settlement but also give u her gains in the east.

In 1914 men had rather lightheartedl gone to war in support of their nation glory and prestige. By 1918 eleven mil lion had died, and the horror and waste c it all were clear to many.

¶ HOARE, ROBERT J. *World War One.* 1973; SCOTT DANIELL, DAVID. *World War I.* 1965

See also BALKANS; BELGIUM; CONVO SYSTEM; DARDANELLES; TSAR; VERSAILLES TREATY OF; etc.

World War II (1939–45): war fought t limit the ambitions of Hitler's German in Europe and of Imperial Japan in Eas Asia and the Pacific. At first there wer two separate conflicts, which merged int a world war in 1941, when the Britis mmonwealth and USA were involved both theatres of war.

he European war began in 1939, when itain and France tried to stop Hitler's adual extension of German territorial wer. Throughout the 1930s both coun- es were worried at the rise of Italian, rman and Spanish dictatorships, but red that the only alternative was the read of Soviet communism. Only after tler's destruction of Czech indepen- nce in March 1939 and his invasion of land in September, in spite of British d French diplomatic opposition, did ey feel they must act.

he Asian conflict began in 1937 with a panese invasion of China. Japan's grow- g population and shortage of land in- eased her need for raw materials and arkets for her manufactures. She had ready moved into Manchuria six years fore and now she wanted total control China. A quarrel with the USA veloped and, when American oil to pan was cut off in 1941, Japan attacked S naval power at Pearl Harbour and unched a campaign to seize all south- st Asia's riches in oil, food and metals.

Both German and Japanese military rces gained spectacular successes. The uropean continent as far east as the iburbs of Moscow and the Caucasian lfields came under German control, as ell as North Africa as far as the Nile elta. The Japanese conquests extended to e Indian frontier and over the Pacific lands to just north of Australia and west f Hawaii. Yet both aggressors took on n impossible task. Their ruthless and ometimes atrocious treatment of the eoples they conquered ended any hope f a quick and acceptable peace, and ecret resistance movements engaged in uerrilla warfare against Germany's and apan's "New Order". The tremendous esources and determination of their four nain enemies, the USA, the Soviet

Street fighting in Stalingrad, 1942.

Union, the British Commonwealth and China, meant that in a prolonged war they had little hope of victory, despite the earlier conquests.

The seeds of German defeat were already clear in the failure to win control of air and sea power in the Battles of Britain and the Atlantic, but the turning point came in 1942–43. At Stalingrad and El Alamein the German military advance was checked, whilst the Japanese were halted at Midway and Guadalcanal in the Pacific and at Imphal in India. There followed a gradual, three-year destruction of their power. Hitler's "Fortress Europe" was invaded, first through Italy and Normandy by Commonwealth-American armies, and then from the east by Soviet forces. As the Russians fought their way into Berlin Hitler committed suicide and Germany surrendered unconditionally. The Japanese, too, lost control of the sea to the Americans, who forced them out of key islands such as Saipan and Okinawa. In the climax of the struggle in 1945 the Americans faced the desperation of the Japanese "Kamikaze" suicide pilots. In August two atomic bombs were dropped on Hiroshima and Nagasaki and the Japanese government immediately surrendered.

There were over 30 million deaths in World War II. Some people were killed in battle, others in air raids; but more

World War 2
PRINCIPAL SEATS OF WAR 1939 to 1945
Pacific
MIDWAY Is.
HAWAIIAN Is.
PEARL HARBOUR
SAIPAN
PACIFIC OCEAN
GUADALCANAL
AUSTRALIA
Far East
MONGOLIA
MANCHURIA
CHINA
JAPAN
OKINAWA
INDIA
PHILIPPINES
MALAYA
N. Africa
MEDITERRANEAN SEA
BENGHAZI
TOBRUK
SIDI BARRANI
ALAMEIN
SUEZ CANAL
CAIRO
LIBYA
EGYPT
Burma
KOHIMA
INDIA
IMPHAL
LASHIO
MANDALAY
MEIKTILA
AKYAB
Irrawaddy R.
Sittang R.
Europe 1939
0 600 Miles
0 800 Km
KEY: A. ALBANIA
BEL. BELGIUM
B. BULGARIA
D. DENMARK
E. ESTONIA
E P. EAST PRUSSIA
G. GREECE
H. HUNGARY
LIT. LITHUANIA
LAT. LATVIA
N. NETHERLANDS
P. PORTUGAL
S. SWITZERLAND
Y. YUGOSLAVIA
FINLAND
NORWAY
SWEDEN
E
LAT.
LIT.
E.P.
MOSCOW
U. S. S. R.
UNITED KINGDOM
D
N
BEL
GERMANY
POLAND
STALINGRAD
FRANCE
S
H
ROMANIA
CAUCASUS
BLACK SEA
P
SPAIN
ITALY
Y
B
A
G
TURKEY
MEDITERRANEAN SEA

ere victims of Japanese and German rsecution. Prisoners-of-war in the Far ıst were ill-treated, whilst in Europe illions of Jewish and Slav civilians died concentration camps such as Ausch-itz. The war had been successfully ught to end this type of tyranny but ıd created many new problems. Wide-read destruction by bombing added the ɔmeless to the already vast number of fugees. There were renewed fears of ɔmmunism, with the Russians intent on nposing their own rule on areas they had eed from German control. Over-ıadowing all was the destructive power f the atomic bomb.

HOARE, ROBERT J. *World War Two*. 1973; SCOTT-ANIELL, DAVID. *World War II*. 1966

ee also ALAMEIN, BATTLE OF; ATLANTIC HARTER; AXIS; BATTLE OF BRITAIN; EISEN-OWER, DWIGHT DAVID; HITLER, ADOLF; EASE-LEND BILL; MIDWAY, BATTLE OF; IUSSOLINI, BENITO; NAZI; PAPEN, FRANZ ON; PEARL HARBOUR; YALTA CONFERENCE.

Vren, Sir Christopher (1632–1723): ne of England's greatest architects. He vas also sufficiently skilled in mathematics nd astronomy to have been elected rofessor of astronomy at Oxford. The Great Fire of London (1666) provided Wren with his great opportunity. Earlier, Charles II had asked him to prepare a plan for the restoration of old St Paul's. As a result of the fire Wren designed a new St Paul's and fifty-one parish churches in addition. Unfortunately for London, his splendid scheme for a comprehensive replanning of the entire city was not adopted. Other buildings designed by Wren include the Royal Exchange and Greenwich Hospital. A famous inscription over the interior of the north door in St Paul's is attributed to Wren's son: *Si monumentum requiris, circumspice* (If you would see his monument, look around).

¶ GOULD, HEYWOOD. *Sir Christopher Wren*. 1972

t Paul's Cathedral by Christopher Wren.

Wright, Frank Lloyd (1869–1959): American architect who was one of the first to use architectural features – wide windows, open-plan interiors, etc. – which have become extensively adopted in modern design. Among his best-known buildings are the Imperial Hotel, Tokyo, and the Guggenheim Museum, New York, as well as private houses which seem to have grown out of the landscape, so much are they in sympathy with it.

¶ In CANNING, JOHN, editor. *100 Great Modern Lives*. 1965

See also INTERNATIONAL STYLE.

Shop front in San Francisco by Frank Lloyd Wright.

Wright, Orville (1871–1948) and **Wilbur** (1867–1912): American aircraft engineers (brothers) who built the first stable and controllable heavier-than-air machine. Beginning with a modest bicycle repair business, they developed a passionate interest in mechanical flight and brought their experiments to a successful conclusion on 17 December 1903 when, at Kitty Hawk, North Carolina, a machine powered by a four-cylinder petrol motor of 12 horsepower made four free flights, the longest of 59 seconds, the maximum speed 30 miles [48 km] per hour, the greatest height 852 feet [260 metres]. The original machine is in the Science Museum, London.

¶ GLINES, CARROLL V. *The Wright Brothers*. 1970
See also AVIATION.

Wyclif or **Wycliffe, John** (*c.* 1320–84): English philosopher, theologian and religious reformer who sought to purge the Church of those who held office for private enrichment rather than the glory of God. With his band of 'poor priests" he preached a Christianity that ordinary people could understand. He published many learned works in Latin, but his chief service to literature was the first English translation of the Bible, to which he contributed probably the whole of the New Testament as well as part of the Old.

¶ STACEY, JOHN. *John Wyclif and Reform*. 1964

X

Xenophon (*c.* 430–*c.* 354 BC): Athenian soldier and author. In the confused state of the times he lent his services on occasions to the Spartans (*see* SPARTA) and to Cyrus, who claimed the Persian throne. His best known work, the *Anabasis*, describes the latter's expedition into Asia with an army of Greek mercenaries, of whom Xenophon was one. He also wro on philosophy, history and countr pursuits.

Xerxes I, called **"the Great"** (*c.* 519 *c.* 465 BC): King of Persia 485–465 BC. H attempted to revenge his father's failur to subdue Greece, but his large fleet wa destroyed at Salamis (480) and his va army defeated at Plataea in the followin year (*see* PERSIAN WARS).

X-ray: At the end of the 19th century German scientist, Wilhelm Roentgen was engaged in experiments with elec tricity. He discovered that if an electri current were passed through a black tub containing certain gases a very powerfu greenish glow resulted. This glowin light, or radiation, could be used i photography. It could illuminate th body, showing what was inside it, bu would not pass through metal. Roentge did not know what this radiation was, s he named it the "X" ray. Doctors soo realised that it could be used to photo graph the interior of the body, revealin diseased bones and other internal mal formations. The technique of makin X-ray photographs is known as radio graphy.

The first precise x-ray photograph of a man' hand, made by Wilhelm Roentgen in 1907.

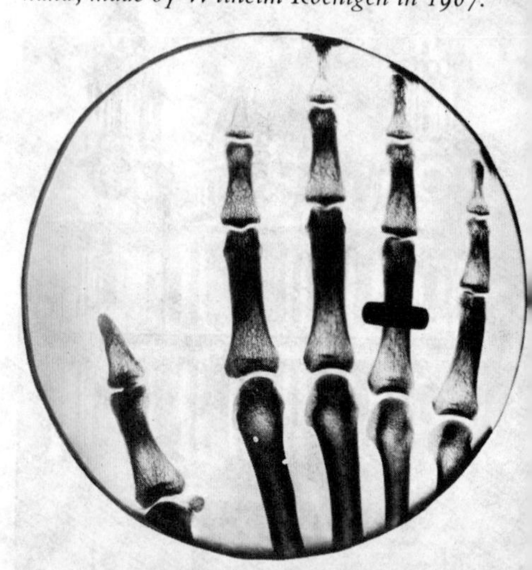

Y

ale University: the third oldest uni-rsity in the USA, situated in New aven, Connecticut. Founded in 1701 was named, in 1718, after Elihu Yale 649–1721), son of one of the first ttlers in New Haven. Elihu Yale became e governor of the East India Company's *ee* separate entry) settlement in Madras nd made a fortune in the Indian trade. hrough his generosity the university 'as able to expand greatly from its nodest beginnings. Together with Har-ard (at Cambridge, Mass.) and Princeton NJ), Yale today occupies a position of igh prestige and scholarly esteem.

'alta Conference (4–11 February 1945): neeting at Yalta, in the Crimea, between talin (USSR), F. D. Roosevelt (USA) nd Churchill (Britain) to discuss the final lefeat of Germany and the problems vhich would follow that country's sur-ender. This was to be unconditional and Germany would then be split into four ones for occupation by US, British, 'rench and Russian forces, with head-quarters in Berlin. Arrangements to lestroy German military power for ever would be made at a future conference. Some details of the new United Nations Organisation were agreed, including the power of veto in the Security Council. The "Big Three" renewed their resolve to create "a world order under law, dedicated to . . . the general wellbeing of all mankind". Ironically, the conference marked the end of much of the wartime unity, since there were serious disagree-ments with Stalin over such things as the proposed all-communist Polish govern-ment and the drawing of the Oder–Neisse Line.

See also INDIVIDUAL ENTRIES.

Yangtze Kiang: the most important river (3,340 miles; 5,374 km long) in China, passing through the cities of Ipin, Chungking, Wan-hsien, Ichang, Kiang-ling, Wu-ch'ang, Hankow, Wuhu and Nanking. The great port of Shanghai is near its mouth.

¶ SPENCER, CORNELIA. *The Yangtze, China's River Highway*. 1966

Yankees: among its various meanings, any citizen of the USA; earlier, a native of one of the northern states or a soldier in the Union forces in the American Civil War (*see* separate entry), as opposed to those of the Confederate states. The origin of the word is doubtful.

Yemen: republic of south-western Arabia. The area had a highly developed civilisation as early as the 8th century BC. The Romans took possession at the end of the 1st century AD, and later the Abyssinians. Judaism and Christianity were established in the 4th century. Under Persian and Islamic rule, Yemen had its own dynasty from the 11th century. Turkey occupied it in 1538 and

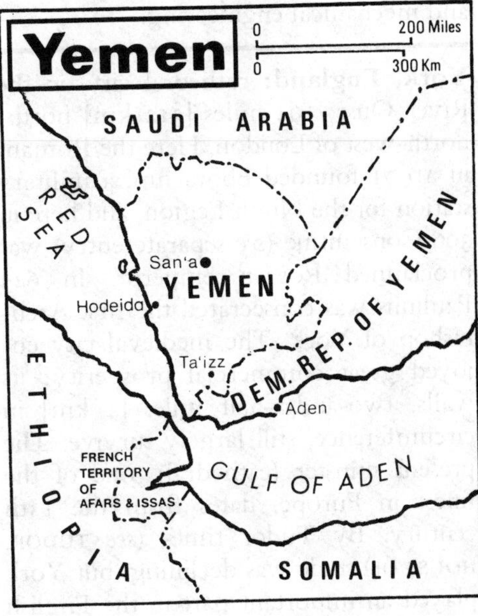

1849. When it was invaded by Saudi Arabia in 1934, Yemen was supported by Britain. Becoming a member of the United Nations in 1947 and a republic in 1962, Yemen has been the scene of conflict between Saudi Arabia and the United Arab Republic.

Yiddish: the language of about six million Jews. It developed from the 12th century AD, based mainly on German (jüdisch = jewish), but about 10 per cent of its vocabulary comes from Hebrew and another 10 per cent from Slav languages. A literature developed from the 16th century and includes many modern novels. *See also* JEWS; JUDAISM.

Yokohama: Japan's chief seaport and second largest city, adjoining Tokyo. It was only a fishing village when the American Commodore Perry landed there in 1854, opening Japan to the western world. Destroyed by earthquake and fire in 1923 and heavily bombed in World War II, it is now a major industrial city, with extensive shipyards and manufactures in steel, chemicals, motor cars and mechanical engineering.

York, England: cathedral city on the River Ouse, 194 miles [312 km] north-north-west of London. Here the Romans in AD 71 founded Eboracum, a military station for the Ninth Legion, and here in 306 Constantine (*see* separate entry) was proclaimed Roman emperor. In 625 Paulinus was consecrated the first Archbishop of York. The medieval city enjoyed great commercial prosperity: its walls, two-and-a-half miles [4 km] in circumference, still largely survive. The present minster (cathedral), one of the finest in Europe, dates from the 13th century. By Tudor times (*see* TUDOR, HOUSE OF) trade was declining, but York played an important part in the English Civil War of 1642–49, and still retai some of the characteristics of Englanc "northern capital".

York, House of: royal house whi occupied the English throne from 1461 1485. It traced its ancestry from Edwa III. Edward IV was the son of Richar the grandson of Edmund, fifth son Edward III and of Anne, great-gran daughter of Lionel, third son of Edwa III. The rival House of Lancaster de cended from John of Gaunt, fourth son Edward III.

Edward IV has been described as "th first English Prince of the Renaissanc type" (*see* RENAISSANCE). Unlike the Lar castrians, Edward was rich. A new kin of extortion, benevolences or force loans, yielded large sums of mone which enabled him to "live of his own without recourse to taxes voted b parliament, which met only once be tween 1475 and 1483.

On Edward's death in 1483, his rightfu heir, Edward V, was displaced by hi uncle, Richard III, about whom historian have little good to say, although th parliament of 1484 did some useful work The dynastic history of the House o York ended with the marriage of Henr VII to Elizabeth of York, thus uniting th houses of Lancaster and York. The badg of the House was the white rose.

See also LANCASTER, HOUSE OF.

Yorktown: small town of south-easter Virginia, USA, founded in 1691 as a por of entry for York County. In 1781 it wa the scene of the surrender of the British forces under General Cornwallis at the end of the American War of Independence (*see* separate entry). Yorktown is now the centre of a national historical park containing original and reconstructed buildings, remains of the War of Independence earthworks, guns, etc.

ıger Klondike gold prospectors pitch their tents along the ledge below the treacherous icy trail over the hilkoot Pass in the Canadian Rockies.

oung, Brigham (1801–77): American Mormon leader who headed the migraon to Utah in 1847 and founded Salt ake City. *See also* MORMONS.

'oung Turks: early 20th-century revoıtionary/political movement in the 'urkish empire. After a rising in Maceonia in 1908 the reformers obtained ower in 1909 under Enver Bey, deposing he Sultan. A surviving member of the novement was Kemal Ataturk (1880–938), who modernised Turkey after Vorld War I.

see also ATATURK; WORLD WAR I.

Yukon: territory in north-west Canada, constituted a separate political entity in 1898, and sending one member of parliament to Ottawa. The 1897–98 Klondyke gold rush temporarily inflated the population. Mining remains important, alongside furs, forestry and fishing. The Yukon River, first explored by Schwatka in 1883 and navigable in summer from Whitehorse, the capital, to the Bering Sea, formerly provided the chief means of transport. The construction and strategic importance of the Alaskan Highway, the railway from Whitehorse to Alaska, air transport, the oil pipeline to Norman Wells and oil potential, have combined to improve the Yukon's economy and attract population.

Z

Zaire, The Republic of: central African republic, formerly Belgian Congo, bounded in the north and north-west by the Central African Republic and Republic of the Congo; north-east by the Sudan; east by Uganda, Rwandi Burundi and Tanzania; south-east by Zambia; south-west by Angola. The total area is 904,990 square miles [2,343,915 square kilometres], and its population in 1983 was 30,730,000.

The central tableland has an average altitude of 3,000 feet [914 metres] and is largely wooded savannah, with forest country in the river valleys. A great forest region stretches from Lake Albert to the mouth of the Aruwimi River, and is inhabited by the Pygmies. Agriculture is underdeveloped, but rubber, teak, ebony, mahogany, cotton, coffee, rice, tobacco, caoutchouc and oil palms are grown. There are rich deposits of copper, cobalt, iron, zinc, uranium and radium in Katanga, gold at Ruwe, Kilo and the Mboga district, and diamonds in the Kasai district.

Cameron's expedition of 1875 led to the formation of the *Association Internationale Africaine*, under the personal auspices of Leopold II of Belgium, which was given its status in 1885 by the treaty of Berlin. Its original object was to suppress slavery and civilise Africa, but before any real progress could be made war broke out between Belgium and the Arabs under Tippoo Tib. The postwar economy, based on a system of concessions for development and the exploitation of natural resources, led to abuses, and the territory was formally annexed by Belgium in 1908, administered by a Governor General representing the King. As a result of Congolese pressure and world opinion it became the independent Democratic Republic of the Congo in June 1960, renamed the Republic of Zaire in October 1971. The country suffered much civil strife, with spasmodic intervention by UN forces, Belgian paratroopers and foreign mercenaries, but achieved some measure of stability under General Mobutu who became President in 1965 ar has remained head of state ever since. *See* CENTRAL AFRICA for map.

Zambia: republic, formerly Northe Rhodesia, bounded in the north by Zai and Tanzania, in the south by the Zambe which forms its boundary with Zin babwe and the Caprivi Strip, and in t east by Angola. The chief exports a copper, cobalt, vanadium, zinc, lead an tobacco, with copper predominating s greatly that the economy is dependent o it. The greater part of the country li 4,000 feet [1,220 m] or more above se level, which tempers what would other wise be a tropical climate. It is watered b great rivers, among them the Zambe which thunders a mile wide over the 36 foot [110 m] Victoria Falls, near Living stone, spreads into Lake Kariba, the shoots through the great sluices of th Kariba Dam on its way to Mozambique

The country has a very long history an important prehistoric settlements hav been discovered. The Bantu people, wh now form the majority of the population invaded from the 17th century onwards to be followed by Arab, Zulu and Basut tribes. Portuguese expeditions in the 18th and early 19th centuries led to a great dea of slave traffic. Livingstone explored the territory in the 1850s and came upon the Victoria Falls. Later the British South Africa Company (1889–1900) virtually took over control. The British Crown assumed administration in 1924, following unification of the country as Northern Rhodesia.

Northern Rhodesia, with Southern Rhodesia and Nyasaland, formed the experimental Central African Federation in August 1954. This broke up in 1963, however, and on 24 October 1964 Northern Rhodesia became the independent Republic of Zambia, with Dr Kenneth Kaunda as head of state.

anzibar: former British protectorate, ɔw part of the United Republic of anzania, comprising the islands of Zanzi-ır, Pemba, Lamu, Manda, Patta and Siu. he principal town is Zanzibar. The lands supply most of the world's cloves ıd clove oil.

Γhe islands probably served South rabian traders as a staging and trading ost for many centuries, and were also isited by traders from the east coast of ıdia. In the 10th century the population ppears to have been Muslim, and by the ıd of the 15th century each island was ıled by a chief of mixed African and siatic blood. At the beginning of the 6th century the Portuguese dominated ıe islands but were deposed by the Arabs ı 1698. In 1829 the Sultan of Oman ıoved his capital from Muscat to Zanzi-ar, and when he died in 1856 his son Aajid became Sultan of Zanzibar. In 888 Sultan Khalifa granted the lease of a ırge part of his territory to Germany, ut when Count von Caprivi was the German Foreign Minister, 1890–93, he vithdrew Germany's claim to Zanzibar nd negotiated a deal with Britain in vhich Zanzibar was exchanged for Heli-goland and the Caprivi Strip (a long nar-ow wedge of land between Zambia and Botswana). Zanzibar was a British pro-ectorate until 1963 when it became inde-endent. Zanzibar joined Tanganyika to orm the United Republic of Tanzania n April 1964.

See CENTRAL AFRICA for map.

Zeppelin: type of cigar-shaped airship developed by the German inventor Count Ferdinand von Zeppelin (1838–1917). His first airship (1900), wrecked on landing, remained in the air for 20 minutes. These dirigibles were used in bombing raids in World War I (*see* separate entry) and, later, on transatlantic voyages.

See also AIRSHIP.

Zionism: political movement begun in 1897 by Theodor Herzl (*see* separate entry) to secure a national home for Jews in Palestine, an objective achieved in 1948 with the establishment of the republic of Israel. Zionism takes its name from the hill in Jerusalem on which the ancient palace of King David and, later, the Temple, were built.

See also ISRAEL, JEWS.

Zulus: a proud Bantu tribe whose ancestors probably migrated from East Africa, settling in Natal in South Africa, where, under their chief Chaka, they terrorised a large area, conquering other Nguni Bantu tribes and forming themselves into a great warrior nation. Chaka was killed by his brother Dingaan in 1829. The Zulus were as great a threat to the Dutch farmer settlers (Boers; *see* separate entry) as the Red Indians were to the settlers of the western states of America, and in 1838 the Boers fought a pitched battle against them, defeating them heavily at Blood River. Dingaan was succeeded by Umhanda and Cetewayo, and in 1887 Zululand was annexed by the British, who brought peace to the region. Early in the 19th century a rebellious regiment of Zulus under Mzilikazi fought its way north and settled in the western half of Zimbabwe, where they founded the Matabele nation.

Zurich: largest city and administrative canton in Switzerland, on Lake Zurich in the upper Rhine valley. Following even earlier settlements it was founded as a Roman customs station called Turiam, and has always been an important trading and craft area. During the Reformation Zurich, like Geneva, became a refuge for people fleeing Catholic persecution. In recent years it has gained newspaper prominence as an influential banking and financial centre ("the gnomes of Zurich").

Index

Key to Index
Bold numbers (eg. **130–31**) refer to page numbers of named articles.
Italic numbers (eg. *271*) refer to page numbers of illustrations.
Map 7 refers to page number of map.
Words in bold (eg. *See* **Flemish Art**) refer to articles within Index entries.

armorial bearings, **40–41**, *41*
armour, **41–4**, *43*
arms, **44–5**
Armstrong, Neil (b. 1930), 9
army, **46**
Arnold of Brescia (d. 1155), 801
Arras, Netherlands, 903
Arsaces, King of Parthia (247–246 BC), 701
art, *see* **Flemish art**; **Fresco painting**; **Gothic art and architecture**; **Impressionists**; **Landscape painting**; **Mural painting**; **Portrait painting**. *See also* individual painters
Artaxerxes II, King of Persia (AD 404–359), 701
Arthur, King (b. 5th cent. AD), **47**, *47*
artillery, **47–8**
Aryans, 448, 456–7
Asam, Cosmas Damian (1686–1739), 84
Asam, Evid Quirin (1692–1750), 84
Ashanti empire, 361
Ashdown, Battle of (AD 871), 16
Ashley, Anthony Ashley Cooper, 1st Earl of Shaftesbury (1621–83), 129. *See also* **Shaftesbury**
Ashmole, Elias (1617–92), 609
Ashton, Frederick, 223
Ashur, Asshur, 54, 581. *Map 55*
Ashurbanipal, Asshurbanipal, *or* Assur-bani-pal (d. *c.* 633 BC), **48**, *49*, *54*
Asia, **49–53**. *Maps 50*, *51*
Asia Minor, **53–4**
Asiento, **54**
Asoka (*c.* 273–232 BC), 52, **54**, 122
Asquith, Herbert Henry, 1st Earl of Oxford and Asquith (1852–1928), 536
assassination, **54**, 281
Asser, Bishop of Sherborne (d. AD 909), 15–16, 97
Assisi, 319
Assyria, **54–5**, 72–3, 700. *Map 55*
Assyrian language, 405
Astrakhan, 481
astrolabe, **55–6**, 236, 563–4, *56*, *563*
astrology, 56
astronomy, 55, **56–8**, *56*
Aswan Dam, 221, 617
Atahualpa (*c.* 1502–33), 265, 446, 720, *720*
Ataturk, Kemal (Mustafa Kemal, *c.* 1880–1938), 54, **58**, 670, 946, 999
Athanasians, 207
Athanasius (*c.* AD 296–373), Bishop of Alexandria, 410
Athelstan (AD 895–940), 213
Athens, **58–9**
Athens (ancient), **58–9**, 282, 375–8, 407, 963; Parthenon, 59, 707, *58*; struggle against Persia (490–479 BC), 58; war with Sparta, 291. *Map 376*
Atlantic, Battle of the (1939–43), **59**
Atlantic Cable, **59**
Atlantic Charter, **59**
Atlantis, 19, **59**
atomic bomb, **59–60**, *60*; Japan, 488, 614, 941. *See also* **Nuclear power**
Atomic Energy Authority Act (1954), 960
Attalids, 377, 407
Attic pottery, 380
Attica, 696. *Maps 376*, *696*
Attila (*c.* AD 406–53), 81, 330, 355, 434, 665
Aubrey, John (1626–97), 97, *97*
Augsburg, Religious Peace of (1555), 921
Augustine, St (d. AD 604), **60**, 142, 380, 595
Augustine of Hippo, St (AD 354–430), **60–61**, 301, 340
Augustus Caesar, Gaius Julius Octavianus (63 BC–AD 14), **61**, 220, 291, 313, 411, 735, *61*
Aungier, Gerald, President of Surat (1669–77),
Aurangzeb, Mogul Emperor (d. 1707), 450, 59 966
Aurelian, Lucius Domitius, Roman Emperor (AD 270–75), 680
Auschwitz, 732
Austerlitz, Battle of (1805), 66, 615, 616
Australia, **61–5**, 119, 690, *62*; Aborigines, 246, 317; Cook's voyage, 61, 201. *Maps 63*, *64*
Australian Colonies Act (1850), 624
Austria, **66**, 336, 359–60; rule of Italy, 478–9; war with France (1792), 338
Austria-Hungary, Austro-Hungarian Empire, 66, 385, 500–01
Austrian Succession, War of (1741–48), 54, **67**, 489, 557, 623. *Map 66*
Austro-Prussian War (1866), 420
auto-da-fe, **67**
Avars, 76, 126–7. *Map 127*
Avebury, **67–8**, *67*
aviation, **68–70**, *68*, *69*, *70*
Avignon, 186, 684, *684*, 778
Axis, **71**
Azores, 443
Aztecs, **71**, 196, 205, 206, 322, 329, 366, *71*

Baalbek, *see* **Heliopolis**
Babar *or* Babur (1483–1530), 12, **72**, 228, 448, 59 855
Babbage, Charles (1792–1871), 131; Babbage's card, *132*
Babington Plot (1586), 978
Babylon *and* Babylonia, 54, **72–3**, 349, 430, 494, 700; astronomy, 56; baking, 74; calendar, 133; civilisation, 507; language, writing, 8. *Maps 15*, *72*
Bach, Johann Sebastian (1685–1750), 273
Bacon, Francis, 1st Baron Verulam (1561–1626), **73**, 115, 175, *73*
Bacon, Francis (painter, b. 1910), 742
Bacon, Roger (*c.* 1214–92), 68, **73**, 383
Bactria, 512. *Maps 15*, *701*
Badajoz, Battle of (1811), 697. *Map 398*
Baden-Powell, Agnes (1858–1954), 363
Badr, Battle of (AD 624), 596
Baekeland, Dr Leo (1863–1944), 725
Baghdad, **73–4**, 395, 429, 475, 922. *Map 32*
Baghdad Pact (1955), 469–70
Baglione family, 702
Bagratunis, 40
Bahadur, Mogul Emperor (1701–12), 596
Bahrain, 647
bailey, **74**, *151*
Bailey, Sir Donald (Bailey bridge), 116
Bakewell, Robert (1725–95), 10
baking, **74–5**
Baku, 647
Balaclava *or* Balaklava, Battle of (1854), **75**, 211, 428, *75*
balance of power, **76**
balance of trade, **76**
Balanchine, George (b. 1904), 223

Florence, 224, **318–19**, 477–8, *477*
Florentine art, **319–20**
Florey, Howard (1898–1968), 574
Florida, 650–51. *Maps 22, 23*
Fokine, Michael (1888–1943), 223
Folger, Henry Clay (1857–1930), 529
font, **321**, *321*
Fontainebleau, **321**
Fontainebleau Decree (1810), 200
Fontenoy, Battle of (1745), 67. *Map 66*
food preservation, **321–2**
fool, **322**, *322*
football, **322–3**
Ford, Henry (1863–1947), **323**, 606, *323*
Foreign Legion, **324**
forgery, **324–5**
forging (of metals), **325–6**, *326*
Formosa, 487, 512. *Map 167*
Forrest, General Nathan Bedford (1821–77), 511
Fort Knox, 367
Fort Sumter, 20. *Map 23*
forum, **326**
fossils, **326–7**, *327*
Fouché, Joseph (1758–1820), 736
Fourdrinier, Henri (1766–1854), 756
Fourteen Points, **327**, 969, 987
Fourteenth Amendment, **327**
fourteenth century, **327–9**
Fox, Charles James (1749–1806), 254, **329**, 399, 660, *329*
Fox, George (1624–91), **329–30**, 340, 766, *330*
France, **330–32**. *Map 292*; African colonies, 481; Canadian colonies, 21, 136, 520, 634; electoral system, 275; Reign of Terror (1793–94), 483, **786–7**; Republic, 332; rule in Italy, 477–8; Second Empire, 104; Second Republic, 104; taxation, 446; wars with Britain, 373–4 *See also* **Bonaparte**, **Bourbon**, **Capet**, **Valois**
Francis I, King of France (1515–47), 149, 306, **332**, 526, 666, 855, 966, *332*
Francis Joseph I, Emperor of Austria (1848–1916), **332**, 565, *332*
Francis of Assisi, St (*c.* 1181–1226), **332–3**, 338–40, 664, *333*
Francis Borgia, St (1510–72), 491
Francis I, Duke of Lorraine (1745–65), 385
Francis Xavier, St (1506–52), **333**, 486, 491
Franciscan Order, 948
Franco, General Francisco (1892–1975), 111, 129, **333**, 877
Franco-Prussian War (1870–71), 105, **333–4**, 360, 414, 666, 688. *Map 334*
Frankfurt, Treaty of (1871), 334
Franklin, Benjamin (1706–90), 275, **334–5**, 745, *335*
Franklin, Sir John (1786–1847), **335**, 637, 733
Franks, 303, **335**, 352, 357, 585; Ripuarian, 330, 335; Salian, 330, 335, 815
Franz Ferdinand, Archduke (d. 1914), 332, 501, *990*
Fraunhoffer, Joseph von (1787–1826), 57
Frederick I Barbarossa, Holy Roman Emperor (1155–90), 216, **335–6**, 419, 423, 849, 920
Frederick I, Holy Roman Emperor (1220–50), 217, 381, 420, 423, 463, 919–20
Frederick William, the Great Elector (1640–88), 359, 748, 762, 833, 921
Frederick I, King of Prussia (1701–13), 420
Frederick William I, King of Prussia (1713–40), 336
Frederick II, the Great, King of Prussia (1740–86), 67, 157, 271, **336**, 359, 557, 748, 763, 833, *33*
Freemasons, 863, *863*
free trade, **336–7**
Fremont, John C. (1830–90), 664
French Indo-China, 971
French language, 518
French Revolution (1789–9), 271–2, 276, 299, 331, **337–8**, 906; calendar, 134; Committee of Public Safety, 189; Directory, 235. *See also* **Reign of Terror**
French Revolutionary Wars (1792–1802), 331, **33**
fresco painting, **339**
Freud, Sigmund (1856–1939), **339**, 501, 575, *339*
friars, **339–40**, 664, 920, *340*
Friedland, Battle of (1807), 615, 616
Friendly Societies, **340**
Friends, Religious Society of, 330, 329, **340–1**, *330*, *341*. *See also* **Quakers**
Froben, Johann (d. 1527), 755
Frobisher, Sir Martin (*c.* 1535–94), 237, 387, 637,
Froebel, Friedrich (1782–1852), 703
Froissart, Jean (1337–*c.* 1410), 125, 175, 211, **341–2**, *342*
frontier, **342**
Froude, J. A. (1818–94), 415
Fry, Elizabeth (1780–1845), 341, 640, 759, 783, 938, *783*
Fugger, Family of, **342–3**
Fujiwara family, 486
Fuller, Thomas (1608–61), 97
Fulton, Robert (1766–1815), 893
Furneaux, Tobias (1735–81), 177, 210, 905
fur, **343**
furniture designers, **343–5**, *344*

Gaberone, 111
Gabon, *Map 7*
Gadsden Purchase, *Map 22*
Gaelic, 470; Gaelic alphabet, 18
Gagarin, Yuri (1934–68), 871, *873*
Gainsborough, Thomas (1727–88), 273, 742
Gaiseric, *see* **Genseric**
Galatians, 53, 81
Galicia, 954
Galilee, 411
Galileo *or* Galileo Galilei (1564–1642), 57, **346**, 371, 677, 835, 909, *346*
galleon, **346**, *347*, *842*
galley, **346–7**, *347*, *842*
Gallipoli, **347**. *Map 225*
Galton, Sir Francis (1822–1911), 289, 310
Gama, Vasco da (1460–1524), **347–8**, 367, 607, 855, 930; voyage to Calicut (1497), 206, 236, 308. *Map, see endpapers*
Gambia, 119. *Map 7*
Gandhara, 703
Gandhi, Mohandas Karamchand (1869–1948), 178, **348**, 451, 621, *348*
Gandhi, Mrs Shrimati Indira, 452
Ganges River, 49, **348**, 713
gangsters, **348–9**
gardens, **349–51**, *350–1*. Plate 23
Gardiner, S. R. (1829–1902), 416
Garfield, James A., US President (1881), 25
Garibaldi, Giuseppe (1807–82), **351**, 479, 567, 678, *793*
Garnerin, A. J. (1770–1823), 78–9, 687, *687*

McGill University, Canada, 529, 600
Machiavelli, Niccolo (1469–1527), 109, 194, **544**, *544*
Machu Picchu, **544**, *544*
McIntire, Samuel (1757–1811), 345, *344*
Mackenzie, Sir Alexander (1763–1820), 136
McKinley, William, US President (1897–1901), 25, **544**
Madagascar, *see* **Malagasy Republic**
Madeira, 409, 443, **545**, 894. *Map 545*
Madison, James, US President (1809–17), **545**, 754
Madras (Fort St George), 67, 181, **545**
Madrid, **545**, 837
Maecenas, Gaius Cilnius (*c.* 70–8 BC), 61
Mafia, 349, **546**, 864
Magdeburg, Battle of (1629), 921
Magellan, Ferdinand (*c.* 1480–1521), 177, 237, **546–7**, 674, *178. Map, see endpapers*
Magna Carta (Great Charter, 1215), 164, 198, 305, **547**, 827, 920–1
Magnesia, 275
magnetism, 275
Magonid family, 149
Magyars, 435, **547**, 859
Maharaja, Maharajah, **547**, *547*
Mahdi, the (Mohammed Ahmed, 1844–85), 367
Mahomet, *see* **Mohammed**
Mahrattas, Marathas, **547**, *547*
Maiden Castle, 260, *260–1*
Maillart, Robert (1872–1940), **547–8**, *548*
Maine, USA, *Maps 22, 23*
Mainz (Mentz), 446–7, **548**
Maitland, F. W. (1850–1906), 416
Malagasy Republic (Madagascar), 548. *Maps 7, 565, 607*
malaria, **548**
Malawi (Nyasaland), 119, **549**, 791. *Maps 7, 791*
Malaya, 475, 487, 854; Malay language, 518
Malaysia, 119, 455, **549–50**, 697. *Maps 549, 818*
Malcolm II, King of Scotland (1005–34), 144
Mali (French Sudan), 6, **550**. *Map 7*
Mallory, George Leigh (1886–1924), 293
Malplaquet, Battle of (1709), 175, **550**
Malta, 119, **550–1**. *Map 576*
Mamelukes, 31, 130, 153
mammoths, **551**, *551*
Mamun, Caliph (*c.* 786–833), 74
Mance, Sir Henry Christopher (1840–1926), 852
Manchester, **551**, *551*
Manchu Dynasty (1644–1912), 168, 272, 509, 833, 855, 900
Manchukuo, 552, 854. *Map 552*
Manchuria, 487, **551–2**, 854. *Map 552*
mandarin, **552**
mandates, **552–3**
Mandeville, Sir John (14th cent.), **553**
Manet, Edouard (1823–83), 444
Manila, **553**, 708. *Map 675*
Manitoba, 136. *Map 138*
Mannerheim, General (1867–1951), 311
Manning, Cardinal Henry (1808–92), 673
Manson, Patrick (1844–1922), 574
Mantegna, Andrea (1431–1506), 553
Mantua, 338, **553**, *553*
Manuel, King of Portugal (1495–1521), 546
Manutius, Aldus (1449–1515), 106
Manzikert, Battle of (1071), 53, 128. *Map 127*
Manzoni, Alessandro (1785–1873), 418
Maori, 353, **553–4**, 627–29, 976
Mao Tse-tung (b. 1893), 165, 168–9, 192, 512, **554**, *554*
map, **554–6**, *555*
Maquis, **556**
Marat, Jean Paul (1743–93), **556**, *556*
Marathon, Battle of (490 BC), 87, 226, 290, 375, **557**, 701. *Map 376*
Marconi, Guglielmo (1874–1937), **557**, 769–70
Marcus Aurelius, Roman Emperor (AD 161–180), 800
Marengo, Battle of (1800), 338, 428, **557**
Margaret of Parma, Regent of the Netherlands (1559–67), 622
Maria Theresa (1717–80), 385, **557**
Marie Antoinette (1755–93), 184, 190, 337, 493, **557**, *557*
Maria Feodorovna (1847–1928), **557–8**, *558*
Mariana Islands, *Map 675*
Marines, **558–9**
marionettes, **559–60**, *559*
Maritza, Battle of the (1371), 76
Mark Antony *or* Marcus Antonius (*c.* 82–32 BC), 61, 220, 269
Marlborough, Duke of, *see* **Churchill**
Marlowe, Christopher (1564–93), **560**
Marne river, **560**
Marrakesh, Marrakech, **560**
Marsden, Samuel (1765–1838), 627
Marseillaise, **560**
Marseilles, **560**
Marshall, George C. (1880–1959), 561
Marshall Islands, 676. *Map 675*
Marshall, John (1755–1835), 414, **560–1**
Marshall Plan, **561**, 665
Marston Moor, Battle of (1644), 243, 806
Martello towers, 183, 280
Martial (*c.* AD 80), 105
Martinique, **561**, 616, 975
martyrs, **561–2**, *561*
Marx, Karl (1818–83), 147, 192, 463, 525, **562**, 631, *562. See also* **Economics, Imperialism, Socialism**
Marxism, 53
Mary, Queen of Scots (1542–87), 39, 159, 825, 892, 978, *892*
Mary I (Mary Tudor), Queen of England (1553–58), 131, 204, 210, 708, 943, 988, *942*
Mary II, Queen of England (1689–94), 365, 390, 483, 659
Maryland, USA, 21, 919. *Maps 22, 23*
Masaccio (*c.* 1401–28), 319, 516, 608
Masaryk, Jan (1886–1948), 219, **562**
Mason-Dixon Line, **562–3**. *Map 563*
Massachusetts, USA, 21, 919. *Maps 22, 23*
Masséna, André (1756–1817), 338
Matabele tribes, 938
mathematical instruments, **563–4**, *563*
Matilda, Queen (d. 1167), 633
Matisse, Henry (1869–1954), 516
Matthias I Hunyadi *or* Matthias Corvinus, King of Hungary (1458–90), King of Bohemia (1478–90), **564**
Mau Mau, 504, **564**
Maurice of Nassau (1567–1625), 617, 658
Mauritania, *Map 7*
Mauritius, 119, **565**, 616. *Map 565*

Phoenicia, 708–9. *Map 55*
Phoenician alphabet, 17, 375, 412; Phoenician language, 405–6
Phoenicians, 129, 148, 308, 550, **708–9**, 936, *709*
photography, **709–11**, *711*
Phraates III, King of Persia (70–37 BC), 701
Phrygia, *Map 55*; Phrygians, 53, 945
Phyfe, Duncan (1768–1854), 345
Picardy, **712**
Picasso, Pablo (1881–1973), 287, 516, **712**, 742
Piccard, Auguste (1884–1962), 79, 644, **712**, *712*
Pickford, Mary (1893–1979), 604, *605*
Piedmont, **713**
Piero della Francesca (*c.* 1415–92), **713**
Pilate, Pontius, Governor of Judaea (AD 26–30), 491, 495, **713**
pilgrimage, **713–15**, *714–15*
Pilgrim Fathers, 195, **715–16**, 729, 917, *715*. *See also* **American Colonies, The**; **Cape Cod**; **"Mayflower"**; **New England**
Pillnitz, Declaration of (1791), 337
Pilsudski, Jozef (1867–1935), **716**
Piltdown Man, 324–5
Pindar (518–438 BC), 975
Pinel, Philippe (1745–1826), 574
Piraeus, The, **716**
Pirandello, Luigi (1867–1936), 250
Piranesi, Giovanni Battista (1720–78), 287
pirates, **716–17**, *717*
Pisa, 354, **717–18**, *718*
Pisarro, Camille (1830–1903), 44
Pisistratids, 375
Pisistratus (5th cent. BC), 58
Pitcairn Island, 613, **718**, 908. *Map 675*
Pitman, Isaac (1813–97), 849
Pittsburgh, USA, 588, **719**
Pitt, William, 1st Earl of Chatham, "the Elder" (1708–78), **718**, 766, *718*
Pitt, William, "the Younger" (1759–1806), 254, 446, 450, 616, **719**, *719*
Pius V, Pope (1565–72), 527, 571, **719**, *719*
Pius VI, Pope (1775–90), 684
Pius VII, Pope (1800–23), 491, 802
Pius IX, Pope (1846–78), 685, **720**
Pius XI, Pope (1922–39), 685
Pius XII, Pope (1939–58), **720**, *720*
Pizarro, Francisco (*c.* 1475–1541), 237, 445, 582, **720**, 856, *720*
Pizarro, Gonzalo (1502–48), 196, 274, 768
place-names, **720–2**
plagues, 328, 402, 700, **722–3**, *723*. *See also* **Black Death**
Plains States, The, USA, **723**. *Map 23*
planetarium, **723–4**, *724*
Plantagenet, House of (1154–1399), 724–5. *Map 725*
Plassey, Battle of (1757), 85, 181, **725**
plastics, **725**
Plataea, Battle of (479 BC), 376, 448, 702, 996
Plato (*c.* 427–348 BC), 59, 276, 291, 377, **726**
Plautus (*c.* 254–184 BC), 249
playing cards, **726–7**
plebian, **727**
plebiscite, **727**
Pleistocene, 752
plimsoll line, **727**, *727*
Plimsoll, Samuel (1824–98), 580, 727
Pliny the Elder (d. AD 79), 970
Pliny the Younger (*c.* 61–113), 233, 313, 740
plough, **727–9**, *728*
Plutarch (AD 46–120), 96
Plymouth, England, **729**
Plymouth, USA, 729
Pocahontas *or* Matoaka (1595–1617), **729**
pocket battleship, **729–30**, *729*
poison gas, **730**
Poitiers, **730**. Plate 54; Battle of (1356), 45, 267, 328, 331, 429, 435, 730
Poland, 224, 495, 676–77, **730–2**. *Maps 224, 731*; Polish Corridor, 732, 969. *Map 731*
polar expeditions, 26, 70, 321, 732–34, 826, 835. *Map 733*
police, **735–6**
political parties: (general), **736–7**, 861–2; Britain, **737–8**; USA, **738–9**
poll tax, **739**
Polk, James K., US President (1845–49), 582
Pollaiuolo, Antonio (1429–98), 320
pollution, 953
Polo, Marco (1254–1324), 52, 236, 243, 426, **739–40**, *739*. *Map 50*. *See also* **Cathay**; **Kublai Khan**
Poltava *or* Pultowa, Battle of (1709), 87, 731
Polygnotus (*c.* 475–447 BC), 741
Polynesia, **740**. *Map 675*; Polynesians, 644, 674
Pomerania, *Map 358*
Pompeii, 34, 345, 379, **740**, 975. *See also* **Herculaneum**; **Vesuvius**
Pompey (Gnaeus Pompeius Magnus, 106–48 BC), 130, 494, **740**
Pondicherry, **740–1**
"poor whites", **741**
Poona, 228
Pope, Alexander (1688–1744), 106
Popes, *see under individual names. See also* **Papacy**
Port-of-Spain, **741**
portrait painting, **741–2**
Port Royal, **742**
Portsmouth, Treaty of (1905), 811
Portugal, 437, **742–3**, *743*. *Maps 292, 875*; colonies, 308, 451, 455, 504, 744, 925–6; exploration, 52, 114, 236–7, 293, 856; trade routes, 930. *Map 7*
postal history, **744–7**, *745–7*; stamps, 412–13
Potemkin, Grigori Aleksandrovich (1739–91), **747**
Potomac River, **747–8**
Potsdam, **748**; Potsdam Conference (1945), **748**, 884
pottery, 257–8, **748–9**, *748*, *749*
Poussin, Nicolas (1594–1665), 516
power politics, **749**
Pozzo di Borgo, Count (1764–1842), 683
pragmatic sanction, 67, **749–50**
Prague *or* Praha, 102, **750**, *219*; Peace of (1635), 921–2
Praxiteles (4th cent. BC), 59, 379
Pre-Cambrian period, 355
prehistoric, **750**; Prehistoric Age, 8; prehistoric animals, **750–1**, *750*, *751*; prehistoric art, **752–3**
Prejvalsky, Nikolay (1839–88), 426
premier, **753**

Acknowledgements

The publishers wish to thank the following for allowing us to reproduce copyright illustrations in black and white: Aerofilms Ltd: page 2, 538, 551, 688; Aldus Books Ltd: page 856; J. Allan Cash Ltd: page 165, 168, 229, 488, 524, 547, 609, 623, 643, 652, 667, 679, 684, 718, 749, 785, 794, 801, 804, 806, 814, 816, 839, 857, 886, 890; Edizione Alinari: page 320, 333; Courtesy of the American Museum of Natural History: page 974; Architect of the Capitol: page 196; Archives Photographiques: page 172; Art-Wood Photography: page 115; Associated Press: page 179, 768; Atlantic Press: page 20; Australian News and Information Bureau: page 412, 467; Austrian National Tourist Office: page 971; Barnaby's Picture Library: page 6, 8, 12, 26, 28, 36, 41, 154, 244, 282, 298, 406, 413, 467, 599, 777, 787, 792, 795, 823, 849, 871, 873, 878, W. F. Meadows 976; Barnardo Photo Library: page 784; B. T. Batsford: page 71, 555; Bethnal Green Museum: page 245; Blenheim Palace: page 100; The Curators of the Bodleian Library, Oxford: page 97, 159, 739; British Aircraft Corporation Ltd: page 70; British Library Board: page 169, 222, 256 MSS Royal 15E III f269-690; British Lion Films Ltd: page 605; Trustees of the British Museum: page 33, 47, 49, 54, 71, 72, 94, 110, 120, 257, 258, 268, 272, 289, 294, 297, 298, 342, 344, 351, 379, 390, 440, 447, 490, 492, 508, 515, 519, 529, 566, 586, 591, 600, 625, 633, 690, 705, 720, 748, 807, 896, 913, 935; Trustees of the British Museum (Natural History): page 235; British Olivetti Ltd: page 295; British Railways Board: page 773; British Red Cross Society: page 778; Camera Press Ltd: page 4, 165, 221, 259, 277, 352, 419, 445, Mike Andrews 466 and 968, Karsh of Ottawa 504, 522, 526, 543, 544, 570, 573, 589, 617, 693, 694, 696, 714, 720, 748, 754, 847, Paul Almasy 995; Campagna dei Giovani: page 251; Canadian Pacific Railroad: page 140; Central Press Photos: page 190; Church Information Service: page 143; Church of Jesus Christ of Latter-Day Saints, USA: page 602; Colorsport: page 881; Master and Fellows of Corpus Christi College, Cambridge: page 586; Council of the Institution of Mechanical Engineers, from "Engineering Heritage": page 92; Courtauld Institute of Art: page 284, 517; Courtaulds Ltd: page 915; Crown Copyright: page 205; Culver Pictures: page 388, 485, 580; Dominic Photography: page 657; Esso: page 648; Mary Evans Picture Library: page 182, 188, 542; Fishbourne Roman Palace and Museum: page 34; Fort Ticonderoga Museum Collection: page 599; Fox Photos: page 231, 245; John R. Freeman and Co.: page 485, 625; Lucie Freud: page 339; The Frick Collection, New York: page 601; Genehmigung des Museums für Volkerkunde: page 90; Stanley Gibbons Ltd: page 746; Government Information Service, Crown Copyright: page 424; Greater London Council Fire Brigade: page 313; Guildhall Record Office: page 383; Hale Observatories: page 643; Paul Hamlyn: page 15; Fritz Hansen, Denmark: page 344; B. J. Harris (Oxford) Ltd: page 99; Frederick Hill Reserve Collection, courtesy American Heritage: page 533; Hirmer Fotoarchiv, München: page 58; Historical Pictures Service, Chicago: page 370; Historical Society of Pennsylvania: page 698; Michael Holford Picture Library: page 285; Dr L. H. Hurrell: page 715; Hydatum, J. Baker and J. Scheerbohm: page 743; Imperial War Museum: page 200, 253, 729, 992; Instituto Nacional de Antropologia e Historia, Mexico: page 71; Israel Museum: page 227; Italian State Tourist Office: page 304; The House of Thomas Jefferson, Monticello: page 489; Jodrell Bank, Cheshire: page 643; A. F. Kersting: page 154, 246, 255, 480, 497, 995; Keystone Press Agency: page 538, 546, 554, 566, 605, 644, 653, 712, 758, 776, 796, 802, 837, 873, 884, 891, 926, 955; The Library of Congress, Washington: page 110, 529, 625; Lloyd's of London: page 536; London Express: page 178; The London Planetarium: page 724; Los Angeles County Museum of Natural History: page 453; Lowell Observatory: page 387; The Mansell Collection: page 3, 4, 5, 9, 11, 12, 13, 14, 18, 38, 39, 61, 68, 69, 75, 78, 94, 103, 104,

7, 109, 115, 124, 129, 130, 144, 146, 147, 152, 154, 156, 175, 176, 177, 178, 179, 180, 186, 195, 197, 201, 2, 211, 227, 231, 237, 247, 251, 254, 262, 272, 295, 303, 307, 310, 314, 320, 332, 340, 344, 348, 357, 5, 401, 410, 418, 423, 425, 427, 439, 452, 456, 477, 479, 481, 487, 499, 505, 511, 512, 526, 544, 553, 567, 1, 583, 586, 596, 598, 602, 603, 661, 666, 672, 673, 693, 695, 703, 705, 711, 715, 717, 719, 723, 728, 747, 2, 773, 779, 789, 804, 813, 819, 823, 827, 832, 833, 835, 836, 840, 851, 858, 863, 864, 881, 885, 887, 888, 9, 893, 925, 934, 935, 936, 937, 970, 989; Mercedes Benz (GB) Ltd: page 606; The Monotype Corpora-on: page 756; Montagu Motor Museum: page 323; Musée Cantonal d'Archeologie, Neuchatel: page 13; Musée des Arts Decoratifs: photo Giraudon: page 344; Musée Royale des Beaux-Arts: page 556; Museo del Prado: page 256; Museum of Fine Arts, Boston: page 110, gift of Maxim Karolik: page 344; Museum of Modern Art, New York, gift of Edgar Kaufmann, Jr: page 344; NERC copyright. Repro-uced by permission of the Director, Institute of Geological Sciences: page 285, 327; National Film rchives: page 427; National Galleries of Scotland: page 508, 825; National Lifeboat Institution: page 31; National Maritime Museum, London: page 40, 163, 398, 839, 840, 843; Maritime Museum of weden and the warship *Wasa*: page 957; National Portrait Gallery: page 73, 88, 181, 210, 213, 242, 48, 267, 329, 364, 367, 515, 535, 621, 626, 645, 659, 673, 682, 690, 695, 700, 718, 719, 754, 775, 779, 83, 807, 826, 836, 837, 861, 892, 942, 987; National Theatre: page 251; National Tourist Organisation f Greece: page 251; The Nobel Foundation, Stockholm: page 632; Novosti Press Agency: page 205, 44, 301, 510, 809, 810, 831, 873, 993; Ore Mining Corporation: page 592; Overseas Containers Ltd: age 580; P. and A. Photos: page 680, 681, 687, 706; Phaidon Press Ltd: page 88; Photographie Giraudon: age 307, 332, 390, 492, 540, 557, 615, 650, 665, 686, 692, 709, 765, 786, 792, 805; Popperfoto: page 363, 05, 677; Port of London Authority: page 240; From *The Darien Disaster* by John Prebble, by courtesy of Simon Prebble: page 226; Public Archives of Canada: page 139; Public Record Office, London, Crown Copyright: page 760, 780, 827, 828, 901; *Punch*: page 277; By gracious permission of Her Majesty the Queen: page 390, 942; Radio Times Hulton Picture Library: page 27, 29, 62, 83, 84, 107, 125, 212, 253, 36, 354, 374, 381, 399, 403, 412, 473, 485, 506, 510, 527, 534, 536, 558, 562, 573, 602, 608, 613, 641, 645, 70, 672, 683, 745, 746, 758, 776, 778, 786, 793, 802, 839, 899, 911, 912, 932, 934, 944, 990; RIBA Library: age 350, 351; Rijksmuseum, Amsterdam: page 436, 659; H. Roger-Viollet: page 466; Royal Com-mission of Historical Monuments: page 528; The Salvation Army: page 815; Crown Copyright, Science Museum, London: page 56, 60, 89, 266; Science Museum, London: page 10, 89, 132, 193, 233, 274, 275, 346, 430, 617, 711; Shell: page 647; Skyfotos: page 532; E. A. Sollars: page 586; Staatliche Museen zu Berlin: page 14; Staatsbibliothek, Berlin: page 996; Städtische Galerie in Lenbachhaus München: page 98; Statens Sjonistouska Museum, Sweden: page 957; Syndication International: page 501; Swiss National Tourist Office and Swiss Federal Railways: page 548; TMM (Research) Ltd Museum: page 206; TWA/Photri: page 812; The Tate Gallery: page 419, 517; E. Piccaglioni, Teatro alla Scala: page 656; Tennessee Valley Authority: page 221; Tourisme-Franceschi: page 467, 524; United Kingdom Atomic Energy Authority: page 436; United Nations: page 390; United Press International: page 219; United States Coast Guard: page 532; USIS: page 221; University of Reading Museum of English Rural Life: page 525; University of Washington, USA: page 507; Victoria and Albert Museum, Crown Copyright: page 122, 173, 245, 248, 278, 287, 344, 365, 414, 450, 481, 492, 559, 561, 767, 914, 981; Volkswagen Motors Ltd: page 295; Weidenfeld & Nicolson Ltd: page 245; Fraser, *History of Toys*, 311, 344; Dean and Chapter of Westminster: page 268; Roger Wood: page 917; WHO: page 404.

The illustrations by Anthony Colbert are based upon information from the following sources: *Age of Kings*, Time Life Books (Time Life International); *Annals of Printing*, Turner and Poole (Blandford); *Armour and Weapons*, Paul Martin (Herbert Jenkins); *Arms and Armour*, Vesey Norman (Weidenfeld & Nicolson); *Assyrian Palace Reliefs*, R. D. Barrett (Batchworth); Bibliotheque Nationale, Paris; British Museum; *British Trade Marks and Symbols*, David Caplan and Gregory Stuart (Peter Owen); *Castles, An Introduction* (HMSO); *Country Life*; *The Early Motor Bus*, Charles E. Lee (British Rail); *Encyclopedia Brittannica*; *A Glossary of Arms and Armour*, G. Cameron Stone (Jack Brussel, NY); *Greek Pottery*, Arthur Lane (Faber and Faber); *Greek and Roman Life* (British Museum Publications); *A History of Architecture*, Bannister Fletcher (Batsford); *History of Mankind*, J. Hawkes and L. Woolley (Allen and Unwin); *The Horse Bus as a Vehicle*, Charles E. Lee (British Rail); *I See All*, Arthur Mee (Amalgamated Press); *Illustrated English Social History*, G. M. Trevelyan (Penguin); *Industry and Technology*, Chaloner and Musson (Studio Vista); *Life and Work of the People of England*, P. Hartley and M. Elliot (Batsford); *Life Science Library* (Time Life International); *The Making of Books*, Sean Jennet (Faber); *Musical Instruments Through the Ages*, A. Bains (Penguin); *New Architecture of London*, Sam Lambert (British Travel Asso-ciation); *Odhams Illustrated Encyclopedia*; *Pictorial Knowledge* (International Learning Systems); *Plough and Pasture*, E. C. Curwen (Colwell Press); *Scientific Instruments in Art and History*, Henri Michel (Barrie & Rockliff); *Soldiers Soldiers*, Richard Bowood (Paul Hamlyn); *The Styles of Ornament*, Alexander Speltz (Dover Publications); *The Universal Encyclopedia of Machines* (Allen & Unwin); Victoria and Albert Museum; *Watermarks in Paper*, W. A. Churchill (Menno Hertzburger and Co).